British Romanticism

Including classic essays and lively debates, *British Romanticism* shows that Romantic literature is an interesting and exciting topic to read and study. Combining key pieces from the last 25 years alongside newly written essays offering fresh takes on the area, this book covers the essential topics but with a contemporary and dynamic twist.

Each section includes a detailed introduction and covers issues which are as relevant to current readers as to those in the Romantic period, such as media, science, religion, politics, ethics, gender, sexuality, race and nationalism. The book contains additional features such as suggestions for further reading and an introduction to the history of interpreting Romantic literature. Designed to appeal to both undergraduate and postgraduate readers, this distinctive volume reflects the vibrant debates across Romantic studies from the 1990s to the present.

Mark Canuel is Professor in the Department of English at the University of Illinois at Chicago, USA.

Routledge Criticism and Debates in Literature

The *Routledge Criticism and Debates in Literature* series offers new perspectives on traditional and core subjects from Medieval Literature to Postmodernism. Exploring different approaches and critical directions, essays range from 'classic' and newer criticism to brand new papers. Sections give an essential overview of key topics and inspire lively debate, enhancing subjects through modern takes, angles or arguments against classic debates.

Ideal for students approaching a topic for the first time, the volumes are also useful for those looking for important critical background. Each contains section introductions that usefully situate the topic within wider debates, and glossaries of key terms, people and places. Challenging and provocative, the *Routledge Criticism and Debates in Literature* series shows how subjects and their criticism have travelled into the twenty-first century in an intelligent and accessible way.

Available in this series:

Medieval Literature
Edited by Holly Crocker and D. Vance Smith

British Romanticism
Edited by Mark Canuel

Coming soon:

Victorian Literature
Edited by Lee Behlman and Anne Longmuir

Nineteenth-Century Poetry
Edited by Jonathan Herapath, Erin Lafford and Emma Mason

British Romanticism

Criticism and Debates

Edited by Mark Canuel

Routledge
Taylor & Francis Group

LONDON AND NEW YORK

First published 2015
by Routledge
2 Park Square, Milton Park, Abingdon, Oxon OX14 4RN

and by Routledge
711 Third Avenue, New York, NY 10017

Routledge is an imprint of the Taylor & Francis Group, an informa business

British Library Cataloguing in Publication Data
A catalogue record for this book is available from the British Library

Library of Congress Cataloging in Publication Data
British Romanticism: Criticism and Debates/edited by Mark Canuel.
pages cm. — (Routledge Criticism and Debates in Literature)
Includes bibliographical references and index.
1. English literature—18th century—History and criticism.
2. Romanticism—England. I. Canuel, Mark, editor.
PR447.B746 2014
820.9'145—dc23
2014019837

ISBN: 978-0-415-52381-3 (hbk)
ISBN: 978-0-415-52382-0 (pbk)

Typeset in Baskerville
by Swales & Willis Ltd, Exeter, Devon, UK

Printed and Bound in the United States of America by

Edwards Brothers Malloy on sustainably sourced paper.

Contents

List of figures   x
Notes on contributors   xi
Acknowledgements   xviii

General introduction: the criticism of Romantic literature
from the Victorians to post-historicism   1
MARK CANUEL

PART 1
Politics, ideology, and the literary   **17**

Introduction   19

1 Insight and oversight: reading "Tintern Abbey"   23
MARJORIE LEVINSON

2 Keats and critique   33
PAUL HAMILTON

3 Byron's causes: the moral mechanics of *Don Juan*   46
JAMES CHANDLER

4 Stealing culture in the shadow of revolutions   57
DANIEL O'QUINN

PART 2
Aesthetics and literary form   **69**

Introduction   71

5 Local transcendence: cultural criticism, postmodernism, and the
romanticism of detail   75
ALAN LIU

6 Historicism, deconstruction, and Wordsworth   88
FRANCES FERGUSON

7 Legislators of the post-everything world: Shelley's *Defence* of Adorno   102
ROBERT KAUFMAN

8 Utility, retribution, and Godwin's *Caleb Williams*   114
MARK CANUEL

PART 3
Audiences and reading publics   **127**

Introduction   129

9 The sense of an audience   133
LUCY NEWLYN

10 Theater as the school of virtue   146
ANN K. MELLOR

11 Study to be quiet: Hannah More and the invention of
conservative culture in Britain   158
KEVIN GILMARTIN

12 Audience, irony, and Shelley   170
ANDREW FRANTA

PART 4
Authorship and authority   **181**

Introduction   183

13 From "national tale" to "historical novel":
Edgeworth and Scott   187
INA FERRIS

14 Keats's prescience   198
ANDREW BENNETT

15 De Quincey's imperial systems   209
ANNE FREY

16 *Milton* unbound   222
MARGARET RUSSETT

PART 5
Gender, sexuality, and the body   **243**

Introduction   245

17 Gendering the soul   249
SUSAN WOLFSON

18 The domestication of genius: Cowper and the rise of
    the suburban man   265
    ANDREW ELFENBEIN

19 Sensibility, free indirect style and the Romantic
    technology of discretion   280
    CLARA TUITE

20 Writing/righting gender   294
    JACQUELINE M. LABBE

PART 6
Racism, nationalism, imperialism   **303**

Introduction   305

21 Was Frankenstein's Monster "a man and a brother"?   309
    H.L. MALCHOW

22 Blake and Romantic imperialism   323
    SAREE MAKDISI

23 "Voices of dead complaint": colonial military disease narratives   336
    ALAN BEWELL

24 Anna Letitia Barbauld and the ethics of free trade imperialism   349
    E.J. CLERY

PART 7
Affects and ethics   **361**

Introduction   363

25 Phantom feelings: emotional occupation in
    The Mysteries of Udolpho   367
    ADELA PINCH

26 Female authorship, public fancy   382
    JULIE ELLISON

27 The art of knowing nothing : feminine melancholy and
    skeptical dispossession   395
    JACQUES KHALIP

28 The force of indirection: "Tintern Abbey" in the literary history
    of mood   409
    DAVID COLLINGS

PART 8
Religion and secularization   **419**

Introduction   421

29 The unknown God   425
    ROBERT RYAN

30 Wordsworth's chastened enthusiasm   438
    JON MEE

31 Godwin, Wollstonecraft, and the legacies of Dissent   451
    DANIEL E. WHITE

32 The entangled spirituality of "The Thorn"   464
    COLIN JAGER

PART 9
Modernity and postmodernity   **473**

Introduction   475

33 The romantic movement at the end of history   479
    JEROME CHRISTENSEN

34 Everyday war   494
    MARY FAVRET

35 Modernity's other worlds   505
    IAN DUNCAN

36 Two pipers: romanticism, postmodernism, and the cliché   518
    ORRIN N.C. WANG

PART 10
Sciences of mind, body, and nature   **527**

Introduction   529

37 Coleridge and the new unconscious   533
    ALAN RICHARDSON

38 John Clare's dark ecology   547
    TIMOTHY MORTON

39 The monster in the rainbow: Keats and the science of life   557
    DENISE GIGANTE

40 Romantic transformation: literature and science   571
    SHARON RUSTON

PART 11
Literature, media, mediation   **581**

Introduction   583

41 Ballads and bards: British romantic orality   587
    MAUREEN MCLANE

42 Processing   601
    ANDREW PIPER

43 If this is Enlightenment then what is Romanticism?   615
    CLIFFORD SISKIN AND WILLIAM WARNER

44 Romantic long poems in Victorian anthologies   625
    TOM MOLE

    Index   635

Figures

16.1   Blake, William. Milton, a Poem. Title page. This item is
reproduced by permission of The Huntington Library,
San Marino, California   223

16.2   Blake, William. The [First] Book of Urizen. Title page: Urizen
bound. Lessing J. Rosenwald Collection, Library of Congress.
© 2014 William Blake Archive. Used with permission   228

16.3   Blake, William. Milton, a Poem, pl. 29, 33. "William." These
items are reproduced by permission of The Huntington Library,
San Marino, California   234

16.4   Blake, William. Milton, a Poem, pl. 29, 33. "Robert."
These items are reproduced by permission of
The Huntington Library, San Marino, California   235

16.5   Blake, William. Milton, a Poem, pl. 30 (detail).
Contrary epigraphs. This item is reproduced by permission
of The Huntington Library, San Marino, California   236

16.6   Blake, William. Milton, a Poem, pl. 15. Milton unbinding
Urizen. This item is reproduced by permission of
The Huntington Library, San Marino, California   237

16.7   Blake, William. Milton, a Poem, pl. 45. Ololon; or,
the unbound book. This item is reproduced by permission
of The Huntington Library, San Marino, California   238

21.1   The Negro Revenged by Henry Fuseli, 1807. Published by
Joseph Johnson; Print made by Abraham Raimbach.
© The Trustees of the British Museum   314

41.1   William Blake, Male figure and cherub
© The British Library Board, C.71.d.19 page 2   591

41.2   William Blake, Songs of innocence and experience
© The British Library Board, C.71.d.19 page 3   592

43.1   An abstract in the form of an argument   617

43.2   An abstract in the form of a thought experiment   623

44.1   Number of extracts from Don Juan reprinted in anthologies
surveyed, by canto   632

Contributors

Andrew Bennett is Professor of English at the University of Bristol. He is the author of numerous books, including *Ignorance: Literature and Agnoiology* (2010), *Wordsworth Writing* (2007), *Romantic Poets and the Culture of Posterity* (1999), and *Keats, Narrative and Audience: The Posthumous Life of Writing* (1994). In addition to Romanticism, his research focuses on twentieth- and twenty-first-century writing, and on literary theory. He is currently editing *William Wordsworth in Context* and working on a study of the representation of suicide in literature.

Alan Bewell is Professor and Chair of English at the University of Toronto. He is the author of *Romanticism and Colonial Disease* (1999) and *Wordsworth and the Enlightenment: Nature, Man, and Society in the Experimental Poetry* (1989) as well as editor of *Medicine and the West Indian Slave Trade* (1999). He is working on a book entitled *Romanticism and Mobility*. He has received grants from the Social Sciences and Humanities Research Council of Canada (*SSHRC*) and is a Fellow of the Royal Society of Canada and a Guggenheim Fellow.

Mark Canuel is Professor of English at the University of Illinois at Chicago. He is author of *Justice, Dissent, and the Sublime* (2012), *The Shadow of Death: Literature, Romanticism, and the Subject of Punishment* (2007), and *Religion, Toleration, and British Writing, 1790-1830* (2002).

James Chandler is Barbara E. & Richard J. Franke Distinguished Service Professor at the University of Chicago. His publications include *An Archaeology of Sympathy: The Sentimental Mode in Literature and Cinema* (2013), *England in 1819: The Politics of Literary Culture and the Case of Romantic Historicism* (1998), and *Wordsworth's Second Nature: A Study of the Poetry and Politics* (1984). He is the editor of *The New Cambridge History of English Romantic Literature* (2008) and co-editor with Maureen McLane of *The Cambridge Companion to Romantic Poetry* (2008) and with Kevin Gilmartin of *Romantic Metropolis: The Urban Scene in British Romanticism, 1780–1840* (2005).

Jerome Christensen is Professor of English at the University of California, Irvine. He is the author of *America's Corporate Art: The Studio Authorship of Hollywood Motion Pictures* (2012), *Romanticism at the End of History* (2000; rept. 2004), *Lord Byron's Strength: Romantic Writing and Commercial Society* (1992), *Practicing Enlightenment: Hume and the Formation of a Literary Career* (1987), and *Coleridge's Blessed Machine of Language* (1981). He is working on a study of postmillennial Hollywood and the financialization of American culture.

E.J. Clery is Professor of English at the University of Southampton, where she is also Director of the Southampton Centre for Eighteenth-Century Studies. She is author of *The Feminization Debate in Eighteenth-Century England: Literature, Commerce, and Luxury* (2004), *Women's Gothic: From Clara Reeve to Mary Shelley* (2000), and *The Rise of Supernatural Fiction, 1790–1820* (1995). She is co-editor of *Authorship, Commerce, and the Public: Scenes of Writing, 1750–1850* (2002) and *Gothic Documents: A Sourcebook* (2000). She is currently working on a book on Anna Barbauld's *Eighteen Hundred and Eleven.*

David Collings is Professor of English at Bowdoin College. He is the author of *Stolen Future, Broken Present: The Human Significance of Climate Change* (2014), *Monstrous Society: Reciprocity, Discipline, and the Political Uncanny, c. 1780–1848* (2009), and *Wordsworthian Errancies: The Poetics of Cultural Dismemberment* (1994). His current project is tentatively entitled *Disastrous Subjectivities: Romanticism, Catastrophe, and the Real.*

Ian Duncan is Florence Green Bixby Professor of English at the University of California, Berkeley. He is the author of *Scott's Shadow: The Novel in Romantic Edinburgh* (2007) and *Modern Romance and Transformations of the Novel* (1992); editor of several novels, including *Kidnapped* (2014) and *The Private Memoirs and Confessions of a Justified Sinner* (2010); and co-editor of *The Edinburgh Companion to James Hogg* (2012), *Approaches to Teaching Scott's Waverley Novels* (2009), and *Scotland and the Borders of Romanticism* (2004). He is presently researching a study of the novel and the "science of man" from Buffon to Darwin.

Andrew Elfenbein is Professor of English at the University of Minnesota, Twin Cities. He is the author of *Romanticism and the Rise of English* (2009), *Romantic Genius: The Prehistory of a Homosexual Role (1999)*, and *Byron and the Victorians (1995)*, as well as editor of *Bram Stoker's Dracula (2010)* and *The Picture of Dorian Grey (2007).*

Julie Ellison is Professor of American Culture and English at the University of Michigan and a Faculty Associate in the Department of African and Afroamerican Studies and the Stamps School of Art and Design. Her books include *Cato's Tears* (1999), *Delicate Subjects: Romanticism, Gender and the Ethics of Understanding* (1990), and *Emerson's Romantic Style* (1984). She co-authored *Scholarship in Public: Knowledge Creation and Tenure Policy in the Engaged University* (2008).

Mary Favret is Professor of English at Indiana University, Bloomington. She is the author of *War at a Distance: Romanticism and the Making of Modern Wartime* (2009) and *Romantic Correspondence: Women, Politics and the Fiction of Letters* (1993), as well as co-author with Nicola J. Watson of *At the Limits of Romanticism: Essays in Cultural, Feminist and Materialist Criticism* (1994).

Frances Ferguson is Ann L. and Lawrence B. Buttenwieser Professor of English at the University of Chicago. Her books include *Pornography, The Theory: What Utilitarianism Did to Action* (2005), *Solitude and the Sublime: Romanticism and the Aesthetics of Individuation* (1992), and *Wordsworth: Language as Counter-spirit* (1977). She is currently working on two book-length studies: *Designing Education* about the rise of mass education and how it affected our conception of both individuals and society and *A Brief History of Reading and Criticism.*

Ina Ferris is Professor of English at the University of Ottawa and author of *The Romantic National Tale and the Question of Ireland* (2002), *The Achievement of Literary Authority: Gender, History, and the Waverley Novels* (1991), and *William Makepeace Thackeray* (1983). She has edited *The Old Manor House (2006)* and *Rayland Hall* (2006), and co-edited with Paul Keen *Bookish Histories: Books, Literature and Commercial Modernity 1700–1850 (2009)*. Her current research focuses on the intersection of antiquarianism, bookishness, and print culture in the Romantic period.

Andrew Franta is Associate Professor of English at the University of Utah. He is the author of *Romanticism and the Rise of the Mass Public* (2007) and is currently completing a book on narratives of systems failure from Johnson to Austen.

Anne Frey is Associate Professor of English at Texas Christian University. She is the author of *British State Romanticism: Authorship, Agency, and Bureaucratic Nationalism* (2010) and has published articles in *Studies in Romanticism, The Wordsworth Circle,* and *Novel.*

Denise Gigante is Professor of English at Stanford University. She is the author of *The Keats Brothers: The Life of John and George* (2011), *Life: Organic Form and Romanticism* (2009), and *Taste: A Literary History* (2005), as well as the editor of two anthologies: *The Great Age of the English Essay* (2008) and *Gusto: Essential Writings in Nineteenth-Century Gastronomy* (2005). She is currently working on *The Book Madness: A Story of Book Collectors in America.*

Kevin Gilmartin is Professor of English at the California Institute of Technology. He is the author of *Writing against Revolution: Literary Conservatism in Britain, 1790–1832* (2007) and *Print Politics: The Press and Radical Opposition in Early Nineteenth-Century England* (1996). *William Hazlitt: Political Essayist and* an edited volume, *Sociable Places: Locating Enlightenment* and *Romantic Culture in Britain,* are forthcoming. He is co-editor, with James Chandler, of *Romantic Metropolis: The Urban Scene of British Culture, 1780–1840* (2005).

Paul Hamilton is Professor of English at Queen Mary University of London. His books include *Realpoetik: European Romanticism and Literary Politics (2014), Coleridge and German Philosophy: The Poet in the Land of Logic* (2007), *Metaromanticism: Aesthetics, Literature, Theory* (2003), and *Historicism,* 2nd ed. (2003).

Colin Jager is Associate Professor of English at Rutgers University. He is the author of *The Book of God: Secularization and Design in the Romantic Era* (2007) and of *Unquiet Things: Secularism in the Romantic Age* (2014), and co-editor of *Working with a Secular Age* (forthcoming, 2015). He is working on a book on the political possibilities of romanticism, and is the recipient of a fellowship from the American Council of Learned Societies.

Robert Kaufman is Associate Professor of Comparative Literature and Co-Director of the Program in Critical Theory at the University of California, Berkeley. His research interests in experimental poetry and poetics since Romanticism, and in aesthetic, cultural, and literary theory, have led to three interrelated book projects, including *Negative Romanticism: Adornian Aesthetics in Keats, Shelley, and Modern Poetry* (forthcoming).

Jacques Khalip is Associate Professor of English and Associate Professor of Modern Culture and Media at Brown University. He is the author of *Anonymous Life:*

Romanticism and Dispossession (2009) and co-editor of *Releasing the Image: From Literature to New Media* (2011). Currently, he is working on a book entitled *Dwelling in Disaster*, a study of romantic reflections on extinction and wasted life.

Jacqueline M. Labbe is Professor and Pro-Vice-Chancellor for Arts and Humanities at the University of Sheffield (UK). She is the author of, most recently, *Writing Romanticism; Charlotte Smith and William Wordsworth, 1784–1807* (2011) and three other monographs. She is editor of *The History of British Women's Writing, 1750–1830* (2010) and several other collections and editions. She has published more than 40 articles on the complexities of Romantic-period gender identities and their relation to art and form, and on nineteenth-century children's literature. She is currently working on a study of the resonances between Charlotte Smith and Jane Austen.

Marjorie Levinson is F.L. Huetwell Professor of English at the University of Michigan. She is the author of *Keats's Life of Allegory: Origins of a Style* (1988), *Wordsworth's Great Period Poems* (1986), and *The Romantic Fragment Poem: Critique of a Form* (1986) as well as editor of *Rethinking Historicism* (1989).

Alan Liu is Professor of English at the University of California, Santa Barbara, and an affiliated faculty member of UCSB's Media Arts & Technology graduate program. He is the author of *Local Transcendence: Essays on Postmodern Historicism and the Database (2008), The Laws of Cool: Knowledge Work and the Culture of Information* (2005), and *Wordsworth: The Sense of History* (1989).

Maureen McLane is Professor of English at New York University. Her scholarly publications include *Balladeering, Minstrelsy, and the Making of British Romantic Poetry* (2008), *Romanticism and the Human Sciences: Poetry, Population, and the Discourse of the Species* (2000), and *The Cambridge Companion to British Romantic Poetry*, co-edited with James Chandler (2008). She has also published books of poetry and non-fiction, including *This Blue: Poems* (2014), *World Enough: Poems* (2010), *Same Life: Poems* (2008), and *My Poets* (2012).

Saree Makdisi is Professor of English and Comparative Literature at the University of California, Los Angeles and the author of *Making England Western: Occidentalism, Race and Imperial Culture* (2014), *Palestine Inside Out: An Everyday Occupation* (2008; revised and updated, 2010), *William Blake and the Impossible History of the 1790s* (2003), and *Romantic Imperialism* (1998). He is the co-editor of *The Arabian Nights in Historical Context* (2008) and *Marxism Beyond Marxism* (1996).

H.L. Malchow is Walter S. Dickson Professor of English and American History at Tufts University. He is the author of *Special Relations: The Americanization of Britain?* (2011), *Gothic Images of Race in Nineteenth Century Britain* (1996), *Gentlemen Capitalists: The Social and Political World of the Victorian Businessman* (1991), *Agitators and Promoters in the Age of Gladstone and Disraeli* (1983), and *Population Pressures: Emigration and Government in Late Nineteenth-Century Britain* (1979).

Jon Mee is Professor of Eighteenth-Century Studies in English at the University of York. His publications include *Conversable Worlds: Literature, Contention, and Community 1762–1830* (2011), *Romanticism, Enthusiasm, and Regulation: Poetics and the Policing of Culture in the Romantic Period* (2003), and *Dangerous Enthusiasm:*

William Blake and the Culture of Radicalism in the 1790s (1992). He is also the editor or co-editor of a number of volumes, including *Romanticism and Revolution: A Reader (2011), Blake and Conflict* (2008), *Trials for Treason and Sedition, 1792–4,* 8 vols (2006–7), and *The Selected Letters of John Keats* (2002).

Ann K. Mellor is Distinguished Professor of English and Women's Studies at the University of California, Los Angeles. Her books include *Mothers of the Nation: Women's Political Writing in England, 1780–1830* (2000), *Romanticism and Gender* (1993), *Mary Shelley: Her Fiction, Her Life, Her Monsters* (1988), *English Romantic Irony* (1980), and *Blake's Human Form Divine* (1974). She is the editor of *Romanticism and Feminism* (1988) and co-editor of *Passionate Encounters in a Time of Sensibility* (2000), *British Literature 1780–1830* (1996), and *The Other Mary Shelley* (1993).

Tom Mole is Reader in English Literature and Director of the Centre for the History of the Book at the University of Edinburgh, and an Adjunct Professor of Languages, Literatures and Cultures at McGill University. He is the author of *Byron's Romantic Celebrity* (2007) and the editor of *Romanticism and Celebrity Culture* (2009) and (with Michelle Levy) the *Broadview Reader in Book History* (2014). He led the Interacting with Print research group in 2008–2013 and won the International Byron Society's Elma Dangerfield Prize in 2009. He is currently researching the reception of Romantic writing in Victorian Britain.

Timothy Morton is Rita Shea Guffey Chair in English at Rice University. His books include *Nothing: Three Inquiries in Buddhism and Critical Theory* (forthcoming), *Hyperobjects: Philosophy and Ecology after the End of the World* (2013), *Realist Magic: Objects, Ontology, Causality* (2013), *The Ecological Thought* (2010), *Ecology without Nature* (2007), *The Cambridge Companion to Shelley* (2006), and *Shelley and the Revolution in Taste: The Body and the Natural World* (1995).

Lucy Newlyn is A.C. Cooper Fellow and Professor of English Language and Literature at Oxford University. She is the author of *William and Dorothy Wordsworth: 'All in Each Other' (2013), Reading, Writing, and Romanticism: The Anxiety of Reception* (2000), *"Paradise Lost" and the Romantic Reader* (1993; 2nd ed. 2001), and *Coleridge, Wordsworth, and the Language of Allusion* (1986; 2nd ed. 2001) and the editor or co-editor of several volumes, including *Branch-Lines: Edward Thomas and Contemporary Poetry* (2007), *Edward Thomas, Oxford* (2005), and *The Cambridge Companion to Coleridge* (2002).

Daniel O'Quinn is a Professor in the School of English and Theatre Studies at the University of Guelph. He is the author of *Entertaining Crisis in the Atlantic Imperium, 1770–1790* (2011), and *Staging Governance: Theatrical Imperialism in London, 1770–1800* (2005). He is also the co-editor of Lady Mary Wortley Montagu's *Turkish Embassy Letters* (2012) with Teresa Heffernan, and of the *Cambridge Companion to British Theatre, 1730–1830* (2007) with Jane Moody. He has also edited the *Travels of Mirza Abu Taleb Khan* (2008), and Lady Craven's *Travels through the Crimea to Constantinople* (2007). He is currently working on new book entitled *After Peace: Modernity and the Geo-politics of Emotion.*

Adela Pinch is Professor of English and Women's Studies at the University of Michigan. She is the author of *Thinking about Other People in Nineteenth-Century British Writing* (2010) and *Strange Fits of Passion: Epistemologies of Emotion, Hume to Austen* (1996) and editor of Jane Austen's *Emma* (2003).

Andrew Piper is Associate Professor in the Department of Languages, Literatures, and Cultures at McGill University. He is author of *Book Was There: Reading in Electronic Times* (2012) and *Dreaming in Books: The Making of the Bibliographic Imagination in the Romantic Age* (2009), and co-founder of the research group *Interacting with Print: Cultural Practices of Intermediality, 1700–1900*.

Alan Richardson is Professor of English at Boston College. His publications include *The Neural Sublime: Cognitive Theories and Romantic Texts* (2010), *British Romanticism and the Science of the Mind* (2001), *Literature, Education, and Romanticism: Reading as Social Practice, 1780–1832* (1994), and *A Mental Theater: Poetic Drama and Consciousness in the Romantic Age* (1988). He is the editor or co-editor of several volumes, including *Early Black British Writing* (2004) and *Romanticism, Race, and Imperial Culture* (1996). His current research involves Romantic theories and representations of sub-jectivity, embodied agency, and language in relation to eighteenth- and early nineteenth-century neuroscientific speculation and experimentation.

Margaret Russett is Professor and Chair of English at the University of Southern California. Her books include *Fictions and Fakes: Forging Romantic Authenticity, 1760–1845* (2006) and *De Quincey's Romanticism: Canonical Minority and the Forms of Transmission* (1997). She is currently at work on a book that combines her interests in Romanticism and translation studies with reflections on multilingualism, adop-tion, and *ostranenie*. She has been the recipient of fellowships and grants from the Guggenheim, Fulbright, and Mellon Foundations and has held visiting appoint-ments at Bogazici University and the Bread Loaf School of English.

Sharon Ruston is Professor and Chair in Romanticism at Lancaster University. She has published *Creating Romanticism: Case Studies in the Literature, Science and Medicine of the 1790s* (2013), *Shelley and Vitality* (2005), and *Romanticism: An Introduction* (2007), and has edited *Literature and Science* (2008) and co-edited with David Higgins *Teaching Romanticism* (2010). She is currently co-editing *The Collected Letters of Sir Humphry Davy*. She has received grants from the AHRC, British Academy and other bodies and is a Fellow of the English Association.

Robert Ryan is Professor Emeritus of English at Rutgers University – Camden. He is the author of *The Romantic Reformation: Religious Politics in English Literature, 1789–1824* (2004) and *Keats: The Religious Sense* (1976).

Clifford Siskin is Henry W. and Albert A. Berg Professor of English and American Literature at New York University and Director of The Re:Enlightenment Project at New York University and the New York Public Library. He is the author of *Blaming the System: Enlightenment and the Forms of Modernity* (forthcoming), *The Work of Writing: Literature and Social Change in Britain 1700–1830* (1998), and *The Historicity of Romantic Discourse* (1988) and, with William Warner, co-editor of *This Is Enlightenment* (2010).

Clara Tuite is Head of English and Theatre Studies at the University of Melbourne. She is the author of *Romantic Austen: Sexual Politics and the Literary Canon* (2002) and the co-editor of *A Companion to Jane Austen* (2009) and *Romantic Sociability: Social Networks and Literary Culture in Britain, 1770–1840* (2002).

Orrin N.C. Wang is Professor of English and Comparative Literature at the University of Maryland at College Park. He is the author of *Romantic Sobriety: Sensation, Revolution, Commodification, History* (2011) and *Fantastic Modernity: Dialectical Readings in Romanticism and Theory* (1996), and the series editor of the *Romantic Circles Praxis Series*. His current project investigates the historical and transhistorical dimensions of Romantic media. *Romantic Sobriety* was awarded the Jean-Pierre Barricelli Prize in 2011.

William Warner is Professor of English at the University of California, Santa Barbara. He is the author of *Protocols of Liberty: Communication Innovation and the American Revolution* (2013), *Licensing Entertainment: The Elevation of Novel Reading in Britain (1684–1750)* (1998*), Chance and the Text of Experience: Freud, Nietzsche, and Shakespeare's Hamlet* (1986), and *Reading Clarissa: The Struggles of Interpretation* (1979). He is co-editor, with Clifford Siskin, of *This Is Enlightenment* (2010) and, with Deirdre Lynch, of *Cultural Institutions of the Novel* (1996).

Daniel E. White is Professor of English at the University of Toronto. His teaching and research address Romantic literature, the history of the book, religious nonconformity in the long eighteenth century, and the culture of the early British Empire. Author of *From Little London to Little Bengal: Religion, Print, and Modernity in Early British India, 1793–1835* (2013) and *Early Romanticism and Religious Dissent* (2006) and co-editor of *Robert Southey: Later Poetical Works, 1811–1838* (2012), he is now working on a new book, *Bengal Annuals and Orient Pearls: Imperial Print Culture in Circulation*.

Susan Wolfson is Professor of English at Princeton University. She is the author of *Romantic Interactions: Social Being & the Turns of Literary Action* (2010), *Borderlines: The Shiftings of Gender in British Romanticism* (2006), *Formal Charges: The Shaping of Poetry in British Romanticism* (1997), *Women in the Curriculum: British Literature: Discipline Analysis* (1997), and *The Questioning Presence: Wordsworth, Keats, and the Interrogative Mode in Romantic Poetry* (1986). She has edited or co-edited several volumes, including *Northanger Abbey: An Annotated Edition* (2014), *The Annotated Frankenstein* (2012), *Reading for Form* (2007), and *Felicia Hemans: Selected Poems, Letters, & Reception Materials* (2000).

Acknowledgements

The publishers have made every effort to contact authors/copyright holders of works reprinted in *British Romanticism* and to obtain permission to publish extracts. This has not been possible in every case, however, and we would welcome correspondence from those individuals/companies whom we have been unable to trace. Any omissions brought to our attention will be remedied in future editions.

Part 1: Politics, ideology, and the literary

1   Cambridge University Press and the author for kind permission to reprint an abridged version of Marjorie Levinson, *Wordsworth's Great Period Poems: Four Essays* (Cambridge UP, 1986), chapter 1, "Insight and Oversight: Reading 'Tintern Abbey'," pp 14–57, and notes. © Cambridge University Press 1986, reproduced with permission.

2   Wiley Blackwell and the author for permission to reprint an abridged version of Paul Hamilton, "Keats and Critique" in Marjorie Levinson, Marilyn Butler, Jerome McGann, and Paul Hamilton, *Rethinking Historicism: Critical Readings in Romantic History* (Oxford: Blackwell, 1989). pp 108–115, 120–123, 124–128, 127–137 with cuts.

3   University of Chicago Press and James Chandler for kind permission to reprint an abridged version of *England in 1819: The Politics of Literary Culture and the Case of Romantic Historicism* (Chicago UP, 1999), chapter 6, "Byron's Causes: The Moral Mechanics of Don Juan," pp 350–388.

Part 2: Aesthetics and literary form

5   University of California for permission to reprint an abridged version of Alan Liu, "Local Transcendence: Cultural Criticism, Postmodernism, and the Romanticism of Detail," *Representations*, 1990: pp 77–78, 80–113 with cuts. Copyright © 1990, The Regents of the University of California.

6   Taylor and Francis Group LLC Books for permission to reprint an abridged version of Frances Ferguson, *Solitude and the Sublime: Romanticism and the Aesthetics of Individuation* (Routledge, 1992), chapter 7, "Historicism, Deconstruction, and Wordsworth," pp 146–157 with cuts, 163–169.

7   Kaufman, Robert. "Legislators of the Post-Everything World: Shelley's Defence of Adorno," ELH: English Literary History 63:3 (1996), 707–733. ©1996 The Johns Hopkins University Press. Reprinted with permission of Johns Hopkins University Press.

Part 3: Audiences and reading publics

9   Oxford University Press for permission to reprint an abridged version of Lucy Newlyn, *Reading, Writing, and Romanticism: The Anxiety of Reception* (New York: Oxford UP, 2000), chapter 1, "The Sense of an Audience," pp 3–48.

10 Indiana University Press for permission to reprint an abridged version of Ann K. Mellor, *Mothers of the Nation: Women's Political Writing in England. 1780–1830* (© Indiana UP, 2000), chapter 2, "Theater as the School of Virtue," 39–51; 61–68, and notes with cuts. Reprinted with permission of Indiana University Press.

11 Gilmartin, Kevin. "Study to be Quiet: Hannah More and the Invention of Conservative Culture in Britain," ELH: English Literary History 70:2 (2003). pp. 493–501, 511–512, 515–516, 523, 528–530, 534–540. © 2003 The Johns Hopkins University Press. Reprinted with permission of Johns Hopkins University Press.

Part 4: Authorship and authority

13 Reprinted from *The Achievement of Literary Authority: Gender, History, and the Waverley Novels*, by Ina Ferris. Copyright © 1991 by Cornell University. Used by permission of the publisher, Cornell University Press.

14 Edinburgh University Press and the author for kind permission to reprint an abridged version of Andrew Bennett, *Romantic Poets and the Culture of Posterity* (Cambridge UP, 1999), chapter 6, "Keats's Prescience," *Romanticism*, 1996 Volume 2, Page 9–26.

15 Trustees of Boston University for permission to reprint an abridged version of Anne Frey, "DeQuincey's Imperial Systems," *Studies in Romanticism* (2005): 41–61.

Part 5: Gender, sexuality, and the body

17 Abridged version of Susan Wolfson, "Gendering the Soul," in *Romantic Women Writers: Voices and Countervoices*, edited by Paula R. Feldman and Theresa M. Kelley (U Press of New England, 1995). pp 33–38, 52–67 with cuts. © University Press of New England, Lebanon, NH. Reprinted with permission pp 33–68.

18 Abridged version of "The Domestication of Genius: Cowper and the Rise of the Suburban Man," pp. 63–89, from *Romantic Genius: The Prehistory of a Homosexual Role*, by Andrew Elfenbein. Copyright © 1999 Columbia University Press. Reprinted with permission of the publisher.

19 Cambridge University Press and the author for permission to reprint an abridged version of Clara Tuite, *Romantic Austen: Sexual Politics and the Literary Canon* (Cambridge UP, 2002), chapter 2, "Sensibility, Free Indirect Style, and the Romantic Technology of Discretion," 56–97, and notes. © Clara Tuite 2002, published by Cambridge University Press, reproduced with permission.

Part 6: Racism, nationalism, imperialism

21 Oxford University Press Journals for permission to reprint an abridged version of H.L. Malchow, "Was Frankenstein's Monster 'a Man and a Brother'?" *Past & Present* 139 (1993): 90, Copyright © 1993, Oxford University Press.

22 The University of Chicago Press and the author for permission to reprint an abridged version of Saree Makdisi, *William Blake and the Impossible History of the 1790s* (U of Chicago P, 2003), chapter 5 "Blake and Romantic Imperialism," pp 204–259.

23 Bewell, Alan. *Romanticism and Colonial Disease.* pp. 96–108,119–125,127–128, 319–322. ©2000 Johns Hopkins University Press. Reprinted with permission of Johns Hopkins University Press.

Part 7: Affects and ethics

25 *Strange Fits of Passion: Epistemologies of Emotion, Hume to Austen* by Adela Pinch, Copyright © 1996 by the Board of Trustees of the Leland Stanford Jr. University.

26 The University of Chicago Press and Julie Ellison for permission to reprint an abridged version of *Cato's Tears and the Making of Anglo-American Emotion* (U of Chicago P, 1999), chapter 4, "Female Authorship, Public Fancy," 97–122, and notes.

27 Reprinted from "A Disappearance in the World: Wollstonecraft and Melancholy Skepticism" by Jacques Khalip in *Criticism: A Quarterly for Literature and the Arts*, Vol. 47, No.1. Copyright © 2005 Wayne State University Press, with the permission of Wayne State University Press.

Part 8: Religion and secularization

29 Cambridge University Press and the author for permission to reprint an abridged version of Robert M. Ryan, *Romantic Reformation: Religious Politics in English Literature. 1789–1824* (Cambridge UP, 1997), chapter 7, "The Unknown God," pp 193–223, and notes. © Cambridge University Press 1997, reproduced with permission.

30 Oxford University Press and the author for permission to reprint an abridged version of Jon Mee, *Romanticism. Enthusiasm. and Regulation: Poetics and the Policing of Culture in the Romantic Period* (Oxford UP, 2003), pp 214–217, 236–256.

31 Cambridge University Press and the author for kind permission to reprint an abridged version of *Early Romanticism and Religious Dissent* (Cambridge UP, 2006), chapter 4, "Godwin, Wollstonecraft, and the Legacies of Dissent," pp 87–118. © Daniel E. White 2006, published by Cambridge University Press, reproduced with permission.

Part 9: Modernity and postmodernity

33 The University of Chicago and the author for kind permission to reprint an abridged version of Jerome Christensen, "The Romantic Movement at the End of History," *Critical Inquiry* (1994): pp. 452–476.

34 Favret, Mary A. "Everyday War," *ELH: English Literary History* 72:3 (2005), 605–608, 618–633. © 2005 The Johns Hopkins University Press. Reprinted with permission of Johns Hopkins University Press.

35 Duncan, Ian; Scott's Shadow. © 2007 by Princeton University Press. Reprinted by permission of Princeton University Press.

Part 10: Sciences of mind, body, and nature

37 Cambridge University Press and the author for kind permission to reprint an abridged version of *British Romanticism and the Science of Mind* (Cambridge UP, 2001), chapter 2, "Coleridge and the New Unconscious," 39–65, and notes. © Alan Richardson 2001, published by Cambridge University Press, reproduced with permission.

38 Trustees of Boston University for permission to reprint an abridged version of Timothy Morton, "John Clare's Dark Ecology," *Studies in Romanticism* 47 (2008): 179–193.

39 Reprinted by permission of copyright owner, the Modern Language Association of America, from "The Monster in the Rainbow: Keats and the Science of Life," PMLA (2002): 433–448

Part 11: Literature, media, mediation

41 The University of Chicago Press and the author for kind permission to reprint an abridged version of Maureen McLane, "Ballads and Bards: British Romantic Orality," *Modern Philology* (2001): 423–443.

42 The University of Chicago Press and the author for permission to reprint an abridged version of Andrew Piper, *Dreaming in Books: The Making of the Bibliographic Imagination in the Romantic Age* (U of Chicago Press, 2009), chapter 3, "Processing," 85–120, and notes.

43 An abridged version of Clifford Siskin and William Warner, "If This is Enlightenment Then What is Romanticism?," *European Romantic Review* 22.3 (2011): 281–291. Copyright © 2011 Routledge. Reprinted by permission of the publisher Taylor & Francis Ltd, http://www.tandf.co.uk/journals.

General introduction

The criticism of Romantic literature from the Victorians to post-historicism

Mark Canuel

What is Romanticism? What does it mean to be Romantic? Is Romanticism a state of mind, a collection of beliefs, a set of social practices? Are those mental states, beliefs, and practices associated with a specific historical period? If so, how does a historical view of the term differ from our conventional definition of "romantic" today – that is, our way of describing people, places, experiences, or relationships as romantic?

Questions about exactly what it means to be "Romantic" lie behind a great deal of recent critical interpretations of works written during the 1790s and early 1800s (what historians have come to call the Romantic period), but they were also very much alive during that period of years. William Wordsworth briefly distinguished the "classic lyre" from the "romantic harp" in the Preface to his 1815 *Poems*. The distinction, perhaps suggesting something like a Romantic epoch in music and song, drew on a common contrast between the pagan lyre and Judeo-Christian harp (the harp was also associated with Irish and Scottish bards). Wordsworth's point in his Preface, however, was to say that, for most of his lyrical poems, an instrument was not required, only "an animated or impassioned recitation, adapted to the subject" (Wordsworth 1984: 629). The French novelist and critic Madame de Staël gave this distinction more historical precision in her *De l'Allemagne*, in which she contrasted a neoclassical admiration of Greek and Roman models with a Romantic admiration for chivalric Christian romance. More than merely indicating a preference for one canon of literature over another, she understood "Romantic" to refer to a distinct set of tastes and aesthetic practices (loosely derived from chivalric romance), one that emphasized heightened personal "feelings" and inspiration over imitation, "native" culture over antiquity, and religious faith over a submission to "fate" (de Staël 1987: 301).

At least some aspects of de Staël's account of "Romantic" (itself an adaptation of the German philosopher Friedrich Schlegel's) are not far from English usage of the same period to describe a range of images, texts, people, and situations. William Hazlitt used the term to describe a current style of writing that was "wild and expansive" (Hazlitt 1983: 306). In his poem "Kubla Khan," Samuel Taylor Coleridge referred to a "deep romantic chasm" as the mysterious place where the "mighty fountain," and the "sacred river" Alph, had its origin. The peculiar feature of Coleridge's diction – the chasm "slanted / Down the green hill athwart a cedarn cover," as if vacancy or negative space could be credited with an action – suggested that in this poem "romantic" described the mysterious and exotic powers of poetic inspiration to which the speaker ultimately alluded in his desire to recapture the song of the "Abyssinian Maid" in the last stanza. "Romantic" also connected to a sense of spirituality – the place was "holy," the river was "sacred" – that the poet attempted to recover or remember (Coleridge 1912: 297–8).

The word "romantic" was used by writers of the day in a sense that was not always admiring or positive. Mary Wollstonecraft seemed to give an entirely negative view of the "romantic" in her *Vindication of the Rights of Woman*. Opposing the influence of male writers from John Milton to Jean-Jacques Rousseau, she criticized women's "romantic wavering feelings" and a "romantic twist of the mind" that compromised their ability to exercise reason (Wollstonecraft 1994: 146, 271). Jane Austen's *Sense and Sensibility* was also somewhat similar in its judgments on the flaws of Marianne Dashwood, which were "romantic" insofar as they demonstrated only the "charms of enthusiasm and ignorance of the world" (Austen 2002: 43).

The examples of Coleridge and Wollstonecraft alone suggest a great deal of complication that attends any attempt to define what is "romantic" in Romanticism. The two authors seemed to be using "romantic" in ways that nearly opposed each other. Coleridge's use appeared to be about the poet's autonomous power, acquired but distanced from the song of the maid even as it was likened to the quest of the sovereign Khan. It was a quest that appeared to depend upon the abstract and performative power of language. Wollstonecraft seemed to use the term to describe a state of being (and also a practice of reading and writing) that was not abstract but embodied; it appeared to be a synonym for "sentimental," and it conjured up images not of autonomous power but of subjection or even enslavement (Wollstonecraft 1994: 271).

In her *Memoirs of Modern Philosophers*, Elizabeth Hamilton added a revealing dimension to Wollstonecraft's account of the "romantic" turn of mind. She made one of her heroines in her satirical novel into an enemy of domestic attachment and conventional female sentiment (in the manner of Wollstonecraft, Mary Hays, and William Godwin), but she was also a "romantic" proponent of impractical political projects and metaphysical speculation (Hamilton 2000: 178). Of course, Hamilton's rhetoric indicated the degree to which "romantic" could be, as it is today, applied as a slur to anyone who didn't accept the author's reality. But there was also something more subtle going on in Hamilton's portrayal, suggesting that perhaps Wollstonecraft was a certain kind of romantic figure despite her own efforts to avoid an overly romantic sensibility. That is, while Wollstonecraft resisted a romantic emphasis on mere sentiment, her emphasis on the use of reason to imagine new social relations and institutions – democratic governments, gender equality, and national education, for instance – bore a greater resemblance to Coleridge's "romantic" lyricism than we might initially think.

We have drifted from "Romantic" to "romantic" – from an account of a movement to an account of individual images and characters. But the abstracting, idealizing, and imaginative powers connected with these individual "romantic" instances still help us to get a sense of at least one very prominent way of thinking about what it meant to be Romantic even to writers of the day. (Readers should note that there are many ways of defining Romanticism, and this has long been a subject of debate at least since the 1920s [Lovejoy 1924: 235]). It was these powers in particular, furthermore, that were of crucial significance to later generations who sought to describe and analyze the works immediately preceding and following the French Revolution. Indeed, in these brief introductory remarks, I would particularly emphasize how an interest in the powers of literary imagination made a great many works written in the 1790s to the early 1800s not merely into subjects of literary criticism but into emblems of what it meant to be literary.

These powers caused much discomfort, for instance, among Victorian writers who were only children at the height of Lord Byron's fame. Admittedly, Matthew Arnold (1922) admired William Wordsworth's poetry and even edited a selection of his poems with an appreciative preface in 1879. John Stuart Mill also praised Wordsworth and credited his poetry with turning him against what he regarded as the narrow calculations of utilitarian philosophy, and toward "a greatly increased interest in the common feelings and common destiny of human beings" (Mill 1874: 148). But this kind of praise was severely qualified. Arnold looked back at the English poets from Wordsworth to Byron and criticized them for having a lack of "data," "materials," and "ideas" about the world (Arnold 1914: 13, 18); he restricted his admiration even for Wordsworth by eliminating *The Prelude* from serious consideration and praising him only insofar as he was a moral writer (Arnold 1914: 13). In related ways, other Victorians criticized a whole range of Romantic writers for their inattention to the human and natural world. Mill faulted Byron for cultivating "vehement and sensual passion" and "sullenness" as a result of having "worn out all pleasures" and rendered life itself "vapid" and "uninteresting" (Mill 1874: 147, 146). John Ruskin accused writers like Keats of imposing their emotion and imagination on, and thus denying the truth of, nature (Ruskin 1965: 77).

Early in the twentieth century, T.S. Eliot echoed Mill's concern with the degree to which poetry could address human interest when he claimed that Wordsworth and Coleridge's achievement was to theorize poetry as "an expression of a totality of unified interests" (Eliot 1933: 72). But in this maneuver, related to his praise for William Blake as well, Eliot in fact refocused the concerns of earlier critics, turning his attention away from a worry about the Romantics' lack of relation to worldly knowledge, and toward poetry as a "totality." Thus he converted poetic abstraction into an object of admiration rather than anxiety or derision. Later critics – especially adherents of "New Criticism" (a term first used by John Crowe Ransom in 1941 to describe critical trends since Eliot) – went still further and quite nearly inverted the priorities of Arnold and many of his contemporaries. If Arnold argued that Romantic poetry's deficiency was that it lacked the information that could be provided to it by the work of criticism, the New Critics argued that even the most enigmatic poems' terms were, on their own, sufficient. A poem, in the words of poet Archibald MacLeish and later quoted by critics W.K. Wimsatt and Monroe Beardsley, "should not mean / But be" (MacLeish 1985: 107).

With versions of the claim that poetry was about abstract "being" rather than about moral, political, or emotional "meaning," critics in the first half of the twentieth century frequently found Romantic literature to provide particularly compelling defenses for their views. As it increasingly placed the highest value on the integrity of the individual literary work, the modernist appreciation of Romantic writing, even though seemingly far more generous than that of the Victorians, ended up adopting a highly restrictive view of what was actually written during the late 1790s and early 1800s. Such inclusions and exclusions should be noted very carefully. Eliot had little patience for Byron or Scott; he considered both to be "society entertainers" rather than writers of great literature (Eliot 1933: 78). He also dismissed Shelley's poetry (as Arnold had done) as juvenile, muddy, and didactic (Eliot 1933: 80–4); the inverse of Byron, Shelley seemed, in his view, to write poetry solely as a vehicle for his passionately held but incoherent beliefs.

The New Critics, following in Eliot's footsteps, were also rigidly selective in their view of what was worth careful study. The elegant symmetries of Keats's odes and the serene meditations of Wordsworth's nature poetry won the most admirers. Allen Tate saw Keats as a poet who was attracted to embodied experience but also aesthetically distanced from it; the idealizing impulse made the poet "among the few heroes of literature" and made his poetry an appropriate object for literary critics. This was because critics themselves, he argued, should also restrict their concerns to literature rather than science or politics (Tate 1955: 210). W.K. Wimsatt, with similar grounds for evaluation, admired the nature lyrics of Wordsworth and Coleridge because they showed a concentrated form of imaginative attention freed from religious and moral "association" extrinsic to the observed scene (Wimsatt 1954: 107). Wordsworth and Coleridge made Cleanth Brooks's opening case for the centrality of "paradox" in the structure of great poetry in his book *The Well Wrought Urn*, which also contained one of the most celebrated appreciations of Keats's "Ode on a Grecian Urn" from the twentieth century (Brooks 1947: 1–8, 151–66).

Some of these critics, we must admit, occasionally worked strenuously to make surprising instances fit their theories. Even when faced with a poetic fragment like Coleridge's "Kubla Khan," that is, Wimsatt and Beardsley still found a "unity" present in the poem (Wimsatt and Beardsley 1954: 12). Tate saw Keats's *Lamia* – considered by some of today's critics to be noteworthy for its jarring departures from poetic propriety – as a model of aesthetic perfection on a par with the odes (Tate 1955:197). But the many works excluded from consideration by this generation of scholars were also significant, and these choices made a long-lasting mark on the history of criticism. This was at least partly because New Criticism claimed to be an objective and disinterested criticism even while it passionately yet surreptitiously attached itself to restricted poetic embodiments or demonstrations of its practices. Indeed, when Romanticism was defined by such critics, the examples, only slightly more generous than Eliot's, seldom strayed from a list of poets beyond Wordsworth, Coleridge, Keats, and occasionally Blake and Shelley. When New Critics and like-minded formalists turned to study the novel, most of them – searching for models of aesthetic perfection that they also located in George Eliot and Henry James – saw Jane Austen as the only writer worthy of attention. F.R. Leavis's appreciation for Austen's mastery of form and "impersonalize[d]… moral tensions" – which he could not find anywhere else among other novelists of her day – could stand as a representative instance (Leavis 1963: 7). Many writers in both poetry and prose represented in the present volume – including Anna Letitia Barbauld, Maria Edgeworth, and Charlotte Smith – suffered from a critical neglect motivated by distinct tastes for sublime contemplation over quotidian observation, or for lyrical selfhood over communal histories. This neglect, furthermore, was clearly reflected in the fact that works by many writers out of favor with twentieth-century critics were not made available in easily accessible paperback editions for students until the late twentieth century.

New Critical methods and theories, it should also be noted, had a profound influence on other critics of the Romantic period, even when their claims departed slightly from the New Critical formalist idiom. For instance, M.H. Abrams (whose work is cited by critics in this volume) was far more interested than New Critics were in mapping out models of intellectual history. His influential study *Natural Supernaturalism* argued that Romanticism internalized the human relation to God so that poets in the Romantic tradition worshipped the mind, or man himself (Abrams 1971). Even so, his work here and in *The Mirror and the Lamp* owed a great deal to New Critical methods of close reading (Abrams 1953); theoretically, Abrams's work argued – in historical and philosophical terms – for Romanticism's emphasis on, if not discovery of, self-sufficient literary forms. For these reasons alone, it is hardly surprising that some critics described him simply as a New Critic despite Abrams's own discomfort with that association and general reluctance to align his work with a specific theoretical camp (de Man 1986: 6). A similar point about New Criticism's far-reaching influence could be made about Earl Wasserman's reading of Shelley's idealism in *Shelley: A Critical Reading,* and about his reading of Romanticism's emphasis on poetry as "cosmic wholeness" in *The Subtler Language* (Wasserman 1971, 1959: 186).

In the work of some New Critics and those who were influenced by them we can observe a certain degree of slippage in terms occurring in critical thought: a slippage between accounts of poems and accounts of the minds of the makers of poems. Thus New Criticism occasionally seemed to be associated with some degree of emphasis on an individual's psychology or mental process. But a careful study of this history (like Frances Ferguson's [1991]) would reveal that one claim did not necessarily imply the other; in fact (as we have seen), many New Critics were often hostile to a discussion of anything that looked like the author's beliefs or attitudes beyond what could be found in the literary work. Harold Bloom, another influential critic of the Romantic period whose works are quoted in this volume, studied with Abrams and turned Abrams's emphasis on the human soul into what appeared to be a more full-blown psychoanalytic theory. In the 1950s, Lionel Trilling had described Romantic writing as a triumph of heroic selfhood, but Bloom's vision was significantly more complicated than Trilling's emphasis on a merely individual assertion of will (Trilling, 1955: 3–49, 118–50). Bloom's account, rather than emphasizing the ego or subjectivity of the poet, construed readings that were psychological only because they formally rehearsed an Oedipal struggle between the father and son, the precursor and ephebe. Poems are "necessarily about *other poems*," he claimed, and relations between earlier poems and later poems always involve the later poem powerfully "misreading" the first in order to establish "priority" over it (Bloom 1975: 18, 51).

In Bloom's account of this struggle for priority – which he memorably called the "anxiety of influence" – John Milton, author of *Paradise Lost,* loomed the largest as a father-figure. This was because, as a poet who was able to incorporate precursors from Ovid to Shakespeare while also correcting them, he seemed like an archetype of literary authority itself. And the Romantics loomed the largest as rebellious poets, because of their powerful awareness of Milton's influence matched with their Satanic overturning of it. The insight that Bloom offered was certainly important for revising ideas about individual subjectivity, but it was even more important for revising ideas about unitary poetic form espoused by the New Critics. For the meaning of an individual work, in Bloom's view, was to be found not only in itself but also somewhere else, making poetic meaning "radically indeterminate" (Bloom 1975: 69). Any reading of a poem might eventually get bent out of shape by turning to a previous author's work, which was also revising the work of another, and so on.

This was one of the points of connection between Bloom's work and the work of deconstructionist critics such as Paul de Man and Geoffrey Hartman with whom he was associated (Bloom dedicated *A Map of Misreading* to de Man; de Man had written an insightful review of Bloom's earlier book *The Anxiety of Influence* that coaxed it into a position closer to his own [de Man 1983: 273]). Indeed, the sense of a relation between one poet and a precursor in Bloom's work related to a more extreme point – moving beyond the interest in agonistic psychological relations – that de Man made about the way that all language works. For de Man, the unity of the natural world – and the further unity of mind and nature that New Critics and other mid-twentieth-century formalists found in Romantic writing – was visible in Romantic texts only as a defense against a deeper inauthenticity and dissolution at work in the operations of linguistic signs. Thus de Man, in a well-known reading of the "Blessed be the infant Babe" passage from Wordsworth's *Prelude*, claimed that the "totalizing" power of language was palpable not as a guarantee of unity but rather as a "part of a process of endless differentiation" that was the "undoer of unity." Language – particularly poetic language – produced a "logic," he claimed, quoting *The Prelude*, which could "find no surface where its power might sleep" (de Man 1984: 90–2).

Romanticism continued to occupy a starring role among these deconstructionist critics. But the reasons for the centrality of Romantic texts were now different; poems of the period were valued not because meaning came from formal unity but because meaning came from "endless differentiation" produced by the figurative interconnections produced by poetic language. The anthology *Deconstruction and Criticism*, featuring essays by leading critics of the Yale School (the name applied to the group of deconstructionist critics there), provided a case in point. It consisted of a series of essays primarily on Percy Shelley's *The Triumph of Life*, and this prominent position – a reversal of many generations of judgments about Shelley's poetry – said much about precisely what it was that deconstruction is critics saw and valued in Romantic writing. The poem's dizzying succession of visions frustrated rather than assured understanding, leading Jacques Derrida to find it an instance of a text that "overruns all the limits assigned to it," and de Man to describe its language as demonstrating a "performative power" wrought from the "madness of words" (Bloom et al. 1979: 69, 54, 56).

It is far beyond the scope of this introduction to speculate on the reasons for general changes across the landscape of literary theory and criticism – that is, to explore in any kind of detail *why* it is that trends have developed at specific times. Some critics have suggested that in fact the changes in critical theory and practice in the past 20 years or more have still depended upon assumptions inherited from New Criticism. In *After the New Criticism*, Frank Lentricchia suspected Bloom and de Man of aestheticizing tendencies that repeated assumptions of earlier critics they hoped to overturn (Lentricchia 1980: 313, 326). More recently, Mary Poovey wrote in equally provocative ways about the sustained appeal of the New Critics' organic accounts of literature, which were themselves derived from Romantic organic accounts. An assumption about organic form as self-contained "continues to organize most of the strains of criticism that now dominate U.S. practice" (Poovey 2001: 432). Practices of close reading and narratives of generic development (among other things), she argued, inadvertently support the very traditions of New Critical formalism that contemporary criticism may be attempting to overturn.

Even if we proceed with some caution about exaggerating shifts in critical temper as radical departures, it is hard to deny that "new historicist" critics of the 1980s and 1990s, several of whom are represented in this volume, set out in very explicit ways to distinguish their practices and theoretical approaches from critics in the previous several decades of the twentieth century. Critics and theorists have suggested that new historicism's dissatisfaction with formalism and deconstruction was at least in part inspired by larger shifts in the structure of the academy and other social institutions. Brook Thomas and Paul Hamilton, for instance, locate new historicism within other forms of institutional dissatisfaction, resistance, and demographic change in the 1980s (Thomas 1993: vi–xvi; Hamilton 2003: 131). Informed by the work of theorists such as Michel Foucault and Louis Althusser, new historicists sought to consider literary works not as autonomous entities but as ineradicable parts of the cultural contexts in which they emerged. Still more specifically, they sought to consider literary works as part of the generation and maintenance of power structures within social institutions and groups of individuals marked by the features of race, gender, and class. As in all instances of critical "schools," there was significant variation among practitioners. Catharine Gallagher and Stephen Greenblatt – among the founding new historicist critics at UC Berkeley – nevertheless generalized among methods, claiming that they shared a dissatisfaction with the traditional methods of "close readings" of literary forms, which resulted in "a sense of wondering admiration, linked to the celebration of genius." A new generation of scholars sought to remedy the apparent abstraction of such approaches with a study of "the mutual embeddedness of art and history" (Gallagher and Greenblatt 2001: 9, 7).

In this sense, new historicists wanted to be arguing not only against New Critics, but also against older methods of history-making. Earlier scholars like Abrams, Wasserman, and even Bloom mention historical details in their works, but late twentieth-century historicists sought to differentiate their cultural and materialist histories from earlier "intellectual" histories or "histories of ideas." This shift from intellectual to cultural history entailed analysis of writers in terms of their relation to a host of social realities: the French Revolution, political dissent and unrest, conservative and repressive British reactions to the Revolution, and urban and rural poverty. Among the many important works of historicist criticism on Romanticism, there could be found a cluster of closely related claims about the connection between literature and its historical context. Marilyn Butler's important study *Romantics, Rebels, and Reactionaries* took aim at Abrams and Bloom, showing how their "hazy" versions of history depended upon a false notion that Romanticism depended only upon revolutionary forms of individualism; she encouraged instead a greater attention to "the community which generated art and provided its public" (Butler 1981: 9–10). To do anything other than see the poet as a "citizen" rather than a "solitary" would be to accept Romanticism's own deluded version of itself – a version accepted by the critics from the Victorians to the Yale School (Butler 1981: 9).

There had certainly been some important earlier works on Romanticism that discussed literature and its connection to more concrete political positions and movements: David Erdman and Carl Woodring, among others, did historical work that could be contrasted with the more intellectual historicism of Abrams or Bloom; they traced the politically radical or conservative beliefs of Romantic writers as they expressed them in their work (Erdman 1954; Woodring 1970). Crucial to the work of new historicists, however, was not merely the suggestion that critics needed to understand history as it was expressed in and through literature, but rather that they needed to understand literary works as mythologized versions of history, or even as denials of it. And thus the interpretation of literature, in Jerome McGann's influential study *The Romantic Ideology*, needed to move beyond the "idealized localities" of literary construction in order to study the "actual human issues with which the poetry is concerned" (McGann 1985: 1).

In one sense, works of Romantic writing continued to be central in this increasingly dominant mode of academic literary theorizing, which inflected literary scholarship at campuses across the country. As many have noted, new historicism grew to prominence in Renaissance Studies and American Studies, but historicism's ambition to distance itself from any abstract "celebration of genius" would seem to find its most trenchant occasion for analysis in works of Romantic art and its ideology – its false consciousness, that is, about the poet's ability to "transcend" the world of "politics and money" (McGann 1985: 13). In her essay on Wordsworth's "Tintern Abbey" excerpted in this volume (appreciatively cited by McGann before its publication [McGann 1985: 86]), Marjorie Levinson argued eloquently against Wordsworth-worship by appraising the material conditions behind the poem's idealizing gestures. She did this by producing a thick description of Wordsworth's historical circumstances, which included the particular political climate of the moment and the features of the English landscape that Wordsworth would have seen when he composed his poem "Tintern Abbey." Other historicist critics, including John Barrell, Alan Liu, and David Simpson made important contributions to the study of Romantic literature's tendency to abstract itself from historical circumstance – an abstraction that both New Critics and deconstructionist critics, with their exclusive attention to the forms and figurative language of poetry, had (new historicists claimed) uncritically incorporated into their methodology.

Even with their criticism of conventional genius-worship, historicist critics of the past few decades continued to focus on many of the same writers that occupied formalist and deconstructionist literary analysis. Austen, Blake, Wordsworth, Coleridge, Shelley, and Keats endured as the focus of many a distinguished work of criticism by scholars already mentioned here. Furthermore, the most casual glance at current publications in the field of Romanticism would confirm that these writers continue to attract spirited commentary. At the same time, however, the new historicist emphasis on context, which necessarily included the context of other writers of the Romantic age, distributed critical attention beyond an established canon of works solidified by a century of critical appreciation. Criticism of the later twentieth century extended into a range of works "outside the proper circles of interest" (Gallagher and Greenblatt 2001: 9). This move to address works and authors previously marginalized only begins to suggest the ways in which historicist trends in the late twentieth century need to be considered not merely as an insulated movement but instead in close connection with advances in other theoretical currents within and beyond literary studies in the academy, including African American Studies, feminism, postcolonial theory, queer studies, and multiethnic studies. In particular, new historicism appropriated theoretical paradigms from such fields as African American Studies and feminism, both of which involved critiques of conventional raced and gendered power structures; new historicism in turn enriched those areas of study. H.L. Malchow's essay on race in *Frankenstein* in this volume, for instance, shows how a critical study of race and a historicist emphasis on Mary Shelley's cultural context can be tightly woven together in order to reveal the novel's relation to a power structure at work at a specific moment in time, and defended within specific contemporary texts.

The influence of new historicism and related trends upon canon-formation was visible at several levels. Critics studied lesser-known works by authors who had occupied critical attention for two centuries: for instance, William Galperin (1989), Alison Hickey (1997), and Peter Manning (1990) studied works by

Wordsworth – particularly later works like *The Excursion* – that had been rarely ana-lyzed even by the most adventurous critics in the field. Still more, a range of writ-ers neglected since the early twentieth century were brought into publication and included within scholarly arguments. As James Chandler's chapter in this volume indicates, historicist critics had only just initiated a "Byron revival," retrieving this writer from negative judgments and neglect from the New Critics to deconstruction. The work of Walter Scott has seen a similar kind of revival. Serious work also emerged on such poets as William Cowper, John Clare, and Robert Southey, who had often been relegated to asides and footnotes. Entire books of biography and criticism in the wake of new historicism were also devoted to Jane Austen's many other fellow novelists – including Maria Edgeworth, Lady Morgan, and Charlotte Smith – who critics began to consider as important authors making crucial innovations in their own right. Excellent editions of work like Olaudah Equiano's *Interesting Narrative* and lesser-known novels by William Godwin and Mary Shelley attracted scholarly atten-tion and discussion; still more, literary criticism embraced a range of works in politics, aesthetics, economics, and other disciplines not conventionally considered "literary." Jeremy Bentham, Edmund Burke, and Thomas Malthus are only a few such authors that seldom received notice in literary analyses until the past few decades. The canon-expansion extended still further into literary reviews, newspapers, and magazines, which gave scholars an increasingly accurate sense of Romantic literature's reception history and cultural milieu.

This proliferation of new objects of study, to some extent, simply meant that "Romanticism" had many more components to it than people had previously believed. But even more interesting implications followed. From an empirical stand-point, the objects being considered raised intriguing challenges for interpretation, since many newly exposed writings could not easily be analyzed within some of the reigning paradigms for interpreting the period. Works by Barbauld, Edgeworth, Southey, and Charlotte Smith (just to name a few authors) seemed ill-suited to theo-ries that understood Romanticism's self-conception as secular, individualist, or aes-thetically impersonal. Far more frequently, the study of these new entrants into the canon (including lesser-known works by Wordsworth like the *Ecclesiastical Sonnets*) linked them to discourses of manners and sentiment from the eighteenth century, or to institutional and imperial ambitions of the nineteenth century. The inclusion of these new and very different works raised still other more profound disciplinary questions, in that the very resources for explaining Romanticism more fully seemed (at least for some critics) to challenge the validity of studying Romanticism as a dis-tinct and separate field. Indeed, as the implications of new historicism continued to play out over the late 1990s and 2000s, many scholars – while nominally writing in the rubric of Romantic studies – seemed less devoted to defending the integrity of the category than previous generations of critics had been. We could point to the work of Julie Ellison, Kevin Gilmartin, Clifford Siskin, and William Warner (among oth-ers) as examples of critics whose work has not only expanded the authors and areas of inquiry for Romanticists, but also helped to raise questions about the distinctive-ness of Romanticism in relation to eighteenth- and nineteenth-century literary and cultural history.

The influence of historicist critics can be felt virtually everywhere in this volume's essays – and many critics would continue to call themselves historicists, although perhaps without considering themselves to be part of the loosely affiliated group of new historicists. But there are many ways in which criticism of the 1990s and 2000s has reassessed, revised, and contested some of the central historicist paradigms. For instance, the eagerness to place literary works in cultural contexts seems, for some critics, to make it difficult to account for literature as literature: that is, to account for its particular generic significance. Paul Hamilton's and Robert Kaufman's selections are among several essays in the volume that move beyond contextualizing literature within history to articulate literary form's critical *relation* to that history.

Some other views may share broad agreement with new historicist criticism, but they focus on aspects of it that expand upon or trouble its conclusions. Work on both authority and readership provides examples of how new historicist accounts of Romanticism's urge for individual transcendence are not universal; Lucy Newlyn's account of the Romantic writer's nervousness about the reception of their work or Anne Frey's account of De Quincey's view of state authority complicate those accounts by showing how deeply aware Romantic writers actually were of their surrounding social contexts. In a similar spirit of questioning, critics writing on issues of gender, sexuality, and race show how writers were not only aware of their surrounding discourses and institutions but sometimes actively argued against or subverted them.

Another group of critics represented here explores a range of topics that seemed to be ignored or even suppressed by previous generations of scholars. Recent writing on religion shows that new historicism inherited some assumptions about the secular character of literature from the New Critics; this recent work corrects the historical record but also occasionally proposes different theoretical approaches that can capture complex connections between belief and political structures during the Romantic period. In a related way, work on affects shows how previous generations of historicists, concentrating on somewhat abstract issues of power and domination, tended to leave little room for exploring the more local, emotive relations between persons and the communal affiliations they construct or occupy. In many senses, then, critics continue to be interested in the political work of Romantic writing, but they seek new paradigms or methodologies for explaining it.

The approaches just mentioned often (but not always) continue to examine, through new subjects and new analytical lenses, the dynamics of political organization and affiliation. The sections on science and media, however, open up opportunities for thinking about literary production that occasionally lie still further from the questions that were central for new historicists. With their attention to the material configurations of bodies, or the material conditions for literary texts in terms of their publication, these areas of concern tend to show some other limits of 1980s and 1990s historicism, which often tended to think of historical context as an articulation, however distanced, of a political position. Both of these growing areas of inquiry adopt a series of new objects for analysis, and these new objects have in many senses changed the process and endpoint of analysis itself. Work on the sciences, by showing how literary meaning is connected to the structure of human and non-human bodies, exposes how many historicists continued to share a New Critical assumption about the opposition, or at least the strong distinction, between literary and scientific work. Investigation of the media cultures of the Romantic period points out the degree to which many previous generations of critics frequently saw the details of print as a transparent and stable medium for literature's messages, rather than as a component or generator of message-making itself.

Most scholars would probably agree that criticism in the most recent years has not revealed a dominant trend that would compare with New Criticism in the 1950s and 1960s, deconstruction in the 1970s and 1980s, and new historicism in the 1980s and 1990s. But we are still in an adequate position to assess a prominent trend. Some recent scholarship represented here could be called post-historicist, in that motivations for criticism are now being located outside the restricted attempt to locate authors within their historical contexts and to account for the blindness or insight of literary work in relation to those contexts. For instance, Andrew Elfenbein's reading of Cowper, while in a sense historicist in that it acknowledges the context in which Cowper's writing appears, links him to postmodern accounts of identity and thus to a more salutary approach to gender politics: one that challenges conventional structures and boundaries. In related ways, Timothy Morton's essay on Clare – and indeed all his work on the environment – not only explains a Romantic relation to the world but advocates it. And Mary Favret's essay on war finds a connection between violence and the everyday that characterizes the Romantic age but also our own moment. Beyond her essay selection here, Denise Gigante suggests that her attention to the interdisciplinary project of attending to "living form" can help boost the "institutional status" of literary criticism within and beyond the academy (Gigante 2007: 270).

For many years, "presentism" was taken to be a criticism applied to historicism that was guilty of not being historical enough. Alan Liu shows (in this volume and elsewhere) how attempts at establishing "context" often contain covertly transcendent, ahistorical, or formalist moments, and (as I have already suggested) recent scholarship has often corrected these errors by grasping the precise texture of literature's historical embeddedness. But some of the scholarship I describe as post-historicist moves beyond history in a way that shuns the kind of embarrassment over presentism that Liu may wish to encourage. The move we are seeing is often explicit and intentional, making Romantic literature into something that can speak directly to our own moment. In closing, there are two observations that could be made about this shift in criticism on the Romantic period. First, Gigante's concern with the institutional position of literary criticism provides a particularly useful way for us to provide a context for the recent trend in criticism. The ability to connect the study of past literary and cultural movements to current beliefs and practices seems directly to respond to our present age, in which the academy has been – now more than ever – subject to enormous political and economic pressures. Longstanding suspicions of academic radicalism or liberalism are now accompanied by demands not only from governments but from an educated public to make both public and private universities more suited to a world dominated by global capitalism. Higher learning, such critics say, can perform its proper function by making individuals into effectively trained workers in this economy. In order to achieve that goal, universities continue to shrink their commitments to supposedly non-useful areas of interest and to further expand their commitments to STEM (science, technology, engineering, and mathematics) disciplines. We might very easily conclude that some recent criticism, dissatisfied with the results of new historicism, is now asking what – under these present conditions – literary criticism can contribute to new demands and how it can thereby justify itself.

The second observation to be made takes a longer historical view, in that the post-historicist trend represents a postmodern revision of the Victorian mindset about literature. Like the Victorians, many recent critics are valuing literature for the contributions that it contains for the present, and a recent book on *Wordsworth's Ethics* by Adam Potkay is a particularly forthright example of a work of criticism that aims to recover the moral weight of criticism from the eras of New Criticism, deconstruction, and new historicism, arguing for Wordsworth's sense of "morality without moralism" (Potkay 2012: 5). Unlike the Victorians, however, most recent critics collectively convey the sense that the present is necessarily fragmented. While literature is claimed to be valuable, it is not valuable because it contains the common interest of humanity, as Mill thought it was. It is valuable because of very specific insights, political positions, and professional interests. Nearly the opposite of Mill's account of Wordsworth, these critics find value for the literary according to the logic of the division of labor: one group of texts performs one function, another group performs another. In the wake of postmodern criticism, literary criticism has found it impossible to argue for abstract human value. But the institutional pressures on literary study itself have resulted in a widespread attempt to seek out current value even when it cannot be considered as generalized as the Victorian model. Another term for post-historicism, then, might be post-humanist humanism, an attempt to produce a shared but restricted value in the wake of extreme skepticism.

Construction of the volume and teaching ideas

I end here with a brief discussion of the construction of this volume for the benefit of students and teachers, followed by a note on the text. In all sections in this volume, works on the same topic give contrasting views of the 11 subjects in those sections. The aim has been to show significantly different approaches with different theoretical assumptions and implications. The volume thus highlights debates in topic areas rather than providing coverage of works of authors, and in this sense it departs from many other critical anthologies. Although each of the 11 sections features a series of four contrasting views – three previously published pieces followed by an essay newly commissioned for this volume – the views are not meant to represent a simple progress in critical understanding from an earlier to a later moment. Instead, the views demonstrate contrasting positions, outlined briefly in a set of prefatory remarks to each section, that continue to animate scholarly debate in Romantic studies (and in other areas of literary studies as well). There are several different ways in which this collection of texts can be used for upper level undergraduate and graduate teaching, and I briefly outline a few of them here.

1   Debates in Romantic Studies. The volume perhaps most obviously can be used to focus on a series of debates in the field of Romanticism. As in each of the following teaching ideas, this text would be most effectively used in combination with an anthology or series of literary texts that pairs the literary texts with appropriate essays. Since the goal of the volume is to dramatize larger critical and theoretical debates, however, instructors will most likely find it fruitful also to use the claims in the essays to interpret texts that lie beyond their view.

2   Broader themes or areas of debate. Although the volume ranges over 11 sections, there are many interrelated sections which will help instructors to craft rubrics of their own that combine topic areas and essays in this anthology. For instance, courses on aspects of literary form, nationalism and state formation, reading and media cultures; gender and patriarchy, and many other topics will be found to

cut across several different sections in the volume. The section introductions give an indication of many of these points of contact among the essays and sections. Thus, course designs that aim to encompass fewer topic areas, or broader ones, can combine essays and sections in different ways to emphasize debates that have been of interest to Romanticists.

3   Romantic literature and culture. The volume includes a range of essays on authors and texts that are likely to be taught in many courses on Romantic literature. Thus, it can be used as an accompaniment for a class that may actually focus on literary traditions and authors rather than on scholarly debates. Even in a course of this kind, the essays – with the section introductions – can nevertheless help students to get a sense of the variety of perspectives that have been brought to bear on the literature they are studying.

4   Criticism and literary theory. Because the volume is set up to magnify points of debate, this collection of essays could be used in a course on literary theory; if combined with an anthology of Romantic literature and a series of works of literary theory (or an anthology of literary theory), this volume could allow students to see different theoretical positions put into practice within theoretical essays.

A note on the text

The previously published selections in this volume were often taken from their original form as journal articles before they appeared in book form; when book versions of the essays made substantial changes that were conducive to appearing in this volume, the later version was chosen over the earlier one. In each case, moreover, selections required excerpting, and deletions from the text are marked by ellipses. Students who wish to engage fully with these arguments in a research paper are encouraged to consult the full essays, articles, or books from which the excerpts are taken. Occasional editorial additions have been made, and notes reordered, for ease of reading. Other changes were made only to correct occasional typographical errors in the original text. Editorial changes or additions are made in brackets.

Acknowledgments

I wish to thank the careful and steady guidance of Polly Dodson and Ruth Moody at Routledge for supporting this project from start to finish. Andrew Franta gave me helpful advice on the introductions, and Kate Short did a superb job with copyediting. Finally, I wish to express my sincerest thanks to Amy Gates for the preparation of the final manuscript; the book simply would not have been completed without her expert assistance.

Works cited

Abrams, M.H. (1953) *The Mirror and the Lamp: Romantic Theory and the Critical Tradition*, Oxford: Oxford University Press.

Abrams, M.H. (1971) *Natural Supernaturalism: Tradition and Revolution in Romantic Literature*, New York: W.W. Norton.

Arnold, Matthew. (1914) *Essays in Criticism*, Oxford: Oxford University Press.

Arnold, Matthew, ed. (1922) *Selected Poems of William Wordsworth*, New York: Harcourt Brace.

Austen, Jane. (2002) *Sense and Sensibility*, ed. Claudia Johnson, New York: Norton.

Bloom, Harold. (1975) *A Map of Misreading*, Oxford: Oxford University Press.

Bloom, Harold, Paul De Man, Jacques Derrida, Geoffrey H. Hartman, and J. Hillis Miller. (1979) *Deconstruction and Criticism*, London: Continuum.

Brooks, Cleanth. (1947) *The Well Wrought Urn: Studies in the Structure of Poetry*, New York: Harcourt Brace.

Butler, Marilyn. (1981) *Romantics, Rebels, and Reactionaries: English Literature and its Background, 1760–1830*, Oxford: Oxford University Press.

Coleridge, Samuel Taylor. (1912) *Poetical Works*, ed. Ernest Hartley Coleridge, Oxford: Oxford University Press.

de Man, Paul. (1983) *Blindness and Insight: Essays in the Rhetoric of Contemporary Criticism*, 2nd edn, revised, Minneapolis: University of Minnesota Press.

de Man, Paul. (1984) *The Rhetoric of Romanticism*, New York: Columbia University Press.

de Man, Paul. (1986) *The Resistance to Theory*, Minneapolis: University of Minnesota Press.

de Staël, Germaine. (1987) *Major Writings of Germaine de Staël*, trans. and intr. Vivian Folkenflik, New York: Columbia University Press.

Eliot, T.S. (1933) *The Uses of Poetry and the Uses of Criticism*, Cambridge: Harvard University Press.

Erdman, David. (1954) *Blake: Prophet Against Empire*, Princeton: Princeton University Press.

Ferguson, Frances. (1991) "On the Numbers of Romanticisms," *ELH* 58: 471–88.

Gallagher, Catherine, and Stephen Greenblatt. (2001) *Practicing New Historicism*, Chicago: University of Chicago Press.

Galperin, William. (1989) *Revision and Authority in Wordsworth*, Philadelphia: University of Pennsylvania Press.

Gigante, Denise. (2007) "Zeitgeist," *European Romantic Review* 18: 265–72.

Hamilton, Elizabeth. (2000) *Memoirs of Modern Philosophers*, ed. Claire Grogan, Peterborough: Broadview Press.

Hamilton, Paul. (2003) *Historicism*, 2nd edn, London: Routledge.

Hazlitt, William. (1983) *The Spirit of the Age, or Contemporary Portraits*, ed. Harold Bloom, New York: Chelsea House.

Hickey, Alison. (1997) *Impure Conceits: Rhetoric and Ideology in Wordsworth's* Excursion, Stanford: Stanford University Press.

Leavis, F.R. (1963) *The Great Tradition*, New York: New York University Press.

Lentricchia, Frank. (1980) *After the New Criticism*, Chicago: University of Chicago Press.

Lovejoy, Arthur O. (1924) "On the Discrimination of Romanticisms," *PMLA* 39: 229–53.

MacLeish, Archibald. (1985) *Collected Poems, 1917–1982*, Boston: Houghton Mifflin.

Manning, Peter. (1990) *Reading Romantics: Texts and Contexts*, New York: Oxford University Press.

McGann, Jerome J. (1985) *The Romantic Ideology: A Critical Investigation*, Chicago: University of Chicago Press.

Mill, John Stuart (1874) *Autobiography*, New York: Henry Holt.

Poovey, Mary. (2001) "The Model System of Contemporary Literary Criticism," *Critical Inquiry* 27: 408–38.

Potkay, Adam. (2012) *Wordsworth's Ethics*, Baltimore: Johns Hopkins University Press.

Ransom, John Crowe. (1941) *The New Criticism*, Norfolk, CT: New Directions.

Ruskin, John. (1965) *Literary Criticism of John Ruskin*, ed. Harold Bloom, New York: W.W. Norton.

Tate, Allen. (1955) *The Man of Letters in the Modern World: Selected Essays, 1928–1955*, New York: Meridian.

Thomas, Brook. (1993) *The New Historicism and Other Old-Fashioned Topics*, Princeton: Princeton University Press.

Trilling, Lionel. (1955) *The Opposing Self: Nine Essays in Criticism*, New York: Viking.

Wasserman, Earl R. (1959) *The Subtler Language: Critical Readings of Neoclassic and Romantic Poems*, Baltimore: Johns Hopkins University Press.

Wasserman, Earl R. (1971) *Shelley: A Critical Reading*, Baltimore: Johns Hopkins University Press.

Wimsatt, William. (1954) "The Structure of Romantic Nature Imagery," in W. Wimsatt, *The Verbal Icon: Studies in the Meaning of Poetry*, Lexington: University Press of Kentucky, 103–16.

Wimsatt, William, and Monroe Beardsley. (1954) "The Intentional Fallacy," in W. Wimsatt, *The Verbal Icon: Studies in the Meaning of Poetry*, Lexington: University Press of Kentucky, 3–18.

Wollstonecraft, Mary. (1994) *A Vindication of the Rights of Woman and a Vindication of the Rights of Men*, Oxford: Oxford University Press.

Woodring, Carl. (1970) *Politics in English Romantic Poetry*, Cambridge: Harvard University Press.

Wordsworth, William. (1984) *The Oxford Authors William Wordsworth*, ed. Steven Gill, Oxford: Oxford University Press.

Part 1

Politics, ideology, and the literary

Introduction

The essay excerpts in this section offer an introduction to the other selections in this volume; this is because so much work in recent decades has built upon, modified, or reacted against historicist criticism. The selections here present different ways of thinking about literature as historical, but, more particularly, about the relationship between literature and politically relevant features of the author's world. These excerpts also present different ways of understanding the degree to which literature is (by virtue of that relationship) "ideological" – insofar as ideology is understood as an imaginary relationship to specific material conditions in that world. To what extent, these excerpts ask, does literature represent, defend, or further the interests of specific groups or classes of people at specific moments in time? To what extent does it understand this relationship, or to what extent does it deny or suppress it?

Such questions, approached in different ways by the authors in this section, continue to provoke urgent discussion among critics of Romantic literature and of other literatures as well. The continued engagement with these questions – displayed in other essays throughout this volume – conveys the sustained power of historicist inquiry's central preoccupations. More specifically, it conveys the sustained power of "new historicist" inquiry, which took an interest in analyzing the specific contexts in which works were produced and in interrogating the ways in which those works imaginatively participated in, and supported, dominant structures of power and authority. We begin with one of the most important instances of new historicist criticism, a selection from Marjorie Levinson's excerpt on Wordsworth's poem "Lines Written a Few Miles Above Tintern Abbey, On Revisiting the Banks of the Wye During a Tour, July 13, 1798"; the complete chapter appeared in her book *Wordsworth's Great Period Poems*. The essays that follow, by Paul Hamilton and James Chandler, represent two ways in which scholars have reconsidered the theoretical assumptions behind Levinson's essay – assumptions that are extended or pressured in numerous other selections in this volume.

Historicist critics of the 1980s, as explained in the general introduction, departed from two prominent ways of talking about literature and history – one emphasizing "intellectual" history, and the other emphasizing the political alliances formed through literary texts. These two forms did not entirely disappear: books by Seamas Deane on Romanticism and the Enlightenment and by Nicholas Roe on the political alliances of John Keats are only two examples of excellent work in these areas (Deane 1988; Roe 1997). But for the most part new historicists sought more thoroughly to account for the "context" of literary work than intellectual historians were able to do. And – particularly in the field of Romantic studies – they sought to show not only the explicit political ambitions of writers, but also the manner in which literary works insisted, however covertly, on an imaginative distance from the objects, events, and persons they represented. A great deal of historicist criticism was devoted to identifying this distance and analyzing the consequences of it.

Levinson's essay carefully reads the particular "occasion" of Wordsworth's famous poem, a lyric meditation that assesses the poet's thoughts and feelings when revisiting a landscape after an absence of five years. Levinson suggests that Wordsworth's "sense sublime" celebrated throughout the poem is an "escape from cultural values." Viewing a landscape that is not merely "natural" but filled with the marks of industrialization and poverty, Wordsworth both reminds us of those details and then erases them in order to achieve his transcendent vision. The "mind" functions in his poem not as a way of perceiving what is in front of him, but rather as a "barricade to resist the violence of historical change and contradiction." This provocative reading of Wordsworth's poem was joined by a range of other influential historicist interpretations, such as Jerome McGann's *The Romantic Ideology*, David Simpson's *Wordsworth's Historical Imagination*, and Alan Liu's *Wordsworth: The Sense of History*; all of these works in their different ways approached Wordsworth as the quintessential example of how Romantic writing was historical precisely insofar as it avoided overt acknowledgment of its "limiting or enabling conditions of time and place" (Simpson 1987: 1)

Levinson's reading of Wordsworth attracted many thoughtful arguments, however. From an empirical perspective, for instance, Charles Rzepka challenged the accuracy of Levinson's representation of the landscape that Wordsworth would actually have encountered (Rzepka 2003); David Bromwich insisted that Wordsworth was advocating for a more generous human sympathy than in her account (Bromwich 1998); Thomas Pfau argued that, far from escaping history, Wordsworth demonstrated and enacted a specific, historically identifiable position – that of the poet as a literate (and literary) bourgeois individual (Pfau 1997). This is only a snapshot of responses to one argument, but it could be said that these, and many others like them, argued against a prominent historicist line of inquiry yet still worked within historicist paradigms.

From two different positions, Paul Hamilton's and James Chandler's selections press somewhat harder on the theoretical underpinnings of historicism. In Hamilton's "Keats and Critique," later appearing as chapter 4 in his book *Metaromanticism*, Hamilton takes up yet another argument of Levinson's – about the connections between John Keats's poetry and his class standing (Levinson 1988) – and shows how the poet's "lapses from poetry," ridiculed by Keats's hostile reviewers, are the basis for a critique of aesthetic idealizations and the political conservatism that such idealizations might entail. These cracks in aesthetic perfection reveal "the relativism inherent in its essentialist claims."

The selection on Byron from James Chandler's book *England in 1819* argues quite differently that any view insisting on Romanticism's imaginative distance from historical reality is improperly historicized. Chandler's book in general shows how historicism is mistaken insofar as it attempts merely to unearth a hidden or denied historical context; readers must also consider how Romantic works demonstrate their own awareness of history. The implications of this argument are fully visible in "Byron's Causes." The eponymous hero of *Don Juan* seems to demonstrate a case in which a character is part of his age, and Byron even sees himself as a writer and narrator in these terms. At the same time, however, the poem subtly undermines the very idea of periods or phases with explanatory networks that scramble attempts to assign clear relations of causality. Apparently universal erotic passions are complicated by Byron's own sexuality, for instance; *Don Juan* as a poem dramatizes, rather than answers, questions about whether poetic form is caused by history or history by form.

Daniel O'Quinn's new essay for this collection continues an aspect of Chandler's argument in that it aims to unearth the way that Romantic texts positioned themselves and participated in their historical moments. His analysis, however, partakes of recent attention to media, performance, and audience. His focus on Richard Brinsley Sheridan's theatrical production and composition insists that our view of historical awareness must take account of "the repetitive temporality of performance"; close attention to evidence of successive performances reveals how meanings of any given work change over time. Examining the production history and media reception of Thomas Otway's *Venice Preserv'd* and Sheridan's *The Rivals*, O'Quinn shows how these theatrical works magnetized competing radical and conservative political readings, and even competing readings of Sheridan the playwright and politician himself. The reigning metaphor for understanding literature's relation to its historical moment is thus theft, as interpreters "steal" culture in order to give the past new meanings in the present and future.

Works cited

Bromwich, David. (1998) *Disowned by Memory: Wordsworth's Poetry of the 1790s*, Chicago: University of Chicago Press.

Deane, Seamus. (1988) *The French Revolution and the Enlightenment in England*, Cambridge: Harvard University Press.

Levinson, Marjorie. (1988) *Keats's Life of Allegory: The Origins of a Style*, Oxford: Basil Blackwell.

Liu, Alan. (1989) *Wordsworth: The Sense of History*, Stanford: Stanford University Press.

McGann, Jerome J. (1983) *The Romantic Ideology: A Critical Investigation*, Chicago: University of Chicago Press.

Pfau, Thomas. (1997) *Wordsworth's Profession: Form, Class, and the Logic of Early Romantic Cultural Production*, Stanford: Stanford University Press.

Roe, Nicholas. (1997) *Keats and the Culture of Dissent*, Oxford: Oxford University Press.

Rzepka, Charles J. (2003) "Pictures of the Mind: Iron and Charcoal, 'Ouzy' Tides and Vagrant Dwellers at Tintern, 1798," *Studies in Romanticism* 48: 155–85.

Simpson, David. (1987) *Wordsworth's Historical Imagination: The Poetry of Displacement*, New York: Methuen.

Further reading

Barrell, John. (2000) *Imagining the King's Death: Figurative Treason, Fantasies of Regicide: 1793–96*, Oxford: Oxford University Press.

Butler, Marilyn. (1981) *Romantics, Rebels, and Reactionaries: English Literature and its Background, 1760–1830*, Oxford: Oxford University Press.

Collings, David. (2009) *Monstrous Society: Reciprocity, Discipline, and the Political Uncanny*, Lewisburg, PA: Bucknell University Press.

Cronin, Richard. (2000) *The Politics of Romantic Poetry: In Search of the Pure Commonwealth*, New York: St. Martin's Press.

Friedman, Geraldine. (1996) *The Insistence of History: Revolution in Burke, Wordsworth, Keats, and Baudelaire*, Stanford: Stanford University Press.

Galperin, William H. (1993) *The Return of the Visible in British Romanticism*, Baltimore: Johns Hopkins University Press.

Mahoney, Charles. (2003) *Romantics and Renegades: The Poetics of Political Reaction*, New York: Palgrave Macmillan.

Moody, Jane. (2000) *Illegitimate Theater in London, 1770–1840*, Cambridge: Cambridge University Press.

Russell, Gillian. (1995) *The Theatres of War: Performance, Politics, and Society, 1793–1815*, Oxford: Clarendon Press.

Siskin, Clifford. (1988) *The Historicity of Romantic Discourse*, New York: Oxford University Press.

Smith, Olivia. (1984) *The Politics of Language, 1791–1819*, Oxford: Clarendon Press.

Williams, Nicholas M. (1998) *Ideology and Utopia in the Poetry of William Blake*, Cambridge: Cambridge University Press.

Worrall, David. (1992) *Radical Culture: Discourse, Resistance, and Surveillance, 1790–1820*, London: Harvester Wheatsheaf.

Zimmerman, Sarah. (1999) *Romanticism, Lyricism, and History*, Albany: State University of New York Press.

1   Insight and oversight

Reading "Tintern Abbey"

Marjorie Levinson

It is a curious fact that nowhere in the poem does Wordsworth mention Tintern Abbey itself, though we know that he must have admired it, for they returned from Chepstow to spend a second night there. Gilpin describes its condition; the grass in the ruins was kept mown, but it was a dwelling-place of beggars and the wretchedly poor. The river was then full of shipping, carrying coal and timber from the Forest of Dean. This also Wordsworth does not mention . . .

Mary Moorman, *Wordsworth's Early Years*
(London: Oxford Univ. Press, 1957), pp. 402–3

I

In a note to "Tintern Abbey," 1800, Wordsworth calls attention to the poem's odal transitions and versification; he hopes that the reader will find in these features "the principal requisites of that species of composition."[1] Inasmuch as our criticism judges "Tintern Abbey" a work peculiarly comparable to the Intimations Ode, Wordsworth's formal hopes would seem to have been realized. We note, however, that the association of these poems probably has less to do with transition and versification than with the more general businesses of theme and procedure. "Tintern Abbey"'s subject is, like the Ode's, profound and universal, its mode of address lofty and abstract, and its questions and answers seem to originate in textual space.

I produce the comparison so as to bring out an interesting difference. Whereas the Intimations Ode explains its discursive procedures by reference to a determinate genetic problem, textually rehearsed, "Tintern Abbey"'s 'wherefore' is, strictly within the poem, strangely elusive. Its 'whereby,' consequently, assumes an independent interest and one that contains or engenders its own philosophic rationale. Most readers observe that an object does not materialize in the poem before it is effaced or smudged; a thought does not find full articulation before it is qualified or deconstructed; a point of view is not established before it dissolves into a series of impressions.[2] These textual facts are typically situated as the semantic matter of the poem and as criticism's point of departure. To put this another way, it is easier and far more courteous to explicate "Tintern Abbey" than it is to explain it. So rich, coherent, intellectually strenuous, and moving a reading does the poem enable that the *writing* dimension – the order of authorial and contextual urgencies – fades from view.

The representational tendencies noted above – all of which diminish the determinacy of Wordsworth's poetic subject *and* object – seem to me referable to a single but far reaching textual maneuver: Wordsworth's erasure of the occasional character of his poem. One does not generally expect an ode or odal form to incorporate into its utterance its contextually genetic conditions. One does, however, anticipate from a poem entitled "Lines Written a Few Miles Above Tintern Abbey, *on revisiting the banks of the Wye during a tour, July 13, 1798*" – by that title, a loco-descriptive poem – some allusion or attention to the time and place of composition. "Tintern Abbey" does *allude*, although it does not attend, to the dimension designated by its title. Lines 1–22 – to all appearances, a series of timeless, spiritually suggestive pastoral impressions – in fact represent a concretely motivated attempt to green an actualized political prospect and to hypostatize the resultant fiction, a product of memory and desire.

Students of Wordsworth commonly refer to the poem as "Tintern Abbey"; it even seems to have been something of a convention in late nineteenth- and early twentieth-century textbooks and anthologies to print engravings of the Abbey alongside the poem.[3] I suspect that at some point, many readers have wondered why Wordsworth is so specific in the title about the circumstances of his visit, and so vague in the poem. Why would a writer call attention to a famous ruin and then studiously ignore it, as it were repudiating its material and historical facticity?[4] Why not situate his utterance in the bower or dell and avoid the cynosure altogether? Certainly it is noteworthy that Wordsworth's chosen focus is a tract of woodland rather than the monument at hand. And, given the emergence of the religious house as a subject of considerable importance in the later verse, its absence from "Tintern Abbey" looks uncomfortably like a suppression. It seems inadequate merely to suggest, as one critic has done, that had Wordsworth written "Tintern Abbey" after 1805, the Abbey would have been the "centerpiece" of the poem.[5] In order to make sense of Wordsworth's advertised exclusion, one would infer some problem – in the poet's mind, in the prospect, or in both – that the poem at once solves and conceals.

We notice as well that the date so suggestively featured in the title announces a conjunction of themes no less public nor problematic than Wordsworth's location. While the poet underlines the strictly personal import of that date (it demarcates a five-year interval during which the narrator's responsiveness to Nature's vital influences seems to him to have diminished), the contemporary reader could have read in the date some far more dramatic meanings. July 13, 1798, marked almost to the day the nine-year anniversary of the original Bastille Day (the eight-year anniversary of Wordsworth's first visit to France), and the five-year anniversary of the murder of Marat, also the date of Wordsworth's first visit to Tintern Abbey.

Why Wordsworth composed for his lofty, psychically searching meditation a title so burdened with topical meanings is the question that motivates this essay. [. . .] I will suggest that what "Tintern Abbey" presents as, if not natural values, then undetermined and apolitical ones, define a negative ideal: the escape from cultural values.[6] "Tintern Abbey" 's Nature is a place – a concept – to fly to, not to seek, and the poem's developmental psychology serves a primarily extrinsic remedial intention: the de- and reconstruction of the scene of writing.

I will show that what Wordsworth offers under the sign of the picturesque is a portion of rural England (overdetermined by his knowledge of urban England), in 1798. What Wordsworth presents as mythic, uninterpretable givens – e.g., "vagrant dwellers in the houseless woods" – are the result of socioeconomic conditions whose causes were familiar to the poet and his readers. By attending to these conditions, we find that "Tintern Abbey" is a rather anomalous ode – its model more "Winds or Forest" (political allegory) than "Eton College," and its object the translation of ideological contradiction into natural variety, national myth, and psychic opportunity.

The poem's prospect is as "determined by events of political history" as is Denham's in *Coopers Hill.* In each case, the poet occupies a "real hill with a view of an actual stretch of English landscape authentically rich in historical associations," and both vistas include the "ruins of a chapel despoiled by Henry VIII."[7]

We note as well that Wordsworth's selection of a prospect and his representation of it are neither entirely individual nor, of course, natural. While the first 22 lines of "Tintern Abbey" do not construct a scene that *any* man might see, they depict a landscape that any number of poets of Wordsworth's political persuasions might have selected in 1798 for their artistic sightings. The moral to be drawn from all this is that in "Tintern Abbey" as in *Coopers Hill,* "it is not the landscape that counts, so much as the use made of it," and as with Denham's georgic, "Tintern Abbey" "treat{s} a rural scene as the paradigm for a hortatory political discourse."[8] The doctrine delivered by "Tintern Abbey" is not, of course, a lesson about the Puritan Revolution but about both the French and Industrial Revolutions.

As long as we subscribe to the belief that "a Wordsworthian landscape is inseparable from the history of the poet's mind," we will never really see Wordsworth's mind or his landscapes.[9] What the poet sees is, of course, conditioned by how he sees, but we should add that the equation is reversible: what he sees *determines* how he sees, as do the when and the whence of his seeing. Let us, then, hold Wordsworth to his claim, that he "endeavoured to look steadily at {his} subject." What were the circumstances surrounding Wordsworth's 1793 and 1798 visits to the Wye Valley; what bearing had these facts upon Wordsworth's particular structure of feeling and belief, and upon the more general ideological conditions of that structure? [. . .] I assemble material long familiar to Wordsworth scholars and culled from the most general of nineteenth-century histories. By using this material in a systematic way and for the purposes of textual intervention, I hope to explain the poem's transformational grammar. By going outside the work, we may produce, I think, a closer reading of it.

II

[. . .]

For whatever reasons, Wordsworth found himself at Tintern Abbey in mid-July (11–14). As I noted, the date marked the eight-year anniversary of Wordsworth's first visit to France, the nine-year anniversary of the original Bastille Day ("that great federal day," *Prelude* 6, 346), and the five-year anniversary of the murder of Marat. Marat's execution marked the beginning of the Terror, and in the contemporary mind, Marat figured as the first Revolutionary martyr. In him, the age read the image of the true cause destroyed by the false, the republic betrayed by the tyrant.

[. . .]

By 1798, Wordsworth had to some degree established himself as an adult: he had become an identifiable element in English society (a published poet), a member of a class (the {barely} leisure class), head of a household, and a potential agent in his country's ideological governance (member of a small intelligentsia). Wordsworth had much more to leave in 1798 than he had had in 1790 and 1791. And beyond these attachments, there is the natural reaction of a man who sees his country threatened by a foreign power. His own, familial critique typically gives way to a defensive posture.

[. . .]

"Tintern Abbey"'s Nature is a guardian of ground hallowed by private commemorative acts – Mnemosyne, a deeply conservative muse. Wordsworth approaches this presence in a spirit of worship. The poem leaves no doubt about this. It is far less explicit, though, about the occasion for this homage, an occasion that might be reconstructed in the following way. Wordsworth, finding himself at Tintern Abbey on a day marking four troubling anniversaries and bearing its own immediate freight of sad significance, experiences a need for rededication: to his past, to his country, and to his own hopeful self projections. Before embarking on an estrangement that would objectify his political status at home, Wordsworth would secure his birthright as an Englishman – the paternal blessing, so to speak. "Tintern Abbey" evinces the poet's desire to house his experience, past and future, in a mental fortress[.]

[. . .]

The narrator achieves his penetrating vision through the exercise of a selective blindness. By narrowing and skewing his field of vision, Wordsworth manages to "see into the life of things." At the same time and quite casually, so it seems, he excludes from his field certain conflictual sights and meanings – roughly, the *life* of things. This exclusion is, I believe, the poem's 'wherefore.'

[. . .]

What did Tintern look like to Wordsworth in 1798?

Tintern was a singularly appealing ruin due to its isolated situation in a lush green valley threaded by the Wye. Its state of preservation added to its appeal: all walls standing, open to the sky, it had then as now, the look of a classical temple. But perhaps the best explanation of Tintern Abbey's charm is the contrast it offered to the surrounding countryside. In 1798, the Wye Valley, though still affording prospects of great natural beauty, presented less delightful scenes as well. The region showed prominent signs of industrial and commercial activity: coal mines, transport barges noisily plying the river, miners' hovels. The town of Tintern, a half mile from the Abbey, was an iron-working village of some note, and in 1798 with the war at full tilt, the works were unusually active. The forests around Tintern – town and Abbey – were peopled with vagrants, the casualties of England's tottering economy and of wartime displacement. Many of these people lived by charcoal burning, obviously a marginal livelihood. The charcoal was used in the furnaces along the river banks. The Abbey grounds were crowded with the dispossessed and unemployed, who begged coins of the tourists anxious to exercise their aesthetic sensibilities. The cottage plots noted in the poem are "green to the very door" because the common lands had been enclosed some time back and the only arable land remaining to the cottager was his front garden.[10]

[. . .]

[Here Levinson quotes from poetry and several guidebooks to the region, demonstrating a contrast between the abbey and its impoverished and industrial surroundings.]

[Works written at around the same time as *Lyrical Ballads* celebrate] the advance of industry into erstwhile "indolent glades"; the guidebooks sharply regret the despoliation. The evidence [. . .] would strongly suggest that Wordsworth and his readers were alike cognizant of the contrast between Abbey and town, inwardness and industry, and all the attendant emotional, historical, economic, and intellectual complexities. We might observe in this context that Wordsworth's explanation of his position *above* Tintern (note, 1798: "The river is not affected by the tides a few miles above Tintern") strikes a disingenuous note. Had he situated himself downstream [from the Abbey] – within the tidal field – the river would not have "reflected the several objects on its banks" with a clear grandeur. Wordsworth would have instead observed an "ouzy, and discoloured," that is, polluted surface.[11]

[. . .]

To a man of Wordsworth's experience and inclination, Tintern Abbey would have represented a retreat from the commercial interests so clearly figured by its neighborhood, the Abbey's cultural value sharply defined by the visual opposition and the destiny it inscribed. A poet given to historical perspectives could not but remark the Abbey's continuity of function. From its inception, this building had sheltered those who refused or were excluded from the dominant exchange interests of the day: monk, hermit, tourist, pauper, poet.

[. . .]

"Tintern Abbey"'s celebrated mysticism, that I associate with its Protestant, progressive theme, produces the deathly isolation of the mind that would find this "the image of the sole self."[12] By its morbid representational aura, this persona confesses its divorce from an order of collectivity that might validate poetic achievement, or confirm the poet's social and therefore individual being. Monks seek the thing they love and they seek it in the company of their fellows. Hermits are in flight from a dreaded reality, a social way of life felt to oppose interiority. The private, meditative poet is not, one feels, a credibly satisfying substitute for that older form of worship. And it is *certainly* not, as the poem argues, an evolutionary improvement on that 'primitive' model.[13]

[. . .]

By constructing that idyllic landscape, lines 1–22, Wordsworth not only exorcizes the soulless image on the eye, he establishes a literary immortality for the endangered farms and woods. Or, what we witness in this poem is a conversion of public to private property, history to poetry. In 1793, preoccupied with 'forward-looking' political thoughts, Wordsworth did not know to cherish – to preserve by internalizing – Abbey and farms. Now that he feels his need for these mental resorts and at the same time sees them past and passing, he brings to bear the massive imagination that is "Tintern Abbey."

"Tintern Abbey" originates in a will to preserve something Wordsworth knows is already lost. At the same time, it arises from the will to deny this knowledge.

[. . .]

III

Given the sort of issues raised by "Tintern Abbey"'s occasion, it follows that the primary poetic action is the suppression of the social. "Tintern Abbey" achieves its fiercely private vision by directing a continuous energy toward the nonrepresentation of objects and points of view expressive of a public – we would say, ideological – dimension: that knowledge which is neither natural nor individual but which defines and hides within the former and constructs a certain kind of consciousness as the latter. The poem defines its utterance as a natural history dictated to the poet in a natural language ("inland murmur"), and offering a natural lesson "of moral evil and of good" ("The Tables Turned"). What is 'good,' the poem tells us, is organically sublative evolution. We realize this process when we refuse that willfulness which binds us to a fetishized past, as to our particular dreams of the future, forcing us thereby to live a discontinuous, inauthentic present. The audience consists of one person, the poet's 'second self,' and even she is admitted into the process a third of the way through, a decidedly feeble gesture toward externality. Wordsworth cancels the social less by explicit denial and/or misrepresentation than by allowing no scope for its operation.[14]

[. . .]

The success or failure of the visionary poem turns on its ability to hide its omission of the historical. It must present culture as Nature and Nature as a landscape framed but not altered. And of course, the framing itself must figure an innocent, inert procedure. Consider in this light the narrator's randomly descriptive musings – sylvan historiography, as it were, that tells no story but that of its own unfolding. The definition of objects and of a representational style must proceed continuously and impersonally so as to remain imperceptible. In this way, the figure appears to exclude nothing of the real. By these remarks, we might guess that the near seamlessness of "Tintern Abbey" is proportional to the number and strength of the spirits it must suppress.

Consider the opening lines. "Five years have passed; five summers, with the length / Of five long winters!" While the statement seems more than slightly tautological, I think we can all agree that the opening clause offers an apparently objective (as well as abstract and formulaic) statement and that the following phrase presents the same phenomenon as a subjective experience. The years *felt like* five blocks of lived time (summer is, for Wordsworth, a seme for freedom, holiday, happiness, see *Prelude* 6, 190–203, 322) separated by five of endured time, the two portions seemingly of unequal size ("the *length* / Of five *long* winters"). The syntax, diction, punctuation, and lineation of this sentence, however, strongly urge the commutability of objective–quantitative and subjective–qualitative experience. Or, the device works to conceal the difference between an object and an object of knowledge. What we can see only with difficulty is that in the conversion of objective to subjective, formulaic to felt, something is lost: spring and fall. Or, the realities (discursive and experiential, if we can make this distinction) produced by objective and subjective processes do not in fact account for all the matter in question. In adding the two modes of representation, Wordsworth subtracts something – in this case, nothing of great moment. There is a place held open by the semicolon and in that aperture an act of selection has taken place. That which is not consecrated by private experience is eliminated and the blank is covered over. That is, in his subjective analysis of the objective fact, Wordsworth liberates a quantum of negative energy that, by resisting, reinforces the positive charge or expressed subjectivity. When we respond to the "length" of those "long winters," we have unconsciously tacked on to them spring and fall.

The most significant omission of this sort is found in the phrase, "all thinking things, all objects of all thought." One tends to read this as an exhaustive statement touching both poles of possibility. The poem argues that "thinking things" largely construct the object world, so that the latter, while its first cause is "a motion and a spirit," is subject to an efficient cause as well. There is, however, no indication of reciprocity. "Thinking things" and their products, thoughts, apparently suffer no interference from the material and social world. Thought is free – the mind is its own place, the world is another.

[. . .]

The poem employs other, no less disarming discursive strategies. We notice, for example, that Wordsworth's pastoral vision actually foregrounds features that encode potent historical meanings. To the contemporary reader (or viewer) – and in any context but "Tintern Abbey" – these details would have indicated the effects of concrete social relations. "These pastoral farms, / Green to the very door" helps establish the monochromatic blend of the separate elements in the scene (one principle of the picturesque), the visual material suggesting a conceptual sequence and affective continuity. As I noted above, however, the green lawns, that figure in the poem as an image of psychic and material wellbeing, are the miserable product of an economic fact and its charged history, as are the attractively, 'sportively' sprinkled lines of hedges, another emblem of enclosure. Ironically, Wordsworth corrects his initial statement ("these hedgerows") as if to acknowledge its inaccuracy, the result of its objective (here, nonsensational, socially mediated) provenance. [. . . E]vincing scrupulous sincerity, the narrator converts substance into formal property, reality into design, the end result being the suppression of the historical significance of those lines: their cause and effect. This is empiricist idealism of a most seductive kind. Ignorance provides no counterargument.

[. . .]

In this context, we observe that the smoke wreathes, which figure in the passage as a kind of natural sacrifice to the benevolent God responsible for the rich harmony of the scene, are perversely demystified by those curious lines, "as might seem, / Of vagrant dwellers in the houseless woods." The curiosity of the phrase is, of course, its gratuitous allusion to the vagrants. The strictly notional being of these figures ("as might seem . . . ") marks an attempt to elide the confessed factual intelligence. Or, while the passage explicitly associates the smoke with the cozy pastoral farms, and situates the image as an instance of natural supernaturalism, the 'surmise' identifies the smoke as the effects of charcoal burning. More to the point, it identifies those idealized vagrants – a sort of metonymic slide toward the hermit/poet – as the actual charcoal burners who migrated according to the wood supply and the market. Or, more simply, Wordsworth reverses objective and subjective knowledges: he presents real vagrants as hypostatized (archetypal) figures, and positions the scene all gratulant – an idea *tout court* – as unmediated sensory impression. Moreover, we observe that by equating the wanderers with the hermit – one who possesses even less than they but whose spirit is inversely enriched and exalted – Wordsworth further discredits the factual knowledge hiding in his representation. Following the text, we forget that hermits choose their poverty; vagrants suffer it. [. . .] Finally, lest we focus too closely on the meaning of these scenic elements – lest we perversely insist on reading them as cultural features – Wordsworth classifies them in summary as "beauteous forms."

[. . .]

Perhaps it is appropriate to say that Wordsworth's visual/conceptual field cannot sight/think the *unlovely* forms – the *contents, shapes* – of that landscape. The speaker looks on Nature through the spectacles of thought; mixing metaphors, the "still, sad music of humanity" drowns out the noise produced by real people in real distress. Even as we see this, we should be careful to observe that the visionary authenticity of "Tintern Abbey" *is a function* of its authentic visual restrictions.

[. . .]

"Tintern Abbey"'s narrator makes no secret of his blindness; we all know the light of sense has gone out by line 22. Because he defines himself as an individual spirit, dependent only on Nature and on his own responsiveness for his sense of meaning and attachment (ll. 108–111), he cannot conceive himself as anything other than a role (the recluse) – or, what amounts to the same thing, a past and a future projection. The turn to Dorothy, then, is a move toward otherness, or toward a social reality, albeit a greatly complaisant (cathected) instance of that order. Dorothy functions in the poem as a final surface, the condition for the poet's ongoing reflective life. Lacking this screen – a kind of alienated *tabula rasa* – the speaker knows himself only as a fixture of the landscape; unable to reflect upon it, and therefore, by his problematic, produced by it, and, as its creature, incapable of self-reflection.

[. . .]

IV

Wordsworth's glancing awareness of alternative problematics could explain the poem's general, structural (as opposed to local, stylistic) procedures. The movements which Hartman designates as turns and counterturns might also be conceived as approaches to and withdrawals from the object of address. By this Pindaric allusion, so to speak, Wordsworth suggests the ultimately elusive, ineffable nature of his subject, and the necessity of an approach-avoidance relation to it. We see the scene and its meanings by glimpses and peripherally, probably the only way we ever start imagining what we know, which is to say, knowing our imaginations. Not to put too enlightened an edge on it, though, we must also observe that Wordsworth's invocation of the conventionally numinous presence effectively marginalizes the orders of actuality we have been focusing here.

[. . .]

"Tintern Abbey" invents and idealizes a procedure whereby the mind's extension (denotation, object representation, quantitative knowledge) is experienced as intension (connotation, valorization, qualitative knowledge). The pun is well meant; the narrative project of "Tintern Abbey" is to intentionalize matter, and matter-of-fact. The functional agency is, of course, memory. Under its direction, the return to a place is experienced as the passive creation of it (ll. 4–7: "Once again / Do I behold these . . . cliffs, / That on a wild secluded scene impress / Thoughts of more deep seclusion"). Recognition (a self–other, subject–object dynamic) is felt as reproduction of the inner life, the valorized order of "beauteous forms." Yet the expressive modality assumed by this experience is description: a discourse in praise of Nature and not in competition with it.

[. . .]

By suggesting that we find our thoughts "impressed" upon Nature, Wordsworth denies that we make our thoughts, that we are made by those thoughts, and that a good deal of social thinking gets done, for good and ill, through our most private reflections. Moreover and more deliberately, Wordsworth dissociates thoughts from their effects, canceling in this manner thinking responsibility at a certain practical level. Wordsworth's thoughts and purposes – his adult pragmatic structure, so to speak – betrayed him, and Tintern Abbey's appearance holds him to that treason. Wordsworth escapes by denying culture's perfidy – that is, by placing that perfidy or its manifestations under the sign of Nature-Psyche and their redemptive operations. By this transposition, this testimony – "Knowing that Nature never did betray / The heart that loved her" – Wordsworth brings forth the *sententium* that crystallizes the poem's self-understanding: *sic requiescat gloria mentis.*[15]

[. . .]

"Tintern Abbey" finally represents mind, and specifically memory, not as energy – a subtle psychic ongoingness – but as a barricade to resist the violence of historical change and contradiction. With the displaced but certain elaboration of this figure, Wordsworth overrides his own defenses against the sighting of Tintern Abbey, The ruin enters the poem and not by the backdoor but as the divine subject of the odal apostrophe. Knowing as we do the genetic conditions of this topos, we can grasp at once its deeply historical character and at the same time, its archetypal power.

[. . .]

Notes

1 [References to Wordsworth's poetry, except *The Prelude*, are to *The Poetical Works of William Wordsworth*, ed. Ernest de Selincourt, Helen Darbishire, Thomas Hutchinson, 5 vol. (Oxford: Clarendon Press, 1940–49). References to *The Prelude* are to *The Prelude, 1799, 1805, 1850*, ed. Jonathan Wordsworth, M.H. Abrams, Stephen Gill (New York: Norton, 1979).]
2 Geoffrey Hartman observes in "Tintern Abbey" a "peculiar type of redundance {which} indicates resistance to abrupt progression." Geoffrey Hartman, *Wordsworth's Poetry 1787– 1814* (New Haven: Yale Univ. Press, 1964), p. 26.
3 And conversely, English guidebooks and ecclesiastical histories often embellish their remarks about and drawings of Tintern Abbey with quotations from Wordsworth's poem. [. . .]
4 [. . .] For a line of argument consonant with my own, see Kenneth Johnston's "Wordsworth and *The Recluse*: The University of Imagination," *PMLA* 97, no. 1 (January 1982, pp. 60–82). [. . .]
5 Laurence Goldstein, *Ruins and Empire: The Evolution of a Theme in Augustan and Romantic Literature* (Pittsburgh: Univ. of Pittsburgh Press, 1977), p. 179.
6 "Whenever we attempt to define the romantic nature it is always helpful to enquire to what this nature is being opposed, what is *not* nature." E. P. Thompson, "Disenchantment of Default? A Lay Sermon," in *Power and Consciousness*, ed. Conor Cruise O'Brien and William Vanech (London: Univ. of London Press, 1969), p. 151.
7 Karl Kroeber, *Romantic Landscape Vision*, (Madison: Univ. of Wisconsin Press, 1975), pp. 91, 92, 103.
8 See Brendan O Hehir, *Expans'd Hieroglyphicks: A Critical Edition of Sir John Denham's Coopers Hill* (Berkeley: Univ. of California Press, 1969), pp. 3–24; pp. 9, 11, 13.
9 Karl Kroeber, *Romantic Landscape Vision*, p. 103. [. . .]
10 Goldstein, *Ruins of Empire*: Chap. 10 "The Auburn Syndrome; Change and Loss in Grasmere," pp. 163–83; J.H. Plumb, *England in the Eighteenth Century, 1714–1815* (Baltimore: Penguin, 1950), p. 153.
11 [William Gilpin, *Observations on the River Wye* (1792).]
12 Hartman, p. 175.
13 The very literal Dr. Charles Burney sniffs out the ghosts in the poem; he, for one, remarks the significance of Wordsworth's selected vantage. (Donald Reiman, comp., *The Romantics Reviewed; Contemporary Reviews of British Romantic Writers*, 9 vols (New York: Garland, 1972), Part A, vol. 2, p. 717. From *Monthly Review*, 2nd series (June 1799).
Although Burney admires "Tintern Abbey," he finds it

somewhat tinctured with gloomy, narrow, and unsociable ideas of seclusion from the commerce of the world: as if men were born to live in woods and wilds, unconnected with each other! Is it not to education and the culture of the mind that we owe the raptures which the author so well describes as arising from the view of beautiful scenery, and the sublime objects of nature enjoyed in tranquility, when contrasted with the artificial machinery and "busy hum of men" in a city?

14 M.H. Abrams, "Structure and Style in the Greater Romantic Lyric," in *Romanticism and Consciousness,* ed. Harold Bloom (New York: Norton, 1970). Abrams describes "Tintern Abbey" as a poem remarkably "complete, self-sufficient, and endless," p. 206.

15 The image – not *of* Tintern Abbey but of its dissolution into an influence or essence – "discovers the restoration as opposed to the depredations of time" [Michael Cooke, *Acts of Inclusion: Studies Bearing on an Elementary Theory of Romanticism* (New Haven: Yale Univ. Press, 1979), p. 205.]

2   Keats and critique

Paul Hamilton

> The beautiful forms displayed in the organic world all plead eloquently on the side of
> the realism of the aesthetic finality of nature in support of the plausible assumption
> that beneath the production of the beautiful there must lie a preconceived idea in the
> producing cause – that is to say an *end* acting in the interest of our imagination.
>
> Kant, Critique of Judgement, 58

> In this relation [of Romantic art] the inner, so pushed to the extreme, is an expression
> without any externality at all; it is invisible and is as it were a perception of itself alone,
> or a musical sound as such without objectivity and shape, or a hovering over the waters,
> or a ringing tone over a world which in and on its heterogeneous phenomena can only
> accept and re-mirror a reflection of the inwardness of soul.
>
> Hegel, Aesthetics, 527

I

In a letter of 16 August 1820, Keats wrote to Shelley:

> A modern work it is said must have a purpose, which may be the God – *an artist*
> must serve Mammon – he must have 'self-concentration' selfishness perhaps.
> You I am sure will forgive me for sincerely remarking that you might curb your
> magnanimity and be more of an artist, and 'load every rift' of your subject with
> ore. The thought of such discipline must fall like cold chains upon you, who
> perhaps never sat with your wings furl'd for six months together, And is this not
> extraordina[r]y talk for the writer of Endymion? whose mind was like a pack of
> scattered cards – I am pick'd up and sorted to a pip. My Imagination is a Monastry
> and I am its Monk – you must explain my metap^{cs} [metaphysics] to yourself.

Keats's readers inherit a critical tradition in which his own language is regarded as
being everywhere as loaded and mixed in its blessings as that recommended here to
Shelley. His 'metap^{cs} [metaphysics]', as he told Shelley in the same letter, 'you must
explain . . . to yourself' (II, 323). [. . .] [W]hen Keats asks Shelley to curb his presumably political 'magnanimity' in the interests of being 'more of an artist', he characterizes this aestheticism as devotion to 'Mammon' rather than to 'God', paradoxically
(so it seems) recalling the material interests of politics through his very appeal to
artistic idealism. By shifting the accents in that unexpected verbal conjunction, we
realize that Keats's metaphysics, or his writerly situation *within* rather than reference
to a current metaphysical configuration, has been ignored as much as his politics. In

working them out 'for yourself', 'you' find that the aura of 'metaphysical conceit' apparently unrealizing Keats's politics is the clue to their nature.

This is one of the pioneering insights of Marjorie Levinson's book, *Keats's Life of Allegory – the Origins of a Style*. At last one can see clearly the conceitfulness with which Keats's poems double and displace their political concerns. Furthermore, we learn to read these concerns not as something under Keats's conscious control, but as part of an exercise in 'doing to himself what others do to him'. At the same time, Levinson's work discovers in the prescribed perversity that this social effect reveals, the absence of that collective life which would, conventionally, explain the unfreedom of Keats's self-fashioning. Keats suffers the 'scandal of a man without a class', the 'neither-nor' of someone stationed between the lower and middling orders. In a doubly effacing movement, then, the Keatsian poet is subjected to a social determination which stems from an indeterminate social provenance. Moreover, Levinson shows that the bourgeois culture to which Keats aspires shares his uncertainty of origin and recognizes its prototype in him. *His* visibly disadvantaged perspective on bourgeois aesthetics thus accentuates *its* characteristic nothingness in a subversive parody, betraying its poverty, as Hyperion does the misery of the Titans, 'To the most hateful seeing of itself'. Levinson's interest in developing a sociology of Keatsian literariness requires a de-emphasis of the familiar semantic questions: 'Keats's solutions *do* solve metaphysical and epistemological problems, but it is the others that need explaining.'[1]

My own return to 'metaphysical and epistemological problems' tries to capitalize on the new visibility which the old problems have gained as a result of Levinson's study. Re-immersion in these problems may weaken the sense of Keatsian parody, but, as Levinson asserts, metaphysical problems *are* solved in Keats's writings; and an analysis like mine, which shows the poverty of these successes, may help us see what happened to the idealist aesthetic when submitted to those pressures which Levinson's cultural materialism has identified. To work within the scheme of Romantic idealism in relation to Keats is not, then, to forgo critique. It is, rather, to explore from within a frustrated and inhibited critique which is transformed into effective parody as soon as its strict immanence is abandoned. Thus do we start to explain the mutual displacement of the political and the metaphysical within the discursive economy of Keats's time. We consider the means by which Keats and his early critics hid from themselves the substantive issues cultural materialism reveals. Finally, we relate the subversive implausibility of this containment, a weakness sensed but of necessity protected by Keats's contemporaries, to the productive and absorptive aporiae of the Kantian aesthetic.

The 'metaphysical conceit' of Keats's politics is a way to name the manner in which two discourses reciprocally disguise each other. The fact that Keats's metaphysical is political and his political metaphysical makes each invisible and accounts for the proverbial absence of both from his work. The word for this common vanishing-point is the 'aesthetic'. In the Kantian tradition, the aesthetic is what is left of reality after the critical philosophy has performed its task. A critique which, like Keats's poetry, operates under the sign of the aesthetic might therefore be expected to remain fairly well hidden. The aesthetic is also the area in which politics consolidates itself as culture; in which, again in line with Kantian practice, universals are imaginatively negotiated rather than deduced, and the political character of such transactions is both masked and validated as the exposition of what is metaphysically possible.[2]

My argument is that the interchangeability in Keats's poetry of its ideal status and its political reticence gradually begins to expose the contemporary politicizing of the ideal and the idealizing of the political. Moreover, in speaking that aesthetic function, the poetry breaks the silence on which that function's effectiveness depended, raising considerable problems for the criticism of Keats, both hostile and sympathetic. Hostile critics, in this sense, are neither heterodox nor antithetical but share the aesthetic under critique. Their complicity means that they cannot say what Keats is doing without joining in blowing the whistle on the common aesthetic's political function. Their criticism serves this political interest by becoming theoretically muted; my point is that such reticence still has *its* ideological point, and is thus indirectly expressed by the language of social animus which rushes in to fill the theoretical vacuum. [. . .]

The political is [. . .] revealed by the way in which Keats's apparent lapses from poetry into supposedly lower, extra-literary registers are contained by the aesthetic, in accordance with its idealizing function. The fact that these lapses are not recuperable, or that the idealizing function becomes visible, means that the poetry's political, 'objective' critique immanently invokes a disabling self-critique. [. . .]

What is objective about criticism here is that it is problematic. It cannot find an independent *point d'appui*, and what it unveils is a series of non-identities between aesthetics and politics: not an object but that object's dissolution through its immanent critique of its own consistency. The historical content in what follows consists of the failure of criticism, like the Kantian/Keatsian aesthetic, to secure its object. Therefore we must be vigilant to restore to these deconstructive victories their historical specificity. We are confronted with two heuristic modes which are equally aporetic *and* recuperative. The undermining of history through the deconstruction of its specificities is retrieved as a precisely historical experience of uncertainty – the historicity of history. The determination of the shape of deconstructive practice by historical circumstance is yet another productive defeat on which deconstruction thrives – the deconstruction of deconstruction. Because we cannot decide between these oppositions, both can claim the victory. The practical pay-off of this intellectual dilemma is that the reader can utilize whatever information emerges without having to adjudicate. To be outside one approach is to be inside both. [. . .] We will see that Keats's writing dissolves a comparable opposition, revealing how the aesthetic betrays (semiotically and polemically) the political and vice versa, each bringing the other to our notice as its dishonourable disguise.

[. . .]

[Keats's] poetry exposes its limitations by doubling. It demonstrates its critical remove from what its aesthetic ideology obliges it to do by exhibiting the relativism inherent in its essentialist claims. This is a self-wounding critique, but possible none the less, and one which reflects upon the foundational model of all critique, Kant's critical philosophy. It does so by showing that the aesthetic remaining when critique has done its work is hermetic. It resists discursive parallels in so far as it lays claim to a universal humanism. [. . .] Keats, I think, lays bare a contradiction in the radical bias of Kantian aesthetics, [. . .] [His] famed sensuousness is fuelled by an art which releases in us the desire that it *not* possess that imaginary function, the sphere of undetermined universality which allows it authority to educate our desires, but that it be, rather, a determinate judgement. Keats puts this point with a directness that courts the philosophical scandal involved: 'O for a Life of Sensations rather than of Thoughts!' (I, 185). [. . .] Keats's poetry makes us want to possess the aesthetic experience it offers on terms which do not allow it to have generated such a desire. Once discovered in Keats's 'Monastry', 'Mammon' could never have belonged there. This impasse is at the heart of what I am calling Keatsian critique.

[. . .]

[A section of this essay in its original form summarizes attacks on Keats by reviewers, including John Wilson Croker and John Gibson Lockhart]

[II]

[John Wilson] Croker's difficulties with the opening of *Endymion* arose from his resistance to the poem's invitation that we join in a fiction whereby the flagrantly anecdotal is projected as the essential, and the full import of an idealist poetry is exposed. 'This', runs the fiction, 'is what fulfilment is like' – a symbolic adequacy of thought to object, the unproblematic assumption of necessity as one's own freedom, the experience of the random or miscellaneous as a significant catalogue, the whole rhetoric of comfort which directs the opening scenes of *Endymion*. Croker, I would suggest, disguises the poverty of this ideal by in effect claiming it has not happened: that it is not there to be observed and so cannot be judged. Keats's poem has, for him, the appearance of having been produced by 'an immeasurable game of *bouts-rimés*': this is to say, its equivalences are arbitrary and pat, the random result of auditory associations, risible as a Cockney parody of the heroic couplet and meaningless on the poem's own account.[3] The undoubted difficulties, however, in following the opening of *Endymion* arise from the effort of understanding a further possibility encompassing the qualities which Croker rightly senses, but allotting to them a place within another argument which he would have thought could not be formulated coherently. Since the theme of fulfilment is usually thought to exclude critique (critique being properly limited to the policing of the desire whereby fulfilment is to be achieved), the ultimate discontent suggested by a Keatsian critique of fulfilment can only appear to Croker as incompetence, ruled out of court by its successes. But, as I shall emphasize later, the critique of value is a common feature of contemporary economic discourse. Its bind is inescapable if you want to say something like the following: within Romantic aesthetics fulfilment, which only works as an idea in the normative, prescriptive realm, none the less has as its rationale the dissolution of that distinctiveness. Fulfilment is when an 'ought' becomes an 'is', but actually to present it as an 'is' may render it so ordinary as to make its previous, legislatory function quite incredible – hence the dissatisfied 'Was it for this . . . ' which Wordsworth uses all his resources of poetic revision to restore. To preserve that legislative function, the power of aesthetic jurisdiction, it is best to keep fulfilment as the invisible endpoint of desire. It is this contradiction within the realist logic of fulfilment (in Kant's dialetic, 'the realism of the aesthetic finality of nature') which is exposed in Croker's and [John Gibson] Lockhart's twin accusations of *Endymion's* unintelligibility and vulgar sensuousness.[4]

The poem's provocative dedication to Chatterton is a guide to the way Keats might have been thinking his way through his own abrasiveness. The dedication invites the reader to remember how Chatterton's youthful fraud is to create a language not natural to him, 'the strechèd metre of an antique song'. This strange and insincere tongue is assimilated to the Romantic aesthetic when Chatterton is welcomed, as in Coleridge's 'Monody', as 'the young-eyed Poesy / All deftly mask'd as hoar Antiquity'.

In Chatterton's case, the predominant taste *has* found it possible to escape the bind that if he is original, he is not antique; and if he is the genuine thing, he is not original. The parallel escape for Keats, given *Endymion's* first reviews, would be from the certainty that if he is using a vocabulary of satisfaction, he cannot be critical of it; and if the effect *is* critical, he cannot be in command of his vocabulary.

The double-think required to escape the Keatsian bind is present at the start of *Endymion*, in its difficult opening transition:

> A thing of beauty is a joy for ever,
> Its loveliness increases; it will never
> Pass into nothingness, but still will keep
> A bower quiet for us, and a sleep
> Full of sweet dreams, and health, and quiet breathing.
> Therefore, on every morrow, are we wreathing
> A flowery band to bind us to the earth,
> Spite of despondence, of the inhuman dearth
> Of noble natures, of the gloomy days,
> Of all the unhealthy and o'er darken'd ways
> Made for our searching – yes, in spite of all,
> Some shape of beauty moves away the pall
> From our dark spirits.
>
> (I, 1–13)

The pivotal 'Therefore, on every morrow, are we wreathing' is puzzlingly reflexive. Who is doing the wreathing? Who is the narrator incorporating in the royal 'we' wreathing the 'thing of beauty'? The poem already appears tied to the task of simulating an image of aesthetic success – a poem about the experience of having read an aesthetically finished poem (good Wordsworthian precedents here). This is the Keatsian logic of catching up on an already poeticized landscape, a wilderness already 'dressed' by thought to facilitate the arrival of consciousness.

> And now at once, adventuresome, I send
> My herald thought into a wilderness –
> There let its trumpet blow, and quickly dress
> My uncertain path with green, that I may speed
> Easily onward, thorough flowers and weed.
>
> (I, 58–63)

The effect is to continue the earlier sonnets' view of the creation of poetic language as a place of repose: not a characterization of anything but, as in the 'Ode to Psyche', the dwelling on apprehension, the treatment of it as a place of arrival, John Jones's 'end-stopped feel'.[5]

[. . .]

Cosmology in *Endymion* is inseparable from cosmetics, the 'known Unknown' carnally remystified by the poem's romance as 'Such darling essence' (II, 739–40). The opening passage of *Endymion* continues with a substantial, paratactic passage concluding in the unequivocal ascription of essence to its individual clauses, including the sequence which drove Croker to think of *bouts-rimés*:

> Such the sun, the moon,
> Trees, old and young, sprouting a shady boon
> For simple sheep; and such are daffodils
> With the green world they live in; and clear rills
> That for themselves a cooling covert make
> 'Gainst the hot season; the mid-forest brake,
> And such too is the grandeur of the dooms
> We have imagined for the mighty dead,
> All lovely tales that we have heard or read –
> An endless fountain of immortal drink,
> Pouring unto us from the heaven's brink.
>
> Nor do we merely feel these essences
> For one short hour . . .
>
>   (I, 13–26)

Pan soon becomes the poem's principle of such a catalogue, a physical 'leaven' which dodges all conception and so escapes being part of mental 'dress', remaining the object of 'address' in the shepherds' hymn to him:

> Be still the unimaginable lodge
> For solitary thinkings – such as dodge
> Conception to the very bourne of heaven,
> Then leave the naked brain; be still the leaven,
> That spreading in this dull and clodded earth
> Gives it a touch ethereal, a new birth;
> Be still a symbol of immensity,
> A firmament reflected in a sea,
> An element filling the space between,
> An unknown – but no more!
>
>   (I, 293–302)

Pan is the 'element filling the space between', the idea of a yeasty consistency behind differences, taken up in the indiscriminate stream of apostrophes to which the bright, essential Cynthia provokes Endymion in Book III (III, 52–102, 163–75), which raises also the idea of a benevolent nature. The paganism which reportedly offended Wordsworth's religious sensibilities seems too a convention under which a realism of fulfilment can be contemplated, and its unstable condition examined. Endymion, imagining 'happiness' as 'A fellowship with essence', is to be 'Full alchemized, and free of space' (I, 780), a solution that could be entirely ethereal, or, which might involve his transformation into a material form of infinite extension. The meaning will not settle and remains as oxymoronic as Endymion's dream of an archetypal union with Cynthia – 'O unconfined / Restraint! imprisoned liberty!' (I, 455–6). To have succeeded in writing a language which raises such equivocations about 'that completed form of all completeness . . . that high perfection of all sweetness' (I. 606–7) is by implication to have questioned the idea of fulfilment as the adequation of desire and, conversely, of desire as the Striving for fulfilment. This conclusion either suggests an ideological component which can use the aesthetic idea of fulfilment for its own legislative ends, manipulating people's desires under false pretences which nevertheless seem inherent in the very logic of desire, and thus safe from criticism, their falsity expressible only as a kind of nonsense. Or else it suggests a willingness to accept the conventionally aberrant and unnatural as imaginative possibilities: following Adorno, we can experience in art the non-identity of things with their labels, an experience which promises the 'emancipation' of the aesthetic subject.[6] *Endymion's* hostile critics drew both implications in their charges of nonsensical voluptuousness. Keats's own revision of the 'fellowship with essence' passage inspires his most explicit image of a critique of pleasure working through human variables.

[. . .]

[III]

So far, the possibilities for Keatsian critique have been largely passive, given shape through the accusations of the first hostile critics of his poems. But the reciprocal, revealing provocation which his writings offer to idealism should now be more visible. *Endymion* is a poem in which Keatsian intensity crowns the narrative far too soon. Endymion finds that he has 'raught / The goal of consciousness' early in the second of four books, and the precocious sexual continuation rather than realization of this achievement takes place before the end of book two. Yet the poem forestalls any straightforward discontent with its apparent structural mismanagement by foregrounding this intensity and overriding other disappointments through its claim to hold in focus a fugitive climax, and so to nudge us beyond the pleasure principle and into a critique of pleasure. The effect is to say: this is the goal of narrative, usually unquestioned, here brought forward for examination. The poem's psychological defence against critical discontent is a phenomenology of the *tristitia* consequent on pleasure.

Endymion's language of cultural acquaintance, in contrast to the deferential modesty of the published Preface, is strikingly ambitious in the possessiveness of its portrayal of 'the beautiful mythology of Greece'. This presumption takes the form of an intimate inwardness, physical and psychological, by which the empirical reach of Keats's poetic language exceeds its pictorial licence, at the same time foregrounding its poeticity. [. . .] Alternatively, Keats's self-signifying cultivation translates into endless circumscription which never closes on a classical centre because such closure is in general epistemologically impossible. Possession is inherently vicarious – Phoebe in place of Cynthia – and poetry is the aesthetic recognition or polemical redemption ('beauty is truth') of that otherwise unhappy fact. Both these versions of Keatsian sensuousness have had their skilful expositors.[7] What they return us to is the notion of a putative endpoint at which we are encouraged to apply what we take to be natural standards of experience to something we cannot have on those terms at all. This is a political as well as an epistemological point, and we have already discussed the politically advantageous self-deception which might be involved. But to expose such a tactic is to impugn the aesthetic collaborator, and in doing so Keatsian critique begins to go on the offensive. On the one hand, *Endymion's* exaggerations suggest that such satisfaction is an impossible ambition of all art, and one which is, as a rule, decently repressed. On the other, Keats's importunate hyperboles conspicuously disguise the fact that if this view of art had its way, poetry would aspire to the condition of kitsch: an art which meets with no external resistance because it has been purified of all critical difference. This is the moral consequence of the Hegelian reading of the rhetoric of Kantian *aisthesis* quoted at the head of this chapter, a reading to which, Adorno concedes, Kant's formalism makes him vulnerable. The replicatory motives of *aisthesis* are so innocent – so disinterested – that they appear completely complacent in any but the most brazenly self-serving world. For readers who consider themselves cultivated, to meet with the implication that this is what they desire from their reading is highly insulting. It is as if Keats imagines a sudden access of expertise in which the esoteric reflexivity of avant-garde art becomes indistinguishable from the effortless self-evidence of kitsch: caviare for the general at last.[8]

Idealist bourgeois culture legitimates itself by constructing Keats as the *arriviste*, the importunate consumer of what is not for sale. He cannot buy into this culture because it is presented as the system which makes buying possible. This system is analogous to the ubiquitous symbolic order of exchange or credit which, from Simmel through Saussure to Foucault, rationalizes the *paroles* of individual monetary transactions; or, to the psychological blueprint which the Kantian tradition deduced and aesthetically savoured as the logical prerequisite of every act of determinate judgement or specific cognition. On either of these descriptions, political interest is disguised as the conditions under which a metaphysic is possible. The specifics of high bourgeois taste pose as an absolute regime – a universal – and it is the unchallengeable quality of this acculturation which converges embarrassingly with the self-exonerating logic of kitsch. One cannot change someone's taste for kitsch by pointing out the easiness or cheapness of the experience on offer, because it is just this facility of possession which is prized as the distinctive quality of the art.[9] To value kitsch knowingly, on the other hand, can be to express scepticism about any alternatives and, also, contempt for the naïve belief that more than an 'aura' survives of a sincerely humanist art claiming to escape comparison with kitsch. This is a modernist disingenuousness, reworked in postmodernism of all kinds from Warhol to Lyotard, which is not at all Keats's position. The modernist reader of Keats, however, is bound to see the connection and to find it useful in demonstrating the ways in which his writing escapes the straightforward recuperations of Romantic irony without simply amounting to the ineptitude and gaucheness attributed to it by his contemporary critics.

Writing of his suppressed Preface to *Endymion*, Keats describes his 'Public' as 'a thing I cannot help looking on as an Enemy', and claims that 'if there is any fault in the preface it is not affectation: but an undersong of disrespect to the Public'. In this context, the more a poet risks, not personally but on his own professional behalf, the further he pushes his readers into a position reflecting the endemic discomfiture of an audience positioned by an idealist aesthetic. It is hard, after all, to see how the Prefaces, published and unpublished, could be more modest on their author's part – the true function of a preface according to Keats's original version. Rather than a laboured and straightforward irony, Keats's persistent wish 'to conciliate men who are competent to look, and who do look with a zealous eye, to the honour of English literature' suggests that in so far as these critics represent public taste, to allow them to have their way – genuinely to conciliate them – is insult enough.

The provocation Keats offers to an idealist Romantic aesthetic makes it reveal its ideological basis in the analogy it bears to capital as a whole. As is the case with Schiller, the universals which are the stuff of aesthetic legitimacy are symbolic, like Kantian symbols, not just of morality but also inadvertently of the unquestionable efficacy of the credit on which bourgeois culture subsists. Keats's writing throws in relief the self-defeating character inflicted on art by this uncritical role. He does not produce independent critique but uncovers the equivalent of an uncritical moment in the critical philosophy, a disabling contradiction in the mastery with which art promotes its authoritative humanism. In this way he turns aesthetic success into its opposite, and symbolically calls into question the universals of which art is the acceptable expression and legitimating front. The possession of capital is, by analogy, made to seem accidental and disputable rather than the essential, unarguable right of the landed and mercantile classes.

This analogical reading adds to the picture of dominant members of a culture anxiously confronting in Keats's work the diminished importance their culture attributes to art. Art serves not as something which presents the content of fulfilment, but provides the excuse to go on believing in the possibility of utter satisfaction precisely because of the fact that it is never there. To propose, as Keats seems to do, a phenomenology of the ends of art is to reveal precisely that lack by visibly exploiting art as the discourse in which the relation of this discovery leaves us untroubled and reconciled. Art is given credit for what it cannot redeem; and to question this credit – to cause a 'run' on art – would be analogous to undermining confidence in the basic fiction by which those in possession of capital possess it by virtue of a universal interest in which all share. The force of Keats's conciliatory critique becomes even more palpable if we consider the contemporary crises of confidence in capital itself, crises whose character offers reinforcement to the aesthetic analogy from the other direction.

This happens especially where controversies over paper money are concerned. In economic debates of the time, value-making was not a Nietzchean overcoming of humanity, but a routine choice between contested options.[10] There is a long tradition in English philosophy and literature of distrust for and ridicule of the gradual ascendancy of paper money over coin, dating from the establishment of the Bank of England in 1694 onwards. [. . .] As Levinson has observed, [. . . during] Keats's lifetime [. . .], faced with the additional demands of financing the Napoleonic Wars, the government passed a Restriction Act prohibiting the Bank of England from redeeming any of its notes in gold, legislation which held from 1797 until 1819. Even in 1819, only the palliative measure of David Ricardo's Ingot Plan was adopted, and none but relatively large amounts of cash could be redeemed, and then only in bullion, not in coin. Of the 2,028 bars made for this purpose, nicknamed 'Ricardoes', only thirteen were sold, mainly because the market price fell below the mint price and buyers in the short term lost money. Full convertibility resumed only in 1823. By a striking corroboration, therefore, in Keats's productive years 'the realms of gold' would provide the perfect image of the imaginary wealth of literary inheritance, while showing that it would be wiser to stay in credit there, on paper, than to seek a more tangible and realistic standard of value.[11]

Most economic historians [*sic*] seem agreed that it is, after all, very doubtful if the English economy could have borne the financial burdens imposed by the Napoleonic Wars had it not adopted the device of the Restriction Act and declared Bank of England notes to be legal tender irrespective of the availability of securities. The *Edinburgh Review* opposed Ricardo and the 'bullionists' who wanted to limit the domestic money supply and thus facilitate a return to the gold standard. Ricardo took Adam Smith's disapproval of devaluation as precedent, and could have cited Franc[i]s Hutcheson in support.[12] In *Queen Mab*, the young Shelley shows himself an out and out bullionist. In *The Mask of Anarchy* he continues to attack paper credit as another form of disenfranchisement, straightforwardly opposing its exchange-value to workers' labour-value [. . .] (xlv). Keats, on the other hand, is a poetic inflationist; one whose work suggests that 'the inheritance of the earth' will become more available through the spread of credit [. . .].[13] Logically, however, Ricardo made it as embarrassing as possible for the anti-bullionists to defend the expansion of paper credit. In his Appendix to *The High Price of Bullion*, he asks his opponent from the *Edinburgh Review*: 'is it conceivable that money should be sent abroad for the purpose merely of rendering it dear in this country and cheap in another, and by such means to ensure its return to us?'[14] Clearly it was, and, transposed to the economics of the aesthetic, such pragmatism could be equally sophistical and compromising. Arguably, Keats, in the eyes of *Endymion's* hostile reviewers, had demonstrated the perversity of Ricardo's logic to the letter. First, he showed that the aesthetic experience of ultimate good depended for its unique value on having been 'sent abroad', deferred to some ideal, irredeemably exemplary realm. Second, through his 'promiscuous' exploration of these aesthetic ends (that is, the hedonistic phenomenology of satisfaction and fulfilment), Keats cheapened them sufficiently to remind readers of their justifiable expectation of enjoying them back in the here and now. Keats's 'speculative Mind', as a passage in his letter to the George Keatses of February–May 1819 shows, carries a Wordsworthian universal, 'one human heart', to its shockingly democratic conclusion without fear of debasement – 'the pity is that we must wonder at it; as we should at finding a pearl in rubbish' (II, 80). Not to accept the reality of 'speculations', and to lack the courage 'to put down his halfseeing', is how Keats's poet 'makes a false coinage . . . poetry that has a palpable design upon us – and if we do not agree, seems to put its hand in its breeches pocket'. Bad poetry, that is, abandons credit to buy readers off in kind (I, 223–4).[15]

[. . .]

[IV]

Keats's immanent critique of the Romantic aesthetic is powered by his writing's exposure of the fact that its hedonistic credit is irredeemable, and that attempts to redeem aesthetic promise are treated as misunderstandings of the best way to put its fictional wealth to work. The Keatsian example shows that this defence cuts both ways, since the use of art to preserve the idea of transcendental imperatives with categorical claims on our essential nature is now married to a disreputable, inflationary disregard for an economy which thus balances the normative and the natural in opposite columns. Keats's sensuousness and vulgarity dispense with the niceties of idealist bookkeeping and propose phenomenological satisfactions in the speculative field. This is the unacceptable face of an aesthetic which in theory sanctions this proposal, but always under the semblance of economic responsibility. In (Kantian) theory, adventures in the intelligible world can only be recalled in terms which judge without determining a universality bathetically fitting the world of natural appearances; and natural desire is similarly policed by this hypothetical convergence with its regulative ideals. However, to cash the bond by innocently imagining a fulfilment realized threatens the economy's credit by placing under scrutiny the value of its redemption. At best, a cosmetic gloss is spread over its tautologies and parataxes, making them more acceptable but still showing how plenitude can shade into kitsch. To ignore the economy's assumed security of *specie* is, then, to beat it at its own game, enjoying on credit what could never possibly be paid for in kind – kind, that is, as defined according to prescriptions of the natural before the ideal spending-spree began.

[. . .]

[T]he 'Hyperion' poems [. . . can be] read as a resumé of Keats's immanent critique of the sublime redundancy of the Romantic aesthetic, the divine sameness by which it recuperates the aporetic, simultaneously inside and outside its own rhetorical project. 'Hyperion' conjures up the availability of a heroic tradition, the enormity of whose imminence has a petrifying effect. The shape of this pressure is initially given through the poem's temporality, or rather its atemporality, in anticipation of that paralysing *nunc stans* which freezes and monumentalizes the kinetic efforts of its actors and narrators in a series of achieved moments and sculpted poses. The isolation which the opening sentence of 'Hyperion' exposes grows more intimate and assured as, again almost in parody of Wordsworth's 'Ode', it slips into an inwardness 'Far' from the common coordinates of everyday experience – 'morn', 'noon', 'eve'. This interiorization does not consequently take on the temporal form of inner sense: there has been no Wordsworthian movement through memory to arrive at this place and so measure its depth. Rather, the vale pictures what it is to obviate all motion, all desire. The landscape apparently described is in fact telescoped into images of its own lack of identifying temporal or spatial perspective. To be 'quiet as a stone' is to be so unsurprisingly quiet as to be quiet *simpliciter*: a stone without a dynamic moment or an energizing context because it has absorbed all such as qualities of its own massive equilibrium. The rhetoric of this state is sheer tautology, as in the extended pleonasm with which Thea evokes the Titans' inner life as one of undifferentiated externalization: 'O moments big as years! / All as ye pass swell out the monstrous truth, / And press it so upon our weary griefs / That unbelief has not a space to breathe.' Truth so protracted can only reiterate its own mass or extension; there is no room for the temporal or spatial progression necessary to Wordsworthian revision. We now realize that what we are 'far' from, what we are distanced from, is again distance itself.

[. . .]

The rest of 'Hyperion' works on the possibility of something else, something strained for in the early move from pleonasm into the chiasmus describing Thea's expression: 'But O! how unlike marble was that face, / How beautiful, if sorrow had not made / Sorrow more beautiful than Beauty's self.' Rhetorically flexed in this way, the tautologies of 'Hyperion' try to curb their own self-sufficiency and restore a meaningful difference between themselves and their object, impossibly revealing themselves 'frail / To that large utterance of the early Gods'. Yet the outcome, tragically, falls once more into repetition, and in 'The Fall' the further internalization of action within Moneta's brain can only resume the same old Titanic story, the start of 'Hyperion'. However, the cul-de-sac is already sketched in the openings of both poems, in the show of a criticism trapped within the ironic elaboration of what it cannot distance, possessing a conscious but unforthcoming insincerity. This dilemma is developed by Saturn's apparent recourse to another perhaps only closer language, the 'mother tongue' taken up in the opening of 'The Fall'. With hindsight, the reader can take Saturn 'listening to the Earth, / His ancient mother, for some comfort yet' as listening for a story different from that of the 'high tragedy', in which the poet of 'The Fall' has to be initiated and which has brought him to this low and deep realization of its archetype. The 'Hyperion' poems can easily appear to blend into the common currency of Romantic irony; but, closely read, the poems expose irony's impoverished fulfilment and incorrigible reflexivity. They begin to negotiate the surrender of such self-identity for something less assured, something not inevitably recuperable through the ironies of poetic self-criticism. By the opening of 'The Fall', the 'mother tongue' has become the democratic franchise of 'every man whose soul is not a clod', in explicit contrast to elitist, a priori prescriptions of who can and cannot be a poet. Fanatic, savage and poet differ only in powers of articulation, and the resources of articulateness lie in the *mamaloschen*. The only content ascribed to the poet's 'dreams' and 'visions' comes from the utopian impulse of others, of fanatics who 'weave / A paradise for a sect' or the savage who 'Guesses at Heaven'. Poetry has no content of its own, hence its inability to legislate on its own account and its deference to posterity for its definition. Poetry is nothing but the name given to the effective expression of something better than there is by those who have been educated ('nurtured') in their native language. The narrator's concession at the end of the paragraph – 'Whether the dream now purposed to rehearse / Be Poet's or Fanatic's will be known / When this warm scribe my hand is in the grave' – is a paradox which appears covertly to reinforce the nothingness attributed to poetry by the logic of the argument so far. In other words, whatever happens, 'the dream now purposed to rehearse' is in language, and any subsequent soubriquet of 'poetry' can only appear honorific or supernumerary. Abandoning the whole 'Hyperion' project, Keats writes that it is 'English', not an 'artful' poetry, which 'ought to be kept up' (II, 167).

To read the opening of 'The Fall' in this way seems to go against the grain of Keats's poetic ambitions, ambitions caught in that final dedication to posterity, however vulnerable. But again it is worth emphasizing that even this bid for retrospective legislation masks or euphemizes a present lack. [. . .] Keats dramatizes in this way the impossibility of his own parabasis and the gains and losses of a historical appreciation which will be able to see the poetry, but only at the cost of being able to take the aesthetic crisis seriously.

We cannot take idealism at its own estimation of itself, and so we fail to be limited by and thus true to the constraints of Keats's aesthetic. We see the manner in which his critique and its self-censorship are bound together. We see too what Keats could not when his conspicuously euphemistic and cosmetic style negates his writing's ostensible ideological conformity. By then, however, his aesthetic credit is exhausted. We have to move on to another critical standard. In socially genetic terms, the 'Hyperion' poems situate Keats closest to a class whose radical moment has passed with the French Revolution, and whose effaced sign of a former radical interest is the commercial credit it enjoys as a result of the same economic shifts more peacefully achieved in England. As critique, Keats's poetry portrays the ersatz establishment thus created 'To the most hateful seeing of itself'. But, above all, what is peculiar about such inauthenticity is the inscribed suggestion that there is no alternative; and the tragic strength of the 'Hyperion' poems is their euphemistic betrayal of the historical fact that, within their aesthetic, criticism and creation, disownment and renewal, abandonment and progress have to take place in the same words, through the same effects, powered by the same talents, clenched in the same narratives.

Notes

References to Keats's poems are to *The Poems of John Keats*, edited by Miriam Allott (London and New York: Longman, Norton, 1970). Quotations from the letters come from *The Letters of John Keats: 1814–21*, edited by Hyder E. Rollins, 2 vols (Cambridge, MA: Harvard University Press, 1958).

1 Marjorie Levinson, *Keats's Life of Allegory – the Origins of a Style* (Oxford: Basil Blackwell, 1988), pp. 291, 23, 5–6, 141.
2 I am here following Hannah Arendt's interpretation of Kant's third *Critique* as containing:

> perhaps the greatest and most original aspect of Kant's political philosophy . . . Culture and politics, then, belong together because it is not knowledge or truth which is at stake, but rather judgement and decision, the judicious exchange of opinion about the sphere of public life and the common world.
> *Between Past and Future* (New York: Viking Press, 1961), pp. 219–24

[. . .]

3 [*Keats: the Critical Heritage*, ed. G.M. Matthews (London: Routledge & Kegan Paul, 1971), p. 112]; see William Keach's useful discussion of Keats's couplets, 'Cockney Couplets: Keats and the Politics of Style', in 'Keats and Politics: a Forum', *Studies in Romanticism*, vol. 25, no. 2 (Summer 1986), pp. 182–96.
4 [*Critical Heritage*, p. 111.]
5 John Jones, *John Keats's Dream of Truth* (London: Chatto & Windus, 1969).
6 Theodor Adorno, *Aesthetic Theory*, trans. C. Lenhardt, ed. Gretel Adorno and Ralph Tiedemann (London and New York: Routledge & Kegan Paul, 1984), p. 113.
7 C. Ricks, *Keats and Embarrassment* (Oxford: Clarendon Press, 1974), pp. 13ff; M. Aske, *Keats and Hellenism: an Essay* (Cambridge: Cambridge University Press, 1986).
8 See Clement Greenberg's discussion in 'Avant-garde and Kitsch' (1939) in *Art and Culture* (London: Thames & Hudson, 1973), p. 14; for Keats's use of 'caviare' see [Jerome] McGann, *The Beauty of Inflections* (Oxford: Clarendon Press, 1985), pp. 32–9.
9 I am trying here to expand on Adorno's remarks in *Aesthetic Theory* – 'Implicit in the concept of art is the phenomenon of kitsch' (p. 175), 'It lies dormant in art itself' (p. 339), 'A critique of kitsch, if it is radical and unrelenting, passes beyond kitsch and encompasses art *per se*' (p. 435), and also pp. 53, 70–1; see also Stephen Bungay's brief but helpful discussion in *Beauty and Truth: a Study of Hegel's Aesthetics* (Oxford: Clarendon Press, 1984), p. 95.
10 See, for example, [David] Ricardo's summary of the problem in the chapter on 'Value and Riches, their Distinctive Properties', in *The Principles of Political Economy and Taxation* (1817), introduced by Donald Winch (London: Dent, 1973) [p. 183]. [. . .]
11 See Michael J. Gootzeit, *David Ricardo* (New York and London: Columbia University Press, 1975), pp. 2, 22.
12 Ricardo, *Economic Essays*, ed. E.C.⬚. Gonner (London: Frank Cass, 1923), p. 40; see also W.L. Taylor, *Francis Hutcheson and David Hume as Predecessors of Adam Smith* (Duke, NC: Duke University Press, 1965).
13 See Douglas Vickers, *Studies in the Theory of Money 1690–1776* (London: Peter Owen, 1960), p. 133; Gareth Stedman Jones, *Languages of Class, Studies in English Working Class History 1832–1982* (Cambridge: Cambridge University Press, 1983), pp. 137–40, discusses the relevance of Shelley's bullionism to the Chartists.
14 *Economic Essays*, p. 45.
15 For Keats's use of 'speculative' and 'speculation', see *Letters*, vol. I, pp. 175, 184–5, 223–4, 243, 277, 387; vol. II, pp. 80–1, 115. [. . .]

3   Byron's causes

The moral mechanics of *Don Juan*

James Chandler

[The opening sections of this chapter explore Byron's interest in, and complication of, causal explanation throughout *Don Juan*.

[F]rom the very first stanza of the dedication, *Don Juan* represents the genre of its poetic enemies as, precisely, epic – the pretentious, renegado, modernizing, anti-Popean verse productions on a grand scale such as [Robert] Southey's *Thalaba the Destroyer* (1801) and [William] Wordsworth's *The Excursion* (1814). There was, however, another version of modernized epic available to [Lord] Byron, a version, as it happens, for which he showed nothing less than a passion. This is the version of "modern epopée" available to Byron in [Walter] Scott's Waverley novels. Though the topic of Byron's connection with Scott has enjoyed some recent attention, and although the notion of *Don Juan* as "novelistic" has long been a commonplace in the commentaries, the precise relation of Byron's epic to the new form of the historical novel has remained curiously unexplored.[1]

This is curious for several reasons. The first is that Byron's letters for the period of the composition of *Don Juan* make it clear that he is a man obsessed with reading Scott's fiction. References to Scott are nearly as numerous as those to Shakespeare, and show a far greater degree of absorption. Less than two weeks after Byron sent off to John Murray the packet containing cantos 3 and 4 of *Don Juan,* he wrote Murray as follows (on March 1, 1820):

> Pray send me W. Scott's new novels – what are their names and characters? I read some of his former ones at least once a day for an hour or so. – The last are too hurried – he forgets Ravenswood's name – and calls him *Edgar* – and then *Norman* – and Girder – the Cooper – is – styled now *Gilbert* and now *John* – and he don't make enough of Montrose – but Dalgetty is excellent – and so is Lucy Ashton – and the bitch her mother. . . . Don't forget to answer forthwith – for I wish to hear of the arrival of the packets – viz. the two Cantos of Donny Johnny. . . .
>
> (BLJ, 7:48–49)[2]

Writing again to Murray less than two months later on April 23, he resumes:

> My love to Scott – I shall think higher of knighthood ever after for his being dubbed – by the way – he is the first poet titled for his talent – in Britain – it

has happened abroad before now – but on the continent titles are universal & worthless. – Why don't you send me Ivanhoe & the Monastery – I have never written to Sir Walter – for I know he has a thousand things & I a thousand nothings to do – but I hope to see him at Abbotsford before very long, and I will sweat his Claret for him – . . . I love Scott and Moore – and all the better brethren – but I hate & abhor that puddle of water-worms – whom you have taken into your troop in the *history* line I see.

(BLJ, 7:83)

That Byron invidiously compares Scott, and even [Thomas] Moore, with Murray's "troop in the *history* line," betrays a recognition on Byron's part that the "history" that is being made in this age of historicism is not in the genre of historiography as such. Byron's own work, by extension, deserves such comparison. This particular sequence closes, unsurprisingly, with Byron's acknowledging receipt of, and offering simple emphatic praise for, Scott's longed-for last novel of 1819: "I have received *Ivanhoe; – good*" (June 7 – p. 113). But his letters of this period often show the process by which Byron's appetite is whetted for other novels – *The Monastery* and *The Abbott,* for example – and then gratified when the desired books have been delivered and perused.

In those instances, furthermore, where Byron expresses even the slightest disappointment with Scott's novels, as in his criticisms of *The Bride of Lammermoor,* it is often the case that his opinions improve with continued and compulsive rereading. Here is Byron's subsequent response to *The Bride*:

[January 5, 1821] Read the conclusion, for the fiftieth time (I have read all W. Scott's novels at least fifty times) of the third series of 'Tales of my Landlord', – grand work – . . . wonderful man! I long to get drunk with him.

(BLJ, 8:13)

Although it is safe to assume exaggeration in these numbers – Byron has a stanza-long joke, after all, about the number "fifty" (BLJ, 1:108) – it is worth recalling that this passage is not from a letter but from the journal Byron kept during his time in Ravenna, where hyperbole seems less in order. And while the fact that the character of Ravenswood in *The Bride of Lammermoor* was modeled on Byron's characters (and even his character) clearly might have influenced his judgment, just as clearly the entire series of "Landlord" tales struck a responsive chord with Byron. In the two critical essays he wrote during the period 1820–21, for example, Byron cited both of the early series, alluding to David Deans's deathbed lamentation on his time at the close of his public response to *Blackwood's* and borrowing an epigraph from *Old Mortality* for his *Letter to **** ****** [John Murray] on the Pope Controversy.[3]

Not only does Byron laud Scott in private writings and related prose essays, but he also praises him openly in the stanzas of *Don Juan* itself. In the poem's dedicatory stanzas, Scott is the first of the contemporary writers offered by Byron in lieu of the renegado trio "Wordsworth, Coleridge, Southey" (DS:7).[4] He is cited as Byron's "buon camerado" when it comes to the question of representing aberrant morals (12:16). He also figures prominently in the famous passage where Byron, while discussing the *Edinburgh Review,* comes to terms with his own Scottishness (10:17–19). Beyond the fact of the praise incorporated into the poem, though, there is the further issue of what Scott is praised for. Late in the poem, when he calls Scott "the superlative of my comparative," the particular talent that Byron identifies is Scott's way with comparative description: "Scott, who can paint your Christian knight or Saracen, / Serf, lord, man with such skill" (15:59). One could argue (as Byron seems to recognize) that Scott's innovations in historical epic are built on a power to describe the typical characters and elements of various cultures, past and present, and to see the connection between such a literary mode and those popular travel books that Moore would have seen advertised in his *Morning Chronicle* for New Year's Day 1819.

This sort of comparativist cultural representation is a literary technique Byron seeks to redeploy to his own epic purposes, and nowhere more evidently, Byron being Byron, than in the canto where he denies that he will do so:

> I won't describe; description is my forte,
>> But, every fool describes in these bright days
> His wond'rous journey to some foreign court,
>> And spawns his quarto, and demands your praise –
> Death to his publisher, to him 'tis sport;
>> While Nature, tortured twenty thousand ways,
> Resigns herself with exemplary patience
> To guidebooks, rhymes, tours, sketches, illustrations.
>> (5:52)[5]

Canto 5, written in the fall of 1820, marks the beginning of the third major block of the poem's composition-publication, and arguably the block where its comparative scheme of national-cultural critique begins to emerge. On February 16, 1821, soon after completing it, Byron confronted a jittery John Murray and addressed the possibility of the poem's being suspended while Murray assessed public reaction. At this point, he stressed that the five completed cantos formed "hardly the beginning," and outlined a scheme in which Juan would be taken on "the tour of Europe – with a proper mixture of siege – battle – and adventure – and to make him finish as *Anarcharsis Cloots* – in the French revolution" (BLJ, 8:78). Byron writes that he is uncertain of the number of cantos he would live to write but adds that he also "meant to have made him [Juan] a Cavalier Servente in Italy and a cause for divorce in England – and a Sentimental 'Werther-faced man' in Germany – so as to show the different ridicules of the society in each of those countries" (BLJ, 8:78). It is in cantos 3 and 4, and then more dramatically in canto 5, where "description" is formally abjured, that Byron begins with steadily increasing deliberateness to move his protagonist into determinate cultural contexts that require the extraordinary descriptive virtuosity, the Scott-like "skill," to paint your Greek pastoral, Turkish harem, your English military, your Russian court, your English manor – those diverse scenes where Juan acts and is acted on.[6]

In establishing the relation of Byron to Scott, it is important to understand that they were not only the two recognized "kings" of the literary realm but that they had also, in a sense, been taking turns appropriating each other's readerships. Scott built an unprecedented public taste for romantic poetry in the first decade of the century, when he emerged as far and away the most widely read and acclaimed verse writer in Britain. Byron capitalized on this newly established audience with the first cantos of *Childe Harold* and with the early Oriental verse tales. Meanwhile, Scott turned his talents to the innovative series of Waverley novels, which reached their zenith just in the years (1818–19) when Byron composed and published the early cantos of his most "novelistic" verse production to date. Byron's use in *Don Juan* of so many elements of the Waverley format results in a poem in which it is hard not to see the general stamp of Scott's new form of "modern epopée."

In Juan we confront a distinctively and notoriously "passive" or "mediocre" hero, very much in line, in spite of his famous name, with such cipher-ish protagonists as young Waverley and Ivanhoe.[7] Byron traces the historically conditioned and conditioning education of Juan in some detail, paying close attention to the culture of private or everyday life. He deftly steers Juan through situations that are identified in relation to stages of society – from the most "primitive" to the most "advanced." Further, as we have seen, if there is one Romantic-era project that is as fully absorbed in the problematics of explanation as *Don Juan* is, it is surely Scott's attempt in the Waverley novels to bring Edinburgh "philosophical history" to bear on the practice of fiction. Scott's is the literary form in which the problem of what it means to "be of one's age" was given the fullest and certainly its most influential realization, and this certainly included the new mode of explanation in which, as [Georg] Lukács wrote of Scott, we understand the "specifically historical" as the derivation of the individuality of characters from the historical peculiarity of their epoch.[8] This in turn [. . .] involved a new notion of typification – the moral exemplification of historical or age-specific "peculiarity" – and thus both a new sense of the historical situation and a concomitant transformation of casuistry.

I want to suggest, then, that *some* of the difficulties of the epic riddle that is *Don Juan,* some of its causal conundrums in particular, can be helpfully addressed in relation to the Waverley model. One such difficulty is the kind of contradiction that seems to be implicit in the relation of Byron's own literary practices in *Don Juan* and those of the figures he denounces, such as [Viscount] Castlereagh and Southey. To the extent that Byron is understood to be working within a "spirit-of-the-age" model of literary culture of the sort implicit in the Waverley novels, or in [Percy Bysshe] Shelley's contemporary observation that all writers must willy-nilly participate in the spirit of the age in spite of their avowed doctrines and systems, to that same extent must Byron see himself, like Shelley and Scott, as in some sense a party to contemporary developments he professes to abhor. On such an account, Byron would be inscribing himself into the representation of an epoch in which, much as he might wish to lampoon his fellow representative men, we can make out a dim recognition that he is of their number.

It may be well to recall in this connection what Byron said on the subject of contemporaneity at about this time, when he took part in the controversy that erupted in 1819 over the canonical status of [Alexander] Pope. Here [. . .] the issue is broached by way of a problem about intelligibility, although here Byron is more explicit in seeing it as a problem in his own writings. The rhetorical crescendo of his *Letter to **** ******* [John Murray], published in 1821, occurs as an elaboration of his charge that the present enemies of Pope

> have raised a mosque by the side of a Grecian temple of the purest architecture; and, more barbarous than the barbarians from whose practice I have borrowed the figure, they are not contented with their own grotesque edifice, unless they destroy the prior, and purely beautiful fabric which preceded, and which shames them and theirs for ever and ever.[9]

Byron then answers the charge of hypocrisy on this score by conceding its truth: "I shall be told that amongst these – I *have* been – (or it may be still *am*) conspicuous; – true – and I am ashamed of it. I *have* been amongst the builders of this Babel, attended by a confusion of tongues. . . . "[10] The appositeness of this passage to *Don Juan* is punctuated by Byron's castigation of those disciples of Wordsworth who, understanding his poetry, "would be able / To add a story to the Tower of Babel" (DS:4). What Byron goes on to say in his own defense – i.e., that at least he has not been among the detractors of the pure classical temple erected by Pope – is no more directly relevant here than his acknowledgment that when it comes to the production of romantic unintelligibility he cannot escape being of his age any more than Pope could have escaped being of his.[11] Byron, Scott, Moore, Shelley, Southey, Wordsworth, Coleridge, and even Castlereagh (insofar as his speeches would have been taken as "literature" and thus susceptible to poetic analysis) – each becomes a case *in relation to* the normative scheme of the epoch, the "common case" of degenerate Babel.

Don Juan is thus haunted by a historicism with which it can neither dispense nor quite come to terms. To see how this poem poses a kind of case for the new Romantic historicism, it is useful to ask exactly how, reading *Don Juan,* we best construct the poem's "historical situation." In [Jerome] Christensen's study, as its subtitle suggests, the "historical situation" of *Don Juan* is "commercial society."[12] In McGann's, especially in the coda essay he published after *Don Juan in Context,* the answer is somewhat more chronologically specific. The poem's historical situation, for McGann, is defined by "the period 1789–1824," and it offers the "history" or "*wholeness* of [this] period," at the same time that it dramatizes its participation in its repetition compulsions.[13] What I wish to emphasize here is the way in which the poem offers an implicit critique of the very idea of the "commercial" phase of society or of a "period" like 1789–1824 even as it so crucially deploys such conceptions. It is useful here to reconsider one of the standard exhibits in talking about Byron's grand scheme for his poem.

Responding to a review of the poem about a year after spelling out his vision of the poem for Murray, Byron rearticulated his plan of *Don Juan* for his friend [Thomas] Medwin:

> [W]hat the Writer says of DJ is harsh – but it is inevitable – He must follow – or at least not directly oppose the opinion of a prevailing & yet not very firmly seated party – a review may and will direct or "turn away" the Currents of opinion – but it must not directly oppose them – D Juan will be known by and bye for what it is intended a *satire* on *abuses* of the present *states* of Society – and not an eulogy of vice.
>
> (BLJ, 10:68)

Byron's echo of the Scottish-Enlightenment idiom – "states of society" – clearly establishes Byron's assimilation of the cultural-historical model and identifies his resistances to it. First, Byron seems willing to see society itself in global terms, rather than positing a relation between a "state of society" and a "state of the world" of the sort we [trace] back to John Millar in Scottish-Enlightenment theory. Second, in his curious phrase "present *states* of society," Byron emphasizes the simultaneity of such states with each other in his scheme of things. In the *Letter to **** ******* [John Murray], this simultaneity of states is figured in the fact that Byron has the romantic poets of his own age building their grotesque mosque "by the side of" the temple erected by Pope. In *Don Juan,* this simultaneity is figured in the fact that Byron has Juan traverse the states of society in just a brief interval of a relatively short lifetime. That Juan is young at the Siege of Ismail (late 1790) but will die in the Reign of Terror (1793–94) conveys a strong sense of the copresence of the "states" through which he passes in the contemporary world order. Indeed, after his flight from polite Spanish society in canto 1, Juan is taken through a series of social arrangements corresponding at least *roughly* to the kind of sequence familiar from the schemes of the philosophic historians: a bucolic natural state on the island with Haidée, an eastern despotic state in canto 5, a medieval siege in cantos 6–8, an absolutist court in Catherine's Russia, a commercial oligarchy in the English cantos.[14] Finally, Byron's satirical emphasis on the "abuses" of these states of society, like his insistence on the "degeneracy" of the age of Southey and Castlereagh in Britain, suggests a stronger emphasis on decline and decay in the course of history than we have seen in the Scottish Enlightenment accounts of the "progress" and (albeit uneven) development of societies.

What Byron's comments to Medwin help to highlight, then, are the ways in which *Don Juan* manages to reopen the question of what counts as "a society" in the discourse on the "State of Society" and, what amounts to the same thing, to expose the aporia in the relationship established by writers like Millar between the "state of society" and the "state of the world." The problem, in a sense, has to do with the question of what you hold constant as part of an explanatory framework and what you allow as variation to be explained. The problem also marks the contradiction between the first and last chapters of *Waverley* – turning on the question of whether Scott undertook this experiment with historical narrative to preserve evanescent manners or to identify the unchanging features of human nature. Significantly, when Scott seems to be arguing the latter point, as he does in the opening chapter of *Waverley,* he identifies the explanatory substratum as the domain of "the passions." Taking his metaphor from the language of heraldry, the narrator distinguishes between the changing colors by which the passions are differently expressed in different times from their underlying "bearings":

> The wrath of our ancestors, for example, was coloured *gules;* it broke forth in acts of open and sanguinary violence against the objects of its fury. Our malignant feelings, which must seek gratification through more indirect channels, and undermine the obstacles which they cannot openly bear down, may be rather said to be tinctured *sable.* But the deep-ruling impulse is the same in both cases; and the proud peer who can now only ruin his neighbour according to law, by protracted suits, is the genuine descendant of the baron who wrapped the castle of his competitor in flames, and knocked him on the head as he endeavoured to escape from the conflagration. It is from the great book of Nature, the same through a thousand editions, whether of black-letter, or wire-wove and hot-pressed, that I have venturously essayed to read a chapter to the public.
>
> (Wav, chap. 6)[15]

To focus on the subtext in this palimpsest, the book of human nature, the same through all editions, is presumably to operate in a code that is always already evened out. It is not a respecter of the unevennesses of cultural development. Byron, how-ever, has his own way of flattening the emergent sense of historical specificity into the grammar of the passions. To see how, and to conclude with *Don Juan*, I would like to turn briefly now to the representation of Juan's encounter with Catherine the Great, who, like Castlereagh, is a world-historical individual in *Don Juan*, and who is perhaps the only character in the poem to surpass Castlereagh in demonic power. This episode, perhaps more obviously derivative of one of Scott's inventions than any other in the poem, also points to Byron's crucial departure from Scott's narrative practice in the Waverley novels, especially in regard to explanation.

Catherine and Castlereagh: worst cases, worst causes

To consider the kind of episode from the Waverley novels on which Byron partially modeled his encounter between Juan and Catherine the Great, one need only think of Edward Waverley's meeting with Bonnie Prince Charles, Henry Morton's with Claverhouse (in *Old Mortality*), or Jeanie Deans's with the Duke of Argyle (in *The Heart of Mid-Lothian*). All show how this sort of incident is handled in Scott. The reason that this sort of episode – the encounter between the mediocre protagonist and the "world-historical individual" – recurs so often in Scott's fiction is that, as Lukács has explained, it is so crucial to the fundamental representational dynamics of Scott's new form. In such episodes, Scott tends to draw the historical figure in such a way as to typify a specifically historical formation or sociological group of the cultural epoch in question; the encounter serves to place the mediocre hero in connection with such forces. Certain residual tendencies of this narrative strategy survive in Byron's handling of the Juan–Catherine episode. Seeing the poem as moving through a series of "stages of society," from the barbarism of the shipwreck episode to the commercial manners of the English cantos, we might say that Catherine and her modernized court typify something about the social structure of Europe's developing nation states in the eighteenth century. Something of this historical particularity is suggested in the way in which Byron dresses Juan for the part he will play in this meeting. We are asked to "suppose" Juan as "Love turned a Lieutenant of Artillery":

> His Bandage slipped down into a cravat;
>   His Wings subdued to epaulettes; his Quiver
> Shrunk to a scabbard, with his Arrows at
>   His side as a small sword, but sharp as ever;
> His bow converted into a cocked hat;
>   But still so like, that Psyche were more clever
> Than some wives (who make blunders no less stupid)
> If She had not mistaken him for Cupid.
>
>   [(9:45)]

But, just as the particularity of Juan's role as late-eighteenth-century military officer is overshadowed by the mythic type he is said to embody, so Catherine will be made to play Psyche to his Cupid here, as well as Helen to his Paris.

Nor does Byron quite observe the kind of relations Scott tended to portray between mediocre protagonist and world-historical individual as those relations were set forth and analyzed by Scott. Indeed, when it comes to issues of explanation and causality, which are intensely foregrounded here, explanation from period specificity tends to give way to an overriding explanatory axis, just as the third-person narrative decorum of the passage gives way to an apostrophe that is extraordinary even by the wide-ranging standards of this poem:

> Oh, thou 'teterrima *Causa*' of all 'belli' –
>   Thou gate of Life and Death – thou nondescript!
> Whence is our exit and our entrance, – well I
>   May pause in pondering how all Souls are dipt
> In thy perennial fountain – how man *fell*, I
>   Know not, since Knowledge saw her branches stript
> Of her first fruit, but how he falls and rises
> *Since, thou* hast settled beyond all surmises.
>
> Some call thee 'the worst Cause of war,' but I
>   Maintain thou art the *best:* for after all
> From thee we come, to thee we go, and why
>   To get at thee not batter down a wall,
> Or waste a world? Since no one can deny
>   Thou dost replenish worlds both great and small:
> With, or without thee, all things at a stand
> Are, or would be, thou Sea of Life's dry Land!
>
> Catherine, who was the grand Epitome
>   Of that great Cause of war, or peace, or what
> You please (it causes all the things which be,
>   So you may take your choice of this or that) –
> Catherine, I say, was very glad to see
>   The handsome herald, on whose plumage sat
> Victory; and, pausing as she saw him kneel
> With his dispatch, forgot to break the seal.
>
> Then recollecting the whole Empress, nor
>   Forgetting quite the woman (which composed
> At least three parts of this great whole) she tore
>   The letter open with an air which posed
> The Court, that watched each look her visage wore,
>   Until royal smile at length disclosed
> Fair weather for the day. Though rather spacious,
> Her face was noble, her eyes fine, mouth gracious.
>
> (9:55–58)

The addressee of the apostrophe in stanzas 55 and 56, the *causa* in question, as the Latin allusion makes clear, is the Horatian *cunnus,* and Byron's figurings of it at this key juncture in the poem mark some of the most complex poetry he ever composed. Stylistically, these lines comprise one of those rare passages in his work where his Augustan sensibility fully merges with both a Cavalier poetic subject matter and Metaphysical poetic talent for complicating the witty conceit. The conceit itself, the female genitalia as *cause* or case, is a familiar one in seventeenth-century bawdy comedy of the sort that Byron knew and often cited.[16]

Some of the complications of the metonymy in question here are elaborated by an ostentatious logic that seems to call attention to Byron's "wish to be perspicuous."

Although the *cunnus* is the worst cause of war, he argues, it is also the best, since of all causes of war this at least can also replenish the populations that war destroys. In stanza 57, which returns from apostrophic to narrative mode, Byron extends the analysis of the *cunnus* as the cause of war by an implicitly syllogistic line of thought that runs thus: if the *cunnus* is the cause of all things, and if war is a thing, then it is necessarily the cause of war as well. And yet the complications generated here are not so easily held in check. In the passage leading up to these lines, Byron has prepared the undoing of Catherine's historical specificity by the strong suggestion that the Siege of Ismail is a replay of the Homeric account of the Siege of Troy, a siege he represents as carried out on very much, as it were, the same grounds. At first, one might take Byron's dehistoricizing move here as a simplification of Scott's practice in such episodes. Where Scott makes such scenes occasions for the applications of his explanatory frameworks for relating characters to one another, Byron turns one of his characters, Catherine, into the "Epitome" of what he insists on calling the cause of all things, the great (w)hole itself. This is Catherine as Woman, Woman as Eve, Eve as the absent cause [. . .] of all of Man's fallings and risings. This very reduction, however, is articulated in terms of tropes that seem to defy it and to recomplicate the question with a vengeance. In Kenneth Burke's terms, the passage might be said to conflate the dramatistic functions of scene and agent (GM, 7–20).[17] For the *cunnus* in this passage is figured both as a part of the scene – the gate of our exits and our entrances – and as a part played in the scene, in the person of Catherine, who is said to be epitomized by it. The *cunnus* as *causa,* in other words, shares a structural principle with the *causa* as case: the sense of being ambiguous as to the question of frame and subject, container and thing contained.[18]

One of the obvious problems with Byron's taking the *cunnus* as what Burke would call the "representative case" of his philosophic casuistry, however, is that it inadequately engenders generality in respect to the question of gender itself. The problem shows in Byron's deployment of the first-person-plural pronoun, which seems to wobble along an axis very close to that which can been seen in Byron's self-conscious paranomasia with "man" as marking both gendered and ungendered humanity.[19] In calling the *cunnus* the scene of "our exits and our entrances," he even seems to be giving himself away on this point, since (in view of Catherine's notorious heterosexuality) the first "our" indicates a nongendered first-person plural and the second a gendered one. The representative case of the *cunnus* likewise has limited application in the domain of sexuality and sexual preference, a limitation that seems particularly acute in view of recent studies of Byron's own homosexuality. The notion that the *cunnus* might not mean the world to a man of passion, might not be (to paraphrase Wittgenstein) "all that is the case," ought to have been available to a writer of Byron's experiences – a writer so well-versed in what Andrew Elfenbein, applying D.A. Miller's term to the case of Byron, calls the "open secret" of Regency sodomy.[20] Thus, on the one hand, the case of Catherine is elaborated as a prophylactic measure to sustain the myth of heterosexual normativity embodied in the figure of Juan/Byron. On the other (though it may be the same hand), it becomes a kind of Byronic escape hatch from history, a passage into unproblematized passion as such, the element of pure unintelligibility that is supposed to lend meaning to all around it. For Byron, Catherine lacks sense because she embodies it.

It is here, I think, that the great bogey figure of Castlereagh returns to haunt that of Catherine. In *Byron and Greek Love*, Louis Crompton actually deals at some length with the case of Castlereagh, but his concern is chiefly with the "historical" Castlereagh, and with the possibility that his suicide in 1822 was occasioned by attempts to blackmail him for (actual or contrived) homosexual liaisons. Oddly, Crompton does not address the "textual" Castlereagh, the character whose sexuality is made an issue in *Don Juan* three years before either the suicide of Castlereagh or the arrest of Bishop Clogher on charges of homosexuality. Does Byron's Castlereagh become the epitome of all that lies beyond the causal field of the all-causing *cunnus* of which Catherine is the epitome? In calling Castlereagh an intellectual eunuch, can he be suggesting that the explanatory confusions of this monstrous sphinx are what they are because "it" has attempted to place itself beyond the power of what the poem represents as the *primum mobile*? And if so, then where does this sort of placement leave "Byron" itself in the poem's epic framework of erotics and explanations?[21]

Perhaps the most vexing questions of all for the poem, in the end, have to do precisely with the way in which "Byron" figures as a site of motivation for what we read in *Don Juan*. At the beginning and the end of the long set-piece description of Donna Julia there are editorial interjections: "Her eye (I'm very fond of handsome eyes) / Was large and dark" and "Her stature tall – I hate a dumpy woman" (1:60–61). Causal relations are very much in play here but it is hard to judge how they run: are the editorial comments occasioned by the picture of such charms, or are they meant to explain why the character is drawn that way in the first place? To put it another way, do such comments explain Byron's masquerade of masculinity or does it tend rather to explain them? We are still early in the Byron revival, and criticism has only begun to broach such questions for the perspicuous perplexity of this text. When they are pursued further it may prove that the poem does covet probability after all, but that it is confused by this very desire and quite at a loss to explain it. Meanwhile, the question of whether the case of *Don Juan* may be said to have a cause remains suspended in its contradictions. Perhaps the poem is too quick to take refuge in the very charm of contradiction:

> If people contradict themselves, can I
>   Help contradicting them and everybody,
> Even my voracious self? But that's a lie;
>   I never did so, never will. How should I?
> He who doubts all things nothing can deny,
>   Truth's fountains may be clear, her streams are muddy
> And cut through such canals of contradiction
> That she must often navigate o'er fiction.
>
> (15:88)

Here Byron's casuisty reaches its limit, not by attaining resolution but by giving way to Pyrrhonian skepticism. Forsaking the possibility of rational deliberation, the poem can no longer, in such a view, continue to suspend our judgments or prolong our work of explanation.

Notes

1 There are two brief biographical essays in *Byron and Scotland,* ed. Angus Calder (Totowa, N.J.: Barnes and Noble, 1989): P.H. Scott, "Byron and Scott," pp. 51–64, and J. Drummond Bone, "Byron, Scott, and Scottish Nostalgia," pp. 119–131; and a footnote in [Jerome] McGann's "The Book of Byron and the Book of a World," p. 269, n. 21. Andrew Rutherford

takes up the question of Byron's relation to Scott's fiction toward the latter half of his "Byron, Scott, and Scotland," in *Lord Byron and His Contemporaries,* ed. Charles Robinson (Newark: University of Delaware Press, 1982), pp. 43–65. Perhaps the most provocative discussion of the subject, especially in respect to their mutually constructed relation to the literary market, is Sonia Hofkosh's "The Writer's Ravishment: Women and the Romantic Author – the Example of Byron," in *The Romantic Woman,* ed. Anne K. Mellor (Bloomington: Indiana University Press), pp. 99–104.

2   [*Byron's Letters and Journals.* Edited by Leslie A. Marchand, 12 vols. Cambridge, MA: Harvard University Press, 1973–82. (BLJ).]

3   [Lord Byron, *The Complete Miscellaneous Prose,* ed. Andrew Nicholson (Oxford: Clarendon Press, 1991), pp. 119, 120.]

4   [Citations of Byron's poetry are taken from George Gordon, Lord Byron, *The Complete Poetical Works.* Edited by Jerome J. McGann, 7 vols. Oxford: Clarendon Press, 1980–93. (CPWB).]

5   Cf. "I won't describe – that is, if I can help / Description" (10:28).

6   In August 1819, when Byron told Murray he had "no plan" for *Don Juan,* he also had no plan to continue it: "If it don't take I will leave it off where it is with all due respect to the Public" (BLJ, 6:207). In the seventeen months that follow, apparently the period of his most intense engagement with Scott, he reaches a point where he can already describe the plan of the poem in the past tense.

7   See Alexander Welsh, *The Hero of the Waverley Novels* (1963; Princeton, NJ: Princeton University Press, 1993), pp. 21–39.

8   [Georg] Lukács, *The Historical Novel,* trans. Hannah and Stanley Mitchell (London: Merlin Press, 1962), p. 19.

9   *Works of Lord Byron,* ed. R.E. Prothero and E.H. Coleridge, 13 vols. (London: 1898–1904), 5:559.

10   Ibid., 5:559.

11   Byron's chief ally in the defense of Pope was Isaac Disraeli, whose contributions to the campaign Byron knew and praised. [. . .] For a more detailed account of Byron's position on this subject see my "The Pope Controversy: Romantic Poetics and the English Canon," *Critical Inquiry* 10 (spring 1984): 481–509.

12   [Jerome Christensen, *Lord Byron's Strength: Romantic Writing and Commercial Society* (Baltimore: Johns Hopkins University Press, 1993).]

13   McGann, "The Book of Byron and the Book of a World," in *The Beauty of Inflections: Literary Investigations in Historical Method and Theory* (Oxford: Clarendon Press, 1985), pp. 287, 291, 288.

14   None of these "states" is pure, the way that Pope's temple is supposed to be. Thus, notoriously, the idyllic largesse of Haidée's apparently innocent island proves to be supported by a particularly ambitious and violent network of piracy.

15   [Walter Scott, *Waverly; or, 'Tis Sixty Years Since,* 1st ed. Edinburgh: Constable, 1814. (Wav.)]

16   Eric Partridge cites Shakespearean puns on *case* as "pudend" in both *The Merry Wives of Windsor* and *All's Well that Ends Well* – in *Shakespeare's Bawdy* (London: Routledge, 1947), pp. 84–85. [. . .]

17   [Kenneth Burke, *A Grammar of Motives,* Berkeley and Los Angeles: University of California Press, 1969. (GM).]

18   And there is the further issue of whether *tetterima causa* is not better translated as "worst case," making Catherine's scene the worst-case scenario of war.

19   There are a number of passages in *Don Juan* that acknowledge the problem of the gender specificity of humanist idiom. Even in the stretch between this encounter with Catherine and the "Man fell with apples" passage at the start of the next canto, we find one that marks this semantic wobble, a stanza in which the Shakespearean epicene idiom – "what a strange thing is man" – is immediately undercut: "and what a stranger / thing is woman!" (9:64). For a good discussion of related gender questions in the poem, see Susan Wolfson, "Their She-Condition: Cross-Dressing and the Politics of Gender in *Don Juan,*" *ELH* 54 (fall 1987): 585–613.

20   Elfenbein, *Byron and the Victorians* (Cambridge: Cambridge University Press, 1995), pp. 209–10.

21   Louis Crompton, *Byron and Greek Love* (Berkeley: University of California Press, 1985).

4   Stealing culture in the shadow of revolutions

Daniel O'Quinn

Within the highly social Georgian playhouse, multiple forms of embodied acts engaged with the constitutive forces that defined life in London. However, because well over half the plays on offer at the patent theatres were from the stock repertoire, theatrical audiences and performers engaged in a complex form of cultural work, much like the work of memory itself, that rigorously took place in the present but pertained to forms and expectations whose relation to the past was crucial to their signification. Diana Taylor's expansive definition of the repertoire as "all those acts usually thought of as ephemeral, non-reproducible knowledge" emphasizes that

> performances . . . replicate themselves through their own structures and codes. This means that the repertoire, like the archive, is mediated. The process of selection, memorization or internalization, and transmission takes place within (and in turn helps constitute) specific systems of re-presentation. Multiple forms of embodied acts are always present, though in a constant state of againness. They reconstitute themselves, transmitting communal memories, histories, and values from one group/generation to the next. Embodied and performed acts generate, record, and transmit knowledge.
>
> (Taylor, 2003: 20–1)

Although performance continually modifies cultural memory, there are moments when the lived experience of the repertoire, its simultaneous relationship to the present and the past, makes itself available for political intervention. This essay is about a pair of such interventions and it demonstrates how the dynamic relationship between the theatre and the press in Georgian Britain allowed not only for the recognition of the volatility of political life in times of grave crisis, but also for the valuation of social and theatrical performance itself as a crucial instantiation of political affiliation.[1] Over the space of a few days, three historically distinct revolutions – one Glorious, one American and one French – permeated the repertoire in a manner that forces us to reconsider, among other things, the shadowy relations among past political dispositions, the potential to steal tradition for the present moment, and the importance of Richard Brinsley Sheridan for Romanticism's future.

Curs'd be your Senate; curs'd your constitution

In the fall of 1795, William Pitt's government was under increasing pressure to change its policy with regard to the counter-revolutionary war with France. There was widespread public consensus, especially among the lower orders, that the famine sweeping through the country was a result of the economic hardships incurred by the war. Public protest was mounting throughout the period leading up to George III's speech from the throne on 29 October 1795. The speech was heavily scrutinized both because the war with France was going badly and people were starving and because the Ministry had failed to convict radicals associated with the London Corresponding Society. The acquittal of Thomas Hardy, Horne Tooke, and John Thelwall buoyed the forces of reform both in Parliament and in the streets. In short, the Ministry was losing the propaganda war against reform and was desperate for a means to justify not only its foreign policy, but also its incursion on the rights of dissident citizens.

"The opportunity that the ministry . . . may have been preparing for, eventually came . . . on 29 October, the day of the state opening of Parliament" (Barrell, 2000: 554). On its journey from St. James's Palace to Parliament, the King's coach was surrounded by

> a hostile crowd chanting "Down with George!", "No king!", "No George!", along with some less treasonable prayers and imprecations, "Peace, peace!", "Bread, bread!", "No famine!", "No war!", "No Pitt!" Some of the protestors brandished loaves on sticks, draped in black crêpe.
>
> (Barrell, 2000: 556)

A projectile shattered the glass of the Royal coach and the King reportedly told Lord Chancellor Loughborough, "My Lord, I have been shot at!" The King's coach was surrounded again on his return from Parliament and attempts were made to physically remove the King from the coach. The assaults on the King's coach were immediately figured by the Ministry as an assassination attempt organized by the LCS. These events would now be used to justify the introduction of the Treasonable Practices Act, legislation aimed at "'modern' treason and seditious meetings, which had been anticipated since the acquittals of [Hardy, Tooke and Thelwall] the previous year" (Barrell, 2000: 559).

That Act was deemed necessary not because anyone really feared for the safety of the King, but rather because the conventional tools of governance enshrined in the British Constitution were insufficient to curb political dissent. The Ministry's propaganda organs represented the assault as a threat to monarchical government by an organized political entity intent on overthrowing the British Constitution, and thus the introduction of the Treasonable Practices Act was figured as an act of preservation of British liberty by the state. However, during the debate on the Act, the Whig opposition argued fiercely that the legislation squelched the most sacred elements of British liberty and that the tradition of the King-in-Parliament was being gutted by ministerial absolutism ratified by an ambitious King. This is why Richard Brinsley Sheridan and others could then represent the events of 29 October as a ministerial plot – indeed Sheridan claimed that ministers privately referred to it as a "providential" event. It doesn't matter whether the Ministry staged the assault or simply attributed treasonous intention to someone else's actions. Intention does not precede the destruction or preservation of tradition, but rather is retroactively constituted from the repertoire.

Sheridan addressed these issues in his passionate speeches against the suspension of Habeas Corpus, but his role in the debate regarding intention and tradition at this juncture extends beyond Parliament. On the day that the King's carriage was attacked, Sheridan and John Philip Kemble's production of Thomas Otway's *Venice Preserv'd* was given its third and final performance at Drury Lane Theatre. After three nights of unrest, in which radical members of the audience attempted to "steal" the play, the Lord Chamberlain revoked the play's license. The theft and counter-theft demonstrate how the repertoire's dynamic relation to received notions of culture and sociability allowed audiences and performers to mobilize the repetitive temporality of performance and its complex remediation in the press to evaluate the potential futures inscribed in figurations of the present political disposition.

For eighteenth-century theatre goers, *Venice Preserv'd* had been traditionally understood as a deeply loyalist and patriotic play. First performed in February 1682 following Charles II's dissolution of Parliament and the arrest of the Earl of Shaftesbury in 1681, the play's political narrative focuses on a plot to assassinate the entire Senate of Venice that is foiled when one of the conspirators, Jaffier, betrays his friend Pierre because of his competing love for Belvidira. Because the play was framed by a royalist prologue and epilogue and because the play's subtitle, "A Plot Discovered", echoes pamphlets denouncing the Popish Plot, *Venice Preserv'd* was understood to be a triumphant Tory play and was conventionally revived for patriotic ends.[2] However, this factional reading owes a great deal to retroactively defined intention, for the play is far more ambivalent than its initial reception would suggest. Otway's dedication explicitly aligns the corrupt senators of Venice with the Whigs and the epilogue draws parallels between the play's conspiracy and Whig factionalism (Owen, 2002: 121). But how do these Tory attacks on the Whigs square with the fact that Jaffier's betrayal saves the Whiggish Republic? As Bywaters states, "Since neither the senate nor the conspiracy against is politically respectable, neither can be Tory; yet since the two factions are violently opposed, both cannot be Whig" (Bywaters, 1983: 256).

As the play entered the repertoire, its specific allegorization of the Exclusion Crisis became less and less important, except as a vague harbinger of the Glorious Revolution. The play's complex politics became vestigial, but the she-tragedy's complex affective economy allowed for the slow re-calibration of the play's signification across the century that ultimately allowed for a re-activation of topical allegory. From 1782 onwards, the play was inseparable from Sarah Siddons's electrifying performance as Belvidira.[3] However the sympathy generated for Belvidira and for Jaffier by Siddons's formidable mobilization of affect in the famous dagger scene and in the closing scene of her madness was complemented by a corresponding demonization of Belvidira's father, Priuli. Belvidira's filial piety saves her father from the conspirators' knives and he repays her by falsely promising to save Jaffier. His duplicity results not only in Jaffier taking both Pierre's and his own life, but also in Belvidira's subsequent madness and death. The former action is understood by Pierre as a form of successful resistance to the Senate and the latter event results in Priuli castigating himself for cruelty. The more powerfully that the audience is moved by Belvidira's predicament and death, the more resolutely does the Senate and Priuli become the focus of disapprobation. By the 1790s, both Otway's complex intentions and the patriotic tradition of the play were increasingly overthrown by audience factions wilfully ascribing their own heterodox intent either to wrest tradition from the stranglehold of the state or to invent a new tradition altogether.[4]

Sheridan and Kemble's production of *Venice Preserv'd* in October of 1795 was "presented . . . in a style of uncommon magnificence" (*Morning Post and Fashionable*

World, 22 October 1795). If the pathos generated by Siddons emphasizes the cruelty of Priuli and the Senate, then Kemble's introduction of "a tableau of the conspirators being led to their execution, to the sound of tolling bells and muffled drums" late in Act IV, scene ii would have presented the audience with a sudden still moment for contemplation of the conspirators' culpability.[5] However, as Genest reports, after the following speech, Pierre was "rapturously applauded"[6]:

> Pierre: Curs'd be your Senate; curs'd your constitution.
> The curse of growing factions and divisions
> Still vex your councils, shake your public safety,
> And make the robes of government you wear
> Hateful to you, as these base chains to me.
>
> (Kemble [Otway], IV.ii. 40)

The rupture of the tragic action by the tableau after this speech drew attention to the conspirators' situation before the law. Thus the tableau's status as an interruption opens the scene of treason and punishment to heterodox interpretations – permeated by the 1794 treason trials – that would have been otherwise regulated by the tragic plot.

It is difficult to read Sheridan and Kemble's intervention except through the lens of Thelwall's attempt to "steal" the play in February of 1794. Thelwall's admiration for the republican language of Pierre and Jaffier's speeches in Act I led him to believe that the play could be successfully pulled over to the radical cause.[7] In a production of *Venice Preserv'd* at Covent Garden in February of 1794, Thelwall and his associates noisily applauded the republican passages and the play was removed from the stage after only two performances because it was too politically embarrassing. A similar campaign was waged at Drury Lane on the opening night of Sheridan and Kemble's production in October of 1795. Outraged pro-Ministry papers such as *The Sun* and the *True Briton* argued that the audience members applauding Pierre and Jaffier failed to correctly ascertain the play's loyalist intent. In response to "the most marked and violent approbation to the democratical remarks of the principal Conspirator *Pierre*", *The Sun* made the following observation:

> these sagacious Politicians seem wholly to have mistaken the object of the Author, and the tendency of his play:–They were not aware that the sentiments which they most applauded were chiefly put into the mouths of men of infamous characters, foreigners of different nations, who could not be supposed to have any attachment to the country, nor any laudable motive for attempting to subvert its Government and Constitution.
>
> The *avowed* object of *Pierre* and his Friends is, "the destruction of a whole people". – Men who have the assurance openly to applaud a project of such a description . . . should have remembered too, that the Author has displayed a strict regard to *Justice*, poetical and moral, by bringing all the Traitors who conspired against the safety of the State – *to the Block*.
>
> (22 October 1795)

For *The Sun*, those audience members happy to associate themselves with the foreigners Pierre and Renaud, whose very names indicate a connection to France, are seditious.

Following the alleged assassination attempt on 29 October, a different narrative of intention emerged in which Sheridan and Kemble were folded into a plot to assassinate George III. According to the *Times*, the production was staged to incite the audience to kill the King by inspiring them with a "thirst for blood". The reconstruction of Sheridan's intention here has everything to do with his double status as theatrical manager and Whig parliamentarian. John Barrell's discussion of the importance of this commutability between theatre and politics re-frames the issue in a way that draws attention to the broader intentions of the kind of oppositional reading staged by Thelwall and his associates in the Pit of the Theatres Royal:

> The *Times* claim, if it makes sense at all, does so only in terms of the publicity which would be attracted by a demonstration in the theatre . . . the appropriation of Otway at Covent Garden and Drury Lane were media events, performances staged for the newspapers, as much examples of the theatricalization of politics as of the politicization of theatre.
>
> (Barrell, 1998: 14–15)

If one turns to the papers to measure the effects of this kind of media protest, what one discovers is a very complex negotiation over tradition and intention that allows us to see the volatility of the repertoire in times of social crisis.

In its opening night review, the *Morning Post and Fashionable World*, a paper with an aristocratic and largely Whig address, reported that

> the manly sentiments of *Pierre*, the declared enemy of those
>> "*Domestic traitors,*
>> "*Who make us slaves, and tell us 'tis our Charter*"
> were received with by shouts of applause from *all parts* of the House, which lasted many minutes.
>
> (22 October 1795)

That *all* parts of the House applauded this speech was challenged by the loyalist papers. *The Sun* reported that "a very considerable majority of [the audience], by judicious direction of their applause, evinced a determination to counteract the evil designs of those, who endeavoured to render the . . . amusements of the Theatre a subject of political dissention" (22 October 1795). But radical demonstration staged in the government-controlled playhouse not only asserted a counter-tradition, but also declared that intention does not inhere over time. In spite of loyalist arguments that Otway's patriotic intent trumps all subsequent interpretations, the conflict emphasized that the repertoire was a site of contention within which tradition and intention were always in historical flux. But this was more than a matter of arguing that the politics of *Venice Preserv'd* were more complex than evinced by conventional productions; Thelwall's intervention cannily understood that any intervention on the part of the Ministry would only confirm radical critique.

Taking its cues from Otway's ostensible allegorization of the Popish Plot, the pro-Ministry faction extended that allegory to the Pop-Gun Plot and the assault on George III's carriage.[8] Hence, Otway's retroactively declared intention is supplemented and ultimately supplanted by the political intentions of the Ministry. But this implies that the Venetian Senate is the model of good governance. That the pro-Ministry press says nothing about the allegorical links between the Senate and Pitt's Ministry in favour of ridiculing the play's "democratical passages" is symptomatic, for the disapprobation heaped on the audience members applauding Pierre requires the activation of this larger allegory. This enacts precisely what radicals and Whigs alike had been saying for some time: that Pitt's government was not only corrupt, but also a perversion of the notion of King-in-Parliament. Priuli's deceit and his cruelty make him an easy figure for Pitt or even the King, thus pro-Ministry accounts of the play also verify anti-ministerial sentiments. Driving the point home, the *Morning Chronicle* published a satire entitled "A Modest Defense of the Minister Against Jacobins and Democrats", which concluded with the following stanza clearly aligning Pitt and Priuli:

> Since, then, our MINISTER of State
> Is CUNNING, SHAMELESS, OBSTINATE,
> HARD-HEARTED–He's beyond dispute
> A MINISTER most ABSOLUTE.
> > (2 November 1795)

In "preserving" Otway's play, the Ministry had re-enacted Priuli's duplicity: it had co-opted insurgency to consolidate its own power; for its part, the Whig press was hoping to activate the feelings of betrayal and anger embodied by Siddons in the repertoire of Georgian life.

There are "two kinds of tradition – the sustaining, identity-shaping ones and the invented tools of state power that sustain the nation at the expense of others and of its own historical awareness" (Bal, 2002: 251–2). The Lord Chamberlain's withdrawal of the license for *Venice Preserv'd* following the performance of 29 October 1795 was an attempt by the state to obliterate the former by the latter. Thus it was the action of the state through the Lord Chamberlain that confirms Pierre's account of governance, for it was the Ministry, and not the democratic audience, that finally re-constructed an icon of loyalty and patriotism into an expression of Jacobinical desire. In Thelwall's words, "the play . . . notwithstanding its original intention, was . . . converted into a provocative, not an antidote to jacobinism", but this conversion was achieved through a startling joint effort. Thelwall and his associates put forward a counter-reading of the play's intent in the form of a performative proposition and the government confirmed the proposition when it declared the play a dangerous incitement to treason. The Ministry had effectively stolen the *Venice Preserv'd* from itself and thus had isolated itself from the long-standing patriotic repertoire.

Evidence of this crisis in the attribution of intent can be found in the days following the revocation of Drury Lane's licence to present *Venice Preserv'd*. On 5 November, both *The Sun* and the *True Briton* print identical "historical accounts" of the play with scholarly-looking citations of Dryden's prologue and a full quotation of Otway's epilogue. This reiterates their earlier suggestions that "those designing men, who had perverted particular passages to *political* purposes, had entirely mistaken the tendency of the Play and the meaning of the Author" (5 November 1795). Conceding that Otway's intention was "to expose the villainy and imbecility of rebellion . . . which a Government willing to repress sedition would desire to bring forward", Whig papers simply asked why the play was to be thrown aside (*Morning*

Chronicle, 2 November 1795). The implication was not only that the government needed to confirm the performance of sedition in the relatively safe space of the theatre to justify its own treasonous assault on the constitution in Parliament and on the streets, but also that the government was itself transforming in ways that alienated it from the constitutional precepts of King-in-Parliament established during the Glorious Revolution and historically linked to Otway's play. In other words, the Whig press declared that the absolutist Ministry had every intention of separating itself from the sustaining traditions enacted in the patriotic repertoire and thus were arguably more dangerous than the radical constituencies who were acting on the repertoire in the name of reform.

I serve the King

In its harshest invective against the censorship of *Venice Preserv'd*, the *Morning Chronicle* not only argued that the government "now daily affirms that Plots and Conspiracies exist" so that it can justify the Treasonable Practices Act, but also asserted that it is not above "attacking individuals on the side of their private concerns" – i.e. the Managers' investment in the production (*Morning Chronicle*, 3 and 2 November 1795). This insinuated that the damage being inflicted on the finances of Drury Lane was an emblem for the damage being sustained by the economy and the constitutional ideals of the nation in the government's prosecution of war. Despite the *Morning Chronicle*'s warning to the King not to give "a marked, uniform, and intentional preference of the one Theatre to the other", George III chose to frequent Covent Garden exclusively during this period (3 November 1795). On the day following the assault on the Royal Coach, he once again ventured into the streets in order to attend a performance of Sheridan's *The Rivals* at Covent Garden. Press coverage of this trip to the theatre was far more extensive than the controversy elicited by *Venice Preserv'd* because

> the aim of the king's visit . . . may have been partly to give official expression to . . . ministerial disapprobation of Sheridan's management of Drury Lane, as well as to demonstrate his own refusal to be intimidated by the events of the previous day.
>
> (Barrell, 2000: 568).

The radical press represented the King's heavily guarded procession to the theatre as "the conveyance of a *Criminal* to the place of *Execution*".[9] As Barrell notes, the Royal Coach was not only guarded, but took an unusual route to the theatre: "The Public were barred from the streets adjacent to the route, but still there seems to have been some hooting and hissing, and some of the crowd were trampled under the hooves of the cavalry and wounded by sabre-cuts" (Barrell, 2000: 569). *The Sun* represented the evening at the theatre rather differently:

> "Upon the whole, we never witnessed a more general, and a more cordial attestation of LOYALTY; and friends of the BRITISH CONSTITUTION have evidently no reason to fear the Principles of *Jacobinism*, and the arts of *Sedition*, as MONARCHY appears to reign in the hearts of Englishmen"
>
> (31 October 1795)

But despite the presence of the King himself and a largely loyalist audience – assembled by issuing special tickets to officers of the government and the police – even *The Sun* had to admit that the audience was not universally loyal to George III:

> a few solitary hisses, indeed, issued from a dozen or two of democratic serpents, distributed in the Pit and the Gallery, whose dark heads appeared like a few scattered poppies in a rich bed of tulips. But they were so completely overpowered by a general burst of loyalty, as to be scarcely audible.–In short, the audience felt, like honest and loyal subjects, the recent escape of a beloved SOVEREIGN, from the base attempts of a hired Assassin.
>
> (31 October 1795)

The loyal garden is of course Eden and it is threatened by democratic serpents; but this clumsy attempt to figure the conflict in the theatre as one rooted in class and demeanour failed to capture the complexity of political affiliation in this place at this moment in time. When one moves away from the pro-Ministry press, it becomes clear that the performance of patriotism during this production of Sheridan's play was exceedingly volatile:

> Their Majesties and the Princesses went last night to see the Comedy of The Rivals, and the Entertainment of *Hartford-Bridge*. The croud [sic] in the streets to see the sovereign pass, was very great; and the Theatre was full in every part. The loyal songs, "God save the King," and "Rule Britannia," were both sung and both encored. Near the end of the play, a great degree of clamour was excited, by *Captain Absolute* repeating, as his reason for fighting a duel, the words "*I serve the King*". In the midst of it, Mr. Macmanus walked on the stage, no one knew why, and placed himself opposite to the King's box. The noise then increased to an almost alarming degree, till Mr. Macmanus retired; and then it subsided. An odd accident happened as his Majesty went to the Theatre: one of the Horse Soldiers pistol, in the holster, went off, and shot the next horse in the shoulder. This gave rise to a false, and perhaps malicious report, for it was industriously circulated, that his Majesty had been fired at.
>
> (*Morning Chronicle*, 31 October 1795)

Aside from indicating that the King's passage to and from the theatre was itself a form of political theatre susceptible to "malicious" – i.e. ministerial – interpretation, the *Morning Chronicle*'s account of the unrest during the play re-engages the question of intention for its own ends. Just as the loyalist press ridiculed the failure of radicals to apprehend Otway's intent, so now the *Morning Chronicle* questions the audience's response not only to Sheridan's intent in *The Rivals*, but also to the intent ascribed to the play by the audience. Because it does not specify the political inflection of the "clamour", the report forces the reader to work through the possibilities.

Like many comedies before it, "elderly relatives in *The Rivals* prescribe for their heirs marital fates that the latter seek to resist" (Cordner, 1998: xi). This is given a political valence because Sir Anthony Absolute, as his name suggests, is a figure for patriarchal tyranny not at all distant from George III's manifestation of tyranny at the moment of the play's first performance in 1775 on the eve of the American war. Sir Lucius O'Trigger is the focus of Sheridan's Whig critique of bellicosity – the

Irishman's incoherent advocacy of violence and his manipulation of the rhetoric of honour allegorizes the North Ministry's policy of war and re-conquest in America. That policy effectively incited resistance in order to brutally suppress it; is there a more damning critique of the Coercive Acts than Sir Lucius's specious coercion of Captain Absolute into a duel? Because colonial relations were embedded in a familial rhetoric, Sheridan's play evinced the historical incoherence of the father's demands on the son and thus allegorized the American crisis.[10] The American colonists were demonstrating this incoherence in their own way, but in *The Rivals* Sir Anthony desires that his son should both "obey him implicitly" and "have the spirit to show defiance". Audiences in 1775 would have clearly heard the impasse because it constitutes precisely the merging of servility and liberty that colonists were resisting at this moment. As the play drives towards the violent extirpation of the son, the only way out of this double-bind is for Sir Anthony, the King in this story, to intervene and for Sir Lucius to be shamed. This is why Captain Absolute declares that he has no choice but to duel "because he serves the King". To translate the allegory, the King must change his policy, recognize the colonists as equal governmental subjects before King-and-Parliament, and North and his Tory supporters must be ejected. And this is not simply a Whig power play but a recognition that the phantasmatic accommodation of liberty and sovereignty at the heart of the British Constitution requires this precarious adjustment. Needless to say there is a certain commutability to the moment in 1795 when Sheridan, Fox, and more radical politicians were again openly criticizing the absolutism of the state, its prosecution of war to preserve monarchy from democratic critique, and the specious incitement to "sedition" in the realm of both legislation and propaganda. The re-performance of *The Rivals* in 1795 had the potential to link two moments of democratic revolution and suggest that any rehearsal of Britain's earlier bellicose posture would result in a similar historical humiliation.

When Munden, who played Captain Absolute, repeats "I serve the King", how are we to interpret the reported clamour? The speech is from Act V, scene iii, in which it is revealed that the various duels in Sheridan's play arise either from Absolute's attempt to deceive both his beloved Lydia Languish and his father so that he can retain her fortune when he marries her, or from an even more ridiculous misunderstanding between Absolute and Sir Lucius O'Trigger. Absolute's claim to be serving his Majesty because he is a soldier is at best a rationalization for deceit and greed staged to appease his father. Are the words "I serve the King" spoken by a man in uniform sufficient to elicit loyalist approbation in spite of the fact that Sheridan's play gently ridicules the character who expresses them as both impulsive and deceitful? If the crowd is applauding the phrase as a sign of loyalty, then their approbation is comparable to that expressed for Pierre's democratic principles on the previous evening at Drury Lane for it reverses the traditional view of the author's intention and detaches the character from the dramatic action. For the *Morning Chronicle,* such a reversal is a sign that loyalism is itself unable to discern the distinction between satire and panegyric and thus stands as a form of delusion akin to that described by Pierre in the controversial speech from Act I of *Venice Preserv'd.*

But theatregoers would also have known that the duel in *The Rivals* closely followed events in Sheridan's own life and that Captain Absolute stands for Sheridan himself.[11] In this light, the Covent Garden production is figuratively forcing "Sheridan" to state his loyalty. This would have been seen as a burlesque on Sheridan's hypocrisy by loyalist audience members, fully convinced that his resistance to the suspension of the Habeas Corpus Act and his staging of *Venice Preserv'd* were signs of treason.[12] In response to such an interpretation, anti-loyalist members of the audience could applaud Captain Absolute's statement of loyalty as a re-iteration of Whig assertions that Sheridan and Fox serve the constitution with more integrity than the Ministry, here figured by Sir Anthony and Sir Lucius O'Trigger. Even the speciousness of Captain Absolute's service to the King suits this latter interpretation for it implies that, with a corrupt or delusional monarch like George III on the throne, the only true service to the notion of Kingship would have to be specious. In short, the clamour could well be over competing accounts of Sheridan's politics.

It is important to remember that Pitt was regularly satirized for his absolutism, his greed, his bellicosity, and his ostensible manipulation of George III. In this light, Captain Absolute's name and his defence of his duelling as service to the King also operate as an allegory for Pitt's absolutism and his specious rationalization for continued war with France. Traditional readings of *The Rivals* tend to argue that the authoritarian Sir Anthony Absolute is duped by his adventurous son, but it is important to remember that all of Captain Absolute's deceptions are also aimed at deceitfully securing Lydia's immense fortune.[13] If we turn this into a topical allegory, then the play has the potential to allegorize the authoritarian George III being manipulated by his Minister. If we understand Lydia to be a figure for the nation, itself willing to be deluded, then the allegory expands to suggest that Pitt and the King were using the war with France to defraud the nation. One can imagine the "poppies", highly attuned not only to the traditional understandings of Sheridan's ostensible intention in the scene, but also to the reformist critique of the Pitt Ministry, applauding Munden's repetition of "I serve the King" as an unwitting attack on Pitt and the King. Because Covent Garden was seen as the more loyal of the Theatres Royal, it is hard to imagine Munden intentionally attempting to elicit this response, but the very fact of repetition opens the way for a rigorously traditional reading of the scene's dynamics, but with an intent unforeseen not only by the Manager and players at Covent Garden when they mounted the production, but also by Sheridan when he wrote *The Rivals* twenty years earlier.

Whether Captain Absolute is Pitt or Sheridan depends upon how the audience engages with the repertoire. A similar undecidability is registered by the *Morning Chronicle* when it declares that Macmanus's actions before the King are incomprehensible: is he protecting the King from the threat posed by a heterodox reading of the scene? Or is he authorizing the suppression of such a reading as an expression of the will of the management? Macmanus's performance escalates political conflict in the theatre not only because it links response to the play and response to the sovereign and thus confirms the political allegory it would seem to proscribe, but also because it recognizes, and thus legitimizes, the constituency (including Sheridan) predisposed to publicly criticize the King. Whether the latter is done out of fear, or out of confidence that the threat will be easily quelled and thus appropriable by loyalist rhetoric, it serves the purpose of enabling political turbulence. And as we have seen, the *Morning Chronicle*'s analysis of governmental affairs at this juncture consistently accuses the Ministry of promulgating unrest, much like Lucius O'Trigger, in order to justify even more draconian and absolutist actions.

But the entire performance of loyalism here re-enacts both sides of the controversy surrounding *Venice Preserv'd* and thus is itself in dialogue with the repertoire of theatrical and political performance. Here in Covent Garden, *The Rivals* is stolen from Sheridan to critique both his past and his present resistance to George III, but in the process crucial parallels are drawn not only between present French policy and the historical failure to govern judiciously during the American crisis, but also between past and present moments of George III's predilection for absolutism. In that sense, Sheridan's critique becomes only more vital because in 1795 the war with France was haunted by the spectre of the American war. In spite of the fact that the Ministry has control of the means of production in the form of theatrical licensing and royal approbation, it cannot control the repertoire itself because its performative manifestation in the present, its engagement with the past, and its postulation of yet to be realized futures are equally transient and available for appropriation in the next remediated performance.

Notes

1 See O'Quinn (2011: 1–39).
2 For the political context of Otway's tragedy, see Owen (2002: 121–46), Harth (1987–8: 345-62) and Solomon (1986: 289–310).
3 See Backscheider (2012: 52–69) for a discussion of Siddons's performance in the role.
4 See Taylor (1950: 143–223) for a stage history of *Venice Preserv'd* in the long eighteenth century.
5 Kemble was known for these suspensions of dramatic action, but in his Shakespearean adaptations they were generally deployed to defend and promote monarchy. See Moody (2000: 122).
6 Genest (1832: VII, 229).
7 See Barrell (2000: 567–9), Russell (1997) and Scrivener (2001: 40–1, 170–1, 294–5).
8 For a discussion of the Pop-Gun Plot, see Barrell (2000: 445–503).
9 *Truth and Treason!*, 7. Quoted in Barrell (2000: 568).
10 For treatments of how the American war permeates Sheridan's comedies, see Taylor (2012: 24–5) and Jones (2011: 159–94).
11 For a helpful summation of the complex allegorical relation between events in *The Rivals* and elements of Sheridan's life, see O'Toole (1997: 86–96).
12 See Freeman (2002: 183–92) for an illuminating analysis of Jack Absolute's hypocrisy.
13 Lydia explicitly states that Absolute's masquerade as Beverly is a complex ruse to gain her fortune. See *The Rivals*, 70–1.

Works cited

Backscheider, Paula. (2012) "Politics and Gender in a Tale of Two Plays", in Tiffany Potter (ed.) *Women, Popular Culture, and the Eighteenth Century*, Toronto: University of Toronto Press.

Bal, Mieke. (2002) *Traveling Concepts in the Humanities*, Toronto: University of Toronto Press.

Barrell, John. (1998) "'An Entire Change of Performances?': The Politicization of Theatre and the Theatricalisation of Politics in the mid-1790s", *Lumen* 17, 11–50.

Barrell, John. (2000) *Imagining the King's Death: Figurative Treason, Fantasies of Regicide, 1793–1796*, London: Oxford University Press.

Bywaters, David. (1983) "Venice, Its Senate, and Its Plot in Otway's Venice Preserv'd", *Modern Philology* 80(3), 256–63.

Cordner, Michael. (1998) "Introduction", in Richard Brinsley Sheridan, *The School for Scandal and Other Plays*, London: Oxford University Press.

Freeman, Lisa. (2002) *Character's Theater: Genre and Identity on the Eighteenth-Century English Stage*, Philadelphia: University of Pennsylvania Press.

Genest, John. (1832) *Some Account of the English Stage from the Restoration in 1660 to 1830*, 10 vols, Bath: H.E. Carrington, vol. 7.VII,

Harth, Philip. (1987–8) "Political Interpretations of *Venice Preserv'd*", *Modern Philology* 85, 345–62.

Jones, Robert W. (2011) *Literature, Gender and Politics in Britain during the War for America 1770–1785*, Cambridge: Cambridge University Press.

Kemble, John Philip. (1795) *Otway's Tragedy of Venice Preserv'd; Or, A Plot Discovered*, revised by J.P. Kemble, London: C. Lowndes.

Moody, Jane. (2000) *Illegitimate Theatre in London, 1770–1840*, Cambridge: Cambridge University Press.

O'Quinn, Daniel. (2011) *Entertaining Crisis in the Atlantic Imperium, 1770–1790*, Baltimore: Johns Hopkins University Press.

O'Toole, Fintan. (1997) *A Traitor's Kiss: The Life of Richard Brinsley Sheridan*, London: Granta Books.

Owen, Susan J. (2002) *Perspectives on Restoration Drama*, Manchester: Manchester University Press.

Russell, Gillian. (1997) "Burke's Dagger: Theatricality, Politics and Print Culture in the 1790s", *Journal for Eighteenth-Century Studies* 20(1), 1–16.

Scrivener, Michael. (2001) *Seditious Allegories: John Thelwall and Jacobin Writing*, University Park: Pennsylvania State Press.

Sheridan, Richard Brinsley. (1998) *The Rivals*, in Michael Cordner (ed.) *The School for Scandal and Other Plays*, London: Oxford University Press.

Solomon, Harry M. (1986) "The Rhetoric of 'Redressing Grievances': Court Propaganda as the Hermeneutical Key to *Venice Preserv'd*", *ELH* 53, 289–310.

Taylor, Aline Mackenzie. (1950) *Next to Shakespeare: Otway's Venice Preserv'd and The Orphan*, Durham: Duke University Press.

Taylor, David Francis. (2012) *Theatres of Opposition: Empire, Revolution, and Richard Brinsley Sheridan*, London: Oxford University Press.

Taylor, Diana. (2003) *The Archive and the Repertoire: Performing Cultural Memory in the Americas*, Durham: Duke University Press.

Part 2

Aesthetics and literary form

Introduction

There is ample evidence for seeing the Romantic age as the moment in which many aspects of the "literary" are defined with greater specificity than ever before in literary history. The Augustan poet Alexander Pope defended the idea of poetic art in his *Essay on Criticism* as "nature" that coincided with a standard inherited from ancient practice: "Those rules of old discover'd, not devis'd, / Are nature still, but nature methodized" (Pope 1963: lines 88–89). The methods of nature, in turn, applied not only to poetry but also to every aspect of human conduct – to the task of criticism, for instance, and to the cultivation of general good conduct. But in Samuel Taylor Coleridge's account of poetry in the *Biographia Literaria* as that to which we return and reread with pleasure, and that which cannot be translated into "other words in the same language" (Coleridge 1983: 23), we find one among many attempts by writers of the Romantic age to understand and describe poems or novels as distinct entities or forms. Although the term "aesthetics" arose in German philosophy, twentieth-century critics have often appropriated the term to describe, among other things, the appreciation and analysis of these distinct entities or forms.

The general introduction to this volume explains how various aspects of literary form were of great interest to critics in the first half of the twentieth century. Deconstructionist critics are sometimes considered to be formalists: a work like Paul Fry's study of the English ode, despite its essentially poststructuralist attention to textual failure and insufficiency, claimed to be analyzing the complexities of a specific generic form (Fry 1980). Ian Balfour adds a note of complication to that picture as he remarks on how this strain of formalism radicalized and reversed traditional formal claims so that "close reading" resulted in "rhetorical reading"; rhetorical reading pointed to the instabilities rather than the internal unity of literary works (Balfour 2005: 10). Still, historicist critics of the 1980s tended to see deconstruction itself as far too "courteous," as Levinson puts it in her selection in the previous section; those critics, she says, mobilized that courtesy to "explicate" the complications of poetry rather than "explain" them. To "explain" works of literature, in the view of many historicists, was to see the context for literature not within patterns of language but within specific material human experiences. The true nature of "authorial and contextual urgencies" (again, quoting from Levinson) was to be unearthed by analyzing the literary work in relation to its historically specific "occasion."

Historicists, in other words, often tended to treat deconstructionist critics as if they were New Critical formalists. Such strongly worded characterizations notwithstanding, historicists shared with deconstructionists a deeper common ground: both camps had a commitment to unraveling the stabilities of literary meaning with reference to a materiality that – when exposed by the critic – enabled the reader to avoid the errors of transcendence and idealism. The struggle to maintain this position, and the problems associated with that struggle, are analyzed in many essays by Alan Liu – including the one excerpted in this volume, which later appeared in chapter 3 of his book *Local Transcendence: Essays on Postmodern Historicism and the Database.* Liu's commentary understands form as a problem that criticism must attempt to overcome because form is false "transcendence." Even in the most apparently un-transcendent "detailism" which he locates in new historicism (as well as in cultural criticism and new pragmatism), Liu finds an implicit aspiration for transcendental form, and he sees in this aspiration a covert connection to Romanticism. "As Coleridge might phrase it," he writes, "cultural-critical 'detail' is the part through which the whole shines through translucently." The solution that Liu offers, however, is not to move beyond (or under) the logic of local transcendence; the witty irony of Liu's essay, which critiques lists and details even while providing them, is that it knowingly practices the logic it critiques. He encourages us at the end of his argument to adopt a greater self-consciousness about the critical and theoretical enterprise – to acknowledge that historical and cultural "context" is a "grid" or aesthetic construction imposed upon material, historically specific culture.

Critics have continued to be wary of forms and formal readings. In this volume, Andrew Bennett's selection challenges the idea of poetic authority as a unitary intention, for instance; beyond these pages, Tilottama Rajan's work on Romantic narrative shows how Romantic narrative "unbinds" the idea of plot as "closure" (Rajan 2010: xv); Alexander Regier has drawn renewed attention to Romanticism's interest in literary fragmentation (Regier 2010). Still other critics, however, are reviving interest in analyzing literary forms, inaugurating what some have termed a "new formalism" (Levinson 2007). Stuart Curran's *Poetic Form and British Romanticism* and Susan Wolfson's *Formal Charges* make strong arguments for acknowledging the centrality of formalist techniques of "close reading" in literary criticism (Curran 1986; Wolfson 1997); many essays in different areas of this volume (aside from Wolfson's own contribution) practice these techniques and attend to varied aspects of literary form. Examples of these include Clara Tuite's concept of Jane Austen's "formal mechanisms" of free indirect style, Jerome Christensen's idea of a "Romantic formalism on the move," and Maureen McLane's study of the literary mediations of orality in "the book form."

The fact that "form" can refer to transcendence, to large narrative structures, to local uses of figurative language, and even to the book or printed page only begins to suggest that there are considerable disagreements about exactly what form is and does. Frances Ferguson's essay excerpt, from her book *Solitude and the Sublime: Romanticism and the Aesthetics of Individuation,* offers an account that opposes Liu's view that form presents a problem for literary theory, and this is because of her profound disagreement with Liu's theoretical understanding of form as such. Rather than seeing form as false transcendence, she considers it as more essential for literary meaning because it is fundamental to linguistic meaning. Taking aim at both deconstructionist and historicist criticism, she questions the attempts that both lines of thought (here exemplified in the work of Jerome McGann and Paul de Man) make to locate meaning in human or linguistic materiality apart from formal systems. Her reading of William Wordsworth's "We are Seven" demonstrates, in contrast to these views, how the poem depends for its meaning upon formal and material properties of language being translatable into each other. The poem in a sense dramatizes the fact that language can function abstractly or concretely, as both formal structure – "the patterning of language" – and concrete naming.

There are some ways in which Robert Kaufman's account of aesthetics connects with Ferguson's. Both critics emphasize the centrality of aesthetic form in a way that reaffirms the weight that the philosopher Immanuel Kant placed upon aesthetic judgments, particularly insofar as those judgments inform our basic understanding of the world and our ethical and political relations to it. Other critics who have taken Kantian aesthetics seriously as a way of discussing Romantic literature include Steven Knapp and Vivasvan Soni (Knapp 1993; Soni 2006); Kaufman's account is distinctive among these for stressing a congenial relationship between Kantian aesthetics and an influential strain of Marxist thought. Whereas many critics tend to see the line of thinking found in the Frankfurt School philosopher Theodor Adorno to be very much at odds with the impassioned defenses of aesthetic form in Percy Shelley's poetry and prose, Kaufman (whose reading connects on some levels with Hamilton's account of Keats in the previous section) brings these thinkers very close together, showing how both explore the emancipatory potential within aesthetic contemplation. Shelley anticipates Adorno in his defense of a "critical aesthetics," Kaufman argues, because Shelley's "artistic structure" holds together an "emancipatory gesture" and a "formal constraint."

My own essay contribution to this volume extends work that I have done on Romantic aesthetics and politics, particularly in my book *The Shadow of Death* (Canuel 2007). Like Kaufman, I emphasize political aspects of literary form; however, I focus more steadily on understanding how literary forms participate in and comment on particular political discussions rather than general literary theoretical trends. In my reading of William Godwin's novel *Caleb Williams*, I show how Godwin's work is deeply immersed in competing accounts of punishment that were debated during the author's day. While focusing in many respects on reforming retributive justice, the novel also goes further to overturn its legitimacy in more profound ways. Still, even the utilitarian modes of assessment that the novel mobilizes to criticize the logic of retribution are in themselves exposed as compromised or insufficient. This is dramatized in the uneasy shifts in the novel from first-person to third-person "free indirect" style.

Works cited

Balfour, Ian. (2005) "History Against Historicism, Formal Matters, and the Event of the Text: De Man with Benjamin," *Romantic Circles Praxis Series*, 23 pars.

Canuel, Mark. (2007) *The Shadow of Death: Literature, Romanticism, and the Subject of Punishment*, Princeton: Princeton University Press.

Coleridge, Samuel Taylor. (1983) *Biographia Literaria, or Biographical Sketches of My Literary Life and Opinions*, eds James Engell and W. Jackson Bate, Princeton: Princeton University Press.

Curran, Stuart. (1986) *Poetic Form and British Romanticism*, New York: Oxford University Press.

Fry, Paul. (1980) *The Poet's Calling in the English Ode*, New Haven: Yale University Press.

Knapp, Steven. (1993) *Literary Interest: The Limits of Anti-Formalism*, Cambridge, MA: Harvard University Press.

Levinson, Marjorie. (2007) "What is New Formalism?" *PMLA* 122: 558–69.

Pope, Alexander. (1963) "An Essay on Criticism," *The Poems of Alexander Pope*, ed. John Butt, New Haven: Yale University Press.

Rajan, Tillottama. (2010) *Romantic Narrative: Shelley, Hays, Godwin, Wollstonecraft*, Baltimore: The Johns Hopkins University Press.

Regier, Alexander. (2010) *Fracture and Fragmentation in British Romanticism*, Cambridge: Cambridge University Press.

Soni, Vivasvan. (2006) "Communal Narcosis and Sublime Withdrawal: The Problem of Community in Kant's Critique of Judgment," *Cultural Critique* 64: 1–39.

Wolfson, Susan. (1997) *Formal Charges: The Shaping of Poetry in British Romanticism*, Stanford: Stanford University Press.

Further reading

Duff, David. (2009) *Romanticism and the Uses of Genre*, Oxford: Oxford University Press.

Kucich, Greg. (1991) *Keats, Shelley, and Romantic Spenserianism*, University Park: Pennsylvania State University Press.

Milnes, Tim. (2003) *Knowledge and Indifference in English Romantic Prose*, Cambridge: Cambridge University Press.

Pyle, Forest. (1995) *The Ideology of Imagination: Subject and Society in the Discourse of Romanticism*, Stanford: Stanford University Press.

Rawes, Alan, ed. (2007) *Romanticism and Form*, Houndmills: Palgrave Macmillan.

Redfield, Marc. (2003) *The Politics of Aesthetics: Nationalism, Gender, Romanticism*, Stanford: Stanford University Press.

Rei Terada. (2009) *Looking Away: Phenomenality and Dissatisfaction, Kant to Adorno*, Harvard: Harvard University Press.

Whale, John. (2000) *Imagination Under Pressure, 1789–1832: Aesthetics, Politics, and Utility*, Cambridge: Cambridge University Press.

5   Local transcendence

Cultural criticism, postmodernism, and the romanticism of detail

Alan Liu

I wish in this essay to criticize cultural criticism in what may be called its high postmodernist forms: cultural anthropology, new cultural history, New Historicism, New Pragmatism, new and/or post-Marxism, and finally that side of French theory – overlapping with post-Marxism – that may be labeled French pragmatism (i.e., the "practice" philosophy and/or semiotic "pragmatics" of the later Michel Foucault, Pierre Bourdieu, Michel de Certeau, Jean-François Lyotard). These aggressively "new" forms of contextualism do not exhaust the field of postmodern cultural criticism, and a fuller study would need to include the different emphases of ethnic, gender, and area studies as well as of British cultural materialism. But for now we can stay high. "High" distinguishes neither the theoretical from the practical, the high cultural from the populist, nor the neoconservative from the leftist. Rather, it indicates a shared mode of cultural engagement that undercuts all such polemics dividing the field to project an increasingly generic discourse of contextualism. This mode of engagement may be called *detached immanence.* Detached immanence amid worlds of context is the distinctively postmodern, the "new," in cultural criticism.

But we must descend to particulars. I refer to a tenet so elementary, pervasive, and insistent in all the high cultural criticisms that it appears foundational (despite the method's avowed philosophical antifoundationalism). The basis of high cultural criticism is its belief that criticism can, and must, engage with context in a manner so close, bit-mapped, or microbial (to use some of the method's paradigms) that the critic appears no farther from the cultural object than a cybernetic or biological virus from its host at the moment of code exchange. We live in an age of "detailism" characterized by the "pervasive valorization of the minute, the partial, and the marginal," Naomi Schor says in her intriguing *Reading in Detail,* a study of the genealogy of detailism leading up to modernist and post-structuralist aesthetics.[1] High cultural criticism is an aesthetics – and much more – of specifically postmodern detailism. Or to name the method's related leading concepts: it is particularism, localism, regionalism, relative autonomism, incommensurabilism, accidentalism (or contingency), anecdotalism, historicism, and – to draw attention to a set of curiously prominent Greek prefixes in the method – "micro-," "hetero-," and "poly-"ism. "All these," we may say in words borrowed from Clifford Geertz's *Local Knowledge,* "are products of a certain cast of thought, one rather entranced with the diversity of things."[2] Or as Richard Rorty sums it up, "All that can be done to explicate 'truth,' 'knowledge,' 'morality,' 'virtue' is to refer us back to the concrete details of the culture in which these terms grew up."[3] And most succinctly, that unofficial motto repeated several times in Jerome McGann's *Social Values and Poetic Acts:* "I make for myself a picture of great detail."[4]

[Here Liu lists a "matrix of cultural-critical phrases," emphasizing the importance of location, fragmentation, and detail throughout cultural and literary criticism.]

[. . .]

Detail is the very instrument of the antifoundational and anti-epistemological imperative in high cultural criticism: its contention is that there is no reason (other than fidelity to quaint notions of philosophy) why contexts of discretely perceived particulars should resolve into culture as a single, grounded, and knowable order. The empirics, pragmatics, and dialogics of high cultural criticism are finally methodologies as much *against* as of knowledge – a methodical antimethod.

But there is a danger in antimethod, of course. It is possible to discern in the all too often trenchant formulations of cultural criticism precisely an incipient method or meta-way (*meta/hodos*) of alternative knowledge. This is the criticism of hidden foundationalism that has long haunted Marxist criticism, for example. Or again, we can think of the polemical hard edges of other cultural criticisms: Geertz's antifunctionalism, New Historicism's antiformalism, or the anti-*Annales* movement in New Cultural History – all of which wear their dissent, perhaps, with too heightened a sense of the sanctity of their meta-way.[5] [. . .] The picture of great detail, as it were, threatens to become a *great picture* of detail.

How to discern [. . .] a "thought" or "idea" of culture, then, without being too knowing even in the way of antiknowing? The answer, I suggest, lies precisely under the sign of a very old antifoundationalism or sophistry: rhetoric. [. . .] [T]he methodology of high cultural criticism is really an incoherence of three rhetorical "moments." For ease of reference, these may be called *immanence, commitment*, and *detachment*. It is immanence that speaks within cultural criticism's empirics of the Real; commitment within its pragmatics of variously oppositional or neoconservative "practice"; and detachment within its cool dialogics of improvised conversation or *petits récits* [. . .]. Each such rhetorical moment at the core of the method, I suggest, is not an integral discourse but the site of an instability or turning in rhetoric. After all, only inner troping allows method to be perceived *as* rhetoricity in the first place – as a way of knowing prevented from hardening into dogma (*especially* when it is being most polemical or rhetorical) by the arbitrary intervention of its media.

Of course, our most recent avatar of rhetoricity certainly holds to its own meta-way. But deconstructive method will serve as a salutary corrective to cultural-critical method so long as we persist in seeing rhetoric as mediational to the end – that is, as perpetually a media or means rather than end. Rhetoric will be our means of referring cultural-critical method to the ultimate antifoundationalism or endless end: history. History, or "elsewhereness" as I have called it elsewhere, is alienated foundation.[6] It is what orders the thought and, within thought, rhetoric of cultural criticism into a characteristic sequence whose logical necessity is subordinated to the phantom necessity of contingency.

What I mean here may be educed from the detectable tug of diachrony in high cultural-critical argument, the tendency in the method to marshal reasons and discourses in a certain order unpredictable from within the system. As "thought," to begin with, cultural criticism follows a logical order that is pseudo-syllogistic. Consider as evidence, for instance, the strong drift in Geertz's cockfight essay *from* counting bets *to* meditating on aesthetics; or, again, witness the glide in Rorty's *Contingency, Irony, and Solidarity* toward a culminating discussion of literature.[7]

[. . .]

The romanticism of detail

The present essay focuses on the "first" or opening rhetoric of high cultural criticism: immanence. Here we are closest to foundationalism. Like pitons driven by the climber into a mountain face, details in the rhetoric of immanence are points of attachment where we experience such hands-on knowledge of the gritty cultural mass that we seem to feel the very quiddity of culture, the Real.

[. . .]

What such empirics projects is a view of cultural matter (economic, social, political, or ideological) so objective that materialism seems to obey the dynamics of literal matter. We can take as our explanatory paradigm the sometimes explicit conceit in cultural criticism that details are "atoms." Observe that our matrix of phrases repeatedly isolates "atoms," "tiniest, indivisible elements," "elementary particulars," "highly charged phenomena," and ultimately "molecules" akin to what Arthur O. Lovejoy's history of ideas once called "unit-ideas." Details, that is, are elementary particles engaged in an overall systemics of combination much like the molecularism for which Louis O. Mink once criticized Lovejoy.[8] But a discrimination is in order. As calibrated by such pervasive cultural-critical modifiers as "determinate" and "specific" ("deeply specific," Marjorie Levinson says), elementary particularism is innocent of the fuzzy probabilities of current particle science.[9] [. . .] [C]ultural criticism remembers in the detail something like Democritan atomism as well as the geopolitical insularity of Greek city-states. The atom of detail is a classically hard, discrete unit. Or put *neo*classically: the unit-detail analytic indicates the residual hold of Newtonian physics and of the emergent philosophy of Newton's age: Locke's program of elementary "ideas" and/or social-contract individuals associating in compound aggregates. With associational mechanics in mind, indeed, we might reinforce that great pillar of materialism throughout cultural criticism: the "concrete." Phrases in our matrix such as "concretely situated," "the concrete, the material, and the particular," or "ordinary, retail, detailed, concrete" build a world that is exactly concrete: a cement aggregate of specific and determinate particularity.

Such unit-detail atomism is ubiquitous, affecting even the most sophisticated interpreter whenever argument turns in the direction of empirical investigation. To come directly to the heart of the "matter," we need only foreground what our matrix of phrases has already enacted: the strangely overdetermined role of matrix forms throughout cultural criticism. Matrices are the method's great aggregates of atomistic detail. To read at any length in cultural criticism, after all, is often precisely to read *at length* – an effect consisting not so much in the actual number of pages as in the wet-cement quality of the reading experience. Cultural criticism dilates discourse through interpolated arrays of particulars, a sort of *blason* of the mundane or what Rorty (inspired by a Philip Larkin poem) calls "lading lists" of the world.[10]

[. . .]

The science of the list may be stated: wholes are knowable only as aggregates in which the detail *has no interior detail*. Cultural-critical detail, that is, is as much a resistance to, as enactment of, the more radical detailism of fractal and chaos theory in postmodern science proper. It is clear that the particulars gathered by [Robert] Darnton and Geertz, for example, have no visible interior detail – no more so than the "*And, And moreover, And nevertheless*" in Lyotard's great work of/about lists (what he terms phrases "linked" in disconnection by their "differends"). "Frame, figures of speech," "size, bone thickness," and, and, . . . exist at that lower event horizon known to all empirical investigators of culture where evidentiary authority must at last rest upon sketchy, borrowed, or otherwise uncooked "facts" collected without linkage in a notebook.[11] At that event horizon there is no substantive difference between traditional empiricists and such *outré* "scientists" of culture as structural anthropologists or structural Marxists. "Structure" itself reduces to lists. However much [Louis] Althusser's overall theory is structural, for example, it is evident that his "empirical list" cements rough-hewn institutions *en bloc* in an essentially aggregate social whole. Similarly, the few details he does offer about the internal practices of religious and educational institutions accrue in an essentially mechanistic manner. "Apparatus," we may say, is the bureaucratization of the Lockean aggregate. "Thus Schools and Churches use suitable methods of punishment, expulsion, selection, etc.," Althusser says at one point, checking off the particulars of superstructure on a lading list of undetailed details punctuated by an *etc.*[12]

And with this *etc.* we come to the heart of the matter: the strange interface where the science of the list reveals its rhetoricity and, indexed by rhetoricity, its historicity. Seen one way, after all, the science of lists depends on a convention of figuration rather than of induction: a syntagmatics or metonymics whose illusion is that wholes are polymers of parts. What makes such figuration visible is an interior instability where saying one thing – in this case, listing atoms – suddenly seems equivalent to saying something else. What else does high cultural criticism have to say in the very act of reciting lists as if syntagm were its only discourse?

It has a lot to say, namely "etc."

[. . .]

Etc., I suggest, is a *trope* of inexpressibility that introduces within atomism a rhetoric-within-rhetoric. Besides metonymy, after all, there is also that variant, more expansive play on particulars: synecdoche. It is synecdoche that redeems the *etc.* from the wasteland of endless syntagm (which some cultural criticisms also call consumerism) by transforming incompletion into the figure of fulfillment: a symbolics or iconic metaphorics putting the part *for* the cultural whole.[13] I refer to the implicit rhetorical turn heard in such phrases from our matrix as "some fragment of a lost life," "my vision is necessarily more fragmentary," or "the fragments, the incommensurable levels, the heterogeneous impulses." Such rhetoric clearly confesses incompletion, but, at last, also the unmistakable sign of synecdoche. Fragments, after all, are by definition not "particles" (which exist whether or not they join in a larger unit); they can only be parts-of-a-whole. [. . .] The fragmentary atomism of cultural-critical detail harbors a huge error or trope: "microcosm" in the old sense.[14]

Or rather, the detail is big with a slightly more recent, if still premodern, rhetoric of microcosm – with the rhetoric of parts-become-wholes, indeed, that originally arose to combat Lockean systemics. Here I advance the historical complement to rhetorical analysis. The moment of immanence is "first" in cultural criticism, as I have said, not because it is a priori but because it initiates an embedded historical sequence of rhetorics. [. . .] [I]t is now culture that is ambiguous and paradoxical in its tense complexity of particularity, its texture of "local irrelevance." It is culture that should not mean, but – with all the ontological zing of the Real – be. Thus arises our new concrete universal: the *cultural* rather than verbal icon. But instead of bringing us back to the regime of Eliotic fragments shored against ruin, I will here drink deeply from the source. Let me refer postmodern cultural criticism to the movement that modernist aesthetics itself – together with such parallels as Deweyan philosophy – so aggressively sublated: romanticism. Cultural criticism is "first" of all an allusion to the moment when the rhetoric of empiricism confronted the early regime of the fragment: an emerging romantic rhetoric.

Witness [. . .] the broad, deep, and explicit remembrance of high romanticism – both literary and philosophical – in high postmodern cultural criticism. Without exaggeration, it may be said that romanticism is the most common ancestor of the various cultural criticisms: more basic, more shared than such polemically charged and relatively recent parent figures as Marx, Nietzsche, Dewey, Braudel, or Malinowski. Romanticism, as it were, is the grandparent or grandmuse: a grand-matrix of thought that, precisely because it is more distanced from current struggles for and against Marx, Nietzsche, Dewey, etc., indulges the most uncritical statements. A first evidence consists in such unabashed allusions in our matrix as "minute particulars," "grains of sand in which the world may be seen," "minute particulars of time, place, and circumstance," and (in imitation of Wordsworth's spots of time) "phenomenal spots of history."[15] But the evidence runs deeper than spot allusions. There is a whole subgenre in cultural criticism of sustained and egregiously adventitious uses of romanticism – gorgeous insets of romantic consciousness so well wrought, so self-sustaining, that we wonder whether cultural criticism is at last something like Keats's Grecian Urn: a mere fretwork of culture (some "little town by river or sea shore . . . emptied of [its] folk") silhouetted against an ideal ground.

A prime example is the New Historicism, whose frequent dependence on assumptions of romanticism and nineteenth-century historicism I have discussed elsewhere. In its many invocations of Hegelian "dialectic" together with its master-servant or "containment/subversion" analytic of power, for instance, Renaissance New Historicism is big with Spirit.[16] [Stephen] Greenblatt's massively antithetical notion of Renaissance self-fashioning (outlined in his introduction) could thus be mapped directly over a previous, celebrated work about self-fashioning: [Geoffrey] Hartman's *Wordsworth's Poetry*.[17] But it is in romantics New Historicism that romanticism redux is most brazen. McGann's *Social Values and Poetic Acts*, for example, is an exhilaratingly polymorphous, heterocosmic, or – Americanizing the prefix – coon-curious work that chases the argument of cultural detailism through many fields of inquiry. Two fields, however, stand out: romantic literature and postmodernism. Whether these two are polymorphs or isomorphs is open to question: there is a strong presumption throughout the book that Blakean, Byronic, and other aspects of romanticism simply *are* postmodern. "Insofar as works like [Blake's] *Songs* and *Marriage* are nonnarratives which do not involve themselves in forms of atonement," McGann can thus say, "they resemble various kinds of poststructural discourse, in particular the work now commonly known as L = A = G = U = A = G = E Writing."[18]

[. . .]

Similarly, romanticism exerts an inordinate influence on the New Pragmatism. It is intriguing, for instance, to consider the infamous setpiece at the center of Steven Knapp and Walter Benn Michaels's "Against Theory."[19] When that Lucy poem ("A Slumber Did My Spirit Seal") washes up on the beach as if by natural process without "intention," we are certainly being instructed in the manner of the philosophical traditions succeeding original pragmatism: analytical philosophy and its strong revision, "ordinary language" philosophy. Compensating for a bluntly denotative style with loony, pure thought-experiment examples ("The universe has expanded to twice its original size this night," "Suppose that in a distant galaxy there is the twin of our earth," "1227 is a rhombus," "Caesar is a prime number," "Should unusual, brilliant patterns suddenly appear in the sky – even if they took the form of letters which seemed to compose a sentence . . . "), analytical and ordinary language philosophy formed New Pragmatism in its image.[20] Plain, blunt, and trenchant to the point of exaggeration, New Pragmatist discourse also favors "pure" examples – paradigms so denotatively complex but connotatively insensitive that they resemble Rube Goldberg contraptions. "Suppose that you're walking along a beach and you come upon a curious sequence of squiggles in the sand," Knapp and Michaels begin, and then set up their contraption: "You step back a few paces and notice that they spell out the following words: 'A slumber did my spirit seal'. . . . "[21]

But if we attend to the undertow of allusion, we will recognize that the contraption washes up on a berm of romanticism. Surely, after all, we are in the wake of *Lyrical Ballads* with its original "ordinary language."[22] Surely (to allude to *The Prelude*) we stand by some glimmering lake where a boy halts his owl songs to feel with shock the "voice" and "imagery" of the landscape sinking "unawares into his mind."[23] Or again, to invoke "The Sensitive-Plant," we pause by some Shelleyan ocean "whose waves never mark, though they ever impress / The light sand which paves it – Consciousness." What hidden romantic current, after all, washes a *Lucy* poem onto Knapp and Michaels's shifting sands of antifoundationalism?[24] [. . .] [W]hen Knapp and Michaels state that "the meaning of a text is simply identical to the author's intended meaning" such that "the project of *grounding* meaning in intention becomes incoherent," what does "simple" mean?[25] Does the standard New Pragmatist argument by dismissal (of the sort: "It simply *is* this way," "Nothing interesting can be said; they just *are* that way") mean that the premise of authorial intention is so natural that it could be an appendix to that romantic theory of simplicity: the Preface to *Lyrical Ballads*? (Wordsworth on intention: rustic existence is paradigmatic because "in that condition of life our elementary feelings co-exist in a state of greater simplicity" and because rustics "convey their feelings and notions in simple and unelaborated expressions.")[26] Is intention, in sum, as "simple" as Lucy, whatever Wordsworth intended by that name?

[. . .]

The full significance of such romantic vignettes set within New Pragmatist discourse only comes to view when we peruse the broad wash effects of romanticism in an extended corpus of cultural criticism such as Richard Rorty's (and, in the background, John Dewey's and William James's).[27] There are Rorty's direct quotations and allusions, for example: "something far more deeply interfused," "murder to dissect," "negative capability," "clerisy of the nation," "create the taste by which he will be judged," "I must Create a System, or be enslav'd by another Man's," and so forth.[28] [. . .] And there is Rorty's consistent use of "romantic" as a period concept designed at once to instruct philosophy in the imaginative groundlessness of romantic world making and to criticize the too idealist goal of the original romantic world makers.

[. . .]

Finally, I invoke just one other side of high postmodern cultural criticism: French postmodern/pragmatist theory as represented, for example, by Lyotard's *The Differend: Phrases in Dispute*.[29] *The Differend* is emphatically a work of cultural criticism not only because it draws its semiotics from the "pragmatics" tradition launched by C.S. Peirce, G.H. Mead, and Charles Morris[30] but because it sets its finally *post*semiotic world of splintered phrase universes on a primal scene of (post) culture: Auschwitz. Auschwitz – and, since this remains an ineluctably French work, secondarily the terror of the French Revolution – is where old philosophers come to dispute their final truth-solutions: epistemological, metaphysical, even syntactical "realities." Is there a speakable and verifiable truth communicable between phrase universes? How can there be such "linkage" if some final solutions silence an entire class of speakers, an entire testament of phrases? In truth, did the Final Solution, did Auschwitz really happen?[31] Philosophers come to offer their judgments. And two of the philosophers who walk most largely are Kant and Hegel. Tutelary geniuses of some of Lyotard's most sustained "Notices," Kant and Hegel are the bookends of Enlightenment and romanticism between which the "differend" is the book burning. The differend is a "feeling" for the unspeakability of any Truth about final solutions, a noncognitive reaching after unspeakable words, a silent grasping for . . . As Lyotard says immediately after his third Kant Notice:

> Is this the sense in which we are not modern? Incommensurability, heterogeneity, the differend, the persistence of proper names, the absence of a supreme tribunal? Or, on the other hand, is this the continuation of romanticism, the nostalgia that accompanies the retreat of . . . , etc.?
>
> (Lyotard's elision)[32]

More such fragments of romanticism could be gathered. Cultural criticism's pragmatics of "everyday" or "ordinary" "experience," for example, is in part certifiably romantic. So, too, there is romanticism in the dialogics of cultural criticism: the view that culture is no more than a series of conversational improvisations, stories, or *petits récits*. The ordinary and the storied, after all, is the heartland of *Lyrical Ballads*. But perhaps our fragments already limn the whole. To view cultural-critical atomism in historical perspective is to discover precisely what I earlier called an iconic metaphorics, or, to use the romantic rather than modernist concept, the symbol. As Coleridge might phrase it, cultural-critical "detail" is the part through which the whole shines translucently.[33]

[. . .]

In the picture of great detail, in sum, the local threatens to go transcendental: detailism becomes what [Jean] Baudrillard calls "molecular transcendence," the "idealism of the molecule."[34] Cultural critics, we note, recognize this witching moment of local transcendence in their works. In some of their most meditative passages, they pause on the threshold of transcendence aware that Keatsian magic casements of detail are about to open on a foam of perilous seas, in faery lands forlorn. In this moment ("Forlorn! the very word is like a bell / To toll [them] back . . . "), they become critics of cultural criticism. Only so does their *critical* sense survive, in a self-reflexive rather than social gaze. Leah Marcus thus observes reflexively in the epilogue to her fine book on topical or local reading: "The project for localization sets itself resolutely against the general and the universal, but has its own ways of creating generalities, leaping over difference in order to construct an alternative order of 'essences' out of the materials of history"; and again, "Generating a plenitude of particulars is not the same as appealing to a realm of ultimate truths, yet there may be important ways in which the two activities are functionally similar."[35]

[. . .]

[W]e can take a page from Naomi Schor's *Reading in Detail*. The "threshold" of transcendence on which high cultural criticism pauses is the sublime. In a series of chapters tracing the tradition of detailism from Sir Joshua Reynolds through Hegel, Freud, Barthes (and others), Schor comes to the crucial insight that detailism overthrew neoclassical generalization to dominate in the age of romanticism and the realistic novel only because it was made subservient to the aesthetics of sublimity.[36] The spot-of-time detail was a help (and, in Schor's gender argument, helpmeet) to transcendence. It is our own modernist and poststructuralist age, she argues, that at last "desublimates" the "detail ideal."[37] Addressed specifically to the postmodern, my own argument diverges in a direction suggested by Lyotard's "What Is Postmodernism?" Lyotard argues:

> Modern aesthetics is an aesthetic of the sublime, though a nostalgic one. . . . The postmodern would be that which, in the modern . . . searches for new presentations . . . in order to impart a stronger sense of the [sublimely] unpresentable.[38]

Postmodernism, that is, re-presents modernism but is continuous with it and its romantic predecessor: the moment of sublimity is there at the root.

[. . .]

Cultural criticism looks out on perilous seas of detail, but – blocked from any overview by its casement view or local perspectivism – experiences a crisis of incompletion, of significance drowned in insignificance. The details are so many details. Only the reactive phase of the romantic sublime (specifically, Kant's "mathematical sublime") can intervene: insignificance becomes the trope of transcendental meaning. By this trope, the least detail points to total understanding; as we say, history is in the details. Culture, that is, can be understood in its totality only if we believe that our inability to understand totality *is* the total truth.

And with this copular *is* we at last come to the Real. The Real in cultural criticism is indistinguishable from figure. How else could we understand what *is* by what *is not* except by synecdoche, metaphor, or symbol so extreme that it is catachresis? To change our own figure from perilous seas to high sierras: when we face the massif of detail piled up by high cultural criticism, we at last truly climb mountains. We end on some cloud-wrapped Snowdon or nimbus-noumenon where any visible detail – say the way a rift in the clouds sublimes all the underlying voices of the world – marks the threshold of the visionary.[39] The visionary "is" the Real.

[. . .]

To complete this picture of great detail, we need now only rename the "atom" so as to restore the discourse of scientism and immanence to the sphere of culture proper. Other names in high cultural criticism for the atom are "individual" and "community" – the progressively enlarged horizons of local detail.

What is the "subject," that vexed unit of identity in cultural criticism? In one view, the subject is the immanental individual: the "individual" who fends off totalism in de Certeau's *The Practice of Everyday Life* and that [Frank] Lentricchia in his "The Return of William James" calls "the particular, the local, the secret self," the "*isolatos* . . . at the frontier."[40] In its reverence for detail, I suggest, cultural criticism reveals a hidden agenda of Western individualism not clearly distinguished from what Lentricchia recalls to us in his essay on James: an original-pragmatist nostalgia for the colonial or nineteenth-century frontiersman of can-do sufficiency. Such is true also of all the more-or-less Marxist authors in our matrix. It may be said about the materialist side of New Historicism, for example, that detailism is in part a sustained allegory for individualism: when we subscribe to "the concrete, the material, and the particular" or "the particular and particularly constrained," we are really rewriting the biography of what old-line Marxism made taboo: individualities behaving with all the relative autonomy of "real" people in the ideal Western democracy. People, as it were, are personified details.

The highest stakes involved in mapping the atomistic detail over the individual then appear if we enlarge our horizons to "community." Here I refer to what may be the single most promising, if also problematic, front of cultural criticism: its exploration of the communally "parochial," "local," and "regional." These latter terms, which criss-cross our matrix, herald worlds of research.[41] Leah Marcus's and Richard Helgerson's works about localism, for instance; Bourdieu's project of *habitus*; or Geertz's essays on local knowledge focus "localism" as the underexplored zone between the discretely individual and the massively collective.[42] But localism is assuredly also problematic. We can witness such phrases from our matrix as "the experience of particular communities," "individual autonomy . . . communal autonomy," "a reader situated in a particular social space," or "daily life in a particular community." By defining hyperdiscrete communities that behave as if they were particular individuals, these phrases indicate what sometimes seems a too resistless mapping of the person-concept *over* localism. The regional community functions as if it were a solidarity of one, as if, in other words, it were immanent with identity.

[. . .]

[I]n all the cultural criticisms, there resides [to varying degrees] a deeply troubled Us-versus-Them problem that is not resolved by the bare recognition that the interpretive community of Us *does* confront Them. The very denomination or pronomination of an Us (and "I") by which to make statements about Us and Them is the blindness of cultural criticism's insight. It leaves in darkness all that is truly of moment about the Us-versus-Them, self-versus-other, problem: the procedures of emigration/immigration, border inspection/recognition, confrontation/negotiation, and ultimately terror/desire creating an Us *from* Them. What assures "us," after all, that the local, regional, or parochial community we study *is* a community – or collective "unity" – in the first place? Nothing but a direct mapping of the *isolatos* concept over community (in a spirit directly contrary to Lentricchia's intention in "The Return of William James" to challenge imperialist appropriations of world identity). And the possibilities for then multiplying such implicitly imperialist mappings by creating even larger communities such as "nation" or "world" are fearsome.

The detail, we might say, is as small as Napoleon.

[. . .]

Toward a practiced detachment: a prospective conclusion

When high postmodern cultural critics sing the detail, I have argued, they rehearse a rhetoric of immanental reality descended most famously from romanticism. But that is not all there is to the romance of contextualism.

There is also the *rhetoric of commitment* to detail. Commitment is not neutral attachment to "reality" but partisanal attachment to one side or the other in the existential combat, the essential *binarism,* of culture – of culture, that is, conceived as local Us versus Them and, within any Us, as less versus more powerful subcultures.[43] Or more fully, since not all cultural critics express political sympathy with one side or the other: high postmodern cultural criticism is committed to the antitotalistic vision of culture as the "or" or "versus" of struggle itself. For high cultural critics, that is, culture is a tragedy, an eternal agon. Details are the supporting cast. [. . .] Yet however high the pile [of details], such details evidencing the agony of the dominated-versus-the-dominating remain strangely faceless, anonymous. They are never more than throwaway markers, representations, "symbols" of a contest enacted in the *name* of detail but greater than any particular detail. While high cultural critics may commit themselves to an agonist in the contest, in sum, the very facility with which they process interchangeable details argues their greater commitment to "struggle," "resistance," "opposition," "subversion," "transgression" as abstract, perfect forms of contest.

The logic that issues from such commitment to the idea of contest is "practice." Increasingly heard in high cultural criticism across all its denominations, practice is the analytic of culture as digital rather than atomic – as a field of zero versus one, dominated versus dominating. According to this logic, cultural contestants are essentially "bits," and the function of bit-people is to enact through myriad "micro-tactics" and "-techniques" of resistance what [Michel] de Certeau calls "the practice of everyday life" and what Foucault, gazing reciprocally upon repression, calls the practice of "power."

A question for high cultural criticism: What is the common denominator of "practice" as spoken on both sides of the Atlantic and across the political spectrum that makes the details of practice at once so fulsome and faceless? Why does the very word *practice* at times seem so overdetermined – so overstrong, repetitive, and at last ritualistic that it threatens to become compulsory? And in our post- or against-theory ambience, is there such a thing as a "resistance to practice" akin to resistance to theory?

A further question that an extended version of this essay would need to ask: What *about* that moment of remove when the critic views the perfect form of cultural agony as if from across the proscenium? How is it that the detailed and practical battles of culture can finally seem as distantiated as little, regional wars glimpsed on the television screen or in a computer war game? If postmodern culture is agonic, in short, it is also ironic and aesthetic: commitment to a staged scene of resistance lasts until the show is over and the critic touches the control to bring up the next riveting *petit récit* on the cable. The rhetoric of commitment ends in the *rhetoric of detachment.* And the logic that this latter, ironic rhetoric makes possible is dialogism: the view that every set of cultural practices is finally just the outcome of a local "vocabulary," "perspective," or "simulation" whose conversational improvisations, little stories, "spatial stories," styles, and so on make culture – from the view of the ironist rather than those trapped in the simulation – all a detachable facade.[44] High cultural criticism, we may say vulgarly, is a culture-*spiel* as determinedly depthless in its play with representational surfaces, facades, screens, and media of all sorts as a vinyl LP hand spun by a rap artist, that master of *culture-spiel* able to fragment long-play metanarrative into *petits récits.*

Cybernetic, televisionary, rhapsodic: such models of mediated and detached cultural experience could be multiplied. The array of surfaces that is the cultural matrix grows thick all about us, and it comforts more than disturbs. Once we insulated ourselves from reality in universals and totalisms. Now we wrap ourselves in detailed layers of context as thick and multiform as cotton [. . .]. If I had to put my criticism of high postmodern cultural criticism in brief, it would come to this: "context" is not the same as "culture." Context throws over the surface of culture an articulated grid, a way of speaking and thinking culture, that allows us to model the scenes of human experience with more felt significance – more reality, more practicality, more aesthetic impact – than appears anywhere but on the postmodern version of romantic "nature": a screen.

Notes

1 Naomi Schor, *Reading in Detail: Aesthetics and the Feminine* (New York, 1987), 3.
2 Clifford Geertz, *Local Knowledge: Further Essays in Interpretive Anthropology* (New York, 1983), 232.
3 Richard Rorty, *Consequences of Pragmatism: Essays, 1972–1980* (Minneapolis, 1982), 173.
4 Jerome J. McGann, *Social Values and Poetic Acts: The Historical Judgment of Literary Work* (Cambridge, Mass., 1988), 7, 122, 124. McGann quotes the phrase from Milman Parry's *The Making of Homeric Verse: The Collected Papers of Milman Parry*, ed. Adam Parry (Oxford, 1971), 411. [. . .]
5 For Geertz on functionalist sociology, see, for example, *Interpretation of Cultures*[*: Selected Essays*, (New York, 1973)], 206, 448. For the effort of the New Historicism to distance itself from formalism (in some regards counterfactually), see, for example, Jean E. Howard, "The New Historicism in Renaissance Studies," *English Literary Renaissance* 16 (1986): 14–15. For the complex reaction of the New Cultural History against *Annales* historiography (particularly its sociological tendencies), see François Furet, "Beyond the *Annales*," *Journal of Modern History* 55 (1983): 389–410; Lynn Hunt, "French History in the Last Twenty Years: The Rise and Fall of the *Annales* Paradigm," *Journal of Contemporary History* 21 (1986), esp. 213ff.; and "Introduction: History, Culture, and Text," in *The New Cultural History*, ed. Hunt (Berkeley, 1989), 6–7; and [Roger] Chartier, *Cultural History* [*: Between Practices and Representations*, trans. Lydia G. Cochrane (Ithaca, N.Y., 1988)], 19–52. ("Reaction" against the *Annales* movement could also be called revisionism, since Chartier and others descend with variation from the "mentalities" side of *Annales* method.)
6 On "elsewhereness," see [Alan] Liu, *Wordsworth* [*: The Sense of History* (Stanford, Calif., 1989)], 5, 467, 497, and passim.
7 [Richard Rorty, *Contingency, Irony, and Solidarity* (Cambridge, 1989).]
8 Louis O. Mink, "Change and Causality in the History of Ideas," *Eighteenth-Century Studies* 2 (1968): 7–25.
9 [Marjorie Levinson, *Wordsworth's Great Period Poems: Four Essays* (Cambridge, 1986), 12.]
10 Rorty, *Contingency, Irony, and Solidarity*, 23–7. Cf. Roland Barthes on "The Blazon," in *S/Z*, trans. Richard Miller (New York, 1974), 113–14.
11 [Robert Darnton, *The Great Cat Massacre and Other Episodes in French Cultural History* (New York, 1985), 20. Geertz, *Interpretation of Cultures*, 427, n. 13. Jean-Francois Lyotard, *The Differend: Phrases in Dispute*, trans. Georges Van Den Abbeele (Minneapolis, 1988), 67.] For economy, I have used lists of categories or concepts as my examples. The point would also be true if Darnton and Geertz (as they do elsewhere) were to itemize not categories but factual particulars ordered by number, dimension, location, or chronology. For a splendid thematization (but also enactment) of the problem of matrix making and listing, see Darnton's chapter "A Police Inspector Sorts His Files" in his *Great Cat Massacre*.
12 [Louis] Althusser, *Lenin and Philosophy* [*and Other Essays*, trans. Ben Brewster (London, 1971)], 138.
13 Cf. Schor on synecdoche and detail, *Reading in Detail*, 28–9.

14 Cf. Schor on the relation between the detail and the microcosmic fragment (ibid., 28); and
Theodor Adorno on "fragmented transcendence" (*Aesthetic Theory*, ed. Gretel Adorno and
Rolf Tiedemann, trans. C. Lenhardt [London, 1984], 184). [. . .]
15 [McGann, *Social Values and Poetic Acts*, 127. Liu, *Wordsworth*, 47.]
16 [Alan] Liu, "[The] Power of Formalism [: The New Historicism," *English Literary History*
56 (1989):] 764, n. 35. See also Alan Liu, "Wordsworth and Subversion, 1793–1804," *Yale
Journal of Criticism* 2, no. 2 (Spring 1989): 55–100.
17 [Stephen Greenblatt, *Shakespearean Negotiations: The Circulation of Social Energy in Renaissance
England* (Berkeley, 1988). Geoffrey H. Hartman, *Wordsworth's Poetry, 1787–1814* (New
Haven, 1975).] [. . .]
18 McGann, *Social Values and Poetic Acts*, 207.
19 Steven Knapp and Walter Benn Michaels, "Against Theory," in W.J.T. Mitchell, ed., *Against
Theory: Literary Studies and the New Pragmatism* (Chicago, 1985). Knapp and Michaels's essay,
of course, confines itself to literary theory. But I include it in my discussion of cultural criticism both as a *cause célèbre* of New Pragmatism and as a lead-in to Rorty's cultural criticism.
[. . .]
20 Friedrich Waismann, *The Principles of Linguistic Philosophy*, ed. R. Harré (New York, 1965),
326; John R. Searle, *Intentionality: An Essay in the Philosophy of Mind* (Cambridge, 1983),
62; J.L. Austin, *Philosophical Papers* (Oxford, 1961), 186; Rudolf Carnap, "The Elimination
of Metaphysics Through Logical Analysis of Language," trans. Arthur Pap, in *Logical
Positivism*, ed. A.J. Ayer (New York, 1959), 67; Carnap, "Psychology in Physical Language,"
trans. George Schick, in *Logical Positivism*, 179. [. . .]
21 Knapp and Michaels, "Against Theory," 15. The full example runs to p. 17.
22 A discussion of the Preface to *Lyrical Ballads* in the light of twentieth-century British philosophy would be instructive. Wordsworth's "philosophy of language," if it may be so called,
blends the compulsions of analytical and ordinary-language philosophies. Thus rural discourse is at once a "more permanent, and a far more philosophical language" and "a selection of language really used by men"; *The Prose Works of William Wordsworth*, eds W.J.B. Owen
and Jane Worthington Smyser, 3 vols (Oxford, 1974), 1: 125, 123.
23 [William] Wordsworth, [*"The Prelude," 1799, 1805, 1850: Authoritative Texts, Context and
Reception, Recent Critical Essays*, ed. Jonathan Wordsworth, M.H. Abrams, and Stephen Gill,
Norton Critical Edition (New York, 1979), 1805 version], 5. 389–413.
24 In this regard, Knapp and Michaels's footnote is misleading: "Wordsworth's lyric has been
a standard example in theoretical arguments since its adoption by Hirsch; see *Validity in
Interpretation*, pp. 227–30 and 238–40" ("Against Theory," 15n.). As specified in the pages
cited here, Hirsch was himself improvising upon earlier theorizers of the Lucy poem,
including Cleanth Brooks [. . .]. And once we reach back to the New Criticism, we must
attend to the strongly overdetermined presence in modernist aesthetics of romanticism. It
is no accident, for example, that the first poems mentioned in Brooks's *Well Wrought Urn*
are two Wordsworth sonnets, that [John Crowe] Ransom spent so much time in his chapter
"Wanted: An Ontological Critic" [*The New Criticism* (Norfolk, Conn., 1941)] deriding the
romantics, and, of course, that such high old modernists as T.E. Hulme and T.S. Eliot were
so archly postromantic. Knapp and Michaels's claim that they are following a "standard"
example does not register the overdetermination that made the example standard in the
first place (nor, it must be said, the sheer bizarreness of their own improvisation on the
example).
[. . .]
25 Knapp and Michaels, "Against Theory," 12. [. . .]
26 For "simplicity" in the Preface, see Wordsworth, *Prose Works*, 1: 125. [. . .]
27 Cf. [Frank] Lentricchia on Rorty and romanticism, *Criticism and Social Change* [(Chicago,
1983)], 17–19.
28 [Richard] Rorty, *Philosophy and the Mirror of Nature* [(Princeton, N.J., 1979)], 105, 190;
Consequences of Pragmatism, 67, 149; *Contingency, Irony, and Solidarity*, 97, 109.
29 A variant example here would be Baudrillard, whose controversial "silent majority" thesis
has been called a "populist neo-romanticism" by Michael Ryan, "Postmodern Politics,"
Theory, Culture, and Society 5 (1988): 566. To read Baudrillard and Lyotard together in the
context of romanticism may well require thinking the relationship between the former's
"silent majority" and the latter's "silent" "feeling of the different" [. . .].

30 For the connection between Lyotard's semiotic pragmatics and the tradition launched by Peirce and Morris, see [*The*] *Postmodern Condition* [*: A Report on Knowledge*, trans. Geoff Bennington and Brian Massumi (Minneapolis, 1984)], 9, 87, n. 28.

31 Lest there be any unclarity, I am here ventriloquizing Lyotard, who is himself ventriloquizing an investigator skeptical of the facticity of the gas chambers. On Auschwitz and the Final Solution as verification problem, see *Differend*, 3–4, 87–106, and passim.

32 Ibid., 135.

33 We might apply here Paul de Man's comment in "The Rhetoric of Temporality": "The world is then no longer seen as a configuration of entities that designate a plurality of distinct and isolated meanings, but as a configuration of symbols ultimately leading to a total, single, and universal meaning. This appeal to the infinity of a totality constitutes the main attraction of the symbol as opposed to allegory"; in *Blindness and Insight: Essays in the Rhetoric of Contemporary Criticism*, 2nd ed., revised (Minneapolis, 1983), 188. [. . .]

34 [Jean] Baudrillard, ["The Structural Law of Value and the Order of Simulacra" (excerpts from *L'Échange symbolique et la mort*, 1976), trans. Charles Levin, in *The Structural Allegory: Reconstructive Encounters with the New French Thought*, ed. John Fekete (Minneapolis, 1984), 66.]. Cf. Adorno on "fragmented transcendence," *Aesthetic Theory*, 184–5.

35 [Leah S.] Marcus, *Puzzling Shakespeare* [*: Local Reading and Its Discontents* (Berkeley, 1988)], 213, 218.

36 Schor, *Reading in Detail*, 5, 17–41, 141–7. "The detail," Schor writes, "was to become, as Blake had predicted it would, the very 'Foundation of the Sublime'" (22).

37 [. . .] I take the apt phrase *detail ideal* slightly out of context from Schor's chapter on Freudian detail; ibid., 70.

38 Lyotard, *Postmodern Condition*, 81.

39 Wordsworth, 1805 *Prelude*, 13. 52–65.

40 [Michel] De Certeau, e.g., [*The*] *Practice* [*of Everyday Life*, trans. Steven Rendall (Berkeley, 1984)], xxiii–xxiv; [Frank] Lentricchia, "[The] Return of William James," [in *The Current in Criticism: Essays on the Present and Future of Literary Theory*, ed. Clayton Koelb and Virgil Lokke (West Lafayette, Ind., 1987)] 191, 193. [. . .]

41 Indeed, it may be predicted that the effort to redefine "locality" or "region" will continue to offer cultural criticism room for innovation – both empirical and theoretical – long after its neo-individualist and often virtually biographical experiments have passed (I refer to the obsessional studies in the New Historicism, New Pragmatism, New Marxism, or French pragmatism of "More," "Tyndale," "Elizabeth," "Wordsworth," "Marx," "Kant," and so forth).

42 [Marcus, *Puzzling Shakespeare*. Richard Helgerson, "The Land Speaks: Cartography, Chorography, and Subversion in Renaissance England," *Representations* 16 (Fall 1986). Pierre Bourdieu, *Outline of a Theory of Practice*, trans. Richard Nice (London, 1977). Geertz, *Local Knowledge*.]

43 For the term "commitment," cf. Adorno on "artistic commitment," *Aesthetic Theory*, 349–52.

44 A full consideration of this topic would need to take up an especially thorny aspect of the pragmatist problem of "belief": whether it is possible to view or imagine other people's beliefs *qua* beliefs. [. . .]

6   Historicism, deconstruction, and Wordsworth

Frances Ferguson

I shall begin by isolating a largely indifferent instance, Wordsworth's, of a very general late eighteenth- and nineteenth-century phenomenon, the walking tour. Wordsworth, like many others in the latter part of the eighteenth century, occasionally toured the country – and did so on foot, either by accident or by design. In 1793, as Paul Sheats recounts it:

> Wordsworth and Calvert left the Isle of Wight in August, bound for the west of England. An accident to their carriage abruptly ended the trip; Calvert rode off on the only horse, and Wordsworth was left alone in the midst of Salisbury Plain. For the next three weeks he was once again a pedestrian traveler, as he made his way northward toward Wales along the valley of the Wye, where he viewed Tintern Abbey, met the little girl of *We Are Seven*, and walked for several days with the wild rover who became Peter Bell.[1]

I want to use this example to raise questions about sequence and personification as they have figured in recent Romantic criticism. For if the simple iterative gesture of putting one foot in front of another represents sequence for the walking tour, the questions that have loomed largest for the criticism are how – and whether – such a sequence can have faces attached to it.

It is easy enough to see that Wordsworth's walking tour, with its commitment to the accidental, or at least something like planned accident, has its affinities with the picturesque discovery of the motif in landscape. In painting and drawing, the notion of motif, through a geometrical reading of natural forms and their interrelationships, supplanted the notion of motive or motivation as an individual and psychological phenomenon. But if a natural motif instructed "the picturesque eye" on where to stand, in Wordsworth's pedestrian tours the motif that provides a stance for the poet is the appearance of another person, someone whose words operate as the opening strokes of a linguistic geometry. Wordsworth's frequent use of conversations and dialogues in the poems associated with his pedestrian tours (poems such as "We Are Seven") thus might appear less as the excessively realistic gesture that Coleridge chided him for and more as a way of seeking a linguistic motif (understood not as a theme but as a formal perspective).

There are two problems with this suggestion, however. First, the treatment of language as assimilable to formal pattern raises different issues from those that emerge when natural objects are treated as assimilable to formal pattern; if found objects can become formal only in being supplied intentionality, "finding" human speech produces competitive intentionality. Second, one does not know how to determine the linguistic equivalent of pictorial perspective; grammatical structure, particularly its rendering of personhood as number (first, second, third, singular and plural), perhaps represents the closest approximation to perspective. Yet even a grammatical account of number provides only the sketchiest version of linguistic perspective, a positioning by virtue of having eliminated two or three other possibilities.

These problems – and their combined effect – have made it seem both obligatory and impossible to represent persons in literary works. Obligatory because of the moral discomfort aroused by taking literary works and their pretexts for granted, impossible because of the imperfect transmissibility of literary works and language. While one school of recent Romantic criticism tends to suggest that representations of other people constitute a means of suppressing them, the other claims that such representations essentially do not – and cannot – intersect with persons and could not suppress them even if they tried.

This problem of the presence – or absence – of other people seems to me the central one in Jerome J. McGann's account *The Romantic Ideology*, although he frequently identifies the issues rather differently – in terms of the Romantic desire for transcendence, the view that knowledge is an abstract rather than a social pursuit,[2] and the movement toward internalization which has been seen as characteristically Romantic. In his diagnosis, the "polemic of Romantic poetry . . . is that it will not be polemical; its doctrine, that it is not doctrinal; and its ideology, that it transcends ideology" (70). And although he repeatedly urges a critical criticism upon his readers, critique sounds less like a panacea when we realize that we can never know when we are standing apart from ideology and when we are merely instantiating it. The commitment to returning "poetry to a human form" (160) thus proceeds in terms of the assertion that "no adequate [literary] criticism can occur which does not force itself to take . . . into account" the reality that it is today "practiced under the aegis of very particular sorts of Ideological State Apparatuses" and the conclusion that "criticism must analyze, self-critically, the effect which those apparatuses have in shaping, and distorting, our critical activities" (159). On the one hand, ideology prevents the self from knowing itself: "for the cooptive powers of a vigorous culture like our own are very great" (2). On the other hand, the self that has been deluded is enjoined to move from its position of abject powerlessness to one of absolute power in being able to isolate and eject the alien power of ideology. The major problem is that the self can never know when it's done with this project of casting out ideology, and a subsidiary difficulty is that it is hard to see how the process of critique will not itself become a version of the very self-involvement it was designed to repudiate.

Thus, McGann sees the limits of Wordsworth's ideology becoming apparent in a poem like the Immortality Ode, of which he observes that "between 1793 and 1798 Wordsworth lost the world merely to gain his own immortal soul" (88), but he does not suggest that his own opposition between self and ideology might recapitulate the opposition between self and world that he has been describing. For in McGann's schema the only way to gain one's soul or oneself is to separate from one's world and its ideology. Critique is, then, consciousness imagined as an Archimedean lever; where ideology was, there ego shall be.

Far from eschewing a supposedly Romantic preoccupation with the self, thus, McGann recasts it in salvific terms. The chief difference between his version of self-consciousness and the Romantic one that he would repudiate is that he imagines a self-conscious self that achieves its transcendence through particularity. His "general argument," as he identifies it in his introduction to *The Romantic Ideology*, is that "artistic products, whatever they may be formally, are materially and existentially social, concrete, and unique." [. . .] McGann thus seems to encourage an historical criticism that would involve a recovery of the specificity of individual authors and their labor. And he explicitly claims that the process of categorizing literary products as "works" rather than "texts" is one aspect of the project of returning "poetry to a human form" and seeing "that what we read and study are poetic *works* produced and reproduced by numbers of specific men and women" (160).

Yet the particularity of individual poems emerges in a very peculiar way in an essay like "Keats and the Historical Method in Literary Criticism." [. . .] As McGann's readings of various Keats poems show, he would substitute an account of textual production for an account of texts. The social statements that a poem makes must continually be teased out by establishing contexts in terms of reference (the kind of enterprise that biographical criticism sets itself) and in terms of reception (the kind of approach that publication history may sketch out). Moreover, McGann's critic should identify his own context: "One of the principal functions of the socio-historical critic is to heighten the levels of social self-consciousness with which every critic carries out the act of literary criticism."[3] That is, the socio-historical critic has three sets of contexts to provide: that in which the poem originated, that into which the poem was received, and that in which the critic situates him- or herself.

On the face of it, this project sounds fine, in that it seems aimed at a literary version of truth in advertising. But only one of these contexts – that of a poem's reception very narrowly construed as the most basic facts of its publication history – can be delimited enough for one to say much of anything about it. And thus the multiplication of particulars that these very contexts provide does not so much enable us to recognize distance and difference from ourselves as insist upon the preeminence of difference as opposed to similarity. That is, McGann offers his method as an effort to avoid collapsing our contemporary views into those of Romantic poets in a disingenuous self-projection that hides behind the text, but this attempt to acknowledge differences – between then and now, authors and readers, and so on – challenges the very notion that any claim might be seen to apply to more than one case.

McGann's target, then, is any form of abstraction in which the terms of similarity (homogeneity) are allowed to obscure the differences among the individual works that have been grouped together. Thus, while generalizations about Romanticism rely on a process of abstraction from a collection of individual literary works, McGann would demonstrate the inadequacy of the generalizations to any individual case. On one level, he is of course right. Periodization and the counting that produces it do not personalize. The kind of operation that enables one to see things as part of a sequence or series does not preserve the distinct individuality of each individual or unit in the series. When one counts students, for example, one recognizes a basic similarity – their being students – that enables one to put them together for the purpose of making the count. But only by considerably exaggerating the claim being made by such a count can one suggest that such an operation involves taking the various terms to be identical – or even similar – in all respects. [. . .] McGann, in repudiating the claims that appear to be made when one generalizes about the Romantics on the basis of a Wordsworthian model, does not in fact argue so much against that particular model as he does against the notion of any definition by intension, because he sees the fact of putting the various texts together as an illegitimate assertion of their identity. Thus, while he is most comfortable when defending Austen and Byron as distinct from Wordsworth, his argument becomes shakiest when he moves from Byron or Austen to the abstract "human face" of poetry. What McGann sees as the secondary "unmasking" of primary "illusions"[4] has plausibility then in so far as the "unmasking" constitutes the critic's prerogative not to understand something in the terms that he or she takes the poet or novelist to have provided. The "unmasking" does not, however, constitute a counterargument but rather the attempt to repudiate the very notion of abstraction or generalization, which for McGann is coterminous with formalism.

What he takes as formalism's hegemonic tendencies to elide differences thus yields a positive program of dispersion. Therefore, he criticizes not only literary critics who conflate themselves with the writers who produced the texts they read, but also editors who emphasize a definitive version of a text at the expense of other versions. [. . .] McGann essentially argues for removing an element from the counting series every time one can see *any* heterogeneous feature, whether in terms of the words on the page or the audience that read those words. [. . .] Literature, that is, should be recognized as personalized, in McGann's account, so that it can be seen as different whenever the particular combination of writer, text, and reader changes. Personification is, on this account, not so much a trope deployed by poets in poems; it is the very function of literature and criticism – to make individuals of us all.

In adopting this version of personification, in which poems are, because of their didactic function, responsible for making people (and enabling people to make themselves the right way), McGann thus revives a time-honored account of the relationship between poetry and society. Poetry is, in this account, an antidote to the values of society, and McGann's only real variation on this essentially Arnoldian position is to claim that criticism can (or must) now assume the role that poetry used to achieve on its own. Now that it has been shown that poetry may itself represent (or be coopted into) the dominant values of the society, the critic must become a critical critic, identifying the values of poetry and choosing among them.

[. . .]

A multiplicity of contexts, poems, and readers ends up dissolving the question of how the words of a poem can come to seem like an expression of anyone's intention, because the very question of interpretation has been suspended by the commitment to taking a stand, to having the critic see the poem as an occasion for him or her to personify virtue. Thus, McGann rehearses a portion of Marjorie Levinson's argument about "Tintern Abbey" – that Wordsworth sets it up to be a poem that substitutes a landscape with social and political implications for an exclusively mental landscape. While "the ruined abbey had been in the 1790s a favorite haunt of transients and displaced persons," Wordsworth "observes the tranquil orderliness of the nearby 'pastoral farms' and draws these views into a relation with the 'vagrant dwellers in the houseless woods' of the abbey."[5]

What McGann and Levinson take to be the Romantic project of internalization becomes suspect in this schema, because Romantic internalization is equated with privacy, and specifically with a commitment to privatization which is willing to impose itself no matter what the consequences for other people. As soon as the homeless become the palimpsest on which the individual meditation is superimposed, the privacy of Romantic thought becomes clear – and clearly corrupt; the personal meditation comes to look like a willful refusal to see a world outside of oneself, an engagement of alternately weary and triumphant self-scrutiny when there are people with real problems. On this account, the poet's apparent isolation – not just from Dorothy but also from the homeless vagrants at Tintern Abbey – itself implicates poetry in a lethal attack on other people. The presence or absence of the representation of persons in a poem, that is, becomes the personal responsibility of the poet who did not put them in, or who edited them out.

[. . .]

Against this effort to reclaim literature for the human, let us set Paul de Man's account, in his essay on Rousseau's *Confessions*, "Excuses," of the way persons enter literary texts.[6] Although McGann almost never mentions de Man directly, his dark comments about critics who have chosen to enter the prison house of language suggest that de Man ought to be one of his targets, whether he is, in fact, or not. The account of linguistic agency in "Excuses" gives particular scandal to McGann's position in both thematic and argumentative terms. There de Man analyzes Rousseau's description in the *Confessions* of his having committed an act of theft and then blamed it on someone else, Marion, a servant girl who worked in the household with Rousseau and of whom he was enamored. De Man's entire account rests on the argument that there is a difference between Rousseau's intentions toward Marion and the formal expression of those intentions which gets interpreted in such a way as to cause Marion harm. Thus, although de Man traces possible connective links between Rousseau's thoughts and his representation of them to those who have caught him with the ribbon, he focuses particularly on the moment at which Rousseau abandons – or attenuates – his causal explanations. That is, de Man patiently traces the metaphorical structures in which Rousseau's desire to possess Marion becomes substitutable for his possession of the ribbon and in which Marion becomes substitutable for Jean-Jacques in the reciprocal relationship that Rousseau equates with "the very condition of love" (283). He chiefly engages, however, Rousseau's explanation that his accusation was not intentional but rather accidental. Thus he points to "the use of vocabulary of contingency ('le premier object qui s'offrit') within an argument of causality" that allows "for a complete disjunction between Rousseau's desires and interests and the selection of this particular name":

> Marion just happened to be the first thing that came to mind; any other name, any other word, any other sound or noise could have done just as well and Marion's entry into the discourse is a mere effect of chance.

(288)

The chief point here is that the existence of representations of persons is not coextensive with the empirical existence and actions of those persons – either those (such as Rousseau) who might appear to commit those actions or those (such as Marion) who might appear to be their objects. The entire drama rests on the difference between, on the one hand, taking names and persons as substitutable for one another and, on the other, recognizing names and persons as nonequivalent. Rousseau can thus say the name "Marion" in a way that implicates the actual person Marion in a criminal act that she did not commit and that he knows she did not commit. He can do so, moreover, without having meant it. Having a name thus far makes one hostage to the accidents of other people's uses of the name. But de

Man describes two victims here. [. . .] The mechanical operation of the form [. . .] dispatches two characters at once: Marion, whose control of her own fate has been definitively eliminated by the false personification of the reception of Rousseau's act of naming, and Rousseau, whose control of his own story has degenerated into a story of the implacable operation of reception to empty itself of original intention.

On de Man's account, Rousseau's personal feelings about an actual person begin to lose their relevance as soon as the text begins to operate upon the "actual event." And any interpretative gesture toward empathy or motivational conjectures may produce the "human face" that McGann calls for, but it does so only by insisting upon an abject projection of formal notions of persons upon the pure operation of matter. De Man's discussion thus far coincides with Kant's aesthetics in imagining form as continually enabling a movement in excess of experience precisely because of its ability to proceed beyond what can be empirically perceived. Yet, like Kant's account of the natural sublime, and unlike his account of the beautiful with its artificial objects, de Man's reading converts writing into a version of accident: as the formal reveals itself as material it becomes as unavailable for human purposes as nature. Thus, this procedure does not merely avoid anthropomorphizing nature. It also naturalizes the human, not by making it seem more normal but rather by making it seem unhuman. [. . .] Because accident is always equally unintelligible to all persons, intelligible, that is, only when it happens to say "nothing" and therefore to coincide with a materiality that is itself not something but nothing, language might well be defined as prelinguistic rather than linguistic.

This is to say that de Man analyzes ambiguity, the ability of language to be taken in more than one way, in order to read a multiplicity of meanings as annihilating the possibility of reconciling those meanings with one another. In doing so he is thus essentially challenging the basic assumptions implicit in the notion of ambiguity, which, along with allegory and irony, has been a basis for Romantic and post-Romantic claims about literariness itself. Whereas these terms once figured in Romantic and phenomenological arguments about the ambivalence of material form (and thus about the insufficiency of the material in accounts of meaning), de Man's point here (in what I take to be a repudiation of his well-known essay "The Rhetoric of Temporality" with its consideration of allegory and irony) is that seeing the stakes of naming is recognizing that neither allegory nor irony is genuinely possible. For ambiguity, like allegory, like irony, emphasizes the changes that can be rung on material equivalence. They depend, that is, on emphasizing the perception of identity even as it is transformed, made to look like difference. By contrast, the nominalism of de Man's position on naming is that not merely universals but names should exist genuinely in name alone – without the persistence that would make identity (even the identity imputed by auditors) a relevant issue. Once this position is really taken seriously, moreover, it becomes clear that referentiality (or nonreferentiality) is only the beginning of the problem of linguistic nominalism. Every word becomes a name.

[. . .]

Whereas ambiguity, allegory, and irony revolve around the ability to mean different things with the same words, accounts of them have typically centered on reference, the names of things. De Man, however, emphasizes the nameness of names, in which the generalization of names lies not in their referring to things but in their being names that are incidentally rather than inherently repeated. The precise nature of this shift may become apparent if we compare de Man's account of the diverse meanings attached to the word "Marion" with a more traditional example of two diverse and even opposed names, "morning star" and "evening star," applying to the same thing. This case relies on having a referent as the focal point of a triadic relationship. While de Man sets up a similarly triadic relationship, he inserts the name (or word or "noise") "Marion" as the focal point. With such a shift, he is able to argue that there is a fundamental asymmetry in the relationship between language and things. That there always seem to be words that correspond to things does not apply in reverse; there are not always things that correspond to words. "Marion," seen from the standpoint of the persons interrogating Rousseau, makes sense in a referential system, but "Marion," from the standpoint of the contingent and merely contiguous series that de Man traces in Rousseau's narrative, makes sense as "nothing." Marion and "nothing" are, for de Man, equivalent in being terms that stand in equidistant relationships to "Marion" (just as "morning star" and "evening star" can be said to stand in equidistant relationships to the same physical body). While the convergence of two names on one object creates the paradoxical situation in which two such palpably different terms as "morning star" and "evening star" refer to the same thing while meaning different things, the convergence of one human referent and "nothing" on the name "Marion" yields a greater contradiction. For while the relative stability of the referent in the "morning star"–"evening star" example creates the possibility of continually arriving at "morning star" from "evening star" by way of the referent, de Man describes a case in which the fact of competing versions of the "same thing" is seen to bracket that thing as different from the various equidistant terms that would refer to it. That is, it functions in terms of pure positionality, having counted only to bring the other terms into proximity with one another. Thus, the account of the referential or cognitive – the connection between "Marion" and Marion – is juxtaposed with the performative – the connection between "Marion" and "nothing" which is laid out by the narrative. And the process of juxtaposing these two different meanings for "Marion" makes them look as though they resemble one another more than either of them resembles "Marion." Thus, the competing claims of cognitive and performative, epistemological and narrative, Marion and "nothing" are forced into a positional equivalence. The effort at equivalence (Marion = "nothing") quickly reveals itself as a *contradiction* (Marion ≠ "nothing") because de Man, having isolated the term that provided a rationale for each of the two divergent series, explicitly sees that term as self-dividing rather than a hinge between two different accounts.

The "morning star"–"evening star" case could be represented in numerical terms – as if you were to say that the number 7 could be represented as 10 if you were counting in a base of 7 and as 7 if counting in a base of 10. The apparent homology between the number 7 and its representation as 7 in a base of 10 counts neither as an absolute justification of the validity of this particular representation nor as a statement of the invalidity of other possible representations. Rather, it provides a context that enables the divergent procedures of representation to converge. It is, in other words, formal in imagining reference as a focal point for different explanatory systems. And it is precisely such a formal account of reference as a focal point that de Man is attacking. For in his account, the various ways of rendering "Marion" are put into a positional equivalence that relies upon the sense of identity but involves only the appearance of identity: that one could plausibly mean to be uttering a mere noise and that one could plausibly be understood to have named a thief by saying "Marion" does not mean (as it might in an extrapolation of formal idealism) that name is the linguistic equivalent of the *Ding an sich*, the unexperienced projection of the various possible versions of the experiential object. It means, instead, that name is the material unit of the illusion of succession.

The construction that de Man's deconstructive materialism would confute insists, that is, upon name specifically as name functions as an alternative to any notion of narrative sequence that emerges in an account of numerical series. While it is certainly the case that one can treat numbers as if they were names (according to the principle identifying randomness with non-heritability on which the access numbers for automatic teller machines are based), the question is whether the notion of sequence has really been defeated when one treats numbers as names. Whether, in other words, one can make all language be as conveniently performative as de Man would like. De Man, and Andrzej Warminski in exposition of him,[7] must resort to the claim that "zero . . . is heterogeneous to the number system" to make the operation of zero in numerical series look as though it is the (random) name upon which number depends. Yet this account of zero, which de Man and Warminski take from Pascal, treats number exclusively in terms of reference (toward things that might be counted) rather than in terms of system.[8] Now one can state with some confidence that the status of zero changed in 1888, when J.W.R. Dedekind declared, in the first of five axioms for the natural numbers, that "0 is a natural number."[9] When number was seen to involve the ability to produce another number by adding one to the previous number, zero could, like one, be recognized as a number. [. . .] I introduce [this] because the assumption that zero could have been – and was – incorporated into the number system indicates more clearly than any other specific example what is at stake in my doubts about de Man's account of materiality in general and zero in particular.

[. . .]

[Ferguson here discusses de Man's essay "Pascal's Allegory of Persuasion," in which de Man concludes that the number system emphasizes heterogeneity, materiality, and infinity.]

If McGann would present us with literary works that continually accommodate human form and purpose, de Man makes the literary the arena of the nonhuman, in that literature is asked to make only "natural" statements, that is, statements (in an intensification of I.A. Richards's notion of pseudostatements) in which linguistic matter is given a face by its utterer, but only to be given additional faces by its reception. But the drive to discount the merely personal, or the psychological motivation, oddly reinstates the personal as the occasion of an otherwise arbitrary connection. In de Man's account of Rousseau, the operation of naming began with a kind of panic reaction. To be confronted with other people's demand that you explain yourself is to have a panic reaction that causes you to blurt something, anything, out. And the substitution of the accident of apparently formed matter for the accident of other people's presence and pressure is therefore less than an out-and-out renunciation of knowledge. For it can claim to escape mistakenness only by insisting that there is nothing to be shared.

In this account (and in a line of argument that de Man develops more fully in "Pascal's Allegory of Persuasion"), number appears superior to name because the connection between numbers and the persons they correlate with can continually be reordered, reshuffled, and redirected. But de Man here insists upon a peculiarly naturalized version of number, in that he wants it continually to be detached from any of the operations performed with number and the inevitable directionality that those operations provide. For him to emphasize the claims of materiality and the progress of number toward name (the move he achieves with the zero and the one) is for him to delineate the aesthetic as the impossibility of aesthetic intersubjectivity by having made materiality look as though it were always, everywhere and equally, at odds with formality. Having created the illusion that language is essentially material and uninheritable because one can arrive at a word through different routes, de Man recuperates identity on the level of form that is no less form for its being presented as if it were matter. For in his reading of Rousseau's *Confessions* and in that of Kant's Third Critique ("Phenomenality and Materiality in Kant"), linguistic structures imitate the world they cannot represent only in aping their form, that is, in becoming just as material (and, thus, in his view as unintelligible) as the things they seem to (or seem to want to) represent.[10]

From McGann's standpoint, the multiplication of one's categories should continue infinitely so that one can register the variety of humans and their literary products; from de Man's, a nonphenomenal materiality represents the only possibility of recognizing that sequence and matter will never coincide. For McGann, there should be a name for everything; for de Man, names are names by virtue of looking simultaneously singular and infinite. And in the context of these positions, I should like to look at Wordsworth's treatment of counting in "We Are Seven," one of the poems that is connected with his walking tour of 1793.[11] The most frequently mocked poem by the most frequently parodied writer in English, "We Are Seven" notoriously depicts a standoff between a young girl and a man who is traveling through her village. She claims that she, together with her six siblings, makes up a family of seven children; he, for his part, tries to explain to her that one does not customarily count the dead. In other words, this poem takes up the question of personification, of the way persons appear in language, by staging a direct debate on the issue.

In the preface to *Lyrical Ballads*, Wordsworth distances himself from the personification of abstract ideas (on the grounds that "such personifications" do not "make any regular or natural part of" "the very language of men"), and he goes on to assert that he wishes to keep his reader "in the company of flesh and blood."[12] But, of course, the interest of 'We Are Seven' lies in the girl's being able by counting to personify persons – which in this case represent neither abstract ideas nor flesh and blood. Her personifications take their plausibility and their strangeness from the mere fact that they attempt to cancel out the difference between past existence and present existence.

Had the girl said, "We were seven," or some version of "my parents had seven children," her statement would have been unexceptionable, and her chance interlocutor would never have had anything to quiz her about. Seeing how easily their disagreement could have been avoided, one can see that perhaps the most curious aspect of poem is not how much the girl and the man disagree on but instead how much they agree on. From his question, "'Sisters and brothers, little maid, / How many may you be?'" he establishes an equivocation about the relation between one person and many persons. The possibility for the word "you" to apply in the singular or the plural continues to operate unchecked and strangely undisambiguated, because his words conflate possession with existence, *having* sisters and brothers with *being* sisters and brothers.[13] Thus, the girl's apparent surprise in registering his question – "'How many? seven in all,' she said / And wondering looked at me" – occurs almost as a question about the traveler's powers of perception. "How many are you?" receives the reply "We are seven" as if it were just a version of "I am seven." Her wonderment appears to revolve around the fact that her being seven in being one is to her as readily apparent as the fact that she has thick curly hair.

This equation between "we are seven" and "I am seven" becomes clearer by stages, as the child's ability to count her siblings first merely involves her ability to place them despite their physical absence from this place ("'And two of us at Conway dwell, / And two are gone to sea'"). In this particular progression, death simply figures a distance greater than that from her to Conway, or from here to the sea. And yet the child cites the existence of her dead siblings' graves as proof of their continuing existence. Being farther away than if one were at sea reconciles itself with its exact opposite, its proximity: "Twelve steps or more from my mother's door."

The child can know that one sister and one brother are dead and can also claim the opposite – that they still live and therefore count so that "we are seven." And she can thus produce the possibility of speaking of absent things as if they were present by what looks like a simple development of the logic of naming. If names such as Jane and John – the names of the dead siblings – enable one to represent persons as existing even when they cannot be seen, they also enable one to insist upon the existence of those names beyond their loss of referents. In "We Are Seven," only the dead siblings have names (except for the speaker's "dear brother Jem," who appears in the first line of the first version of the poem). Their names hold their places. Ordinary enough, these names sound almost excessively like generic names when "Jane" and "John" follow upon "dear brother Jem." When the child cites these names, their familiarity – the familiarity of particular names made virtually general through frequent use – creates an opposition between the generic names and the particularized names, the man's and the girl's different apprehensions of these same words. For the girl, names function as if they could never lose their referents, their connection to persons who can be pointed to, even in the absence of their bodies. For the man, what is there now is what counts, and signs of persons – be they names or graves – bespeak bodily absence. Yet the importance of their conflict has tended to be obscured by criticism that has treated the poem on the plausible assumption that the poem, being a dialogue, enacts the exchange much as drama would. Thus, critics have tended to defend the child and abuse the man. The traveler, acting from a certain callowness, tries to force on the child a knowledge for which she is not prepared as he promotes efficiency with arithmetic in the best modern way. Or, in a development of such a position, he tries to impose his hegemonic system upon an innocent victim. And from such a perspective, the traveler's explanation of his calculation sounds like a crude enough empirical distinction.

> "You run about, my little maid,
> Your limbs they are alive;
> If two are in the church-yard laid,
> Then ye are only five."

But his insistence upon counting what is there, what one can point to, and not to count what isn't, identifies not so much his world view as a crucial characteristic of numbers when they are used for counting. Counting, that is, always takes numbers to have references that are available to be pointed to. As Russell puts it, "The act of counting consists in establishing a one-one correlation between the set of objects counted and the natural numbers (excluding 0) that are used up in the process."[14] As the little girl of "We Are Seven" puts it, the act of counting consists in using number to preserve the integrity of the amalgam, the set of numbers that have been counted. And if William Wordsworth would say of his brother John's death in 1805, "the set is now broken," the girl of the poem speaks as if sets could never be broken. That is, she uses number as if it were name, as if it never counted down as it lost reference, as if none of the "objects" in the set could be exhausted.

Recalling the circumstances of the composition of "We Are Seven" in his notes to Isabella Fenwick, Wordsworth tells of having written the poem backward:

> while walking to and fro I composed the last stanza first, having begun with the last line. When it was all but finished, I came in and recited it to Mr. Coleridge and my Sister, and said, "A prefatory stanza must be added, and I should sit down to our little tea-meal with greater pleasure if my task were finished." I mentioned in substance what I wished to be expressed, and Coleridge immediately threw off the stanza thus:
>   A little child, dear brother Jem,
>
> – I objected to the rhyme, 'dear brother Jem,' as being ludicrous, but we all enjoyed the joke of hitching-in our friend, James Tobin's name, who was familiarly called Jem. . . . I have only to add that in the spring of 1841 I revisited Goodrich Castle, not having seen that part of the Wye since I met the little Girl there in 1793. It would have given me great pleasure to have found in the neighbouring hamlet traces of one who had interested me so much; but that was impossible, as, unfortunately, I did not even know her name.[15]

Wordsworth later deleted "dear brother Jem," that ludicrous rhyme, leaving the first line of the poem shortened by two feet. But the "joke of hitching-in our friend, James Tobin's name" counts as a joke, partially for demonstrating the ludicrousness of the accidents of rhyme and partially for demonstrating the accidents of meter. Like "I travelled among unknown men," "To the Cuckoo," and many other early Wordsworth poems, "We Are Seven" is cast in Common Measure, or ballad meter derived from the "split-up septanarius." That is, it has seven feet for every two-line segment. In this meter, "Dear brother Jem" makes seven, as form adapts name to the purposes of number.

The introduction of this detail risks suggesting that any formal ordering proceeds on its own, so that reference is ultimately either a matter of indifference or a private joke or pang. And on such a generally deManian account name is always on the verge of being assimilated to (one version of) number, which achieves its formality by virtue of its indifference to retaining the specificity of its reference. But if Wordsworth decides that "Jem" makes one name too many, his other recollection about the hazards of naming involves having one name too few. He can't, when he revisits Goodrich Castle in 1841, seek out the woman who had been the eight-year-old girl in 1793 because he never got her name. That lack of a name, moreover, underscores an oddness of naming in the poem, that the only siblings who have names are the dead ones. Wordsworth never got the girl's name, that is, because she was there, because her being there to be counted seemed to render her name irrelevant.

The 1841 retracing of the 1793 walking tour thus throws into relief the importance and the limitation of counting as ostensiveness. The girl in 1793 needed no name because she was one, the one who could be pointed to. But her having been pointed to is no more useful to Wordsworth in relocating her than the multiplication of texts, contexts, and critical criticism is to McGann. It does not make it possible to relocate the girl any more than McGann's self-proliferating inventories would make it possible for him to show the way one gets from here to there in sketching out a genetic narrative that would humanize literary works.

That is, we can see McGann focusing on the sense of materiality that one derives from the empirical situation of counting, pointing to things and persons. De Man meanwhile has been pointing to the materiality of naming and number as their formal persistence directly establishes the irony of the notion of a memory of counting. McGann's socio-historical method would point to how one gets from here to there, or from Salisbury Plain to Tintern Abbey, but it can do so not by deriving a course from the things one can point to but only by a sudden act of definition: this poem is for human value. He can, that is, stipulate the value for people of literary works with a human face, but he can never show the way one could arrive at that value on the basis of an argument about how many things or people there are. And de Man, less interested in making literature serve society, continually dramatizes the implausibility of imagining that there is an explicable connection between persons – be they authors or objects – and their representations. What is, however, ultimately most interesting is that they both resolve interpretative issues in favor of an insistence on a more explicit (McGann) and a more covert (de Man) empiricism. McGann's nominalistic commitment to recognizing an ever-proliferating plurality and de Man's treatment of name and number as if they always involved (failed or limited) acts of reference – as if they were always a version of counting what there is – demonstrate the achievement of an empirical sublime, the ability to lose a sense of one in the process of producing yet more.

Opposed on everything else, they agree in seeing a fundamental conflict between the individual and collection, the specific number and the amalgam. "We Are Seven," in its pitting of numbering against number, does not so much invalidate their approaches as suggest that they move too far toward resolution of the conflict between what there may be and what may be represented. The traveler's initial direct question to the girl is "What's your number?" rather than "What's your name?" And this way of seeing it establishes the representation of persons as a conflict between a numbering that can say who is there and a conception of name and number that always treats the representation as an amalgam both more extensive and more untraceable than that empirical count. The opponents of a bill that would have inaugurated an English census in 1753 claimed that a count was "totally subversive of the last remnants of English liberty," that it would "reveal the weakness of England to her enemies, and that it concealed tyrannical schemes for compulsory military service."[16] As in Rousseau's account of the way metaphorical language precedes literal language, the proposal to say what there is – whether by naming or counting – appears as a threat. If naming a "man" like oneself first involves taking him to be a "giant," someone larger and stronger than oneself, fear of the census likewise takes self-enumeration as a potential disclosure of one's weakness. By 1800 the prospect of this count seemed at least unthreatening enough for a bill of census to be passed, for self-enumeration had come to be identified with the possibility of planning, of seeing other people as something other than accidents.

Numbering, that is, had come to be just another version of naming, not just a way of saying what there is, but largely a way of making it possible to anticipate one's future. It was, in that sense, simply the inverse of the process of numbering individual houses that had begun in London in 1764, an articulation that made it that much easier to retrace one's steps, because house numbers combine ostensiveness (a correlation between number and object) with the identification of a house as a part of a series. Thus, while counting is indifferent to sequence (in that it does not matter which of, say, seven things one counts first), an operation like the numbering of houses insists on the sequence of houses and numbers so as to enable various persons to arrive at a place (even by different routes). That is, it coordinates individual meanings by systematizing the notion of place.

The convergence of these uses of number in the late eighteenth century suggests the possibility of reading a poem like "We Are Seven" in terms of a more general movement to coordinate meanings among individuals. For however much an individual number may slough off reference, the narrativizing of numbers in such projects as the numbering of houses represents a process of developing names as if they could function like numbers (with the heritability and successiveness that involves a regular interval between one term and the next). This coordination of meanings in numbering thus allows for representational divergence that can, for all its difference, be registered as comprehension. That is, despite the divergent arithmetics that yield "one" and "seven" for the problem of how many "you" are, the poem is less about the girl's incorrigibility or the man's obtuseness than about reconciling numbers to unity, or understanding another way of conceiving persons. Where modern criticism sees a gap, that is, the understanding of mathematics that I have associated with Kant sees an interval. And that sense of interval epitomizes the way in which Romantic formalism rescues language from a fundamental empiricism, by making it clear that the relationship among the terms supplements empirical reference. Just as the natural sublime comes to stand for an experience of something that does not already exist, the interval represents the formalist discovery of the patterning of language as at least as important as its ostensible referents. The problem of "We Are Seven" is that the girl speaks what ought, on an empiricist or crypto-empiricist account, to be an incomprehensible language. Yet what I take to be the chief point of the man's abandoning the exchange and walking away is to acknowledge that he understands what the girl has said. The poem is, then, a representation in miniature of the spirit animating paraphrase, an exchange of what you mean for what I would say, and in which the coordination of meaning counts neither as oppression nor as formal accident.

Notes

1 Paul Sheats, *The Making of Wordsworth's Poetry: 1785–1798* (Cambridge, Mass.: Harvard University Press, 1973), 83.
2 Jerome J. McGann, *The Romantic Ideology: A Critical Investigation* (Chicago: University of Chicago Press, 1983), 5.
3 McGann, ["Keats and the Historical Method in Literary Criticism," *MLN* 94 (1979),] 994.
4 See Clifford H. Siskin, *The Historicity of Romantic Discourse* (New York: Oxford University Press, 1988), 62 ff., for a particularly cogent critique of McGann.

5 McGann, *Romantic Ideology*, 86. See Marjorie Levinson, *Wordsworth's Great Period Poems* (Cambridge: Cambridge University Press, 1986). Although McGann's book appears three years before Levinson's, he summarizes the argument of her unpublished work.

6 Paul de Man, "Excuses (*Confessions*)," *Allegories of Reading* (New Haven: Yale University Press, 1979), 278–301. My exposition of this passage coincides with, and relies on, that of Steven Knapp and Walter Benn Michaels in "Against Theory," *Critical Inquiry* 8 (Summer 1982): 134.

7 For a somewhat different version of this debate between Andrzej Warminski and myself, see Frances Ferguson, "Historicism, Deconstruction, and Wordsworth," *Diacritics* 17 (Winter 1987), 32–45; Andrzej Warminski, "Response," *Diacritics* 17 (Winter 1987), 46–8; and Frances Ferguson, "Response," *Diacritics* 17 (Winter 1987), 49–52.

8 See Paul de Man, "Pascal's Allegory of Persuasion," *Allegory and Representation*, ed. Stephen Greenblatt (Baltimore: Johns Hopkins University Press [English Institute], 1981), 1–25.

9 See the discussion in H. Behnke, F. Bachmann, K. Fladt, W. Suss, eds, *Fundamentals of Mathematics*, 3 vols (Cambridge, Mass.: M.I.T. Press, 1986), 1:72, which includes an accidentally interesting remark on naming: "The best-known system of axioms for the natural numbers is due to Dedekind (1888) but is named after Peano (1889)."

10 See Paul de Man, "Phenomenality and Materiality in Kant," in *Hermeneutics: Questions and Prospects*, ed. Gary Shapiro and Alan Sica (Amherst: University of Massachusetts Press, 1984), 121–44.

11 Elaine Scarry, in her introduction to *Literature and the Body: Essays on Populations and Persons* (Baltimore: Johns Hopkins University Press [English Institute], 1988), writes wonderfully about counting as an operation that is simultaneously the most and the least referential of activities.

12 William Wordsworth, *The Prose Works of William Wordsworth*, ed. W.J.B. Owen and Jane Worthington Smyser, 3 vols (Oxford: Clarendon Press, 1974), 1:130.

13 This conflation has its point, because *having* brothers and sisters is bound up with *being* a brother or sister oneself.

14 Bertrand Russell, *Introduction to Mathematical Philosophy* (London: Allen, 1963 [1919]), 16–17.

15 William Wordsworth and Samuel Taylor Coleridge, *Lyrical Ballads*, ed. R.L. Brett and A.R. Jones (London: Methuen and Co., 1963), 280.

16 Quoted in Paul Mantoux, *The Industrial Revolution in the Eighteenth Century: An Outline of the Beginnings of the Modern Factory System in England*, rpt. (Chicago: University of Chicago Press, 1983), p. 342.

7   Legislators of the post-everything world

Shelley's *Defence* of Adorno

Robert Kaufman

To speak of Percy Shelley's "*Defence* of Adorno" is perhaps to invoke Jorge Luis Borges and his wonderful claim for Kafka's influence on Robert Browning.[1] But my purpose here is not to make the case for Shelley simply by reading his High Romantic argument through dark Adornian lenses, presumably a corrective prescription for our post-Modern glare. Instead, the Borgesian injunction to cross-wire the circuits of historical understanding – of reading, really – is heeded with the intent of more accurately plotting the relationship between German metaphysics and British literature since Wordsworth. It is also heeded with the intent to present the case for seeing in Shelley and Adorno the lineaments and trajectory of a critical aesthetics that is already a working-through, and ultimately a rejection of, what is today called "the critique of the ideology of the aesthetic." Reading Shelley together with Adorno – who seems to have written only a few words about the British poet – finds its justification in more than the playful coupling of different or succeeding historical *geister*.[2] Because as if in historical recompense for Coleridge's stealings from Kant, Adorno's work rather than that of any comparable English-language critic has come to be treated as an indispensable reference point for investigations of the vexed "aesthetics and politics" question in British letters (as opposed to the "culture and society" issue, where Raymond Williams and his successors figure most prominently). And given that for British literature the modern "aesthetics and politics" question is first broached during Romanticism, there turns out to be unexpected and specific historical warrant for utilizing Adorno to defend Shelley against cultural materialist, new historicist, and post-structuralist critique. Meanwhile Martin Jay, Fredric Jameson, and others have underscored Adorno's special importance to the development of a Marxian criticism whose themes and procedures, I will show, are almost invented by Shelley (an idea first hinted at by Marx himself).[3]

In what follows I offer a reading of what is probably British literature's most famous proclamation of the revolutionary nature of poetry and the aesthetic. I first rehearse Shelley's polemic in the *Defence of Poetry* against "calculation," his term for the philosophy and practice that has by 1821 brought England to political and economic crisis. Shelley continually asserts that the imaginative and poetical faculty must supersede the calculative principle (an argument that Wordsworth and Coleridge had already made years earlier, and that Adorno would reformulate in the languages of the Modern and post-Modern periods).[4] I establish, however, that at telling moments in his argument, Shelley's use of the term "calculation" indicates a degree of ambivalence about the attack. The ambivalence results from the fact that the most prominent exponents of what Shelley deems an anti-imaginative and anti-poetical "calculation" are *not* classically reactionary; on the contrary, they belong to the progressive and radical pantheon Shelley has until now championed. And this calculative tradition has most recently included not only Shelley's revered Thomas Paine, but also members of his own extended family: William Godwin and Mary Wollstonecraft.

Yet the consequent "anxiety of influence" is crystallized in the *Defence* not in any of these "English Jacobin" rationalists, but in the figure of Milton, Shelley's model for the poet-revolutionary, and, of course, the touchstone of Harold Bloom's theory in the first place.[5] As it happens, the one instance in the *Defence* where the word "calculation" carries a positive valence occurs during a discussion of *Paradise Lost.* I contend that Shelley's offhand, laudatory concatenation of "Milton," "sympathy," and "calculation" signals not just his charged relationship to the earlier poet, but also an otherwise unstated homage to and dependence on the Enlightenment calculators he inveighs against. Shelley is particularly beholden to these figures for his use of their doctrine of the "sympathetic imagination"; their notion of "sympathy," albeit with some Shelleyan variations, plays a prominent role in the *Defence.* This sympathy is connected to the prophetic side of Shelley's aesthetics but is distinct from it. Prophecy, while dependent on auditors, viewers, or readers to receive its messages, involves primarily those who "create" or "make" art.[6] Sympathy, on the other hand, concerns in the most basic sense the aesthetic experience of people who are not literally "makers" of art, but rather, respondents to it.

Provisionally separating the sympathetic from the prophetic, and emphasizing the former, I demonstrate that embedded within Shelley's *Defence* is an alternative or supplement to a primary account of art as inspirational and utopian model of freedom. Moreover, the supplementary account necessarily alters the standard narrative of the Romantic Milton who is rebel, prophet, and demiurge: Shelley's Satanic poet, first trumpeter of the English Revolution, emerges here as anticipatory author of the *Critique of Judgement.* That is, Shelley's *Defence* includes a formal account (linked to Milton) of aesthetic experience quite similar to the one that Kant offers in the Third Critique's Analytic of the Beautiful. But unlike Kant, Shelley wants to describe aesthetic experience in a language of revolutionary partisanship. The self-conscious usage of a vocabulary of revolution allows Shelley to put forward the idea that aesthetic experience has political value because of its potential to generate critical (or at least proto-critical) thought. I frame this contention for Shelley's "Negative Romanticism" as a corrective to the many interpretations that in practice limit the *Defence* to its assertions that poetry and art are prophetic, inspirational, and, almost willy-nilly, transformative.

On the view that will be presented here, Shelley, although recognizing that art is bound to the larger social fabric, decidedly does *not* understand the final work of the aesthetic to be the delivery of quasi-substantive political truths. Nor is its ultimate vocation found in the imaginative mapping, or even negation, of socio-historical constraints on freedom – though of course such gestures are regularly and powerfully instantiated in art, not least in the pages of the *Defence.* Instead, Shelley conceives aesthetic experience as a formal process that produces – in the mind's engagement with the dynamics, textures, and resistances of art – critical thinking itself as a form of truth. Such truth, for Shelley, does not inevitably translate into a progressive politics, but is nonetheless essential to it.

If on the one hand this reading emphasizes the critical rather than the prophetic or utopian Shelley, on the other it necessarily contests recent cultural materialist, new historicist, and post-structuralist judgments that Shelley effectively abandons politics for an elitist or escapist aesthetics. Critics who have aligned the retreat of Wordsworth and Coleridge from revolutionary politics with those poets' adherence to "aesthetic ideology" would be inclined to view skeptically my attempt to align Kantian aesthetics, Shelleyan poetics, and an Adornian argument for the proto-political value of aesthetically derived thought. To such critics it would probably seem that the only way to save Shelley would be to explain why his writing does not partake of aesthetic ideology. At any rate, revisionist criticism has already mooted any possibility of saving Shelley by separating him from "aesthetic culture": Shelley's work has lately been found to be implicated in the aesthetic ideology and its universalizing tendencies. The finding is meant also to indict Shelley for allegedly advocating the replacement of politics with aesthetics, a replacement said to deflect into the latter the energies that would otherwise be channeled into the former. In response to this criticism, I develop the case for the critical, rather than escapist or compensatory, nature of Shelley's aesthetics.

[. . .]

Shelley imagines (as Adorno will imagine) that a critical aesthetics can emerge from the confrontation with art's enactment of impasse, that it can emerge through engagement with an artistic structure that holds emancipatory gesture and formal constraint together in tension. Precisely this brief for the aesthetics ability to enable critical thought is what will link Shelley and Adorno; and so I want to conclude these opening remarks by suggesting a formal and historical relationship, somewhat on the order of two widely separated bookends, between Shelley's dogged post-revolutionary insistence that something useful can be gleaned from the mind's confrontation, in the aesthetic, with impasse, and Adorno's stubbornly paradoxical formulation (at what had seemed to be Modernism's final hour) of the "barbarism" of both the aesthetic and the abandonment of it "after Auschwitz."

[. . .]

Thomas Love Peacock's 1820 essay *The Four Ages of Poetry* calls only half-jokingly for the abandonment of poetic art. Poetry in the modern age is a reactionary pursuit, Peacock maintains. Creative minds should express themselves in the production of truly "useful knowledge," which, "collected, appreciated, and arranged, forms new combinations that impress the stamp of their power and utility on the real business of life." Those who would honor the dynamic poetry of the past should realize that the poetry of modern life lies where dynamism is now to be found: in philosophies and activities "bent on the pursuit and promotion of permanently useful ends." Poetry has become useless "because intellectual power and intellectual acquisition have turned themselves into other and better channels." The classic pronouncements in support of philosophy and history are revived, with the additional twist that poetry is characterized not only as a form of enthusiasm or madness (as in the *Ion*, which figures here as reason's Ur-text), but also as the "backward march of a crab": "While the historian and the philosopher are advancing in, and accelerating, the progress of knowledge, the poet is wallowing in the rubbish of departed ignorance." Finally, Peacock reasons, it was not poetry that inspired the Age of Revolution, but the "subtle skepticism of Hume, the solemn irony of Gibbon, the daring paradoxes of Rousseau, and the biting ridicule of Voltaire" which assaulted "every portion of the reign of authority."[7]

Shelley begins his reply with a classification of two essential mental faculties, reason and imagination; the classificatory scheme is a commonplace, as is Shelley's

Romantic assumption that reason is a subset of the imagination. Shelley describes reason as mathematic, associative, logical; imagination as creative, synthetic, spiritual. In an entirely Vichian manner, Shelley insists that the imagination is originary and transformative; it is a constitutively human power of creating and refashioning the world. Its highest expression is said to be poetry. In an anthropological tour, Shelley then traces the history of the imagination's creation of human society and culture, stopping in each epoch to note how art was the spark for social transformation and revolution.

The tour stops short when he reaches his own time and place. The problem in England in 1821 is that "utility," the rule of "reason," has created inequality, poverty, corruption. Shelley's short-hand epithet for all this is a term Peacock never mentions in *The Four Ages of Poetry*: "calculation." Shelley also gives synonyms for the word – "selfishness," "self-love," "use," "accumulation," "Mammon" – but the favored pejorative remains "calculation."

Now Peacock has plausible grounds to believe, as his encomium for Enlightenment attacks on *ancien régime* authority makes clear, that he and not Shelley stands in the progressive or revolutionary line. And those grounds in turn provide a foundation for us to understand why Shelley introduces the term "calculation" into the debate. For as Peacock launches his broadside, it is but thirty years since the inflammatory proclamations that reason, revolution, and commerce were inseparable. M.H. Abrams observed long ago that Romantic poetry had followed the lead of those eighteenth-century theorists who had turned away "from the rational and calculative ethics of Bentham and the early Godwin" and instead "put sensibility and sympathy at the center of morality."[8] What has not been as authoritatively remarked in literary criticism is the extraordinary role that the term "calculation," along with a severely rationalist antipathy to "imagination," plays in two of the most important documents of English Jacobinism: Paine's *Rights of Man* and Wollstonecraft's *Vindication of the Rights of Men*.[9]

[. . .]

[Kaufman here describes the role that reason plays in opposing "imagination" in Paine and Wollstonecraft, the latter reinforcing "the old, repressive order."]

***

Although others before him had anatomized utilitarianism, Shelley gives the impression that it has fallen to him (and to unnamed fellow-traveling poets) to announce that the career and legacy of revolutionary calculation are exhausted.[10] In fact, it is more than a matter of exhaustion: in accord with the manner in which he opened the *Defence*, he makes reason eternally subservient to imagination, effectively reversing the narrative told by Wollstonecraft and, more recently, Peacock:

> The exertions of Locke, Hume, Gibbon, Voltaire, Rousseau, and their disciples, in favor of oppressed and deluded humanity, are entitled to the gratitude of mankind. Yet it is easy to calculate the degree of moral and intellectual improvement which the world would have exhibited, had they never lived. A little more nonsense would have been talked for a century or two; and perhaps a few more men, women, and children, burnt as heretics. . . . But it exceeds all imagination to conceive what would have been the moral condition of the world if neither Dante, Petrarch, Boccaccio, Chaucer, Shakespeare, Calderon, Lord Bacon, nor Milton, had ever existed. . . . The human mind could never, except

by the intervention of these excitements, have been awakened to the invention of the grosser sciences.

(502)

Not only is it "easy" to perform the mental operations involved in calculation, Shelley implies here, but it is also "easy to calculate" what would have been the effect of not having had the great calculators at all: one just adds a century or so of nonsense, and of murderous immolation. In contrast, far from it being "easy" to imagine the absence of the poetry, it is impossible to do so, it "exceeds" what can be imagined; and just this unrepresentable quality has brought the lesser intellectual powers into existence, by virtue of the human mind's having been "awakened" to "invention." Enlightenment, then, is an awakening, an invention, that is beholden not to reason but to imagination.

And yet this Enlightenment, Shelley charges (*avant* Adorno and Horkheimer), has despite itself turned into its own antithesis, has become a mechanical rather than a reflective process. It has become instrumental reason or, in Shelley's pejorative usage, calculation. In a neoclassical, proto-Marxian language of political economy, Shelley quite explicitly frames all this as a social crisis involving the overproduction and underconsumption of intellectual and material goods, which has been engendered by the extraction of profit from the surplus value produced by, but not re-invested in, human labor and creativity:

> But whilst the sceptic destroys gross superstitions, let him spare to deface, as some of the French writers have defaced, the eternal truths charactered upon the imaginations of men. Whilst the mechanist abridges, and the political oeconomist combines, labour, let them beware that their speculations, for want of correspondence with those first principles which belong to the imagination, do not tend, as they have in modern England, to exasperate at once the extremes of luxury and want. [. . .] The rich have become richer, and the poor have become poorer. . . . Such are the effects which must ever flow from an unmitigated exercise of the calculating faculty.

(501)

Calculation cannot add, it seems, without also subtracting from itself; it perforce works by "exasperating" injurious extremes. Thus the intellectual and social exertions of "the mechanists" round back upon them, reminding them that they are themselves trapped inside the workings of a machine they mistakenly thought they controlled. Without imagination, there is no "outside" to this machine, no perspectival locus from which to take its measure and transform its workings. The rounding back or dialectic of calculation, which now "defaces" the very human creativity that "invented" reason in the first place, arises from the Enlightenment's reliance not on "those first principles which belong to the imagination" (Shelley) but on "those first principles which belong to reason" (Wollstonecraft, Paine). Consequently, Shelley states (again in the vocabulary of political economy), there has been produced

> more moral, political and historical wisdom, than we know how to reduce into practise; we have more scientific and oeconomical knowledge than can be accommodated to the just distribution of the produce which it multiplies. The

poetry in these systems of thought is concealed by the accumulation of facts and calculating processes.

[(502)]

[...]

In a perverse contradiction, the more there is the less there is; the production of facts makes impossible the consumption of facts; mass accumulation produces scarcity. This is so because the creative capacity, and the forms of social life which would correspond to it, have been smothered beneath facts, calculations, and indigestible goods. The words of the opening paragraph of the *Defence* are revealed to have been not just a classification, but also a potential warning: "reason is the enumeration of quantities already known; imagination is the perception of the value of those quantities" (480). Pure enumeration – production or reason or calculation alone – destroys the possibility of value. And this result "must ever flow from an unmitigated exercise of the calculating faculty."

However, there turns out to be one crucial exception to this rule: the calculations of epic poetry. The qualification comes amidst a discussion of epic in general and *Paradise Lost* in particular:

> Milton's poem contains within itself a philosophical refutation of that system of which, by a strange and natural antithesis, it has been a chief popular support. Nothing can exceed the energy and magnificence of the character of Satan in Paradise Lost. It is a mistake to suppose that he could ever have been intended for the popular personification of evil. . . . Milton has so far violated the popular creed (if this shall be judged to be a violation) as to have alleged no superiority of moral virtue to his God over his Devil. And this bold neglect of a direct moral purpose is the most decisive proof of the supremacy of Milton's genius. He mingled as it were the elements of human nature, as colours upon a single pallet, and arranged them into the composition of his great picture according to epic truth; that is, according to the laws of that principle by which a series of actions of the external universe and of intelligent and ethical beings is calculated to excite the sympathy of succeeding generations of mankind.

(498–9)

A strange and natural antithesis indeed. At the exact instant that he famously helps invent the Romantic Milton, Shelley also associates his precursor with both the disease and cure that the *Defence* is written to identify. That is, Milton's epic is associated with the stigmatized term "calculation," as well as with the antidote of aesthetic sympathy, which *Paradise Lost* is said to arouse. A cluster of issues, which need to be disentangled, surrounds this concatenation of Milton's epic, calculation, and sympathy.

It is at first difficult to know just how to regard this use of the word "calculated." It is on its face laudatory, coming amidst effusive praise for Milton and epic, and might be no more than an interesting slip. Yet it is a surprising use of a word that everywhere else in the *Defence* is unambiguously derogatory. It *is* true that not every instance of the term in the *Defence* corresponds to a specifically Enlightenment or Benthamite rationalism; at several points, "calculation" signifies a transhistorical tendency to reason from narrow, selfish premises. Still, from the text of the *Defence* in general, its background, and occasion, it is relatively clear that the main force of the polemic against "calculation" is the historically located situation of early nineteenth-century rationalism.

[. . .]

In epic, calculative reason presumably finds its place; that place is no longer described as subordinate to imaginative sympathy, but as working harmoniously to help create it. Epic truth bears "a defined and intelligible relation to the knowledge, and sentiment, and religion, and political conditions of the age" in which the poet lived "and of the ages which followed it, developing itself in correspondence with their development" [(499)]. Making such truth available is a revolutionary act, so that Dante and Milton are presented together as the two-handed engine that first prepares and then completes the demise of feudalism.

[. . .]

I think that what Shelley is up to in these passages involves the adumbration of an ingenious, socially radical and literarily self-interested narrative. Ventriloquized, it runs along the following lines:

What is "eternal" about poetry is its transformative, or potentially transformative, power, a power expressed differently in different epochs. Accurate historiography has already revealed that the great French *philosophes* and calculators were indebted to the Scottish Enlightenment and English Revolution, which, after all, paved the way for them. What has not heretofore been established is that it was Milton's epic poetry that reinvented a dynamic calculation appropriate for the era of "the third epic poet" [(499)] and the early modern period that would follow him, when such a form of "calculation" did not exist and was needed as a then-revolutionary antidote to feudal and royalist stasis. Milton indeed accomplished this, "making" Enlightenment calculation and projecting its attendant doctrine of imaginative sympathy before the eighteenth century had even thought to name these phenomena. Locke, Hume, Voltaire, and the rest were only the chroniclers of what Milton's epic had instigated. That era of a heroic calculation and reason is over, its discursive and poetic strength exhausted. Imaginative thought must now burrow deep into the calculative vocabulary and diagnoses of political economy, doing justice to them not by jettisoning but by transforming them. Working from materials at hand, poetry must reinvent itself and society; a new poetic must do to capitalism what Milton's poetic did to feudalism: namely, supersede it, through the immanent, imaginative projection of something new and previously inconceivable.

[. . .]

The simultaneous connection and dissociation between Milton and calculation permits Shelley alternately to praise Milton for avoiding or creating it. "Calculation" is here on the one hand the cause of what T.S. Eliot will programatically denounce as the Miltonic "dissociation of sensibility" that was destined to poison British literature and modern life; and on the other hand, it is the last instance of a now-lost paradise where calculation and sympathy, word and thing, signifier and signified, are happily united in epic truth. Shelley can relieve some of his anxiety of influence by subtly casting aspersions on Milton, who, to the extent he did recreate calculation, evidently spawned a monster. Allowing the ostensibly unsullied Milton salutarily to beget a modern, initially progressive, calculating principle in *Paradise Lost*, but elsewhere describing that very principle as "unworthy" of Milton: this effectively lets Shelley have his sympathetic imagination without himself contracting sympathy's attendant virus of calculation (as Milton implicitly contracted it, at least in the historically retrospective view where "calculation," as opposed to "sympathy," has gone bad). Shelley, then, all but announces that he will take up and extend Milton's great experiments in imaginative sympathy, but will isolate or supersede the calculative principle. Furthermore, the construction of this allegory means that Shelley need not acknowledge the degree to which imaginative sympathy springs, in his own era, from the minds of the Enlightenment calculators, including the minds of Paine, Godwin, and Wollstonecraft. Instead, he can impute the modern revivification of sympathy to the poetic forerunner whose epic he is making his own. Which is to say, he ultimately credits the reinvention of sympathy to himself.

Shelley's language, and his sequencing of this mytho-history, *enact* the claim for the Miltonic source of the Enlightenment and its tools; the enactment is also a dramatization of the *Defence's* opening claim, that imagination precedes reason. First, we read that Milton's "great picture" is "calculated to excite the sympathy of succeeding generations" (498–9), and a few pages later, we learn that the poets – "Dante, Petrarch, Boccaccio, Chaucer, Shakespeare, Calderon, . . . Milton" – have with "the intervention" of "these excitements" (poetry) "awakened the human mind to the invention of the grosser sciences." As reason follows imagination, so we are then told that poetry's effects have culminated in the "exertions of Locke, Hume, Gibbon" (502). The great awakeners have themselves been excited and awakened (to the point of being able to "invent" their "grosser sciences") by poetry, and most recently, according to Shelley's list, by Milton's poetry.

Even apart from the taint of calculation, the logic of Shelley's ascribing to Milton the most recent origins of a sympathetic imagination yields some wonderfully Satanic – in the sense of paradoxical or antithetical – results. As we are about to see, Shelleyan aesthetic sympathy becomes a politically inflected Kantianism. Thus in a diabolical reversal, the poet-agitator of the English Revolution must become, despite all odds, the great precursor of a taxonomist of critical faculties. The very creation of aesthetic sympathy that had made Milton Satanic also makes him, with the passage of time, the anticipator of a treatise on taste. But the historical irony really comes more at Shelley's expense than at Milton's, given Shelley's habit of identifying Milton with the Good Old Cause of the English Revolution, on the one hand, and Shelley's avowed reservations about Kantian transcendentalism, on the other.[11] Because in still another turn of the screw, it is precisely Shelley's understanding of the signifier "Milton" as the conjunction of poetry and revolution that enables him to suggest a political value in the capacity of the aesthetic (an essentially *Kantian* aesthetic, it bears repeating) to stimulate critical thought.

In fact, it is not only the *Defence's* odd linkage of *Paradise Lost* and the terms "calculation" and "sympathy" that shadows forth a Third Critique Milton. Actually, the key idea in the passage quoted above is that "the most decisive proof of the supremacy of Milton's genius" – the thing that allows Milton's poem to work according to the "epic truth . . . calculated to excite the sympathy of succeeding generations" – is "bold neglect of a direct moral purpose." Thus Milton has "alleged no superiority of moral virtue to his God over his Devil."

[. . .]

Somehow a simultaneous awareness of, and suspension of instrumental interest in, manifest, moralistic content kindles or inculcates a different kind of interest and thought – one that Shelley will project as critical (or proto-critical). Consequently, the goal is not so much "to tease us out of thought" as it is to tease us out of calculative thought in the restrictive sense; put another way, the process Shelley conceives is meant to tease us *into* thought – into *critical* thought, that is – by means of aesthetic experience. Shelley finds this process available in Milton, and he inflects it with an early nineteenth-century language of revolution.[12]

***

The *Defence* fashions an image of poetry as utopian model in the figure of the poet-prophet, who creates in poetry "the very image of life expressed in its eternal truth," imitating and participating in the "unchangeable forms of human nature, as existing in the mind of the creator" (485). The poet is thus able to approximate or touch a form of divinity. As I mentioned earlier, my emphasis is not on prophecy but on aesthetic sympathy. The two are obviou[s]ly connected; it is axiomatic for Shelley that the poet must sympathize with his or her material, and that the reader must do likewise with the text.

In one of the most famous passages in the *Defence*, Shelley writes that the "great secret of morals is Love; or a going out of our own nature, and an identification with the beautiful which exists in thought, action, or person, not our own" (487). Going out of the self is posited as the counterpoint to the calculative restriction to a "little world of self" (497). As calculation narrows the self, so poetry "enlarges the circumference" of calculation's opposite number, the imagination, "replenishing it with thoughts of ever new delight, which have the power of attracting and assimilating to their own nature all other thoughts, and which form new intervals and interstices whose void for ever craves fresh food" (488).

[. . .]

What Shelley portrays as a going out of the self, a grasping of previously unapprehended relations between things and people, is what since at least Russian Formalism has been called "defamiliarization." Shelley more or less calls it that himself; in a language shared by other Romantics, he says that poetry "strips the veil of familiarity from the world," "lifts the veil from the hidden beauty of the world, and makes familiar objects be as if they were not familiar" (505, 487). Furthermore, all this is deemed "revolutionary." Poetry's work of defamiliarization, its contributions to imaginative empowerment and the going out of self, lead to "social renovation," to the "awakening" of the politically "entranced," to "the struggle for civil and religious liberty" (493, 499, 508). Poetry, in short, is once more heralded as the cause and instrument of true Enlightenment.

While Shelley maintains that poetry makes revolution, he argues simultaneously that it does not determine agency, that the exact relationships between cause and effect are never subject to clear analysis, and that the degree to which art generates or accompanies social change remains mysterious: "We know no more of cause and effect than a constant conjunction of events" (489). The last point is Shelley's riposte to the assumption that any given artistic style or mode can be said to yield a determinate political result.

[. . .]

It follows from the general refusal of certainty about cause and effect [. . .] that the particular *content* of poetry cannot assure a particular ethical or political response on the part of the reader. Since morality is strengthened by the *formal* exercise of the imagination, content itself should be deemed irrelevant: "bold neglect of a direct moral purpose," as we have seen, is Milton's strong suit (498). Finally the tension between the utopian promise and the invisibility of practical payoff, between revolutionary telos and contentless local message, resolves itself into a sustained paradox, one that Shelley figures as a property of achieved form: art is revolutionary, yet in itself non-partisan.[13] Its revolutionary character stems from its potential to stimulate critical thought, without which change is inconceivable.

[. . .]

To put it another, perhaps more Adornian, way: We have to do with the paradox of the simultaneous demand for, and impossibility of achieving, consensus about "the beautiful" – and so we come to discover the *fictive* and, surprisingly enough, *structurally* defamiliarizing, character of aesthetic experience. If for Shelley this is the phenomenology of the subject's apprehension of the artwork, and if it is also what the artwork *teaches* (the proto-political lesson, that is, that among the key conditions for dynamic thought is an apprehension of the constitutive interaction of identity and non-identity), it is just as true of Shelley's vision of intersubjective experience. On this view, Shelley's definition of morality (as "Love; or a going out of our own nature, and an identification of ourselves with the beautiful which exists in thought, action, or person, not our own") charts no endpoint to the going-out of self, no ultimate identification of self and other. Hence "identification" is what the subject at once seeks and, in respect for otherness or non-identity, seeks also to short-circuit or complicate. Hence too the idea that the subject is potentially moved to imagine himself or herself as other and the other as judging subject. Meanwhile, the chastening formalism of this intersubjective *ostranenie* or *Verfremdungseffekt* serves as a reminder, amidst debates over the "aesthetics and politics" question, that there is no royal road between defamiliarization and political (or any other) agency. Although art, criticism, and aesthetics do not themselves necessarily forge a link between perception and action, the stimulus to perception and critical thought that they do afford may be valued, among other reasons, for being a necessary prerequisite *of* effective action.

[. . .]

The claim for Shelley's defense of Adorno is not a claim for the elevation of criticism to the status of poetry. Instead, my undertaking here has involved the reconstruction of Shelley's second-generation Romantic attempt – which anticipates in significant ways what will be Adorno's late Modernist or early post-Modernist attempt – to grapple with the question of aesthetic experience, to investigate what, if any, critical and political function it can serve. In an earlier epoch of the "post," Shelley defends not only the making of poetry and art, but also the value of aesthetic experience for critical thought. Amidst all the declarations these days about "the end of everything," one of the least challenged assertions has been that we now are or should be, at least on the progressive or Left side of things, definitively "post-aesthetic." To be sure, it is often said that influential strains of social critique and political activity seem to have become *merely* aesthetic (or, to make a crucial distinction, that they have become aesthetic*ized*). But my concern (in distinguishing an *aesthetic* from an aesthetic*ized* Left criticism) is the frequent assumption that the aesthetic itself as an enabling category and tool is passé, or worse, hopelessly contaminated, worthy only of ceaseless ideological denunciation and ritual demystification. A glance at the history of Left critical aesthetics, from a Shelleyan Negative Romanticism to an Adornian Negative Dialectics and beyond, may unsettle the certainty that critique should indeed be so post-aesthetic. Whether or not we are living in a post-, pre-, or in-between-everything state of affairs, it is to some extent true that the reader or viewer of an existing text or art object is always "post-" – the work is already made, even if reading or viewing requires, figuratively speaking, a reconstruction. In aesthetic experience, Shelley and Adorno remind us, it is not so much the world that is being legislated, as it is the implements for understanding the world. Whatever this era turns out to be, the first legislative task posed for aesthetics would seem to be the determination of whether it can still provide the tools, or help exercise the faculties, that will be needed to imagine – let alone to answer – the questions that will face us.

Notes

[. . .]

1 "Kafka and His Precursors," in Jorge Luis Borges, *Labyrinths: Selected Stories & Other Writings*, ed. Donald A. Yates and James E. Irby (New York: New Directions, 1962), 199–201.

2 Adorno's published commentary on Shelley seems to be limited to a single, fleeting reference (albeit one made at an important point in a major essay): "Just as for Hölderlin's kindred spirit Shelley Hell is a city 'much like London,' and just as later the modernity of Paris is an archetype for Baudelaire, so Hölderlin sees correspondences between ideas and particular existents everywhere" ("Parataxis: On Hölderlin's Late Poetry," in Adorno's *Notes to Literature*, trans. Shierry Weber Nicholsen, 2 vols [New York: Columbia Univ. Press, 1992], 2:122).

3 Martin Jay, *Adorno* (Cambridge: Harvard University Press, 1984); Fredric Jameson, *Late Marxism: Adorno, Or, The Persistence Of The Dialectic* (New York: Verso, 1990). Both Jay and Jameson portray a quite different Adorno than the one often pressed into service by those commentators whose work focuses on "the critique of aesthetic ideology" from Romanticism through the Modern and post-Modern periods [. . .]

4 I am thinking here not only of the celebrated Adorno-Horkheimer critique of "instrumental" reason (most notably in the 1947 *Dialectic of Enlightenment*), but also, for example, of Adorno's musing that "as calculation thinking itself is defiled" ("Valéry's Deviations," in *Notes to Literature*, 1:173).

5 Chapter 1 of Bloom's "Theory of Poetry" actually begins with Shelley's attempt, in the *Defence*, to write himself into what Bloom identifies as Milton's "strong" visionary line: "Shelley speculated that poets of all ages contributed to one Great Poem perpetually in progress" (*The Anxiety of Influence: A Theory of Poetry* [London: Oxford Univ. Press, 1973], 19).

6 Shelley virtually begins the *Defence* by identifying creation with the imagination, which is said in the second sentence to be the principle of "*poiein*" ("making"); for a loftier version of this idea, he later quotes Tasso's dictum that "none deserves the name of Creator except God and the Poet" (*A Defence of Poetry*, in *Shelley's Poetry and Prose*, ed. Donald H. Reiman and Sharon B. Powers [New York: Norton, 1977] 480, 506). Unless otherwise indicated, all references to Shelley's writing are to this edition and are hereafter cited parenthetically in the text.

7 Thomas Love Peacock, *The Four Ages of Poetry*, reprinted in *Critical Theory Since Plato*, ed. Hazard Adams (New York: Harcourt Brace Jovanovich, 1971), 491–7; quotations are from pages 495–7.

8 Abrams, *The Mirror And The Lamp* (New York: Oxford Univ. Press, 1953), 330.

9 It should be said that at various points, Godwin, Wollstonecraft, and Paine introduce complications and nuances into their generally positive treatments of "calculation," making a place for "bad," "aristocratic" versions of calculation.

10 Although probably not available to Shelley, as were Wordsworth's and Coleridge's critiques of calculative reason, Blake's attacks on "ratiocination" are certainly relevant in this context.

11 Shelley's doubts about Kant are most pronounced, as Stuart Curran has noted, in *Peter Bell the Third*, where study of the philosopher leads to a distressing, if hilarious, outcome. Curran also states that Shelley's reservations stem from what Shelley apparently sees as "the attempt of Kant to resurrect transcendental ideas unrelated to human values" (*Shelley's Annus Mirabilis: The Maturing of an Epic Vision* [San Marino: Huntington Library, 1975], 148, 197).

12 Over a century later, Adorno will perform a similar operation on Kant himself, translating what are still Third Critique principles into another Left vocabulary.

13 My formulation here of the way that Shelley figures *art's* relationship to *society* – as revolutionary, yet non-partisan – might be said to raise to the second power Stuart Curran's analysis of the way that *genre* works, *within* British Romantic poetry, "to supply a geometry for art that is, or can be made to be . . . both morally neutral and a driving force" (Curran's *Poetic Form and British Romanticism* [Oxford: Oxford Univ. Press, 1986], 209).

8   Utility, retribution, and Godwin's *Caleb Williams*

Mark Canuel

To say that the Romantic novel has been overlooked in histories of the novel would only be a mild overstatement. It is not at all the case that great books haven't been written that include Romantic novels. But it is hard to deny a peculiar feature of our critical history, which is that the more ambitious studies of the "rise of the novel" have tended to focus exclusively on eighteenth-century fiction with an occasional extension into the work of Jane Austen; equally ambitious studies of the nineteenth-century novel, focusing on its connection to modern social theories and institutional developments, have little to say about the fiction written, say, between Ann Radcliffe and Walter Scott. It may be striking enough that this trend seems to hold New Criticism's vision of the novel very much in place – a vision perhaps most vividly mapped out in F.R. Leavis's *The Great Tradition*, which seemed to award serious consideration to prose fiction only insofar as it demonstrated what he understood to be the formal unity of the modern novel (Leavis 1963: 7). But still more remarkable than this is that Romantic studies itself has been more or less comfortable with this enterprise of exclusion, since most scholars have tended to back out of an ambition to formulate the Romantic novel's position with the long history of interconnected social discourses and institutions that stand at the heart of more capacious studies of eighteenth- and nineteenth-century novels. In Romantic studies, by contrast, we have more frequently seen even the most revealing and sophisticated treatments framed in terms of specific themes or specific subgenres. Work on novels, that is, often tends to be incorporated into a treatment of specific subject matter – issues of sympathy, nationalism, and so on – that are often not entirely interested in matters of generic specificity. Or, that work just as often tends to be classified somewhat artificially into different generic categories – the Gothic, the regional novel, the historical novel, the Jacobin novel, and so on. This compartmentalization brings the issue of genre very close to a thematic definition, which is to say that the attention to genre can often seem like the mere expression of a given set of personal or political interests: Gothics are about forbidden sexuality, the national tale is about local attachments, the Jacobin novel is about individual rights, and so on. Attention to genre turns out not really to be about genre at all.

It is not my primary aim in this essay to speculate about why critical history took this turn, but – just to indulge that impulse only for a moment – it is quite possible that the trend to anatomize the novel in the terms I have described is a version of the attachment that Romantic studies has had to lyric poetry and lyricized selfhood, so that treatment of the novel form carried an overtly anti-formal element in it. Of course, formalist analysis of poetry was itself deeply attracted to the lyric. Still, the fact that the mounting interest in Romantic novels (with occasional notable exceptions which, beyond Austen, would most certainly include Mary Shelley's *Frankenstein*) coincided with, and was in fact impelled by, new historicist views of the Romantic age, resulted in a peculiar anti-formalist attachment to lyricism. Historicism, that is, viewed the shape of the Romantic novel in terms that were compartmentalized, thematized, and atomized, and thus in terms that rendered the genre only into slightly more broadly pitched narrative versions of nature lyrics and their various attachments to ideological positions. If many scholars had cause to quarrel with the way critical history marginalized the Romantic era's place within the realist literary tradition, they responded by essentially asserting a justification for that marginality. For the novel thus appeared, to many critics, as personal interest writ large to encompass the sympathies, beliefs, and desires of categories of persons or groups (defined in terms of gender, nation, and so on). From this perspective, it is hardly surprising that Gary Kelly's sweeping account of Romantic fiction repeatedly emphasizes internal emotion and practices of subjectivity across numerous Romantic subgeneric categories (Kelly 1989). And it is also hardly surprising that such an insightful and illuminating reading of the longer history of the novel as Nancy Armstrong's *How Novels Think: The Limits of Individualism from 1719–1900* includes Romanticism precisely as a lyric exceptionalism; she views the place of the Romantic solely in terms of an excessive "expressive individualism" that is at odds with forms of social control that emerge in the nineteenth-century novel (Armstrong 2005: 8).

We might be inclined to take issue with this shape of critical history partly because of its obvious empirical inaccuracy, in that authors writing toward the end of the eighteenth century consider their work to be participating in a much wider circulation of fiction than the separation into specific categories would allow; to think of Austen as merely a departure from Gothic fiction, for instance (the careful distancing from it in *Northanger Abbey* notwithstanding), tends to obscure the degree to which her novels really do draw upon the formal and political preoccupations of Radcliffe's writing. The echoes of Radcliffe in Scott are equally clear and interesting.

There is a more theoretical issue at stake here, though. Whereas many studies of the eighteenth-century rise of the novel and flourishing of nineteenth-century realism have tended to emphasize the interconnection between generic structures and emerging political ones, studies of the Romantic novel – in their concentration on more thematic issues, or at least on treating politics as identity categories – have often seemed too removed from a discussion of the interconnected attributes of subgenres in their eagerness to acclimate those subgenres to a thematic understanding of what Romanticism as a field is supposedly about, from liberty and sympathy to local attachment and nationalism.

I take the example of William Godwin's 1794 novel *Things as They Are; or, the Adventures of Caleb Williams* (usually known simply as *Caleb Williams*) to explore an important feature of British Romantic novels, which is their increasing awareness of, and implication within, a discourse of the common good, or what I will also identify as, in keeping with Godwin's own language in his political treatise *An Enquiry Concerning Political Justice*, a discourse of utility. This is not at all an invention of the eighteenth century, and Peter Miller has usefully traced it back to Cicero (among others), but I want to be placing an emphasis on the way that it begins to exert a new kind of power in later decades of the eighteenth century, especially following the French Revolution (Miller 1994: 21–87). That discourse of utility, common good, or what Jeremy Bentham called "the greatest happiness principle," I would argue, *is not simply a theme* in a great many novels (Bentham 1988: 58). That discourse is inseparable from the Romantic novel's generic self-constitution, in that the narrative identifies with that discourse, producing a generalized assessment of its characters' contributions to each other's prospects that may even reach beyond their immediate intentional, domestic, and contractual alliances.

In Mary Wollstonecraft's fragmentary novel *Maria: or, the Wrongs of Woman*, the primary ambitions that keep getting frustrated by Maria's tyrannical husband are her "plans of usefulness" (Wollstonecraft 1975: 91). In keeping with that thought, Godwin's advertisement to the novel declares that Wollstonecraft's death prevented her from completing the novel, which is itself aligned or compared to "schemes of usefulness, and projects of public interest" (Wollstonecraft 1975: 120). Austen's *Sense and Sensibility*, as far as it may seem from Wollstonecraft's fiction, produces a vision toward the end of the novel in which Elinor's marriage is not to a man with any personal ambition but to a man with a clerical living with communal obligations attached to it; Marianne becomes a perfect utilitarian insofar she is found, after marrying Colonel Brandon, "submitting to new attachments, entering on new duties" and is a "patroness of a village" (Austen 2002: 268). It is not simply that characters make themselves useful to each other at the end of this and all other Austen novels; the characters are awarded a narrative weight or value according to their ability to make such contributions to a public good.

I want to discuss *Caleb Williams* to examine some of the complexities that surround this discourse and its narrative priority. Ultimately this could connect to the way that a very broad range of novels during the Romantic age, often associated with different subgenres, operate as sorting mechanisms according to which beliefs, practices, and alliances can be tested according to axioms of utility. General utility – rather than a dry apparatus of calculation as some have thought it to be – is associated with some of the Romantic novel's most dazzling imaginative resources. But at the same time utility itself – and this is an important dimension of its deployment in the novels throughout the Romantic age and most certainly with *Caleb Williams* – is exposed in terms of its fragility and openness to dissent and revision.

In *Caleb Williams*, the orphaned hero, Caleb, is employed as a secretary with Ferdinando Falkland, a wealthy country gentleman. After observing his employer's strange self-torturing groans in self-enforced solitude, Caleb is told Falkland's history by the house steward, Mr. Collins: once the flower of chivalry, Falkland had engaged in a prolonged dispute with an envious rival in his neighborhood, Barnabas Tyrrel, whose tyranny has led to the ruin of a tenant, Mr. Hawkins, and ultimately to the death of his own niece Emily Melville, who he has thrown in prison merely out of spite for her love for Falkland. After confronting Tyrrel at a rural assembly, Falkland is leveled to the ground by a blow from Tyrrel, and Tyrrel is soon after discovered murdered. Deceptive circumstantial evidence points to Hawkins and his son as the murderers, who are then tried and executed for the crime. But after hearing Mr. Collins's story about his employer, Caleb sets himself up as a spy on him to see what he can uncover about the actual details of the murder. He is all too successful. He finds, among other discoveries, a letter from Hawkins to Falkland that clearly exculpates him. Shortly after that, during a house fire and impelled by his own burning curiosity, Caleb opens a trunk with Falkland's papers and is discovered in the act by Falkland himself, who confesses to the crime – admitting to being the murderer of Tyrrel and indirectly the assassin of the Hawkinses – but Falkland vows to hate and torment Caleb forever. For the remainder of the novel, after Falkland frames him for a theft of his money and jewels and plants evidence in Caleb's own traveling case, Caleb attempts to escape him but is relentlessly pursued. After first being imprisoned (in the same prison that held "the wretched and innocent Hawkinses" [Godwin 1988: 184]), he finds himself captured by a band of thieves. Once he has extricated himself from this misadventure, he tries various disguises and escapes, all of which repeatedly fail because Falkland has so relentlessly employed others on his behalf and so effectively spread news of Caleb's supposed crimes against his gracious and honorable patron. I'll discuss the complications of the novel's ending in a moment, but the version that Godwin published gives Caleb the opportunity at last to bring his case before a magistrate; Falkland confesses, but dies before he is punished, and Caleb ends the narrative where he began, in a condition that he can only describe as "truly miserable" (Godwin 1988: 336).

Godwin's novel intriguingly holds out the possibility during much of its plot that there might be such a thing as a satisfying retributive justice: one in which the innocent will be unharmed and the guilty will receive his just desert, providing a certain kind of poetic closure for the narrative; indeed that is the impulse behind the novel's efforts to "vindicate" the hero's "character" (Godwin 1988: 337). I will examine the ways in which it takes that task rather seriously, but also the ways in which it also frustrates it in several ways. Godwin suggests not only that unequal relations between persons exist in such a way as to render this kind of justice impossible, but also that it may be in fact pointless to find a person who would be able to serve justice and apply punishments with sufficient disinterest. The even more disabling critique of retributive justice, however, comes from the novel's most intriguing interpersonal logic, in which all actions, including acts of retribution themselves, are rigorously scrutinized in terms of their utilitarian value. It is this capacious and agglomerative assessment on behalf of utility, I think, that most clearly aligns the narrative form of *Caleb Williams* with an attempt to imagine and account for the interanimating parts of a social whole. But what makes Godwin's novel especially interesting for us in our account of the history of the Romantic novel is that this work conspicuously demonstrates both the power and the fragility or uncertainty of the very utilitarian assessments that are freighted with a critical potential.

First, then, as critics have so frequently pointed out, the novel routinely portrays problems within a system of retributive justice: a system in which those with the greatest access to wealth and power are able to manipulate the apparatuses of detection, trial, and punishment. Falkland falsely accuses Caleb of stealing from him; he arranges to have evidence for his supposed theft hidden in his trunk; he easily rigs Caleb's trial; he has him thrown in the most miserable of prisons. This only begins the series of sufferings that Caleb endures as Falkland turns the entire nation into a prison in which all people know of his supposed crimes and punish or exclude him accordingly. Early on in his series of struggles, Caleb fears that Falkland could easily kill him and still live with "the applause of his species" (Godwin 1988: 157).

The private control of public justice, a common target for reformers of the day like Samuel Romilly, Bentham, and Godwin himself, in fact abounds in the novel. Tyrrel has no trouble jailing his niece for contradicting his plans to marry her off to his accomplice Grimes; while saving Hawkins from the tyranny of one landlord, he easily manipulates the law to avenge Hawkins, who will not allow his son to be taken into service with him. After dismissing him from his job as bailiff, flooding his crops, and poisoning his livestock, Tyrrel uses every legal expedient to impede Hawkins's search for redress. Indeed, we are told that Tyrrel merely expects the law to serve his own interests: "it would," he argues,

> be the disgrace of a civilized country if a gentleman when insolently attacked in law by the scum of the earth, could not convert the cause into a question of the longest purse, and stick in the skirts of his adversary till he had reduced him to beggary.
>
> (Godwin 1988: 77)

The actions of Falkland and his adversary repeatedly and collectively demonstrate the assertion, as Caleb says, that "wealth and despotism easily know how to engage those laws as the coadjutors of their oppression, which were perhaps first intended (witless and miserable precaution!) for the safeguards of the poor" (Godwin 1988: 75). And the exposure of these actions accompanies a whole range of other implicit criticisms of retributive justice, which have been carefully noted by many critics of the novel (Bailey 2010; Scheuermann 1985: 143–68). The informality of trials in which landowners dispense justice in a practice inherited from the Middle Ages, and the infrequency of courts of assize for appeals, are a common target in the novel. I will have more to say as well about the state of prisons in a moment, since it occupies a disproportionately large section of the narrative and involves complicated layers of attention in Caleb's account. But for now, I simply want to observe that the problem so rigorously identified in the novel's pages at least seems to hold out the tempting possibility that power relations might be equalized so that a more just system of rewards and punishments could be achieved. How might things have turned out differently, we might ask, if an indifferent third party had been involved in order to organize more properly a system of detection and prosecution? What would be the result of a more systematic approach to justice – that is, if those with wealth and power were not able to turn it to their advantage, and if law could be used to serve those for whom, according to the words in the passage cited above, it was first intended?

Questions like these have seemed to make a certain kind of sense to many interpreters of the novel who have tended to analyze it in terms of its more optimistic, revolutionary, or radical messages. Marilyn Butler declares that the novel is "about hierarchy" and what it would take to equalize it (Butler 1995: 355); Scheuermann likewise emphasizes the "mistaken" social codes that Godwin analyzes and criticizes (Scheuermann 1985: 151); Andrew Stauffer traces out the affective implications of tyranny in his reading of "anger" in the novel (Stauffer 2005: 89–109): all of these readings and so many others have a way of looking at the novel's problems as at least an indirect suggestion for a rational, reasonable, and just solution to them. But even while Butler admits that the non-hierarchical system she believes the novel recommends would require some "scaling down of hope" (Butler 1995: 358), the general tendency among these critics is to blur the very delicate ways in which Godwin outlines, explores, and limits the possibilities of correcting the mechanism of justice in the novel.

The very idea of equalizing these relations and setting up a more fair system of rewards and punishments, it turns out, seems deeply problematic because every attempt to achieve a fairer form of retributive justice appears to be only a thin disguise for personal vengeance. When Falkland apes the language of penal reform by declaring "I will never lend my assistance to the reforming of mankind by axes and gibbets" (Godwin 1988: 182), we see that this is only a disguise for Falkland's preference, in the very same passage, for the preservation of his "honor" and thus eventually for his vengeful pursuit of Caleb. Caleb does not fare any better in the reader's eyes. His narrative is said to disclose "plain and unadulterated tale" (334) and a truth that will serve "justice on us both," on Falkland and Caleb (325). But Falkland's appearance before the magistrate at the novel's conclusion is very much a product of Caleb's vengeance. Caleb's aim, after all, is to "crush my seemingly omnipotent foe" (325); the outcome of the trial appears to be the triumph of Caleb's physical strength, will, and sudden advantage over his oppressor. He has "conquered" Falkland, who submits to the "vengeance of the law" (335). In fact, it turns out that almost every opposition that Caleb expresses to Falkland's power is a disturbing repetition of it. And thus there is very little to suggest that there would be any resource for achieving the law's original intent of helping the less fortunate, since Caleb's use of the law at the end of the novel implies that its implementation merely repeats rather than corrects injury.

There is an even more disabling element that makes any attempt to achieve retributive justice look completely unjust. This is because retribution in general attempts to correct injuries that have already been corrected, or it perpetrates more injuries in the process, or both. We are given clues about this dilemma early in the narrative. Before Caleb even knows of Falkland's crime, he sees him groaning in his "closet" with "intolerable anguish" (9); Collins confirms later that he is "inconsolable," that his "sufferings" are "intolerable" (109). Falkland continues to speak in the same terms later: his very attempt to defend himself against detection, prosecution, and punishment is "harrowing and intolerable," the very memory of events leads him, he says, to "despise myself" (142). The point here is that Falkland, in advance of any trial or punishment, is already punishing himself for the crime, and – as Collins says – he "seems to figure to himself by turns every sort of persecution and alarm" (109). Before Caleb's intervention, in other words, Falkland actually seems already reformed from having suffered the very punishment that Caleb might seek to impose.

If punishment seems excessive, redundant, or nearly pointless in relation to the actual conditions that it supposedly addresses, it also appears to set in motion an entire set of processes blinded to their effects. In a sense, Caleb's inflamed "curiosity" (11) about Falkland's criminal actions appears to be an invasion of Falkland's "privacies" (10), as Falkland himself angrily puts it. But it is also quite clearly the case that Caleb's curiosity about Falkland's past – his desire to do "justice" by setting the record straight "in spite of the false colours that may for a time obscure it" (123), is itself a kind of action, so that even what appears to be contained within the realm of knowledge looks strangely injurious. This isn't just because Caleb intrudes in Falkland's personal space, although this is certainly relevant. It is rather because Caleb's curiosity appears to inflict further wounding on an already wounded man. Even when Falkland finally admits his crime to Caleb (after seeing him searching through his trunk), Caleb views the confession not merely as an exposure of the truth but as an injury to Falkland which he immediately regrets: his "soul" yearns for Falkland's "welfare," and begins, at least at first, to be more anxious to excuse than to convict him (143). This, of course, is exactly the fact that Falkland appears to ignore in his pursuit of Caleb: just as Caleb's search for justice appears excessive and injurious, so too does Falkland's retributive action against Caleb. Caleb is already reformed and repentant before Falkland pursues him, while that pursuit produces effects that are injurious even (or especially) to Falkland himself.

The tendency to reframe retributive justice in terms of its larger patterns of effects turns out to be a dominant mode of reasoning in the novel. It characterizes the entire struggle between Falkland and Caleb, in which Falkland's attempt to preserve his honor and Caleb's attempt to uphold the truth seem on both sides to involve a series of actions that only imagine themselves to be disconnected from prior causes and subsequent effects. At the same time, they repeatedly appear – from the novel's analysis of their utility – to have either no value or a purely negative and destructive one.

This aspect of the novel's structure is perhaps nowhere more in evidence than in the prison episode itself, where Caleb's narration allows retributive and utilitarian logics to play off each other. On the one hand, Caleb appreciates how the prison might be organized differently and how people are unfairly punished for their crimes: this is completely consistent with a certain kind of modification of retributive penality popularized by reformers of the period like Cesare Beccaria who argued against cruelty in punishment primarily because it detracted from the sense of the law as a coherent "system" (Beccaria 1986: 47). Godwin's footnotes, moreover, acknowledge the influence of John Howard, whose study of the structure and management of prisons is clearly an influence throughout this episode (Howard 1777). Caleb remarks, in keeping with these accounts, on the indifferently cruel punishment of the innocent and the guilty (186); "three fourths" of those committed to prison are those without evidence "sufficient to convict" (189). Those imprisoned are subjected to a physical environment filled with "squalidness and filth," "dirt," and "putridity and infection" (184). Anyone who would believe that England is without "torture," Caleb tells us, need only look at their own prisons to see "misery" that is even greater than the cruelty of "whips and racks" because of its arbitrariness, chaos, and prolonged "melancholy" (187). Anyone who would think that there is no "Bastille" in England is an "ignorant fool" who need only "visit the scenes of our prisons" to have their national prejudices overturned by scenes of filth, misery, and tyranny (188).

In many ways, then, Caleb's comments on imprisonment resonate with an enlightenment quest to fit punishments to crimes, a project that is attributed to gathering sufficient "information and discernment" to correct the current system of abuses (189). At a particularly grim moment, he even wishes that he could be a condemned man on a scaffold, since at least in that case the nature of his "penalty" would be clear (151). But at other compelling moments in Caleb's account, he openly suggests that the problem with punishment is not simply with its lack of clarity and proportion but with its inutility. Like Falkland and like Caleb, the prisoners are punished for little or no purpose: they think of the past with "insupportable repentance" and each man would be "contented to give his right hand to have again the choice of that peace and liberty which he had unthinkingly borrowed away" (187). The point of course is not that it would make sense to have a thief give away the hand that had once been used to commit a crime, but that the prison redundantly punishes those whose "insupportable repentance" is sufficient to make them feel as if they would do so. Their resignation is a sign of their reform.

The parallels here between Falkland, Caleb, and the prisoners should be more or less obvious at this point. All are being punished for crimes for which they are already remorseful; punishment is less a corrective than a further injury after the correction has already been achieved. It is thus more conspicuous as an incitement rather than a corrective to further "vice" and injury. And Caleb reflects in these terms when his imprisonment in fact encourages his attempts to escape through subterfuge: "in these proceedings it is easy to trace the vice and duplicity that must be expected to grow out of injustice" (201).

Once Caleb does in fact escape and falls into the hands of robbers, the utilitarian critique of retributive penality continues. The trade of the robbers was "terror," he muses, but it is only the vengefulness of the law that keeps them from allowing impulses of "benevolence and kindness" from winning out over more vicious ones (227). Indeed, in one of the novel's most coherent moments of utilitarian speculation, Caleb opines a moment later that "a more just political system" would consider mankind less in terms of good or evil actions that are rewarded or punished, and more in terms of a generalized "energy": such a system "would possess the means of extracting from it . . . its beneficial qualities, instead of consigning it, as now, to indiscriminate destruction" (227). In the current system, he goes on to say, we act like a "chemist who should reject the finest ore, and employ none but what was sufficiently debased to fit it immediately for the vilest uses" (227). Versions of the point are made consistently during this episode with the robbers as Caleb takes note of the benevolence of Raymond and the "uncommon energy, ingenuity, and fortitude" of the criminals with whom he associates, all of whom have qualities or traits that are "thrown away upon purposes diametrically at war with the first interests of human society" (231, 235).

If we skip ahead to the end of the novel, we can see how the critical vantage point on retributive justice informs the events that bring the narrative to a tragic close. Godwin's unpublished manuscript ending for the novel, now published alongside it as an appendix in today's editions, perhaps too easily resolves into a problem with retributive justice. In that version, Caleb is unsuccessful at prosecuting Falkland, who denies his crimes while asserting his uniformly "benevolent and honourable" character (341). His frustration and incarceration lead him to madness. But the published ending more clearly connects to the tensions that I have been describing, between the demand for retributive justice and the conflicting "energy" that precipitates from retributive action. Once brought before the magistrate at the end of the novel's third volume, Falkland admits his guilt for his crime, but he dies three days later before he can receive any punishment for it. The complication in the novel's ending is not only that Caleb now understands himself to be Falkland's murderer. Indeed this is true and makes a certain amount of sense, since the operations of law have partly been subject to his own agency and intervention – he is "author of this hateful scene" [330]. Beyond this, we can see that the operations of conviction and punishment are completely extraneous – Caleb remarks that Falkland is on the verge of death before the trial (329), and Falkland avers that he is suffering "death and infamy" before he receives his sentence (336). Still more, punishment continues to exert harms against its agents (and of course this is perfectly compatible not only with Godwin's views but with a host of writings on capital punishment up into our own day, in which any participation in killing continues to inflict psychological damage). Caleb, that is, continues to feel a penalty for penalty – the penalty of being "truly miserable" that is not calculated into the retributive penalty by which Falkland is convicted (336). We might say that the published ending of the novel perfectly aligns narrative form with a utilitarian account of retribution's terrible fallout.

The manner in which the novel accounts for the inutility – the persistence of pain, torture, and death – following from retributive action, and the way that it imagines some other way of harnessing the "energy" of individuals and communities, might be understood as a kind of biopolitical imperative in the novel, whereby retributive actions get to be ironically recaptured in terms of their consequent effects. On the one hand, what appears biopolitical in the novel is reinforced by the vocabulary of the scientific legislator: Caleb appears to be thinking of a more perfect government, in the passages I quoted earlier, either as a chemist working with elements or a physicist working with energy. On the other hand, however, the logic directs our attention not merely to the physical functions of the given personal body, social body, or natural world. Instead, Godwin's text seems to be pointing to the imaginative, coordinating functions of the utilitarian legislator: functions that Stephen Engelmann has discussed to great effect in his book *Imagining Interest in Political Thought* (Engelmann 2003).

The fact that there is no coherent biopolitical regime in the novel – the fact that there is no utilitarian legislator but only a narrative declaration about the "first interest" of society and "a more just political system" – begins to gesture toward yet another complicating feature of it. As important as these utilitarian modes of assessment may be, Godwin troubles the very sense of aggregation that seems to be implied by utilitarian calculations of harms and benefits.

It is worth at least a brief note here that Godwin's *Enquiry Concerning Political Justice* seems to invite some unsettling of utilitarian assessments. To be sure, it specifies in no uncertain terms that justice is to be understood in terms of utility, and in this sense we could readily see how *Caleb Williams* might be taken to demonstrate this mode of utilitarian assessment in fictional form. At the same time, however, the text's consistent opposition to oath- and test-taking, as well as other forced forms of agreement, makes it clear that utility would be impossible to enforce as a social norm. Justice is utility, but no one can be relied upon to agree upon, much less enforce, exactly what utility is. Of course, Godwin was vilified during his own time and in ours for his few examples of utilitarian calculation, most notably when he recommended that we might save Fénelon from a fire before saving his valet (Godwin 1976: 169–71), prompting Charles Lamb to claim that Godwin set him up as "council for Archbishop Fénelon versus my own mother" (Lamb 1935: 684). But the trouble excited by the example is exactly what should interest us in the context of the novel.

It turns out that *Caleb Williams*, rather than providing a fictional account of the problem of retribution, or a fictional account of the utilitarian solution to that problem, dramatizes the difficulties that attend this apparent solution. The novel, rather than providing an account of utility, gives us a picture of what it might be like to envision a conversation or argument about utility. Perhaps at the conclusion, we might be inclined to take Caleb's claims about his own state of mind – his continued penalty, his continued misery – more or less at face value, although students who approach the novel when I have taught it have been suspicious even of the last statements and suspect him of overdramatizing. This is only the beginning of the problems we encounter. For if the novel seriously questions the justice of retributive justice, it doggedly questions the accuracy of a utilitarian legislator who might claim to get beyond retributive logics by sorting out the social value of actions, thereby making appropriate assessments and recommendations. This is because Godwin keeps setting up occasions in which pleasures and pains are claimed and then disputed. Perhaps the most obvious cases in which this can be observed occur in late portions of the novel, when whole communities of people appear to have secured themselves against Caleb, whom they believe to be a dangerous individual based upon entirely mistaken information. The fact that Caleb has been unjustly accused should not distract us from the fact that those who appear most suspicious of Caleb appear merely to be protecting themselves and honoring the word of someone they believe to be acting in their best interest. The problem, in other words, is not that a person is excluded but that the exclusion is based upon imperfect information that has led to a mistake about who is dangerous and who isn't.

Such instances hold open at least the glimmer of a possibility that more perfect information could lead to better judgments in line with the enlightenment thinking in the novel that I have already talked about. There are less obvious and more troubling instances, however, of the novel's unsettling of utilitarian assessments. In the narrative that Collins conveys about Falkland's early career, Falkland's chivalrous impulses are described as decidedly benevolent ones aimed at producing collective happiness. This may appear to work nicely enough when Falkland gets himself out of an uncomfortable scrape with Count Malvesi and his fiancée, Lucretia. Although Lucretia and Falkland appear to be engaging in some flirtation and the count challenges him to a duel, Falkland defuses the situation in order to procure happiness for all. But the fact that Falkland clearly has the upper hand in that situation, and clearly underlines his benevolence with menace, connects to a series of moments in the novel in which Falkland's beneficial actions seem to be violent, menacing, and exclusionary. The "justice" at this moment is inseparable from the justice in another moment when Falkland saves victims of a fire (including Emily Melville) by tearing down a house, leaving all "astonished" at his "destruction" of property, even while he acts in service of the community as a whole (45–7).

What seems to be happening here is not merely that Falkland's impulses toward benevolence are actually aristocratic, although that is certainly the case. Godwin instead seems to be getting at something even more troubling about the logic of utilitarian reform, and the problems with it punctuate the narrative. When Falkland wants to make peace with Tyrrel in order to secure mutual "happiness" and a life full of "tranquility and enjoyment" (31), Tyrrel dissents from these terms precisely because Falkland's views of happiness, which have gained the upper hand in the community, are so discrepant from his own, to such an extent that Falkland "poisons all my pleasures" (33). The fact that Falkland is identified in this dispute not as an aristocrat but as "pragmatical" and caring only about "consequences" – that is, as a utilitarian – is truly fascinating and points to the way that his pragmatical search for collective good is both consistent with the fervent dreams for political justice in the novel even as they are radically compromised elsewhere in its pages (33).

And there are further instances. When the poet Clare dies, he insists that it is up to people like Falkland to promote "general welfare," which is the "great business of the universe" (36). But the entire scenario surrounding the poet and his death from a "malignant distemper" – a poet declared to be "more than mortal" and beloved by all for his wit, benevolence, and goodness (34) – is fraught with complication. There is more than a bit of wicked humor in the fact that the commitment to general welfare is consistent with his particular death, as if he falls victim to his own doctrines. And when he says that welfare is the task of "younger strengths, such as you" (36) – meaning Falkland – the belief that a new generation could agree on what is best for collective welfare, and that this welfare could be guided (as Clare also suggests) by maxims of "justice and reason" (37), turns out to look more than slightly flawed. And this flaw is only further accentuated by Falkland's own belief in Clare's own "usefulness" and in his ability to have "guided the moral world" (38); Tyrrel, after all, repeatedly shows himself to be immune to his guidance and indifferent to his instruction.

It is not the case that Tyrrel is arguing against the discourse of utility in the novel, however. He seems instead to be adhering to his own version of it which does not coincide with that of others. In his discussion with his rival landlord Underwood, who has tyrannized Hawkins for voting in elections against his wishes, Tyrell in fact agrees with him in his commitment to the "public good," but public good requires conformity and an opposition to "insolence" and insubordination (71). Even while Tyrrel has been victimized by Falkland's "pragmatical" approach to utility, he imposes his own pragmatical utility on others: he claims to want to help Hawkins's son by giving him "lucrative employment in his service" (72), thus ensuring his "future welfare"; but Hawkins declares that his son is "in many ways useful to him" at home (74). And thus the contention between Tyrrel and Hawkins arises precisely around the issues of utility that divide Tyrrel from Falkland.

We are now in a position to say something about one of the peculiar features of the novel, which is that third-person free indirect discourse emerges in first-person narratives as if one could be traded off for another. Much of the history of Falkland's relations with Tyrrel is conveyed by Collins, but the narrative "drop[s]" the "person of Collins" so that Caleb himself becomes "the historian of our patron," which is in turn bolstered by "information which I afterwards received from other quarters," and this information is further supplemented by "certain memorandums I made at the time" (11, 111). This practice shifts toward the end of the narrative about Falkland back to the "words of Mr. Collins" (100). Caleb's strenuous assurances of "fidelity" to the words of Collins is unsettled by the admission that the narrator cannot "warrant the authenticity" of the very narration that he is telling (111). In other words, the narrative insists on the substitutability of Caleb's words for Collins's, and the substitutability of both for an even still wider set of judgments gleaned from "other quarters" or "memorandums." There is a clear insistence here on the idea of a metaphorical relationship between subjects, and in turn their synecdochic relation to a social whole, but at the same time the narrative draws attention to the problematic "authenticity" of that project. The narrative form is thus inseparable from the collectivizing impulses behind utilitarian assessments, but its unsteady wavering between third- and first-person narration connects it to the troubling of those judgments throughout the novel.

Now that we can see this connection between the novel's form and its political positioning, moreover, there are significant adjustments that we can make to two more dominant modes of reading it. John Bender, in an account that has influenced a range of other critics, has viewed the novel in terms of its coherent representation of social discipline on the model of Foucault's Panopticon (Bender 2012: 154–82). Critics like Tilottama Rajan have viewed it as far less unified (Rajan 2010); Emily Anderson takes it to be a narrative about the "multiplicity of narratives," with its contradictions forbidding the discursive coherence that Bender and others (such as Clifford Siskin) have attributed to the novel (Anderson 2009: 112; Siskin 2001). My own view is that what is social about *Caleb Williams* is not its internalized discipline, and not even what Robert Kaufman has understood as its bid for sympathy opposed to despotism (Kaufman 1997) but its commitment to a mode of utilitarian assessment of collective "interest" and "energy" which it simultaneously places under the pressure of conflict. Godwin's point is not to disable those judgments or to disable the project of finding "a more just political system" that depends upon them (and thus I disagree also with Rajan's and Anderson's views). That is, I think that we are supposed to be taking Caleb seriously when he comments on the uselessness of conventional modes of punishment and a better way of imagining society. But at the same time that we take him and his statements seriously, we are led to acknowledge their fragility. We are led to accept the inevitability, indeed the desirability, of contesting those utilitarian assessments with argument and dissent. We are also led to account for the way that those assessments leave pain and tragedy in their wake.

Works cited

Anderson, Emily. (2009) "'I Will Unfold a Tale!': Narrative, Epistemology, and *Caleb Williams*," *Eighteenth-Century Fiction* 22: 99–114.

Armstrong, Nancy. (2005) *How Novels Think: The Limits of Individualism, 1719–1900*, New York: Columbia University Press.

Austen, Jane. (2002) *Sense and Sensibility*, ed. Claudia L. Johnson, New York: W.W. Norton.

Bailey, Quentin. (2010) "'Extraordinary and Dangerous Powers': Prison, Police, and Literature in Godwin's *Caleb Williams*," *Eighteenth-Century Fiction* 22: 525–48.

Beccaria, Cesare. (1986) *On Crimes and Punishments*, trans. David Young, Indianapolis: Hackett.

Bender, John. (2012) *Ends of Enlightenment*, Stanford: Stanford University Press.

Bentham, Jeremy. (1988) *A Fragment on Government*, Cambridge: Cambridge University Press.

Butler, Marilyn. (1995) "Godwin, Burke, and *Caleb Williams*," in Duncan Wu (ed.) *Romanticism: A Critical Reader*, Oxford: Blackwell, 343–58.

Engelmann, Stephen G. (2003) *Imagining Interest in Political Thought: Origins of Economic Rationality*, Durham: Duke University Press.

Godwin, William. (1976) *Enquiry Concerning Political Justice and its Influence on Modern Morals and Happiness*, London: Penguin.

Godwin, William. (1988) *Things as they are, or the Adventures of Caleb Williams*, ed. Maurice Hindle, London: Penguin.

Howard, John. (1777) *The State of the Prisons in England and Wales*, London: T. Cadell.

Kaufman, Robert. (1997) "The Sublime as Super-Genre of the Modern, or Hamlet in Revolution: *Caleb Williams* and his Problems," *Studies in Romanticism* 36: 541–74.

Kelly, Gary. (1989) *English Fiction of the Romantic Period, 1789–1830*, London: Longman.

Lamb, Charles. (1935) *The Complete Works and Letters of Charles Lamb*, New York: Modern Library.

Leavis, F.R. (1963) *The Great Tradition*, New York: New York University Press.

Miller, Peter N. (1994) *Defining the Common Good: Empire, Religion, and Philosophy in Eighteenth-Century Britain*, Cambridge: Cambridge University Press.

Rajan, Tilottama. (2010) "Judging Justice: Godwin's Critique of Judgment in *Caleb Williams* and Other Novels," *The Eighteenth Century: Theory and Interpretation* 51: 341–62.

Scheuermann, Mona. (1985) *Social Protest in the Eighteenth-Century Novel*, Columbus: Ohio State University Press.

Siskin, Clifford. (2001) "Novels and Systems," *Novel: A Forum on Fiction* 34: 202–15.

Stauffer, Andrew M. (2005) *Anger, Revolution, and Romanticism*, Cambridge: Cambridge University Press.

Wollstonecraft, Mary. (1975) *Maria: or, the Wrongs of Woman*, New York: W.W. Norton.

Part 3

Audiences and reading publics

Introduction

Literary criticism has often been nervous about the subject of audiences. W.K. Wimsatt's and M.C. Beardsley's notion of the "affective fallacy" – the fallacy of describing the meaning of a work in terms of its emotional effects on the reader – represents one memorable instance of the kind of aversion that New Critics had when they weighed audience reactions against the formal properties of literature. To read a poem according to the effects on the reader, Wimsatt and Beardsley wrote, would result only in a reading that was either "false" or not based upon those effects at all – because that reading would be focused on "a description of what the meaning of the line [of poetry] *is*" (Wimsatt 1954: 33). Deconstructionist criticism, with its attention to instabilities of language, appeared to continue much of this distance from matters of audiences or readers, to such an extent that reading – as much as it stands at the center of poststructuralist literary theory – was less about any consideration of the reader than about the text's unmasterable indeterminacies.

New historicist criticism in some early instances was not necessarily preoccupied with issues of audiences, but Jerome McGann's work, as Ferguson points out in her essay in the previous section, was indeed attuned to the way that a "context" for a literary work needed to attend not only to circumstances of production but also to those of reception – both the reception at the time of the work's production and during the critic's own present moment. Interest in audiences has continued to grow and attract critical attention. Jon P. Klancher's *The Making of English Reading Audiences, 1790–1832* was an important instance of how historicist commitments continued to move beyond an attempt to specify details of political and institutional situations in order to address a range of important theoretical questions that Romantic literature raises with respect to its relation to a "public" (Klancher 1987). To what extent is literature determined by its reception, and how does literature acknowledge this connection? Do texts have the capacity to discriminate among readers and address specific audiences? How does the literary work's relation to a reading audience connect to a definition of the public in more general terms? Such questions, and the answers that critics have been giving to them, often join literary study to concerns that political theorists such as Nancy Fraser and Jürgen Habermas have had over many years with still larger definitions of the "public" or the "public sphere" (Fraser 1990; Habermas 1994).

A significant piece of the puzzle that moves us toward understanding issues of audience during the Romantic period is the role of literary reviews, which increased in importance with the founding and flourishing of publications such as *Blackwood's, The Quarterly Review*, and the *Edinburgh Review*. The influence of these reviews is documented and studied by historians and critics, including Robert Altick, Marilyn Butler, and Mark

Schoenfield (Altick 1957; Butler 2010; Schoenfield 2009). This context is also important for Lucy Newlyn's selection on "The sense of an audience" from her book *Reading, Writing, and Romanticism: The Anxiety of Reception*. Playing on Harold Bloom's notion of the "anxiety of influence" (discussed in this volume's general introduction), she shows how Romantic writers are anxious not only about past authors who influenced them (as Bloom claimed) but also about their readers – particularly publishing critics who attempted to sway audiences with their judgments. The "politics of reception" she analyzes engage literary writers in both poetry and prose in an array of defensive exercises to protect their own literary authority and the authority of other writers. So combative was the relation between writers and their critics that some authors saw themselves as sacrificial victims to a hostile and even murderous audience.

Newlyn's argument helps to explain a range of statements by writers of the age, like Wordsworth, who – even while supposedly drawing on the popular forms of ballad – nevertheless viewed a politicized "public" with some anxiety, preferring instead to address himself to a far less politically defined "People, philosophically characterized" (Wordsworth 1984: 662). In her analysis, however, Newlyn (modifying claims that Andrew Bennett makes about the lack of interest that women writers took in the reading public [Bennett 1999]) suggests that many women writers of the Romantic period provide a less combative relation to the audience, instead addressing that audience critically yet sympathetically. In the excerpt here from her book *Mothers of the Nation*, Ann Mellor makes a related point about the public in general and about the place of women in it. Her subject is more explicitly the "public sphere" as theorized by Habermas, a sphere of polite public discourse in which discussions of political affairs were dominated by men. Other critics of Romanticism have been interested in this way of analyzing and theorizing the public, including Paul Keen (1999), Paul Magnuson (1998), and Daniel E. White (whose chapter excerpt appears in Part 8). Mellor shows, however, that women were equal participants in this public sphere, and competed with men in it to make their voices heard.

While Mellor's view shows men and women competing for the attention of audiences and thus vying for space within the public sphere, other critics such as Adriana Craciun (Craciun 2005) and Kevin Gilmartin provide yet another view of the audience dynamics at work in the Romantic age – one that is more aggressively inclusive. Gilmartin's essay on Hannah More, later the basis for the second chapter of his book *Writing Against Revolution*, shows how even supposedly conservative writers asserted a "boundless energy" to conscript audiences within the "disciplinary mechanism" of print. And whereas critics like Mellor and even Newlyn wish to see women writers speaking sympathetically to select parts of a public – Mellor sees women addressing other women for the sake of their reform – Gilmartin makes a different claim. He understands this to be an underestimation of the ambitions of a writer like More, who sought to impose "an astonishing range of social, political, and religious controls upon the behavior of men and women alike."

Andrew Franta's new essay shifts attention away from critical conversation that tends to focus on the question of whether literary works do or do not connect with their audiences. He approaches the critical reception of Percy Shelley's work by concentrating at first on the interest many critics like Paul de Man took in irony; Franta's analysis of "ironic self-reflection" in the "Ode to the West Wind," however, does not proceed merely in order to expose the poet's strategy of self-enclosure in order to evade a connection with historical reality (as deconstructionist and historicist critics understood irony to operate). Instead, the "self-reflexivity" enabled by the poem's ironic undercutting of its idealistic assertions indicates one of the most compelling ways in which the poem aims to acknowledge and engage the unpredictability of its reception among present and future audiences. We might see Franta positioned between Newlyn and Gilmartin, then. It is only by ironically troubling the connection between poem and audience that Shelley establishes a novel (but "indirect") form of connection with it.

Works cited

Altick, Robert. (1957) *The English Common Reader: A Social History of the Mass Public, 1800–1900*, Chicago: University of Chicago Press.

Bennett, Andrew. (1999) *Romantic Poets and the Culture of Posterity*, Cambridge: Cambridge University Press.

Butler, Marilyn. (2010) "Culture's Medium: The Role of the Review," in Stuart Curran (ed.) *The Cambridge Companion to British Romanticism*, 2nd ed. Cambridge: Cambridge University Press.

Craciun, Adriana. (2005) *British Women Writers and the French Revolution: Citizens of the World*, New York: Palgrave Macmillan.

Fraser, Nancy. (1990) "Rethinking the Public Sphere: A Contribution to the Critique of Actually Existing Democracy," *Social Text* 25/26: 56–80.

Habermas, Jürgen. (1994) *The Structural Transformation of the Public Sphere: An Inquiry into a Category of Bourgeois Society*, trans. Thomas Burger, Cambridge, MA: MIT Press.

Keen, Paul. (1999) *The Crisis of Literature in the 1790s: Print Culture and the Public Sphere*, Cambridge: Cambridge University Press.

Klancher, Jon. (1987) *The Making of English Reading Audiences, 1790–1832*, Madison: University of Wisconsin Press.

Magnuson, Paul. (1998) *Reading Public Romanticism*, Princeton: Princeton University Press.

Schoenfield, Mark. (2009) *British Periodicals and Romantic Identity: The "Literary Lower Empire,"* New York: Palgrave Macmillan.

Wimsatt, W.K. (1954) *The Verbal Icon: Studies in the Meaning of Poetry*, Louisville: University of Kentucky Press.

Wordsworth, William. (1984) *The Oxford Authors William Wordsworth*, ed. Steven Gill, Oxford: Oxford University Press.

Further reading

Behrendt, Stephen C., ed. (1997) *Romanticism, Radicalism, and the Press*, Detroit: Wayne State University Press.

Bennett, Andrew. (1994) *Keats, Narrative, and Audience: The Posthumous Life of Writing*, Cambridge: Cambridge University Press.

Brantlinger, Patrick. (1998) *The Reading Lesson: The Threat of Mass Literacy in Nineteenth-Century Fiction*, Bloomington: Indiana University Press.

Fairclough, Mary. (2013) *The Romantic Crowd: Sympathy, Controversy, and Print Culture*, Cambridge: Cambridge University Press.

Franta, Andrew. (2007) *Romanticism and the Rise of the Mass Public*, Cambridge: Cambridge University Press.

Gilmartin, Kevin. (1997) *Print Politics: The Press and Radical Opposition in Early Ninteenth-Century England*, Cambridge: Cambridge University Press.

McCann, Andrew. (1999) *Cultural Politics in the 1790s: Literature, Radicalism, and the Public Sphere*, Houndmills: St. Martin's Press.

Rzepka, Charles. (1986) *The Self as Mind: Vision and Identity in Wordsworth, Coleridge, and Keats*, Cambridge, MA: Harvard University Press.

9   The sense of an audience

Lucy Newlyn

[Two opening sections of this chapter review the festering hostility between authors and readers in the late eighteenth century, caused by increasing literacy rates and the growth of literary reviewing.]

I Critics as judges, advocates, and patrons

The survival of poets and critics in the early nineteenth century involved a rather more complex negotiation between public and private spheres of reception than is often remembered. It is the tendency of hindsight to concentrate either on the high points of a writer's rejection or acceptance by the reading-public, or on the more embattled aspects of the relationship between poetry and criticism. Even contemporary accounts can be misleading. Hannah More once complained that:

> Literary patronage is so much *shorn of its beams*, that it can no longer enlighten bodies which are in themselves opake; so much abridged of its power that it cannot force into notice a work which is not able to recommend itself.[1]

But just as literary coteries of a kind survived long after the demise of the coffee-house culture – in the Bluestocking group of which More was herself a member; in families such as the Wordsworths and Coleridges or the Wollstonecraft-Godwin-Shelleys; in groupings such as the 'Lake School' and the 'Cockney School'; and in Dissenting circles like the Warrington Academy – so the traces of a system of patronage were observable in the dependence of writers such as the young Coleridge on private annuities; in the persistence of subscription methods of publication; in various methods of advocacy, whether they took place in public or behind the scenes; in the active promotional role played by influential booksellers; and in the relation between established literary figures and their young protégés.
      [. . .]
   Despite the difficulties to which they sometimes gave rise, the persistence of anachronistic systems of reception was a crucial component in the protective armoury of authorship at this time. Not only did the existence of coteries allow writers to circulate their work before it appeared in print (thus delaying and pre-empting its public reception), it also helped them to establish common aims, intentions, and prejudices; a shared and inevitably exclusive language; and strongly cohesive loyalties. As members of clans, writers were better able to confront what Marilyn Butler calls

the 'dire inveterate partisanship' of the reviewing culture (where, as Peacock puts it, 'The *legatur* of corruption must be stamped upon a work before it can be admitted into fashionable circulation');[2] and to maintain a privacy of address despite emerging into the public domain. It is for this reason that, as Jeffrey Cox has recently argued in respect of Keats, we should consider writers in relation to the immediate circle of colleagues by whom their creativity was sustained, rather than in isolation.[3]

In the absence of patronage proper, favourable critical interventions became increasingly important for ensuring the lasting recognition of writers. Such rites of passage were overseen by public acts of recognition between authors; by the plaudits of reviewing bodies; and by private recommendations between colleagues and friends. In all cases, they could be mutually beneficial to author and critic. Made by a named and recognized writer, such interventions frequently stood out as acts of politesse, solidarity, or proprietorial guardianship. When Anna Barbauld, for instance, allocated eight lines in *Eighteen Hundred and Eleven* to the contemporary dramatist Joanna Baillie – by comparison with a couplet devoted to Shakespeare – she risked being accused of a disproportionate imbalance of praise by her contemporary readers. Doubtless it was one to which she gave careful thought, both as a woman with an interest in promoting women's writing, and as a British writer concerned to warn her readers that London – still considered the thriving centre of European culture it had been in Shakespeare's day – might yet lose its reputation.

[. . .]

Hazlitt was the most powerful writer of his age when it came to anatomizing the politics of reception with a satirical eye. Educated in early life at a Dissenting academy, and therefore debarred from a university education, his stance was that of an embittered outsider to what he called the 'Aristocracy of Letters'. His principled resistance to all forms of patronage derived from his fierce independence, and from a growing resentment towards the privileged institutions from which he was excluded, he felt there was a deep injustice in the affairs of writers, and denounced the practices of puffing and coterie insularity which he saw as discredited anachronisms. Editors he saw as patrons in disguise, borrowing dignity from their situations as arbiters and judges, and increasing their sense of self-importance by abusing the little power they had: 'It is utterly impossible', he lamented, 'to persuade an Editor that he is nobody'.[4]

[. . .]

Whereas the 'man of letters' survived in a form acceptable to polite society, the hack writer was seen as less than nothing:

> Unless an author has an establishment of his own, or is entered on that of some other person, he will hardly be allowed to write English or to spell his own name. To be well-spoken of, he must enlist under some standard; he must belong to some *coterie*. . . . You must commence toad-eater to have your observations attended to; if you are independent, unconnected, you will be regarded as a poor creature.

> (Howe, viii. 211–12)

To Hazlitt's eye, the scurrilous treatment Keats had endured at the hands of *Blackwood's Magazine* was self-evidently the consequence of his cockney origins. The injustice of this treatment came sharply into focus when Keats's abortive career was considered alongside the success of his noble contemporary, Byron. In his essay 'On the Aristocracy of Letters', Hazlitt's anger against this disequity of treatment reaches its pitch. The real butt of his satire is not Byron himself, however, but the spirit of privileged dilettantism for which Byron is a symbolic figurehead:

> Look in, and there, amidst silver services and shining chandeliers, you will see the man of genius at his proper post, picking his teeth and mincing an opinion, sheltered by rank, bowing to wealth – a poet framed, glazed, and hung in a striking light: not a straggling weed, torn and trampled on; not a poor *Kit-run-the-street*, but a powdered beau, a sycophant plant, an exotic reared in a glass-case, hermetically sealed. . . . The poet Keats had not this sort of protection for his person – he lay bare to weather – the serpent stung him, and the poison-tree dropped upon this little western flower: – when the mercenary servile crew approached him, he had no pedigree to show them, no rent-roll to hold out in reversion for their praise: he was not in any great man's train, nor the butt and puppet of a lord.
>
> (Howe, viii. 211)

Hazlitt's prose is full of moments of insight such as this, which reveal the persistence – alongside the Grub Street conditions under which he himself worked – of an outmoded model of gentlemanly authorship. Hazlitt anathematized belletrism of this kind, seeing it as a throwback to an earlier age, when writers were either of independent means or supported by a wealthy patron.

[. . .]

Hazlitt was right in his analysis of the structure and abuse of power. The role of the critic was complicated, at this historical juncture, by being required to fulfil an outmoded role alongside a new one. Criticism rose as patronage fell, yet some of the features of a system of patronage were still discernible in the practices of reviewers, who acquired the status of disinterested judges from their position of anonymity.[5] As a consequence of the realities which lay behind this pretence, the relation between creativity and criticism was in fact a mutual dependency, sometimes collaborative and sometimes competitive, but more often than not a combination of the two.

Consequently, the rhetoric of reviewers reflected a confusion between the roles of judgement and patronage. Summing up the case against Wordsworth's *Poems* (1807) to the 'jury' of the British public, Francis Jeffrey clearly enjoyed his self-arrogated status as the arbiter of public taste: 'Putting ourselves thus upon our country, we certainly look for a verdict against this publication; and have little doubt indeed of the result, upon a fair consideration of the evidence contained in these volumes'.[6] According to Carlyle, Jeffrey 'was always as if speaking to a jury', and Lee Erickson has observed that his 'lawyerly' manner was widely recognized.[7]

[. . .]

In much the same way, the rhetoric used by writers in their dealings with reviewers came to reflect a divided expectation, of sympathy and impartiality, as we see in the letter Byron wrote to Thomas Moore in 1815, attempting to engineer a favourable review for a poet who is represented simultaneously as victim and genius:

> By the way, if C**e [Coleridge] – who is a man of wonderful talent, and in distress, and about to publish two vols. of Poesy and Biography, and who has been worse used by the critics than ever we were – will you, if he comes out, promise me

to review him favourably in the E[dinburgh] R[eview]? Praise him, I think you must, but you will also praise him *well*, – of all things the most difficult. It will be the making of him.[8]

If the advocacy of writers was frequently complicated by private motivations, so there was sometimes a resistance to being publicly acclaimed for personal reasons. When Coleridge included advance praise for *The Prelude* in *Biographia Literaria* as part of a bid to establish Wordsworth's reputation for philosophical poetry, he did so expressly against his friend's own wishes. Wordsworth was wary of receiving praise before it was due, and did not wish *The Prelude* to be retrospectively associated with *Biographia* by this kind of cross-marketing. Nor, one suspects, did he relish the thought that Coleridge might draw sustenance for his criticism from a creative identity that was still in the making – which is how *The Prelude* was regarded until the end of Wordsworth's life. Conversely, Coleridge himself came to regret the way in which 'Christabel' had been systematically promoted by Lord Byron. This behind-the-scenes 'puffing' by a fellow-poet proved ineffectual in the end, and may even have contributed to the reviewers' hostility.

   [. . .]

Whereas anxieties of reception focus in the first instance on the author's ownership, authority, and control of the text he or she has written, they take on a more symbolic significance in the public domain after that text has been circulated in manuscript or published in print, when it becomes subject to political appropriations, themselves reflective of wider struggles for power. [. . .] [T]he friction between two systems – of public judgement and private patronage – sometimes caused a radical split in the reception of a volume, which may be read as paradigmatic of the defensive and embattled culture of the early nineteenth century. The further case of 'poor Keats' has provided a number of recent critics with an instance of the party-political allegiances clearly discernible in acts of critical reception.[9] Interactions of this kind, in which authorial identity was negotiated at the crossing between private and public spheres – or in a sphere where private and political concerns became jumbled – were in all probability widespread. But even where they concerned major canonical authors they are rarely documented, and more often they involved the fortunes of writers whose lasting place in the canon was never secured. Such interactions were, however, the site for successive struggles between authorial and interpretative authority in the Romantic period; and in them we see the ways in which anxieties of reception were reactively produced by the upward mobility of professional criticism.

II Poetry, neglect, and the pursuit of posthumous reputation

Under conditions of dependency on readers who were constructed as hostile others, the question of what constituted the writing-subject's identity became increasingly ambiguous; and a recurrence of the figure of death in the mythology of reception shows that when identity crises were caused by loss of self-esteem, anxieties tended to focus on the threat of extinction. In glamorized images such as those of Chatterton's suicide and Burns's poverty-stricken death, writers found their own worst fears both reflected and sublimated into viable self-exonerating narratives, in which the public's hostility was figurally and causally connected with the poet's demise. These graphic instances of the 'birth of the reader' being at the cost of the 'death of the author' register both the deep hermeneutic anxieties which underlay attitudes to audience at this time, and the defensive strategies which evolved to keep them at bay.

When Wordsworth wrote, in his career-crisis poem, 'Resolution and Independence',

> I thought of Chatterton, the marvellous Boy,
> The sleepless Soul that perished in its pride;
> Of Him who walked in glory and in joy
> Behind his plough, upon the mountain-side
> (ll. 43–6) [10]

The bought into popular myth, at the same time investing it with his own particular brand of wishfulness. Chatterton the temperamental forger, who spent most of his life doing hack work, then killed himself at 17, and Burns, whose drunken debauchery and domestic unhappiness became notorious after the publication of James Currie's *Life*, are here endowed with heroic attributes – made to triumph posthumously over adversity and the public taste for scandal. Fearing that his own talent would go to waste unless he established a successful reputation, that his own private life was open to investigation as theirs had been, and that poverty and death might similarly cut him down in his prime, Wordsworth made these poets into figures of what [Harold] Bloom has called 'capable imagination'. As a corollary to this idealization of creative genius, the public is associatively likened to the leeches whose dwindling numbers are reported by the poet's rustic double, in his turn apotheosized as a kind of surrogate poet. A subliminal connection is made between readers as parasites (sucking the lifeblood out of poets) and readers as a dwindling source of remuneration. Wordsworth here registered how acutely conscious he was of his failure to engage the public's attention as fully as Bloomfield or Burns. Elsewhere it is the largeness, remoteness, and anonymity of the reading-public that overwhelms him; here the increasing scarcity of leeches works as a complex metaphor of his resentful dependence on an audience by whom he was neglected.

[. . .]

In Shelley's *Adonais*, Keats's death is blamed directly on Croker's review of *Endymion*. Andrew Bennett has recently claimed that

> The story has the virtue of a certain dramatic pathos and its apparent implausibility . . . most neatly summed up in . . . Byron's idea of the poet 'snuffed out by an article' in *Don Juan* – is reduced by the suggestion that Keats was already suffering from tuberculosis and the reviews simply weakened his will to live. [11]

Whether or not it contains elements of truth, the story has an extraordinary and enduring potency, as a myth of this particular poet's (feminine) sensitivity to the views of others, and of creativity's vulnerability to criticism. Shelley here successfully packaged Keats's posthumous reception for an audience attuned to the conventions of sensibility, making death at the hands of hostile reviewers the signifier of eternal life at the hands of sympathetic readers. As a piece of defensive marketing, this bore a remarkable resemblance to Keats's own poetic strategies, which involved an emptying out of personality and identity as an inversion of the egotistical sublime. If the poet had 'no identity' – if his genius was characterized by its characterlessness – then perhaps, in this position of impersonality, he could successfully undermine the powerful anonymity of his reviewers.

A complementary myth is to be found in Byron's (masculine) imperviousness to his own popularity. If Keats triumphed over the cult of personality by its negation, Byron's was the opposite course. As John Scott observed in his article on Byron in 'Living Authors' (1821), his unprecedented literary success was almost entirely due to 'adventitious' and 'surreptitious' advantages, 'derived from being considered as too bad for repentance, and too desperate to be pitied'.[12] 'He looks upon [his readers] as sentient existences that are important in his poetic existence', wrote John Wilson, in his review of *Childe Harold*:

> – so that he command their feelings and passions, he cares not for their censure or their praise, – for his fame is more than mere literary fame; and he aims in poetry, like the fallen chief whose image is so often before him, at universal dominion, we had almost said, universal tyranny, over the minds of men.[13]

This view was shared by Hazlitt, who wrote in May 1818, 'Byron would persuade us that the universe itself is not worth his or our notice; and yet he would expect us to be occupied with him';[14] and whose subsequent exposure of Byron in *Table Talk* (1821) focused on the appeal of his class origins to a public eager to claim 'acquaintance with the Lord':

> Is he dull, or does he put off some trashy production on the public? It is not charged to his account, as a deficiency which he must make good at the peril of his admirers. His Lordship is not answerable for the negligence or extravagances of his Muse. He 'bears a charmed reputation, which must not yield' like one of vulgar birth. The Noble Bard is for this reason scarcely vulnerable to the critics. The double barrier of his pretensions baffles their puny, timid efforts.
>
> (Howe, viii. 210)

Hazlitt's judgement of Byron brings into focus some of the animosities (and perhaps envies?) of a writer with stronger allegiances to criticism than to poetry, but with a deep conviction that each is answerable to the other. But it also bears contemporary witness to the successful management of what Jerome Christensen has called 'the literary system of Byronism', which was the collaborative invention of 'a gifted poet, a canny publisher, eager reviewers, and rapt readers', and which worked by selling Byron to the public on the strength of his aristocratic glamour. Furthermore, as Christensen conclusively proves, the commodity 'Lord Byron' was produced *reactively*: first in *English Bards and Scotch Reviewers*, as a belated revenge for Brougham's hostile review of *Hours of Idleness*, and subsequently in *Childe Harold*, where the Byronic persona first appeared. If the first of these poems belonged 'as much to the history of English dueling as to the history of English literature',[15] the third disclosed a subtler mode of counter-attack on hostile reviewers. Constructing 'Lord Byron' first as a persona, and subsequently as an entity indistinguishable from the writing-subject himself, Byron vanished into his charismatic and untouchable disguise, to the delight of his spellbound readers.

The Bloomian category of 'strength' which Christensen resuscitates as the primary characteristic of Byron's self-image is appropriate to the atmosphere of embattled personalities on which the periodical culture of the 1800s thrived: Hazlitt drew on a similar terminology when he referred to 'the defensive and offensive armour of criticism' (Howe, viii. 217), a phrase which updated the courtly language of pugilism used fifty years earlier by Samuel Johnson in *The Rambler*.[16] [. . .] Marlon Ross has shown how metaphors of quest and conquest pervaded critical and poetic discourse at the turn of the eighteenth century.[17] [. . .]

Under these conditions, the language of chivalry had come to seem inadequate to describe the sinister conduct of writers who sold their souls to the periodical press. To John Hamilton Reynolds, reviewers were 'creatures that stab men in the dark' – 'young and enthusiastic spirits are their dearest prey',[18] and John Clare complained, in a letter of 1821, 'is the cold hearted butchers of annonymous Critics to (blast a) cut up everything that escapes their bribery or thinks contrary to them is polotics [sic] to rule genius'.[19] The demonization of reviewers by authors – and particularly by poets – was in some cases well founded; but paranoia was so widespread as to appear almost indiscriminate; and for this reason it became a source of parody. James Hogg, in *The Poetic Mirror, or Living Bards of Britain* (1816), was one of a sequence of writers who made fun of Wordsworth as an over-anxious poet, his eye always on the critics, whose most fervent hope was that he might survive their scorn. In the closing lines of 'The Flying Taylor', Wordsworth is overheard prophesying his immortality. He speaks with the complacent but anxious tone of solemnity which, to an audience sceptical of his objectives, seemed the hallmark of his Prefaces and notes:

> eternally my name
> Shall last on earth, conspicuous like a star
> 'Mid that bright galaxy of favour'd spirits,
> Who, laugh'd at constantly, whene'er they publish'd,
> Survived the impotent scorn of base Reviews,
> Monthly or Quarterly, or that accursed
> Journal, the Edinburgh Review, that lives
> On tears, and sighs, and groans, and brains, and blood.[20]

In an environment of attack and counter-attack, survival was the key enterprise, but not everyone survived, and martyrdom became a recurrent defensive figure in a reception mythology designed to keep the professional reviewers at bay. In an anonymous letter published in the *Alfred*, J.H. Reynolds wrote that 'The Monthly Reviewers . . . endeavoured . . . to crush the rising heart of young Kirk White; and indeed they in part generated that melancholy which ultimately destroyed him.'[21] Susan Wolfson observes that 'the role-call of martyrs had become so routine by the mid-1830s that the *Metropolitan* could invoke it ritualistically, unquestioningly associating Keats with Shelley's mythology'.[22]

[. . .]

Just as the language of victimization was applied to authors who received critical treatment in the press, so vicarious anxieties were frequently expressed by means of interventions on behalf of an author who was seen to be underrated or wilfully marginalized. The hagiographical prefaces and notes which Mary Shelley as editor attached to Shelley's poetry were a retrospective attempt to put the record straight – to show that, 'Shelley did not expect sympathy and approbation from the public; but the want of it took away a portion of the ardour that ought to have sustained him while writing.'[23] In recuperating his reputation for posterity, Mary echoed her husband's stance of proud detachment, while at the same time suggesting the extent to which this very pride was a defence against the cruelty of critics.[24]

[. . .]

John Wilson detected an underlying hypocrisy in this mythology of victimization. In an essay entitled 'An Hour's Talk about Poetry' (first published in *Blackwood's Edinburgh Magazine* in October 1831, then later revised and enlarged for *The Recreations of Christopher North* in 1842), he brought this sharply into focus by contrasting a double standard in the attitudes of English readers towards two figures, Bloomfield and Burns. Both these writers were 'self-taught' poets whose 'native wood-notes wild' earned them the label of genius, and whose popularity brought them a legendary status in their own lifetimes. As Wilson observed, English readers were much readier to sentimentalize Burns as a figure who suffered neglect at the hands of his readers than they were to take responsibility for Bloomfield, a genius of comparable status their own soil had produced. The reception of Burns, in the wake of Currie's *Life*, provoked loyal and impassioned defence; but Bloomfield 'dropt into the grave with no other lament we ever heard of but a few copies of poorish verses in some of the Annuals, and seldom or never does one hear a whisper of his name'.[25] Wilson was not slow to expose the mythology of victimization as a species of scapegoating. There was a veneer of patronizing sentimentality, he implied, which distanced the reader from the grim realities of a poet's occupation: 'Let England then leave Scotland to her shame about Burns; and, thinking of her own treatment of Bloomfield, cover her own face with both her hands, and confess that it was pitiful.'[26] The inwardness and sophistication of Wilson's rhetoric in this essay serves as a reminder of how well developed the mythology of victimization had become by the 1830s. It could be used to reflect ironically on the reading-habits of a nation determined to construct the poet as a figure on the margins of society, but blind to the implications of that construction.

[. . .]

III The threat of modernity: reading, consumption, and overpopulation

Anxiety, which thrives in incestuous conditions, is given a particular inflection by the competitive–collaborative relationship between poets, reviewers, and critics. But its figurative expressions tend to repeat themselves from context to context, transcending specific circumstances even as they powerfully articulate them. These repetitions help to explain the uncanny way in which Romantic texts sound 'modern' – sound, indeed, as if they speak prophetically of the fate of reading in the 1990s – as when Coleridge complains that the enormous stimulant power of events makes the desire to be stimulated almost an appetite; or when he condemns 'general and indiscriminate reading', and 'the habit consequently induced of requiring instantaneous intelligibility'.[27] Such accusations have an all-too-familiar resonance in our multimedia culture, where we are assaulted at every level by unassimilable information. Similarly, De Quincey's 'On the Poetry of Pope', haunted as it is by the twin fears of multiplication and repetition, strikes a chord in our electronic age. The book, some believe, is rapidly being replaced, but fear of an equivalent reduplication has persisted in relation to electronic text, on a scale that De Quincey almost anticipated:

As books multiply to an unmanageable excess, selection becomes more and more a necessity for readers, and the power of selection more and more a desperate problem for the busy part of readers. The possibility of selecting wisely is becoming continually more hopeless as the necessity for selection is becoming continually more pressing. Exactly as the growing weight of books overlays and stifles the power of comparison, *pari passu* is the call for comparison the more clamorous.[28]

This awareness of 'information overload' – of an incommensurability between the amount of data received and the ability to process it – is recognizable as a species of what Kant called the 'mathematical sublime', which involves an overwhelming sense of awe in relation to a magnitude that cannot be comprehended. In one sense, the sublime might be said aesthetically to frame the complex Romantic phenomenon I am terming the 'anxiety of reception'.

Wherever the expansion of reading-matter is at issue, in late eighteenth- and early nineteenth-century discourse, it is figured as having the power to annihilate human capacities of retention and organization. As early as 1795 – three years, that is, before the idea of exponential growth took on political topicality, with the publication of Malthus's *Essay on Population* – Isaac D'Israeli wrote the following passage:

When I reflect that every literary journal consists of 50 or 60 publications, and that of these, 5 or 6 at least are capital performances, and the greater part not contemptible, when I take the pen and attempt to calculate, by these given sums, the number of volumes which the next century must infallibly produce, my feeble faculties wander in a perplexed series, and as I lose myself among billions, trillions, and quartillions, I am obliged to lay down my pen, and stop at infinity.[29]

It was a cry of alarm that periodical essayists over the next century were to echo; and in the context of debates about whether literary standards were improving or on the decline it acquired a note of increasing urgency. [. . .] The insistence with which the question of numbers and standards was raised gave a particularly demographic flavour to nineteenth-century discussions of canon-formation and the poetics of survival.

Harold Bloom has recently claimed in *The Western Canon* that 'Overpopulation, Malthusian repletion, is the authentic context for canonical anxieties'.[30] There is much that bears this out in the metaphorical language that nineteenth-century writers used to figure the reader and the reading-public. It is a discourse characterized by doom-laden prophecy with respect to numerical expansion, and by an almost hysterical sense of unstoppability: 'There never was an age so prolific of popular poetry as that in which we now live', Jeffrey claimed;

and as wealth, population, and education extend, the produce is likely to go on increasing. . . . if we continue to write and rhyme at the present rate for 200 years longer, there must be some new art of short-hand reading invented – or all reading will be given up in despair.[31]

[. . .]

There was a widespread and explicit association of excessive writing with women whose reproductive capacities were seen to be out of control. 'Who are those ever multiplying authors, that with unparalleled fecundity are overstocking the world with their quick-succeeding progeny?', wrote Hannah More, in her *Strictures on the Modern System of Female Education* (1799): 'They are novel-writers; the easiness of whose production is at once the cause of their own fruitfulness, and of the almost infinitely numerous race of imitators to whom they give birth.'[32] The novel, in particular, became the focus for fears of reduplication, in which biological metaphors frequently recurred: 'The press daily teems with these publications which are the trash of the circulating libraries', wrote Burton, in his *Lecture on Female Education and Manners*: 'A perusal of them in rapid succession is in fact a misemployment of time; as, in most novels there is a similarity in the incidents and characters; and these perhaps are unnatural.'[33]

Even Mary Wollstonecraft, a talented novelist herself, shared with her contemporaries an intense disenchantment with the contemporary novel: 'From reading to writing novels the transition is very easy', she complained, in an early and characteristically acerbic review: 'and the ladies, of course, take care to supply the circulating libraries with ever varying still the same productions. "Of making many books there is no end," when talents and knowledge are out of the question.'[34] Typical of this cultural moment was Wollstonecraft's fear that readers were usurping the place of writers, rather than improving their capacity to reflect on what they read.

[. . .]

If the excessive multiplication of literature was metonymically connected with fear of overpopulation, the anonymity of audiences (and of reviewers) was a figurative displacement for more troubling anxieties about loss of self-identity consequent on industrial expansion and the overcrowding of England's great cities.

[. . .]

In addition, Romantic writers experienced Anglocentric fears that the infiltration of foreign literary tastes into national culture might threaten identity on a larger and more pervasive scale. These fears were most famously brought together, in a loosely associative cluster of prejudices, in a passage from the Preface to *Lyrical Ballads* (1800) which would not be out of place in Malthus's 'Essay on Population'. Complaining that 'a multitude of causes, unknown to former times, are now acting with combined force to blunt the mind, and, unfitting it for all voluntary exertion, to reduce it to a state of almost savage torpor', Wordsworth identified the foremost of these as 'the great national events which are daily taking place, and the encreasing accumulation of men in cities, where the uniformity of their occupations produces a craving for extraordinary incident which the rapid communication of intelligence hourly gratifies'. Setting the tone for a subsequent (high Romantic) dissociation of genius from urban conditions, Wordsworth posited a connection between the overcrowding of cities, poverty of intellect, and addiction to stimulants. He also discovered a malignant influence in the 'frantic novels, sickly and stupid German Tragedies, and deluges of idle and extravagant stories in verse' which, he asserted, were driving 'the invaluable works of our elder writers' into neglect.[35] The fears of overpopulation and overstimulation which he associated with contemporary living conditions were thus exacerbated by a xenophobic anxiety with respect to continental literature, which threatened to flood and drown England's treasured national heritage.

Later in the century, De Quincey related an incident in his *Suspiria De Profundis* which gives a special twist to the twin fears of anonymity and overpopulation, amalgamated in a childhood fantasy of literature's endless self-reduplication. Typically, as well as appropriately, the episode is itself prolix – running to six or seven pages, and incorporating a number of digressions and overlapping time-segments to narrate events whose cumulative and associative significance is only gradually disclosed.[36] But the salient narrative features are as follows: when quite a young child, De Quincey claims to have experienced a 'craving' for the 'gratification' supplied by books, much as he would later be addicted to opium. This craving led to his contracting a debt with his local bookseller – a debt which caused him a disproportionate degree of guilt and dread because he had agreed to purchase two books (a History of Great Britain and a History of Navigation), the first of which would appear in sixty or eighty parts, the second in an unspecified number of volumes. He was thus contracted (as he saw it) to infinity:

> Now, when I considered with myself what a huge thing the sea was, and that so many thousands of captains, commodores, admirals, were eternally running up and down it, and scoring lines upon its face so rankly, that in some of the main 'streets' and 'squares' (as one might call them) their tracks would blend into one undistinguishable blot, – I began to fear that such a work tended to infinity. What was little England to the universal sea?
>
> (p. 131)

De Quincey figures his own humiliation in the face of an overwhelming magnitude of yet-to-be-discovered knowledge by way of analogy with England's minuscule size on a globe that is criss-crossed to the point of opacity by voyagers intent on discovery and imperialist expansion. At this stage in the narrative, his anxieties are still relatively controlled by the thought that the volume will run to 'perhaps fourscore parts'; and he is able to diminish the globe's size by imagining it as a city with streets and squares. But as the fantasy develops, his fear amplifies; and when he is told (teasingly, by the bookseller's assistant) that the book might run to 15,000 or so volumes, he reaches a point of crisis in the thought that 'there might be supplements to supplements – the work might positively *never* end. On one pretence or another, if an author or publisher might add 500 volumes, he might add another 15,000' (p. 133). Significantly, at this stage, the image of the city returns, with a new and sinister significance, to reinforce his impression of inconceivable power:

> I saw by the imprint, and I heard, that this work emanated from London, a vast centre of mystery to me, and the more so, as a thing unseen at any time by my eyes, and nearly 200 miles distant. I felt the fatal truth, that here was a ghostly cobweb radiating into all the provinces from the mighty metropolis. I secretly had trodden upon the outer circumference, had damaged or deranged the fine threads and links, – concealment or reparation there could be none. Slowly perhaps, but surely, the vibration would travel back to London. The ancient spider that sat there at the centre, would rush along the network through all longitudes and latitudes, until he found the responsible caitiff, author of so much mischief.
>
> (pp. 133–4)

Where the globe had earlier been likened to a city, the city is now likened to the globe, its web of streets becoming the lines of 'longitude and latitude' that extend out into the provinces, allowing the spider to exact punishment on the terrified child. Significantly, in this arachnophobic fantasy, London is shrouded in 'mystery', its cobweb is 'ghostly' and the spider at its centre is 'ancient': De Quincey here articulates, from a child's perspective, all the terrors that attach to the written book as an embodiment of sacred authority and patriarchal power. The 'dim terrors' he remembers experiencing in connection with the Stationers' Company are not amplified, but are presumably caused by injunctions against copying – as though, by upsetting the balance of power between authors and their readers even minutely, the child is found guilty of a secret desire to plagiarize material he wishes merely to read. Conflating the fears of readers with those of writers, De Quincey here transforms the whole system of authorship, printing, production, and circulation into an image which hauntingly embodies his sense of persecution by mysterious powers-that-be:

> Even, with less ignorance than mine, there *was* something to appal a child's imagination in the vast systematic machinery by which any elaborate work could disperse itself, could levy money, could put questions and get answers – all in profound silence, nay, even in darkness – searching every nook of every town, and of every hamlet in so populous a kingdom.

(p. 134)

[. . .]

Taken as an integrated narrative, De Quincey's fantasy figures the reader as the helpless consumer of books and as the humiliated victim of a powerful machinery of literary production designed precisely to remind him of his anonymous unimportance. This nightmare – of literature wrested from the hands of writers and readers, delivered over to the forces of the market place, divested of spirit and reduced to mere waste-matter in a culture of commodities – characterizes many of the ingredients of the anxiety of reception as it was experienced by high Romantic writers. But although it has elements that are historically determined and specific (the imperialist metaphor of navigation, the parochial emphasis given to De Quincey's fear of the metropolis, and the reference to the Stationers' Company) it can also be seen to prefigure twentieth-century nightmares of centralized power and consumerism, in which the individual's identity and agency are extinguished. Crucially, [. . .] this is a nightmare for which high Romanticism is itself partly responsible.

[. . .]

Notes

1 *The Complete Works* (2 vols, New York: Harper and Brothers, 1855), vol. i, p. vii; quoted in Marlon B. Ross, *The Contours of Masculine Desire: Romanticism and the Rise of Poetry* (Oxford: Oxford University Press, 1989), 229.
2 *Peacock Displayed [: A Satirist in his Context* (London: Routledge and Kegan Paul, 1979)], 277; 'An Essay on Fashionable Literature', in [*The Works of Thomas Love Peacock*, eds H.F.B. Brett-Smith and C.E. Jones (10 vols, London: Constable and Co., New York: Gabriel Wells, 1934)], viii. 273.
3 'Keats in the Cockney School', *Romanticism*, 2/1 (1996), 27–39: 28.
4 [William Hazlitt, *Complete Works*, ed. P.P. Howe (21 vols, London: J.M. Dent and Sons, 1930–4), xvii. 361 (abbreviated as Howe and cited parenthetically in text hereafter).]
5 For Byron's interactions with his anonymous reviewers, and a broader theoretical placing of the practice of anonymity, see Jerome Christensen, *Lord Byron's Strength: Romantic Writing and Commercial Society* (Baltimore: Johns Hopkins University Press, 1993).
6 *Edinburgh Review* (11 Oct. 1807); repr. in *Jeffrey's Criticism: A Selection*, ed. with introd., Peter F. Morgan (Edinburgh: Scottish Academic Press, 1983), 55.
7 Carlyle, *Reminiscences*, ed. Charles Eliot Norton (London: J.M. Dent & Sons, 1932, repr. 1972), 328; Erickson, *The Economy of Literary Form [: English Literature and the Industrialization of Publishing, 1800–1850* (Baltimore: Johns Hopkins University Press, 1996)], 79.

8 *Letters and Journals*, ed. Leslie A. Marchand (12 vols and suppl., London: William Clowes and Sons, 1975), iv. 324.

9 The phrase 'poor Keats' was common currency in contemporary periodicals. It is used by Hazlitt in his essay 'On the Periodical Press' (Howe, xvii. 237). [. . .]

10 [All quotations from Wordsworth's poetry (unless otherwise specified) refer to the Oxford Authors edition, ed. Stephen Gill (Oxford: Oxford University Press, 1984).]

11 *Keats, Narrative and Audience* [*: The Posthumous Life of Writing* (Cambridge: Cambridge University Press, 1994)], 40.

12 Unsigned article in the series 'Living Authors', *London Magazine*, 2 (Jan. 1821); extract in Theodore Redpath, *The Young Romantics and Literary Opinion, 1807–1824* (London: George G. Harrap and Co., 1973), 262–75.

13 Unsigned review of *Childe Harold*, canto IV, *Edinburgh Review* (June 1818); quoted in Redpath, *Young Romantics*, 31.

14 *The Yellow Dwarf*, 2 May 1818; quoted in Redpath, *Young Romantics*, 183.

15 *Lord Byron's Strength*, 33.

16 In *The Yale Edition of the Works of Samuel Johnson*, eds W.J. Bate and Albrecht B. Strauss (New Haven: Yale University Press, 1969), 133–4; quoted in Mary Poovey, *The Proper Lady and the Woman Writer: Ideology as Style in the Works of Mary Wollstonecraft, Mary Shelley, and Jane Austen* (Chicago: Chicago University Press, 1984), 35.

17 *Contours of Masculine Desire*, 27.

18 Review from *The Alfred on* 'The Quarterly Review – Mr Keats' (6 Oct. 1818), in [John Hamilton Reynolds, *Selected Prose of John Hamilton Reynolds*, ed. Leonidas M. Jones (Cambridge, Mass.: Harvard University Press, 1966)], 225.

19 *The Letters of John Clare*, ed. Mark Storey (Oxford: Clarendon Press, 1985), 188–9.

20 In Stones and Strachan (eds), *Parodies of the Romantic Age*, ii. 134. See also George Darley's use of the term 'literary fratricide' in 1836; discussed by Erickson, *Economy of Literary Form*, 91.

21 Repr. by Hunt in the *Examiner* (11 Oct. 1818), 648–9; quoted in [Susan Wolfson, 'Keats Enters History: Autopsy, *Adonais*, and the Fame of Keats', in Nicholas Roe (ed.), *Keats and History* (Cambridge: Cambridge University Press, 1995)], 21.

22 Wolfson, 'Keats Enters History', 21.

23 *The Novels and Selected Works of Mary Shelley*, gen. ed. Nora Crook, with Pamela Clemit, ii. ed. Pamela Clemit (London: William Pickering, 1996), 316.

24 Ibid. 316–17.

25 *The Recreations of Christopher North* (3 vols, William Blackwood: Edinburgh and London, 1842), i, 326.

26 Ibid.

27 [S.T. Coleridge, *Lectures 1808–1819 On Literature*, ed. R.A. Foakes (Bollingen Series; 2 vols, Princeton: Princeton University Press, 1987)], i. 195–6.

28 In [*De Quincey's Collected Writings*, ed. David Masson (14 vols, Edinburgh: Adam and Charles Black, 1890)], xi. 52.

29 Preface to *An Essay on the Manners and Genius of the Literary Character* (London: T. Cadell and W. Davies, 1795), pp. xviii–xix.

30 *The Western Canon: The Books and School of the Ages* (New York: Harcourt Brace and Company, 1995), 15.

31 *Edinburgh Review* (Mar. 1819), 471–2.

32 *Strictures on the Modern System of Female Education. With a view of the principles and conduct prevalent among women of rank and fortune* (2 vols; London: Caddell and Davies, 1799), i. 184.

33 *Lectures on Female Education and Manners* (New York: Samuel Campbell, 1794). Note esp. the recurrence of metaphors relating novels to reproduction (the word 'teeming'; and also the ideas of rapid succession and sameness).

34 *Analytical Review*, 1 (June 1788), article 33. Wollstonecraft is reviewing *Edward and Harriet, or the Happy Recovery: a Sentimental Novel. By a Lady*. See *The Works of Mary Wollstonecraft*, eds Janet Todd and Marilyn Butler (7 vols, London: William Pickering, 1989), vii. 20.

35 [*The Prose Works of William Wordsworth*, eds W.J.B. Owen and J.W. Smyser (3 vols, Oxford: Clarendon Press, 1974)], i. 128.

36 In *Confessions of an English Opium Eater and Other Writings*, ed. with introd., Grevel Lindop (Oxford: Oxford University Press, 1989), 129–35; page refs. will be included in the text.

10 Theater as the school of virtue

Ann K. Mellor

The leading women playwrights of the Romantic era – [including] Joanna Baillie, Hannah More, [. . .] and Elizabeth Inchbald – consciously used the theater to re-stage and thereby revise both the social construction of gender and the nature of good government. They were writing at a time when, as Gillian Russell [(1995)] has recently shown, the theater was an intensely political place and its influence on the cultural and political life of the nation widely recognized. Russell focuses on the ways in which the Georgian theater written and produced by men represented British chauvinist self-affirmations during the French Revolution and subsequent Napoleonic campaigns, celebrating the British army and navy and the freedoms guaranteed by England's constitutional monarchy. Women playwrights engaged in an equally political campaign, using their dramatic writings to challenge a dominant patriarchy by providing counter-examples of "a new woman," a rational, compassionate, merciful, tolerant, and peace-loving woman better equipped to rule the nation than the men currently in power. At the same time they challenged the notion that the English monarchy did in fact protect the liberties of her people, especially those of women. Finally, they argued that the theater was uniquely well situated to promote social reform, since it could function as a public school for females, one that could be used to correct the inappropriate or inadequate education many girls received at home.

Joanna Baillie

In her introductory discourse to *A Series of Plays on the Passions* (1798), Joanna Baillie offered the most detailed theoretical statement of this conception of the theater as a school for female virtue and political empowerment. As Catherine Burroughs [(1997)] has shown, Baillie's theater theory subtly erased the division between the public and the private, formulating the ways in which domestic "closet drama" could be staged in public arenas. Baillie begins her introductory discourse by defining human nature's primary motivation or "great master propensity" as "sympathetick curiosity" ([1990:] 4), a definition that contests the assertions of Hobbes, Locke, Burke, and Bentham, as well as modern "rational choice" social scientists, that human beings are primarily motivated by self-interest. Instead Baillie invokes Adam Smith's concept, in his *Theory of Moral Sentiments* (1759), that sympathy is one of "the original passions of human nature" (Smith [1777:] 2); it is the capacity to *feel* the emotions of another person. Baillie then argues that the subject or self can be constructed only in sympathetic relation to other selves, and that knowledge is produced, not from "objective" or detached observation but rather from empathic identification, an identification that is then articulated through the stories we tell of what and whom we meet, what she calls "tattling." Baillie's epistemology strikingly anticipates contemporary standpoint theory, the belief that valid knowledge can be achieved, not by positing a universal subject removed from local circumstances (as assumed by Habermas [1991] and by many contemporary scientists), but only by acknowledging that all knowledge-producers are historically and culturally located, and by attempting to correct for the inherent biases or limited standpoints of a given set of experimenters or observers. For Baillie, it is the drama that uniquely enables the observer to take up different subject positions, to identify with opposing standpoints, and thus to correct the biases of a single point of view.

Baillie's introductory discourse is specifically to *A Series of Plays in which it is attempted to delineate The Stronger Passions of the Mind*; she further claims that the development of the individual is governed most powerfully by feelings and desires, passions which must be held in check by reason if they are not to become self-destructive. Asserting that human character is organic and developmental, growing not from Locke's "white paper" or blank slate but from an inherent "propensity" or seed, she both anticipates William Wordsworth's influential assertion that "fair seed-time had my soul" and also argues that this growing seed takes its final shape from its interactions with its environment. Each of her tragedies studies the growth of a single passion that, unchecked by the rational advice of others, destroys the hero; her comedies hold that obsessive passion up to the derision of others, laughing its possessor back into a more moderated feeling.

Significantly, in Baillie's plays, it is the *male* characters who are prey to unregulated passion, while the *female* characters are the voices of rational moderation (unless they are driven by hostile external forces beyond the range of reason altogether, as in *Orra*, her Gothic tragedy of female persecution, fear, and madness). She thus denies a patriarchal gender definition of the female sex as irrational, impulsive, and uncontrollable. At the same time, like Mary Wollstonecraft, she insists that there is no significant psychological or mental sex-difference between males and females. As she claims in her introductory discourse,

> I believe that there is no man that ever lived, who has behaved in a certain manner, on a certain occasion, who has not had amongst women some corresponding spirit, who on the like occasion, and every way similarly circumstanced, would have behaved in the like manner.

(36)

The function of drama, Baillie asserts, is to arouse the sympathetic curiosity of the viewer so that the audience will both identify with her characters and learn from their errors. "The theater is a school" (58), she claims, and like the other female literary critics of her day, she wished to use literature to educate her audience to a more responsible morality. In order to do this, she recognized, drama must be probable or "natural" – it must show "the plain order of things in this every-day world" (21), including the way that the passions develop and change *over time*, in their "infant, growing, and repressed state" (59). Despite her claims for the universality of the growth of the human passions, we must recognize that there is a potentially limiting class bias in Baillie's concept of human nature. For Baillie, what is "natural" is what is "middling and lower" class, English, and domestic – she rejects both the "artifice" of the aristocracy and the potentially disruptive "ballad-reading" of the "lowest classes of the labouring people, who are the broad foundation of society, which," she claimed, "can never be generally moved without endangering every thing that is constructed upon it" (57–8).

To achieve a "natural" or probable revelation of the human passions, Baillie devised several specific dramatic techniques: the frequent use of the soliloquy; a focus on but one passion and one plot (with no distracting subplots or unrelated incidents); the staging of processions, balls, banquets, and other social rituals or ceremonies in place of subplots in order to arouse audience attention but avoid distraction; and the confinement of the action to a small, intimate, often domestic space (a house, a town square). Eschewing what she considered to be bad comedy – the rhetorical excesses of satirical comedy, the amorality of witty comedy, the hypocrisies of sentimental comedy, and the contrivances (or "ambushed bush-fighting") of "busy" comedy or farce – Baillie wrote what she called "Characteristick Comedy," a comedy devoted to the representation of the "motley world of men and women in which we live" (49), using ordinary language and focusing on the damage done by emotional excesses.

We must recognize the large cultural authority to which Baillie laid claim. Echoing the sixteenth-century Scottish nationalist, Andrew Fletcher of Saltoun, she suggests that "if I have the writing of its [Drama], let who will make the laws of a nation" (57). Baillie thus positions herself as the unacknowledged legislator of the British nation, superior to the historian, philosopher, and poet. In her view, the dramatist alone can combine an abstract moral lesson with a concrete appeal to our "sympathetic curiosity," an appeal that will – in this first articulation of what we might now call reader-response theory – produce political action, cultural ideology, and meaning itself. Although Baillie employs a conventional modesty topos, craving the "forbearance of my reader" (69), she firmly asserts both the originality and the pedagogical value of her dramatic project: she is the first to attempt to reveal the growth of individual passions, from love and hatred to remorse and sexual jealousy, by writing *paired* plays, a tragedy and a comedy on each passion. By moving the realm of private, psychological feelings from the domestic "closet" to the public stage, Baillie implicitly asserts that a hitherto culturally marginalized "women's realm," the realm of feelings, sympathy, and curiosity, is in fact the basis of all human culture, and especially of political culture. Good domestic management thus becomes her model for good politics; a rational control of passion that produces harmonious and loving family relationships becomes the model for peaceful national and international relations.

Turning now to what I consider to be Baillie's finest play, *Count Basil* (1798), I would like to discuss it briefly as an example of the argument made above. *Count Basil* is Baillie's examination in the genre of tragedy of the passion of love, her response to Shakespeare's interrogation of the conflicting claims of honor and love in *Antony and Cleopatra* and to John Dryden's rehearsal of those same issues in his *All for Love*. Equally important, this play is about the control of the public realm, a debate between two opposing methods of government.

Count Basil begins by staging the meeting of two opposing processions, two genders, two value systems. From one side, accompanied by martial music, comes the military procession of Count Basil and his soldiers, who are hailed for their discipline and military success; from the opposite side, accompanied by "soft music," comes the Princess Victoria and her women, who are hailed for their beauty and their public display of filial devotion and religious duty. Two bodies are here presented for the specular desire both of the audience and of Count Basil: the wounded body of the old soldier Geoffrey and the "splendid" body of Victoria. Overtly, this display stages the tension between military honor and erotic love, between masculine heroism and feminine graciousness. But Baillie is not simply rewriting *Antony and Cleopatra*. Instead, she insists in this opening scene on what is *absent*: Geoffrey's arm ("this arm . . . / Which now thou seest is no arm of mine" [76]) and Victoria's mother ("She is fair, / But not so fair as her good mother was" [79]).

This absence at the center of the public realm is further identified, as the play proceeds, with the amoral, Machiavellian policies of Victoria's father, the Duke of Mantua, who schemes to keep Basil in his court long enough for his secret ally, the King of France, to defeat Basil's Austro-Hungarian Emperor. Pretending hospitality, the Duke employs his daughter as a pawn in his policy. Unknowingly, Victoria graciously urges Basil to stay with her and Basil, infatuated with her beauty, acquiesces.

Basil stays in Mantua one day, two days, three days, despite the urgent demands of his cousin, fellow officer, and chief advisor, Count Rosinberg, that he continue on his march at once. Rosinberg's motives are called into question, however, both by his misogyny (the only woman he knows whose love will never change is his "own good mother" [88]), and by his erotic infatuation with his younger cousin. His "foolish admiration" claims that "when Basil fights he wields a thousand swords" (80–1), and he embraces Basil with the ardor of a jealous lover ("my friend! / I love thee now more than I ever lov'd thee" [161]), when Basil agrees to leave Victoria (Act IV, sc. 3).

As we come to recognize, in *Count Basil* the hero's struggle is not between erotic passion and military duty but rather between three kinds of passion: heterosexual love, homosocial love, and self-love. Basil's heterosexual infatuation with Victoria might well be reciprocated, we are led to believe, as Victoria begins to recognize the difference between Basil's mature devotion and the hypocritical attentions of her previous lovers, and to respond judiciously to Basil's passion for her. But Basil already has another love, as he confesses: "From early youth, war has my mistress been, / And tho' a rugged one, I'll constant prove, / And not forsake her now" (86). As the play unfolds, we see this prior love unveiled as a powerful homosocial bonding of Basil with his men, and especially with Rosinberg, who is passionately devoted to Basil and hostile to any woman who might interrupt that bond. Two bodies are here displayed for Basil's specular desire: the "divine" body of the beautiful Victoria and the scarred body of the old soldier Geoffrey. Weeping with his men over the body of Geoffrey, Basil manifests his deeper emotional bond, with his men. When Basil betrays that bond, when his men mutiny, Basil's self begins to split apart. The "wounded soldier" whose mask Basil wears at the ball is not only the rejected lover of Victoria, as he claims, but also the rejecting lover of his own wounded men.

But the wounded love which drives Basil to suicide is finally neither heterosexual nor homosocial. It is, as Basil admits, "his great love of military fame" (81): the wound to his own "glorious name." His failure to fight at Pavia did no harm to his own men or to his emperor's cause, since the French King was soundly defeated by another general. Nor did it, as Old Geoffrey tells him, do any lasting damage to Basil's own military career, since his previous victories remain untouched and his "soldier's fame is far too surely raised / To be o'erthrown with one unhappy chance" (179). Only Basil's self-love is fatally wounded, and it is that unregulated self-love that causes his self-destruction. Thus Baillie uncovers the dominating passion of the masculine public realm: an egotistic self-love that seeks only its personal aggrandizement, whether through Machiavellian policy or military success. Both the Duke's policy, the profit-and-loss calculations of a "petty tradesman" (107), and Basil's desire for military glory finally overwhelm their possessors: the Duke is betrayed by his own followers, especially Gauriceio, while Basil is betrayed by his own love of fame. Basil's self-love can thus be seen as the ghostly, absent arm of Old Geoffrey: what men seek and most admire is that heroic arm which is but an empty sleeve.

Opposed to this conception of masculine honor in Baillie's play is an alternative sphere of action and value, what we might think of as the female public sphere, the space assigned to the absent mother. This space is filled by the Countess Albini, who "stands in" for Victoria's mother, as Victoria acknowledges: "Still call me child, and chide me as thou wilt. / O! would that I were such as thou couldst love! / Couldst dearly love! as thou didst love my mother" (111). The Countess Albini is Baillie's homage to Mary Wollstonecraft, the ideal woman Wollstonecraft envisioned in *A Vindication of the Rights of Woman* published six years before Baillie wrote this play. She is the embodiment of rational judgment, the one who sees Victoria's faults, the one who unmasks at the ball, the one who can advise all the characters honestly and judiciously, the one who urges Rosinberg to persuade Basil to leave before permanent harm is done (131). She engages in the same revisioning of gender roles as did Wollstonecraft, advocating not the "poor ideal [i.e., "most unreal"] tyranny" of feminine beauty but rather the domestic "duties of an useful state" (109) and a love grounded in "sincerity and truth" (130). In effect, she argues for what both Hannah More and Mary Wollstonecraft defined as a family politics: the model of the well-managed home and a family harmoniously united by the domestic affections as the paradigm for successful political government. As even the misogynist Rosinberg acknowledges, of all women, only the "brave Albini" can "so wisely rule, / Their subjects never from the yoke escape" (163).

But the Countess Albini "disdains" (163) to rule a nation founded solely on self-interest; her reign is over an alternative public sphere, which in this play is associated with the interior or "closeted" spaces of the bedroom, where she advises Victoria, and the ballroom, where she rightly warns Rosinberg. Her rule of reason and the "fettered" control of the emotions does not yet extend to the militarized spaces of the ramparts where Basil meets his mutinous soldiers or to the savage, uncivilized forest where Basil declares his passionate love for Victoria. Significantly, it is in these "wild" or open spaces (of the town street, of the forest) that uncontrolled emotions reign. Basil brings his rebellious men to tears by threatening to shoot himself, while his own heart, as he leads Victoria aside during the hunt, is "bursting" (169) as he "walks up and down with hurried step, tossing about his arms in transport" (stage direction, 171). And it is outdoors, during a dark night, first in a graveyard and then in a hidden cave, that Basil, having learned that General Piscaro has alone defeated the King of France at Pavia, flings aside the sensible arguments of Old Geoffrey and rushes off in a frenzy of wounded self-love to kill himself.

The ending of the play is ambiguous. Basil dies, as his men weep beside him and Rosinberg passionately declares his love for him. Excessive masculine emotion is thus explicitly identified with death, as all who admired Basil "love him fall'n" (192) – love him who has fallen, but also, these concluding words subtly imply, love him *because* he has fallen, because those who endorse a masculinist code of honor can love only themselves or that which is finally not there, the empty sleeve of Geoffrey's arm.

Victoria vows to spend her days grieving in a "dark, shaded cloister" (190), both assuming responsibility and doing penance for having aroused but failed to control Basil's unregulated passion: "I've wrecked a brave man's honour" (175); "I have murder'd thee!" (189). But since we know Victoria to be innocent of any conscious effort to deceive Basil – and even suspect that she might well have returned his love sincerely in time, we cannot endorse her self-blame. While Victoria defines her coming life in a convent as "sad and lonely" and "cheerless" (190), might we not also see it as a possible affirmation of a female public sphere, a space where women reign? At the very least, her cloistered life endorses Albini's view that the female pursuit of the "worthless praise" and "silly adoration" of a male lover does "degrade a noble mind" (167). Finally, I would argue, Baillie suggests that it is men who destroy themselves through an excess of emotion and women who have the ability to free themselves from the follies and prejudices of their youth, to take up all standpoints, and to see a larger truth. As in *De Montfort, The Alienated Manor*, and many other plays by Joanna Baillie, it is finally the wise *woman* who combines rational prudence with sympathetic understanding and thus acts best for the nation.

Hannah More

Hannah More's hostility to the "pernicious ribaldry" ([1834] I: 109) and dangerously corrupting influence of the theater, as proclaimed in the preface to her plays first included in her collected *Works* in 1801, has been often cited. Yet she began her writing career as a playwright, continued to revise her plays for performance throughout her life, and included them in every edition of her collected *Works*. What might seem a contradiction is not so if we recognize that More enthusiastically endorsed a drama that would actively reform the morals of the nation, but denounced the actual plays performed on the stages of England during her lifetime [. . .]. When she first wrote for the stage, in 1773, she believed fervently that "the stage . . . might be converted into a school of virtue" (V: vi). Even in her mature view, drama remained a far more potent agent of moral reformation, one might even say propaganda, than prose or poetry.

[. . .]

More came to believe that the moral efficacy of the theater could be realized only after the audience – rather than the plays themselves – had been "purified" (V: viii), that her contemporary English playgoers took no delight in sacred plays or virtuous protagonists, preferring the "holy mummery" of comic medieval mystery plays and the "promiscuous pleasure" of comedies of manners (V: ix, x), and that sincere Christians who attended the popular plays of the day would be forced to spend an unjustifiable amount of time and energy counteracting the pernicious temptations set before them. She therefore urged her peers to stay at home and *read* plays that conveyed moral improvement, to prefer the quiet pleasures afforded by closet drama to the unregulated passions roused by the spectacles of the public theater (V: xxv–xxxi).

Recognizing that the stage possessed a "decided superiority in point of mental pleasure," an ability to "charm the imagination and captivate the senses" provided by no other genre (V: xvi), Hannah More first turned to playwriting to carry out her educational project of useful and moral "instruction as well as pleasure" (V: vii). *The Search after Happiness*, written in 1773 to be performed by an all-female cast at the girls' school in Bristol she ran with her sisters, went through several significant revisions, as Patricia Demers has shown (Demers [1996:] 26–35). The prologue for the eleventh edition in 1796 emphasizes that More is writing a new kind of drama, one not intended to represent the existing (and corrupt) manners of the age but rather to promote "simple truth and common sense," "plain virtue," and "useful thought" (VI: 228). The final version of the play consciously promotes the new concept of female education that More described at length in her *Strictures on the Modern System of Female Education* in 1799. So sympathetic were the teachers at girls' schools to More's revolutionary program of female educational reform that *The Search after Happiness* became the most widely performed play in England between 1780 and 1830 (admittedly in performances limited to schoolrooms), as well as the most often chosen prize book for girls, second only to the Bible, judging by the number of copies that survive, prize gift-plates intact, in both British and American libraries.

In *The Search after Happiness,* four girls escape the corruptions of the city and the "disease of state" to seek happiness in "pure" Nature (VI: 229–30). More quickly establishes that these four girls are middle class, neither "vulgar" (working class) nor vitiated aristocrats. They visit the wise woman (and Milton's former muse) Urania, a woman who has lost her former rank and fortune and now "shuns the public eye," but who embodies both "maternal love" and genuine wisdom. Urania asks each girl to define her "ruling passion," and also to confess what has most troubled her as she sought to gratify that passion: for Euphelia it is the "pleasures," "pomp," and "dress" of high society, which have only aroused "envy" in her; for Pastorella it is the desire for romance, inspired by the novels of sensibility (such as Charlotte Lennox's *The Female Quixote*), which has led her to live in a fantasy world and loathe "the offices of real life"; for Laurinda it is the pleasures of indolence which have left her with "no principle of action" and no "character" of her own; and most problematic, for Cleora it is fame as a writer and scholar, which has aroused "wonder" but not "affection" (VI: 236–43).

Urania, with the help of Florella, a shepherdess who has sustained the artless simplicity and natural piety of her innocent youth, then counsels each girl. She urges Euphelia to combine her love of beauty and fashion with intelligent mental effort and conscious virtue. She tells Pastorella that she must act, not daydream, and similarly urges the lazy Laurinda to undertake a vigorous program of self-education and religious charity. And she urges Cleora to seek, not learning for the purposes of public admiration, but rather the *domestic* virtues of good sense, practical knowledge, taste, and usefulness, "for woman shines but in her proper sphere" (VI: 251).

Patricia Demers has read this play as a contradiction between a humanist concept of knowledge as a process of organic growth, "a combination of trial and error with amenability to instruction," and a "retrograde," "anti-educational manifesto" that urges women to settle for Florella's pious simplicity rather than to seek learning ([1996:] 32–4). But this very early play may be more coherent, more subtly feminist, and hence more revolutionary than Demers allows. More does not suggest that women either cannot or should not attain a high degree of learning – indeed, Cleora presents herself as a female who has acquired a competent knowledge of British literature, physics, geometry, metaphysics, and the philosophy of John Locke. Rather, More argues that one should not desire learning merely for the purposes of *display*, merely to flaunt one's pedantry and win a spurious public fame. Instead one should combine the pursuit of knowledge with modesty, with the desire to serve others, and thus with a life of active charity. It is not Cleora's learning that More condemns, but the way she uses it. Not fame, but a life of dedicated benevolence, domestic good works, and conscious self-approbation are what both Urania and More advocate for women.

The evangelical principles that inspire Urania's counsel to young women are also applied to men in More's dramas written for the legitimate public theater. As Christine Krueger has perceptively shown, More's three tragedies – *The Inflexible Captive* (1774), *Percy* (1778), and *The Fatal Falsehood* (1779) – all condemn those heroic or patriarchal codes which violate a Christian concept of domestic responsibility and active care (Krueger [1992:] 97–104).

[. . .]

Throughout her tragedies, More, like Baillie, consciously uses drama to stage both the greater wisdom and virtue of women and the superiority of a Christian ethic of forgiveness and self-discipline over a Roman republican or medieval chivalric code of honor and fame. As she proclaims in the prologue to *The Fatal Falsehood*, "*self-conquest* is the *lesson* books should preach" (VI: 172; More's italics). And it is her female characters – Attilia, Barce, Elwina Raby in *Percy*, Emmelina and Julia in *The Fatal Falsehood* – who embody that virtue of generous self-control.

[. . .]

[A section of this chapter, not included here, interprets the plays of Hannah Cowley.]

Elizabeth Inchbald

In some ways the most overtly political of the major female playwrights of the Romantic era, Elizabeth Inchbald drew subtle parallels in her plays between the prisons of the state and the constraints of institutionalized marriage. By revealing these connections, she hoped to reform both the political institutions and the marital practices of her day. As she confidently asserted in her prologue to *All on a Summer's Day*, the female playwright may be better suited to this task than the male:

> When haughty man usurp'd fair learning's throne
> And made the Empire of the stage his own
> He rul'd a realm where Genius seldom smil'd
> And Nonsense hail'd him as her darling child. . . .
> Bard follow'd Bard, yet few coud [sic] justly claim
> The laurell'd trophies of a lasting name
> 'Till gentle woman seiz'd the pen and writ
> And shone not less in beauty than in wit.
> Woman! by honest emulation fir'd
> Sportive, yet elegant; tho' pointed, chaste,
> To mend our manners & refine our taste:
> Man from her learnt the fascinating art
> To please the fancy, captivate the heart
> And paint the scenes of happiness and strife
> The various scenes that chequer human life.

Inchbald's more overtly political dramas focus on the prisons of the state: debtors' prison, the French Bastille, criminal prisons. Again and again she shows how unjust these institutions are; how their inmates do not deserve to be there; yet how difficult it is to free oneself from them once one is incarcerated. In her view, it is not an appeal to the legal system or institutionalized justice but only an appeal to the quality of mercy that enables the wrongly imprisoned to escape their chains.

In *Next Door Neighbours* (1791), the father of the beautiful, well-bred Eleanor is in debtors' prison. Her neighbor Sir George Splendorville, catching a glimpse of her, offers her one hundred guineas to release her father – at the price of her chastity. She is saved from rape only by the pity of Sir George's compassionate butler, Mr. Bluntly; at the same time her father refuses the money, preferring prison to his daughter's (even suspected) dishonor. When Sir George loses his estate at gambling and his fair-weather friends desert him, his lawyer, Mr. Blackman, urges him to lie to the court, to present falsified documents that his long-lost half-sister is dead, so that he can collect her inheritance. Here Inchbald suggests how easily lawyers can corrupt the judicial process. Only when the honest barrister Mr. Manly produces evidence that Eleanor is that long-lost sister does her father leave prison. It is the good will of Bluntly and Manly that saves Eleanor and her father, not the workings of the law.

[. . .]

Inchbald turns her attention to the most famous prison of the time, the French Bastille, in *The Massacre* (1792), a play set sixty miles outside Paris. Here the violent and unjust cruelties of the leaders of the Terror are vividly portrayed: the well-born Eusebe's wife's family have been slaughtered in Paris during the St. Bartholomew's Day massacre; his entire family, including his old father, Tricastin, a model of charity and good sense, are arrested; and all are condemned to death by the Montagnard Dugas and his men. Only the last-minute intervention of the benevolent judge Glandeve saves them from execution. Glandeve refuses to participate in a travesty of justice, and insists that "my first object is, freedom of *thought*" and "liberty joined with peace and charity" ([1980:] 26). While Inchbald here represents all of revolutionary France under the Terror as a prison, she also suggests that mercy and benevolence may still be able to preserve a space for freedom (although not until after Eusebe's wife and children are murdered in the streets). Whether such benevolence could be found in an *English* court of law remains an open question.

Inchbald's most extended treatment of prisons occurs in one of her finest plays, *Such Things Are* (1787), which is explicitly based on the work of John Howard, the prison reformer. By displacing the action to "India," literally Sumatra in Dutch Indonesia, Inchbald leaves open the question whether the capriciousness of the Sultan's methods of incarceration is greater or less than that of Britain's. On the one hand, the Sultan is guilty of numerous acts of arbitrary cruelty: he beheads a wife who dares to say "I won't" to him; he arrests and sells into slavery anyone who is merely suspected of disaffection from his reign, without proof; he keeps prisoners locked up without fresh air for decades at a time, never permitting others to visit them or to examine their cases. On the other hand, as the Sultan confesses to Haswell (John Howard), he is a Christian, converted by his love for the Christian Arabella who was killed (or so he thinks) by his rival (whom the Sultan then killed and is now impersonating). When Haswell gains permission to visit the Sultan's prisons, he discovers that many are there only because they lack the funds to bribe their jailers, that several have been falsely accused, and that one European woman has been kept in solitary confinement for fourteen years. Haswell persuades the Sultan to allow him to free six prisoners – among them is the European, Arabella. Devastated by the suffering he has inflicted on his own beloved, the Sultan promises to adopt every measure of prison reform that Haswell shall lay out. Moreover, he will govern his nation with the Christian benevolence, mercy, and forgiveness of the long-suffering Arabella, to whom he gives the ultimate political authority to "redress the wrongs of all my injured subjects" (71).

One might accuse Inchbald of promoting a "home-office mentality" in *Such Things Are* – the Christian Europeans, Haswell and Arabella, display a universal benevolence and willingness to turn the other cheek that is notably lacking in the Sultan and his compatriots, until they are converted by the example of the Christians. But this triumph of Christian mercy does not occur at home in England, only abroad. The implication is that Turks may make better Christians than do Europeans. In *Such Things Are*, the ferocious and vengeful Muslim prisoner Zedan steals Haswell's purse as he passes by, but after having experienced Haswell's pity, immediately returns it, feeling for the first time "something that I never felt before – it makes me like not only you, but all the world besides. – The love of my family was confined to them alone – but this sensation makes me love even my enemies" (28).

[...]

Set back in England, Inchbald's domestic comedies focus on domestic tyranny, specifically the plight of the *married* woman – the consequence, perhaps, of Inchbald's own seven-year marriage to the womanizing, gambling, and much older actor Joseph Inchbald (see Boaden [1833] I: 32–59). In *Wives as They Were, and Maids as They Are* (1797), Inchbald portrays marriage as an oppressive feudal institution in which wives are prisoners. Lord Priory exacts absolute obedience from his wife. He proudly claims the title of an "unkind husband," insisting that he has always treated his wife "according to the antient mode of treating wives. . . . The antients seldom gave them the liberty to do wrong; but modern wives do as they like," and boasting of his violent temper, which is "rather of advantage to me as a husband – it causes me to be obeyed without hesitation – no liberty for contention, tears, or repining. I insure conjugal sunshine, by now and then introducing a storm" (5–6). Moreover, he keeps his wife at home under lock and key, never permitting her to attend operas, balls, or appear in public places, preventing her from having company at home or spending the night at another's house, and making sure she is in bed by 10 o'clock every night. When he breaks his rule and brings his wife to Lord Norberry's home for one evening while his furniture is moved into his London apartment, Lady Priory is exposed both to the attractions of high society, as embodied in the attractive young "heedless woman of fashion," Miss Dorrillon, and to the libertine attentions of the fop Mr. Bronzeley, who tries to seduce her. But Lady Priory foils Bronzeley's plans, first by obtaining her husband's "permission" to meet Mr. Bronzeley alone and then by steadfastly resisting his sexual advances even after he has tricked her into an "elopement." Lady Priory returns in triumph to her husband, her chastity intact, but a far wiser woman. As she observes:

> I should have continued those [primitive] manners, had I known none but primitive men. But to preserve antient austerity, while, by my husband's consent, I am assailed by modern gallantry, would be the task of a Stoic, and not of his female slave.
>
> (93)

At the same time Lady Priory resubmits to this feudal marriage: "Not all the rigour of its laws has ever induced me to wish them abolished" (78). Even though several of the older men are uneasy with Lord Priory's patriarchal tyranny, the play offers no escape from this patriarchal construction of marriage. Mr. Bronzeley turns to Lady Mary Raffle, asking "if, in consequence of former overtures, I should establish a legal authority over you, and become your chief magistrate – would you submit to the same control to which Lady Priory submits?" To which the hitherto spirited, independent Lady Raffle responds, "Any control, rather than have no magistrate at all." And Miss Dorrillon ends the play by responding to *her* lover's query as to what she thinks of this, "Simply one sentence – A maid of the present day, shall become a wife like those of former times" (78).

Did Elizabeth Inchbald herself endorse this affirmation of feudal marriage? Throughout *Wives as They Were, Maids as They Are*, the female characters have been treated brutally by those very patriarchs who claim to cherish and protect them. Lady Priory has been irresponsibly exposed to the predations of a libertine rapist. Even worse, Miss Dorrillon has been arrested and taken to jail at her disguised father's behest, in order to "teach her a lesson" about the dangers of indebtedness. Only her innate generosity and filial devotion (she tells Mr. Mandred – her disguised father – to send the thousand pounds he has brought to pay her debts instead to her supposedly impoverished, dying father in India) pierces through her father's hardened heart. Many members of the audience, both male and female, may have seriously asked themselves if the domestic tyrannies practiced in this play were indeed morally defensible.[1]

[. . .]

In the world of Inchbald's domestic comedies, there is no escape from the prison of an unhappy marriage. Divorce, as Inchbald's play *I'll Tell You What* (1785) suggests, only plunges one into a second marriage more painful than the first. Unmarried women are repeatedly portrayed as unhappy with their status in life. Either they are embittered old maids desperate to marry[2] or discontented widows. In *Every One Has His Fault*, for instance, Miss Spinster eagerly accepts the reluctant proposal of Mr. Solus, even though he is "a man, of all others on earth, I dislike" while he thinks her "peevish, fretful, and tiresome" (11). Even very wealthy widows are represented as secretly unhappy. In *The Widow's Vow* (1786), the widowed Countess, despite her arranged marriage to a "bad husband" whom she hated, and despite the vow of celibacy which she has since taken, is easily fooled into meeting and then marrying her neighbor, the Marquis, who appears before her implausibly disguised as a girl. In these domestic comedies, Inchbald's only solution to the agonies of marital incompatibility, mutual distrust, betrayal, and patriarchal tyranny is an ineffective placebo: a call for tolerance and forgiveness within marriage which only her female characters seem able to answer.

Implicit in Inchbald's plays is the argument that Britain is not the land of liberty it claims to be, that its wives are prisoners, its subjects the victims of an oppressive class system that sends many honest workers to debtors' prison, and its ruling classes the slaves of dissipation and folly. Only through the agency of benevolent sensibility can social improvement come, but in Inchbald's plays the most empowered of these humanitarians tend to live elsewhere – in the East, in France, or "next door." Thus it is left to her, a female dramatist, to rouse the conscience of the British nation. [. . .]

Throughout these plays by Joanna Baillie, Hannah More, [. . .] and Elizabeth Inchbald, the voices and bodies of women dominate the stage. Whether we are observing Baillie's female exemplars of rational self-control and wise advice, or

More's embodiments of Christian virtue, useful learning, and compassion, [. . .] or Inchbald's ironic vision of a more enlightened, benevolent, and just government beyond the domestic and state tyrannies of the England of her day – we see women putting forth a claim to ultimate moral, cultural, and political authority. Even when the settings of these plays are domestic, the very act of transferring to the public sphere of the legitimate stage the tyrannies and freedoms of the private sphere works to *publicize* women's capacities for rational control and virtuous behavior. Finally, these powerful female dramatists and their characters assertively occupy the discursive public sphere in order to stage intellectually and emotionally persuasive versions of a New Woman, a rational, just, yet compassionate, benevolent, and peace-loving woman, the person best suited to govern the new British nation.

Notes

1 Paula Backscheider has drawn attention to Inchbald's fascination with "the stern, nearly tyrannical, father-figure" in both her fiction and her drama (Backscheider 1980: xxxii).
2 Inchbald's essays on British drama [. . .] take a far more positive view of the spinster, as Anna Lott has observed (Lott [1994:] 639–40).

Works cited

Backscheider, Paula R. Introduction to *The Plays of Elizabeth Inchbald*. 2 vols. New York: Garland, 1980.

Baillie, Joanna. *A Series of Plays: in which it is attempted to delineate the Stronger Passions of the Mind. Each Passion being the Subject of a Tragedy and a Comedy*. London: T. Cadell, 1798. Facsimile reprint, Oxford: Woodstock Books, 1990.

Boaden, James. *Memoirs of Elizabeth Inchbald*. 2 vols. London: Richard Bentley, 1833.

Burroughs, Catherine B. *Closet Stages: Joanna Baillie and the Theater Theory of the British Romantic Women Writers*. Philadelphia: University of Pennsylvania Press, 1997.

Demers, Patricia. *The World of Hannah More*. Lexington: University Press of Kentucky, 1996.

Habermas, Jürgen. *The Structural Transformation of the Public Sphere: An Inquiry into a Category of Bourgeois Society*. Translated by Thomas Burger with the assistance of Frederick Lawrence. Cambridge, Mass.: MIT Press, 1991.

Inchbald, Elizabeth. *The Plays of Elizabeth Inchbald*. 2 vols. New York: Garland, 1980.

Krueger, Christine L. *The Reader's Repentance: Women Preachers, Women Writers, and Nineteenth-Century Social Discourse*. Chicago: University of Chicago Press, 1992.

Lott, Anna. "Sexual Politics in Elizabeth Inchbald." *Studies in English Literature, 1500–1900* 34 (1994): 635–48.

More, Hannah. *The Works of Hannah More*. 6 vols. London: H. Fisher, R. Fisher, and P. Jackson, 1834.

Russell, Gillian. *The Theaters of War: Performance, Politics, and Society, 1793–1815*. Oxford: Clarendon Press, 1995.

Smith, Adam. *The Theory of Moral Sentiments* (1759). 6th ed. Edinburgh: Constable, 1777.

Wollstonecraft, Mary. *A Vindication of the Rights of Woman* (1792). Edited by Carol Poston. New York: Norton, 1988/1975.

11 Study to be quiet

Hannah More and the invention of conservative culture in Britain

Kevin Gilmartin

Although not as widely known and anthologized as *Village Politics*, Hannah More's 1795 *History Of Tom White the Postilion* and its sequel, *The Way to Plenty*, are in many respects more typical of the kind of writing through which her Cheap Repository Tracts (1795–1798) achieved a leading role in the antiradical and antirevolutionary campaigns of the 1790s.[1] For this reason, *Tom White* can provide a useful preliminary map of More's reactionary fiction, and of the challenge it presents to our understanding of the literary history of Romantic-period Britain, particularly the impact that reactionary movements had upon cultural politics in an age of revolution. The *Tom White* series is typical, to begin with, in its heterogeneous narrative form (the dialogue of *Village Politics* is less characteristic of More's work), and in the pressure it brings to bear upon the social world More believed her readers inhabited. Like many of the Cheap Repository Tracts, *Tom White* serves up a moral parable that rests, in the first instance, upon a precisely situated sense of rural virtue:

> Tom White was one of the best drivers of a post-chaise on the Bath road. Tom was the son of an honest labourer at a little village in Wiltshire: he was an active industrious boy, and as soon as he was old enough he left his father, who was burthened with a numerous family, and went to live with farmer Hodges, a sober worthy man in the same village. He drove the waggon all the week; and on Sundays, though he was now grown up, the farmer required him to attend the Sunday-school, carried on under the inspection of Dr. Shepherd, the worthy vicar, and always made him read his Bible in the evening after he had served his cattle; and would have turned him out of his service if he had ever gone to the ale-house for his own pleasure.
>
> (5:219–20)

While a sober employer and the weekly round of labor and piety would seem to be adequate security for Tom's virtue, the attractions of the nearby "Bath road" soon lure the young hero from the simple discipline of the wagon to a more glamorous career as a postchaise driver, and from there to the Black Bear public house and a litany of corrupt habits: "oaths and wicked words," "drunkenness," "fives, cards, cudgel-playing, laying wagers, and keeping loose company" (5:221–4). Taverns and public houses, strung out along the avenues of transport and communication that linked village and metropolitan life, occupy a critical position in the distinctive cultural geography of the Cheap Repository Tracts. In the Black Bear of reality and imagination, the residue of morally offensive popular recreations catalogued in *Tom White* met emerging patterns of popular literacy and radical organization, which More had noticed earlier in *Village Politics*, in the form of the "mischief" introduced by the Painite Tim Standish when he threatened to "corrupt the whole club" at the Rose and Crown tavern (1:347).[2] For this reason, antipathy to the plebeian tavern underworld provided More with a ready meeting point for her own evangelical moral reform project and the more narrowly political campaigns of loyalist organizations like John Reeves's Association for Preserving Liberty and Property against Republicans and Levellers.[3] If Tom White's departure from village honesty begins at the Black Bear, it culminates at another public house, when a "foolish contest" among the young post-chaise drivers to see who "would be at the Red Lion first – for a pint"(5:225) ends in catastrophe. Tom emerges from the wreck with a broken leg and a chastened conscience, and the period of his recuperation at a London charity hospital brings to a close the tract's initial sequence of lively incidents, opening up a very different narrative and spiritual "space for repentance" (5:230). As his early Sunday school education returns to him with the added force of experience, "Tom began to find that *his strength was perfect weakness*," and remorse quickly yields conversion and reform. From London, he retraces the course of his decline, returning first to the Bath road, where as *"careful Tom"* (5:235) he "soon grew rich for one in his station" (5:235), and then "to his native village" (5:235), where he purchases a farm and marries "a young woman of excellent character, who had been bred up by the vicar's lady" (5:238). By the end of the first part of the tract Tom has returned to Dr. Shepherd's fold and become the respectable Farmer White.

Thus far, the parable of fall and redemption that forms the core of *The History of Tom White* only implies the range of moral categories and social controls that More would extend to her characters and her readers, yet this is by no means the end of the story. Like most of the ballads, tales, hymns, and allegories that she published over the course of a counterrevolutionary decade, *Tom White* is informed by the serial design of the Cheap Repository, and as the second part, *The Way to Plenty*, more closely engages the immediate famine conditions of 1795, narrative assumes a more heterogeneous form.[4] The ordered plot of the first part – circular in structure, focusing on the spiritual development of an individual, and punctuated by scriptural quotations and pious reflections – gives way to a less coherent series of separately titled episodes: "The Roof-Raising," "The Sheep Shearing," "The Hard Winter," "The White Loaf," "The Parish Meeting," "Rice Milk," "Rice Pudding," and "A Cheap Stew." The first of these programmatic incidents opens with a perfunctory gesture towards Tom's life and narrative continuity – "Some years after he was settled, he built a large new barn" (5:249) – but subsequent transitions from section to section convey the tract out of the timeless world of the moral parable, and into a more immediate and circumstantial present day. "The Hard Winter" brings the reader down to "the famous cold winter of the present year, 1795" and "The White Loaf" then explores the consequences of that disastrous season within the context of a government and social hierarchy contending with unprecedented economic distress and popular discontent:

> One day, it was about the middle of last July, when things seemed to be at the dearest, and the rulers of the land had agreed to set the example of eating nothing but coarse bread, Dr. Shepherd read, before sermon in the church, their public declaration, which the magistrates of the county sent him, and which they had

also signed themselves. Mrs. White of course was at church, and commended it mightily. Next morning the Doctor took a walk over to the farmer's, in order to settle further plans for the relief of the parish.

$$(5:265–6)^5$$

Eventually, the narrative energy derived from a tale of Tom's spiritual fall and redemption dissipates entirely, and is replaced in the climactic "Parish Meeting" episode by the polemical force of Dr. Shepherd's spirited harangue against the prevailing "*bad management*" of cottage households, apparently the real reason for popular distress (5:271). As the logic of the tract becomes increasingly programmatic and pedagogical, More exercises her remarkable powers of discursive assimilation, taking on everything from actual public resolutions about poor relief to Mrs. White's "dainty receipts" (5:277) for rice milk, rice pudding, and cheap stews and soups (5:268–9). The nominal hero of the tract series increasingly yields the foreground to his wife and Dr. Shepherd, and in the final episodes he must literally "beg leave to say a word to the men" (5:278) in order to advance community reform. Ironically, his address to the men neither reaffirms the centrality of his experience nor reclaims his patriarchal authority, but instead provides clear evidence of the way that feminized controls upon household management, the central issue in the tract's denouement, will dissolve the moral risks of his own masculine domain: "If you abstain from the ale-house," he tells the assembled men, "you may, many of you, get a little one-way beer at home" (5:278). In gesturing from public house to private home, Tom also makes explicit the political stakes of moral reform. His claim that "the number of public houses in many a parish brings on more hunger and rags than all the taxes in it" (5:279) is a calculated refutation of the radical view that popular misery resulted from the excessive taxation required by corrupt government.

What More has done in the second half of *Tom White*, through the collaboration of vicar, housewife, and husband in organizing locally what the "magistrates" and "rulers of the land" have determined nationally, is to shift her writing away from the narrative conventions of a moral parable, and towards a dense fictional representation of her own public enterprise.[6] Plot gets subordinated to schematic treatments of the material and institutional conditions for moral reform, nowhere more clearly than in the recipe sections ("Rice Milk," "Rice Pudding," "A Cheap Stew") with which *Tom White* concludes. Put another way, where the first part of the tract explored Tom's moral and spiritual experience, with only passing attention paid to the institutional agents (schools, publishers, associations, hospitals) conditioning that experience, the second part is concerned above all with the social mechanisms that frame Tom's newly acquired agency in determining the experience of others, an agency that is increasingly shared out to his wife and the vicar. In More's fictional universe, this condition of having acquired moral influence over the lives of others turns out to be the surest index of individual regeneration. To be sure, the concern for personal agency in *Tom White* does sometimes mystify the institutional operations of the Cheap Repository and the Sunday school movement by fictionally privileging less formal networks for communication and social change. [. . .] The tract closes, too, under the nostalgic sign of a popular proverb that valorizes individual initiative and inherited wisdom: "Let us now at last adopt that good old maxim, *every one mend one*" (5:282). Yet as so often in More, such gestures towards the authority of the past and the integrity of the individual or local are overwhelmed by the emphatic positioning of her characters within the present framework of an aggressive national movement to reform the social order. The maxim about individual initiative may be old, but its adoption would evidently count as an innovation, since it is "now at last" achieved through the collaborative and institutionally orchestrated work of the narrative agents of moral reform.

The shift from conventional parable to a more ambitious fictional synthesis of the whole machinery of moral reform involves More in a complex and frankly promotional set of references to her own activity. In lending its support to an evangelical campaign against luxuries like white bread in periods of distress, *Tom White* indexes More's other printed works: "Our blessed Saviour ate barley bread, you know, as we are told in the last month's Sunday reading of the Cheap Repository, which I hope you have all heard" (5:270). There is more subtle evidence, too, of the way that informal practices and haphazard village conversations about moral propriety might assume a more organized and disciplinary form, quite unlike the fantasy of a world remade through a casual call at the vicarage for a neighbor's recipe. Dr. Shepherd's "common custom" (5:239) of visiting the celebrations that follow a wedding ceremony, for example, is recommended as a form of community surveillance, since "the expectation that the vicar might possibly drop in, in his walks, on these festivities, often restrained excessive drinking, and improper conversation" (5:239–40). Evangelical enterprise surfaces as a form of discipline again later in the tract, when those cottagers "who wished to buy" rice at the "reduced rates" made possible by subscription "were ordered to come to the farm on the Tuesday evening" for a ritual disbursement. The shift here from the volition of the poor ("wished") to the command of the wealthy ("ordered") indicates with unusual clarity how middle-class provision worked to establish material incentives (in this instance, cheap rice) which, if accepted, implied a form of consent to the revised social hierarchy that Dr. Shepherd and the Whites embody.

[. . .]

The culmination of *Tom White* in a systematic reform of cottage management, which aligns Mrs. White's domestic expertise with Dr. Shepherd's pastoral authority, and with a "public declaration" about diet issued by "the rulers of the land," provides compelling evidence for the case made by a number of feminist scholars that More's decisive intervention in British society was to advance responsible household management, a feminized version of the ancient model of *oikonomia,* as the central principle for the management of national affairs.[7] When these principles of reform are applied to domestic matters, as at the close of *Tom White,* they often arrive under the nostalgic sign of restoring lost or corrupted household practices, in part to mitigate the challenge that a new feminine authority posed to masculine conventions about politics and public life. Yet there were limits to More's accommodating spirit, and in the last analysis the Cheap Repository made little real effort to represent household reform as the recovery of some past phase of cottage life. In the sequence of tracts that opened with *The Cottage Cook, or Mrs. Jones's Cheap Dishes,* the recently widowed middle-class reformer, Mrs. Jones, determines "that baking at home would be one step towards restoring the good old management" (4:342) among local cottagers, which would in turn allow the community to negotiate a period of high food prices without popular unrest.[8] However, because "the new bad management" has left most cottages without ovens, Mrs. Jones procures subscriptions for "a large parish oven" (4:342), and the result looks less like a restoration of the old order than the introduction of a new system of central community provision: "To this oven, at a certain hour, three times a week, the elder children carried their loaves which their mothers had made at home, and paid a halfpenny, or a penny according to their size, for the baking" (4:347–8). Breadmaking now begins in the privacy of the laborer's cottage, but is completed within the institutional framework of middle-class moral reform. This hybrid ritual (public and private, common and elite) may seem curious, but it is typical of the way female evangelical enterprise participated in "the inevitable re-negotiation of the apparently fixed public/private, male/female division," by intruding its own quasipublic operations into the domestic life of the poor, and by inventing collective rituals which drew that life out into a public arena, making the manners and habits of ordinary subjects regularly available to the inspection and supervision of their superiors.[9]

If the proper management of the domestic household was More's model for national affairs, this was in part because the cottage or home (stipulated now as an observable domain) seemed to her the safest place for labor and leisure. The consumption of alcohol provides a revealing case in point: recall the suggestion in *Tom White* that men who ought to "abstain from the ale-house" might with less risk "get a little one-way beer at home." As she and her fictional proxies moved outside the domestic sphere and targeted riskier public habits, their interventions became more aggressively revisionist and controlling, without even modest gestures towards the authority of the "good old." Here we can usefully return to the career of Tom White himself. I have so far emphasized the way the second part of the tract loses interest in his life and departs from the conventions of a redemption narrative in order to encompass wider institutional and material considerations (in the form of recipes, sermons, speeches, publications, and subscriptions). Yet the first part of the tract is by no means innocent of the collective conditions for individual development. The role of Tom's Sunday school education in his conversion provides the occasion for the tract's first openly self-promotional gesture, as the author interrupts the tale to call the reader's attention to this "encouragement . . . for rich people to give away Bibles and good books" (5:230). And while a lineage of rural virtue is no doubt the point of Tom's first appearance, as "the son of an honest labourer at a little village in Wiltshire," this rural world has from the outset been penetrated by the enterprising spirit associated with "the Sunday-school, carried on under the inspection of Dr. Shepherd." The entire course of the conversion narrative is determined by More's commitment to cosmopolitan middle-class enterprise as a remedy for the moral lapses of the rural poor. [. . .] When he returns at last to the village of his birth, Tom does not discover the untainted source of his own virtue, but rather a profoundly compromised social order upon which to unleash his own newly acquired zeal for reform. Before yielding the stage to the collaborative enterprise of Mrs. White and Dr. Shepherd, Farmer White undertakes his own vigorous campaign against the residual evils of rural popular culture:

> He had sense and spirit enough to break through many old, but very bad customs of his neighbours. If a thing is wrong in itself, (said he one day to farmer Hodges,) a whole parish doing it can't make it right. And as to its being an old custom, why, if it be a good one I like it the better for being old, because it has the stamp of ages, and the sanction of experience on its worth. But if it be old as well as bad, that is another reason for my trying to put an end to it, that we may not mislead our children as our fathers have misled us.

(5:248–9)

There can be no more compelling expression of the way moral principle trumps historical process in More's fiction. Far from offering a reliable guide for human conduct, the pattern of inherited transmission so venerated by Edmund Burke threatens to "mislead" past, present, and future generations alike.[10] The "Roof-Raising" and "Sheep Shearing" episodes that occur in the early phases of the second part of the tract are suffused with Farmer White's iconoclastic determination "to break through a bad custom," and in each case the communal traditions of "ribaldry, and riot, and drunkenness," associated with the agricultural calendar, give way under his strong hand to more "orderly and decent" invented traditions of collective psalm singing and sober feasts for the poor (5:249–61).[11] It is this aggressive revisionism, rather than any simply nostalgic or conservative response to radical innovation, that distinguishes the political project of the Cheap Repository, and links its treatment of a public, masculine sphere of alehouses and barn raisings with the feminine domain of housekeeping and domestic management.

[. . .]

[Omitted sections of this chapter expand on More's participation in an "improving campaign" in conservative politics.]

I would distinguish my treatment of the Cheap Repository from that of a number of feminist scholars who have argued, each in distinctive ways, that More's effective redefinition of the possibilities available to women, in her own career and in her influence on others, meant that her project was essentially liberating rather than reactionary or disciplinary in nature. She was, in Anne Mellor's provocative phrase, a "revolutionary reformer."[12] The Hannah More presented here is a more compromised though, I hope, no less complex figure, a reformer no doubt, but in important respects, a reactionary as well. While I share an interest in the transforming cultural work of the Cheap Repository and have learned a good deal from these feminist scholars about More's attention to women's work and her provocative redefinitions of gender, domesticity, education, and public life, it seems to me crucial that we not lose sight of the ways in which the evangelical enterprise of middle-class women imposed an astonishing range of social, political, and religious controls upon the behavior of men and women alike, and insisted, above all, upon the rigorous subordination of the lower orders.[13]

[. . .]

The heterogeneous structure of the two-part *Tom White*, with its opening narrative of fall and redemption, followed by a sequence of more discrete programmatic episodes, certainly yields something less than seamless fiction. Yet taken together, and considered in relation to More's wider project, the series does represent an impressive attempt to comprehend, in fictional form, the whole evangelical reform of manners. This comprehensive scope was a chief feature of the Cheap Repository. If the economy of the evangelical penny tract was by definition marginal, and its target audience impoverished, More's expectations for it were never modest, and she later boasted of having circulated over two million tracts within the first year of the establishment of the project (5:viii). There is ample evidence within these tracts, and in the letters and memoirs that surround them, of her restless campaign for increased subscriptions and more extensive circulation, and her ambition was evidently contagious: the Religious Tract Society, founded on More's model within a year of the formal termination of the Cheap Repository, accounted for sales of more than four million tracts by 1808, and ten million by 1824, and the group maintained a regular catalogue of hundreds of tracts in a variety of formats and series throughout the early decades of the nineteenth century.[14] Historians have long recognized More's achievement as a watershed event in the history of print, since it was through the Cheap Repository "that influential middle-class Englishmen got their first experience in the mass production and distribution of reading matter."[15] Yet the tension between the announced modesty of the project ("cheap") and its immodest ambitions could only be managed through the commercial sleight of hand that allowed tracts nominally priced at "one penny" to be distributed, in fact, through massive charitable subsidy and bulk sales. The peculiar print economy that resulted generated further tensions. Just as Tom White's reform left him eager to reform others, so the print economy of the Cheap Repository was an endless exercise in self-propagation, which seemed always to risk exhausting its own resources.

[. . .]

Given [the] comprehensive design upon reading audiences [. . .], and the sheer scale of the publishing enterprise, one of the most striking rifts within the Cheap Repository involved the tension between a desire to incorporate every reader and every text within a single print economy, and an insistence that differences of privilege and function within that economy be strictly enforced.

[. . .]

The willingness of the Cheap Repository to measure its success in the proliferation of millions of printed tracts invites a more pointed interrogation of the whole tract system. Who or what ensured the value of all of this printed material? And particularly for elites who were enjoined to participate as subscribers and distributors, and who therefore lent their credit to a network of effects they could not possibly witness, where was the guarantee that any of this reading material did any good in the world? In an era in which the threat of a French invasion had compelled Britain after 1797 to suspend specie payment, and thus to undertake an anxious, extended experiment with a currency not guaranteed by gold, these questions may have acquired an added urgency, since any scheme for unlimited textual production and circulation risked playing into anxieties about an inflationary currency unmoored from intrinsic standards of value.[16] If pressed for some guarantee of the credit of the entire system, the Cheap Repository had an advantage over its equally prolific but relatively secular counterpart, Reeves's Loyalist Association, where the production of counterrevolutionary propaganda often stood in tension with a blunt insistence that the British constitution was invulnerable to any challenge. By contrast, More's evangelical version of a counterrevolutionary project not only assumed the corruption of human nature and the imperfection of human institutions, but it could invoke the primary authority of scripture to underwrite its own print enterprise. Even the formal tendency of evangelical discourse to stray from narrative into catalogues of scriptural reference can be taken to confirm the fundamental authority of the Bible in the formation of these tracts. This was, as Robert Hole has indicated, a position with deep political implications: for all her evangelical leanings, More shared with her Anglican establishment friends like George Horne, Bishop of Norwich, a "politico-religious" commitment to "the divine authority of the established order" in church, state, and society, which "not only provided them with a Biblical foundation of political obligation, it also sanctified the existing social hierarchy as the work of Divine Providence."[17]

Yet as the Cheap Repository perfected a system of charitable provision that multiplied titles, editions, and series, and as it seconded the manageable convention of scriptural allusion with a more unruly network of references to other Cheap Repository Tracts (later editions of these works often display the further accretion of such promotional self-reference), there was a danger that the project might appear to supersede, rather than simply reinforce, the original authority of scripture. It is not surprising, then, that More was not consistent in her treatment of Biblical authority. "The grand subject of instruction with me is the bible itself," she once assured a correspondent, and while this claim was meant to reassure supporters that Sunday-school literacy would not exceed the limits of Christian piety, it seemed to indicate that scripture could by itself produce orderly, submissive, and industrious subjects.[18] Recommending the Bible to her readers in the opening paragraph of *The History of Hester Wilmot*, More's narrator reflects that "it is a pity people do not consult it oftener. They direct their ploughing and sowing by the information of the Almanack, why will they not consult the Bible for the direction of their hearts and lives?" (5:284). Yet despite this confidence in scriptural sufficiency, More was keenly aware that available forms of piety and loyalty were not adequate grounds for antirevolutionary culture, and she spent her career supplementing the Bible as moral almanac with an elaborate system of prayers, catechisms, schoolbooks, devotional tracts, and pious tales and ballads, along with supervised reading practices to manage textual reception.

[. . .]

The Cheap Repository could not have been more deliberate about its departure from localized, contained, or nostalgic approaches to managing the lives of the working poor in the face of revolutionary challenges. The ballad poem *Dame Andrews*, a 1795 Cheap Repository broadsheet that was not written by More, provides a vivid case in point. The opening lines are firmly embedded in a local community – "Near Lechlade Town, in Glostershire, / Upon the Banks of Thame" – but the narrative then conveys its heroine through a series of "mishaps" that require outside intervention. As the impoverished Dame Andrews prepares to feed her children their last loaf of bread, she hears a noise at the door, significantly not a knock, but the rattling of one "who tried to move the pin." Again, the Cheap Repository rescues the dispossessed by opening their private lives and domestic circumstances to the inspection of their superiors. Anticipating relief from a "friendly neighbour," Dame Andrews finds instead a woman "lately come / Within this town to live," who turns out emphatically to be a neighbor of another kind – "A friendly Neighbour sure it was!" – by virtue of her willingness to reward virtue by enlisting it in the cash nexus of evangelical reform: "I an offer to you make / My Schoolmistress to be; / To teach poor children and for this, / You shall be paid by me."[19] The double substitution here is crucial: as the condition for neighborhood shifts from proximity to charitable motive, so a recruitment to evangelical enterprise replaces bread, alms, or respectability as the reward of virtue. This conscripting mode of recompense allowed More and her collaborators to legitimate their own ambitions by representing the indigenous pious poor and the mobile, reformist middle class as interdependent social forces and reciprocal narrative effects.[20] It also sustained the pattern by which a print economy of charitable provision managed its own inflationary pressures by channeling redundant energy (and money) back into further charitable enterprise. The fact that episodes of this kind of reward often occur in a sequel, or in the later phases of a multipart publication, suggests an important formal consideration: Cheap Repository narrative tended to secure converts to the endless, serial task of moral reform at precisely that point where its own publishing operations were supplemented through the device of the sequel or final part.[21] Where conservative reactions to radical protest in this period often involved grub street nightmares of an exploding print culture, the evangelical economy of print sought to allay such fears by demonstrating an unlimited capacity to recycle its own boundless energy as a disciplinary mechanism.[22]

[. . .]

The full range of Cheap Repository narrative certainly complicates the impression, derived largely from *Village Politics*, of More as a narrow anti-Painite polemicist. At the same time, an appreciation of the literary complexity and cultural density of her later work can enrich our understanding of *Village Politics*. This widely reprinted dialogue was arguably her most influential fiction, and in many ways it provides the clearest index of the range of her ambitions, and of the contours she would assign to plebeian life and literacy. From the outset, the conversation "between Jack Anvil, the Blacksmith, and Tom Hod, the Mason" is very much a case of village politics, firmly embedded in English rural life and vernacular idioms, and pitched against the cosmopolitan abstractions of French "*organization* and *function*, and *civism*, and *incivism*, and *equalization*, and *inviolability*, and *imperscriptible*, and *fraternization*" (1:324). Paine's *Rights of Man* has intruded upon this world, via the intoxicated political sociability of the Rose and Crown tavern, but the radical challenge remains an alien language, both in its French associations and in its remoteness from the concrete experience of village life: the deluded Tom Hod can articulate his discontent only by "*looking on his book*" (significantly, the dialogue's first stage direction), and Jack Anvil, who secures the loyalist half of the conversation, considers it "a good sign" that "you can't find out you're unhappy without looking into a book for it!" (1:323–4). More's effort to weave her later Cheap Repository Tracts into the rhythms of popular life is negatively anticipated here by an attempt to pry the revolutionary text away from the life and world of its audience. The revolutionary lexicon cited above ("*organization* and *function*, and *civism*, and *incivism*") does not enter any real analysis of republican political theory, since Jack makes no effort to explain or demystify his terms. Instead, the simple act of reiterating the language of revolution within a village dialogue becomes an adequate critique, since the encompassing rhythms of vernacular speech serve to mark and cast out the supposed otherness of revolutionary discourse.

The initial act of the dialogue, Jack's interruption of Tom's reading, announces an evident ideological pressure in *Village Politics* away from printed texts and towards ordinary speech and the real world of things. Yet, as his alertness to "a good sign" indicates, Jack is nothing if not an expert reader of his world, and he shares his author's skepticism that concrete facts or real experiences might by themselves counteract Tom's acquired disaffection. On the contrary, the fundamental aim of the tract, as its full title indicates, is to use the medium of cheap print to make local orthodoxy available on a national scale: *Village Politics. Addressed to all the Mechanics, Journeymen, and Labourers, in Great Britain*. Nor is More content with the well-fed, well-governed logic that informed much of the reactionary discourse of the early 1790s, and issued in such crude dictums as, "None but a fool would rebel against beef and pudding."[23] *Village Politics* is from the outset a text generated out of another text, and Jack's opening gambit, "What book art reading?" (1:323), is very much the author's own. The tract achieves its orthodox narrative trajectory not by departing from the revolutionary empire of signs for the loyal comforts of "beef and pudding," but rather by succumbing to the inexorable force of other texts and other discourses, which are taken to be more securely embedded in the village world. In a characteristic concession to elites more interested in plebeian industry than orthodoxy, More has Jack confess that his work leaves him "little time for reading," but he goes on to answer Paine's *Rights of Man* with Richard Allestree's *Whole Duty of Man*, and to delineate a series of oral and printed authorities – scripture, sermons, English law, popular songs and sayings, "a story-book from the charity-school" (1:330) – that leave the village so hemmed in by discursive orthodoxy that there is simply no room for radical expression. The local squire, Sir John, enters the dialogue first as an equal, in Jack's conventional anti-French boast about English equality before the law: "I may go to law with Sir John at the great Castle yonder; and he no more dares lift his little finger against me than if I were his equal" (1:327). Yet as the discussion proceeds, this leveling gesture loses its force, and the same Sir John becomes the upper limit in a discursive hierarchy that secures the village against revolution. His sayings are local legend, and versions of the formula, "Sir John, who is wiser than I, says," have persuaded Jack, as they will soon persuade Tom, that "the whole [French] system is the operation of fraud upon folly" (1:340–1). Even the private letters of the Squire contribute to a common network of loyal discourse, as his foreign correspondence filters out through his servants into the village, to expose the bleak reality behind a Jacobin lie: " 'Tis all murder and nakedness, and hunger" (1:340).

If this last claim seems to offer a negative version of the material fact as antidote to revolution (French hunger rather than British beef), my point is to notice also the communicative circuit along which More imagines that such disenchanting truths get transmitted, so that Tom can make them available to Jack and to the reader: "Sir John's butler says his master gets letters which say" (1:340). This active exercise of counterrevolutionary orality and literacy, rather than any repressive prohibition of seditious texts, becomes the principal mechanism for contesting and defeating popular discontent in More's fictional world. As if to confirm that the stakes here are dangerous reading practices, not dangerous texts, let alone the experience of poverty or injustice, the dialogue closes as Jack first dissuades Tom from burning the book he has agreed to disown – "let's have no drinking, no riot, no bonfires" (1:348) – and then leads him off to the more important work of breaking up the tavern gatherings that have given rise to his phantom Painite discontent. The message is clear, and entirely consistent with More's dual role as Sunday school educator and founder of the Cheap Repository: control how books are distributed and where they are read, and there will be less to fear from seditious writers and texts. Tom's rousing chorus of "*[t]he roast beef of old England*," a blunt register of material satisfaction and fit accompaniment to a popular riot, gives way in the end to Jack's less nostalgic and subtly revisionist, though still scriptural, motto: "Study to be quiet, work with your own hands, and mind your own business" (1:347–8). The phrase belies the historical inertia of one of Jack's own earlier anti-French dictums about liberty: "We've no race to run! We're there already!" (1:335). Instead, "study to be quiet," and work to acquire habits of contentment and subordination. For More, popular loyalty and civil order were neither given conditions nor available inheritances; instead, they had to be aggressively taught and actively learned, through the procedures developed in her educational and publishing schemes, and then relentlessly thematized in her fiction.

[. . .]

Notes

1 The tracts were published under these titles by the Cheap Repository in March and September of 1795; in the first collected edition of Hannah More's work, *The Works of Hannah More*, 8 vols (London: T. Cadell and W. Davies, 1801), they were reprinted as *The History of Tom White the Post Boy. In Two Parts.* More's work for the Cheap Repository appeared in a dizzying array of editions and formats over the course of her life, and for the purposes of uniformity, I will refer to this 1801 Cadell and Davies edition (hereafter cited parenthetically by volume and page number), except where particular variations in content or presentation are relevant to my argument. I also refer to several Cheap Repository Tracts not written by More; since these were not collected in any uniform edition, I cite them in their original form. Such tracts were subject to More's approval and appeared under the Cheap Repository title, and can therefore be treated as integral to the project. For the authorship of the tracts, see G.H. Spinney, "Cheap Repository Tracts: Hazard and Marshall Edition," *The Library* 20 (1939–1940): 310–11.

2 For the public house as "central transmitter of . . . plebian custom," see Mitzi Myers, "Hannah More's Tracts for the Times: Social Fiction and Female Ideology," in *Fetter'd or Free? British Women Novelists, 1670–1815*, ed. Mary Anne Schofield and Cecilia Macheski (Athens: Ohio Univ. Press, 1986), 272. [. . .]

3 Though widely applied to Hannah More by critics and historians alike, "evangelical" is in some respects an imperfect term. In using it, I accept Robert Hole's caution that, while the term usefully indicates her concern for personal salvation and her social activism with respect to slavery and poverty, it should not obscure her dislike for Methodism and her firm commitment to social hierarchy and the established church [. . .] See Hole's introduction, *Selected Writings of Hannah More*, ed. Hole (London: William Pickering, 1996), xx–xiv.

4 The precise circumstances of the title are glossed in later editions of More's work: "Written in 1795, the Year of Scarcity" (5:244).

5 *The History of Tom White, the Postillion. In Two Parts* (London and Bath, [no date]), 25. In the 1801 edition of her works, the word "present" was dropped from this phrase (5:261).

6 In an intriguing discussion of providential causality in the Cheap Repository Tracts, Catherine Gallagher identifies what I take to be a related gap between the moral agency of More's characters and the narrative episodes they occupy, though Gallagher's concern is finally the priority of divine providence rather than the institutional framework within which moral reform occurs. See Gallagher, *The Industrial Reformation of English Fiction: Social Discourse and Narrative Form, 1832–1867* (Chicago: Univ. of Chicago Press, 1985), 38.

7 See [Dorice Elliott, "'The Care of the Poor Is Her Profession': Hannah More and Women's Philanthropic Work," *Nineteenth-Century Contexts* 19 (1995): 194–5]; Anne Mellor, *Mothers of the Nation* (Bloomington: Indiana Univ. Press, 2000), 28–32; and Kathryn Sutherland, "Hannah More's Counter-Revolutionary Feminism," in *Revolution in Writing: British Literary Responses to the French Revolution*, ed. Kelvin Everest (Milton Keynes, Eng.: Open Univ. Press, 1991), 53–61.

8 In collected editions of More's work, the tract was renamed *A Cure for Melancholy: Shewing the Way to Do Much Good with Little Money*, emphasizing the way Mrs. Jones's introduction to evangelical enterprise corrects her excessive grief after the death of her husband; by contrast, the earlier title, consistently used for Cheap Repository editions beginning in early 1797, calls attention to the practical guidance contained in a closing section of recipes and domestic advice, removed in the collected *Works*.

9 Sutherland, 27, 51.

10 More does take her epigraph for volume 5 of the 1801 collected works from "Burke on the French Revolution," but it is significant that the passage she selects from the *Reflections* involves a discussion of the established church, and therefore presents Edmund Burke as the defender of faith rather than custom [. . .].

11 I borrow the notion of an invented tradition from *The Invention of Tradition*, ed. Eric Hobsbawm and Terence Ranger (Cambridge: Cambridge Univ. Press, 1983).

12 Mellor, 13; [Christine L. Krueger, *The Reader's Repentance: Women Preachers, Women Writers, and Nineteenth-Century Social Discourse* (Chicago: Univ. of Chicago Press, 1992)], 85, 112–15;

Elliott, 179–204; Sutherland, 27–63; Myers, "Hannah More's Tracts for the Times," 264–84; and Myers, "Reform or Ruin: 'A Revolution in Female Manners.'" *Studies in Eighteenth-Century Culture* 11 (1982): 199–216. For a less sympathetic feminist response, see Elizabeth Kowaleski-Wallace, *Their Fathers' Daughters: Hannah More, Maria Edgeworth, and Patriarchal Complicity* (New York: Oxford Univ. Press, 1991), 56–93.

13 Gallagher has written suggestively about the potential "friction" (40) between More's commitment to a "rule of providential necessity" (38) and her effort "to portray people in all conditions of life as free moral agents" (38). [. . .]

14 See *An Account of the Origin and Progress of the London Religious Tract Society* (London, 1803), 6; *Report of the Committee of the Religious Tract Society* (London, 1808), 5; and *The Twenty-Fifth Annual Report of the Religious Tract Society* (London, 1824), xv.

15 Richard Altick, *The English Common Reader: A Social History of the Mass Reading Public, 1800–1900* (Chicago: Univ. of Chicago Press, 1957), 76.

16 For a suggestive account of the shift to a nonconvertible paper currency in the work of nation making, see Jerome Christensen, "The Detection of the Romantic Conspiracy in Britain," *South Atlantic Quarterly* 95 (1996): 603–27.

17 Hole, introduction to *Selected Writings of Hannah More*, xx.

18 *Mendip Annals: Or, A Narrative of the Charitable Labours of Hannah and Martha More in Their Neighbourhood. Being the Journal of Martha More*, ed. Arthur Roberts (London: James Nisbet, 1859), 8.

19 *Dame Andrews, A Ballad* (Bath, 1795).

20 Of course the force of obligation moved primarily in one direction along the social hierarchy: "Indeed, the rich have been very kind," Betty Plane observes at the end of *Tom White*, as the villagers gather under Dr. Shepherd's direction to cope with the effects of the high price of provision, "I don't know what we should have done without them" (5:280).

21 Dorice Elliott has written perceptively about the way that More's charitable enterprise, more broadly considered, sustained itself by generating obligations as well as further demands. [. . .]See Elliott, 185–7.

22 For conservative anxieties about the explosion of radical print culture, see [Kevin Gilmartin, *Print Politics: The Press and Radical Opposition in Early Nineteenth Century England* (Cambridge: Cambridge Univ. Press, 1996)], 68–9.

23 "Think a Little," in Association for Preserving Liberty and Property against Republicans and Levellers, *Association Papers* in *Part the Second: Containing a Collection of Tracts Printed at the Expence of the Society* (London, 1793), Number 8:14.

12 Audience, irony, and Shelley

Andrew Franta

Shelley has been regarded as perhaps the least ironic of the romantic poets. This was T.S. Eliot's judgment, for example, when he called Shelley's ideas "ideas of adolescence." Eliot finds Shelley's views "repellant" and describes him as "humorless, pedantic, self-centered." But he also points to a different, and deeper, issue. Eliot's most powerful objection to "Shelley's abuse of poetry" – which distinguishes him from Wordsworth, who, Eliot remarks, "does not present a very pleasing personality either" – has to do with "the difficulty of separating Shelley from his ideas and beliefs" (Eliot 1964: 80). The problem with Shelley, Eliot argues, is not merely that his views are wrong but that they present an obstacle to the appreciation of his poems. By contrast, we can reject the views of Lucretius or Dante but still appreciate the poetry, because "when the doctrine, theory, belief, or 'view of life' presented in a poem" is "coherent, mature, and founded on the facts of experience, it interposes no obstacle to the reader's enjoyment, whether it be one that he accept or deny, approve or deprecate" (Eliot 1964: 87). If we strip away Eliot's palpable dislike of Shelley's moral and political opinions (as he suggests we should), his difficulty with Shelley is that his views are impositions – on the poems and the reader.

Eliot's assessment goes a long way toward explaining the New Critical antipathy toward Shelley. In *Modern Poetry and the Tradition*, Cleanth Brooks argued that Shelley's incoherence was not only intellectual and moral but aesthetic. Shelley is betrayed by his "tone and attitude" and his "sometimes embarrassing declarations – 'I die, I faint, I fail' or 'I fall upon the thorns of life! I bleed!'" (Brooks 1939: 237). Shelley lapses into sentimentality, but, as with Eliot, the real problem for Brooks is not content but form – or, more precisely, the lack thereof. "The characteristic fault of Shelley's poetry," Brooks says, "is that it cannot bear ironical contemplation. What Shelley's regenerated world of *Prometheus Unbound* really has to fear is not the possible resurrection of Jupiter but the resurrection of John Donne. Grant that, and chaos comes again" (Brooks 1939: 50). Shelley's metaphysics are not metaphysical – or not metaphysical enough. For Brooks, this is a failure of form rather than merely a matter of preference because irony, along with verbal paradox, is the defining feature of poetry.[1]

With the emergence of deconstruction, by contrast, the critical interest in irony – and the tendency to associate its effects with literariness as such – led toward rather than away from the romantic poets. Unlike Eliot and Brooks, deconstructive critics did not segregate Shelley from Keats and Wordsworth. Commenting on Northrop Frye's characterization of irony as "a pattern of words that turns away from direct statement or its own obvious meaning" (Frye 1957: 40), Paul de Man suggests that irony "seems to be the trope of tropes," an intensification or special case of figuration which "involves a little more, a more radical negation than one would have in an ordinary trope such as synecdoche or metaphor or metonymy" (de Man 1996: 165). In the wake of this reassessment, we tend to see irony in romantic poetry as what Deborah Elise White has called "a stand in . . . for the romantic *topoi* of self-consciousness and self-division: contradiction, fragmentation, dissolution" (White 1999). De Man's irony is not the irony of Eliot or Brooks; New Critical paradox stops short of "radical negation." In "Irony as a Principle of Structure," for example, Brooks argues that irony "acknowledges the pressures of context"; it is a feature of "a poetry which does not leave out what is apparently hostile to its dominant tone, and . . . is able to fuse the irrelevant and the discordant" (Brooks 1951: 732). At the same time, however, while their value judgments diverge – where Brooks wants "balance" (Brooks 1951: 733), de Man finds "a little more" – deconstruction and the New Criticism both regard irony as an index to poetry's essentially formal significance.

Is it possible to construe Eliot's strictures on taste, the New Critical insistence on paradox, or deconstruction's linguistic turn in a way that makes them sound anything but old-fashioned? Even with the resurgence of theory, de Man's deep formalism seems to speak from a different era. If romantic scholars tend not to pay much attention to irony these days (and I don't think we do), it is perhaps because we associate it with a critical moment before the rise of historicism. One could argue that the new historicism pushed irony to the side in the study of romantic poetry. But it would perhaps be more accurate to say that new historicists viewed irony as among romantic poetry's myriad resources of displacement – one of the tools poets used to fashion "a world elsewhere" and perform the "acts of exclusion" designed to transcend their social reality (McGann 1979: 57; Levinson 1986: 32).[2] The new historicism did not turn its back on form. It sought instead to displace the formalist project of definition evident in both Eliot's and Brooks' policing of the literary and de Man's identification of theory and reading rendered as the rhetorical critique of the ontology of the literary text (de Man 1986: 15). The desire to delve into the social and political contexts of romantic poetry and to insist upon the referential stakes of romantic writing was thus an effort to renew our critical appreciation of how poetry's formal engagements find their ultimate point of reference in the world rather than the poem or language itself.[3]

If the new historicism aimed to redirect and expand the scope and stakes of formal analysis – to assert that such inquiry should not be bounded by the borders of the literary text – the recent return to theory has tended to understand the relationship between history and form in oppositional terms. This renewed attention to the formal dimension of the literary text – even, perhaps especially, when it does not take the form of a critique of the turn to history or a polemic about the "return" of form – can give the impression that historical and formal analysis are incompatible and that the critic must choose between them. For better or worse, it seems to me that this is where we are now, which is to say that the field of romantic studies, like the romantic subject of high theory, is self-divided.[4] In part, recent calls for a return to the text, to form, and to theory are an effect of what we might term "history exhaustion" – the not unjustifiable feeling that, to the extent that the field possesses an accepted methodology, it entails the conjunction of "romanticism" with a seemingly endless series of historical contexts (which, we reflexively add, are in fact constitutive rather than merely contextual). It is an objection, that is, not to the critical procedures of the new historicism but a model of cultural studies which regards history in almost entirely material terms – as content rather than form, content as opposed to form.[5]

But what this assessment misses, I think, is the serious sense in which the twin legacies of formalism and historicism remain at once deeply relevant to the literature and the period we want to understand and frustratingly difficult to reconcile with one another.[6] However convinced we might be, looking back, that the distance between high theory and the new historicism wasn't nearly as great as we might once have imagined, it is hard not to acknowledge the sense that history and form are locked in some kind of allegorical conflict – a battle played out over the prostrate body of romantic poetry. This contest often seems rhetorical; it turns on questions of priority and emphasis rather than starkly antithetical claims. If our primary analytical framework is historical, we still make room for form. If our emphasis is formal, we rarely argue that history simply doesn't matter. What I'm suggesting is that what might look like a matter of a critic's particular disposition, in the larger context of the recent history of romantic scholarship represents the effect of an unfinished conversation between formalism and historicism. That we can now choose between history and form – and are sometimes enjoined to declare our allegiance to one side or the other – isn't the sign of a healthy scholarly pluralism. It is evidence of a critical impasse.

Despite what Eliot had to say about him, Shelley is an ironic poet. And, despite de Man's "madness of words," Shelley's irony is not a turn away from history (de Man 1984: 122). Indeed, to talk about Shelley's irony in this context is to register the ways in which the kind of self-conscious formalism that we still associate with romantic poetry can be as much about the world as the world of poetry. In turning to the "Ode to the West Wind," I want to suggest that the questions raised by ironic self-reflection in this poem, and much romantic poetry, emblematize the poet's difficult engagement with the reading public and the idea of audience. It is my hope that paying attention to this kind of self-reflexivity might allow us to rethink (or think our way out of) our persistent tendency to understand the relationship between history and form as antagonistic. Shelley's irony is not merely self-conscious; it reflects a consciousness of audience as at once a condition of possibility for literature and a limit to authorial control. Understood in this way, romantic irony represents more than a self-enclosed linguistic moment or purely critical posture. Instead, it is a means of addressing an uncertain audience and an attempt to engage the reader in a dialogue or dialectic that is less Hegelian than Socratic. In his self-reflexive framing of instances of reading, Shelley articulates a form of self-consciousness oriented not only inward but outward and conceptualizes reception as an integral feature of poetic address. Romantic self-reflexivity is thus a double gesture which reveals the reciprocity between romantic poetics and the history of the reading public. Shelley's conception of history is instructive, and perhaps especially so for us now. It is not history as event, but history as practice.

***

The last line of the "Ode to the West Wind" is structured by an opposition between assertion and negation. Read as a rhetorical question with an affirmative response, the Ode's final line – "If Winter comes, can Spring be far behind?" (70) – celebrates the success of the poem's vision of change. The correspondence between the natural and human worlds the speaker has worked so hard to create has been established; the connection between seasonal change and a revolution in human affairs has been forged. To this way of thinking, the Ode's closing question is an affirmation that the work the speaker has invoked the wind to perform will be done. Taken as a real question, however, one that admits the possibility of a negative reply or at least acknowledges that obstacles still stand in the way of the transformation the poem imagines, the Ode's closing line broaches an ironic critique of its project. The question in its bare form remains rhetorical – of course if winter comes spring will follow. But attending to the possibility that the question might in fact "bear ironical contemplation" (Brooks 1939: 50) suggests that the speaker's effort to map human affairs onto an "Uncontroulable" natural force is at best provisional or equivocal (47) – perhaps renovation will follow repression as spring follows winter. At worst, as an instance of "radical negation" (de Man 1996: 165), the question is an admission of failure and an acknowledgement of the limits of the imagination's capacity to effect the kind of change toward which the poem so powerfully gestures.

Placing these two readings side by side, as phrases in dispute rather than mutually exclusive alternatives, suggests radical contradiction rather than resolution (Lyotard 1988). The Ode's rhetorical question produces the "state of suspended ignorance" that de Man identifies as the condition of literature itself (de Man 1979: 19).[7] As Shelley's fervent anticipation of change gives way to, or oscillates with, its negative, we once again encounter "the romantic *topoi* of self-consciousness and self-division" (White 1999). The abstraction of the question, as well as its recourse to an analogy the poem has not only worked very hard to forge but shown itself to be laboring to establish, sets the speaker at odds with himself and stages a drama played out in his psyche – a contest between idealism and skepticism. In addition to reanimating this familiar Shelleyan conflict, a reading along these lines effectively rehearses de Man's account of the development of the relationship between mind and nature in romanticism, in which "the relationship with nature has been superseded by an intersubjective, interpersonal relationship that, in the last analysis, is a relationship of the subject toward itself" (de Man 1983: 196). In fact, one could argue that the story de Man tells is the subject of stanza IV of the Ode, where the speaker makes an explicit attempt to establish an analogy that would secure him to the natural world. We could go further and observe that it is precisely the speaker's articulation of his felt distance from the external power he strives to internalize that prompts one of the declarations Brooks found so embarrassing: "I fall upon the thorns of life! I bleed!" (54). What looks from one perspective like the genesis of a self-divided subject, from the other represents the pronouncement of a troublingly unified, and self-pitying, self. Divergent formal readings arrive at antithetically opposed evaluations of the same state of textual affairs: on the one hand, ontological pathos; on the other, mawkish sentimentality. One man's radical idealism is another's solipsism.

Neither of these readings takes seriously the prospect that Shelley is joking. Or not joking exactly, but "being ironic," in a familiar sense. The passage Brooks criticizes is self-dramatizing, to a degree that makes it difficult to read. Brooks understands this difficulty as an embarrassment, but he is perhaps too quick to credit Shelley's sincerity. (Shelley's speaker does, after all, respond to his failure to internalize nature by impaling himself on it.) In *The Visionary Company*, Harold Bloom responded to the New Criticism's "aesthetic condemnation" of Shelley by arguing that it was "a mask for . . . moral and religious outrage." For Bloom, "The spirit of urbanity is so prevalent in Shelley that one learns to distrust the accuracy of any critic who finds Shelley's poetry shrill, without humor, self-centered, or exhibiting only 'primary impulses'" (Bloom 1971: 284). "Usually intense," he writes, "Shelley is yet always at ease, though few of his critics want to note this. Shelley's irony is neither the 'romantic irony' of pathos . . . nor the 'metaphysical' irony so valued in the generation just past." Instead, "Shelley's irony is gentler and relies on incongruities that can suddenly startle us in the midst of the sublime without dropping us into the bathetic" (Bloom 1971: 283). The effect Bloom describes depends on a particular mode of address, and its power derives from the juxtaposition of vehement expression and a conversational tone. It has to do with the ability not to separate Shelley from his ideas and beliefs, as Eliot wanted to do, but to gauge his relative distance from them.

The line in the Ode to which Brooks so strenuously objects turns on just this kind of calculation. The fourth stanza of the poem begins as an attempt at the kind of intensification and transformation of the invocation of the wind undertaken in stanza V; what will become a command ("Make me thy lyre . . . " [57]) is first articulated provisionally, as a conditional ("If I were a dead leaf . . . " [43]). The speaker's initial effort to identify himself with the wind is derailed by the existential distance that separates him from it ("only less free / Than thou, O Uncontroulable" [46–7]), and the aborted identification turns instead into an expression of powerlessness. But the speaker's lament, his account of his subjection to the "heavy weight of hours" (55), however deeply felt and vividly (or embarrassingly) expressed, is also an allusion to Wordsworth's account of a very similar anxiety in "Tintern Abbey." Like Wordsworth, Shelley's speaker turns to his "boyhood" for an image of a unified self (48), a self that exists in harmony with nature, but he is in no better position than Wordsworth to "paint / What then I was" (75–6); in each case, the speaker's distance from his past self echoes rather than repairs his separation from nature. As in "Tintern Abbey," the image of the speaker's youthful relation to nature is less a vehicle that enables him to overcome self-division than a particularly cruel reminder of his alienation. Beyond these basic similarities, however, Shelley's radical distillation of Wordsworth's hesitations and equivocations ("If this / Be but a vain belief . . . " [49–50]) transforms the passage into a kind of parody of "Tintern Abbey"; in the Ode, the intensity of the speaker's "sore need" provokes hysteria rather than mature reflection (52).[8] The allusion to Wordsworth, which serves as a kind of shorthand for the speaker's existential crisis, undermines his sincerity by exposing his powerful feeling as a pose and a performance – emotion quoted rather than felt.

That the Shelley of the "Ode to the West Wind" is at odds with Wordsworth comes as no surprise. (Given his hostility toward Wordsworth in poems like "To William Wordsworth" and "Peter Bell the Third," it would be shocking if he took "Tintern Abbey" straight.) What I'm suggesting, by contrast, is that what looks to Brooks like sentimentality in fact lies closer to sarcasm – and that this cynicism is directed at the idea of the divided self. Paying attention to the Ode's irony reveals the way the transition from stanza IV to stanza V brackets the fragmentation of the self and reframes it, self-reflexively transforming an image of internal conflict into a gesture directed outward. In "The Rhetoric of Temporality," de Man describes such moments, in which "the dialectic between subject and object" is rejected or suspended, as examples of the "allegorizing tendencies" of late eighteenth-century European literature more generally (de Man 1983: 204). He argues that the reemergence of allegory in romanticism demonstrates that the confrontation of subject and object "does not designate the main romantic experience, but only one passing moment in a dialectic, and a negative moment at that" (de Man 1983: 204–5). This "rediscovery" of allegory represents a rupture in the "continuous development from allegory to romantic naturalism," and, in writers like Rousseau and Wordsworth, the turn away from symbol, the ascendant metaphorical style of modernity, "implies the discontinuity of a renunciation, even of a sacrifice" (de Man 1983: 205).

For de Man, "the prevalence of allegory always corresponds to the unveiling of an authentically temporal destiny" (de Man 1983: 206). This temporality links allegory and irony: "in both cases, the sign points to something that differs from its literal meaning and has for its function the thematization of this difference" (de Man 1983: 209). But if the return to allegory exposes the dialectic between subject and object as "a major mystification" (de Man 1983: 214), the "duplication," or "*dédoublement*," on which irony depends "is a relationship, within consciousness, between two selves, yet it is not an intersubjective relationship" (de Man 1983: 212). The frame of reference remains the self, even as it is renounced or sacrificed, and the authentic temporality that allegory and irony reveal is ultimately that of literary language itself. De Man's account is illuminating with respect to the structure and trajectory of the "Ode to the West Wind"; the poem's movement from the analogical correspondences of the first three stanzas through the crisis of the fourth to the narrativizing turn of the last seems to recapitulate the literary-historical development he describes. In an important sense, Shelley's allegory, like de Man's, is an allegory of reading (de Man 1979). But Shelley departs from de Man in that the kind of reading figured in the final stanza of the Ode is the product not only of language on the page but of the dissemination of those pages. When Shelley's speaker imagines a correspondence between his "leaves" and the forest's and asks the wind to "Drive" and "Scatter" his "thoughts" and "words" (58, 63, 66, 63, 67), he conceives of his thoughts and words as language embodied in text. The Ode's allegory of reading is a myth of textual transmission.[9]

What we discover when we attend to Shelley's irony in the Ode is the presence in the poem's final stanza of an audience – the readers whose "incantation of this verse" is capable of realizing the transformative change the poem imagines (65). In lending their voices to its verses and animating the breathlessly long periods of stanzas I-III, the poem's readers become the "breath of Autumn's being" (1).[10] The spirit addressed in the Ode, in other words, looks forward to the spirit invoked in the last paragraph of the *Defence of Poetry*. De Man begins "The Rhetoric of Temporality" by alluding to "the possibility of a rhetoric than would no longer be normative or descriptive but would more or less openly raise the question of the intentionality of rhetorical figures" (de Man 1983: 187–8). In the Ode and the *Defence*, Shelley's figures redistribute the ascription of intentionality by calling attention to the effects that poems have on their readers and the role of reception and transmission in the creation of poems. His claim, for example, that "our own will be a memorable age in intellectual achievements" – "a new birth" – is grounded in not only the works of contemporary "philosophers and poets" but their reception by a future audience. In fact, poets and philosophers are themselves alienated from the "comprehensive and all-penetrating spirit" that animates their writing: "they are themselves perhaps the most sincerely astonished at its manifestations, for it is less their spirit than the spirit of the age." If, as Shelley claims, "it is impossible to read the compositions of the most celebrated writers of the present day without being startled with the electric life which burns within their words," the sincere astonishment of "the person in whom this power resides" – "even," he adds, "whilst they deny and abjure" – marks the moment at which writers become readers (535). This is as true, moreover, of Shelley as it is of Wordsworth (to whom Shelley's remarks clearly allude). That the power that works through the poet is not subject to "the determination of the will" (531), that writers "may often, as far as regards many portions of their nature, have little apparent correspondence with that spirit of good of which they are the ministers" (535), makes it clear that the transformation of agency Shelley describes entails the attenuation of authorial control. Unlike Dorothy in "Tintern Abbey," whose voice allows Wordsworth to "catch / The language of my former heart" (116–17) and in whose "wild eyes" he can "read / My former pleasures" (119, 117–18) or the "youthful Poets" of "Michael," "who . . . / Will be my second self when I am gone" (38–9), the readers Shelley imagines in the Ode are as "Wild" and "Uncontroulable" as the wind itself (13, 47). The power he invests in the audience is predicated on the possibility of errancy – refusal, critique, or misreading – rather than the assurance of a positive response.

I have argued elsewhere that this idea of reception is the product of romantic poets' responses to the emergence of the mass reading public. *Romanticism and the Rise of the Mass Public* contends that the perceived antagonism between romantic poetry and the reading audience – the longstanding conviction that "there is, in fact, something singularly fatal to the audience in the romantic point of view" (Abrams 1953: 25) – has led even those critics most concerned with exploring the historical conditions of romantic writing to overlook the powerful sense in which poets' anxieties about the reading public fueled the conviction that, as Shelley puts it in the *Defence*, a poem might be "the source of an unforeseen and an unconceived delight" (528). The formative influence of the kind of ungovernable reception Shelley describes in the Ode is one of the key effects of what Lucy Newlyn has called "the rise of the reader" in early nineteenth-century England (Newlyn 2000: 3). The better part of Shelley's account of poetry in the *Defence* is devoted to describing "its effects upon society" (516): what begins as a work of definition turns into a work of literary history whose focus is reception. In his remarks on Dante and Milton, in particular, Shelley presents himself as the sort of reader he envisions in the Ode. His reading of the tradition's greatest Christian poets does not, as Eliot would have it, bracket their views of life. Instead, Shelley refigures reading and reception as a process of transformation. Dante's "very words," like the "Ashes and sparks" of the Ode (67), "are instinct with spirit; each is as a spark, a burning atom of indistinguishable thought" (528). But, because "many yet lie covered in the ashes of their birth, and pregnant with a lightning which has yet found no conductor," it is up to new ages and new readers to animate them with the energy that "their peculiar relations enable them to share" (528).

These "peculiar relations" are historical, but Shelley conceives of history as an engine of formal transformation rather than its background. His description of poetry as "the most unfailing herald, companion, and follower of the awakening of a great people to work a beneficial change in opinion or institution" equivocates about the relationship between history and form, but this equivocation, or temporization, is antithetical to the idea that form and history are opposed (535). Shelley's orientation to the future, to put it bluntly, is the measure of his historicism. His formalism is not a turn inward or away from the world, but an attempt to engage it by "defeat[ing] the curse which binds us to be subjected to the accident of surrounding impressions"

(533). The irony of the last line of the "Ode to the West Wind," the sense in which it is at once an exhortation and an expression of doubt, opens the poem to the reader, and to reading.

It would not be going too far to say that, for Shelley, history is made as much by the practice of reading the past as the unfolding of sequences of actions and events. History as action and event conforms to the *Defence*'s understanding of story: it "is a catalogue of detached facts, which have no other bond of connexion than time, place, circumstance, cause and effect" (515). History conceived as practice, by contrast, looks particularly modern: it is at once progressive and unpredictable. Shelley's account of poetry is idealizing – "The story of particular facts is as a mirror which obscures and distorts that which should be beautiful: Poetry is a mirror which makes beautiful that which is distorted" (515) – but it also discloses a temporality that makes the source of poetry's power puzzlingly obscure. Poetry is "herald, companion, and follower"; poets are "the mirrors of the gigantic shadows which futurity casts upon the present" (535). These are oblique formulations, but their ambiguity points to a conception of history much more capacious than our current critical practice often allows. For Brooks, modern poetry's "commitment to metaphor" entailed both "a principle of indirection" and "a principle of organic relationship" (Brooks 1951: 729). For Shelley, the power of poetic form has to do with the indirect access it affords to relationships that extend beyond the poem – the "peculiar relations" between writers, texts, and readers; past, present, and future.

Notes

1 For an insightful contemporary response to the New Critical evaluation of Shelley, see Ford (1960).
2 Much of the crucial new historicist work in romanticism focused, like Levinson's, on the analysis of what David Simpson called Wordsworth's "poetry of displacement" (Simpson 1987). See also Chandler (1984) and Liu (1989).
3 For appraisals of the place of formal analysis in the new historicism along these lines, see Wolfson (2000) and Levinson (2007).
4 This is an observation rather than a criticism. One of the striking things about such exemplary, and varied, recent studies as Rei Terada's *Feeling in Theory: Emotion After the 'Death of the Subject'* (Terada 2001) and *Looking Away: Phenomenality and Dissatisfaction, Kant to Adorno* (Terada 2009), Anne-Lise François' *Open Secrets: The Literature of Uncounted Experience* (François 2008), and Jacques Khalip's *Anonymous Life: Romanticism and Dispossession* (Khalip 2009) is how their canons of criticism diverge from those of historicist studies. This deviation, which has to do not only with the critics cited but how they are treated, reflects a divided field.
5 In an incisive essay, Richard Strier takes aim at this strain of cultural studies, in which "the fact that some item . . . is mentioned in a text . . . is sufficient to get the machinery of 'archeology' and archive-churning going" and texts are treated "almost entirely in terms of content" (Strier 2002: 213).
6 Despite illuminating efforts, from divergent perspectives, demonstrating the crucial place of formal analysis in historicist and cultural studies. See Liu (1990) and Chandler (1998).
7 The Ode thus performs the kind of reading de Man describes at the end of "Semiology and Rhetoric":

> Any question about the rhetorical mode of a literary text is always a rhetorical question which does not even know whether it is really questioning. The resulting pathos is an anxiety (or bliss, depending on one's momentary mood or individual temperament) of ignorance, not an anxiety of reference. . .
>
> (de Man 1979: 19)

8 I do not intend to endorse Shelley's reading of Wordsworth but to note the use to which
   he puts this parody of "Tintern Abbey." For a reading of the poem that finds a common
   ground between Wordsworth and Shelley as I describe him here, see Canuel (2012).
9 For a reading of the Ode along these lines, see Franta (2007: 111–36).
10 Chandler notes the "strong sense in which the West Wind's inspiration has been interchangeable with the readerly audience from the start" (Chandler 1998: 553).

Bibliography

Abrams, M.H. (1953) *The Mirror and the Lamp: Romantic Theory and the Critical Tradition*,
   New York: Oxford University Press.
Bloom, Harold (1971) *The Visionary Company: A Reading of English Romantic Poetry* (1961), rev.
   edn, Ithaca, NY: Cornell University Press.
Brooks, Cleanth (1939) *Modern Poetry and the Tradition*, Chapel Hill, NC: The University of
   North Carolina Press.
Brooks, Cleanth (1951) "Irony as a Principle of Structure," in *Literary Opinion in America*,
   Morton Dauwen Zabel (ed.), rev. edn, 729–41, New York: Harper and Brothers.
Canuel, Mark (2012) "Historicism, Formalism, and 'Tintern Abbey,'" *European Romantic Review*
   23: 363–72.
Chandler, James K. (1984) *Wordsworth's Second Nature: A Study of the Poetry and Politics*, Chicago,
   IL: University of Chicago Press.
Chandler, James K. (1998) *England in 1819: The Politics of Literary Culture and the Case of Romantic
   Historicism*, Chicago, IL: University of Chicago Press.
de Man, Paul (1979) "Semiology and Rhetoric" (1973), in *Allegories of Reading: Figural Language
   in Rousseau, Rilke, Nietzsche, and Proust*, 3–19, New Haven, CT: Yale University Press.
de Man, Paul (1983) "The Rhetoric of Temporality" (1969), in *Blindness and Insight: Essays
   in the Rhetoric of Contemporary Criticism*, 2nd edn, 187–228, Minneapolis, MN: University of
   Minnesota Press.
de Man, Paul (1984) "Shelley Disfigured" (1979), in *The Rhetoric of Romanticism*, 93–123, New
   York: Columbia University Press.
de Man, Paul (1986) "The Resistance to Theory," in *The Resistance to Theory*, 2–20, Minneapolis,
   MN: University of Minnesota Press.
de Man, Paul (1996) "The Concept of Irony," in *Aesthetic Ideology*, Andrzej Warminski (ed.),
   163–84, Minneapolis, MN: University of Minnesota Press.
Eliot, T.S. (1964) *The Use of Poetry and the Use of Criticism*, Cambridge, MA: Harvard University
   Press.
Ford, Newell F. (1960) "Paradox and Irony in Shelley's Poetry," *Studies in Philology* 57: 648–62.
François, Anne-Lise (2008) *Open Secrets: The Literature of Uncounted Experience*, Stanford, CA:
   Stanford University Press.
Franta, Andrew (2007) *Romanticism and the Rise of the Mass Public*, Cambridge: Cambridge
   University Press.
Frye, Northrop (1957) *Anatomy of Criticism: Four Essays*, Princeton, NJ: Princeton University
   Press.
Khalip, Jacques (2009) *Anonymous Life: Romanticism and Dispossession*, Stanford, CA: Stanford
   University Press.
Levinson, Marjorie (1986) *Wordsworth's Great Period Poems: Four Essays*, Cambridge: Cambridge
   University Press.
Levinson, Marjorie (2007) "What is New Formalism?" *PMLA* 122: 558–69.
Liu, Alan (1989) *Wordsworth: The Sense of History*, Stanford, CA: Stanford University Press.
Liu, Alan (1990) "Local Transcendence: Cultural Criticism, Postmodernism, and the
   Romanticism of Detail," *Representations* 32: 75–113.
Lyotard, Jean-François (1988) *The Differend: Phrases in Dispute* (1983), Georges Van Den
   Abbeele (trans.), Minneapolis, MN: University of Minnesota Press.

McGann, Jerome (1979) "Keats and the Historical Method in Literary Criticism," *Modern Language Notes* 94: 998–1032.

Newlyn, Lucy (2000) *Reading, Writing, and Romanticism: The Anxiety of Reception*, Oxford: Oxford University Press.

Shelley, Percy Bysshe (2002) *Shelley's Poetry and Prose*, Donald H. Reiman and Neil Fraistat (eds), 2nd edn, New York: Norton.

Simpson, David (1987) *Wordsworth's Historical Imagination: The Poetry of Displacement*, New York: Methuen.

Strier, Richard (2002) "How Formalism Became a Dirty Word, and Why We Can't Do Without It," in *Renaissance Literary and Its Formal Engagements*, Mark David Rasmussen (ed.), 207–15, New York: Palgrave.

Terada, Rei (2001) *Feeling in Theory: Emotion After the 'Death of the Subject,'* Cambridge, MA: Harvard University Press.

Terada, Rei (2009) *Looking Away: Phenomenality and Dissatisfaction, Kant to Adorno*, Cambridge, MA: Harvard University Press.

White, Deborah Elise (1999) "Introduction: Irony and Clerisy," in *Irony and Clerisy*, Romantic Circles Praxis Series, College Park, MD. Online. Available www.rc.umd.edu/praxis/irony/white/ironyintro.html (accessed 15 August 2013).

Wolfson, Susan (2000) "Reading for Form," *Modern Language Quarterly* 61: 1–16.

Wordsworth, William (1984) *William Wordsworth*, Stephen Gill (ed.), The Oxford Authors, Oxford: Oxford University Press.

Part 4

Authorship and authority

Introduction

In many respects – especially in Lucy Newlyn's essay in Part 3 on the anxiety that Romantic writers felt about the reception of their work – criticism on the role of Romantic audiences has been concerned with the role of authors, asking how audiences either threaten or reinforce a writer's "authority." The fact that texts are written by someone at some point in time might seem brutally obvious, but what has attracted the notice of critics is the set of shared beliefs and assumptions about what (if anything) this fact really means. The French literary theorist Roland Barthes famously and provocatively proclaimed the "death of the author" in his essay of 1968. What he meant was that, although authors had "always" been dead in a sense because they were usually absent when a reader encounters a work, the "sense" of this absence had grown over time, so that writers like Proust and Mallarmé deployed their works stylistically to conquer the "tyranny" of believing in a unitary and stable author established since the seventeenth century (Barthes 1977: 142, 143). Michel Foucault's influential essay "What is an Author?" added historical focus to this kind of argument. He urged that authorship – once considered beyond the controlling influence of the will or intention of the writer – needed to be considered as the result of historical construction. Authority derived from beliefs about authorial "status," "systems of valorization," and specific cultural "conditions" that enable "the fundamental critical category of 'the man and his work'" (Foucault 1977: 115). Many historians and critics, such as Catherine Gallagher (1994), Robert Griffin (1999), and Mark Rose (1993), have heeded this call over the past several decades, giving us crucial insights into the way that changes in copyright legislation, book printing, authorship attribution, and other such conditions gave shape to the author in the Romantic age not as a natural entity but as a culturally constructed one.

The impulse to study matters of literary authority – the cultural constructions that create authorship as a social function rather than merely a fact – seems particularly urgent for the study of Romanticism, a period in which many authors have been said to promote ideas of solitary genius, even while that notion could be harshly criticized by those like Keats, who admonished Wordsworth for his "egotistical sublime" (Keats 1891: 184). Ina Ferris's chapter excerpt on Maria Edgeworth and Sir Walter Scott from her book *The Achievement of Literary Authority* shows how attention to the way that authors participate in the history of genres can give us a sense of how and why certain authors achieved a triumphant canonical status. As she traces the relation between the "national tale" and the "historical novel," Ferris shows how Scott's decisive position in the history of the novel was achieved by his taking advantage of uncertainties and instabilities in the national tale's narrative technique. While Edgeworth's work (in its complete form, Ferris's chapter also includes a discussion of Lady Morgan) lacks a keen seen of "historical time," Scott establishes his own work as an absorption and recreation of "official" historical narratives, trumping them with his own ostensibly more sensitive view of transient history in need of preservation. The historical novel marks the shift from fiction as competing narratives in Edgeworth to fiction as a more stable "document" in Scott.

The spirit of Foucault's work clearly influences the work of Ferris, who, in the scope of her project as a whole, shows how Scott's work was notable not merely for its individual effort but for its attempt to shape and discipline a reading public according to the norms of proper manly authority. Other critics that share in this impulse to show how Romantic authorship came to establish itself include Zachary Leader (1996) and Peter Murphy (1993), who give careful attention to the self-conceptions and generic practices of poets and novelists of the period. Still other critics approach the issue of authority from different perspectives that either complicate or expand the idea of authorship. Some critics like Susan Eilenberg (1992) and Margaret Russett (2006), for instance, show how Romantic writers experienced considerable anxiety about their power and authenticity. Andrew Bennett's contribution is related to these points of view, although he suggests that the very nature of Romantic authority consists of a commitment to a dissolution of subjectivity. In a sense, this argument echoes the work of deconstructionist critics, and Bennett elsewhere shows how many notions of Romantic writing anticipate the literary theories of Jacques Derrida (Bennett 1999). In his selection on Keats from his book *Romantic Poets and the Culture of Posterity*, he shows how the poet cannily anticipates Barthes's claims about the death of the author, although with a heightened sense of paradox. The author's death guarantees, rather than compromises, the author's genius: for "to talk about Keats's character or his genius . . . is to talk about his sickness and ultimately his bodily dissolution."

Another group of critics tends to retain an interest in the cultural formation of authorship in a way that theoretically echoes but also broadens Ferris's perspective. They take an interest in expanding notions of authority to include ways of writing that go beyond the author as a single personality or source of intention, even though they have resisted the idea of death or dissolution in their conceptual models. Jeffrey Cox's work on the "Cockney School" of poets has emphasized the need to consider collaborative authorship in the Romantic age (Cox 1998); other critics such as Alison Hickey and Daniel E. White have investigated collaborations between Samuel Taylor Coleridge and Robert Southey, for instance, or between Anna Barbauld and John Aikin (Hickey 1998; White 2006). Anne Frey's essay on Thomas De Quincey takes these ideas even further to include an idea of corporate or systemic authorship. In her account, which eventually appeared in chapter 5 of her book *British State Romanticism: Authorship, Agency, and Bureaucratic Nationalism*, De Quincey's view of authorship is connected to the authority of the nation-state. This authority, neither personal nor even human, is created by "technological structures" – structures that support, and are supported by, De Quincey himself. In her view, authority is not so much an intentional collaboration between individuals as an impersonal imperial "system."

In her new essay for this volume, Margaret Russett adds a further dimension to her previous work on the tenuous authority of Romantic literary texts. She argues that Blake, unlike Wordsworth (and many other Romantic authors for that matter), in fact sought to understand his own work less as an "author" and more as an "artisan." He took his elaborately engraved books to be "performances of the art and craft of writing as embodied action" rather than commodities imprinted with the godlike power of a single author. While in some ways destabilizing the idea of authorship as Bennett and others have done, she shows how this strategy is very much part of Blake's intention and practice. Unitary authorship emerges in Blake's writing as poisonous philosophical and religious "illusion"; he satirizes and criticizes the illusion of sole authorship, representing author-figures absorbed into books and into the "pedestrian" art of book-making.

Works cited

Barthes, Roland. (1977) *Image, Music, Text*, trans. Stephen Heath, New York: Hill and Wang.

Bennett, Andrew. (1999) "On Posterity," *Yale Journal of Criticism* 12: 131–44.

Cox, Jeffrey. (1998) *Poetry and Politics in the Cockney School: Keats, Shelley, Hunt, and their Circle*, Cambridge: Cambridge University Press.

Eilenberg, Susan. (1992) *Strange Power of Speech: Wordsworth, Coleridge, and Literary Possession*, Oxford: Oxford University Press.

Foucault, Michel. (1977) *Language, Counter-Memory, Practice: Selected Essays and Interviews*, trans. Donald F. Bouchard, Ithaca: Cornell University Press.

Gallagher, Catherine. (1994) *Nobody's Story: The Vanishing Acts of Women Writers in the Marketplace, 1670–1820*, Berkeley: University of California Press.

Griffin, Robert J. (1999) "Anonymity and Authorship," *New Literary History* 30: 877–95.

Hickey, Alison. (1998) "Coleridge, Southey, 'and Co.,'" *Studies in Romanticism* 37: 305–49.

Keats, John. (1891) *Letters of John Keats*, ed. Sidney Colvin, London: Macmillan.

Leader, Zachary. (1996) *Revision and Romantic Authorship*, Oxford: Clarendon Press.

Murphy, Peter. (1993) *Poetry as an Occupation and an Art in Britain, 1760–1830*, Cambridge: Cambridge University Press.

Rose, Mark. (1993) *Authors and Owners: The Invention of Copyright*, Harvard: Harvard University Press.

Russett, Margaret. (2006) *Fictions and Fakes: Forging Romantic Authenticity, 1760–1845*, Cambridge: Cambridge University Press.

White, Daniel E. (2006) *Early Romanticism and Religious Dissent*, Cambridge: Cambridge University Press.

Further reading

Manning, Peter. (1990) *Reading Romantics: Texts and Contexts*, New York: Oxford University Press.

Siskin, Clifford. (1988) *The Historicity of Romantic Discourse*, New York: Oxford University Press.

Woodmansee, Martha. (1994) *The Author, Art, and the Market: Rereading the History of Aesthetics*, New York: Columbia University Press.

13 From "national tale" to "historical novel"

Edgeworth and Scott[1]

Ina Ferris

> To Sir Walter Scott belongs the honour of having first shown how history ought to be made available for the purposes of fiction.
>
> T.H. Lister, *Edinburgh Review* (1832)

[...]

[Sir Walter] Scott's innovation [...] depended on a form of fiction already in place, on what came to be called the "national tale." And in transforming national tale into historical novel, Scott was working within a contemporary female genre. An Anglo-Irish creation, the national tale was founded by Maria Edgeworth in *Castle Rackrent* (1800), and it was transformed into national romance by Morgan's *Wild Irish Girl* (1806). Morgan, in fact, came to be more firmly linked to the category than Edgeworth herself. As a narrative form, the national tale was symptomatic of what John Wilson Croker saw as the definitive characteristic of the contemporary novel. According to Croker, contemporary fiction was distinguished from that of the previous century in taking as its object of representation "men of a peculiar nation, profession, or temper, or, to go a step further – of *individuals*." So, he claims, Tom Jones

> might have been a Frenchman, and Gil Blas an Englishman, because the essence of their characters is human nature ... while, on the other hand, the characters of the most popular novels of later times are Irish, or Scotch, or French, and not in the abstract, *men*.[2]

As a sign of the new importance beginning to be granted to national distinctiveness in the late eighteenth and early nineteenth centuries, the national tale takes its place in the matrix of (mostly) counter-Enlightenment forces that converged to form the nationalism that was to mark nineteenth-century Europe.

The Waverley Novels themselves, of course, were to play a significant role in that formation not only in Scotland but in countries as diverse as Italy and Poland where historical fictions modeled on Scott quickly assumed the status of national epics in the nationalist struggles of the nineteenth century.[3] And the national tale provides the immediate novelistic context for the reception of *Waverley*, which is consistently placed in relation to Edgeworth's work.

[...]

In so doing, they follow Scott's own example in the postscript to *Waverley*, which defines the novel's attempt to represent the Scots as an emulation of "the admirable

Irish portraits drawn by Miss Edgeworth, so different from the 'dear joys' who so long, with the most perfect family resemblance to each other, occupied the drama and the novel."[4] Reiterating the point in private but under cover of his anonymity, Scott wrote to Matthew Weld Hartstonge that the author of *Waverley* "must have had your inimitable Miss Edgeworth strongly in his view, for the manner is palpably imitated while the pictures are original."[5] These early tributes received powerful confirmation in the 1829 general preface when the now canonical Sir Walter Scott credited Edgeworth with having revived his interest in the unfinished manuscript of *Waverley* and so of having played a catalytic role in the formation of the Author of Waverley. Where the novel itself had stressed her innovative role in undermining standard modes of cultural representation, the late preface sets her up as the model of the politics of conciliation that always attracted Scott: "she may be truly said to have done more towards completing the Union than perhaps all the legislative enactments by which it has been followed up."[6] In his own writing, he adds, he sought to achieve a similar reconciliation between the Scots and the English by introducing the "natives" of Scotland "to those of the sister kingdom in a more favourable light than they had been placed hitherto." His goal was to "procure sympathy for their virtues and indulgence for their foibles" (*Wav. Nov.*, 1:9–10).

Such reconciliation was soon to become suspect, and both Edgeworth and Scott have come under serious criticism, especially by twentieth-century Irish and Scots nationalists.[7] But the practice of fiction by this Anglo-Irish woman and this Scotsman was instrumental in initiating the historically significant process of authorizing cultural margins in nineteenth-century Europe, a process that depended on but was not always congruent with the nationalist drive. Admittedly, the early national novel typically sought recognition for colonized groups within the current imperial arrangement of things. [. . .] For her part, Edgeworth sought principally to create a more responsible attitude on the part of the landlords, and Scott himself (however ambiguously) affirmed the Union. But in introducing cultural difference – in language, habits, attitudes – the national novels of the early nineteenth century challenged assumptions of cultural homogeneity and superiority, opening up important new spaces within – and through – their own conservative fictions for "other" questions. And here it was the Waverley Novels, rather than the Irish fictions on which they built, that became the effective medium of literary and cultural innovation. What follows sets the first novel[] of Edgeworth [. . .] in relation to Scott's own first novel, asking questions about discursive authority [. . .], in an attempt to explain why this should have been so.

[. . .]

Both *Castle Rackrent* and *Waverley* make the realist claim to nonfiction, more precisely to historical value, and each couches the claim in a narrative frame. Edgeworth encloses Thady Quirk's first-person memoir of the Rackrents within a preface, coda, and glossary;[8] and Scott makes his historical claim after the conclusion of Waverley's story in the final chapter, "A Postscript, which Should Have Been a Preface."[9] In making their realist claim, both writers exchange fictional for historical discourse in a very specific way by diminishing the distance between actual author, implied author, and narrator.

Paul Hernadi's argument about the distinction between historical and fictional narrative is pertinent here. Hernadi posits that it is possible to derive a "workable theoretical distinction" between the two discourses on the basis of the different relationships they prompt the reader to postulate between the implied author and the narrative *persona* of a text. Fiction demands a distinction between the two, whereas history precludes it. Of special interest is Hernadi's point that the narrator of a work of fiction is fictional because the particular narrator "has been created for the purpose of narrating a given work of fiction."[10] One could, of course, say something similar about the narrator of a work of history, who is equally constructed in terms of a specific discourse and hence in a sense equally fictional. Nevertheless, there is an important difference in the "pledge" (to use Scott's metaphor in *Waverley*) between writer and reader that is involved in fiction and in history. And that difference has less to do with the status of the referent (X really happened) than with the status of the speaker mediating between reader and referent. This does not mean that the referent is either unimportant or fictional but simply that it is the speaker who establishes for the reader which referential and hermeneutical rules are in place. The speaker of history implicitly claims identity with the author of the text, as a fictional narrator does not, and in so doing the speaker of history grants to what is spoken a status distinct from that of fiction.

Two key self-reflexive moments in *Waverley* help clarify the point: the opening and the closing of the text. In chapter 1 the narrator establishes his credentials as a *novelist*, demonstrating in a playful and self-deprecating manner his familiarity with novelistic genres and conventions. Following his list of the types of novels he has chosen not to follow, for example, he remarks:

> I could proceed in proving the importance of a title-page, and displaying at the same time my own intimate knowledge of the particular ingredients necessary to the composition of romances and novels of various descriptions. But it is enough, and I scorn to tyrannize longer over the impatience of my reader, who is doubtless already anxious to know the choice made by an author so profoundly versed in the different branches of his art.
>
> (4; chap. 1)

What follows this passage is rather more serious as the narrator sets out the "object" of his tale, but the discourse remains firmly within literary, and more specifically, novelistic tradition. Hence when the hidden term of the preface – "history" – finally surfaces in the last few lines of the chapter ("at the period of my history"), it is read in the novelistic context evoked by the narrative voice. "My history" is received as a standard fictional device familiar to novel readers since the early eighteenth century. While the gap between narrator and implied author opened up by irony in the first pages is not sustained over the entire narrative, this initial evocation of the rules of fiction governs the overall reading of the narrator as a fictional device. His primary function is to serve the fiction – to tell the story – and questions about his relationship to the author do not, in the normal course of reading, arise.

But in the postscript of chapter 72 the rules change, and *Waverley* moves decisively out of the fictional contract. That contract is recalled at the very beginning of chapter 72 by the Fieldingesque image with which it opens:

> Our journey is now finished, gentle reader, and if your patience has accompanied me through these sheets, the contract is, on your part, strictly fulfilled. Yet, like the driver who has received his full hire, I still linger near you, and make, with

becoming diffidence, a trifling additional claim upon your bounty and good nature.

(339; chap. 72)

But the Fieldingesque tone is reintroduced only to be abruptly abandoned when the narrative voice announces: "There is no European nation which, within the course of half a century, or little more, has undergone so complete a change as this kingdom of Scotland" (340; chap. 72). This statement signals the end of fiction and the beginning of another kind of discourse. In contrast to chapter 1, the narrative voice is now located in a specific place and in a specific historical period, and its particularization continues as it speaks of "my younger time" and "my accidental lot . . . to reside during my childhood and youth" among Highlanders. This is the voice less of a novelist than of a Scotsman, a shift to autobiography whose rules invoke a different understanding of who is speaking and of how (or what) he speaks. No longer the playful, stylized novelist of the introductory chapter, this voice draws on the conventions of personal, serious discourse as it reflects on cultural change and on the sources and production of the fiction that has just been concluded.

Here, in other words, is an authorial voice, and it is read as such whether or not one knows that the author is Walter Scott, and whether or not Walter Scott is lying or otherwise acting in bad faith. In fact, it is the possibility of making such charges that distinguishes the kinds of generic contracts evoked in the opening and concluding chapters (and accounts, perhaps, for the vehemence with which a critic like David Craig could indict Scott's novels).[11] To accuse the narrator of chapter 1 with something like betrayal, for example, would be to read inappropriately, whereas it would not be inappropriate to aim such a charge at the authorial voice of the final chapter. The difference lies in the kind of responsibility that the author-narrator takes for what he says, the kind of referential authority that he wants his words to have for the reader. Because of this voice the "Scotland" of the final pages falls under the category of history in a way that the "northern part of the island" referred to in chapter 1 does not.

The history-effect of both *Waverley* and *Castle Rackrent* depends in large part on such shifts in narrative voice. Interpretive authority in both texts is finally granted through a nonfictional voice that identifies the aim and referent of the fiction as historical. Edgeworth first indicates her historical project through the subtitle, a technique that Scott was to imitate effectively in the teasing subtitle to *Waverley*, "'Tis Sixty Years Since." *Castle Rackrent* is subtitled "An Hibernian Tale Taken from Facts, and from the Manners of the Irish Squires, before the Year 1782." The terms "Facts," "Manners," and "Irish Squires" suggest a social, nonfictional intent, but novels of the period routinely claimed such an intent, and it is only with the very specific date that Edgeworth's text begins to distinguish itself (though still not decisively) from standard procedures. The year 1782 figures prominently both in the personal history of the Edgeworths (the year of their move from England to Ireland) and in the public history of the nation (the year of the establishment of the Irish Independency). For Maria Edgeworth herself, then, the year stood as a watershed in several ways, not least in the sense that "before 1782" marks a time in Ireland that she could know only as history. In public terms, the adoption of the constitution in that year meant that it served to divide former days from these days, a point stressed in the preface: "The Editor hopes his readers will observe, that these are 'tales of other times;' that the manners depicted in the following pages are not those of the present age."[12]

Despite the short chronological gap between the date noted in the subtitle and the date of actual publication (a mere eighteen years compared with the almost seventy years of *Waverley*), Edgeworth identifies her tale as an account of the vanished past; hence it falls into the category of historical narrative. But *Castle Rackrent* is rarely classified as a historical novel. More commonly, as with George Watson's edition for Oxford's World's Classics, it is recognized as "the first regional novel in English" (vii). Marilyn Butler allows that because of its material, it is "one kind of historical novel," but she argues that "at a more serious level it is the least historical of Maria's tales. There is no sense of impending future in it – no clash between the Rackrents' values and those of the people replacing them."[13] Butler's contrast is with *Waverley*, whose sense of historical process as the painful replacement of one cultural order by another has been much commented on, and it is certainly true that the history-likeness of Scott's novel depends crucially on his peculiar sense of cultural collision and transition. It depends, that is, on a certain narrative thematization or configuration, but it also depends – and this is where Edgeworth is especially useful as a contrast – on the way it merges its discourse with that of history. Where Scott absorbs the authority of official discourses like that of history, even as he modifies and on occasion subverts them, Edgeworth challenges such discourses but betrays an uneasiness in so doing that in effect leaves their authority in place.

Edgeworth's preface takes official history as its target, criticizing "the professed historian" and the critics who support his claims to authority by scorning the public taste for "anecdote." Edgeworth makes two related main points: official history is full of "fine fancy," and even "the best authenticated antient or modern histories" contain "much uncertainty." Those who love truth, therefore – and this is the interesting and important conclusion of the preface – look to "secret memoirs and private anecdotes": "We cannot judge either of the feelings or of the characters of men with perfect accuracy from their actions or their appearance in public; it is from their careless conversations; their half-finished sentences, that we may hope with the greatest probability of success to discover their real characters" (1). Edgeworth's notion of the "real" is classically logocentric: its discovery depends on a set of binaries that privilege speech over writing, private over public, the careless over the careful, and so on. For one so committed to rationality – and her rationality [. . .] was much recognized and often lamented by her contemporaries – Edgeworth grants an odd primacy to the secret, the hidden, and the half-finished. It is even odder if we allow that the arch-rationalist Richard Lovell Edgeworth had a hand (as he probably did) in writing this preface.

But it all proves to be somewhat less strange than it seems at first, for the downgrading of the conscious, public, and writerly sphere turns out to be a way of privileging the domestic, which for the Edgeworths stood as the measure of virtue and the source of rational social value. Noting the public interest in autobiographies, familiar letters, and diaries, the preface maintains that

> we are surely justified in this eager desire to collect the most minute facts relative to the domestic lives, not only of the great and good, but even of the worthless and insignificant, since it is only by a comparison of their actual happiness or misery in the privacy of domestic life, that we can form a just estimate of the real reward of virtue, or the real punishment of vice.

(2)

Because the historian can seldom "consistently with his dignity, pause to illustrate this truth," we have to turn to the (presumably less dignified) biographer.

[. . .]

In all this, Edgeworth is following novelistic tradition, which had long claimed not only that the novel was a form of history but that it was a more authentic form of history than official history. Authenticity for the novel, Mikhail Bakhtin has argued, always resides in the unofficial genres,[14] and one does not have to turn Edgeworth into a carnivalesque figure in order to align her with his insight. In this preface in particular there emerges a strong sense of the value of a writing outside the official and dignified genres. What is stressed about the historian is "his dignity"; to be outside the sphere of dignity, the preface repeatedly urges, is to be authentic. Valorization of the unofficial genres reaches its height not, as might be expected, with the defense of the use of dialect but with the notion that gossip represents the model for biography. Speaking through the male voice of the editor and taking as a specific target Dr. Johnson's biography of Richard Savage, Edgeworth argues that an uneducated and untalented writer makes a better biographer because such a writer will be less capable of deceiving the reader. He will not sacrifice truth to style, nor will he be able to disguise as easily his prejudices and biases. For Edgeworth, the public is right to countenance those who "simply pour forth anecdotes and retail conversations, with all the minute prolixity of a gossip in a country town" (3). This argument is mounted to prepare the reader not only for the voice of Thady Quirk (identified here as "an illiterate old steward") but also for distance from that voice. Thady's prejudices on behalf of the Rackrents, Edgeworth declares, "must be obvious to the reader" (3–4). But the "must," hovering between indicative and imperative senses, betrays a certain anxiety about exactly how obvious it all is, and *Castle Rackrent*, notoriously, has yielded to contradictory readings: as a nostalgic lament for and as a devastating critique of the world it represents.[15]

To Edgeworth, the limitations of Thady should be "obvious" because truth is obvious to all right-minded persons. It is Edgeworth's Enlightenment belief in the clarity, rationality, and uniformity of truth that allows her to fictionalize and to argue for unofficial genres like gossip. At the same time, her faith in the homogenous world of reason, as that uneasy "must" suggests, is somewhat porous. Two points in the preface are suggestive here: the definition of the role of "vernacular idiom" in the text, and the admission that to "the *ignorant* English reader" the memoirs may be unintelligible. Both acknowledge difference and discontinuity. In admitting Thady, Edgeworth has admitted not only an obviously prejudiced person (and hence a target for irony) but also one who is culturally particular. The editor notes that he has recorded Thady's "vernacular idiom" even though he had thought of translating it into "plain English." Two perceptions prevented translation, and both effectively unsettle the rationalist assumptions that the preface has also been urging: first, Thady's idiom is "incapable of translation"; second, the "authenticity" of his story would be exposed to doubt "if it were not told in his own characteristic manner" (4). To admit that a language is incapable of translation and to tie the judgment of authenticity to a characteristic manner is in an important way to question assumptions about human uniformity. It is not necessarily to deny those assumptions, but it is to make them more problematic. Like Scott, who opens *Waverley* on a Fieldingesque note affirming uniform human nature (despite historical differences) and closes it on a historicist note foregrounding radical historical difference (despite general human nature), Edgeworth struggles with opposing models of cultural understanding, and out of their friction generates the novelistic innovation of *Castle Rackrent*.[16]

Her innovation – and this is the second point unsettling the assumption of homogeneity – was directed at the English reader. As with the admission that Thady's idiom is untranslatable and essential, so the admission that the English reader will need a few notes in order to understand the story foregrounds cultural heterogeneity rather than the ideal homogeneity of the literary republic. The point is made even more strongly at the end of the narrative in the editor's coda and by the glossary. At the conclusion of Thady's narrative, the voice of the editor returns, reiterating his decision not to varnish "the plain round tale of faithful Thady": "He [the editor] lays it before the English reader as a specimen of manners and characters, which are perhaps unknown in England. Indeed the domestic habits of no nation in Europe were less known to the English than those of their sister country, till within these few years" (96–7). Even more strongly than in the preface, the editorial voice here merges with the authorial voice as it goes on to single out for commendation *A Tour of Ireland* by Arthur Young as "the first faithful portrait of [Ireland's] inhabitants" and adds that its own sketches "were taken from the life" (97). Concluding with some inconclusive comments on the impending union of Ireland and Scotland, the narrative proper is followed by an "Advertisement to the English Reader." Since this consists of a simple announcement that the glossary is added in order to explain terms and idiomatic phrases that might be unintelligible to "the English reader," the advertisement is oddly redundant. The point has been made several times before, and it will continue to be made throughout the commentary of the glossary, which distances itself not just from "the lower Irish" (the main subject) but also from "the English reader" (the main object). Mediating between the subject and object is a voice apart from both, providing information and linking past and present.

Edgeworth insists that the narrative of the Rackrents is a tale of other times, that the manners are not those of the present, that the race of Rackrents has long been extinct. This insistence signals not so much a historical understanding (as it will do in *Waverley*) as an ethical and political hope. Referring to the impending union at the end of the preface, she imagines the present as analogous to "a time when individuals can bear to be rallied for their past follies and absurdities, after they have acquired new habits and a new consciousness. Nations as well as individuals gradually lose attachment to their identity, and the present generation is amused rather than offended by the ridicule that is thrown upon their ancestors" (5). The final paragraph of the preface reads: "When Ireland loses her identity by a union with Great Britain, she will look back with a smile of good-humoured complacency on the Sir Kits and Sir Condys of her former existence" (5). But the coda at the end is not quite so hopeful, for here the editor admits that "it is a problem of difficult solution to determine, whether an Union will hasten or retard the amelioration of this country" (97). Written when Edgeworth's father was in Dublin voting on this very question of union, *Castle Rackrent* is permeated with a sense of change, of the end of an order – and with ambivalence about the future.

Strangely enough, this sense of temporality does not create a sense of historical process. Instead, Thady's recital of the fall of the Rackrents over successive generations (and the rise of his own family) takes on the static, spatial contours of the rise-and-fall pattern of older histories, fables, and didactic tales. Despite her own ambivalence to historical changes and despite her techniques of local color and historical reference, Edgeworth's narrative (and this remains true of her later Irish tales as well) lacks a sense of historical time.[17] And this has a great deal to do with the way in which narrative voice in *Castle Rackrent* is awkwardly split between the first-person, specifically located Thady Quirk, and the third-person, unlocated editor. Between the two is simply a gap; they seem to exist in the same narrative space but in noncontiguous portions of it. They do not exist in different times. In order for *Castle Rackrent* to register as *historical* in its approach to cultural change, Edgeworth has not only to create a third-person perspective to give the sense of temporal distance but to make that third-person perspective an active mediation. Through the editor and his apparatus she attempts something like this, but this narrative device, prompted by the valorization of the private and domestic that underlies the use of Thady's view of things, fails to effect the connections and to generate the sense of process that historical narrative requires. Not surprisingly, her later Irish tales turn to a third-person narrator even as they abandon the attempt to record historical change.

When Scott praised Edgeworth as his model in the postscript to *Waverley,* he was probably thinking more of her *Absentee* than of *Castle Rackrent.*[18] *Waverley* certainly has a great deal in common with the later novel (from the plot centered on a journey out of England to third-person narration), but to see *Waverley* in relation to *Rackrent* is to stress the self-consciousness with which both writers approached the cultural project of their novel writing. Only in their first novels is either so explicit and so tentative about what she/he is trying to do. Furthermore, Scott's postscript provides an important contrast to Edgeworth's preface and coda, suggesting why his, rather than her, approach to "a tale of other times" registered as historical with nineteenth-century readers.

Scott's postscript, as noted earlier, quickly drops the editorial role that Edgeworth maintains in her preface, and its primary concern is less literary than cultural. Where Edgeworth worked through literary notions of genre to develop a formal justification of her choice of narrative mode, Scott justifies his narrative by abandoning literary concerns (the concerns of *his* prefatory chapter) and directly entering historical and political discourse. History as change is the first problem and the main concern of the postscript, which asserts that no European nation has undergone "so complete a change" in the last half century as Scotland:

> The effects of the insurrection of 1745, – the destruction of the patriarchal power of the Highland chiefs, – the abolition of the heritable jurisdictions of the Lowland nobility and barons, – the total eradication of the Jacobite party, which, averse to intermingle with the English, or adopt their customs, long continued to pride themselves upon maintaining ancient Scottish manners and customs, commenced this innovation.
>
> (340; chap. 72)

With its list of public causes, the passage establishes the authority of the author-narrator as historian and social analyst. The postscript cites references (e.g., Lord Selkirk's *Observations on the Present State of the Highlands of Scotland*) and types of change (e.g., "extension of commerce") that count as part of historical discourse in a way that the private memoirs privileged by Edgeworth do not. Where her preface attempts to discount official history, Scott's postscript (like his preface with its reluctance to engage in "unnecessary opposition") signals acceptance of generic codes and demonstrates its own historical competence.

But even more than Edgeworth, Scott effectively undermines official history, and he does so because of his ambivalence about the paradigm of progressive historical change standard in his day. Scott's much-noticed dualism comes into prominent play in the contrasting – even contradictory – notions of change articulated in the postscript. The change in Scotland in the last century is characterized as both a violent rupture ("so complete a change") and a "gradual" evolution. The "present people" of Scotland, for example, are said to be "a class of beings as different from their grandfathers, as the existing English are from those of Queen Elizabeth's time." But the radicalness of the change suggested here is softened by the insistence that this change has "nevertheless, been gradual." Where the first model draws attention to cultural loss, the second compensates for loss with cultural gain, but Scott's emphasis typically falls on the former, as in this description of the Jacobites:

> This race has now almost entirely vanished from the land, and with it, doubtless, much absurd political prejudice; but, also, many living examples of singular and disinterested attachment to the principles of loyalty which they received from their fathers, and of old Scottish faith, hospitality, worth, and honour.
>
> (340)

The contrast with Edgeworth's sense of the vanished past in *Castle Rackrent* is striking. If for her the "former existence" of Ireland ideally evoked "a smile of good-humoured complacency," for Scott the vanished Scottish past evokes neither smiles nor complacency. Its absurdities, while admitted, are of far less interest to him than the loss of the valuable code of conduct with which he associates the displaced social order. The point is not that Edgeworth somehow feels superior to the past or that Scott engages in easy romantic nostalgia. Both writers have a complex and troubled response to historical change even as they affirm its fundamental direction. But they stand differently in relation to the country whose history is their concern, and that difference produces a markedly different narrative motivation.

When Scott introduces the idea of change as gradual, he adopts a simile to make his point clear: "like those who drift down the stream of a deep and smooth river, we are not aware of the progress we have made until we fix our eye on the now-distant point from which we set out" (340). The simile suggests a position similar to that of Edgeworth's editor when he argues that the present generation is secure enough and distinct enough from the past to be able to look complacently at the past. But this image of the smooth river of history which allows one to look back at ease and measure one's progress is soon disrupted not only by the insistence on what has been lost but by the shift to a highly personal definition of preservation as the aim of the preceding narrative. Informing the reader that it was "my accidental lot" to spend much of childhood and youth among Highlanders, Scott explains:

> and now, for the purpose of preserving some idea of the ancient manners of which I have witnessed the almost total extinction, I have embodied in imaginary scenes, and ascribed to fictitious characters, a part of the incidents which I then received from those who were actors in them.

The historian and scholar of the previous paragraph now speaks the language of autobiography and personal witness, a shift into unofficial genres that is all the more effective for its placement after two different "official" roles: the novelistic role of good-humored guide, and the historical role of cultural analyst.

The incorporation of unofficial genres, prompted by the unprogressive notion of preservation, continues as the authorial voice turns to its sources. The accounts of the military battles in the novel, he tells us, are "taken" from the stories of "intelligent eye-witnesses" and "corrected" from John Home's *History of the Rebellion in the Year 1745*, so that the narrative base lies in unofficial genres but gives final authority to an official one. As for the representation of the Lowlands, it comes both from personal witness ("I have witnessed some remnants in my younger days") and from tradition ("partly gathered from tradition"). This account of sources is then followed by the tribute to Edgeworth, who enters as a literary model once the sources for the historical material have been acknowledged. The acknowledgment of Edgeworth raises the issue of cultural purpose and intended audience. Scott seeks to "emulate" Edgeworth in breaking the stereotypes of the Scots that have been internalized by the English (and in part by the Scots themselves) through literary representations in the drama and the novel. Two "female authors," he notes, anticipated him while the unfinished manuscript of *Waverley* lay where it had been mislaid among "other waste papers." During this time, Elizabeth Hamilton published her novel of rural Scotland, *The Cottagers of Glenburnie* (1808), and Anne Grant published her collection of Highland material, *Account of Highland Superstitions: Essays on the Superstitions of the Highlanders of Scotland* (1811). Neither, however, offers quite the "fictitious narrative" that he contemplated. Female rivals thus out of the way, Scott turns directly to the question of audience. The audience he has in mind seems to be primarily Scottish, for he affirms his hope that *Waverley* will "recall" for "elder persons . . . scenes and characters familiar to their youth," and "present" to the younger generation "some idea of the manners of their forefathers" (341). In contrast to Edgeworth, then, he aims his narrative at cultural insiders as well as at the outsiders on whom she concentrates her attentions. The whole notion of "preserving some idea of the ancient manners" of Scotland makes sense primarily for a Scottish audience, so that Scott's motivation dictates a different attitude not just to the subject of representation (Scottish manners) but to its intended recipient as well.

Preservation, moreover, implies an acute sense of time as an agent, and such a sense is the basis for (if not a guarantee of) historical awareness. Certainly, the postscript to *Waverley* is permeated with images of the working of time, whereas the preface to *Rackrent* is not. Infused with a sense of the precariousness of cultures, Scott's final image of his narrative attempt is "the task of tracing the evanescent manners" of his "own country." His novel, then, comes into existence under the sign of transience: it traces what is itself evanescent. Historically, of course, the novel (as its very name suggests) has been linked to the temporary and the fleeting; at the same time, its link to print culture has enabled it to fix and to preserve. Building on both associations, Scott founds his historical mode of fiction. If novels, as critics like John Dunlop were arguing at this time, were valuable cultural indexes and hence gained through time a nonfictional, documentary value,[19] *Waverley* anticipated the generic shift granted by time and marked itself from the beginning as a document.

    [. . .]

Notes

1 The original chapter also included a discussion of Lady Morgan and was entitled "From 'national tale' to 'historical novel': Edgeworth, Morgan, and Scott."
2 Review of *Waverley*, *QR* [*Quarterly Review*] 11 (1814): 355.
3 I have in mind texts like Alessandro Manzoni's *I Promessi sposi* and Adam Mickiewicz's *Pan Tadeusz*, both of which became (and to some extent still are) nationalist icons in Italy and Poland, respectively.
4 [Sir Walter Scott, *Waverley*, Claire Lamont ed. (Oxford: Clarendon, 1981), 341; chap. 72. For ease of reference, the citation of the page number is followed by the chapter as consecutively numbered in most modern editions. Future references to this book will appear in the text.]
5 *The Letters of Sir Walter Scott*, ed. H.J.C. Grierson et al., 12 vols (London: Constable, 1932), 4:465.
6 [Sir Walter Scott, *Waverley Novels*, 25 vols (Edinburgh: Adams and Charles Black, 1870), 1:9. Future references to this book will appear in the text, indicated by *Wav. Nov.*]
7 As the more successful creator of national myths, Scott has been attacked more vehemently and consistently than Edgeworth. In the course of setting up his own argument that Scott deserves to be celebrated as a pioneer of modern Scottish nationalism, P.H. Scott gives a good sense of the nationalist attack in "The Malachi Episode," prefaced to his edition of Walter Scott's *The Letters of Malachi Malagrowther* (Edinburgh: Blackwood, 1981), ix–xxxiv. The *Malachi Malagrowther* papers themselves, written in 1826, show Scott at his most nationalist, and they were instrumental in forcing the English government to change its policy on abolishing the issue of Scottish bank notes.
8 I leave aside the notes as a secondary device, and I am also leaving aside the problem of Richard Lovell Edgeworth's contributions to the narrative frame and the documentation. Not only does his specific role seem impossible to determine, but my interest is in authorship as a discursive sign in the text.
9 Here too I leave aside the notes since these, along with Scott's introductions, were added later.
10 "Clio's Cousins: Historiography as Translation, Fiction, and Criticism," *New Literary History* 7 (1976): 252.
11 *Scottish Literature and the Scottish People, 1680–1830* (London: Chatto & Windus, 1961).
12 *Castle Rackrent*, ed. George Watson (New York: Oxford University Press, 1964), 4. All references are to this edition, which is based on the first edition of the novel.
13 *Maria Edgeworth: A Literary Biography* (London: Oxford University Press, 1972), 357.
14 The most convenient collection of Bakhtin's essays on the novel is *The Dialogic Imagination*, trans. Caryl Emerson and Michael Holquist, ed. Michael Holquist (Austin: University of Texas Press, 1981).
15 Thomas Flanagan, for example, inclines to the nostalgic and Marilyn Butler to the critical reading. [Flanagan, *The Irish Novelists, 1800–1850* (New York: Columbia University Press, 1958); Butler, *Maria Edgeworth.*]
16 On the ambivalence of Edgeworth's narrative, see Robert Tracy, "Maria Edgeworth and Lady Morgan," *Nineteenth-Century Fiction* 40 (1985): 1–22.
17 [Barry] Sloan disagrees, finding in *Castle Rackrent* an "astonishing sense of historical process" [*The Pioneers of Anglo-Irish Fiction, 1800–1850* (Totowa, N.J.: Barnes and Noble, 1986), 3].
18 Butler, *Maria Edgeworth*, 394–95.
19 Dunlop's whole study is motivated by the notion of fiction as cultural index. He notes in his preface:

> By contemplating the fables of a people, we have a successive delineation of their prevalent modes of thinking, a picture of their feelings and tastes and habits. In this respect prose fiction appears to possess advantages considerably superior either to history or poetry.
>
> (*History of Fiction*, 3 vols [London, 1814], 1:ix)

14 Keats's prescience

Andrew Bennett

> I am literally worn to death, which seems my only recourse.
>
> (Keats to Fanny Brawne)

> Had there been no such thing as literature, Keats would have dwindled into a cipher.
>
> (De Quincey, 'John Keats')

We read Keats too quickly. I am not referring to the possibility of performing the kind of langorous, indolent reading that a certain Keatsian discourse appears to demand or to the way in which, you might say, there is never enough time for Keats. Nor am I making an unlikely claim about critical attention to the complexities and ambiguities of a poem such as 'Ode on a Grecian Urn'. In saying that we read Keats too quickly, I am referring to the way in which we hurry through our reading of what Derrida calls that 'little, insignificant piece of the whole corpus', the name.[1] While the name of every author is no doubt transformed by metonymic substitution into his or her writing, I want to suggest that reading John Keats provokes particularly difficult and unavoidable, if unanswerable questions. Keats – his name and renown, his body, writing and life – is multiply inscribed in whatever it is that we think we are doing when we read 'Ode to a Nightingale', for example, or 'Isabella', or 'Hyperion'. This chapter concerns the renaming of Keats, his renown.[2]

In the early reviews and commentary on Keats and his poetry, the poet's name was, literally, a site of disturbance and conflict. In the first place, there is Leigh Hunt's moniker 'Junkets', suggested by its phonetic congruence with John Keats but also, no doubt, by its sense of 'a dish consisting of curds sweetened and flavoured, served with a layer of scalded cream' (*OED*). More aggressive mis-nominations include repeated references to 'Mr K'[3] and his name repeatedly misspelt as 'Keates';[4] John Croker appears to disbelieve in his name: 'Mr Keats, (if that be his real name, for we almost doubt that any man in his senses would put his real name to such a rhapsody,)' (*KCH* 111); in *Blackwood's* he is 'Pestleman Jack';[5] John Gibson Lockhart refers to 'Mr John', 'Johnny Keats' and 'Johnny';[6] Byron variously refers to Keats as 'Johnny Keats', 'Johnny Keates', 'Mr John Ketch', and 'Jack Keats or Ketch, or whatever his names are' (*KCH* 129, 130); and writing in 1854, James Russell Lowell comments that 'You cannot make a good adjective out of Keats, – the more the pity, – and to say a thing is *Keatsy* is to condemn it' (*KCH* 359).[7] Nowadays, by contrast, the renowned John Keats is always properly named, twentieth-century criticism having become immune to the instability of the poet's name. In fact, the name has undergone a transformation such that, as with other canonical poets, it is ubiquitously used to denote a body of work. Two recent books on Keats exemplify this change: on the first page of *The Sculpted Word*, Grant Scott claims that we 'often feel, in Keats, that we are wandering through a museum . . . ',[8] and many of the contributors to Nicholas Roe's collection of essays *Keats and History* use a similar short-hand: 'a diversity of critical and theoretical approaches to Keats'; 'subsequent readers of Keats . . . our understanding of Keats today'; 'I wish to avoid this way of reading Keats . . . the reading of Keats'; 'by applying the historical method to Keats . . . Keats is one instance of . . . the Romantic ideology'; 'other applications of literary history in Keats'; and, slightly differently, 'The Keats of *To Autumn*'.[9]

This chapter concerns the question of the name, and what it denotes: what are we reading when we 'read Keats'? 'We always pretend to know what a corpus is all about', Derrida remarks.[10] In order to rethink the corpus of Keats, this chapter will culminate in a reading of his sonnet written at the birth-place of Robert Burns in the summer of 1818, especially its first line, 'This mortal body of a thousand days'. I want to suggest that this line – with its scandalous deixis, with its unequivocal assertion of the presence, here and now, of the body that writes, the body that speaks, of, in short, 'Keats' – that this line has been both central to and largely obliterated in the critical tradition: this line, and the poem as a whole, suppressed by Keats himself, is what we might term the repressed of Keats criticism. What little commentary there is on the line turns on whether it should be read 'literally' or 'figuratively' – in other words, on the question of what Keats can possibly mean by 'This'. The alternative readings are polarised in two biographies. While Aileen Ward argues that the line represents Keats 'staring at the prospect of his own death, less than three years ahead', Robert Gittings claims that it is 'a purely rhetorical opening line'.[11] Furthermore, the question of the relationship between life and the literal is overdetermined in recent criticism on Keats's life as allegory and by Keats's famous letter in which he argues that 'A Man's life of any worth is a continual allegory' and that 'Lord Byron cuts a figure – but he is not figurative' – a letter in which Keats baldly states that 'above all . . . they are very shallow people who take every thing literal'.[12] It is within this space of biography and criticism, of rhetorical and somatic figuration, of the literal and the figurative, of writing lives and writing death, of prospective and retroactive reading, of Keatsian prescience and the scandal of deictic and nominal reference that this chapter will attempt to read, all too quickly, 'John Keats'. 'John Keats', I want to suggest, is determined by a certain prescience of posthumous renown. It is in this figure that the Romantic culture of posterity might be said to find its proper referent. Supremely aware of the kinds of shifts in the relationship between poet and audience encountered by Wordsworth and Coleridge and theorised by Isaac D'Israeli, Hazlitt and others, the figure of 'John Keats' is produced within and produces this new poetic dispensation. The present chapter attempts to think through the relationship between the reception of Keats and his prescient prefiguration of that reception.

We might start with Keats's first life. What is Richard Monckton Milnes's *Life, Letters, and Literary Remains, of John Keats* (1848)? Both biography and collected works, this inaugural Keats book presents both the body of Keats – his life – and his corpus – his letters and literary remains. In a gesture from which criticism has never fully recovered, the book conflates, undecidably, the life with the writing. The first sentence of the narrative of Keats's life reads as follows:

> To the Poet, if to any man, it may justly be conceded to be estimated by what he has written rather than by what he has done, and to be judged by the productions of his genius rather than by the circumstances of his outward life.[13]

The life of Keats, then, in the first, unequivocal sentence of this first life is conceived as supplementary to the writing. But by the end of the paragraph, this proposition has curiously shifted its ground so that instead of the life being obliterated by the poetry, the writing becomes an *expression* of, and therefore in turn supplementary to, the poet's life. By contrast with that of historians, novelists and philosophers, Milnes argues, the writing of poets constitutes a direct transcription of an authentic and confessional voice:

> the Poet, if his utterances be deep and true, can hardly hide himself even beneath the epic or dramatic veil, and often makes of the rough public ear a confessional into which to pour the richest treasures and holiest secrets of his soul. His Life is in his writings, and his Poems are his works indeed.[14]

To the extent that we take Milnes's biography as an authoritative and prescriptive nineteenth-century framing of the life, letters and literary remains of John Keats, the inaugural biography as a decisive factor in the inscription of Keats into the poetic canon, then these comments are crucial to any understanding of what I shall call, after Sidney Colvin, Keats's 'after-fame'.[15] The specificity of poetry, its singularity and marked difference from other discursive regimes, is constituted in Milnes's analysis by its elimination of the mediating and distorting elements of form or generic convention – in short, the 'epic or dramatic veil' – and by its direct articulation, representation or what we might term, after Milnes, 'confession', of the poet's self. The 'full speech' implied by Milnes's extravagant metaphor of confession is achieved by means of its *biographical* revelation: 'His Life is in his writings.' As Keats himself ambiguously comments in a letter to J.H. Reynolds, with regard to Robert Burns, 'We can see horribly clear in the works of such a man his whole life, as if we were God's spies' (*LJK* 1.325).

The opening – indeed the very title – of Milnes's *Life, Letters and Literary Remains of John Keats* is, however, traversed by death as an inescapable determinant of life. 'These pages', comments Milnes in the second paragraph, 'concern one whose whole story may be summed up in the composition of three small volumes of verse, some earnest friendships, one passion, and a premature death'.[16] It is this death, its fact and its structural anachronism, its prolepsis, which defines and regulates this and any biography of John Keats. Indeed, as Milnes's next, most extraordinary sentence suggests, it is in dying that the character of Keats – his personality, self or soul – is expressed or represented. Keats's death and his life in posterity determines, for Milnes, our 'impression' of Keats. Milnes's sense of Keats's after*life*, his living on, is expressed both in his assertion that Keats 'walk[s] among posterity', and in a hallucinatory grammatical presence produced by the uncanny suspension of Milnes's present participles:

> As men die, so they walk among posterity; and our impression of Keats can only be that of a noble nature perseveringly testing its own powers, of a manly heart bravely surmounting its first hard experience, and of an imagination ready to inundate the world, yet learning to flow within regulated channels and abating its violence without lessening its strength.[17]

Milnes canonises a certain oppositional rhetoric of power and masculinity against the feminising and attenuating representation of the early reviewers which has marked criticism and biography of Keats up to the present day.[18] At the same time, Milnes defines Keatsian nature in terms of the containment of revolution – a violence and inundation regulated within the context and rhetoric of 'channels' and 'strength'. But, most importantly perhaps, Milnes institutes a rhetoric of posthumous *life* for Keats, his 'walking among posterity', which saturates later criticism and biography of the poet. It is this effect of living on, of surviving – what we might call Keats's after-effect, or after-affect – which may be said to characterise the corpus known as 'Keats'.

In the next paragraph, Milnes develops this rhetoric of posterity when he argues, by a conventional comparison of Keats with Chatterton, that early death acts as an enobling substitute, an empowering supplement to a 'fulfilled poetical existence'. It is precisely because Keats died young that he is a poet. Milnes proposes:

> The interest indeed of the Poems of Keats has already had much of a personal character: and his early end, like that of Chatterton, (of whom he ever speaks with a sort of prescient sympathy) has, in some degree, stood him in stead of a fulfilled poetical existence.

To say that Keats's early death has 'stood him in stead of a fulfilled poetical existence' involves the recognition that such an end works as a redemptive supplement, an alternative to life. Keats, who could have been living when this was written, could have been (although it is the premise of the present chapter that this is unthinkable) in his early fifties, has another life, the life of a *poet*, through his death. But Milnes goes further than this, in parenthesis, to suggest that Keats articulates the fact of his own death in terms of what Milnes calls a 'prescient sympathy' with Chatterton. Keats is sympathetic to Chatterton, we are led to conclude, because he knows that he too will die neglected and young. This rhetorical figure – the coincidence of Keats's constitutive poetic act of dying with a certain prescience of that death – is a fundamental concatenation in the reception of Keats in the nineteenth and twentieth centuries, in his after-fame. Our understanding of Keats as a poet, I am suggesting, is determined, in multiple and complex ways, by Milnes's insistence on the relationship between his early death and a certain prescience. Crucial to the figuration of Keats as Poet is an early death which is presciently inscribed within the poet's life and work – an early death which he *knows about*.[19] Milnes elaborates Keats's prescient sympathy with Chatterton a few pages later when he introduces Keats's poem 'Oh Chatterton! how very sad thy fate' and suggests (via an allusion to Wordsworth's 'Resolution and Independence') that Keats's poem involves a proleptic intertextual reference to the end of Shelley's *Adonais* – that Keats's poem includes a reference to another poet's yet-to-be-written elegy on his own death:

> The strange tragedy of the fate of Chatterton 'the marvellous Boy, the sleepless soul that perished in its pride', so disgraceful to the age in which it occurred and so awful a warning to all others of the cruel evils, which the mere apathy and ignorance of the world can inflict on genius, is a frequent subject of allusion and interest in Keats's letters and poems, and some lines of the following invocation bear a mournful anticipatory analogy to the close of the beautiful elegy which Shelley hung over another early grave.[20]

Both the tenor of Keats's poem on Chatterton (the sense that the earlier poet lives on in a transcendental afterlife) and the vehicle of the sidereal metaphor (Keats's figuration of Chatterton as 'among the stars' and that 'to the rolling spheres' he 'sweetly singest') echo, in prescient sympathy, Milnes suggests, the sense of Shelley's *Adonais* as 'like a star' which, in the last line of his elegy, 'Beacons from the abode where the Eternal are' (*SPP* 406).[21] In this respect, Milnes's biography frames Keats in terms of an aesthetics of prescience, in terms of the poet's proleptic articulation of his own death. The afterlife of Keats's reputation, that is to say, is regulated by a sense that it has been prophetically inscribed within the poet's life and writing. In this respect, Keats's relationship with Chatterton is fundamental, since it provides the critic and biographer with a way of talking about this recognition by means of the figure of identification. Critics can talk about Keats's prescience – what Susan Wolfson has recently termed his 'weirdly prophetic intuition'[22] without talking nonsense.

[. . .]

The corpus of Chatterton, [. . .] that fetishised body of the self-poisoned poet and the fetishised image of the poet's corpus, his work, is transformed into the very stuff of Keats's canonical writing [in 'To Autumn', 'Ode on a Grecian Urn', 'Bright Star' and other poems]. It is not necessary to align Keats's poetry with the specific intertextual resources of either Chatterton's poetry, as critics have done, or with the Chatterton myth, [. . .] nor to appeal to the various direct references in both Keats's poetry and letters[23] – to perceive Keats acting out, in his life and writing, a Chattertonian figuration of writing and the writer. The figure of the neglected young poet, in particular the sick, poisoned or dead poet, is overdetermined in the early nineteenth century by the image of Chatterton. The sheer number of the comparisons of Keats to Chatterton by critics, friends and enemies both before and after Keats's death would suggest that the parallel cannot but have been apparent to Keats. But my point is that the very texture of the corpus of Keats is constituted in part by that other body, that other life and writing. In other words, we cannot help but read Keats through the corpus of Chatterton – a corpus visualised in commemorative handkerchiefs, in engravings such as 'The Death of Chatterton' by Edward Orme (1794), and in later paintings such as Henry Wallis's 'The Death of Chatterton' (1855–56). Chatterton's life provides an early version of the myth of neglected genius which is distilled in the life and writing of Keats: Keats's prescience is, in part, the trace of another poetic life and death, another body, name and corpus.

As this might suggest, one way to talk about the inscription of Keats's death in his writing is to talk about the poet's failing body. In his review of Milnes's *Life* in *The North British Review*, Coventry Patmore articulates the intimate relation that the nineteenth-century critical and biographical tradition asserts between the poet's 'genius' and his sickness: 'In almost every page of the work before us, the close connection between the genius of Keats and his constitutional malady pronounces itself.'[24] Patmore goes on to suggest that a true assessment of Keats's character is made particularly difficult by

> the necessity of constantly distinguishing between signs of character and the products of a very peculiar physical temperament, always subject to the influences of a malady, which, in its earliest stages, is frequently so subtle as to defy detection, and to cause its identification for a long period, with the constitution that it is destroying.[25]

In this telling passage, Patmore presents the Keatsian body as a site of semiotic disturbance in which malady and genius, sickness and character, or disease and the body are largely indistinguishable: to talk about Keats's character or his genius, and thus to talk about his poetry, is to talk about his sickness and ultimately his bodily dissolution. In this respect, I suggest that Keats's prescience is, first of all, somatic. 'Perhaps', as Aubrey de Vere suggests in another review of Milnes's biography, 'we have had no other instance of a bodily constitution so poetical' as that of Keats – and, famously, 'His body seemed to think'.[26]

In his review of Keats's 1820 volume, Josiah Conder argues that 'The true cause of Mr Keats's failure' involves the 'sickliness' of 'his productions', 'his is a diseased state of feeling' (*KCH* 238). To read Keats in this way, to read Keats through his body, and with that body figured as both weak and sickly, would be to go against the grain of much recent criticism and biography. Such writing would protect or, rather, cure the Keatsian body of a morbid and unhealthy nineteenth-century figuration. The most remarkable instance of bio-critical body-building is, no doubt, Lionel Trilling's claim that Keats 'stands as the last image of health at the very moment when the sickness of Europe began to be apparent';[27] but more recently, in a study of the early biographies, William Marquess has stated that 'The notion of an all-pervasive illness that casts a fatally Romantic pall over Keats's entire career is, of course, simply wrong';[28] and in her study of Keats and medicine, Hermione de Almeida has asserted moral and physiological well-being for Keats: 'Keats points the way through sickness, sorrow, and pain – through the medium of a poetry of life – to spiritual wholeness and imaginative health.'[29] Without simply rejecting such pronouncements,[30] I want to suggest that one of the most pressing aspects of Keats's engagement with his own after-fame is his articulation of the fragility and vulnerability of the poet's body. The poet, in his exploration of the possibility that he will live on, figures himself, his body, as *sick*.[31]

The most obvious example of this trope is Keats's sonnet 'On Seeing the Elgin Marbles', which presents the poet as a sick eagle looking longingly at the sky:

> My spirit is too weak – mortality
>   Weighs heavily on me like unwilling sleep,
>   And each imagined pinnacle and steep
> Of godlike hardship tells me I must die
> Like a sick eagle looking at the sky.
>   Yet 'tis a gentle luxury to weep
>   That I have not the cloudy winds to keep
> Fresh for the opening of the morning's eye.
> Such dim-conceived glories of the brain
>   Bring round the heart an undescribable feud;
> So do these wonders a most dizzy pain,
>   That mingles Grecian grandeur with the rude
> Wasting of old time – with a billowy main –
>   A sun – a shadow of a magnitude.

This is one of the least coherent of Keats's well-known poems, a poem impelled by a sense of 'wasting' – most clearly figured in the fragmentary dissolution of the last lines. Keats's bodily response to the immortality of Grecian sculpture is a proleptic experience of death, of wasting, fragmentation and dissolution. The poet not only acknowledges that he 'must die', but enacts that wasting, sickness and death in the poem.[32] This death is not only in the future but is incorporated or embodied in the inscription – in the act of inscribing – itself. The second sentence (lines 6–8), for example, enacts or embodies, in its wasted syntax, its semantically and grammatically indeterminate acedia, a figurative wasting of the poet himself. This is the poetry of failure, poetry which *works* precisely in and through its acknowledgement and articulation of a certain deficiency. The 'glories of the brain' are 'dim-conceived', the 'feud' is 'undescribable', the 'wonders' produce a 'dizzy pain', and the magnitude is but a shadow of itself. And the poem fails, in the second sentence, by producing the 'gentle luxury' of unmeaning, the failure of communication. But if this sentence resists reading, resists the sense-making demands of reception, it does so in accordance both with the necessities of the principle of posterity, and with a poetics of what, in a different context, Leo Bersani and Ulysse Dutoit term 'impoverishment'.[33] And it is the weight of this poem, its mortal oppression by a somatic and semantic *heaviness*, that reminds us proleptically of that other Keats poem which begins in a first-person possessive pronoun ('My heart aches') and records multiple bodily failures and fadings – 'Ode to a Nightingale'. These are failures which also occur in Keats's second sonnet on the Elgin marbles, 'To Haydon with a Sonnet Written on Seeing the Elgin Marbles', where the poem's language wastes away in a wasting evacuation of sense – 'Forgive me, Haydon, that I cannot speak / Definitively on these mighty things; / Forgive me that I have not eagle's wings – / That what I want I know not where to seek' (lines 1–4). 'That what I want I know not where to seek' describes the failure of desire, the failure of not achieving one's desire and of not even knowing where to look for it. And it also articulates a failure of language, it expresses somatic failure in a devastation of semantic acuity: the line is remarkable for a flatness of diction which hardly rises from the commonplace and for an emphatic semantic and alliterative repetition – I, I; what, want, where – which allows little scope for imaginative or linguistic flight. It is difficult to find another line of Keats's poetry which achieves failure with such consummate acumen. The poet asks Haydon to forgive him that he 'cannot speak / Definitively on these mighty things', but our line – 'That what I want I know not where to seek' – is the very evacuation of the definitive, undefines, wastes language away.

It is a condition of Keats's, poetic success that he fails.[34] This is evident from numerous moments of professed failure in his poems. The odes, for example, are a catalogue of inability, weakness, insufficiency, ignorance, and so on. 'Ode on a Grecian Urn' is full of unanswered questions and ends by articulating the wasting of the living – 'When old age shall this generation waste, / Thou shalt remain'; 'Ode to a Nightingale' figures the poet imagining himself drugged or drunk, disabled in consciousness, while the climactic moments of aesthetic apprehension are those of sensory failure – 'I cannot see', 'I have ears in vain' – and the poem ends with the failure of somnolent discrimination, an epistemological uncertainty which constitutes a defining moment in the development of Keatsian aesthetics – 'Do I wake or sleep?'; 'Ode on Indolence' concerns the poet's 'Benumb'd' senses, a poet who imagines 'drowsy noons', 'evenings steep'd in honied indolence' and 'an age . . . shelter'd from annoy'; and 'Ode to Psyche' is a poem which is too late properly to pay homage to the poet's goddess, 'too late for antique vows, / Too, too late for the fond believing lyre'. The poetry of failure is central to Keats's project, central to the success of his poetry.

Success for Keats, then, involves a failure of inscription, success promulgated on the possibility that this writing, now, is inadequate or insufficient. But this failure of success also involves the wasting of the poet's body, its weakness, dissolution or fainting – what I call, borrowing the word from its exemplary occurrence in 'Ode to a Nightingale', 'fading'. Most commonly in Keats, this involves sensory degradation or deprivation – forms of fading in which the world fades as a result of the fading of the senses. The Keatsian body – the poet's body, his corpus or corpse – is repeatedly inscribed in the poetry in terms of the characterological body dissolving and disempowered, as weak, wasted or failing. There is Endymion's repeated bodily failing, his swooning, for example; Saturn's deathly stillness in the opening to 'Hyperion', his scriptive right hand lying 'nerveless, listless, dead' (1.18); Porphyro's climactic melting in 'The Eve of St. Agnes'; the palely loitering knight in 'La Belle Dame sans Merci'; Lamia's dissolution and Lycius's immediate lifelessness; the poet's 'slow, heavy, deadly' pace as he mounts the steps to Moneta in 'The Fall of Hyperion' (1.128); as well as the 'Ode on a Grecian Urn' imagining a heart 'high-sorrowful and cloy'd, / A burning forehead, and a parching tongue', the 'Ode to a Nightingale' presenting a catalogue of sensory dissolution and 'fading', and 'Ode on Melancholy' producing a very thesaurus of sickness and homeopathic cure. Each of Keats's major poems, that is to say, may be read as centred around a moment of bodily failure, of mortal fading. But I also want to suggest that this wasted corpus of Keatsian writing is the very condition of the afterlife of that corpus. Keats's corpus – his body/of work – is also his failed body, his corpse. If immortality for Keats is associated with a failure of the body, a corporeal fading or dissolution, this failing body is precisely the condition of Keats's success in his afterlife, the necessary correlate of his afterfame.[35] The failed or failing body in or of Keats is a condition of the poetry's permanence; without the wasted or dissolved, dispensed-with but indispensable body, Keats's poetry, his corpus, does not live. Without the dysfunctional Keatsian body, the body failed or failing, there is no after-fame.

As I suggested at the beginning of this chapter, one of the most important and overlooked poems in the context of Keats's prescience is his sonnet on Robert Burns, 'This mortal body of a thousand days'. [. . .] As in so much of Keats's writing, the poem articulates a narrative of bodily failure – the speaker's 'head is light', his 'eyes are wandering', and 'cannot see', his 'Fancy is dead and drunken', and [. . .] the poet imagines a dissolution of consciousness, of thought, thinking 'till thought is blind'. [. . .] The poem's multiple identifications of the living with the dead poet, Keats with Burns, the bodily replacement of one poet by another, presciently inscribe the living poet into a posthumous life, into after-fame. [. . .]

'In literature', declares Jean-Luc Nancy in an essay on the literary body, 'there is nothing but bodies'. But this assertion is made on condition that, at the same time, 'the body is not a locus of writing':

> No doubt one writes, but it is absolutely not where one writes, nor is it what one writes – it is always what writing exscribes. In all writing, a body is traced, is the tracing and the trace – is the letter, yet never the letter, a literality or rather a lettericity that is no longer legible. A body is what cannot be read in a writing.[36]

For Keats – for every poet – writing poetry takes place as a certain embodiment in which inscription both bodies forth and disembodies, makes literal and figures: the body as what Nancy calls 'the last signifier, the limit of the signifier'.[37] But from a very early stage in the life of Keats such embodiment signifies a proleptic autobiographical inscription, albeit largely illegible – of the poet's own bodily dissolution: the writing of the Keatsian body figures what, in a different context, Louis Marin has termed the 'autobiothanatographical'.[38] Keats's mortality is figured in a body which increasingly takes on the status of a signifier of dissolution. And this dissolution also affects or infects the distinction between body and writing, corpus and corpus. Gittings, by his rejection of the Keatsian body in his judgement of the pure rhetoricity of 'This mortal body of a thousand days' – repeated by Morris Dickstein in his assertion that Aileen Ward's is an 'excessively literal reading of the poem'[39] – paradoxically *literalises* the Keatsian body. By refusing to read the body in the poem, by effacing, disembodying or *figuring* the corpus of writing, Gittings guarantees a reading of the body, of 'what cannot be read in writing': he reinstates, re-embodies, like a ghostly prosopopoeia, the dying corpus, the corpse, of Keats. Gittings's articulation of the unreadability of the literal body re-figures John Keats, re-embodies the poet – a poet whose writing, according to Coventry Patmore in his review of Milnes's biography, can never, with his particular 'physical organization', be anything other than 'sensual, or literal'.[40]

The exemplary inscription of the Keatsian body is, precisely, 'This mortal body of a thousand days' – the phrase and the poem – just as the exemplary figuration of the body writing in Keats is the performing hand in that haunting and grasping poem 'This living hand', and just as the exemplary figuration of Keatsian reading is that of the only other Keats poem to begin in 'This' – 'This pleasant tale is like a little copse'. In each case, the uncanny presence of the written and writing body and its uncanny prescience, too, is indicated by the opening deictic reference – '*This* mortal body', '*This* living hand' and, less obviously, '*This* pleasant tale'.[41] But this involves a deictic opacity of language, language which goes beyond language, which points and refuses to point, deixis as a figure which refuses figuration. Inscription is *this*: *this* body, here, now, not here, not now. But I have also tried to suggest that the Keatsian body has a further dimension, that posthumous existence for Keats, the reading of his work since his death, is irreducibly bound up with the dissolute body – that the death of John Keats, the dissolution of the poet's body, is an inescapable element of any reading of his work. [. . .]

Notes

1 Jacques Derrida, *Signéponge/Signsponge*, trans. Richard Rand (New York: Columbia University Press, 1984), p. 116.
2 On the congruence of 'renown' and 'renaming' (both *renommée* in French, from which 'renown' derives), see Derrida, *Signéponge*, pp. 2/3.
3 See, for example, [*Keats: The Critical Heritage*, ed. G.M. Matthews (London: Routledge and Kegan Paul, 1971)], 71, 73, 115, 204, 205, 213, 227. [Hereafter abbreviated *KCH*.]
4 For example, *KCH* 21, 22, 24.
5 *Blackwood's Edinburgh Magazine* xiv (July 1823), 67.
6 *KCH* 98, 110; 100, 109; 102; see J.R. MacGillivray's comment in *Keats: A Bibliographical and Reference Guide with an Essay on Keats' Reputation* (University of Toronto Press, 1949), p. xxii, that 'whenever the name "Johnny" is given to the poet . . . the writer is not merely being jocular or contemptuous; he is making it plain . . . that he shares Lockhart's opinion'.
7 On the origins of the name Keats, see Robert Gittings, *John Keats* (Harmondsworth: Penguin, 1971), p. 23.
8 Grant F. Scott, *The Sculpted Word: Keats, Ekphrasis, and the Visual Arts* (Hanover, NH: University Press of New England, 1994), p. xi.
9 Nicholas Roe (ed.), *Keats and History* (Cambridge University Press, 1995); the authors are as follows: Roe, p. 5; Daniel P. Watkins, p. 93; Kelvin Everest, pp. 111, 125; Theresa M. Kelly,

p. 212; Nicola Trott, p. 272; John Kerrigan, p. 304. My *Keats, Narrative and Audience: The Posthumous Life of Writing* (Cambridge University Press, 1994) also wantonly employs such locutions (*passim*). Compare Daniel Watkins on the question of Keats's name in 'History, Self, and Gender in "Ode to Psyche"', in Roe (ed.), *Keats and History*, p. 88.

10 Derrida, *Signéponge*, p. 24.

11 Aileen Ward, *John Keats: The Making of a Poet* (London: Seeker and Warburg, 1963), p. 200; Gittings, *John Keats*, p. 333; compare Andrew Motion's mediating comments on the line's 'uncanny premonition': it 'may have been intended as a purely rhetorical phrase: we cannot read it without realising that Keats died almost exactly a thousand days after writing it' (*Keats* [London: Faber and Faber, 1997], p. 283). The fullest treatment of this neglected poem that I am aware of is John Glendening's 'Keats's Tour of Scotland: Burns and the Anxiety of Hero Worship', *Keats–Shelley Journal* 41 (1992), 76–99, especially 92–5; Glendening, however, refrains from commenting on the first line.

12 [*The Letters of John Keats, 1814–1821*, 2 vols. ed. Hyder Edward Rollins (Cambridge, MA: Harvard University Press, 1958),] 11.67. [Hereafter abbreviated *LJK*.] On Keats's life as allegory, see especially Marjorie Levinson, *Keats's Life of Allegory: The Origins of a Style* (Oxford: Basil Blackwell, 1988).

13 Richard Monckton Milnes (ed.), *Life, Letters, and Literary Remains, of John Keats*, 2 vols (London: Edward Moxon, 1848), 1.1.

14 Milnes, *Life*, 1.1–2.

15 Sidney Colvin, *John Keats: His Life and Poetry, His Friends, Critics, and After-Fame*, 3rd edn (London: Macmillan, 1920).

16 Milnes, *Life*, 1.2.

17 Ibid.

18 Hazlitt, for example, complains that Keats's poetry suffers from 'a deficiency in masculine energy of style' and that 'all he wanted was manly strength and fortitude' (*KCH* 248), while Leigh Hunt, by contrast, argues that Keats 'was a very manly, as well as delicate spirit' (*KCH* 249). On the gendering of the corpus of Keats in the nineteenth century, see George H. Ford, *Keats and the Victorians: A Study of His Influence and Rise to Fame, 1821–1895* (1944; repr. Hamden: Archon Books, 1962), p. 68; and Susan J. Wolfson, 'Feminizing Keats', in Hermione de Almeida (ed.), *Critical Essays on John Keats* (Boston: G.K. Hall, 1990), pp. 317–56.

19 It should be noted, however, that Milnes is far from the first to remark on such prescience: see, for example, L.E.L.'s 'Lines on Seeing a Portrait of Keats' (apparently written in 1822), in *Critical Writings by Letitia Elizabeth London*, ed. F.J. Sypher (New York: Scholars' Facsimiles, 1996), pp. 183–4: 'the seeds of death / Are sown within thy bosom, and there is / Upon thee consciousness of fate' (lines 10–12).

20 Milnes, *Life*, 1.12.

21 [*Shelley's Poetry and Prose*, ed. Donald H. Reiman and Sharon B. Powers (New York: Norton, 1977), 406.]

22 22 [Susan J. Wolfson, 'Keats Enters History: Autopsy, *Adonais* and the Fame of Keats', in Roe (ed.) *Keats and History*], p. 18

23 References include Keats's sonnet on Chatterton, his dedication to *Endymion* and his comment on associating Chatterton with autumn and his being 'the purest writer in the English Language' (*LJK* 11.167; see also 11.212).

24 The *North British Review*, 10 (1848), 70.

25 Ibid., 72.

26 *KCH* 343; compare David Masson's comments in an 1860 article in *Macmillan's Magazine* on the overriding importance of the Keatsian body in his writing (*KCH* 375–7, 379). For a consideration of Keats's body and last sickness, see Jennifer Davis Michael, 'Pectoriloquy: The Narrative of Consumption in the Letters of Keats', *European Romantic Review* 6 (1995), 38–56.

27 Lionel Trilling, *The Opposing Self: Nine Essays in Criticism* (London: Secker and Warburg, 1955), p. 49.

28 William Henry Marquess, *Lives of the Poet: The First Century of Keats Biography* (University Park, PA: Pennsylvania State University Press, 1985), p. 41.

29 Hermione de Almeida, *Romantic Medicine and John Keats* (New York: Oxford University Press, 1991), pp. 12–13.

30 Although we might question what is involved in, for example, 'spiritual wholeness and imaginative health': such an assertion sounds unhealthily close to what Leo Bersani analyses in *The Culture of Redemption* (Cambridge, MA: Harvard University Press, 1990), as the repressive modernist ideologies of 'art's beneficently reconstructive function in culture' which 'depend on a devaluation of historical experience and of art' (p. 1).

31 On the tradition of reading Keats as weak and sickly, see Marquess, *Lives of the Poet*, pp. 40, 63–4, 66 [. . .].

32 See Scott, *The Sculpted Word*, pp. 55–6, on the way that Keats is 'paralyzed by the marbles and oppressed by their spirit', and on the poem's 'structural weakness'; see also Marjorie Levinson, *Keats's Life of Allegory*, p. 248, on the way that Keats 'attenuates himself'.

33 Leo Bersani and Ulysse Dutoit, *Arts of Impoverishment: Beckett, Rothko, Resnais* (Cambridge, MA: Harvard University Press, 1993).

34 For a similar comment, on Keats and his poetry as *wanting*, see Levinson, *Keats's Life of Allegory*, p. 6.

35 Critics have often noted the fetishised corpulent particularity of Keats's writing – for example, the way that, as Christopher Ricks shows, blushing generally or engorged *foreheads* more particularly carry such an extraordinary weight of Keatsian pathos and intellectual and sensuous intentionality, or the way that, as Susan Wolfson has recently suggested, the dismembered hand is a crucial Keatsian inscriptor, or finally the way that the masturbating body calls for the assertion of an onanistic poetics for Keats elaborated by Byron and more recently by Marjorie Levinson. See Christopher Ricks, *Keats and Embarrassment* (Oxford University Press, 1974), Susan J. Wolfson, 'The Magic Hand of Chance: Keats's Poetry in Facsimile', *Review* 14 (1992), 213–17; Levinson, *Keats's Life of Allegory*; Byron's comments are conveniently collected, although in expurgated form, in *KCH* 128–32.

36 Jean-Luc Nancy, 'Corpus', in *The Birth to Presence*, trans. Brian Holmes, *et al.* (Stanford University Press, 1993), pp. 193, 198; it is Nancy's argument that the body is 'both sense and the sign of its own sense . . . *Sign of itself* and *being-itself of the sign*' (p. 194).

37 Ibid., p. 195.

38 Louis Marin, 'Montaigne's Tomb, or Autobiographical Discourse', *OLR* 4 (1981), 45.

39 Morris Dickstein, *Keats and his Poetry: A Study in Development* (University of Chicago Press, 1971), pp. 175–6.

40 *KCH* 331; see also Patmore's comment on Keats's characteristic faults as 'extreme literalness of expression' (*KCH* 337).

41 'This pleasant tale' does, in fact, articulate a corporeal intensity of reading such that, by the end of the poem, the opening deixis marks both the inscription of the speaker's (/reader's) body into the act of reading and the uncanny heart-stopping mortality of that act: the reader 'full hearted stops; / And oftentimes he feels the dewy drops / Come cool and suddenly against his face'.

15 De Quincey's imperial systems

Anne Frey

Much of the best recent criticism of Thomas De Quincey has focused on the relationship between De Quincey and his erstwhile friend and mentor, William Wordsworth. Charles Rzepka and Alina Clej, for instance, read De Quincey's friendship and subsequent hostility to Wordsworth as an anxiety of influence, an attempt to upstage the more illustrious writer.[1] Margaret Russett, in contrast, argues that De Quincey does not attempt to avoid Wordsworth's influence, but to parasitically profit from it: De Quincey befriends the poet, inhabits his former house, and claims to interpret his genius for the popular magazine audience.[2] I find Russett's account especially compelling because it explains De Quincey's continual tendency to stake his own literary authority on other people and agencies, whether Wordsworth, Ricardo, opium, or, as this essay will argue, the English mail.[3] While the attention to the Wordsworth–De Quincey relationship provides illuminating readings of De Quincey's early career, however, focusing on the relationship between the writers has prevented critics from noticing that De Quincey's later works shift from dependence on a person such as Wordsworth to dependence on vast, impersonal national organizations.

One example from De Quincey's revised *Confessions of an English Opium Eater* can quickly illustrate this shift from an interpersonal to a national context. In the 1821 *Confessions*, when De Quincey explains his strong attraction to the Lake District, he credits Wordsworth: Wordsworth's poetry has so amazed and intrigued him that he wants not only to meet the poet, but to wander the very hills depicted in his poetry. When De Quincey revised and expanded the *Confessions* in 1856, however, he diminished the role of Wordsworth and of poetry more generally in drawing him to the Lakes. In 1856 Wordsworth appears (along with Anne Radcliffe and the landscape painters) as merely one of many influences provoking his curiosity. De Quincey ultimately attributes his interest in the Lakes to English administrative divisions: due to the "mere legal fiction" that the southern section of the Lakes was part of De Quincey's Lancashire home, the Lakes held "a secret fascination, subtle, sweet, fantastic, and even from [his] seventh or eighth year spiritually strong."[4] He cannot claim acquaintance with the lake region, and he cannot claim that any similarity between landscapes or peoples connects this portion of the Lakes to Lancashire. Still, writing retrospectively, De Quincey allows the legal identity of the Lakes to assign them a "spiritual" meaning even before he reads Wordsworth's poetry. Even more than literature, local culture, or any author's personal charisma, "the eccentric geography of English law" identifies De Quincey as a native of the Lakes.

In moving from Wordsworth to "English law," De Quincey refuses the organic relationship to the Lakes that Wordsworth claimed for his boyhood in *The Prelude*. Equally crucially for my argument here, De Quincey shifts his interest in the Lakes out of the psychological register. [. . .] I will argue [that] De Quincey identifies with national bureaucracy because by 1856 he locates authorship within a national system of information rather than in individual genius. This redefinition of authorship culminates in De Quincey's 1849 essay, "The English Mail-Coach."

De Quincey's turn to the mail follows a growth in the importance of such organizations in Britain following the Napoleonic wars. As imperial historian C.A. Bayly has argued, in the years following the Napoleonic wars the British government not only founded organizations to launch sociological and statistical studies of the newly expanded colonial territories and populations, but also expanded such bureaucratic organizations at home, investigating the numbers of men available for armed service, effecting a rationalization of the army (containing largely Scottish, Irish, and Indian troops), and standardizing bank notes and customs.[5] Far from simply responding to a historical and social growth in the number and importance of state organizations, however, De Quincey turns to the mail to find an alternative means to achieve literary authority. In locating himself in the English mail, I will argue, De Quincey moves from disseminating the ideas of an illustrious predecessor to disseminating English nationality. To do so, however, requires redefining both what constitutes nationalism and how individuals identify with nations. In "The English Mail-Coach," De Quincey insists that an ethnic understanding of nationality must be combined with an imperially defined nationality that imposes Englishness upon its own people. Only those with English blood can truly share in the joy of English victory, but even those of English blood must have that blood stirred by the conquering force of the English mails.

Even if De Quincey proves far from a disinterested historical observer, I find his version of national identification interesting because of the challenge it offers to our current models of nationalism. First, De Quincey's appeal to a specifically English national identity and his insistence on the primacy of English blood contradict Linda Colley's argument that the eighteenth and early nineteenth centuries saw the development of a British national identity.[6] Second, De Quincey's model of a top-down transmission of national identity reverses our understanding of how national identity rises and spreads. Both Benedict Anderson and Linda Colley locate the origins of national identity in the middle classes rather than in their rulers, and suggest that the British royalty in particular began to claim British nationality only when the people demanded it. [. . .] In "The English Mail-Coach," in contrast, nationalism descends onto the English people rather than arising from them. De Quincey's portrayal of the mail's agency suggests that Colley's model of national identification as a moment of specular exchange neglects the role that organizations play in determining the very categories with which people identify. Indeed, for each of Colley's sources of national pride, we could identify a corresponding national bureaucratic institution: for Protestantism, the English church; for trade, the East India Company and other trading organizations; for liberty, the courts.

We can read De Quincey's insistence on the need for state intervention to incite even popular feelings of nationalism as part of the "official nationalism" identified by Benedict Anderson.[7] [. . .] De Quincey's model of nationality, [. . .] goes [. . .] further [than Anderson's] in marking the government as the origin of all popular feelings.

In doing so, he makes the nation look increasingly like the empire it governs. Both Anderson's model of "official nationalism" and Hannah Arendt's study of imperialism point to a core contradiction in the definition of the imperial nation, but they site this contradiction in the contrast between the nation's projects at home and abroad: a nation rules over like individuals, whereas empire places one people in conquest over an ethnically different people.[8] [. . .] De Quincey undoes this contradiction by insisting that even national identity is imperial because nationality imposes upon a citizen's other identities. The nation must imperially conquer its own people in the name of the king, even if only through a battle of information.

De Quincey finds the imperial model of national identity so compelling because it serves his literary ambitions. Only when national identity is imposed in a central system of information can De Quincey claim to be the author of Englishness. Locating his authority in a government organization therefore challenges the high Romantic models of authorial genius. When riding the English mail, De Quincey finds literary authority in the position in which he sits and in the message he distributes rather than in his own capabilities; terms such as "sympathy" and "imagination" refer not to the author, but to the vast system whose center he occupies. Transmitting national identity through a government organization also supports De Quincey's Tory politics; no radical reforming voices will offer rival claims to speak for the nation. If De Quincey's top-down model of nationality offers the possibility of nullifying potential discord, he also fears that joining a nation requires the sacrifice of persons as well as personal allegiances. In "The English Mail-Coach," De Quincey finds a position of personal and authorial safety, imagining that the official authority of the mail protects all those who ride it. Turning in conclusion to his final revised *Confessions,* however, I argue that the terrors, rather than the benefits, might prove predominant if the authority granted him by his position on the mails cannot protect him from the sacrifice that national identification potentially demands.

Over thirty years after the end of the Napoleonic wars, De Quincey nostalgically remembers riding on the mail coaches as they carried across the countryside the first news of English victory over France. De Quincey describes riding on the outside seat of the mail as a theatrical experience. Sitting on the outside, he can watch the passers-by at the very moment when they see the laurelled coach and learn of victory. Moreover, he knows that these passers-by also see him on the coach, part of the spectacle conveying the news. He not only shares in the observers' exultation, but feels that he has played a role in arousing it. On the outside of the coach, he becomes not merely a passenger, but actually part of the medium that conveys information to the people along the coach's route.

De Quincey turns back to the era of the Napoleonic wars to remember a time of national unity. He attributes this national unity, however, not only to the message of victory that the mails carried, but to the system of its dissemination. De Quincey argues that the mail coaches presented information in a manner that unified, rather than dispersed, the English people. He prefers the old mails to the modern rails because

> the gatherings of gazers about a laurelled mail had one centre, and acknowledged one sole interest. But the crowds attending at a railway station have as little unity as running water, and own as many centres as there are separate carriages in the train.[9]

De Quincey requires that the crowd have a center because it is only when he rides at the center of the crowd's attention that he himself feels a part of the news he carries. Only when every eye looks at him and the mail can De Quincey feel connected to the entire nation. On the mail, the laurels celebrating victory recall the laurels that bedecked classical poets: the mail proves the successor of the poets, because it stirs the sentiments of a nation. And when riding the mail, De Quincey can earn these laurels by virtue simply of his position: when he finds himself at the center of the distribution of the news, a part of the message he carries, De Quincey claims a status equivalent to "laurelled" poets such as Wordsworth or Milton.

De Quincey prefers the mails to the rails not only because the mails place him in a position from which he can join in the dissemination of the news of victory, but because he feels connected to its source. De Quincey argues that only the mail allows passengers to experience their "imperial natures." First, only on the mails, and not on the rails, could passengers feel the speed at which they traveled. On the railways, De Quincey insists, it is impossible to ascertain how fast the coach is traveling without a watch; even if the rails move more quickly than the mail, the passenger experiences this velocity "not . . . as a consciousness, but as a fact of our lifeless knowledge, resting upon *alien* evidence" (193). On the mails, in contrast, every passenger can witness the speed in the exertion of the horse, and know that this speed began as an order from the driver. [. . .] Not only does the horse give more visible signs of its exertion, it also allows the passenger to sympathize with this effort in a way one cannot sympathize with the rails' "blind insensate agencies, that had no sympathy to give" (194). For De Quincey, sympathy does not imply concern for the horse, as much as an awareness that the horse's exertion stems from man's actions. On the rails,

> iron tubes and boilers have disconnected man's heart from the ministers of his locomotion. Nile nor Trafalgar has power to raise an extra bubble in a steam-kettle. The galvanic cycle is broken up for ever; man's imperial nature no longer sends itself forward through the electric sensibility of the horse.
>
> (193–4)

The horse is more "imperial" than the rails because the horse can better promulgate the thrill of victory. Unlike the mechanical rails, the horse can respond to its driver's excitement with increased speed and exertion, and can therefore carry this excitement to both passengers and observers who note the horse's effort. Once again, man's nature proves "imperial" not only because of its grand reach, to Nile and Trafalgar, but because he experiences his own power in directing and observing the exertion of another. In De Quincey's imperialist discourse, sympathy does not oppose imperialism (as it might in anti-imperial discourse, where an individual's suffering would be used to suggest a system's immorality), but fuels the empire's mechanism: the connection of horse to man allows the individual to experience his connection to empire as a feeling of exhilaration.

Even when De Quincey insists that passengers can only feel their "imperial nature" through animal nerves rather than mechanical technologies, he still relies on technological structures to authorize his position. In other words, even if De Quincey prefers that the mail's messages travel through human and animal nerves, he still requires the centralized bureaucracy of the mail system to direct the flow of information across these nerves to the waiting English people. De Quincey needs the mail to place him at the center of every crowd in order to enable him to transmit national identity. And in transmitting information from a single center, the mail imposes an analogously central political system: power flows from the king to the provinces, because the king and his agents control the movement of information. Indeed, the mail proves a "medium" in Friedrich Kittler's sense of the word because the way in which it organizes and transmits information transforms the social and political structure of its society by dictating who will hold information and how they will gather and transmit it.[10] The very power of technology to determine social structures and authorial possibilities, however, ironically propels De Quincey's attempt to return to a past era. Only in the "discourse network" of the Napoleonic wars can he find the technological and political conditions that support his authorial position.

De Quincey's 1834 essay "Travelling in England in Old Days" also considers the role of transportation networks in developing patterns of communication that ultimately underwrite political systems. The 1834 essay, however, imagines a more democratically structured civic order. If technology improved to the point of allowing instantaneous communication, De Quincey suggests, a new political system might arise:

> Action and reaction from every point of the compass being thus perfect and instantaneous, we should then first begin to understand, in a practical sense, what is meant by the unity of a political body, and we should approach to a more adequate appreciation of the powers which are latent in organization. . . . Then every part of the empire will react upon the whole with the power, life, and effect of immediate conference amongst parties brought face to face. Then first will be seen a political system truly *organic* – i.e., in which each acts upon all, and all react upon each: and a new earth will arise from the indirect agency of this merely physical revolution.
>
> (*M* 1.270)

De Quincey imagines a technological revolution that would create a cultural revolution: a change in the movement of information (specifically its velocity) would indelibly join vast expanses of territory, and create a "new earth." He describes this transformation, however, with a word we have come to associate with a much less technological Romanticism, suggesting that technical and organizational advances will create "a political system truly *organic.*" In crediting an organic society to a revolution in technology, De Quincey revises Samuel Taylor Coleridge's strict opposition between organic and mechanic forms.[11] [. . . A]lthough for Coleridge [. . .] organic and mechanic forms are opposites, for De Quincey the "indirect agency" of a mechanism reveals society's "latent" organic form. [. . .]

De Quincey imagines the organic system as latent in a representative rather than monarchical government. In the organic model that "Travelling in England in Old Days" envisions, no single place or person controls the empire. Instead, when communication moves instantaneously, "each acts upon all, and all react upon each." The revolution De Quincey imagines here would remove the need for a center because every part would be linked to every other part. Such a model diffuses agency: it is difficult to suggest where the action or movement might begin; we can only be sure that any movement or idea will spread across the empire. The movement of the whole simply follows the sum of the actions and reactions of all of its parts, with each part voting in a representative assembly, as it were, of parts. De Quincey introduces his expectation of technological revolution with the assertion that he has

> always maintained, that under a representative government, where the great cities of the empire must naturally have the power, each in its proportion, of reacting upon the capital and the councils of the nation in so conspicuous a way, there is a result waiting on the final improvements of the arts of travelling, and of transmitting intelligence with velocity.
>
> (1.270)

The telegraph ends this "wait" because its instantaneous communication allows every part of the empire to immediately "act and react" and to weigh its reacting, according to its appropriate "proportion," in the voice of the whole.

[. . .]

Although De Quincey relies on communication technologies to produce a "new earth," however, he indicates some dissatisfaction with this "merely physical revolution": he suggests that looking back on these lines (written twenty years previously), he found that

> already, in this paragraph . . . a prefiguring instinct spoke within me of some great secret yet to come in the art of distant communication. At present I am content to regard the electric telegraph as the oracular response to that prefiguration. But I still look for some higher and transcendent response.
>
> ("English Mail-Coach" 219)

The telegraph can tie together the empire, but it is not sufficiently "transcendent." The mail system, in contrast, corrects this failure of "transcendence" in two ways. First, as I have discussed, De Quincey states that the mail operates on animal and human nerves, rather than on electric wires, and thus allows passengers to feel their own power over the horse, and to imagine that news travels solely through human agency. More importantly, however, the mail coach enables both passengers and spectators to "transcend" their individual identities when they recognize their national identity and join the celebrations of victory.

De Quincey's model of national identity compromises between a latent "organic" and an imposed "mechanic" derivation: the organizational system of the mail mechanically imposes an English identity that lies organically latent in the English people. Riding the mails, De Quincey can be confident that *he* speaks for the nation, as the author of national identity. When the communication system spreads in straight lines from a single center, De Quincey can place himself at that center.

[. . .]

> The half-slumbering consciousness that all night long, and all the next day – perhaps for even a longer period – many of these mails, like fire racing along a train of gunpowder, will be kindling at every instant new successions of burning joy, has an obscure effect of multiplying the victory itself, by multiplying to the imagination into infinity the stages of its progressive diffusion. A fiery arrow seems to be let loose, which from that moment is destined to travel, without

intermission westwards for three hundred miles – northwards for six hundred; and the sympathy of our Lombard Street friends at parting is exalted a hundredfold by a sort of visionary sympathy with the yet slumbering sympathies which in so vast a succession we are going to awake.

(204–5)

Riding the mails and watching the passers-by, De Quincey finds himself at the center of a crowd's attention. As he watches the mails depart from Lombard, his sense of self-importance is of the same kind but proportionally greater, for he imagines himself at the center of the English nation. De Quincey determines his personal importance from the "infinite" number of people who will hear the news he carries: here imagination verges on mathematical calculus, in which each instantaneous moment of a line is taken to infinity.[12] De Quincey need not see every person who hears the news in order to imagine that he is responsible for conveying it; instead, he simply imagines the reach of the mails. When he terms this imagination "visionary sympathy," sympathy becomes not a matter of knowing and feeling for individuals, but of envisioning the system of which one is a small part; envisioning the system links one with each individual in it. De Quincey redefines "vision," "sympathy," and "imagination" as aspects of one's placement within a system of information and communication rather than as poetic qualities requiring a special sort of mind.[13] When De Quincey rides the mails, his imaginative reach extends beyond his physical movement, for he identifies himself with the outward movement of the news he carries.

In describing the English people as gunpowder, De Quincey implicitly resorts to an ethnic model of national identity, suggesting that some Englishness is necessary in order to take pride in English victory: those not made of gunpowder cannot be lit aflame. In De Quincey's model of nationality, English ethnicity is necessary to share authentically in the glory of victory even if the battles were fought by a united Britain. At the moment of victory, "one heart, one pride, one glory connects every man by the transcendent bond of his English blood" (203). De Quincey uses the term "English" rather than "British" deliberately. "The English Mail-Coach" never considers imperial subjects, and most of the essay only imagines the English people receiving the news of victory, and therefore only imagines a population that should rise together in glorious sympathy with the spread of empire.

[. . .]

Even if Englishness lies latent as an ethnic category, stirring it to the surface proves coercive. Although the news of English victories brings joy, this joy takes each individual violently. After the battle is over, the dissemination of news figuratively continues the fighting. Information appears as "fiery arrows," and moves like "fire racing along a train of gunpowder . . . Kindling at every instant new successions of burning joy." People are merely the "gunpowder" and require a spark to flare. Setting individual emotions aflame, the mail's "fiery arrows" seem almost as powerful as actual munitions, but it is the English people (rather than the colonies) that they conquer.

To understand why De Quincey insists that national identity imposes itself upon the English people and cannot simply rise up within them, we need to consider De Quincey's political as well as authorial concerns. In restructuring the national communication system around a single center, De Quincey insists upon an imperial center–periphery political structure rather than the more "democratic" inter-regional organization seen in the telegraph system. As I have argued, De Quincey finds in such a centralized structure a surer authorial position: he can only be certain that every man, woman, and child in England listens to his message when he joins his message to the king's mail. An 1836 political essay, however, demonstrates a second reason for seeking both a centralized structure and an imperial context for national identity. "Toryism, Whiggism, and Radicalism" considers the question of who can speak for the nation, and worries that the reform movement claims to rise above partisan politics to speak with a national voice. [. . .] De Quincey admits that the reformers do indeed achieve the numbers to win a democratic contest for the national voice. Within this democratic system, however, De Quincey imagines the power of the people as "despotic" because their sheer numbers co-opt even those like himself who disagree with the goals of reform (*M* 9.347).

De Quincey and his fellow Tories cannot defeat the reformers in any fairly contested election or contest of voices. Instead, he counters the reformers first by suggesting that there is no room for a third party in the British government: in a division of labor, the Whigs "tak[e] charge of the popular influence" and the Tories "tak[e] charge of the antagonist or non-popular influence" leaving no position for reform (*M* 9.337). Second, and more interesting in the context of "The English Mail-Coach," he turns outward from a contest for the national voice to the battle for empire, attributing the essay to "a letter to a friend in Bengal." [. . . He] addresses the essay specifically to Bengal in a deliberate attempt to restore himself to the English political center. By admitting that the English government of Bengal needs reform, even if such reform is currently too "perilous" to attempt, he claims the position of a moderate: he desires some reforms (in Bengal), but not others (in Britain). And addressing the essay to Bengal makes De Quincey's Englishness more important than his Toryism. When speaking to the colonies, he becomes a member of the center in a way he does not while participating in English partisan debates. In a version of what John Barrell has termed "this, that, and the other," he incorporates the near other, the British working classes, by opposing both to a more distant other, Bengal.[14] One way to counter the reformers' claim to speak on behalf of the nation is to address himself to a colonial.

In "The English Mail-Coach," De Quincey again uses the imperial context to unite the nation and restore himself to the political center. "The English Mail-Coach," however, does not face the English people to a colonial other, but rather to a united vision of the English nation. In questioning how the nation can speak and feel as one, "The English Mail-Coach" raises the same question as "Toryism, Whiggism, and Radicalism": who speaks for the nation? The mail coach, however, need not worry over rhetorical positioning, but decisively overruns all opposition. In turning to the mail, De Quincey's memory serves his politics. He looks to the Napoleonic war era rather than to some other moment of mass union (such as the rallies for the Reform Bill) to epitomize the national imagination at a moment when the nation thinks like a Tory. Only at such a moment can De Quincey be supremely sure that no individual citizen will break the chain of "burning joy" (205). De Quincey figures this unified vision, however, as a consequence not only of the historical moment, but of the action of the mail. The mail stirs a consensual national identity among all English people.

[. . .]

"The English Mail-Coach" most decisively combats the figure of reform by figuring any opposition to its message of patriotism as personal, not political. The individuals who cannot share in national joy do not seek an alternative national voice. Instead, they have "suffered some deep personal affliction," perhaps losing sons or brothers or husbands in the war, that prevents them from celebrating national glory. The news of victory merely reminds them of their loss, or causes them to sympathize with other families now experiencing similar tragedy. [. . .] De Quincey portrays the moment of national pride as a forgetting of one's self. In "The English Mail-Coach," English identity lies dormant until awakened by news of victory; only at the moment of victory do people give up their individual identities to identify themselves as members of a nation. In describing the joy of national identity, De Quincey argues that the mail is generous; it elevates even the basest spectator to greatness by demonstrating the glory of his English blood: "The beggar, rearing himself against the wall, forgets his lameness – real or assumed. . . . The victory has healed him, and says – Be thou whole!" (205). The poor charwomen "for this one night . . . feel themselves by birthright to be daughters of England, and answer to no humbler title" (206). Identifying with the nation makes the beggar and charwomen whole because it allows them to forget their poverty and social position.

[. . .]

In the cases of the beggar and the charwomen, the requisite forgetting seems benign: each forgets pain. When we set "The English Mail-Coach" alongside De Quincey's more explicitly political writings, however, we can see that the advent of national identity is not always so innocent. Indeed, in De Quincey's Tory logic the generous glory of the mail almost removes the need for reform by elevating the poor, in spirit if not in social class. And in every citizen it reaches, patriotic joy appears violently because it comes at the cost of an individual's other identifications. De Quincey does not imagine that it would be possible to identify oneself in more than one way at a time, and so even those with English blood can only experience national pride as a conquering of national over individual feeling. National identification can never be neutral. Most, like one woman whom De Quincey meets, the mother of a soldier in a regiment that has just won a bloody victory, forget the uncertain fates of friends and relatives in the moment of joy. Not considering that the crucial role played by her son's regiment likely meant his death, she "blindly allowed herself to express an exultation so unmeasured in the news, and its details" (207). In one respect, the woman's exultation is far from "blind": she responds to the visual spectacle of the mail coach, which only announces victory, and does not foretell its costs.

[. . .]

De Quincey figures this conquering of all feeling as the mail's utter indifference to any unofficial persons. The motion of the coach itself threatens to destroy whatever humans might step into its path, and De Quincey initially argues that such unresponsiveness cannot be helped:

> Tied to post-office time, with an allowance in some cases of fifty minutes for eleven miles, could the royal mail pretend to undertake the offices of sympathy and condolence? Could it be expected to provide tears for the accidents of the road? If even it seemed to trample on humanity, it did so, I contended, in discharge of its own more peremptory duties.
>
> (191)

[. . .]

But even if De Quincey accepts the constraints of the coach – and even thanks the mail for "regulating" his love affair with a girl at one stop, limiting his acquaintance with her to the short time necessary to change the horses – he nevertheless remains haunted by the individual sacrifices that the mail, both in its own terms and as a figure for the motion of England's imperial expansion, demands.[15]

The horrific danger of the mail's speed and the profundity of the sacrifice that national identification potentially demands climax in "The Vision of Sudden Death." As the mail travels at increasing speeds through the dark, its driver asleep and De Quincey the only passenger, it veers into the wrong lane and heads straight for a young couple in a small cart. Absorbed in each other, the couple is unaware of the impending danger, and they take no action to remove their coach from the mail's path. De Quincey tries to sound the horn, but his reach is blocked by a large stack of foreign mail. Luckily, he says, he remembers a passage from the *Iliad*, and thinks to shout a warning to the cart. The man looks up, sees the approaching mail, and is able to pull himself and the woman just out of reach. When De Quincey looks back, he sees the young woman raising her arms to heaven, in fear and in acknowledgment.

[. . .]

In portraying the near-victims of the mail as a young couple in love, De Quincey once again figures any English resistance to national progress as personal – or more exactly in this passage, sexual – rather than political. The young couple in the cart is so absorbed in their private conversation that they do not notice the approach of the bolting mail:

> Ah, young sir! What are you about? If it is necessary that you should whisper your communications to this young lady – though really I see nobody at this hour, and on this solitary road, likely to overhear your conversation – is it, therefore, necessary that you should carry your lips forward to hers?
>
> (221)

[. . .] By reading private relationships as sexual rather than political, he can suggest the power of the mail over all individual concerns without evoking either the threat of reform or his own Toryism. A "whisper" in the dark signals romance, not sedition. Once again, "The English Mail-Coach" imagines only isolated and non-ideological resistance to the encroaching force of a centrally distributed nationalism.

The incident haunts De Quincey, I would suggest, because it illustrates the potential threat of national identity.[16] If the nation demands sacrifice, no other temporal authority can intervene. In replaying the incident in his "Dream Fugue," De Quincey appeals to religion to rehabilitate any sacrifice to the nation as Christian resurrection. In the dream fugue, the young woman reappears as a baby who quickly grows into a woman who must be sacrificed as "the ransom for Waterloo" (230). But her angel intervenes, the woman is saved, the war ends, and the people wait to celebrate the secret word, "Waterloo and Recovered Christendom." [. . .] Neither the end of the war nor his Christian rehabilitation of sacrifice, however, ends De Quincey's worries over the cost of national allegiance. If remembering a moment of victory solves the problem of what the nation thinks, the increasing importance to De Quincey of the nation and its imperial project also increases the peril they pose to individuals. Riding the mail coach offers to protect De Quincey from such dangers.

Although the dream fugue recounts the potential sacrifice of the young woman, in the dream neither the mail coach nor the national identity that it represents threaten De Quincey himself. As in the Malay incident in the *Confessions,* danger threatens only the innocent person at the end of the communication chain. When national identity demands a sacrifice, or when communication fails, it sacrifices those on the outskirts – the colonial subject, the young woman.

[. . .]

In the 1856 *Confessions of an English Opium Eater* [. . .], De Quincey worries that [. . .] a position of national authority cannot protect him from the personal cost of national identification. He figures these concerns in recurring references to the Whispering Gallery in St. Paul's Cathedral. De Quincey introduces the Whispering Gallery as a symbol of a related set of fears, his fears that he will later regret his current words and actions. Recalling a visit to the Whispering Gallery during his youth, he remembers his horror at the thought that a "solemn whisper" at one end of the gallery could turn into a "volleying thunder" at the other. The very idea that his words or actions could have consequences beyond what he intended is enough to make De Quincey "nervous[ly] recoil from any word or deed that could not be recalled" (*M* 3.296). In "The English Mail-Coach," the mail offers protection from these worries: as long as De Quincey rides the mail, the king's authority will sanction his words and actions and protect his person. Such protection, however, lasts only as long as he maintains his position on the moving coach. De Quincey remembers the Whispering Gallery with the retrospective knowledge that the very chamber in which he had seen "pompously floating to and fro in the upward space of a great aisle running westward from ourselves, many flags captured from France, Spain, and Holland . . . solemn trophies of chance and change among mighty nations," would five years later witness the burial of Lord Nelson (*M* 3.296). In his first visit to the Whispering Gallery, De Quincey identifies his own position in the cathedral with that of his nation; the flags "run[] westward from ourselves" as if he and his friend were the point of origin of their movement. In contrast, Lord Nelson's casket – in "pretty nearly the very spot" in which they had stood to watch the flags – suggests that position, whether physical location or professional status, cannot protect the individual. The same physical position that temporarily marked De Quincey as the center of English military power, with the flags of the vanquished nations arrayed before him, sees Lord Nelson's casket. The juxtaposition of De Quincey's national identification and Lord Nelson's burial suggests the precariousness of any attempt to identify with a physical position, like De Quincey's position on the mail coach: without any diminution of national glory, the same position that in one instance signaled triumphant victory (and authorized by association anyone who stood there), in another brings death.

[. . .]

In addition to demonstrating that national authority cannot save the individual, Lord Nelson's fate suggests to De Quincey the dangers of fame. In associating Nelson's death and the seeming center of world history, or "chance and change among mighty nations," De Quincey suggests Nelson's prominence means stasis. Nelson's position as Admiral of the Navy – at the origin, as it were, of the national glory De Quincey and the mail coach celebrate – ties his name and his person too firmly to a single national role. De Quincey's position while riding the mail differs from Nelson's situation in several important respects: De Quincey's authority is temporary, impersonal, and non-functional; he performs no task for the mail or for the nation – the news would travel just as well without him on board the coach – and the vision he imagines descending upon him would fall to any English person sitting in his position. Furthermore, the mail grants De Quincey rhetorical protection: the speed of the coach insures he travels ahead of any personally specific news, and the evanescence and impersonality of his position on the mail protects him from any significance in the public eye. However, publishing his autobiography – for all that he signs with a pseudonym – poses a danger similar to Lord Nelson's public identity. Only by refusing to locate his self and his literary persona can De Quincey claim to publish English identity, and also protect his person from dissolution.

After "The English Mail-Coach," De Quincey continued revising his autobiographical *Confessions*. In the context of De Quincey's meditations in the Whispering Gallery, these revisions serve two contrary purposes. On the one hand, his work records the personal identity the nation could annihilate. On the other hand, his continued expansions to his autobiographical *corpus* keep that very subject in constant motion, eliding any fixed identification of his authorial persona. De Quincey remains flexibly available to place himself within whatever information system may authorize his discourse and provide a speaking position. But the mail provides the most certain authority that De Quincey will find because it underwrites an impersonal and ever-moving position before a national audience it forcefully, if briefly, constitutes.

Notes

1 Alina Clej, *A Genealogy of the Modern Self: Thomas De Quincey and the Intoxication of Writing* (Stanford: Stanford UP, 1995). Charles Rzepka, *Sacramental Commodities: The Gift and the Text in Thomas De Quincey* (Amherst: U of Massachusetts P, 1995).
2 Margaret Russett, *De Quincey's Romanticism: Canonical Minority and the Forms of Transmission* (Cambridge: Cambridge UP, 1997). Russett also helpfully locates De Quincey's authorial strategies within the contemporary magazine industry.
3 Josephine McDonagh argues that De Quincey uses Ricardo to redefine debt (including literary debt) as central to all social interaction (*De Quincey's Disciplines* [Oxford: Oxford UP, 1994] 42–65). De Quincey's opium addiction figures both the power and the danger of literary dependency; on opium, see Clej and Alethea Hayter, *Opium and the Romantic Imagination* (Berkeley: U of California P, 1968).
4 *The Collected Writings of Thomas De Quincey*, ed. David Masson (London, 1897), vol. 3: 282. Further references to the Masson edition will be cited parenthetically as *M*.
5 See *Imperial Meridians* (New York: Longman, 1989) and *Empire and Information: Intelligence Gathering and Social Communication in India 1780–1870* (Cambridge: Cambridge UP, 1996).
6 *Britons: Forging a Nation* (New Haven: Yale UP, 1992).
7 Benedict Anderson, *Imagined Communities: Reflections on the Origin and Spread of Nationalism* (London: Verso, 1991) 109–10.
8 Hannah Arendt, *Origins of Totalitarianism* (New York: Harcourt Brace, 1973) 123–34. In Anderson, see especially 92–4.
9 Quotations from "The English Mail-Coach" are from the Oxford edition edited by Grevel Lindop (New York: Oxford UP, 1984), 194. Subsequent references will be cited parenthetically in the text.
10 See *Discourse Networks, 1800/1900*, tr. Michael Metteer with Chris Cullens (Stanford: Stanford UP, 1990).
11 Cited in *Biographia Literaria*, ed. James Engell and W. Jackson Bate (Princeton: Princeton UP, 1983) 2: 84, editor's note.

12 John Plotz terms this stage-by-stage reach of the mails "fractalization," and argues that for De Quincey the gradual accretion of the "national crowd" presents an important contrast to the newspapers which distribute news simultaneously [. . .] (*The Crowd: British Literature and Public Politics* [Berkeley: U of California P, 2000] 107, 119).

13 Redefining authorship as placement within a system therefore also frees De Quincey from comparing himself to Wordsworth. [. . .]

14 John Barrell, *The Infection of Thomas De Quincey: A Psychopathology of Imperialism* (New Haven: Yale UP, 1991), see especially 8–15.

15 See also Eva-Lynn Alicia Jagoe's discussion of De Quincey's regulated love affair in her essay ["Degrading Forms of Pantomime: Englishness and Shame in De Quincey," *Studies In Romanticism* 44.1 (2005): 23–40].

16 See also Jagoe's argument, in her article ["Degrading Forms"], that identifying with the nation causes shame.

16 *Milton* unbound

Margaret Russett

Thou also, man, hast wrought,
For commerce of thy nature with itself,
Things worthy of unconquerable life;
And yet we feel – we cannot chuse but feel –
That these must perish. Tremblings of the heart
It gives, to think that the immortal being
No more shall need such garments. . .
The consecrated works of bard and sage,
Sensuous or intellectual, wrought by men,
Twin labourers and heirs of the same hopes,
Where would they be? Oh, why hath not the mind
Some element to stamp her image on
In nature somewhat nearer to her own?
Why, gifted with such powers to send abroad
Her spirit, must it lodge in shrines so frail?

(Wordsworth 1979: 152–4 [5: 17–23, 41–8])[1]

I begin this essay on Blake with an epigraph from Wordsworth to highlight the tropes of "book" and "author" which both poets inherited from the literary property debates of the eighteenth century, and which were linked, for both, with the figure of John Milton. Book Fifth of *The Prelude*, the book of "Books," begins by lamenting the temporality of the "shrines" which house the "spirit[s]" of bard and sage. To publish a book, Wordsworth suggests, is not in fact to achieve vicarious immortality but to exchange one form of embodiment for another: book is to "consecrated works" as "garment" is to "immortal being," or as "element" is to "mind." Books, that is, share the dual ontology of the persons who write them: at once matter and spirit, body and soul. Indeed, the "mind. . . stamp[s]. . . her image" on paper just as "the speaking face of earth and heaven" once impressed upon that mind the language of the "sovereign Intellect," and thereby "diffuse'd / A soul divine which we participate": the "deathless spirit" of the canonized author (Wordsworth 1979: 152: [5: 12–17]). Wordsworth's lament suggests not only the reciprocal dependency of "author" and "book," but also how book production recapitulates subjectivity – and vice versa – in a world of "standardized texts" where "paper and body, writing and soul fall apart" (Kittler 1999: 14). This, to be sure, is not Blake's world: in nothing is Blake more consistent than in his hostility to the miniature selfhoods, called books, which anchor the Lockean conception of authorship. To put this point a little differently, I will describe Blake as a *media* critic of authorship. His argument, waged

Figure 16.1 Blake, William. Milton, a Poem. Title page. This item is reproduced by permission of The Huntington Library, San Marino, California

at the levels of poetic theme and artistic production, addresses the dual reifications of author as immaterial spirit, and book as lifeless matter. It culminates in the late prophecy *Milton a Poem*, a book whose very title suggests its preoccupation with the "name of an author" (Foucault 1977: 121).[2]

The title page of *Milton* presents its readers with a heroic male nude, seen from the rear, but identifiable as "John Milton" by his long hair and "manly grace" (Hayley 1796: 195; Figure 16.1). This figure's right hand is raised in exhortation or entreaty, like that of the narrative persona who, in the proem, asks the "Daughters of Beulah" to "come into my hand / By your mild power; descending down the Nerves of my right arm / From out the Portals of my Brain, where by your ministry / The Eternal Great Humanity Divine planted his Paradise" (Blake 2008: 148 [2: 1–8]). Or perhaps this hand is pushing its way through the capitalized proper name which it splits into two constituent syllables, MIL/TON, the second of which descends down the right margin of the page. The name "Milton" is thus placed under erasure, as is the subtitle, "a Poem in [either] 12 [or] 2 Books," depending on which of the four existing copies of *Milton* we consult. "Under erasure" is a fair summary of Milton's status in the poem, whose main action consists in its protagonist's willing descent from Heaven, where he has resided for the past 100-plus years, into "annihilation" – a *felix culpa* prompted by his belated discovery of the harm he has wrought by propagating a false account of Satan's fall in *Paradise Lost.* The title illustration depicts Milton at the moment of beginning his descent, surrounded by a vortex of clouds (heaven) or flames (hell), and leading with his right foot so that the left one lifts off the caption "To Justify the Ways of God to Men," a provisional iteration of the poet Milton's vow to "assert Eternal Providence, / *And* justify the ways of God to men" (Milton 2003: 3 [1: 25–6]). Naked though he be, the graphic emphasis on his upraised *hand* suggests his identity as an epic poet, while his striding *feet* pun visually on the metrical "feet" which, in the prefatory hymn known as "Jerusalem," "walk[ed] upon England's mountains green" (Blake 2008: 147 [i {E 1}: 1–2]).

In the fourth quadrant of the page is inscribed "The Author and Printer W Blake 1804." This byline is ironically juxtaposed with the preeminent authorial name "Milton," whose appearance on a book not *written* by John Milton might lead us to expect a biography – such as the one published by Blake's patron, William Hayley, in 1796 – or a critical study, perhaps even a tributary ode, but hardly a poem in which the author Milton has become a character, the protagonist of a fictional story. Yet the form of Blake's inscription is recognizably Miltonic, for "The Author John Milton" was Milton's own way of styling himself on title pages, though this was not typical seventeenth-century practice and implied "an idea of authorship – especially for himself – that departs markedly from early modern norms" (Lewalski 2006: 54).[3] It follows that a poem about "Milton" is a poem about authorship, the more so if Blake uses the uncharacteristic (after *Thel* and the *Songs*) term "author" to describe his own role in its production. Before we return to *Milton,* this point may be elucidated by a detour through Blake's first engagement with the legacy of John Milton in *The Marriage of Heaven and Hell.*

The Marriage is at once the single work in Blake's oeuvre which most directly concerns book-making, and itself a text without an "author." While the illuminated books usually name one "Will" or "William" or "W" Blake as "printer," *The Marriage* lacks any byline at all. This is a telling omission in the book which, along with *Milton,* is Blake's most explicitly self-referential. There, in a passage long understood as manifesto for his own method of "relief etching," Blake's narrator describes the unorthodox techniques of "a Printing House in Hell."[4] Briefly, since many will already be familiar with this term, relief etching was a method for producing an image by painting with a viscous substance on copper, then submersing the plate in an acid bath which ate away the untreated surfaces and left raised lines or planes where the substance had been applied. Relief etching was the reverse of the standard "intaglio" method Blake had learned as a commercial engraver, and in which lines were incised *into* a copper plate with a stylus. In intaglio etching, images are reproduced by first inking the entire plate, then wiping it off so that ink remains only in the incised lines. When pressure is applied to the plate, ink from those incisions bonds to the receiving surface. In relief etching, by contrast, ink is applied to the raised planes of the metal plate, and then transferred by gentle application to a piece of paper. For Blake, the great aesthetic advantage of relief etching consisted in its "autographic nature" (Essick 1989: 169), the painterly freedom of line that allowed him to incorporate text and image into a single organic design. Its disadvantages included loss of fine detail and a shorter life for the plate, since each successive printing would slightly abrade the surfaces to be inked.

Blake scholars have explained in compelling detail how the technique of relief etching allowed Blake to become his own publisher of books which were each unique works of art.[5] Because he controlled every aspect of production, from composition to design to layout to coloring, Blake could conceive of his work as exempt from the mechanized world of commercial publication, in which the writer so revered in theory was, in practice, a contractor with little influence over the visual form of his book. Blake could and did treat successive printings as distinct events, making changes both large and small to each "edition" of the poems he printed. No two copies of any Blake book are precisely alike, their differences ranging from variations in coloring and hand-drawn details to major reshufflings of page sequences, as well as the inclusion or omission of individual plates. By contrast with the author of conventionally printed books, whose name on the title page guaranteed "content" but not form, "W Blake" functioned more like a *signature*, the graphic mark identifying a single artistic performance such as a painting or sculpture.[6] Even as a poet, Blake was in certain ways more artist or artisan than "author," if authorship implies the fixity and interchangeability of a book's textual contents, as well as the distance between the writer's originating consciousness and the commodity bought by the reader. Blake's books, by the same token, were less objects – "garments" or "shrines" – than performances of writing as a mode of embodied action.

I rehearse these familiar points to provide a backdrop for the announcement by Blake's narrative persona, in plate 14 of *The Marriage*, that

> First the notion that man has a body distinct from his soul, is to be expunged; this I shall do, by printing in the infernal method, by corrosives, which in Hell are salutary and medicinal, melting apparent surfaces away, and displaying the infinite which was hid.
>
> If the doors of perception were cleansed every thing would appear to man as it is, infinite.
>
> For man has closed himself up, till he sees all things thro' narrow chinks of his cavern.
>
> (Blake 2008: 75 [*Marriage* 14])

Of particular interest here is the rapid slide from theology – heaven and hell, body and soul – to phenomenology and thence to technical questions of medium. How can any means of production "expunge" the governing binary of Christian thought? One clue is supplied by Blake's jibe at the closed doors and narrow chinks of the perceptual "cavern," a clear allusion to the reviled John Locke's account, in his *Essay Concerning Human Understanding*, of the mind as an "empty Cabinet" or a "*dark Room* . . . wholly shut from light, with only some little openings left" for the admission of "Ideas" through the "Windows" of "external and internal Sensation." Elsewhere, Locke imagines the inexperienced mind as a "white Paper, void of all Characters" until it receives the "imprint" of Experience (Locke 2008: 23, 96 [I:ii, II:xi]).[7] The inconsistency of these metaphors, according to which mind is at once a three-dimensional space and a two-dimensional surface, does not go unnoticed by Blake – and will, along with Locke's concomitant elision of medium, be explicitly thematized in the later prophetic books. Either way, however, the mind begins as something "meerly *passive*"; ideas come *to* it as "impressions" from the external world, the "reflection" upon which mysteriously animates this matter with self-consciousness (Locke 2008: 63 [II:i]). Locke's is thus not merely a textual figure for consciousness but one specifically modeled on print technology, and one that assumes a sexual division of labor between vehicular matter and ideational content. "Impression," a term of art in printing, evokes the mechanical procedure by which, according to Locke, "archetypes" are transferred from the external world to the blank page. This terminology also recalls the intaglio method of engraving, by which "Characters" are etched *into* a *tabula rasa*. In *The Four Zoas* and its spinoffs, Blake takes up the gender implications of both Lockean theory and publishing practice by depicting "Emanations" as feminine imprints of the presumptively masculine Zoas.

According to Locke, each mind precisely resembles all others, inasmuch as the sameness of archetypes points to their origin in the transcendental printing-press that he calls God. It is easy to see why this assumption is so offensive to Blake, and why he could imagine his "corrosive" method, which reveals inert "surface" to be the deceptive outer circumference of poetic form, as a practical rebuttal of Locke's argument. In Blakean terms, relief etching offers a productive "contrary" to mechanical printing and intaglio etching, whereas blank paper is merely the "negation" of typeface. Even so, we may notice that Blake attacks Locke's model of consciousness by reversing tenor and vehicle – by making books in a different way than Locke envisioned, not by contesting the metaphor of mind-as-print. Robert Essick suggests that "by making books with a physical presence, a body, that we cannot ignore, Blake tries to prevent his readers from separating out a 'soul' of verbal meaning and leaving the body behind" (Essick 1986: 210). Blake, that is, attacks epistemology via ontology, refusing the bookish dualism of "matter" (paper, ink, and cardboard) versus linguistic "spirit," notionally indifferent to the matter it animates.

The idea of human nature as a war between matter and spirit is older than Christianity, but that of the book as a *container* for spirit is an artifact of print capitalism, more specifically of the eighteenth century. I allude here to the series of Parliamentary Acts and high-profile piracy cases, beginning with the Statute of Anne and culminating in *Donaldson v. Becket* of 1774, which established the modern concepts of copyright and intellectual property in the Anglophone legal tradition. As scholars including Mark Rose and myself have pointed out, it was only by abstracting writing into incorporeal "spirit" that it could be imagined as distinguishable from "its Appendage or Adjunct, the corporeal Part" distributed by booksellers (William Warburton, qtd. Russett 2006: 77). Only by sloughing off its materiality, in other words, could writing be conceived as literary *property* – and only literary *properties* have "authors," in the sense associated with possessive individualism and famously critiqued by Foucault. There is a rich series of Blakean paradoxes to be unfolded here, beginning with the fact that the evanescence of texts was occasioned by their treatment as real estate. The presumptive stability of the ideal text, however, rested on a mystification of technological advances such as the stereotype. Those familiar with Blake's late prophetic books will anticipate where this is going, but let us pause to notice the fearful symmetry by which Locke, author of the printing-press model of consciousness, is also the founder of *personal* property, or property in oneself, which supplied the alibi for literary property as the individual writer's "improvement" of the linguistic commons by investing words with the expression of a unique personality (Rose 1993: 64–5, *passim*).

Returning from this excursus to *The Marriage*, we can see that Blake's corrosive critique addresses itself at once to Locke's mechanistic derivation of personality from the imprint of sensory experience, and to the analytical division of paper body from textual soul that underwrites literary property – and which gave rise to that infamous oversoul, the "author" as transcendental origin of the immaterial text. Such "spirits" or "personalities" are indeed, for Blake, not souls at all, but bodies in the fallen, restricted sense dramatized in *The Four Zoas*. Essick is surely right to describe Blake's technique as an insistence on the *embodiedness* of his books, but the opposite is also true. The differences of these books from one another – differences that follow inevitably from the means of their production, and in which happenstance played a large role, but which were also deliberately exaggerated by Blake's finishing work – invest each "body," such as the four extant copies of *Milton*, with the uniqueness and unrepeatability which pertain to "souls." The "notion" to which Blake objects, after all, is not that there are souls but that there are bodies, if by body we mean anything other than "the portion of Soul discerned by the five senses" (Blake 2008: 70 [*Marriage* 4]). This is to suggest that illuminated printing constituted a new *medium* (not just a new form), whose message was the redemption of negations into mutually productive contraries.

It remains for the reader of *The Marriage* to "discern" its authorial personality, or soul, in the "sensual enjoyment" of its riotous designs, exuberant coloring, polygeneric form, and erratic personae who occasionally recall the historical William Blake. That Blake is never named as author makes a certain sense, considering how the work's incoherence problematizes any assumption of an originating personality, and how this formal critique correlates with explicit attacks on two *authors* – most immediately, Emmanuel Swedenborg, but most especially, John Milton. Milton is an author not merely in the formal sense posited by eighteenth-century copyright law, but in the specialized sense Foucault reserves for the "initiators of discursive practices" who "made possible a certain number of analogies that could be adopted by future texts" and "also made possible a certain number of differences. They cleared a space for the introduction of elements other than their own, which, nevertheless, remain within the field of discourse they initiated" (Foucault 1977: 132). To Blake, Milton is not just the poet of *Paradise Lost*, and not even just the greatest of the eighteenth century's canonical trinity (with Spenser and Shakespeare). For it is to Milton, as Blake's narrative persona claims, that we owe the pernicious conflation of psychology, theology, and politics according to which "desire" is doomed to a losing contest with "the restrainer or reason," which "usurps its place and governs the unwilling" (Blake 2008: 70 [*Marriage* 5]).

Blake's personification of this usurper is often depicted precisely as an author: as the author, in fact, of *The [First] Book of Urizen*, on whose title page he is seen squatting atop the open pages of the folio he is simultaneously composing (Figure 16.2). One hand holds a pen, the other the stylus used for intaglio engraving. Behind Urizen are the twin tablets of Mosaic law, the stony or reified form of the book he sits on, and which, by "inclosing" and "improving" it in the manner of a Lockean claimant to land ownership, he marks as his own "real property." The "abstracted" author

Figure 16.2 Blake, William. The [First] Book of Urizen. Title page: Urizen bound. Lessing J. Rosenwald Collection, Library of Congress. © 2014 William Blake Archive. Used with permission

"refus[es] all Definite form" for himself, even while scheming to present the other Eternals with the "books formd of metals" in which he has "written. . . / The secrets of dark contemplation" (Blake 2008: 149, 117–20 [*Milton* 3: 9; *Urizen* 4: 24–6]). Blakean pretenders to immaterial authority always meet the ironic fate of becoming stonified or "bonified." Urizen's "enormous labours" (Blake 2008: 115 [*Urizen* 3: 22]) succeed in the Miltonic feat of "restrain[ing] desire" only by bringing death into the world, with all our woe: the willows arching over Urizen's head make the title page into a tombstone, announcing, one might say, the "death of the author" just as he is born. If authorship is the quintessentially Urizenic activity, with lifeless metal books as its product, that is darkly in keeping with Milton's characterization of God as "Author of all being," himself "invisible" (Milton 2003: 62 [3: 374–5]).

Pridefully styling "himself the Sole author / Of all his wandering Experiments in the horrible Abyss" (Blake 1988: 356 [*Four Zoas* 80: 51–2]), Urizen *mistakes* himself for Milton's God. In fact, his assertion of authorship is precisely Satanic – for it is Satan, in *Paradise Lost*, who refuses the definite fact of having been created, haughtily insisting that he is "self-begot, self-raised / By [his] own quick'ning power" (Milton 2003: 123 [5: 860–1]). But while *Paradise Lost* presumes the existence of one true Author, no such authority exists in Blake. Neither Urizen nor the other Zoas can rightfully claim sole authorship of *The Four Zoas*, yet each authors the others, in the unending drama of division that begins with "Emanation." The Emanation both extends and undercuts the Zoa's authority, somewhat as the multiplication of textual copies, in standardized book production, both amplifies and abstracts the identity of the writer. We may be reminded here of Freud's textual metaphor for "transferences" – "tendencies or phantasies" which, belonging properly to the past, are "aroused and made conscious" as "new editions or facsimiles" of those earlier tendencies. Transferences can, Freud avers, reproduce past emotions with the typographical accuracy of "reprints," or they may, by means of "sublimation," reconstitute themselves as "new editions" (Freud 1997: 106–7). This is not at all to suggest that we read other people "like a book," but rather that, by stereotypically "impressing" old scenarios onto them, we turn them *into* books, copies of some presumptive original that we falsely believe ourselves to have authored. In Blake's mythos, transference gives rise to feminine entities who personify the "meerly *passive*" matter on which ideas are imprinted. This matter itself then develops "consciousness" in an occult twist that recalls how, according to Marx, commodities come to mistake themselves for social agents (Marx 1979: 319–21).

Emanations begin by emanating from their originals. In a primal scene repeated from *Urizen* to *The Four Zoas*, "a globe of life blood" oozes "trembl[ing]" from the Eternal (Blake 2008: 123 [*Urizen* 17: 59; 18: 1) before assuming human form. At this point the Emanation is a "book" in the idealized Miltonic sense, "the precious life-blood of a master spirit" (Milton 1974: 150). But no sooner does she take shape than she devolves into "a shadowy form now Separate" from her author (Blake 1988: 320 [*Four Zoas* 30: 46]). When, for instance, Los sets out to "bind" Urizen into form, he finds that he has unwittingly created a new entity:

> The globe of life blood trembled
> Branching out into roots:
> Fib'rous, writhing upon the winds:
> Fibres of blood, milk and tears. . .
> At length in tears & cries imbodied
> A female form trembling and pale
> Waves before his deathy face.
>   (Blake 2008: 123 [*Urizen* 18: 1–8];
>   see also Blake 1988: 338
>   [*Four Zoas* 56: 24–7])

The fibrous, pale female form that confronts Los with his own "death[iness]" tropes the gender dynamics implicit in Locke's metaphor of mind-as-paper. This division likewise suggests the devaluation of "paper and print" as mere "vehicles" for the "immaterial" combination of "style" and "sentiments" that define authorship in eighteenth-century law (William Blackstone, qtd. Rose 1993: 89). Enitharmon the weaver,

Los's lost page, is gendered feminine as the textilic vehicle of Los's self-alienation. And while the cultural identification of matter with mater long predates the eighteenth century, Blake emphasizes how the mechanics of book production recapitulate the metaphysical division of masculine mind and feminine medium.

The bound Urizen's transformation into a parody of the Lockean mind, whose "fountain of thought" becomes "inclosd / In an orb," corresponds with the hardening of his body into "Bones of solidness" and "a vast Spine" that "writh[es] in torment / Upon the winds" (Blake 2008: 120–1 [*Urizen* 10: 33–41, 11: 1]). With his "binding" and "jointed spine," Urizen has become what he purported to author, suggesting a diffuse satire on the Judeo-Christian aggrandizement of the faithful as "peoples of the book." But if Blake demonizes authorship in the fate of Urizen, we must remember that, as Foucault remarks, authorship "is not formed spontaneously through the simple attribution of a discourse to an individual," but proceeds from "a complex operation whose purpose is to construct" the author via "projections," or transferences, "of our way of handling texts" (Foucault 1977: 127, 130–1). Authors, in other words, are not born but made. They are the bonified byproducts of a dissemination system that both builds upon and sponsors a "plurality of egos" – beginning with compositors and engravers, but extending into editors, biographers, and readers. It might be said, in a Blakean turn on Foucault's argument, that the division of poetic labor into writing and reading, and the corresponding division of egos into Emanations and Spectres, produces the illusion of a sole originating subject.

At this point we may return for a second look at the title page of *Milton*, and notice that, in some copies, Milton appears to be spurning a book under his left foot. Milton's parting of his own capitalized name, and his passage *through* that name, suggests a passage *into* the book that bears it. By leaving Heaven he is entering the Book of Milton, turning its first page with his extended right hand. But this will be a "corrosive" book, full of "flaming fire raging around & melting the metals into living fluids" (Blake 2008: 76 [*Marriage* 15]), rather than the puny paper object he disowns. To brave these flames is to accept the unexampled fate, for a revered poet, of becoming a character in someone *else's* book. This is in effect to relinquish the status of author, a sacrifice Milton-the-character describes as going "down to self-annihilation and eternal death" (Blake 2008: 162 [*Milton* 15 {E 14}: 22]). At the level of plot, he is annihilated by his entry into the body of *Milton's* narrative persona, named as "William" or as "Blake," and residing at a cottage in "Felpham's Vale" – Blake's home during his closest association with Hayley, author of the *Life of Milton* (Blake 2008: 203 [*Milton* 49 {E 42}: 7]). In the phenomenological terms of *The Four Zoas*, Milton must renounce the illusion of Urizenic – here explicitly "Satanic" – authority, recognizing himself *as* and *in* Emanation. Only by accepting "Eternal Death" can he reunite with Ololon, the "six-fold" personification of Milton's wives, daughters, and female characters – both his *women* and his *books* (Blake 2008: 162 [*Milton* 15 {E 14}: 30, 14]). With her he will enter the "Void Outside of Existence," recapitulating Blake's journey in *The Marriage* "thro' a stable & thro' a church" to a "mill" and thence to a "void boundless as the nether sky" (Blake 2008: 202, 77 [*Milton* 48 {E 41}: 37; *Marriage* 17]).

Blake and the Angel of *The Marriage* tread the *via negativa* from the chapel (printers' slang for a press-room) to the "infinite" space of Hell's printing-house. Milton's journey will likewise accomplish both a spiritual and a material redemption of the work of writing. When he passes through "MIL TON," we discern the mill that lurks within his name and suggests his secret affinity with the Satan of *Milton,*

"Prince of the Starry Hosts," whose appointed task is "to turn the Mills" of Reason (Blake 2008: 150 [*Milton* 4: 9–10]). Confessing his own Satanism, Milton resolves "to loosen [Satan] from my Hells / To claim the Hells, my Furnaces." By confronting his "Spectre," the Satanic author who "weav[es] the Woof of Locke" (Blake 2008: 162 [*Milton* 15 {E 14}: 31–2; 4: 11]), Milton willingly accepts the fate of *being* his books – their artifact as much as their maker (Blake 2008: 162, 150 [*Milton* 15 {E 14}: 31–2; 4: 11]).

To say this much is to offer a brief plot summary of *Milton*. More specifically, Milton is prompted to the "unexampled deed" of leaving Heaven by "a Bard's prophetic Song," which occupies the following ten plates of the poem (Blake 2008: 149 [*Milton* 2: 21–2]). This song retells the familiar Blakean story of creation and division, but alerts Milton to his culpability for these horrors by introducing his most memorable character into a redaction of *The Four Zoas*. *Milton*'s "mild" Satan, no fiery ideologue but merely a plausible insinuator, wreaks havoc in Eternity by coveting the job allotted to his brother, Palamabron. The Bard's Song details the disastrous consequences. Upon hearing the song to its close, Milton declares his intention to descend from Heaven, lest he be given into "the hands of [his] own Selfhood" (Blake 2008: 162 [*Milton* 15 {E 14}: 22–4]). Blake's point is presumably that Satan's "self-imposition" – his failure even to recognize his own duplicity – is of a piece with the poet Milton's official endorsement of the mild Son of God while he cleaves unconsciously to the "Devil's party." Yet it is not clear what in this Song leads Milton to connect Satan with himself, or to see himself as Satan's author, unless it is his recognition of the words uttered by a new character, "Leutha," who makes her appearance when Satan has been brought before the Assembly of the Immortals for judgment. When, says the Bard, Leutha "beheld Satan's condemnation," she offer[ed] herself a Ransom for Satan, taking on her[self], his Sin." This apparent self-sacrifice is rendered as a *coup de theatre* stunning in its grandiosity:

> I am the Author of this Sin! by my suggestion
> My Parent Power Satan has committed this transgression. . .
>
> O wherefore doth a Dragon-form forth issue from my limbs
> To sieze her new-born son? Ah me! the wretched Leutha!
> This to prevent, entering the doors of Satan's brain night after night
> Like sweet perfumes I stupified the masculine perceptions
> And kept only the feminine awake. . .
>
> I weeping hid in Satan's inmost brain;
> But when the Gnomes refus'd to labour more, with blandishments
> I came forth from the head of Satan! back the Gnomes recoil'd.
> And call'd me Sin, and for a sign portentous held me.
> (Blake 2008: 159–60 [*Milton* 12 {E 11}: 28–30, 34–6;
> 13 {E 12}: 2–6, 36–9])

The Gnomes "call'd me Sin," we may assume, because they recognize Leutha for what she is, a quotation from *Paradise Lost*. Satan's encounter with Sin and Death was clearly among Blake's favorite passages of Milton's epic, and inspired the most memorable painting in a series on *Paradise Lost* that he executed around 1805. Like its Miltonic model, the Bard's story of Leutha parodically anticipates the genuine self-sacrifice that is to come: in *Paradise Lost*, this is the Son's willing acceptance of mortality; here it is Milton's descent into Ulro and reunion with Ololon. Leutha's presumption in naming herself "author" of her Parent Power's sin is signaled by her blithe unawareness of her own citationality. By the lofty standards of *Milton*'s Preface, where Blake avows his disdain for classical *imitatio* as fit only for the "Daughters of Memory," Leutha herself ought to count as a plagiarism – or at least, to reinvoke Freud's neo-Lockean account of "transferences," as a "second edition" of Milton's greatest imaginative flight. Here is the corresponding story in *Paradise Lost*, as told by Sin to the Parent Power she obsequiously calls *her* "Author":

> All on a sudden miserable pain
> Surprised thee, dim thine eyes, and dizzy swum
> In darkness, while thy head flames thick and fast
> Threw forth, till on the left side opening wide,
> Likest to thee in shape and count'nance bright,
> Then shining Heav'nly fair, a goddess armed
> Out of thy head I sprung: amazement seized
> All th' host of Heav'n; back they recoiled afraid
> At first, and called me *Sin*, and for a Sign
> Portentous held me.
>
> (Milton 2003: 45–6
> [2: 864, 749–61])

Hearing his own words in the mouth of a rechristened character, Milton might well be prompted to exclaim, "I am the Author of this Sin!" For Sin's ascription of authorship to Satan, like Eve's prelapsarian deference to her own "author and disposer," Adam, underscores the sexual division of labor at stake in Miltonic originality (Milton 2003: 90 [4: 635]). Emanation, the endless iteration of Sin's birth from Satan, is Miltonic authorship rewritten as Blakean history of the book. The afterlife of Milton's Sin in copyright law is suggested by Eaton Drone's remark, in his 1879 *Treatise on the Law of Property in Intellectual Productions*, that "an intellectual creation without material form may exist in the mind of the author" even before being "embodied in written or spoken language" (qtd. in Russett 2006: 80). Drone, for his part, simply inverts the complaint of Justice Yates, in the 1769 piracy case *Millar v. Taylor*, that the "incorpo-reality" of ideas renders them inaccessible to "identification"; because "their whole existence is in the mind alone," Yates opines, they cannot be appropriated but by "mental possession" – and yet "these are the phantoms which the author would grasp and confine to himself" (qtd. in Russett 2006: 77). The original sin of authorship is this conscientious confusion of "immateriality" with a textual "body," as when Leutha insists that she planted the first seed of Satan's transgression by "entering the doors of [his] brain night after night" (Blake 2008: 159 [*Milton* 13 {E 12}: 4]).

Leutha's absurd boast of being "the Author of this Sin" casts her in the Urizenic mold of would-be originals who have forgotten whence they emanated. As a Daughter of Beulah (memory), she is patently *not* the author of the words she speaks, much less of the "intellectual creation" spawned by Milton/Satan in *Paradise Lost*. By inverting Sin's mistaken reverence for authorship, she merely travesties the agonism invoked and renounced in *Milton*'s title. Blake's path through the poem, both paralleling and intersecting with Milton's descent, gradually evacuates the authority of his neo-Miltonic invocation, where the Daughters of Beulah are exhorted to descend "down the Nerves of my right arm / From out the portals of my brain" (Blake 2008: 148 [*Milton* 2: 1, 5–7]). Can we be sure that these "Muses who inspire the Poet's Song" will indeed become "Daughters of Inspiration" if they enter the poet's body through the doors of Satanic (or Lockean) intellection? Milton's journey through *Milton* contrarily depicts inspiration as a "literally pedestrian" affair (Balfour 2002: 159). First glimpsed "in the Zenith as a falling star, / Descending perpendicular, swift as the swallow or swift," Milton enters "Blake" through his left foot in a bizarre scene of investiture repeated several times to index its deferred action. The moment itself does not register as "mental possession," for Blake "knew not that it was Milton" (Blake 2008: 164, 171 [*Milton* 17 {E 15}: 46–50, 23{E 21}: 8]). From this point Milton ceases to be "Milton," incarnated in a (metrical) foot, the "pulsation of the artery" which is "equal in its period & value to Six Thousand years" and in which "the poet's work is done" (Blake 2008: 183 [*Milton* 30 {E 28}: 63–4; 31 {E 29}: 1–3]).[8] Annihilated, not disembodied: as foot or pulse or period, Milton is redeemed from the pernicious dualism of mind and dead matter represented by the book he left behind in Heaven. Such feet as these tread "the Wine-presses of Luvah," where "the Human grapes. . . / . . . howl & writhe" in the torments of annihilation (Blake 2008: 181 [*Milton* 29 {E 27}: 24, 30–1]). "Call'd War on Earth," this "is the Printing-Press / Of Los: and here he lays his words in order above the mortal brain / As cogs are formd in a wheel to turn the cogs of the adverse wheel" (Blake 2008: 181 [*Milton* 29 {E 27}: 8–10]). In Luvah's unLockean press, "mortal brain[s]" are not passive and do not *receive* imprints; rather, as "adverse[s]" or contraries to the word-cogs that turn them, they are imprinted with the ink of their own blood. The implications of this figure become clear in the apotheosis to which we now hasten.

The scene of Milton's entry is depicted several times in *Milton*, most notably in two full-page illustrations, spaced four plates apart and captioned respectively "William" and "Robert," though the face of neither is visible in the moment of his selfhood's erasure (Figures 16.3 and 16.4). To place these images side by side is to be reminded of other visual contraries in *Milton*, particularly the first page of Book 2, where appear, in mirror writing, the two inscriptions: "How wide the Gulf & Unpassable! between Simplicity and Insipidity" and "Contraries are Positives A Negation is not a Contrary" (Blake 2008: 187 [*Milton* 33 {E 30}]; Figure 16.5). Writing backward is of course one way of embodying the contrariety without which "there can be no progression," but the irony is sharpened by the fact that relief etching, *like* letter-press in this one respect, required that Blake write backward on his copperplates to approximate conventional left-to-right handwriting on paper. Therefore, the assertion that "contraries are positives" must have been written "positively," left to right, to print as a contrary. Here Blake puns visually on the positive (raised) copperplate sketch, contrasted with the "negative" substance on which it is printed; when it is the plate rather than the paper that is legible, which is the masculine original, which the emanation? These mottoes frame the book devoted to the journey of Milton's contrary, Ololon, and in which Milton also learns from "Hillel who is Lucifer" that

> We are not Individuals but States: Combinations of Individuals
> We were Angels of the Divine Presence: & were Druids in Annandale
> Compelld to combine into Form by Satan, the Spectre of Albion,
> Who made himself a God &, destroyed the Human Form Divine. . .

Figure 16.3 Blake, William. Milton, a Poem, pl. 29, 33. "William." These items are reproduced by permission of The Huntington Library, San Marino, California

Distinguish therefore States from Individuals in those States.
States Change: but Individual Identities never change nor cease:
You cannot go to Eternal Death in that which can never Die. . .
Judge then of thy Own Self: thy Eternal Lineaments explore:
What is Eternal & what Changeable? & what Annihilable!
(Blake 2008: 189–90 [*Milton* 35 {E 32}: 10–14, 22–4, 30–1)

In explaining how Milton can cast off "Selfhood" without fear, Hillel is talking like a printmaker: "states" are drafts of a usable image, printed off to assess the engraver's finishing work on the plate. The seeming contradiction between an annihilable "self" and an eternal "identity" may resolve, then, into artisanal decisions about the detailing – for example, the distinctive white-line etching used in *Milton* – by which "form"

Figure 16.4 Blake, William. Milton, a Poem, pl. 29, 33. "Robert." These items are
reproduced by permission of The Huntington Library, San Marino, California

is evoked from "lineaments" that, while themselves durable, never print exactly the
same way twice. By extension, we may consider the four copies of *Milton* as four
"states" of the poem, none of which can be identified as its final version. States, then,
are energetic contraries to the fixed form posited by eighteenth-century copyright
law, and the Platonic author from which that form emanates.

To explore the lineaments of this claim, let us backtrack to plate 15 of Book 1, just
after the lines in which Blake's persona describes his first vision of Milton as a falling star.
Here Blake inserts a full-page image depicting Milton's reconstruction of authorship.
A figure reminiscent of *Urizen*'s title illustration is being strangled, or reshaped, or
embraced by a heroic nude again seen from the rear, this time with hair shorn, or

Figure 16.5 Blake, William. Milton, a Poem, pl. 30 (detail). Contrary epigraphs. This item is reproduced by permission of The Huntington Library, San Marino, California

pulled into a chignon (Figure 16.6). The stone tablets which served as Urizen's wings in the earlier image are toppling to each side, and his robes are merging into the pages of a giant book, which this time appears face-down, with Milton's left foot supporting the open spine. If Milton is murdering his Spectre, he is also liberating that Spectre from his binding – releasing him into another state, as the downward sequence of stone tablet to fibrous page to watery medium implies. Meanwhile, Milton's *right* foot divides the spectral word "Self-Hood" into its two halves, much as his hand cleft the word "Milton" on the title page. The death of the author occasions a musical performance – a Bard's prophetic song, accompanied by female musicians.

This last detail reminds us that Blake's critique of authorship encompasses the gendered division of authorial labor. *Milton* accordingly closes with Ololon's assimilation into "Milton" when they meet in Blake's garden. Milton, still not fully

Figure 16.6 Blake, William. Milton, a Poem, pl. 15. Milton unbinding Urizen. This item is reproduced by permission of The Huntington Library, San Marino, California

redeemed, vows to "purge away with Fire" the "Sexual Garments" that have veiled prophetic poetry (Blake 2008: 202 [*Milton* 48 {E 41}: 25–7]). His "Feminine Portion" "tremble[s]," as well she might, protesting all the while against his implication that "we [are] Contraries O Milton, Thou & I" (Blake 2008: 202 [*Milton* 48 {E 41}: 25–35]). With that,

> the Virgin divided Six-fold & with a shriek
> Dolorous that ran thro all Creation a Double Six-Fold Wonder!
> Away from Ololon she divided & fled into the depths

Figure 16.7 Blake, William. Milton, a Poem, pl. 45. Ololon; or, the unbound book. This item is reproduced by permission of The Huntington Library, San Marino, California

Of Miltons Shadow as a Dove upon the stormy sea
Then as a Moony Ark Ololon descended to Felphams Vale
In clouds of blood, in streams of gore, with dreadful thunderings
Into the Fires of Intellect who rejoic'd in Felphams Vale
Around the Starry Eight: with one accord the Starry Eight became
One Man Jesus the Saviour. wonderful! round his limbs
The Clouds of Ololon folded as a Garment dipped in blood
Written within & without in woven letter & the Writing
Is the Divine Revelation in the Litteral expression:
A Garment of War, I heard it named the Woof of Six Thousand Years
(Blake 2008: 202–3 [*Milton* 49 {E 42}: 2–15])

Despite Milton's hostility to the "rotten rags" of "Albion's covering" – books as abject matter – *Milton*'s apotheosis does not spell the end of materiality. Instead, the Starry Eight combine into a new state, the Book of Revelation, or *Milton*'s Eternal form. Written "within and on the backside" (Revelations 5.1), this book is translucent to the Immortals, like the motto of *Milton*'s Book 2; or it is a "Garment dipped in blood," recalling the incarnational ideal of language conjured by Wordsworth in his "Essays Upon Epitaphs."⁹ But the redeemed *Milton*'s immediacy is indistinguishable from its *hyper*mediacy: the garment, "a traditional figure" for language; the clouds which "mediate and. . . even obscure"; the name only "heard" by the speaker (Balfour 2002: 170). The contraries of immediacy and hypermediacy finally meet here because their "negation," blank paper, has been destroyed by a book "written within & without." *Milton*'s apotheosis conjures nothing so much as the interwoven pixels of an electronic screen: how do we know matter from spirit in the "woven letters" of a *web* page?

The Litteral expression is envisioned in *Milton*'s final plate, a trinity centered on a cruciform figure, clearly feminine if not certainly female, whose body is coextensive with her outstretched "garments" (Figure 16.7). "Where is Milton?" asks David Erdman of this image, and answers: "in Blake. Where is Blake? One Man with Los – in Jesus" (Erdman 1974: 266). More precisely, *Milton*'s "Finis" evokes the "Void Outside of Existence, which if enterd into / Becomes a Womb" (Blake 2008: 202 [*Milton* 48–9 {E 41–3}: 38, 1]).¹⁰ The womb delineated in Ololon's bloody garments is *Milton* as "vortex": the book which, according to Northrop Frye, demands to be read "from its own point of view" (Frye 1962: 350) or, as W.J.T. Mitchell glosses this insight, the book as "a transmitter and receiver," a "system which contains numerous subworlds within itself" (Mitchell 1978: 71–2). As a utopian evocation of hypermedia, Mitchell's phrasing could hardly be improved. Our passage into these subworlds requires us to read *Milton* unbound. Erdman avers that to glimpse the "state of spousal *preparation* at the end of the poem," we "must hold the volume open to its first and last plates to see Milton striding forward in self-annihilating wrath. . . and Ololon in pity removing her garment and stepping forward to the embrace of 'Resurrection and Judgment'" (Erdman 1974: 267). What he recommends is physically impossible unless the text he imagines is not a "volume" at all: the book into which Milton disappears on the title page must itself have been annihilated, leaving us to recombine its individual pages into an infinitude of states. Would such a book be the triumph of the godlike author, or would it be the end of authorship as the eighteenth century knew it? Blake's own postscript on *Milton* leaves this an open question: "I may praise it, since I dare not pretend to be any other than the Secretary; the Authors are in Eternity" (Blake to Thomas Butts, 6 July 1803, qtd. Damon 1988: 276).

Notes

1 Quotations from works of poetry are cited by page numbers keyed to the quoted editions, with Book or Plate and line numbers noted in brackets. Where there is disagreement on the order of Blake's plates, Erdman's numeration is referenced in the form {E –}.
2 While Jones's concern with authorship runs broadly parallel with mine (Jones 2010), this essay more specifically concerns the relation between ideology and medium.
3 On Milton and authorship, see also Fallon (2007, *passim*).
4 For a detailed practical exegesis of this passage, see Viscomi (2003).

5 The most important works on this subject include Essick (1980, 1989), Viscomi (1993), and Eaves (1982, 1992).
6 On the temporality of the artistic signature, see Baudrillard (1981).
7 On *The Marriage* and Lockean epistemology, see Glausser (1998: 160–2). Blake claimed to have read and annotated Locke's *Essay* "when very young," but his copy has never been found.
8 On "pulsation" and "period," see Goldsmith (2013: 231–6).
9 See Balfour (2002: 170–1) on Blake's dense allusions to Revelations and Ezekiel in this passage.
10 I thank Sarah Vap and Diana Arterian for alerting me to the pervasive visual motif of the womb in Blake's late work.

Works cited

Balfour, I. (2002) *The Rhetoric of Romantic Prophecy*, Stanford: Stanford University Press.

Baudrillard, J. (1981) *For a Critique of the Political Economy of the Sign*, trans. Charles Levin, St. Louis: Telos Press.

Blake, W. (1988) *The Complete Poetry and Prose of William Blake*, ed. D.V. Erdman, New York: Random House.

Blake, W. (2008) *Blake's Poetry and Designs*, eds M.L. Johnson and J.E. Grant, New York: Norton.

Damon, S.F. (1988) *A Blake Dictionary: The Ideas and Symbols of William Blake*, Hanover, NH: University Press of New England.

Eaves, M. (1982) *William Blake's Theory of Art*, Princeton: Princeton University Press.

Eaves, M. (1992) *The Counter-Arts Conspiracy: Art and Industry in the Age of Blake*, Ithaca, NY: Cornell University Press.

Erdman, D.V. (1974) *The Illuminated Blake*, Garden City, NY: Doubleday.

Essick, R.N. (1980) *William Blake, Printmaker*, Princeton: Princeton University Press.

Essick, R.N. (1986) "How Blake's Body Means," in N. Hilton and T.A. Vogler (eds) *Unnam'd Forms: Blake and Textuality*, Berkeley: University of California Press.

Essick, R.N. (1989) *William Blake and the Language of Adam*, Oxford: Clarendon Press.

Fallon, S.M. (2007) *Milton's Peculiar Grace: Self-Representation and Authority*, Ithaca, NY: Cornell University Press.

Foucault, M. (1977) "What is An Author?" in D.F. Bouchard and S. Simon (trans.) *Language, Counter-Memory, Practice*, Ithaca, NY: Cornell University Press.

Freud, S. (1997) *Dora: An Analysis of a Case of Hysteria*, ed. Philip Rieff, New York: Simon and Schuster.

Frye, N. (1962) *Fearful Symmetry: A Study of William Blake*, Boston: Beacon Press.

Glausser, W. (1998) *Locke and Blake: A Conversation Across the Eighteenth Century*, Gainesville: University Press of Florida.

Goldsmith, S. (2013) *Blake's Agitation: Criticism and the Emotions*, Baltimore: The Johns Hopkins University Press.

Hayley, W. (1796) *The Life of Milton, in three parts*, 2nd edn, London: T. Cadell.

Jones, J.H. (2010) *Blake on Language, Power, and Self-Annihilation*, New York: Palgrave Macmillan.

Kittler, F.A. (1999) *Gramophone, Film, Typewriter*, trans. G. Winthrop-Young and M. Wutz, Stanford: Stanford University Press.

Lewalski, B. (2006) "Milton's Idea of Authorship," in M. Lieb and A. C. Labriola (eds) *Milton in the Age of Fish: Essays on Authorship, Text, and Terrorism*, Pittsburgh: Duquesne University Press.

Locke, J. (2008) *An Essay Concerning Human Understanding*, ed. P. Phemister, Oxford: Oxford University Press.

Marx, K. (1979) "The Fetishism of Commodities and the Secret Thereof," in R.C. Tucker (ed.) *The Marx-Engels Reader*, 2nd edn, New York: Norton.

Milton, J. (1974) "Areopagitica," in K.M. Burton (ed) *Milton's Prose Writings*, New York: Dutton.

Milton, J. (2003) *Paradise Lost*, ed. J. Leonard, London: Penguin.

Mitchell, W.J.T. (1978) *Blake's Composite Art: A Study of the Illuminated Poetry*, Princeton: Princeton University Press.

Rose, M. (1993) *Authors and Owners: The Invention of Copyright*, Cambridge, MA: Harvard University Press.

Russett, M. (2006) *Fictions and Fakes: Forging Romantic Authenticity, 1760–1845*, Cambridge: Cambridge University Press.

Viscomi, J. (1993) *Blake and the Idea of the Book*, Princeton: Princeton University Press.

Viscomi, J. (2003) "Illuminated Printing," in M. Eaves (ed.) *The Cambridge Companion to William Blake*, Cambridge: Cambridge University Press.

Wordsworth, W. (1979) *The Prelude 1799, 1805, 1850*, eds. J. Wordsworth, M.H. Abrams, and S. Gill, New York: Norton.

Wordsworth, W. (1988) "Essays Upon Epitaphs," in J.O. Hayden (ed.) *Selected Prose*, London: Penguin.

Part 5

Gender, sexuality, and the body

Introduction

In recent decades, critics have increasingly taken an interest in issues of gender and sexuality – especially following in the wake of groundbreaking work in feminist and queer criticism and theory published from the 1970s through the 1990s. Sandra Gilbert and Susan Gubar demonstrated the importance of a women's literary tradition responding to the stifling confines of "patriarchal" literature (Gilbert and Gubar 1979); Gayle Rubin alerted critics to how gender inequality was the product of a "social system" constructed within a specific culture and historical moment (Rubin 1975: 205); and Judith Butler showed how the constructedness of gender roles might actually destabilize normative gender functions and hierarchies (Butler 1990).

Such important contributions within and beyond literary criticism were actually late developments of a very strong tradition in the analysis of gender and sex that is still being researched and brought to light. In the fifteenth century, Christine de Pizan aimed to correct the common male belief in women's natural vices (de Pizan 1997: 116–55); Ann Finch criticized the male-centered judgments of woman writers in the late seventeenth century (Finch 1903); and Anne Ingram, Viscountess Irwin, fought back against the witty barbs of Alexander Pope in the early eighteenth century when she celebrated women's ambitions and education (Lonsdale 1989: 150–1). Considerations of gender, sexual relationships, and literature reached a fever pitch during the Romantic age, moreover. The explosion of readership among women, the equally striking increase in the number of female authors across all genres of literary production, the heightened interest in the education of young women, and the increasingly public role that women took in schools, churches, and other institutions helped to alter the sense that public life and public voices were dominated by men. Long before Oscar Wilde, moreover, authors from Coleridge to Byron hinted subtly and not-so-subtly at the reality of desires that did not fit into conventional heterosexual couplings. The upsetting of some traditional roles, though, only provided further motivation for determined reaction – for policing the boundaries around those roles, and for regulating the conduct of men and women within and beyond the home. We should not in any sense get the impression that Romanticism was a period of unproblematic erotic freedom. Mary Wollstonecraft, intent on challenging the prejudices of her day, nevertheless considered motherhood and the "rational" care of "infants, parents, and husbands" (Wollstonecraft 1994: 264) to be among the most important duties that women had to their families and to the nation; Jeremy Bentham, certainly enlightened in his belief that homosexuality should be decriminalized because of its contribution to human happiness, still worried about the supposedly unhealthy practice of masturbation (Bentham 1978).

Scholars in Romanticism, aligning themselves with historicism, feminism, and queer theory, have taken very different approaches to addressing the complex ways in which Romantic writers negotiated with social norms. Susan Wolfson's "Gendering the Soul," forming the basis for chapter 9 of her book *Borderlines: The Shiftings of Gender in British Romanticism,* builds upon work by critics such as Stuart Curran and Anne K. Mellor that had identified differences between male and female literary traditions in the Romantic age (Curran 1998; Mellor 1993). But she sees Romantic authors positioning their gender identity in problematic ways. The artist's "soul" is a primary concern in Romantic poetry, in her view, and that soul is shaped according to gendered hierarchies. She claims that many male poets viewed women's souls as their (inferior) complements, but women poets – who wish to claim their status as women but also claim poetic genius for themselves – confront a contradiction between claiming authority and inscribing themselves within a gender hierarchy.

The constructedness of gender roles, and the opportunities or constraints that these constructions pose for Romantic writers, has also been studied by a range of other critics, including Julie Carlson and Sonia Hofkosh, although there are significant differences in these perspectives as well (Carlson 1994; Hofkosh 1998). Toward the end of Wolfson's selection, she shows how Felicia Hemans attempts to move well beyond conventional roles and hierarchies; this may provide a connecting link between her account and the selection on Cowper from Andrew Elfenbein's *Romantic Genius: The Prehistory of a Homosexual Role.* His contribution is an instance of work by many critics – Susan Matthews and Richard Sha among them – who, influenced by theoretical work in queer studies, are interested in the way that heterosexualized or hierarchized gender roles may be subverted (rather than reinforced) by a self-conscious, and even playful, approach to traditional categories of difference (Matthews 2011; Sha 2008). Elfenbein shows not only how gender hierarchies are questioned but also how the very concept of gender itself is destabilized by William Cowper's representation of his own bodily identity in his poem *The Task.* The speaker in the poem, in Elfenbein's view, demonstrates a mysterious ambiguity in gender identity or sexuality: this ambiguity is connected to the sublimity of Romantic "genius" but it also provoked the ostracism and hostility imposed by public homophobia.

Wolfson's feminist approach and Elfenbein's queer approach to Romanticism address questions about whether gender and sexual identity are stable or unstable, expressed or contained. Clara Tuite's approach differs from both of these in that "female subjectivity," neither wholly expressed or contained, is the product of internalized "discipline." The theoretical influence of Michel Foucault's work (and also the work of other literary critics such as Deidre Lynch [1998] and Clifford Siskin [1998]) is particularly evident in this selection in that the articulation of female subjectivity is considered to be the effect of shared discursive and institutional structures. Rather than opposing sexual and sentimental "excess" with male or heterosexual dominance, Austen – Tuite argues – normalizes subjectivity through socialization and the acquisition of taste and "cultural capital."

There are some ways in which Jacqueline M. Labbe's new contribution to this volume continues the argument that Tuite makes about the emphasis on proper gender roles in Austen, and she sees this logic operating in Mary Shelley's novels as well. At the same time, however, Labbe sees this as a late phase in Romanticism, and not necessarily representative of the period in general. Whereas historian Drohr Wahrman argues that the end of the eighteenth century witnesses a stabilization and naturalization of roles (Wahrman 2004), Labbe examines novels by Charlotte Smith, Mary Robinson, and Maria Edgeworth in order to tell a different story in which characters "work outside a set of gendered expectations." With women who display conventional male stoicism, or men who display a conventional feminine sensibility, the novels she examines show gender to be not only destabilized but often "unfixed."

Works cited

Bentham, Jeremy. (1978) "Offenses Against Oneself," *Journal of Homosexuality* 3(1978): 389–405.

Butler, Judith. (1990) *Gender Trouble: Feminism and the Subversion of Identity*, New York: Routledge.

Carlson, Julie. (1994) *In the Theater of Romanticism: Coleridge, Nationalism, Women*, Cambridge: Cambridge University Press.

Curran, Stuart. (1988) "The I Altered," in Anne K. Mellor (ed.), *Romanticism and Feminism*, Bloomington: Indiana University Press.

Finch, Anne, Countess of Winchelsea. (1903) "The Introduction," in *Poems*, Chicago: University of Chicago Press.

Gilbert, Sandra M., and Susan Gubar. (1979) *The Madwoman in the Attic*, New Haven: Yale University Press.

Hofkosh, Sonia. (1998) *Sexual Politics and the Romantic Author*, Cambridge: Cambridge University Press.

Lonsdale, Roger. (1989) *Eighteenth Century Women Poets: An Oxford Anthology*, Oxford: Oxford University Press.

Lynch, Deidre Shauna. (1998) *The Economy of Character: Novels, Market Culture and the Business of Inner Meaning*, Chicago: University of Chicago Press.

Matthews, Susan. (2011) *Blake, Sexuality, and Bourgeois Politeness*, Cambridge: Cambridge University Press.

Mellor, Anne K. (1993) *Romanticism and Gender*, New York: Routledge.

de Pizan, Christine. (1997) *The Selected Writings*, ed. Renate Blumenfeld-Kosinski, New York: Norton.

Rubin, Gayle. (1975) "The Traffic in Women: Notes on the 'Political Economy of Sex,'" in Rayna Reiter (ed.), *Toward an Anthropology of Women*, New York: Monthly Review Press.

Sha, Richard. (2008) *Perverse Romanticism: Aesthetics and Sexuality in Britain, 1750–1832*, Baltimore: Johns Hopkins University Press.

Siskin, Clifford. (1998) *The Work of Writing*, Baltimore: Johns Hopkins University Press.

Wahrman, Drohr. (2004) *The Making of the Modern Self: Identity and Culture in Eighteenth-Century England*, New Haven: Yale University Press.

Wolfson, Susan. (2006) *Borderlines: The Shiftings of Gender in British Romanticism*, Stanford: Stanford University Press.

Wollstonecraft, Mary. (1994) *A Vindication of the Rights of Woman and A Vindication of the Rights of Men*, ed. Janet Todd, Oxford: Oxford University Press.

Further reading

Clarke, Eric O. (2000) *Virtuous Vice: Homoeroticism and the Public Sphere*, Durham: Duke University Press.

Gross, Jonathan David. (2000) *Byron: The Erotic Liberal*, London: Rowman and Littlefield.

Haggerty, George. (2006) *Queer Gothic*, Urbana: University of Illinois Press.

Hobson, Christopher Z. (2000) *Blake and Homosexuality*, Houndmills: Palgrave Macmillan.

Jacobus, Mary. (1989) *Reading, Writing, and Sexual Difference: Essays on The Prelude*, Oxford: Oxford University Press.

Johnson, Claudia. (1995) *Equivocal Beings: Politics, Gender, and Sentimentality in the 1790s: Wollstonecraft, Radcliffe, Burney, Austen*, Chicago: University of Chicago Press.

Keane, Angela. (2000) *Women Writers and the English Nation in the 1790s*, Cambridge: Cambridge University Press.

Kipp, Julie (2003) *Romanticism, Maternity, and the Body Politic*, Cambridge: Cambridge University Press.

Labbe, Jacqueline. (2003) *Charlotte Smith: Romanticism, Poetry and the Culture of Gender*, Manchester: Manchester University Press.

Lokke, Kari E. (2004) *Tracing Women's Romanticism: Gender, History, Transcendence*, London: Routledge.

Ross, Marlon. (1989) *The Contours of Masculine Desire: Romanticism and the Rise of Women's Poetry*, Oxford: Oxford University Press.

Sedgwick, Eve. (1993) *Tendencies*, Durham, NC: Duke University Press.

Swann, Karen. "Harassing the Muse," in Anne K. Mellor (ed.), *Romanticism and Feminism*, Bloomington: Indiana University Press.

17 Gendering the soul

Susan Wolfson

I Sex in souls and the gender of the soul

So repeatedly does *A Vindication of the Rights of Woman* refer to a notion of soul that is not sex-differentiated that it seems to authorize its case on this ground alone. "Surely," insists Wollstonecraft, "she has not an immortal soul who can loiter life away merely employed to adorn her person, that she may amuse the languid hours" of any man whose "serious business of life is over."[1] She herself expresses gratitude "to that Being who impressed . . . on my soul" the falsity of giving "a sex to morals" that would authorize different standards of behavior for men and women (36). For "if the dignity of the female soul be as disputable as that of animals," she proposes to any potential antagonist, then women "are surely of all creatures the most miserable" (45; cf. 63). In light of Coleridge's esteem in modern feminist criticism for speculating that "a great mind must be androgynous," it may seem an easy transition from Wollstonecraft's rationalist brief for the moral equality of men's and women's souls to the Romantic-Coleridgean liberalism of a double-sexed genius.[2] Yet Coleridge's textual site reveals that he was thinking only of male minds with feminine qualities; in other texts, we find him rather less sanguine about the invasion of male political and aesthetic territory by actual women. And [. . .] unlike Wollstonecraft, he eagerly insisted on the sex of souls.

Sexing of soul for Romantic men was critical in the poetics of inspiration, for the master trope was the analogy of creation with a female muse, and the implicit ideological alliance was with a long-standing "masculinist" tradition of appropriating and subordinating the feminine.[3] Yet the tradition in Romanticism is hardly stable, and this essay will show the consequences [. . .] by investigating the poetics of gender in some (perhaps unfamiliar) soul stories by two women, Maria Jane Jewsbury and Felicia Hemans. The ideological value of telling such a story is evident enough in Wollstonecraft's concern to argue for the rights of woman through reference to, or what amounts to a polemical construction of, the female soul. For all its transcendental reference, the idea of "soul" had substational sociohistorical resonance. Quaint as this term may seem today, it saturated the cultural languages of the Romantic age and was vitally theoretical for its writers. As such, it offers us a historically situated discourse through which to negotiate our present concerns with gender and Romanticism. Moreover, as Wollstonecraft's conversation with tradition demonstrates, its discourse involves the composite text of men's and women's writing; thus, it is the field that most forcefully reveals how the terms of sexual difference matter, both in individual perception and in reflections of cultural values. As we shall see, gendering the soul is vexed on both sides of the divide. Romantic men write stories that contend with uneasy sensations of their souls being or becoming feminine, the difference of gender often naming a decentered power and so bearing important questions about male poetic authority. And Romantic women, as eager as Wollstonecraft was to claim a dignity of soul that the central literary and cultural tradition has reserved for men, do not find easy ways to address this tradition or to imagine enabling alternatives.

I want to return briefly to Coleridge's remarks on the question because some contradictions in his theorizing of sex in souls will alert us to important dilemmas, both in canonical Romantic poetry about the soul and, not coincidentally, in the (not always coherent) critiques emerging in women's texts. Coleridge's idea of sex in souls is involved in a comprehensive theory about what drives creative desire. Noting that "in her homely way the Body tries to interpret all the movements of the Soul" (for example, in the sign of tears or a quickened pulse), he wonders about the strongest of the body's desires, its "yearning to compleat itself by Union." This is what moves him to ask, "Is there not a Sex in Souls?" and to elaborate:

> We have all eyes, Cheeks, Lips – but in a lovely woman are not the eyes womanly – yea, every form, every motion, of her whole frame *womanly?* Were there not an Identity in the Substance, man & woman might *join*, but they could never *unify* – were there not throughout, in body & in soul, a corresponding and adapted Difference, there might be addition, but there could be no combination. One *and one* = 2; but one cannot be multiplied into one. 1 x 1 = 1 – At best, it would be an idle echo, the same thing needlessly repeated –[4]

His conviction is such that he is willing to project the impression of the sexed soul beyond the contours of anatomy into an aura or affect, what may command description as *womanly,* even in features not only common to both sexes but susceptible to androgynous impression – eyes, cheeks, lips.[5] This reading of non-sex-specific features as reflections of a sexed soul is radical in implication. If one tradition of metaphysics opposes soul to body and designates a categorical difference, Coleridge's desire-based theory treats soul as an agent of body, part of the same continuum of identity.

Union of difference is a Coleridgean signature, most famously inscribed in the theory of "poetic Imagination" elaborated in chapter 14 of *Biographia*: this is a "power" that works a "balance or reconciliation of opposite or discordant qualities" (2:16–17). For this generative interaction of difference, the most appropriate metaphor may be the naturally given (and guaranteed) ground of sexual difference.[6] But something else is at work in the text that Coleridge summons to gloss this process. Slightly misquoted from Davies, it gives a story of the soul that is gendered rather than sexed:

> she turns
> Bodies to spirit by sublimation strange,
> As fire converts to fire the things it burns,
> As we our food into our nature change.
>
> From their gross matter she abstracts their forms,
> And draws a kind of quintessence from things;

Which to her proper nature she transforms
To bear them light, on her celestial wings.

This does she, when from individual states
She doth abstract the universal kinds . . . [7]

Measured by the analogy of "Imagination," this is a feminine soul with a difference. The process described in these lines is not a uniting of equal poles, a wedding of "Feminineness" and "Masculineness" at points where they "are one in spirit, a unity in duplicity" (so Coleridge sketches one abstract of sex and souls in his notebooks [3:3308]). Davies's female soul has no such equivalence; it is a subordinate agent of a general metaphysics that, following his subtitle, creates *the Soule of Man*. The she-soul, and implicitly its service to the Coleridgean scheme of "Imagination," is that of a secondary medium.

Coleridge's conscription of this hierarchical gendering is in conflict with his idea of sex in souls. If he proposes sexual difference to explain the creative desire of equal opposites, he tends to deploy the language of gender, as in the lines he quotes from Davies, in tandem with unequal distributions of function and privilege. Even when he is theorizing sex in souls, this contradiction may appear.[. . .] What Coleridge's texts show us is that sex in souls and gendering the soul are different, often contradictory, matters. This ambivalence – experienced both psychologically and as cultural logic – informs some key but hardly stable or coherent soul-stories in Romantic writing. In male-authored texts, gendering the soul as feminine is endorsed by classical paradigms and the linguistic precedent of the feminine *anima* of Latin. Yet the enactments are tensed in ways that have not received adequate attention in some of the more programmatic arguments about Romanticism and gender.[8] For women writers, moreover, the sexed soul is inherently unstable. Their texts both disclose the contradictions of gendered definitions and reflect the ambivalence of their own desires. Must women regard their intellectual souls as Wollstonecraft is tempted to do, as "*male* spirits, confined by mistake in female frames," and so wrestle with the burden of this contradiction and alienation? Or does alienation offer a position from which to query the very idea of a determining sexual identity in the soul?

[. . .]

[A section of this essay in its original form details the gendering of the soul in Wordsworth, Shelley and Keats.]

II Romantic women and the politics of gender and soul

[. . .] So what happens when the writer [formulating a poetics of the soul] is a woman? One answer, which amounts to a sustained display of ideological tensions and contradictions, appears in Maria Jane Jewsbury's "History of an Enthusiast," an account of a young woman's thirst for artistic fame. Rejecting the culturally saturated advice that "the only celebrity that can increase a woman's happiness is that which results from the esteem excited by her domestic virtues," Julia Osborne is convinced that "Fame . . . would make amends for being a woman – I should not pass away and perish" (25–6). How this involves her soul is spelled out by Jewsbury's epigraph for chapter 5, a verse credited to "Professor Wilson":[9]

As far as human soul may be let loose
From impositions of necessity, –
Forgetting oft, in self-willed fancy's flight,
All human ties that would enchain her dreams
Down to a homelier bliss; and loving more
The dim aerial shadow of this life,
Even than the substance of the life itself.

(43)

In this image of necessity, not only is this errant, "self-willed" soul gendered feminine, but the gendering is reinforced by the fact that its necessary enchainment is to the sentimentalized place that culture has assigned to women, home.

Jewsbury's tale of restless female enthusiasm shifts the professor's traditional wisdom into a new perspective. The chapter headed by the lines above concludes with Julia yearning to be kindled with "boundless, glorious energy" and dedicating herself to artistic "Fame" as the only possible embodiment of such energy (47). Eventually, she writes a satiric poem that frankly names home in all of its guises, "the present, new, and near," as "fetters to our souls" (149). To counter the cultural authority of the professor with another male poet, Jewsbury summons Percy Bysshe Shelley, though a Shelley converted to the uses of female enthusiasm. The texts that Jewsbury interpolates into her female history, that is, are not the ones that gender the soul but ones whose schemes are potentially available to or revisable for female interest.

One such text infuses the voice of Julia's early enthusiasm. When Cecil Percy, a friend from adolescence whom she is convinced she loves, tells her that the books she cherishes "will be productive of more loss than gain," she retorts with Asia's song at the close of act 2 of *Prometheus Unbound* (2.5.72–81, 88–90):

My soul is an enchanted boat,
    Which, like a sleeping swan, doth float
Upon the silver waves of *their* sweet singing.
    And each doth like an angel sit
    Beside the helm conducting it,
Whilst all the winds with melody are ringing.
    It seems to float, ever, for ever,
    Upon that many-winding river,
Between mountains, woods, abysses,
A paradise of wildernesses!
. . . .
And we sail on, away, afar,
Without a cloud, without a star,
But by the instinct of sweet music driven.

(*History*, 59)

Julia's emphatic *their* shifts the reference of Asia's *thy*, a voice in the air, to the voices of her books, the feeders of her intellectual soul. Her rewording not only challenges the prescriptions for conduct that Cecil would impose upon her, it also revises Shelley's script for her own ends, namely, a story of female desire that is not subordinate to the urgencies of men in crisis.

We can see the force of this revision by recalling that in Shelley's scene, Asia's soul is tuned to a masculine theomachia; her celebratory song follows her interview of Demogorgon, in the previous scene, about Prometheus's fate.[10] [. . .] For [. . .] Shelley in *Prometheus Unbound*, the female soul is circumscribed by masculine culture and agenda.

[. . .]

Jewsbury's history tacitly reconceives Asia's interview as a kind of interval for the female soul in this larger action and makes her song into a hymn of intellectual energy for Julia. It is not long after that Julia's diary records her "enchantment" at the thought of a "communion of spirit" with "a superior being . . . not so much stronger than myself, as wiser, better, gentler, graver; the idea that I may some time or other find such a being . . . seems to give my soul wings" (64). In relocating Asia's song in the history of a female enthusiast, Jewsbury revises what is culturally conservative in Shelley's visionary revolution: its distribution of aspiration and expectation along lines of male privilege. She similarly revises the Shelleyan language that she uses to describe Julia's enjoyment of the energies of her mind: "emparadised in dreams of intellectual beauty" (103). This evocation of "Hymn to Intellectual Beauty" is as important for its contextual revision as for its Shelleyan echo, for it makes the implicit argument (whatever the latent and later ironies for Julia of "emparadised in dreams") that there is a common intellectual soul in men and women and that in women's dreams this soul is drawn to the paradise of intellectual satisfaction denied to them by their material existence in this world.

As a term of intersexual provenance, "intellectual beauty" is particularly resonant, for it accrues value not only from Shelley but also from a female-authored work that he and Jewsbury knew well, Wollstonecraft's *Vindication*. Complaining that the "prevailing opinion of sexual character" does not allow "the soul of woman" to perfect itself "by the exercise of its own reason" (53), Wollstonecraft puts forth the notion of an "intellectual beauty" capable of inspiring in men something "more sublime" than the "sensual homage" paid to physical beauty (47). Beginning her treatise by urging opportunities for women to exercise "ambition and those nobler passions that open and enlarge the soul" (10), Wollstonecraft assumes a sexual equality, a claim for the "soul of woman" (53) that she sets corrosively against that "Mahometan strain" that would "deprive [women] of souls, and insinuate that we were beings only designed . . . to gratify the senses of man when he can no longer soar on the wing of contemplation." If women are allowed by Christian Providence "to have souls," she contends, then they should be "allowed to have sufficient strength of mind to acquire what really deserves the name of virtue" (19). Emphasizing her debt to this text, Jewsbury concludes her *History* with Julia speculating in similar terms about "soul of no sex – versatile powers" (144) and worrying her friends about the likely consequence of touring the Continent alone: "how excessively improper! – well, the reviewers will certainly leave off their compliments about her womanliness" and start regarding her as a "second Mary Wolstonecroft" (*sic*, 143). For inspiration in this adventure, Julia returns to the first feeders of her soul, her books, quoting on the last page "Ode to the West Wind" and, in effect, once again pointedly claiming Shelley's voice as her own: "O lift me as a wave, a leaf, a cloud; / I fall upon the thorns of life – I bleed; / A heavy weight of hours has chained and bowed / One too like thee, tameless, and swift, and proud" (160).

Although this exuberance occupies the last page of Jewsbury's *History*, the ideological restraints with which it contends are apparent enough in the internal economy of Julia's narrative. Before committing herself, not totally joyously, to her final adventure, Julia's life as a London celebrity so pales after five years that she feels the pull of conservative cultural prescriptions: "Ah, what is genius to woman, but a splendid misfortune! What is fame to woman, but a dazzling degradation" (112). This melancholy exacts a price on her soul: she laments the utter absence of any "child-like abandon of the soul to fresh and vigorous impulses" and is gripped by a "sense of present loneliness [that] paralyzes all the finer functions of the soul" (114–15). As if to confirm these sensations in social fate, Jewsbury plots her history to have Julia's enthusiasms alienate the man she secretly loves, Cecil Percy, losing him to a proper English wife. Even so, Jewsbury's ambivalence about this cultural wisdom troubles these conservative correctives in two ways. For one, and despite the regret she gives to Julia, she writes the character of Cecil to suggest that he is not much of a loss, never quite escaping the contour of a dull, conservative twit. A "cold and simple spirit . . . passionless," Julia herself describes him, even as she is excited by a visit from him in the midst of her jaded celebrity (117); he exposes himself as such in his pallid poetics of the soul, exhorting Julia to leave her life of "vanities" and enter "that solemn chamber of the soul wherein conscience sits enthroned as judge" (122). For another, Jewsbury closes Julia's *History* not with her enthusiast exposed and doomed as a figure of emptiness nor recuperated to domesticity but revitalized by a decision to leave England and travel on the Continent. If the female enthusiast's precise future is left untold, what is most evident in the close of her history is that England in the 1830s seems to have no place for such souls.[11]

As a woman of intellect and artistic fame, Hemans figures into Jewsbury's *History* as one of its models – or rather, two. She appears first as the transgressive, unfeminine girl reader of Shakespeare in the apple tree (11–22) and then as the voice of sentimental poetry (58, 86, 116).[12] This double figuration is a shrewd reading of Hemans, for like Jewsbury, her writing, despite its overt commitment to orthodox sentiments, takes on the question of sex in souls, especially to question the cultural norms for women. Hemans's sensitivity to constrictions and contradictions in these norms is compelling in light of her general adoration in Regency and high Victorian cultures as the soul of femininity. The terms are baldly stated in Francis Jeffrey's 1829 review: the natural concerns of women writers epitomized by Hemans, he says, are "tenderness and loftiness of feeling, and an ethereal purity of sentiment, which could only emanate from the soul of a woman."[13]

[. . .]

Much in Hemans's poetry justifies these impressions, and their conservative infusions are strengthened by the religious pieties of Hemans's last poems, which, in the burden of her fatal ill health, seek the traditional consolation of a dualism that anticipates the soul's release:

> Come to the land of peace!
> Come where the tempest hath no longer sway,
> The shadow passes from the soul away,
> The sounds of weeping cease!
> ("The Angels' Call")[14]

In this spirit, these poems also produce more than a few meditations on the vanity of fame as nurture to the female soul. "Women and Fame," a poem that the Gall and

Inglis edition prints on the same page as "The Angels' Call," concludes in tones that resonate with Julia Osborne's most depressed meditations:

> Fame! Fame! thou canst not be the stay
>   Unto the drooping reed,
> The cool fresh fountain, in the day
>   Of the soul's most feverish need.
> Where must the lone one turn or flee? –
> Not unto thee, oh! not to thee!

Yet even this caution emerges from a rhetoric that constantly has to face the attractions against which it guards: "Thou hast a voice, whose thrilling tone / Can bid each life-pulse beat." In earlier poems, moreover, when Hemans was alive to her prospects in this world, the soul is a much less stable and much more temptable site of desire.

Like Jewsbury, Hemans wonders about the soul of female desire, whose fevers are not allayed – and are often aggravated – by domestic stays. The tensions of her ambivalence unsettle even a poem with so unpromising a title as "The Domestic Affections," the summary piece in *The Domestic Affections and Other Poems* (1812).[15] If its opening verses seem a hornbook of Jeffrey's "Mrs. Hemans," the poem as a whole compels attention for the way its very effort to formulate such terms hints at a terribly corrupt economy for a woman's soul. It begins with standard polarities – material and spiritual life, worldly and domestic scenes – all opposed in ways for which the language of gender supplies universal, transcendent sense. Home is the realm of the female soul; under its sway, the domestic affections restore world-weary men's souls and, beyond this service, remind us all of the soul's true home:

> Her angel voice his fainting soul can raise
> To brighter visions of celestial days!
> And speak of realms, where virtue's wing shall soar
> On eagle plume – to wonder and adore!
> And friends, divided here, shall meet at last,
> Unite their kindred souls – and smile on all the past.
>
>   (*DA*, 164–5)

Yet these unities, kindred and divine, contend with some subversive lines in Hemans's poem that limn the restrictions and deeper poverties of its schemes of gender.

One point of stress, though its ideological commitments cannot allow the poem to treat it as such, is a contradiction between the terms of this spiritual function for women, and those that convey the extradomestic expansions of male genius. Hemans means to anchor genius and its attendant "Fame" in the nurture of the domestic affections, even gendering "Fame" and "Freedom" as feminine, as if to make them co-nurturers. But her larger and more emphatic division of masculine genius and feminine nurture reveals conflicting values. Consider the emblem of the aspiring eagle:

> On Freedom's wing, that ev'ry wild explores,
> Thro' realms of space, th' aspiring eagle soars!
> Darts o'er the clouds, exulting to admire,

Meridian glory – on her throne of fire!
Bird of the sun! his keen, unwearied gaze,
Hails the full noon, and triumphs in the blaze!
But soon, descending from his height sublime,
Day's burning fount, and light's empyreal clime;
Once more he speeds to joys more calmly blest,
'Midst the dear inmates of his lonely nest!
Thus Genius, mounting on his bright career,
Thro' the wide regions of the mental sphere . . .

(*DA*, 157)

Sustained by a feminine muse of Freedom and nurtured by the mother birds of the domestic nest, masculine Genius enjoys a freedom and energy in these lines for which the descent to the "lonely nest" of home, however calmly blest its joys, seems a death-in-life.

Indeed, the word *lonely* here has a deconstructive pressure. For in domestic bliss devoted to female healing of male souls, the result for women, Hemans finds herself saying (first in subordinate clauses and then in sustained meditations) is too frequently a depletion of her spiritual reserves. The praise of the woman's "angel voice" for its power to raise a man's "fainting soul" "to brighter visions of celestial days" (quoted above) is tellingly preceded by a notation that even as she "whisp[ers] peace" to these world-battered men, she must "conceal, with duteous art, / Her own deep sorrows in her inmost heart." A parenthesis a few lines later inscribes the necessary suppression of her own soul's pangs: "(Still fondly struggling to suppress *her own*)" (*DA*, 164). The italics are also Hemans's, a second graphic sign that presses hard against the parentheses that would contain their stress. By the end of the poem, her imagination is concentrating on the unequal economy that sustains gendered souls. In a significant shift, Hemans projects soul's ease for women – when gentle spirits "sooth her soul, / With soft enchantments and divine control" – into the world beyond death. Her "parting soul" becomes an "exulting spirit" as it "leaves her bonds of clay" (*DA*, 170–1).

This anticipation evokes traditional Platonisms that affect male poetics of the soul, too: this is the fundamental allegiance of *Alastor*, we recall, and it is an evolving one in Wordsworth's Christian orthodoxies. But where the schemes of their poems tend to reject the inconstancies of the feminine and nature together (reading one in terms of the other), the strains of "The Domestic Affections" keep both terms in view, exposing a culturally specific release for women from the "naturalized" domestic sphere that is supposed to ground their sense of soul. It is revealing that the poem ends with a celebration of the "Elysian clime" of heaven that is for women what the blessings of home are for men: an escape from the ravages of the world – but more specifically for the female soul, a delivery from the disappointments of the domestic sphere that cultural orthodoxy tells her is her heaven on earth:

Yes! in the noon of that Elysian clime,
Beyond the sphere of anguish, death, or time;
Where the mind's bright eye, with renovated fire,
Shall beam on glories – never to expire;
Oh! there, th'illumin'd soul may fondly trust,

More pure, more perfect, rising from the dust;
Those mild affections, whose consoling light
Sheds the soft moon-beam on terrestrial night;
Sublim'd, ennobled, shall for ever glow,
Exalting rapture – not assuaging woe!

(*DA*, 171–2)

The affections of the soul on which women's social and cultural value is based now
at least have a spiritual, if not a material, correlative and scope. It is only here that
"th'illumin'd soul" enjoys a rapture paralleling that of masculine Genius in the mortal world.

[. . .]

If a Woman's soul is moved [. . .], say, into civic heroism, Hemans's cultural
orthodoxy tends to contain the potential transgression within an expanded field for
the affections and to "correct" the expansion with tragic depletions. In "The Indian
City," Maimuna, a Muslim widow on a pilgrimage to Mecca, is moved to passion when
her son is slain by Brahmin children for having inadvertently wandered on to holy
grounds.[16] Hemans evokes her grief in the image of a stilled, seemingly resigned
soul – "her soul sat veil'd in its agony" (89) – and then turns this soul into a double
soul whose division marks a site of transformation:

And what deep change, what work of power,
Was wrought other secret soul that hour?
How rose the lonely one? – She rose
Like a prophetess from dark repose!
And proudly flung from her face the veil,
And shook the hair from her forehead pale,
And 'midst her wondering handmaids stood,
With the sudden glance of a dauntless mood.
Ay, lifting up to the midnight sky,
A brow in its regal passion high,
With a close and rigid grasp she press'd
The blood-stain'd robe to her heaving breast,
And said – "Not yet – not yet I weep,
Not yet my spirit shall sink or sleep,
Not till yon city, in ruins rent
Be piled for its victim's monument.

(90)

As compelling as this transformation is Hemans's insistence on representing it in the
language of the soul, using this term to chart an emergence from veiled stillness and
passivity to an unveiled regal passion and a spirit committed to violent action.

At the same time, Hemans's inhibition in the face of this kind of emergence impels
her to stabilize this eruption of energy by reinscribing the gender of this secret soul
of power. Although Maimuna's passion inspires a war that wreaks the havoc she had
pledged, her female soul cannot survive its lost affections, "the yearning left by a
broken tie." Even as the city that destroyed this tie is itself destroyed, her fate joins
that of the vanquished city rather than the victorious armies; and the barometer

of this fate is her soul, now imaged as the prisoner of a walled city on the verge of collapse:

> Sickening she turn'd from her sad renown,
> As a king in death might reject his crown;
> Slowly the strength of the walls gave way –
> *She* wither'd faster, from day to day.
> All the proud sounds of that banner'd plain,
> To stay the flight of her soul were vain;
> Like an eagle caged, it had striven, and worn
> The frail dust ne'er for such conflicts born,
> Till the bars were rent, and the hour was come
> For its fearful rushing thro' darkness home.
>
> (93–4)

In one stroke, this passage rewrites the gender and the fate of the aspiring eagle of Genius and Freedom in "The Domestic Affections." Here, the eagle is the caged soul, longing for release from the agonies of the worldly triumph it had kindled; its most deeply desired soaring is a flight from life to death. Escalating the conflict that strains "The Domestic Affections," "The Indian City" posits not the domestic nest but female life itself as the prison from which the female soul seeks release. The only energy Hemans leaves to the woman warrior's soul is its brief arousal to a final expression of maternal love. Mourning her son's death on her own deathbed issues "a fitful gust o'er her soul again" that urges her to beg that they be laid to rest together (95).

Jewsbury's more heroic, "Roman" story of the female soul in grief is "Arria," but it is revealing that her cultural syntax, even so fortified, yields a similarly fatal figure.[17] Arria, "a Roman Matron," is imprisoned with her husband Pætus, whom she means to help die with Roman honor "by his own right hand." But already "[i]n soul and strength subdued" by his fetters, he merely expires, and it is left to "the wife and woman high" symbolically "to teach *him* how to die." This is the essential demonstration, Jewsbury implies, of "woman's soul" in its mode of heroic love.

   [. . .]

Whether in heroic sacrifice or in the meeker idioms of domestic affection, "woman's soul," in Jewsbury's imagining, bears a transhistoric and transcultural identity, [as] fundamental stasis [and] endurance. [. . .] Burke, in a famous text that is the tacit backdrop for Jewsbury's emblem, hoped for no less heroism from the imprisoned "queen of France," whom he depicts as a "Roman matron" with both the dignity and the opportunities for suicidal honor borne by the compliment.[18]

For Hemans, the self-sacrificing passions of "a woman's soul" persist even when domestic affections are forsaken for life as an artist, and it is a sign of the conflict she herself felt that she repeatedly subverts her cultural identity as a poet with representations of women's art as a debased or impotent achievement. In "The Domestic Affections," woman's art is delimited to the "duteous art" of self-effacement in the nurture of others, and Hemans's uneasiness about her work as artist yields more than one poem in which the soul of the woman artist accomplishes little more than discoveries of emptiness. The eponym of "The Sicilian Captive" (*Records*, 172–9) is merely a singer, not an artist in any primary character; the trajectory is still one of self-cancelation, and her soul is the register. At first, as she sings of her lost home for her captors, her soul is invigorated by its theme:

> Faint was the strain, in its first wild flow,
> Troubled its murmur, and sad, and low;
> But it swell'd into deeper power ere long,
> As the breeze that swept over her soul grew strong.
>
> (174)

Enchanting to her audience, the ultimate force of her art is its fatal effect on her. If singing evokes memories that inspire her soul – let "[t]hy soul flow o'er my lips again," she cries to Sicily (176) – such inspiration always contends with a soulful mourning that cannot be redeemed by a home so far away: "my sunny land! . . . Doth not thy shadow wrap my soul?" (175). The soul of the artist steadily declines and weakens in these shadows; when, recalling the "sweet sounds" of Sicily, the captive exclaims, "the soul to hear them faints in dreams of heaven away!" (177), the denouement is all but guaranteed. At the close of the song we are told (in the poem's last lines), "She had pour'd out her soul with her song's last tone; / The lyre was broken, the minstrel gone!" (179).

In the monologue of the sculptor, "Properzia Rossi" (which appears earlier in *Records* [45–54]), artistic creation emerges as a less than abundant recompense for the "deep affections that o'erflow / [Rossi's] aching soul" (51). Hemans's linear poetics write the story. The overflow of sense from line to line conveys this affectional force, while the grammatical richness of the word *o'erflow* itself utterly absorbs the artist's soul in a comprehensive grammar: the affections seem both to overflow from the aching soul and to flow overwhelmingly into it. An unsigned epigraph heralds this economy, its tenor explicitly diminishing any power of the soul devoted to genius and fame against the measure of all that has been lost:

> ——————————Tell me no more, no more
> Of my soul's lofty gifts! Are they not vain
> To quench its haunting thirst for happiness?
> Have I not lov'd, and striven, and fail'd to bind
> One true heart unto me, whereon my own
> Might find a resting-place, a home for all
> Its burden of affections? I depart,
> Unknown, tho' Fame goes with me . . .
>
> (47)

The contradictory strains of "The Domestic Affections" are here submitted to adamant evaluation by cultural norms. While the opposition between "happiness" and "lofty gifts" is a stock Romantic trope for the pains of genius, even of consciousness (everyone "understands" Manfred), Hemans unsettles the cliché by giving it a female voice. Rossi is exiled from happiness not just by genius but by the cultural contradiction of gender and genius.[19] In this contradiction, she, like the Sicilian Captive, can imagine no art for her soul purchased without her annihilation, and her monologue begins thus:

One dream of passion and of beauty more!
And in its bright fulfilment let me pour
My soul away!

(47)

Again, Hemans's enjambment nicely tropes the flow of the soul-effacing desire.

For Romantic men, [. . .] sex in souls typically involves schemes in which the feminine is evoked to nurture and complete a masculine soul – or if not, to suffer slander as the gender of every bafflement to such desire. Hemans and Jewsbury find themselves at cross purposes with these arrangements, but in their attempts to engage soulful discourse for their own poetics of desire, the dissonance of speaking as a woman entails a price. For Jewsbury's Julia, this is cultural alienation: Her love unrequited and her fame unsatisfying, yet still eager for adventure, she has to leave England for the sake of her soul. For Hemans, alienation is of the affections: Her poems not only repeatedly present women's souls as sites of frustrated affection, both lacking and yearning for the creative complement of a male soul, but their female epipsyches such as Rossi tend to reflect this desire in what Coleridge's letter describes as an "idle echo," a sterile "addition" rather than creative "combination."

Even so, the fuller narrative in which Hemans frames Rossi's dream of art subtly interrogates the negative cultural economy of woman's affection and the artist's soul. This has to do, in no small part, with the fact that Rossi's dream is not for art per se, but for art as the remedy and record (so a title-page note informs us [45]) of a fatally "unrequited attachment": "A painting by Ducis, represents her showing her last work, a basso-relievo of Ariadne, to a Roman Knight, the object of her affection, who regards it with indifference." This knightly shrug, while pathetic in the immediate narrative of Rossi's desire, is also, in the rhetoric of the poem's address to its reader, a stark sign of what a vain sacrifice art for affection would have been. Not only would abandoning her art not win happiness for her soul, but it would deny the only resource through which her soul gains, however fleetingly, a sense of self-possession and creative power. Although the poem devolves into a lament of the "aching soul," its middle section marks a brief interval of this access. Hemans softly but tellingly shifts Rossi's language into this register as Rossi describes her art taking shape (49):

It comes, – the power
Within me born, flows back; my fruitless dower
That could not win me love. Yet once again
I greet it proudly, with its rushing train
Of glorious images: – they throng – they press –
A sudden joy lights up my loneliness, –
I shall not perish all!

Despite the brief bitterness about the "fruitless dower" of this lovelorn power, Rossi's language moves energetically into the lexicon of genius enjoyed by the aspiring eagle of "The Domestic Affections." And as she continues to express this enthusiasm, some of her terms (the work of the hand, the definition of the line, the infusion of self into art) seem to include not just the sculptor but also the poetry in which she is rendered:

The bright work grows
Beneath my hand, unfolding, as a rose,
Leaf after leaf, to beauty; line by line,
I fix my thought, heart, soul, to burn, to shine,
Thro' the pale marble's veins. It grows – and now
I give my own life's history to thy brow,
Forsaken Ariadne! thou shalt wear
My form, my lineaments; but oh! more fair,
Touch'd into lovelier being by the glow
Which in me dwells, as by the summer–light
All things are glorified.

(49)

While Rossi's statue of forsaken Ariadne is clearly her mournful epipsyche and Rossi herself is such for Hemans, the unity of "thought, heart, soul" that Hemans briefly imagines for her work poses a tenuous suggestion of a different psychic economy: what women may create if the affections can inform and enjoy the bright work of art.

One of Hemans's last poems, written in the frustration of sickness, elevates and explicitly identifies with this imagined moment in Rossi's work. The "soul" of "Design and Performance" is given entirely to artistic inspiration and labor and, significantly, it is not gendered. The frustration is not of any domestic affection but of mortality itself:

They float before my soul, the fair designs
Which I would body forth to life and power,
Like clouds, that with their wavering hues and lines
Portray majestic buildings: – dome and tower,
Bright spire, that through the rainbow and the shower
Points to th'unchanging stars; and high arcade,
Far-sweeping to some glorious altar, made
For holiest rites. Meanwhile the waning hour
Melts from me, and by fervent dreams o'er-wrought,
I sink. O friend! O linked with each high thought!
Aid me, of those rich visions to detain
All I may grasp; until thou see'st fulfilled,
While time and strength allow, my hope to build
For lowly hearts devout, but *one* enduring fane![20]

If, as Coleridge argues, there is a sex in souls, Hemans's design of the soul richly reconceives the ideologies of gender that grant only men's souls the privilege of desire and a claim to power. An important element of this design, in fact, is her incorporation of male-authored poetry. There are strains of Shelley's "Ode to Liberty," not only its language of the soul ("my soul spurned the chains of its dismay, / And in the rapid plumes of song / Clothed itself, sublime and strong" [5–7]) but also its visionary architecture: "a city such as vision / Builds from the purple crags and silver towers / Of battlemented cloud" (61–3). And at her sonnet's turn, there is a more resigned repetition of the crisis of vision at the end of *Epipsychidion* ("The winged words on which my soul would pierce / Into the height of love's rare Universe, / Are chains of lead around its flight of fire. – / I pant, I sink . . . " [588–91]).[21] There are also anterior recollections of Wordsworthian imaginings: "Earth has not any thing to shew more fair: / Dull would he be of soul who could pass by / A sight so touching . . . towers, domes, theatres, and temples" ("Composed upon Westminster Bridge"); and a subdued version of the heart-swelling vision given to his despondent Solitary ("Clouds of all tincture, rocks and sapphire sky . . . composing thus . . . that marvellous array / Of temple, palace, citadel, and huge / Fantastic pomp of structure without name" [*The Excursion*, 2.854–9]).[22] These strains seem to some readers to mark Hemans as unoriginal, even "highly derivative,"[23] but we can grant their audibility a conscious design – something like a muted but no less resonant version of Jewsbury's appropriation of Shelley for Julia's voice. In this perspective, the prior texts participate in an intertextuality in which poetic performance is always engaged with something external. If Romantic men gender the soul as feminine in order to explain and contain a decentered soul of inspiration, Hemans's intertextual inspirations amount to a similar acknowledgment of externality but without a troping in gendered terms. Other texts, like a soul outside, offer sources of inspirations that – to recall the terms by which Coleridge justifies a sex in souls – solicit a generative union with difference.

For a woman to write of sex in souls is to take on the question of what it means to write of the soul as a *woman*, to confront a literary tradition in which the female soul is contained by paradigms that mean to serve male privileges and interests. Some women are so impressed by this tradition that they internalize it as personal and cultural truth. To Wollstonecraft's biological heir, for example, who felt herself "nothing" in consequence of paternal disapproval and her husband's death, her mother's progressive speculations are unconvincing. "You speak of women's intellect," Mary Wollstonecraft Shelley writes to her friend Maria Gisborne,

> I know that however clever I may be there is in me a vaccillation [*sic*], a weakness, a want of "eagle winged["] resolution that appertains to my intellect as well as my moral character – & renders me what I am – one of broken purposes – falling thoughts & a heart all wounds. – My Mother had more energy of character – still she had not sufficient fire of imagination – In short my belief is – whether there be sex in souls or not – that the sex of our material mechanism makes us quite different creatures – better though weaker but wanting in the higher grades of intellect. –
>
> (11 June 1835)[24]

Yet if she recoils from earlier Romanticism to retreat to the poorer safeties and comforts of orthodox hierarchies and the determinism of material mechanism (or what today we call essentialism), Jewsbury and Hemans put pressure on the terms that shape such understandings. Their writing shows how the very dislocation of female interest can also prove a productive ground for Romantic women: from a point of alienation, they may find themselves able to wonder about releasing spiritual poetics from a politics of gender, even enabled to imagine forms of desire neither dependent on nor limited by a sex in souls.

Notes

1 [Mary Wollstonecraft, *A Vindication of the Rights of Woman*, ed. Carol H. Poston, 2nd ed. (New York: Norton, 1988), 29; cited hereafter parenthetically.]

2 [Coleridge's speculation about androgyny is in *Table Talk*, 1 September and 17 March 1832, in *Table Talk* (recorded by Henry Nelson Coleridge and John Taylor Coleridge), ed. Carl Woodring, 2 vols (Princeton, N.J.: Princeton University Press, 1990), 2:190, 2:158.]

3 See, for example, the first chapter of Margaret Homans's *Women Writers and Poetic Identity* (Princeton, N.J.: Princeton University Press, 1980); Irene Taylor and Gina Luria, "Gender and Genre: Women in British Romantic Literature," in *What Manner of Woman: Essays on English and American Life and Literature*, ed. Marlene Springer (New York: New York University Press, 1977), esp. 113–15; Alan Richardson, "Romanticism and the Colonization of the Feminine," in *Romanticism and Feminism*, ed. Anne K. Mellor (Bloomington: Indiana University Press, 1988), 13–25; the first chapter of Marlon Ross's *The Contours of Masculine Desire: Romanticism and the Rise of Women's Poetry* (New York and Oxford: Oxford University Press, 1989); and Anne K. Mellor, *Romanticism and Gender* (New York and London: Routledge, 1993).

4 12 March 1811; *Collected Letters of Samuel Taylor Coleridge*, ed. Earl Leslie Griggs, 6 vols (Oxford: Clarendon Press, 1956–71), 3:305; cited hereafter parenthetically.

5 It is Coleridge, moreover, who helped develop a vocabulary for this effect, proposing, for example, that there is "something feminine – not *effeminate*, mind – discoverable in the countenances of all men of genius" (*Table Talk*, 17 March 1832 [2:158]). [. . .]

6 Coleridge, *Biographia Literaria, or Biographical Sketches of My Literary Life and Opinions* (1817), ed. James Engell and W. Jackson Bate, 2 vols (Princeton, N.J.: Princeton University Press, 1983), 2:16–17; cited hereafter parenthetically.

7 Bate and Engell identify these lines from Sir John Davies's *Nosce Teipsum: Of the Soule of Man and the Immortalitie Thereof* (1599), 4, sts. 11–13, and provide the correct text.

8 Thus, Homans argues that only women's poetry is pressured by a sensation of the "apparent otherness of [the] mind's powers," the "alien centers of imaginative power," a dislocation in which "the sources of poetic power are not to be felt within the self" (*Women Writers*, 104).

9 This is John Wilson, after 1820 professor of philosophy at Edinburgh University and as "Christopher North," a regular contributor to *Blackwood's Edinburgh Magazine*. Quotations of Jewsbury's "History" follow "The History of an Enthusiast" in *The Three Histories. The History of an Enthusiast. The History of a Nonchalant. The History of a Realist.* (1830; Boston: Perkins & Marvin, 1831).

10 As Marlon Ross remarks, she has no function in the poem separate from Prometheus's fate: "Asia acts in his behalf since he is bound. . . . She serves as an extension of him" (*Contours*, 144).

11 This severing (and implicit concession to the cultural contraction) of domestic romance from female spiritual quest at the conclusion of Jewsbury's *History* is one of the ideologically fraught narrative patterns of nineteenth-century women's fiction, according to Rachel Blau DuPlessis (*Writing beyond the Ending: Narrative Strategies of Twentieth-Century Women Writers* [Bloomington: Indiana University Press, 1985], 1–19). The removal of Julia to Europe predicts the "critical dissent from the dominant narrative" that DuPlessis sees as an emergent strategy of twentieth-century women's writing (5).

12 Jewsbury would have known the anecdote of the apple tree from Hemans herself. It became a staple in memoirs. See Henry F. Chorley, *Memorials of Mrs. Hemans, with Illustrations of Her Literary Character from Her Private Correspondence*, 2 vols (London: Saunders and Otley, 1836), 1:17–18 (cited hereafter as "Chorley"); and Harriett Mary [Browne] Hughes (later Owen), *Memoir of the Life and Writings of Felicia Hemans: By Her Sister; with an Essay on Her Genius: By Mrs. Sigourney* (New York: C. S. Francis/Boston: J. H. Francis, 1845), 34; this memoir was first published as vol. 1 of *The Works of Mrs. Hemans*, 6 vols (London: Thomas Cadell; Edinburgh: William Blackwood & Sons, 1839).

13 *Edinburgh Review* 50 (October 1829): 37.

14 [*The Poetical Works of Mrs. F[elicia]. Hemans* (London and Edinburgh: Gall and Inglis, 1876)], 574.

15 Felicia Dorothea Browne, *The Domestic Affections and Other Poems* (London: T. Cadell and W. Davies, 1812); cited by *DA* and page number.

16 Hemans, *Records of Women: With Other Poems* (Edinburgh: William Blackwood, London: T. Cadell, 1828), 83–96; references are to page numbers.

17 Jewsbury, *Phantasmagoria; Or, Sketches of Life and Literature*, 2 vols (London: Hurst, Robinson/ Edinburgh: Archibald Constable, 1825), 1:122–4.

18 Burke, *Reflections on the Revolution in France, 1790;* in *Two Classics of the French Revolution* (New York: Anchor/Doubleday, 1973/1989), 88–9.

19 For an interesting survey of Romantic alignments of "gender and genius," see Christine Battersby, *Gender and Genius: Towards a Feminist Aesthetics* (Bloomington: Indiana University Press, 1989), 13, 35–8, 46–7, also chaps. 8 and 10.

20 My text follows [*The Poetical Works of Mrs. Hemans* (London: Frederick Warne, n.d. [c. 1889]),] (656–7).

21 [*Shelley's Poetry and Prose*, ed. Donald H. Reiman and Sharon B. Powers (New York: Norton, 1977), cited by line number.]

22 [*William Wordsworth: The Poems*, ed. John O. Hayden, 2 vols (Middlesex U.K.: Penguin, 1977).]

23 This is Angela Leighton's evaluation (*Victorian Women Poets: Writing against the Heart* [New York and London: Harvester/Wheatsheaf, 1922]), though our views are more congruent in her sense that Hemans's "verse achieves another kind of originality in the persistent and ostentatious gendering" of these recognizable voices (21).

24 *The Letters of Mary Wollstonecraft Shelley*, ed. Betty T. Bennett, 3 vols (Baltimore: Johns Hopkins University Press, 1980–88), 2:246. Thanks to Theresa Kelley and Stephen Behrendt for calling this letter to my attention.

18 The domestication of genius

Cowper and the rise of the suburban man

Andrew Elfenbein

[. . .]

[William Cowper] demonstrated what I will call the domestication of genius, a translation of the rebellious originality and autonomy of genius into the coziness of the domestic sphere. This domestication proved fundamental to the developing role of the suburban man, for which Cowper provided a model to generations of readers. Yet the role of the suburban man was highly vexed because it was never clear how original and autonomous a man might be in his own house without stepping over the line, as Cowper had, into unacceptable behavior. In particular, given Cowper's bachelorhood, the suburban man was especially vulnerable to fears that his perceived specialness might be interpreted as the wrong kind of specialness, sexual deviance. Life in the suburbs had as a precondition the ability to distinguish sharply between the respectable character of the suburban man and the deviant character of the homosexual.

Not coincidentally, the nineteenth century witnessed a marked increase both in suburban populations and in the systematic surveillance and persecution of men who had sex with other men. As Louis Crompton notes, "During the period 1805–1835, when the annual number of executions for all crimes dropped from about seventy to thirty, sodomy was the only crime for which the number of hangings remained more or less constant."[1] By 1885, while sodomy was no longer a capital crime, the Labouchère amendment to the Criminal Law Amendment Act increased the courts' ability to punish sex between men by making acts of "gross indecency" illegal when they occurred not only in public, as had been the case previously, but also in private.[2]

[. . .]

William Cowper and the suburban man

To develop the history of the suburban homophobia and the domestication of genius, I turn to [. . .] Cowper and to his most famous poem, *The Task* (1785). Cowper may seem a strange choice for a discussion of nineteenth-century masculinity since he is an eighteenth-century writer whose poetry has traditionally been read in the context of eighteenth-century literary developments. I base my choice on the work of Leonore Davidoff and Catherine Hall in *Family Fortunes*. According to them, Cowper and Hannah More were the most influential writers on members of the nineteenth-century middle class. While More concentrated on female behavior, Cowper, especially as he presented himself in his most famous poem, *The Task*, became the most widely loved role model for middle-class men. By citing a variety of archival sources, Davidoff and Hall create an impressive portrait of the range of Cowper's appeal. He was accessible as an ideological paragon to virtually all who could read or who could have others read to them.[3]

I am struck by the sheer unlikeliness of Cowper as a model suburban man. He had no job, wife, or children; suffered paralyzing bouts of religious mania; lived as a virtual recluse in rural England; and was supposedly a hermaphrodite. Yet legions of readers looked to him and his work to help them understand what a man's happy home should be. My purpose [. . .] is not to offer a literary analysis of *The Task*. Rather, I want to draw on Raymond Williams's characterization of the dynamic interrelations of a cultural system in terms of dominant, residual, and emergent elements to examine aspects of Cowper's work most important for middle-class masculinity.[4] Since the study of Cowper generally has fallen to scholars of the eighteenth century, they have treated his work in terms of its dominant elements, such as its Evangelicalism or sensibility, or its residual elements, such as its indebtedness to Augustan satire.[5] Yet, except for Davidoff and Hall, scholars of the nineteenth century have overlooked the emergent elements of Cowper's work at the cost of ignoring a formative writer for nineteenth-century manhood.

Nineteenth-century reactions to Cowper repeatedly emphasized that he provided the perfect image of domestic life. In 1800, *The Monthly Magazine* noted that *The Task*'s most memorable passages were those "in which the charms of rural life, and the endearments of domestic retirement are described." The poem's reputation was "established by universal consent." For Francis Jeffrey in 1803, Cowper was popular because of "the minute and correct painting of those home-scenes and private feelings with which every one is internally familiar."[6]

[. . .]

Cowper's home in *The Task* was not in the suburbs but in the rural village of Olney. Yet, as Robert Fishman demonstrates, Cowper's domestic ideal inspired the Evangelical founders of Clapham, the "prototypical suburban community" and model for later British suburbs. They organized a living environment that balanced closeness to the city with what Cowper had represented as the desirable solitude of the country.[7] [. . .]

In discussing Cowper, Davidoff and Hall overlook an important and unexpected aspect of his writing: he was a bachelor. Work on domesticity has so emphasized the role of middle-class women that it comes as a surprise to note that neither wife nor children appear in *The Task*. Although some analyses of bachelors assume that they threatened gendered norms of domesticity, *The Task*'s representation of a bachelor's life, surprisingly, became *the* model for the English home.[8] *The Task* presents no father reading to or playing with children, no husband counseling his wife, and no family enjoying meals together, and yet it came to define domestic life. The poem does occasionally mention Cowper's female companions. Mary Unwin appears as his friend in Books I and IV, but Cowper never names her, never gives her voice, and barely sketches her. Lady Austen inspires the poem by suggesting that Cowper write about the sofa, but she, too, vanishes from the poem after his opening invocation. He treats his female friends in such a cursory way that he increases rather than decreases the impression of his solitude.

In representing himself as a solitary, Cowper was not being radical: he drew on the long Horatian tradition recounting a single man's pleasure in rural retirement.[9] Nevertheless, it might seem that other eighteenth-century works would have provided more suitable models for nineteenth-century middle-class men, especially books emphasizing the importance of husbands and fathers to the domestic unit. Yet the overwhelming evidence of Cowper's popularity suggests that the roles of husband and father were not the only ones available to men for their home lives. While Davidoff and Hall suggest that "the real reward for the private man would, of course, be in the world to come," *The Task* showed instead that men might find internal, spiritual rewards in homes that belonged to this world.[10] Cowper's self-portrayal was an emergent representation of the suburban home's supposed ability to nurture a man's sense of privileged distinction from the outside world.

In accordance with the Horatian tradition, Cowper locates his home on a moral map that associates the city with luxuriousness and effeminacy and the country with health and truth. London has some virtues, but for the most part is a sink of iniquity, the seat of "ambition, av'rice, penury incurr'd / By endless riot; vanity, the lust / Of pleasure and variety" (3.811–13).[11] In the country, "virtue thrives as in her proper soil" (1.600). Its purest essence appears in Cowper's home, where "domestic happiness" is the "only bliss / Of Paradise that has survived the fall!" (3.41–2). It contrasts in every way with London's corruptions and violence.

Cowper describes how he learned to value the blessings of home in what became the poem's most famous passage. Rather than being a joyful account of domestic pleasure, his story is one of personal trauma and partial recovery:

> I was a stricken deer, that left the herd
> Long since; with many an arrow deep infixt
> My panting side was charged when I withdrew
> To seek a tranquil death in distant shades.
> There was I found by one who had himself
> Been hurt by th'archers. In his side he bore,
> And in his hands and feet the cruel scars.
> With gentle force soliciting the darts
> He drew them forth, and heal'd and bade me live.
> Since then, with few associates, in remote
> And silent woods I wander, far from those
> My former partners of the peopled scene,
> With few associates, and not wishing more.
> Here much I ruminate, as much I may,
> With other views of men and manners now
> Than once, and others of a life to come.
>
> (3.108–22)

Cowper draws on the familiar story of Christian conversion, a shortened version of the exodus narrative that dominates English spiritual biography.[12] Yet if he conforms to the conventional role of the Christian man, what is most striking about the passage is how subdued his promised land is. The joy and comfort in Christ and incorporation into the church that the redeemed man should conventionally find in his salvation are eerily absent. Christ is at the center of the episode, yet as the passage describes it, he functions less as the center of Cowper's spiritual life than as a liminal figure carrying Cowper into a new understanding of his isolation. Though Cowper proudly reconceives of himself as a man whose solitude authorizes his "other views of men and manners" and "others of a life to come," an undercurrent of mysterious loneliness persists. His haunting repetition of the phrase "with few associates" (a Miltonic effect put to utterly un-Miltonic uses) emphasizes "few" so as to make the associates figures of absence, not presence.

Part of Cowper's mystery derives from his use of the stricken deer emblem itself, which implies that he could narrate a more detailed history than the one he shares with the reader. In masking the specifics of his situation, he seems to be holding back details that might explain the full truth of the situation. Why did he have to leave "the herd"? What were the "arrows" that wounded him? Why has he not returned to society? Why, if he has been saved, does he still refer to himself as if he suffered from depression? If Cowper is a domestic everyman, then the history of the domestic everyman is markedly secretive. Not everything about the passage is mysterious: the deer is obviously Cowper and the "one" who rescues him is obviously Christ. Yet Cowper does not reveal how or why he was wounded and what the historical reference for the allegorical darts might have been.

The Task intensifies the secrecy of the stricken deer passage by suggesting that Cowper has not fully recovered from his experience. For example, he praises writing poetry for its ability to "steal away the thought / With such address, from themes of sad import" (2.299–300) without explaining what the themes are. In the middle of a description of England's climate, he notes that its gloom "disposes much / All hearts to sadness, and none more than mine" (5.463–4) without explaining why. When faced with "fierce temptation," he claims that "to combat may be glorious, and success / Perhaps may crown us, but to fly is safe" (3.684, 687–8). These lines set up the expectation that he will describe the true Christian's ability to resist temptation, but he startlingly concludes by recommending flight. For unknown reasons, naked fear blanks out more exalted theological considerations. While such scattered references to Cowper's distress appear as diversions from topics at hand, they cumulatively heighten the sense that he is withholding key aspects of his personality.

Throughout *The Task*, Cowper lets his audience know enough about himself to suggest that he is harboring secrets. At a general level, Cowper's secrecy effect anticipates a "deep" selfhood never fully available to language that would become a nineteenth-century commonplace, typifying a major strand in the romantic representation of subjectivity from Wordsworth and Byron to Freud. Michel Foucault's work has provided the most influential account of the construction of this subjectivity. In *The Order of Things*, he traces a shift from eighteenth-century "order" to nineteenth-century "history," which involved the construction of "a depth in which what matters is no longer identities . . . but great hidden forces developed on the basis of their primitive and inaccessible nucleus, origin, causality, and history." In *The History of Sexuality*, Foucault argues that the discourse of confession gave such depth to subjectivity itself. [. . .][13]

While I agree with Foucault about the rise of a "deep" model of subjectivity, I question the assertion that the truth of this subjectivity arose solely through a discourse about sex. [. . .] If psychic knowledge was in the first place sexual knowledge, it was also true that knowledge of sexuality did not necessarily exhaust knowledge of subjectivity.

I note the possible distinction between knowledge and sexuality to avoid the too hasty reduction of Cowper's secrecy effect in *The Task* to sexual secrecy. Instead, it is useful to explore its significance quite apart from its potential sexual associations, although I will turn to these later in the essay. In itself, the association between confession, secrecy, and inner depths was not new to the late eighteenth century. Yet it had new effects in Cowper's work because his poem was so overtly autobiographical. While many eighteenth-century poets wrote about themselves and their feelings, they often did so within the conventional lyric decorum of a generalized "I." Cowper, unlike such writers as [Thomas] Gray or [William] Collins, exchanges the lyric "I" for an autobiographical narrator who describes his daily activities, his opinions of the world, and even, as in the stricken deer passage, his past. Personal self-revelation led Cowper to be loved for what were perceived to be his personal qualities even more than for his verse.

As Cowper presents himself in the stricken deer passage, what he has gained from his mysteriously traumatic conversion experience is a sense of being different. Without ever invoking the cult of genius, he has achieved the domestication of genius that I described earlier, in which his finest accomplishment is the creation of himself as a unique and special individual. Cowper is privileged because he can believe that he is better than the larger community from which he has set himself apart. In the Horatian tradition, the mere fact of being in the country gave the solitary man a sense of privileged superiority. But since Cowper eventually finds that even the country is imperfect because "the town has tinged the country" (4.553), he internalizes the privileged vision of the rural solitary.[14] For him, his distinction arises from the internal changes he underwent after the experience described in the stricken deer passage, not from his location in Olney. His secrecy effect is a continual reminder of the mysterious process whereby a man who was once a member of a herd has developed in solitude "other views of men and manners now / Than once, and others of a life to come.' However painful his experience was and still is, it allows him to claim a sense of distinction because he knows that his perspective is different from and superior to that held by merely ordinary men.

Cowper's domestication of genius reveals itself not in how he creates art but in how his sense of his own specialness permeates all his activities, down to the most mundane. For example, when he reads the newspaper, he feels how fully his "other views" separate him from the public world that it represents:

'Tis pleasant through the loop-holes of retreat
To peep at such a world . . .
Thus sitting and surveying thus at ease
The globe and its concerns, I seem advanced
To some secure and more than mortal height,
That lib'rates and exempts me from them all.
It turns submitted to my view, turns round
With all its generations; I behold
The tumult and am still. The sound of war
Has lost its terrors 'ere it reaches me,
Grieves but alarms me not. I mourn the pride
And av'rice that make man a wolf to man,
Hear the faint echo of those brazen throats
By which he speaks the language of his heart,
And sigh, but never tremble at the sound.
(4.88–9, 94–106)

The newspaper, by translating the public world into a network of textual signs, allows him to imagine it as something from which he is cut off but which provides him with material for reflection. Cowper resembles the reader that Jon Klancher describes as being fashioned by early nineteenth-century periodicals:

> The individual reader must be defined as a textual presence in a discourse where he constitutes himself as a "reader" by becoming aware of his distinction from all social, collective formations that he learns to "read" as a social text.[15]

Not only is Cowper separate from the social text of the newspaper; he is also superior to it, "advanc'd / To some secure and more than mortal height." He revalues his social marginality as a position that earns him privileged interpretive power. Because he is not involved in the morass of politics, he can see the true littleness of contemporary leaders in ways that commonplace men who lack his depth of mysterious experience cannot.

Cowper in *The Task* is a specifically masculine model. When he reads the newspaper, the action belongs to him and not to his female companions. He is "fast bound in chains of silence, which the fair, / Though eloquent themselves, yet fear to break" (4.53–4). Reading the paper becomes a peculiarly masculine form of self-discipline and concentration, a chaining in silence, that women are forbidden to interrupt.
[. . .][16]

Although when Cowper wrote in the 1780s, modern suburbs had not yet appeared in England, for his later audiences the suburban home provided the ideal space in which to develop and refine the domestication of genius, since it valued privacy above all else: "The most satisfactory suburb was that which gave [the Englishman] the maximum of privacy and the minimum of outside distraction."[17] Whereas previously men had sought distinction by proving themselves in the public world, Cowper suggested that a man gained his true distinction only at home. Since few men had the financial resources to take Cowper literally and abandon public life altogether, the suburbs allowed them both to earn the money necessary to maintain a suburban home and to live far enough away from the city that it could be perceived as a refuge. At home, they might follow Cowper's example, which suggested that the home could soothe the secret wounds produced by the public world's demands for conformity. Whether or not men actually thought that their public lives hurt them as Cowper says his life did, *The Task* taught them that the private sphere was a space of compensation.
[. . .]
While I earlier suggested that his secrecy did not necessarily have to be interpreted in sexual terms, I want now to turn to the aspects of the poem that encouraged such an interpretation in the nineteenth century. The domestication of genius brought with it the aura of possible sexual deviance that eighteenth-century writers had attributed to genius. Just as one sign of the genius's rebellion against convention lay in his rebellion against fixed gender categories, so the domestic genius might find his privileged specialness arising from sexual nonconformity. Yet such nonconformity was never a conscious strategy for Cowper, as it was for a writer like [William] Beckford. Instead, if Cowper's secrecy anticipated romantic subjectivity, it also anticipated the homosexual closet in ways that had important effects for the suburban man's relation to homoeroticism. In a complex definition, [Eve Kosofsky] Sedgwick notes that

"closetedness" itself is a performance initiated as such by the speech act of a silence – not a particular silence, but a silence that accrues particularity by fits and starts, in relation to the discourse that surrounds and differentially constitutes it.[18]

Cowper's secrets in *The Task* surrounded him with many silences, not solely ones about his sexuality. Yet certain aspects of his self-representation provided clues for later readers about his possible sexual deviance.

As critics have long recognized, Cowper's self-presentation in the stricken deer passage has much in common with the eighteenth-century man of feeling, such as his "virtually helpless, passive, 'feminine'" characteristics.[19] [... T]he man of feeling's putative femininity did little to challenge heteronormative sexual roles.[20] Cowper, however, differed from men of feeling like Laurence Sterne's Yorick and Henry Mackenzie's Harley by avoiding displays of heteroerotic attachment. *The Task* begins with his taking up his friend Lady Austen's challenge to write about the sofa, a piece of furniture associated in eighteenth-century literature with illicit or violent sex. Cowper's mock-epic history drains the sofa of its sexual associations, an act characteristic of his desire for "a world in principle as chaste / As this is gross and selfish" (6.836–7). He is a bachelor markedly uninterested in the possibilities of women as objects of erotic sympathy.

No eighteenth-century writers that I have discovered found any scandal in Cowper's self- representation as a bachelor, probably because the reflective, solitary man was such a literary commonplace after the success of such works as John Milton's "Il Penseroso," Edward Young's *The Complaint; Or, Night Thoughts on Life, Death, and Immortality*, and Thomas Gray's "Elegy Written in a Country Churchyard." Yet Cowper differed from these writers in one respect: by placing his solitary in a setting so closely associated with women, marriage, and the family, he drew attention to his anomalous celibacy. While this anomalousness did not affect his eighteenth-century reception, perceptions about Cowper changed dramatically in the nineteenth century. In the next section, I will trace how reactions to him point to a crisis in the formation of the suburban man's identity. Cowper's link between secrecy and distinction could be read as one between secrecy and sexual deviance in ways that made the violent repudiation of homosexuality necessary for the suburban man to maintain his masculine authority.

The stricken deer and the hermaphrodite

In the years following *The Task*'s publication, Cowper's readership spread as he was taken up by the Evangelicals and their periodicals, reprinted in numerous editions, acquired by lending libraries, excerpted in schooltexts, copied in commonplace books, and generally treated as an unexceptional author for the respectable home. From the start, readers wanted to know the answers to the mysteries with which he surrounded himself. The *Gentleman's Magazine*'s comment in 1785 held true for readers at least until the end of the nineteenth century: "All who read [Cowper] must be curious to know him and his communication, and grieve that such a writer, such a man, ever had an 'arrow' in his side."[21] The solution to the identity of the mysterious "arrow" that received most attention from early biographers was not Cowper's sexuality but his insanity. Almost immediately after his death, accounts of his madness began to appear, which provoked a stormy controversy between Evangelical and anti-Evangelical readers about whether Evangelicalism had created or cured it.[22]

Part of Cowper's success depended on his readers' assimilation of him to the role of poetic genius. Even though he never used the word to describe himself, it quickly became a standard part of descriptions of him, as when John Blain Linn included Cowper in his poem *The Powers of Genius*. The publication of William Hayley's *Life and Posthumous Writings of William Cowper* did the most to place Cowper in the cult of genius. First, hoping to calm the argument among religious groups about Cowper's madness, Hayley printed hundreds of Cowper's letters for the first time. He commented that they "must render all who read them intimately acquainted with the Writer, and the result of such intimacy must be . . . an increase of public affection for his enchanting character."[23] [. . .]

Yet Hayley also produced what looks at first like a curious split in Cowper's reception. Even as Cowper was the model domestic man in his letters, he also became, in Hayley's hands, a tortured genius:

> The smothered flames of desire uniting with the vapours of constitutional melancholy, and the fervency of religious zeal, produced altogether that irregularity of corporeal sensation, and of mental health, which gave such extraordinary vicissitudes of splendor and of darkness to his moral career, and made Cowper at times an idol of the purest inspiration, and at times an object of the sincerest pity.[24]

After Hayley's biography, calling Cowper a genius was no longer simply a casual word of praise. It signified instead that Cowper manifested all the melodramatic traits with which the eighteenth century had endowed genius. Poetic responses to Hayley revealed how deeply his portrait of Cowper's madness touched contemporary readers. For example, while addressing the "Ill-fated Minstrel!" Bernard Barton lamented that "the feverish dream / Of mental anarchy, with dreadful gloom, / Obscur'd the light of hope's celestial beam." By 1833, Cowper had become a standard example of mad genius, as the nearly one-hundred-page analysis of him in R.R. Madden's *Infirmities of Genius Illustrated* demonstrates. His supposed personality had become inseparable from his work.[25]

Discomfort at the split between Cowper as a masculine role model and Cowper as insane genius became especially pronounced with the 1816 publication of his *Memoirs*. Although many late twentieth-century critics have found this text to be his most compelling, early nineteenth-century readers disliked the specificity with which Cowper described his madness and his suicide attempts:

> We do not like to be carried back to all the particulars of his early offences. . . . When they are pressed once more upon our notice, with all their minuteness, they have a tendency . . . to detract somewhat from our respect.
>
> The secret sufferings of the gifted but most unhappy subject . . . were detailed with a minuteness, which nothing but the unsocial and indelicate taste of *methodism* could for one instance have endured.[26]

Just as [John] Bowdler had warned, if a man told too much about what made his suffering distinctive, he would not be admired. Cowper's memoir strained the ability of his audience to distinguish between the glamorous insanity of genius and the sheer wretchedness that Cowper described.

One might suppose that such a strain would have ended Cowper's popularity. If Cowper the bachelor seems an unlikely model for suburban masculinity, Cowper the mad genius seems impossible. Yet the actual reactions of nineteenth-century readers were more complex. Among Evangelicals, he remained an irreproachable standard of piety. While Southey's 1837 anti-Evangelical edition of Cowper sold 6,000 copies, the Rev. T.S. Grimshawe's 1835 Evangelical edition sold 32,000.[27] For William Blake, the Romantic link between madness and inspiration encouraged him to see Cowper as an inspired visionary.[28] What prevented Cowper from losing his audience entirely was the increasing perception of his femininity. Rather than seeing him as a sharp satirist, as his first readers tended to do, he came to seem a man who for various reasons appeared interestingly feminine. This femininity prevented the potential division between Cowper the domestic model and Cowper the lunatic. Those who admired Cowper the domestic man could praise his feminine meekness, gentleness, and domesticity. At the same time, they could admit that, at certain moments, Cowper's feminine side had unfortunately become too strong and had allowed him to descend into madness. Those who wanted to see Cowper less as a moral model and more as an aesthetic genius could praise his feminine side, which eighteenth-century treatises had insisted was part of the genius's character. Not all readers were happy with Cowper's supposedly feminine side. [William] Hazlitt complained of the "effeminacy about [Cowper], which shrinks from and repels common and hearty sympathy." Frederick Denison Maurice worried that the "gentleness of [Cowper's] life might lead some to suspect him of effeminacy," but he assured them that "the old Westminster school-boy and cricketer comes out in the midst of his Meditation on Sofas."[29] For both writers, "effeminacy" had lost its older associations with civic humanism and had come to mean a man who has the characteristics of femininity in civil humanist discourse [. . .]. In defending Cowper, Maurice did not suggest that Cowper really possessed adult masculine characteristics. Instead, he projected backwards into the eighteenth century the aggressive masculinity associated with Victorian public schools. Better for Cowper to be a boy than to be effeminate.

Yet the distaste that Hazlitt and Maurice felt for Cowper's effeminacy was far less common among readers than a recuperation of Cowper as a man who, while flawed in many ways, still remained a model. Toward his "feminine" aspects, critics who treated him as a model domestic man maintained an amiable condescension. Jeffrey praised his "feminine gentleness and delicacy of nature, that shrank from all that was boisterous, presumptuous, or rude," and George Saintsbury commented on his "slightly feminine" nature.[30] Even those who did not use "feminine" used feminizing phrases to describe him, such as "delicate in constitution, and timid in his disposition"; they praised his "peculiar naïveté" and "tender, generous and pious sentiments."[31] The long-term effects of this condescension are still evident, as in the *Norton Anthology*'s description of him as a poet whose "sensibility" is "delicate" and whose "gentle talk" can "re-create for us the serenity and simplicity of life in an English village."[32]

This condescension reveals more about uncomfortable perceptions of relations between masculinity and domesticity than it does about Cowper. Labeling Cowper as feminine let nineteenth-century writers imply that they, in contrast, were masculine. Nevertheless, they respected Cowper's femininity insofar as it distinguished him from vulgarity. Nor did they ever treat Cowper exclusively as feminine, but as a man who had masculine and feminine qualities: he united "the playfulness of a child, the affectionateness of a woman, and the strong sense of a man."[33] The only supposedly masculine quality with which readers were eager to associate him was his patriotism: "Cowper is the poet of a well-educated and well-principled Englishman"; "When the shame of England burns in the heart of Cowper, you must believe him; for through that heart rolled the best of England's blood."[34] Likewise, Cowper's love of domesticity and his strong faith earned him "many simple and honest readers who turn to books for sympathy and fellowship" because "Cowper is one of the strongest instances, and proofs, how much more qualities of this kind affect Englishmen than any other."[35] If Cowper's gender identity was unusual, his national representativeness was not, since identifying with this vulnerable and feminized man was a mark of English manhood.

For those interested in Cowper's genius, his femininity might be recuperated as the source of his aesthetic distinction. [. . .] Nevertheless, Cowper's perceived mixture of masculine and feminine qualities had within it the seeds of scandal that haunted the character of genius. There was always the possibility that this mixture would be recognized not as distinctive and even admirable eccentricity but as alarming deviance. The most dramatic evidence for this possibility arose in the 1830s while Robert Southey was writing his Cowper biography. He heard of a letter supposedly by Cowper's mentor John Newton that disclosed "something regarding Cowper much more remarkable than anything that is publicly known concerning him."[36] According to the memoirs of Charles Greville, the letter claimed that Cowper "was an Hermaphrodite; somebody knew his secret, and probably threatened its exposure."[37] Southey pondered the significance of the letter, but did not include the rumor in his biography. It leaked out through "the sensation-mongering editor of a small journal, the *Literary Times*," though it received little public attention.[38] Later in the century, it resurfaced with the publication of Southey's letters and of an expurgated version of Greville's memoirs, which changed Greville's language to say that Cowper had "some defect" in his "physical conformation."[39]

The most intriguing aspect of this incident is trying to understand precisely what these men thought was wrong with Cowper. The 1874 editors of Greville's memoirs assumed that Cowper's hermaphroditism was a physical condition, presumably of the sort that Alice Domerat Dreger has shown received considerable attention from Victorian doctors.[40] Yet Southey decided otherwise. According to Southey, if Cowper possessed an actual physical deformity, "no parent would or could have sent him to a boarding school," as Cowper's parents had done.[41] Instead, Southey treated Cowper's hermaphroditism as evidence not of biological deformity but of mental instability: "He fancied that he was an androgyne"; "It occurs to me that the most probable solution is to suppose it a mere conception of madness, not the real and primary cause of his insanity, but a hypochondriacal and imaginary effect of it."[42] By treating hermaphroditism as a figment of Cowper's mind rather than a fact about his body, Southey suggests that Cowper's gender deviance was a psychological rather than a physical trait. He assimilates Cowper to the role of the mad genius whose imagination overpowers his reason. For Southey, Cowper's delusion that he had a body combining male and female biological traits must have stemmed from a prior confusion about gender identity related to his mental illness.

Greville's remark in his memoir that Cowper was a "hermaphrodite" with a "secret" that might have been exposed suggests that, for him, Cowper's "hermaphroditism" had a different significance. Since the Renaissance, the term *hermaphrodite* had hovering around it an ambiguity similar to that surrounding the adjective *effeminate* in the eighteenth century. If applied to a man, it might mean that he was a man who had sex with other men, but it did not necessarily do so. In the case of the quotation from Greville, the association of "hermaphrodite" with same-sex passion seems probable because of its link to secrecy and exposure. By the 1830s, a series of scandals had accustomed the British public to understand sex between men as the most shameful secret that could possibly be exposed. Crompton discusses the most famous of these in his accounts of William Beckford, the Bishop of Clogher, and Lord Byron.[43] These cases took place against the backdrop of many lesser-known examples of men forced to flee the country because of their "disgraceful conduct," as well as cases in which men who had sex with other men submitted to blackmail to keep their behavior secret.[44] Such events suggest that Greville understood Cowper as a man worried about keeping his sexual desires closeted. For him, Cowper looked more like a closeted homosexual than like a model suburbanite.

The history of the hermaphrodite rumor took a surprising turn in 1837 after Southey had seen the supposedly incriminating letter about Cowper. He was shocked to discover that it referred not to his Cowper but to one of Cowper's relatives with the same name:

> I obtained from Ingles a sight of the sealed letter. How little are men's memories to be trusted upon points of which they have no cause to take particular notice at the time! . . . The facts of the disappearance, the tracing of the lost person to France, and the supposed cause of his thus absconding, relate to the *other* William Cowper, as clearly ascertained by the date. What then becomes of all the collateral traditional evidence respecting *my* Cowper's real or supposed malformation? . . . Did *my* Cowper apply to himself what was reported of his kinsman, and engraft this miserable imagination upon his other delusions?[45]

Presumably the other William Cowper disappeared and fled to France after a homosexual scandal. In any case, this letter makes clear that the hermaphrodite rumor about Cowper the poet arose from a case of mistaken identity. No evidence existed for it whatsoever.

It may look as if the hermaphrodite rumor should be dismissed as telling more about Southey and later readers than about Cowper. Yet doing so would lose the insight that the rumor provides into the nineteenth century's use of the poetic genius to construct masculinity in relation to homosexuality. Southey, once he learned that the rumor was groundless, still wondered about the "collateral traditional evidence" of Cowper's "supposed malformation." Even without the specific evidence of Cowper's hermaphroditism, Southey still suspected that Cowper harbored a secret about gender deviance. He even thought that it was possible that Cowper believed himself to have engaged in same-sex passion, as the earlier Cowper evidently had. Even more remarkably, twentieth-century scholars have entirely overlooked the evidence of Southey's letter and proceeded as if the hermaphrodite rumor really applied to Cowper the poet. It persists in the most recent and authoritative accounts of Cowper, even though it arose from a mistake. Scholars have produced a wealth of theories and denials in relation to the rumor, including the possibility that Cowper was a latent homosexual.[46]

The rumor's durability is no mere accident. It reveals how little distance might exist in the nineteenth century between the model suburban man and the sexual deviant. In Cowper's case, his supposed feminine qualities overdetermined the possibility of seeing him as having a secret identity as a "hermaphrodite" or "androgyne." Tellingly, Southey and Greville never described him as a "sodomite" or a "bugger," but used words that pointed specifically to feminine traits in a man. For Greville, if Cowper were a "hermaphrodite," he had sex with other men. For Southey, Cowper the "androgyne" might at least have thought, in his insanity, that he had homoerotic desires.

In terms of Cowper's larger significance to the history of masculinity, the hermaphrodite rumor reveals the potential danger in the domestication of genius as a model for male behavior. In the 1780s, Cowper had defined himself as a stricken deer who had earned his unique perspective on the world through painful but mysterious experience. The secrets with which Cowper surrounded himself could by the 1830s be taken as evidence of homosexuality, or at least of gender dysfunction. *The Task* taught nineteenth-century suburban men that any man who wished to aspire to the special viewpoint fostered by the domestic sphere needed to have his share of secrets. Yet this secrecy effect could seem potentially scandalous after "one particular sexuality . . . was distinctively constituted as secrecy," as Sedgwick notes of homosexuality.[47] Although the hermaphrodite rumor was not widely known in the nineteenth century, it reveals the anxieties for nineteenth-century men lurking beneath the model for the suburban man represented by Cowper. The question marks potentially surrounding masculine secrecy as the mark of a distinctive inner life meant that the suburban man had to find a way to differentiate his secrecy from the kind that could make him look "hermaphroditic."

The solution to these anxieties in nineteenth-century writing was to recreate the stricken deer narrative as a specifically masculine story of achievement. Like Cowper, nineteenth-century heroes underwent secret inner struggles that earned them a distinctive, individual perspective on the world and separated them from the supposedly less sensitive mass of commonplace men. Yet far from feminizing them, this process gave them masculine character. [. . .]

Once [. . .] the stricken deer could be rewritten as a masculine model, the secret of homosexuality had to be connected not to men of individual character but to men who lacked such character. Writers located such homosexuals in cities, far from the isolating world of the suburban home:

> These wretches have many ways and means of conveying intelligence, and many signals by which they discover themselves to each other . . . by means of these signals they retire to satisfy a passion too horrible for description, too detestable for language.[48]

A Victorian work entitled *The Yokel's Preceptor* warned those new to London to beware of groups of men who "generally congregate around the picture shops, and are to be known by their effeminate air, their fashionable dress."[49] Reactions to Oscar Wilde treated him likewise as the leader of a cult. *Punch* noted that when Wilde's plays were performed, "nightly the stalls were fulfilled by Row upon Row of neatly curled Fringes, surmounting Buttonholes of monstrous size."[50] When testimony at his trials revealed his involvement with same-sex activity, the newspaper commented that "this curse of an outrageous cult" had at last been exposed.[51] Even in British colonial experience, the homoerotic anxieties surrounding the possibility of "going native" can be seen as a version of the paranoia surrounding secrecy. As in the attacks on Wilde or the Tractarians, anxieties about masculinity arose when men faced the possibility of submerging their individual personality within an eroticized, larger body, such as the secretive mass that writers like Kipling represented as India.

This mode of homophobia remains familiar today in the attacks by the religious right on the gay agenda. Homosexuals supposedly threaten the fundamental value of individualism insofar as they are represented as a cult eager to recruit new members rather than as an oppressed minority. The suburban domestication of genius continues, with the proviso that the required uniqueness never be the wrong kind of uniqueness. At the same time, a gay man's story can be acceptable if it follows an archetypal individualist narrative, as in Jonathan Demme's film *Philadelphia* (1994). Its hero is a latter-day Cowperian stricken deer whose secret is not madness but AIDS. The contradiction whereby a violently homophobic culture can praise and reward a film that sympathetically represents a gay man has its roots in Cowper's model of suburban masculinity and the discomfort surrounding its nineteenth-century reception. Cowper's poem installed the structure of the closet at the center of the middle-class suburban psyche in ways that made homophobia more useful than ever as a means of reinforcing the fragile borders of bourgeois masculine subjectivity.

Notes

1 Crompton, *Byron and Greek Love: Homophobia in Nineteenth-Century England* (Berkeley: University of California Press, 1985), 38.
2 On the Labouchère amendment, see H. Montgomery Hyde, *The Love That Dared Not Speak Its Name: A Candid History of Homosexuality in Britain* (Boston: Little, Brown, 1970), 134–7; Ed Cohen, *Talk on the Wilde Side: Toward a Genealogy of a Discourse on Male Sexualities* (New York: Routledge, 1993), 491–3.
3 Davidoff and Hall, *Family Fortunes[: Men and Women of the English Middle Class, 1780–1850* (Chicago: University of Chicago Press, 1987)], 162–7.
4 For these terms, see Williams, *Marxism and Literature* (Oxford: Oxford University Press, 1977), 121–7.
5 For standard works on Cowper, see Patricia Meyer Spacks, *The Poetry of Vision: Five Eighteenth-Century Poets* (Cambridge: Harvard University Press, 1967), 178–94; Vincent Newey, *Cowper's Poetry: A Critical Study and Reassessment* (Totowa, N.J.: Barnes and Noble, 1982); Marvin Priestman, *Cowper's Task: Structure and Influence* (Cambridge: Cambridge University Press, 1983); Bill Hutchings, *The Poetry of William Cowper* (London: Croom Helm, 1983); Marshall Brown, *Preromanticism* (Stanford, Calif.: Stanford University Press, 1991), 58–81.
6 "Additional Particulars Relative to Mr. Cowper," *Monthly Magazine* 9 (1800): 498–500 (500); Jeffrey, "Hayley's *Life of Cowper*," *Edinburgh Review* 2 (1803): 64–86 (84).
7 Fishman, *Bourgeois Utopias[: The Rise and Fall of Suburbia* (New York: Basic Books, 1987)], 51–62.
8 On bachelors as threats, see [Eve Kosofsky] Sedgwick, *Epistemology [of the Closet* (Berkeley: University of California Press, 1990)], 189–95.
9 On Cowper's use of this tradition, see Newey, *Cowper's Poetry*, 83–4; see also Dustin Griffin, "Redefining Georgic: Cowper's *Task*," *ELH* 57 (1990): 865–79.
10 Davidoff and Hall, *Family Fortunes*, 112.
11 All quotations from *The Task* are from volume 2 of *The Poems of William Cowper*, ed. John D. Baird and Charles Ryskamp, 3 vols (Oxford: Clarendon Press, 1980–1995); refs. to book and line numbers.
12 On this tradition, see Linda H. Peterson, *Victorian Autobiography: The Tradition of Self-Interpretation* (New Haven: Yale University Press, 1986), 34–40.

13 Foucault, *The Order of Things: An Archaeology of the Human Sciences* (New York: Random House, 1970), 251; Foucault, *The History of Sexuality*, [vol. 1, *An Introduction*, trans. Robert Hurley (New York: Vintage, 1990)], 59, 61.

14 For a complete discussion of this process, see my "Cowper's *Task* and the Anxieties of Femininity," *Eighteenth-Century Life* 13 (1989): 1–17.

15 Klancher, *The Making of English Reading Audiences, 1790–1832* (Madison: University of Wisconsin Press, 1987), 173.

16 On the importance of self-discipline to eighteenth-century understandings of masculinity, see Carolyn D. Williams, *Pope, Homer, and Manliness: Some Aspects of Eighteenth-Century Classical Learning* (London: Routledge, 1993), 9–26.

17 [Donald J.] Olsen, [*The*] *Growth of Victorian London* [(London: Batsford, 1976)], 214.

18 Sedgwick, *Epistemology*, 3.

19 Patricia Meyer Spacks, *Desire and Truth: Functions of Plot in Eighteenth-Century English Novels* (Chicago: University of Chicago Press, 1990), 124.

20 See Claudia L. Johnson, *Equivocal Beings: Politics, Gender, and Sentimentality* in *the 1790s* (Chicago: University of Chicago Press, 1995), 1–22; Judith Frank, "'A Man Who Laughs is Never Dangerous': Character and Class in Sterne's A *Sentimental Journey*," *ELH* 56 (1989): 97–124.

21 "Review of Cowper's Poems," *Gentleman's Magazine* 55 (1785): 985–8 (987). [. . .]

22 On the controversy, see Lodwick Hartley, "Cowper and the Evangelicals: Notes on Early Biographical Interpretations," *PMLA* 65 (1950): 719–31.

23 Linn, *The Powers of Genius, A Poem* (Philadelphia: Asbury Dickens, 1801), 36; William Hayley, *The Life and Posthumous Writings of William Cowper*, 3 vols (London: John Johnson, 1803–1804), 1:206.

24 Hayley, *Life of Cowper*, 2:222.

25 Bernard Barton, "Verses on Reading Hayley's Life of Cowper," *Metrical Effusions; Or, Verses on Various Occasions* (Woodbridge: S. Loder, 1812), 212–15 (214); R.R. Madden, *Infirmities of Genius Illustrated*, 2 vols (London: Saunder and Otley, 1833), 2:1–104.

26 "Cowper's Poems and Life," *Quarterly Review*, [16 (1816): 117–29 (123)]; "The Rural Walks of Cowper," *Monthly Review* 100 (1823): 111–12 (111). [. . .]

27 Newey, *Cowper's Poetry*, 1–2.

28 For Blake and Cowper, see my "Cowper, Blake, and the Figure of the Invader," *The Friend* 1, no, 4 (1992): 10–19.

29 Hazlitt, *Lectures on the English Poets* (1818) in [*The Complete Works of William Hazlitt*, ed. P.P. Howe, 21 vols (New York: AMS, 1967)], 5:91; Maurice, *The Friendship of Books and Other Lectures*, ed. Thomas Hughes, 2nd ed. (London: Macmillan, 1874), 28.

30 Jeffrey, "Hayley's *Life of Cowper*," 80; Saintsbury, *Short History of English Literature* (New York: Macmillan, 1898), 590.

31 Madden, *Infirmities of Genius*, 2:99; "Private Correspondence of William Cowper," *Somerset House Gazette 1* (1824): 297–300 (298); "Cowper's Poems and Life," *Quarterly Review*, 120.

32 Samuel Holt Monk and Lawrence Lipking, in M.H. Abrams, ed., *The Norton Anthology of English Literature*, 6th ed., 2 vols (New York. Norton, 1993), 1:2502.

33 "Private Correspondence of Cowper," *Quarterly Review* 30 (1823):185–99 (185).

34 [Thomas Frognall] Dibdin, *The Library Companion*, [2nd ed. (London: Harding, Triphock, and Lepard, 1825),] 735*n*; John Wilson, "North's Specimens of the British Critics, No. VIII: Supplement to MacFlecnoe and the Dunciad," *Blackwood's* 58 (1845): 366–88 (388).

35 Maurice, *Friendship of Books*, 28.

36 *The Correspondence of Robert Southey with Caroline Bowles*, ed. Edward Dowden (London: Longmans, Green, 1881), 296.

37 *The Greville Memoirs, 1814–1860*, ed. Lytton Strachey and Roger Fulford, 8 vols (London: Macmillan, 1938), 3:85.

38 Charles Ryskamp, *William Cowper of the Inner Temple, Esq.: A Study of His Life and Works to the Year 1768* (Cambridge: Cambridge University Press, 1959), 140.

39 Greville quoted in ibid., 139.

40 Dreger, "Doubtful Sex: The Fate of the Hermaphrodite in Victorian Medicine," *Victorian Studies* 38 (1995), 336–70.

41 *New Letters of Robert Southey,* ed. Kenneth Curry, 2 vols (New York: Columbia University Press, 1965), 2:432.

42 Southey's letter printed in Ryskamp, *William Cowper,* 141; Southey, *Correspondence,* 300; see also Southey, *New Letters,* 433.

43 Crompton, *Byron and Greek Love,* 118–23,196–235, 300–1.

44 On these cases, see Rictor Norton, *Mother Clap's Molly House: The Gay Subculture in England, 1700–1830* (London: GMP, 1992), 169–86, 226–31.

45 Southey, *Correspondence,* 346.

46 For the most complete account, see Ryskamp, *William Cowper,* 135–44; for a discussion of Cowper's possible homosexuality, see David Perkins, "Cowper's Hares," *Eighteenth-Century Life* 20 (1996): 57–69.

47 Sedgwick, *Epistemology,* 73.

48 George Parker, *Views of Society and Manners in High and Low Life,* quoted in Norton, *Mother Clap's Molly House,* 185.

49 *The Yokel's Preceptor,* quoted in Hyde, *Love That Dared Not Speak Its Name,* 120.

50 *Punch,* quoted in Matthew Sturgis, *Passionate Attitudes: The English Decadence of the 1890s* (London: Macmillan, 1995), 226.

51 *Daily Telegraph,* April 6, 1895, quoted in Cohen, *Talk on the Wilde Side,* 172.

19 Sensibility, free indirect style and the Romantic technology of discretion

Clara Tuite

> the first question on entering the shop I found to be universally – Have you anything new?
>
> > (Vicesimus Knox, in a circulating library, as a reluctant patient under doctor's orders at a 'watering place')[1]

> a New Novel . . . an Extraordinary Novel! . . . an interesting Novel.
>
> > (Advertising puffs for *Sense and Sensibility*, in *The Morning Chronicle*)[2]

> The story may be thought trifling by the readers of novels, who are insatiable after something new. But the excellent lesson which it holds up to view, and the useful moral which may be derived from the perusal, are such essential requisites, that the want of newness may in this instance be readily overlooked.
>
> > (1812 anonymous review of *Sense and Sensibility*, in *Critical Review*)[3]

The want of newness

As an antisentimental novel begun in the late 1790s and not published until November 1811, *Sense and Sensibility* is dated by its own datings. A work which is very much *of* its antisentimental 1790s moment of production, it nonetheless forfeited that context of reception because of its belated publication. The anonymous review of *Sense and Sensibility* which appeared in the February 1812 *Critical Review* is significant not only because it is the first review of Austen's first published novel, but because it claims that *Sense and Sensibility* demonstrates a 'want of newness'.

Contradicting the puffs which proclaim *Sense and Sensibility* as 'a New Novel', this review implicitly locates *Sense and Sensibility* under the sign of the 'old'. However, given that the category of the new is reproduced satirically in the review, the assertion that *Sense and Sensibility* has a 'want of newness' cannot be taken at face value. For despite the fact that the *Critical Review* would seem effectively to contradict the successive October and November 1811 *Morning Chronicle* puffs of the novel as 'a New Novel', an 'Extraordinary Novel!' and an 'interesting Novel', its claim that the novel will disappoint those 'insatiable after something new' is clearly ironic. For the *Critical Review*, the generally Tory journal established by Tobias Smollett in 1756, the 'new' signifies merely an insatiable, feminine-identified appetite for *novelty*, the cliché of more of the same. Unlike the vast 'multiplicity' of novels which proffer a debased form of novelty, *Sense and Sensibility* boasts a rarer combination of 'both amusement and instruction . . . *Sense and Sensibility* is one amongst the few, which can claim this fair praise' (Southam [ed.], *Casebook*, p. 80).

This review marks an important moment in Austen's contemporary reception, appearing just a few years before the enthusiastic receptions of Austen by Sir Walter Scott in 1816 and Richard Whately in 1821, both of which produce Austen unequivocally under the sign of the new. This category of the new is critical to the early reception of Austen. [. . .] What the review in the 1812 *Critical Review* suggests is that the perception of Austen as new occurred after an initial perception of her as old, or as more of the same, and that this transition in the perception of Austen from being old to new occurred over a relatively short space of time. My primary concern in this chapter will be to map the terms of this transition: to consider this moment of reception before Austen was perc[e]ived as new, and to relate it to the question of when, how and why it was that her work was perceived as new. As I will argue, the issue of Austen's newness is critically implicated in the changing status of the novel of sentiment.

We can draw a number of conclusions from the *Critical Review*'s review: that literary innovation is not necessarily recognized at the moment of a text's first production and reception, that innovation is not the same as what is recognized at the time as new, and that a work which might later come to be recognized as innovative can be perceived at the time as having 'a want of newness'. The *Critical Review*'s attribution of 'want of newness' instantiates important distinctions between newness and innovation and between contemporaneity and canonicity.

Readings of Austen which assume her canonical status have always overlooked *Sense and Sensibility*'s 'want of newness', despite its position as a minor novel within the Austen canon. Take, for example, Margaret Doody's introduction to *Sense and Sensibility*, which claims that the contemporary reviews of the novel 'do not note that a distinctive genius has entered the literary scene'.[4] Why is it that contemporary reviewers do not note the arrival of a genius? The only plausible answer implied by Doody's account is that the particular reviewers are unobservant or insufficiently sensitive. Doody thereby enacts a post-Romantic version of what Margaret Russett has recently referred to as 'the *Romantic* institution of the institution's absence'.[5] Doody's reading ignores the way in which the category of genius is retrospectively attributed and indeed constructed by a history and a set of historical institutions – the idea of genius itself being one of these Romantic institutions. Doody's claim enacts the overlooking of history which marks canon-forming criticism, and overlooks the distinction between canonicity and contemporaneity which informs the historical processes of literary production and reception.

A vast expanse of literary-institutional history has been comprehended in the move from the *Critical Review*'s review to Doody's claim, and this raises several questions. How does *Sense and Sensibility* move from being a relatively unnoticed, unspectacular and unremarkable novel upon first publication, to being a novel of 'genius'? How does it move from having 'a want of newness' to being both a canonical antisentimental or antisensibility novel? How does it come to be an initiatory text of British domestic realism?[6] Finally, how is it that Austen, and *Sense and Sensibility*, moved from being unremarkable to being almost the only version of sensibility which was told in English literary history?

Sense and Sensibility is both the least canonical of Austen's 'mature' fictions and the one which most explicitly situates itself in relation to contemporary literary fashion. As [Eve Kosofsky] Sedgwick has pointed out, *Sense and Sensibility* is 'at once germinal and abjected', in the Austen canon and hence in 'the history of the novel'.[7]

Sedgwick's formulation of the 'at once germinal and abjected' encapsulates the distinction between retrospective 'newness' as innovation and contemporary 'want of newness' which is registered both in the *Critical Review*'s original review of the novel and in the trajectory of reception from the *Critical Review* through Watt to Doody.

Sense and Sensibility has held an 'abjected' position in the Austen *oeuvre* partly because of its explicit relation to the genres of sensibility and sentiment. It has nonetheless been the Austen novel's retrospectively constituted historical and canonical mission to abject and expel sensibility and sentiment from the British novelistic repertoire. And therein lies its claim to 'germinal' status. For if we *read* – rather than overlook – the specific claims both of the *Critical Review*'s review, and of its historical context, this attribution of 'want of newness' can be read as an effect partially of *Sense and Sensibility*'s status as an antisentimental novel. It has a 'want of newness' because the antisentimental novel is more properly read in its contemporary context as a specific form within the genre of sentiment and sensibility, rather than as a distinct genre. *Sense and Sensibility*'s 'want of newness' derives at least in part then from the co-reproductive relationship between the sentimental and the antisentimental novel, in their interminable efforts to distinguish true from false and virtuous from self-interested sensibility, and in the circular and mutually implicating relationship between sensibility and its parodic others. [. . .]

Since its novelistic inception in the 1740s, sentiment's claims to virtue, sincerity and propriety had always been parodically subverted and inverted. In parodic rewritings of sentiment such claims were cast as the insincere ruses of a style of writing which worked to inflame the passions and encourage impropriety. Sentimental productions had always in a sense been partially constituted by and received through their parodic others, in critical writings, imitations and pastiches.

[. . .]

During the 1790s this interimplication reached a land of impasse which weakened the claims of sentiment as a social and moral code, and rendered the distinction between sentiment and antisentiment far more tenuous. Having become overdetermined politically, sensibility comes to have exhausted its capacity for generating any stable kind of meaning. The exhaustion of the will to discriminate between the sentimental and the antisentimental accounts partially for *Sense and Sensibility*'s contemporary reception as having a 'want of newness' and for its later 'abjected' status within the Austen *oeuvre*.

Nonetheless, not only 'abjected' but also strangely 'germinal', *Sense and Sensibility* is perceived retrospectively to have overcome this impasse of indistinguishability between the sentimental and the antisentimental. Indeed, the *Critical Review*'s ironic conjurations of the discourse of novelty seem to announce a contemporary scene which is receptive to the antisentimental project of *Sense and Sensibility*. This project is that of outdating sentiment and of outdating sentiment as a symptom of fashion. In this way, the 'want of newness' is the accusation which *Sense and Sensibility* makes against the cult of sensibility; the rhetorical and polemical project of *Sense and Sensibility* is an outdating of sensibility as a stock of social and cultural capital.

There is at least one significant way, then, in which *Sense and Sensibility* can be seen to move beyond sentiment, to overcome the impasse over anti/sentimental definition which marked the 1790s, and to reconfigure or to undertake the discursive management of a social and ethical vocabulary which had become unruly. Austen's novel attacks the cult of sensibility by outmoding and outdating it, casting it as a symptom of fashion. But this very strategy of course frames the text itself within the claims of the current, the fashionable, the novel. For if Austen takes on this predominant mode of writing on its own terms, in order to outmode it and to present it as a fashion, this very repudiation relies itself upon the code of fashion which it targets in its attack on sensibility.

[. . .]

[A]s a transitional novel, *Sense and Sensibility* occupies the curious position of occupying the ground of the novel of sensibility which it outdates. It outdates sensibility in its parodic reproduction of sensibility as a fashion, and through its own innovatory form of the probable. It offers a view of what came before. Canonical Austen is *the* bourgeois novel's retrospective and parodic view of sensibility. The prominence of Austen's parodic backward look, which institutes a hygienic barrier in the development of the novel between sensibility and realism, is the means by which, as the novel was becoming a canonical form, sensibility became sealed off as an antiquarian curiosity or 'a fugitive literary tendency [of] little intrinsic merit'.[8]

Sensibility is retrospectively divorced in canon-forming literary histories from the localized, politicized context of the 1790s, as is Austen's *oeuvre* itself. Austen's canonicity attests to her successful transformation of counter-revolutionary didacticism to discretion: the movement from politics to style. By 'style', I mean style understood as that which transcends fashion. Austen's style in *Sense and Sensibility* involves a highly aestheticized discretion which resists localization as a 1790s antisentimental and anti-Jacobin text. Before discussing how the contemporary identification of sensibility with the French revolutionary threat is nonetheless legible in *Sense and Sensibility*, despite the text's discreet abstention from political commentary, I wish to engage Austen's discretion in some detail in terms of its centrality to her canonical positioning.

Free indirect style: the novel genre's lyric technology of discretion

Austen's discretion is the form, tactic or strategy by which the Austen novel makes its bid for the new, and is inserted into literary history as a break with the old. *Sense and Sensibility* moves beyond the novel of sentiment not only by outdating it, representing it as a sign and symptom of fashion. This is not enough on its own, because this strategy is always subject to the claims of fashion itself, as I have suggested. More significantly, it moves beyond sentiment by correcting and revising it through new strategies of reading, representation and through the representation of reading. This technology of discretion, both as a novelistic generic technique and as a specific kind of pleasure as novelistic reading experience, comes to be identified as the primary distinguishing feature both of the Austen novel and of the realist novel in its development away from the excesses of sensibility. *Sense and Sensibility* is a germinal text within literary history because it begins to offer a series of formal mechanisms through which an older and more archaic style of didactic and romance fiction is displaced. These new mechanisms are the subtle, nuanced and formidably ideological strategies of realist narrative: irony, ambiguity and free indirect discourse as a language of sympathy.

Sense and Sensibility is not the first Austen novel to use the technique of free indirect discourse, nor, more importantly, is it a technique which Austen invented. Free indirect discourse is a defining feature of Austen's realism, and a technique which Austen finessed, but it is also a technique Austen would have encountered in the work of other novelists such as Frances Burney and Ann Radchiffe.[9] Indeed, we can see this encounter between Austen and Radcliffe's free indirect discourse being played out in *Northanger Abbey*, where Austen engages Radcliffe's work in the form of Gothic parody. A defining feature of Radcliffe's pioneering form of 'female Gothic' is the use of free indirect discourse. And *Northanger Abbey*'s parody of the Gothic involves a parody specifically of Radcliffe's use of this technique. Radcliffe's female Gothic can be characterized as a mode of representing female interiority, and it is precisely this interiority that distinguishes Radcliffe's female Gothic from the male Gothic of Matthew Lewis, for example, which is characterized by a materialist aesthetic in the production of sensation and spectacle. [. . .] Austen's parody can be read as a drama of literary apprenticeship that turns on the identification of Radcliffe as the mistress of a certain form of interiority and negotiates the inheritance of this technique from Radcliffe.

One way of characterizing the development in Austen's fiction from the parodic texts of the juvenilia and *Northanger Abbey* is to identify the free indirect discourse of the later novels as an internalization of an externalized process of doubling which defines parody. The primary feature of free indirect discourse is a form of doubleness, where the character's thoughts cannot be distinguished from those of the narrator; and this structure is very similar formally to what occurs with parody, which presents a double voice, in terms of which the parodied object (Radcliffe) cannot be distinguished from the parodying subject (Austen).

To refine this idea of externalization, we might engage Pierre Bourdieu's definition of parody as a form of 'appropriation'.[10] *Northanger Abbey*'s parodic 'appropriation' of Radcliffe, or what we might further refine as a form of parodic 'channelling' of Radcliffe, is an exercise in free indirect style, itself a form of channelling. *Northanger*'s parody of Radcliffe's female Gothic – 'Could it be possible? . . . It was the air and attitude of a Montoni'[11] – depends to a large extent upon the reader identifying the free indirect style *as* a style associated with Radcliffe. The parody spectacularizes a style which has been successfully appropriated, to use Bourdieu's term. In Austen's later fiction, the free indirect style is refunctioned or refashioned within a new form of novel – 'Yes, novel!' (*Northanger Abbey*, p. 22) – which is free of the stigma attached to the sentimental or Gothic genres. This form of novel involves a discretion achieved by the free indirect style, a discretion explicitly thematized in *Sense and Sensibility*.

[. . .]

One of the ways in which *Sense and Sensibility* engages [. . .] sentimental genealogies is by offering a generic allegory of discretion. It does this by setting up a negative exemplum between the romance form and what the *Critical Review* terms 'genteel' fiction (quoted in Southam [ed.], *Casebook*, p. 79). One thing that characterizes the polite or bourgeois novel, both in its development away from the more scandalous genres of romance, and in its simultaneous attempt to capitalize on the popular appeal of romance elements, is the domestication of the scandal tale within the novel. This takes the form of the relegation of the tale of scandal to the margins of the larger narrative of proper courtship and transmission, as in the intergenerational revision of the scandalous mother's tale by the daughter that occurs in Frances Burney's *Evelina* (1778) and Elizabeth Inchbald's *A Simple Story* (1791).

In *Sense and Sensibility*, the scandalous tale is the inset tale of Eliza, narrated by Colonel Brandon. In his first appearance in the text, Brandon initiates a conversation with Elinor on the subject of 'second attachments', which he uses to launch the tale of a young woman who 'resembles' Marianne.[12] [. . .] This gesture emplots Brandon within the novel as a kind of sentimental narrator. Significantly, of course, Brandon's tale is interrupted.

Appearing early in the text, just after the meeting with Willoughby, it is not continued until near the end of the text. By this later stage in the text, the similarity between Marianne and Eliza has been unfolded by the narrative. Brandon's tentative prolepsis is no longer faintly indecorous – as the reader is subtly enjoined to suspect it might be earlier, when Brandon demonstrates his discretion in breaking off the tale, lest the similarity with Marianne prove too painful for Elinor. When Brandon later tells Elinor, 'Use your own discretion, however, in communicating to her what I have told you' (p. 183), he has already demonstrated his own powers of discretion. Elinor's discretion dictates that she wait until the danger has been averted before 'communicating' the story to Marianne. Discretion is thereby explicitly invoked and implicitly enacted through the figure of Brandon as a reluctant narrator, who puts discretion into circulation in the text as a positive value and model of narration. Brandon's narrative discretion is a synecdochic model of Austen's own stylistic discretion in *Sense and Sensibility*, as is the modest discretion of Anne Elliot in *Persuasion*. [. . .]

Brandon's discretion is the example that enables Austen discreetly to repeat by reformulating Richardson's didactic preface to *Clarissa*:

> it is one of the principal views of the publication: to caution parents against the undue exertion of their natural authority over children in the great article of marriage: and children against preferring a man of pleasure to a man of probity, upon that dangerous but too commonly received notion, *that a reformed rake makes the best husband.*[13]

Brandon is discreetly and ironically instantiated as the sentimental narrator who cautions – in relation to the Marianne and Willoughby romance plot – against the idea that the reformed rake makes the best husband. As this example suggests, Austen's protocols of invoking and revising paternal models of canonical authority are themselves subtle and discreet.

Brandon is so discreet that he prefaces his own tale of the misfortunes of a young woman with the self-conscious disclaimer, 'You will find me a very awkward narrator' (p. 178). With Brandon as Richardson as male narrator of female misfortunes, Austen revises the novel of sensibility by turning the sentimental narrator into the 'man of probity', and reforming the male sentimental narrator and reader by turning him into a model of discretion. Nonetheless, Brandon carries out this Richardsonian function of man of probity awkwardly and unconvincingly. He is too compromised by his own knowledge of the sentimental plot, as he stands back and watches it unfold in Marianne's life. Brandon anticipates every move, demonstrating a mastery of the sentimental plot, despite his disavowal of the knowledge implied by reading, 'You will find me a very awkward narrator.' This disclaimer both announces Brandon's association with the positive value of discretion (in this germinal novel of discretion) yet it also positions him ambivalently as a kind of rake figure and voyeur. Brandon himself is to some extent a reformed rake, a man with a past.

Like the sentimental narrator, and its other, the libertine, both of whom derive their own mastery from the fiction of innocence, the only really *knowing* reader in

Sense and Sensibility is Brandon. Suspended ambivalently as the man of feeling, the sentimental narrator/reader/spectator/voyeur, who finds 'something so amiable in the prejudices of a young mind' (p. 48), Brandon occupies a problematic position in relation to the text's critique of sentiment and sensibility and masculine libertinism. It is through Brandon that *Sense and Sensibility* awkwardly and counter-intuitively signifies this novel's abjected status in the Austen canon, ambivalently acknowledging its own generic forebears in the novel of sensibility.

Free indirect discourse and the rhetoric of sympathy

As Brandon's reading of Marianne comes to be countenanced by the narrative, and formalized by the marriage plot, Brandon is made to occupy a kind of privileged, post-sentimental status. This is one way in which Austen attempts to transform a discredited sensibility into a respectable sympathy. Such a move restages the philosopher David Hume's transformation of sympathy from a mode of excess into a principle of correction.

[. . .]

Sympathy is not an explicit term within the vocabulary of Austen's novel, but it is invoked repeatedly in critical work on Austen, and is significant in contemporary moral-philosophical discourse in the work of Francis Hutcheson, Shaftesbury, David Hartley, Adam Smith and David Hume, *Sense and Sensibility* can be seen to manoeuvre towards sympathy as a synthesizing, stabilizing third term that lies between 'sense' and 'sensibility'. It institutes a rhetoric of sympathy in the character of Brandon, and a mechanism of sympathy through the technique of free indirect discourse, which mainly focalizes the sympathetic character of Elinor. Austen's text transforms the suspect, contagious principle of sensibility into a more sober principle of sympathy through free indirect discourse.

[. . .]

Free indirect discourse [. . .] can be seen to be *the* novelistic technique that enables the development of sympathy as a formal strategy. As John Bender has argued in *Imagining the Penitentiary*, his groundbreaking and justly influential account of the development of the realist novel:

> Sympathy, operating through the medium of impersonal spectatorship, fuses the subjectivity of the beholder with other equally isolated but seemingly accessible consciousnesses. This staging of speech and thought in the third person, as if it were immediately present, is accomplished technically in the novel through free indirect discourse.[14]

Working against the grain of formalist criticism, in its examination of the strategic and ideological status of fictional technique, Bender's account also tends to overstate the case for the self-disavowal of realist discourse. It does not sufficiently historicize free indirect discourse in relation to specifically novelistic generic strategies. Bender's account relates free indirect discourse to earlier forms of realism, like Defoe's and Fielding's, but gives it no sense of self-consciousness as a strategy. Bender's ingenious use of the figure of the penitentiary to represent free indirect third person narrative tends to overstate and overdetermine the extent to which realist fiction involves a disavowal of its own fictional status; and this works to efface this ironic relation between realism and romance or sensibility genres.

I read free indirect discourse, particularly in Austen's work, as a highly self-conscious strategy, implicated within the project of counter-romance. Bender's account can be complicated by historicizing the dialectical movement of free indirect discourse within the moment at which late eighteenth-century realism establishes itself in opposition to romance. *Sense and Sensibility* involves a dramatization of this initiatory polemical, self-conscious moment of realism in opposition to sentimental romance. Another way of putting this would be to say that *Sense and Sensibility* represents that moment in the history of the novel before realism and realist strategies are naturalized, that is, before these strategies are so naturalized as to make the realist novel seem to be transparent. *Sense and Sensibility* suggests a way in which the 'reality effect',[15] to use Roland Barthes' term, is both preceded historically and present for the historical reader by an effect of inescapable irony directed at and in opposition to sentimental fiction or romance.

Free indirect discourse replaces the epistolary technique and its method of disclosure through the 'spontaneous' and reproductive flow of communication as sensibility, with a form of sympathy which simultaneously coerces, controls and corrects, as Bender points out. However, in order for the fiction of mimesis or verisimilitude to be established as a coherent, naturalized protocol of reading, whether constituted historically or in the individualized act of reading, the narrative transparency through which mimesis came to be achieved has to be read as being preceded by and implicated within an ironic and polemical relation to sentimental fiction. This polemical relation to the sentimental predecessor is there as a trace in the ironic distance of free indirect discourse.

In traditional Austen criticism, the categories of ambiguity and sympathy are essentialized [. . .]. However, a more cultural-materialist account would stress ambiguity and sympathy as textual effects produced by the historically specific formal strategy of free indirect discourse.[16] Free indirect discourse constructs a fiction of correspondence whilst maintaining distance and irony, passes off as 'free' what is tightly synthesized. Whilst it can be useful to identify free indirect discourse through the absence of formal or grammatical identifying marks to distinguish it from and/ or as authorial statement, it is significant not merely as a technique to be defined and identified in terms of noticeable grammatical anomalies, but as a strategy that bears the traces of a moment of polemical opposition to romance. In the necessary undecidability as to whether it is the narrator or the character who 'speaks', free indirect discourse dramatizes the paradox of the realist aesthetic, which is that it achieves verisimilitude through the disavowal of its own fictionality, that the narrative is the most self-referential when it is the most invisible. This pervasive irony is so enmeshed in the texture of the fiction that we might refer to the text as having a kind of 'ironicity'.

I would like to consider the ironic character of the following passage from *Sense and Sensibility*, where the text presents its characteristic critique of sensibility in the form of Elinor's reflections on the sentimental sufferings of her sister:

> But whatever might be the particulars of their separation, her sister's affliction
> was indubitable; and she thought with the tenderest compassion of that violent

sorrow which Marianne was in all probability not merely giving way to as a relief, but feeding and encouraging as a duty.

(p. 66)

This passage features the free indirect presentation of the conventional antisentimental attack on the sentimental aestheticizing of morality in terms of which the display of feeling is a duty. Strictly speaking, the passage moves from the free indirect to the indirect and back to the free indirect modes: after the free indirect phrase of 'her sister's affliction was indubitable', the indirect mode is introduced with grammatical marker 'she thought', but this quickly shifts back to the indirect narrative voice through the attribution of 'with the tenderest compassion'.

The novel's free indirect focalization through the sympathetic sister Elinor is a technique that softens the critique of the sentimental young woman, whose 'violent' feeling is mitigated because naively indulged as a 'duty'. The free indirect technique here uses Elinor's reading of Marianne to present its own mediated reading of Elinor. Elinor's reading of Marianne is a foil for the text's presentation of Elinor's feelings. The effect of this subtle indirect presentation of Elinor's 'tenderest compassion' is to suggest that 'sense' of course can feel too, that feeling is not confined to sensibility. Such a 'sense' which can feel is precisely the kind of chastened, regulated and regulating feeling which Austen cultivates in her readers through Elinor as the model of a new kind of female propriety and sensitivity. The mode of feeling that Austen proposes through the figure of Elinor involves a return to that model of virtue and feeling associated with an earlier form of sentiment, where virtue and feeling are mutually regulating. The actual term 'sentiment', however, is not available to the novel to name this feeling because it has by the late 1790s been almost thoroughly discredited. Sentiment and sensibility and sensibility fiction are for this reason critiqued and replaced by a fiction of sympathy in which criticism is effortlessly and seamlessly superimposed as irony.

Austen's form of third-person narration, and the fiction of this technique as an absolute entrance into the sentiments of others, is significant not so much as an opposition to the principle of sensibility or sentimental discourse, but as a discreet or 'genteel' refinement of it, to use the *Critical Review*'s term. Sensibility as a mechanism is naturalized and domesticated as discretion, 'tenderness'. Elinor's 'sense' is the narrator's controlling sympathy that subsumes and ironizes 'sensibility', domesticating sensibility by subjecting it to the sympathetic patronage of the sensible sister's anxious concern. As a technique of counter-romance, which in this case overwrites the originally epistolary novelistic technique of 'Elinor and Marianne',[17] free indirect discourse inscribes within the novel genre a new model both of feminine authorship and feminine authority in the exercise and refinement of feeling and discretion.

[. . .]

[A section of the chapter interprets Austen's novel *Persuasion*.]

In *Sense and Sensibility*, free indirect discourse operates as a complex mechanism which inscribes the surveilling instructress as a formal answer to the problem of pedagogy raised by sentimental novel-reading. [. . .] [The novel's] free indirect discourse chastens its sentimental heroine, but also vicariously recuperates some of the pleasure of sentimental excess through what Sedgwick refers to as Elinor's 'rapt attention' to her sister and the:

undeviating consistency with which Elinor's regard is in turn vectored in the direction of her beloved. Elinor's self-imposed obligation to offer social countenance to the restless, insulting, magnetic, and dangerous abstraction of her sister constitutes most of the plot of the novel.

(Sedgwick, 'Masturbating Girl', pp. 830–1)

For Sedgwick, Marianne's 'dangerous abstraction' refers to the masturbatory condition associated with sensibility in its incapacity to distinguish the real from the fictional.

This feature of Austen's work in chastening sensibility, but also recuperating, a vicarious form of sentimental excess accounts for why, as [Clifford] Siskin points out, 'Austen's work . . . was received not only as pleasurable, but as comfortable'.[18] There is of course nothing exceptional in Austen's attempt to make the novel safe. [. . .]

What is unprecedented about Austen is that she offers a domestic novel which is aestheticized and aestheticizing: a domestic novel as a polished, finished, aesthetic artefact. This is a domestic novel which turns moral, ethical and prudential problems into problems of aesthetic interest: the exquisite suspensions of point of view between the character and the narrator, such as can only be enabled through a highly sustained mode of free indirect discourse, gives the experience of reading a character's self-examination and examination by a narrator, and the relations between these, a new level of complexity. This is what other novelists did not achieve, at least not with the same degree of intensity. And it is the intensification of the effect which characterizes the increased aesthetic resources of Austen's fictions. It is the success of this enterprise which made early twentieth-century criticism reach for idealized categories like 'Augustan' to attempt to describe the highly aestheticized nature of Austen's texts: the transformation of pedagogical irony into something so stylized and formal and abstract that it does not even appear to resemble moralizing or 'instruction'. This refinement of moral questions into aesthetic objects of interest is also what characterizes the most important feature of the relationship between the domestic and the aesthetic in the canon-forming process we might call the coming to power of Austen's fiction.

The 'threat of writing' (Siskin) that Austen helps to solve is a threat named most emphatically by the sentimental novel[. . . . T]he threat that sentimental novels present to stable narratives of development and socialization is most emphatically figured in antinovel discourse as a form of masturbation. It is the 'discretion' with which these masturbatory threats, anxieties and pleasures are named and managed and redirected in Austen's work that marks it with what Whately calls the 'tameness of the scene' of the 'genteel' novel, and marks it as an exorcism of what Sedgwick has referred to as the sentimental novel's 'Muse of Masturbation' ('Masturbating Girl', p. 819).

One of the most explicit contemporary relations of sentimental novel-reading to masturbation is produced by the Reverend Vicesimus Knox, who succeeded his father as headmaster of Tonbridge School in 1778 until 1812, in his 'On Novel-Reading' (1778):

If it be true, that the present age is more corrupt than the preceding, the great multiplication of Novels has probably contributed to its degeneracy . . . The sentimental manner seems of late to have supplanted it. But it is matter of doubt, whether even this manner is not equally dangerous. It has given an amiable name to vice, and has obliquely excused the extravagance of the passions, by representing them as the lovely effect of sensibility . . . A softened appellation has given a degree of gracefulness to moral deformity . . . [Books] often pollute the heart in the recesses of the closet, inflame the passions at a distance from temptation, and teach all the malignity of vice in solitude.[19]

As the headmaster of an elite public boys' school, Knox would have had a very familiar knowledge of the material effects of inappropriate reading matter upon the bodies of little boys. It would have been his professional responsibility to police and curb these corporeal effects. It is not surprising, then, that Knox's knowledge of the relations between novel-reading and physical degeneracy should manifest itself in such explicit terms. The task of policing and regulating such masturbatory effects – as we now know from Foucault – cannot but avoid the discursive *production* of such effects.

Austen's text obliges Knox by inventing for the novel genre 'the discreet reader' demanded by Knox's critique. The discreet reader is, like Marianne herself, 'born to an extraordinary fate' (p. 333). She is the sociable reader, reborn from the social death of sentimental reading. Austen creates this 'discreet reader' through free indirect discourse, a Romantic technology of depth and discretion. In her account of free indirect discourse in *Sense and Sensibility*, Deidre Lynch complicates the association between free indirect discourse and depth by suggesting that free indirect discourse is not only a technology of depth but also a technology of sociability. Lynch argues that free indirect discourse involves a strategy by which:

> the narrator seems to hand over her text to the voice of the cultural context. The narrator moves over to make room not only for a rendering of subjective consciousness in its own idiom, but also for the rendering of the secondhand idiom of a vox populi.

In this way, the fact that 'Elinor's mind is full of other people's feelings . . . suggests how Austen renders interiority as a social space' (Lynch, *Economy*, p. 238). This rendering of interiority as a social space is, therefore, a critical strategy for Austen in resocializing sentiment, in reconstituting sentiment as a disciplining mode of sympathy.

In arguing that 'Austen, in disciplining the threat of writing, helped turn writing into a discipline' (Siskin, *Work of Writing*, p. 206), Siskin locates Austen in terms of the burgeoning discipline of Literature. However, there is another kind of 'discipline' which is critical here: the 'discipline' which names the cultural functions of socialization, didacticism, pedagogy, instruction – functions which continue to be undertaken by the novel genre during the nineteenth century as the intellectual discipline of Literature is being institutionalized. It is in these terms that Austen makes her mark producing a form of discipline or 'instruction' which is not punishment or 'imprisonment', but a form of 'discreet' instruction within a form of fiction that is assuming a greater 'sense' and 'taste' – to use the terms of Whately's 1821 analysis (quoted in Southam [ed.], *Casebook*, p. 39). This is not to say that instruction ceases to have any importance as a practice or category of analysis of fiction in this period. Rather, Austen is significant precisely because she continues to offer a form of instructive fiction – albeit a highly aestheticized one – even as the novel genre assumes a higher status within the generic hierarchy and becomes increasingly legitimated as a form within the practices of writing and reading which are being consolidated and autonomized as the discipline of Literature.

The novel genre becomes disciplined by offering a discreet version of the disciplining of its female subjects: it disciplines its own disciplining strategies. The novel no longer bears heavy marks of its proximity to the conduct book. Nor is it required merely to balance amusement and instruction. In the early nineteenth century, particularly in the post-Waterloo period, with the proliferation of specialist literary journals, the novel starts to develop as a sophisticated kind of cultural technology, one which is encouraged to display to a certain extent its own aestheticizing impulses, and to make good its claims for its own 'taste' and cultural capital and that of its readers.

Novel genealogies

[A section of the chapter relates Austen to the tradition of the French novel.]

> Pedigree can never be a guarantee.
> (Wilson Stephens, *Gundog Sense and Sensibility*, p. 115)[20]

[. . .]

Sense and Sensibility is clearly working within the genre of the female-authored female 'quixote' fiction exemplified in works such as Lennox's *The Female Quixote* (1752), Burney's *Evelina* (1778) and Inchbald's *A Simple Story* (1796), which chastise their heroines for excessive sensibility, but also sympathize with them. Like Lennox's fiction, *Sense and Sensibility* stages a kind of cure of masturbatory romantic excess, and does this whilst making claims for both female subjectivity and the novel genre. Inasmuch as Austen is attempting to raise the status of a genre which is vilified or held in low critical esteem because of its association with a predominantly female readership, part of the project of gaining generic respectability for the novel involves making claims for and on behalf of a particular kind of female subjectivity. It is a responsive but sensible – in the sense of thinking and feeling – and properly educated, upwardly mobile, upper middle-class or gentry female subjectivity. The differences between the marriage plots of *Sense and Sensibility* and Lennox's original female quixote fiction index changing patterns of marriage and social mobility. Lennox's *Female Quixote* (1752) coincides with the period debate predating the 1754 Marriage Act. Like the Act, Lennox's fiction seems to offer the 'cure' or solution to what became known as 'the heiress problem': specifically, the threat posed to landed families of the downward social mobility of the heiresses through marriages of choice. Lennox's quixote is the heiress, with grand delusions about her own power – in realistic terms, the heiress who is cured of an allegedly excessive estimation of her own power and prerogative for choice in the marriage market. The reason why Lennox's heiress has such an elevated sense of her own power is because she had historically become a powerful player in the transmission of property. So whilst *The Female Quixote* discountenances the downward female mobility of heiresses, *Sense and Sensibility*, on the other hand, needs to vindicate the upward social mobility of bourgeois women. [. . .]

In *Sense and Sensibility*, the vindication of upward mobility occurs, nonetheless, through a tropology of the fall. The structural logic of *Sense and Sensibility*'s parody of the novel of sensibility is informed by the narrativization of the trope of the fall of woman. This trope underpins the text's revision of the sentimental plot and the critique of sensibility, in which literal and symbolic falls are continually repeated and interimplicated. Austen narrates the economic fall of the Dashwood women, ironically exposing and implicating the operations of primogeniture through the pointed genealogy which opens the text. Whilst the ironic narration of the disinheritance of a family of women would seem to enunciate a 'wrongs of woman' thesis, a radical critique of the institution of primogeniture is not involved. Rather, in keeping with the tactics of neoclassical misogynist satire, the decisive moment in the economic fall of the Dashwood women occurs when the Dashwoods are dispossessed by one of their own sex, Mrs John Dashwood. The representation of the wrongs of primogeniture involves not the strategies of radical critique, but those of conservative satire, in which the representation of the victims of primogeniture occurs through a lament for the paternal aegis which is finally restored in the figure of Brandon. At the level of narrative telos, the repetition of the fall and the instantiation of rebirth and marriage gradually undercut the irony of the framing genealogy so that the 'wrongs of woman' are those wrongs for which women must be held accountable. This version of the 'wrongs of woman' distinguishes Austen from Mary Wollstonecraft, in a way which marks Austen's conservative status and complicates any simple or ahistorical claim for Austen's form of feminism. It aligns her with a form of Tory feminism, which validates female independence but within the limits of the paternally authorized and authorizing structures of social hierarchy, church and family.[21]

Just as Marianne is reborn, and that rebirth stages the disciplining and professionalization of the British novel, Brandon and the paternal aristocratic class he represents are also reborn and professionalized. Brandon would seem to win Marianne on account of his proficiency at negotiating safe boundaries between the fictive and the real-life heroine – a proficiency demonstrated by his reading and narration of the sentimental plot. There is, however, another strategy open to him, which he also exploits: this is the classic male sentimental aristocratic gesture of sympathy as benevolence. By bestowing the 'favour' (p. 313) of the living at Delaford on Edward Ferrars, Brandon buys Elinor off and rewards her for her collaboration in wooing Marianne. For she is in a sense a kind of marriage-broker. The granting of the favour offers Brandon another opportunity for sentimental display – the benevolent display of wealth.[22] And it is yet another testimony to Austen's discretion that by this point in the text Colonel Brandon has been sufficiently rehabilitated as a member of the aristocracy for such a display to seem innocuous.

Typically, as in other Austen novels, the recuperative cultural labour of celebrating the wealthy aristocracy is disavowed by satirically relegating it to the more vulgar characters, such as Mrs Dashwood: 'His fortune too! . . . and though I neither know, nor desire to know, what it really is, I am sure it must be a good one' (p. 297), and then John Dashwood 'But, I confess, it would give me great pleasure to call Colonel Brandon brother. His property here, his place, his house, every thing in such respectable and excellent condition – and his woods!' (p. 330). In granting the living, Colonel Brandon's desirability as a sympathetic man coincides with his desirability as a member of the landed aristocracy. This gesture conflates the two significant and discrete contemporary moral categories of benevolence and sympathy. Whilst sympathy is reproductive, benevolence presupposes distance, effectively reinscribing the class differences that are rhetorically erased in sentimental discourse through the idealized current of sympathetic correspondence that flows across classes. Through this benevolent gesture, Brandon is made to figure the rehabilitation of the paternal aristocratic class *as* a paternalizing class.

   [. . .]

Notes

 1 Vicesimus Knox, 'On Reading Trifling Literature Called Summer Reading', *Winter Evenings: or, Lucubrations on Life and Letters* (1788, 3 vols, New York: Garland, 1972), iii, p. 151.
 2 Quoted in R.W. Chapman, 'Introductory Note to *Sense and Sensibility*', *The Novels of Jane Austen*, ed. R.W. Chapman, 3rd edn, 5 vols (Oxford, Clarendon Press, 1946) i, p. xiii.
 3 [Quoted in B.C. Southam (ed.) *Jane Austen: 'Sense and Sensibility', 'Pride and Prejudice' and 'Mansfield Park': A Casebook* (London: Macmillan, 1987), p. 80.]
 4 [Margaret Anne Doody, Introduction, *Sense and Sensibility*, by Jane Austen, ed. Margaret Anne Doody (Oxford University Press, 1990), p. viii.]
 5 Margaret Russell, *De Quincey's Romanticism: Canonical Minority and the Forms of Transmission* (Cambridge university Press, 1997), p. 238.
 6 For Ian Watt, *Sense and Sensibility* is a leading example of the 'domestic comedy [which is] a characteristically English genre' (quoted in Southam [ed.], *Casebook*, p. 118).
 7 [Eve Kosofsky Sedgwick, 'Jane Austen and the Masturbating Girl', *Critical Inquiry* 17 (1991), pp. 817–37, p. 826.]
 8 [Ian Watt, *The Rise of the Novel: Studies in Defoe, Richardson, and Fielding* (1957; Harmondsworth: Penguin, 1963), p. 302.]
 9 For a persuasive account of Burney's 'production of a brave new world of female interiority', see Deidre Lynch, [*The Economy of Character: Novels, Market Culture, and the Business of Inner Meaning* (University of Chicago Press, 1998)], pp. 164–206 at p. 167. For an earlier argument on Burney's pioneering use of free indirect discourse, see Margaret Anne Doody, *Frances Burney: The Life in the Works* (New Brunswick, NJ: Rutgers University Press, 1988), p. 256.
10 Pierre Bourdieu, 'The Field of Cultural Production', *The Field of Cultural Production[: Essays on Art and Literature* (Oxford: Polity Press, 1993)], p. 31.
11 [Jane Austen, *Northanger Abbey, Lady Susan, The Watsons*, and *Sanditon*, ed. John Davie (Oxford University Press, 1980), p. 150.]
12 [Jane Austen, *Sense and Sensibility* (1811), ed. James Kinsley and Claire Lamont (Oxford University Press, 1984), p. 47–9.]
13 [Samuel Richardson,] *Clarissa or The History of a Young Lady* (1748), ed. Angus Ross (Harmondsworth, Penguin, 1985), p. 36.
14 [John Bender, *Imagining the Penitentiary: Fiction and Architecture of the Mind in Eighteenth-Century England* (University of Chicago Press, 1987), p. 227.]
15 The 'effet de réel' is Roland Barthes' coinage for the textual motivation of nineteenth-century French realism; see 'The Reality Effect', in *The Rustle of Language*, trans. Richard Howard (London, Basil Blackwell, 1986), pp. 141–8.
16 For traditional accounts of free indirect discourse in Austen, see Graham Hough, 'Narrative and Dialogue in Jane Austen' (1970), *Selected Essays* (Cambridge University Press, 1978), pp. 46–82; David Lodge 'Jane Austen's Novels: Form and Structure', in David Grey (ed.), *Jane Austen Companion* (New York, Macmillan, 1986), pp. 175–7. [. . .]
17 ['Elinor and Marianne' is first referred to as an early version of *Sense and Sensibility* in notes by Cassandra Austen; see *Minor Works*, ed. R.W. Chapman, revised by B.C. Southam (Oxford, Clarendon Press, 1967), plate facing p. 242.]
18 [Clifford Siskin, *The Work of Writing: Literature and Social Change in Britain, 1700–1830* (Baltimore and London: Johns Hopkins University Press, 1998), p. 202.]
19 [Vicesimus Knox, 'On Novel-Reading', *Essays, Moral and Literary*, 2 vols (1778; London: printed for W. Baynes and Son, 1822), I, p. 96.]
20 [(2001) Shrewsbury: Swan Hill Press.]
21 For an explanation of Austen's Tory feminism, see Marilyn Butler, Introduction, [*Jane Austen and the War of Ideas* (1975) (Oxford: Clarendon Press, 1989)], p. xxiii.
22 On this strategy, see Robert Markley, 'Sentimentality as Performance: Shaftesbury, Sterne, and the Theatrics of Virtue', in Felicity Nussbaum and Laura Brown (eds), [*The New Eighteenth Century: Theory, Politics, English Literature* (New York: Methuen, 1987)], pp. 210–30.

20 Writing/righting gender

Jacqueline M. Labbe

Recent work by Dror Wahrman (2004), Elisabeth Krimmer (2004), and others has sought to place just when the familiar literary and social constructions of femininity and masculinity solidified into their modern forms, by which I mean stereotypes: strong, silent, repressive, sexualized men; passive, docile, submissive, expressive women.[1] For Warhman, this has been effected by about 1780; for Krimmer, 'around 1800' is the preferred moment. Thomas Laqueur's charting of the substitution of the two-sex for the one-sex model also focuses on the eighteenth century as a period of flux wherein science and culture decided that women and men were not obverses but complements (1992). The ongoing desire to establish the exact nature of the male/female construct stutters, in this period; *something* happens in the period we have labelled Romantic, but there has been no real consensus about when it happens or, indeed, what it constitutes. This essay contributes to the speculation, building on the idea that the period can be seen as an Age of Experimentation and an Age of Classification, simultaneously. Clifford Siskin's ongoing work (1998, 2001) exploring what he calls 'System' illustrates how the philosophy and knowledge matrices of the late eighteenth and early nineteenth centuries pull inexorably towards order and the creation of categories while at the same time acknowledging and relying on disruptions of both. Gender and gendering are expressions of a desire and need to classify and stabilize male and female behaviour, but the fact that the period cannot agree on a standard narrative belies the idea of consensus or even stasis. What does it mean to be a manly man or a womanly woman, when presented with Lord Orville, Delamere, at least three Willoughbys, at least three Walsinghams, Caleb Williams, Darcy; or Evelina, Emmeline, Rosalie, Belinda, or the many Charlottes, Janes, and Catherines? While literature is not required to speak with one voice, nonetheless there is a striking variety present in the novels of the period resonant with experimentation and classification, with anxiety and hopefulness, with avenues that open and shut themselves repeatedly.

Experimentation and Classification underpin a working hypothesis that the gender flux evident in the novels of the period reflects the lack of a general theory of subjectivity that is itself inflected by the uncertainties and anxieties of Revolution.[2] Wollstonecraft's revolution in female manners is only one such expression. Although the Romantic period saw the flourishing of conduct manuals and other texts that sought to regularize gender roles, and subsequent studies of Romantic-period literature have clarified the ways in which authors maintain gender convention through imagery and metaphor (especially in relation to the construction of Nature), the earlier years of the Napoleonic wars saw the publication of novels in which characters continually strayed outside these boundaries. In novels by Smith, Robinson, and Edgeworth, men were not-masculine and women were not-feminine in intriguing ways, suggesting that the social turmoil occasioned by war was creeping into fiction, creating new behavioural subsets. However, what is even more intriguing is the lack of a lasting effect this had. By the 18-teens, the moment of flux, and opportunity, has passed; gender (especially but not exclusively femininity) begins to be righted, with its punishments and rewards realigned. In novels by Austen and Shelley, the gendered identities of men and women are reified.

This is not to suggest that within these general movements there were not countervails; indeed, at the heart of the idea that 'something happens' in the eighteenth century is the uncertainty about exactly what that something is. For every Chevalier D'Eon, there is a Harriot Freke, with cross-dressing not used to empower the subject and to upset expectations but rather to act as a corrective, a signifier of error that is suitably punished and order restored. And yet even Harriot Freke disallows easy assignments of praise and blame: for all her meanness, she also reminds Edgeworth's readers of the constraints men and women both assumed: she is neither not-woman nor not-man. She is, in fact, an unsuccessful enacter of gender, unable to convince either her fellow-characters or the reader that she is what she isn't. Indeed, while the OED provides a definition of 'freak' as 'whim', 'vagary', or 'caprice', it should be noted that 'freke' also appears, intriguingly (albeit obsolete), as a Middle English word for a 'warrior, champion; but usually a mere poetic synonym for "man"'. Even etymologically, then, Harriot Freke both *is* and *isn't*. And cross-dressing is only the most obvious form of gender-bending; behaviour, as described in the novels of the period, presents an altogether more nuanced picture. When placed within a context of revolution, both political and cultural, novelists responded to the possibilities for change as well as the desire for order and classification. Something happened, then: gender stabilizes, and it doesn't; sex is recognized as essential to gender, but it's not; behaviour becomes inextricable from a sexed identity, or it doesn't.

Wahrman's reliance on a binary system of gender means that the various examples he draws on: the Chevalier, cross-dressed women warriors, breeches roles, must always fall on one side or the other, by about 1780. Even sensibility loses its destabilizing power, since, as he notes (following Claudia Johnson), 'sentimental traits that had previously been considered feminine were redefined as masculine, thus disarming sensibility of its potential to disrupt gender categories' (Wahrman 2004: 39). Describing the 'hasty retreat of the moist-eyed man of feeling' as marked by *The History of Sandford and Merton*, he asserts that any display of emotion after this was made meaningful by its masculinized restraint. Is it so clear that representations of behaviour conformed so readily to a binary depiction? It is true, of course, that public declarations of correct conduct often relied on modifiers like manly and womanly, and yet the behaviour described, and ascribed separately to men and women, nevertheless often featured the same actions and reactions: tears, fortitude, restraint, enthusiasm. Consider Charlotte Smith's panoply of hysterical yet lovable men. Delamere's passion for Emmeline drives him throughout the novel. He is introduced to the reader as a typical dissolute young nobleman, sure that the Orphan of the Castle is his for the taking. Confronted with her strength of character and of mind, he spends the rest of the novel in hot (literally: he even develops a fever) pursuit of Emmeline. His passion often breaks out in tears and his lack of self-control eventually leads to his death in a duel. Charles Montgomery in *Ethelinde* expresses his love for the heroine through an exaggerated physical and emotional reliance on her, even as he leaves the country to make his fortune and earn his right to marry her. Then there is Montague Thorold in *Celestina*, whose overwhelming desire for the heroine transforms him from a rather nondescript undergraduate to a writer of sentimental poetry, who shadows Celestina from the Highlands to the rural South-West of England, and whose attachment never wavers in the face of public suspicion of her virtue. Orlando Somerive, perhaps Smith's most famous hero, pays court to two women: his patron, Mrs Rayland, and his lover, Monimia. Mocked for his courtliness by his rakish older brother, he finds regular reasons not to pursue his intended courses of action so that he may spend more time with his beloved, whom he regularly oppresses with his extreme emotional responses.

Throughout her corpus, Smith writes heroes whose emotionalism belies Wahrman's 'hasty retreat', but more importantly these heroes are sustained and rewarded for their sensibility. Delamere wins Emmeline's promise of marriage to the extent that she agrees to a binding contract (she does not love him, but submits to his love for her). Montgomery gains the economic independence that allows him to claim Ethelinde. Thorold, it is true, does not marry Celestina, but he gets the next best thing: her French cousin Anzoletta, as alike to her as a twin. Orlando triumphs doubly in love, by marrying Monimia even without economic security, and by winning the Rayland estate via testament from his courted patron, Mrs Rayland. The Man of Feeling, in other words, exists well into the 1790s in Smith's novels, and he is rewarded as such; his emotionalism is treated as an intrinsic part of his manly attractions and exerts a control over the heroines and the plots that, in these four novels, suggests a general condoning of his excesses. Then Smith does something interesting: she continues the characterization but begins to vary the morality. The hinge is *Montalbert*, where the hero's emotionalism is so uncontrolled that it leads him into the extreme error of assuming his virtuous wife's infidelity and nearly costs her her life. Smith is clear that Montalbert's behaviour is unwarranted and uncondoned – and yet apart from its ramifications, the behaviour itself is the same hysterical over-reaction to events that gained the eventual nod in the other novels. If it is true, as Chris Mounsey suggests, that 'gender was unstable in a society that did not wish it to be so and demanded ideological support from its fictions' (2001: 14),[3] then Smith demonstrates both sides of this instability: first, she constitutes feeling as indicative of a manliness that her novels will support; then, she constitutes feeling as indicative of a manliness that her novels will not support. The flux is located in the impact of the feeling; in other words, it is not a problem that men feel strongly and act on that strong feeling. They must simply feel *rightly*. 'The urgency and the persistence of the rhetoric used to reinforce traditional gender roles', says Conrad Brunstrom, in itself indicates the flexibility of such roles in the period; gender is both 'precious' and 'insecure' (Brunstrom 2001: 29, 47). Smith's men of feeling demonstrate, contra Wahrman, that the 1790s featured masculinities whose primary mover was emotional susceptibility.[4]

Of course, Smith wrote feeling women as well, although never simply: Emmeline sets the tone with her reliance on reason and self-sufficiency; Ethelinde complicates all notions of womanliness with what can only be called her performativity[5]; Celestina makes use of her emotional reactions to situations to produce art in the form of poetry; Monimia evolves from a superstitious and frightened child-woman to an Emmeline-like self-sufficiency (and coincidentally an enabler of Orlando's sensibility). Womanly sensibility in the earlier novels is characterized by strength and autonomy. Again, the hinge text is *Montalbert*, wherein Rosalie's immersion in full-on textbook sensibility means she is unable to withstand the importunities of Montalbert that they marry secretly, unable to defend herself when he conceives an irrational conviction that she has been unfaithful (compare a similar scenario in both *Emmeline* and *Celestina*, where the heroines proudly reject such suspicions), and nearly unable to survive his tyrannical treatment.[6] Rosalie's victimization is the result not of Montalbert's manner of feeling, but of her own surrender to a womanly model that has done away with any form of strength or independence. In *Belinda*, Edgeworth will write a character whose devotion to a literary mode of sensibility is encouraged, indeed created, by a male author-figure, Clarence Hervey, who has read too much Rousseau and seeks to create the perfect wifelet. But although Virginia St. Pierre's sensibility causes her to fall in love with a portrait and to subsume her own wishes to those of her 'author', the most she risks is unhappiness. Rosalie's extreme sensibility nearly costs her her reason and her life. The novel suggests that this most womanly of feelings, with its self-sacrificial devotion to another, is a life-threatening condition on a literal level. Far from condoning it, *Montalbert* inaugurates Smith's authorial unease with such a mode and subsequent novels balance it with strong, reasonable, and fully independent women such as Althea in *Marchmont*.

Sensibility is, however, only one aspect of a gendering that is more complicated than a simply binary model would allow. Sexuality, for instance, following the binary, would seem to be the province of male characters and 'fallen' female ones. But Smith makes an artful use of doubles in *Desmond*, with the English Geraldine Verney and the French Josephine de Boisbelle creating a composite woman who is both mother and lover. Although the novel is epistolary, the overarching point of view is maintained by Desmond, who simultaneously desires Geraldine and desires to maintain her purity. Josephine functions as Geraldine's stand-in sexually, providing a bed and a body, and eventually a child, thus allowing Desmond to engender his own binary. But the novel does not fully endorse Desmond's point of view – the ending ambivalently portrays his acquiring of Geraldine in the light of possession, aligning him with Geraldine's abusive and villainous first husband – and moreover it does not condemn Josephine for her actions. Josephine carries on the sexual activity Lady Adelina Trelawney begins in *Emmeline* and which varied secondary characters undertake throughout Smith's corpus. The significance lies in the novels' refusal to present such women as morally suspect or culpable. Although the women themselves might be overcome with regret – Adeline indulges in complete self-abasement, for instance – the plots carefully present characters like Betty Richards in *The Old Manor House* and Emily Cathcart in *Celestina* as key to the successful denouement of the stories. As such, they are morally responsible and respectable; what they are *not* is punished. Again, Smith's novels work outside a set of gendered expectations: her men can be manly and emotional wrecks, her women can be sexual and respectable, sensibility can be a very bad thing indeed. The underlying experimentation refuses the ordered classification of persons and behaviours.

It is easy to concentrate on Smith; her novels provide a variety not always apparent in other writers, and her output spans the decade with a regularity that supports the sense that the 1790s make a difference to the period as a whole. But Robinson's *Walsingham* provides one of the most striking examples of a not-man/not-woman from the period: the cross-dressed Sidney Aubrey who, as Julie Shaffer notes in her essential article on the novel, is neither 'contain[ed]' nor 'punish[ed] . . . for her transgressions', but 'remains convincing until her mother makes her secret public' (Shaffer 2001: 137). Like Smith, Robinson allows her counter-creation a full existence within the story, unhemmed-in by convention or adherence to a binary. Sidney occupies both subject positions, and in doing so blurs and smears the very idea of gendered boundaries. *Walsingham*, published in 1797, closely follows, chronologically, the 1795 publication of the hinge-text *Montalbert*, which also features not one but two characters named Walsingham: one a dissolute rake, the other (his cousin) his nobler namesake who acts as Rosalie's knight-errant while pining for the love of another.[7] Robinson's Walsingham begins the novel embittered at what he perceives as the usurpation of his rightful inheritance by his cousin Sidney, and ends the novel endowed with said inheritance once Sidney is revealed to be female (and hence ineligible to inherit). Shaffer argues that the novel 'tolerates what [Dianne] Dugaw and Wahrman demonstrate was widely culturally intolerable' in the late eighteenth century (2001: 138); more than that, the novel demonstrates the continued fluidity of gender assignment. It comes, again, down to behaviour: Sidney acts (and dresses) male, and hence his masculinity is unchallenged. When 'he' dresses female, the only change is in costume: 'he appears desirable as a male . . . for precisely those reasons that also apparently make him desirable as a woman' (Shaffer 2001: 158). As Shaffer establishes, Sidney's 'gender' is tied entirely to surface qualities of dress and what might be called dressage: he performs male in breeches and performs female in skirts. But *who* and *how* he is remains stable. Although Shaffer concludes that the novel 'destabilize[s]' 'both gender and sexuality' (2001: 160), it could also be said that *Walsingham* participates in the trend to experiment with and query exactly those categories of gender and sexuality that rely on or assume a straightforward binary.[8] Instead of destabilizing what was fixed, it pursues a further avenue in positing the positively *unfixed*.

When Edgeworth publishes *Belinda* in 1801, sensibility has become enough of a comic trait that she can, as noted, present its potential for vagary in the character of Virginia. The affectionate way in which Virginia is rewarded with her 'true love' suggests that such overblown sensibility calls out for protection and support rather than condemnation, an effective contrast to Smith's Rosalie and a firm indication of its dwindling favour as an aspect of womanliness. And yet the very fact that Virginia achieves her girlish dream of love within a novel where the other characters are required to work very hard indeed to achieve theirs indicates a lingering sense that passively awaiting one's prince may, after all, be easier than actively seeking him out. Belinda, famously cold, reveals her passions only involuntarily, in her propensity to blush. She is used to demonstrate the pros and cons of making an intellectually considered choice of marriage partner, and her eventual reunion with Clarence Hervey satisfies the dramatic instincts of Lady Delacour, at least: the novel's conclusion *en tableau* captures a moment of clarity in a plot that has explored the ramifications of a series of misunderstandings and miscommunications. Rational Belinda, however, begins the novel as Miss Portman, husband-hunter, who learns to hide her feelings by observing the results of display by others: Clarence's flirtations with Lady Delacour, Lady Delacour's flippant disregard for the feelings of others, Lord Delacour's self-protective layer of drink. And the novel itself undercuts its seeming reliance on such 'wise' characters as Lady Anne Percival by showing her partiality for Mr Vincent as Belinda's marriage-partner to be founded on a truly stunningly uninsightful assumption of his virtue based on his social position.

Belinda's portrayal of the womanly and the manly is focalized in the character of Harriot Freke, who as discussed unsuccessfully cross-dresses in that her disguise is always already transparent, but whose very presence upsets a gender binary by allowing her to exist at all. Her identity as female is always undercut by her performances as male, and the very visibility of the performance ensures a constant comment on her very obvious freakishness. And although she is usually discussed as an unreservedly unpleasant character, it must be noted that her very repulsiveness proves attractive in that she seduces Lady Delacour and other characters into the cross-dressing game, and that her interest in Belinda verges on the sexual and proves fascinating for Belinda, who can't look away. It may be impossible to rehabilitate Harriot Freke, but by including her Edgeworth draws our attention to the fact that there is no easy assumption of the traits of either manliness or womanliness. Her mirror-image, and perhaps the most womanly character, in the end, is Lady Delacour, if we define the gender through the lens of caring for others: Lady Delacour, unlike Belinda, completes a journey from disappointed love (for Mr Perceval) to marital and maternal rapprochement via a heavily symbolic breast cancer scare. Lady Delacour occupies the 'heart' of the novel as well as its 'court', its central setting. Her elaborate personality provides another thread to the experimentation with gender identities that so occupies the period, and *Belinda* as a whole parades its competing models across the page: even Harriot Freke has her moment. In the end, while various marriages have been arranged and/or assumed, what is left unfixed is any preferred mode of gendering: rational and reserved, exuberant and emotional, thoughtless and unreflective, complacent and self-assured all occupy the same space, literally, in the *tableau vivant*.

In the background, and forming the historical context for these experiments in gender, is the ongoing war and its concomitant social ructions. The 1790s' willingness to take risks gives way to a new century's generally subdued acceptance of restriction and limitation. Austen is drafting and redrafting her novels in this period, from the early 1790s onwards, and her texts contain striking examples of men who are manly and women who are womanly and who are rewarded as such. Austen is adept at leading her readers to 'right' conclusions, so that we understand that we are to admire Elizabeth, for instance, and feel regretful at the deficiencies of Mary Crawford. If we simply compare their characters, however, their personalities are interestingly similar: both are independent, both speak their minds, both are spirited, sparkling, sexually attractive women. Louisa Musgrove, who fancies herself spirited, sparkling, and sexually attractive, is made to learn otherwise. Models of sensibility are reimported and made newly attractive: Jane Fairfax and Jane Bennet receive their due rewards. Equally, it is plain that Maria must be punished for her sexual transgression, even if the punishment has its comic undertones: to be banished in the company of Mrs Norris is not quite as deadly as the confinement in a convent brought about by a *lettre du cachet* suffered by Maria's predecessor, Lady Frances Crofts in Smith's *Emmeline*, for instance.[9] And despite Austen's documented lack of enthusiasm for Fanny Price, we understand that her self-sacrifice, timidity, and deference are part of her charm.

Similarly, the strong and silent Darcy claims the status of hero, who must be led to emotional literacy by Elizabeth and his own heart. Mr Knightley wins Emma by being as much a father-figure as a lover. Charming and rakish Wickham, charming and rakish Willoughby, charming and rakish Henry Crawford: all are duly outed and then sidelined as cads. Emotional display is always suspect: Frank Churchill manipulates his own emotional vulnerability by allowing his love for Jane to be translated by others as desire for Emma. Henry Tilney attracts the inexperienced Catherine mainly by virtue of being more experienced, and the narrator makes us fully aware that her main attraction is the pleasant way she finds him attractive. And one suspects that Marianne's main attraction for Colonel Brandon is her youth: that is, her external form, face, and aspect. It may be that as a latter-day Eliza who only just barely escapes Eliza's fate, she represents a second chance for him, but even this means that Marianne is symbolic rather than real, and that the essence of the person, that which Smith and Robinson, and to a certain extent Edgeworth, spent many pages establishing via lengthy adventures and plot developments, has been replaced by external markers of identity. An experimental attitude which allowed men to be feeling and women to be rational, which thereby detached such essences from the gender of the person and allowed them to free-float, is righting itself, culturally, by the time Austen writes her undoubtedly attractive and readable characters whose gender identity is, by and large, stable and typical.

Which brings us to Mary Shelley and a very brief comparison of *Frankenstein* and *The Last Man*. The Creature has been the subject of too many feminist readings for those to be covered here: suffice to say the maternal, the wifely, the daughterly, the desperate, the outsider, the disrupter and more have been explored as aspects of its 'thing[ness,] put together'. But the Creature, however central to Victor and by extension to Walton, is mainly marginal to the text; even its direct speech is bookended at the story's close. Embedded in the core of the story is Safie, a character utterly without personality but absolutely smothered in a fully feminised gendering. Her function is to be attractive to Felix and to contrast, as do Elizabeth and Justine, with the Creature's oversizedness. *Frankenstein* thus pivots on a character whose gendered identity could not be less experimental even as it explores the ramification of creating a being *without* gender, a Creature made from male bodies but whose subjectivity is pointedly *uncivilized*. Ten years later, in *The Last Man*, Shelley writes a plot fantastic in its outline and yet utterly gendered; even its cross-dressing character Evadne does so only in abjected desire to follow her man and who, as Shaffer notes, 'dies in battle as a (fe)male warrior' (2001: 137): that is, exposed as a woman and regendered as womanly. Lionel and Lord Raymond are typically manly, as is Adrian, even if he displays a Shelleyan delicacy; Perdita, Idris, and Evadne are typically womanly. The men do battle, with each other and the elements; the women love their men. It is dispiritingly conventional in its gender dynamics, however experimental it is in its futuristic vision. Gender has been thoroughly righted.

Linda M. Shires tells us that what was a positive possibility, in terms of gendering, in the 1790s has become a social threat by the 1830s (Shires 1992). Indeed, by surveying the portrayals of women and men and their grapplings with womanly and manly behaviour in this period, what is striking is not what stops happening at the end of the eighteenth century, but rather the variety with which things keep happening. The Age of Experimentation, with its excitation derived from flux and change, in the end acted in service to a move to re-order, create classes, categories, and systems: even the word 'gender' as it applies to 'classifying', 'dividing', or 'differentiating' human behaviour appears in the OED as current by the 1820s. Possibilities, supported by the social uncertainty and disruption caused by war and conflict, subside to consolidation and retreat, and a validation of systems and categories with hard boundaries. The end of war brought with it social recalibration, ironically enough informed by the scientific developments that exploited new tools and discoveries to posit new Truths. Something had, indeed, happened.

Notes

1 For the purposes of this essay, I will use the terms 'womanly' and 'manly' as aligned more closely with ideals and practicalities of behaviour and identity in the Romantic period.
2 Robin Ikegami (1997) is not alone in noting that the 'principles of the French Revolution, the questions it raised about previously unquestionable ideas, challenged the basic fabric of British society' (225). As she argues, one aspect of this basic fabric is stable gender identities: the 'concern over the instability of gender was a very real one . . . for thinkers and activists on both sides of the Channel. . . . [T]he greatest threat is the levelling of the status of men and women in relation to each other' (224). Vivien Jones (1993) had earlier made a similar point, that there was a concern 'to maintain national stability through sexual propriety and a traditional division of gender roles' (300). And Lisa Wood (2003) reflects a general consensus when she argues that, by the end of the 1790s, 'it had become not only unpopular, but also dangerous to vindicate "revolutionary and jacobinical notions" in print since a series of parliamentary acts made such publications treasonable' (82). It is thus all the more intriguing that the period saw such variations in condoned gendered behaviour in the novel.
3 Mounsey derives this from Patricia Meyer Spacks; see 13 passim.
4 Jan Wellington (2001) argues that stereotypes of national identity also draw on patterns of feeling, to oppose 'the English character as reserved (but impassioned), serious, deep, artless, original, and independent' with 'the French character which was seen as effusive, lighthearted, shallow, changeable, artful, and slavish' (35). Interestingly, the 'French' style of feeling accords almost directly with Smith's mode of manly emotionalism, while the 'English' maps nicely onto Smith's depiction of womanly behaviour.
5 For a nuanced and sophisticated reading of *Ethelinde* in terms of (en)acted gender, see Joseph Morrissey (2013).
6 Smith continues to write such susceptible heroines after *Montalbert*, culminating in the raped and imprisoned wife Elizabeth in Volume I of *The Letters of a Solitary Wanderer*.
7 Walsingham, of course, is a familiar historical English name, which makes it all the more interesting that both Smith and Robinson choose it for their characters.
8 As Elisabeth Krimmer (2004), in *In the Company of Men: Crossed-Dressed Women Around 1800*, says, 'stories about cross-dressers were employed to work through competing concepts of the body and to imagine different models of gender identity' (1–2). This requires the 'reveal' as in *Walsingham*: if no-one knows that someone cross-dresses, then in actual terms the binary is maintained.
9 There are multiple intriguing overlaps and links between Smith's and Austen's works. See Labbe (2008, 2010) for initial discussions of these.

Works cited

Brunstrom, C. (2001) ' "Be male and female still": An ABC of hyperbolic masculinity in the eighteenth century', in C. Mounsey (ed.) *Presenting gender: Changing sex in early-modern culture*, Cranbury, NJ: Rosemont Publishing.
Ikegami, R. (1997) 'Femme-hommes, she-bishops, and hyenas in petticoats: Women reformers and gender treason, 1789–1830', *Women's Studies: An Inter-disciplinary Journal* 26: 223–239.
Jones, V. (1993) 'Femininity, nationalism and romanticism: The politics of gender in the revolution controversy', *History of European Ideas* 16: 299–305.
Krimmer, E. (2004) *In the company of men: Cross-dressed women around 1800*, Detroit: Wayne State University Press.
Labbe, J. (2008) 'Narrating seduction: Charlotte Smith and Jane Austen', in J. Labbe (ed.) *Charlotte Smith in British Romanticism*, London: Pickering and Chatto.
Labbe, J. (2010) 'What happens at the party: Jane Austen converses with Charlotte Smith', *Persuasions Online* 30.2, www.jasna.org/persuasions/on-line/vol30no2/labbe.html.

Laqueur, T. (1992) *Making sex: Body and gender from the Greeks to Freud*, Cambridge: Harvard University Press.

Morrissey, J. (2013) 'Gentry women and work and leisure 1770–1820', unpublished thesis, University of Warwick.

Mounsey, C. (ed.) (2001) *Presenting gender: Changing sex in early-modern culture*, Lewisburg: Bucknell University Press.

Shaffer, J. (2001) 'Cross-dressing and the nature of gender in Mary Robinson's *Walsingham*', in C. Mounsey (ed.) *Presenting gender: Changing sex in early-modern culture*, Lewisburg: Bucknell University Press.

Shires, L.M. (1992) 'Of maenads, mothers, and feminized males: Victorian readings of the French revolution', in L.M. Shires (ed.) *Rewriting the Victorians: Theory, history, and the politics of gender*, New York and London: Routledge.

Siskin, C. (1998) 'Novels and systems', *Novel* 34: 9–31.

Siskin, C. (2001) 'The year of the System', in R. Cronin (ed.) *1798: The year of the Lyrical Ballads*, Basingstoke: Macmillan.

Wahrman, D. (2004) *The making of the modern self: Identity and culture in eighteenth-century England*, New Haven: Yale University Press.

Wellington, J. (2001) 'Blurring the borders of nation and gender: Mary Wollstonecraft's character (r)evolution', in Adriana Craciun and Kari Lokke (eds) *Rebellious hearts: British women writers and the French Revolution*, Albany: SUNY Press.

Wood, L. (2003) 'Bachelors and "old maids": Antirevolutionary British women writers and narrative authority after the French revolution', *Tulsa Studies in Women's Literature* 22: 81–98.

Part 6
Racism, nationalism, imperialism

Introduction

One of the most prominent registers of new historicism's impact over the past several decades can be observed in the increasing interest that critics have taken in the way that British Romantic literature represents the shifting and consolidating boundaries of the British nation and empire, and in the way that literature represents ruling and subject populations. So crucial are these issues of how community is constructed and how its members are identified and policed, included or excluded, that concerns in this section routinely emerge in other contexts: in Mellor's discussion of women's writing and the public sphere in Part 3, for instance, or in Ann Frey's discussion of literary authority and the state in De Quincey in Part 4. The British nation and its imperial dominions have a long history, and critics have drawn on important historical and theoretical work by Benedict Anderson and Linda Colley on nationalism (Anderson 1983; Colley 1992), and by Edward Said on cultural histories of imperialism (Said 1978), in addition to many other works by scholars who have elaborated on the process of nation- and empire-formation in great detail.

The representation of specific places, and persons associated with those places, has been considered one of the hallmarks of Romantic writing for quite some time. Geoffrey Hartman's work on Wordsworth is well known for analyzing the poet's commitment to a "genius loci" or "spirit of the place" which binds people to emotionally charged locations (Hartman 1964). But historicist criticism has focused more intently on these places of attachment, and on the particular political terms in which attachments are understood and regulated. Scholars have increasingly understood the literary alignments with places to involve communities rather than individuals; communities are often understood to be defined by specific interests or shared categories of identity. Even this critical standpoint is far from new: in *The Roots of Romanticism*, based on his Mellon lectures in 1965, philosopher and historian Isaiah Berlin connected British Romanticism with fervent nationalism, because nationalism was able to provide a commitment to freedom that avoided abstractions and universalisms associated with the French Revolution (Berlin 1999). But later historicist accounts of the Romantic age added greater depth to this kind of argument: Anne Janowitz connected the English interest in ruins and landscapes with a desire to anchor nationality in nature and tradition (Janowitz 1990); David Simpson showed how such impulses composed part of a collective British revolt against "theory" that was associated with enlightenment rationality (Simpson 1993: 4). These and other accounts contributed to a growing consensus that circumstances in the late eighteenth and early nineteenth centuries combined to make the issues of nationalism and imperialism – and the definitions and exclusions of persons within these entities – into particularly urgent subjects. Persistent military conflicts across the world, debates over colonial expansion and administration, and the struggle over the abolition of the slave trade (and ultimately slavery itself) are among the developments during the Romantic age that are relevant for the discussions in this section.

H.L. Malchow's selection on Mary Shelley's *Frankenstein* from his book *Gothic Images of Race in Nineteenth-Century Britain* places Mary Shelley's celebrated novel in the context of enlightenment rationalism and universalism. He shows how Frankenstein's monster shares characteristics with a black slave, and how Shelley sides with a prominent strain of abolitionism. As a whole, he argues, the novel reveals tensions in the abolitionist treatment of black bodies: it "mirror[s] contemporary difficulties in maintaining universal humanistic ideals in the context of the slave economy of the West Indies and an expanding empire over nonwhite populations in Asia and Africa." Shelley's work critiques injustices but repeats or reinforces them with racial stereotypes; Malchow describes this logic as the "paradox" of abolitionist humanitarianism. Debbie Lee and Anne K. Mellor have also discussed issues of race in *Frankenstein* (Lee 2002: 171–93; Mellor 2001); more generally, the connections between race and empire are explored in work by Moira Ferguson and Helen Thomas, among others (Ferguson 1992; Thomas 2000).

There is an important point of agreement between Malchow's account of *Frankenstein* and Saree Makdisi's contribution on Blake from his book *William Blake and the Impossible History of the 1790s*. Both critics consider the rational humanitarianism of enlightenment thinkers to be complicated by contradictory habits of thinking. Makdisi sees much of the radical writing in England as dependent upon an "Orientalist" logic that separates the Western "self" or "subject" from its Eastern "other" or "object." But Makdisi's attention to a different author also conveys a different theoretical interest in the way that literary texts can present alternative, or "impossible," modes of thought outside existing power structures. Readers of his work may want to compare it to work by Hamilton and Kaufman in this volume, who make connecting (but also quite different) arguments on behalf of literary representation. Blake employs his texts "to emphasize . . . *all* human cultures," he writes. "Such a notion of sharing and being in common – not withstanding important differences" must be seen in contrast with the "imperialist rhetoric" that dominated the literature and politics of the day.

Divisions between British and other identities – even in the context of an expanding empire – continue to occupy Alan Bewell in his account of Coleridge and Wordsworth in the following selection from his book *Romanticism and Colonial Disease*. His approach differs from both Malchow's and Makdisi's, however, in that he sees far more internal division, disruption, suffering, and trauma at the heart of the imperial enterprise (his approach bears some resemblance to Mary Favret's selection in Part 9 of this volume). He thus explicitly takes aim at new historicist readings of Romantic writing that tend to see it as a suppression of the historical record. In contrast to those accounts, Bewell concentrates on the identity of British subjects and their works as necessarily "hybrid" identities. Individuals, families, and nations reverberate with the traumas and injuries that are perpetrated abroad, and this complex awareness resonates throughout literary works of the period.

In her new contribution to this volume, E.J. Clery also aims to correct historicist accounts that tended to view literature in terms of an opposition between imperial administration and subject populations. Her reading of Anna Letitia Barbauld's poem

Eighteen Hundred and Eleven shares some motivations with Alan Bewell's selection, but her theoretical assumptions are quite different. Rather than focus on psychological trauma, Clery focuses on a very specific connection that Barbauld established with a prominent discourse of patriotism during her day. This fine-grained historicism could be compared to Daniel O'Quinn's essay contribution in Part 1 of this volume, in that both selections show an increasing attention to the audiences and discourses circulating at the moment of a work's composition and reception. Clery's account shows how Barbauld shrewdly makes freedom coincide with (rather than oppose) the expansion of empire; this is because Barbauld's patriotism supports a "new age of cooperative global commerce in which economic and political freedom are mutually supporting and war has no place."

Works cited

Anderson, Benedict. (1983) *Imagined Communities: Reflections on the Origin and Spread of Nationalism*, London: Verso.

Berlin, Isaiah. (1999) *The Roots of Romanticism*, Princeton: Princeton University Press.

Colley, Linda. (1992) *Britons: Forging the Nation, 1707–1837*, New Haven: Yale University Press.

Ferguson, Moira. (1992) *Subject to Others: British Women Writers and Colonial Slavery, 1670–1834*, London: Routledge.

Hartman, Geoffrey H. (1964) *Wordsworth's Poetry, 1787–1814*, New Haven: Yale University Press.

Janowitz, Anne. (1990) *England's Ruins: Poetic Purpose and the National Landscape*, Cambridge: Basil Blackwell.

Lee, Debbie. (2002) *Slavery and the Romantic Imagination*, Philadelphia: Pennsylvania University Press.

Mellor, Ann. (2001) "Frankenstein, Racial Science, and the Yellow Peril," *Nineteenth-Century Contexts* 23: 1–28.

Said, Edward. (1978) *Orientalism*, New York: Pantheon Books.

Simpson, David. (1993) *Romanticism, Nationalism, and the Revolt Against Theory*, Chicago: University of Chicago Press.

Thomas, Helen. (2000) *Romanticism and Slave Narratives: Transatlantic Testimonies*, Cambridge: Cambridge University Press.

Further reading

Baum, Joan. (1994) *Mind-Forg'd Manacles: Slavery and the English Romantic Poets*, North Haven: Archon Books.

Carey, Brycchan. (2005) *British Abolitionism and the Rhetoric of Sensibility: Writing, Sentiment, and Slavery, 1760–1807*, Basingstoke: Palgrave Macmillan.

Doyle, Laura. (2008) *Freedom's Empire: Race and the Rise of the Novel in Atlantic Modernity, 1640–1940*, Durham: Duke University Press.

Fulford, Tim. (2006) *Romantic Indians: Native Americans, British Literature, and Transatlantic Culture, 1756–1830*, Oxford: Oxford University Press.

Jarvis, Robin. (2012) *Romantic Readers and Transatlantic Travel*, Farnham: Ashgate.

Leask, Nigel. (1992) *British Romantic Writers and the East: Anxieties of Empire*, Cambridge: Cambridge University Press.

Schmitt, Cannon. (1997) *Alien Nation: Nineteenth-Century Gothic Fictions and English Nationality*, Philadelphia: University of Pennsylvania Press.

Scrivener, Michael. (2007) *The Cosmopolitan Ideal in the Age of Revolution and Reaction, 1776–1832*, London: Pickering and Chatto.

Wood, Marcus. (2002) *Slavery, Empathy, and Pornography*, Oxford: Oxford University Press.

21 Was Frankenstein's Monster "a man and a brother"?

H.L. Malchow

> The Black stripp'd, and appeared of a giant-like strength,
>
> Large in bone, large in muscle and with arms a cruel length.[1]

It is now commonly accepted that the gothic literary genre of the late eighteenth and early nineteenth centuries represented, if remotely and unconsciously, the central tensions of an age of social liberation and political revolution. The themes of unjust persecution and imprisonment that are central to works like Matthew Lewis's *The Monk*, Charles Maturin's *Melmoth*, and Eugène Sue's *The Wandering Jew*, together with the dilemmas of identity facing the liberated that permeate William Godwin's *Caleb Williams* and Mary Shelley's *Frankenstein*, obviously resonate with the events of an age that, as Chris Baldick has finely observed, witnessed humanity seizing responsibility "for recreating the world, for violently reshaping its natural environment and its inherited social and political forms, for remaking itself."[2] Criticism in this vein has, however, focused almost exclusively on domestic themes – the "demonizing" of the proletariat in an era of industrial and political revolution, or the self-exploration and "nascent feminism" of authors like Mary Shelley and Charlotte Brontë. In contrast, I shall offer a racial reading of Mary Shelley's *Frankenstein* as an important level of interpretation that meshes with Marxist and feminist efforts to locate the novel in its social and psychological context.

In the portrayal of her monster, it is at least as plausible that Mary Shelley drew upon contemporary attitudes toward nonwhites – in particular, on fears and hopes of the abolition of slavery in the West Indies – as upon middle-class apprehension of a Luddite proletariat or her own "post-birthing trauma."[3] Indeed, the peculiar horror of the monster owes much of its emotional power to this hidden, or "coded," aspect, and the subsequent popularity of the tale through several nineteenth-century editions and on the Victorian stage derived in large part from the convergence of its most emotive elements with the evolving contemporaneous representation of ethnic and racial difference. Of necessity, such an argument rests on evidence that is indirect, circumstantial, and speculative. There is no clear proof that Mary Shelley consciously set out to create a monster explicitly suggestive of the Jamaican escaped slave or maroon, or that she drew directly from any personal knowledge of either planter or abolitionist propaganda. That she did so is certainly not impossible. It is not, in any event, my purpose to prove explicit connections and direct sources. Nor is it my purpose to discover a hidden "key" that will unlock every level of meaning, intended or otherwise, in the novel. What does interest me is how closely Shelley's fictional creation in many respects parallels the racial stereotypes of the age, and how her exploration of the limits of the thinking of Rousseau and William Godwin on man and education, surely the most important subtheme in the novel, mirrors contemporary difficulties in maintaining universal humanistic ideals in the context of the slave economy of the West Indies and an expanding empire over nonwhite populations in Asia and Africa.

[. . .]

[In two omitted sections – here and at the end of the selection – Malchow contextualizes Shelley's novel within Romantic ideas about race, and interprets the racial dimensions of Victorian appropriations of *Frankenstein*.]

As is well known, *Frankenstein; or, The Modern Prometheus* had its origins at a house party near Geneva in June 1816 at which the eighteen-year-old Mary Wollstonecraft Godwin (she married Shelley the following December) was challenged to produce a ghost story. The resulting tale was published anonymously in March 1818, and was surprisingly successful. In the form of a gothic horror romance, it recounts, through the letters of Walton, an Arctic explorer, the tortured history of Victor Frankenstein, the young son of a Genevan magistrate, who, as a Faustian university student, aspired to create life, and whose creation – his monster, fiend, or demon – rejected by his creator, flees to the wilderness, where he lives rough on nuts and berries. His appearance produces violent revulsion in all who meet him, however, in spite of the Creature's earnest attempts to make friends and do good. Educated vicariously and surreptitiously, he develops a sense of the injustices heaped upon him and turns to vengeance. He first murders Frankenstein's child brother, then causes the judicial murder of an innocent young woman, and finally, half-repentant, tracks down his creator to demand that he create a mate for him, vowing that they will live apart from mankind. This Frankenstein at first agrees to do, but he betrays his promise after reflecting on the dangers of a race of creatures arising from the union of two such monsters. The enraged Creature exacts a further terrible vengeance, first killing Frankenstein's friend Clerval, and then his bride Elizabeth on their bridal bed. The novel concludes with a determined Frankenstein pursuing his creation into the Arctic, only to die before confronting the Monster, who mourns his maker and disappears into the northern darkness with a vow of self-immolation.

A reading of this text that attempts to draw out an embedded racial message must begin where racism itself begins, with physiognomy. The Monster, it will be seen, is not merely a grotesque, a too-roughly cobbled-together simulacrum of a man. He is, first, larger and more powerful than his maker, and, second, dark and sinister in appearance. This suggests the standard description of the black man in both the literature of the West Indies and that of unfolding West African exploration. Mungo Park's *Travels*, which Mary Shelley had ready to hand, described the Mandingoes as "commonly above the middle size, well-shaped, strong, and capable of enduring great labour." A Negro guide who "mounted up the rocks, where indeed no horse could follow him, leaving me to admire his agility" indicates both great strength, and perhaps the simian dexterity with which the Monster eludes Frankenstein in the Alps.[4] The Jamaican Bryan Edwards described the Mandingoes as "remarkably tall," while the Eboes were, he averred, a sickly yellow in complexion with eyes that appeared to be "suffused with bile."[5]

By the early nineteenth century, popular racial discourse managed to conflate such descriptions of particular ethnic characteristics into a general image of the

Negro body in which repulsive features, brutelike strength and size of limbs featured prominently. Frankenstein's creature, when we first see him, is defined by a set of clichés that might be picked out of such literature. His eyes are "dull yellow" and "watery," hair "a lustrous black" and "ragged," and his black lips contrast with "teeth of pearly whiteness." His skin was "in colour and apparent texture like that of a mummy."[6] Mummies are, of course, ordinarily dark brown or black in color, a fact that led to speculation about the racial origin of the ancient Egyptians following the Napoleonic excavations. There was already a tradition drawn from classical authors that the civilization of ancient Thebes had originated in Ethiopia. The comte de Volney made use of this in his *Ruins*, a book Mary Shelley knew and used as one of the Monster's textbooks in the novel; Volney wrote of "the black complexion of the Sphinx."[7] This is not to say that Shelley intended to create a specifically Negro monster – elsewhere she writes of the Monster's yellow skin[8] – but rather that, reaching into childhood fantasy and imagination, she dredged up a bogeyman that had been prepared by a cultural tradition of the threatening Other – whether troll or giant, gypsy or Negro – from the dark inner recesses of xenophobic fear and loathing.

This seems to me to be at least as reasonable a reading as the claim that the Monster is a feminine-masculine composite that transcends gender,[9] or that his alien hideousness reflects bourgeois fears of a threatening working class. The physical lineaments of the Creature suggest little that can be construed as feminine, nor do they explicitly raise the image of the wan and bowed pauper or proletarian laborer, often small in stature and poor in health. Frankenstein's Monster is robust and larger than life, ostentatiously rural rather than urban. Of course, the Monster as industrial worker does not have to be a literal image, but rather the enlarged fear of a collective threat. Nevertheless, at the level of physiognomy at least, a racial reading seems to me to be closer to the mark than a Marxist one.

Beyond size and repulsiveness, the most striking physical attributes of the Monster are his apelike ability to scamper up mountainsides and his endurance of temperatures that European man would find intolerable: "I was more agile," he says, "than they and could subsist upon coarser diet; I bore the extremes of heat and cold with less injury to my frame."[10] This description closely parallels the claims of the apologists for West Indian slavery. The Negro, it was said, had more brute strength than the white man and could stand the heat of the tropics, which would enervate, perhaps kill, a European.[11] One might, without stretching imagination very far, see in Frankenstein's futile chase after his creature in the Alps or the frozen waste of the Arctic a displaced image of the white planter's exhausting, and in Jamaica often futile, search for the runaway slave in the opposite extreme of the equatorial tropics.[12] Moreover, some apologists for slavery defended a subsistence slave diet of maize and water by claiming that the race did not require the white man's luxuries of meat and drink. This draws on a long European tradition that imagined wild men or natural men of the woods as, like Frankenstein's Monster, colossal vegetarians, images eighteenth-century naturalists helped to melt into that of more primitive races of men abroad, far down the ladder of racial hierarchy. Mungo Park commented on the largely vegetable diet of many Negroes.[13]

Shifting from the image to the story, however, we see that Shelley's Monster is no mere ape-man. He has an innate desire for knowledge, a capacity to learn, and feelings of right and wrong. He is, notwithstanding his hideous appearance, dreadfully wronged by a society that cannot see the inner man for the outer form. Here one might argue quite plausibly for an abolitionist rendering of the image of the Monster as "a man and a brother." However, Shelley's Creature is, if not a masculine and feminine composite, a compound of both sides of the slavery debate. He *is* wild and dangerous, unpredictable and childlike, but at the same time has perhaps (as the Creature himself says) been made such by the circumstances of an unjust exclusion. And yet the depth of his rage and destructiveness seems to stem from more than environment and frustration; it suggests an inherent bestiality lurking somewhere. How much the Monster's excitable character is the result of his unique physiology, and how much of his environment, is an ambiguity exactly paralleling the central conundrum of the antislavery debate. Something of this ambiguity might even be said to be buried unconsciously in Godwin's own good-natured telling of the fable about washing the blackamoor, which he intended no doubt as an abolitionist, homily that skin color mattered only to the ignorant. But it would more commonly have been read with another message, that the black could no more be educated into whiteness than a leopard could change his spots, that there were basic and ineradicable racial differences, of which skin color was but an outward sign.[14]

[. . .]

Violently contradictory and unbridled emotions were characteristics commonly associated with the Negro. Mungo Park, who was killed by natives in the upper Niger region, related numerous examples of violence – "The Jaloffs (or Yaloffs) are an active, powerful, and warlike race" – and "savagery": "The Negro carried the body [of a deceased boy] by a leg and an arm, and threw it into the pit with a savage indifference, which I had never before seen." Edwards describes the blacks of Jamaica who originated on the Gold Coast, "the genuine and original unmixed Negro," as having a

> firmness of body and mind; a ferociousness of disposition; but withall, activity,
> courage, and a stubbornness . . . of soul, which prompts them to enterprises
> of difficulty and danger; and enables them to meet death, in its most horrible
> shape, with fortitude or indifference.[15]

Many writers, like John Leyden in 1799, made much not only of the violence of native Africans and slaves, in particular their thirst for revenge, but also of their contrasting capacity for gratitude and affection:

> The understanding is much less cultivated among the Negroes than among
> Europeans; but their passions, whether benevolent or malevolent, are
> proportionately more violent. . . . Though addicted to hatred and revenge, they
> are equally susceptible to love, affection, and gratitude.[16]

It will be apparent how closely Leyden's choice of description – passionate revenge and loving gratitude – echoes Shelley's own characterization of her Monster. It was a common theme, which Mungo Park voiced in his observations, for example, of the "Feloops" near the Gambia River: "They are of a gloomy disposition, and are supposed never to forgive an injury. . . . This fierce and unrelenting disposition is, however, counterbalanced by many good qualities: they display the utmost gratitude and affection toward their benefactors." This combination of vengefulness and affection was, in fact, a stereotype commonly applied to any savage or primitive race.[17]

[. . .]

Mary Shelley's addition of *cruel* vindictiveness to the portrait of the natural savage accords with a contemporary shifting of attitude from that of Dr. Johnson's savage ("a man untaught, uncivilized") to the egregiously cruel as well as ignorant black, which was well established in mid-nineteenth-century opinion.[18] Writing in the 1790s, Edwards ascribed a particular cruelty to both the ancient Caribbees (an "unnatural cruelty") and the mulattoes and Negroes of his time:

> It serves to some degree to lessen the indignation which a good mind necessarily feels at the abuses of power by the Whites, to observe that the Negroes themselves, when invested with command, give full play to their revengeful passions; and exercise all the wantonness of cruelty without restraint or remorse.[19]

It is possible to find in contemporary abolitionist representation positive images of the black as a powerful force for *justifiable* vengeance rather than a mere supplicating child, although this perspective remained somewhat exceptional. In 1811 the abolitionist artist George Dawe exhibited at the British Institution a larger-than-life painting, *A Negro Overpowering a Buffalo*, which depicted a massive black body tensed with brute strength. A few years earlier, Henri Fuseli, also an abolitionist, had given the public a towering, elemental, and heroic black in his *The Negro Revenged*. If Dawe's message was oblique, Fuseli's was direct, suggested perhaps by lines from Thomas Day's poem "The Dying Negro": "For Afric triumphs! – his avenging rage / No tears can soften, and no blood assuage." A black male, larger than the white woman clinging to him, erect rather than kneeling, calls down the wrath of God on a foundering slave ship (Figure 21.1).[20] More commonly, however, the image of the black as a destructive force – with a suggestion of irrational bestiality – drew from the propaganda of the Jamaica planter class, and was echoed by their parliamentary defenders. For example, in 1796 *The Parliamentary Register, The Annual Register*, and presumably other London publications as well, gave ample space to Henry Dundas's reply in the House of Commons to humanitarian concerns over the use of bloodhounds to hunt down Negro men, women, and children in Jamaica:

> The Maroons were accustomed to descend from their fastnesses at midnight, and commit the most dreadful ravages and cruelties upon the wives, children, and property of the inhabitants, burning and destroying every place which they attacked, and murdering all who unfortunately became the objects of their fury.[21]

One might note here the coincidence that Shelley's implacably vengeful Monster murders both a woman and a child, and burns the De Lacey cottage to the ground. Such images were common to the literature on the West Indies with which Mary Shelley was recently familiar. She would, for instance, have read Edward's rather more explicit description of the horrors of a slave rebellion that saw widespread "death and desolation," he claimed:

> They surrounded the overseer's house about four in the morning, in which eight or ten White people were in bed, every one of whom they butchered in the most savage manner, and literally drank their blood mixed with rum. . . . [They] then

The Negro revenged.

*Hark! he answers — Wild tornadoes,
Strewing yonder sea with wrecks,
Wasting towns, plantations, meadows,
Are the voice with which he speaks.*

Pub. by J. Johnson London March 1 1807.

Figure 21.1 The Negro Revenged by Henry Fuseli, 1807. Published by Joseph Johnson; Print made by Abraham Raimbach. © The Trustees of the British Museum

set fire to the buildings and canes. In one morning they murdered between thirty and forty Whites, not sparing even infants at the breast.[22]

[. . .]

This essentially gothic image of frenzied blacks drinking the blood of their victims (Frankenstein accuses the Monster of being "his own vampire")[23] makes use of a common trope for a depraved and irrational lust for vengeance. It also brings together two characteristics of the racial primitive – a manic preoccupation with avenging grievances and cannibalism – that were gaining currency by the end of the eighteenth century. Conflicting European traditions of the vegetarian wild man and the cannibalistic savage parallel other contradictions – like that between affectionate gratitude and indifferent, casual cruelty – that were held to coexist in primitive natures. The notion of cannibalism as a characteristic of primitive peoples had been passed down from well-elaborated, if largely fanciful, sixteenth-century accounts of the Caribbean, and was lodged in popular culture by Defoe's *Robinson Crusoe* (recommended by Godwin for the education of children).[24] It was a tradition that, although often discounted in the early Enlightenment, was powerfully reinvested as a universal mark of primitivism in the late eighteenth and nineteenth centuries and received apparent empirical corroboration in explorers' accounts of the South Pacific and Africa. Bryan Edwards, who believed that cannibalism had once been widespread in the West Indies, drew attention to the debate on the extent of the practice in his *History*.[25]

While Mary Shelley's Monster cannot actually be charged with cannibalism, the subject is certainly raised, if obliquely, in the novel. William Frankenstein, the child whom the Monster strangles, his most horrific crime, charges him at first sight with this savage intention: "Ugly wretch! You wish to eat me and tear me to pieces."[26] The charge is, of course, unjust; it is part of the prejudice the Creature meets wherever he turns. Although Victor Frankenstein metaphorically associates his Monster with vampirism, it is Frankenstein himself who is the cannibal, who tears "to pieces" both the corpses from which he assembles his creature and the female mate he had begun to construct. Similarly, he also takes on the savage's thirst for vengeance, and dedicates himself to revenge the deaths of his brother and bride, to a relentless pursuit of his own creation. As Anne Mellor and other critics have noted, Frankenstein and his Monster become indistinguishable: "The creator has become his creature."[27]

There remains a further aspect of the Monster's physical appearance and character that bears emphasizing in any search for a racialized image. A strong tradition, already familiar by the late eighteenth century, and insisted upon by racist propagandists for slavery like Edward Long, had it that Negroes were both particularly libidinous and possessed of unusually large genitalia. William Godwin himself had written that:

> The heat of the climate obliges both sexes [of the Negro] to go half naked. The animal arrives sooner at maturity in hot countries. And both these circumstances produce vigilance and jealousy, causes which inevitably tend to inflame the passions.[28]

Edwards related that Negroes were promiscuous, and possessed a strong sexual passion, which "is mere animal desire."[29] The threat that white women might be brutalized by oversexed black men of great strength and size became a cliché of racist writing, ready for appropriation in the creation of gothic horror and given an extra charge by the recently dramatized and exaggerated stories of the plight of white women in revolutionary Haiti.

Mary Shelley's Monster, because of his great strength and his unpredictable moods, his alternate plaintive persuasiveness and fiery rage, is suffused with a kind of dangerous male sexuality. [. . .] Shelley describes her creation as not only eight feet tall but "proportionably large." Frankenstein's shocked reaction to his first sight of the living creature seems to invoke the image of a great, engorged, and threatening phallus: "Great God! His yellow skin scarcely covered the work of muscles and arteries beneath."[30] A similarly threatening masculinity may be suggested in his later awakening to find the Monster nakedly towering above him as he lies in his bed.

The murder of Elizabeth, Frankenstein's bride, would seem almost certainly to draw, either consciously or otherwise, upon the classic threat of the black male. The sharp contrast between the hazel-eyed, auburn-haired, high-browed, fragile white woman and the dark Monster was sharp in the 1818 version, but was made much starker in Mary Shelley's revision of 1831. Here we can see the construction of both race and a vulnerable femininity, the "angel in the house," progressing together toward the Victorian age. Elizabeth is described in this third edition as not only of aristocratic, but of stereotypically northern, Teutonic beauty:

> Her hair was the brightest living gold . . . her brow was clear and ample, her blue eyes cloudless . . . none could behold her without looking on her as of a distinct species, a being heaven-sent, and bearing a celestial stamp in all her features. . . . Her mother was a German.[31]

It is this master-race maiden whom the Monster, her racial negative – dark-haired, low-browed, with watery and yellowed eyes – violently assaults in her bedroom and strangles as Othello smothers Desdemona.[32] The scene is emotionally and suggestively that of rape as well as of murder, or rather, as murder in lieu of rape.

Finally, the racial threat of an oversexed, rapidly propagating, monstrous Other is practically made explicit in Frankenstein's hesitation to create a mate for his Monster:

> Even if they [the Monster and his bride-to-be] were to leave Europe [as the Monster had suggested] and inhabit the deserts of the new world, yet one of the first results of those sympathies for which the daemon thirsted would be children, and a race of devils would be propagated upon the earth who might make the very existence of man a condition precarious and full of terror. Had I a right, for my own benefit, to inflict this curse upon everlasting generations?[33]

Two interesting allusions are possible here. First, the idea of exile from Europe was already available in the Sierra Leone experiment in sending destitute blacks "back to Africa." By the time Mary Shelley was writing, this much-advertised experiment had come to be regarded largely as a failure. But, more pointedly, there was a strong parallel to the fear of "a race of devils" in conditions of autonomy in the recent history of Haiti and in highly exaggerated stories about the escaped or freed slave communities of mulattoes in the West Indies and the threat they posed to the white planter society, and in particular to its women. Once again, this was a fear the slaveowning class encouraged in their loud protests against humanitarian intervention. The year Shelley began her novel, there were reports that rebellious blacks in Barbados flew a flag portraying "a black chief, with a white woman, with clasped hands, imploring mercy."[34]

The image of blacks free from the discipline of a white master, in an environment where nature provided unlimited sustenance, breeding at a rate unrestrained by decency or prudence, was already available well before Carlyle's essay on the "Nigger Question." And in it lay much of the basis for the prediction of the inevitability of race war that is the preoccupation of much late-nineteenth-century racist literature. *Frankenstein* prefigures this racial Armageddon as much as it does the mad scientist of twentieth-century fiction and film.

Education and moral dilemma

The education of Frankenstein's monster occupies an important, indeed central, part of the story, involving a complicated and lengthy subplot at the De Lacey cottage.

This has drawn the attention of literary critics, who see in it not just a digression that allows Mary Shelley to parade her grasp of Lockeian ideas on the acquisition of knowledge by sensory association (the Monster as tabula rasa), but also a sophisticated means of introducing the Rousseauian critique that true instruction must engage the emotions and requires loving contact. It is precisely this, of course, that the Monster is denied both by his creator and ultimately by the family from whom he secretly learns language and history. This is a reasonable view, which accords well with what we know of Mary Shelley's own reading of both Locke and Rousseau. It should not, however, preclude an examination of the novel as at some level also a comment on sharply focused and pragmatic contemporary issues, as well as on past educational theory.

It is apparent that the success of Victor Frankenstein's hubristic experiment immediately poses the central problem of the novel, the hinge upon which the moral of the tale turns. This is the dilemma of whether he is willing to acknowledge his responsibility to nurture and educate his creation in the ways of humankind, thus not only making his progeny safe for society but admitting the fact of his paternity and responsibility to both himself and the world at large. This he cannot force himself to do, and his flight from moral obligation has terrible consequences for all concerned. This ethical problem can be generalized. Can any parent, slave master, patron, or employer escape, without retribution, the moral obligation of providing for the welfare and education of those who are dependent upon him and who have been in some sense at least called into being, shaped, and perhaps deformed to serve his needs. This was a powerful and demanding issue, which not only hints at a common critique of Rousseau's own notorious avoidance of the obligations of paternity, but directly targets a central, perhaps the central, social question of the postrevolutionary, early-industrial age.

Frankenstein's refusal to admit responsibility for the creature he has made or to help it to achieve a full integration into the society of men, coupled with the potential threat of the brute strength of the Monster, has led some critics to the view that the story is a metaphor for domestic class relations in the era of early mechanization and Luddism. In such a reading, Frankenstein's refusal to ameliorate the condition of his Monster roughly anticipates the coming liberalism of the age of laissez faire and individualism. The Monster's later discovery of social injustice through his effort at self-education comfortably conforms to this interpretation. But these issues of accountability, paternalism, and the dangerous self-awareness of a subordinate class emerge with equal, if not greater and more immediate, force in nineteenth-century race relations.

Like Frankenstein, the white, gentlemanly abolitionist sought to give reality to an [ideal], the potential humanity of the degraded slave. The slave, like the Monster, was in the eyes of some philanthropists indeed a tabula rasa, a cultureless creature ready to receive their moral teaching and their theology. In the optimism of the movement, others assumed that the abolition of the institution of slavery alone – in Frankenstein's story the mere act of creation – would be followed by inevitable improvement as the liberated black man found his place as a fully responsible, self-improving citizen. By the time Mary Shelley was writing, however, there were already deep misgivings. In Sierra Leone, the projectors of a free and self-respecting black colony had had to retrench their expectations, impose discipline, and withhold self-governance. By the second decade of the century, there must have been many even within the abolitionist camp who also harbored doubts about at least the immediate result of wholesale abolition in the West Indies, and who were anxious to deny their own responsibility for any horror that might emerge. Denial is, of course, Frankenstein's first reaction to his own creation. Furthermore, the leaving of the Monster to his own devices in the wilderness results in brooding grievance and childlike rage. Already malformed by his creator, he does not rise to full humanity but reverts to the beast, in part because of the prejudice of those he encounters, in part because real self-improvement without an education involving discipline and a nurturing paternalist connection was as unlikely for him as it seemed to many to prove unlikely for blacks in the West Indies.

Here it will be seen that *Frankenstein* strongly resonates with a great and pressing social concern much in the mind of the upper- and middle-class public. As with Frankenstein's Monster, there was a dual aspect to the problem of education in the early nineteenth century: the advancement, moral well-being, and happiness of those to be educated, but also the safety of the society into which, in some degree, either the new urban citizen of the "dangerous classes" or the freed slave of the plantation was to be admitted.

In Mary Shelley's world, these issues of responsibility and discipline were sharply debated. The same evangelicals who advocated abolition and missionary activity abroad pressed for Sunday schools and philanthropic instruction at home. The issue of the education of factory children, of women, and of slaves in the West Indies emerged in much the same terms. Where did responsibility lie? What ought to be taught? What was the (clearly anomalous) social role of an educated black or worker or woman? Clearly, the problem facing the rejected Monster, how to educate himself, and the disappointment he experiences on discovering that his efforts at self-tuition are of little use in winning acceptance, closely approximates the issues raised both by abolitionists and by domestic educational reformers of either a Benthamite, radical, or evangelical persuasion. Behind this were the frustrations inherent in the formal education of subordinate persons in a society that remained intensely patriarchal, class-bound, and color-prejudiced.

Like race prejudice and class snobbery, the racial and domestic educational issues were tightly intertwined. The two discourses drew from and reinforced each other, and share the key questions of appropriateness, responsibility, social control, and social danger. The historians of education in this period have neglected the degree to which the "problem" of Negro education, a debate that raged at least in abolitionist and proslavery quarters from the late eighteenth century until well after the American Civil War, influenced the tenor and substance of the domestic European debate over the educability of the poor and women. A further consideration of aspects of the novel in this light will be of some interest.

In the first place, it is appropriate to recall that the issue of whether black slaves ought to receive any education – enough, at least, to read the edifying homilies of religion – had long been a bone of contention between the Jamaican planters and the humanitarians. Knowledge is power, and the withholding of instruction was a highly symbolic entrenchment of the master–slave relationship. This suggests another debate: whether slaves ought to be baptized into a Christian church, which would bring them into the brotherhood of Christ and pose problems in their disposal as chattels. It is not a far-fetched reading of the novel to see some reflection of these issues in Frankenstein's refusal either to instruct or to name his creature. Mary Shelley's Monster is not only denied education; he is also denied a Christian name.[35] Frankenstein thus retreats from a commitment to a relationship, an attachment of sentiment and parentage, which is as repugnant to him as it would have been to the white slave master. The Monster's thirst for knowledge is, in fact, a thirst for deliverance from the condition of "a vagabond and a slave." What education he is able to glean from the conversation of the De Laceys (like that a "house-nigger" might have picked up from those he served) teaches him that one such as himself, lacking "unsullied descent" and even a name, is "doomed to waste his powers for the profits of the chosen few!"[36]

It might be thought that the Monster's articulateness, his precocious quickness of intellect in learning at second hand from overheard conversation, belies a close comparison with the slave stereotype. Certainly the most brutal stereotype, from, say, the pages of Edward Long, would deny the Negro sufficient intelligence to learn, but liberal opinion, that read by Mary Shelley, held otherwise. Edwards claimed that he had "been surprised by such figurative expressions [from his slaves], and (notwithstanding their ignorance of abstract terms) such pointed sentences, as would have reflected no disgrace on poets and philosophers. . . . Negroes have minds very capable of observation."[37]

"Observation" is the Monster's only means of self-education. Like the Negro slave, he is kept an outsider. In what is clearly a sense of self-recognition, he responds with weeping to Volney's tragic history of "the helpless fate" of the native inhabitants of America.[38] However, he not only identifies with the sufferers of this racial injustice, but, although protesting that "mine shall not be the submission of abject slavery," finally acknowledges to himself his own inferiority and despairs:

> I became fully convinced that I was in reality the monster that I am. . . . I abhorred myself . . . I was the slave, not the master. . . . I, the miserable and the abandoned, am an abortion, to be spurned at, and kicked, and trampled on. . . . Your abhorrence cannot equal that with which I regard myself.[39]

His response is at first rebellion, but this turns to despair and, ultimately, to suicide. The Monster's "education" has taught him self-contempt, just as the little education of the plantation black or freed slave served merely to reinforce his own awareness of inferiority. This mentality conforms to that observed by Edwards among the mulattoes in Jamaica, where an official system of racial identification "tends to degrade them [freed blacks and mulattoes] in their eyes, and in the eyes of the community to which they belong."[40]

It was a commonplace of the literature of slavery that the recently enslaved experienced deep depression and were, particularly those from some proud, warlike tribes, prone to either rebellion or suicide. Edwards remarks on the frequent suicides among the Eboes of West Africa and comments elsewhere that it was widely believed (although he disagreed) that "Negroes consider death not only as a welcome and happy release from the calamities of their condition, but also as a passport to the place of their nativity."[41] Matthew Lewis echoes this in his *Journal* of his visit to Jamaica in 1815–16.[42] The Monster's intended self-immolation brings together three clichés of this tradition: the low self-regard of the slave, slave suicide (a form of impotent rebellion), and destruction by fire (the common image of real rebellion).

From overheard conversations and readings, the Monster also learns the ethnic stereotyping of which he himself, as an alien, is ironically also a victim – of slothful

Asiatics, degenerate Romans, and *ungrateful*, wicked Turks.[43] Indeed, the idea of gratitude, and its opposite, the corrosive sense of resentment, feature strongly throughout the novel. There is the story of the Christian Arab Safie and her Turkish father, who unnaturally rewards his Christian deliverer with treacherous ingratitude. When Justine, a poor relation living as a servant in the Frankenstein household, is unjustly accused of the murder of Frankenstein's brother, the charge of murder is made more horrible in the eyes of the public by its suggestion of "ingratitude" to the Frankenstein family, which has protected her. Then there is the repeated assertion of the Monster himself that if treated by someone with kindness, he "would bestow every benefit upon him with tears of gratitude" at his acceptance; "my virtues will necessarily arise when I live in communion with an equal," for his heart, the Creature says, "was fashioned to be susceptible of love and sympathy."[44] Again, this is a theme that features prominently in the literature on African and West Indian blacks with which Mary Shelley was familiar. Edwards, like others, was eager to affirm that, however violent and passionate the black or mulatto might be, there was a counterbalancing tendency to affection, and he speaks of "their disinterested gratitude and attachment where favours are shown them"; "if their confidence be once obtained, they manifest as great fidelity, affection, and gratitude as can reasonably be expected from men in a state of slavery."[45]

This projection of gratitude invokes the classic colonizer mentality, evident in the middle-class humanitarian as well as in the paternalist slaveholder. Those who are the receivers of liberation, protection, or education in the Christian virtues of patience and forbearance are expected to repay benevolent condescension with self-abasing thankfulness and loyalty. The cardinal sin in this system is "ingratitude," a failing Mary Shelley herself at one point calls "blackest ingratitude,"[46] and that the Victorians were later quick to ascribe to sepoy troops and Jamaican freed slaves. This discloses the paradox at the center of the humanitarian abolitionist enterprise: that while the *gift* of liberation transforms the slave into a freed man, it does so only through the good offices of white, middle- and upper-class patrons rather than by self-help. In this relationship, the idealized black, although a "man and a brother," is inevitably still on his knees as a grateful man and a younger brother.

[. . .]

Notes

1 Anonymous English ballad inspired by the contest between the British boxing champion Tom Cribb and the Negro challenger Thomas Molineaux in 1811. See [Peter] Fryer, *Staying Power*[: *The History of Black People in Britain* (London: Pluto Press, 1984)], 447–8.
2 [Chris] Baldick, *In Frankenstein's Shadow* [: *Myth, Monstrosity, and Nineteenth-Century Writing* (Oxford: Clarendon Press, 1987)], 5.
3 For the novel as allegory of the class struggle, see [Paul] O'Flynn, "Production and Reproduction [: The Case of *Frankenstein*," *Literature and History* 9, 2 (1983):] 194–213; and, less convincingly, [Franco] Moretti, *Signs Taken for Wonders* [: *Essays in the Sociology of Literary Forms*, ch. 3, "Dialectic of Fear" (London: Verso, 1983)]. For the feminist interpretation, see [Ellen] Moers, "Female Gothic," [in *The Endurance of Frankenstein: Essays on Mary Shelley's Novel*, eds G. Levine and U.C. Knoepflmacher (Berkeley: University of California Press, 1979), 77–87, reprinted from *Literary Women* (1974); Sandra Gilbert and Susan Gubar, *The Madwoman in the Attic: The Woman Writer in the Nineteenth-Century Literary Imagination*, ch. 7, "Horror's Twin" (New Haven, Conn.: Yale University Press, 1979); Mary Poovey, "My Hideous Progeny: Mary Shelley and the Feminization of Romanticism," *PMLA* 95, 3 (1980): 332–47; and Gayatri Chakravorty Spivak, "Three Women's Texts and a Critique of Imperialism," *Critical Inquiry* 12 (Autumn 1985): 243–61.] Moers argues that

the novel is a dream both of awakening sexuality and of the horror of maternity, while Gilbert and Gubar assert that Mary Shelley took the male cultural myth of *Paradise Lost* and rewrote it into a mirror of female experience. Poovey emphasizes the dilemma of the female artist expected to produce literature with a moral, while Spivak offers a deconstructionist perspective on the novel as "a text of nascent feminism," where the binary male–female opposition is undone in Frankenstein's womb-laboratory.

4 [Mungo] Park, *Travels* [*in the Interior Districts of Africa: Performed under the Direction and Patronage of the African Association in the Years 1795, 1796, and 1797* (London: W. Bulmer, 1799)], I: 21, 239.

5 Bryan Edwards, [*The History, Civil and Commercial, of the British Colonies in the West Indies.* (Dublin: Luke White, 1793),] 2: 58, 69.

6 [Mary Wollstonecraft] Shelley, *Frankenstein* [*; or, The Modern Prometheus.* 1831 ed. Introduction by Maurice Hindle (London: Penguin Books, 1985)], 105–261. All following references, except where indicated, are to this version. The 1831 edition was the one most commonly available in the nineteenth century and, although Mary Shelley made some significant alterations of the 1818 text, for our purposes these changes are not ordinarily of much significance.

7 [Constantin François Chasseboeuf comte de] Volney, *Ruins* [*; or, A Survey of the Revolutions of Empires* (London: J. Johnson, 1795)], 331. One should also note in this context that Bryan Edwards attempted to associate the West Indian superstition of Obeah with ancient Egyptian sources (*History*, 2: 83).

8 Although [...] some writers drew attention to the yellowish skin and eyes of some Negroes.

9 [David E.] Musselwhite [...] argues that "the lustrous black hair and pearly white teeth suggest 'feminine' attributes, contrasted with the straight black lips and the prominent musculature, which suggest predominantly 'masculine' traits" [*Partings Welded Together: Politics and Desire in the Nineteenth-Century Novel* (London: Methuen, 1987), 60.] Also see [William] Veeder, *Mary Shelley* [& "Frankenstein": The Fate of Androgyny (Chicago: University of Chicago Press, 1986)].

10 Shelley, *Frankenstein*, 166.

11 A point made by [John] Davis [in *Travels of Four Years and a Half in the United States of America; During 1798, 1800, 1801, and 1802* (London: Edwards, 1803)], 95, among many others.

12 An inversion perhaps suggested to Mary Shelley by her father's discussion of the impact of climate on character: "In their extreme perhaps heat and cold may determine the character of nations, of the negroes for example on the one side, and the Laplanders on the other" [(William Godwin, *An Enquiry Concerning Political Justice.* 1793. (London: Penguin Books, 1985), 151)]. It may also be relevant to note that Edwards described the snow-covered mountains of South America in his history of the West Indies, and the lesser mountains of the islands that "have never yet, that I have heard, been fully explored" (1: 20). Davis in the American South alludes to the Alps when in sight of the Blue Ridge Mountains, and associates both with escape and melancholy (376).

13 [U.C.] Knoepflmacher, " 'Face to Face' [: Of Man-Apes, Monsters, and Readers," in *The Endurance of Frankenstein*, eds G. Levine and U.C. Knoepflmacher (Berkeley: University of California Press, 1979)], 317–24, 319. Park, *Travels*, 1: 279–80.

14 [William] Godwin, *Fables*, [*Ancient and Modern, Adapted for the Use of Children* (London: Thomas Hodgkins, 1805)], 165–8.

15 Park, *Travels*, 1: 16, 235. B. Edwards, *History*, 2: 59.

16 [John] Leyden, *Historical and Philosophical Sketch*, 98, as quoted by [Philip D.] Curtin, [*The Image of Africa: British Ideas and Action, 1780–1850* (London: Macmillan, 1965),] 223.

17 Park, *Travels*, 1: 15–16.

18 See [Douglas A.] Lorimer, *Colour* [*, Class and the Victorians: English Attitudes to the Negro in the Mid-Nineteenth Century* (Leicester: Leicester University Press, 1978)], who cites (147) Joseph Hooker (to John Tyndall, 15 Feb. 1867):

> It depends on the definition of the term "SAVAGE." Johnson defined savage as "a man untaught, uncivilized"; in general parlance the world now super-adds CRUELTY to the above. Now I hold the Negro in W. Africa and Jamaica is untaught, uncivilized, and CRUEL TOO.

19 B. Edwards, *History*, 1: 33–6, 2: 74.
20 [Hugh] Honour, [*Slaves and Liberators*, Vol. 4, part 1, of *The Image of the Black in Western Art* (Cambridge, Mass.: Harvard University Press, 1989), 93, and *Black Models and White Myths*, Vol. 4, part 2, of *The Image of the Black in Western Art* (Cambridge, Mass.: Harvard University Press, 1989), 25–6.]
21 *Parliamentary Register*, 44: 337.
22 B. Edwards, *History*, 2: 60–1.
23 Shelley, *Frankenstein*, 124.
24 [Anne K.] Mellor, *Mary Shelley* [*: Her Life, Her Fiction, Her Monsters* (London: Routledge, 1989)], 9. On cannibalism and the Colombian Caribbean, see [Peter] Hulme, *Colonial Encounters* [*: Europe and the Native Caribbean, 1492–1797* (London: Methuen, 1986)], and [Stephen] Greenblatt, *Marvelous Possessions* [*: The Wonder of the New World* (Chicago: University of Chicago Press, 1991).]
25 B. Edwards, *History*, 1: 29–30, where he attempts to refute Labat's claim that cannibalism had been rare.
26 Shelley, *Frankenstein*, 187.
27 Mellor, *Mary Shelley*, 135–6.
28 Godwin, *Political Justice*, 152.
29 B. Edwards, *History*, 2: 76.
30 Shelley, *Frankenstein*, 105.
31 Ibid., 83. For the 1818 description, see *Frankenstein* (University of California Press, 1968), 31.
32 Shakespeare gave Othello the "bloody thoughts" of "a capable and wide revenge," suggesting not only the fury of male jealousy but also the racialized characteristic of the African slave.
33 Shelley, *Frankenstein*, 210–11.
34 *Annual Register . . . for the Year 1816*, 77.
35 Something emphasized by the playbills advertising the popular stage adaptation of the novel in 1823, where the Monster is designated only by "——."
36 Shelley, *Frankenstein*, 165.
37 B. Edwards, *History*, 2: 78.
38 Shelley, *Frankenstein*, 165. The De Laceys read Volney's *Ruins*.
39 Ibid., 159, 262–4.
40 B. Edwards, *History*, 2: 20.
41 Ibid., 69–70, 80.
42 [Matthew Gregory] Lewis, *Journal* [*of a West India Proprietor, 1815–17.* 1834. (London: George Routledge & Sons, 1929)], 89–90.
43 Shelley, *Frankenstein*, 164–5, 171.
44 Ibid., 131, 190, 192, 262.
45 B. Edwards, *History*, 2: 25, 69–70.
46 Shelley, *Frankenstein*, 131, with reference to public opinion of Justine.

22 Blake and Romantic imperialism

Saree Makdisi

1 Introduction

At that momentous historical turning point, toward the end of the eighteenth century, in which almost every attempt to represent otherness seemed to slip into the exoticizing political aesthetic that would enable and justify imperial conquest, it was a matter of some urgency to be able to think of the foreign without resorting to (or sliding into) the language and figures of exoticism. What I want to suggest is that [William] Blake drew on and reformulated for the exigencies of his own time a heterogeneous underground tradition that stressed the continuity of European and Afro-Asiatic cultures, rather than the sharp differentiation between Europe and its others which would prove essential to modern imperialism. For, as we shall see, Blake's interest in certain mystical currents which had plunged deep underground long before his own time offered him a way to articulate a logic of cultural heterogeneity that refused the discourse of exoticism. Indeed, his simultaneously political and aesthetic stance on otherness must be seen to enable a carefully articulated position on the cultural politics of imperialism, as well as a discourse of freedom contesting the internal imperialism of the state. Or, rather, Blake's elaboration of a form of religious and political freedom that would defy what he called "state religion" was also an elaboration of a form of political and cultural freedom from the discourse and practice of imperialism. In the following pages I will elaborate Blake's position with reference to the greatest imperial exoticism of all – Orientalism – to try to explain why his position has not been adequately recognized by most earlier scholarship, and to suggest what significance all this has for our understanding and interpretation of the rest of Blake's work in relation to 1790s radicalism and the culture of modernization that emerged with it. What I want to propose is that through this investigation of Blake's anti-imperialism we will discover how he found a way to produce a critique for his own time, rather than as a quasi-reactionary attempt to return to some lost original fullness, both of the ancien régime and of the bourgeois radicalism which attacked it – a way to refuse the logic of the state and of the discourse of sovereign power itself in the name of what he would call "Immortal Joy."[1]

2 Romantic Orientalism

Few English writers or artists of the 1790s with an interest in the "foreign" were able to approach, or even to imagine, foreignness in terms other than exoticism (whether superficial or extravagant, critical or adulatory), which tended to magnify difference into the mark of insurmountable alienation. Of all the exoticisms that blossomed in the two decades before and after 1800, Orientalism had the greatest cultural and political significance. For in those years Orientalism began to take on new significance as Britain's imperial project slowly reemerged (following the debacles of the 1770s and 1780s, and in particular the sensational trial of Warren Hastings) in a properly modern form and with a new set of approaches – informed and sustained by the emergent cultural logic of modernization – to colonized and subject peoples.[2] Especially given these changes, and given the emergence of an altogether new imperial mission fully coinciding with a modern worldview developing in the 1790s, it is in terms of the Orient that we can most clearly locate Blake's divergence from the emergent culture of modernization as that culture was articulated both in romanticism and in the radical movement alongside which it appeared. The Orient and Orientalism provide us with an important index of the distance between the aesthetic and political position articulated by Blake and the one being elaborated by other writers of the 1790s, including Tom Paine, Constantin Volney, Mary Wollstonecraft, John Thelwall, and William Wordsworth.

The hegemonic radical critique of the ancien régime and its "traditional culture" of despotism, patronage, ritual, corruption, and privilege helped to define an emergent culture of modernization based on a universalist discourse of rights and duties, rather than inherited privileges; a discourse of merit, rather than religious inspiration; and, above all, a discourse of sturdy rational frugality, control, virtue and regulation, rather than emotional (let alone sensual) excess. By 1800 the Orient would be definitively recognized as the imaginary locus par excellence of the culture of excess – despotic, enthusiastic, sensual, exotic, erotic – that was the target of bourgeois radicalism. Hence, it served as the ideal surrogate target for radical critique, an imaginary space on which to project all the supposed faults of the old regime and then subject them to attack, scorn, condemnation, repudiation – a cultural and ideological process that cannot meaningfully be separated from the simultaneous change in paradigms of imperial rule, which were already preparing the way for the enormous expansion of imperial activity later in the nineteenth century.

[. . .]

[Two omitted sections of this chapter excerpt describe the reliance on Orientalist representations in the political radicalism of Paine and Wollstonecraft. Such representations support "the power and knowledge of the self-controlling, self-knowing, self-representing sovereign subject" at the heart of Romantic aesthetics.]

3 Blake and the politics of "Immortal Joy"

[. . .] The Blakean landscape of *The Marriage of Heaven & Hell* [. . .] lacks the all-determining structural and structuring opposition of subject and object. But if the vertiginous landscapes visited by the narrator of *The Marriage* and his angelic enemy/friend do not exist in an objective sense, that is not because they are merely the idealistic projections of a viewing subject, for the subject himself does not exist as such, either (which is what prevents Blake from sliding into an idealism predicated on a viewing subject).[3]

Whereas the relation of spectator and spectacle in Wordsworth is one of essential alterity (enabling the mutual dialectical constitution of self and other), in Blake one cannot speak of a spectator that is in any way essentially different from the spectacle being viewed. The "landscapes" being viewed and the "subject position" from which they are viewed are both as unstable as the wildly unbalanced poetry, prose, and art constituting Blake's notoriously unstable text. The point here is not, of course, to contrast an "unstable" text with some fantasy of a normative textual "stability." It is, rather, to consider the ways in which Blake's text plays on – exaggerates – its own instability; and in particular to consider the political implications of this instability in the historical context of the 1790s, when such instability was considered by the hegemonic radical movement to be not only a bad thing, but the worst and most dangerous thing, the telltale warning sign of dangerous plebeian enthusiasm, aristocratic indulgence, feminine licentiousness, Oriental seductiveness, wiliness, treachery.

The impossible landscapes traversed by the many narrators of *The Marriage* are – like the verbal and visual material form which they constitute – incompatible with a self-centered viewing subject. [. . . T]he explicit task of the highly regulated and law-obeying language of Wordsworth's poetry is to "temper" and "restrain" the possibility of an "unusual and irregular state of the mind," in which "ideas and feelings" do not "succeed each other in accustomed order," so that excitement can be prevented from being "carried beyond its proper bounds."[4] Similarly, the explicit task of Wollstonecraft's or Paine's polemical prose is to be "useful" rather than "elegant," to be concerned with "things, not words!" and hence to manifest a forthright "manly" honesty grounded on the incontrovertible security of clear, obvious, manifest *things*, supposedly unencumbered by any dangerously excessive signifying capacity.[5] On the other hand, "That which can be made Explicit to the Idiot," as Blake wrote, "is not worth my care," and indeed the task of the insanely excessive language of Blake's composite art involves an unleashing of signifying potential in as many different forms (verbal, visual, material, spiritual) as possible, bypassing, we might say, the individual consciousness and instead "rouzing" the sub- or trans- or meta-individual "faculties to act."[6] If, for Paine, Wollstonecraft, and Wordsworth [. . .] rhetorical or linguistic stability serves as an analogue for the stability of the sovereign subject, for Blake linguistic and visual instability undermine the false stability of any solitary subject position. But, more than that, they also require an entirely new way of conceiving being and belonging; that is, they require a radically different aesthetic mode – call it a "style" – and a political stance appropriate to it. Without recognizing this, Blake cannot be understood: his work will look like the gibberish so many people have found it to be.

For the hegemonic radicals, [. . .] self-knowledge and self-determination depend upon, among other things, one's capacity to construct an elaborate argument by "establishing, admitting, or denying" certain "facts, principles, or data to reason from" rather than merely asserting whatever one pleases, "on the presumption of its being believed, without offering evidence or reasons for so doing," which is what Paine accuses Burke of [. . .].[7] Blake, on the contrary, pushes us to consider how or to what extent such "Perswasion" actually *does* produce reality ("Does a firm perswasion that something is so, make it so?" the narrator of *The Marriage* asks Isaiah, who replies, "All poets believe that it does, & in ages of imagination this firm perswasion removed mountains").[8] As we see here and throughout Blake's prophetic books, this kind of "Perswasion" [. . .] is not, however, the prerogative of the individual subject or the lonely artist, but rather a collective endeavor, whose potential is amplified by the ever greater joining together of bodies and minds.

For what Blake calls "poetic genius" can be understood – if it can be understood at all – only as a collective process. If language and art here offer lines of flight away from the apparent certainty of knowledge grounded in the viewing subject, they do so by allowing an approximation of the "poetic genius," whose true "subject-position" could be occupied only by that infinite being in common which Blake calls God. This is why throughout his work Blake would contrast, on the one hand, the subject-grounded "philosophic and experimental" knowledge of "man" as a "natural organ subject to sense," that is, man as a "natural body," with, on the other hand, man as a "spiritual body" defined by that capacity for the infinite opened up by poets and prophets activating the "poetic genius."[9] The former, experimental knowledge, is produced through controlled and disciplined discourse. It involves not simply the confrontation of a knowing mind with a material object world over which it seeks "power, of which knowledge is the effect,"[10] as Wordsworth puts it, but also, ultimately, the subjection of that mind to a set of material circumstances which are understood as given once and for all time, determining a human mind which is understood to be equally given once and for all time – hence Wordsworth's project to reconnect the "indestructible" human mind with the "great and permanent objects that act upon it, which are equally inherent and indestructible."[11]

Although Blake himself is often thought of in terms of Napoleonic, Byronic, or Wordsworthian romantic genius and was certainly notoriously prone to angry bouts of paranoia – which were not always unjustified – it is important to remember the extent to which he relentlessly removed himself as the grounding authority, even the author figure, in his own texts. For on his own account, his work is little more than dictation inspired by Jesus Christ, or John Milton, or "the eternals," or fairies (like the one who dictated *Europe*), or his dead brother Robert, with whom Blake claimed to "converse daily & hourly in the Spirit," and who, supposedly appearing to Blake in a vision, taught him how to combine words and pictures in the special method for which he is now known.[12] Blake's work may in this sense be said to have been collectively authored. [. . .]

Many scholars are familiar with those lines in his annotations on Wordsworth in which Blake writes that "Natural Objects always did & do now Weaken deaden & obliterate Imagination in Me," adding that Wordsworth's supplementary "Essay" seems to have been written not by a true poet but by a "Landscape Painter."[13] For, Blake insists, the imagination "is the Divine Vision not of The World nor of Man nor from Man as he is a Natural Man but only as he is a Spiritual Man."[14] Thus, as against the "philosophic and experimental" knowledge of Paine or Wordsworth, with its class- and race-defined requirements for what we can now recognize as a stable Western subject (adequately learned, prepared, disciplined, and "cultivated"), and with its quest for moral virtue and domination over the other, Blake proposes the prophetic power precisely of the unlearned, of his "fellow labourers,"[15] and especially of children, who, he tells Trusler, "have taken a greater delight in contemplating my Pictures than I even hoped."[16] Jesus, Blake writes, "supposes every Thing to be Evident to the Child & to the Poor & Unlearned Such is the Gospel." For, he adds,

> the Whole Bible is filld with Imaginations & Visions from End to End & not with Moral virtues that is the baseness of Plato & the Greeks & all *Warriors* The Moral Virtues are continual Accusers of Sin & promote Eternal Wars & *Domineering over others*.[17]

Thus, rather than the imperial "warrior" discourse of Wordsworth and the hegemonic liberal-radicals – a discourse obsessed with sovereign power and domination of the other – Blake proposes an opening out away from the discourse of sovereign power and toward the mode of being in common appropriate to the spiritual man – that is, a mode of being which recognizes that "God is Man & exists in us & we in him."[18] Infantilization, and especially the infantilization of women, is the disaster that Wollstonecraft seeks to avert, but for Blake, we might say that infantilization – for example, the unity of body and mind that we see in young children, whose impulses Wollstonecraft seeks to bring under control in her training manual for children – actually presents a mode of power precluded by the cultural politics of sovereignty. But Blake's is a radically different conception of power – and his brand of Ranterish plebeian enthusiasm would have made Paine or Wollstonecraft uncomfortable (to say the least). And indeed Blake had occasion elsewhere to apologize for his "Enthusiasm which I wish all to partake of Since it is to me a Source of Immortal Joy."[19] In the remainder of this chapter, I wish to explore not only what Blake meant by this "Immortal Joy," but to consider what a politics built on such joy might look like in an age already dominated by the political aesthetics of empire.

[. . .]

4 Blake's Orient

[. . .] In the *Descriptive Catalogue* of his 1809 exhibition. Blake compares his work not to the earliest European classics of Greece and Rome, but rather to Persian, Indian, and Egyptian art. The traces of those ancient arts are, he says, still preserved on monuments,

> being copies from some stupendous originals now lost or perhaps buried till some happier age. The Artist having been taken in vision into the ancient republics, monarchies, and patriarchates of Asia, has seen those wonderful originals called in the Sacred Scriptures the Cherubim, which were sculptured and painted on walls of Temples, Towers, Cities, Palaces, and erected in the highly cultivated states of Egypt, Moab, Edom, Aram, among the Rivers of Paradise, being originals from which the Greeks and Hertrurians copied Hercules, Farnese, Venus of Medicis, Apollo Belvidere, and all the grand works of ancient art.[20]

Just a few years after Blake wrote these lines, Shelley would famously proclaim in *Hellas*,

> we are all Greeks. Our laws, our literature, our religion, our arts have their roots in Greece. But for Greece – Rome, the instructor, the conqueror, or the metropolis of our ancestors, would have spread no illumination with her arms, and we might still have been savages and idolaters; or, what is worse, might have arrived at such a stagnant and miserable state of social institution as China and Japan possess.[21]

Shelley's rhetoric, of course, has not only an aesthetic motive, but also a very clearly articulated political one as well. It serves to distinguish an emergent European world of modernity from a premodern world of savages, barbarians, and Orientals, all of whom were much in need of "our" glorious civilization.[22] Shelley, in other words, consolidates in *Hellas* an imperial worldview that had only begun to emerge in the radical discourse of the 1790s – and would be transmitted to the Cromers and Balfours of coming generations, serving, in making its all-important distinction between Europe and its others, as one of the crucial ideological underpinnings of nineteenth-century British imperialism. What is being marked here is the transition, explored at length by Martin Bernal, toward a Hellenocentric model of Western European identity, which involves the repudiation and denial of the Afro-Asiatic sources of the earliest European cultures.[23]

Blake's position, on the other hand, involves something more than merely a rhetorical disdain for "the silly Greek & Latin slaves of the sword" and dismissal of "the Stolen and Perverted Writings of Homer & Ovid: of Plato & Cicero, which all Men ought to contemn."[24] For if Blake refuses the Hellenocentric move, he does so not only in order to stress the Afro-Asiatic origins of European culture (a notion also stressed, for quite different purposes, by East India Company officials including William Jones and Thomas Maurice as well as artists like Luigi Mayer), but also in order to emphasize the of *all* human cultures. Such a notion of sharing and being in common – notwithstanding important differences – must be seen to be quite drastically at odds with the imperialist rhetoric both of his own time and of the coming decades. In his work of the 1790s, Blake contests the political aesthetics of empire which were emerging in Wordsworthian romanticism as well as in the liberal-radical writings of Paine and Wollstonecraft, and which would pit self against other, West against East.

Whereas the political aesthetic of empire is predicated on the dialectics of otherness, what Blake attempts in his work is the resurrection of a lost common being which might reunify humankind *along with* all its differences. We can see this political aesthetic at work, for example, in *A Divine Image* in *Songs of Innocence.*

To Mercy Pity Peace and Love,
All pray in their distress:
And to these virtues of delight
Return their thankfulness.

For Mercy Pity Peace and Love,
Is God our father dear:
And Mercy Pity Peace and Love,
Is Man his child and care.

For Mercy has a human heart
Pity, a human face:
And Love, the human form divine,
And Peace, the human dress.

Then every man of every clime,
That prays in his distress,
Prays to the human form divine
Love Mercy Pity Peace.

And all must love the human form,
In heathen, turk or jew.

> Where Mercy, Love & Pity dwell,
> There God is dwelling too.

Written at a moment of intense political and military interest in foreign cultures, these lines present a radical challenge to the emergent cultural politics of British imperialism. Only through the most superficial and banal of readings, which have often been proposed, could this expression of Blake's intense antinomian faith – and its underlying political stance – be assimilated into the ideology of the established church. Indeed, although Blake bound the plates constituting the various copies of *Songs of Innocence and of Experience* in widely divergent and seemingly random sequences, one of the rare consistencies among the different editions is that in the majority he paired *A Divine Image* with either *Holy Thursday* or *The Chimney Sweeper*.[25] All three of these songs share a highly critical attitude toward the religious conventions of the established church, which Blake identified elsewhere in unambiguous terms as the "state religion" that he associated with such notorious "state tricksters" as the bishop of Llandaff, and, moreover, with that version of the Bible which had been repeatedly deployed as "a State Trick, thro which tho' the People at all times could see they never had the power to throw off."[26] Nor, for that matter, could *A Divine Image* rightly be seen as anything like an approximation of the supposed "humanism" of evangelical abolitionists such as William Wilberforce or Hannah More. The evangelical challenges to the slave trade were quite readily compatible with highly repressive attitudes regarding domestic politics and an aggressively proimperial stance on foreign affairs, both of which would have been profoundly offensive to Blake.[27]

In *A Divine Image*, the orthodox Christianity of the established church and state (as articulated, for example, in Isaac Watts's fervent lines, "Lord, I ascribe it to thy Grace / And not to Chance, as others do, / That I was born of *Christian* Race, / And not a *Heathen,* or a *Jew*")[28] is challenged by Blake's affirmation that all religions are one, a position that he had already elaborated in his first work in illuminated printing the year before (1788): "As all men are alike (tho' infinitely various) So all Religions."[29] [. . .]

[T]he essential being in common of Christian, Heathen, Turk (i.e., Muslim), and Jew [in *A Divine Image*] is constituted by their *heterogeneity*, rather than by their *sameness*. The relationship of essence and identity formulated by Blake is something like the relationship of substance and mode in Spinoza. In both cases, essential unity is sharply differentiated from homogeneity, and [. . .] in both cases this opens up the possibility of a kind of freedom that is far less constraining than the emergent discourse of "liberty" constructed around the position of a supposedly transcendent bourgeois subject, whose freedom could be worked out only in a network of relations with "others" who are more or less free. Especially in the context of empire (which is the context in which the 1790s advocates of liberty were working) these others would generally have been less free rather than more free.

In Blake's account, there is no contradiction between being "infinitely various" and being "alike," no contradiction between one essence and many identities, or, to use Spinoza's language, one substance and many modes. Rather, the "alike" for Blake is perfectly consistent with infinite variety: "As all men are alike in outward form, So (and with the same infinite variety) all are alike in the Poetic Genius," he writes in *All Religions are One*. Indeed, such variety and infinity in Blake's antinomian conception are what *immanently* define being, and what define God: "the desire of

Man being infinite the possession is Infinite & himself Infinite," he writes in another early copy engraving; "Therefore God becomes as we are, that we may be as he is." What would threaten our infinite and ever-differentiated being is, on the contrary, constant identity, conformity, nullity, and death, since "the same dull round even of a univer[s]e would soon become a mill with complicated wheels."[30] Infinite variety is in other words what makes being possible and desirable, while a uniform identity (turning all difference into sameness, all others into the self, and indeed hardening the self itself into an atom-like monad) would turn the world into a predictable mechanism like a clock or a mill.

If what I am calling the political aesthetic of empire distinguishes one person from another, one culture from another, Blake's religio-political aesthetic is an attempt to resurrect a lost immanent unity – identified in those "stupendous originals now lost or perhaps buried till some happier age" – without placing one culture in a position superior to that of another. "The antiquities of every Nation under Heaven," he writes, "are the same thing as Jacob Bryant, and all antiquaries have proved." For, he adds, "all had originally one language, and one religion, this was the religion of Jesus, the Everlasting Gospel."[31] Here the everlasting gospel – the central organizing concept in the underground antinomian tradition going back at least to the seventeenth century – is sharply distinguished from the Judeo-Christian tradition of the established state religion, which would so ably serve the imperial culture of the nineteenth century as a way to distinguish savages from civilized men.

Blake must be seen here to be articulating his own autodidactically cobbled-together and highly radicalized version of a very old tradition of pantheistic thought, which claimed its origins in pre-Christian antiquity, when all humankind is supposed to have shared one language and one religion (Blake's "everlasting gospel"), which was copied, appropriated, and perverted by later religions and cultures. [. . .]

Blake, however, would have inherited this tradition – whose lineage was traced as long ago as the 1950s by A.L. Morton,[32] but seemingly forgotten by Blake scholars – after its regeneration in the middle of the seventeenth century, when, following Isaac Casaubon's repudiation of the antiquity of the Hermetic texts, the Hermetic tradition went underground and was highly radicalized during England's revolutionary years. From then on, the Hermetic tradition can be seen to have diverged, one line of thought leading to an elitist notion of hidden knowledges and mysteries, which would be most fully elaborated in Rosicrucianism and Freemasonry, and the other line of thought plunging deeper underground in a lineage of antinomian dangerous enthusiasm, one of whose end points would be William Blake, who stood out in his own time as a freak, a crazy Orientalized Cockney, trying to sell crazy picture books. [. . .] Put back in this context, from which it emerged, one of the lines that is repeatedly reiterated in Blake's illuminated books – "every thing that lives is holy" – suddenly takes on new meaning, for we are reminded that Blake was not alone in his beliefs, however bizarre they may have seemed in his own time, let alone in our own. He was part of a long tradition of what appears from the standpoint of the dominant dualistic philosophical and political tradition deriving from Locke as a series of "savage anomalies."[33]

However, in the context of the 1790s, Blake's reactivation and rearticulation of the old panthetistic and antinomian tradition takes on particular political significance. Somewhere in the hidden core of this tradition was the belief that European civilization is not essentially different from Afro-Asiatic civilization, or, in other words, the belief that, in spite of all their differences, "All Religions are One." Modern imperialism could emerge really only with, or after, the recognition that Europe was essentially different from its others, that is, with the recognition of an insurmountable distinction between East and West ("East is East and West is West"). Blake's emphasis on the common essential unity of humankind would, quite clearly, have been radically incompatible with the emerging imperialist worldview, including the version of that worldview which we can see in the work of evangelical writers who sought to affirm a common humanity by turning all cultures into the same. For Blake, as we have seen, essential unity was quite readily compatible with enormous heterogeneity and difference.

In tracing a lost being in common, of course, Blake sometimes runs the risk of seeming to collapse all cultures into each other. Whereas the Oriental scenes of Montesquieu, Byron, or Southey are structured in terms of radical difference from some Western norm, the kings and counselors of "Asia" in *The Song of Los,* for example, look and sound rather like their European counterparts, seeming particularly indistinguishable when they seek "to fix the price of labour" and "to cut off the bread from the city, / That the remnant may learn to obey," charges which were frequently leveled at the Pitt regime in England all through the 1790s.[34] Various critics have pointed to the reference to the "darkness of Asia" awaiting the "thick-flaming, thought-creating fires of Orc" in *The Song of Los,* suggesting that Blake here participates in Eurocentric or Orientalist discourse in a depiction of Oriental ignorance awaiting Western enlightenment.[35] Yet *all* the continents of Blake's 1790s prophecies are described (for whatever such "descriptions" are worth) as "dark," including revolutionary America itself, which is repeatedly shown wrapped in "thick clouds and darkness."[36]

If anything, all the continents and all the peoples of Blake's world are equally subject to the same forces of oppression, all together waiting for the fires of freedom and deliverance from a common enemy – the Urizenic codes, which take on different forms in different places but nevertheless share underlying continuities. For, just as Blake traced an original language and religion immanently and heterogeneously uniting humankind via "the poetic genius" (since "the Religions of all Nations are derived from each Nations different reception of the Poetic Genius"), the perversion of the common poetic genius and its usurpation by a hierarchizing state is also shown to be a universal occurrence, manifested differently from place to place. Thus in *The Song of Los* there is an ongoing systematic relationship between the "Abstract Philosophy" given to "Brama in the East," the "abstract Law" given to "Pythagoras, Socrates & Plato," the "loose Bible" given to "Mahomet," the "Code of War" given "in the North, to Odin," and the "Philosophy of Five Senses" which Urizen places in the hands of "Newton & Locke."[37] So while Blake's great idol Milton had declared – like many of the radicals of Blake's own time – that "the people of Asia" are "much inclinable to slavery,"[38] Blake's Asians are neither more nor less servile than his Europeans, and they certainly do not seem particularly different. Actually, their appearance never really registers as an issue, and in this context we should bear in mind Blake's tendency to de-exoticize as much as possible many of the images of otherness that were involved in his commissioned work.

[. . .]

It has recently been suggested, however, that Blake's representation of non-Europeans amounts to a denial of cultural difference. For example, Blake's *Little*

Black Boy in *Songs of Innocence* is in many copies of the plate indistinguishable from the little white boy with whom he appears (though, as Morris Eaves points out, too few readings of *Little Black Boy* pay sufficient attention to that plate's relationships to *The Chimney Sweeper*, in which skin color has nothing to do with matters of race or culture). Anne Mellor sees this as evidence that, although in his visual artwork (including his commissioned work, notably the Stedman illustrations) Blake may indeed have made an effort to portray African or Asian bodies as more noble and heroic by making them seem more "European," this is because he "participated in a cultural erasure of difference between races and individuals that gave priority to Western, white models."[39]

[. . .]

[I]n examining texts and images from the late eighteenth and early nineteenth centuries, we need to be careful to distinguish between, on the one hand, attitudes toward other cultures and, on the other hand, positions on imperialism. [. . .] Warren Hastings and William Jones admired Indian culture as much as Thomas Macaulay and James Mill would revile it – but all of them were committed imperialists. The problem is that they were committed to quite different imperialist projects, or perhaps to different moments of the same imperialist project. In the late eighteenth and early nineteenth centuries it was therefore possible to mobilize what we would today recognize as racist arguments in order to oppose imperialism, just as it was also possible to justify one's support for the empire's civilizing mission on the basis of one's profound and genuinely felt concern for other peoples and cultures, one's sense of their desperate need for the "gift" of what has been called civilization. Indeed, such contradictions persist into our own time. While, for example, it is easy enough to recognize that Victorian imperialists tended to express hostility toward what they regarded as inferior cultures, we sometimes have to pinch ourselves to remember the extent to which, for all its celebration of "otherness" and "difference," twenty-first century multiculturalism – in an era of truly globalized capitalism – is in fact a by-product of the most aggressively acquisitive exploitation of other cultures in the history of the world.

For similar reasons, the suppression – rather than the emphasis – of racial and cultural difference need not, in itself, be taken as evidence of the visual discourse of modern European colonialism.[40] At certain moments in its history, as we have seen, European colonialism itself celebrated difference and otherness; at others it denigrated them. The mere suppression or expression of racial difference, in themselves, therefore do not automatically indicate positions for and against colonialism itself. It has, in fact, been the central argument of the present chapter that by the end of the eighteenth century a sense of radical cultural difference (real, exaggerated, or otherwise) would provide the new form of the British imperialist project that began to emerge during the 1790s with one of its essential ideological underpinnings, which is why, even in its most benign guise, the period's widespread interest in – or really obsession with – exoticism would have such an immediately political character. In this context, Blake's systematic avoidance of such exoticism suggests a very different attitude toward other cultures and peoples than the ones rising to dominance at the dawn of the nineteenth century.

If "the Religions of all Nations are derived from each Nations different reception of the Poetic Genius," what that suggests is not that "all Religions are One" in the sense that they are all homogeneous, but rather that "all Religions are One" in the sense that they are all quite different. From the normative notion of identity and difference evoked by Mellor, this proposition could amount to little more than a flat contradiction in terms. But for Blake this proposition offers a line of flight away from the normative discourse of "warrior" aesthetics. The work of Jacob Bryant, to which Blake often refers, is a monumental attempt to chart out the common ancestry of humankind, to locate in every distinct cultural tradition "some shattered fragments of original history; some traces of a primitive and universal language"[41] The "Jewish & Christian Testaments," Blake writes in *All Religions are One*, "are An original derivation from the Poetic Genius."[42] But each religion, each nation, each people, has its own version of the same – but immanently differentiated – lost original, which was the object of Bryant's enquiry. "The Religions of all Nations," Blake writes, "are derived from each Nations different reception of the Poetic Genius which is every where call'd the Spirit of Prophecy."[43] Blake is able to avoid collapsing all nations and peoples into a bland homogeneous sameness, while at the same time he is able to preserve each nation's distinctiveness, since each nation's distinct identity does not prevent it from sharing in a common essence. Blake here must be seen to be trying to preempt or perhaps subvert the monadic politics of sovereign power – which, as he could already see, was threatening to reduce the world to a homogeneous machine and to preserve the possibility of the political aesthetics based on "immortal joy."

Blake's refusal of Orientalism, in offering an escape from the models of normative self-regulating subjectivity, proposes not only a different way of regarding otherness, however, but above all a different way of living, sharing, belonging, loving, being in common. All of this is not to say, though, that Blake was unique in his disengagement with Orientalism. To find his nearest equivalents, however, we have to look not among the canonical romantic poets but rather among the many appeals to working people around the world issued by members of the insurrectionary underground of the 1790s, especially those members of the underground who were more concerned with fighting the state than with insinuating themselves into it, such as Thomas Spence, or Daniel Isaac Eaton, who – in response to Burke's reference to "a swinish multitude" – wrote in one issue of his *Politics for the People* that

> we, the swine of Great Britain, have no right to esteem ourselves superior, in the scale of beings, to the swine of France, or any other country; we regard our brethren, whether they be found in the East or Western Indies, or on the burning plains of Africa, with true fraternal affection.[44]

The common cause among the peoples of Africa, Asia, America, and Europe in Blake's Lambeth books – including *The Song of Los* – must be understood in this context: it requires much more adaptation, and a great sacrifice of its political significance, to fit it into the Eurocentric discourse of romantic Orientalism.

Nor, clearly, were all radicals as quick as, say, Paine or Wollstonecraft or Thelwall to reject the charge of belonging to the "swinish multitude," or to try to lay claim to respectability and moral superiority over others. However subversively, Eaton, Spence, and many others eagerly embraced Burke's dismissive epithet in their stories and publications ("Pig's Meat," "Salmagundy for Swine," "Swineherd's Remonstrance," "Advice to Swine," etc.). Without conforming to the agenda of either Eaton or Spence, Blake – whose library, as Frederick Tatham pointed out, included many "mystical" titles[45] – was also interested in an altogether different kind of political culture from the one so zealously championed by the hegemonic radicals. It is no coincidence that Oriental exoticism held little interest for him as he tried to imagine a world in which the all-important distinctions between Orient and Occident – or self and other – had no role to play, and in which supposedly essential distinctions among the continents were put to one side rather than mobilized as the explanation and indeed the root cause of all cultural and political differences among people.

Blake must be seen to be trying to rescue against all odds the possibility of a political aesthetic of immortal joy, which we can understand as an affirmation of joyous unity and collective freedom. This amounts to a refusal of the very logic of domination, of warrior power over others. More precisely, the quest for such immortal joy can be seen to involve two distinct components: first, a struggle against transcendence and domination in all of their political and religious and military forms, and second, a struggle for a form of being in common that would not require authorization by a transcendental principle such as the king, or the state, or the transcendent god of the established church.

Notes

1 Blake, letter to Hayley, 6 May 1800 [in *The Complete Poetry and Prose of William Blake*, ed. David Erdman (New York: Doubleday, Anchor Books, 1988), E705. Unless otherwise noted, all references to works by Blake are to this edition, identified by the letter *E* preceding the page number].
2 This is a point that I discuss at much greater length in *Romantic Imperialism: Universal Empire and the Culture of Modernity* (Cambridge: Cambridge University Press, 1998).
3 Blake, *Marriage of Heaven & Hell*, E41.
4 See [William] Wordsworth, "Preface" [in *Lyrical Ballads*, by William Wordsworth and Samuel Taylor Coleridge (1800; reprint, London: Routledge, 1991)], p. 264.
5 See [Mary] Wollstonecraft, [*A Vindication of the Rights of Woman* (1792; reprint, Harmondsworth: Penguin, 1992),] p. 82.
6 Blake, letter to Dr. Trusler, 23 August 1799, E702.
7 [Thomas Paine, *Rights of Man* (1790–92; reprint, Harmondsworth: Penguin, 1985) pp. 66–7.]
8 Blake, *Marriage of Heaven & Hell*, E38–9.
9 See Blake, *There is No Natural Religion*, E2–3.
10 Wordsworth, "Preface."
11 Ibid., pp. 249–50.
12 See G.E. Bentley, ed., *Blake Records* (Oxford: Oxford University Press, 1969), pp. 32–3, 406; also see Blake, letter to Hayley, 6 May 1800, E705.
13 See Blake, annotations to Wordsworth, E665–6.
14 Ibid., E666.
15 Blake, *Public Address*, E580.
16 Blake, letter to Dr. Trusler, E703.
17 Blake, annotations to Berkeley, E664. Emphases added.
18 Ibid., E664.
19 Blake, letter to Hayley, E705.
20 Blake, *Descriptive Catalogue*, E531.
21 Shelley, preface to *Hellas*.
22 I discuss this at length in the chapter on Byron and Shelley in *Romantic Imperialism*.
23 [Martin] Bernal, *Black Athena* [*: The Afroasiastic Roots of Classical Civilization* (New Brunswick, N.J.: Rutgers University Press, 1987)], esp. pp. 161–308.
24 Blake, *Milton*, E95.
25 In *Songs of Innocence*, copies A–H and K–M, *Chimney Sweeper* and *Divine Image* appear together on facing pages; in copies I, O, P, Q, and S, *Divine Image* and *Holy Thursday* appear together; in the complete *Songs of Innocence and of Experience*, in copy A, all three appear in sequence,

and then in copies B–F, I, M, and P, *Divine Image* is paired with or appears sequentially after either *Holy Thursday* or *Chimney Sweeper.* See G.E. Bentley, *Blake Books: Annotated Catalogues of William Blake's Writings in Illuminated Printing, in Conventional Typography, and in Manuscript* (Oxford: Oxford University Press, 1977), pp. 375–80.

26 See Blake's annotations to the bishop of Llandaff's *Apology for the Bible* (E612–16). Of course, as Blake points out in *The Everlasting Gospel,* "Both read the Bible day & night, / But thou readst black where I read white." See Blake, *Everlasting Gospel,* E524.

27 The abolitionist movement's object of concern was the slave as an individual ("am I not a man and a brother?"), and in particular the slave as a potential Christian, rather than the slave as a representative of a particular alien culture.

28 Isaac Watts, *Divine Songs,* quoted in the editor's notes in the Blake Trust edition of *Songs of Innocence and of Experience,* ed. Andrew Lincoln (Princeton, N.J.: Princeton University Press, 1991), p. 159.

29 Blake, *All Religions are One,* E2.

30 Blake, *No Natural Religion,* 2d ser., E2.

31 Blake, *Descriptive Catalogue,* [E]543.

32 See A.L. Morton, *The Everlasting Gospel: A Study in the Sources of William Blake* (London: Lawrence and Wishart, 1958).

33 See Antonio Negri, *The Savage Anomaly: The Power of Spinoza's Metaphysics and Politics,* trans. Michael Hardt (Minneapolis: University of Minnesota Press, 1991).

34 See Blake, *Song of Los,* E68–9.

35 See, for example, [Marilyn] Butler, "Orientalism," [in *The Romantic Period,* ed. David Pirie (Harmondsworth: Penguin, 1994),] esp. pp. 408–9. Also see Blake, *Song of Los,* E68.

36 Blake, *America,* E54.

37 See Blake, *Song of Los,* E67–8.

38 John Milton, *The Tenure of Kings and Magistrates,* in *John Milton: Critical Edition of Major Works* (Oxford: Oxford University Press, 1991), p. 279.

39 See [Ann] Mellor, "Sex, Violence, and Slavery[: Blake and Wollstonecraft," *Huntington Library Quarterly* 58, nos. 3, 4 (1997): 345–70], esp. pp. 350–9.

40 Mellor, "Sex, Violence, and Slavery," p. 359.

41 Jacob Bryant, *A New System, or Analysis of Ancient Mythology; wherein an Attempt is made to divest Tradition of Fable; and to reduce the Truth to its Original Purity* (London, 1774).

42 Blake, *All Religions are One,* E1.

43 Ibid., E1.

44 Daniel Isaac Eaton, ed., *Politics for the People: Or, A Salmagundy for Swine,* no. 5 (London, 1794), p. 60.

45 See Bentley, *Blake Records,* p. 41 n. 4.

23 "Voices of dead complaint"
Colonial military disease narratives

Alan Bewell

[Five sections omitted from this excerpt provide background on the connection between colonialism and disease in eighteenth-century political and literary writing.]

The Ancient Mariner's "ghastly tale": tropical disease as punishment

At the end of a century largely silent about the enormous number of servicemen being lost in military and colonial ventures, the 1790s saw the emergence of debate, especially with the greater public role being played by military physicians and the reports of the casualties in the British attempt to occupy St. Domingue. [. . . T]he appearance of a literature focused on dead and dying soldiers and their abandoned wives may have less to do with literary fashion than with a growing need to understand and speak about the epidemiological cost of colonialism, especially when we realize that throughout most of the eighteenth century about one-quarter of British battalions were in or bound for the West Indies.[1] The ongoing warfare on the Continent was causing equally disastrous losses by disease, though public concern did not develop substantial momentum until the scandalous losses at Walcheren, where in six months, out of an original force of 39,000 men, almost 4,000 died of malaria and over 11,000 returned sick.

One gauge of the depth of this concern is that even the more conservative voices in the British Parliament were beginning to question the cost of colonial policy in the West Indies. Edmund Burke, for instance, was arguing that it was not military might but a combination of race and climate that was the true enemy of the British:

> In carrying on the war in the West Indies, the hostile sword is merciful; the country in which we engage is the dreadful enemy. There the European conqueror finds a cruel defeat in the very fruits of his success. Every advantage is but a new demand on England for recruits to the West Indian grave. In a West India war, the Regicides have for their troops, a race of fierce barbarians, to whom the poisoned air, in which our youth inhale certain death, is salubrity and life. To them the climate is the surest and most faithful of allies.[2]

Burke powerfully captures the growing public perception of the Sugar Islands as a deadly pathogenic space. It is not the people but the environment that the English are fighting, a gigantic graveyard or miasmatic space of death incessantly swallowing up new recruits. "It was not an enemy we had to vanquish, but a cemetery to conquer," he declares. Whereas throughout the eighteenth century the high mortality of Europeans in tropical regions was a justification for slavery in the New World, over the nineteenth century it raised more and more questions about the feasibility of empire.

Romantic poets, writing in the midst of this public debate, lacked neither knowledge nor examples of the terrible impact of war and colonial expansion on the lives of both indigenous peoples and the European "casualties" who served in the military.[3] On 5 May 1796, for instance, in a passage that anticipates the "Rime," [Samuel Taylor] Coleridge writes:

> About 70 men of the 20th regiment landed at Plymouth on Tuesday last from on board a transport lately arrived from the West-Indies. Many of them are in an unhealthy state. They are the remains of 700 fine fellows, who have been thus reduced by the ravages of the yellow fever.[4]

As poets sought to respond to the staggering epidemiological cost of empire, however, they simultaneously faced the problem that by 1795 the discourse of protest was itself becoming commonplace. Sentimentalism's appeal to the generalized sympathy of an educated audience had lost its power. In the midst of suffering on an unprecedented scale, the rhetoric of the philanthropic observer seemed just that – rhetoric.
[. . .]
In this context Coleridge wrote the "Rime" not as a displacement of "history" but to express the enormous suffering produced by colonialism in a more imaginative and emotionally engaging language.[5] Like the sentimental magazine poetry of the day, the poem is structured as an encounter between a vagrant (one of those "wretches that sadden every street in this City")[6] and an English gentleman. Coleridge, however, overturns the sentimentalist paradigm by giving us a Wedding Guest who feels he has better things to do than listen to a wandering, perhaps mad, vagrant. Nor are we asked to adopt the Mariner's point of view, even though his account dominates the poem. Their meeting is staged as a forced encounter: the Mariner cannot refuse to speak, nor can the Wedding Guest refuse to hear. The story must be told.

Jerome J. McGann has made a strong case for reading the "Rime" as an "imitation of a culturally redacted literary work."[7] He argues that it is about the historical reception of salvific narratives, as the original story told by the Mariner in the early 1500s is made into a ballad by an Elizabethan minstrel and then published during the late seventeenth century as an edited text complete with a Neoplatonic prose gloss. According to McGann, the poem is an imitation of higher criticism's concept of Scripture; it

> is, as it were, an English national Scripture; that is to say, the poem imitates a redacted literary text which comprises various material extending from early pre-Christian periods through a succession of later epochs of Christian culture, and the ultimate locus of these transmissions is England.
>
> (57)[8]

It should be stressed, however, that the time frame of the narrative and its successive retellings, from the early sixteenth century to its publication as a literary imitation in 1798 (or to its revised form in 1817), is also that of the colonial period. The poem is very much a colonial narrative, "a supreme crystallization of the spirit of maritime expansion" (Ebbatson 175). Yet as an interpolated narrative, a story that has undergone interpretive transformations over 300 years, it is more than simply an account of colonial experience – *it also enacts the historical reception of colonial narratives*. In the "Rime," Coleridge made his own frustration at representing colonial suffering – obvious in the lecture "On the Present War" – itself the subject of the narrative. For the Wedding Guest, who is but one of a long line of people who hear, sing, or read this tale, the events narrated are fantastic and frightening. They document an experience that is almost totally beyond comprehension, yet "he cannot choose but hear."[9] As the final stanza of the poem suggests, the narrative has transformed him:

> He went like one that hath been stunned,
> And is of sense forlorn:
> A sadder and a wiser man,
> He rose the morrow morn.
>
> (622–5)

The Ancient Mariner has been more than "stunned" by colonial experience; he has been traumatized. Recourse to the supernatural seems the only way to explain it. As Charles Lamb suggested, he has undergone "such trials as overwhelm and bury all individuality or memory of what he was – like the state of a man in a bad dream."[10] Telling the tale thus becomes a partial means of expiating his own guilt:

> Since then, at an uncertain hour,
> That agony returns:
> And till my ghastly tale is told,
> This heart within me burns.
>
> (582–5)

Even though the tale is told in Britain, the radical differences between the experience of the Mariner and that of the Wedding Guest seriously undermine the claim that the poem takes on the status of a "national Scripture" because a coherent interpretive community is lacking. Coleridge may have been attempting to write a Christian "saving history," one that would make sense of an otherwise pointless nightmare of suffering. Yet within the framework of the poem, the "salvific narrative" is itself another redaction, which does not fully displace the world and experience of the Ancient Manner, whose conversion has been largely based on his sense of being in a world where "God himself / Scarce seemèd there to be" (599–600). What remains a priority throughout the poem is the necessity to tell the tale and to force someone to listen. Although in literal terms the "silent sea" (106) of the poem refers to the Pacific, it also evokes the silent world of death that the tropics had become by the end of the eighteenth century.

The "Rime" is typical of the kind of colonial narrative that Coleridge and Wordsworth were writing at this time because it is less about "colonial encounter" than about "colonial return." The epidemiological cost of colonialism returns in the form of "tropical invalids" who wander through the landscape as vagrants or frightening pariahs. Through his encounter with the Ancient Mariner, the Wedding Guest confronts colonialism registered not in the experience of indigenous populations, but in that of those Europeans who played a key role in the expansion of empire. He fears what he sees, and rightly so, because the Mariner embodies sickness and death. As in [Richard] Glover's "Admiral Hosier's Ghost" the disease experience of the common sailor is anonymous and spectral, voiced by the background appearance of silent ghosts – "these mournful spectres sweeping / Ghastly o'er this hated wave."[11] The Ancient Mariner's voice draws its being from this spectral world; it taps into the dark cultural unconscious of an England that recognized its fundamental link to these pariahs even as it disowned them. To the Wedding Guest he is almost a figure of the colonial landscape itself, the beaches of the New World – "thou art long, and lank, and brown, / As is the ribbed sea-sand" (226–7). "I pass, like night, from land to land" (586), the Ancient Mariner declares, as if he were death itself and a force that moves across the globe, recognizing no geographical boundaries. Sara Suleri suggests that "colonial facts are vertiginous," that "they move with a ghostly mobility to suggest how highly unsettling an economy of complicity and guilt is in operation between each actor on the colonial stage."[12] Coleridge's narrative of the encounter between the Wedding Guest and Britain's disowned son, the Mariner, profoundly enacts this economy of "complicity and guilt."

Like Smallpox in the legend of the Kiowas, the Ancient Mariner is mythologized. Nevertheless one should not ignore the social and historical reality he embodies. James C. McKusick has suggested that his "ominous, shadowy presence" (106) can already be seen in the 1795 "Lecture on the Slave-Trade," where Coleridge claims that the West Indian slave trade has been an epidemiological catastrophe not only for blacks, but also for the sailors engaged in it:

> From the brutality of their Captain and the unwholesomeness of the Climate through which they pass, it has been calculated that every Slave Vessel from the Port of Bristol loses on an average almost a fourth of the whole Crew – and so far is this Trade from being a nursery for Seamen, that the Survivors are rather shadows in their appearance than men and frequently perish in Hospitals after the completion of the Voyage. . . . In Jamaica many rather than re-embark for their native Country beg from door to door, and many are seen in the streets dying daily in an ulcerated state – and they who return home, are generally incapacitated for future service by a complication of Disorder[s] contracted from the very nature of the Voyage.
>
> (*Lectures* 238–9)

In drawing attention to the many sailors invalided or reduced to beggary or "shadows" by the slave trade. Coleridge was greatly indebted to the work of Thomas Clarkson, who made the high mortality rate of sailors a key justification for abolishing it. Although the British had long recognized the high mortality suffered by blacks – in Africa, during the "middle passage," and after their arrival in the West Indies – it was not until the late 1780s that attention was drawn to slavery's cost in sailors' lives. [. . .] Clarkson, working for the Society for the Abolition of the Slave Trade, made the health of sailors working in the trade a public issue. To support his arguments, he did something extraordinary for the time: by personally interviewing sailors in the major slaving ports of London, Bristol, and Liverpool and examining ship muster lists, he attempted to compile a detailed record of what happened to *every* sailor employed in the trade. He notes that by 1788 "I had already obtained the names of more than 20,000 seamen, in different voyages, knowing what had become of each."[13] Clarkson was thus able to demonstrate, for instance, that "of 5000 sailors on the triangular route in 1786, 2320 came home, 1130 died, 80 were discharged in Africa and unaccounted for and 1470 were discharged or deserted in the West Indies."[14] In the *Essay on the Impolicy of the African Slave Trade* (1788), in a passage cited by Coleridge, Clarkson asserted that contrary to prevailing opinion the slave trade was not "a nursery for [British] seamen" but "a Grave" that destroyed "more in one year, than all the other trades of Great Britain when put together destroy in two."[15] "If we refer it to the number of seamen employed" in each slave-trading voyage, Clarkson concluded, "more than a fifth perish" (the rates for Bristol, Coleridge notes, were higher) (57). Clarkson also pointed out another surprising fact: mortality rates for seamen on the middle passage were higher than those of slaves! As the French trader P. Laberthe remarked in 1805, with some exaggeration, some "parts of the Guinea Coast were so unhealthy that the slave trade there was 'an exchange of whites for blacks.'"[16]

Although Clarkson's disease statistics may appear extreme, they have been confirmed by recent historians. [Philip D.] Curtin observes that "the death rate per voyage among the crew was uniformly higher than the death rate among the slaves in transit at the same period."[17] He adds another surprising statistic, that even as the death rates for slaves fell throughout the eighteenth century, those "of the crew remained fairly at the same level" (284). [. . .] This historical context informs the Mariner's story as it explores how the racial violence directed toward blacks recoils on the enslavers. In [Captain George] Shelvocke's *Voyage* (1726), from which the central event in the poem was taken, it is the color of the albatross that disturbs Hatley, the second captain and justifies his destruction of it:

> a disconsolate black *Albitross* . . . accompanied us for several days . . . till *Hatley* . . . imagined from his colour, that it might be some ill omen. . . . [He] at length, shot the *Albitross*, not doubting (perhaps) that we should have a fair wind after it.[18]

Agreeing with Clarkson, Coleridge recognizes that although sailors seem to have greater control over their destinies, they are treated no better than those they victimize.[19] The "Rime" produces a similar symbolic conflation of these two groups, as many images used to describe the Ancient Mariner's disease experience could just as easily have been drawn from descriptions of slaves during the middle passage. The Mariner undergoes a symbolic "blackening" throughout the poem. There is a striking emphasis on his brown skin: "I fear thee, ancient Mariner . . . thou art long, and lank, and brown . . . I fear . . . thy skinny hand so brown" (224–9).[20] In describing the Ancient Mariner's entrance into the "tropical Latitude of the Great Pacific Ocean" (Argument), Coleridge reinforces the contemporary expectation that such spaces are pathogenic, for it is a depopulated world of corruption, disease, and death. Yet he also asserts that the institution of slavery has made this space what it is. The old sailor does not come upon an "other" but instead, as William Empson has observed, meets the "naked hulk" (195) and "rotting planks" of a European slaver.[21] What the Mariner sees, he sees through the eyes of the slaves of the middle passage:

> With throats unslaked, with *black lips* baked,
> We could nor laugh nor wail;

. . . .
I bit my arm, I sucked the blood
And cried, A sail! a sail!
      (157–61, emphasis added)

Thus the Mariner's experience extends across the determinacies of race, as it draws parallels between the maritime experience of sailors and slaves; through his own violence he has been given the ability to see the world differently.[22] Where the Kiowas personified disease in the figure of Smallpox, Coleridge locates it in a slave ship, whose reach now extends to the limits of the known world. "There was a ship" (line 10) are the Mariner's first words.

As the hulk approaches, it is portrayed as a force that imprisons, its naked ribs appearing like a "dungeon-grate" (179) standing "Betwixt us and the Sun" (176). On board are two allegorical figures, who represent the two primary aspects of colonialism – "Death" and "Life-in-Death." The latter is described as a prostitute:

Her lips were red, her looks were free,
Her locks were yellow as gold:
Her skin was as white as leprosy,
The Night-mare Life-in-Death was she,
Who thicks man's blood with cold.
      (190–4)

Although prostitution, in a colonial context, has a massive range of meanings, Coleridge is here drawing extensively on the discourse of luxury, which plays such a key role in his understanding of colonial slavery. "The pestilent inventions of Luxury," he argues, are the fundamental basis of the West Indian slave economy (*Lectures* 236). [. . .] Coleridge portrays Life-in-Death as having "leprosy," a disease that was associated not only with the Middle East and Africa but also with the impact of European colonialism on the people of the Pacific.[23] [. . .] Since the sailors themselves were also afflicted by many of the same diseases, Life-in-Death is the allegorical embodiment of colonial epidemiology.[24] Leprosy also brings into focus the importance of race and skin color within the economics of colonialism. "Her skin was as white as leprosy" suggests both an artificial whitening of the skin and a disease of "white" society.[25] In the *Watchman* essay "On the Slave Trade," Coleridge emphasizes the link between luxury, cosmetics, and leprosy when he writes that the various reasons that have been brought forward to justify the slave trade "have been the cosmetics with which our parliamentary orators have endeavored to conceal the deformities of a commerce, which is blotched all over with one leprosy of evil" (136). Coleridge's Life-in-Death represents this "leprosy of evil." Like the "painted ship" and the "painted ocean" (*Complete Poems* 117–18), she personifies what the world the Mariner moves in has become.

This encounter produces one of the most vivid representations of tropical death in British literature. In "On the Slave Trade," Coleridge speaks of the West Indian trade as "more often a losing than a winning trade – a Lottery with more blanks than prizes in it" (*Watchman* 135). In the poem this gamble is literalized, as the mariners watch Death and Life-in-Death rolling dice to decide their fate. Although Life-in-Death wins the Mariner, the other two hundred sailors will die with the rapidity frequently ascribed to epidemic fevers:

> Four times fifty living men,
> (And I heard nor sigh nor groan)
> With heavy thump, a lifeless lump
> They dropped down one by one.
>   (216–19)

They die silently, cursing the Ancient Mariner with their eyes, their only sound the "heavy thump" of their bodies falling to the deck, which is made even more gruesome by the "homely" diction in which it is purveyed.[26] Conditions on the ship evoke the worst in contemporary descriptions of slave ships:

> I looked upon the rotting sea,
> And drew my eyes away;
> I looked upon the rotting deck,
> And there the dead men lay.
>   (240–3)

A passage like this one, for instance, might be compared to Olaudah Equiano's description of the "stench" in the hold of the slave vessel:

> Now that the whole ship's cargo were confined together, it became absolutely pestilential. The closeness of the place, and the heat of the climate, added to the number in the ship . . . almost suffocated us. This produced copious perspirations, so that the air soon became unfit for respiration, from a variety of loathsome smells, and brought on a sickness among the slaves, of which many died.[27]

Coleridge hoped the imagination would cure itself, that the faculty that creates the desire for West Indian luxuries would also lead human beings beyond them, as "sensual wants / Unsensualize the mind" ("On the Slave Trade," *Watchman* 131). Telling the tale serves a similar purpose in the "Rime," as the vagrant sailor's account of the horror and the guilt connected with the death of the albatross makes the Wedding Guest (and through him, contemporary readers) realize the cost of colonial commerce. It demonstrates that living in harmony with nature is inseparable from living in harmony with each other. In one of the more extraordinary episodes of the poem, which might be said to enact "the psychopathology of empire,"[28] the dead mariners are brought to life, as if, indeed, they have been redeemed:

> The mariners all 'gan work the ropes,
> Where they were wont to do;
> They raised their limbs like lifeless tools –
> We were a ghastly crew.
> The body of my brother's son
> Stood by me, knee to knee:
> The body and I pulled at one rope,
> But he said nought to me.
>   (337–44)

In this image of the mariner working alongside the dead, "knee to knee," we are once more in the haunted world of "Admiral Hosier's Ghost." The viewpoint, however, is no longer that of the Admiral, appealing for patriotic retribution, but instead is that of the spectral Mariner. The episode might seem to recover the voices of the forgotten, yet they remain silent throughout: these corpses are no longer inhabited by the guilty spirits of the mariners but are occupied by a new "troop of spirits blest" (349) who produce "sweet sounds . . . slowly through their mouths" (352). Eventually their voices will be symbolically dissolved into the "sweet jargoning" (362) of nature. The horrors of the slave trade, the deaths of innumerable sailors and slaves, are thus poetically transformed into a utopian image of nature under divine protection, though even here the gruesomeness of these spectral warblers powerfully emphasizes the tensions within this poetic recovery. When the Mariner returns to his native home the dichotomy between the abjected corpses of the sailors and the drive for a salvific conclusion is once more apparent. "Each corse" continues to "lay flat, lifeless and flat" (488), yet on each stands "A man all light, a seraph-man" (490), and the light from this angelic crew guides the ship into the harbor:

> This seraph-band, each waved his hand,
> No voice did they impart –
> No voice: but oh! the silence sank
> Like music on my heart.
> (496–9)

Now, not only the voices of the anonymous crew but also the angels that have displaced them are silent, yet Coleridge hopes this silence will speak as music to the heart of a transformed Mariner and reader.

Throughout history, disease has frequently been understood as a *punishment* for sin, from biblical explanations of the link between leprosy and lust, through Renaissance explanations of syphilis as a divine retribution for sexual promiscuity, to contemporary accounts of AIDS as a punishment for homosexuality. The "Rime" powerfully suggests how far colonial disease and death were understood as fitting retribution for the crime against nature (both human and natural) implicit in colonialism. The experience of the sailors remains unredeemed, for they can speak only once their bodies have been taken over by new recruits, the "troop" of angelic spirits. Nevertheless, their experience continues to be articulated as narrative, through the pariah Mariner whose frightening tale continues to exert its power over listeners long after the voices of his fellow crew members have become silent. Indeed, Coleridge seems to be suggesting that if there is any redemption at all, it lies in telling the tale. Our relation to the "Rime," as modern readers, is not significantly different from that of Coleridge's audience. Through retelling the tale, these events are repeated over and over, the "silent sea" is "burst" into again, thus demanding that readers take a stance in regard to the actions recounted. The poem narrativizes the meeting of worlds, as we are asked to confront the colonial world and to understand the trauma that continues to lie within its silence. The "Rime" is among the first great Romantic narratives to question colonialism by interrogating not a colonized other but the "otherness" that colonialism produced within Britain itself. The Mariner is a hybrid double, at once a phantasmic other who voices colonial experience as in a glass darkly and also the most common of colonial others, the vagrant and displaced sailor. Homi Bhabha describes how colonial authority is structured and subverted in the scene of the "discovery [and reading] of the English Book."[29] The "Rime" presents a similar yet opposite scene, as those at "home" are taught the text of colonialism, in a reading in which identities are riven by difference and anxiety.

[...]

[An omitted section discusses the role of violence and trauma of colonialism in Wordsworth's *Salisbury Plain* poems and "The Discharged Soldier."]

In seeking to understand colonialism in terms of the disease experience of a group of people who had been largely ignored, Coleridge was responding not only to historical events but also to the poetry of Wordsworth, who, as an original collaborator on the "Rime," first suggested the killing of the albatross and the re-animation of the sailors. The writings of the two poets during this period are very much a "lyrical dialogue," as each found his voice in relation to the other's work.[30] How to represent colonial disease was also a central concern of Wordsworth's, giving rise to a series of experimental narratives, each based on the same story yet all strikingly different in their approach to the problem.

[...]

"The Ruined Cottage"

While composing "The Discharged Soldier" and revising *Adventures on Salisbury Plain* [two works responding to the colonial predicament], Wordsworth was [...] writing "The Ruined Cottage." [...] I want [...] to see ["The Ruined Cottage"] in terms of Wordsworth's ongoing reflection on how colonialism affected the rural poor of Britain. [...] Wordsworth articulates a range of contradictory attitudes toward his subject by employing differing viewpoints – those of the narrator, the Pedlar, and Margaret. [...T]he extensive revisions the poem underwent before finally being published as book I of *The Excursion* suggest a continuing struggle and dissatisfaction with how these events are to be understood.[31] Here Wordsworth shifts his view from the diseased bodies of English servicemen returning from the tropics to demonstrate that colonialism produces disease landscapes at home just as easily as elsewhere. For Wordsworth, colonialism was not restricted to "somewhere else" but was also actively reshaping British landscapes and dispossessing the English rural population.

Although the poem presents three biographies, only two usually receive attention. In its early stage, from 1797 to 1798, as "the story of Margaret,"[32] the poem was about the psychology of loss. Margaret's decline leads with tragic inevitability to a stark conclusion, as if there were nothing to say in the face of such suffering: "in sickness she remained, and here she died, / Last human tenant of these ruined walls" ("*Ruined Cottage*" 527–8). In 1798 the poem doubled in size as Wordsworth increased the role of the Pedlar, who now provides a philosophy of nature that makes healing sense of this tragedy. Dorothy Wordsworth writes, on 5 March 1798, "The Pedlar's character now makes a very, certainly the *most*, considerable part of the poem."[33] In this version the emphasis has shifted to how to interpret these events. A third biography nevertheless resides at the heart of the poem – the story of Margaret's husband, Robert. This history remains a fragment, for we never learn what happened to him.

Robert's story follows a familiar pattern. A weaver, after a long illness he falls among the ranks of "casualties" in the 1780s, when war and drought combined to make employment scarce. He is forced to search for "any casual task" (219), "pointing lame buckle-tongues and rusty nails," "braiding cords or weaving bells and caps / Of rushes" (226–9). David Simpson remarks that Wordsworth shows "a complex awareness of the terrible effect of unemployment on the moral and domestic life."[34] Poverty leads to erratic behavior and aimlessness. Eventually Robert enlists with "a troop of soldiers going to a distant land" (327–8), leaving behind a "purse of gold" (323) to support his family. This is the last that is ever heard of him.

In the face of these events Margaret's grief is natural, but the intensity of her suffering and her inability to relinquish the need to know what happened to Robert constitute an enigma. In depicting Margaret's inability to forget Robert, Wordsworth drew on contemporary literary sources, such as the Crazy Kate episode in Cowper's *The Task*, which tells of a maid who fell in love

> With one who left her, went to sea and died.
> Her fancy followed him through foaming waves
> To distant shores, and she would sit and weep
> At what a sailor suffers . . . [35]
>
> (1.538–41)

Through Margaret readers are forced – like Coleridge's Wedding Guest – to address what they might otherwise prefer to forget. From the Pedlar's first encounter with the abandoned Margaret, when "she inquired / If I had seen her husband" (315–16), to our final image of her, she is obsessed with learning what happened to Robert:

> Yet ever as there passed
> A man whose garments shewed the Soldier's red,
> Or crippled Mendicant in Sailor's garb,
> . . . .
> she with faltering voice,
> Expecting still to learn her husband's fate,
> Made many a fond inquiry.
>
> (498–504)

For the Pedlar, Margaret's questioning is a *psychological* enigma, a "fond" "sickness" (527) or madness. Its very persistence disturbs him: "any heart had ached to hear her [beg] / That wheresoe'er I went I still would ask / For him whom she had lost" (480–2). Unable to learn whether Robert is dead, Margaret lives in a state of permanent paralysis, in "unquiet widowhood, / A wife, and widow" (483–4) until she finally dies. Like the contemporaneous "Baker's Cart" passage, Margaret's is a case study in psychopathology, an example of "a mind / Which being long neglected and denied / The common food of hope was now become / Sick and extravagant" ("*Ruined Cottage*" 463, lines 18–21). Unable to bury the dead, she joins them.

[. . .]

"The Ruined Cottage" is quite clearly "the story of Margaret," but even more, it worries about the history of an entire range of people whose lives and actions many readers would prefer to forget. Read from a social rather than a psychological perspective, Margaret's questions produce an unsettling *unease*, because we cannot but feel they do deserve an answer. "Forget Robert," the Pedlar seems to say, even as he recognizes his own impotence in the face of a narrative whose very openness suggests a final indignity directed toward Robert. One of the strengths of the poem, a strength that postcolonial criticism can learn from, is that it idealizes neither Margaret's resistance nor Robert's status as a subaltern, nor does it forget Robert because he supposedly *deserves* oblivion. Margaret's answer to Robert's disappearance, her continuing state of critical grieving, is shown to be just as unsatisfactory. We are left, then, not with an answer to the problematic link between colonial disease and forgetting, but with a dramatic structuring of the problem. Wordsworth simultaneously asks readers to occupy a position between grief and its denial, between acceptance of the past and a continuing critique of it, between the absence of a recoverable history for a large number of colonial victims and our insistence on the need to know. Denied the "last rites" provided by burial and narratives, Robert haunts this text, and Margaret takes on his ghostly status. The Pedlar seeks to bury both these ghosts by burying one of them. One of the strengths of the narrative, however, is that it recognizes their continuing presence, the unwillingness of those who have suffered indignity during life to rest easy in death.

[. . .]

"The Ruined Cottage" examines the social production of English "casualties." Yet even more powerfully, it talks about colonialism and British social space, arguing that the separation between colonial and British life is both unstable and no longer valid. Even as it represents a specific "domestic tragedy" (14), its link to other narratives about dead soldiers and abandoned women suggests that Wordsworth was seeking to depict more than an isolated tragedy. It should be read as a "depopulation narrative," in which the ruin of a single cottage is intended to stand for a general social situation. How many Roberts and Margarets were there? As I have suggested, there were many.

[. . .]

Notes

1 In 1792, of Great Britain's eighty-one battalions of foot soldiers, nineteen were stationed in the West Indies; nine were in India, and twenty-five were in Gibraltar, Nova Scotia, and Ireland, leaving only twenty-eight for service in Great Britain [T.H. McGuffie, "The Short Life and Sudden Death of an English Regiment of Foot." *Journal of the Society for Army Historical Research* 33 (1955): 16–25. 16].

2 [Edmund Burke, *The Writings and Speeches of Edmund Burke*. Ed. Paul Langford. Oxford: Clarendon, 1991. 9: 273.]

3 For English Romantic interest in the West Indies, see [Alan] Richardson ["Romantic Voodoo: Obeah and British Culture, 1797–1807." *Studies in Romanticism* 32 (spring 1993): 3–28]. M[oira] Ferguson provides a detailed discussion of English feminist responses to events in St. Domingue [*Subject to Others: British Women Writers and Colonial Slavery, 1670–1834*. New York: Routledge, 1992] (209–48).

4 [Samuel Taylor Coleridge, *The Watchman*. Ed. Lewis Patton. *The Collected Works of Samuel Taylor Coleridge*. Princeton: Princeton UP, 1970. 332.]

5 Although discussions of the important impact of colonialism on the "Rime" can be traced back to [John Livingston] Lowes, [(*The Road to Xanadu: A Study in the Ways of the Imagination*. 1927. New York: Vintage, 1959)], the most developed and strongest political readings are those of [William] Empson, ["The Ancient Mariner." *Critical Quarterly* 6 (1964): 289–319] and [J.B.] Ebbatson ["Coleridge's Mariner and the Rights of Man." *Studies in Romanticism* 11 (1972): 171–206]. See also B[ernard] Smith ["Coleridge's Ancient Mariner and Cook's Second Voyage." *Journal of the Warburg and Courtauld Institutes* 19 (1956): 115–54];

[Patrick J.] Keane [*Coleridge's Submerged Politics: "The Ancient Mariner" and "Robinson Crusoe."* Columbia: U of Missouri P, 1994]; [James C.] McKusick [" 'That Silent Sea': Coleridge, Lee Boo, and the Exploration of the South Pacific." *Wordsworth Circle* 24 (1993): 102–6]; and [Joan] Baum [*Mind-Forg'd Manacles: Slavery and the English Romantic Poets.* North Haven, CT: Archon Books, 1994.] 1–56.

6 [Samuel Taylor Coleridge, *Lectures 1795 on Politics and Religion.* Ed. Lewis Patton and Peter Mann. *The Collected Works of Samuel Taylor Coleridge.* Princeton: Princeton UP, 1971. 59–60.]

7 [Jerome J. McGann, "The Meaning of The Ancient Mariner." *Critical Inquiry* 8 (1981): 35–67. 51.]

8 See also H[untington] Brown ["The Gloss to *The Rime of the Ancient Mariner.*" *Modern Language Quarterly* 6 (1945): 319–24].

9 [Samuel Taylor Coleridge, *The Complete Poems.* Ed. William Keach. London: Penguin, 1997. 38.]

10 [Charles Lamb and Mary Lamb. *The Letters of Charles and Mary Anne Lamb.* Ed. Edwin W. Marrs Jr. 3 vols. Ithaca: Cornell UP, 1975–78. I: 266.]

11 [John Masefield, *A Sailor's Garland.* New York: Macmillan, 1928. 131.]

12 [Sara Suleri, *The Rhetoric of English India.* Chicago: U of Chicago P, 1992. 3–4.]

13 [Thomas Clarkson, *The History of the Rise, Progress, and Accomplishment of the Abolition of the African Slave-Trade by the British Parliament.* 2 vols. 1808. London: Cass, 1968. 1: 412.] Coleridge wrote a review of this book when it appeared.

14 [Alexander Wilson, *Some Observations Relative to the Influence of Climate on Vegetable and Animal Bodies.* London: Cadell, 1780. 40.]

15 [Thomas Clarkson, *An Essay on the Impolicy of the African Slave Trade.* 2nd ed. London: Phillips, 1788. 53–4.]

16 [qtd. in Gerald W. Hartwig and K. David Patterson. "The Disease Factor: An Introductory Overview." *Disease in African History: An Introductory Survey and Case Studies.* Ed. Gerald W. Hartwig and K. David Patterson. Durham: Duke UP, 1978. 3–24. 7.]

17 [Philip D. Curtin, *The Atlantic Slave Trade: A Census.* Madison: U of Wisconsin P, 1969. 282–3.] See also [Herbert S.] Klein, [*The Middle Passage: Comparative Studies in the Atlantic Slave Trade.* Princeton: Princeton UP, 1978.] 197; [Marcus] Rediker, [*Between the Devil and the Deep Blue Sea: Merchant Seamen, Pirates, and the Anglo-American Maritime World, 1700–1750.* Cambridge: Cambridge UP, 1987.] 43; and K.[G.] Davies ["The Living and the Dead: White Mortality in West Africa, 1684–1732." *Race and Slavery in the Western Hemisphere: Quantitative Studies.* Ed. Stanley L. Engerman and Eugene D. Genovese. Princeton: Princeton UP, 1975. 83–98].

18 [Captain George Shelvocke, *A Voyage Round the World by the Way of the Great South Sea.* London: Senex, 1726. 73–4.]

19 In the verse of the 1790s, the slave and the soldier are regularly associated with each other, as in Robert Merry's "The Wounded Soldier," which speaks of the "savage hearts" of those who send "the *slave* to fight against the *free*" in colonial regions (B[etty T]. Bennett [*British War Poetry in the Age of Romanticism: 1793–1815.* New York: Garland, 1976.] 242–5).

20 John Stedman displays a similar fear in seeing a group of newly landed slaves in Suriname [John Gabriel Stedman, *Narrative of a Five Years' Expedition against the Revolted Negroes of Surinam.* Ed. Richard and Sally Price. Baltimore: Johns Hopkins UP, 1988.] (166).

21 [William Empson, Introduction. *Coleridge's Verse: A Selection.* Ed. William Empson and David Pirie. London: Faber, 1972. 28–32.]

22 For a valuable discussion of yellow fever in the poem, especially its dissolution of the boundaries of race, slavery, and empire, see [Debbie] Lee, "Yellow Fever [and the Slave Trade: Coleridge's *The Rime of the Ancient Mariner.*" *Journal of English Literary History* 65 (1998): 675–700.]

23 [Nora] Crook and [Derek] Guiton suggest that the poet may have been drawing on the belief put forward by Giolamo Fracastor and by the orientalist William Jones that leprosy was a tropical form of syphilis, caused by heat and sun [*Shelley's Venomed Malady.* Cambridge: Cambridge UP, 1986.] (120–1).

24 Jonathan Lamb, in " 'The Rime of the Ancient Mariner,' a Ballad of the Scurvy" (unpublished), provides persuasive evidence that Coleridge drew on medical representations of scurvy in his representation of "Life-in-Death."

25 In discussing the *Journal* of Janet Schaw, [Elizabeth A.] Bohls notes that an extreme whiteness of skin was valued by West Indian plantation women. (["The Aesthetics of Colonialism: Janet Schaw in the West Indies, 1774–1775." *Eighteenth-Century Studies* 27 (1994): 363–90.] 386).

26 [J.R. de J. Jackson, *Poetry of the Romantic Period*. London: Routledge and Kegan Paul, 1980. 75.]

27 [Olaudah Equiano, *The Life of Olaudah Equiano or Gustavus Vassa the African*. Ed. Paul Edwards. London: Dawsons, 1969. 78–9.]

28 I am drawing this term from [John] Barrell [*The Infection of Thomas De Quincey: A Psychopathology of Imperialism*. New Haven: Yale UP, 1991.]; see also [Nigel] Leask's broader employment of the term [*British Romantic Writers and the East: Anxieties of Empire*. Cambridge: Cambridge UP, 1992].

29 [Homi K. Bhabha, *The Location of Culture*. London: Routledge, 1994. 102.]

30 [Paul Magnuson, *Coleridge and Wordsworth: A Lyrical Dialogue*. Princeton: Princeton UP, 1988. 16–32.]

31 The revision of the poem is discussed by [James] Butler, ([William] Wordsworth, *"The Ruined Cottage" and "The Pedlar."* Ed. James Butler. Ithaca: Cornell UP, 1979.] 3–35) and by J[onathan] Wordsworth [*The Music of Humanity: A Critical Study of Wordsworth's "Ruined Cottage" Incorporating Texts from a Manuscript of 1799–1800*. London: Nelson, 1969].

32 See, for instance, Charles Lamb's comment to Wordsworth on 9 August 1814, that he had "known the story of Margaret . . . even as long back as I saw you first at Stowey" (3: 95).

33 [William Wordsworth, *The Letters of William and Dorothy Wordsworth*. Ed. Ernest de Selincourt. 2nd rev. ed. 6 vols. Oxford: Clarendon, 1967–82. I:199.]

34 [David Simpson, *Wordsworth's Historical Imagination: The Poetry of Displacement*. New York: Methuen, 1987. 192.]

35 [William Cowper, *The Poems of William Cowper*. Ed. John D. Baird and Charles Ryskamp. 3 vols. Oxford: Clarendon, 1980–95. I. 538–41.] [. . .]36.

24 Anna Letitia Barbauld and the ethics of free trade imperialism

E.J. Clery

1

At the moment when postcolonial theory was consolidated in the field of Romantic studies, a passage from *Eighteen Hundred and Eleven*, a protest against war by the veteran Unitarian poet Anna Letitia Barbauld, began to circulate as a classic articulation of 'cultural imperialism'. The poet addresses her country:

> Wide spreads thy race from Ganges to the pole,
> O'er half the Western world thy accents roll:
> . . .Thy stores of knowledge the new states shall know,
> And think thy thoughts, and with thy fancy glow;
> Thy Lockes, thy Paley's shall instruct their youth,
> Thy leading star direct their search for truth;
> Beneath the spreading Plantain's tent-like shade,
> Or by Missouri's rushing waters laid,
> 'Old father Thames' shall be the Poet's theme,
> Of Hagley's woods the enamoured virgin dream,
> And Milton's tones the raptured ear enthrall,
> Mixt with the roar of Niagara's fall.
>
> (ll. 81–2, 87–96)

These lines are cited by the editors at the start of *Romanticism and Colonialism* (1998), and have since been more fully discussed in essays specifically addressing the 'colonial subtext' discovered in the poem, notwithstanding the fact that it is best known, and was at the time most controversial, for its powerful prophetic vision of Britain's inevitable decline and ruination.[1] There is no doubt that these critics have identified a crux in the moral and political rationale of the text. It is acknowledged that the work is elliptical, allusive, and at times downright cryptic. I suggest that its relation to the question of empire is chiastic. This apparently open-and-shut case of 'cultural imperialism' connotes not patriotic complacency but risk-taking opposition to loyalist ideology. At the same time, the privileging of elements in the poem identified as 'anti-imperialist' by other critics has tended to mask an ethic of free trade and 'informal empire' that, it will be argued, actually drives its polemic.

It is striking that one of the things that detractors found most disturbing about *Eighteen Hundred and Eleven* was not the implicitly defeatist attitude towards France, but its eulogising of America. Fellow-poet Elizabeth Cobbold and critics from the

Universal Magazine, the *Quarterly Review* and the *Anti-Jacobin Review* all make comment on this aspect, the latter declaring:

> Whatever consolation may be experienced by the dissenting patriots of the Monthly Review, from the reflection that America may become free and rich from the destruction of England, we can assure them, it affords us not the smallest particle of comfort.
>
> (Anon 1812: 42, 203)

The poem was written and published at a point when Britain stood on the verge of war with the United States; a probability referred to on line 60 as 'The tempest blackening in the distant West'. Tensions had been building since America had been drawn into the economic battleground which had been the main theatre of the European conflict since 1806. The American republic had retaliated against the effect of trade blockades by issuing its own non-intercourse acts, attempting to force Britain and France into more liberal policies towards neutral trading partners by threatening to cut off one or the other from the transatlantic market. Relations with Britain were complicated by the ideologically hostile stance of the Tory government, and by the British habit of impounding American ships and imprisoning or pressganging American sailors as renegade Britons. The Perceval government was apparently deaf to pleas for a more conciliatory line from the manufacturing and trading interest, dependent on transatlantic commerce and facing financial collapse as a result of the embargoes. The crisis was particularly acute in Lancashire, a region to which Barbauld retained ties both social and emotional.

Yet, setting aside this imminent conflict early in the poem, Barbauld imagines a melting away of the national boundaries dividing Britain and America in a manner as dreamlike and surreal, in its way, as Blake's vision *America*. 'Not like the dim, cold crescent shalt thou fade', she addresses her country; which could be taken to imply the British Empire trumps the Ottoman empire, even in its eclipse; or it could mean, as I suggest, that what is being described is not a facet of imperialism at all. It is a dream of dispersion ('Wide spreads thy race from Ganges to the pole') without the name of empire, or the power, or the prospect of gain. It resolves itself into a transmigration of mind and language westwards, to a former colony that has won its freedom from the mother country. The poet sees a process of unstinting and inexhaustible exportation of art, science, and law, regardless of the destruction of Britain as an economic or military power:

> If westward streams the light that leaves thy shores,
> *Still* from thy lamp the streaming radiance pours.
>
> (my emphasis; 79–80)[2]

Many critics have been content to identify these passages as an application of the classical theme *translatio imperii*, the movement of civilisation from East to West. Certainly it is a presence here. Barbauld wants the reader to pick up her revisions of a meta-narrative which had passed through the hands of triumphalist British precursor poets. James Thomson, who himself makes a cameo appearance in her poem as a cultural export, struggled with the problem of how the westward passage could be halted with the British Empire forever in the ascendant in *Britannia* and *Liberty*.

The idea that the transition was inevitable is regretfully but courteously accepted by sympathetic reviewers of *Eighteen Hundred and Eleven* from the *Monthly Repository* and the *Monthly Review*; they simply express the wish that this event might take place in the very distant future, obscuring the polemical purpose. Hostile critics are a better guide; their heat is a measure of the urgency of issues she addressed. For Barbauld is not engaged here in a general critique of enlightenment faith in progress, nor in offering a recuperative vision of cultural imperialism. Her rhetoric is pragmatic: maximum provocation, not elegiac reflection. The poem was published in early February 1812 at the moment of decision, with the Peninsular campaign stagnating, the north of England in a state of social collapse, and war with America imminent. There is strong evidence, internal and external, that it formed part of a concerted campaign led by the Friends of Peace and on 23 June brought to a triumphant conclusion in Parliament by Henry Brougham, to overturn the 'Orders in Council', the policy of imposing punitive trade blockades.[3] The primary aim of *Eighteen Hundred and Eleven* is to voice opposition to economic warfare and to subvert the consensus over patriotism that facilitates it.

By emphasising the cultural kinship of Britain and the United States, Barbauld is countering government belligerence towards America. She is also alluding to the economic significance of transatlantic trade, put at risk by the Tory ministry. But more fundamentally, she is bringing into play a central aspect of the original, oppositional language of patriotism shared by Dissenters and 'True' Whigs. Pro-Americanism had been a fixture in this discourse since the first organised stirrings of rebellion in the colonies in the 1760s. Her friends and fellow-Unitarians Joseph Priestley and Richard Price had made their names as political writers with treatises in defence of the American Revolution. Dissenters recognised in the grievances of the colonials the mirror of their own concern with equality, freedom of conscience, and political representation. They also saw America as a barometer: British oppression across the Atlantic was a warning of the temper of times in Britain itself, soon realised in the suspension of *habeas corpus*, giving the state powers of imprisonment without trial. Their case against war, then as in 1811–12, centred on economic factors, the crippling expense of prolonged military action, and the damage to trade, in both instances giving rise to a sustained campaign of petitions to Parliament. The lessons they learned from the colonial conflict helped to forge their identity and their programme as a unified pressure group.[4]

The distinction between the Dissenters and the 'independent' Whigs such as Edmund Burke on this issue may have its source in the intensity of the continuing attachment of non-conformists to the idea of the United States as the asylum of liberty; and indeed, as a potential place of refuge. For Dissenters, independent America retained the true spirit of British freedom. By this token Priestley's relocation to Pennsylvania in 1794 was as much a homecoming as an exile. When Coleridge and Southey the same year developed their Pantisocracy scheme to settle nearby on the banks of River Susquehanna, they too were briefly subscribing to this transnational ideal.

Leah Greenfield has pointed to the apparent paradox that Americans sought independence *because* they were 'loyal and proud Englishmen'. Their English identity and loyalty to fundamental national values motivated the 'drive for secession' and legitimated it (1992: 412). One could argue reciprocally that 'national loyalty', patriotism in its 'idealistic or abstract' original form, allowed British radicals to continue to see the United States as part of their homeland, regardless of material differences and geographical distance. Lucy Aikin, in her *Memoir* of her father, John Aikin, Barbauld's brother and literary collaborator, wrote that the war with America brought about 'a gradual but complete and permanent revolution' in his view of politics, from unthinking loyalty to Britain to a new identity as 'strenuous supporter of the cause of civil liberty, in whatever quarter of the world her banner was displayed'. Although Barbauld did not share his fervour at this stage, she was apprised of it: 'The change is dated by a letter to his sister as having taken place in the year 1778' (Aikin 1823: I, 46). His outlook remained unchanged throughout the most repressive years of the French wars and beyond. Milton had, before his death in 1666, written to a friend, 'one's Patria is wherever it is well with him', a translation of the Latin motto *ubi bene ibi patria* (cit. Viroli 1995: 54). This statement can be taken to mean not a retreat from politics, but a broadened engagement: 'The place of Milton's liberty after the Restoration – his true *patria* – was the widening universe of his readers'(Shifflet 1998: 154).

In *Eighteen Hundred and Eleven*, there is a movement from what Maurizio Viroli calls 'natural patriotism' – 'an attachment to the native soil understood as a place of memory' (1995: 46) – towards something that could be described as an 'imagined community', distinct from physical territory. The poem's nationalism is at its most conventional in the passage,

> Yet, O! my Country, name beloved, revered,
> By every tie that binds the soul endeared,
> Whose image to my infant senses came
> Mixt with Religions' light and Freedom's holy flame!
> (ll. 67–70)

These were the lines that her defenders quoted routinely. They seem to indicate a reassuringly spontaneous, reflexive attachment to place, founded on memory. But already she is preparing to move to an abstract definition of nation as *patria*: although she refers to the experience of early childhood, 'Country' is a 'name', a verbal sign and not a place, and it is inscribed in the soul by process of association, mixed with the ideals of nonconformity and liberty. By an implicit connection, she moves from memory to present and future time with the prompt of 'Freedom's holy flame'. In his influential study of the rise of modern nationalism, Benedict Anderson (1991) emphasises the growth of national identity based on the power of media and the creation of 'cultural artefacts'. Barbauld's brand of transatlantic patriotism takes precisely this shape. Patriots in both countries are joined by their inheritance of books. The 'virgin' and the 'ingenuous youth' will go through the same process that Barbauld underwent, internalising the philosophy of Locke and William Paley and the poetry of Milton, Thomson, and Shakespeare, and most recently, Joanna Baillie. Baillie's plays, popular in the United States, serve as synecdoche for the vitality of the 'Dissenting public sphere' spanning 'transatlantic realms' (l. 111). By locating this process amid the natural wonders of the New World – 'the spreading Platan', 'Niagara's fall' – she emphasises the precedence of idea over place. The poet's vision of 'Old Father Thames' (from Pope's *Windsor Forest*, l. 330) overwrites 'Missouri's rushing waters'.

Barbauld's transnational perspective had resonances beyond the traditions of British Dissent and Whig opposition, and participated in the Enlightenment ideal of cosmopolitanism. Adriana Craciun, in her study of the self-identification of women writers during the French Revolution as 'citizens of the world', has described Barbauld as exemplary (2005: 16–26). Stoic doctrines familiar to Barbauld were in accord. Stoics professed a form of cosmopolitanism which held the state to be a less significant bond than shared humanity and a collective standard of virtue.[5] The cosmopolitan principle was most influentially restated in recent memory by a Dissenter, Richard Price, in his sermon 'On the Love of Our Country', which sparked the Revolution debate in 1789. There he had argued that 'a narrower interest should always give way to a more extensive interest', the precept so controversially enacted by *Eighteen Hundred and Eleven* (1789: 10).

2

In contrast to the postcolonial position on the poem, feminist scholars have described *Eighteen Hundred and Eleven* as an anti-imperialist text, and have even suggested that this was the cause of the critical backlash at the time.[6] A sententious section near the close has licensed this view:

> But fairest flowers expand but to decay;
> The worm is in thy core, thy glories pass away;
> Arts, arms and wealth destroy the fruits they bring;
> Commerce, like beauty, knows no second spring.
> Crime walks thy streets, Fraud earns her unblest bread,
> O'er want and woe thy gorgeous robe is spread,
> And angel charities in vain oppose:
> With grandeur's growth the mass of misery grows.
> (ll. 313–20)

But to assert the over-riding authority of this passage is to negate other moral positions in the poem. This is a work full of disjunctions, ambiguities, and tonal shifts. Its multi-voiced quality indicates the presence of 'parodic stylization' (Bakhtin 1981: 312). Lines 313–16, for instance, mimic the opinions of William Cobbett, an uneasy ally in opposition to the war, rabidly opposed to commerce. Evidence both internal and circumstantial suggests not only that Barbauld condoned a strand of thinking about empire largely unrecognised within Romantic criticism, but that the poem derives its ethical force from it.

Eighteen Hundred and Eleven represents the convergence of poetic and economic arguments for the moral value of global trade. Within Barbauld's alternative patriotic idiom, commerce is a trope combining national pride with the promise of international peace. The needs of commerce were the main plank of the ant-war arguments of the Friends of Peace and the commercial argument is central to her poem. Yet the pro-commerce poetic language, as it develops from Dryden to Cowper, was a deeply compromised inheritance, and Barbauld would need to find a strategy for stabilising it. The figure of 'Old Father Thames', who we saw surfacing in quotation marks in line 93, dates from 1714, featuring in the revised version of Pope's *Windsor Forest*. Like the speaker in Barbauld's poem, Father Thames is a prophet.

> The time shall come, when free as seas or wind
> Unbounded Thames shall flow for all mankind,
> Whole nations enter with each swelling tide,
> And seas but join the regions they divide.
>
> (ll. 397–400)

Some of his words are cryptic, not to say contradictory. On the one hand he declares that 'suppliant States' will 'be seen / Once more to bend before a BRITISH QUEEN' (ll. 383–4) and on the other commands, 'Conquest cease and Slav'ry be no more' (l. 408). The solution to this riddle is the 1713 Peace of Utrecht, which represented a new stage in the gradual dismantling of Spain's empire at the close of the War of the Spanish Succession. Abjuring conquest is an easy sacrifice when another nation's overseas possessions are undergoing decolonisation; the only slaves mentioned are pointedly the 'Indians' of South America. Britain was to be granted trading privileges in the Spanish colonies, including (incredibly, given the assurances of Father Thames) a 30-year Asiento: the right to sell African slaves. And yet the poem insists of Britain's' rising power: 'The shady empire shall retain no trace / Of war or blood . . . ' (ll. 371–2).

From the 1720s, this rhetoric was taken up by the Patriot opposition to Walpole. In James Thomson, there is the same combination of self-serving nationalism with the vision of international peace: the 'blue-water' policy of the disaffected Tories and 'True' Whigs will enable the alchemy which transforms maritime aggression and colonial expansion into global harmony. Britain must turn its back on political involvement in Europe, extricate itself from the military commitments entailed by the Hanoverian dynasty, and turn instead to its true destiny as an island nation, across the oceans. Where Isaac Kramnick and J.G.A. Pocock emphasised the nostalgic, anti-luxury strand in opposition discourse, Christine Gerrard has identified the 'Patriot' as typically a supporter of 'war with Spain which would open up new prospects for British merchants in the expanding Atlantic markets' (1994: 6). Such is certainly Thomson's position in *Rule Britannia* and *Liberty*, and there, as in *Windsor Forest*, imperialist combativeness sits side by side with ardent pacifism. John Barrell and Harriet Guest use the term 'economic theodicy' to convey the 'knotting together of economic amoralism and theodicy in a hybrid discourse', a device serving to smooth over the moral contradictions in long poems by Pope, Thomson, and Goldsmith (1988: 83).[7]

Contradictions there certainly are, in tone as well as content. For in spite, or rather because, of the protestations of manifest destiny and divine mission, the poetic language of global unification which characterises the blue-water theory is constantly poised to convert into a war cry. The flipside of world peace is justified combat. Any who would block or divert the path of British merchants must suffer the consequences. Trade barriers, monopolies, protectionism arising from the claims of rival empires; all these are intolerable, an assault on British liberty.

The poetic language of British liberty, of 'Patriot' opposition, was born out of belligerent antagonism to the overseas empires of rival nations, above all the empire that emerged from the explorations of Columbus. By the mid-nineteenth century, the old call for commercial freedom had been transmuted and rationalised into the doctrine of free trade, upheld with spiritual fervour by Richard Cobden and his disciples, and combined with a pacifism that was active rather than largely rhetorical. Barbauld's poem is part of this transition, informed by Montesquieu's claim in *Spirit of the Laws* (1748) that the 'natural effect of commerce is to lead to peace', the demonstration by the Scottish historical school of the inevitable passage from militarism to peaceful commercial competition, and the insistence of William Paley (whose name appears pointedly alongside Locke's in line 89) that capitalism was next to godliness.[8]

The poem presents the antithetical relation of commerce to war in the form of the amicable sociability of the 'crowded mart' and the downcast 'princely merchants' who look with dread towards the outbreak of conflict with America. The Biblical affirmation 'merchants are princes' (*Isiah* 23:8) is also recalled in a later passage of retrospect, after the calamity, remembering London's vanished 'glories' in terms that anticipate but markedly diverge from the twinned image of the diseased metropolis in the closing lines. Here 'plenty' is presented not as corrupting but 'spontaneous' and inclusive, the flow of commerce equated with healthy circulation, the city a harmonious multi-ethnic meeting-place, and its

> . . . merchants (such the state which commerce brings)
> Sent forth their mandates to dependent kings.
>
> > (ll. 163–4)

By contrast with the actuality of Napoleonic suzerainty, this picture of the subordination of national sovereignty to the laws of economics is an endorsement of the humanitarian benefits of 'informal empire', also known as the 'imperialism of free trade': commercial dominion without military conquest, settlement, or direct political rule.[9]

However problematic the imperialist ideal of global peace might appear in retrospect, it provided Barbauld with a rhetorical tool with which to oppose her political enemies and enabled her to avoid the paralysing doubts that afflicted some fellow-radicals by the late 1790s. Coleridge's 'Fears in Solitude' is a case in point; a dramatisation of pro- and anti-war sentiments that should be considered beside *Eighteen Hundred and Eleven*. There can be no doubt that Barbauld knew it. There were personal links with Coleridge even beyond their personal acquaintance, begun the summer before it was published, in 1798, by Joseph Johnson, Unitarian, radical, and Barbauld's publisher of long standing. Certainly, when the *British Critic* complained of the author's 'preposterous prejudices against his country' (49–50), she would have sympathised with the younger poet.

In lines 41–86 of 'Fears in Solitude', Coleridge adopts the Dissenting conventions of thunderous denunciation along with Barbauld's particular poetic rendition of the language of national disease; as in *Epistle to William Wilberforce*, the practice of slavery is seen as a 'pestilence' (*FS*, l. 48). It is clear from *Eighteen Hundred and Eleven* that she studied Coleridge's poem in turn, and incorporated the device that provides the crucial turning-point of his meditations. His extravagantly comprehensive condemnation of his countrymen (barely mitigated by the pronoun 'we') constituting nearly two-thirds of the poem, abruptly breaks off in line 175. Critique of extremes of radicalism and loyalism is followed by abrupt submission to the force of 'natural' patriotism:

> . . . all
> Who will not fall before their images,
> And yield them worship, they are enemies

Even of their country!

Such have I been deemed. –
But O dear Britain! O my Mother Isle!
Needs must thou prove a name most dear and holy
To me, a son, a brother, and a friend,
A husband, and a father! Who revere
All bonds of natural love, and find them all
Within the limits of thy rocky shores.
O native Britain! O my Mother Isle!
How shouldst thou prove aught else but dear and holy
To me, who from thy lakes and mountain-hills,
Thy clouds, thy quiet dales, thy rocks and seas,
Have drunk in all my intellectual life,
All sweet sensations, all ennobling thoughts,
All adoration of the God in nature,
All lovely and all honourable things.

(ll. 171–89)

This is unmistakably the model for the hinge of Barbauld's preliminary reflections. More concisely than Coleridge, she too performs an abrupt tonal and mental shift from criticism of the nation to patriotic apostrophe. In Barbauld's poem, a train of thought involving barbed reference to Britain's wartime 'guilt' and the consequent inevitable loss of 'thy Midas dream' of commercial empire is capped by effusive description of the spontaneous internalisation of the name of 'Country' in childhood accompanied by religious and political ideals, in the same way that Coleridge relates that he has 'drunk in' all that is good in conjunction with the sense of place; a geographical 'fixing' of personal identity. In each case, the turn anticipates and responds to the charge that the poet is anti-patriotic, though Barbauld, in her compact rendering, leaves this implicit.

The difference lies in where Coleridge and Barbauld then go, following the affirmation of patriotic feeling. For Coleridge, the hiatus, appearing towards the end, is the signal for a return to the here and now, to the peaceful rural scene at Nether Stowey with which it began. The preceding agonies of conscience and national shame are set aside with a devout wish that 'My filial fears, be vain!' (markedly different from Barbauld's Stoic insistence that, though future efforts towards peace are 'in vain', yet protest must continue), and the poet retreats homewards, even further from public debate, to 'my own lowly cottage, where my babe / And my babe's mother dwell in peace!'. For Barbauld, by contrast, the personal affirmation does not lead back to locality and the private self. Quite the reverse. It motivates a series of leaps in space and time, first to America, then to the Britain of the future, culminating in a historical journey that traces the movement of civilisation from East to West, only pausing in Britain before passing on to South America. The personal voice is never heard again, studiously avoided in the course of this sequence of bold outward-bound imaginings.

In a letter to his brother from this time, Coleridge seems to lay out a new political programme to be furthered by poems dwelling in and on retirement: the depiction of nature is to be the foundation of a revised patriotism, an instrument of the spread of benevolence as a method more effective than direct political engagement.[10] He would go on to find philosophical confirmation for this impulse in the work of Herder and Fichte, proponents of a spiritual and emotional attachment to nation.

Invasion evidently meant something very different for Coleridge and for Barbauld. To Coleridge's way of thinking, it was a threat both intimately personal and cosmic in its purport: a divine punishment for a benighted land; a worm that had already threaded its way into his brain and caused havoc there, confusing his loyalties and provoking vivid fantasies of rapine and destruction to be enacted right here, in a remote corner of the West Country. Barbauld feels none of this. She rejects alarmism, but is not averse to spreading it ('Nor distant is the hour', l. 47).[11] In place of Coleridge's 'Mother Isle' she counterposes a self-deluding 'island Queen' who imagines the storms that shake the Continent 'but kiss thy shore', and that the 'grassy turf' of Britain will ever remain 'unbruised by hostile hoof'. Invasion is a weapon in her rhetorical armoury. It is perhaps worth making the obvious point here that it is the male poet who imagines invasion as rape, and not the female. Barbauld did not respond imaginatively to borders or boundaries, or the possibility that they might be transgressed. She conceptualises Britain not as an island but, ideally, as the hub of international systems of exchange in which the unimpeded flow of raw materials, manufactured commodities, art works, texts, and ideas among nations will bring about an era of perpetual peace, in place of the current era of perpetual war.

At the conclusion of *Eighteen Hundred and Eleven*, the 'Genius' who gives and withdraws prosperity and civilisation 'turns from Europe's desolated shores' and reappears on the summit of mount Chimborazo in Ecuador. He 'bids the nations rise', addressing not individual states but a Continent, interdependent, 'mingled tribes from sea to sea'. The final words of the poem, the spirit's promise, 'Thy world, Columbus, shall be free', contains irony heaped on irony; its meaning less transparent and timeless than the lapidary form and sublime location as the Last Word would suggest. Like *anamorphosis*, the optical device used in Holbein's painting *The Ambassadors* (a not inapposite intertext), it produces an effect that becomes visible only from a specific perspective. The apostrophic address to South America is a feint. *Eighteen Hundred and Eleven* is a carefully targeted political satire and deliberate provocation, and with this realisation the old *canard* about its reception ending her career can be finally laid to rest.[12] The required viewpoint is in fact that of the Tory government, the new-style patriots, the jingoists, the loyalist *literati* that use the *Quarterly Review*, the *Anti-Jacobin Review*, and the *British Critic* as the ideological support structure for what Barbauld regarded as a bloody and senseless war. They are best positioned to understand the teasing mixture of warning and promise.

South America is the real prize, she reminds them; ministers were at that moment were hamstrung by their simultaneous desire to exploit independence movements in the colonies in order to gain access to new markets and their commitment to the Spanish Regency to preserve the old empire, while the British trade lobby clamoured for action. 'Free' operates as a politico-economic pun. Not until 1825 would George Canning be able to state: 'Spanish America is free, and if we do not mismanage our affairs sadly, she is *English*'.[13] This is in part the fulfilment of Barbauld's prophecy; along with it, she envisaged a new age of cooperative global commerce in which economic and political freedom are mutually supporting and war has no place.

Notes

1 In addition to Fulford and Kitson (1998: 5), see Birns (2005: 545–62), Crocco (2010: 91–4), and Heinowitz (2010a: 142–4).
2 See James Thomson's *Britannia*, ll. 222–7 for the jingoistic origins of the term 'bright stream', revised by Barbauld.
3 This is the subject of my forthcoming monograph, with the working title '*Eighteen Hundred and Eleven*: Poetry, Protest, and Economic Crisis'. For a detailed discussion of the campaign which makes mention of Barbauld as the sole female participant, see Cookson (1982).
4 On all these points, see Bonwick (1977).
5 See McCarthy (2008: 51–8) and Clery (2013).
6 Mellor (2000: 80); Bradshaw (2001: 12–15); Craciun (2005: 19, 24).
7 Excellent recent studies in this field are David Shields (1998), Kaul (2000), and Griffin (2002).
8 On political economy and morality, see notably Winch (1996) and Searle (1998).
9 For valuable reconsideration of the term, see Brown (2008). For the original debate, see Shaw (1970) and Semmel (1970). Cf. Wordsworth's *Prelude*, VII. 211–28, for a more ambivalent representation of the metropolis as fulcrum of empire, discussed by Makdisi (1998: 30–6).
10 Coleridge (1956–71, I: 397); see Fulford (1996: 218–36).
11 For her cool response to the threat of invasion at its height in 1802–3, see her letter to Susannah Taylor, cit. McCarthy and Kraft (1994: 302).
12 See new research on Barbauld's pattern of literary production, before and after 1812, supporting this revised view: Looser (2008: 136–8) and Levy (2013: 37–58).
13 cit. Kaufmann (1951: 178).

Bibliography

Aikin, L. (1823) *Memoir of John Aikin, M.D., with a Selection of His Miscellaneous Pieces, Biographical, Moral, and Critical*, 2 vols, London: Baldwin, Cradock, and Joy.
Anderson, B. (1991) *Imagined Communities: Reflections on the Origin and Spread of Nationalism*, rev. edn, London and New York: Verso.
Anon (1812) 'Reviewers Reviewed' (on *Eighteen Hundred and Eleven*), *Anti-Jacobin Review*, 42: 203–9.
Bakhtin, M.M. (1981) *The Dialogic Imagination: Four Essays*, trans. C. Emerson and M. Holquist, Austin: University of Texas Press.
Barrell, J. and Guest, H. (1988) 'The Uses of Contradiction: Pope's *Epistle to Bathurst*', in *Poetry, Language and Politics*, ed. J. Barrell, Manchester: Manchester University Press.
Birns, N. (2005) '"Thy World, Columbus!": Barbauld and Global Space, 1803, "1811", 1812, 2003', *European Romantic Review*, 16(5): 545–62.
Bonwick, C. (1977) *English Radicals and the American Revolution*, Chapel Hill: University of North Carolina Press.
Bradshaw, P. (1998) 'Gendering the Enlightenment: Conflicting Images of Progress in the Poetry of Anna Letitia Barbauld', *Women's Writing*, 5(3): 353–71.
Bradshaw, P. (2001) 'Dystopian Futures: Time-Travel and Millenarian Visions in the Poetry of Anna Barbauld and Charlotte Smith', *Romanticism on the Net*, 21: 12–15.
Brown, M. ed. (2008) *Informal Empire in Latin America: Culture, Commerce and Capital*, Oxford: Blackwell.
Clery, E.J. (2013) 'Stoic Patriotism in Barbauld's Political Poems', in *Anna Letitia Barbauld: New Perspectives*, eds W. McCarthy and O. Murphy, Lewisburg PA: Bucknell University Press.
Coleridge, S.T. (1956–71) *Collected Letters*, ed. Earl Leslie Griggs, 6 vols, Oxford: Clarendon Press.
Cookson, J.E. (1982) *The Friends of Peace: Anti-War Liberalism in England 1793–1815*, Cambridge: Cambridge University Press.
Craciun, A. (2005) *British Women Writers and the French Revolution: Citizens of the World*, Houndmills, Basingstoke and New York: Palgrave Macmillan.

Crocco, F. (2010) 'The Colonial Subtext of Anna Letitia Barbauld's *Eighteen Hundred and Eleven*', *Wordsworth Circle*, 41(2): 91–4.

Fulford, T. (1996) *Landscape, Liberty and Authority: Poetry, Criticism and Politics from Thomson to Wordsworth*, Cambridge: Cambridge University Press.

Fulford, T. and Kitson, P.J. eds (1998) *Romanticism and Colonialism: Writing and Empire, 1780–1830*, Cambridge: Cambridge University Press.

Gerrard, C. (1994) *The Patriot Opposition to Walpole: Politics, Poetry, and National Myth, 1725–1742*, Oxford: Clarendon Press.

Greenfield, L. (1992) *Nationalism: Five Roads to Modernity*, Cambridge Mass: Harvard University Press.

Griffin, D. (2002) *Patriotism and Poetry in Eighteenth-Century Britain*, Cambridge: Cambridge University Press.

Heinowitz, R.C. (2010a) *Spanish America and British Romanticism, 1777–1826: Rewriting Conquest*, Edinburgh: Edinburgh University Press.

Heinowitz, R.C. (2010b) 'The Spanish American Bubble and Britain's Crisis of Informal Empire, 1822–1826', in *Romanticism and the Anglo-Hispanic Imaginary*, eds J.M. Almeida, New York and Amsterdam: Rodopi.

Kaufmann, W.W. (1951) *British Policy and the Independence of Latin America, 1804–1828*, New Haven: Yale University Press.

Kaul, S. (2000) *Poems of Nation, Anthems of Empire: English Verse in the Long Eighteenth Century*, Charlottesville and London: University Press of Virginia.

Levy, M. (2013) 'Anna Letitia Barbauld's Career in Script and Print', in *Anna Letitia Barbauld: New Perspectives*, eds William McCarthy and Olivia Murphy, Lewisburg PA: Bucknell University Press.

Looser, D. (2008) *Women Writers and Old Age in Great Britain, 1750–1850*, Baltimore: Johns Hopkins University Press.

McCarthy, W. (2008) *Anna Letitia Barbauld: Voice of the Enlightenment*, Baltimore: Johns Hopkins University Press.

McCarthy, W. and Kraft, E. eds (1994) *The Poems of Anna Letitia Barbauld*, Athens and London: University of Georgia Press.

Makdisi, S. (1998) *Romantic Imperialism: Universal Empire and the Culture of Modernity*, Cambridge: Cambridge University Press.

Mellor, A.K. (2000) *Mothers of the Nation: Women's Political Writing in England, 1780–1830*, Bloomington IN: Indiana University Press.

Price, R. (1789) *A Discourse on the Love of Our Country*, London: T. Cadell.

Searle, G.R. (1998) *Morality and the Market in Victorian Britain*, Oxford: Clarendon Press.

Semmel, B. (1970) *The Rise of Free Trade Imperialism: Classical Political Economy, the Empire of Free Trade and Imperialism, 1750–1850*, Cambridge: Cambridge University Press.

Shaw, A.G.L. ed. (1970) *Great Britain and the Colonies 1815–1865*, London: Methuen.

Shields, D. (1998) *Oracles of Empire: Poetry, Politics, and Commerce in British America, 1690–1750*, Chicago: University of Chicago Press.

Shifflet, A. (1998) *Stoicism, Politics and Literature in the Age of Milton: War and Peace Reconciled*, Cambridge: Cambridge University Press.

Viroli, Maurizio (1995) *For Love of Country: An Essay on Patriotism and Nationalism*, Oxford: Clarendon Press.

Winch, D. (1996) *Riches and Poverty: An Intellectual History of Political Economy in Britain, 1750–1834*, Cambridge: Cambridge University Press.

Part 7

Affects and ethics

Introduction

Some of the earliest accounts of literature involve passions, emotions, or affects. Plato's famous opposition to poetry in the *Republic* derived partly from its too-easy association with emotions (Plato 1961: 830). Aristotle designated an important role for emotions in dramatic poetry when he understood tragedy to induce pleasure "by means of pity and fear"; the generation of "*pathos*" was central to the tragic plot (Aristotle 1967: 37–8). Critics and writers of literature continued to take an interest in the relationship between different genres and the emotions – for instance, in the way that the realist novel represented and induced sentiment – but at least some statements by writers during the Romantic age betray uneasiness about this relationship. Mary Wollstonecraft's feminism often defined itself against what she understood as a stereotyped feminine sensibility; she considered sensibility to be the construction of a patriarchal culture that limited women's independent reasoning and personal ambition (Wollstonecraft 1994). Samuel Taylor Coleridge was likewise suspicious of sentimental feeling and expression, which (he thought) deflected attention from more urgent concerns such as slavery and foreign war (Coleridge 1969: 259).

This uneasiness is reflected in many facets of the critical tradition described in the general introduction to this volume. W.K. Wimsatt was notoriously opposed to characterizing poems according to the "intensity of emotions" aroused by them (Wimsatt 1957: 33). Geoffrey Hartman's formalist account of the Romantic imagination as "anti-self-consciousness," through which the mind relieves itself of its own burdens, most certainly followed in this tradition (Hartman 1970: 51), and his account demonstrates how even treatments of internal mental states could eschew consideration of the emotions. Historicist critics such as G.J. Barker-Benfield and Jerome McGann, however, began to expose how many previously neglected writers of the Romantic age were actually interested in, and dependent upon, emotion (Barker-Benfield 1992; McGann 1996). And they also revisited many canonical writers to show how emotions or affects – grounded in bodily "sensibility" and generalized into shared "sentiment" or "sympathy" – played a larger role in their work than many critics had previously recognized. Selections in this volume by Clara Tuite in Part 5, Jon Mee in Part 8, as well as many others, offer evidence for the influence that studies of emotion have had on critical work throughout Romantic studies. The essays in this section can provide a useful context for approaching the treatment of affects in the other sections, where references to them may be theoretically significant even where they are less thematically central.

Although recent critics have rekindled interest in emotional states, considerable debate has arisen about what emotions are and how they are related to literary language. If feeling seems to be something that comes before, or outside of, language, it is nevertheless also true that emotion may be influenced by it, serve as a conduit for it, or even be a product of it. In Adela Pinch's essay selection on the Gothic novelist Ann Radcliffe, taken from her book *Strange Fits of Passion*, Pinch emphasizes the paradoxical position of emotions. While deeply felt, she argues, they may not actually be one's own. For her, the fact that the language of emotion is public and circulated means that emotion itself is radically separated from the subject who expresses it. In Radcliffe's fiction, she argues, "feeling attaches itself . . . not to persons or to causes but to the novel's language itself."

Although Julie Ellison credits Pinch in her work for recognizing the way that emotion depends upon representations, there are important differences in the perspective of her book, *Cato's Tears and the Making of Anglo-American Emotion*, from which her selection on Anna Letitia Barbauld is excerpted. (The complete chapter includes a discussion of the poet Phyllis Wheatley as well.) Ellison's aim in her book is to provide a wide-ranging study on "the cultural history of public emotion," but what is "public" in her account about emotion differs from Pinch's. Rather than disconnected representation, the language of emotion carries ethical and political efficacy, and similar claims about this instrumentality and effect of sympathy have occupied many Romanticists in their work in recent years, including Kevis Goodman, Thomas Pfau, and Adam Potkay (Goodman 2010; Pfau 2005; Potkay 2012). For her, emotion is in the possession of individuals and then shared in an aestheticized "transaction" of sensibility. Sensibility, in turn, furthers Barbauld's race politics by allowing her to extend her own subjective feeling to others, imagining a "heterogeneous" community of differently racialized subjects.

Toward the end of her selection on Radcliffe, Pinch makes an important point about the way modern psychoanalysis, like the Gothic novel itself, investigates the phenomenon of "being occupied by feelings that are not one's own." This abstraction from the self might seem to have a tragic dimension to it, in the same way that all psychoanalysis does in its story of the subject's position as one that suffers irretrievable loss. Jacques Khalip's selection here takes up this melancholy position of the subject, but modifies Pinch's argument to show how ethically and politically significant this sense of loss might be (as in work by McGann and Potkay, the analysis of affect leads into an analysis of ethics). While recovering the public impact of emotion from Ellison's argument, Khalip shows how melancholy affect in Wollstonecraft is "the condition for a revisionary form of social critique." In the strenuous work of evaluating and repositioning female subjectivity, that is, Wollstonecraft registers an embodied sense of subjectivity that both measures its distance from political structures – political structures that contradictorily provide the means for visibility and threaten the subject with anonymity.

In " 'Tintern Abbey' in the Literary History of Mood," David Collings revisits the tradition of the Romantic nature lyric viewed through the arguments that Pinch and Khalip make. In this new essay written for the volume, Collings shows how Wordsworth's "sense sublime" may involve a considerable abstraction, or a "radical suspension of affect." But – modifying the reading of "Tintern Abbey" that Levinson pursues in Part 1 – he demonstrates that this suspension gestures toward the actual affective and historical dimensions of experience that were (in the new historicist argument) supposedly denied. While not directly expressed, the "depths" of personal affect and experience are "felt at the mind's edge"; thus Collings claims that the very ability to make the world visible, in Wordsworth's reckoning, depends upon the poem's maintenance of sharable conventions of emotional and linguistic communication. In this sense, his essay makes the study of affect into an argument against, rather than an extension of, many assumptions behind new historicist scholarship.

Works cited

Aristotle. (1967) *Poetics*, trans and intr. Gerald F. Else, Ann Arbor: University of Michigan Press.

Barker-Benfield, G.J. (1992) *The Culture of Sensibility: Sex and Society in Eighteenth-Century Britain*, Chicago: University of Chicago Press.

Coleridge, Samuel Taylor. (1969) *Poetical Works*, Oxford: Oxford University Press.

Goodman, Kevis. (2010) "Nostalgia, Pathologies of Motion, Practices of Reading," *Studies in Romanticism* 49: 197–227.

Hartman, Geoffrey. (1970) "Romanticism and Anti-Self-Consciousness," in Harold Bloom (ed.), *Romanticism and Consciousness: Essays in Criticism*, New York: Norton, 46–56.

McGann, Jerome. (1996) *The Poetics of Sensibility: A Revolution in Literary Style*, Oxford: Clarendon Press.

Pfau, Thomas. (2005) *Romantic Moods: Paranoia, Trauma, and Melancholy, 1790–1840*, Baltimore: Johns Hopkins University Press.

Plato. (1961) *The Collected Dialogues of Plato*, ed. Edith Hamilton and Huntington Cairns, Princeton: Princeton University Press.

Potkay, Adam. (2012) *Wordsworth's Ethics*, Baltimore: Johns Hopkins University Press.

Wimsatt, W.K. (1957) *The Verbal Icon: Studies in the Meaning of Poetry*, Lexington: University of Kentucky Press.

Wollstonecraft, Mary. (1994) *A Vindication of the Rights of Woman and a Vindication of the Rights of Men*, ed. Janet Todd, Oxford: Oxford University Press.

Further reading

Benedict, Barbara M. (1994) *Framing Feeling: Sentiment and Style in English Prose Fiction, 1745–1800*, New York: AMS Press.

Chandler, James. (2013) *An Archaeology of Sympathy: The Sentimental Mode in Literature and Cinema*, Chicago: University of Chicago Press.

Ellis, Markman. (1996) *The Politics of Sensibility: Race, Gender, and Commerce in the Sentimental Novel*, Cambridge: Cambridge University Press.

Fisher, Philip. (2002) *The Vehement Passions*, Princeton: Princeton University Press.

Marshall, David. (1998) *The Surprising Effects of Sympathy: Marivaux, Diderot, Rousseau, and Mary Shelley*, Chicago: University of Chicago Press.

Mullan, John. (1988) *Sentiment and Sociability: The Language of Feeling in the Eighteenth Century*, Oxford: Oxford University Press.

Phillips, Mark Salber. (2000) *Society and Sentiment: Genres of Historical Writing in Britain, 1740–1820*, Princeton: Princeton University Press.

Reddy, William. (2001) *The Navigation of Feeling: A Framework for the History of Emotions*, Cambridge: Cambridge University Press.

Sedgwick, Eve Kosofsky. (2003) *Touching Feeling: Affect, Pedagogy, Performativity*, Durham: Duke University Press.

Soni, Vivasvan. (2010) *Mourning Happiness: Narrative and the Politics of Modernity*, Durham: Duke University Press.

25 Phantom feelings

Emotional occupation in
The Mysteries of Udolpho

Adela Pinch

The gothic novel is the genre that is most devoted to exploring and adjudicating the proportions of emotional response. This is especially true of Ann Radcliffe's novels, for her notorious eleventh-hour "natural" explanations of supernatural appearances imply that her characters' emotional responses – to the pile of old clothes they mistake for a ghost, for example – are disproportionate to their causes. Disciplining and demystifying her characters' terrors, Radcliffe's novels suggest that there are ultimately standards of suitable emotional response. At the same time, of course, her novels glorify and cultivate all kinds of excessive feeling in both her characters and her readers.

The Radcliffean gothic's double-edged attitude toward extravagant feeling – both indulgent and disciplinarian – reminds us that the politics of feeling in the gothic decade of the 1790s often turned on precisely such claims to distinguish excessive from "natural" feelings. Every participant in the great debate over the French Revolution accused his or her opponents of exhibiting either too much emotion or not enough. [Edmund] Burke distinguished between the "natural" feelings that bind a country to its past and the unnatural "enthusiasms" of his republican opponents. Pondering the revolutionary sermon of the dissenting Dr. [Richard] Price, Burke reflects upon his own emotions:

> Why do I feel so differently from the Reverend Dr. Price, and those of his lay flock, who will choose to adopt the sentiments of his discourse? – For this plain reason – because it is *natural* I should; because we are so made as to be affected at such spectacles with melancholy sentiments . . . ; because in those natural feelings we learn great lessons; because in events like these our passions instruct our reason.

In this passage from his *Reflections*, Burke asserts that a political vision is underwritten by standards of suitable emotional response, which are personally verifiable; at the same time, this passage leaves Burke vulnerable to the charge that he glorifies passion over reason. Thus, while Burke, like other anti-Jacobin writers, found his opponents alternately to be dangerous enthusiasts or fundamentally unfeeling, writers sympathetic to reform and revolution turned their response to Burke in the same terms. In *A Vindication of the Rights of Man*, [Mary] Wollstonecraft finds Burke's own feelings false, referring ironically to the "compassionate tears" he "elaborately laboured to excite": "You foster every emotion till the fumes, mounting to your brain, dispel the sober suggestions of reason." She denounces his "sentimental exclamations," his "pampered sensibility," and the sentimental nostalgia of his political vision: his "gothic" view that "our *feelings* should lead us to excuse . . . the venerable vestiges of ancient days." But Burke's feelings are not only false and regressive; they also fail where real feeling is due: "Your tears," Wollstonecraft admonishes, "are reserved . . . for the declamation of the theatre, or for the downfall of queens . . . whilst the distress of many . . . were vulgar sorrows that could not move your commiseration." For all sides of the revolution controversy, both the naming of feelings and the naming of feelings' sources – as an excess of sensibility, perhaps, or a false theatricality – carried great ethical weight.[1]

The novels of Ann Radcliffe take the judgment of passion as their territory, giving philosophical scrutiny and narrative form to the ethics and politics of the naming of feelings. Thus in the decade in which the stakes of declaring feelings to be either extravagant or natural responses to political "terrors" were high, her long, complex plots told stories about the philosophical and aesthetic discussions of feelings' origins [. . .]. Her novels question how one might verify the claims of emotional rhetoric.

We might find an example of *The Mysteries of Udolpho's* accounting for emotion in its most canonical image, the black veil. [. . .] A black veil hanging in the castle of Udolpho is thought to cover a painting. In a brave moment, Emily lifts the veil but drops it when she realizes it hides something else: "– perceiving that what it had concealed was no picture, and, before she could leave the chamber, she dropped senseless on the floor."[2] This brief encounter prompts one fainting fit, several close calls, a "thousand nameless terrors" (240), and a chain of mysterious, affectively charged associations that recur to Emily throughout the novel. Conditioned to presume that something which is "no picture" must be the opposite – something "real" – Emily concludes that the veil conceals the corpse of the murdered Lady Laurentini. We can bracket temporarily the hypothetical contents of the veil: as a figure for the unveiled, the thing behind the veil stands throughout most of the novel as an empirical cause for an authentic, reverberating emotional shock. It stands as an example of an object that naturally causes terror, according to the sensationalist reasonings to be found, for example, in Burke's earlier treatise, the *Philosophical Enquiry into the Origin of Our Ideas of the Sublime and Beautiful*. In that treatise, Burke rejects the view that the feelings occasioned by a sublime object are the result of associations in our minds and locates them instead "in the natural properties of things." [. . .] Burke explains [. . .] that in confronting such an object the self aspires to the object's power, as our feelings follow the principles of ambition and self-preservation. The black veil's associations between terror, nature, and the real are thus corroborated by the Burkean thinking that accompanies Emily's approach to the dreaded veil:

> But a terror of this nature, as it occupies and expands the mind, and elevates it to high expectation, is purely sublime, and leads us, by a kind of fascination, to seek even the object, from which we appear to shrink.[3]

A strong emotion, such as a sublime terror, seems to be not only a natural response to the real; it also enables an approach to the real, a lifting of the veil.

At the end of the novel, the mysterious object behind the veil is disclosed, famously, to be not a corpse but only a wax representation of one. Emily's responses are inauthenticated: her willingness to find Montoni capable of the most horrid crimes is blamed for her delusion; and, as in other instances of Radcliffean demystification, the episode teaches a lesson about both the fallibility of individual senses and the need to discipline the emotions. The narrator affirms that experience can indeed instruct one how to feel: "Had she dared to look again, her delusion and her fears would have vanished together" (662). Once one knows what something is, Radcliffe implies, one's feelings will be appropriate to it. However, while most of her demystifications work by revealing the "real" behind the deluded impression that caused the reaction – the ghost was only a bandit, the clothes belonged to a perfectly real person, the knock on the door was really a servant's – here, in the space of the real, is another veil of illusion. The object is not exactly "no picture." Unlike the other demystifications that replace the object of terror with a natural object and thus reduce the object of terror to a "nothing," the scary thing in this case turns out to be a replica of a scary thing, naturalistically rendered. Thus this object and its effects require a different kind of explanation. Had Emily "dared to look again" and perceived the object to be an imitation, what should have been her response? Does a picture of something horrible lie somewhere between a "something to be scared of" and a "nothing"? Does the object behind the veil confirm that emotions are proportionate to their empirical objects, or does it scramble the narrator's ability to deauthenticate Emily's feelings?

Udolpho's adjudication between spurious terrors and authentic emotions thus takes it into the realm of aesthetic theory's views of its objects. Late eighteenth-century aesthetic theory frequently pondered how an emotional response to an image of a thing should be like and unlike a response to the thing itself. For [David] Hume, the "*feelings* of the passions" caused by poetical fictions are fainter than those caused by the same objects in reality: the passion "feels less firm and solid"; it is but a "mere phantom" of the passion caused by reality. Frequently, however, imitation itself is seen as adding an emotional power all its own. In Hume's discussion of tragedy, for example, imitation – which is "always itself agreeable" – converts into pleasure the disagreeable emotions we would feel if the objects on the stage were real.[4] [. . .] Burke questioned the power of imitation itself: the fact that a tragedy "is a deceit, and its representations no realities" could not for him be a "considerable part" of its power.[5] As for a representation of an object, Burke asserts that how much of its power belongs to the object, how much to imitation itself, depends upon the nature of the object.[6]

[. . .]

Though Burke admits [. . .] that imitation has a power of its own, it is a "mere effect"; the object has the power to dictate how imitation shall affect us. In Burke's analysis, moreover, we will "run to see" all kinds of dreadful objects – a criminal executed, London in ruins.[7] The tendency of the *Enquiry* as a whole is to treat the pleasures and pains caused by things and by representations as equivalent; and the same is true, though for different reasons, of [Henry Homes, Lord Kames's] *Elements of Criticism*. In his discussion of "Emotions caused by Fictions," Kames explains that representations affect us to the extent that the objects of representations take on an "ideal presence" in our minds, affecting us as if we were "spectators" of the things themselves. "The idea of a thing I never saw, raised in me by speech, by writing, or by painting," according to Kames, causes emotion when it produces a species of reverie that places the object before us.[8]

According to late eighteenth-century theorists, then, the emotions inspired by an image or effigy find their causes and their intensities somewhere along a wide spectrum. They are derived from the power of natural objects or the powers of imitation; they either are in excess of real emotions or are real emotions' paler "phantoms." [. . .]

[I]f at its most canonical moment, *The Mysteries of Udolpho* discloses something that seems to question the notion of a "real" cause, the novel nevertheless repeatedly looks for feelings' empirical origins, hunting after – as Emily poses it – "the remote cause of this emotion" (73). In Radcliffe's inquiries into feelings, appeals to the order of experience and appeals to the order of representation closely accompany each other. This chapter will try to account for why this doubled appeal recurs in the gothic novel. It will consider whether the logic that attributes real causes to emotions in experience can turn out to be just as deluded as that which causes false terrors. I will be focusing less on the properly gothic terrors of the novel than on its gentler emotions, its seductive representations of an ideal world of melancholy, nostalgia, and tearful exchanges.[9] Doing so will affirm that the events of the 1790s elicited other emotional rhetorics as complex as the claims and counterclaims about feeling in the Revolution debates. Gothic nostalgia might seem to locate the origins of emotion in an empirical past – a historical past, or a familial past. However, nostalgia's circuitous narrative paths disclose instead the political, philosophical, and formal benefits of casting the origins of feelings as attenuated and difficult to know. I will begin and end by discussing the naming of feelings.

***

As much as *Udolpho* focuses our attention on the origins of feelings, it expresses special interest in feelings whose sources are remote, attenuated, and diffuse. Radcliffe is lavish in her attentions to feelings that can barely be named: though we think of her work as providing us with a whole taxonomy of emotion – discriminating between "horror" and "terror," for example – the book as frequently engages in a process of *de-naming* emotions. The most glamorous and touching feelings are those which are named negatively, such as that behind the tears Emily sheds on first returning to her family's home, La Vallée, toward the end of the book: "While she contemplated, with tempered resignation, the picture of past times, which her memory gave, the tears she shed could scarcely be called those of grief" (591). This kind of formulation occurs several times at important moments in the text, suggesting that the best emotions are those that can "scarcely" be called anything at all. The relationship between emotion and language here should be distinguished from a gesture toward the ineffable, the more conventional notion that powerful emotions belong to the realm of the unsayable beyond the reach of language. The pleasure in Radcliffe's "gently euphemistic" prose seems to be in endlessly discriminating between fine feelings rather than in pointing to the beyond.[10] To euphemize is to speak not of what one cannot spell out but rather precisely of what one can but would prefer not to. Euphemism pronounces that there are, in fact, words that are unbearably close to the things to which they are attached. Radcliffean melancholy is inseparable from a prose style whose glamour lies in the way it brushes up against the referential status of feelings. Through this naming and un-naming of emotions – through the prose's dramatization of its ability to refer or not to refer to feeling – feeling attaches itself most of all not to persons or to causes but to the novel's language itself.

Melancholy is embodied in a certain kind of language in *The Mysteries of Udolpho*, and it seems as well to be almost literally in the air. After Emily has listened to some songs in Venice,

> she then remained sunk in that pensive tranquillity which soft music leaves on the mind – a state like that produced by the view of a beautiful landscape by the moon-light, or by the recollection of scenes marked with the tenderness of

friends lost for ever, and with sorrows, which time has mellowed into mild regret.
Such scenes are indeed, to the mind, like "those faint traces which the memory
bears of music that is past."

(177–8)

This state of mind seems distinguished most of all by its ability to evoke a multiplying
chain of associations; Radcliffean melancholy is among other things a medium of
metaphorizing, and thus a way (as in Charlotte Smith's poetry) of eliciting remarkably hackneyed poetical phrases, allusions, and quotations. "Melancholy" would
seem to function teleologically rather than referentially, to be about recognizing
clichés rather than about experiencing the things to which these images refer. The
associative drift of the passage ends by coming full circle: the scenes marked by
tenderness and sorrow which were at first simply in the service of a comparison
become the subject of the next sentence, where they are compared to the original
subject, music. Present scenes (a view of a landscape by moonlight) and recollected
scenes, music present and music past, are seen as acting identically, leaving the same
trace or mark on the mind. The absence or presence of an object of feeling seems
immaterial.

As this example suggests, melancholy in *The Mysteries of Udolpho* always reverts to
the past. To remember is to feel sad; and if a character is feeling sad it is because
she or he is remembering. Objects of nostalgia seem to maintain their melancholic
aura of perpetual loss even when they are restored to presence. When St. Aubert
moves back to his childhood home, La Vallée, it is already an object thought of with
"enthusiasm and regret" (2), and it remains so. Feeling melancholy is the form of
cognition where the past is concerned, and the past that is the object of melancholy
feelings is not limited to a character's own personal past: memory in this book
exceeds personal memories. After their escape from Udolpho, Emily and Du Pont
pass by the river Arno and contemplate "the remembrances, which its classic waves
revived" (460). Needless to say, neither Du Pont nor Emily has seen the Arno before;
the remembrances revived are cultural ones. This nostalgia for a cultural past could
provide one way of thinking about Radcliffe's characters' melancholy fixation on
all kinds of pasts, personal, fictional, and historical: it could be linked to the gothic
novel's nostalgia, as a genre, for an idealized, preindustrial, chivalric past. That the
characters' objects of nostalgia are so varied and extrapersonal suggests indeed that
their feelings are never simply their own feelings. It is as if the characters were oddly
aware of and acting out the book's own generic longings.

It is easy to imagine what a popular novel of the 1790s might be nostalgic for:
a landscape different from the changing countryside of agrarian capitalism; a
landscape in which peasants danced, rather than a countryside in which relations
between classes displaced and threatened many; a world in which one could travel
freely (Radcliffe's own journey on the continent in the summer of 1794 was, as
we shall see, thwarted and shaped by the Revolution); an idealized, unanxious
leisure. It is important, however, to see nostalgia in *The Mysteries of Udolpho* not
simply as a conservative, Burkean sentiment (I am thinking of Wollstonecraft's
attack on that writer's "gothic" attachment to "the venerable vestiges of ancient
days"). Nostalgia is a cultural practice that has no determinate content. A structure
that opens up a space between a "once was" and a "now," nostalgia can provide
a framework for the making of meanings, a road map for navigating a changing
landscape.[11]

One of the ways in which nostalgia may create a possibility of meaning is through its claims to rewrite the contingencies of history. The gothic novel is an instance of what Susan Stewart – preeminent theorist of nostalgia – calls "distressed genres," the archaic genres such as ballad, fairy tale, and romance that were revived and imitated as "new antiques" in the eighteenth century. For Stewart the popularity of the "new antique" is the appeal of a cultural form that invents "its own temporal grounds," that represses its cultural context in order "to conceive of its own context as being encapsulated within the form of representation."[12] [. . .] Nostalgia poses a circular relationship between event and emotion. It looks back to a lost object in order to generate desire, inventing contexts for its own emotions. At the same time, the nostalgic mode uses the feelings it generates in looking back as evidence with which to canonize the lost object or event as an origin.

[. . .]

[T]he 1794 novel [*The Mysteries of Udolpho*] invents its own events through feeling. Almost any given moment in the novel earns its significance in relationship to other moments, past, future, or both: while sometimes the past or future will seem to be the true origin for the significance of that present, often a series of moments will be linked together through a temporalizing that is purely relational, without a single origin. The death of the mother, Mme St. Aubert, at the beginning of the novel is the occasion for one of these series. After M. St. Aubert's own illness, he spends an afternoon with his wife and daughter at the family's fishing house at the river's edge. Everybody admires the beauties of nature and looks at each other through veils of tears as St. Aubert luxuriates in acute anticipatory nostalgia:

> He felt the tender enthusiasm stealing upon himself in a degree that became almost painful; his features assumed a serious air, and he could not forbear secretly sighing – "Perhaps I shall some time look back to these moments, as to the summit of my happiness, with hopeless regret. But let me not misuse them by useless anticipation; let me hope I shall not live to mourn the loss of those who are dearer to me than life."
>
> (8–9)

When Madame is, later in the same chapter, on her deathbed, St. Aubert

> remembered the feelings and the reflections that had called a momentary gloom upon his mind, on the day when he had last visited the fishing house, in company with Madame St. Aubert, and he now admitted a presentiment, that this illness would be a fatal one.
>
> (18)

Looking back to those earlier feelings, in other words, allows him to look forward to the future. And a short time after her death, while nostalgically looking at a landscape that resembles the view from the fishing house, the earliest moment is finally canonized as a premonition: "St. Aubert remembered the last time of his visiting that spot in company with her, and also the mournfully presaging thoughts, which had then arisen in his mind, and were now, even thus soon, realized!" (29). An earlier feeling is now grounded and identified ("premonition of death") not simply retrospectively, at the time of death, but later through nostalgic reminiscence.

Later in the novel, two paragraphs link this kind of temporalizing to an aesthetic dilemma [. . .]. The family that dominates the post-Udolpho section of the novel, the Villeforts, repeats both the St. Aubert family's perpetually nostalgic relation to an old family place and their strange way of relating to each other by imagining each other dead. [. . . T]hey travel to a castle marked by time. Returning to the scenes of his youth at Chateau-le-Blanc in the company of his daughter, the Count ruminates on his own aging, and looks forward to when Blanche will have the same experience of looking back:

> The landscape is not changed, but time has changed me; from my mind the illusion, which gave spirit to the colouring of nature, is fading fast! If you live, my dear Blanche, to re-visit this spot, at the distance of many years, you will, perhaps, remember and understand the feelings of your father.
>
> (474)

This invocation to anticipatory nostalgia of course provokes Blanche to weep as she imagines the death of her father, who in turn must go to the window to conceal his own emotion. Here a present moment of bonding between daughter and father (they join hands) is constituted not simply by looking back or looking forward, but both.

This moment of family sentiment, moreover, is followed by one of cultural nostalgia. Blanche leaves her "fading" father and goes to her antique, tarnished room in the chateau, dwelling in particular on a "faded" tapestry representing the scenes from the Trojan Wars,

> though the almost colourless worsted now mocked the glowing actions they once had painted. She laughed at the ludicrous absurdity she observed, till, recollecting, that the hands, which had wove it, were, like the poet, whose thoughts of fire they had attempted to express, long since mouldered into dust, a train of melancholy ideas passed over her mind, and she almost wept.
>
> (474)

As Eve Sedgwick has noted, the "almost colourless" fabric here is typical of Radcliffe's predilection for the faded, her distrust of color.[13] But this is not simply an aesthetic of pastness: these fading colors take on significance in relation to a more persistently robust and colorful "past," the glowing actions of Troy. The passage reverses the idea that art lives long and preserves human action, which does not last: here art becomes "distressed" by time. The relation between representation and action – really, between representation (the tapestry) and representation (Homer) – manifested here becomes more complicated in the last sentence, in which Blanche recollects that the "hands" who wove the carpet are as dead as Homer. (I will return to the synecdochic hand in the next section.) In one sense this doesn't seem like such a bad way to be dead: to be as dead as Homer is to be memorialized in marble. This passage is indicative of the ways in which almost anything can be made into a memorial in Radcliffe's book. [. . .][14]

The juxtaposition of the fading father with the fading tapestry asks us to try to join the book's obsessive anticipatory nostalgia in human relationships with Radcliffe's meditations on the movingly nonmimetic in art and writing. Each takes meaning from the other: the fading father borrows from the fading tapestry some of its consolatory aura, its capacity to elicit a mourning or commemoration. At the same time, this juxtaposition reveals the extent to which Radcliffe's aesthetic depends on the invention of a temporal gap between artifacts and their origins.

The attractions for Radcliffe of nostalgia, of fading fathers and fading tapestries, are evident in the context of her relationship to the genre in which she writes. Such nostalgia could be seen as an effect of the book's worries about the legitimacy of its own terrifying events. Radcliffe's novels are supremely concerned with their own repetitions. Their most familiar tropes all bespeak the novels' knowledge of their belatedness, their highly formal nature. The novels frequently begin in atmospheres of great self-consciousness about their own return upon the familiar; places their characters think are most their own, as we shall see, bear traces of other inhabitants. Characters hear mysterious yet familiar music coming from unlocatable sources; they return to spots that have meant something in the past; they discover themselves in dramas of recognition: these scenarios constitute the gothic novel's acknowledgment that they – and we – have all been here before.

The fundamental mystery of *The Mysteries of Udolpho* concerns how to explain the repetition of its forms. We can see the book's notorious need for elaborate explanations – how the voice and the music got to be there, for example – as an attempt to wed the book's highly formal aesthetic with a more empiricist one.[15] While the melancholy that frames the book can seem to express the novel's sense of belatedness, the characters' moody nostalgia also invents and canonizes its own origins. The gloomy feelings that frame the novel's gothic terrors may be a symptom of Radcliffe's sense of the illegitimacy of her plots and terrors, but, as I have been arguing, melancholy often plays a teleological role. Nostalgia appears both as a way of representing the conventional gothic plot as a return, and as a way of retreating from its repetitive nature. If extravagant emotion is often, in *The Mysteries of Udolpho*, what needs to be explained, it can also serve *as* explanation.

Meanwhile, it is the gothic heroine who stands as the figure for the recipient of these returns. Robert Kiely has shrewdly remarked of Radcliffe:

> What her heroines must do during their ordeals is not simply preserve their lives and their virginity – that they would do so is taken so much for granted it is hardly at issue – but they must "hold fast" in every way, keep every old idea and emotion intact.[16]

Kiely's remark is apt because it links what is most conventional (and hardly worth remarking) in the gothic heroine's plot – her struggle to preserve life, chastity, and love – with what produces some of the novel's most deviant effects. There is indeed a profound conservatism in Emily's emotional life, an effort to preserve former feelings and ideas. She is often returning to places, and "remembering the emotions, which she had formerly suffered there" (501). Emily frequently keeps the idea of the past before her eyes so firmly that she barely sees what is before her. [. . .] In fact, it would be possible to see the emotional excesses of *The Mysteries of Udolpho* as effects of the gravitational pull of [its] conservative impulse. Rather than seeing the gothic novel as taking an old plot – the embattled virgin – and adding to it new extremes, we might see its new extremes as the effects of a wholesale effort to preserve, at all levels, the old. The conservatism of the gothic heroine, her efforts to "hold fast," is in fact what produces the most extravagant aspects of the genre.[17]

***

The phenomenology of feeling described thus far has been associated with the structure of nostalgia, with an emptying out of the present and an attenuation of feelings located in the past. People's affective lives seem emptied of anything proper to the present itself. Concomitantly, another pattern of images in the book depicts characters *as filled in* by feelings that may or may not be theirs. The characters' emotional lives turn out to be occupied territory; and we can begin to establish this pattern by noticing it at all levels.

In *The Mysteries of Udolpho*, the places one thinks are most one's own never are: they always turn out to be occupied by someone else. This is true not only of the variously haunted rooms and recesses of the castle of Udolpho but also of the place that is truly home, La Vallée. The fishing house that is Emily's – and her parents' – "favourite retreat" and setting of the musical and melancholy exchanges that establish the St. Aubert family's identity in the first section of the novel is from the beginning filled with the traces of an other. A sonnet, addressed to Emily, appears penciled on the wainscot (7); someone plays her lute there (9); the crucial miniature of Emily disappears there (10). This other is revealed to be the insignificant Du Pont, who serves in the book only as a shadow for Valancourt, or later on as an utterly banal source of mysteries. The home's occupation by traces of another, however, is an ontological condition in this novel, essential to the way it represents identities. From this perspective, the typically gothic episodes in which intruders break into one's room at night or find one's secret mountain hiding place (see 596–618) could be seen as illustrations of a self always occupied, rather than as trials and assaults which the inviolate self must resist. Lovers are particularly prone to invading and occupying the home of the beloved. Wandering through the estate at Toulouse that she has now inherited, Emily is mentally occupied with the image of Valancourt: "Sometimes, indeed, she thought, that her fancy, which had been occupied by the idea of him, had suggested his image to her uncertain sight" (586). It turns out that he is, in fact, trespassing on her estate, where he is mistaken by a servant for a common poacher and shot. That Valancourt can be seen as threatening Emily with territorial encroachment makes the lover's approaches seem dangerously close to those of her persecutor, Montoni, who pursues Emily chiefly for her estates.

The feelings the lover expresses, moreover, may be feelings that are not his: indeed it is difficult to know whose language is the language of the beloved's heart. In a crucial scene shortly after Valancourt parts company with Emily and St. Aubert, she begins to think about reading one of her books:

> She sought for one, in which Valancourt had been reading the day before, and hoped for the pleasure of re-tracing a page, over which the eyes of a beloved friend had lately passed, of dwelling on the passages, which he had admired, and of permitting them to speak to her in the language of his own mind, and to bring himself to her presence. On searching for the book, she could find it nowhere, but in its stead perceived a volume of Petrarch's poems, that had belonged to Valancourt, whose name was written in it, and from which he had frequently read passages to her, with all the pathetic expression, that characterized the feelings of the author. She hesitated in believing, what would have been sufficiently apparent to almost any other person, that he had purposely left this book, instead of the one she had lost, and that love had prompted the exchange; but, having opened it with an impatient pleasure, and observed the lines of his

pencil drawn along the various passages he had read aloud, and under others more descriptive of delicate tenderness than he had dared to trust his voice with, the conviction came, at length, to her mind. For some moments she was conscious only of being beloved; then, a recollection of all the variations of tone and countenance, with which he had recited these sonnets, and of the soul, which spoke in their expression, pressed to her memory, and she wept over the memorial of his affection.

(58)

Emily's experience of finding someone else's book where she expected to find her own is reminiscent of her experiences of finding the fishing house already occupied. The novel's plot encourages us to see these episodes as parallel, insofar as it suggests that Valancourt is also the perpetrator of the fishing house transgressions. As a writer of gothic romance, moreover, Radcliffe knows to what extent books are occupied: we can see this passage as a typically Radcliffean instance of taking a canonical trope – the lovers who fall in love through reading books (Paolo and Francesca) – and temporalizing it, separating the lovers in time and making one already think of the other as an object of nostalgia. The presence of the beloved is once again a violation; and indeed here the language of the passage ("lost" rather than stolen books) and its elegiac tone associate the consciousness of being beloved with a fall. [. . .] The passage suggests that the language of the heart is never really one's own.

[. . .]

That people are occupied by alien feelings suggests that they are highly susceptible to catching other people's. A key figure for emotional transmission in *The Mysteries of Udolpho* is the image of someone's tears falling on someone else's hands. Emily's tears fall on her father's hands (67); his "warm tear" falls on hers (46). Emily weeps "over the hand she held there" (78); Valancourt holds Emily's hand, which is "wet with . . . tears" (101). In a characteristic moment (characteristic because in it the novel identifies its own semiotic codes), this exchange – tears falling on hands – is called a language: "Valancourt sighed deeply, and was unable to reply; but, as he pressed her hand to his lips, the tears, that fell over it, spoke a language, which could not be mistaken, and to which words were inadequate" (668). The tear-bathed hand undergoes a kind of baptism: it is the way Emily imbibes her father's melancholy, the way she and Valancourt communicate love. To have feelings transmitted through this bodily exchange of fluids revises the sentimental trope [. . .] in which one imbibes feelings by *seeing* the tears of another. The tears-on-hands trope makes the exchange more magical, immediate, and contagious. In this ambiguously gendered exchange of bodily fluids, moreover, unlike in the sentimental tableau, feeling can flow in both directions.

Why is a hand a receptacle of tears? The trope foregrounds the physicality of emotional exchange, the hand representing the body as a whole. But the hand also especially represents the seat of emotion, the "heart," which itself has only a metaphorical existence. The hand is thus simultaneously more physical and more metaphorical than the eye. Further, the hand as a figure in *Udolpho* is especially susceptible to the ambiguities of synecdoche, which can both connect, and detach, the figure and its referent. In the tapestry scene discussed earlier, for example, the pathos of the pastness of the tapestry-weaver is reinforced by the sense of loss that is built into synecdoche: the weaver is already only a hand, the rest of him or her having faded away, Cheshire cat-like, with the tapestry itself. Hands appear elsewhere in the novel as images of decay, and synecdoches of hands, moreover, are associated not only with the figuration of loss or severing but with figuration and writing itself. In addition to the weaving hand of the tapestry passage, there is the writing hand of the novel's last paragraph:

> And, if the weak hand, that has recorded this tale, has, by its scenes, beguiled the mourner of one hour of sorrow, or, by its moral, taught him to sustain it – the effort, however humble, has not been vain, nor is the writer unrewarded.
>
> (672)

What interests me here is the "weak hand" of the writer. Once again, the structure of synecdoche – a hand detached from, as well as standing in for, the subject – seems to add to the debility of the professed hand (and whose hand wouldn't feel weak after writing *The Mysteries of Udolpho?*). The symmetry between the weak writerly hand and the mourning reader links this passage to the "tears-on-hands" exchanges, suggesting that reader and writer are ideally bound together much as the characters are. However, the mourning reader's tears fall not into an open hand but into an open book, where the hand has disappeared into tiny marks of print.

The conjunction of hands, loss, and figuration can be seen as well in the novel's central figure for representation itself, the wax figure behind the black veil. Located behind the veil, and thus in the space identified as the space of the unrepresentable real, this memento mori – constructed in penance by an earlier inhabitant of the castle of Udolpho – suggests, as we've seen, that it's representation all the way down. Revealed for what it is at the end of the novel, the narrator points out as one of the horrors of the spectacle the "worms" that disfigure the face, "which were visible on the features and hands" (662). Disfiguring markings highlight the most legible features of this image that fills the space where we most expect the real. Because hands have already been linked with tearful exchange, hands such as these (even such grotesque ones) which are associated with loss and figuration are rendered objects of some pathos. But this vacillation of the hand, from organic, living conduit for the transmission of feeling to cut-off figure of decay, can also cast doubt on the tears-and-hands affirmations of the successful, spontaneous transmissions of feeling: the different uses of the hand reveal the hand in the text as precisely a figure, cut off by the movement of synecdoche and proliferating throughout the novel.

***

It is tempting to see the two directions in which the uses of hands appear to go – the one hand invoking the contagious transmission of feeling, the other hand severed, signifying the detached, figurative repetition of feeling – as pointing to a model for two general modes of emotional transmission in the novel. In the first case a person's feelings have their origins in an observable relationship to another empirical person; in the second, feelings pass to persons in mysterious ways. We could test this hypothesis by focusing on the relationship of Emily and M. St. Aubert, between whom many of these tears-on-hands exchanges take place. The fading father is the novel's primary locus for investigations into the causes of feelings. Recollecting her ailing father's inexplicable response to the environs of Chateau-le-Blanc, Emily feels "strongly interested concerning the remote cause" of his emotions (73). Emily gets her most explicit lessons about emotional susceptibility from her father in his famous deathbed speech about the dangers of sensibility:

> Above all, my dear Emily . . . do not indulge in the pride of fine feeling. . . . Those,
> who really possess sensibility, ought early to be taught, that it is a dangerous
> quality, which is continually extracting the excess of misery, or delight.
>
> (79–81)

If, like her fishing house, Emily is persistently occupied by things that may belong to
other people, it would make sense to point to the father.

The attractions of seeing "the father" – or "the mother" – as the explanation for
Emily's emotions are compelling. We could begin with the scene in which Emily
enters her father's room at night and sees him reading and weeping: "She could not
witness his sorrow, without being anxious to know the subject of it; and she therefore
continued to observe him in silence, concluding that those papers were letters of her
late mother." What Emily soon discovers is that her father is weeping and sighing
convulsively over a miniature: "She perceived it to be that of a lady, but not of her
mother" (26). We could then move to the episode in which Emily returns to the
scene and burns – at her father's dying injunction – the papers, but not before she
has found the miniature of the lady and seen some dreadful words:

> She was unconscious, that she was transgressing her father's strict injunction, till
> a sentence of dreadful import awakened her attention and her memory together.
> She hastily put the papers from her; but the words, which had roused equally her
> curiosity and terror, she could not dismiss from her thoughts.
>
> (103)

The miniature her father wept over is found at the bottom of a hidden purse along
with some coins that Emily now weeps over: "'His hand deposited them here,' said
she, as she kissed some pieces of the coin, and wetted them with her tears, 'his hand
– which is now dust!'" (104). Here, we could say, we have the coming together of the
tears-on-hands trope with the hand as figure for death: the tears-on-hands is mediated
by the coin that Emily wets with tears. The transmission of feeling has become the
transmission of both paternal responsibility (he leaves her some money) and sexuality.
The miniature and the dreadful words awaken memory and canonize the first scene as
a primal scene: and behind the vision "my father is weeping over someone who is not
my mother" is the fantasy "my father is sleeping with someone who is not my mother."

From this point we could see the novel as telling a certain kind of story, suggesting
that Emily's extravagant emotional sensitivity is symptomatic of a returned, repressed
fantasy about her father's sexuality, specifically about the classic primal scene, the
scene of her own conception. The novel's gothic horrors – the lifting of a veil, the
pulling back of bedclothes, anxious bedrooms and anxious nights – can thus be
seen as repetitions of the fantasized bedroom scene between the father and "a lady."
Emily's progress through the novel is thus a search for her origins, a search that
repeatedly casts before her horrifying bedroom images: as one critic has argued, "the
more Emily investigates her origins, the more such mementi she comes upon in the
form of progressive, replicated corpses"; "behind the veil is an image of the generating
marriage bed of her parents, of the violence and 'death' of the sexual act."[18]

But as some of Freud's best readers have pointed out, an original fantasy –
especially when it is a fantasy about origins – is a strange kind of origin.[19] Primal
fantasies are subject to and constructed by strange chronologies similar to the

deferred temporalities surrounding St. Aubert's response to the death of his wife in *Udolpho*. They are never a fixed point of origin but are constructed retrospectively. [...]

What if Emily's feelings were her father's? if the tears he sheds on her hands and those she sheds on his coins were in fact the same? if these scenarios – scenes of seeing the father reading and weeping, for example – had truly involved the transmission of his gloomy preoccupation, his melancholy to her? [...] Hysterically seeing women murdered in beds (her aunt at Udolpho, the mysterious figure in the bed at Chateau-le-Blanc), Emily is in fact obsessed with her *father's* secret fear: that his sister has been murdered. We could propose that *The Mysteries of Udolpho* is indeed haunted by a phantom, the kind described by the very gothic psychoanalysis of Nicolas Abraham and Maria Torok. They describe patients haunted in their words and feelings not by the *presence* of a ghost but precisely by a *gap* left within the patient by a concealment or secret not in their own life but in the life of a loved one. They thus propose the possibility of persons being subject to feelings that are fundamentally gratuitous in relation to themselves but rather belong to someone else.[20]

The question of how a secret pain in a father is transmitted to a child – as in a number of Abraham's case studies – is one that, in their analysis, resists being answered by other psychoanalytic explanations. The mode in which the interpersonal phantom passes, for example, is evidently to be distinguished from the dynamics of repression: "The phantom's periodic and compulsive return lies beyond the scope of symptom-formation in the sense of a return of the repressed; it works like a ventriloquist, like a stranger within the subject's own mental topography." The phantom is "radically heterogeneous" in relation to the subject, "to whom it at no time bears any direct reference. In no way can the subject relate to it as his own repressed experience, not even as an experience by incorporation."[21] The result is a subject who – in an earlier formulation – "experienced (unaccountably for himself and, for a long time, for the analyst) affects that were not his own."[22] [...]

The theory of the phantom and of endocryptic identification suggests that psychoanalysis makes in itself a place for gothic, uncanny stories about being occupied by feelings that aren't one's own, that belong to another. It is a theory of affective movement that bypasses the subject in order to speak of transgenerational and social practices; of mental processes fixed on words that work *against* oedipal stories;[23] and it is connected, for Abraham, to the theory of the death drive. [...] My point here is not to offer Abraham and Torok's theory as an explanation of the gothic but to note the similarities between its stories and the gothic's, between its scattered limbs and Radcliffe's weak and faded hands. Readers have often drawn parallels between gothic literature and psychoanalysis: most comparisons between the two modes have focused on their common fascination with the recovery and repetition of primal, illicit, uncanny material.[24] Perhaps these common materials, however, can be seen as effects of psychoanalysis's central debt to the gothic: a compulsion to tell often conflicting stories about feeling's origins in experience.

Notes

1 [Edmund] Burke, *Reflections on the Revolution* [*in France* (Ed. Conor Cruise O'Brien. Harmondsworth: Penguin, 1968)], 175; for other accounts of radicals' emotional insensitivity see *The Anti-Jacobin; Or, Weekly Examiner* (Nov. 20, 1797): 7; (Dec. 4, 1797): 28, 31; [Mary]

Wollstonecraft, [*A Vindication of the*] *Rights of Men* [(London, 1790)], 2, 5, 6, 10, 27. Most accounts of the relationship between the gothic novel and the French Revolution focus on the genre's themes and iconography; see, for example, [Ronald] Paulson, [*Representations of Revolution, 1789–1820* (New Haven: Yale University Press, 1983),] 215–47. For discussion of the political connotations of "enthusiasm," see [Susie I.] Tucker, [*Enthusiasm: A Study in Semantic Change* (Cambridge: Cambridge University Press, 1972),] 93–106; for a study of the language of the Revolution debates, see [James T.] Boulton, [*The Language of Politics in the Age of Wilkes and Burke* (London: Routledge and Kegan Paul, 1963)].

2   [Ann] Radcliffe, [*The*] *Mysteries of Udolpho*, [(Ed. Bonamy Dobrée. Oxford: Oxford University Press, 1966),] 248–9. Subsequent page references to this text will be in parentheses.

3   [Edmund] Burke, [*A*] *Philosophical Enquiry* [*into the Origin of Our Ideas of the Sublime and Beautiful* (Ed. James T. Boulton. Notre Dame: University of Notre Dame Press, 1958)], 131, 50–1, 248.

4   [David Hume, *A Treatise of Human Nature* (Ed. L.A. Selby-Bigge. 2nd edn, Ed. P.H. Nidditch. Oxford: Oxford University Press, 1978), 630–1; Hume, "Of Tragedy," in *Essays, Moral, Political, and Literary* (Eds T.H. Green and T.H. Grose. 2 vols. London, 1882), 1:261.]

5   Burke, [*Enquiry,*] 47.

6   Ibid., 49–50. For an account of the Burkean sublime which sees as central Burke's tendency to render objects and images indistinguishable, see [Frances] Ferguson, *Solitude and the Sublime*[*: Romanticism and the Aesthetics of Individuation* (New York: Routledge, 1992)].

7   Ibid., 47–8.

8   [Lord Henry Home] Kames, [*Elements of Criticism*. 7th edn (2 vols. Edinburgh, 1788),] 1:92.

9   [Terry] Castle's essay "The Specialization of the Other" is one of the few sustained approaches to the pre- and post-Udolpho sections of the novel. I find Castle's phenomenological description of the novel's representations of others excellent. ["The Spectralization of the Other in *The Mysteries of Udolpho*" (In Laura Brown and Felicity Nussbaum, Eds, *The New Eighteenth Century: Theory, Politics, English Literature*. New York: Methuen, 1987).]

10 [Robert] Kiely, [*The Romantic Novel in England* (Cambridge, Mass.: Harvard University Press, 1972),] 65. Kiely's phrase seems a more apt description of Radcliffe's prose than Castle's assessment of her language as "vulgar": she speaks of the need "to restore to view the powerful current of feeling in her work, however awkwardly or crudely this feeling is expressed" (307, n. 3). If Radcliffe's prose is crude or vulgar, it is precisely because it so dramatically attaches feeling to itself, not because "genuine feeling" is hidden under it.

11 I am indebted here to the anthropologist K[athleen] Stewart's eloquent essay, "Nostalgia – A Polemic" [*Cultural Anthropology* 3 (1988): 227–41]. For a view of the historical displacements of eighteenth-century gothic fiction, see [David] Punter [*The Literature of Terror: A History of Gothic Fictions from 1765 to the Present Day* (London: Longman, 1980)]. *Udolpho's* meditations on time may be seen as meditations on its own length and status as a time occupier (or waster) in a context in which increased leisure time for middle-class women was accompanied by prohibitions against wasting time; see [Leonore] Davidoff and [Catherine] Hall, [*Family Fortunes: Men and Women of the English Middle Class, 1780–1850* (Chicago: University of Chicago Press, 1987),] 225–8. The author of the "Memoirs of the Life and Writings of Mrs. Radcliffe" (published with Radcliffe's posthumous *Gaston de Blondeville*) makes much of her predicament as the wife of a busy newspaperman (William Radcliffe owned and edited *The English Chronicle*); he claims that she wrote in order to fill up her evenings in her husband's absence [in *Gaston de Blondeville; or the Court of Henry III Keeping Festival in Ardenne and St. Albans Abbey: A Metrical Tale*. 4 vols (London, 1826),] (1:6).

12 Susan Stewart, "Notes on Distressed Genres" [in *Crimes of Writing: Problems in the Containment of Representation* (Oxford: Oxford University Press, 1991), 67, 73].

13 [Eve Kosofsky] Sedgwick, "The Character in the Veil[: Imagery of the Surface in the Gothic Novel." *PMLA* 96 (1981): 255–70], 264.

14 The author of the "Memoirs of the Life and Writing of Mrs. Radcliffe" alludes to the possibility that Radcliffe's own prestige and glamor at a certain point in her life were inseparable from the rumors that she was herself dead (in *Gaston de Blondeville* 1:3–83).

15 In *Solitude and the Sublime,* Ferguson argues that the Gothic novel specializes in staging a conflict between the claims of experience and the claims of a systematic or formal world view; see 97–8.

16 Kiely, 79.

17 In her essay on the relationship between the heroic epistle and the gothic romance, [Gillian] Beer argues that it is the gothic's indebtedness to some of the characteristics of a very old form that allowed women writers to express certain kinds of emotions. ["Our Unnatural No-Voice: The Heroic Epistle, Pope, and Women's Gothic." *Yearbook of English Studies* 12 (1982): 125–51.]

18 This argument belongs to [Mary Laughlin] Fawcett's "*Udolpho's* Primal Mystery," [*Studies in English Literature* 23 (1983): 481–94] 487, 488.

19 See, for example, P[eter] Brooks, "The Fictions of the Wolf Man," in *Reading for the Plot[: Design and Intention in Narrative* (New York: Knopf, 1984)]; [Jean] Laplanche and [J.B.] Pontalis, "Fantasy and the Origins of Sexuality." [*International Journal of Psycho-analysis* 49 (1968): 1–18.]

20 [Nicolas Abraham and Maria Torok, "A Poetics of Psychoanalysis: The Lost Object-Me." *SubStance* 43 (1984): 3–18.]

21 [Nicolas] Abraham, ["Notes on the Phantom: A Complement to Freud's Metapsychology." *Critical Inquiry* 13 (1987): 287–92] 291. For a literary critical use of Abraham and Torok's notion of the phantom, see [Esther] Rashkin, [*Family Secrets and the Psychoanalysis of Narrative* (Princeton: Princeton University Press, 1992)].

22 Abraham and Torok, 8.

23 Abraham, 292.

24 The literature on gothicism and psychoanalysis includes [William Patrick] Day, [*In the Circles of Fear and Desire: A Study of Gothic Fantasy* (Chicago: University of Chicago Press, 1985)]; [Michelle] Masse, [*In the Name of Love: Women, Masochism, and the Gothic* (Ithaca, N.Y.: Cornell University Press, 1992)]; and [David B.] Morris, ["Gothic Sublimity." *New Literary History* 16 (1985): 299–319].

26 Female authorship, public fancy

Julie Ellison

From deathbed to death song

"Invention is perhaps the most arduous effort of the mind," declares Judith Sargent Murray in "On the Equality of the Sexes" (1790). Claiming the arts and public life for women, Murray answers her own rhetorical question: "Is the needle and kitchen sufficient to employ the operations of a soul thus organized? I should conceive not."[1] Fancy is a female "creative faculty," specializing in "continual variation," "playfulness," "exuberance," and "prolifick imagination." Fancy is both a point of entry into the public culture of sensibility and a device for mapping power relations within the space and time of that culture. Fancy is crucial to the gendered poetics of race in the long eighteenth century, and it is worth moving carefully from one body of poetry to another in order to establish why that is so.

[. . .] The master plot of the [eighteenth-century] republican hero proved to be extraordinarily accommodating, extending not just to [. . .] Romans [such as Cato] or their functional equivalents in tragic drama but also to the deathbed or graveyard scenes of eighteenth-century poetry by men.

But melancholia was not just associated with masculinity. It was also thoroughly conflated with the imagined subject of the internationally self-conscious nation and its margins. The literary history of eighteenth-century masculine pathos was demonstrably inseparable from the racial imagination of a colonial and imperial culture. Sensitive subjectivity could be represented as either British (or Roman, or European) or Native American (or African, or Arab). The attribution of deeply felt suffering to racial "others" was critical to the dissemination of sensibility after the Treaty of Utrecht in 1713. Racial, ethnic, and national differences became efficient vehicles for translating sensibility into narratives of inequality. The ideological malleability of sentiment, as a relationship available to conservatives, liberals, and radicals of the right and the left, relies on the ubiquity of race. Race and empire, then, are key factors in the story of how sensibility becomes central to the historical vision of women poets.

That sensibility is a transaction, not a character type, is never more clear than the way in which it is distributed on both sides of interracial encounters and portioned out to the dying man, or his friend, or both. The whole encounter is charged with the intimate tension of social equality – equality that often registers the struggle to invest narratives of cross-racial imperial relationships with the legitimizing rhetoric that evokes friendship between peers. Sensibility inspired by manly death joins empire to elegy. This is especially important in the close connections in eighteenth-century literary texts between elegy and Indians. The British fascination with the

Native American "death song" fused the lyric mode with the figure of the "vanishing Indian." The violence of European occupation is rewritten as conveniently voluntary deaths or removals undertaken by native inhabitants themselves. The literary Indian suffers or elects his (or occasionally her) own death, and the song that bears his spirit forth blends stoicism with pathos – especially when sung during torture.

The Indian death song thrived among British and Euro-American poets in the late eighteenth century, and a rigorous study of the genre's origins in response to early ethnographic feedback from traders and missionaries would certainly yield even earlier examples. Literary death songs were composed by female poets about male Indians and by male poets about female Indians. They formed part of a cluster of lyric types that include Indian songs other than death songs and lyrics that rely on the persona of the Indians' white captive. Hester Thrale Piozzi recorded Anne Hunter's "North American Death Song, Written for, and adapted to, An Original Indian Air" in her journal in 1782.[2] This is the well-known and much-circulated song of Alknomook performed by the female lead in Royall Tyler's drama of the Early Republic, *The Contrast*, having apparently made its way from London to New York.

Hunter's lyric expresses Alknomook's defiance under torture, and his pathos-laden refusal to speak the language of pain or lament. The refrain is a series of variations on "the son of Alknomook will never complain." The son of Alknomook reminds his Indian enemies of his ruthless exploits against them, but the song ends with gestures of filiopiety, friendship, and stoicism rewarded:

> I go to the land where my father is gone,
> His ghost shall rejoice in the fame of his son:
> Death comes like a friend to relieve me from pain;
> And thy son, O Alknomook, has scorned to complain.[3]

In the 1802 preface to *Lyrical Ballads*, Wordsworth recalled his interest in tracing how "maternal passion" "cleave[s] in solitude to life and society" when composing his 1798 poem, "The Complaint of a Forsaken Indian Woman." For Wordsworth, "maternal passion" is a form of affective projection, a social expression of fancy that is receptive, as this lyric shows, to the genre of complaint. This poem arose, Wordsworth explained, from having read "with deep interest" Samuel Hearne's *Journey from Prince of Wales's Fort in Hudson Bay to the Northern Ocean* (London, 1795). The speaker of the poem, "unable to continue" her journey with her "companions," is left to recover or die, as Wordsworth's ethnographic note states. She oscillates between stoicism – "No pleasure now, and no desire. / Then here contented will I lie! / Alone, I cannot fear to die" – and mourning her parting from her "poor, forsaken Child":

> I should not feel the pain of dying,
> Could I with thee a message send;
> Too soon, my friends, ye went away;
> For I had many things to say.
> (lines 18–20, 65, 47–50)[4]

Wordsworth's poem shows the close affiliation of the deathbed scene and the figure of the Native American with the power of fancy. A favorite form of eighteenth-century lyric action, fanciful thinking or meditative projection is compatible with loss as well as with the pleasures of appropriation. The exotic vignette of the North American wilderness and the activity of fancy join forces, for example, in Charlotte Smith's *Elegiac Sonnets* of 1797 and 1800. Two of the sonnets turn on conceits derived from captivity narratives and other accounts of the North American wilderness. In Smith's "Sonnet LVI," "The Captive Escaped in the Wilds of America," the "breathless Captive," disoriented and terrified by "the war-whoop howl" in the distance, is shaken by every motion of the forest that "Speaks to his trembling heart of woe and death." The sestet introduces the image of a light at the end of the tunnel: "far streaming, a propitious ray" emanates from "some amicable fort." At the last minute – in the last line – and with a crucial "As," we learn that this has all been an elaborate conceit. The saved captive represents the English-woman's gratitude toward her friend: "He hails the beam benign that guides his way, / *As I*, my Harriet, bless thy friendship's cheering light" (emphasis added).⁵ Danger becomes figurative, not literal, and the protagonist turns from a man into a woman. The speaker, it turns out, has worked herself up to a gothic fantasy of capture, escape, pursuit, and rescue.

"America" is the setting for a similarly overwrought mood – a mood in which racial images float to the surface of the mind – in Smith's "Sonnet LXI," "Supposed to Have Been Written in America." The sonnet is a precursor of Poe's "The Raven," tracing the speaker's hysterical reaction to the call of an "Ill-omen'd bird." The state of "shuddering fancy" yields the image of a susceptible Native American, signifying the speaker's powerful imagination of exotic scenarios and also drawing on the Indian as a trope of pathos. The bird is heard by "the Indian" as well as by the speaker, and this phantasmic Indian, too, is overcome by the "Dark dread of future evil":

> O'er my sick soul thus rous'd from transient rest,
> Pale Superstition sheds her influence drear,
> And to my shuddering fancy would suggest
> Thou com'st to speak of every woe I fear.⁶

These lyrics by Hunter, Wordsworth, and Smith show how both male and female poets absorb the cluster of related terms that includes the Stoic, the Man of Feeling, and the Indian. They also reveal how a poem can slip from a commitment to the discourse of Whiggish civic sensibility to the condition of fancy, gothic atmospheres, and complaint. The slip occurs by way of elegy, for "the deathbed of the just" is genetically related to the literary "death song." Fancy forms a key part of the aesthetics and politics of sensibility. It represents subjectivity that is at once ungrounded – liberated from or deprived of territory – and mobile, committed to ambitious itineraries through international space and historical time. As a motion of escape and mastery, fancy lends itself to complex ambitions for public-minded poets of both sexes and of different races. As such, it plays a crucial role in the fundamental reorientation of sensibility to the needs of global culture. In order to understand the shifty politics of aestheticized emotion, I will focus in this chapter on recurring connections among race, melancholia, artfulness, and empire – all in relation to gender and the career of the woman poet. Because fancy is at the heart of this cultural matrix, I will emphasize the ways in which this faculty performs the management of sensibility.

"Sovereigns of the regions of fancy"

By the late eighteenth century, fancy was well established as an inferior but therapeutic faculty. Definitions of fancy catalog verbs for operations performed on images and ideas: associating, collecting, combining, embellishing, mixing.[7] According to the usual explanations, fancy treats experience, including feelings, as material that can be managed but not transformed. It draws unsystematically on the processes of intellectual sorting that comprise the methodologies of the early modern human sciences. When accelerated, these pleasurable and empowering mental acts give fancy its dynamic structure. Fancy's rapid substitutions, in turn, give it its ephemeral or "airy" quality. As pure motion from one image to another, it claims no substance of its own, despite the materiality of the particular representations in which it deals.[8]

[. . .]

As a form of motion, fancy's spatial or geographical dimension connects it to the poetics of the prospect. The view from mental heights induces fancy to stage "the magnitude of prospect a rising empire displays" and then to entertain visions of imperial time ranging from elegy to celebration, from apocalypse to panegyric.[9] In these historical or geographical prospects, fancy meets politics. The mental trajectory of the fanciful poet dramatizes an engagement with historical process. Situated in retirement but ascending to survey international or even cosmic change, these speakers often rely on the conventions of the poetry of rural retreat in order to launch a more inclusive perspective. Panoramas of the progress of empire and of poetry, the big pictures of civilization's ebb and flow, bring into fancy's view vignettes of the national or racial other. And with the appearance of a stereotypical sufferer, fancy modulates into sensibility directed toward the alienated figure of the slave, the Indian, the oriental, the poor, the homeless, and – persistently combined with all these other identities – the female.

The texts of sensibility register the awareness of a political connection between pleasurable emotion and real suffering. In the tradition of literary victimization, melancholy combined with otherness leads to art. Indeed, we know that liberty, love, and suffering are invested so persistently in figures of the other by Anglo-American and European writers that such figures come to stand for emotion itself, while the specifically racial difference of the alien subject correspondingly diminishes. The mode of reflective address that reaches beyond the local situation to international subject matter and cosmopolitan audiences is as important to the dynamics of sensibility, therefore, as the pathos surrounding its familiar types of victims. The activities of "fancy," "reflection," "meditation," and "imagination" structure the reader's progress. While these choreographies of invention play a part in many poems that have nothing overtly to do with race, they are bound up even then with the speaker's desire to conceive a world and to move actively within it. [. . .]

Fancy is available in different ways for male and female poets. Writing in the *Massachusetts Magazine* of March–April 1790, Murray conflated imagination and fancy in order to make a case for female mental power:

> [S]uffer me to ask in what the minds of females are so notoriously deficient, or unequal. . . . The province of imagination hath long since been surrendered up to us, and we have been crowned undoubted sovereigns of the regions of fancy.[10]

Some male writers, especially those who subscribed to a more familiar, romantic theory of the imagination, considered fancy a form of slumming, a trivial recuperative interlude with children, animals, the working class, and women. But for many writers of both sexes, fancy retained the vertical, almost sublime associations implied by the phrase flight of fancy. Fancy became one idiom of authorial ambition by virtue of its metaphors of ascent and expansion. It could also serve the language of collective aspiration, including ambivalent or oppositional aspiration.[11] What, then, are the affinities between fancy and specific political content?

[. . .]

I stay focused on poetry [. . .] in order to introduce the category of fancy. Taking fancy seriously expands our understanding of the repertoire of sensibility over a long stretch of literary history. Because fancy is a mode in which gender dynamics are unabashedly overt, it allows us to examine the negotiations by female authors with masculine sensibility in politically serious poetry by women.

Anna Letitia Barbauld's first verse collection [. . . was . . .] published in London in 1773. [It was] fostered [. . .] by the community of intellectuals centered in English Dissenting academies [. . .]. The idioms [. . .] of Barbauld['s poetry] – specifically fancy – point to a broadly disseminated literary vocabulary that connects the growth of female authorship to racial politics.

Fancy in "transatlantic realms"

Barbauld's poetry demonstrates the way fancy can lead both to and away from questions of public policy. In many instances, her sensibility is more reflexive than social. What is other to the self takes the form of transcendental or descendental motion, an altered state of consciousness, the spirit's own spatial or temporal prospects. In "A Summer Evening's Meditation" (1773), the relationship between fancy and sympathy is narrated by a contemplative female speaker. Impelled by fancy's vertical energy, the speaker rises from the "green border of the peopled earth" past Jupiter's "huge gigantic bulk" and beyond to "the dim verge, the suburbs of the system," where Saturn presides "like an exiled monarch."[12]

In other poems by Barbauld, the structure of meditative action matches the drama of historical vision. Fancy brings before the reader vignettes of slavery, trade, and cultural transmission. In "A Summer Evening's Meditation," however, fancy leads lyric subjectivity through the cosmos in search of its own powers and limits. Here fancy finds vistas that connect it to epic aspiration through a resemblance to Milton's tours of space. But such extravagances, even in the poetry of retirement, link fancy to the history of Europe's geopolitical prospects, as well. There is a clear correlation between cosmic place and power relations: Jupiter is central and dominant; Saturn is dethroned and suburban, in the longstanding negative sense of "the suburbs." Even more striking than the political geography of center and suburb are the implications of another term, "the system." For sensibility is bound up with notions of interdependent structures and economies, the circulatory systems that no liberal author feels able to escape.

The culture of vicariousness includes experiences – of desire, projection, and substitution – that complicate the whole spectrum of subject positions. We are tempted to consider a writer like Barbauld to be almost within the system [. . .]. But, as R. Radhakrishnan has observed, both "mobilizing the inner/outer distinction" and choosing "radical relationality" pose problems for the late twentieth-century scholar.[13] We can extend this dilemma backward. The dynamics of eighteenth-century sensibility rely on the logic of center and margin while simultaneously incorporating both positions into a relational field.

"A Summer Evening's Meditation" dramatizes an encounter between the poetry of contemplation and the poetry of prospects. Fancy emerges from a fostering nocturnal environment to undertake a prospective mission. Such endeavors derive in part from Thomson's poetry of British prospects and polite indolence; they also descend from *Paradise Lost*, where elevated surveys are prophetic or satanic.[14] The action of "A Summer Evening's Meditation" centers on the figure of Contemplation. Emerging from her grotto, Contemplation directs the poet/speaker, who has already narrated the displacement of Apollo by an "impatient" Diana, to gaze on the night sky. "With radiant finger," Contemplation "points / To yon blue concave swelled by breath divine." When her "unsteady eye . . . wanders unconfin'd / O'er all this field of glories," the speaker describes the "spacious field" of starry "hieroglyphics" as a "tablet" that has been "hung on high / To public gaze." Human viewers are characterized collectively as the "public" that looks upon "the Master." The Master's directive specifies a required attitude: "Adore, O man! / The finger of thy God." The public, then – including the speaker – is defined by its distance from and attraction to elevated power. And in this gesture, the female poet refuses to be idiosyncratic by virtue of her sex and joins the general, or public, culture. Contemplation needs the authority of the celestial text in order to create a spatial arena vast enough for the subjective expansion that follows. The upward wanderings of the "restless and dazzled" eye require the "blue concave swelled by breath divine" (9, 23–4, 28–34).

But this vertical thought is followed by the downward gaze of maternal stars, "pure wells / Of milky light," "friendly lamps" that "light us to our home." The speaker is almost back where she began, in Nature's "thick-wove foliage," Contemplation's "lonely depth / Of unpierc'd woods." Down here the proper language is not the hieroglyphic text spread before the public eye. Despite the stars' mediation, the speaker, instead of intensely looking, is "[i]ntensely listening": "the raised ear . . . drinks in every breath" and hears nature's praise in the voice of silence itself and a "tongue in every star that talks with man." The starry tongues, perhaps, constitute a counterpublic to human viewers. "Wisdom mounts her zenith with the stars" and we expect the speaker to ride along. Deep space and deep time are now interior to the subject, however, or, in Barbauld's phrase, interior to "the self-collected soul":

> At this still hour the self-collected soul
> Turns inward, and beholds a stranger there
> Of high descent, and more than mortal rank;
> An embryo God; a spark of fire divine,
> which must burn on for ages, when the sun
> . . . .
> Has closed his golden eye.
> (36–9, 18–20, 46–9, 52–9)

This passage marks another surge of agency. Masculine fire is taken into the female subject. In this annunciation scene, the meditative faculty turns inward to behold an alienated self-image. The soul is pregnant with itself. But this fiery selfhood has to be a "stranger" of "high descent" in order to give the speaker genealogical access to the "ages." This strange son, the soul's soul, enables a passionately speculative episode.

Apostrophizing the "citadels of light" once more, the recharged speaker links herself temporally and spatially to them, imagining herself there rather than at home in the starlit plane of earthly nature: "Perhaps my future home, from whence the soul / Revolving periods past, may oft look back." But this hypothetical vista is inadequate to the soul's ambitions, and Barbauld collapses the time frame from the "future" to "now" in the next phrase: "O be it lawful *now* / To tread the hallow'd circle of your courts" (emphasis added). After a deferential nod to the "seats of Gods," the speaker gives herself over to fancy's most grandiose possibilities:

> Seiz'd in thought,
> On fancy's wild and roving wing I sail,
> From the green borders of the peopled earth,
> And the pale moon, her duteous fair attendant;
> From solitary Mars; from the vast orb
> Of Jupiter, whose huge gigantic bulk
> Dances in ether like the lightest leaf;
> To the dim verge, the suburbs of the system.
>
> (61–78)

Here, as in so many other fanciful poems of the period, "wild and roving" fancy generates figures of dancing and ethereality, with both of these compressed into the merely seasonal and almost weightless wind-driven leaf. We know this is still the aesthetic of fancy rather than the sublime because Jupiter's "huge gigantic bulk" is perspectively transformed into familiar diminutives.

The strength of the feminine lyric subject's ego rises and falls in relation to space and scale. Immensity is a trope for women's public ambition and for the doubts to which ambition is prone. Barbauld's fancy could not rove without a "gigantic" cosmos. In her tour of the "system," she passes one patriarchal form after another, from "solitary Mars" to Jupiter and finally "cheerless Saturn." Having passed these depressing hulks, the contemplative soul is further exhilarated: "fearless thence / I launch into the trackless deeps of space." Among "ten thousand suns . . . / Of elder beam," she reaches the first of two crises of confidence. "Here must I stop," she thinks, then asks, "Or is there aught beyond?" To ask about "aught beyond" is already to be in the grip of its "hand unseen," already a seer. And here the soul finds itself in a version of the womblike space that had represented subjective coherence at the beginning of fancy's galactic voyage. She is impelled onward

> To solitudes of vast unpeopled space,
> The desarts of creation, wide and wild;
> Where embryo systems and unkindled suns
> Sleep in the womb of chaos.

Fancy travels through its own reproductive zone, its chaotic womb, where the systems that consciousness will continue to explore take shape. Passages like this make it difficult to determine what is internal and what external, what psychological and what "public" in this poem. And it is difficult not just for the twentieth-century reader, but also for Barbauld. Confronted with its own inside as the ultimate outside, or vice versa, the soul reaches its second, and decisive, crisis of confidence: "fancy droops, / And thought astonish'd stops her bold career" (75–81, 89–98).

In fact, fancy doesn't just "droop"; it all at once abases itself. "Where shall I seek Thy presence," she queries of "thou mighty mind!" Still disoriented, she wonders how, "unblamed," she is going to "[i]nvoke thy dread perfection?" The only thing the soul can be blamed for is its vertical approach to divinity, a conclusion verified by the rapidity with which the meditative speaker now places herself below the divine:

> O look with pity down
> On erring, guilty man; not in thy names
> Of terror clad: not with those thunders armed
> That conscious Sinai felt, when fear appalled
> The scatter'd tribes;

The poem concludes rapidly in a chastened and not much comforted key. The "bold career" of fancy reaches its limits when "thought" cannot go further back than the generative "desarts of creation." Creation marks the point of transgression, and the chaotic womb is superseded by a single origin, the "mighty mind." The speaker collapses "appalled" before the deity's "names / Of terror," then reminds divinity that it possesses a "gentler" internal voice of heart-intuited "whispers." The "soul, unused to stretch her powers / In flight so daring, drops her weary wing." She plants herself firmly in "the known accustomed spot" that sheltered the figure of Contemplation at the beginning of the poem. Here she will "wait" for death and immortality, when "splendors" of the "world unknown" will come to her, rather than she to them (99–122).

[. . .]

The tension between masculine authority and feminine ambition is played out in the field of cosmic perspectives. The idea of the system provides an opportunity for the woman writer to expand her scope, but then turns into a conceptual frame from which she cannot escape.

Barbauld entertains the class-inflected perspective for which the elevated view is the goal of educated thought. For her, this strategy offers access to or agency within a large cultural universe. Such agency can take the form of mobile spiritual cognition in "A Summer's Evening's Meditation," but this is not the only use to which fancy may be put by sensibility. And in her 1773 essay, "An Enquiry into those kinds of Distress which excite Agreeable Sensations," Barbauld clearly expresses her opinion that sensibility should be morally useful.[15] Fancy reveals the logic of human systems and economies in the culture of sensibility. "Epistle to William Wilberforce, Esq. on the rejection of the bill for abolishing the slave trade" (1791) is a critique of sentimental portrayals of slaves as victims. That is, Barbauld criticizes the antislavery campaign mounted by many women writers, among others, in the 1780s. She argues that the rhetoric of victimization has failed and should be replaced by the systematic logic of moral economy. She declares that the conventions of abolitionist sensibility are obsolete. They persist as structural elements of Barbauld's own revisionist alternative, but with a crucial shift in tone from pity to indignation.[16] Both pathos and protest share fancy's systematic overview and rely on emotion to establish the poet's right to cultural citizenship.

The "Epistle" opens with an exasperated catalog of speakers who have used the bodily rhetoric of sensibility on British audiences to no avail:

> The Preacher, poet, Senator, in vain
> Has rattled in [Britain's] sight the Negro's chain;
> . . . .
> Forc'd her averted eyes his stripes to scan,
> Beneath the bloody scourge laid bare the man,
> Claim'd Pity's tear, urged Conscience' strong controul
> And flash'd conviction on her shrinking soul.

Barbauld's account of abolitionist writing makes clear the link between vicarious suffering and political criticism. Indignation causes abolitionists to torment their readers with depictions of "the Negro's" tormented flesh in order to coerce identification with the victim. The "scene of distress" "forces" the reader to gaze on the beaten slave and "assails" the audience with his groans. Barbauld characterizes the rhetoric of sensibility as itself a scourge that, like the whip, "lays bare" the suffering body of the reader. Barbauld values the language of Wilberforce and his allies insofar as it amplifies the groans and tears of slaves for the resistant British public. But, while praising the attempt to make the guilty suffer, she zeroes in on the shortcomings of rhetorical flagellation. Poetry designed to make the nation know slavery proved that knowledge, however visceral, is not enough: "She knows and she persists – Still Afric bleeds, / Unchecked, the human traffic still proceeds" (3–17).

Barbauld attributes the failure of sensibility to inspire legislative action to the systematic effects of slavery itself. Wilberforce's cause is hopeless in the face of Britain's immunity to feeling guilty. "Wit, Worth, and Parts and Eloquence" – poets, writers, and rhetoricians – have rallied to Wilberforce's cause: "All, from conflicting ranks, of power possest / To rouse, to melt, or to inform the breast." But against the language of "Avarice," the "Nation's eloquence" fails: "th'unfeeling sneer / . . . turns to stone the falling tear" and "[f]ar from the sounding lash the Muses fly." Sentimental representations of pain duel with conscious cynicism and lose: "In Britain's senate, Misery's pangs give birth / To jests unseemly, and to horrid mirth." "Seek no more to break a Nation's fall," Barbauld urges Wilberforce. Just give up. Britain has accepted itself as a profit-driven society, and against this self-knowledge, "[t]h'acknowledged thirst of gain," the appeal for vicarious suffering is useless (21–33, 85, 41–2, 117–18).

Barbauld prophesies Africa's revenge on Britain through the systematic, impersonal operations of empire. This retaliatory logic is set in motion by "Heaven's impartial plan," not by the "injur'd" themselves, despite the attribution of agency to the oppressed continent:

> injur'd Afric, by herself redrest,
> Darts her own serpents at her Tyrant's breast.
> Each vice, to minds depraved by bondage known,
> With sure contagion fastens on his own.

The suburbs of this system poison the capitol reflexively, through the numbed emotions and degraded appetites of the slave economy. The loop of vice and disease hastens the venom's progress through the body of Great Britain. Drawing on a familiar convention, Barbauld shows how slaveholding turns women into tyrants. The mistress embodies the "monstrous fellowship" of "Scythian, and ... Sybarite," of "indolence to fierceness join'd."[17] The East Indian trade, meanwhile, evicts the figures of "Simplicity," "Stern Independence," and "Freedom" from rural England: "By foreign wealth are British morals chang'd, / And Afric's sons, and India's, smile avenged."[18]

Barbauld replaces the conventions of sensibility, which rely on vicarious emotion to induce pity, with the threat of contagious corruption. African slaves and colonized Indians become spectators, as England's free population sinks to the condition of slaves: "Shrieks and yells disturb the balmy air, / Dumb sullen looks of woe announce despair, / And angry eyes thro' dusky features glare" (44–9, 62–6, 101–6, 82–5). This process of role reversal or poetic justice seems to abandon moral judgment to the impersonal reflexes of economic logic. The shift makes possible a change of tone from pity, directed at generic victims, to prophetic, almost Blakean, exasperation. The "angry eyes" glaring out of the sullen faces of degraded British citizens mark the extent to which sensibility could be revised in the disinhibiting aftermath of 1789. The victim's body houses rage, not the slave's "constant tear."

Barbauld's most remarkable work combines the tense connection between sensibility and system with the power of fancy. It does so, furthermore, through an explicitly transatlantic vision. "Eighteen Hundred and Eleven" joins the strengths of "A Summer Evening's Meditation" and the "Epistle to Wilberforce." In "Eighteen Hundred and Eleven," the logic of systematic moral correction again prevails in declarations that irritated some of Barbauld's original readers: "Britain, know, / Thou who has shared the guilt must share the woe."[19] The speaker surveys the empire from India to "the Apalachian [*sic*] hills," evoking the spread of British culture "o'er transatlantic realms." When the visionary tour speeds up and shifts into an apocalyptic tone, Fancy materializes both to suffer and to stage the show, and finally to offer commentary on it. Weeping Fancy represents the fusion of sensibility and mental voyaging. Fancy, a sentimental reader or, perhaps, theatergoer, travels through time, which takes the form of "imaged" events.

> Where wanders Fancy down the lapse of years,
> Shedding o'er imaged woes untimely tears?
> Fond, moody power! as hopes – as fears prevail,
> She longs, or dreads, to lift the awful veil,
> On visions of delight now loves to dwell,
> Now hears the shriek of woe or Freedom's knell:
> Perhaps she says, long ages past [*sic*] away,
> And set in western wave our closing day,
> Night, Gothic night, again may shade the plains
> Where Power is seated, and where Science reigns;
> England, the seat of arts, be only known
> by the gray ruin and the mouldering stone;
> That Time may tear the garland from her brow,
> And Europe sit in dust, as Asia now.
>
> (83, 111–26)

The poem begins by detailing the contemporary Napoleonic wars and their human cost abroad and to British families at home. With the accusation of Britain's guilt,

Barbauld starts to prophesy the future doom of the empire, moving between tones of rebuke, bitter fantasy, and elegiac regret.[20] She no longer refuses pathos, but embraces its theatrical power. With the long passage quoted above, increasingly agitated emotions find a vehicle in Fancy. Fancy's emotional volatility transforms prophecy into a series of competing fictions. Oscillating between "fond" or "moody" feelings – depending on whether hope or fear, longing or dread, delight or woe is "imaged" – the figure of Fancy abandons the narrator's dignified tonalities and overreacts. Her "untimely" passion over unrealized events climaxes in the vision of a new dark age, a "Gothic night." The trope refers both to the gothic genre of Fancy's sentimental trepidation and to the historical return of the feudal, or gothic, past. Fancy utters a vision of the orientalization of the West, relying on the topos of the progressive westering of empire that leaves lands further east in ruins: "'Perhaps,' she says, long ages past away," Europe may "sit in dust, as Asia now."

After speaking as passionate historian in the British present, Fancy becomes the agent of American inspiration. And the thought of America brings with it a Utopian scene of harmonious racial and ethnic variety. Ages hence, fanciful young Americans will tour the ruins of empire "just as our young noblemen go to Greece."[21] With "throbbing bosoms" and "musing mind[s]" but most of all with Fancy's "mingled feelings," these "wanderers" will visit the remnants of London. Animated by the fantasies of tourists, the lost capitol will be remembered as the center of an internationally dominant but generously multiracial empire. The mixed population of the city and the mingled feelings of the travelers both exemplify Fancy's heterogeneous aesthetic:

> The mighty city, which by every road,
> In floods of people poured itself abroad
> Ungirt by walls, irregularly great,
> No jealous drawbridge, and no closing gate;
> Whose merchants (such the state that commerce brings)
> Sent forth their mandates to dependent kings;
> Streets, where the turbaned Moslem, bearded Jew,
> And woolly Afric, met the brown Hindu;
> Where through each vein spontaneous plenty flowed,
> Where Wealth enjoyed, and Charity bestowed.

As Barbauld's retrospective, then prospective, narrative continues to unfold, history appears to be the random consequence of "changeful fancy." The "Spirit" that roams the earth, "Moody and viewless as the changing wind," governs the progress of empire in its passage through Babel, Egypt, and Troy (177, 187, 157–68, 215–17, 259–65). In a fine example of how historical prospects celebrate heterogeneity, then convert it into unity, a long passage surveying the complicated mix of cultures from Syria to Scandinavia climaxes in praise of modern British refinement.

At this juncture, Barbauld's "Spirit" acts in accord with teleological westerly movement. As "the Genius soars" toward South America – executing a striking swerve away from the devotees of British culture in North America – the systematic justice of imperial decay sets in: "Arts, arms, and wealth destroy the fruits they bring. . . . With grandeur's growth the mass of misery grows." As the Genius of history "pours through feeble souls a higher life," shedding its transcendental influence on "Andes' heights,"

"Chimborazo's summits," and La Plata's "roar," it seems to promise both cultural multiplicity and manifest destiny. The Genius "Shouts to the mingled tribes from sea to sea / And swears – Thy world, Columbus, shall be free" (315, 320–34). What kind of resolution is effected by these paradoxical lines, and in what tone? The Genius unifies "mingled tribes" through the imperial singular ("Thy world, Columbus"), but the energetic new world mix is never wholly homogenized.

The personified spirit of historical change has multiple relationships with the poetics of fancy, then. The personification itself is invented by Barbauld's fancy. The vistas of past empire created by fancy turn the faculty itself into a spectator, and fancy crystallizes briefly as the temporally fluid and overemotional audience of projected historical scenes. Britain's cultural heirs in North America exhibit a more temperate but still fanciful connoisseurship as they re-imagine, among London's future ruins, its present flawed glories. History itself, finally, is an artist in fancy's mode, insofar as it repeatedly creates empires out of "mingled tribes." Racial heterogeneity is a sign of health and energy for Barbauld, as long as she can channel the diverse, lively origins of great cultures into a single historical meaning. "Mingled tribes" are infused with the "higher life" of cultural purpose, with its intrinsic tendencies toward self-destruction.

Barbauld, who refused to take a stand in favor of female authorship, uses the language of fancy to engage the pathos of public time.[22] This strategy characterizes authors of both sexes who mourn the violence of the systems they analyze, who cannot think systematically without pity, or mourn without analysis. Yet when women relied on the politics of fancy, criticism of their positions collapsed into attacks on their sex. Reactions to "Eighteen Hundred and Eleven" conformed to party lines. The reviewer for the *Anti-Jacobin* argued that the *Monthly Review* praised the poem only because Barbauld expressed Dissenting views. Croker's article in the *Quarterly Review* lumped Barbauld with "her renowned compatriot," William Roscoe, whose two pamphlets on parliamentary reform are critically, though affectionately, reviewed in the same issue. But while the *Anti-Jacobin* categorized the poem's genre as prophecy and dismissed it as Dissenting propaganda, the *Quarterly* called it satire and attacked it on grounds of gender: "Our old acquaintance Mrs. Barbauld turned satirist! . . . We had hoped, indeed, that the empire might have been saved without the intervention of a lady-author." And Croker goes on to deplore the "irresistible impulse of public duty – a confident sense of commanding talents" that "induced her to dash down her shagreen spectacles and her knitting needles, and to sally forth . . . in the magnanimous resolution of saving a sinking state, by the instrumentality of . . . a pamphlet in verse."[23] In order to oppose the Dissenter, Croker excoriates the woman. In order to turn a poem into a pamphlet, he shrinks fancy to polemic. And in the process, he marks off political prose as the preserve of men. Fancy becomes the emotional excess that allows Croker to claim that "Eighteen Hundred and Eleven" fails because of a mismatch of gender and genre. But whatever he had wrong, Croker had one thing absolutely right: it is precisely the "irresistible impulse of public duty" and "a confident sense of commanding talents" that fuels the hallucinatory rage of "Eighteen Hundred and Eleven."

Notes

1 Judith Sargent Murray. "On the Equality of the Sexes," in *Selected Writings of Judith Sargent Murray*, ed. Sharon M. Harris (New York: Oxford University Press, 1995), 4–5. Written in 1779, the essay was first published in *Massachusetts Magazine* 2 (March 1790): 133.

2 See Lora Romero. "Vanishing Americans: Gender, Empire, and New Historicism," *American Literature* 63 (September 1991).

3 Roger Lonsdale, ed. *Eighteenth-Century Women Poets: An Oxford Anthology* (Oxford and New York: Oxford University Press, 1989), 364.[. . .]

4 William Wordsworth, *The Poems*, ed. John O. Hayden (New Haven, Conn.: Yale University Press, 1981), 1:871. 275–6, 945.

5 Charlotte Smith, "Elegiac Sonnets and Other Poems," in *The Poems of Charlotte Smith*, ed. Stuart Curran (New York: Oxford University Press, 1993), 50.

6 Ibid., "Sonnet LXI," 54, lines 1, 3–4, 9–12.

7 James Engell, *The Creative Imagination: Enlightenment to Romanticism* (Cambridge: Harvard University Press, 1981), 172–96.

8 Here I paraphrase my characterization of fancy in " 'Nice Arts' and 'Potent Enginery': The Gendered Economy of Wordsworth's Fancy," *Centennial Review* 33 (fall 1989): 442, 446–7.

9 *The Plays and Poems of Mercy Otis Warren*, ed. Benjamin Franklin V (Delmar, N.Y.: Scholars' Facsimiles and Reprints, 1980), 100. The passage cited is taken from "To a Young Gentleman in Europe" (1784), Warren's prefatory letter to *The Ladies of Castile*, which appeared in *Poems, Dramatic and Miscellaneous* (1790).

10 Murray, "On the Equality of the Sexes," 4–11.

11 Ross Chambers explores the politics of the melancholy or "suicidal" text in terms that illuminate the status of otherness in the literature of sensibility.[. . .] "The Suicide Tactic: Writing in the Language of the Other," chap. 3 in *Room for Maneuver: Reading (the) Oppositional (in) Narrative* (Chicago: University of Chicago Press, 1991).

12 Anna Letitia Barbauld, "A Summer Evening's Meditation," *The Works of Anna Letitia Barbauld, with a Memoir by Lucy Aiken* (London: Longman, 1825), p. 126, lines 73–8. Subsequent references are cited by line in the text.

13 R. Radhakrishnan, "Nationalism, Gender, and the Narrative of Identity," in *Nationalisms and Sexualities*, ed. Andrew Parker et al. (New York: Routledge. 1992), 81–4.

14 John Barrell, "An Unerring Gaze: The Prospect of Society in the Poetry of James Thomson and John Dyer," chap. 1 of *English Literature in History, 1730–80: An Equal, Wide Survey* (New York: St. Martin's Press, 1983).

15 John Aiken and A. Aiken, *Miscellaneous Pieces in Prose* (London, 1773), 190–214.

16 For a detailed discussion of antislavery poetry by women, focusing on contributions to the 1787 parliamentary campaign for abolition, see Moira Ferguson, *Subject to Others: British Women Writers and Colonial Slavery, 1670–1834* (New York: Routledge, 1992).

17 Ferguson points out that the character of the corrupted mistress of a slave-owning family would have been familiar from Sarah Scott's novel, *Sir George Ellison* (1766), set in Jamaica (Moira Ferguson, "British Women Writers and an Emerging Abolitionist Discourse," *The Eighteenth Century: Theory and Interpretation* 33 [spring 1992]: 17).

18 Marlon Ross, *The Contours of Masculine Desire: Romanticism and the Rise of Women's Poetry* (New York: Oxford University Press, 1989), 221–4.

19 Barbauld, *The Works*, 232–50.

20 The attack on "Eighteen Hundred and Eleven" in the *Anti-Jacobin* of 12 August 1812 counters the favorable notice of the *Monthly Review*. Quoting the *Monthly's* approving claim that "poets are prophets as well as satirists," the *Anti-Jacobin* expresses its "sovereign contempt for the prophetic powers of Mrs. Barbauld," especially because those powers depict "the ruins of England with so much more spirit than . . . her beauties."

21 *Quarterly Review* 7 (June 1812): 311.

22 On "Eighteen Hundred and Eleven," Marlon Ross comments,

> In a sure, strong voice, Barbauld predicts England's fate as irreversible. How ironic that this tour de force should be executed by a woman who believes that women should not become authors and should refrain from entering the masculine world of politics and knowledge.
>
> (*The Contours of Masculine Desire*, 226)

23 *Quarterly Review* 7 (June 1812): 281.

27 The art of knowing nothing

Feminine melancholy and skeptical dispossession

Jacques Khalip

> There is nothing I shrink from more fearfully than publicity – I have too much of it – & what is worse I am forced by my hard situation to meet it in a thousand ways – Could you write my husband's life, without naming me it were something – but even then I should be terrified at the rouzing the slumbering voice of the public – each critique, each mention of your work, might drag me forward. . . . Now that I am alone in the world, [I] have but the desire to wrap night and the obscurity of insignificance around me. This is weakness – but I cannot help it – to be in print – the subject of *men's* observations – of the bitter hard world's commentaries, to be attacked or defended! – this ill becomes one who knows how little she possesses worthy to attract attention – and whose chief merit – if it be one – is a love of that privacy, which no woman can emerge from without regret. . . . But remember, I pray for omission – for it is not that you will not be too kind too eager to do me more than justice – But I only seek to be forgotten.
>
> (Mary Shelley, letter to Edward Trelawny, April 1829)

As she shrinks away from the glare of the public sphere, how do we characterize Shelley's refusal of recognition in this letter?[1] On the one hand, there are palpable fears and terrors of involuntary exposure, of being dragged forward into the light and having one's agency wrested away as a condition of forced submission to the will of another. There are also longings here of a more domestic kind, longings for the securities of seclusion that banally translate into privacy and retirement. On the other hand, Shelley's refusal testifies to something more profound – a wish for disengagement, for an anonymity or invisibility of self beyond "the bitter hard world's commentaries," where personal intimacies and strategies are given room to maneuver despite their apparent "insignificance," far afield from prying eyes. Are these wishes, however, as Shelley maintains, signs of weakness? Her resistance to the "slumbering voice of the public" doesn't so much reject social participation altogether as intimate an alternative social presence. It thus comes as no surprise that by backing away from the writing of her husband's life, Mary Shelley wants a different history for herself, one that radically disavows the kind of fellowship and narrative plenitude her husband's biography promises: "I only seek to be forgotten."

On one level, Shelley's disavowal might be read as symptomatic of what Julie Ellison has persuasively identified as a gendered vanishing point within traditional critical narratives of romanticism:

The invention of the romantic subject as the hero of desire is therefore wholly bound up with the feminine. At the same time, romantic writers suspect that desire may be a form of power, understanding a form of science, and woman a form of sabotage. Objects of desire are lost or violated in ambivalent allegories of the domestic and the maternal. Ultimately, the feminine becomes, first, wholly figurative or non-referential and then invisible.[2]

Building upon the work of several critics who have pointed to tensions between feminist thought and romantic ideology,[3] Ellison seeks to return women as the absent causes to a philosophical tradition they had already partly inaugurated, taking the "language of mood" (of intuition) to describe one kind of romantic hermeneutic that can be "marked as a feminine quality."[4] A suggestive implication of her argument is that the receding or lost figure of the feminine signifies the crucial object of loss or aporia at the core of romanticism's epistemological and ethical concerns, and in this sense, femininity throws into sharper relief the melancholic structure of the romantic enlightenment of which it is a constitutive part. However, if the representation of women is bound to a volatile series of tropological substitutions through which women are initially rendered "wholly figurative or nonreferential and then invisible," it would appear that the nonrecognition Shelley longs for staunchly resists all progressive attempts at her critical rescue. After all, by refusing publicity and its attending conferrals of meaning and reputation, Shelley's wish for anonymity seems to resemble an act of bereavement: falling away from memory and representation, she embodies the loss that cannot ever be thought of or recuperated *as* loss – "the loss of loss," as Alan Liu diagnoses the critical fears of a suggestively "romantic" postmodernism.[5] And yet, what would it mean to read Shelley's refusal here as a radical negativity that takes loss as the condition of *possibility* (rather than failure) of subjectivity? In other words, loss would be the constitutive expression of a dispossessed relation to the world, one that assumes the absent character of the "unmemorable" female melancholic as its rising yet recessive star, forfeiting identification.

[. . . R]omantic culture approaches subjectivity as dispossessed and anonymous: whether it is protectively erased through political narratives, lyrically negated, or rendered virtual as a result of its sympathetic identifications, anonymity is less a mystic and embryonic state of being than it is a predicament that broadly testifies to certain affects or modes of cognition that challenge the tidiness of claiming an autonomous "I" as the core to our moral actions. What the subject *is* remains a permanently suspended question for romanticism, and this toleration for the self's apartness – its reluctance to accede to categorization and display – inaugurates an ethics of engaged withdrawal or strategic reticence. In this [. . .] chapter, I want to consider how the figure of the female melancholic, as she appears in Mary Wollstonecraft's *A Vindication of the Rights of Woman* and *A Short Residence in Sweden, Norway, and Denmark,* [. . .] dramatizes multiple concerns about the problems of skepticism in relation to selfhood, agency, and knowledge. I interpret melancholy less as an affective pathology than as an extension of skeptical thought, or, to borrow Tilottama Rajan's phrase, a "figure of understanding" that characterizes the feminine self as intelligible at the very point at which she appears most alienated from her own thoughts and actions.[6] For Wollstonecraft, [. . .] the female melancholic is perceived as ambivalently participating in and challenging what Wollstonecraft will call "making an appearance in the world,"[7] or the project of developing the social terms under which one makes oneself known and available to others. I argue that the female melancholic rethinks this incentive to declare oneself, to make oneself known as a properly civic subject, and finds in loss a state of being that lends itself to an ethics of dispossession, one that fundamentally disarticulates personal fulfillment from self-presentation and self-assertion. [. . . H]ow and *what* one thinks about is inextricable from questions of social embodiment and knowledge, and the challenges of (re)presenting the anonymous female subject foreground the degree to which a kind of negativity is at work in the structure of melancholy itself, one that Mary Jacobus has described as typifying a certain feminine refusal of masculinist structures of Enlightenment revelation.[8][. . .]

Building on Kristeva's recuperation of Freudian melancholy as a form of resistance to the monumentalizing imperatives of patriarchal culture,[9] Jacobus reads the negativity of female melancholy as part of a wider claim launched by writers like Inchbald, Radcliffe, Wollstonecraft, and Edgeworth to produce, not simply a rival discourse of feminine subjectivity, but a discourse that measures "the Enlightenment's refusal to accommodate the very discourse of sexual difference that its inquiries into the nature and rights of personhood, bodies, and passions had seemed to initiate." In claiming that the negativity of melancholy marks a "limit of [enlightenment] discourse,"[10] femininity comes to figure for an obstacle or interruption in certain linear narratives of the "empire of Reason" that promote progressivist ideologies of the self. What Jacobus doesn't notice, however, is the way in which her recasting of feminine negation comes to mark a cognitive plenitude: as a categorical limit of sorts, femininity assumes a special self-privileging knowledge to itself in the very instant that it contests "Reason," thus reaffirming (instead of redefining) the transparent autonomy of Enlightenment thought. In contrast, I want to argue that Wollstonecraft [. . .] conceive[s] the female melancholic as a recessive and complex character who explores, practices, and displaces various anxieties about alterity, moral obligation, and self-determination – anxieties that evoke a toleration for the subject's apartness and the ethical aspect of dispossession.[11]

As a "structure of feeling,"[12] melancholy in its eighteenth-century incarnation evolves out of Enlightenment discourses of the sentiments, conflating social, aesthetic, and philosophical factors. To the extent that it partakes of the language of sensibility, it rhetorically manages a subject whose experiences of loss are related to a wider public culture that values sentiment as a "transaction, not a character type."[13] Melancholy represents (as it did for earlier writers of the Renaissance and Baroque periods) a surplus of knowing that seemingly fails to provide enlightenment; in this sense it defines a self-consciousness that repudiates discursive systems even as it finds itself to be implicated in them – an "unhappy consciousness," as Hegel intuited, that in its alienation acquires a critical renunciatory force.[14] Antedating Hegel, the degree to which sadness and philosophizing are often of a piece is eloquently exemplified in the section "On Personal Identity" in Hume's *Treatise Of Human Nature,* where Hume famously amends the fantasy of self-motivated *Bildung* by intimating that the self can only come into its own if it can be taught to remember and reexperience its identity by deliberately standing away from itself. Hume demonstrates that what we consider to be "intimate" in fact marks our strongest estrangement from both ourselves and others, because self-consciousness is by definition permeated by otherness [. . .].[15] The mind's sense of its own vertigo soon gives rise to the deep melancholy at the conclusion of "On Personal Identity":

Where am I, or what? From what causes do I derive my existence, and to what condition shall I return? Whose favour shall I court, and whose anger must I dread? What beings surround me? and on whom have I any influence, or who have any influence on me? I am confounded with all these questions, and begin to fancy myself in the most deplorable condition imaginable, inviron'd with the deepest darkness, and utterly depriv'd of the use of every member and faculty.

(175)

Hume's melancholic exhortation reads like an embedded soliloquy, occasioned by the conflagrating pressures of his reflections. Indeed, the profundity of his crisis evokes a powerful, idealistic remainder that retains the governing presence of mind in the wake of disembodiment. In this sense, Hume doesn't so much obliterate the self as dramatically rethink it as a consequence of a spiraling skepticism, one that construes identity to be distributed along various possible points in time.

In just this way, Hume is able to emphasize the *cognitive* value of dispossession, and in turn, his work of mourning redeems dispossession as a viable subjectivity-effect: the self (re)appears as an impersonal, reflexive entity that is subject to exchange and transfer, and its melancholic bent becomes a symptom of a probabilistic culture that forever depends on loss [. . .]. For writers such as Wollstonecraft [. . .], however, the problem of melancholic skepticism is gendered: experienced by female characters who deal with loss as the experience of their social marginalization but also as an agonistic refusal (rather than a Humean reaffirmation) of specific kinds of participatory identity. [. . .] Wollstonecraft perceives the melancholic female subject as cultivating a being-in-the-world that evokes an ontological *and* cognitive "failure" of enlightenment, but ironically, it is precisely this failure which characterizes the historical predicament of melancholy subjectivity tout court: at once the subject and the object of self-bereavement over which it claims reflective agency, such a subjectivity figures for the (im)possibility of an Enlightenment culture of skepticism as well as the cause of that culture's precarious instabilities.[16]

Because skepticism, in a fundamentally Hegelian sense, is embedded in the very operation of reflection – it is the affective correlate of self-awareness that can never be expunged or otherwise overcome – it dramatically destabilizes the self through the act of reflection meant to announce its presence in the discursive public sphere. This latter point echoes in Freud's theory of melancholy [. . .] as the affect of a grieving subject who, in her unwillingness to absorb the termination of loss, *becomes* the site of self-cancellation: "The inhibition of the melancholic seems puzzling to us because we cannot see what it is that is absorbing [her] so entirely."[17] For Wollstonecraft, it is precisely the unintelligibility of the female melancholic that imperils her, casting self-reflection as a potential indulgence that violates the female subject's claims to knowledge and social participation.

[. . .]

What is significant about the "performances" of the female melancholics described by Wollstonecraft [. . .] is the manner in which femininity becomes for [her] in varying ways the productive site of lack; in this sense, [her] notio[n] of dispossessed femininity resemble[s] Judith Butler's theorization of the performativity of "gender melancholy." [. . .][18] Gender identity *is* melancholic for Butler, insofar as melancholy thematizes the noncoincidence of the subject's gender and sexual identities; subjectivity, then, is "produced" through a series of disavowals and losses.

Although Butler's remarks are brought to bear on the homosexual prohibitions of heterosexual identity, her theory allows us to understand gender as an embodied, skeptical performance of identification, one that testifies to the "nothingness" of the subject.[19] In this way, gender as an epistemological category becomes inscribed with a sense of dispossession that is thought and felt to be an *ethical* imperative – "the recognition," as Stanley Cavell observes in connection with his meditations on the "philosophical" genre of the "melodrama of the unknown woman," "that the terms of one's intelligibility are not welcome to others," and that such a recognition entails a consideration of the pressures of an ethico-intellectual disposition that goes by the name of skepticism.[20]

Critical explorations of romantic femininity in terms of dispossession have often misunderstood the epistemological and ethical implications of this latter point, conceiving self-loss either as the basis for a reaffirmation of interpersonal agency or as the total, paralyzing evacuation of agency and identity. Wollstonecraft [. . .] see[s] the anonymous effects of skeptical melancholy as sustaining specific engagements with agency and identity; [she] conceive[s] the dispossessed self's moral obligations in terms that are deeply critical of self-presence and demonstrable action. Furthermore, the epistemic and ethical shape of the projects of self-description for Wollstonecraft [. . .] depend[s] on the different narrative forms [she] use[s] to explore the anonymity of melancholy. [. . .]

Disappointment in this world

"Most women, and men too, have no character at all," writes Wollstonecraft in the essay "The Benefits Which Arise from Disappointments," from her early work *Thoughts on the Education of Daughters* (1787). "Just opinions and virtuous passions appear by starts. . . . It is reflection which forms habits, and fixes principles indelibly on the heart; without it, the mind is like a wreck drifted about by every squall."[21] Wollstonecraft organizes her defense of rationalism by emphasizing its formative value on female character – thinking shapes, renders habitual, and fixes certain "principles to our minds and hearts" that eventually contribute to self-presence and appearance. And yet, as Wollstonecraft concedes in the same essay, reflection can very well evoke losses of a unique kind that cannot be simply recuperated by the intellect alone:

> when a person is disappointed in this world, they turn to the next. Nothing can be more natural than the transition; and it seems to me the scheme of Providence, that our finding things unsatisfactory here, should force us to think of the better country to which we are going.
>
> (117)

In this instant, the force of thought disavows the putative materiality of the empirical world: by conceiving it as insufficient, the female thinker is reoriented or turned away by her sadness from present surroundings and made to solicit a providential world that promises an end to loss altogether. In this sense, melancholy corresponds to a mode of self-consciousness that promises unknown, future hope, yet it also throws into relief a predicament in which the female subject can only achieve self-consciousness through renunciation. It is the substance of that turn from the empirical world that concerns me here since it defines Wollstonecraft's understanding of melancholy as linked to the question of one's being-in-the-world, and the kinds of abstractions and alienations that it is subject to. What will emerge in the *Vindication of the Rights of Woman* is a critique of melancholy as both the calcification *and* the abandonment of identity: "Women have seldom sufficient serious employment to silence their feelings," she writes in the *Vindication*;

> a round of little cares, or vain pursuits frittering away all strength of mind and organs, they become naturally only objects of sense. In short, the whole tenour of female education (the education of society) tends to render the best disposed romantic and inconstant; and the remainder vain and mean.
>
> (153)

For Wollstonecraft, feeling threatens to monopolize the female self because it absorbs her in an experience that has no apparent "object of sense" and thus forecloses the possibility of subject formation. Thus, in the *Vindication* melancholy names one kind of sentimental experience (along with romantic love, for example) that deprives female subjectivity of its rational self-ownership.

Despite her arguments against melancholy, however, Wollstonecraft's most significant difficulties emerge out of her attempts to discriminate a certain pensive skepticism that abstracts the female subject into a virtual, civic-minded identity from the more damagingly excluding (and possibly fatal) effects of unreflective melancholy:

> The passions which have been celebrated for their durability have always been unfortunate. They have acquired strength of absence and constitutional melancholy. – The fancy has hovered round a form of beauty dimly seen – but familiarity might have turned admiration into disgust; or, at least, into indifference, and allowed the imagination leisure to start fresh game.
>
> (101)

The cultural stereotype of women as emotionally (and thoughtlessly) absorbed in reveries that spirit them away into nothingness brings to mind Hume's descriptions of the kinds of losses that buoy identity through skeptical negation. For Wollstonecraft, however, it is precisely the self-differentiating turn of melancholy that ends up alienating female consciousness from itself. The pernicious effects of that turn register in the chapter in the *Vindication* "The Effect Which an Early Association of Ideas Has upon the Character," where Wollstonecraft seeks to demonstrate how the "determinate effect an early association of ideas has on the character" unravels female consciousness in a way that structurally resembles loss. According to the logic of associationism, proper reflection consists in storing and acquiring knowledge by linking sense impressions and memories – in other words, it appears serial. At the same time, associationism threatens to enslave women by literally stranding them in an unhealthy attachment to their own thoughts [. . .]. Associationism theoretically presumes that we are never fully in possession of our thoughts because we can only know ourselves in proportion to the expansion and linkage of proximate ideas and impressions. Mental self-possession, then, like financial inheritance, accrues to us in fits and starts by means of thoughtful recollections through time. As Wollstonecraft herself remarks, it is only in "glowing minds" that the full force of these associations is felt: "Education thus only supplies the man of genius with knowledge to give variety and contrast to his associations," and "when the intellectual powers are not employed to cool our sensations, [the mind] retraces them with mechanical exactness" (201).

What Wollstonecraft seeks to discern is the point at which reflection can fail the self and derealize it. For her, the problem of women's "habitual slavery, to first impressions" underscores the fact that improper reflection is irrevocably tied to the loss of self-presence and freedom:

> Business and other dry employments of the understanding, tend to deaden the feelings and break associations that do violence to reason. But females, who are made women of when they are mere children, and brought back to childhood when they ought to leave the go-cart for ever, have no sufficient strength of mind to efface the superinductions of art that have smothered nature.
>
> (201)

Women's arrested or interrupted development – "made women of when they are mere children, and brought back to childhood when they ought to leave the go-cart for ever" – is evidence of a certain self-estranging temporal process that never fully reaches maturity as a result of the irreparable effects of broken associations. It is this attachment to broken associations that characterizes, for Wollstonecraft, an alienated and melancholic female character who is steeped, as it were, in lost time. [. . .]

Wollstonecraft will argue that the inability to advance in one's reflections ends up negatively hyperrealizing the female body as the physical materialization of a cognitive regression:

> Every thing that they see or hear serves to fix impressions, call forth emotions, and associate ideas, that give a sexual character to the mind. False notions of beauty and delicacy stop the growth of their limbs and produce a sickly soreness, rather than delicacy of organs.
>
> (201–2)

The crude deterioration of the female subject is the gross physical equivalent of her passive intellectual absorption of a culturally prescribed and calcified discourse of femininity. As Wollstonecraft implies, the melancholic female subject absorbs the masculine gaze as a form of self-regulation, her "femininity" less an actual condition than what Judith Butler has described as "a process of reiteration by which both 'subjects' and 'acts' come to appear at all . . . *a process of materialization that stabilizes over time to produce the effect of boundary, fixity, and surface we call matter.*"[22] Being is the belated manifestation of a self-knowledge it has never been able to completely assimilate, and melancholy forcefully gives a name to that experience of belatedness and marginalization. Tethered to sense impressions, the female body is thus the symptom of an excess of materiality or signification that can be rescued only through a "revolution in time" (204).

Oddly enough, self-loss or anonymity for Wollstonecraft typifies the excessive visibility of the female body: being is imprisoned within a belated body that is the melancholic site of temporal accumulation; left behind, it is consigned to the anonymous life of a forgotten relic. The kind of revolution in time, however, that Wollstonecraft longs for – a revolution that evokes a desire for change, deracination, and becoming – suggests a longing *for* longing that structurally resembles melancholy insofar as both longing and loss figure for the plenitude of an ideal self-identity that forever eludes each as an originary lack. The providential futurity that Wollstonecraft evokes in the *Education of Daughters* precisely defines such an unattainable ideal, and it initiates a certain self-berating longing that persists indefinitely. This ideal, moreover, echoes in the pages of the *Vindication* as a withering hope on the horizon:

> She who can discern the dawn of immortality, in the streaks that shoot athwart the misty night of ignorance, promising a clearer day, will respect, as a sacred temple, the body that enshrines such an improvable soul. True love, likewise, spreads this kind of mysterious sanctity round the beloved object, making the lover most modest when in her presence. So reserved is affection that, receiving or returning personal endearments, it wishes, not only to shun the human eye, as a kind of profanation; but to diffuse an encircling cloudy obscurity to shut out even the saucy sparkling sunbeams. Yet, that affection does not deserve the epithet of chaste, which does not receive a sublime gloom of tender melancholy, that allows the mind for a moment to stand still and enjoy the present satisfaction, when a consciousness of the Divine presence is felt – for this must be the food of joy!
>
> (210)

Wollstonecraft anticipates and loquaciously exaggerates the futurity of female being by conceptualizing it as poised on the brink of self-revelation and discovery, but her logic mandates that the "future time" of women be indissociable from their abstraction: the "encircling cloudy obscurity" that keeps them within the parameters of gender norms precisely works to regulate their pure ascension in the world.[23]

At best, Wollstonecraft wants to spiritualize and abstract the female subject at the expense of the mind's apogee – a complex ethical position which suggests that a trace of the lost body always haunts reason as a specter of its own renunciations. As Claudia L. Johnson has observed, because "Wollstonecraft's political writings insist again and again that virtue has no sex," the female body becomes a "strategic non-issue" in the *Vindication*, ultimately suppressed as a result of severe social surveillance.[24] Johnson is correct to point out the virtuality of gender in Wollstonecraft's thought, and I want to further suggest that the thematic (dis)embodiment of the female body in her writings is tied to a desire to equate reflection with self-abstraction and remasculinization – a point she presses home in the following passage from the *Vindication*, where the impersonalizing effects of melancholy are recast as the privileges of masculine mobility and abstraction:

> For though moralists have agreed that the tenor of life seems to prove that *man* is prepared by various circumstances for a future state, they constantly concur in advising *woman* only to provide for the present. Gentleness, docility, and a spaniel-like affection are, on this ground, consistently recommended as the cardinal virtues of the sex; and, disregarding the arbitrary economy of nature, one writer declared that it is masculine for a woman to be melancholy. She was

created to be the toy of man, his rattle, and it must jingle in his ears whenever, dismissing reason, he chooses to be amused.

$$(103-4)^{25}$$

The arrested development of women's presentness is contrasted with the futurity of men's perfectibility. Feminine "being" is slighted with regard to masculine "becoming," underscoring the degree to which the moodiness of skeptical reflection often characterizes the elite and mobile masculine mind – the intellect on holiday from the body or dispersed into an aggrandized omniscience.[26] Mary Jacobus has argued that Wollstonecraft's ambivalence about the masculinization of melancholy resulted in attempts to appropriate it for a "feminine counter-culture – a contestatory position from which to vindicate the rights of woman – while at the same time providing the basis for the (de)formation of Romantic feminine subjectivity in the face of enlightenment sexual indifference."[27] Thus Wollstonecraft's half-hearted reclamation of melancholy aims at a cross-wiring of gender privileges: if "making an appearance in the world is the first wish of the majority of mankind" (153), appropriating melancholy *for women* means short-circuiting the paths of social and psychic identifications through which gender identities are constructed, thereby reclaiming skepticism for a radically different kind of "female" character.[28]

In answer to her own question, "When do we hear of women who, starting out of obscurity, boldly claim respect on account of their great abilities or daring virtues? Where are they to be found?" (133), Wollstonecraft draws upon Smith's *Theory of Moral Sentiments*, in order to amplify her argument in the *Vindication* that solitary reflection lends itself to an intersubjective mode of self-fashioning or becoming. Thinking about oneself and others demonstrates an ability to participate in social and public forums, and consequently gain mutual confirmation and recognition in the eyes of others. Following Smith, the kind of "reasonable" sympathy that Wollstonecraft promotes for women implies a powerful, cognitive straining beyond the limitations of the self – an extension of female consciousness outside of its set boundaries and toward an imaginative communion with others. Reflection promises a much sought-after social privacy that enables intersubjectivity and works as an antidote to the kind of oppressive crowding the female subject frequently experiences [133] [. . .]

Close company breeds improper sympathies: it forecloses personal motivation at the expense of spurious group welfare. Thus the supposedly protective atmospheres of social circles circulate a negatively contagious form of sympathetic energy that culturally disables women.[29]

Wollstonecraft's referencing of Smith's own complex reflections on sympathy demonstrates her attentiveness to the ways in which fantasies of pure communication through transparently sympathetic bodies are accomplished at the expense of denying the complex disavowals and coercions through which social attachments manipulate and produce selfhood in the first place. But as we have already seen, Smith's model of sympathy precisely abstracts the self, a maneuver that echoes in Wollstonecraft's melancholic spiritualization of the female subject. On the one hand, Wollstonecraft's appropriation and amendment of sympathy furthers the broader ideological critique in the *Vindication* against the impostures of false modesty and chastity, which spuriously regulate the visibility of the female self. On the other hand, her argument continues to characterize subjectivity as the site of irreparable loss or anonymity, straining toward an originary wholeness it cannot ever fully gain.

For Wollstonecraft, the difference between a brooding, skeptical reflectiveness and a paralyzing melancholy rests in what each takes to be its object of longing:

> I own it frequently happens that women who have fostered a romantic unnatural delicacy of feeling, waste their lives in *imagining* how happy they should have been with a husband who could love them with a fervid increasing affection every day, and all day.
>
> (102)

Whereas skepticism is marked by a "healthy" attention to lack as the incentive for intellectual agility and social mobility, melancholy fosters a love for the void. Marriage, for example, is a dispossessing symptom of a romanticized imagination that imperils the female subject because it denotes an ideological fantasy or illusion which, as Žižek notes, "consists in overlooking the illusion which is structuring our real, effective relationship to reality."[30] The imagination engenders the kinds of demoralizing abandonments of identity that are part and parcel of numerous ecstatic myths of romantic love:

> Love, such as the glowing pen of genius has traced, exists not on earth, or only resides in those exalted, fervid imaginations that have sketched such dangerous pictures. Dangerous because they not only afford a plausible excuse, to the voluptuary who disguises sheer sensuality under a sentimental veil; but as they spread affectation, and take from the dignity of virtue.
>
> (151)

The attending sorrows of love mark the unreasonableness of the imagination's impoverished fantasies: produced by enfeebled minds that imitate the cultural discourses of female emotional dispossession and devastation, love constrains women to an unreflective form of unhappy thought, one that buoys them on vaporizing sentiments.

So far, I have been attending to the arguments of the *Vindication*; but the kinds of vacillations that Wollstonecraft experiences in her reflections on unhappy reason also powerfully resonate in her *Letters Written During a Short Residence in Sweden, Norway, and Denmark* (1796), where the undoing effects of her crises, tinged with feelings over her failed love for Gilbert Imlay, express a hope that dispossession might signal a more pensive and acute form of (dis)appearance in the world, one that recognizes the belatedness of female identity as the condition for a revisionary form of social critique. This possibility in large part is due to the form of Wollstonecraft's *Letters*, which Mary Poovey has described as

> enabl[ing] her to objectify her tumultuous emotions in a form that does not demand an integrated persona. In such a form, writing can become an act of self-creation rather than self-assertion, the uninhibited revelation of the *process* of seeking inner equilibrium.[31]

The generic "hybridity" of the *Letters*, then, mixing autobiography with fiction, attests to the epistolary mode's capacity to critique, evaluate, and reposition the female self in time.

Reflecting on the vagaries of the self in the context of her sojourn in Tønsberg, during which time internal disquiet is almost cinematically projected into "the soft freshness of the western gales," soon to die away leaving "the aspen leaves [trembling] into stillness," Wollstonecraft expresses a tellingly Wordsworthian attachment to the seasonal cycles:

> If a light shower has chanced to fall with the sun, the juniper the underwood of the forest exhales a wild perfume, mixed with a thousand nameless sweets, that, soothing the heart, leave images in the memory which the imagination will ever hold dear.
>
> (99)

These thoughts, however, also intimate the subtle way in which personal identity is imagined, recalled, and then lost as it embarks upon the drift of its own sensory impressions. Wollstonecraft follows her description of nature by remarking on

> what misery, as well as rapture, is produced by quick perception of the beautiful and sublime, when it is exercised in observing animated nature, when every beauteous feeling and emotion excites responsive sympathy, and the harmonized soul sinks into melancholy, or rises to extasy, just as the chords are touched like the aeolian harp agitated by the changing wind.
>
> (99)

Recasting in a more pensive and agreeable tone her earlier disparagements of the female melancholic's bereft and petrified body, Wollstonecraft identifies herself as affectively vulnerable to the felt disturbances of her environment, and she positions herself as courting the very danger of "foster[ing] these sentiments in such an imperfect state of existence" (99) – imperfect because reflection might well expose the self to the corroding, temporal risks of sentimentality:

> When a warm heart has received strong impressions, they are not to be effaced. Emotions become sentiments; and the imagination renders even transient sensations permanent, by fondly retracing them. I cannot, without a thrill of delight, recollect views I have seen, which are not to be forgotten, – nor looks I have felt in every nerve which I shall never more meet. The grave has closed over a dear friend, the friend of my youth; still she is present within me, and I hear her soft voice warbling as I stray over the heath. Fate has separated me from another, the fire of whose eyes, tempered by infantine tenderness, still warms my breast; even when gazing on these tremendous cliffs, sublime emotions absorb my soul.
>
> (99–100)

Wollstonecraft's melancholic reminiscences point to a loss at the core of thought itself, as she retreads the "grounds" of her consciousness, recalling her dead friend Fanny Blood who is like a stand-in for a Wordsworthian "Lucy" character. On the one hand, Fanny awakens Wollstonecraft to the depths of her own "personal" reflections, but more subtly, the memory of her provokes a difference within the melancholic mind between the deeply individualistic authority Wollstonecraft seeks, and the apparently "private," anonymous, and belated (yet no less public) form of her passing memories. The tug between retained, accumulating memories and their evanescence into perturbing feelings perplexes Wollstonecraft throughout the writing of the *Letters*, where the self isn't so much resolutely abstracted as it is granted a temporary reprieve from presence and publicity – temporary because [. . .] Wollstonecraft can never fully relinquish her embodied sense of identity [(109)].

[. . .]

Throughout the *Letters*, Wollstonecraft struggles to turn the melancholic belatedness of subjective experience into a stance of principled selfhood, despite its threat to personal integrity. For example, in a subsequent passage that is strongly reminiscent of the boat scene in Rousseau's *Reveries of the Solitary Walker*, Wollstonecraft consciously reacts to the impersonalizing effects of sentimental reflection in a way that violently contrasts with the Rousseauian mood of anonymous contemplation. Having decided to take up the oars and row out to sea off Tønsberg with a female companion, Wollstonecraft abandons her "train of thinking" to the lulling rhythms of the oars, suffering "the boat to be carried along by the current, indulging a pleasing forgetfulness, or fallacious hopes." The drift of the current, however, fails to indulge Wollstonecraft for too long:

> How fallacious! yet, without hope, what is to sustain life, but the fear of annihilation – the only thing of which I have ever felt a dread – I cannot bear to think of being no more – of losing myself – though existence is often but a painful consciousness of misery; nay, it appears to me impossible that I should cease to exist, or that this active, restless spirit, equally alive to joy and sorrow, should only be organized dust – ready to fly abroad the moment the spring snaps, or the spark goes out, which kept it together. Surely something resides in this heart that is not perishable – and life is more than a dream.
>
> (112)

Selfless reflection in this passage fails to incite the anonymous pleasures of a body singularly detached from all debts and obligations. The drift of thoughts signals fears of an overpowering self-loss, turning the scene of solitary reflection into one of uneasy containment and oppression. The flow of impressions and ideas evokes the "annihilating" associationist logic that Wollstonecraft critiqued in the *Vindication*, and which she now perilously experiences herself: "but the fear of annihilation – the only thing of which I have ever felt a dread – I cannot bear to think of being no more – of losing myself – though existence is often but a painful consciousness of misery." Wollstonecraft here performs her identity as an effect of skeptical reflection – after all, reflection can only proceed through loss, despite the painful knowledge that one might lose oneself entirely.

Jacobus has pointed out that Wollstonecraft's misery in the *Letters* signals a revisionary outlook on her part, singularly aware of the ideological failures of the French Revolution that sought to install revolutionary time through carnage and violent warfare.[32] Conflating the revolution's masculinist onslaught with Imlay's own manipulative love for her, Wollstonecraft's "complaint" demonstrates how the positional "powerlessness" of anonymous witnessing can amount to reflection on (rather than an outright assumption of) historical agency:

> An ardent affection for the human race makes enthusiastic characters eager to produce alteration in laws and governments prematurely. To render them useful and permanent, they must be the growth of each particular soil, and the gradual fruit of the ripening understanding of the nation, matured by time, not

forced by an unnatural fermentation. And, to convince me that such a change is gaining ground, with accelerating pace, the view I have had of society, during my northern journey, would have been sufficient, had I not previously considered the grand causes which combine to carry mankind forward, and diminish the sum of human misery.

(198)

The prematurity of revolutionary hope is exposed as a naive faith in a violent, vindicatory future – a faith that, like longing, resembles loss in its appeal to an impossibly authentic wholeness that can be recuperated only in the most apocalyptic of tones. If Wollstonecraft arrives at the belief that it is in fact the seemingly unforced record of unacknowledged change that achieves the most effective political momentum, she does so by also recognizing the extent to which dispossession itself, or one's withdrawal from the stages of the world, can amount to a kind of historical intervention. For the *Letters*, in tracing the relationship between personal misery and public declaration, have us consider what kind of history can now be imagined in the absence of any "great" events and characters. The feminine self evoked in the *Letters* defends itself precisely by remaining defenseless in its evocative, melancholic suspension.

Wollstonecraft's epistolary cultivation of her anonymity intimates a subtle hermeneutical identification for her readers: by refusing to define herself according to the terms of a historical progressivism that threatens to annul the desisting feminine self, Wollstonecraft provides an ethical meditation on the extent to which melancholic subjectivity expresses a being-in-the-world that disengages from the status quo only to better conceptualize it, and finds itself rhetorically caught between social insertion *and* desertion.

[. . .]

[The original chapter includes readings of Mary Shelley's *Matilda* and Jane Austen's *Persuasion*.]

Notes

1 Mary Shelley to Edward Trelawny, April 1829, *The Letters of Mary Wollstonecraft Shelley*, ed. Betty T. Bennett, 2 vols (Baltimore: Johns Hopkins University Press, 1983), 2: 72.
2 Julie Ellison, *Delicate Subjects: Romanticism, Gender, and the Ethics of Understanding* (Ithaca, N.Y.: Cornell University Press, 1990), 11.
3 Sandra M. Gilbert and Susan Gubar, *The Madwoman in the Attic* (New Haven, Conn.: Yale University Press, 1979); Margaret Homans, *Women Writers and Poetic Identity* (Princeton, N.J.: Princeton University Press, 1980); Cora Kaplan, *Sea Changes* (London: Verso, 1986); Jan Montefiore, *Feminism and Poetry* (London: Pandora, 1987).
4 Ellison, *Delicate Subjects*, 10, 11.
5 Alan Liu, "The New Historicism and the Work of Mourning," *Studies in Romanticism* 35.4 (1996): 553–62.
6 Tilottama Rajan, *The Supplement of Reading: Figures of Understanding in Romantic Theory and Practice* (Ithaca, N.Y.: Cornell University Press, 1990).
7 Mary Wollstonecraft, *A Vindication of the Rights of Men* and *A Vindication of the Rights of Woman*, ed. Sylvana Tomaselli (Cambridge: Cambridge University Press, 1999), 153.
8 Mary Jacobus, "'The Science of Herself': Scenes of Female Enlightenment," *Romanticism, History, and the Possibilities of Genre: Re-forming Literature, 1789–1837*, eds Tilottama Rajan and Julia M. Wright (Cambridge: Cambridge University Press, 1998), 241.
9 See Julia Kristeva, *Black Sun: Depression and Melancholia*, trans. Leon S. Roudiez (New York: Columbia University Press, 1989). Also of interest are *New Maladies of the Soul*, trans. Ross

Mitchell Guberman (New York: Columbia University Press, 1995), and *Powers of Horror: An Essay on Abjection*, trans. Leon S. Roudiez (New York: Columbia University Press, 1982).

10 Jacobus, " 'Science of Herself,' " 242.

11 Amanda Anderson has used the term *aggrandized agency* to describe the way in which some feminist critics conceive certain female subjects in literature and history as unusually attuned to and performing those acts of systematic resistance to which they are otherwise utterly bound. See *The Powers of Distance: Cosmopolitanism and the Cultivation of Detachment* (Princeton, N.J.: Princeton University Press, 2001), 36–46.

12 Raymond Williams, *Marxism and Literature* (New York: Oxford University Press, 1977), 129 ff.

13 Julie Ellison, *Cato's Tears and the Making of Anglo-American Emotion* (Chicago: University of Chicago Press, 1999), 98.

14 As Thomas Pfau notes, melancholy has had this definition since at least the sixteenth century [. . .] (*Romantic Moods: Paranoia, Trauma, and Melancholy, 1794–1840* [Baltimore: Johns Hopkins University Press, 2005], 315–16).

15 David Hume, *A Treatise of Human Nature*, eds David Fate Norton and Mary J. Norton (Oxford: Oxford University Press, 2001), 165.

16 See Wolf Lepenies, *Melancholy and Society*, trans. Jeremy Gaines and Doris Jones (Cambridge, Mass.: Harvard University Press, 1992), where he elucidates melancholy as a historical and class-based phenomenon that arose parallel to the ascendancy of the (German) bourgeoisie in the late-eighteenth century. See esp. chap. 4, "On the Origins of Bourgeois Melancholy: Germany in the Eighteenth Century," 55–86.

17 Sigmund Freud, "Mourning and Melancholia," *The Standard Edition of the Complete Psychological Works of Sigmund Freud*, trans. James Strachey, 24 vols (London: Hogarth, 1957), 14: 245–6.

18 Judith Butler, *The Psychic Life of Power: Theories in Subjection* (Stanford, Calif.: Stanford University Press, 1997), 144, 145–6. In addition, see *Gender Trouble: Feminism and the Subversion of Identity* (New York: Routledge, 1990), 57–72.

19 "As a mode of relation," writes Butler, "neither gender nor sexuality is precisely a possession, but, rather, is a mode of being dispossessed, a way of being *for* another or *by virtue of* another" (*Precarious Life: The Powers of Mourning and Violence* [London: Verso, 2004], 24).

20 Stanley Cavell, *Contesting Tears: The Hollywood Melodrama of the Unknown Woman* (Chicago: University of Chicago Press, 1996), 12. [. . .]

21 Mary Wollstonecraft, *Thoughts on the Education of Daughters* (New York: Woodstock, 1994), 111.

22 Judith Butler, *Bodies That Matter: On the Discursive Limits of "Sex"* (New York: Routledge, 1993), 9 (italics in original). The discussion of the temporality of sedimentation appears in an extended footnote, 244–6.

23 See John Krapp, "Female Romanticism at the End of History," *Texas Studies in Language and Literature* 46.1 (Spring 2004): 73–91, which considers the anachronistic potential of romantic women's poetry as a challenge to progressive movements in masculinist narratives. [. . .]

24 Claudia L. Johnson, *Equivocal Beings: Politics, Gender, and Sentimentality in the 1790s: Wollstonecraft, Radcliffe, Burney, Austen* (Chicago: University of Chicago Press, 1995), 48, 49.

25 In *Cato's Tears*, Julie Ellison discusses the connections between the privileges of male sentimentalism and geographical mobility in the chapter "Walkers, Stalkers, Captives, Slaves," 148–70. [. . .]

26 See Juliana Schiesari, *The Gendering of Melancholia: Feminism, Psychoanalysis, and the Symbolics of Loss in Renaissance Literature* (Ithaca, N.Y.: Cornell University Press, 1992), for a consideration of this argument. [. . .]

27 Jacobus, " 'Science of Herself,' " 258.

28 Frances Ferguson makes this argument in her essay, "Wollstonecraft Our Contemporary," *Gender and Theory: Dialogues on Feminist Criticism*, ed. Linda Kauffman (Oxford: Blackwell, 1989), 51–7. [. . .]

29 For a study of the history of privacy, see Lawrence Stone, *The Family, Sex, and Marriage in England, 1500–1800* (New York: Harper and Row, 1977).

30 Slavoj Žižek, *The Sublime Object of Ideology* (London: Verso, 1999), 32–3.

31 Mary Poovey, *The Proper Lady and the Woman Writer: Ideology as Style in the Works of Mary Wollstonecraft, Mary Shelley, and Jane Austen* (Chicago: University of Chicago Press, 1984), 91.

32 Mary Jacobus, "In Love with a Cold Climate: Travelling with Wollstonecraft," *First Things: The Maternal Imaginary in Literature, Art, and Psychoanalysis* (New York: Routledge, 1995), 63–82.

28 The force of indirection

"Tintern Abbey" in the literary history of mood

David Collings

One of the most canonic evocations of "deep" feeling in romantic literature is William Wordsworth's "Lines Written a few miles above Tintern Abbey, on revisiting the banks of the Wye during a tour, July 13, 1798," commonly known as "Tintern Abbey" (Wordsworth 1984: 131–5; henceforth cited by line number). Few poems of the period better capture a mode of affect which still resonates today. Yet it would be amiss of readers to assume that this poem states a natural evocation of emotion. On the contrary, its strategies arise within a particular moment in the formation of the literary codification of feeling. The poem bears in nearly every feature an impress of the complex figuration of emotion that had developed over the previous several decades, even as it modifies that figuration in several ways. Yet because the affective subjectivity captured in the poem has become so naturalized as common sense, it is no easy matter to decipher what strategies helped form that subjectivity.

In the discussion that follows, I will argue that the poem creates a distinctive language of affect by means of a strategy of deliberate indirection. By adopting that strategy, the poem designates a mode of response that is not, and can never become, entirely visible or legible, an affect that is less an emotion in its own right than a not fully conscious, and thus only partly discernible, capacity for feeling. In doing so, the poem inherits and modifies the conventions of sensibility and the Gothic which precede it, producing a distinctive rhetoric of indirection by which it evokes emotional depth.

Because the poem relies so heavily on the strategy of indirection, its reader might easily fall into several interpretive traps. One might wish, for example, to read its indirections as evasions, denials of the literal (e.g., Levinson 1986: 14–57). But reading it in this vein ultimately leads one to treat it as a denial of history, as if history is found in a literal reality outside it, rather than locating it within a history to which it belongs, the history of the lyrical codification of affect.[1] In a similar manner, out of a wish to contest the poetics of depth, one might claim that it evades a more direct rendition of emotion – a version one might therefore seek in alternative texts of the moment (e.g., Henderson 1996). But in doing so, one would once again read the poem as a refusal of something outside itself, rather than comprehending it as a text that inherits a range of strategies familiar in those alternatives. Finally, in a converse move, one might wish to celebrate the poem's achievement and claim that it enabled literature to arrive at a mature, superior mode of emotional articulation. But doing so would treat prior works as mere preparations for this text, designating it as the destination of a history rather than placing it in an open process in which the questions it addresses are never fully answered. One reads the poem best when one refuses the temptations of moralism or triumphalism and sees it instead as exploring further possibilities in the poetic articulation of affect.

The poem clearly belongs to the broad history of the literature of sensibility, which emerged in the early eighteenth century and became increasingly dominant in the decades after 1750. In her analysis of this literature, Adela Pinch argues that it arose in part as a response to the difficulty of knowing what others feel. That difficulty, she argues, speaks of the fact that the literature of sensibility is caught between opposed intuitions: an awareness of the universality of emotion and a sense that emotion arises from within individual experience. Is feeling uniquely our own, or is it on the contrary our share of what everyone feels? The literature of sensibility lingers over situations in which protagonists are overwhelmed with emotion when confronting the misery or distress of another, pondering whether such a response shows how the emotions of others might truly be universal, almost too easily becoming one's own (Pinch 1996). Yet scenarios of this kind can be so often repeated, and be codified in a series of easily recognized conventions, that they ultimately raise the question of their artifice.

Exploring this question, Pinch discusses a moment when Charlotte Smith, a poet of sensibility, reassures her readers that she actually feels the emotion that one of her poems represents. In doing so, Smith does not so much align poetic language and actual feeling as show that the two can never fully intersect, that they occupy different registers. But in that case, Pinch argues, the literature of sentiment does not falsify genuine feeling (as the charge of "sentimentality" suggests) but rather codifies emotion in a domain distinct from lived experience. It belongs, as it were, to a universe of affective *signs*, not to a space in which words transparently express feeling (Pinch 1996: 69–71). Yet the fact that Smith must reassure her readers that she actually feels what she writes points to a certain dissatisfaction with that gap, a wish to break out of the conventions of sensibility even as she marks out their terrain.

Such resistance, however, is widespread in this literature; authors so often register their unease with extravagant feeling that, as Barbara M. Benedict argues, they constructs further conventions "that induce and endorse readerly detachment," balancing the wish to identify with the emotions of fictional characters and the demand to evaluate them according to the standards of moral duty or social norms. The spectacle of emotion, then, remains "firmly a fictional phenomenon," for in these texts feeling is futile "unless it is socialized by being observed, unless, that is, it is useful to or used by others" (Benedict 1994: 9, 12). This contrast between feelings and norms, in turn, points to a question about the ethical effects of sympathy: one might feel for others without necessarily being moved to take action on their behalf. The attempt to ensure that readers take action, however, might inspire a poetry of feeling to appropriate its depiction of suffering others for the use of readers, operating as Julie Ellison argues through "vignettes of the national or racial other," especially "the alienated figure of the slave, the Indian, the oriental, the poor, the homeless, and – persistently combined with all these other identities – the female" (Ellison 1999: 102). As it turns out, then, the literature of sensibility revolves around a series of intractable epistemological, political, and ethical disjunctions – between the universal and individual, the conventional and spontaneous, as well as between the affective and the normative, the sympathetic and the political.

This set of interlocking concerns undergoes a further development in the mode of the Gothic, which is often interwoven with sensibility over most decades of the eighteenth century but becomes culturally dominant in the vogue for Gothic fiction in the 1790s. The Gothic innovates on sensibility by bringing into view a series of darker emotions – a dubious interest in imprisonment, blasphemy, encounters with ghosts, and unspeakable violations. Furthermore, it takes a fascination with the affective resonances of the visible so evident in sensibility and expands it, seeking out what is hidden behind the surface of the face in the secret desires and actions of characters, or behind the surface of things in the dungeons of castles, the vaults of monasteries, or the caverns of the earth. Yet because it implies or demonstrates that these hidden depths could become visible, it creates a powerful interplay not so much between surface and depth as between surface and a second surface, as it were – between what we see at first and the scandalous force of what could eventually be revealed. In this respect, it at once questions the regime of the visible and expands it, finding a sensationalist version of the visible even in those murky depths that the visible hides.

Within these innovations on sensibility emerge the fairly subtle explorations of Ann Radcliffe, the most influential Gothic novelist of the 1790s. In her novels, characters who encounter strange events imagine possibilities (hidden crime, the prospect of assault or theft, the visitation of ghosts) that eventually have rather mundane explanations. One could thus argue that Radcliffe insists on the integrity of the surface, reproving the temptation to imagine that much, if anything, takes place in the depths. Yet the fact that the surface of things provokes her characters to imagine so continuously suggests otherwise; for them the phenomenal world hums with possibilities which, even if untrue, still come to mind thanks to its inexhaustible openness and suggestiveness. Radcliffe detaches affective life from the force of immediate experience, introducing an element of indirection into the emotional practices of sensibility.

Looking closely at this dimension of Radcliffe's work, Pinch shows how *The Mysteries of Udolpho*, Radcliffe's most canonic novel, frames the heroine Emily's affective life through her tendency to hold fast to all that happens to her and even to what has happened to those who came before. She is a truly preoccupied character – both by what she remembers and by aspects of herself which, it turns out, are already occupied by others. As Jacques Khalip would suggest, this heroine exemplifies the aesthetics of dispossession or anonymity: Emily is haunted less by imaginary fears or dreads than by a range of realities or emotions from other times, places, and people, as well as by various representations that subsist within herself (cf. Khalip 2009: 34–5). While Radcliffe may explain away extravagant fictions, then, she does not produce a flat, easily interpreted world, but rather maps out the space of a multilayered subjectivity, one so affectively rich that it can compete with the visible world; as Pinch points out, "Emily frequently keeps the idea of the past before her eyes so firmly that she barely sees what is before her." In a novel pervaded by nostalgia, anticipation, and even anticipatory nostalgia, the present serves as a point of intersection between temporalities that can eclipse its force (Pinch 1996: 111–36; 124, 122).

One might thus conclude that precisely because Radcliffe cancels an agency outside the empirical reality her protagonists inhabit – the alterity of the dead, of evil, perhaps of transcendence itself – she can with unusual force elaborate on the multiple levels within immanence, finding in that terrain a host of features that, through their indirect force, can complicate and challenge the sway of the world's visible signs.

"Tintern Abbey" draws on a similar set of conventions, elaborating them in lyrical rather than narrative form – drawing, for example, on the conventions of poems about retiring from active life or of Coleridge's conversation poems – but in doing so makes certain implications even more explicit (Collings 2000: 57–79). The poem's speaker is quite preoccupied by his memory of his previous visit to this landscape – and indeed by his anticipation of remembering it again in the future (see 64–6). The poem elaborates on this preoccupation in several surprising ways. First, it does so while positioning the speaker within the landscape he remembers, as if to heighten the tension between the affective force of what preoccupies him and its literal presence. That landscape, of course, triggers his thoughts about what it has meant to him in the intervening years. But once he begins to meditate on its significance for him, he loses sight of the scene around him. Once he returns to it, the poem emphasizes this gap explicitly, stating that his return to "the picture of the mind" takes place "with gleams of half-extinguished thought, / With many recognitions dim and faint, / And somewhat of a sad perplexity" (59–62), as if the speaker's seeing the mind's picture within the immediate space of the world before him is painful for him. Wordsworth thus heightens Radcliffe's practice, in the process dismantling what might seem to be a formidable gender opposition, elucidating an affective terrain that Radcliffe's heroines and this poem's speaker share.

He does so, moreover, in a mode which is not explicitly narrative but which maps out a brief, schematic narrative of the speaker's affective life nevertheless – a sequence from an initial phase of the "coarser pleasures of [his] boyish days" with their "glad animal movements," through one in which nature's forms were "An appetite: a feeling and a love," a set of "aching joys" and "dizzy raptures," to his maturity, when he feels in nature's presence "a sense sublime / Of something far more deeply interfused" (81, 82; 85, 86; 96–7). He does so to provide a broadly representative account of the stages of emotional life through which he can build on the conventions of preoccupation. Here, as in Radcliffe's novels, the text circles around a protagonist whose emotional states might be taken to represent a moral subjectivity available to all. But because Wordsworth writes in first person, drawing on the biographical fact of his visit to the landscapes in the Wye Valley with his sister, he tacitly draws greater attention to the gap between the conventions on which he draws and the more complex facts of actual lives, hinting at a further disjunction in the articulation of sensibility.

In its final verse paragraph, "Tintern Abbey" opens up the question of preoccupation in still another way, focusing on how that notion bears on the relationship between people who know each other intimately. The speaker first proposes that his sister embodies his own past mode of responsiveness, as if he can encounter "what [he] was once" in "the shooting lights / Of [her] wild eyes" (121, 119–20), seeing in her face the signs of a prior state of his own mind. It then reverses this scenario, for it imagines a future moment when this scene, which is new to her, his presence in the scene with her, and his words will inhabit *her* memory (138–52). Relationship, it turns out, is a process of *mutual* preoccupation, such that each person carries one's memory of the emotional state of the other and, in turn, serves to inspire and provoke further transformation in the other. This passage thus sketches out a scenario of relationship as it transpires over time, through a sequence of mutual embeddings and layerings that will continue indefinitely.[2]

By exploring these further implications of preoccupation so explicitly, "Tintern Abbey" takes seriously the possibility, broached in Radcliffe's novels, that experience can evoke emotions for which the visible signs of the world or of affect cannot fully account. The poem delves into this possibility with such attention in the second verse paragraph – which I will explore at length in what follows – that it constructs a provocative account of affective depth on its basis. In that passage, Wordsworth suggests that such a memory could occupy the mind so thoroughly that it might do so beyond one's own conscious awareness, giving rise to "feelings . . . Of unremembered pleasure," which, in turn, may influence "nameless, unremembered acts / Of kindness and of love" (31–2, 35–6). Such a memory may be "unremembered," though not exactly forgotten; if it may be triggered by an event at any moment, then it must inhabit the mind at all times, influencing one's action in ways one could never reconstruct. In this account, the mind may consist of nothing other than an anonymous web of memories that inspire an array of inner sensations and ethical impulses, which in turn lead to one's acts of kindness or love: memory, sensation, affect, and ethical action are inextricably interwoven here.[3] Indeed, the poem takes its rendition of such anonymity quite far, for it suggests that memory can lead to "sensations sweet, / Felt in the blood, and felt along the heart" (28–9), sensations that are felt not *in* the heart, but *along* it, as if they are too elusive to appear directly in the seat of emotions but are best found adjacent to it, perhaps even *in the blood*, in what the heart pumps – in what the seat of emotion circulates throughout affective subjectivity overall. These sensations, then, may not take shape in any specific feeling, in anything that can be codified in a regime of signs, but in the feel of affective life itself.

Thus the strategy of indirection, which led Radcliffe at times to specify that her heroine pondered the memory of one scene while faced with another, here makes the retention of experience so indirect that it eludes conscious memory but as a result ultimately forms the matrix of all the mind's activities. The poem's sense of the mind closely resembles a theory of mood that appears contemporaneously in the work of several German writers, including Kant, Novalis, Hölderlin, and Hegel, which influences a similar account in Martin Heidegger, a theory that has received exemplary treatment in Thomas Pfau's *Romantic Moods*. These thinkers posit that *Stimmung*, or mood, is a "quasi-cognitive" state that underlies conscious experience; irreducible to any positive emotion or feeling, it cannot be captured in the field of representation or of signs but is best evoked or awakened indirectly (Pfau 2005: 7–12, especially 10). By extending Radcliffe's aesthetic of indirection, Wordsworth radicalizes sensibility's attention to the unknowability of affect, proposing a similar possibility that what eludes knowledge or explicit formulation may become the enabling precondition for one's entire affective and intellectual life.

The second verse paragraph hints at a further implication of this notion of mood: it gives solace to those who might otherwise be caught within a resolutely empirical domain. Referring to the "forms of beauty" before him, the speaker writes that "oft, in lonely rooms, and mid the din / Of towns and cities, I have owed to them, / In hours of weariness, sensations sweet" (24, 26–8). These lines no doubt refer to how these memories restored him in specific moments of weariness. But the contrast between the confines of those lonely rooms and the comparatively expansive space of the sensations to which his memories give rise also suggests that this speaker suffers from the pressure of what is too evident, whose signs are too easily heard. Those sensations, precisely because they are in part unremembered, have the power to dissolve that threat, to alleviate the din of the empirical world.

This reliance on what indirection makes possible may help to explain a feature of this poem that has long puzzled its readers: its gestures toward realities it does not fully designate. Critics have pointed out, for example, that the date in the subtitle – July 13, 1798 – *almost* names an anniversary of the fall of the Bastille on July 14, 1789, much as the title refers to the ruined Tintern Abbey while locating the poem a few miles above it (Levinson 1986: 14–16). These and other moments elaborate further on the strategy of indirection that it explores in the second verse paragraph, as if the poem wishes not to be contained within the lonely rooms of any particular geographical or historical reference. Once again, one might find an exemplary counterpart to the poem's stance in Pfau's elaboration of mood. In his account, human existence registers its historicity – not its location in a particular historical moment, but its vulnerability to the hazards of historical experience as such – in mood; furthermore, one only falsifies the impress of this historicity by representing it as a specific historical situation, which can exemplify only aspects of that condition. For Pfau, this historicity arises in western Europe within the late eighteenth century, when the political and cultural transformations in the wake of the French Revolution undermined any apparent foundation and subjected everyone to a "perilous historical situatedness" that persists throughout the modern era (Pfau 2005: 11, 25, 1–2).[4] One could infer that through its referential indirection, "Tintern Abbey" helps formulate a modern condition whose impress we still feel today.

No doubt this poem, by delineating such a historicity and evoking it in mood, marks out a new phase in the elaboration of affect, signaling the further elaboration of sensibility and the Gothic into romanticism. Yet rather than attributing that innovation to the emergence of a new historical condition, one might find instead that it arises from the poem's *construction* of a particular account of affective life. Historicity, one might say, arises not from an event in the world but from certain discursive interventions. This text, like others, might hope to justify its sense of historicity by indirectly evoking the broader contours of its historical moment, but in the end this gesture projects onto history the precondition it would find there.

It does not follow, however, that one should once again denounce this poem for falsifying its moment; on the contrary, it shapes history in its very rhetoric of indirection – in its displacement from history to historicity, from remembered to unremembered emotion, from the feelings in the heart to the feel of affective life itself. This poem is indeed historical, through and through, exactly when it resists the regime of signs to produce a language of evocation.

Yet the second verse paragraph in "Tintern Abbey" does not end with this intervention; it pushes further, innovating not only within the conventions of sensibility but of the Gothic as well. In its final lines, it depicts a

> serene and blessed mood,
> In which the affections gently lead us on,
> Until, the breath of this corporeal frame,
> And even the motion of our human blood
> Almost suspended, we are laid asleep
> In body, and become a living soul:
> While with an eye made quiet by the power
> Of harmony, and the deep power of joy,
> We see into the life of things.
>
> (43–50)

Here the movement of affect which earlier alleviated the din of the empirical world takes the speaker to the very limit of embodiment, as if a mind constituted by the unremembered is still too confining. This passage's references to a sleeping body and living soul draws on a traditional Christian language of death and resurrection, except that in a more Gothic vein it depicts a similar process taking place within mortal life itself, resisting too direct an invocation of religious belief.[5] Invoking the metaphor of blood that it used earlier, the poem suggests that affect can "gently lead us on" into a *second* indirection or displacement – this time, from the movement of blood to its near-suspension, from the feel of affective life to the entrancement of near-death. This mood, it seems, arises when the affections *suspend feeling*, taking one, as it were, *beyond mood itself* into a quieter, deeper joy. Underlining this possibility, the passage suggests that this moment nearly suspends the motion of "our *human* blood" – as if to suggest that an inhuman, or more-than-human, blood, and by extension a more-than-emotional affect, flows through the living soul. In this moment of suspension, it seems, we nearly leave the domain of humanity and enter another mode of being, which, following Khalip, we might designate as an even more anonymous condition than before – and by the same token leave behind singular personhood and enter, as the passage's pronouns suggest, a plural state.[6] Yet because in this moment the poem does not cross the threshold but hovers upon it, in the zone of the "almost," like Radcliffe's fictions refusing what is truly outside empirical experience, it treats death not as a force opposed to life but as a metaphor for the limit of experience. It seems that when the supernatural is explained away, as in Radcliffe's novels, or resisted, as in this passage, it does not vanish but becomes an attribute of lived experience, indeed of the movement of affect itself – for if mood can "gently lead" to its own suspension, then a more-than-human element is present within it from the start.

This development, it turns out, bears on more than affect alone. The state of suspension gives the living soul, animated by a "deep power," the capacity to "see into the life of things." This entire sequence, then, leads the subject *back* to the literal world, enabling one to see *into* it anew.[7] The full force of this passage becomes even clearer in a later moment which depicts how the speaker draws on his "deep" power to feel "a sense sublime / Of something far more deeply interfused" throughout all objects in the world (96–7). That sense sublime, it seems, is not only seen or witnessed, for it is *felt*: by this point, the speaker feels his deep mood and that of the world at the same time. The world, too, has a mood – one that the speaker may discern, as it were, through the medium of his own.

All this is possible, according to the poem, not because of the unremembered dimension of subjectivity but because of the near-suspension which brings death into life, for only after the latter does the poem begin to speak of a certain "deep power." This reading is confirmed later in the poem, where something deeply interfused is felt by one who "hear[s] oftentimes / The still, sad music of humanity" (91–2) – a music whose sorrow and stillness bear the imprint of something like a deathly suspension. Only death's equivalence within life, it seems, can lead to the depths. Here the full force of the poem's indirection bears upon the Gothic, for those depths refer to no secret or scandal, no unspeakable scene, no hidden signs, but what nearly eludes affective life itself. Yet because only the radical suspension of affect can lead to these depths, it is no wonder that the speaker suggests that the "deep power of joy" is a feeling that "*disturbs* [him] with the joy / Of elevated thoughts" (95–6, emphasis added). Strangely enough, then, if the depths are felt at the mind's edge, what is deepest inside is also at the outermost verge, and vice versa – for both are "far more deeply *interfused*," blended together inextricably, so that as with a Möbius strip, inside and outside become indistinguishable.[8] The immanent and its limit, sensibility and the Gothic, here interfuse to become that volatile, difficult ensemble that is romantic affect.

Nothing this poem proposes is definitive; it occasionally pauses to strike a tentative note, to wonder "If this / Be but a vain belief" (50–1) or to allow the speaker to explain that he "would believe" what it offers (88). Even in its level of confidence, the poem pursues its strategy of indirection (cf. Wolfson 1986; Quinney 1997). Yet through the range of its explorations, it makes clear that this strategy, taken through multiple phases, may construct an extraordinarily forceful account of mood. In doing so, however, it does not in fact finally elude the regime of signs, for it perforce must rely on those signs, and the conventions it inherits, to construct a strategic use of signs in a poetics of indirection. By the same token, precisely through its attempt to propose an account of historicity, rather than history, it contributes to the history *of* the articulation of historicity.[9] In the end, "Tintern Abbey" does not surpass, but greatly complicates and extends, the conventions it inherits.

Notes

1 Reading in this vein might also exaggerate the poem's falsification of its setting; for a crucial argument that it does not, see Rzepka (2003).
2 On the intricacies of the poem's depiction of relationship, see Thomson (2001).
3 The poem thus relies on an associationist theory of the mind; see Craig (2007: 99–100).
4 On the contradiction in Pfau's argument between regarding historicity both as a condition underlying any specific historical event and as a condition emerging within the historical context of the late eighteenth century, see Collings (2009: 377).
5 The poem thus applies its strategies of indirection to the British confessional state; for an exemplary discussion on this score, see Canuel (2012).
6 For a brief discussion of anonymity in Wordsworth, see Khalip (2009: 7–8). The poem's evocation of the plural here touches on themes best addressed in Nancy (2000).
7 On the ethical import of this feature of the poem, see Potkay (2012: 71–89).
8 The poem thus relies on the logic of the internal limit, whereby the sign of a canceled transcendence inhabits, and perpetually disrupts, the operations of immanence. For an exemplary discussion of this logic, see Copjec (2002: 94, 96).
9 For a relevant treatment of the history of representations of history, especially as they shift in the late eighteenth century, see Koselleck (2004).

Works cited

Benedict, B.M. (1994) *Framing Feeling: Sentiment and Style in English Prose Fiction, 1745–1800*, New York: AMS Press.
Canuel, M. (2012) "Historicism, Formalism, and 'Tintern Abbey,'" *European Romantic Review*, vol. 23, 363–71.
Collings, D. (2000) "The Harsh Delights of Political Duty: Thelwall, Coleridge, Wordsworth, 1795–1799," in P. Shaw (ed.), *Romantic Wars: Studies in Conflict and Culture, 1793–1822*, Aldershot: Ashgate, 57–79.
Collings, D. (2009) "Troping Mood: Pfau, Wordsworth, Hegel," *Literature Compass*, vol. 6, 373–83.
Copjec, J. (2002) *Imagine There's No Woman: Ethics and Sublimation*, Cambridge, MA: MIT Press.
Craig, C. (2007) *Associationism and the Literary Imagination: From the Phantasmal Chaos*, Edinburgh: Edinburgh University Press.

Ellison, J. (1999) *Cato's Tears and the Making of Anglo-American Emotion*, Chicago: University of Chicago Press.

Henderson A. (1996) *Romantic Identities: Varieties of Subjectivity, 1774–1830*, New York: Cambridge University Press.

Khalip, J. (2009) *Anonymous Life: Romanticism and Dispossession*, Stanford: Stanford University Press.

Koselleck, R. (2004) *Futures Past: On the Semantics of Historical Time*, trans. Keith Tribe, New York: Columbia.

Levinson, M. (1986) *Wordsworth's Great Period Poems: Four Essays*, New York: Cambridge University Press.

Nancy, J.-L. (2000) *Being Singular Plural*, trans. Robert D. Richardson and Anne E. O'Byrne, Stanford: Stanford University Press.

Pfau, T. (2005) *Romantic Moods*, Baltimore: Johns Hopkins University Press.

Pinch, A. (1996) *Strange Fits of Passion: Epistemologies of Emotion, Hume to Austen*, Stanford: Stanford University Press.

Potkay, A. (2012) *Wordsworth's Ethics*, Baltimore: Johns Hopkins University Press.

Quinney, L. (1997) "'Tintern Abbey,' Sensibility, and the Self-Disenchanted Self," *ELH*, vol. 64, 131–56.

Rzepka, C. (2003) "Pictures of the Mind: Iron and Charcoal, 'Ouzy' Tides and 'Vagrant Dwellers' at Tintern, 1798," *Studies in Romanticism*, vol. 42, 155–85.

Thomson, H. (2001) "'We Are Two': The Address to Dorothy in 'Tintern Abbey,'" *Studies in Romanticism*, vol. 40, 531–46.

Wolfson, S. (1986) *The Questioning Presence: Wordsworth, Keats, and the Interrogative Mode in Romantic Poetry*, Ithaca: Cornell University Press.

Wordsworth, W. (1984) *The Major Works*, ed. S. Gill, New York: Oxford University Press.

Part 8

Religion and secularization

Introduction

Although the topics of religion and religious belief have been explored with particular urgency in criticism of the past two decades, Romanticists have acknowledged the religious influences on Romantic poetry for generations. Hoxie Neale Fairchild provided a blueprint for many years of literary interpretation when he claimed that Romanticism aimed to bypass the need for external redemption and concentrate on "limitless self-expansion" (Fairchild 1939: 8). It was only a slight modification of this that Harold Bloom offered decades later in *The Visionary Company* when he emphasized the importance of "Protestant dissent" in Romantic poetry, which resulted in an attempt to "formulate personal religions" in poetic forms (Bloom 1971: xvii). Still later, M.H. Abrams provided yet another modification – perhaps the most enduring one for later generations of critics – when he claimed that Romantic writers shifted their attention from the supernatural world to the natural world, and thus secularized imagination by turning it from the worship of God to the worship of "the heights and depths of the mind of man" (Abrams 1971: 25).

Marjorie Levinson's selection in Part 1 of this volume subtly deconstructs this worship as "a barricade to resist the violence of historical change and contradiction"; her view has been appropriated by many recent critics who have sought to avoid an equation between Romanticism and generalized individualism or private imaginative vision. At the same time, however, a growing number of critics now believe that new historicism's opposition to abstract spiritualizing nevertheless requires further analysis and contextualization. For even while correcting the account of individualized spirituality that Fairchild, Bloom, and Abrams offered, critics more lately are giving some account of the dense religious culture and theological debate that typified Romantic-era writing. Specifying the religious context for this writing has been important for all of these writers. The Church of England continued to maintain its cultural importance throughout the eighteenth and nineteenth centuries; a battery of oaths and tests restricted participation in politics and civil life for Catholics and Protestant dissenters (Protestants who did not adhere to the Thirty-nine Articles of the Church of England). At the same time, however, this authority was continually challenged by poets, novelists, and parliamentary reformers.

All of the critics represented in this section of the volume coincide in their basic commitment to the idea that Romantic writers had powerful religious beliefs that found their way into their writing. But interrelated questions continue to provoke debate. What effect does religious belief have on literary representation? How much of a challenge (if any) do those beliefs pose to traditional religious cultures and political institutions? Robert Ryan's book *The Romantic Reformation: Religious Politics in*

English Literature, 1789–1824 sees Romanticism as a revision of Christianity because of its renewal of religious commitment and feeling. This significantly alters the view of critics like Abrams, but it also sharpens the historicist account of Romanticism so that our understanding of the period can include an account of religion's impact on literary works. In this selection on Percy Shelley, Ryan shows that even Shelley's atheism is not entirely opposed to certain currents within Christianity; it is opposed, however, to corruption in established religions. Shelley's early work, he argues, demonstrates an admiration for the practical utility of Jesus's teachings; this matures in *Hellas* into an endorsement of Christian idealism and humanism.

Ryan's emphasis in his work is on the religious underpinnings of ethical perspectives and spiritual community; Jon Mee's emphasis, in his selection on Wordsworth's *Prelude* from his book *Romanticism, Enthusiasm, and Regulation: Poetics and the Policing of Culture in the Romantic Period*, is on religion's urgent conflict with British disciplinary institutions. The influence of Michel Foucault's writing on the connection between institutional and internal discipline is quite palpable here (Foucault 1977): Mee shows how religious "enthusiasm" emerges as an "unstable force" that must be refined by internal methods of control. Mee's account connects (but modifies) some other views of religious culture in the Romantic age by Shaun Irlam and David Riede in identifying Romantic imagination with a visionary religious "enthusiasm" (Irlam 1999; Riede 1991). But it also connects with critics such as Jasper Cragwall and Michael Tomko (Cragwall 2013; Tomko 2011), who have followed Mee's lead in identifying a variety of religious cultures of the Romantic period with a dangerous element that must be controlled by institutional structures allied with literary forms.

There is yet another direction that Daniel E. White takes in the selection on William Godwin from his book *Early Romanticism and Religious Dissent*. Like Mee, he shows how religious dissent has deep political implications rather than only spiritual ones (as Ryan most often suggests). But White's view of the relationship between religion and politics is theoretically very different from Mee's because of his interest in a bourgeois "public sphere" as it has been explained in the work of Jürgen Habermas (Habermas 1994). White concentrates on religious dissent insofar as it coincides with two contrasting views of a public. Godwin's shifts in perspective are not about opposing, or conceding to, social norms: they are about re-imagining them. Godwin, influenced by Mary Wollstonecraft, accommodated his earlier "rational" dissent to a public discourse of sensibility. Affect is what enables, rather than obstructs, the poet's relations with a wider public. Thus White's account could be usefully read with Julie Ellison's in Part 7, and also with the essays in Part 3 on audiences and the reading public.

All three of these accounts, because of their pronounced emphasis on human thought and affect, appear to work within what Colin Jager understands as a "secular" account of religious belief. In his new contribution to this volume on Wordsworth's "The Thorn," Jager shows that it is insufficient merely to attend to what the "objects and actions" in Wordsworth's celebrated poem "mean" for the human agents represented there. After providing an account of a "secular age" created by eighteenth-century methods of literary reading that emphasized the imaginative role of the reader, Jager complicates that view by exposing the persistence of "entangled" spirituality. Entangled spirituality involves and connects human agents with objects in the world rather than separating and privatizing them. "The Thorn" moves us away from the idea of religion as either shared or unshared (as in Ryan, Mee, and White) and toward an idea of religion as intense (and sometimes mysterious) spiritual involvement with the world.

Works cited

Abrams, M.H. (1971) *Natural Supernaturalism: Tradition and Revolution in Romantic Literature*, New York: Norton.

Bloom, Harold. (1971) *The Visionary Company: A Reading of English Romantic Poetry*, rev. ed., Ithaca: Cornell University Press.

Cragwall, Jasper. (2013) *Lake Methodism: Polite Literature and Popular Religion in England, 1780–1830*, Columbus: Ohio State University Press.

Fairchild, Hoxie Neale. (1939) *Religious Trends in English Poetry*, New York: Columbia University Press.

Foucault, Michel. (1977) *Discipline and Punish: The Birth of the Prison*, trans. Alan Sheridan, New York: Vintage.

Habermans, Jürgen. (1994) *The Structural Transformation of the Public Sphere: An Inquiry into a Category of Bourgeois Society*, Cambridge: MIT Press.

Irlam, Shaun. (1999) *Elations: The Poetics of Enthusiasm in Eighteenth-Century Britain*, Stanford: Stanford University Press.

Riede, David G. (1991) *Oracles and Hierophants: Constructions of Romantic Authority*, Ithaca: Cornell University Press.

Tomko, Michael. (2011) *British Romanticism and the Catholic Question: Religion, History, and National Identity, 1778–1829*, Houndmills: Palgrave Macmillan.

Further reading

Fulford, Tim. (2002) *Romanticism and Millenarianism*, New York: Palgrave Macmillan.

Jager, Colin. (2007) *The Book of God: Secularization and Design in the Romantic Era*, Philadelphia: University of Pennsylvania Press.

Jones, Tod E. (2003) *The Broad Church: A Biography of a Movement*, Lanham, MD: Lexington Books.

Prickett, Stephen. (1976) *Romanticism and Religion: The Tradition of Coleridge and Wordsworth in the Victorian Church*, Cambridge: Cambridge University Press.

Ragussis, Michael. (1995) *Figures of Conversion: "The Jewish Question" and English National Identity*, Durham, NC: Duke University Press.

Spector, Sheila A. (2005) *The Jews and British Romanticism: Politics, Religion, Culture*, New York: Palgrave Macmillan.

29 The unknown God

Robert Ryan

The phrase "religious reformer" may sound paradoxical as applied to Percy Bysshe Shelley, whose ideas about reformation usually involved eradication of what most people call religion. Yet Shelley's theological dispositions were always subtler than his polemic stances suggested – a situation that has produced the critical anomaly of a self-proclaimed atheist who has been admired in every generation as a profound religious poet.[1] From the beginning, Shelley's readers have tended to divide into those who take his assertions of atheism as the deepest truth about him and those who find a contrary tendency to religious affirmation present in his poetry from the start. An attempt to mediate these conflicting readings may tempt a critic to qualify or sentimentalize the meaning of religion until the term is broad enough to accommodate atheism – too often the tactic of readers who want their religion and their favorite lyric poet too. A better solution to the problem involves reconsidering the meaning of atheism, a word that in Shelley's time had no precise definition beyond polemical ones formulated by those to the right of the "atheist" on the spectrum of religious opinion.

One hesitates before attempting to mitigate the reality of Shelley's atheism or qualify his contempt for the Christian religion as it was embraced by most of his contemporaries; it is a stance that he maintained with unrelenting passion and vigor, and one for which he willingly suffered considerable personal hardship, beginning with his expulsion from Oxford for publishing and refusing to retract *The Necessity of Atheism*. To diminish its importance would be to betray his memory. But an observation made by James Thrower in connection with ancient religion seems to me appropriate to Shelley's own position:

> The majority of thinkers whom later writers designated *atheoi* are found upon closer examination to deny only the notion of the gods as expressed in popular belief, and this more often than not as a prelude to the putting forward of a more sophisticated and developed conception of the divine.[2]

Shelley made just such a qualification when he said of himself to Godwin, "I became in the popular sense of the word 'God' an Atheist."[3] As to the word atheist, the poet explained to Trelawny, "I used it to express my abhorrence of superstition; I took up the word, as a knight took up a gauntlet, in defiance of injustice."[4] [. . .]

Even at his most militantly irreligious, Shelley's expressions of atheism were always carefully qualified. For example, Queen Mab's bold assertion, "There is no God!"

is immediately modified in a footnote: "This negation must be understood solely to affect a creative Deity. The hypothesis of a pervading Spirit coeternal with the universe remains unshaken."[5] Shelley was always distinguishing in this manner false conceptions of God from others that he allowed to be true, if only for the sake of argument. The deity whose existence Shelley denied was the one he called "the god of human error,"[6] a god that had little to do with the high conception of divinity that he entertained as an ideal all his life. My argument here is that Shelley himself cultivated such an exalted idea of what a Supreme Being might be that he was intolerant of any inadequate or distorted representation of it. He set himself up as a critic of religion not from a position outside the realm of belief, but from a position of higher authority and insight within that sphere. [. . .] Shelley's atheism, his intolerance of all religion, can be seen as an expression of respect for a purer conception of divinity than most of the world was able or willing to imagine. Similarly, he made a point of distinguishing the authentic character of Jesus Christ from the misconstructions of it fostered by what he called "the popular religion." The actual teachings of Jesus, he said, "afford an example and an incentive to the attainment of true virtue, whilst the [erroneous interpretation of them] holds out a sanction and apology for every species of mean and cruel vice."[7]

When his angry political sonnet "England in 1819" characterized the religion of his country as "Christless, Godless, a book sealed," the poem was evidently imagining a Christlike, godly religion that British Christianity had failed to approximate, apparently because the national religion did not understand or could not accept the true character of God and Christ. [. . .]

Shelley was more articulate when criticizing religious error than when characterizing the true, godly, Christian faith from which the religion of his country had deviated. In religious discourse he was disabled rhetorically by a philosophical reticence arising from his belief that ultimate reality was beyond the reach of human comprehension and human language. Shelley's skepticism has been traced through William Drummond to the influence of David Hume,[8] but he could have learned a similar epistemology from Plato. [. . .]

The safest course for the religious reformer [. . .] was a *via negativa* that identified religious error rather than affirming religious truth. [. . .] One can see Shelley using his talent for such reformational purposes in one of the great religious poems of our literature, "Mont Blanc," the central purpose of which is precisely to create such a vacancy in a place where religious error had previously gone unchallenged.

Shelley arrived at Chamounix in the summer of 1816 in the wake of a procession of pilgrims who had come there anticipating a religious experience – the kind of metaphysical *frisson* that the poet Thomas Gray had reported in letters whose publication helped make the valley a fashionable religious resort. "Not a precipice," Gray wrote, "not a torrent, not a cliff, but is pregnant with religion and poetry. There are certain scenes that would awe an atheist into belief without help of other arguments."[9] A more formidable precursor than Gray was a poet who had visited Mont Blanc more recently, but only in imagination – Samuel Taylor Coleridge. His "Hymn Before Sunrise, in the Vale of Chamouni" (first published in 1803 and reprinted in *The Friend* in 1809) seems to have been consciously offered as a contribution to the pious literary fashion inaugurated by Gray. In an introductory note to the poem as originally published in the *Morning Post*, Coleridge shows Gray's influence when he writes: "the whole vale, its every light, its every sound, must needs impress every mind not utterly callous with the thought – Who *would* be, who *could* be an Atheist in this valley of wonders!"[10] It was this kind of conventional and coercive religiosity that provoked Shelley, when he arrived in the valley, to register as an atheist in one or more of the local inns – a prank that, when it was reported in England, did permanent damage to his reputation.

Shelley probably knew that Coleridge had never in fact seen Mont Blanc, although he may not have known that much of his response to Chamounix was borrowed, without acknowledgment, from the German writer Friederike Brun, and therefore that his pious emotion was secondhand in more senses than one.[11] [. . .] Shelley's poem contains what sound like deliberate allusions to Coleridge's; gazing upon the same mountain, the same fierce, ceaselessly raving river, the same black, jagged rocks, the poets ask similar questions: "Who called you forth from night and utter death?" "Who gave you your invulnerable life?" The questions are similar; the answers are strikingly different.[12]

Coleridge/Brun find positive religious meaning everywhere[, but . . . their] account doesn't notice, as Shelley's does, that the garlands of "living flowers" at the feet of the mountain are being crushed by the inexorable glacier, which has not been completely stopped by divine command; and the older poet seems unaware of any theological ambiguity or irony in his statement that the ruinous avalanche thunders the name of God. Shelley, by contrast, sees and laments the relentless "flood of ruin . . . that from the boundaries of the sky / Rolls its perpetual stream":

> The dwelling-place
> Of insect, beasts, and birds, becomes its spoil;
> Their food and their retreat forever gone,
> So much of life and joy is lost. The race
> Of man flies far in dread; his work and dwelling
> Vanish, like smoke before the tempest's stream,
> And their place is not known.

Shelley details the brutal, destructive side of the natural phenomena that Coleridge's absent-minded piety attributes placidly to a benevolent deity. [. . .]

He had himself been impressed by the "magnificence" and "radiant beauty" of the glaciers (*Letters* I: 496–9) but his poem, as though in refutation of the argument from design, insists on the deformity and menace of the landscape and on its inability to proclaim any religious truth distinctly. Indeed, his description raises religious questions, in both a mythopoeic and a scientific manner, only to refrain from answering them:

> Is this the scene
> Where the old Earthquake-demon taught her young
> Ruin? Were these their toys? or did a sea
> Of fire envelop once this silent snow?
> None can reply – all seems eternal now.
> The wilderness has a mysterious tongue
> Which teaches awful doubt, or faith so mild,
> So solemn, so serene, that man may be,
> But for such faith, with nature reconciled;

> Thou hast a voice, great Mountain, to repeal
> Large codes of fraud and woe; not understood
> By all, but which the wise, and great, and good
> Interpret, or make felt, or deeply feel.

The doubt (it would have been "awful" even to the author of *Queen Mab*, who liked to imagine the creative power as a nurturing principle) is the inability to believe in the existence of a benevolent creator. The mild faith that keeps mankind from being reconciled with nature is that of observers like Gray and Coleridge, who cannot see nature for what it really is because it would disturb their religious security.

Commentators struggling with Shelley's syntax in lines 77–9, which speak of "awful doubt, or faith so mild, / So solemn, so serene, that man may be, / But for such faith, with nature reconciled," have attempted to eliminate his precise equivocality,[13] not seeing that the point of the poem is its two-edged skepticism, its genuine agnosticism. Shelley is deliberately asserting that humanity may become reconciled with nature *except for a* too serene faith. Faith in general was suspect in Shelley's eyes. [. . .] Religious preconceptions distort our vision of nature. The "mild faith" of natural religion selects only what can be accommodated to its serene confidence in the benevolent God it likes to worship. This complacent assurance, based on selective perception of reality, is what allows us to create gods in our own image and subscribe to those "large codes of fraud and woe" that have ravaged history. [. . .] Looking without preconceptions at a landscape like the one surrounding Mont Blanc, what can one say with certainty of its Creator? What moral attitudes can one predicate of the Maker of that conflict of beauty and ruin? How can we invoke such a Being to sanction or sanctify our religious and political systems?

Shelley is not underwriting either the awful doubt or the mild faith of "Mont Blanc." What the mountain "says" to the adverting mind is that the Power present in nature is incomprehensible and that surrender to intellectual uncertainty might help to repeal the codes of fraud and woe that have resulted from the anthropomorphizing tendency that leads people, in Leigh Hunt's words, to "palm their bad and vindictive passions on Heaven."[14] Shelley was to illustrate this kind of fraud and woe at its most brutal in *The Cenci*, in which the worst crimes are justified (whether by Count Cenci or the Pope or Beatrice) by a presumption of divine authorization.

Coleridge illustrated Shelley's principle that "where indefiniteness ends idolatry and anthropomorphism begin"[15] when he concluded his "Hymn" with an apostrophe personifying the mountain, and he demonstrated the political consequences of this kind of projection by falling into the language of monarchy and hierarchy:

> Thou kingly Spirit throned among the hills,
> Thou dread ambassador from Earth to Heaven,
> Great Hierarch! tell thou the silent sky,
> And tell the stars, and tell yon rising sun
> Earth, with her thousand voices, praises God.

[. . .]

As Coleridge's poem was bold enough to command the "Great Hierarch," to obey his will, Shelley also assumes a position of authority in his confrontation with the Power of the mountain. From the start of the poem he has insisted in a Berkeleyan manner that his own mind substantiates whatever he seems to perceive in this landscape, and at the end, having spoken of Mont Blanc as the symbol of ultimate power dwelling apart in its tranquility, "remote, serene, and inaccessible," and after conceding even that "The secret Strength of things / Which governs thought, and to the infinite dome / Of heaven is as a law, inhabits thee!" he turns upon the Power and reminds it that his own mind determines their relationship, insofar as any relationship exists. He has attributed religious significance to the mountain by an act, by a gift, of his imagination. The human mind, ultimately, is where religion is made, as "it peoples with its wishes vacancy & oblivion" (*Letters* 2: 60). "And what were thou," he finally asks, "If to the human mind's imaginings / Silence and solitude were vacancy?" The mind infuses with significance what would otherwise be mere vacancy. The kind of significance it attaches to its projections depends on its preconceptions and its psychic needs. We can create regal, authoritarian gods, like Coleridge's, or we can imagine more liberating and loving divinities if we so choose. The suggestion that silence and solitude may be mere vacancy – that the Coleridge who "worshipped the Invisible" was worshiping a nonentity (a "sovran Blanc," as Coleridge wrote, apparently without any sense of irony) contributes to the ambiguity of the poem's attribution to a transcendent power of "the secret strength of things / Which governs thought, and to the infinite dome / Of heaven is as a law." Evidently belief in a transcendent order is possible, but it must be tendered carefully, indeed skeptically. [. . .]

In "Mont Blanc" Shelley emphasized the absolute otherness of supreme power in order to rescue the concept of divinity from anthropomorphisms that, in his view, have corrupted religion from the start. His insistence on the unknowable otherness of God did not abate as he grew older, but he became increasingly willing to risk the dangers of anthropomorphism in order to imagine a Divine Being whose essence is love and whose creative power is directed toward the enhancement of human life in a manner concordant with our own highest ideals. His earlier, stricter metaphysics, scrupulous in its avoidance of anthropomorphic indulgence, may be seen in *Queen Mab* when the Fairy speaks of the "Spirit of Nature" [. . .] (6: 200–19). This is admirably guarded speculation, but a moralist with a social conscience as sensitive as Shelley's, whose metaphysics, as Kenneth Neill Cameron observed, were always subordinate to his ethics,[16] could not long remain content with the restrained religiosity of *Queen Mab*, or with a deity that is unable to choose between an upas and an oak, that is too detached from human values to prefer a good man over a sensual slave, love over hate, or joy over pain. As alert as he was to the danger of anthropomorphizing God, he finally could accept, even in theory, only a divinity that was humane in sympathy and purpose, one who promoted the ethical and political ideals to which Shelley himself subscribed. As it endorsed positive human emotions like love and justice, such a Being must also be understood to sponsor the human champions of love and compassion – such as Jesus Christ, for whom Shelley's admiration increased as he grew older.

The younger Shelley was not likely to attribute any enlightened thinking to Jesus, against whom he harbored a fierce personal grudge because the Galilean had, among other offenses, alienated the affections of Harriet Grove, the poet's first love. "Oh how I wish I *were* the Antichrist," he wrote in 1810, "that it were *mine* to crush the Demon, to hurl him to his native Hell never to rise again – I expect to gratify some of this insatiable feeling in Poetry. You shall see, you shall hear" (*Letters* I: 35).

By 1814, his feelings about Jesus had become ambivalent, if not contradictory. In *Queen Mab* while Ahasuerus is describing Jesus as a malignant being who promoted intolerance and persecution, Shelley's notes speak of him as "a man of pure life, who desired to rescue his countrymen from the tyranny of their barbarous and degrading superstitions" and acknowledge the importance of distinguishing

> between the pretended character of this being as the Son of God and the Saviour of the world, and his real character as a man who, for a vain attempt to reform the world, paid the forfeit of his life to that overbearing tyranny which has since so long desolated the universe in his name.[17]

[...]

As he grew older, Shelley [...] displayed two conflicting dispositions toward Christianity, one that "burned toward heaven with fierce reproach and doubt" (*Prometheus Unbound* III.i.6), waging relentless mental warfare against the religion he considered the archenemy of human liberty and progress, and another that searched for what was originally and truly beneficial in this faith that now dominated the European mind. It seemed necessary for one part of Shelley's consciousness to resist and repudiate "impious" conceptions of God while another part strove to articulate a worthier theology. His most ambitious poem, *Prometheus Unbound*, might be read as an allegory of these two responses.

Prometheus's role is to defy and resist a repressive, authoritarian image of God until it is finally abandoned by mankind. Yet while Prometheus may be "the type of the highest perfection of moral and intellectual nature, impelled by the purest and the truest motives to the best and noblest ends" (Preface), he evidently lacks certain important mental qualities that one may observe in his female counterpart, Asia. While Prometheus, bound, is resisting and scorning Jupiter, Asia sets out on a journey of discovery and uses her sensitive metaphysical intuition to discern an alternative theology to the one Jupiter personifies. She learns to distinguish (or to make her interlocutor, Demogorgon, distinguish) the God "who reigns" from an "almighty" and "merciful" God who is "eternal Love" (II.iv.120). Asia brings about the downfall of Jupiter not by challenging his power directly but by imagining and then appealing to a worthier conception of Deity that makes it impossible for the inferior one to endure.[18] Prometheus himself seems unable to see beyond the Jupiter who reigns as "God and Lord" (I.282), and he remains imprisoned in his own defiance. His very hatred of his conception of God is debilitating and self-destructive. This helps to explain why Shelley prefaces his drama with a rejection of what we have learned to call Romantic Satanism. Rebellious defiance of God, he says, may be admirable but ultimately it has deleterious effects on the rebel's character. Prometheus's hatred of God inhibits his imagination; only when the hero adopts a more magnanimous attitude to Jupiter does Asia become free to set out on her quest for a clearer understanding of what Divinity ought to be.

Evidently, incessant reproach and doubt and insurrection cannot by itself bring down the empire of Jupiter, so securely is that empire pillared on faith and fear (3: 1–17). Change in theology is brought about most effectively not by mere denial but by the articulation of alternative beliefs. In the *Defence of Poetry* Shelley suggests that "dispersing the grosser delusions of superstition" is the accomplishment of an inferior mental power. While the rational faculty is useful for discrediting erroneous conceptions of

God, the imaginative faculty is the one that intuits more authentic conceptions as it sifts "the evidence of things unseen" for fresh insight. In his early life Shelley had insisted that conceptions of ultimate reality must be reasonable and logical; he was always on guard against his own propensity to believe what his reason could not countenance, conscious that "belief is but desire."[19] Later, he came to trust desire as an expression of imagination and, as such, an avenue to truth. In religious matters he would have agreed with Keats that "what the Imagination seizes as Beauty must be truth."[20]

As Shelley's idealistic politics eventually accommodated themselves to the realities of history, one can see his religious principles likewise acquiring an alloy of pragmatism as he grew older. His ultimate goal might continue to be the radical purification or, failing that, the eradication of Christianity, but he was coming to see that the Christian religion even in its present state could generate beneficial effects in society, serving as a kind of homeopathic antidote to belief systems with worse social consequences. [. . .] Events in Europe in 1821 seem to have encouraged Shelley in this new optimism regarding the social utility of Christianity. In April he could have read a letter in the *Examiner* which reported the presence of priests among the Carbonari: "This society is at once political and religious. Its principles have their foundation in the purest maxims of the Gospel, from which they derive eternal hatred to political and religious tyranny."[21] When later in that year revolution broke out in Greece, Leigh Hunt, laboring under the mistaken impression that the Greeks were treating the Turks with "generosity of spirit," attributed this forbearance to their Christian principles.

> The noble spirit which the Greeks have evinced . . . is evidently the same as that which has actuated the Reformers in Spain and Portugal, and proceeds from the same causes. It is the growth of the philosophical part of Christianity, as distinguished from the dogmas that have hitherto been confounded with and perverted it.[22]

While Shelley does not seem to have joined fully in this effort to transmogrify the Greeks into Unitarians, he was able to convince himself that "the chiefs of the Greeks are almost all men of comprehension and enlightened views on religion and politics."[23] [. . .]

Shelley welcomed the Greek rebellion of 1821 as signaling the revival of the spirit of freedom in the post-Napoleonic world. As the Greeks with their ancient democratic heritage provided a suitable embodiment of the libertarian spirit, their antagonists in the Ottoman Empire offered an especially appropriate incarnation of the principle of repression. The Turkish Sultan was a monarch more absolute than any European king, and his power had a sacred dimension that offered a single focus for Shelley's contempt of kingcraft and priestcraft. Four years earlier he had located an imaginary popular revolution in "Islam" and named his tyrant "Othman" – a word that is used in *Hellas* as an alternate spelling for "Ottoman" (l. 1019). Now current events had transformed his visionary revolution into historical reality – the revolt of Islam had begun in the real world and had begun with satisfying poetic propriety in the very birthplace of democracy.

[. . .]

Hellas is an extended meditation on the possibility that the Greek rising might inaugurate such a "period of regeneration and happiness," and it anticipates this millennium in language borrowed from the apocalyptic literature of the Bible. When the Sultan, Mahmud, says:

> take this signet,
> Unlock the seventh chamber in which lie
> An Empire's spoil stored for a day of ruin.
> O spirit of my sires, is it not come?

any contemporary reader would have instantly recognized that conjunction of a signet, the opening of a seventh chamber, and the prophecy of a day of ruin as an allusion to the opening of the seventh seal which precipitates the destruction of the earth in the Book of Revelation.

As an account of a final decisive struggle between Islam and the forces striving to effect a religious and political revolution in Greece, *Hellas* is charged with apocalyptic urgency. A dying Greek Christian becomes possessed by the spirit of prophecy and cries out to the Turks:

> Time has found ye light as foam.
> The Earth rebels; and Good and Evil stake
> Their empire o'er the unborn world of men
> On this one cast; – but ere the die be thrown,
> The renovated genius of our race,
> Proud umpire of the impious game, descends,
> A seraph-winged Victory, bestriding
> The tempest of the Omnipotence of God,
> Which sweeps all things to their appointed doom,
> And you to oblivion!
>
> (442–51)

The Sultan himself becomes obsessed with reading the portents of impending apocalypse, finding signs in the heavens and the earth of the fall of Islam and the triumph of Christianity [. . .] (337–47). The star of freedom that rises against the Turkish crescent, and in which Mahmud finds an "insolent" emblem of universal insubordination (351–5), is elsewhere identified as the "folding star of Bethlehem" (231). It may be surprising, even disconcerting, to find Shelley thus representing Christianity as an ideology of liberation, but in the religio-political order established in the play, and in Shelley's maturing vision of history, the teaching of Christ had come to represent a truly revolutionary vision, advocating "doctrines of reform" far more radical than any which had been advanced by others – more daring than those of Plato before him or Godwin after him.[24]

The struggle for Greek freedom is called in *Hellas* "the Christian cause" (1. 554), and the drama becomes as much a meditation on religion as on politics, on the rebels as Christians as on the rebels as Greeks. The revolution was in fact a religious war, its passion and its rhetoric (whether in battle cries or in official proclamations) deriving special intensity from the centuries-old antagonism between a Christian people and their Islamic rulers. The conflict provided Shelley with an occasion to give imaginative expression to his theory that Christianity was, or ought to be, fundamentally antithetical to political and religious tyranny. As the modern Greeks in his drama incarnated the spirit of the eternal Hellas even in their present degraded condition, he allowed Greek Christianity, in all its superstition and corruption, to serve as a representation of the liberating faith originally taught by Jesus, that pure religion that Shelley acknowledged might never be realizable on earth but which could still serve as an enduring inspirational ideal. The Christianity of the Greek rebels thus functions in the play as a kind of Coleridgean symbol representing what it cannot itself adequately express.

By the time he wrote *Hellas*, Shelley was in the habit of treating earthly realities as emblematic of higher things. [. . .] But even the glorious Greeks did not represent the highest ideals that humanity was capable of conceiving. Ancient Greek society, with all its magnificent intellectual and cultural achievements, was a radically flawed civilization, contaminated by some deadly Shelleyan sins [. . .].[25] The decline of Greek civilization into autocracy and militarism indicated that something was lacking in the Hellenic spirit, an inadequacy that jeopardized and finally vitiated their great achievements in art and philosophy. What was missing, *Hellas* suggests, was the nobler vision of human potential that was later articulated by Jesus.

[. . .]

The most important contribution to civilization of the religion of Jesus was its central emphasis on charity, mercy, and forgiveness. Warning against the brutality and bloodshed that the Greek rebellion would inevitably provoke, the chorus in *Hellas* sings,

> In sacred Athens, near the fane
> Of Wisdom, Pity's altar stood:
> Serve not the unknown God in vain,
> But pay that broken shrine again,
> Love for hate and tears for blood.
>
> (733–7)

Shelley is alluding here to the passage in *Acts of the Apostles* (17: 16–23) narrating the disturbance caused in Athens when the apostle Paul "preached unto them Jesus, and the resurrection."

> Then Paul stood in the midst of Mars' hill, and said, Ye men of Athens, I perceive that in all things ye are too superstitious. For as I passed by, and beheld your devotions, I found an altar with the inscription, TO THE UNKNOWN GOD. Whom therefore ye ignorantly worship, him I declare unto you.

Shelley was nearly paraphrasing the last sentence of Paul's address when he called Christianity "the exoteric expression of the esoteric doctrines of the poetry and wisdom of antiquity." But his assertion is qualified: only in its "abstract purity" does Christianity surpass the Greek achievement. This pure Christianity was a religion that had never yet existed on earth and perhaps never could. The chorus's reference to the "unknown God" expresses Shelley's painful consciousness that the God who joins wisdom and pity, who prefers love to hate and tears to blood, is a God whom humanity seems incapable of serving, incapable even of knowing. This is the "almighty, merciful God" of *Prometheus Unbound* whose existence is veiled by the reign of the usurping Jupiter.

Shelley's understanding of the Greek revolution as a critical moment in the perpetual struggle between liberty and tyranny, between ideals of freedom and justice on one hand and on the other a persistent antithetical tendency in mankind to deny or despair of those ideals, is expressed most clearly in what is called the "Prologue to *Hellas*," a fragment that seems to have been intended to introduce the drama but which was not published with it in 1821. [. . .]

Within the drama itself, advocacy of the pessimistic, Satanic viewpoint is provided by the somewhat surprising appearance of Ahasuerus, the Wandering Jew who had figured so prominently in Shelley's early poetry. Most interpreters have assumed that the Ahasuerus of *Hellas* is the same sympathetic figure who is called to testify against religion in *Queen Mab*, that he is still in 1821, as Neville Rogers put it, the "incarnation of accumulated Shelleyan philosophy."[26] But as Shelley's attitude to Jesus Christ had altered since *Queen Mab*, one might also expect a change in his opinion of this ancient scorner and repudiator of Christ – whom he would now see as one of the multitude that misunderstood his character and his mission. When Jesus came, as the chorus sings in *Hellas*, "a Power from the unknown God," treading "the thorns of death and shame" (lines 211–14) he was mocked by Ahasuerus, very much as Christ is mocked by Satan in the "Prologue to *Hellas*." In fact, in the terms of the Prologue Ahasuerus has to be seen as a Satanic figure. When he says to Mahmud: "The Past / Now stands before thee like an Incarnation / Of the To-come" (lines 852–54), he aligns himself with the Satan of the Prologue, to whom Christ says: "Obdurate spirit! Thou seest but the Past in the To-come."[27] Ahasuerus denies any real distinction between past and future:

> All is contained in each.
> Dodona's forest to an acorn's cup
> Is that which has been, or will be, to that
> Which is the absent to the present.[28]

In the running debate in *Hellas* between fate and freedom, Ahasuerus denies the possibility of any real progress in human affairs. He represents in his own history the inability to change or conclude, "condemned to behold for millenniums that yawning monster Sameness, and Time, that hungry hyaena, ever bearing children, and ever devouring again her offspring."[29] His primary dramatic action in *Hellas* involves raising the phantom of Mahomet II, the sultan who conquered Constantinople in 1453. Mahomet II's return from the dead reinforces the pessimistic theme that the present and future are fated to repeat the past. When Ahasuerus says, "The Future and the Past are idle shadows / Of thought's eternal flight – they have no being," his denial of humanity's potential and of its responsibility for creating its own future reinforces the resigned fatalism articulated by Satan and the Sultan.

The central struggle in *Hellas*, then, is between two competing religious ideologies, one redemptive, insisting on the possibility of radical alteration in mankind's situation, the other fatalistic, denying the possibility of any significant change for the better in the human condition. Inadequate attention to this conflict accounts for some of the difficulty critics have had in interpreting the best known lines in the drama – the great concluding chorus, "The world's great age begins anew" – a lyric that encapsulates the tension in the drama between its longing for a "brighter Hellas" that will revive the spirit of Athens in her prime and its dread of a return of the kind of violence that has been an integral part of Greek history and literature from the beginning. Even if a brighter Hellas were to emerge from the present political struggle, the chorus acknowledges that the Greek story could once again end in hatred, brutality, and "fruitless ruin," for want of an ideal that goes beyond the ethics of revenge.

[. . .]

The last stanza [of the drama's chorus] has caused consternation among some critics because it has seemed to them an abrupt auctorial intrusion rather than an organic, dramatically appropriate development in the poem.

[. . .]

The problem of interpretation has arisen [. . .] because critics want to read the chorus as an optimistic poem, then object to it because it is not sufficiently or consistently optimistic. But what sounds like optimism in the poem is really a kind of wishful thinking that is then undercut by the ironic historical consciousness of the Greek women who sing the chorus – a captive people and, as women, doubly enslaved by the Turks. Misreading tends to begin with an interpretation of the word "great" in the first line as celebratory, paralleling "golden" in the next line, when it actually means great in length or duration. Shelley is referring to Plato's sense of earthly time as a cycle eternally returning upon itself. [. . .] From the beginning, [. . .] Shelley's chorus expresses as much dread of historical recurrence as optimism about renewal. Mahmud had earlier suggested that cycles of loveliness come accompanied by cycles of desolation (lines 746–7) and predicted, "Come what may, / The Future must become the Past." This grim suggestion of an equation between past and future, with the possibility that the terms of the equation are reversible, is what the chorus's final stanza protests. The Sultan and Ahasuerus, like Satan in the Prologue, have been saying, in the language of the chorus, that hate and death must return, that men must continue to kill and die. It is fear of that fatality – fear that the absence of pity and forgiveness will make a revival of "the tale of Troy" just as likely as a resurrection of Periclean Athens – that inspires the chorus's weary exclamation, "Oh Cease!"

But it is too much to say with John Hodgson that "*Hellas* ends, despairingly, with a lamentation over all cyclicity."[30] To lament cyclicity is not necessarily to despair. To demand an end to recurrent, predictable evil is to reject the fatalist vision of Satan in the "Prologue" for the optimistic ideal articulated by Jesus Christ. What Jesus offers is the possibility of escape from historical determinism. If Shelley indulged in a longing for such a redemption from history, it would not necessarily have been a betrayal of radical principles. That there will be a final conflict, a war to end all wars, has been the dream of political visionaries for centuries.

[. . .]

Hellas concludes with [an] eschatological yearning for a way out, a final, absolute redemption. Multiple allusions to the Biblical apocalypse suggest a hope that the Greek rebellion might prove to be a kind of Armageddon in which "Good and Evil [would] stake / Their empire o'er the unborn world of men / On this one cast." If the Greeks could embrace the Hellenic ideal, if the Christian rebels could accept as their program the genuine ethical and political teachings of Jesus, then Greece might be changed forever and provide a pattern of revolution for the rest of the world to follow. But as Shelley's drama ends, the chorus of Greek women is still enslaved and the world stands waiting for a redemption, an apocalyptic revelation, that does not come. To serve the unknown God of pity and forgiveness apparently remains beyond the capacity of the Greek revolutionaries, whose imaginations have apparently surrendered to the fatalist vision of Satan and the ethic of revenge that it justifies.

Christian eschatology offers an alternative to historical fatalism, but it offers such hope on terms that Shelley evidently could not bring himself to accept, even in a visionary work like *Hellas*. He could take no comfort from the prospect of a glorified Christ coming to transform the world. In his drama Shelley alludes specifically to the prophecies of the second coming in Matthew 24: 29–30; and Mark 13: 24–6 ("they shall see the Son of man coming in the clouds of heaven with power and great glory") and revises them:

> The Greeks expect a Saviour from the West
> Who shall not come, men say, in clouds and glory:
> But in the omnipresence of that spirit
> In which all live and are.

(598–601)

Here the image of the returning Christ fades into a universal transformative power like the one in *Adonais* that "sweeps through the dull dense world, compelling there / All new successions to the forms they wear" and "wields the world with never-wearied love." This universal renovation of the human spirit, Shelley suggests, should be the object of the Greeks' messianic hope, not the Christ who is worshiped in the Christian churches and invoked as the sponsor of half the atrocities generated by the war in Greece. This Christ, Shelley insists, represents no improvement over the old gods of Greece.

> Saturn and Love their long repose
>   Shall burst, more bright and good
> Than all who fell, than One who rose,
>   Than many unsubdued:
> Not gold, not blood their altar dowers
> But votive tears and symbol flowers.

This apparent repudiation of the Christianity he has been celebrating, and even of Jesus Christ himself, is at first confusing, but Shelley here is insisting once again on his distinction between the Jesus of history and the Christ of faith. When he says that the revived Saturn and Love would be more bright and good "than One who rose," he is referring not to Jesus as he actually lived but as he was revised by those who fabricated the story of his resurrection – the primary fiction on which the religion called Christianity was founded. Shelley would have agreed with Thomas Paine's description of the resurrection account as a "wretched contrivance . . . with every mark of fraud and imposition stamped upon the face of it."[31] The poet is insisting here at the end of *Hellas*, as he had always done, that historical Christianity was a betrayal of the teaching and example of Jesus Christ.

[. . .]

Notes

1 In 1828, F.D. Maurice declared Shelley to have been the preeminent religious poet of his generation [(*Athenaeum*, March 7, 1828)], and, in our own day, Stuart Curran has called him "the greatest religious poet in the English language between Blake and Yeats." *Shelley's Annus Mirabilis: The Maturing of an Epic Vision* (San Marino, CA: Huntington Library, 1975), p. 205.
2 *The Alternative Tradition: Religion and the Rejection of Religion in the Ancient World* (The Hague: Mouton, 1980), p. 17.

3 *The Letters of Percy Bysshe Shelley*, ed. Frederick L. Jones, 2 vols (Oxford: Clarendon Press, 1964), 1: 228. All further references to this edition will be included in the text.

4 Edward John Trelawny, *Records of Shelley, Byron, and the Author*, 2 vols (London: Pickering, 1878), 1: 92–3.

5 *Shelley: Poetical Works*, ed. Thomas Hutchinson, 2nd edn, corrected by G.M. Matthews (London: Oxford University Press, 1971), p. 812. The most careful and helpful analysis to date of Shelley's shifting conceptions of this transcendent "Spirit" as they were influenced by his reading of Berkeley, Hume, Holbach, Spinoza, Drummond, and others, is offered by Jerrold E. Hogle in *Shelley's Process: Radical Transference and the Development of His Major Works* (New York: Oxford University Press, 1988). It will be evident that I do not concur with Hogle's central thesis – that Shelley's apparent theism is only a metaphor for an unceasing process of linguistic transference.

6 *Queen Mab* 6: 199, in *Shelley's Poetry and Prose*, eds Donald H. Reiman and Sharon B. Powers (New York: Norton, 1977), p. 50. Unless otherwise indicated, all quotations from Shelley's poetry are taken from this edition and references will be cited in the text.

7 "Essay on Christianity" in *The Complete Works of Percy Bysshe Shelley*, eds Roger Ingpen and Walter E. Peck, 10 vols (New York: Scribner, 1926–30), 6: 240.

8 C.E. Pulos, *The Deep Truth: A Study of Shelley's Skepticism* (University of Nebraska Press, 1954), pp. 24–41.

9 *The Correspondence of Thomas Gray*, eds P. Toynbee and L. Whibley (Oxford: Clarendon Press, 1935), 1: 125.

10 *The Poems of Samuel Taylor Coleridge*, ed. Ernest Hartley Coleridge (London: Oxford University Press, 1912), p. 377n.

11 See Norman Fruman, *Coleridge: The Damaged Archangel* (New York: Braziller, 1971), pp. 26–30. See also Keith G. Thomas, "Coleridge, Wordsworth, and the New Historicism: 'Chamouny: The Hour Before Sunrise. A Hymn' and Book 6 of *The Prelude*," *Studies in Romanticism* 33 (Spring 1994): 81–117.

12 He wrote at this time from Geneva, "Coleridge is in my thoughts" (*Letters* 1: 490). Harold Bloom offers a provocative examination of the contrasts between these two poems in *Shelley's Mythmaking* (Cornell University Press, 1959), pp. 11–19. See also Hogle, *Shelley's Process*, pp. 79–86.

13 Timothy Webb says that the standard reading "But for such faith" "can only be justified by the most tortuous explanations." *Shelley: A Voice Not Understood* (Atlantic Highlands, NJ: Humanities Press, 1977), p. 137.

14 [*The*] *Examiner: A Weekly Paper on Politics, Literature, Music and the Fine Arts* (London, 1808–81)], Sept. 6, 1818, p. 563.

15 *Complete Works* 6: 232.

16 *Shelley: The Golden Years*, [(Harvard University Press, 1974),] p. 115.

17 *Poetical Works*, ed. Hutchinson/Matthews, p. 820.

18 I am particularly indebted here to F.A. Pottle, "The Role of Asia in the Dramatic Action of Shelley's *Prometheus Unbound*," reprinted in *Shelley: A Collection of Critical Essays*, ed. George M. Ridenour (Englewood Cliffs, NJ: Prentice-Hall, 1965), pp. 133–43.

19 The phrase is Jerrold Hogle's in *Shelley's Process*, p. 29.

20 *The Letters of John Keats*, ed. H.E. Rollins (Harvard University Press, 1958), 1: 184.

21 *Examiner*, April 1, 1821, p. 195.

22 *Examiner*, October 7, 1821, p. 631.

23 Shelley's note to *Hellas*, in *Poetical Works*, ed. Hutchinson/Matthews, p. 458.

24 "On the Moral Teaching of Christ," *Complete Works* 6: 255.

25 *Complete Works* 6: 237–8.

26 *Shelley at Work* (Oxford: Clarendon, 1967), p. 293.

27 *Poetical Works*, ed. Hutchinson/Matthews, 452.

28 A perceptive analysis of these lines is offered by William A. Ulmer in "*Hellas* and the Historical Uncanny," *ELH* 58 (1991): 618–19.

29 Note to *Queen Mab* 7: 67. *Poetical Works*, ed. Hutchinson/Matthews, p. 819.

30 *Coleridge, Shelley, and Transcendental Inquiry: Rhetoric, Argument, Metapsychology* (University of Nebraska Press, 1989), p. 90.

31 *The Age of Reason*, ed. Moncure Daniel Conway (New York: Putnam, 1896), p. 27.

30 Wordsworth's chastened enthusiasm

Jon Mee

[Two omitted sections explain Wordsworth's regulation of 'enthusiasm' – sensation and passion associated with religious inspiration – in his prose and early poetry.]

'Extraordinary calls'

By the time [William] Wordsworth wrote his Preface to the *Lyrical Ballads*, [. . . he] was involved in an uneasy and uneven journey away from his own earlier radicalism, and away from the less regulated idea of poetic enthusiasm to be found in *An Evening Walk*. The version of *The Prelude* completed in 1805 was in part an attempt to make sense of this journey, and to present his qualifications as the kind of regulated poet outlined in the Preface to the *Lyrical Ballads*. [. . . T]his chapter is concerned with the ways that the discourse of enthusiasm structured Wordsworth's representation of his poetic development. [. . .] Wordsworth's idea of poetic enthusiasm was closer to [Anthony Ashley Cooper, the third Earl of] Shaftesbury and [Mark] Akenside's than [Samuel Taylor] Coleridge's because of the omission of an explicitly religious context for the word. For Coleridge, as for John Dennis at the beginning of the century and Richard 'Citizen' Lee at the end of it, the highest raptures of enthusiasm were always to be reserved for religious matters, dangerous though they might be in themselves. For Wordsworth, in 1798 at least, as for Shaftesbury, Nature and the 'Spirits of the Mind' are sufficient both as sources of enthusiasm itself and of its regulation. The situation is rather different in *The Prelude*, perhaps reflecting the growing influence of Coleridge, and his concern that Wordsworth was too prone to construct a sense of mind out of the combustible matter it was meant to be regulating. Not that the 1805 version of *The Prelude* allows much of an explicit role either for the institutions of the Church or for a particularly Christianized language. What does emerge is a language powerfully inflected with the strains of biblical prophecy. Obviously identifying the poet as strongly with the prophet as Wordsworth's poem does is an attempt to claim a certain kind of cultural authority.[1] Yet the claims made on prophecy brought with them a deficit that Wordsworth had to respect. Especially where this language seemed relatively free of the direct controlling influence of the Church, as it was in *The Prelude*, it was likely to seem a sort of presumption that threatened to confound poetic with unrulier forms of enthusiasm. After all, even *The Excursion*, a poem more explicitly Christian than *The Prelude* of 1805, was for Francis Jeffrey too much like the enthusiasm of the Methodist in this respect.[2] Wordsworth himself [. . .] was no less conscious than Jeffrey of the dangers of '. . . false imagination, placed beyond / The limits of experience and of truth' (*Prelude* 1805, x. 845–7).[3] Indeed as a poem of apprenticeship (Clifford Siskin calls it the longest résumé in literary history), *The Prelude* is constantly attempting to show that its prophetic pretensions are properly disciplined, that is, assuring his readers that his enthusiasm is meant 'not in a mystical and idle sense' (II. 235). Such reminders are attempts at confirming the status of his writing as poetry and so as qualitatively different from 'mystical verbiage'.

The language of prophecy is a particularly unstable element in this process, because of the long-standing historical memory of its role in stirring up religious enthusiasm, and there were plenty of contemporary examples, as we have seen, of the continuation of this aspect of the popular imagination. Thus, contrary to the suggestions of critics such as [David] Riede, for Wordsworth to create an 'oracular self' is not in itself a guarantee of poetic authority. Undisciplined prophetic pretensions invited at best ridicule and at worst contempt. Looking at the language of prophecy from this point of view means that we have to reconsider the widely accepted but recently much-contested claim that Romanticism in general and Wordsworth in particular were involved with a process of displacing public history onto private apocalypse. For critics such as M.H. Abrams, this 'imaginative transformation of the self' is to be celebrated as the basis of a great poetic achievement.[4] For New Historicist critics such as Alan Liu, the same movement is an evasion of history. I would argue that the dichotomy between History and Apocalypse accepted by both sides of the argument is itself a Romantic construction. Perhaps its currency even indicates the eventual success of Coleridge and Wordsworth in rewriting these terms for literary criticism. Yet this success in terms of our understanding of Romantic enthusiasm should not be allowed to obscure either their own anxieties or the immediate reservations of critics such as [Francis] Jeffrey. The process of rehabilitation [. . .] was a long and uneven one. It neither began nor ended with Coleridge and Wordsworth. Alongside their rewriting of the poetics of enthusiasm there still existed a troubling other in the enthusiastic public sphere, associated with Methodism and popular excesses of all kinds. The continuing presence of this unregulated species of enthusiasm made possible attacks such as Jeffrey's. [. . .]

Wordsworth does not simply assume a language of prophecy. No such stable language was available to be assumed in poetry. Wordsworth had to participate in an uneasy process of rehabilitation that had much to do with the fear of the dangerous nature of enthusiasm, a response which was itself part of a broader unease about public spaces becoming infected by 'the discomforting proximity of the lower orders'.[5] In this context then, the Romantic Apocalypse of the Imagination represents not so much a displacement of History as the rewriting of prophecy. *The Prelude* is the key text in the rehabilitation of enthusiasm in the Wordsworthian canon, for it is here that the language of prophecy is most clearly subjected to reworking. The 'spots of time' that recur through the poem are the laboratories of this process. M.H. Abrams argued that these spots of time transform 'the Christian paradigm of right-angled change into something radically new'.[6] The outcome is 'a pattern . . . in which development consists of a gradual curve back to an earlier stage, but on a higher level incorporating that which has intervened'.[7] What Abrams rather casually ignores is that such 'right-angled irruptions' were widely identified in Wordsworth's time with the delirium of enthusiasm. Ideas of 'instantaneous regeneration, assurance, and sinless perfection' (*Life of Wesley*, ii. 23)[8] were what [Robert] Southey disapprobated most about [John] Wesley's teaching, even after he had decided that the general effects of the Methodist movement had been towards disciplining the lower classes, but Wesley himself tried to lay down the role of such ideas in the movement. Distancing oneself from such sudden irruptions of the unworldly was essential to most definitions of true piety at the time in both Anglican and dissenting traditions. Southey decried the tendency to make religion 'a thing of sensation and passion, craving perpetually for sympathy and stimulants, instead of bringing with it peace and contentment' (*Life of Wesley*, ii. 217). He was not seeking to distance the spiritual life from feeling as such, only – as [Anna Lætitia] Barbauld had done in the 1770s – attempting to distinguish 'the quiet regularity of domestic devotion' from the tastelessness of 'public performances' (ii. 218). Any appeal to the authenticating power of enthusiasm in the period always had to distance itself from such right-angled disruptions of coherent subjectivity.

Wordsworth's case is no different in these general terms from the ongoing requirements of the rehabilitation of enthusiasm. Affective appeals to the influx of the spirit had to distance themselves from any claim to *immediate* intercourse with the divine presence. Whereas prophetic enthusiasm was traditionally identified with the distracted subject, Wordsworth exploits the process of unworlding in the interests of discovering an abiding self beyond the fluctuations of the world as it is, but the allied process of folding spots of time back into a continuous sense of self-identity is part of a long English tradition of making sure that the transports of the sublime come with a return ticket back to a coherent subjectivity. His situation was in some respects not very different from Wesley's.[9] Although *The Prelude* seems consciously to avoid making its interest in spiritual agency too explicitly Christian, both Wesley and Wordsworth were faced with the problem of representing their prophetic faith as more than a dangerous enthusiasm. Wordsworth was careful to present his spiritual ecstasies as the product of a serious preparation as Siskin and other critics have pointed out recently.[10] Moreover both men laid a stress on the productiveness of spirituality against the dangers of revelling in the intoxication of the moment of conversion. The fruits of conversion and notions of steady stages of spiritual growth are privileged over the sudden ecstasies of the spirit in their writing as a means of distinguishing themselves from those who laid too ready a claim to spiritual enlightenment:

> Them the enduring and the transient both
> Serve to exalt. They build up greatest things
> From least suggestions, ever on the watch,
> Willing to work and to be wrought upon,
> They need not extraordinary calls
> To rouse them: in a world of life they live
> By sensible impressions not enthralled,
> But quickened, rouzed, and made thereby more fit
> To hold communion with the invisible world
>   (*Prelude* 1805, XIII. 97–105)

'Extraordinary calls' – a phrase at the very centre of disputes about the 'enthusiasm' of Methodism – implied a sudden and perfect apprehension of truth. Spiritual transports were disavowed absolutely by neither Wordsworth nor Wesley, but their effects are worked out gradually. Ecstasies of conversion, for both Wesley and Wordsworth, are the beginning not the end of a disciplinary process. Unworlding is a necessary component of the ideas of regeneration promoted in the writing of both men, but its benefits are lost if they are not reinscribed into a continuous sense of the productive subject.[11]

   [. . . T]his disavowal of 'extraordinary calls' is not simply a matter of distancing the language of prophecy from supernatural agency. Wordsworth's 'spots of time' are also distanced from the sensuousness that Wordsworth routinely identified with the 'soulless eye'. Part of the scandal of vulgar enthusiasm [. . .] was the perception that it was too eager to claim to be able to comprehend (and in turn represent) the spiritual world. Distinctions between the spiritual and carnal eye were routine in popular religious writing, but to commentators such as Leigh Hunt these distinctions were not properly observed by those who drew them. The heat and passion of Methodist discourse suggested to observers such as Hunt and Southey that popular religious feeling remained in the thrall of 'sensible impressions'. *The Prelude* may affirm the possibility of 'communion with the invisible world', but not immediately. Nor does it claim to be able to represent directly that world with any particularity. [. . .]

   The discourse of regulation that Wordsworth would have found in Shaftesbury and poets such as Akenside offered one route through which prophecy could be disciplined into poetry. *The Prelude* certainly exploits the techniques of self-division outlined in [Shaftesbury's] *Characteristics*. The spots of time are opportunities for self-division in which the mature self looks back on a previous version and sees a deeper continuity in the development of an organic subjectivity beneath the surface of the world as it is. The natural self that is actually created or 'discovered' in these moments is a paradox of artifice, the product of a 'rigorous inquisition' (I. 159) through the self that had also been essential to Shaftesbury's ideas of natural self-fashioning. Wordsworth throughout his poem seeks to demonstrate his own ability to move beyond 'present joy' (I. 109) into a narrative of personal development that qualifies him as a poet. Ironically enough, true authenticity of being in Wordsworth, as in Shaftesbury, is predicated on the ability to divide the self. One cannot be authentic without enthusiasm, but only enthusiasm that has been worked upon can provide a durable basis to identity. *The Prelude* begins with just such a moment of 'unworlding' that it proceeds to refine and discipline:

> Trances of thought and mountings of the mind
> Come fast upon me. It is shaken off –
> As by miraculous gift 'tis shaken off –
> That burden of my own unnatural self,
> The heavy weight of many a weary day,
> Not mine, and such as were not made for me.
>   (1805 *Prelude*, I. 20–5)

Certain parts of Book I may seem unapologetically to identify the poet with the prophet in this ability to see beyond the world as it is:

> . . . To the open fields I told
> A prophecy: poetic numbers came
> Spontaneously, and clothed in priestley robe

> My spirit, thus singled out, as it might seem,
> For holy services.
>
> (I. 59–63)

Yet the reader is quickly made aware of a potential error even in the moment of release: 'Or shall a twig, or any floating thing / Upon the river, point me out my course?' (I. 31–2) Poetry such as Robert Merry's, [. . .] building perhaps on the idea of self-annihilation found in Hartley and Priestley, seems more willing to abandon the self upon the stream of experience and consciousness in order to harvest new associations and emotional responses. Wordsworth figures such abandonment as a serious diminution of possibility, becoming a mere 'twig or any floating thing'. Unworlding is the sign of a healthy return to nature in the poem, but also brings with it the spectre of a mindless play of sensation. There is a voice that tempts the prophet to think only of 'present joy':

> So, like a peasant, I pursued my road
> Beneath the evening sun; nor had one wish
> Again to bend the sabbath of that time
> To a servile yoke.
>
> (I. 110–13)

The figure of the peasant here is ambiguous, and one that is ultimately disavowed in *The Prelude* in favour of a more regulated (and by implication professional) self-image. The comparison with the simplicity of the peasant may function as the sign of an authentic and uncomplicated relationship to nature in these lines, but it is haunted by the idea of a weak surrender to the temptation of 'present joy'. Ultimately, the model of the carefree peasant is disavowed. Such joys are subsumed in Wordsworth's poem to a process of development in which the poet incorporates but also transcends the knowledge of the peasant. *The Prelude*, no less than the *Lyrical Ballads*, will distinguish Wordsworth from the peasants with whom he seems to consort. He marks himself by his ability to bend 'present joy' towards higher purposes. He will not shirk from the 'service' outlined in the earlier reference to the prophetic task, that is, he must 'brace [himself] to some determined aim' (I. 124). The unworlding experience cannot simply stand as a spontaneous event, important though the recovery of the power to feel is to the poem, but has to be written into a narrative of improvement that sets his apart from those who can *only* feel. Wordsworth, like Shaftesbury, will do productive work on his enthusiasm, and 'through myself / Make rigorous inquisition' (I. 158–9). What might be a mere matter of 'animal delight' – as such experiences among peasants and Methodists alike were usually deemed to be – turns into a process of 'sanctifying by . . . discipline' (I. 439). 'Extraordinary calls' are valuable only if they are worked into a true faith by those with the cultural capital to undertake such work.

  Francis Jeffrey was hard on those he thought abandoned their true social station to follow such calls, whether in religion, poetry, or politics, throughout his reviewing career. John Thelwall he dismissed as someone incapable of regulating his enthusiasm into a productive form. Indeed his 'enthusiastic virtues' are simply to be dismissed as 'an impatience of honest industry'. Not only is Thelwall's poetry useless, but it has distracted him from the sphere of life where he could be useful. Jeffrey's attacks on Wordsworth are part of the *Edinburgh's* more general campaign against popular enthusiasm. [. . .]

One of the ways in which *The Prelude* seeks to distinguish itself from this kind of vulgar enthusiasm, for all its involvement with the language of prophecy and conversion, is by de-corporealizing the senses, that is, by uncoupling the visionary from the visible.[12] Wordsworthian calm betokens a meditative frame of mind that is able to separate the bodily passions from the nobler kinds of enthusiasm:

> Oft in those moments such a holy calm
> Did overspread my soul that I forgot
> That I had bodily eyes, and what I saw
> Appear'd like something in myself, a dream,
> A prospect in my mind.
>
> (II. 368–71)

Nature, on the one hand, offers a guarantee that Wordsworth's enthusiasm is a response to permanent and substantial forms, not the ideal dreaming of the fanatic, but, on the other, a process of rhetorical de-corporealization also functions in *The Prelude* as a way of distancing Wordsworth's feel for stocks and stones from the 'electrick' energy of the senses that critics regularly deprecated in poets such as Thelwall and Merry (not to mention the enthusiasm of Methodism). [. . .] The experiences that Wordsworth feels in 'solitude' are not the delusions of enthusiasm. They do not 'Speak to my eye' (iv. 391); they have not become fouled with the sensual, but they really were, he insists, at the same time, 'heard and felt' (ibid.). The attempt is to separate the instinctual or the 'mechanical' from spiritual experience marked as genuine, but it is one that is constantly circling round its own terms, anxious to rescue them from associations with the twin polarities of enthusiasm, that is, on the one hand, an unworlding that abandons the world too completely, or, on the other, a sensuousness that mires the spiritual with the passions. The intercourse with nature is only the worthless spasming of the enthusiast if it is not disciplined with an idea of the regulating mind that the poem identifies with Coleridge's philosophy, but cut free from the world of nature entirely such ideas represent an unworlding without any anchor in the world as it is.

Because of the infectious nature of enthusiasm, liable to intensify the passions and even overwhelm its own source, solitude itself is one form of regulation, as it was for Shaftesbury, insofar as it creates the conditions for quiet meditation. The product of habitual acts of self-regulation in solitude in his childhood, Wordsworth represents himself as able to sift the beneficent from dangerous enthusiasm. At the beginning of Book VII, for instance, journeying to London, Wordsworth describes himself as 'self-willed, / Yet temperate and reserved, and wholly free / From dangerous passions' (VII. 70–2). Solitude was not without dangers of its own when it came to enthusiasm, as poems such as Wordsworth's 'Lines written on a Yew Tree' suggest, but the infectious conditions found in urban centres seem more threatening to Wordsworth's sense of wholeness. Book VII of *The Prelude* tells of the dangers facing even a well-regulated subjectivity when confronted with the infectious proximity of the crowd. Just as [William] Godwin's account of Thelwall's oratory represented him as a well-intentioned man liable to be swallowed up by the enthusiasm he had stirred in those around him, so Wordsworth represents himself as deeply troubled and almost undone by the 'colours, lights, and forms; the Babel din' (VII. 157). Only a deep training in a version of Shaftesbury's techniques of regulation, above all, an ability gained through habitual practice in solitude to relate the confusion of the senses to a larger harmonious whole, ultimately preserves Wordsworth from the 'endless stream of men and moving things' (VII. 158):

> But though the picture weary out the eye,
> By nature an unmanageable sight,
> It is not wholly so to him who looks
> In steadiness, who hath among least things
> An under-sense of greatest – sees the parts
> As parts, but with a feeling of the whole.
> (vii. 707–12)

Whereas a poet such as Merry continually throws the self into hazard in relation to the social in order to reap 'a feeling of the whole', Wordsworth's habitual stance is one of self-preservation in the face of such external dangers. Both positions owe something to Shaftesbury. Merry's is related to but much extends Shaftesbury's notion of 'amicable collision' (*Characteristics*, 31)[13] as a means of developing the self towards benevolence. Wordsworth, of course, follows more closely Shaftesbury's warnings about not exposing one's transports to the public before they are regulated into a relatively safe form. Preserving 'a feeling of the whole' is predicated on the exclusion of vast swathes of affective human experience, and it seems any possibility of regulation for those whose enthusiasm discovers itself in an urban context is denied. Wordsworth's prophetic ardour is regulated in solitude far from the urban centres that Southey and others believed to be the forcing houses of the most dangerous strains of enthusiasm. These solitary acts of 'mental discipline', as James Chandler accurately describes them, are the spots of time disposed throughout the poem.[14] They are essentially apostrophes to Nature as the emblem of a higher harmony of the sort strewn through Shaftesbury's *Characteristics*. The subject is elevated and then reintegrated into an authentic self by the process. The right-angled turn is folded back into a continuous sense of identity progressing through time in a coherent manner. Frequently these moments of elation are described in the grand prophetic manner, but the potential folly of an over-reaching enthusiasm is qualified by a rhetoric of workmanship and professionalism that separates Wordsworth's transports from the extraordinary calls of the Methodist.

Transparence and revolutionary enthusiasm

The language of prophecy also appears as a political discourse in the poem, that is, as a means of representing Wordsworth's youthful responses to the Revolution in France. Given that the coincidence of prophetic language and political discourse was strongly marked as a sign of dangerous enthusiasm in Wordsworth's culture, *The Prelude* sets itself a difficult task in distinguishing his own healthful prophesying from the diseased *transparence* of political zealotry. The crossing of the Alps episode in Book VI of Wordsworth's *The Prelude* is widely regarded as 'the major piece of English apocalyptic poetry in the Romantic period'.[15] It is a passage described by Alan Liu as 'a sustained effort to deny history by asserting nature as the separating mark constitutive of the egotistical self'.[16] Written in 1804, the passage narrates the crossing of the Simplon Pass which Wordsworth had made after having been caught up in the revolutionary enthusiasm of France in 1790. Having looked forward to the crossing as a moment of sublime revelation, the poet meets a peasant who tells him that he is already on his way down the mountain. At this point, the narrative is interrupted as the narrator breaks in with a hymn to the creative power that had anticipated the crossing with such intensity:

> . . . In such strength
> Of usurpation, in such visitings
> Of awful promise, when the light of sense
> Goes out in flashes that have shown to us
> The invisible world, doth greatness make abode,
> There harbours whether we be young or old.
> Our destiny, our nature, and our home
> Is with infinitude, and only there –
> With hope it is, hope that can never die,
> Effort, and expectation, and desire,
> And something evermore about to be
> (VI. 532–42)

For Elinor Shaffer, who objects to the New Historicist emphasis on the evasions of Wordsworth's imagination, there remains in such a passage the possibility of a trans-formative utopia.[17] She is right, I think, to claim that the language of Apocalypse is not *necessarily* to be thought of as operating in a simple binary against history and politics, but she underestimates the extent to which this possibility is cordoned off in Wordsworth's passage. Wordsworth's evasion is not one of displacing History onto the Imagination, but rather one of reconfiguring or rewriting the Apocalyptic moment in quite specific ways:

> . . . the sick sight
> And giddy prospect of the raving stream,
> The unfettered clouds and region of the heavens,
> Tumult and peace, the darkness and the light, –
> Were all like workings of one mind, the features
> Of the same face, blossoms upon one tree;
> Characters of the great apocalypse,
> The types and symbols of eternity,
> Of first, and last, and midst and without end
> (VII. 564–72)

'The theory of denial is Imagination', says Alan Liu; but what is denied here is not History alone, not only the events of the French Revolution or Napoleon's crossing of the Alps, but also the possibility of a different kind of apocalyptic thinking identi-fied by Wordsworth and his contemporaries with the counter-public of enthusiasm.[18] Strictly speaking, the rhetorical swerve made by Wordsworth is not one of denial at all, for the apocalyptic does not necessarily deny the historical and political, but one of disciplinary regulation that distances his poetic enthusiasm from its more political forms (whether inflected with religion or not). [. . .] The problem faced by Coleridge in 'Religious Musings' of laying claim to the prophetic experience is addressed in *The Prelude* by a process of internalization that reinforces the process of de-corporealization described in the previous section. [. . .] In *The Prelude*, no less than in Coleridge's conversation poems, the language of prophecy came to be safely separated from public political utterance by the poetic reconstruction of apocalyptic unveiling as an intensely private experience. The spots of time are incorporated into Wordsworth's development in another sense too. They are precisely sublimated into a higher realm by the act of recollection that pulls them into a narrative of the organic development of the self beyond the exigencies of historical experience. The mind that feels sympathy with the rocks and stones of the Alps [. . .] is not denied as such, but it is reconstituted in terms of a 'higher' level of experience: one that defines Wordsworth's enthusiasm less in terms of the material experiences of crossing the mountain, but as a de-corporealized mental apocalypse. Such experiences are moments of enthusiasm that Wordsworth builds into himself in order to move beyond them into maturity.

If Wordsworth's disciplining of the prophetic keeps alive any utopian possibility, his Apocalypse of the Imagination is what Ernst Bloch called an 'abstract utopia', that is, one that does not provide 'an historical alternative – a utopia to be translated into reality'.[19] [. . .]

When it comes to describing his own political enthusiasm of the 1790s in Book x, Wordsworth uses specifically prophetic terms:

> But as the ancient prophets were inflamed,
> Nor wanted consolations of their own
> And majesty of mind when they denounced
> On towns and cities, wallowing in the abyss
> Of their offences, punishment to come;
> Or saw like other men, with bodily eyes,
> Before them, in some desolated place,
> The consummation of the wrath of Heaven;
> So did some portions of that spirit fall
> On me, to uphold me through those evil times,
> And in their rage and dog-day heat I found
> Something to glory in, as just and fit
> And in the order of sublimest laws.
> And, even if that were not, amid the awe
> Of unintelligible chastisement
> I felt a kind of sympathy with power –
> Motions raised up within me, nevertheless
> Which had relationship to highest things . . .
>
>   (x. 401–18)

The treatment of prophecy in this passage is far from straightforward. While the validity of the republican enthusiasm represented here is ultimately disavowed in the poem, the idea of a specific prophetic insight dwelling within Wordsworth's radicalism is not cast away, but now transferred to an intimation of 'higher things'. Wordsworth's youthful enthusiasm is no bad thing in itself, one might say, but its validity depends on a work of regulation of which the French revolutionaries are not capable. Coleridge explored a parallel understanding of his own youthful 'enthusiasm' in the essays he wrote in *The Friend* after reading Wordsworth's long poem. Wordsworth's youthful revolutionary zeal is represented as the anticipation of another, more disciplined and mediated kind of prophetic insight, the kind of Apocalypse that bursts into the narration of the Simplon Pass episode from the mature present as a hymn to the Imagination.[20] Although there is much that is positive about the representation of Wordsworth's pro-revolutionary friend Michel Beaupuy, there is a structural significance to the emphasis on his early death. For Beaupuy, who is 'enthusiastic to the height / Of highest expectation' (ix. 300–1), is not able to provide a sustainable form of regulation that will preserve his sense of self from the dangers of his own enthusiasm. His feverishness is the disease that kills him rather than a symptom of it. He is almost too good for this world in the immediate strength of his enthusiasm. Wordsworth's own youthful enthusiasm, in contrast, is incorporated and transcended by the older poet.

A similarly complex strategy of desire and discipline is evident later in Book x, when Wordsworth discusses his youthful response to French military expansion:

> And now, become oppressors in their turn,
> Frenchmen had changed a war of self-defence
> For one of conquest, losing sight of all
> Which they had struggled for – and mounted up,
> Openly in the view of earth and heaven,
> The scale of liberty. I read her doom,
> Vexed inly somewhat, it is true, and sore,
> But not dismayed, nor taking to the shame
> Of a false prophet; but, roused up, I stuck
> More firmly to old tenets, and, to prove
> Their temper strained them more. And thus in heat
> Of contest, did opinions every day
> Grow into consequence, till round my mind
> They clung, as if they were the life of it.
>
> (x. 791–804)

The 'false prophet' in this passage is one who would foretell the doom of France and proclaim failure to fulfil millenarian hopes, while the true prophet holds 'firmly to old tenets'. Needless to say that at the perspective from which these events are being related, that is, from the narrator's position looking back from 1804, these old political tenets have already been discarded, but Wordsworth credits himself with a resolution to be contrasted with what Coleridge had called 'dough-baked patriots' (*L1795* 8).[21] Ultimately this resolution allows him to discover a more permanent kind of insight within his earlier political enthusiasm, Wordsworth implies, even if he discards its transient political content. The dim sense of a higher unity becomes the kernel of the experience even as, paradoxically, its political content is put aside. This discovery itself is not a sudden conversion. Other stages of apprehension form a prelude to this higher knowledge, and these too he represents in terms of a prophetic power that Wordsworth disavows in its specific political form, even as he builds it into his sense of his higher poetic enthusiasm:

> This was the time, when, all things tended fast
> To depravation; the philosophy
> That promised to abstract the hopes of man
> Out of his feelings, to be fixed thenceforth
> For ever in a purer element,
> Found ready welcome. Tempting region that
> For zeal to enter and refresh herself,
> Where passions had the privilege to work,
> And never hear the sound of their own names!
>   (x. 805–13)

Nicholas Roe has argued that these lines specifically allude to the 'tempting region' of Godwin's ideas, but prior to ascribing a particular referent to them it is worth dwelling on the language that Wordsworth uses here.[22] For he names his attraction to Godwin's ideas in terms of prophetic 'Zeal'. Implicitly, he is pouring petrol on the flames of his revolutionary enthusiasm. [. . .] Godwinianism is a species of revolutionary *transparence* that shares with religious enthusiasm a refusal to accommodate itself with what Wordsworth calls 'the familiar face of life' (xii. 67). In contrast to the 'abstract hopes' of such philosophy, the evolutionary narrative of progress that provides the larger picture of his development in *The Prelude* appears as a properly regulated use of enthusiasm. [. . .] 'Freedom of the individual mind' [X.825] for Wordsworth consists of a carefully mediated apprehension of a universal harmony roughly parallel to those glimpsed in Shaftesbury's apostrophes to Nature, yet the emphasis on the sanctity of the individual mind does recall Godwin's own anxieties about enthusiasm.

Chris Jones has pointed out that Shaftesbury often spoke of the moral sense 'in terms of the heart and affections'.[23] He might have added 'enthusiasm'. [Francis] Hutcheson's development of Shaftesbury's work, Jones goes on, located the moral sense more firmly in reflective faculties, that is, in a kind of intuitive appreciation of moral qualities brought closer to ideas of conscience in order to distance it from the pejorative associations of 'enthusiasm' with the passions of the crowd. Even so, for all Hutcheson's relative caution, the overtones of sense in the term still gave rise to suspicion that the 'moral sense' was nothing better than enthusiasm. Wordsworth struggles to distinguish his own sympathy for stocks and stones from enthusiasm precisely by stressing the mental discipline of his poetry. Jerome McGann has suggested that Wordsworth's poetics displaces the 'conversational' mode of Della Cruscanism with a 'meditative' poetics.[24] One might say Wordsworth privileges one aspect of the poetic tradition that stemmed from Shaftesbury over another. If the poetics of retirement routinely pointed back to society, as Kelvin Everest has suggested, the social in Wordsworth takes an extremely attenuated and restricted form. Shaftesbury's writing has faith in, as Michael Meehan calls it, 'patterns of untrammelled growth in the natural world, under conditions of freedom'.[25] This free play under liberty in Shaftesbury could be allowed because of a faith in nature's essential and self-righting harmony. If *The Prelude* reassures its readers of the latter, it is cautious over the extent to which the self can be put into play to discover it.

Prophecy in Wordsworth becomes a relatively unsocialized and private discourse. When he represents himself as a true prophet adhering to his 'old tenets', Wordsworth inscribes an idea of prophecy entirely different from the practice of radical prophecy in the 1790s (whether in its religious or Godwinian guise). Thus in terms of the chronology of *The Prelude*, the loyalty of the true prophet seems valued within the chronology of the past being narrated, even while its content is disavowed at the level of the narration, that is, the particular form of Wordsworth's enthusiasm in the 1790s may be disavowed, but the potential for a deeper enthusiasm, produced by disciplinary work on his youthful zeal, is affirmed. In terms of the temporality of the poem as experienced by the reader, the true prophet has already been revealed in Book vi to be the prophet of Imagination, the prophet who has been able to re-collect his transports into a developing subjectivity that is insulated from the violent sympathies of the crowd.[26] Where the latter are all too vulnerable to 'a transport of the outward sense' (xi. 187), as Book vii makes clear, 'vivid but not profound' (188), Wordsworth claims for himself an enthusiasm sanctified by the anchor 'of mind'. The discipline of 'mind' gives 'a substance and a life to what I feel' (xi. 340). 'The spirit of the past' becomes available as part of a continuity for 'future restoration' (xi. 341–2). Rather than the violent unworlding of 'extraordinary calls' Wordsworth offers a vision of 'discipline | And consummation' (xiii. 270–1).

[. . .]

Notes

1 [David G.] Riede, *Oracles and Hierophants*[*: Constructions of Romantic Authority* (Ithaca, NY: Cornell University Press, 1991)], 97, is aware of a tension between 'the poetics of prophecy' and a 'poetics of error' in Wordsworth, but his opposition still rather obscures the cultural history of anxieties surrounding the former (the phrase is originally Geoffrey Hartman's).

2 See Robert Ryan's excellent discussion of the complex attitude to the Church of England in *The Excursion: The Romantic Reformation: Religious Politics in English Literature 1789–1824* (Cambridge: Cambridge University Press, 1997), esp. 100–18.

3 [William Wordsworth, *The Prelude: The Four Texts (1798, 1799, 1805, 1850)*, ed. Jonathan Wordsworth (Harmondsworth: Penguin, 1995). Cited parenthetically in text as *Prelude*; year will follow title in italics.]

4 See Abrams, 'Constructing and Deconstructing', in Morris Eaves and Michael Fischer (eds), *Romanticism and Contemporary Criticism* (Ithaca. NY: Cornell University Press, 1986), 167.

5 See Gillian Russell, *The Theatres of War: Performance, Politics, and Society 1793–1815* (Oxford, Clarendon Press, 1995), 123. [. . .]

6 M.H. Abrams, *Natural Supernaturalism: Tradition and Revolution in Romantic Literature* (New York: W. W. Norton & Co., 1971), 113.

7 Ibid. 114.

8 [Robert Southey, *The Life of Wesley; and the Rise and Progress of Methodism*, 2 vols (London, 1820). Cited parenthetically in text as *Life of Wesley*.]

9 The parallels between Wesley and Wordsworth have been extensively documented in [Richard E.] Brantley, *Wordsworth's 'Natural Methodism'* [(New Haven: Yale University Press, 1975)], but my approach here is more focused on their anxieties about excess, and the disciplinary nature of their responses.

10 See, for example, [Clifford] Siskin, *The Work of Writing*[*: Literature and Social Change in Britain 1700–1830* (Baltimore: Johns Hopkins University Press, 1998)], and Brian Goldberg, ' "Ministry More Palpable": William Wordsworth and the Making of Romantic Professionalism', *Studies in Romanticism*, 36 (1997), 327–47.

11 See Brantley, *Wordsworth's 'Natural Methodism'*, 68–9. For a discussion of Wesley's ideas of limit and extent in relation to religious feelings and the role of reason as a mediating power, see Brantley, *Locke, Wesley, and the Method of English Romanticism* (Gainesville: University of Florida Press, 1984), 68.

12 See William H. Galperin, *The Return of the Visible in British Romanticism* (Baltimore: Johns Hopkins University Press, 1993), esp. in relation to Wordsworth, ch. 7.

13 [Anthony Ashley Cooper, Third Earl of Shaftesbury, *Characteristics of Men, Manners, Opinions, Times*, ed. Lawrence E. Klein, Cambridge Texts in the History of Philosophy (Cambridge: Cambridge University Press, 1999), 31. Cited parenthetically in text as *Characteristics.*]

14 James K. Chandler, *Wordsworth's Second Nature: A Study of the Poetry and Politics* (Chicago: University of Chicago Press, 1984), 199.

15 Elinor Shaffer, 'Secular Apocalypse: Prophets and Apocalyptics at the End of the Eighteenth Century', in Malcolm Bull (ed.), *Apocalypse Theory and the Ends of the World* (Oxford: Blackwell, 1995), 150.

16 Alan Liu, *Wordsworth: The Sense of History* (Stanford, Calif.: Stanford University Press, 1989), 13.

17 Shaffer, 'Secular Apocalypse', 150.

18 Liu, *Wordsworth*, 5.

19 See Ernst Bloch, *The Principle of Hope*, trans. Neville Plaice et al. (Oxford: Blackwell, 1986), 12.

20 Compare the fate of radical 'enthusiasm' in Coleridge's *The Friend*, written after he had read Wordsworth's poem [. . .].

21 [S.T. Coleridge, *Lectures 1795 on Politics and Religion*, eds Lewis Patton and Peter Mann, Bollingen Series (Princeton: Princeton University Press, 1971).]

22 Nicholas Roe, *Wordsworth and Coleridge: The Radical Years* (Oxford: Clarendon Press, 1988), 6–7.

23 [Chris] Jones, *Radical Sensibility*[*: Literature and Ideas in the 1790s* (New York: Routledge, 1993)], 62.

24 [Jerome] McGann, *The Poetics of Sensibility*[*: A Revolution in Literary Style* (Oxford: Clarendon Press, 1996)], 79.

25 See [Michael] Meehan, *Liberty and Poetics* [*in Eighteenth Century England* (Beckenham: Croom Helm, 1986)], 26.

26 See Roe, *Wordsworth and Coleridge*, 6–7.

31 Godwin, Wollstonecraft, and the legacies of Dissent

Daniel E. White

By the mid 1790s, the Dissenting public sphere as lived and represented by liberal Dissenters had begun to dissipate. Three years before his permanent departure in 1794 for the banks of the Susquehanna, Joseph Priestley complained that "rational Dissenters . . . are dwindling away almost everywhere,"[1] and by the middle of the decade the representative figures of Dissenting social and intellectual life, such as Priestley, Richard Price, Timothy Hollis, and Robert Robinson, had either died or emigrated.[2] Furthermore, the principal heterodox Dissenting academies throughout England had closed their doors: Hoxton folded in 1785, Warrington in 1786, Daventry in 1789, and the New College in Hackney in 1796.[3] The Dissenting public sphere thus gradually lost its focused and progressive identity, and rational Dissenters would not project such a coherent public front again until the renewed outburst of propaganda against the Corporation and Test Acts in the 1820s.[4] After 1795, a major year of mortality for prominent members of the nonconformist community,[5] liberal Dissent became increasingly retrospective: *The Protestant Dissenter's Magazine*, published monthly from January 1794 to December 1799 "with the Assistance of several Dissenting Ministers of the Three Denominations," can be read as an epitaph to the active phase of late-eighteenth-century Dissenting public life. Consisting mainly of "Biographical Memoirs" and "Ecclesiastical History," the *Magazine* memorialized Dissenting preachers, educators, and intellectuals, accompanying their "Memoirs" with engraved portraits. Compared with the Dissenting pamphlets, poems, essays, and reviews printed by liberal publishers such as Joseph Johnson and George Robinson during the first movement to repeal the Corporation and Test Acts (1787–90), *The Protestant Dissenter's Magazine* already seems more a pantheon of the dead than a testament of living apostles.

The mid to late 1790s, often understood as the so-called "English Terror," the national battle fought and won by Pitt's administration, Church and King mobs, and anti-Jacobin propagandists against the largely secular radical societies, can thus also be seen as the evening of a coherent and vigorous Dissenting public sphere. In light of this dual interpretation, this chapter examines William Godwin's career during the 1790s as it simultaneously encountered the dissolution of the rational Dissenting community and the rise of new forms of communication, those practiced by the popular political societies which came to dominate moderate to radical political life after 1792. For along with the ascendance of the London Corresponding Society (LCS) and the Society for Constitutional Information (SCI) came new kinds of publicity through which these communities realized their oppositionist identities and expressed their reformist positions, foremost among which were support for a

National Convention, annual parliaments, and universal manhood suffrage.[6] Two important developments occurred along with the shift in radical discourse between 1788 and 1792 from support for the Revolution abroad to calls for reform at home. Central to the French Revolution debate, they involved transformations both in the class and religious make-up of the radical societies and in the print medium of radical literature and propaganda.

After 1792 the source of oppositionist discourse shifted from the London Revolution Society to the LCS and SCI. When the Bastille fell in July 1789, the London Revolution Society represented the most vocal community of moderates and radicals in England. [. . .] By 1792–93, however, control of the moderate to radical movement had shifted away from the largely middle-class and Dissenting Revolution Society to the corresponding societies, chief among which was the LCS, and the SCI.[7] Founded in 1792 by Thomas Hardy, a shoemaker, the LCS built on the successful models already established by corresponding societies in Derby, Manchester, Sheffield, Norwich, and Edinburgh. These groups, unlike the Revolution Society, were largely working-class: "the great majority of the reformers organised in the societies of 1793 were artisans, wage-earners, small masters and small tradesmen."[8] Furthermore, whereas the Revolution Society represented the tempered dissidence of religious Dissent, the LCS in particular was generally a secular community, at times stridently so: when Francis Place, a tailor who joined the LCS in November 1794 and served as one of its leading members until 1797, described the religious cast of the Society in his *Autobiography*, his original draft recalled that "Nearly all the leading members were either Deists or Atheists."[9] Accordingly, in 1796–97 when Thomas Williams was prosecuted for publishing Paine's *Age of Reason*, Place settled on Stewart Kyd to oversee the defense, explaining his selection: "Mr Kyd was an infidel and a man on whom reliance could be placed."[10] Control of the moderate to radical program thus moved from a community of middle-class Dissenters to the predominantly working-class and secular societies.

Second, the shift in radical discourse between 1789 and 1792 from support for the French Revolution, the main thrust of the London Revolution Society, to calls for reform at home, the objective of the LCS and SCI, had material consequences for the dissemination of radical discourse. Although, as Hannah Barker and Simon Burrows have now shown, over the course of the Romantic period "the newspaper began to supersede the pamphlet as the dominant printed form for political discourse and the dissemination of news,"[11] during the 1790s newspapers were only beginning to rival the pamphlet as the major medium of public opinion. For a variety of reasons, other forms remained the focus of independent radical publishing. Whereas the newspapers reported and commented on public meetings and speeches, chapsheets, handbills, and, most importantly, pamphlets brought them to life by announcing, reproducing, and isolating scenes of public oratory. Both the LCS and SCI had their own printing presses, and the SCI in particular counted a good portion of the print industry among its membership; both were thus ideally positioned to produce large numbers of cheap pamphlets at short notice and to distribute them extensively through their wide networks of corresponding divisions.[12] Furthermore, although the four opposition newspapers, the *Morning Chronicle*, the *Morning Post*, the *Gazeteer*, and the *Star*, remained active throughout the decade, by 1793 the other major London dailies and weeklies were all receiving substantial subsidies from the government; readers, in fact, would have immediately understood Godwin's reference to the London papers, in his 1795 pamphlet against the Gagging Acts, as "treasury prints" (*PPW*, ii, p. 136).[13] And newspapers, as Barker and Burrows point out, "by their very nature, were a poor and unlikely medium for truly subversive materials, since they needed to maintain a fixed office and regular impression, and could be suppressed easily or intercepted in the post."[14] Cheap pamphlets thus suited the oratorical medium of radical discourse, the means of the societies, the market for radical literature and propaganda, and the contemporary circumstances of administrative influence and censorship.

In this chapter I will present Godwin's development over the 1790s as an encounter between the legacy of the Dissenting public sphere and the forms of public communication that accompanied populist and largely secular radical culture. In *Godwin's Political Justice* (1986), Mark Philp has persuasively demonstrated that Godwin's revisions of *Enquiry Concerning Political Justice* (1793), published in 1796 and 1798, represent a process of personal and intellectual transformation driven by Godwin's changing social circles and circumstances. The most exciting of Philp's claims is that we need to understand Godwin's utopianism as in a very real sense rooted in the daily life of rational Dissent: "Godwin wrote as if a republic of virtue was possible because he lived in a community which attempted to realise the basic principles of such a republic."[15] It is not my intention here to provide a detailed account of Godwin's changing social circles in the 1790s, a task already admirably undertaken by Philp. Rather, I wish to build on his central argument – that Godwin's faith in the private judgment unfettered by state coercion was "empirically grounded" (p. 173) – by examining the form of moderate to radical communication that replaced [. . .] the tempered dissidence of Dissenting discourse after the decline of rational Dissent at the outset of the decade. For it is against this form of communication that Godwin works out his own self-revisions during the 1790s, a process usually attributed to "retreatism" or "apostasy," to the early Romantic withdrawal from the political into the private, interior, and domestic.

Godwin's *Memoirs of the Author of a Vindication of the Rights of Woman* (1798) has generally been seen as the culmination of that progression by which Godwin distanced himself from the ardent rationalism of his early political philosophy. In the *Memoirs*, as Mitzi Myers has noted, Godwin represents himself and Wollstonecraft as polarities of a collaborative opposition: her intuitive boldness and his methodical skepticism correspond in productive dialectical cooperation.[16] Godwin's biographical depiction directs his readers to attribute the modification of his early self-sufficient rationalism to his brief relationship with Wollstonecraft. It is clear, however, that the moderation of Godwin's earlier position was part of a longer and far more complex reflection upon his own religious as well as literary, philosophical, political, and personal history. Critics have recently connected Godwin's more affective theories of human motivation to his growing investment in the novel, or "romance," as he comes to call it in the important essay of 1797, "Of History and Romance." Marilyn Butler and Mark Philp rightly refer to this essay as "a manifesto for the continuation of *Political Justice* by other means, most notably the novel" (*CN*, i, p. 24).[17] My intention here is to describe another context for our understanding of Godwin's intellectual and artistic development during the 1790s. Throughout the 1780s and into the 1790s Dissent had provided a language, style, and tone – a material habitus – with which to express political aspirations in keeping with Godwin's individualist theory of human motivation. In the absence of this religious language of private judgment, however, Godwin is faced in the mid 1790s with a collective political discourse that threatens both private judgment and rational conversation. Whereas Dissenting publicity assumed a universalized reading audience comprising individuals who would engage rationally and freely with public opinion concerning the common good, pamphlet culture, as Godwin rightly understood, implicitly or explicitly associated readers with particular groups and interests, with speech as opposed to writing, with publics as opposed to the public. In this respect, Godwin's career delineates a distinctive early Romantic encounter between two late-eighteenth-century definitions of the public sphere, the contentious political community of the orator and pamphleteer and the professedly tranquil, literary, and domestic one of the novelist, the author of "romance."

Godwin's self-revision in the *Memoirs*, his representation of his marital conversation with Wollstonecraft as a simultaneously cooperative yet individualist dialectic between reason and sensibility, therefore needs to be understood against both the dissolution of the Dissenting community and the contemporaneous emergence of new radical communities, with their correspondent communicative modes of collective persuasion. Such an understanding indicates that Godwin's *Memoirs*, like Wollstonecraft's writings themselves, at times exceeds the common, almost Manichean opposition between reason and sensibility that informs much literary and political discourse during the revolutionary decade. By attending to Godwin's representation of Wollstonecraft's religious character and to the place of religion in her own work, we can see that Wollstonecraft and Godwin both, in fact, arrive at a new conception of sensibility as the basis for, rather than the counterbalance to, reason. This relation produces a modified rational faculty, a kind of intuitively discriminating intelligence or "taste." In addition to embodying, as Godwin claimed in his own autobiographical notes of 1800, the influence of Hume (*CN*, i, p. 53) – to which we should add that of Rousseau, Smith, and Burke – such a conception may also be interpreted as Godwin's synthesis of Wollstonecraft's thought with his own efforts to accommodate the individuated, conversational models of Dissenting life to the changing political circumstances of the mid to late 1790s.

The legacy of Dissent I: Sandemanianism and *Political Justice*

Godwin's dogged individualism in the early 1790s was the legacy of his experience of Dissenting cultures. If Presbyterian families such as the Aikins descended or ascended, as the case may be, from Calvinism to Arminianism and Arianism over several generations, Godwin underwent this process of religious liberalization in the space of two decades. Godwin's social and religious experiences of Dissent played a substantial role in determining the grounds on which he would encounter the collective discourses of radical oratory and pamphleteering. Before addressing Godwin's Dissenting sociability, we should therefore review his religious development from Independent orthodoxy to his qualified form of atheism in the 1790s.

Godwin, son and grandson of Calvinist Dissenting ministers, experienced a different trajectory away from orthodoxy than did the Aikin family. The Godwins and the Aikins had roots in the same culture – Godwin's grandfather was a personal friend of [Philip] Doddridge, and his father, like [Anna] Barbauld's, was educated by Doddridge at Northampton. But Godwin would become less moderate before turning to heterodoxy. Under the influence of his private tutor in Norwich, Samuel Newton, an Independent minister distinguished by his Wilkite politics and Sandemanian religion, the young Godwin embraced the ultra-Calvinist sect of Particular Baptists known as Sandemanians or Glasites. This sect, originating in Scotland in the late 1720s, took its name from its founder, John Glas (1695–1773), a Presbyterian minister of the Church of Scotland. Glas' son-in-law Robert Sandeman (1718–71) came to be recognized as the leader of the sect, and the name "Sandemanian" became current in England and America. By the end of the century, the major Sandemanian societies were centered in Liverpool, London, Newcastle, Nottingham, and Whitehaven, but they seem to have been few in number, perhaps as few as twenty by the early nineteenth century.[18]

In Godwin's "Of Religion" (1818), he refers to Sandemanian beliefs and practices as "the strictest and severest forms of Christian religion" (*PPW*, VII, p. 63). If the Calvinists would damn "ninety-nine in a hundred of mankind," Godwin claimed, the Sandemanians had "contrived a scheme for damning ninety-nine in a hundred of the followers of Calvin" (*CN*, I, p. 30). For his early religious severity, in April 1773 Godwin was refused admission to the Homerton Academy in London, on suspicion of Sandemanian tendencies, and instead was placed at the Coward Academy at Hoxton under Andrew Kippis, a Socinian, and Abraham Rees. At Hoxton, under the influence of Kippis, Godwin's Calvinism softened, and by the time he assumed the position of ministerial candidate at Ware, in Hertfordshire, 1778–79, he was moving in the direction of heterodoxy: in his autobiographical notes, titled "The Principal Revolutions of Opinion" and dated 10 March 1800, Godwin writes of this period, "I rejected the doctrine of eternal damnation, and my notions respecting the trinity acquired a taint of heresy" (*CN*, I, p. 53). At Ware he also came under the influence of Joseph Fawcett, a republican minister who in addition to sermons wrote anti-war poetry and "was a declared enemy to the private and domestic affections" (*CN*, I, p. 53). In 1780 and 1781 Godwin held a ministry at Stowmarket in Suffolk, where, according to his notes, after reading d'Holbach's *Système de la Nature* he "became a Deist" (CN, I, p. 53). Following a brief stay in London, Godwin moved to Beaconsfield, Buckinghamshire, in late 1782; there he returned to the ministry and, after reading Priestley's *Institutes of Natural and Revealed Religion*, to Protestant Christianity as well: a Deist since 1781, Godwin writes, "I reverted to Christianity under the mitigated form of Socinianism" (*PPW*, VII, p. 64). After leaving Beaconsfield and the ministry in 1783, Godwin remained a heterodox Dissenter throughout the 1780s until 1788 when, as he puts it, he took his "last farewel of the Christian faith" (*CN*, I, p. 53). In his autobiographical notes of 1800 Godwin records that in 1792, under the influence of Thomas Holcroft, he became an "atheist," but these claims about Godwin's unbelief after 1788 bear further examination. Although, according to his own account, since the composition of *Political Justice* in 1792 he had been an "atheist" (*CN*, I, p. 53), in a fragment of 1795 Godwin revealed himself then to have been more of a rational Deist:

> I believe in this being, not because I have any proper or direct knowledge of his existence. But I am at a loss to account for the existence and arrangement of the visible universe . . . I perceive my understanding to be so commensurate to his nature, and all his attributes to be so much like what I know – have observed. As instantly to convert mystery into reason and contradictions into certainty.[19]

It is thus important to follow Philp in suggesting that "we have to view claims about Godwin's atheism," including his own, "with caution."[20] Above all, the question of Godwin's atheism should not obscure the role played by religious thought and experience in his political and aesthetic theory.

When Godwin looked back from 1800 on the "principal revolutions" of his opinions since 1793, he singled out his early Calvinism as the basis for his three principal "errors" in *Political Justice*:

> The Enquiry concerning Political Justice I apprehend to be blemished principally by three errors, I. Stoicism, or an inattention to the principle, that pleasure and pain are the only bases on which morality can rest. 2. Sandemanianism, or an inattention to the principle, that feeling, and not judgment, is the source of human actions. 3. The unqualified condemnation of the private affections.
> It will easily be seen how strongly these errors are connected with the Calvinist system.
>
> (*CN*, I, p. 53)

Much attention has justly been paid to Godwin's claims about his own development, but there are several compelling reasons to question his sweeping attribution of these overlapping errors to "the Calvinist system" and to consider some of Godwin's fundamental and enduring tenets in the context of his early religious austerity. Rowland Weston has recently discussed the ways in which Godwin's early "Enlightenment universalism and essentialism [were] heavily tinctured with Calvinist stoicism and immaterialism," but it remains to be explored in detail how Sandemanian doctrines in particular, as Don Locke has proposed, in fact emerged "as leading themes in the atheistical *Political Justice*."[21]

Godwin's reliance on personal censure as the means by which to persuade the private judgment, and thus to regulate morality, demands individual freedom from all institutional control. Since Glas' schism from the Church of Scotland, Sandemanians had rejected all political and secular interference in the kingdom of Christ, which for Dissenters on both sides of the Calvinist/Arminian divide was essentially spiritual. In *A New Universal History of the Religious Rites, Ceremonies, and Customs of the Whole World* (1788), William Hurd lists "The principal heads of that religion laid down by Mr. Glass [*sic*]," the first of which is that "there can be no civil establishments of religion consistent with the plan laid down in the gospel."[22] A national church thus became an imposition on the unmediated relationship between the individual conscience and God. In accord with this justification for the anti-establishmentarian position held in varying degrees by most Dissenters, Godwin's lifelong principle that any form of institutional coercion of the private judgment constituted an impediment to human progress rested on the primacy of the individual conscience. Although Godwin quickly abandoned his Calvinist upbringing, like Kippis he never relinquished his austere and anti-authoritarian emphasis on the private judgment. In a general sense, in England the Jacobin virtue of candor, of civility and open-mindedness respecting opinions with which one disagrees, was always associated with the laws of free enquiry espoused by religious Dissenters in philosophical and theological debate. Absolute candor, according to this model, could provide a form of control by which wrong would naturally defer to right in the absence of any constraint beyond reason alone. In *Political Justice*, Godwin elevates candor to the level of law itself, envisioning a future that is neither democracy nor anarchy proper but rather a kind of government by opinion in which individuals freely censure one another's conduct, leading irresistibly to right action. In place of law, and of rewards and punishments, "in governments of smaller dimensions opinion would be all sufficient; the inspection of every man over the conduct of his neighbours, when unstained with caprice, would constitute a censorship of the most irresistible nature" (*PPW*, II, p. 316). There is a sectarian spirit associated with this irresistible censorship that goes beyond the denominational openness of rational Dissent and its candid brand of free enquiry. Sandemanian churches in fact placed great emphasis on individual censure as the method of regulating behavior within the congregation. "When any one brother gives offence to another, either by word or deed," writes Robert Adam in his account of Sandemanianism in *The Religious World Displayed* (1809), "the person so offending, whatever his rank or station in civil life, is to be immediately told his fault by the brother offended, whatever may be the rank or station of the latter."[23] Having been recently chosen an elder of the Sandemanian congregation in Aldersgate, Samuel Pike relates that should a member of the fellowship misbehave, "he is to be rebuked and censured for it" individually by another member of the congregation; only if the censured congregant persists in his transgression must he then "be brought before the whole Church, and if he will not hear the Church, he must be cut off."[24] Godwin's imagined polity in *Political Justice*, we might say, seeks to transform the nation into a sect and to regulate the conduct of its citizens through the individualist practices of Sandemanian, sectarian censure.

Although Godwin rejects his early stoicism for what can be described as a theory of sympathetic benevolence, another way in which his Sandemanian legacy continues to inform the conclusions of *Political Justice* lies in the crucial link between the theory of moral duties and Godwin's redefinition of property. If we consider the first error stipulated by Godwin, stoicism, we find a typical example of the liberal progression among many Dissenters away from Calvinism and toward the less rigorous religion of heterodox Presbyterians, General Baptists, and Unitarians. In all editions of *Political Justice*, however, Godwin's important train of thought from the rejection of positive rights to the critique of private property remains rooted in the radical Calvinist tradition. Although he softens his argument in 1796 in order to moderate his radical challenge to property, Godwin persistently refuses to accept the existence of positive rights: thus in the second edition, "Few things have contributed more to undermining the energy and virtue of the human species, than the supposition that we have a right, as it has been phrased, to do what we will with our own" (*PPW*, IV, p. 80). What we think of as our right to behave as we will is "rendered null by the superior claims of justice" (*PPW*, IV, p. 82); that is, our duties to satisfy our own needs and the needs of others supersede our perceived rights to dispose of our own "property." "Strictly speaking," Godwin writes,

> We have in reality nothing that is ... our own. We have nothing that has not a destination prescribed to it by the immutable voice of reason and justice; and respecting which, if we supersede that destination, we do not entail upon ourselves a certain portion of guilt.
>
> (*PPW*, IV, p. 80)

Certainly the incorporation of sympathy and physical sensation into his account of how benevolence becomes habit could involve a Humean rejection of "Sandemanianism, or an inattention to the principle, that feeling, and not judgment, is the source of human actions." But Godwinian benevolence in combination with the theory of duties over rights, with its consequent abstract challenge to private property, still inescapably resembles the most radical component of Sandemanian practices: members of Sandemanian societies, for whom the accumulation of wealth was unscriptural and therefore unacceptable, practiced community of property, within the constraints, of course, of daily life in Liverpool or Newcastle. [. . .] Throughout the eighteenth century it is impossible to dissociate leveling theories against property rights from the radical Calvinist tradition, and enduring elements of the Godwinian notion of justice as a "voice" or a "call" remain indebted to this tradition.

[. . .]

[In three omitted sections, White shows how Godwin's view of rational communication opposed working class "Dissenting sociability," and how Godwin later shifts – partly in response to the vigorous communication embraced by this form of sociability – to a greater emphasis on regulation, politeness, and sensibility.]

Wollstonecraft and anti-sectarian nonconformity

[. . .] Godwin's account of his relationship with Wollstonecraft appears to be less of a retreat than a difficult attempt to conceive a new form of collective discourse. Marriage – or rather the collaborative relationship, unsanctioned by legal or religious institutions, between complementary elements of individual personalities – stands in the *Memoirs* not simply as a retraction of earlier quixotic ideals but as a form of society whose participants converse both as individuals and in a corporate capacity. "Ours was not an idle happiness" (*CN*, i, p. 132), writes Godwin. His narrative of their relationship does not terminate in a conventional novelistic marriage but in a joint authorial identity, a Godwinian variant of Dissenting collaboration. Godwin leaves no doubt that the climax of the *Memoirs* is not the marriage: "We did not marry . . . [C]ertainly nothing can be so ridiculous . . . or so contrary to the genuine march of sentiment, as to require the overflowing of the soul to wait upon a ceremony" (*CN*, i, p. 129). Only after Wollstonecraft becomes pregnant do they marry out of expedience, and thus the emotional climax is not their union but rather Wollstonecraft's death, which emblematizes, for Godwin, the end of "the constancy and uninterruptedness of our literary pursuits" (*CN*, i, p. 133). On "cooperation," Godwin famously wrote in *Political Justice*, "every thing that is usually understood by the term . . . is in some degree an evil" (*PPW*, iii, p. 450). Godwin's description of Wollstonecraft's anti-sectarian religious sensibility constitutes an under-explored aspect of the *Memoirs*, yet it plays a key role in his new advocacy for a cooperative relationship and his dialectical reflection upon reason and sensibility, in the tempering of his austere individualism.

In the *Memoirs*, the "rigid, and somewhat amazonian temper" of Wollstonecraft during the early 1790s gives way to that "softness almost more than human" (*CN*, i, p. 122), that "exquisite and delicious sensibility" of the "female Werter" (*CN*, i, p. 117), or later of Marguerite de Damville in *St Leon*.[25] But Godwin does more than reconstruct Wollstonecraft in terms of the very "*manie* of the day" (*WMW*, v, p. 8),[26] sensibility, against which she had written in *A Vindication of the Rights of Men*. If Godwin's frank discussion of Wollstonecraft's unorthodox sexual morality provoked outrage, the aspect of his account that drew the most ire, as Myers points out,[27] was

Wollstonecraft's lack of religion on her deathbed. By attending to Godwin's treatment of Wollstonecraft's religion and his organization of her writings, we can understand how he can privilege sensibility as the leading feature of Wollstonecraft's character and place *Letters Written during a Short Residence in Sweden, Norway, and Denmark* (1796) and *Maria, or The Wrongs of Woman* (1798) at the head of her canon yet still call his work *Memoirs of the Author of a Vindication of the Rights of Woman*.

Approaching the scene of her death, Godwin boldly if rashly wrote, "Her religion, as I have shown, was not calculated to be the torment of a sick bed; and, in fact, during her whole illness, not one word of a religious cast fell from her lips" (*CN*, I, p. 138). The religion that Godwin did show in various passages throughout the *Memoirs* suggests a perceptive understanding of how Wollstonecraft's religious thought, especially its anti-sectarianism and its emphasis on what I will call affective spontaneity, informed her own political and aesthetic theories and practices. What Myers has termed Wollstonecraft's "aesthetic of spontaneity" is primarily a religious, and specifically a nonconformist, aesthetic.[28] Underpinning Wollstonecraft's writings, however, was a form of anti-sectarianism which for her was theoretically inextricable from that same insistence on spontaneity and originality. A comparison of Godwin's representation of Wollstonecraft's religion with her own writings shows that in this respect his conception of a collaborative dialectic between reason and sensibility at the end of the decade owes much to a genuine conversation with Wollstonecraft, as opposed to a mere revision of her thought to suit the needs of his own gendered narrative.

In the *Memoirs*, Godwin carefully positions her early development simultaneously within and against the rational Dissent of Price, her friend and mentor during the mid 1780s at Newington Green:

> Mary had been bred in the principles of the church of England, but her esteem for this venerable preacher led her occasionally to attend upon his public instructions. Her religion was, in reality, little allied to any system of forms; and . . . was founded rather in taste, than in the niceties of polemical discussion.
>
> (p. 96)

Godwin's terms are clear: on the one side there are the "niceties" of rational, doctrinal debate, and on the other side there is the religion of "taste," a warm faith that needs no forms other than those of the heart, which, often in keeping with Hutcheson's "moral sense," would spontaneously feel and worship what is both divine and right. But these simple terms involve Wollstonecraft in a rich discourse in which the fundamental matters of her feminism in particular and radicalism in general were at stake. Barbara Taylor has persuasively shown that the fulcrum of Wollstonecraft's feminism was a form of faith: "Women's rights . . . are an essential prerequisite to women's redemption."[29] I would supplement this argument, that for Wollstonecraft "Only a free soul can seek and know God,"[30] by proposing that the *means* by which a free soul can seek and know God involve an insistence on extemporaneous feeling that places Wollstonecraft's religion, politics, and aesthetics within the larger field of nonconformist devotion.

The great struggle of Wollstonecraft's career was to transform sensibility from the end into the foundation of female subjectivity. [. . .] Throughout her writings, without sensation there is no "understanding to improve," and thus no possibility of redemption. Sensibility, in fact, becomes the basic mechanism implanted by God in the human heart that allows the understanding to develop. In the *Vindications*, women and the various faces of Burkean ideology are all sensation, as if the means were the end. But in both *The Rights of Woman* and her important late essay "On Poetry, and our Relish for the Beauties of Nature" (1797), Wollstonecraft's combination of affective spontaneity and anti-sectarianism leads her to articulate, and subsequently to represent for Godwin, a nuanced synthesis of the rational and intuitive faculties that exceeds the common opposition found throughout much Jacobin and anti-Jacobin discourse.

Wollstonecraft's lapsed Anglican disposition owed much both to the rational Unitarianism of Joseph Johnson's London circle and *Analytical Review* as well as to the more affective Dissenting traditions which [. . .] appealed to a range of moderate, heterodox nonconformists. But if her devotional taste was akin to that of moderate Dissenters, her anti-sectarianism combined with her feminism to distance her from, and provoke her critiques of, nonconformist communities and practices. Understanding this aspect of her thought, Godwin stresses the personal nature of her faith, insisting that "her religion was almost entirely of her own creation," that "The tenets of her system were the growth of her own moral taste" (*CN*, I, p. 96). Tilottama Rajan is right to propose that Godwin "de-anglicizes Wollstonecraft by stressing sensibility rather than propriety,"[31] but at the same time his account distances her from organized Dissent by insisting that her personal religion took the place of adherence to the practices of any particular sect: "no person . . . [who] is not the zealous partizan of a sect, can bring himself to conform to the . . . regular routine of sermons and prayers" (*CN*, I, p. 96).

Behind Godwin's descriptions is the truth that for Wollstonecraft rational Dissent, like the Church, was limited by its lack of affective spontaneity, a lack she finds conspicuous in so-called women of sensibility as well. It is a too seldom observed fact that the *Rights of Woman* ends with a comparison of "the Dissenting and female world" (*WMW*, v, p. 266):

> From the tyranny of man . . . the greater number of female follies proceed; and the cunning, which . . . makes at present a part of their character . . . is produced by oppression.
>   Were not dissenters, for instance, a class of people . . . characterized by cunning? And may I not lay some stress on this fact to prove, that when any power but reason curbs the free spirit of man, dissimulation is practised, and the various shifts of art are naturally called forth?
>
> (*WMW*, v, p. 265)

"Cunning," "dissimulation," and the "shifts of art" are precisely the modes of expression that disguise affectation as originality, premeditated display as spontaneity, and self-interest as genuine, "rational" sensibility. Just as a preacher should "habitually feel" the matter of the sermon, as Robert Robinson urged, before delivering it spontaneously yet rationally from the heart, so human beings should express devotional feelings without regard to any of the various manifestations of prejudice or patriotism, for nation, family, or sect. The key to Wollstonecraft's mix of religious nonconformity and political radicalism, I think, is this anti-sectarianism: for Wollstonecraft the identification with a sect, like the identification with a family or a nation, is a form of prejudice, unless the sect, family (read "father"), or nation ("King") has earned the love of its members or subjects, as God should be respected because he has earned the love of his creations, not because he is omnipotent. Thus the comparison between women and Dissenters continues: "I know how many ornaments to human nature have been enrolled amongst sectaries; yet, I assert, that the same narrow prejudice for their sect, which women have for their families, prevailed in the Dissenting part of the community" (*WMW*, v, p. 266). The prejudice of women for family and Dissenters for sect stifles the "rational" course of feeling for what is just.

[. . .]

In the *Memoirs*, writes Myers, "Wollstonecraft is treated both as personality and as principle, at once individual woman and symbol of cultural values, even of an alternate cognitive mode," and the narrative is "a marital idyll of complementary reciprocity, mutual interdependence."[32] I wish to stress along with Philp, however, that Godwin's "conversion" to the "new man of feeling" is not a sudden occurrence of 1798–99 rooted in his reflections on the personality and principle of Wollstonecraft.[33] Godwin's "marital idyll," accordingly, should be seen as a moment of clarity within a complex process of political and artistic development, one foundation of which I am placing in the scenes of conversation Godwin scripted for himself and others sympathetic to the cause of reform. Godwin and Wollstonecraft together represent a form of social and intellectual collaboration the polite literary productions of which would engage numerous individuals emotionally and rationally, would communicate to large communities the dynamism of reform along with the ballast of temperate reflection. Although a conjugal conversation, Godwin's representation of himself and Wollstonecraft in the *Memoirs* leaves us with more than a simple gendered opposition between reason and emotion; for both characters, sensibility has to become the individual ground or basis of rational thought. In the narrative, Wollstonecraft's spontaneous and affective yet anti-sectarian religion allows her to achieve this position on her own, and it is conversation with such an individual that renovates the character of Godwin, a renovation we have already seen commencing in the writings of the author Godwin, in his returns to the religious rhetoric of Dissenting conversation and to the sensibility of his nonconformist sermons.

Notes

1 Quoted in [Michael R.] Watts, *The Dissenters[: From the Reformation to the French Revolution*, vol. 1 (Oxford: Clarendon Press, 1978)], p. 487.
2 Robinson died in 1790, Price and Hollis in 1791. Priestley went into permanent exile on 7 April 1794, settling in Northumberland, Pennsylvania.
3 Mark Philp, *Godwin's Political Justice* (London: Duckworth, 1986), p. 162.
4 From January to December 1828, the year in which the Acts were finally repealed, *The Test-Act Reporter* was issued monthly.
5 1795 saw the deaths of Samuel Stennett, Andrew Kippis, Rice Harris, Benjamin Beddome, Samuel Clark, Thomas Toller, Roger Flexman, Henry Beaufoy, and Josiah Wedgwood. Sr. James Fordyce, Thomas Christie, and Stephen Addington followed in 1796.
6 On the radical societies, see [E.P.] Thompson, *The Making [of the English Working Class* (New York: Pantheon Books, 1963)], pp. 17–185, and Albert Goodwin, *The Friends of Liberty: The English Democratic Movement in the Age of the French Revolution* (Cambridge: Harvard University Press, 1979). See also Carl B. Cone, *The English Jacobins: Reformers in Late 18th Century England* (New York: Charles Scribner's Sons, 1968), pp. 187–209; Iain McCalman, *Radical Underworld: Prophets, Revolutionaries and Pornographers in London, 1795–1840* (Cambridge University Press, 1988), pp. 8–14, 114–15; and David Worrall,

Radical Culture: Discourse, Resistance and Surveillance, 1790–1820 (Detroit: Wayne State University Press, 1992), pp. 19–38.

7 Although the SCI was founded in 1780, it was reinvigorated in 1792 with the formation of the LCS, the participation of Thomas Holcroft, who joined in November 1792, and the Scottish Reform Convention of late 1793.

8 Thompson, *The Making*, p. 122.

9 Place, *The Autobiography of Francis Place (1771–1854)*, ed. Mary Thale (Cambridge University Press, 1972), p. 197n. Place joined the LCS at the request of his landlord, a cabinet maker (p. 129).

10 Ibid., p. 162. Although it is generally wise to treat Place's *Autobiography* with reserve as "in part a personal *apologia*, in which the 'sober thinking men' (i.e. Francis Place) are elevated, and the less temperate denigrated" (Thompson, *The Making*, p. 134n), there are instances such as this when Place seems reliable: his discussion of infidelity in the LCS does not further his often revisionary project.

11 Hannah Barker and Simon Burrows, "Introduction," in *Press, Politics and the Public Sphere in Europe and North America, 1760–1820*, ed. Barker and Burrows (Cambridge University Press, 2002), p. 4.

12 Lucyle Werkmeister, *A Newspaper History of England 1792–1793* (Lincoln: University of Nebraska Press, 1967), pp. 21–2, and Richard D. Altick, *The English Common Reader: A Social History of the Mass Reading Public 1800–1900* (University of Chicago Press, 1957), pp. 69–72.

13 [William Godwin, *Political and Philosophical Writings of William Godwin*, gen. ed. Mark Philp, 7 vols (London: William Pickering, 1993), cited parenthetically in the text as *PPW*.] Barker and Burrows, *Press, Politics and the Public Sphere*, provide the apt phrase "contingent autonomy" (p. 14) to describe the typical relationship of newspapers to state power.

14 Ibid., p. 8.

15 Philp, *Godwin's Political Justice*, p. 216. Philp's thesis is anticipated by M. Fitzpatrick, "William Godwin and the Rational Dissenters," *Price-Priestley Newsletter* 3 (1979): 17 [. . .].

16 Myers, "Godwin's Memoirs of Wollstonecraft: The Shaping of Self and Subject," *Studies in Romanticism* 20.3 (1981): 299–316.

17 [William Godwin, *The Collected Novels and Memoirs of William Godwin*, gen. ed. Mark Philp, 8 vols (London: William Pickering, 1992), cited parenthetically in the text as *CN*.] "Of History and Romance" was first published as an appendix to *Caleb Williams*, ed. Maurice Hindle (London: Penguin, 1988). See Evan Radcliffe, "Godwin from 'Metaphysician' to Novelist: *Political Justice, Caleb Williams*, and the Tension between Philosophical Argument and Narrative," *Modern Philology* 97.4 (2000): 528–53.

18 See [David] Bogue and [James] Bennett, *History of Dissenters*, [*from the Revolution in 1688, to the Year 1808*, 4 vols (London, 1808–12),] IV, pp. 327–8. On another Sandemanian, the ultra-radical Thomas Spence, see Thompson, *The Making*, p. 36, and below.

19 Quoted in Philp, *Godwin's Political Justice*, p. 161.

20 Ibid.

21 Rowland Weston, "Politics, Passion and the 'Puritan Temper': Godwin's Critique of Enlightenment Modernity," *Studies in Romanticism* 41.3 (2002): 446. Don Locke, *A Fantasy of Reason: The Life and Thought of William Godwin* (London: Routledge, 1980), p. 17.

22 William Hurd, *A New Universal History of the Religious Rites, Ceremonies, and Customs of the Whole World* (London, [1788]), p. 571.

23 Robert Adam, *The Religious World Displayed; or, A View of the Four Grand Systems of Religion, Judaism, Paganism, Christianity, and Mohammedism; and of the Various Existing Denominations, Sects and Parties, in the Christian World*, 3 vols (Edinburgh, 1809), III, p. 183.

24 Samuel Pike, *A Plain and Full Account of the Christian Practices Observed by the Church in St. Martin's-le-grand, London* (London, 1766), p. 21.

25 On Marguerite de Damville in *St. Leon*, in the context of Godwin's memorialization of Wollstonecraft in the *Memoirs* "as the Revolutionary Feminist in domestic as well as public life," see Gary Kelly, *Revolutionary Feminism: The Mind and Career of Mary Wollstonecraft* (New York: St. Martin's Press, 1992), p. 224.

26 [Mary Wollstonecraft, *The Works of Mary Wollstonecraft*, gen. ed. Janet Todd and Marilyn Butler, 7 vols (London: William Pickering, 1989), cited parenthetically in text as *WMW*.]

27 Myers, "Godwin's Memoirs," p. 314.

28 Myers, "Sensibility and the 'Walk of Reason': Mary Wollstonecraft's Literary Reviews as Cultural Critique," in *Sensibility in Transformation: Creative Resistance to Sentiment from the Augustans to the Romantics*, ed. Syndy McMillen Conger (Rutherford: Fairleigh Dickinson University Press, 1990), p. 123.
29 Taylor, "For the Love of God[: Religion and the Erotic Imagination in Wollstonecraft's Feminism," in *Mary Wollstonecraft and 200 Years of Feminisms*, ed. Eileen James Yeo (London: Rivers Oram Press, 1997)], p. 24.
30 Ibid.
31 Tilottama Rajan, "Framing the Corpus: Godwin's 'Editing' of Wollstonecraft in 1798," *Studies in Romanticism* 39.4 (2000): 514.
32 Myers, "Godwin's Memoirs," pp. 300, 316.
33 Philp, *Godwin's Political Justice*, p. 217.

32 The entangled spirituality of "The Thorn"

Colin Jager

The association of romanticism with religion, or at any rate with a religious impulse, goes back a long way. In the early part of the twentieth century, T.E. Hulme pronounced romanticism "spilt religion" and Irving Babbitt denounced it as "sham spirituality" (Gleckner and Enscoe 1962: 58, 31). By the 1960s, Earl Wasserman was finding in romanticism a "new poetic syntax" suitable to a post-metaphysical age, and M.H. Abrams saw it as a "secularization of inherited theological ideas and ways of thinking." They did not mean that religion was disappearing during the early nineteenth century but that it was being transformed, "assimilate[ed]" into a "world view founded on secular premises," as Abrams explained.

The deconstructive and historicist scholarship of the 1970s and 1980s tended to position secularization as incomplete, and romanticism as a quasi-religious mystification of secular modernity rather than its formal realization. In the 1990s a new round of historicizing studies restored to romanticism a richer and more diversified religious landscape (Roe 1997; Ryan 1997; Priestman 1999). These studies, however, tended to assume that "religion" itself was a stable object. Scholars from other disciplines were meanwhile questioning that very premise, turning their attention to the historical and discursive constructions of both "religion" and "secularism" (Harrison 1990; Asad 1993; Masuzawa 2005). Those scholars reminded us that religion was not some "thing" in the world but rather a mobile discourse that answered particular needs at particular historical moments; that for Europe the crucial moment was an early modern crisis of authority within Christianity, and that around this time a newer, more cognitive definition of religion as belief rose to prominence. And they argued that secularization could not be understood as a simple subtraction story, as though the modern secular self was always there, waiting to be liberated from false beliefs (Taylor 2007); that secularism was not a neutral governance structure but had its own interests, authorizing certain kinds of subjects and marginalizing others (Asad 2003); and that the apparently natural distinction between the religious and the secular was not natural at all but the product of a particular and contingent history (Warner et al. 2010).

These lessons have by now been variously absorbed by scholars working on romanticism and the long eighteenth century (Canuel 2002; Mee 2003; Jager 2007; Cragwall 2013). Indeed, contemporary scholarship directed at the confluence of what used to be called "religion and literature" finds itself in a state of productive disequilibrium, since neither term seems to exist in the stable way that makes investigation easy. The present essay uses Wordsworth's poem "The Thorn," first published in the *Lyrical Ballads* in 1798, as a way to address the shifting boundaries of "religion" and "literature." Wordsworth's poem offers not only an astute meditation on those categories but an alternative approach to them, one closer to archeology than to the usual historical and anthropological investigations.

Historicist questions

"The Thorn" tells the story of Martha Ray, who was jilted at the altar by the lover whose child she was carrying. She goes mad, or partly mad. For the past twenty or more years, she has spent most of her days sitting in a certain place up in the hills and crying, over and over, "Oh misery! Oh misery! / Oh woe is me! Oh misery" (Wordsworth 1992: 79; l. 65–66). A thorn bush, a little hill of moss, and a small pool of water mark the place where she sits. This place has achieved legendary status within the nearby town; no one will go there, but the townspeople are happy to sit around and speculate endlessly about her. These facts are conveyed through a lengthy conversation, probably in a public house, between two men. The narrator has lived in the small rural village for many years, but he is not a native of the place. He turns the various tales he has heard into a roughly coherent narrative, which he retails to an out-of-town visitor. This second man, like a reader passing through on his way to somewhere else, listens to the story and wonders what it all means. He asks the kind of questions a reader typically wants answered:

> "But what's the thorn? and what's the pond?
> "And what's the hill of moss to her?
> "And what's the creeping breeze that comes
> "The little pond to stir?"
>
> (l. 210–213)

Maddeningly, this information is not forthcoming. The hill of moss may be "like an infant's grave in size" (l. 61), yet "if a child was born or no, / There's no one that could ever tell" (l. 159–169). All that the narrator can offer is what people say: that Martha hanged the baby on the tree, or perhaps drowned it in the pond. Or neither. The only fact on which everybody agrees is that Martha sits beside the thorn, weeping and wearing a scarlet cloak. Beyond that, it is all hints and innuendo.

The poem thus distinguishes among three kinds of knowledge. There is the *historical* knowledge of what happened to Martha Ray. There is the *symbolic* knowledge of what the objects and her actions *mean*. And there is the *historicist* knowledge of the habits of mind of the townsfolk, revealed in their endless and mean-spirited discussions of Martha Ray. The poem insists that only knowledge of this last kind is finally possible. Historical knowledge is sketchy at best. Symbolic knowledge is invited but then frustrated: the thorn and the hill of moss and the little pond must mean *something*, but we do not know what. We can, however, learn quite a bit about the townspeople who eagerly retail Martha Ray's story: not just that they are bored, petty, and prejudiced, but also that they perform certain collective rituals, speak in a particular way, and possess a set of folk beliefs that mark them as distinct from their neighbors.

Wordsworth's poem asks the same question that many of Europe's most advanced thinkers had been asking for the past century: in what sense could the various texts collected as the Old and New Testaments be said to be true? For most of its career the Bible had been understood as a repository of divine revelation and an authoritative canon belonging to the Church. In the sixteenth century, however, that same Bible became a site of interpretive and political battles. A fractured post-Reformation church and multiple Bibles meant that there was no longer a central meaning-governing authority: translators introduced subtle differences among versions of the Bible, and increased literacy meant that people began to rely on their own ideas when it came to interpreting Scripture. Textual studies made the Scriptures objects of worldly discussion, and thus a part of the process of disembedding that contributed to a secular phenomenology. By the end of the seventeenth century, the controversial scholarly work of Baruch Spinoza in Holland and Richard Simon in France suggested that the Bible was anything but stable: the original texts had been lost and copyist's errors introduced; there was an obvious time-lag between an event and its written account; in the case of the Old Testament, even the pronunciation of Hebrew itself was uncertain (Harrison 1990; Olender 2002; Legaspi 2010).

In what manner, then, could Scriptural texts still speak across time and offer the kind of eternally relevant instruction they had always offered? One possible answer emerged in the eighteenth century, and it is still with us today. The idea was to read the Bible as a storehouse of culture and of a literary heritage that could hold together a social world (Sheehan 2005). Reading the Bible like this – whether as a repository of poetic resources, an example of what it means to be "inspired," or in the now-familiar manner of University courses in "the Bible as literature" – was an important innovation of the eighteenth century and a balm for the literally dis-spiriting effects of enlightened skepticism and political dispute.

What would a "literary" reading of the Bible tell us? The answer to this question is a complicated one, traversing much of Europe (particularly England, Germany, and Holland) and subject to the kind of intellectual gamesmanship and political intrigue that can take a lifetime to trace. But there are three points worth stressing.

First, in influential writers like Robert Lowth (1710–1787) and Johann Gottfried Herder (1744–1803) we see a shift of emphasis, which sets aside the inspired character of the Old Testament in favor of an analysis of what Lowth called its "machinery" (Lowth 1787: 46). Others had appreciated the literary power of the Scriptures, of course, but none had tried to explain the principles by which that power operated. This is not necessarily to deny its divine inspiration, but because divine inspiration was now analytically separable from poetic genius, it must henceforth be conceived as something other than a typological prefiguration of the Christ event. One might even remain agnostic about the question of divine inspiration and still revere the Bible for its poetry. A way of appreciating the Bible "as literature" had suddenly appeared.

Second, a widespread interest in oral culture emerges during this period. This is in part a reaction to the print revolution that characterized renaissance humanism and that helped to foment a variety of religious conflicts. It is also a reaction to the print saturation of the eighteenth century. The ballad revival (in which *Lyrical Ballads* participates, albeit reluctantly) is the most well-studied literary version of this shift: ballads facilitated the idea of a culturally authentic past accessible through poetry and song. They also modeled the recovery of Scriptural truth in the aftermath of Enlightenment, helping to shore up the authority testimony in the face of skeptical critique by substituting historicism for history: truth now resides in what we can learn about the habits, patterns, and beliefs of earlier folk cultures, as expressed by their most impassioned poets. This may be a loss for theology, but it is a gain for anthropology.

Third, the increasingly literary or autonomous quality of Scriptural language creates a problem of historical distance. Lowth himself had conceded that no contemporary scholars really understood Hebrew grammar or meter, nor did eighteenth-century readers know how the words ought to sound. And even if contemporary readers had a sense of the living language, the Hebrews themselves were radically different: "the manner of living, of speaking, of thinking, which prevailed in those times, will be found altogether different from our customs and habits" (Lowth 1787: 113). The literary or "poetic" reading of the Bible developed as a way of bridging this otherwise enormous gap. In *The Spirit of Hebrew Poetry* (1782), Herder argued that Eastern languages opened up to view "the childhood and youth of the human race" (Herder 1833: 21). These languages were closer to the senses, more concrete, sensuous, and image-laden than modern languages. Their poetic resources were therefore greater. Here the "spirit" of Hebrew poetry plays its most decisive role for the historian. Eighteenth-century protestants could, by a kind of literary magic, become Hebrews for a time, feeling the force of their language, and of the poetic spirit that animated them from within. Thus two hallmarks of the Romantic era emerge together: a method of literary reading that celebrates language for its own sake, and a dizzying awareness of historical time. The pastness of the past and the present power of language are mutually constitutive, both inflicting and healing the wounds that characterize the secular age.

Seekers

The astonishing variety of spiritual practices across the contemporary landscape suggests that these early romantic innovations are still very much with us. Modern life, thoroughly disenchanted in some respects, seems thoroughly enchanted in others: witness not simply the rise of "strong religion" but the continuing salience and proliferation of new spiritualities: neo-pagans, transcendentalists, wiccans, meditators, druids, UFO enthusiasts, shamanic drummers, astrologers, and people variously committed to beliefs and practices that seem a little crazy – in short, an entire landscape of citizens who are "spiritual but not religious" (Nelson 2001; Taylor 2007; Saler 2009; Hollywood 2010).

In her ethnographic account of those she terms the "new metaphysicals" (new age practitioners who reside in and around Cambridge, Massachusetts), the sociologist Courtney Bender resists the impulse to see her subjects as Herderian seekers, adrift on a post-metaphysical sea and in search of authentic expressivity. She argues instead that they are best understood as embodied agents, fitfully and unsystematically aware of how their routines draw them into larger collectives. Bender emphasizes embodied practice and institutional location as themselves a kind of religious experience. "Cambridge's spiritual practitioners lived in worlds of experience shaped . . . by their ongoing, daily engagement with various interpretive and bodily practices" rather than by an expressivist distinction between a spiritual "experience" and its historical, discursive account (Bender 2010: 57). Her new metaphysicals walk the streets of Cambridge and live among the ghosts of Emerson and James, but that tells us less about them than their current habits, meetings, friendships, and webs of connection. Contemporary spirituality, she insists, is not free-floating but almost always institutionally articulated.

In this respect Bender's depiction of spiritual seekers offers a significant provocation to the historicist tradition that I have been tracing here. Historicism learned from Herder that, though matters of fact may be buried under layers of tradition, those traditions themselves could tell the critic a great deal about the cultures in which they arose. Bender's claim is that this shift from the truth of an event to the truth of its attendant discourses (a truth carried, now, in what Herder called the "spirit" of its language) serves to protect the psychological uniqueness of religious experiences: it assumes that once religion becomes the object of discussion, secularization is at hand, and the only way to preserve it is to protect its essence in the form of spirit. In the form of spiritual authenticity – what Charles Taylor (2007) calls "fullness" and romanticists used to call the "spirit of the age" – it liberates experience from institutional articulation and control, making the religious impulse immune to rational analysis. By contrast, Bender argues that institutionally inflected self-narration is part of the practice of contemporary spirituality – the site of its production, rather than the place from which to critically examine it or to uncritically consume it. The word that Bender chooses to describe this phenomenon is of interest to any reader of "The Thorn." She calls it "entangled."

Entanglement

To recap: "The Thorn" presents a spiritual landscape in which there are several options, ranging from skepticism to cruelty to credulity, and in which there is really no way of establishing which one might be empirically correct. At this point the easiest response – much easier than going to the spot itself – is to remain in the pub and ask different questions. First, the expressivist question: what does the site mean to Martha Ray (as though she were a contemporary spiritual seeker)? And second, what does the fact that nobody knows the answer to this question tell us about the particular folk among which we find ourselves? These questions provide an opening for academic theorizing, and yet by encouraging sympathetic understanding they also protect the legitimacy of various spiritual experiences from awkward questions. As the narrator keeps reminding us, "some say" this, and "some say" that. That historicist move (and its correlatives: expressive reading and cultural relativism) has dominated both discussions of contemporary spirituality and such academic disciplines as literary studies, anthropology, and religious studies. Though designed to preserve a sacred history, this might be described as a secular strategy.

One alternative, which I have developed from Bender's work on spiritual seekers, is to assume from the outset that spiritual experiences are not analytically separable from their locations but are in fact entangled in them. I want to suggest now that Wordsworth, like Bender, calls our attention to a kind of spirituality that resides not in minds but that adheres rather to practices, to words, and to things.

We might start with the title of the poem itself. It is named "The Thorn," not "Martha Ray," and its first line ("There is a thorn") suggests that Wordsworth's real interest is not Martha Ray, nor her story, nor the gossipy townsfolk, nor even the process by which stories and tales become attached to places (his avowed interest in other poems of this period). Rather, Wordsworth seems interested here in the things themselves: a small pond, a hill of moss, a thornbush – and a woman who has been rendered thing-like by the very physicality of her words and her bodily reaction to them. If we are to gain any insight into this remarkable behavior, we need a different kind of investigation, hinted at when the narrator closes by wishing that the visitor would stop asking questions and simply go to the spot himself.

One can recast this wish in an ethical register. To focus on the social life of things is to think about them in terms of what they do for us; things become backdrops that "make a specific form of human society possible" (Hodder 2011: 2). Certainly the thornbush makes the gossipy chit-chat of village sociality possible. But by focusing on that, interpretation simply repeats the villager's cruelty to Martha Ray herself. The only way out of this hermeneutic circle is a counterintuitive one: to think not about Martha Ray and what may or may not have happened to her, or how she feels about it, but focus instead on the site where she sits and the things that are there.

Going to the spot, rather than speculating from a distance, is something that archeologists do. Noting the early Wordsworth's interest in stones and his "attention to measurements, locations, and positions," Charles Rzepka has called Wordsworth our "first archeological poet" (Rzepka 2003: 19, 6). Certainly the narrator of "The Thorn," with his attention to detail and penchant for measurement ("I've measured it from side to side / 'Tis three feet long and two feet wide" [l. 32–33]), treats the site where Martha sits in a forensic fashion. Rzepka is correct, I think, to stress how opaque the evidence is; like early archeological excavations near Stonehenge, the site where Martha sits offers "little more than . . . a handful of measurements" (Rzepka 2003: 20). This archeological sensibility, he suggests, rests at the juncture where things "threaten [. . .] to escape altogether into the irrecoverable silence of prehistory" (Rzepka 2003: 14). Archeology, that is to say, is the other option for knowledge after oral and written testimony breaks down. Rather than increasingly elaborate efforts to save testimony by historicizing it, archeology turns to the things themselves.

Rzepka proposes that this kind of history is secular, for it arises in the aftermath of testimonial breakdown. Archeology replaces sacred theories of the earth with secular evidence of its age. But if we take the notion of entanglement seriously, then this kind of stadial history, in which one form replaces another, does not hold up. The archeologist Ian Hodder, for example, argues that human–thing entanglement replaces traditional models of development with a more nuanced sense of how people and things become mutually dependent upon one another. As early humans became more entangled with the materials of their world, they came to see how the world could be changed; by objectifying the world, they became more, not less, invested in it. The domestication of grains is a good example of such mutual entanglement: as certain grains were selected and cultivated, humans gained higher yields, greater convenience, and a more predictable food cycle. But the grains, too, gained much: humans now, in effect, worked for them, cultivating, weeding, and caring for them. Things, Hodder writes, draw us into "various forms of care" (Hodder 2011: 162).

Methodologically, the claim that more material entanglement leads to more objectification, which leads in turn to faster change, acknowledges the material basis of human culture, but in a non-reductive fashion (Hodder 2006: 258). To be sure, such objectification might be seen as evidence of secularization. Marcel Gauchet has argued, for example, that human agency works against the sense of dependence upon external power that is the essence of religion (Gauchet 1997). But that is to assume that the material world gains nothing from human investment in it. In fact, in preindustrial societies the world of things gains a great deal from people; as humans entangle themselves with the material world, the material world entangles itself with humans.

Human–thing entanglement thus suggests a model for religious–secular entanglement. The kind of human agency enabled by entanglement with things can be understood not as a secularizing move (e.g., the transcending of primitive dependence upon higher powers) but rather as a new development within religion. Indeed, entanglement takes us back to the dual etymology of religion itself: to be bound to something (*religare*) and to read over something (*relegere*). We are conditioned by the world, but we also want to transform and renew our relation to it; this is not an escape from the world as it is, nor a secular mastery of it; but rather a tending to the entangled boundaries where the world as it is and the world as it might be intersect. This, at any rate, is the possibility entertained by "The Thorn," which clearly engages such boundary-questions: justice, life, death, what we owe to the living and to the dead. The fact that the villagers manifestly fail to consider these issues suggests that for all their talk they have missed the actual spiritual potential of the events unfolding around them, for that potential includes the capacity not just to feel the force of someone's words but to do something about them. "Humans," writes Hodder, "came to see themselves more clearly as agents able to transform social lives by transforming material objects, artifacts, monuments and environments" (Hodder 2006: 205). By these lights, the community in "The Thorn" is not entangled enough: nothing changes in their social world; they are stuck in the "childhood of the human race" where Herder had placed the Hebrew poets.

But if the community in the valley is not sufficiently entangled, the same cannot be said of the high place where Martha Ray sits. This archeological "site" is entangled with other things: the fog that often rolls in, the path located nearby, the ocean in the distance, the "mossy network" (l. 40) of the small hill, and especially the earth toward which the moss seems determined to drag the thorn "[w]ith plain and manifest intent" (l. 19). The thornbush itself is "a mass of knotted joints" (l. 8), overgrown with lichens and "hung with heavy tufts of moss" that "clasp it round" (l. 14, 17). In contrast to such binding activity, the beautiful hill of moss betrays a hint, or more than a hint, of human care: "As if by hand of lady fair / The work had woven been" (l. 41–42). The gossipy implication may be that Martha cares for this hill of moss because it is actually the grave of her dead child, but that historical conjecture is less relevant than the fact of the entangled relation itself, which holds out the possibility that Martha, or some other human, has been re-working and transforming this material thing, transforming herself and the material world by entangling herself ever more fully within it.

Conclusion

"The Thorn" is an allegory of the uncertainties that attend historical comprehension. Somewhere back in the mists of time is the empirical truth of what happened to Martha Ray. Yet over the years, accumulated oral traditions, tales, legends, and gossip have obscured the facts of the matter. All the poem seems able to do is offer up Martha's responsive body, woeful and weeping, its linguistic marker ("Oh misery! Oh misery!") resonating with greater power as the poem proceeds. As others have noted, it was from Lowth that Wordsworth learned how words gain in force each time they repeat (Prickett 1986: 50, 84; Russell 2005). But when he takes up Lowth's idea of the importance of such "parallelism" for the Biblical writers, Wordsworth focuses less on "spiritual" matters than on the way repetition helps words achieve a kind of physical presence in the world. Repetition, he writes, reveals "the interest which the mind attaches to words not only as symbols of the passion, but as *things*, active and efficient, which are themselves part of the passion" (Wordsworth 1992: 351). Words no longer just point to things; they achieve a kind of resonance that makes them seem to be things themselves.

In this poem, then, words may be things. But things are also things. The current interdisciplinary interest in things (Brown 2001; Latour 2005) is part of a widespread movement in the humanities toward what Bruno Latour (2004) has labeled "matters of concern." As Latour describes it, matters of concern arise in the aftermath of critique, when positivist "matters of fact" have been demolished but we are eager for some solid footing again. How does one live in the aftermath of critique? Or, to bring the question closer to the topic of this essay: How does one live with the knowledge that the Bible is a collection of texts written at different times and by unnamed and untraceable actors, and that its factual truth is no longer a matter that can be taken for granted? This is an Enlightenment problem, and the Enlightenment generated its own answer: together with Lowth and Herder and today's spiritual seekers, we have traced the contours of that answer here. We can call it, for the sake of convenience, "Romanticism."

But it seems to me that the entangled spirituality of "The Thorn" is shadowing forth not Romanticism but something else, perhaps something like what Latour has in mind when he calls for "a multifarious inquiry . . . to detect *how many participants are gathered in a *thing* to make it exist and to maintain its existence*" (Latour 2004: 246). In the case of "The Thorn," we can begin to name those participants: villagers, measuring stick, pathway; Martha Ray, madness, misery; thornbush, moss, scarlet cloak; earth, water, weather. Together, and without perhaps really knowing it, they bind themselves to the thing; in caring for it, they become it, and so transform it.

Works cited

Asad, T., (1993) *Genealogies of Religion: Discipline and Reasons of Power in Christianity and Islam*, Baltimore, MD: The Johns Hopkins University Press.

Asad, T., (2003) *Formations of the Secular: Christianity, Islam, Modernity*, 1st ed., Stanford, CA: Stanford University Press.

Bender, C., (2010) *The New Metaphysics: Spirituality and the American Religious Imagination*, Chicago and London: University of Chicago Press.

Brown, B., (2001) "Thing Theory," *Critical Inquiry*, 28(1): 1–22.

Canuel, M., (2002) *Religion, Toleration, and British Writing, 1790–1830*, Cambridge: Cambridge University Press.

Cragwall, J., (2013) *Lake Methodism: Polite Literature and Popular Religion in England, 1780–1830*, Columbus, OH: Ohio State University Press.

Gauchet, M., (1997) *The Disenchantment of the World: A Political History of Religion*, Princeton, NJ: Princeton University Press.

Gleckner, R., and Enscoe, G., eds, (1962) *Romanticism: Points of View*, Englewood Cliffs, NJ: Prentice-Hall.

Harrison, P., (1990) *"Religion" and the Religions in the English Enlightenment*, Cambridge: Cambridge University Press.

Herder, J., (1833) *The Spirit of Hebrew Poetry*, Burlington, VT: Edward Smith.

Hodder, I., (2006) *The Leopard's Tale: Revealing the Mysteries of Catalhoyuk*, London: Thames & Hudson.

Hodder, I., (2011) "Human-Thing Entanglement: Towards an Integrated Archeological Perspective," *Journal of the Royal Anthropological Institute*, 17: 154–177.

Hollywood, A., (2010) "Spiritual but Not Religious," *Harvard Divinity Bulletin*, 38 (1&2): 19–23.

Jager, C., (2007) *The Book of God: Secularization and Design in the Romantic Era*, Philadelphia, PA: University of Pennsylvania Press.

Latour, B., (2004) "Why Has Critique Run out of Steam? From Matters of Fact to Matters of Concern," *Critical Inquiry*, 30: 225–248.

Latour, B., (2005) *Reassembling the Social: An Introduction to Actor-Network Theory*, Oxford: Oxford University Press.

Legaspi, M.C., (2010) *The Death of Scripture and the Rise of Biblical Studies*, New York: Oxford University Press.

Lowth, R., (1787) *Lectures on the Sacred Poetry of the Hebrews; translated from the Latin of the Right Rev. Robert Lowth, D.D. Late Praelector of Poetry in the University of Oxford*, trans. G. Gregory, London: Printed for J. Johnson.

Masuzawa, T., (2005) *The Invention of World Religions: Or, How European Universalism Was Preserved in the Language of Pluralism*, Chicago: University of Chicago Press.

Mee, J., (2003) *Romanticism, Enthusiasm, and Regulation: Poetics and the Policing of Culture in the Romantic Period*, Oxford: Oxford University Press.

Nelson, V., (2001) *The Secret Life of Puppets*, Cambridge: Harvard University Press.

Olender, M., (2002) *The Languages of Paradise: Aryans and Semites, A Match Made in Heaven*, New York: Other Press.

Prickett, S., (1986) *Words and the Word: Language, Poetics, and Biblical Interpretation*, Cambridge; New York: Cambridge University Press.

Priestman, M., (1999) *Romantic Atheism: Poetry and Freethought, 1780–1830*, Cambridge: Cambridge University Press.

Roe, N., (1997) *John Keats and the Culture of Dissent*, New York: Oxford University Press.

Russell, C., (2005) "A Defense of Tautology: Repetition and Difference in Wordsworth's Note to 'The Thorn'," *Paragraph*, 28(2): 104–118.

Ryan, R.J., (1997) *The Romantic Reformation: Religious Politics in English Literature, 1789–1824*, Cambridge: Cambridge University Press.

Rzepka, C., (2003) "From Relics to Remains: Wordsworth's 'The Thorn' and the Emergence of Secular History," *Romanticism on the Net*, 31. Online. Available HTTP: www.erudit.org/revue/ron/2003/v/n31/008696ar.html (Accessed August 25, 2013).

Saler, M., (2009) *The Re-Enchantment of the World: Secular Magic in a Rational Age*, Stanford, CA: Stanford University Press.

Sheehan, J., (2005) *The Enlightenment Bible: Translation, Scholarship, Culture*, Princeton, NJ: Princeton University Press.

Taylor, C., (2007) *A Secular Age*, Cambridge, MA: Harvard University Press.

Warner, M., VanAntwerpen, J., and Calhoun, C. eds., (2010) *Varieties of Secularism in a Secular Age*, 1st ed., Cambridge, MA: Harvard University Press.

Wordsworth, W., (1992) *Lyrical Ballads, And Other Poems, 1797–1800*, James Butler and Karen Green, eds, Ithaca, NY: Cornell University Press.

Part 9
Modernity and postmodernity

Introduction

Since the work of deconstructionist and new historicist critics in the 1970s and 1980s, critics of Romantic literature have pondered the degree to which Romanticism can be affiliated with the aesthetics, politics, and ideologies of either modernism or postmodernism. The theorist Jean-François Lyotard associated modernism with "grand narratives" about morality, truth, and justice; he associated postmodernism with a skepticism about such grand narratives. The Romantic discourse of the sublime – the encounter with overwhelming magnitude in which the mind struggles with an adequate form to apprehend it – was central in Lyotard's account of postmodernity, because it, like postmodernity itself, "puts forward the unpresentable in presentation itself" (Lyotard 1984: 81). And when Neil Hertz described the technique of *The Prelude*'s book 7 as a welter of unassimilable imagery that challenges narrative progression and closure, he appeared to be arguing in much the same vein as Lyotard by characterizing Romanticism as an anticipation of the postmodern resistance to, or skepticism about, coherent values and forms (Hertz 1985: 58–9).

New historicist criticism began to change this way of viewing Romanticism's relation to the past in remarkable ways. In particular, once critics started interrogating the relationship between Romantic literature and historical developments throughout the eighteenth and nineteenth centuries, the connections between Romanticism and modernity became increasingly more visible. The expansion of global warfare, the early rumblings of the industrial revolution in Great Britain, and the increase of ethnic and racial tensions and inequalities across the expanding empire were only a few features of the Romantic moment that would resonate throughout the "modern" world of the nineteenth and twentieth centuries. This very same line of historicist inquiry also eventually opened up significant theoretical questions about the division between the modern and the postmodern. To what extent was the breakup of conventional narratives an extension of the modern world? To what extent was the modern world fractured by the chaos and uncertainty that is usually ascribed to postmodernity? To what extent was Romanticism (if it indeed resembled some aspects of postmodern thought) critical of, or complicit with, the very historical trends in which it participated?

The excerpt here from Jerome Christensen's essay "The Romantic Movement at the End of History," which became chapter 1 of his book *Romanticism at the End of History*, positions itself against some of the conclusions of historicist critics like Jerome McGann and Marjorie Levinson, who tended to view Romantic literature as an "ideological refuge" from real political action. His viewpoint is not simply anti-historical, however; he aims to be engaging in a method of "post-historical historiography." While engaging with historical context, that is, Christensen aims to uncover Romanticism's "anti-systemic impulses" which cannot be entirely comprehended within a concept of normal historical or "ideological" change resulting in "the naturalization of injustice." Combining features of both deconstruction and historicism, Christensen sees Romanticism as a deconstructive weapon against the normalizing impulses of modern discourses and institutions.

All of the selections in this section of the volume, just like Christensen's, might be considered examples of criticism that react very strenuously to new historicist readings of Romantic writing, but they do so in ways that differ. The distance between Christensen's views and Mary Favret's, in her selection here on Jane Austen, can be glimpsed partly through the title of the book – *War at a Distance: Romanticism and the Making of Modern Wartime* – in which this excerpt appeared as part of its fourth chapter. Unlike Christensen, Favret sees Romanticism as more or less continuous with modernity, and sees modernity as more or less continuous with postmodernity. Drawing on trauma theory by Cathy Caruth (1996) and theories of the "everyday" by Stanley Cavell (1988) and Michel de Certeau (1984), Favret shows in this selection how Romantic literature looks forward in history because of the way that it represents the "everyday" permeated by the pain and trauma of violence and war (her selection thus could be usefully read alongside Alan Bewell's selection on Wordsworth in Part 6). By showing how Austen's characters "cannot find peace in peacetime," she demonstrates how the novel conveys a distinctly modern feel because of its linking of everyday life with the reality of violence and conflict.

The fact that Favret equates the everyday with the trauma of war underlines the degree to which Romanticism's connection with modernity also – or instead – might provoke an effort to re-characterize modernity. Should modernity itself be understood less as a universal development over time and more as an ensemble of troubled and uneven narratives? Many critics, including Paul Keen, Vivavsan Soni, and Ian Duncan have suggested so (Keen 2012; Soni 2010). Duncan stresses this aspect of modernity in his book on Sir Walter Scott and his contemporaries; by doing so, he produces an account that essentially sees Romanticism as neither modern nor postmodern, but as both. Violence is once again crucial for his account of modernity, but he emphasizes modernity as a much more "uncertain" and "cryptic" affair, perhaps, than Favret's account suggests. This is because he locates, in the novels of Scott, a realization about the coincidence or simultaneity of different cultural modes at the same historical moment. Drawing on the work of scholars like James Chandler (featured in Part 1) and Katie Trumpener (1997), and differing from Ina Ferris's account of Scott in Part 4, Duncan shows how Scott's novel *Rob Roy* both recollects progressive views of history but also critiques them from within. The novel's settings and discourses connect with different cultural-historical moments that jostle with each other in the same narrative space. It thus questions the uniform narratives of progress inherited from enlightenment political economy.

Orrin N.C. Wang's new contribution to this volume provocatively takes note of how recent developments in literary and cultural theory appear to have cast aside the term "postmodern" in favor of other terms connected with globalization and biopolitics. But his point is to argue for the continuing relevance of the term, and for its close alliance with Romanticism as well. Drawing most clearly on Christensen's argument, Wang describes Romanticism and postmodernism as historical but also trans-historical – a "radical questioning" of the "onotological ground" of historicist inquiry. His readings of Blake's "Introduction" to his *Songs of Innocence* and of Keats's "Ode on a Grecian Urn" display the continuing relevance of Romanticism's "irresolute energies." Blake's references to actual sound in his *Songs* is complicated by the poet's self-conscious awareness of layered mediation; this awareness is accentuated even further in Keats's famous ode, where the ode's apparently most philosophically resonant statements verge on empty, and endlessly repeated, clichés. The poem's uncanny awareness of mediation as such may link the poem with postmodernism's similar aims to subvert or unsettle meaning.

Works cited

Caruth, Cathy. (1996) *Unclaimed Experience: Trauma, Narrative, and History*, Baltimore: Johns Hopkins University Press.

Cavell, Stanley. (1988) *In Quest of the Ordinary: Lines of Skepticism and Romanticism*, Chicago: University of Chicago Press.

de Certeau, Michel. (1984) *The Practice of Everyday Life*, trans. Steven Rendall, Berkeley: University of California Press.

Hertz, Neil. (1985) *The End of the Line: Essays on Psychoanalysis and the Sublime*, New York: Columbia University Press.

Keen, Paul. (2012) *Literature, Commerce, and the Spectacle of Modernity, 1750–1800*, Cambridge: Cambridge University Press.

Lyotard, Jean-François. (1984) *The Postmodern Condition: A Report on Knowledge*, trans. Geoff Bennington and Brian Massumi, Minneapolis: University of Minnesota Press.

Soni, Vivasvan. (2010) *Mourning Happiness: Narrative and the Politics of Modernity*, Ithaca: Cornell University Press.

Trumpener, Katie. (1997) *Bardic Nationalism: The Romantic Novel and the British Empire*, Chicago: University of Chicago Press.

Further reading

Ferris, David S. (2000) *Silent Urns: Romanticism, Hellenism, Modernity*, Stanford: Stanford University Press.

Goodman, Kevis. (2004) *Georgic Modernity and British Romanticism: Poetry and the Mediation of History*, Cambridge: Cambridge University Press.

Henderson, Andrea. (2008) *Romanticism and the Painful Pleasures of Modern Life*, Cambridge: Cambridge University Press.

Langan, Celeste. (1999) *Romantic Vagrancy: Wordsworth and the Simulation of Freedom*, Cambridge: Cambridge University Press.

Larrissy, Edward. (1999) *Romanticism and Postmodernism*, Cambridge: Cambridge University Press.

McLane, Maureen N. (2000) *Romanticism and the Human Sciences: Poetry, Population, and the Discourse of the Species*, Cambridge: Cambridge University Press.

Wang, Orrin N.C. (1996) *Fantastic Modernity: Dialectical Readings in Romanticism and Theory*, Baltimore: Johns Hopkins University Press.

Wang, Orrin N.C. (2011) *Romantic Sobriety: Sensation, Revolution, Commodification, History*, Baltimore: Johns Hopkins University Press.

33 The romantic movement at the end of history

Jerome Christensen

> We profess it in our Creed, we confess it in our lives.
> (Jeremy Taylor, *Holy Living* [1650])

I profess romanticism, I romantically confess. And if I choose a pretheoretical, prerevolutionary epigraph from [a seventeenth]-century divine to enfranchise this essay rather than a phrase from a more timely master such as Paul de Man or M.H. Abrams, it is because I want to use Jeremy Taylor as Samuel Taylor Coleridge chronically used him: to stage a resistance to theory, to ward off revolutionary utterance, and to keep melancholy at bay. In Taylor's terms, professing romanticism is what I do on each occasion of classroom teaching at Johns Hopkins University or of publishing an article in a specialized journal or a book at a university press. My creed, of course, is not to Coleridge, to Byron, or to Wordsworth. I do not commit belief to what is loosely called a canon but to that discipline which the institutions of education and publication collaboratively authorize and reproduce and which in turn certifies the felicity of my professions. If, as Taylor states, confessing is a matter of living, living ought to be imagined as that structuring activity that Anthony Giddens calls "practical consciousness": an ensemble of repetitive maneuvers, signature gestures, and obsessive themes.[1] Living is for servants and for critics – for those who do not have *texts* in Edward Said's sense of the term but only what Coleridge calls "personalities."[2] This practical, pretextual consciousness assorts the idiosyncratic and the routinized into a compromise formation: something romantic, something like a *biographia literaria*, something which may be at odds or at evens with an institutional warrant. It depends.

I want to address how confessing romantically bears on the profession of romanticism and to argue that its bearing matters. This essay presupposes that romanticism is not an object of study – neither the glorious expression nor the deplorable symptom of a distant epoch and peculiar mentality – but a problem in identification and in practice. As a Christian divine, Jeremy Taylor sought to induce a harmony between creed and life in himself and for others. Romantic writers grandiloquently profess to wish for such a harmony (*poet* is the name that Coleridge gives to the achieved ideal), even as they prosaically confess that what our creeds profess and what our untimely lives confess do not often synchronize.

The advantages of that discrepancy clarify in the light of the "end of history" argument as it has been influentially advanced by Francis Fukuyama in his interrogatory 1989 article "The End of History?" and his recent declarative book *The End of History and the Last Man*.[3] Three features of Fukuyama's "universal history" of the triumph of liberalism are salient here (*EH*, p. 48). First, in line with his all-too-clerical affirmation of the power of ideology to make history, Fukuyama identifies the end of history not with a momentous incident or a sovereign decision but with the prescribed end of what he calls "ideological evolution," consummated in the freshly consolidated global hegemony of the liberal state. For the sake of developing a romantic argument, I am prepared to accept both aspects of that claim: that history is (or rather was) ideological contestation and that ideological conflict has ended. I conclude that if one is looking for something with the strength to challenge commercialist hegemony here at the end of history one should look for something non-ideological – whatever that may mean.

The second arresting feature of Fukuyama's argument is its unembarrassed repetitiveness. Fukuyama freely acknowledges Hegel as his precursor, who announced the end of history in 1806. And Hegel was not alone, probably because he was somewhat premature. Not Europe in 1806 but Europe in 1815 is the better analogy with the worldquake of 1989. [. . .]

Thus the third feature of Fukuyama's universal history: its relentless synchronicity. A fundamental belief in a prevailing synchronicity encourages Fukuyama, like Richard Rorty, to indulge the notion of the history of philosophy as a series of conversations with dead authors. He can imagine that he enters into intellectual exchange with Hegel and that, in his passage through *The Phenomenology of Spirit*, he can come upon the chapter on lordship and bondage and recognize liberalism's glory. [. . .] A pallid scientism, evolution imputes a kind of necessity to the discursive process, subjects change to predictability, and allows for the evidence of "real change" to be stigmatized as monstrous, anomalous, or, worse yet, anachronistic. [Benjamin] Constant was succinct. Writing in 1814 after the abdication of the usurper, he not only trumpeted the end of the era of conquest but also announced that, under the reign of commerce, should some savage fool attempt to conquer, usurp, or dictate he would "commit a gross and disastrous anachronism."[4] Constant got it right. Only a few months after the publication of his book [*The Spirit of Conquest and Usurpation*] Bonaparte returned to France and for a hundred days anachronistically suspended the conventions by which monarcho-liberalism ruled. And therefore Constant got it wrong, for the assumption that an anachronism was a mere nothing that would expire in its appearance proved vain. Although an anachronism does not count in the way that clocks and bank-tellers count, *committing* anachronism romantically exploits lack of accountability as unrecognized possibility.[5]

Posthistorical liberalism's disdain for the anachronistic is exceeded only by a fear of it, which fuels the postmodern drive to abolish the possibility of anachronism. It is because Fredric Jameson, the best Marxist theorist of postmodernism, shares many of the evolutionary assumptions of the neoliberals (the word *revolution* does not appear in the index to his *Postmodernism, or, The Cultural Logic of Late Capitalism*) and adheres to the epochal model of tidy synchrony ("the postmodern must be characterized as a situation in which the survival, the residue, the holdover, the archaic, has finally been swept away without a trace")[6] that his utopian agenda looks less like a challenge to postmodernism than another elegant variation. Jameson's utopia is insufficiently romantic. Considered as a set of doctrines, Marxism does not trouble Fukuyama's reverie, but the emergence of Marx under the Hegelian sun, committing the romantic anachronism of *Das Kapital* in the middle of the nineteenth century, emphatically does.

[. . .]

[This] essay will proceed on the assumption that if we want to discover what possibilities for change remain open now, we might inquire into the untimely back at the beginning of the nineteenth century, when history first ended. Posthistorical historiography suggests that romanticism, which, at least in the British instance, has led a kind of phantomized political existence, crossing among professions conservative, liberal, and Marxist, may, as phantom, confess a political life that is a virtual alternative both to what rules and to what would have inverted ruler and ruled. I will be orienting myself in relation to Coleridge's *Biographia Literaria* for contrary reasons: written in 1815, it is decidedly a Waterloo composition with the Constantian ambition of proclaiming a new dispensation; yet because it was afflicted by near-catastrophic miscalculations in the printing office, the book was not published until 1817 and thus appeared as an anachronism, a ghost at the banquet it had set.

British romantic writing, I shall argue, does not belong with the ideologies but with what [Immanuel] Wallerstein calls the "movements," those political associations on the run which attempted to organize spontaneous antisystemic impulses into an organized "politics of social transformation."[7] Neither sect nor school, the British romantic writers who straggled onto the scene between 1798 and 1802 formed what E.J. Hobsbawm has called a "primitive" social movement.[8] I shall later take advantage of the *re*emergence of the primitive in a post-Jacobin and post-Napoleonic Britain to suggest analogous possibilities for a posthistorical America. Matthew Arnold preferred "prematurity" to primitiveness and diagnosed it in his canonical judgment that Byron and Wordsworth "had their source in a great movement of feeling, not in a great movement of mind."[9] Arnold added mind to feeling with the aim of stopping romantic movement altogether; he was successful insofar as he can be credited with growing precocious writers into Victorian worthies, freezing them as eminent pictures at the Oxbridge exhibition. Arnold's verdict has the unintended consequence, however, of aligning primitive romanticism – turbulent feeling unsubjected by a regulative idea – with Marx's definition of communism: "Communism is for us not a stable state which is to be established, an *ideal* to which reality will have to adjust itself. We call communism the *real* movement which abolishes the present state of things."[10] We shall call romanticism the real movement of feeling that challenges the present state of things, including the consensus that would bury it in the past, whether by omission or by labeling it an ideology. We shall do so in the faith that what was premature then may help revive the possibility of prematurity now – if not to force the spring at least, by heralding, to quicken it.

1 Romanticism and ideology

Not long ago Jerome McGann stigmatized romanticism as a version of what Marx called the German ideology, which "turns the world upside down and sees it from a false vantage because its own point of reference is conceptualized within a closed idealistic system."[11] McGann alludes to Marx's famous metaphor of the camera obscura: "If in all ideology men and their circumstances appear upside-down, as in a *camera obscura*, this phenomenon arises just as much from their historical life-process as the inversion of objects on the retina does from their physical life-process" (*GI*, p. 14). Given that ideology is inversion, the critic's responsibility is clear: he must labor to turn the world right-side up and restore it to its truth.

Roughly speaking, two takes on ideology prevail. The first, shared by Fukuyama and McGann, regards ideology as a set of ideas that you and people like you hold. In this view, ideology is opinion dressed to kill. The second, Althusserian conception of ideology is as a set of representations that holds us, that "*hails or interpellates concrete individuals as concrete subjects*" – concrete subjects being concrete individuals who "work all by themselves."[12] Because ideology has no history (or, as Fukuyama would have it, because its history is universal), it need have no "end" (there is no truth to restore); nonetheless, there are limits to ideology's scope, for there remain "individuals" out of range of its call. Where things work, ideology is; where things do not work, ideology is not, and where ideology is not, *cause*, paradoxically, is. Or, as Lacan aphorizes (thinking of Kant, thinking of Hume) "there is cause only in something that doesn't work."[13] For Althusser *art*, as for Constant *anachronism*, names one of those things that, like an idiot boy or an ancient mariner or a female vagrant, does not work but that does somehow, occultly, *cause*.

Given Lacan's aphorism, it is notable that Marx's artful image of how ideology works does not itself work. Paul Ricoeur has observed that the "unfortunate image" of the camera obscura

> is a metaphor of the reversal of images, but it proceeds as a comparison involving four terms. The ideological reversal is to the life-process as the image in perception is to the retina. . . . But what is an image on the retina

is a puzzle, for, as Ricoeur concludes, "there are images only for consciousness." There may be an image *in* itself, but because there is no image *for* itself, Marx's analogy fails to close and in so failing alludes to something like a supervisory consciousness. Ricoeur goes on to echo Althusser's charge "that the inverted image belongs to the same ideological world as the original. As a result, he claims, we must introduce a notion quite different from inversion, that of an epistemological break."[14] We may suggest that what appears as something like consciousness is a *movement* that disrupts the closure of the optical model and makes Marx's camera obscura metaphor unworkable for the systematic purposes to which Marxists have put it.

W.J.T. Mitchell has observed that

> Marx's use of the camera obscura as a polemical device for ridiculing the illusions of idealist philosophy begins to look even more ungainly when we recall that Locke had also used it as a polemical device – in exactly the opposite way.[15]

Ungainlier still. For if the inversion of the camera image belongs to "the same ideological world" as the original, what are we to make of the common cause of Karl Marx, avowed materialist, and Samuel Taylor Coleridge, supposed idealist? Here is Coleridge's footnoted denunciation of the habits of the contemporary reading public from chapter 3 of the *Biographia*:

> For as to the devotees of the circulating libraries, I dare not compliment their *pass-time*, or rather *kill-time*, with the name of *reading*. Call it rather a sort of beggarly daydreaming, during which the mind of the dreamer furnishes for itself nothing but laziness and a little mawkish sensibility; while the whole *materiel* and imagery of the doze is supplied *ab extra* by a sort of mental *camera obscura* manufactured

at the printing office, which *pro tempore* fixes, reflects and transmits the moving phantasms of one man's delirium, so as to people the barrenness of an hundred other brains afflicted with the same trance or suspension of all common sense and all definite purpose.

[*BL*, 1:48n]

Although both Marx and Coleridge use the camera obscura to illustrate the mechanical projection of inverted images of reality, it is the so-called romantic idealist who connects the mechanism with a system of commodity production. Mitchell likewise adjusts Marx by weaning the camera obscura metaphor away from its Lockean parent, invoking instead the nineteenth-century technological context of photography in order to suture Marx's characterization of ideology with his analysis of commodity fetishism [. . .] [*I*, pp. 189–90]

If Marx echoes Locke, Coleridge, who never saw a photograph, not only anticipates Marx but Mitchell as well by making the connection between ideology and commodity production in the context of an imaginary apparatus that looks like nothing so much as the apparatus of the imaginary we moderns know as the cinema. Projecting his light forward as if a light bestowed, the measure of the distance that Coleridge travels beyond Marx is the romantic's failure accurately to historicize his camera obscura, a neglect symptomatized syntactically by his failure properly to tie the transmitted movement to a stable referent. Is the "moving phantasm" an affecting ghost or the effective flicker of an image on a movie screen? If the "phantasm," an untimely and unaccountable life, is the *figure* of anachronism, Coleridge's "moving" *really* moves – and romantically commits that anachronism to the future.

Whether or not you buy such a fantastic claim, once the fantastic has been reinscribed in the Marxian mechanism (classically by Walter Benjamin or recently by Mitchell), it is difficult to see how Coleridge's "gothic" use of the camera obscura substantively differs from the "mental operation of materialist reversal and demystification," which, according to Jameson, is "alone the feature by which 'materialism' as such can be identified" (*PM*, p. 358). That may be because the image of the camera obscura works *as* a camera obscura, turning upside down reality and dream, idealist and materialist, Coleridge and Marx, Jameson and Fukuyama. Althusser's lesson – which he abstracted from the *German Ideology* but which the Russian masses suffered deep time to learn – would seem to hold: the more the world is turned upside down, the more it stays the same. Such a world seems suited for Fukuyama's spin. [. . .] Not surprisingly, most readers find Fukuyama's moral comforting. But some are unreasonably angry at the message and suspect the messenger. And that's interesting.

2 Romantic resistance to transfer

In the *Biographia Literaria* Coleridge engages the relations among the mechanism of inversion, the possibility of change, and unreasonable anger in his analysis of the reception of *Lyrical Ballads*. He invokes *Macbeth* to epitomize the predicament of the readers of Wordsworth's 1800 preface, who suffer an "unquiet state of mind" and who wonder "at the perverseness of the man, who had written a long and argumentative essay to persuade them, that "Fair is foul, and foul is fair" [*BL*, 1:71–2]. Explaining his explanation, Coleridge appends a complicated footnote that diagnoses and performs the romantic movement:

In opinions of long continuance, and in which we had never before been molested by a single doubt, to be suddenly *convinced* of an *error*, is almost like being *convicted* of a fault. There is a state of mind, which is the direct antithesis of that, which takes place when we *make a bull*. *The bull* namely consists in the bringing together two incompatible thoughts, with the *sensation*, but without the *sense*, of their connection. The psychological condition, or that which constitutes the possibility of this state, being such disproportionate vividness of two distant thoughts, as extinguishes or obscures the consciousness of the intermediate images or conceptions, or wholly abstracts the attention from them. Thus in the well known bull, "*I was a fine child, but they changed me;*" the first conception expressed in the word "*I,*" is that of personal identity – *Ego contemplans*: the second expressed in the word "*me,*" is the visual image or object by which the mind represents to itself its past condition, or rather, its personal identity under the form in which it imagined itself previously to have existed. – Ego contemplatus. Now the change of one visual image for another involves in itself no absurdity, and becomes absurd only by its immediate juxta-position with the first thought, which is rendered possible by the whole attention being successively absorbed in each singly, so as not to notice the interjacent notion, "changed" which by its incongruity with the first thought, "*I,*" constitutes the bull. Add only, that this process is facilitated by the circumstance of the words "*I,*" and "*me,*" being sometimes equivalent, and sometimes having a distinct meaning; sometimes, namely, signifying the act of self-consciousness, sometimes the external image in and by which the mind represents that act to itself, the result and symbol of its individuality. Now suppose the direct contrary state, and you will have a distinct sense of the connection between two conceptions, without that *sensation* of such connection which is supplied by habit. The man *feels*, as if he were standing on his head, though he cannot but *see*, that he is truly standing on his feet. This, as a painful sensation, will of course have a tendency to associate itself with the person who occasions it; even as persons, who have been by painful means restored from derangement, are known to feel an involuntary dislike towards their physician.

[*BL*, 1:72–3]

Coleridge develops a correspondence between Wordsworth as physician and the reviewers *of Lyrical Ballads* as patients. Feeling as if they have been turned upside down by Wordsworth's argument, the reviewers blame the "painful sensation" associated with this revolution in feeling on the author, as patients are wont to blame even that physician who has restored them from derangement. Wordsworth's preface thus made discursive sense where there had been only outlandish poetic sensation but at the cost of transforming everyday sense into the stuff of dream – rough magic guaranteed to antagonize the custodians of conventional wisdom.[16]

Now suppose the direct contrary. Suppose that the "bull," "I was a fine child, but they changed me," anticipates Coleridge's own criticism of Wordsworth's ambitious "Immortality Ode" in the second volume of the *Biographia*. In Coleridge's acknowledged source, Maria and Richard Edgeworth's "Essay on the Irish Bull," the authors feature this resentful expostulation: "'I hate that woman,' said a gentleman, looking at one who had been his nurse, 'I hate that woman, for she changed me at nurse.'" "Change" here signifies "exchange": "our Hibernian's consciousness," the Edgeworths comment, "could not retrograde to the time when he was changed at nurse; consequently there was no continuity of identity between the infant and the man who expressed his hatred of the nurse for perpetrating the fraud."[17] Coleridge queries Wordsworth's "bull" likewise. He has in mind the eighth stanza, which addresses the "six years' Darling of the pigmy size":

> Thou, whose exterior semblance doth belie
>   Thy Soul's immensity;
> Thou best Philosopher, who yet doest keep
> Thy heritage, thou Eye among the blind,
> That, deaf and silent, read'st the eternal deep,
> Haunted for ever by the eternal mind, –
>   Mighty Prophet! Seer blest!
>   On whom those truths do rest,
> Which we are toiling all our lives to find,
> In darkness lost, the darkness of the grave.[18]

In "what sense is a child of that age a *philosopher*?" Coleridge later asks.

> In what sense does he *read* the "eternal deep?" . . . These would be tidings indeed; but such as would pre-suppose an immediate revelation to the inspired communicator, and require miracles to authenticate his inspiration. Children at this age give us no such information of themselves; and at what time were we dipt in the Lethe, which has produced such utter oblivion of a state so godlike?
>
> [*BL*, 2:138–9][19]

Wordsworth's embedded fiction of a Letheward hand corresponds to the Irishman's fanciful notion of a malignant hand that changed him at nurse. Coleridge's "I was a fine child, but they changed me" distills the dependence of Wordsworth's notion of change as alteration on an unreasoned synonymity with exchange as substitution. Coleridge's note thus warns the readers of the *Biographia* – Wordsworth chief among them – that Coleridge's antithetical criticism, designed to set Wordsworth's feet back on the ground of true principle, would likely provoke the poet's "involuntary dislike," which notoriously proved to be the case.

Now suppose we mix in the quotation from *Macbeth*. As physician is to patient, so, it would seem, are the fair-fouling witches (Wordsworth) to Macbeth (reviewers), who, his world overturned, murders the king and usurps the throne. But it is a peculiarity of this matrix that analogies do not multiply symmetrically. In the analogic of Coleridge's note, Macbeth's "involuntary dislike" ought to have been directed against the hags who persuaded him that fair is foul and foul is fair, not against Duncan, the rightful king. Macbeth's "mistake" leads to the primitive violence that Constant called usurpation and that Coleridge identified as the trait of the "commanding genius." History progresses to contain that violence by preventing such mistakes, which entails rationalizing the *inversio* by means of substitution and condensation. If we take the split between witches and king as the difference between those who *know* and that one who *authorizes*, then the modern physician is *one who can authorize because he knows*. Historical progress has the hallmarks of what Freud calls "transference." Not only have "'new editions or facsimiles of the impulses and phantasies [been] aroused and made conscious during the progress of analysis; but they . . . replace some earlier person by the person of the physician.' "[20] Coleridge's note thus assesses the therapeutic possibilities of inversion in the framework of a transition from the feudal era of Macbeth to the modern moment of the professional physician – a transition that reforms the violently discontinuous change of usurpation as the normal change of remediation. History provides a new answer to the question that Macbeth puts to the doctor who comes to treat his maddened Lady: "Canst thou minister to a mind diseased?" *Macbeth's* doctor must answer "no"; the modern psychiatrist professes "yes." But even for the latter, ministration occasionally misfires. Although the transition from usurpation to remediation would seem to be an unambiguous good, the persistence of the "involuntary dislike" – what Wordsworth calls "Obstinate questionings / Of sense and outward things" ("II," 11. 141–4) – is evidence of the holdover of untransferred affect, a movement of feeling that taints the efficiency of the *inversio.* Although the physician has the credentials to summon spirits from the vasty deep of the unconscious, he still cannot guarantee that they will heed his call.

That the professional authority of the physician remains as dubious for the modern as monarchical authority had been for Macbeth suggests to the romantic mind that despite history's progress nothing fundamental has changed. Mistaken ideologies fall as the professions rise in a process of substitution without alteration. Progress through Coleridge's topsy-turvy note induces the same moral. Characteristically, Coleridge has shaped his footnote as a chiasmus (sensation : sense : sense : sensation), a figure indifferent to the cause of truth but well designed to work like a camera lens to invert perception. Both physician and philosophical critic profess to cure. And maybe they do, *generally.* Yet Coleridge's sophistical mimicry of the accredited physician's therapeutic technique supplies a pretext for the outburst of individual hostility directed toward the critic as to the physician: the obtrusion of the rhetorical scheme in the production of the cure confesses a design unavowed and an expertise unshared. Like the posthistorian's mimicry of evolutionary change, such gimmicks seem to turn the world upside down only to return us to where we always were. If the camera obscura illustrates that the ideological reduces to the rhetorical, here the impression of rhetoricity figures the underwriting of the remedial by the coercive: the compulsion applied to the patient reader to choose to recognize himself as subject. That compulsion is not overt, as it is with divining witch and commanding king; it is bound up with the pretense inherent in every profession, whether credentialed or not. This pretense is the chief theme of Coleridge's many attacks on the professions.[21] For Coleridge one must always profess to profess – or, to put it in Jeremy Taylor's terms, professions inevitably confess the pretense of their claims to autonomous power. Twentieth-century readers are less familiar with [the] discharge of affect under Coleridge's phrase "involuntary dislike" than Freud's "negative transference." Nonetheless, the concept had long inhabited the British liberal tradition under the names "negative liberty" and "the right of resistance." J.G.A. Pocock has distinguished between the republican, civic, virtue-based tradition, in which possession of real property grounded a citizen's autonomous political existence, and the liberal, juristic, rights-based tradition.[22] [. . .]

According to C.B. Macpherson, nineteenth-century liberalism internalized the tension between the republican and the juristic traditions as the distinction between economic liberalism, which stresses the "maximization of utilities," and democratic liberalism, which aims at the "maximization of powers." [. . .] Rather than maximize powers, liberal society, obedient to an economic imperative, has consistently promoted a "net transfer of powers," which it executes by allowing some to deny others access to the instruments with which they might develop their natural capacities.[23]

On Macpherson's account, Freud looks like an economic liberal, concerned to maximize utility not power. When, in his essay "The Dynamics of the Transference," Freud asks how it comes about "that the transference is so pre-eminently suitable as a weapon of resistance," his aim is disarmament.[24] [. . .] To cure means to bring up occult, conspiratorial, pointlessly reproductive emotions, to recognize them, and to subject them to the guillotine of analysis, thereby adjusting the patient to the ideological world that Freud calls "real life" ("DT," p. 113).

What Freud called real life, contemporary liberalism has come to call the posthistorical. Fukuyama's universal history tries to reclaim the philosophical vagrants and neurotics of the past (for example, Hegel and Nietzsche) for the "liberal ascent" by adjusting them to a narrative that legitimates the way things are. He supplements the classical, Hobbesian definition of man as driven by the threat of scarcity, fear of death, and an insatiable desire for accumulation with a Hegelian conception of man as motivated by a "totally non-economic drive, the struggle for recognition" (*EH*, p. 135). Hobbes is the scion of economics, Hegel the scion of the political – it is the clerical profession of a universal history to wed them. To seal the bond Fukuyama redescribes affect that is not perceptibly acquisitive as inchoate feelings that *seek*, not, as in Freud, avoid, recognition. [. . .] Nothing resists Fukuyama's redescription, and, as most liberal economists will tell you, nothing is got for nothing.

If Freud circumscribes Fukuyama, Coleridge's account of his early instruction in English composition characterizes Freud. In the *Biographia* he recalls the lessons in Shakespeare and Milton that cost him so much "time and trouble to *bring up*, so as to escape [his teacher James Bowyer's] censure." Drilled in the rigorous logic of poems, Coleridge learned that "in the truly great poets . . . there is a reason assignable, not only for every word, but for the position of every word." Diction fell under the purview of a hanging judge:

> In our own English compositions . . . he showed no mercy to phrase, metaphor, or image, unsupported by a sound sense, or where the same sense might have been conveyed with equal force and dignity in plainer words. Lute, harp, and lyre, muse, muses, and inspirations, Pegasus, Parnassus, and Hippocrene, were all an abomination to him. In fancy I can almost hear him now, exclaiming, *"Harp? Harp? Lyre? Pen and ink, boy, you mean! Muse, boy, Muse? your Nurse's daughter, you mean! Pierian spring? Oh 'aye! the cloister-pump, I suppose!"*
>
> [*BL*, 1:9–10]

Such was learning English composition at Christ's Hospital at the end of the eighteenth century. [. . .] Because the conversational standard of the vernacular has never been simply a diction, given or found, but always a *jurisdiction*, answerable to the imperative of what Benedict Anderson has called "the revolutionary vernacularizing thrust of capitalism,"[25] which peremptorily determines native intelligence by censoring unruly, demotic speech as gibberish (a tale told by an idiot boy), there is no practical difference between moral and political education nor between political education and legal judgment. [. . .] "Certain introductions, similies, and examples," Coleridge recalls, were placed by name on a list of interdiction. Among the similies, there was . . . the example of Alexander and Clytus, which was equally good and apt, whatever might be the theme. Was it ambition? Alexander and Clytus! – Flattery? Alexander and Clytus! – Anger? Drunkenness? Pride? Friendship? Ingratitude? Late Repentance? Still, still Alexander and Clytus! At length, the praises of agriculture having been exemplified in the sagacious observation, that had Alexander been holding the plough, he would not have run his friend Clytus through with a spear, this tried, and serviceable old friend was banished by public edict in secula seculorum.

[*BL*, 1:10]

Coleridge's boyish stereotype reproduced promiscuously.[26] Because it belonged nowhere, the Alexander and Clytus topos could be discharged anywhere. Bowyer interdicted this demotic frenzy by commanding banishment. But, as Freud knows, interdiction is not transference and banishment is not slaying. Having been put away as if the thing of a child, Alexander-cum-Clytus nonetheless thrusts back into Coleridge's biographical composition, where, in the very excess of his prescriptive zeal, Coleridge involuntarily transforms judgment into stereotype and, resisting the transference he wills, tips piety into parody.

3 Romantic politics

As Freud argues, and as my medley of writers illustrates, willful resistance to the cure involves "an inappreciation of time," which manifests itself in the refusal of the patient to meet the requirement that "he shall fit these emotions into their place in the treatment and in his life-history" ("DT," p. 114). As fugitive feelings resist recognition, so they resist being narrativized into the formation of an identity, whether of a person, a people, a nation, a social class, or, in the case of Coleridge, a philosophical critic. From the progressivist perspective shared by Fukuyama and McGann, inappreciation of narrative time looks like a conservative refusal to recognize history. But for the romantic, inappreciation of time is neither position nor attitude but the willful commission of anachronism, the assertion of the historical as that which could not be over because it has not yet really happened.

Coleridge said much the same thing in his unpacking of *Jacobin*:

The word implies a man, whose affections have been warmly and deeply interested in the cause of general freedom, who has hoped all good and honourable things both *of*, and *for*, mankind. . . . Jacobin . . . affirm[s] that no man can ever become altogether an apostate to Liberty, who has at any time been sincerely and fervently attached to it. His hopes will burn like the Greek fire, hard to be extinguished, and easily rekindling. Even when he despairs of the cause, he will yet *wish*, that it had been successful. And even when private interests have warped his public character, his convictions will remain, and his wishes often rise up in rebellion against his outward actions and public avowals.[27]

Coleridge's definition unlinks emancipatory ardor from French principles. Attachment to liberty means resisting the cure of historicization, being locked into synchrony with what the vernacular says can be said. Blind to the vicissitudes of parties and programs, *Jacobin* names a wish that can be fulfilled only in a future toward which, in rebellion against the way things are, the ardent soul moves.

Because *Jacobin* nonetheless imparts the taint of the foreign and ideological, I prefer the term *demotic*. The distinction between vernacular and demotic may be roughly apportioned in terms of the difference between two kinds of disturbance that troubled the social landscape of Great Britain in the 1790s and the early years of the nineteenth century: the riot and the insurrection. A riot involved the hostile, occasionally violent action of the crowd against property or authority, but the rioters observed a traditional protocol that did not, according to John Bohstedt, "normally challenge the arrangement of local power."[28] [. . .] Insurrectionaries can be distinguished from rioters by consciousness, by regional origin, by class, or by anything else you like. They themselves begin to distinguish themselves from rioters as soon as they begin to *produce* their means of resistance, a step that is only conditioned by their symbolic resourcefulness. Demotic utterances challenge traditional systems of social control not with pikes and pistols but with the uncanny repetition of stereotypes circulating without respect to region or kind, resisting protocols of recognition but soliciting acknowledgment of one stranger by another, of United Irishman by United Briton, of United Briton by Yorkshire weaver, of Yorkshire weaver by Lake poet.

The propagation of demotic utterances identifies a species of what Hobsbawm has called "primitive social movements," which historically had been characterized by a ritualistic formalism of ceremonies and symbolism. [. . .] The problem that Hobsbawm never confronts – the problem that dogs every engagement with insurrectionary Great Britain after the coronation of Bonaparte – is the *return* of the prepolitical, a formalism that, because it recurs, cannot be branded as primitive and that, because it is involuntary, cannot be stigmatized as sentimental. The return of the prepolitical or (to romantically equivocate Raymond Williams's famous distinction) the *emergence of the residual* is romantic formalism on the move.[29] Because practiced without good reason in the aftermath of utopian dreams, that movement might be called the politics of hope.

Hobsbawm is inclined to criticize British repressiveness of the post-revolutionary era not for its reactionary ferocity but for its redundancy, for he concludes that "the belief of early 19th-century British governments in the necessarily subversive nature of initiations and secret oaths, was mistaken. The outsiders against which the ritual brotherhood guarded its secrets were not only the bourgeois' and not always the government's." Yet he adds:

> Only insofar as all working men's organizations by virtue of their class membership, were likely to engage in activities frowned upon by employers or the authorities, did the initiation and oath bind their members specifically against these. There was thus no initial distinction between, as it were, legitimately and unnecessarily secret societies, but only between the fraternal activities in which their members were ritually bound to show solidarity, some of which might be acceptable to the law while others were not.
>
> [*PR*, pp. 158–9]

The government's evident overreaction testified not only to a class bias but also to the fact that the initial *in*distinction between the legitimately and the unnecessarily secret societies that was induced by transitive repetition of stereotypes constituted a shared volatility of purpose which *was* insurrectionary without regard to ideology.

That explains why Coleridge's poetry of the late 1790s, which in its supernatural, preternatural, and conversational modes resonates with suggestions of omens and signals ("Frost at Midnight"), strange visitations and conspiratorial understandings ("Christabel"), mysterious symbolism ("The Rime of the Ancient Mariner"), insistent metrical schemes, and arbitrary anachronisms (choose your favorite) did nothing to diminish his reputation for radicalism. It explains why such blatantly bullish ballads of Wordsworth as "We Are Seven," "Simon Lee," "The Idiot Boy," and "The Thorn" could, despite a lack of revolutionary content, seem unsettling, as Coleridge canonically attests in chapter 17 of the *Biographia Literaria*. The production of stereotypes ("Oh misery! oh misery! / Oh woe is me! oh misery!") that initiated strangers into imagined communities unaccountable to the nation-state was dangerous and was branded as such by the Whiggish *Edinburgh Review*. In its inaugural issue of October 1802, which appeared four years after *Lyrical Ballads* but at a time when, as [Roger] Wells demonstrates, insurrectionary activity had strongly revived,[30] the *Edinburgh* both adopted the Enlightenment pose of debunker of conspiratorial theories of the French Revolution and yet succumbed to making hysterically sarcastic charges of sect and conspiracy in its review of the activities of the Lake poets. The issue was not Jacobinism – despite half-hearted attempts, Francis Jeffrey would ultimately agree with the contemporary practitioners of ideology critique that none was detectable – but a kind of insistent formalism, which, because its ideological mission was inapparent, seemed the pretext for a secret bond that could only be defended against by condemning it as "sectual" (Jeffrey's favored ploy) or sexual (the Freudian recourse).

The Edgeworths' "Essay on Irish Bulls" may be taken as another example of the way the legitimately and the unnecessarily secret could be confused. In the bull the joke is always on the Irishman, and the Edgeworths are at pains to argue that he is victimized by the prejudice that the bull represents. Yet the Edgeworths' project, to prove that the bull is not a "species of blunder *peculiar* to Ireland," was finally motivated less by a desire to rescue the Irish from English laughter than to dissipate the English suspicion that there is some kind of essential character or form of thought that binds the Irish together, rejects English reason, and is unassimilable to polite society.[31]

The "depeculiarization" of Irish speech, which meant translating the demotic into the vernacular (both Maria Edgeworth's and Walter Scott's glossaries prosecute the same end), carried forward the Enlightenment project of homogenizing mankind in the guise of the bourgeoisie and, as Mitchell has argued, of restricting character to what can be stamped on a commodity. Yet that strategy could only be partially effective, for insurrectionary signs solicited acknowledgement while eluding recognition by mobilizing borrowed and disposable stereotypes.[32] The difference between the character of the commodity and the character of the demotic is the difference between a trademark, copyrightable and subject to exchange, and what Marx in the *German Ideology* called a "form of activity." The difference is between using a printing press and being one. [. . .]

What was truly peculiar to the insurrectionaries was this form of activity. Hobsbawm comments that "the fantastic nomenclature of the brotherhoods was

totally non-utilitarian unlike later revolutionary organizations which have normally
attempted to pick names indicative of their ideology or programme" (*PR*, p. 166).
"Non-utilitarian" should not be translated as aesthetic. That the nomenclature was
nonutilitarian simply means that it, like the bull, did no work. Because it did no
work, professed nothing, it was therefore without value. It could not be inverted or
transferred, synthesized or evolved. But because it *did* not work it *remains* a cause in
the way that Lacan speaks of cause – a cause untransferred to history's narrative and
therefore untouched by history's end.

[. . .]

For the evolutionary model embraced by Fukuyama, Jameson, and Hobsbawm,
which moves confidently from the archaic to the postmodern, from the prepolitical
to the posthistorical, I would substitute one closer to that proposed by the romantic
paleontologist Stephen Jay Gould in *Wonderful Life*. [. . .] He urges the application
of the thought experiment called "replaying life's tape" as a means to adjudge the
necessity of the way things have turned out. In the cases of the defunct genera
Sidneyia, *Marrella*, and *Opabinia*, replaying life's tape argues for the contingency of
their extinction and therefore the contingency of all that followed.[33] Replaying life's
tape confesses the same contingency in the failure of demotic forms of social life,
of romantic movements. But replaying the tape is only a thought experiment with
organisms that cannot be revived by Gould's song. Because the resources of the
demos were and are symbolic, no such barrier cuts the path between then and now.
The demotic cause lives just because it did not succeed; the romantic movement is
inescapably anachronistic because it is the politics of the future and always will be
until something better comes along. And as contingent analogies between phrases
of address (grips, passwords, meters, motifs, commonplaces) bound each to each in
transient but strong commonalities then, so now *as* then. Sensitive to the strength of
willful analogy in forging a common cause, I ask you to acknowledge that Coleridge's
cliché of the Jacobin's "Greek fire" marks the demotic heat in Wordsworth's
contemporary reference to those "embers" in which there is "something that
doth live" ("II," 11. 130–1) and threads through the political unconscious to link
that insurrectionary glow by analogy with the volcanic *Prometheus Unbound*, with
the fantastically explosive *Don Juan*, as well as with the fire next time of the Greek
Revolution or, perhaps, the 1992 insurrection in LA.

[. . .]

In Arnold's time the notion of romantic expectancy was a sentimental idealism;
in the 1960s it sounded revolutionary; in the 1970s and 1980s things soured as stern-
lipped academics, fortified for history's long haul by strong doses of Marx, denounced
romantic hope as an ideological refuge embraced by apostates to the true cause. Now
that the long haul has been aborted and Marx's beautiful theory withers, the romantic
movement marks time as the reviving possibility of change that is not merely normal,
its historicity the willful commission of anachronism after anachronism linked by
bold analogy. By promiscuously replicating stereotypes that resist recognition and
transfer, the romantic movement rejects the imperial epochalism of the posthistorical
as the sign of the naturalization of injustice. At one point in his writings on ideology
and literature, Raymond Williams wisely warns against what he calls premature
historicization. Until there is justice, all historicization is premature. Until there is
justice the untimely slogan of romantic politics will not be "always historicize" but
"now and again anachronize."

Notes

1 Anthony Giddens, *The Constitution of Society: Outline of the Theory of Structuration* (Berkeley, 1984), p. xxiii.

2 See Edward Said, *Beginnings: Intention and Method* (Baltimore, 1975), pp. 191–7, and Samuel Taylor Coleridge, *Biographia Literaria*, eds James Engell and W. Jackson Bate, 2 vols, vol. 7 of *The Collected Works of Samuel Taylor Coleridge*, gen. ed. Kathleen Coburn (Princeton, NJ, 1983), 1:41n; hereafter abbreviated *BL.*

3 See Francis Fukuyama, "The End of History?" *The National Interest*, no. 16 (Summer 1989): 3–18 and *The End of History and the Last Man* (New York, 1992); hereafter abbreviated *EH.*

4 Benjamin Constant, *The Spirit of Conquest and Usurpation and Their Relation to Civilization*, in *Political Writings*, trans. and ed. Biancamaria Fontana (Cambridge, 1988), p. 55.

5 Wisely or not, this essay abandons the security provided by the so-called anachronism test, which contemporary historians of consequence have argued provides an important criterion for determining that the language identified with a historical agent is not the historian's own fabrication. See Quentin Skinner, "Meaning and Understanding in the History of Ideas," *History and Theory* 8, no. 1 (1969): 3–53, and J.G.A. Pocock, "Concept of a Language and the *metier d'historien*: Some Considerations on Practice," in *The Languages of Political Theory in Early Modern Europe*, ed. Anthony Pagden (Cambridge, 1987), p. 21.

6 Fredric Jameson, *Postmodernism, or, The Cultural Logic of Late Capitalism* (Durham, NC, 1991), p. 309; hereafter abbreviated *PM.* Diane Elam takes a divergent position in her *Romancing the Postmodern* (London, 1992), where she argues that anachronism is an "inevitable" constituent of the genre she calls "postmodern romance" (pp. 68–75).

7 [Immanuel Wallerstein, *Unthinking Social Science: The Limits of Nineteenth-Century Paradigms* (Cambridge, 1991), p. 21.]

8 E.J. Hobsbawm, *Primitive Rebels: Studies in Archaic Forms of Social Movement in the Nineteenth and the Twentieth Centuries* (New York, 1959), p. 151; hereafter abbreviated *PR.*

9 Matthew Arnold, "The Function of Criticism at the Present Time," *Essays in Criticism, First Series*, ed. Sister Thomas Marion Hoctor (Chicago, 1968), p. 13.

10 Karl Marx and Friedrich Engels, *German Ideology, Parts I and III*, ed. R. Pascal (New York, 1947), p. 26; hereafter abbreviated *GI.*

11 Jerome J. McGann, *The Romantic Ideology: A Critical Investigation* (Chicago, 1983), p. 9.

12 Louis Althusser, *Lenin and Philosophy and Other Essays*, trans. Ben Brewster (New York, 1971), pp. 173, 182.

13 Jacques Lacan, "The Freudian Unconscious and Ours," *The Four Fundamental Concepts of Psycho-Analysis*, trans. Alan Sheridan and ed. Jacques-Alain Miller (New York, 1978), p. 22.

14 Paul Ricoeur, *Lectures on Ideology and Utopia*, ed. George H. Taylor (New York, 1986), p. 78.

15 W.J.T. Mitchell, *Iconology: Image, Text, Ideology* (Chicago, 1986), p. 169; hereafter abbreviated *I.*

16 Coleridge is picking up on Wordsworth's warning in the 1800 preface to *Lyrical Ballads* that readers might expect "feelings of strangeness and awkwardness" in their first encounter with the poetry (William Wordsworth, *Wordsworth: Selected Poems and Prefaces*, ed. Jack Stillinger [Boston, 1965], p. 446).

17 Maria and Richard Edgeworth, "Essay on Irish Bulls," *Tales and Novels*, 18 vols in 9 (New York, 1836), 1:102.

18 Wordsworth, "Ode: Intimations of Immortality from Recollections of Early Childhood," *Selected Poems and Prefaces*, p. 189; hereafter abbreviated "II."

19 That children do give us such information is the burden of Wordsworth's "We Are Seven" in *Lyrical Ballads* and of Lacan's version of the bull in "The Freudian Unconscious and Ours":

> Remember the naive failure of the simpleton's delighted attempt to grasp the little fellow who declares – *I have three brothers, Paul, Ernest and me.* But it is quite natural – first the three brothers, Paul, Ernest and I are counted, and then there is I at the level at which I am to reflect the first I, that is to say, the I who counts.
> [Lacan, "The Freudian Unconscious and Ours," p. 20]

Lacan takes the Edgeworths' moral, that there could be no continuity of identity, and runs with it.

20 J. Laplanche and J.-B. Pontalis, *The Language of Psycho-Analysis* (New York, 1973), p. 457, quoting Sigmund Freud.
21 For example:

> Sagacious men and *knowing* in their profession they are not ignorant that even diseases may prove convenient: they remember that Demosthenes, a state-physician, when he wished to finger a large fee from Harpalus, yet was expected by his former connections to speak out according "to the well-known tendency of his political opinions" found a *sore-throat* very serviceable; and they have learnt from their own experience how absolutely necessary in point of "selfish policy" is a certain political palsey in the head, "omnibus omnia annuens."
>
> [Coleridge, "A Letter to Edward Long Fox, M.D.," *Lectures 1795 on Politics and Religion*, eds Lewis Patton and Peter Mann, vol. I of *Collected Works of Samuel Taylor Coleridge*, pp. 326–7]

See also Coleridge, "Lectures on Revealed Religion," *Lectures 1795 on Politics and Religion*, p. 207. An important exception to this programmatic derogation occurs in Coleridge's letters home from Germany in March 1799, written after some study of the German university system, where the term *professor* is treated with uncharacteristic respect.
22 Pocock, "Virtues, Rights, and Manners: A Model for Historians of Political Thought," *Virtue, Commerce, and History: Essay on Political Thought and History, Chiefly in the Eighteenth Century* (Cambridge, 1985), pp. 43–5.
23 C.B. Macpherson, *Democratic Theory: Essays in Retrieval* (Oxford, 1973), pp. 5, [. . .] 10.
24 Sigmund Freud, "The Dynamics of Transference," *Therapy and Technique*, ed. Phillip Rieff (New York, 1963), pp. 113–14; hereafter abbreviated "DT."
25 Benedict Anderson, *Imagined Communities: Reflections on the Origin and Spread of Nationalism* (1983; London, 1991), p. 75.
26 Not least in my own writing, where, I confess, this is the third time I have pulled out this particular plum.
27 Coleridge, "Once a Jacobin Always a Jacobin," *Essays on His Times*, ed. David V. Erdman, 3 vols, vol. 3 of *Collected Works of Samuel Taylor Coleridge*, 1:368.
28 John Bohstedt, *Riots and Community Politics in England and Wales, 1790–1810* (Cambridge, Mass., 1983), p. 5.
29 See Raymond Williams, *Marxism and Literature* (Oxford, 1977), pp. 121–7.
30 See [Roger] Wells, *Insurrection: The British Experience, 1795–1803* (Gloucester, 1983)], pp. 220–52.
31 Edgeworth and Edgeworth, "Essay on Irish Bulls," p. 100.
32 "Where no other organization existed, as after the defeat of a revolutionary movement, masonic lodges were very likely to become the refuge of the rebels" (*PR*, p. 163).
33 See Stephen Jay Gould, *Wonderful Life: The Burgess Shale and the Nature of History* (New York, 1989), pp. 45–52.

34 Everyday war

Mary Favret

> The traumatized, we might say, carry an impossible history within them. Or they become themselves the symptom of a history that they cannot entirely possess (and thus which possesses them).
>
> (Cathy Caruth, Unclaimed Experience:
Trauma, Narrative and History[1])

In her novel *Persuasion*, Jane Austen offers up symptoms of a history not entirely possessed. The past presented in the novel is incomplete, interrupted. Over the narrative hangs the unaccountable weight of "eight years and a half ago," a period of romance which the novel conjures only to dismiss in a few paragraphs. "A short period of exquisite felicity . . . and but a short one. Troubles soon arose."[2] The narrator emphasizes the brevity of a lost love which, now in the form of enduring pain, possesses her heroine, Anne Elliot. "A few months had seen the beginning and the end of their acquaintance" – already the narrator diminishes the affair –

> but not with a few months ended Anne's share of suffering from it. Her attachment and her regrets had, for a long time, clouded every enjoyment of youth; and an early loss of bloom and spirits had been their lasting effect.
>
> (P, 28)

Loss of bloom, loss of spirits, loss of money, loss of status: characters in *Persuasion* are variously in danger of having the past slip away. "Tell me not I am too late, that those precious feelings are gone forever," Capt. Wentworth writes desperately, and he too uses the language of pain to underscore his own share of suffering: "You pierce my soul. I am half agony, half hope" (*P*, 237). In the end, the novel, like Shakespeare's *A Winter's Tale*, reassures us that love can, magically, come back to life. But even that resuscitation remains tenuous, and not without the threat of further pain. The narrator closes the novel by reminding us that the moment of happiness may not last and troubles may arise again. United with her love, Anne Elliot "gloried in being a sailor's wife," but had to "pay the tax of quick alarm" – dread of his being called back to war (*P*, 273). What does endure, filling most of the narrative and more than eight years, testifying to love and its history, is suffering. One name for that history of suffering is the everyday, a term often invoked to characterize the world of Austen's novels. Another name for that history, which cannot be possessed but possesses the novel, is war.

Like other versions of the everyday constructed in the Romantic period, Austen's in *Persuasion* emerges from the reality of worldwide war. Reading these unaccountable histories of pain and loss, one begins to suspect that the everyday is a wartime. In fact, one can follow a distinct strand of thinking about the everyday, from its philosophical and aesthetic roots in Romanticism into twentieth-century critical theory, and find it informed by the language, the features, and the preoccupations of wartime. Modern war – with its national armies, its tendency to erase the line between combatants and noncombatants, its global reach – is the history which possesses, perhaps determines our own current thinking about the everyday. It seems appropriate, at a moment where war appears to have no horizon, to acknowledge this marriage of war and the everyday, but also to call into question, as the best romances do, the inevitability of this marriage.

· · · · · ·

For Austen, the everyday is the elastic form in which she tries to hold the recent history of the Napoleonic Wars; but by understanding the everyday as a record of pain and alienation, as in fact Anne's story, Austen makes it permeable to the suffering of war. The everyday, with its rhythms of routine and accident, of endless waiting and unforeseen returns, provides a chronotope for Austen's novels; in *Persuasion* it reveals itself to be as well the register, the telling surface, on which to read traces of nearly ineffable loss.[3] And reading these traces makes any assumption about Austen's everyday into a problem of history. Distressed, anxious, and punctuated by confusion and pain, the everyday Austen creates for *Persuasion* is, I want to argue, a wartime; more than a container, it is the medium through which she evokes the costs of prolonged war. Shadowing Anne's history, and even more sketchy in its details, is Frederick Wentworth's naval service in Britain's wars with Napoleon. Much of the drama of the novel depends on the reader – and Anne – not having access to Wentworth's "share of suffering" during those years. Even the Musgrove sisters' eager reading about his ships and postings in the navy lists merely points to the scarcity of information. With danger apparently behind him, Wentworth can now affect a nonchalance, who knows how hard-won, and joke about the less than seaworthy ship that was his first command. The satisfaction later afforded by his love letter to Anne, which arrives at the climax of the novel, rests in part in its revelation of how much pain he has borne. Here Austen seems to eclipse the sufferings of warfare with the trials of love, and wipe away both with the romance of her ending. But why then does she leave the novel with the "dread of a future war" and that nagging "tax of quick alarm" (*P*, 252)? And why does she set her novel so carefully in 1814, the year known as the False Peace, after which "troubles soon arose" and Europe found itself again at war?

[. . .]

[An omitted section of this article analyzes William Cowper's *The Task* and twentieth-century theoretical writing; both instances emphasize "the coincidence of war and the everyday."]

[I] *Persuasion*: diverting away the time

Persuasion is Austen's most dated novel, carefully located during the False Peace of 1814, which, like the earlier Peace of Amiens, would prove to be merely another "meantime" or suspension within war. To say what was peace is no longer is to identify the historical but also the emotional and temporal outline of this postwar novel (written in 1817). As Adela Pinch and others have noted, there is often a noise or "buzz" in the air around Anne Elliot which, like the stir and roar [William] Cowper aims to keep at a distance from the "uninjur'd ear," nevertheless infiltrates the insular consciousness Austen has constructed for her heroine.[4] In *Persuasion*, "noises are the means by which other presences make themselves felt" suggests Pinch; they serve as a counter to the heroine's – and the reader's – "soundless absorption in a text."[5] Invasive noise is just one mechanism for the entry of historicity, of the felt experience of wartime, within the novel. Accident, injury, Anne's dizziness, and various knocks to various heads – the hammering away at otherwise impervious defenses – all indicate the historical substance of *Persuasion*.

Try as she might, Anne Elliot cannot find peace in peacetime; the peace she thinks she has achieved during her nearly eight years of limbo is too fragile, too easily broken, and, as events in the novel prove, too illusory to count as true peace. Thus, following her first meeting with Wentworth after his return from the navy, Anne Elliot aims to flee the turbulence.

> She began to reason with herself, and try to be feeling less. Eight years, almost eight years had passed, since all had been given up. How absurd to be resuming the agitation which such an interval had banished to distance and indistinctness! What might not eight years do? Events of every description, changes, alienations, removals – all, all must be comprised in it; and oblivion of the past – how natural and how certain too. It included nearly a third part of her own life.
>
> (*P*, 60)

Like Anne's sense of peace, periodic time, with its clear divisions and oblivions, falls apart through the uncertain chronology of affect: "Alas! with all her reasonings, she found, that to retentive feelings eight years may be little more than nothing" (*P*, 60). Anne's love for Wentworth, in fact, has to break through such false peace and tidy chronology into the stir and roar of a messier, indeed traumatic history. If we recall [Walter] Scott's 1816 assessment of Austen's accomplishment in the novel, we might hear the agitation of that history in his very description of the novel of "ordinary life" with its "striking representation of that which is daily taking place around [one]."[6] What is daily taking place all around *Persuasion*, that is prior to 1814 and afterward, is not at all peaceful; the pains of war overflow into the supposed idyll that is 1814 as they flow into the novel of manners.

Anne Elliot's consciousness, her affective state of simultaneous belatedness and anticipation, and her refined sensibility are designed to register precisely that overflow. Indeed, after keeping her heroine silent for the opening two chapters, while detailing her thoughts, Austen makes these nearly the first words that Anne utters, almost despite herself: "He [Admiral Croft] is rear admiral of the white. He was in the Trafalgar action" (*P*, 21–2). Locked within Anne is the history of a war no one around her seems to acknowledge. The repeated bouts of vertigo and dislocation Anne suffers in Wentworth's presence can be read, then, as a record of the sort of profound *vertige* Paul de Man diagnoses as the sign of self-alienation within history. For de Man, such *vertige* discloses "a truly temporal predicament" or "temporal void" that collapses the sequence and priorities of chronological time so that, in this case, the temporality of the past (the wartime of 1806 and after) and that of the present (the peacetime of 1814) are not at all given or distinct; and, as Anne recognizes, "eight years may be little more than nothing."[7] In this sense, the novelist situates Anne and *Persuasion* within history, suffering history, which is to say that even after Waterloo Austen refuses to let the noise and dust of wartime settle into a clear structure of before and after, now and then. What James Chandler says about vertiginous states and the history of war in W.G. Sebald's novel *Vertigo* (1990) applies directly to Anne's predicament: in the flux of powerful emotions, "[i]t is seldom an easy matter . . . to tell if one is moving in the direction of remembering or of forgetting."[8]

To elaborate my sense of this novel as an everyday record of the felt if not acknowledged experience of war, I read Austen's last novel alongside the diary of John Wetherell.[9] Wetherell does not quite provide the hard evidence to prove my reading of Austen, anymore than Austen supplements Wetherell's account with a home-front perspective. Rather, to a reader alert to the interpellation of wartime and peacetime, everyday domesticity and physical danger, each work sustains and elaborates the other like a conversation – or a marriage. In both texts, war and the everyday fall for each other – a turn of phrase I hope to justify later. Wetherell's account does adumbrate a possibility within the novel: more even than suggesting the contours of Wentworth's life during the lost eight years, Wetherell's account hints at one of the truly lost lives of the novel, that of the dead seaman Dick Musgrave.[10] For *Persuasion* is also, dramatically, a novel of everyday injury and pain, and our ease or difficulty in coordinating the novel's injuries with those of the man at war seems, in the end, crucial to our understanding of any everyday war. Appreciating such inexact alignments suggests to me one way of getting at what can never quite be known about either narrative.

In the broad outline of the text currently in print, we follow Wetherell from his impressment at Harwich in 1803, through various military exploits in the North Sea and North Atlantic, to his shipwreck near Brest and his long journey to the prison at Givet, where Wetherell and his comrades spend many years as prisoners of war. Though I will refer primarily to his years on ship, half the account deals with the prison years in which the sailor adopts a new career as interpreter and nurse. After the prisoners' release in 1814, subsequent to Napoleon's initial defeat, they travel through France (playing everywhere on their fiddles, a skill honed in prison) until their eventual arrival at the sea coast, where they await return to England. Throughout, it is worth mentioning, there is a continual promise and deferral of marriage: Wetherell is engaged before he meets the press-gang, then engaged again before leaving France; one marriage is blocked by the war, the other by the declaration of peace. The penultimate entry finds him comforting himself about this last, lost union by fulfilling his promise to his second fiancée to "write every opportunity" (*W*, 274).[11] Wetherell is clearly proud of his literacy and his attention to the English (and later French) language. Austen herself would appreciate the strenuous manner in which the sailor parses and ironizes the word "duty." His routine use of the word "tyrant" to denominate the British commanding officers, and his unflinching description of their brutality, indicate no small ambivalence about the political aims of the war England is waging against Napoleon's tyranny. Wetherell is a resourceful writer, taking advantage of a range of genres – biblical lament, gothic tale, sentimental romance, even parodic verse – to craft his account of the war years. The literariness of his diary resists any attempt to affirm the priority of the historical over the fictional, or the authentic over the invented. One feature of his work stands out, though, and marks him as a possible companion for Austen. This is his predilection, throughout the years on ship as well as those in prison, to record everyday detail and routine. Together with his attention to small conversations, these registrations disperse any conventional or epic sense of warfare. They do, however, evoke powerfully the felt pains and consolations of an everyday war. Thus, in a witty description of how his fellow prisoners keep busy, Wetherell sketches the man who

> quite busy at his occupations [could] Jump up, take his fiddle, scrape away for some time, then down with it and to work at his book half an hour, then take a walk around the yard, back again, eat a Mouthful if he has any left, and down again to his employment. Then he could hammer or stitch away and settle all the affairs of the two contending nations. In this manner we diverted away the time.
>
> (*W*, 141)

Glimpsed in the brief reference to "his book" is Wetherell's characteristic allegorizing of his own work as writer, which, like Austen's novel, might be said in its attention to the everyday to divert away while recording a time framed by the conflict of two contending nations.

[II] A broken story

> December 22–30, 1803 O England. . . . Did thou but know their cruel treatment to thy brave Seaman on the Ocean, thou woulds't Shudder at the verry name of it. And almost be perswaded to say this cannot be true.
>
> (*W*, 86)

Austen's *Persuasion* is set in motion by the return home of British navy men in 1814 after the apparent defeat of Napoleon, a peace which proves no peace. In its own way *Persuasion* meditates on war and the everyday to see if, like Austen's heroines and heroes, they could remake each other. But in so doing *Persuasion* upsets – or foregoes – peace. I take my cue, then, from [Stanley] Cavell's proposition that the ancient mariner "is a disturber of [the] peace which is no peace."[12] *Persuasion's* Capt. Wentworth, too, is an ancient mariner, a mariner with some connection to the past (whether a distant past or not is partly at stake here); and he too disturbs a peace that is no peace, which is to say, Anne Elliot's day-to-day existence. Unlike Coleridge's "Rime," however, here disruption of peace and movement toward a wedding are not mutually exclusive. One way to approach this topic is to suggest that, ever since Wentworth's release from fighting, ever since the cessation of war, Anne Elliot has quite privately been "pay[ing] the tax of quick alarm" for having him near.[13] Another way is to show how Anne Elliot comes to represent the cultivation of war – or a wartime routine – within the everyday.

> May 25, 26, 27 1803. A smart gale at NW. In a little while we joined the Commodore in the bay and made sail to the eastward . . . where we passed away two days exercising. This was exercising Officers, , , men, , , Ships, , , sails, , , , Guns, , , Yards washing, , , holystoning, , , , , Small arms, , , , Mustering bags. Reefing in two minutes, , , , punishment, , , , Up and down hammocks, , , , Stow them, , , scrub hammocks, Up all chests and bags, , , , sprinkle and scrub, , , , Serve out pursers

Slops and tobacco, , , , serve grog, , , , turn all hands to skylarking, , , , Set the watch. All these little changes were transacted in the course of two days cruise in the North Sea.

(*W*, 46)

It has become a commonplace to note in *Persuasion* Austen's esteem for the navy, registered each time the navy appears as the realm of domestic order as well as real affection. Mrs. Croft proclaims twice, underlining the pun, that she knows "nothing superior to the accommodations of a man of war" (*P*, 69, 70). Anne Elliot admires "all the ingenious contrivances and nice arrangements" of Capt. Harville's house. "[C]onnected as it all was with his profession," she finds it "the picture of repose and domestic happiness" otherwise foreign to her (*P*, 98). The affection and loyalty between the brother officers also contrasts sharply with what Anne has known within her family. As several critics have argued, the novel offers the navy as a more congenial model for living than what Anne Elliot has yet experienced.[14]

Austen is at pains to inform us that life at sea in wartime has its everyday component: the officers mock the young ladies' surprise at learning that meals, prepared by a cook, are served on board.

[Wentworth] was very much questioned . . . as to the manner of living on board, daily regulations, food, hours, etc., and their surprise at his accounts, at learning the degree of accommodation and arrangement which was practicable, drew from him some pleasant ridicule, which reminded Anne of the early days, when she too had been ignorant, and . . . accused of supposing sailors to be living on board without anything to eat, or any cook to dress it if there were, or any servant to wait, or any knife and fork to use.

(*P*, 64)

But what happens to our understanding of warfare, of these men's profession, when we – or Anne – choose it as a happier version of the everyday? An entry from Wetherell's diaries gives an account of dinner aboard a man-of-war that moves beyond what was served and who served it, to record the deep misery of the men expected to eat it. As much as anything, the routine of eating could be a test of the sailors' stoicism.

December 22–30, 1803. By this time it was near six bells in the Afternoon; went to dinner and a poor dinner it was to many, some thro' pain and others through their feelings at such unheard of cruelties. . . . We then Stood out to Sea and on Christmas day had a good Plumb Pudding, and a good piece of beef for dinner, but all this was nothing where contentment had fled; however like old Philosophers we bore all this as patient as possible and of our bad bargain made the best.

(*W*, 86)

What spoils the meal for the sailors, especially the ordinary sailors not mentioned in the dinner conversation at Uppercross, is the everyday brutality of their commanders. In this instance, they had just witnessed the "Savage torture" of a dozen of their crew, whipped till "the deck with human gore was dy'd" (*W*, 85). Physical punishment was routine in the British navy during this period; with Parliamentary hearings into the practice of flogging, no literate person could have been unaware of the prevalence of this practice, though they may have remained persuadable that it could not be true, or truly cruel.[15] When we think about the everydayness of the navy introduced into the novel, we might also recall this more ordinary version of the everyday available in Wetherell's diary. Like Catherine Morland with her "alarms" in *Northanger Abbey*, perhaps the ignorant young ladies who question the "degree of accommodation and arrangement" on board a warship are not absolutely risible.

A more easeful way of bringing together the everydayness of the navy with the world at Uppercross would be to recognize the ethos of care and survival at work in the novel. John Wiltshire has called *Persuasion* the story of "broken bones, broken heads and broken hearts," not quite differentiating between Anne Elliot's suffering and that of, say, Capt. Hayter with his wounded leg.[16] Such a broken-down story calls forth the practice of nursing – think not only of Anne tending her nephew, or Benwick tending Lydia, but of Nurse Ragg and the Musgroves' old nursery maid, Sara, who had been "living in the deserted nursery to mend stockings and dress all the bruises and blains she could get near her" (*P*, 122), as well as Wentworth himself, who spends a week watching over the distraught Capt. Benwick – and calls it forth in such a way that care, a responsiveness to hurt bodies and souls, supplies the ethos of this novel. With this emphasis on care, Austen recognizes the innovations of the "new navy" promoted by Sir John Jervis (later Lord St. Vincent) during the wars with Napoleon. As Monica Cohen has noted, Jervis reorganized the navy along the lines of specialization and professionalization, thus undermining the former hierarchy of class. More immediately, Cohen writes, he "attended to the quotidian life of a naval ship. He bickered with doctors over whether his men should wear warm flannel or cotton weave that could be kept cleaner." Jervis scheduled regular ventilation and fumigation on board; he bothered to order soap for his fleet. And he revised medical procedures so that each fleet was accompanied by a hospital ship. Commenting on Jervis's known attention to hygiene and caring for his men, Cohen notes that "there is a touch of the [domestic] heroine about Jervis."[17] One could also say, in noting her sense of service and care, that there is a touch of the officer in Anne Elliot. Though the Portsmouth episode in *Mansfield Park* may be a better text for demonstrating the intersection of Austen's focus on hygiene and diet with her knowledge of the navy, *Persuasion* shows the coordination of the domestic and the wartime everyday through acts of practical nursing.

Yet, when we hail the navy's everyday as a solution to Anne's situation, or note the interpenetration of the practices of navy and home under the ethos of care, we also need to account for the converse intrusion of alarm and accident into the surface of the peacetime everyday.

> April 27. 1803 [The boy's] resolution was fixed and some time in the night he made his escape overboard. . . . May 12. I made my obedience and then retired in a most horrid state of mind being nearly on the brink of leaping overboard to terminate my cruel treatment. . . . August 25. "What? Shall it be said that Jim Burchell would suffer this from a brat of a boy? No! I will die first!" . . . He sprung up, took the Midshipmen in his Arms, and overboard plunged head foremost, determined to die with him in his ARMS. . . . August 28. We had a very pleasant run out to the Cape, where we had the misfortune to loose one of our messenger boys named Tilford. The night being hot, he got into the Mizn

chains, fell asleep and roll'd overboard; was not heard nor missed until next morning. . . . November 10. Those who had gained hold of the Nettings were all either Shot or run thro' with pikes or sabers and fell back into the Boats or the Sea.

(*W*, 37, 44, 64, 67, 77)

We never learn what killed "poor Richard" Musgrove in *Persuasion*. We simply know "that the Musgroves had had the ill fortune of a very troublesome, hopeless son; and the good fortune to lose him before he reached his twentieth year" (*P*, 50). It is one of the few moments in Austen's fiction at which a reader might flinch. Indeed, the Johnsonian balance of this outrageous sentence later topples over when the narrator expresses distaste over the mother's "large fat sighings over the destiny of a son, whom alive nobody had cared for" (*P*, 68). As D.A. Miller has shown, this moment marks a more than stylistic lapse on the narrator's part: something refuses to fit or be accommodated in this passage about the lost sailor.[18] "Stupid and unmanageable on shore," Dick Musgrove had been shipped off to war where, sometime after serving under Capt. Wentworth, he died unaccountably (*P*, 50). It just happened.

The narrator grudgingly grants us this "pathetic piece of family history" on the way to revealing to Anne Elliot that Capt. Wentworth is back in town (*P*, 50). I imagine that Dick's death involved some sort of fall, because falls – to boys and young women – just happen throughout this novel. Capt. Wentworth's reentry to Anne Elliot's world (he is instantly on "an intimate footing" there) is curiously marked not just by the suddenly upending recollection of Dick Musgrove's death, but by further injuries involving boys (*P*, 73). Anne and the reader first "escape" the possibility of encountering Wentworth when young Charles Musgrove inexplicably falls, dislocating his collarbone and perhaps damaging his spine. Amidst the "alarming ideas" raised up by this falling down, "Anne had everything to do at once": our first glimpse at her effectiveness in an emergency (*P*, 53). Capt. Wentworth's appearance is deferred by this sudden accident, and deferred again when Anne agrees to stay home to nurse the boy while the rest of the family dines at Uppercross. At various moments in the course of the novel, when Anne herself is weighted down or oppressively tired, Wentworth steps quickly to relieve her, retreating as quickly, heightening her sense of "painful agitation" (*P*, 80, 91). Finally, in Lyme, when we and Anne come closest to the fellowship of the navy and all its tidy domesticity, another body falls, this time almost – but crucially not quite – into Wentworth's arms. It is as if this figure of the falling or weighted body were straining to attach itself to him – but cannot quite make contact. What Caruth has said about falling bodies in de Man's writings makes sense as well in *Persuasion*: "In naming a befalling" – or a series of falls that just happen – the "text no longer simply knows what it says, it does more than it knows."[19]

Looking at the socially fallen and invalid Mrs. Smith, Wiltshire argues that, along with care, *Persuasion* promotes "strategies of survival."[20] He finds these strategies epitomized by Mrs. Smith, but also honored in Anne Elliot's resilience after eight years of suffering, which, like Wetherell's "old Philosophers," she has "bor[n] as patient as possible and of [her] bad bargain made the best." But why not assign this survival to Wentworth as well, or to any of the other men we meet who happen to come home from war? The major accident of this novel, the falling bodies seem to suggest, is that Wentworth returns at all. Put another way, the presence of this military man catalyzes the everyday into a zone of quick alarm and harmful accidents demanding both care and the strength to survive. In this sense, and in response to his presence, Anne Elliot cultivates a mode of living every day as if she were at war.

Wiltshire's essay, "*Persuasion*: The Pathology of Everyday Life," focuses our attention on the centrality of accident and injury in this novel, arguing that their everydayness resists "a moral sense which [wants to] discover a narrative rationality in events."[21] Accidents are the fruit of chance and time, simple attributes of mortality, he proposes: they just happen. I would like to suggest instead that an uncanny, unclaimed sense of war rests beneath these accidents, particularly the otherwise avoided sense of war as violent injury. And rather than providing a firm ground or referent for the novel, it undermines any "easy footing" for the everyday (*P*, 59). The tendency in *Persuasion* is to transfer not only the security and familiarity of the everyday to the "man of war," but also the violence and injury of warfare to the space of the everyday, to boys and young women, thereby making them accidental, unaccountable, the natural "miscarriages of life," to use Wiltshire's language.[22] As if the need to cultivate "strategies of survival," like the word "strategies" itself, bore no trace of a circumambient war.

How much weight can be put on the vertigo-inspiring presence of Capt. Wentworth, the falling bodies, and Anne's thwarted desire to find "peace"? Her friend Mrs. Smith, presuming that Anne will marry the smooth Mr. Elliot, proclaims confidently that now "Anne's peace will not be shipwrecked . . . [she will be] safe in all worldly matters" (*P*, 196). But the evening before, when Anne met Wentworth at the concert, her "peace" had been quietly blown to the winds (*P*, 189). Later, after she – and the reader – undergo the "revolution" of reading Wentworth's love letter, Anne is so dazed that Mrs. Musgrove fears her distraction may be the result of her having "at any time lately, slipped down, and got a blow to her head." The older woman must be reassured that "there had been no fall in the case" (*P*, 237, 238). In fact, the narrator describes Anne's nearly shipwrecked state and her supposed blow to the head as approaching the "perfection of her felicity" (*P*, 239). *Persuasion* rewrites the opportunities of war and the so-called pleasures of peace even as it dismisses peace of mind.

> November 10, 1804. . . . as we were endeavoring to bear our boat astern . . . something come in contact with my head. Putting up my hand, I found the muzel of a Frenchman's Musket[,] push'd it on one side just as he fired, saved my own life and nearly shot our first lieut. near enough to graze his skull by the flash of the gun. I saw the man . . . that fired it and drawing my Pistol from my belt gave him the contents through his noodle.
>
> (*W*, 77)

In the end, the head seems the body part most susceptible to the accidents of every-day war in *Persuasion*; and rightly so, if we understand persuasion as the act of getting through to, penetrating, someone's noodle. Austen's response to war may appear more material and personified than, but not unlike, [Sigmund] Freud's tale about "the fragment of living matter"[23]: written in the wake of war, both were trying to narrate the way war invades the mind. Walton Litz has praised Austen's development in *Persuasion* of "a rapid and nervous syntax, designed to imitate the bombardment of impressions upon the mind," specifically Anne's mind.[24] Litz's language – "the bombardment of impressions upon the mind" – intuits the conclusion of my argument; that is, that Austen has brought war home not only to everyday bodies, but also to the rhythms of everyday minds – including that of the reader. *Persuasion* demonstrates one way that the affective structures demanded by war – its peculiar blend of self-alienation, selfless caring for others, alarm, endurance, even a felicity hard to distinguish from pain – migrate into everyday life, becoming so well understood, standing under everything one does, that one hardly knows how or when to account for them.

> June, 1810. From Prison. Buonaparte's wedding was celebrated in Paris. On the 8th of June Mr. Peytavin the Commodant and Mr. Wolfe the British Agent sent for me and they requested me to leave the Commissary and go to the Hospital in order to assist Tho. Stewart attending on the sick. Several of the French and English nurses were dead and the sickness spread such terror thro' all the town and prison that every person was afraid to undertake the unwelcome office of Nurse and interpreter. I obey'd the call and rendered all the assistance in my power.
>
> (*W*, 159)

Notes

1 Cathy Caruth, *Unclaimed Experience: Trauma, Narrative and History* (Baltimore: The Johns Hopkins Univ. Press, 1996), 5.

2 Jane Austen, *Persuasion*, vol. 5 of *The Oxford Illustrated Jane Austen*, ed. R.W. Chapman, 3rd ed. (Oxford: Oxford Univ. Press, 1988), 26. Hereafter abbreviated *P* and cited parenthetically by page number.

3 Nina Auerbach, echoing V.S. Pritchett, made the observation years ago that [. . .] "Jane Austen tells us what an observant, genteel woman has to tell about the Napoleonic Wars: she writes novels about waiting" (Auerbach, *Communities of Women: An Idea In Fiction* [Cambridge: Harvard Univ. Press, 1978], 39.)

4 [William Cowper, *The Task*, in *Complete Works*, ed. H.S. Milford, 4th ed. (Oxford: Oxford Univ. Press, 1967), book 4, line 93.]

5 Adela Pinch, *Strange Fits of Passion: Epistemologies of Emotion, Hume to Austen* (Stanford: Stanford Univ. Press, 1996), 159. [. . .]

6 [Walter Scott], unsigned review of *Emma*, *Quarterly Review*, 14 March 1816, reprinted in *Jane Austen: Critical Assessments*, ed. Ian Littlewood, 4 vols (Mountfield, England: Helm Information, Ltd., 1998), 1:291.

7 Paul de Man, "The Rhetoric of Temporality," in *Blindness and Insight*, 2nd ed. (Minneapolis: Univ. of Minnesota Press, 1983), 222.

8 James Chandler, "About Loss," *South Atlantic Quarterly* 102 (Winter 2003): 245.

9 [John Wetherell, *The Adventures of John Wetherell*, ed. C.S. Forester (Harmondsworth, Middlesex: Penguin Books Ltd., 1994). Hereafter abbreviated *W* and cited parenthetically by page number.]

10 A typical affluent family would have sent the younger son to the navy to give him a career; he would have served among those midshipmen who persecuted the likes of Wetherell, an unwilling recruit. Donald Gray has suggested to me that *Persuasion*, for its part, sheds light on an untold part of Wetherell's account: the story of the fiancée he left behind when he went to war. But again, not only class considerations make the fit inexact.

11 Forester informs us that Wetherell engages himself a third time, in New York, and finally marries there.

12 [Stanley Cavell, *In Quest of the Ordinary: Lines of Skepticism and Romanticism* (Chicago: Univ. of Chicago Press, 1988), 62.]

13 For example: "She could not hear of Capt. Wentworth's sister [coming] to live at Kellynch without a revival of former pains; and many a stroll and many a sigh were necessary to dispel the agitation of the idea" (*P*, 58).

14 Recent examples include Anne Mellor, *Mothers of the Nation* (Bloomington: Indiana Univ. Press, 2000), 121–41; and, with qualifications, Monica Cohen, "Persuading the Navy Home: Austen and Married Women's Professional Property," *Novel* 29 (Spring 1996): 346–66.

15 For more on the navy and *Persuasion*, see Cohen and Jill Heydt-Stevenson, "'Unbecoming Conjunctions': Mourning the Loss of Landscape and Love in *Persuasion*," *Eighteenth-Century Fiction* 8 (Oct. 1995): 51–71.

16 John Wiltshire, "*Persuasion:* The Pathology of Everyday Life," in *Jane Austen and the Body: "The Picture of Health"* (Cambridge: Cambridge Univ. Press, 1992), 192–3.

17 Cohen, 352.

18 See D.A. Miller, "Austen's Attitude," *Yale Journal of Criticism* 8 (Spring 1995): 1–5.

19 Caruth, 89–90.

20 Wiltshire, 186.

21 Wiltshire, 188–9.

22 Wiltshire, 182.

23 [Sigmund Freud, *Beyond the Pleasure Principle*, trans. and ed. Lytton Strachey, intro. Peter Gay (New York and London: W.W. Norton & Company, 1961), 30.]

24 Walton Litz, quoted in Wiltshire, 164.

35 Modernity's other worlds

Ian Duncan

[An omitted section at the beginning of the chapter questions critical arguments about Scott's sense of historical "closure" in his narratives, claiming instead that they critically examine "the project of national romance."]

Topologies of modernization

[Sir Walter] Scott developed his historical scheme from the conjectural historicism of the Scottish Enlightenment, which theorized cultural difference as the effect of historical difference articulated along a universal developmental axis – the set stages of social evolution from savage tribalism to commercial society, formulated by Adam Smith in his *Lectures on Jurisprudence* in the early 1760s and developed by (among others) John Millar, Adam Ferguson, and Smith himself in *The Wealth of Nations*.[1] James Chandler argues that this Scottish sociological history provided Romantic historicism with its fundamental principle of anachronistic or anatopic unevenness within the smooth calendrical time of modernization.[2] The Scottish formulation of "comparative contemporaneity" goes on to generate the Marxist thesis of uneven development (*Ungleichzeitigkeit*) and its variants: Ernst Bloch's nonsynchronism, [Reinhart] Koselleck's noncontemporaneity, Raymond Williams's typology of residual, dominant, and emergent formations, Fredric Jameson's sedimentation. Bloch's and Koselleck's accounts of noncontemporaneity, in particular, show us how the concept might yield the obverse of the linear historicism it is invoked to serve: since the epistemic horizon of modernity that allows a recognition of "the same" cultural stage existing at different times also necessitates the recognition of different cultural stages – different temporalities – inhabiting, and alienating, "the same" historical moment. The violent contemporaneities produced by imperial modernization remain latent within the negative term, noncontemporaneity, that covers them – awaiting their uncanny recognition at any disturbance of the rationalizing order of history.[3] [. . .] The "globe" makes its appearance, as a specifically modern condition of knowledge, through the disjunctive contemporaneity of which noncontemporaneity is the rationalizing inflexion, in the juxtaposition of different cultural "states" rather than in the comparison of one particular state with "universal history." In other words, the historical recognition of modernity itself – commercial society in its world-imperial range – renders the synchronic field of a radical contemporaneity: the present, imbued with strange shadows of the past and of unknown futures through the globalizing mechanisms of contact, exchange, and circulation by which it is constituted.

The argument that Scott's historical novel reproduces the program of Scottish Enlightenment historicism takes its cue from a famous passage in the last chapter of *Waverley*.[4] Scott frames his narrative with a meditation on the modernization of Scotland in the period since 1745:

> There is no European nation which, within the course of half a century, or little more, has undergone so complete a change as this kingdom of Scotland. The effects of the insurrection of 1745, – the abolition of the heritable jurisdictions of the Lowland nobility and barons, – the total eradication of the Jacobite party, which, averse to intermingle with the English, or adopt their customs, long continued to pride themselves upon maintaining ancient Scottish manners and customs, commenced this innovation. The gradual influx of wealth, and extension of commerce, have since united to render the present people of Scotland a class of beings as different from their grandfathers, as the existing English are from those of Queen Elizabeth's time.[5]

Scott identifies the political movement of Jacobitism with a vanished Scottish cultural past, which the preceding narrative (despite the reference to "Lowland nobility and barons") has located especially in the Gaelic Highlands.[6] Second, Scott aligns the perspective of his narrator and his reader with the temporality of the historical process of modernization, an alignment signaled in the novel's subtitle: " 'Tis Sixty Years Since." The title of this last chapter, "A Postscript, which should have been a Preface," spells out the character of a retrospect that sets the terms through which the preceding narrative is to be interpreted.[7]

Rob Roy, however, undoes the rhetorical hinges which articulate that historicist certainty. With the loss of the temporal coordinate, "sixty years since," the tale comes adrift from the linear chronicle of modernization. The "extraordinary mistake" made by [Georg] Lukács, in dating the action of *Rob Roy* (1715) several decades after that of *Waverley* (1745), expresses a profound if inadvertent insight into the later novel's scrambling of the scheme of Enlightenment historicism.[8] Scott refuses the teleological viewpoint of a narrator-editor able to offer us a postscript so sure of itself that it ought to have been a preface. *Rob Roy* is narrated in the first person by a protagonist who "never comes into imaginative possession of himself," or of the story he tells.[9] Frank Osbaldistone fails to give us final access to the meaning of the events he relates; neither his own life nor the public history with which it intersects arrange themselves into a clear pattern in his telling. Resisting the generic imperative of bildungsroman, the narrative never fully emerges from a subjective condition that Scott himself diagnoses as male hysteria. Frank finds himself unmanned by eloquent Amazons: Diana Vernon, whose more authentic "frankness" thwarts his callow lovemaking, and then, at the heart of the story, the terrifying matriarch Helen McGregor, who destroys life in front of his helpless, fascinated gaze. These figures block the course of a masculine heterosexuality that seeks its cue in protective fathers, friendly elder brothers, nurturing mothers, maidens obedient to male desire. The adventure culminates not in any clarity of action or self-realization but in a remarkable sentimental "paroxysm."[10] Diana bids Frank farewell *"for ever"*:

> Heaven knows, it was not apathy which loaded my frame and my tongue so much, that I could neither return Miss Vernon's half embrace, nor even answer her

farewell. The word, though it rose to my tongue, seemed to choke in my throat like the fatal *guilty*, which the delinquent who makes it his plea knows must be followed by the doom of death. . . . I felt the tightening of the throat and breast, the *hysterica passio* of poor Lear; and, sitting down by the wayside, I shed a flood of the first and most bitter tears which had flowed from my eyes since childhood.

(386)

[. . .] Right at the stage where, by the logic of bildungsroman, Scott's hero ought to have realized his masculine agency, he experiences instead the internal irruption of an archaic female organism – a drastic, psychosomatic state of "noncontemporaneity."[11]

Scott uncouples the identification of Jacobitism with Highland culture and blocks both terms from attaining a synecdochical equivalence with "Scotland." The uncoupling makes possible the framing of a new discursive category: the primitive. It is new in that Scott separates the primitive from the past as the product of a linear, teleological historicism, although only after he has evoked the past as a discursive stage through which his narrative may activate the primitive and its uncanny contemporaneity. *Rob Roy* adumbrates the primitive as a category invented by modern culture to allegorize itself: a quality or agency intrinsic to the operations of modernity, but troped as alien to it, moving outside the domestic ideological field of civil society. *Rob Roy* thus dramatizes an internal cleft in the conception of the modern secular collectivity within which the novel circulates, and to which its readers (and its by now transnational machinery of production and reception) belong.

Peter Womack has argued that the wild Highlands and their inhabitants only become visible – valuable – once modernity frames them as figures for its own past, the condition it has extinguished in order to become what it is.[12] But here Scott offers something different from an elegiac surmounting, in that the primitive sheds the trappings of its pastness, its own discursive origin, as soon as it begins to circulate in the narrative. A division of symbolic labor in *Rob Roy* allots the past to that figure now split off from the Highlander – Jacobitism, or the figure of the past as ideology – in order that the primitive may embody another temporal scheme. Scott drives a wedge between two disciplinary categories, anthropology and history, as they emerge from the matrix of the Enlightenment human sciences where they tend to be joined together. *Rob Roy* asserts its generic distinction as a novel in this opening of a gap between the categories. It teases apart the discursive and disciplinary bindings of a rationalist synthesis of the sciences to claim a different kind of imaginative space, one that is not the less a domain of knowledge. In this opening, with its notorious effects of opacity, irrationality, and incoherence, Scott's novel asserts its own modernity, its own contemporaneity. Here the novel claims a cognitive mastery peculiar to itself, rather than justifying fiction as the didactic bearer of some other kind of truth – such as, for instance, political economy.

Inside and outside *The Wealth of Nations*

In *The Wealth of Nations* Adam Smith founded a new discourse of modernity. The famous first chapter closes with an oblique reflection upon the phenomenon of chronotopic unevenness in an immanent world system. Besides expounding the formal principle of a modern economy – the division of labor – Smith establishes the rhetorical conditions of his discourse. He does so by testing its limits: limits that are on the one hand discursive and rhetorical, and on the other hand geographical and anthropological. The implicit question of who shares in the wealth of the nation measures the extent to which the nation itself might constitute an intelligible category.

By means of the division of labor, writes Smith, "a general plenty diffuses itself through all the ranks of society."[13] This general diffusion of plenty turns out to be an imaginary, indeed ghostly condition, realized in the act of reading about it (foreshadowing [Benedict] Anderson's account of the imagined community). It consists in a convergence of globalized metonymic relations, so that the most ordinary everyday object can no longer be conceived as an effect of its phenomenological circumstances, bound to a particular space, visible and tangible against a local ground. Instead it is haunted by an intricate and far-flung network of processes of production and distribution:

> Observe the accommodation of the most common artificer or day-labourer in a civilized and thriving country, and you will perceive that the number of people of whose industry a part, though but a small part, has been employed in procuring him this accommodation, exceeds all computation. The woollen coat, for example, which covers the day-labourer, as coarse and rough as it may appear, is the produce of the joint labour of a great multitude of workmen. The shepherd, the sorter of the wool, the wool-comber or carder, the dyer, the scribbler, the spinner, the weaver, the fuller, the dresser, with many others, must all join their different arts in order to complete this homely production. How many merchants and carriers, besides, must have been employed in transporting the materials from some of those workmen to others who often live in a very distant part of the country! How much commerce and navigation in particular, how many ship-builders, sailors, sail-makers, rope-makers, must have been employed in order to bring together the different drugs made use of by the dyer, which often come from the remotest corners of the world!
>
> (22–3)

The day laborer's woolen coat is no longer just a coat, but a singular, contingent node in a dynamic topology of relations that is – if we trace it far enough – world-wide in its extent. This potentially global topology disintegrates national boundaries as well as the local scene. The perception of such a topology – and of the nature of commodities in a modern economy – requires a special kind of vision, a new kind of discursive mapping, for it to become apparent: an inexhaustible power of metonymy, correspondent to the inexhaustible dynamism of the market. The political economist, Smith himself, aims to provide that mapping: "insisting that society constitutes a *system* visible only to the moral philosopher cum political economist."[14]

The end of Smith's commercial-metonymic sublime takes an odd turn. The smoothly inexorable diffusion of the discourse predicates a homogeneity of "opulence" across all the classes of society. The nation, internally homogenized, secures and stabilizes the scheme. Any economic unevenness between master and worker is a phenomenological illusion which vanishes in the philosophical lens, since the invisible complex relations that signify wealth invest the laborer's coat just as they do the sumptuous garb of royalty:

Compared, indeed, with the more extravagant luxury of the great, [the day laborer's] accommodation must no doubt appear extremely simple and easy; and yet it may be true, perhaps, that the accommodation of an European prince does not always so much exceed that of an industrious and frugal peasant, as the accommodation of the latter exceeds that of many an African king, the absolute master of the lives and liberties of ten thousand naked savages.

(23–4)

Smith affirms the comparative equality of property relations within the national society by invoking a violently exploitative differentiality found outside it: outside Europe, outside civilization and modernity, in Africa. Smith admits this external difference covertly, in another register, that of simile; for it requires little reflection to see that African savagery is nevertheless part of the political economy of the nation, if we trace the metonymic chain far enough. As Smith knew perfectly well, mid-eighteenth-century Glasgow's commercial wealth was founded on the Chesapeake tobacco and (increasingly) West India sugar trades, and thus on slavery.[15] The deflected recognition of that fact occurs here across a syntactical suppression: the European subject (the merchant or citizen who, in Lowland Scotland at any rate, has supplanted Smith's feudal dyad of prince and peasant) *is*, in effect, "the absolute master of the lives and liberties of ten thousand naked savages," whether he owns plantations, has shares in the trade, or consumes sugar or tobacco. Through an analogic skewing, Smith's scheme admits the violent synchronicity of different historical stages – feudalism, savagery, and a suppressed modernity – linked by "savage" political relations of dominance, in the global economy of modern commercial society.

It is unlikely that this distortion, both of Smith's syntax and of the representation of the political economy, marks a "repression" of slavery on Smith's part – its relegation to the text's political unconscious. Later in *The Wealth of Nations* Smith condemns slavery for being economically inefficient, in a critique that would furnish a powerful argument for the antislavery movement. What is at issue is a structure of representation, in the relation of a normative, domestic order (the economic, political, and moral relations that constitute the nation) to another, alien, exterior horizon – one of archaic, savage political relations – which nevertheless permeates the former. Smith's prose admits the shadow of a rhetorical threat: once a system of relations becomes total – global – it reduces all analogies, equivalences between terms inside and outside the system, to homologies: equivalences within the system. Modernity, far from abolishing the difference between civilization and barbarism, preserves it – produces it – inside itself, in a relation of perpetual violence.

Rob Roy opens with a ceremonial duel between commerce and romance. The contest, associated with a filial resistance to paternal discipline, replays another topic – the debate between romance and history – familiar from *Waverley*. Frank Osbaldistone would rather be a poet than succeed his austere father as head of the family firm. But Scott's narrative charges commercial enterprise with the peril and glamor of romance, and sets up the merchant as the proper hero of modern society. Frank's poetry, by contrast, is a dead letter, imitation in the most lifeless, literal sense. Like the youthful Scott, he is translating Ariosto, replicating the forms of the ancien régime in a kind of cultural Jacobitism. Incapable of understanding the dynamic energies of modernity, Frank only dutifully repeats the Smithian maxim:

> [Commerce] connects nation with nation, relieves the wants, and contributes to the wealth of all; and is to the general commonwealth of the civilized world what the daily intercourse of ordinary life is to private society, or rather, what air and food are to our bodies.
>
> (75)

It will take another kind of romance than Frank's verses to be adequate to the forces of connection and circulation that mesh together – and so categorically constitute – nation, world, ordinary life, private society, and our bodies. The romance form of modernity is the novel, exemplified by the book we are reading. It is one of the many subtleties of *Rob Roy* that its poet-*manqué* narrator, in contrast to its author, never quite becomes aware of his vocation as a novelist. Frank does not think of his contemporary, Daniel Defoe, who combined a literary career as "the father of the novel" with the role of economic and political agent, involved, among other enterprises, in the forging of a new multinational state through the Union of Scotland and England; but Scott alludes to him more than once, and makes him the source for the novel's account of the rising economic energies of Glasgow.[16]

Modernity's other worlds

The reader encounters a scientific analysis of history according to Scottish principles of political economy two-thirds of the way through *Rob Roy*, after hundreds of pages in which the historical referent for this historical novel has been all but inscrutable. The analysis is offered by the Glasgow merchant and magistrate Nicol Jarvie, who is the novel's spokesman for an ascendant sociology of commerce, legality, and civic virtue, as well as being the proprietor of a West-India plantation, and thus of slaves (295).[17] Jarvie rehearses the Smithian account of modernity that identifies it with mercantile capitalism and the institutions of a post-1688 national economy: the Stock Exchange, colonial free trade, a national debt. Anticipating a genre that might be called (after Sir John Sinclair's great economic and demographic survey of 1791–99) "the statistical account of Scotland," Jarvie explains the state of the Highlands and the coming rebellion as products of a dynamic relation between population, productivity, and credit. The overpopulated Highlands have become a kind of third-world debtor economy within the new British state, and a national credit collapse will drive the clans into insurrection. Far from marking a resurgence of ancient cultural loyalties, the Jacobite rising is determined by the fluctuations of a modern, imperial economy across a political geography of underdevelopment (300–7).

Jarvie's statistical account appears to occupy a position of authority in *Rob Roy*, identical with the perspective of modernity from which we are reading, and made possible by the very site from which Jarvie, quasi-prophetically, speaks: Glasgow, where Adam Smith – at the time Frank is supposed to be narrating, in the mid-1760s – is delivering the university lectures on jurisprudence out of which will emerge *The Wealth of Nations*. The analysis explains not only historical events but also the novel's private plot, in which Frank's wicked cousin steals the firm's assets, provoking a nationwide financial panic and the Jacobite counterrevolutionary attempt. (We also learn that a credit squeeze lies behind Rob Roy's career in banditry.) Economics would seem to furnish the definitive discourse of the historical novel as well as of history itself, and Jarvie's historical position would seem to grant him the clarity and certainty denied to the novel's first-person narrator.

Scott frames this historical position and its scientific authority within the familiar narrative schema of a tour through the nation that articulates its internal differences. The act of framing, however, historicizes the discourse of historical explanation and deprives it of universal authority. Frank sets out on a northern journey across a series of regional sites, each of which represents a different historical relation to national modernity.

The story opens in London: less thickly described place than abstract premise, the center of the new United Kingdom and its expanding empire. Then the narrative settles, for what seems an inordinate length (chapters 5–18), at a country estate in Northumberland, before moving on to Glasgow (chapters 19–26) and at last the Highlands (chapters 27–36). Respectively, these are the settings of a rustic feudalism (the crucible of Jacobite intrigue), commercial protomodernity, and prefeudal, "savage," clan society. The novel's settings represent not just geographically distinct spaces but anthropologically distinct stages, very much according to Enlightenment conjectural history. We might expect this arrangement of settings to map the historicist scheme exemplified in *The Wealth of Nations*, so that clan society, feudalism, and commerce will describe a developmental progression in which the obsolescence of one stage – its pastness – guarantees the succession of the next. The Northumberland chapters seem to bear this out, their alternating styles of satire and Gothic consigning the feudal, Catholic, and Royalist culture of Jacobitism to a superseded past. The comedy of regional manners, perfected by Maria Edgeworth in *Castle Rackrent*, marks the residual character of a backwoods feudalism. Sir Hildebrand's sons are not characters, inhabitants of the new discourse of the novel, psychologically individuated by the complex specificity of a modern economy. They are types: generic cases of booby-squire decadence, barely distinguishable by their respective humors. Such a representation has nowhere else to go but to record their extinction, which it does in a suitably absurdist key at the end of the novel. As Frank lingers at Osbaldistone Hall, a different stylization of feudal obsolescence takes over, this time drawn from the Gothic novels of Horace Walpole and Ann Radcliffe. Gothic aligns the Jacobites, especially Die's father, not just with psychological themes of repression and sublimation but with a more drastic condition of ghostliness.[18] Both styles, the satiric and the Gothic, suggest a fated fall into the past.

The story's move north into Scotland, however, undoes the teleological certainty – the conviction of pastness – encoded in the Northumberland chapters, and with that the ordering of regional cultural differences along a linear chronology. Scotland is not represented as a unified territorial and cultural entity, a nation, since it is split between the very different worlds of Glasgow and the Highlands; nor, crucially, is it situated as provincial or as past in relation to metropolitan England. The Glasgow of *Rob Roy* is hypermodern and Gothic: the setting for Jarvie's "statistical account" and encomium to commercial society, as well as for a hair-raising series of nocturnal, carceral, and labyrinthine adventures. Glasgow, set just below the Highland line, exemplifies the principle of a contrast of cultures and epochs embodied in Rob Roy himself: a figure like "Robin Hood in the middle ages," as Scott explains in his 1829 introduction, "blending the wild virtues, the subtle policy, and unrestrained license of an American Indian," yet "flourishing in Scotland during the Augustan age of Queen Anne and George I," "within forty miles of . . . a great commercial city, the seat of a learned university" (5). Here Scott specifies the Border topos – the geographical adjacency of different epochs, the historical simultaneity of different worlds – that animates his fiction.[19] However in *Rob Roy* the juxtaposition of savage and commercial stages obliterates instead of clarifying their relation as each other's past and future. Despite their official opposition, savagery and commerce sustain rather than cancel one another, constituting the uncertain, cryptic field of the present.

By the end of *Rob Roy* it will have become clear that particular systems of meaning and value may not always prevail outside the cultural sites where they are produced. The situational specificity that gives Jarvie's "statistical account" its authority – its Glaswegian provenance – also defines its limits. While it is never falsified, the analysis exerts no enlightening force throughout the rest of the narrative. Jarvie's cognitive mastery vanishes (unlike those primitive impulses, his courage and loyalty) once he and Frank enter the Highlands, already denominated in his account "a wild kind of warld by themsells" (300). As the two men cruise on Loch Lomond, Scott gives them set-piece reactions to the scenery: Jarvie speaks for economic improvement, Frank for romantic appreciation (415–16). Jarvie's scheme of development seems grotesquely inappropriate, the crude vision of an economic colonialism that expresses no more than the Glasgow Bailie's provincial foible. This is not just because Frank's aesthetic view seems more authentic, reflecting what he conceives to be the Highlanders' own relation to their setting – "the natural taste which belongs to mountaineers, and especially to the Scottish Highlanders, whose feelings I have observed are often allied with the romantic and poetical" (410). Frank is narrating his adventures in the mid-1760s, the age not just of Adam Smith but of Macpherson's "Ossian" translations, Walpole's Gothic tale, the aesthetic vogue for the sublime, and dissertations on the natural taste of clans and tribes by Hugh Blair and Adam Ferguson. In other words, Frank's aestheticism is no less modern than Jarvie's utilitarianism, and not simply because it yields a prediction of the region's economic future as a destination for picturesque tourism. The two discourses – romance and political economy – persist alongside each other to constitute the contemporary literary culture of Scott's readers, in the Waverley novels, Edgeworth's tales, and the *Edinburgh Review*. Our act of reading acknowledges a romantic aesthetic that is *more* modern than the raw utilitarianism of the primitive stage of capitalism for which Jarvie speaks, since the novel, the up-to-date form of romance, is able to dramatize both perspectives. In contrast to the transcendental authority of a "postscript which should have been a preface," the political-economic analysis remains embedded within the relative cultural spaces of Scott's narrative, framed by it rather than framing it. Scott turns the historicist scheme of Enlightenment political economy against itself, and at the same time fulfils it, by representing the temporal unevenness of the discourses of which the novel is composed, not just of the sites it represents.

This may seem especially paradoxical in the Highland chapters, since the narrative keeps invoking the anthropological equation of Gaelic clan society with a "savage" tribalism, especially of North American Indians, that was one of the set pieces of Enlightenment conjectural history.[20] Rob's kinsman Dougal resembles "a very uncouth, wild, and ugly savage, adoring the idol of his tribe" (258), the Highlanders are "the natives" (324, 345), Mrs. MacAlpine's hut is a "hospitable wigwam" (394). Scott gives this savagery a different kind, not degree, of relation to modernity from that of a Jacobite retro-feudalism. Clan culture enjoys a defiant autonomy rather than a fated obsolescence; it may look marginal and lawless in the eyes of Glasgow or London, but it is the center of its own world, and governed by its own laws. If feudalism and Jacobitism constitute the British nation's socioeconomic and political past, the Highlanders evoke a different order of ancestral relationship to modernity: the order of the primitive. The object of a nascent science, anthropology, the primitive signifies an origin morphologically immanent in modernity – disavowed but persistent – rather than a superseded developmental stage. Charged with original virtues – bravery, loyalty, pathos, but also murderous rage[21] – the primitive belongs to the present as well as to the past, even if it must shift in disguised or (in current jargon of state) deniable forms.

Rob Roy the character embodies the category of the primitive in the tale that bears his name. The outlaw recurs across the narrative's different sites in a sequence of metamorphic appearances and disappearances, gradually uncloaking his shape, as Frank and the reader approach his "native heath," the terminus of this revelation being our glimpses (never more than fragmentary) of his wild body. In the Glasgow jail, Frank observes Rob Roy's freakishly broad shoulders and long arms:

> I afterwards heard that this length of arm was a circumstance on which he prided himself, that when he wore his native Highland garb, he could tie the garters of his hose without stooping; and that it gave him great advantage in the use of the broadsword, at which he was very dexterous. But certainly this want of symmetry . . . gave something wild, irregular, and, as it were, unearthly, to his appearance, and reminded me involuntarily, of the tales which Mabel used to tell of the old Picts who ravaged Northumberland in ancient times, who, according to her tradition, were a sort of half-goblin half-human beings, distinguished, like this man, for courage, cunning, ferocity, the length of their arms, and the squareness of their shoulders.

> (273)

Over the Highland line, Rob's appearance "in the dress of his country" allows Frank to notice the "fell of thick, short, red hair, especially around his knees, which resembled in this respect . . . the limbs of a red-coloured Highland bull" (374). While the allusion to "the old Picts" may echo the account of the MacGregors as the last pure-blooded specimens of "the ancient Celtic race" in one of his sources, Scott develops Rob Roy's primitivism in terms opposite from those of racial purity.[22] Rob is native yet "unearthly," "half-human" and "half-goblin," but also part animal, simian and bull-like: the tropes for his elemental or aboriginal status are not just mixed but contradictory. Through this figure Scott imagines a heretic or outlaw identity at human and cultural origins, both in the miscegenation of categories (human, animal, demonic) and in the appeal to heterodox discourses, folkloric (goblins as the aboriginal inhabitants of the country) and biological (beasts as human ancestors).

Rob Roy's goblinlike power to shift his shape and appear or disappear at will enrolls him within the traditional discourse of "folklore," albeit newly recovered under an anthropological rubric. More striking are the glimpses of him as a kind of anthropoid ape – broad-shouldered, long-armed, covered in a red pelt – and the allusion to a conspicuously new and heterodox scientific hypothesis of subhuman origins. Edinburgh in the late Enlightenment (until the 1830s) was the British institutional center for pre-Darwinian theorizing about human origins, and Scott would have been familiar with the polygenetic thesis of Lord Kames, as well as the notorious claims of Lord Monboddo (ridiculed by Samuel Johnson) that the orangutan was a human subspecies that only lacked speech. This is the kind of ape that Rob Roy resembles. The Romantic vogue for the orangutan – a figure on the threshold of humanity, language, and culture – extended through Scott's own late romance, *Count Robert of Paris*, Peacock's *Melincourt*, and tales by Hogg and Poe.[23] When, in the Northumberland episode, Die Vernon refers to "the Ourang-Outangs, my cousins" (152), the metaphor is absorbed in its satiric context as a joke forecasting the cousins' extinction. But in Rob Roy's case primitivism signifies a rough vitality and cultural integrity ("honour"), the opposite of a destiny of extinction: he is quintessentially a survivor, triumphant over the proscription of his clan. Scott makes the point that Rob dies peacefully in bed long after the end of the adventure, in defiance of Jarvie's prophecy that he will be hanged.

This makes for a striking contrast with *Waverley*, where Scott had identified the failure of the Jacobite rising with the historical end of clan society, ceremonially marked by the state trial and execution of the chieftain Fergus Mac-Ivor. Thanks also, in part, to the earlier novel, Scott's readers knew about the end of the clans; but in this tale they survive, the secret sharers of an imaginary present, strengthened rather than depleted by their station outside the law. Rob Roy's physical energy, his talent for action, puts him at an opposite pole to the wraithlike figures of the Jacobite nobility. He enjoys a preternatural ability to turn up in any scene, or scenario, without being confined to it. Breaking in and out of the story at its crisis points, he inhabits a recursive rather than linear, interruptive rather than continuous, narrative time. Far from typifying the vulnerable savage incarcerated in his "other time" by Western anthropology,[24] this primitive prefigures late-nineteenth-century biological fantasies of organic vitalism and "eternal return." Adept in all cultural sites and roles, the master of appearances and languages, Rob is expert, above all, in the modern arts of commerce and negotiation, which may extend to robbery and homicide – who better than a freebooter should thrive in the new economy? The wild Highlander is also the archetype of economic man, since the new age requires an ideological recovery of "natural man" at the same time that actual savages are being figured into the expanding horizon of an imperial economy. (Mungo Park, the African explorer, had been Scott's friend and neighbor in the Borders.) That is just what theorists of capitalism-as-modernity have wanted to insist, whether they formulate the original principle of human nature as a propensity to exchange or barter (*The Wealth of Nations*) or as an insatiable desire (Ferguson's *History of Civil Society*, Millar's *Origin of the Distinction of Ranks*).[25]

If Scott's novel endows Highland savagery with a specific historical context, it is unmistakably, if only partially, that of colonial empire. More explicitly than just about any other Scott novel, *Rob Roy* represents the Highlands as a colonial frontier. The tale's single episode of military violence follows the historical-romance convention of dramatizing a clash between different worlds, but it is significant (again, in contrast to *Waverley*) that the ambush of Thornton's troop by Helen MacGregor does not belong to the history of the Jacobite rising. This overthrow of disciplined redcoats by a rabble of wild "natives" (most of them women and youths, led not by Rob Roy but his fearsome wife), complete with barbaric atrocity, belongs to the theater of colonial resistance rather than of national history. For Scott's readers, the military role of Highland regiments in the British army would have compounded the episode's allusive force; only a few years earlier, in Wellington's Peninsular campaign, such troops had supported mountaineer guerilla fighters against the Napoleonic empire (a conjunction dramatized by Johnstone in *Clan-Albin*[26]). Scott revives a traditional rhetoric of Highland savagery to insist not on the obsolescence but on the contemporaneity of these figures, "the indispensable atavistic natives," as Womack calls them, "in the Victorian triumph of peace and progress."[27] Here, though, complicating the formula, Scott emphasizes the MacGregors' ferocious resistance to the military and legal apparatus of the state. These Highlanders may not be drafted. Rob Roy's support of Frank, like his kinship with Jarvie, remains private, covert, illicit, unaccountable.

Through the figure of the up-to-date primitive we glimpse instead the shadow of a world system, a sublime, dynamic, outlaw field of force that exceeds the official, public, enlightened boundaries, historical and ideological as well as territorial, of civil society and the nation-state. We intuit, darkly, that the British condition of modernity does not after all consist of an internally unified, civilized "nation," the product of an evolutionary graduation of discrete historical stages. It consists of a global network of uneven, heterogeneous times and spaces, lashed together by commerce and military force, the dynamism of which is generated by the jagged economic and social differences of the local parts. This sublime imperial dynamism, rather than their elegiac absorption by the modern state, invests the aesthetic glamor of the Highlanders in *Rob Roy*.

Rather than opening a window onto the past, Scott's novel shows us the obscure, occult, bewildering shapes and forces of the present – a present not yet amenable to the perspective of historical analysis, and so more authentically sensed through the symbolic techniques of romance. The historicity of the world system becomes legible in the novel's derangement (but not its obliteration) of an Enlightenment historicism by primitive forms and figures. Far from disabling storytelling from the power to represent modernity, Scott's reactivation of these primitive forms produces the cognitive fitness of the novel as the genre of modern life. This fitness relies on those effects that are most notoriously novelistic, least reducible to other discourses: the disclosure of relations and connections through the formal turns of plot (coincidence, reversal, doubling) and symbol (metaphor, allegory); the evocation of psychic states of anxiety, dread, wonder, bafflement, hilarity, longing, all part of the complex of strange pleasures that fiction affords, but officially dismissed from the faculty of cognition. Nassau Senior, the first professor of political economy at Oxford, deplored the plot of *Rob Roy* as a "mass of confusion and improbability":

> The author himself, as he goes on, finds himself so thoroughly involved in the meshes of his plot, that seeing no legitimate extrication, he clears himself at last by the most absolute, we had almost said the most tyrannical, exercise of the empire which authors must be acknowledged to have over their personages and events, which we recollect, even in the annals of that despotic class of sovereigns. C'est un vrai coup d'état – and one which we should have expected rather from an Asiatic writer, than from a novelist "in this free country."[28]

Scott's novel enthralls its readers in the barbaric political psychology of world empire rather than admitting them to the rational transactions of civil society, as a British novel should do. "Despotism is a legitimate mode of government in dealing with barbarians," John Stuart Mill, the great Victorian exponent of civil liberty in the tradition of Smith and Senior, would later declare: "providing the end be their improvement."[29] To be enthralled by *Rob Roy* – as hundreds of thousands of readers have been enthralled – is to find oneself outside the narrative of modernity as a "free country," and with no sure prospect of improvement.

Notes

1 For this tradition see [Duncan] Forbes, "Rationalism of Sir Walter Scott" [*Cambridge Journal* 7 (1953): 20–35]; [P.D.] Garside, "Scott and the 'Philosophical' Historians" [*Journal of the History of Ideas* 36 (1975): 497–512]; [Graham] McMaster, *Scott and Society* [Cambridge: Cambridge University Press, 1981], 49–77; [Kathryn] Sutherland, "Fictional Economies: Adam Smith, Sir Walter Scott and the Nineteenth Century Novel," *ELH* 54, no. 1 (1987): 97–127]; [Cyrus] Vakil, "Walter Scott and the Historicism of Scottish Enlightenment Philosophical History" [in *Scott in Carnival: Selected Papers from the Fourth International Scott Conference*, eds J.H. Alexander and David Hewitt, Aberdeen: Association for Scottish Literary Studies, 1993, 404–18]; [David] Kaufmann, [*The Business of Common Life: Novels and Classical Economics between Revolution and Reform*, Baltimore: Johns Hopkins University Press, 1995] 101–9.
2 [James] Chandler, *England in 1819* [*: The Politics of Literary Culture and the Case of Romantic Historicism*, Chicago: University of Chicago Press, 1998], 107, 127–35.
3 Ibid., 129 (glossing a passage in Millar's *Origin of the Distinction of Ranks*).
4 The passage is cited by several recent commentators, e.g., [Cairns] Craig, *Out of History* [*: Narrative Paradigms in Scottish and English Culture*, Edinburgh: Polygon, 1996,] 38; Chandler, *England in 1819*, 132; Kaufmann, *Business of Common Life*, 107; [Enrica] Villari, "Romance and History in *Waverley*" [in *Athena's Shuttle: Myth, Religion, Ideology from Romanticism to Modernism*, eds F. Marucci and E. Sdegno, Milan: Cisalpino, 2000, 93–111]; [Saree] Makdisi, [*Romantic Imperialism:*] *Universal Empire* [*and the Culture of Modernity*, Cambridge: Cambridge University Press, 1998], 73; [Franco] Moretti, *Atlas of the European Novel*[*, 1800–1900*, London: Verso, 1998], 39.
5 [Walter] Scott, *Waverley*[*; or 'Tis Sixty Years Since*, ed. Claire Lamont, Oxford: Clarendon Press, 1981], 340.
6 See [Murray G.H.] Pittock, [*The Invention of Scotland: The Stuart Myth and the Scottish Identiy, 1638 to the Present*, London: Routledge, 1991], 85.
7 See [James] Buzard, *Disorienting Fiction* [*: The Autoethnographic Work of Nineteenth-Century British Novels*, Princeton: Princeton University Press, 2005], 71.
8 [Georg] Lukács, [*The Historical Novel*, trans. Hannah Mitchell and Stanley Mitchell, Lincoln: University of Nebraska Press, 1983], 57; the phrase is [A.O.J.] Cockshutt's, [*The Achievement of Walter Scott*, London: Collins, 1969], 159 n. 2.
9 [Jane] Millgate, *Walter Scott* [*: The Making of the Novelist*, Edinburgh: Edinburgh University Press, 1984], 149–50; see also [David] Hewitt, "*Rob Roy* and First-Person Narratives" [in *Scott and His Influence: The Papers of the Aberdeen Scott Conference, 1982*, eds J.H. Alexander and David Hewitt, Aberdeen: Association for Scottish Literary Studies, 1983, 372–81.]
10 [Walter] Scott, *Rob Roy*, [ed. Ian Duncan, Oxford: Oxford University Press, 1998,] 387. Further references will be given in the text.
11 See [Mark] Micale, *Approaching Hysteria* [*: Disease and Its Interpretations*, Princeton: Princeton University Press, 1995], 22–3. On sexuality, gender and "politeness" in *Rob Roy*, see [Robert] Irvine, *Enlightenment and Romance* [*: Gender and Agency in Smollett and Scott*, Oxford: Peter Lang, 2000], 153–74.
12 [Peter] Womack, *Improvement and Romance* [*: Constructing the Myth of the Highlands*, Basingstoke, Macmillan, 1989], 147–8.
13 [Adam] Smith, [*An Inquiry into the Nature and Causes of the Wealth of Nations*, eds R.H. Campbell and A.S. Skinner, 2 vols. Edinburgh: W. Creech, 1791–99], 22. Future references are given in the text.
14 [Mary] Poovey, [*A History of the Modern Fact: Problems of Knowledge in the Sciences of Wealth and Society*, Chicago: University of Chicago Press, 1998], 217.

15 Smith notes that the monopolistic profits of the sugar and tobacco plantations were largely responsible for sustaining slavery within the British empire: *Wealth of Nations*, 388–9. See [T.M.] Devine and [Gordon] Jackson, [eds, *Glasgow: Beginnings to 1830*, Manchester: Manchester University Press, 1995], on the tobacco trade, 139–83, and the Caribbean sugar and rum trades: 79, 189–90, 216–18; also [T.M.] Devine, *Scotland's Empire* [, *1600-1815*, London: Allen Lane, 2003], 75–6, 221–49.

16 For Scott's role in canonizing Defoe see [Homer O.] Brown, *Institutions of the English Novel* [: *From Defoe to Scott*, Philadelphia: University of Pennsylvania Press, 1997], 179–92.

17 As [Douglas S.] Mack insists: *Scottish Fiction* [*and the British Empire*, Edinburgh: Edinburgh University Press, 2006], 121–2.

18 On Gothic motifs in *Rob Roy* see [Fiona] Robertson, *Legitimate Histories* [: *Scott, Gothic and the Authorities of Fiction*, Oxford: Clarendon Press, 1994], 178–87.

19 See Moretti, *Atlas of the European Novel*, 35–47.

20 See Womack, *Improvement and Romance*, 20–4; [Robert] Crawford, *Devolving English Literature*, [Oxford: Clarendon Press, 1992,] 16–17.

21 On Scott, Highlanders, and violence see [Ken] McNeil, "Inside and Outside the Nation [: Highland Violence in Walter Scott's *Tales of a Grandfather*," *Literature and History* 8, no. 2 (1999): 1–17.]

22 [Edmund] Burt, *Letters from a Gentleman* [*in the North of Scotland to his Friend in London*, 1754, ed. Robert Jamieson, 5th ed., 2 vols, London: Ogle, Duncan, and Col, 1818], 1:xxii–xxiii.

23 See [Clare A.] Simmons, "[A] Man of Few Words: The Romantic Orang-Outang and Scott's *Count Robert of Paris*," *Scottish Literary Journal* 17, no. 1 (May 1990): 21–34]. In [James] Hogg's "The Pongos" the apes are more humane than European colonists: *Altrive Tales*, [ed. Gillian Hughes, Edinburgh: Edinburgh University Press, 2003,] 160–71.

24 See the classic account by [Johannes] Fabian, *Time and the Other* [: *How Anthropology Makes Its Object*, New York: Columbia University Press, 1983].

25 [John Millar, *The Origin of the Distinction of Ranks*, 4th ed., 1806, Bristol: Thoemmes, 1990.]

26 [Christian Isobel Johnstone, *Clan-Albin: A National Tale*, ed. Andrew Monnickendam, Glasgow: Association for Scottish Literary Studies, 2003.]

27 Womack, *Improvement and Romance*, 60.

28 Originally published in the *Quarterly Review* 26 (October 1821): 109–48; reprinted in [John O.] Hayden, [ed.,] *Scott: The Critical Heritage*, [New York: Barnes & Noble, 1970,] 215.

29 [John Stuart] Mill, *On Liberty*, [ed. Gertrude Himmelfarb, Harmondsworth: Penguin, 1982,] 69.

36 Two pipers

Romanticism, postmodernism, and the cliché

Orrin N.C. Wang[1]

Anachronism and event

Arguably, the time might be past for a discussion of the relation between Romanticism and postmodernism. For a term that seemed to hold much of academic literary studies in its thrall throughout the 1980s and much of the 1990s, discussions about the term postmodernism might very well be exhausted.[2] One could argue that we *should* be calling this contemporary world of empire, globalization, diaspora, biopolitics, and cybernetics the postmodern. The reasons we don't might simply have to do with the constrained demands of intellectual production within the twenty-first century academy, where it is simply impossible to stay with the same cultural analytic, or critical vocabulary, for over twenty to thirty years. It is certainly not as if another term has obviously supplanted postmodernism as a way to understand our world. (Given the vigorous way postmodernism attacked the thought underlying historical periodization, the lack of a clear challenger actually seems appropriate.) And yet it is difficult not to feel as if there is something dated about returning to, yet again, another discussion of the postmodern.

Another more productive way to say this is that postmodernism has become an anachronism. Our hesitation in using this term might then more productively be understood as an intuition of this new torque in the idea of the postmodern. Why productive? Because as an anachronism postmodernism actually converges with the way Romanticism also impinges upon our present, as something that is past but not past. The emphasis of my formulation would thus diverge from Jerome Christensen's idea of the unpredictability of Romantic history as an anachronism, the "lack of accountability as the emergence of unrecognized possibility" (Christensen 2000: 11). For the purposes of this analysis, my interest is focused not so much on how either Romanticism or postmodernism might still unexpectedly occur as how they are still happening, even though they are over. It is the irresolution of Romanticism and postmodernism that makes them actively felt, that makes them not past, when they are.

More specifically, it is the irresolution of whether ultimately both Romanticism and postmodernism can be explained historically, even as the impossibility of history is perceived as one main trait of postmodernism. The argument that most famously squares this circle is Fredric Jameson's, who saw this and other traits of the postmodern – the waning of affect, the loss of the subject, schizophrenia, the spatialization of lived experience, and the rise of the simulacrum – as historical symptoms of late capitalism (Jameson 1991: 1–54).[3] (Curiously, late capitalism itself has become increasingly anachronistic as a subtending critical term, supplanted by such analytic metonyms as globalization and neo-liberalism.) The theoretical *coupure* in Jameson's narrative was basically a twentieth-century affair, focusing on the transition or rupture between high capitalism and modernism and late capitalism and postmodernism. Romanticism was by and large unproblematically linked to an earlier eighteenth and nineteenth-century phase of classical capitalism and the creation of the modern nation state. So one enduring strain of Romanticist postmodernist scholarship has extended but also fundamentally complicated Jameson's model, arguing how the capitalist modernity of English Romanticism is already inflected with the cultural logic of late capitalism; how, for example, in Jerrold Hogle's collision of the increasing abstraction of capital and the rise of Romantic mass culture the gothic simulacrum, or ghost of the counterfeit, comes to be (or not to be) (Hogle 1998).[4] If for many the eighteenth and early nineteenth century is the beginning of modernity in the Western world, for some that narrative is complicated by *historical* energies that already see in modernity a postmodernity, a moment already filled with the traits of the postmodern.

Other classical theories of the postmodern, of course, associate that term with a radical questioning of the very ontological ground upon which Jameson's Marxist analysis depends.[5] Very broadly, though not reductively, this radical questioning is associated with the history of deconstruction in the North American academy, a history very much entwined with a strong form of Romanticism and Romanticist studies in the 1970s. Overlapping with the Jamesonian moment when "postmodernism" seemed to be on everyone's lips, Paul de Man himself eschewed the term, finding it too suspiciously charged with periodizing impulses (de Man 1986: 119–120). But there is no denying that in de Man and others a certain critique comes to be that converges with the radical questioning of ontology, with the attendant implications for politics, aesthetics, and ethics, that we associate with postmodernism.

So in this latter radical questioning, Romanticism and postmodernism converge as a transhistorical event, as something perhaps obsessed with but not absolutely defined by historical identity, while in the previous formulation Romanticism and postmodernism also converge, though this time with Romanticism as a proleptic symptom of a historical narrative tied to the emerging logic of late capitalism. This is a rather wide-ranging description, but a fundamental one, of the relation between Romanticism and postmodernism. And while there have certainly been attempts to work between these two poles, the basic character of this relation most pertinently speaks to the ongoing, irresolute nature of history as an analytic category in Romanticism.[6] Indeed, the paradoxical assertion of Romanticism as both a historical and a transhistorical event becomes yet another way to see in Romanticism the irresolute energies of what we call the postmodern.

For Romanticists, the challenge, and opportunity, is to see this irresolution not simply as an impasse. In what follows, I would like to suggest some specific ways that we might do so, by adding to the conceptual discussion I have just outlined some other terms of analysis, specifically those of *media* and *taste*. Certainly, in our world of brave new technological advancement, the question of (new) media seems intrinsically linked to the category of the postmodern. And one could equally say the same about the relation of postmodernism and the (im)possibility of aesthetic taste.[7] That media and taste are equally central terms in our understanding of Romanticism is an assumption of my essay, as well as something I hope to illustrate. The question of the historical will also run through my piece as an ongoing question of the methodological options we face when thinking about media and taste within Romanticism.[8] This question will also be cathected in another term that will materialize in what follows, that of *the cliché*. The status and meaning of the Romantic cliché will hopefully clarify further the relation of Romanticism and postmodernism as not only a convergence but also, crucially, a divergence.

The analysis begins simply enough as the comparison of two pipers in a pair of well-known Romantic texts.

Two pipers

Readers will immediately know my first piper, the shepherd narrator of the "Introduction" to William Blake's *Songs of Innocence,* who begins the author's collection with the origin myth of poetry. Indeed, because of Claude Levi-Strauss, Jacques Derrida, and most recently Maureen McLane, we know how to describe Blake's myth as a passage out of piped tune into poetry that resonates with a number of other transformations: nature into civilization, speech into writing, rural into urban life, and oral into print culture (Levi-Strauss 1974: 294–304; Derrida 1974; McLane 2001). And we know that at one level this origin myth is *not* a primal scene, in the Freudian sense, insofar as it appears to be a story of generation structured by neither trauma nor antagonism. Written poetry has the plenitude of piped melody; the transformation of nature into culture is not degradation; the natural purity of song transcends the different media, pipe or hollow reed, which express it.

At *another* level, of course, things are not so straightforward. The act of writing poetry "stain[s] the water clear," which, aside from referring to Blake's water colors, also ties together images of purity and pollution, innocence and experience, into a dialectically indeterminate knot. The shepherd turned poet writes down his poem so that "Every child may joy to hear," which can also mean that every child may *not* joy to hear; that and the disappearance of the child on the cloud anxiously hint at the creation of not simply poetry but a mass print audience characterized by the capriciousness of market desire. And the binary between speech and writing is itself destabilized by a slew of intermediating stages – melody, sung ballad, cursive poem, and print poem – that resist the notion of any pure moment of non-mediated expression. As with other songs in *Innocence,* Blake's "Introduction" captivates by showing how innocence is always already structured by experience. That said, in this myth of origins *sound* does occupy the slot of that mystified ontological starting point; the aural, what the shepherd pipes, is this song's originating instant, its assertion, no matter how vexed, of phenomenal plenitude.

Insofar as the piped song is about a lamb even before the shepherd sings anything, one could argue that sound in the "Introduction" never really avoids being contaminated by mimetic reference. Even more obviously, we could complicate the assertion of aural purity by noting the illuminated nature of this and other works of Blake's creations – how the thematized question of the aural in the "Introduction" is also offset by an axis of image versus text that structures Blake's prints, and that has been the occasion for some of the most storied work in Blake scholarship. Sound, image, and text: it is not much of a stretch to say that this poem about the creation of poetry is, like much of Blake's work, a mixed-media event, both literally and figuratively. But this is exactly where I want to shift my focus to another even more famous member of the Romantic canon, John Keats's "Ode on a Grecian Urn," and discuss this work *also* as a mixed-media event.

If not literally, the question of the image is obviously also thematized in the "Urn," as it stands as one of the most well-known examples of ekphrastic poetry in English literature. As others have noted, the poem's title lets us know the ode is in fact *on*, not to or about, the Grecian urn, which invites us to think about a surface either to be read or to be seen. A gender dynamic is also clearly at play in the visual ravishment of a feminized object by an ostensibly male poet narrator. Sound, too, is also signaled as a point of interest in the poem, through the paradoxical interplay of the muteness of the urn and "unheard melodies" that are sweeter than heard ones. Sound seems then to exist figuratively in the "Urn," as opposed to the depiction of sound as an originary source in Blake's "Introduction." More precisely, sound reflexively exists in the "Urn" *as* a figure for the past phenomenal plenitude of an antiquity now emphatically lost to present ears.

Understanding the narrator's mission to be the imaginative recovery of that experience would highlight the familiarity of what I have outlined about the "Urn" so far. But we have gotten to my second piper, the figure (or figures) on the Urn that incites (or incite) the narrator's language of "pipes and timbrels" and "spirit ditties of no tone" that runs through the beginning and middle of Keats's work. More specifically, I am interested in the "happy melodist, unwearied" of stanza three, "For ever piping songs for ever new," who could just as well be the urn itself as a figure painted on it. Even more exactly I am interested in the content of those "piping songs"; determining that might be as ultimately speculative as deciding who the "melodist" really is, but I'd like to suggest to you one particular reading option, that the piping songs play for us the line that immediately follows them in Keats's poem, which happens to be one of the most notorious lines in English poetry: "More happy love! more, happy, happy love!"

What does it mean to understand this line, whose routine excoriation provocatively matches in reverse mirror terms the canonization of Keats's poem, as the *piped song* of the urn or the urn's figures? I have two responses to that question. The first is to note how, unlike in Blake's "Introduction," the piped song would not simply be the sign of phenomenal plenitude but its exact opposite: sound as mechanical white noise, the meaningless repetition of a mindless phrase. In the vigor of its exclamatory expression, the line is certainly unwearied, but to call it "for ever new" is not so much to assert anything like the profundity of an origin as the painful assertion of an endless present enabled by an idiot amnesia that finds freshness in the repetitive, in "more happy, happy love!" Indeed, that aural stupidity explains why the melodist can be playing this line, without putting his pipe down the way the shepherd does in Blake's "Introduction." It is not simply, as with that other tune's invocation of a lamb, a case of referential contamination, of this song already being about happy love before speech or language is introduced. Rather, it is about the emptiness *of* language as meaning, the assertion of "more happy, happy love!" as sheer abstract form that structures the song's idiocy, its literal senselessness. Devoid of semantic sense, "more happy, happy love!" can be piped like any wordless tune. If the song does refer to happy love, it is love as a formal but empty cry or mark, so rote and mechanical it operates as a catachresis or abundance of catachreses – "more happy, happy love!" – troped as repetition, as unwearied, mindless melody.

My second point has to do with what this sonic idiocy then does to our understanding of piped sound in the "Urn" as the poignant sign of a lost plenitude. One tactic to deal with the embarrassment of "happy love" is to see it as reflexively ironic, satirizing the charge of Cockney sentimentality that critics hurled at Keats himself. We can extend that tactic further to see "happy love" virally infecting the elevated eros for a transcendent, eternal aesthetics that would somehow recover the lost meaning of past song. If we cannot read "happy, happy love" with a straight face, neither can we read the well-known alchemy of eternal desire and aesthetics in the "Urn" as anything besides adolescent gush – in that sense, the fact that "happy, happy love" is "panted" as well as piped is entirely appropriate.[9] Rather than simply expressing a desire for elevated aesthetic permanence, Keats's poem exposes this libidinal impulse as something altogether more lowbrow and inane, something that will seamlessly integrate itself into a burgeoning market of getting and spending, "happy, happy love" as idiot consumer joy. Piped song in the "Urn," "happy, happy love" could just as well be the future piped in pop music of a world increasingly lost in the supermarket.[10]

If this seems a curmudgeonly take on the lowbrow, the point that once again needs to be stressed is that the highbrow, a category like the lowbrow that Keats participated in and also unsettled, does not really exist in the "Urn," not even in the afterlife of misreading the poem over the last 200 years as one quintessential emblem of aesthetic ideology. The apotheosis of that ideology is arguably conveyed in the poem's most famous last lines, "Beauty is truth, truth beauty – that is all / Ye know on earth, and all ye need to know." If "more happy, happy love" celebrates an endless expenditure, a ridiculous kind of exorbitance, "Beauty is truth" asserts an aesthetic self-sufficiency, appropriately statute-like in its pithiness and self-containment.[11] But without even entering the question of who or what speaks the poem's last lines and how sincere they are, the history of those last lines upsets any distinction we might like to enforce between them and "more happy, happy love." For if we want to consider a phrase repeated ad infinitum from the "Urn," one that has been routinized as a dictum to the point of being evacuated of meaning, that exists rather as a literal sound byte than as genuine aesthetic experience, as the sign of the literary pedant (you and me) before anything else, that would not be "happy love" but instead "Beauty is truth." The dynamic of the former has become the fate of the latter. "Beauty is truth" has become, if it wasn't already, what "happy love" always was, a cliché.

A linguistic event characterized by the evacuation of meaning through mechanical repetition or emblematized by that repetition; a dynamic where that evacuation inserts itself into issues of distinction and taste; a predicament where that dynamic seems to register a historical narrative of increasingly complex cultural production in both its putatively commercial and non-commercial forms – that would be the realm of the cliché. Indeed, to distinguish between a cliché and a non-cliché – to wonder why, for example, "stained the water clear" resists becoming a cliché the way "Truth is beauty" has – might very well mean mobilizing Pierre Bourdieu's ideas about both restricted and large-scale cultural production in order to describe a material history of the reception of Romanticism (Bourdieu 1993: 112–134).[12] (That history might then also consider the different expectations we now have for a ballad and an ode.[13]) But one might also simply try a more transhistorical approach, to interrogate how the cliché structures the very question of meaning and non-meaning, of the literary and non-literary, that underwrites all our analyses.[14] Indeed, both approaches could yield intriguing answers to the question of Romanticism itself as a cliché, not least because of the contrast in their response. The appositeness of the cliché might very well then be the way it, like Romanticism and postmodernism, opens up the very question of these different approaches. And this is where I want to return to the question of the two pipers, to make the same point about how the question of media is used in the "Introduction" and "Urn."

One might have assumed that by exploring the question of piped sounds in these poems I was making an argument for medium specificity, for the particular character of sound. Rather, I am interested here in *medium reflexivity*, in how a medium as the act of mediation is mobilized to offset claims about purity, about what is mediated. A specific medium is invoked as pure, as in Blake's piped melody, or it is deployed as the evacuation of plenitude, as in Keats's idiot piped song; in either case the result is a dramatization of media as a relational difference that subtends any notion of non-mediated phenomena we might have. (Indeed, this is the biggest problem for the argument for medium specificity, that such an identity exists positively *without* mediation; in that sense medium specificity does exist, but as an impossibility, like de Manian imposition or Derridean justice.)

As Keats's poem especially shows, this dynamic is intimately tied to questions of taste, distinctions attended to by the presence of different media. The question of distinction might then constitute the stuff of a certain history, how the repetition of "Truth is beauty" in a host of academic and non-academic settings turns that phrase into a cliché. But the question of distinction can also incite another kind of analysis, which would see *the trope* of formal repetition itself – of "More happy love! more, happy, happy love!" – as both the cliché *and* the elevated aesthetic form championed by "Truth is beauty"; the moment of that form's full achievement would be the radical disappearance of content, even as the cliché would also assert itself as *simply* form, a mediation with nothing in it. Media in this case would be the event that both wards off and conjures the cliché – song as plenitude and as empty noise.

Its modern usage appearing at the end of the nineteenth century, the cliché referred earlier to a technical term in French printing, to phrases so routinely used that they were cast as a single slug of metal, readymade for printing. (In French, *clicher* means "to print from a stereotype.") Exemplifying the collapse of truth into contentless form, if not beauty, of abstraction into meaninglessness, functionalism into uselessness, convention into calcification, and type into stereotype (in both senses of the word), the cliché literally begins as part of print modernity.[15] As Blake's "Introduction" dramatizes, another name for this print modernity could be Romantic poetry; as Keats's "Urn" shows, the question of distinction that this poetry finds itself entangled with is also fundamentally the question of the cliché. Of course, one can see in Blake as much as in Keats an interest in what we could call clichéd thought, in the poet's warfare against priestly mental forms and, as Mike Goode has argued, in Blake's sendup of the proverb in *The Marriage of Heaven and Hell* (Goode 2006). And my point here certainly is not that a concern about what we might call clichéd language did not exist before Romanticism or its late nineteenth-century formal use. One need only think of, for example, Hamlet's riposte to Polonius, when asked what he read: "Words, words, words."[16] Yet Romanticism does seem to stage an auspicious intersection of a number of vectors – media reflexivity, literariness and non-meaning, aesthetic distinction as both elevated experience and adolescent exuberance – that brings the question of the cliché into sharp focus.

To return to and expand upon what it means to identify the "Introduction" and "Urn" as mixed media creations: Blake and Keats in different ways are among the Romantic poets who most produce poetic works that resist the category of a poem – Blake because of the illuminated nature of his prints and Keats because of how he reflexively thematizes the distasteful reception of his works as something besides poetry. They and others invent our contemporary sense of poetry and simultaneously do away with it. In Keats's case especially this dynamic seems to be about social distinctions that would discipline a certain espousal of poetry, or literature, for being a cliché. The example of Blake's piper, however, allows us to make a further connection. Why do *we* fear our thought, our feelings, our writings, our criticism to be a cliché? Certainly as everyone in the academy intimately knows, a large part of that answer has to do with social distinction. But perhaps our fear of the vagaries of taste is itself a bulwark against, even at this post-postmodern instant, the flatness of the void. We wince, laugh, or feel nausea at "More happy love! more, happy happy love!" because neither hollow reed nor urn can contain what they hold, the non-sound made there. The cliché, then, would be a symptom of how modern we remain even after the anachronism of postmodernism, insofar as invoking the cliché, asserting the ubiquity or endless regress of the cliché, does not quite account for the structure of feeling involved in all our strenuous attempts to avoid being a cliché. (One might more readily admit to being a simulacrum, clone, or automaton than a cliché.) Conversely, perhaps this situation is not so much about remaining modern as signaling, even though it is past, the *forestalling* of postmodernism. More pertinently, if we have yet to be postmodern, we have also yet to be Romantic, insofar as we do find, in at least the Romanticism of Keats, poetry that is defiantly open to the operations of the cliché. From that viewpoint my initial eschewing of the sense of the future – of "the emergence of unrecognized possibility" – in Christensen's understanding of the anachronism would seem premature. Whether openness to the cliché is a strength, resource, or mystification; whether the ruse is to avoid or embrace the cliché; these are some of the future questions that constitute the media song, the cliché of Romanticism. More happy, happy love indeed.

Notes

1 Much thanks to Scott Trudell for his advice on this essay and to my 2012 fall semester undergraduate students for the discussion that generated the Keats section of this piece.

2 One example of the diminished sense of the postmodern is from this footnote of W.J.T. Mitchell's:

> It seems clear that postmodernism has now become a historicist, period term for the era beginning in the sixties and ending somewhere around the fall of the Berlin Wall, roughly 1960–1990. My sense is that it had its greatest leverage on historical thinking in the 1980s, when it served as the rallying point for numerous projects in the critique of politics and culture.
>
> (Mitchell 2005: 318)

On the same page, Mitchell insists the term has value for the present, but by historicizing postmodernism he has also circumscribed it, giving it a heyday and a way for us to see past it.

3 Arguably, the one trait of Jameson's formulation of the postmodern that especially has *not* withstood the test of time is the waning of affect. See, for example, Terada (2001: 1–2, 6). Given Romanticism's longstanding relationship to questions of feeling and sentiment, one could very easily imagine another essay on the relation of Romanticism to postmodernism that would focus on this topic. One could also say that the idea of the cliché in this essay plays a similar role that affect or feeling might in the other piece, by configuring the

relation between Romanticism and postmodernism as one ultimately about what the former might yet have to say about the latter. This is not of course to assume that the connection between affect and cliché is a simple one; elevated feeling as a cliché is precisely a key point in this piece's reading of Keats. One might also ask of Romantic sentiment whether its power comes from being, or not being, a cliché.

4 Another key example of this approach would be the studied analysis of Byronism as both an oppositional and a market force in Christensen (1993). Arguably, as both Hogle and Christensen show, the gothic as an early emerging mass cultural formation in the eighteenth century plays an especially vibrant role in this approach; see also Botting (2005, 2008: 34–59).

5 See, for example, the discussion of grand narratives in Lyotard (1984: 31–39), as well as the theory of the simulacrum posed in Baudrillard (1983).

6 Arguably, both Hogle (1998) and Christensen (1993) could also be seen this way, rather than as simply examples of a purely historicizing model along the lines of Jameson.

7 On the question of media, see Mitchell (2005: 197–356); on aesthetics and postmodernism, see Foster (1983).

8 For a discussion of the relation between Romanticism and postmodernism that remains squarely focused on the question of history throughout – and that also involves a reading of Keats's "Ode on a Grecian Urn" – see Wang (1996: 13–25).

9 I am grateful to James K. Chandler for the connection between "piping songs" and "panted."

10 For one discussion about the relation of the "Urn" to the commodity object, see Collings (2003); for one elaboration of Keats's relation to commodification and some of the scholarship studying this link, see Wang (2011: 180–186, 250–280).

11 In her own discussion of the idiocy of Romantic poetry, Avital Ronell makes a related point about the dynamic of exorbitance, emptiness, and plenitude in Wordsworth's "The Idiot Boy," where Johnny the titular character "functions as the refusal of loss, as the very opposite of the experience of deprivation for which he has been made to stand" (Ronell 2003: 276).

12 For a helpful application of Bourdieu's categories to the question of contemporary aesthetics, see Brown (2012).

13 See, for example, both McLane (2001) and Newman (2007). The question of ballad (or perhaps children's song) versus ode might explain, for example, why Blake's repetitive use of "happy" in his poem, as in "happy pipe" and "happy song," does not draw the critical ire that Keats's "happy, happy love" does.

14 For a key example of this approach, consider the seminal reading of Proust's *Swann's Way* in de Man (1979: 58–67); see also the discussion of hyperbole in Longinus in Hertz (1985: 19–20).

15 The contemporary meanings of cliché and stereotype appear to result from parallel developments coming from French printing terminology. If the modern French and English use of the cliché starts at the end of the nineteenth century, the English use of stereotyping someone or something begins in the early twentieth century, with Walter Lippman credited with using this formulation in 1922 (Kieg 1993: 135–137). Regardless of their more pernicious meanings – one can also refer to a harmful cliché – both seem based on the evacuation of substantial meaning: one can also have a stereotypical day.

16 Hamlet's response is tied to the theme of *sententiae* in Shakespeare's play, one particularly associated with the pedantic nature of Polonius's bureaucratic speech. As sayings encouraged to be written down in a commonplace book, *sententiae* certainly seem to anticipate the late nineteenth-century meaning of the cliché, especially given the scorn characterizing Hamlet's exchange with Polonius (Shakespeare 1974). The degree to which one might still see the two terms diverging speaks exactly to the possibility of a history of the cliché, and perhaps of Romanticism itself. I am grateful to Scott Trudell for bringing the notion of *sententiae* to my attention.

Works cited

Baudrillard, J. (1983) *Simulations*, trans. P. Foss, P. Patton, and P. Beitchman, New York: Semiotext[e].

Blake, W. (1988) *The Complete Poetry and Prose of William Blake*, ed. D.V. Erdman, New York: Doubleday.

Botting, F. (2005) "Reading Machines," in R. Miles (ed.) *Gothic Technologies: Visuality in the Romantic Era, Romantic Circles Praxis Series*, December 2005. Online. Available HTTP: www.rc.umd.edu/praxis/gothic/botting/botting.html (accessed 1 August 2013).

Botting, F. (2008) *Gothic Romanced: Consumption, Gender, and Technology in Contemporary Fictions*, New York and Oxford: Routledge.

Bourdieu, P. (1993) *The Field of Cultural Production: Essays on Art and Literature*, ed. R Johnson, New York: Columbia University Press.

Brown, N. (2012) "The Work of Art in the Age of Its Real Subsumption under Capital," 13 March 2012, *Non-Site*. Online. Available HTTP: http://nonsite.org/author/nicholas-brown (accessed 1 August 2013).

Christensen, J. (1993) *Lord Byron's Strength: Romantic Writing and Commercial Society*, Baltimore: Johns Hopkins University Press.

Christensen, J. (2000) *Romanticism at The End of History*, Baltimore: Johns Hopkins University Press.

Collings, D. (2003) "Suspended Satisfaction: 'Ode on a Grecian Urn' and the Construction of Art," in *"Ode on a Grecian Urn": Hypercanonicity and Pedagogy*, ed. J. O'Rourke, *Romantic Circles Praxis Series*, October 2003. Online. Available HTTP: www.rc.umd.edu/praxis/grecianurn/contributorsessays/grecianurncollings.html (accessed 1 August 2013).

De Man, P. (1979) *Allegories of Reading: Figural Language in Rousseau, Nietzsche, Rilke, and Proust*, New Haven: Yale University Press.

De Man, P. (1986) *The Resistance to Theory*, Minneapolis: University of Minnesota.

Derrida, J. (1974) *Of Grammatology*, trans. G. Spivak, Baltimore: Johns Hopkins University Press.

Foster, H. (ed.) (1983) *The Anti-Aesthetic: Essays on Postmodern Culture*, Port Townsend: Bay Press.

Goode, M. (2006) "Blakespotting," *PMLA*, 121: 769–786.

Hertz, N. (1985) *The End of the Line: Essays on Psychoanalysis and the Sublime*, New York: Columbia University Press.

Hogle, J.E. (1998) "*Frankenstein* as Neo-Gothic: from the Ghost of the Counterfeit to the Monster of Abjection," in T. Rajan and J. Wright (eds) *Romanticism, History, and the Possibilities of Genre: Re-forming Literature, 1789–1837*, Cambridge: Cambridge University Press.

Jameson, F. (1991) *Postmodernism, or the Cultural Logic of Late Capitalism*, Durham: Duke University Press.

Keats, J. (1978) *John Keats: Complete Poems*, ed. J. Stillinger, Cambridge, MA: Belknap Press of Harvard University Press.

Kieg, M. (1993) *Hate Prejudice and Racism*, Albany: SUNY Press.

Levi-Strauss, C. (1974) *Triste Tropiques*, trans. J. Weightman and D. Weightman, New York: Atheneum.

Lyotard, J-F. (1984) *The Postmodern Condition: a Report on Knowledge*, trans. G. Bennington and B. Massumi, Minneapolis: University of Minnesota Press.

McLane, M. (2001) "Ballads and Bards: British Romantic Orality," *Modern Philology*, 98: 423–443.

Mitchell, W.J.T. (2005) *What Do Pictures Want? The Lives and Loves of Images*, Chicago: University of Chicago Press.

Newman, S. (2007) *Ballad Collection, Lyric, and the Canon: the Call of the Popular from the Restoration to the New Criticism*, Philadelphia: University Pennsylvania Press.

Ronell, A. (2003) *Stupidity*, Urbana-Champaign: University of Illinois Press.

Shakespeare, W. (1974) *The Riverside Shakespeare*, ed. G.B. Evans, Boston: Houghton Mifflin.

Terada, R. (2001) *Feeling in Theory: Emotion after the "Death of the Subject,"* Cambridge, MA: Harvard University Press.

Wang, O.N.C. (1996) *Fantastic Modernity: Dialectical Readings in Romanticism and Theory*, Baltimore: Johns Hopkins University Press.

Wang, O.N.C. (2011) *Romantic Sobriety: Sensation, Revolution, Commodification, History*, Baltimore: Johns Hopkins University Press

Part 10

Sciences of mind, body, and nature

Introduction

All of the selections in this section concentrate on the relationship between literary works and nature either as a whole or as particular organisms (including the human body and mind taken together as such an organism). These selections represent different vantage points on an area of interdisciplinary study that has become crucial for understanding the Romantic age and literary history in general. In a sense, this is a recent development in critical history. The French structuralist critic Roland Barthes emphasized the vast separation between literature and science when he claimed that scientific discourse emphasizes language as merely instrumental, whereas literature emphasizes language as language, or the very being of the work (Barthes 1986: 3–10). Other critics, such as American New Critics and those influenced by them, occasionally referred to literary works (following some Romantic accounts) as natural organisms, but they did so with caution and at a great distance from the scientific observation of biological entities. Art's interest in organic form, W.K. Wimsatt wrote in an essay on the subject, was not about a "realistic representation" of such entities (Wimsatt 1976: 210); he agreed with M.H. Abrams that a literary interest in organicism was primarily an interest in a formal integration and interdependence of parts rather than an empirical interest in the fine points of any organism's biological processes (Abrams 1953: 174–5).

The New Critics frequently turned to Samuel Taylor Coleridge in their accounts of the relationship between biological entities and the "synthetic" work of poetic imagination (Abrams 1953: 175); today's critics have taken a still broader and deeper view of the degree to which writers of the period were interested in a startling range of scientific investigations. Percy Shelley and Mary Shelley were fascinated by debates about vitalism; William Wordsworth and Charlotte Smith followed research on geological sciences; Keats drew on his knowledge of human anatomy and physiology for his most sensuous poetic imagery. Critics are now showing how all such interests in the physical world connected Romantic writers more closely with their environments – environments which embraced humans along with plants, non-human animals, geological formations and movements, weather patterns, and so on. It would be impossible to give a balanced sense of what areas of the sciences recent literary critics have focused on; instead, the selections in this section reveal more general theoretical contrasts in approach to the relation between literary works and scientific inquiry.

One way that critics conceptualize the literature–science connection is to emphasize literature's indebtedness to natural processes, or at least to what late eighteenth- and early nineteenth-century science understood of those natural processes. Alan Richardson's selection on Coleridge, excerpted from his book *British Romanticism and the Science of Mind*, points to the way that Coleridge's poems emphasize the activity of the mind as a physical organism. In some respects, his approach is compatible with the materialist emphases of new historicist criticism; this compatibility is clearly pointed out in Noah Heringman's study of Romanticism and geology (Heringman 2004: 22–3). Other critics who have worked roughly in a historicist mode to discuss literature and the sciences include Alan Bewell (2009), Tim Fulford, Peter Kitson, and Debbie Lee (Fulford et al. 2004).

Although a great many critics like those mentioned have been primarily interested in expanding our awareness of science as an important dimension of the historical record, there are other critics who have been more interested in the literature–science connection as a way of investigating theoretical issues surrounding literary form and personal identity (readers could consider this aspect of writing on science in connection with essays on form and identity in this volume). Denise Gigante's selection on Keats formed the basis for chapter 5 in her book *Life: Organic Form and Romanticism*, in which she urges a reconsideration of the relationship between literary forms and living forms as they were understood by writers of the age. She thus revisits the New Critical appropriation of Romantic accounts of organic form, but with a renewed emphasis on the way that Romantics actually understood the science of such entities. Her account of Keats shows how the poet employed his poem *Lamia* to explore the idea of a principle of life within his poetry. He sees "monstrosity" as an "excess of life" which, in its violation of form as "organized," redefines living form (and by extension literary form) itself.

The sense of excess that Gigante ponders in her essay may be connected to the very different mode of analysis to be found in Timothy Morton's essay "John Clare's dark ecology." What lies outside discrete and ordered "organic" forms is precisely what interests him in this essay. In some limited ways, Morton's work – which has also appeared in a range of books on Romanticism and ecology (Morton 2009, 2012) – might seem to join the work of many other critics such as Jonathan Bate and James McCusick (Bate 2000; McCusick 2010), critics who analyze Romantic writers, including John Clare, in light of their connections to their natural or "green" environments. There is also a clear connection between Morton's work and a great deal of recent work on Romanticism and animals or animal rights (Clark 1997; Perkins 2003). But Morton, whose writing shows the clear influence of Jacques Derrida and other deconstructionist accounts of identity, is outspoken in his opposition to ecology as environmentalism or naturalism, since he claims that this commitment too easily reinstates boundaries between self and other, nature and culture, local and global. His opposition to traditional environmentalism, and his embrace of a more inclusive ecological thought, appears throughout this essay. Clare's poetry shows how the narrator is part of a complete ecology, but as a "blank consciousness, filled with ambient noises and disturbing otherness."

In her new contribution to this volume, Sharon Ruston, like Gigante, is interested in the relationship between discourses of science and literary form, but she shows how this relationship is crucial for rethinking the way that an idea of "transformation" can be applied to other aspects of the historical contexts in which Romantic authors are writing. Whereas some earlier writers understand transformation as a re-assemblage of parts whose identities remain the same over time, Romantic writers think of transformation as a re-organization that more profoundly changes the character of its elements. Her essay documents the way that scientific works explored the degree to which physical transformations worked upon their constituent parts, and she suggests that these emerging theories were fundamental for interpreting what is often considered to be the central political transformation of the era – the French Revolution. She thus shows how an exploration of the sciences can help us to reinterpret familiar subjects of historicist inquiry.

Works cited

Abrams, M.H. (1953) *The Mirror and the Lamp: Romantic Theory and the Critical Tradition*, Oxford: Oxford University Press.

Barthes, Roland. (1986) *The Rustle of Language*, trans. Richard Howard, New York: Hill and Wang.

Bate, Jonathan. (2000) *The Song of the Earth*, Cambridge, MA: Harvard University Press.

Bewell, Alan. (2009) "Erasmus Darwin's Cosmopolitan Nature," *ELH* 76: 19–48.

Clark, David L. (1997) "On Being 'the Last Kantian in Nazi Germany': On Dwelling with Animals after Levinas," in Jennifer Ham and Matthew Senior (eds), *Animal Acts: Configuring the Human in Western History*, New York: Routledge, 165–98.

Fulford, Tim, Debbie Lee, and Peter Kitson. (2004) *Literature, Science, and Exploration in the Romantic Era: Bodies of Knowledge*, Cambridge: Cambridge University Press.

Heringman, Noah. (2004) *Romantic Rocks, Aesthetic Geology*, Ithaca: Cornell University Press.

McKusick, James C. (2010) *Green Writing: Romanticism and Ecology*, New York: Palgrave Macmillan.

Morton, Timothy. (2009) *Ecology without Nature: Rethinking Environmental Aesthetics*, Cambridge: Harvard University Press.

Morton, Timothy. (2012) *The Ecological Thought*, Cambridge: Harvard University Press.

Perkins, David. (2003) *Romanticism and Animal Rights*, Cambridge: Cambridge University Press.

Wimsatt, W.K. (1976) *Day of the Leopards: Essays in Defense of Poems*, New Haven: Yale University Press.

Further reading

Allard, James Robert. (2007) *Romanticism, Medicine, and the Poet's Body*, Aldershot: Ashgate.

Armstrong, Charles I. (2003) *Romantic Organicism: From Idealist Origins to Ambivalent Afterlife*, Houndmills: Palgrave Macmillan.

Golinski, Jan. (2007) *British Weather and the Climate of Enlightenment*, Chicago: University of Chicago Press.

Ross, Marlon. (1998) "Reading Habits: Scenes of Romantic Miseducation and the Challenge of Eco-Literacy," in Thomas Pfau and Robert F. Gleckner (eds), *Lessons of Romanticism: A Critical Companion*, Durham, NC: Duke University Press, 126–56.

Wilson, Eric G. (2003) *The Spiritual History of Ice: Romanticism, Science, and the Imagination*, New York: Palgrave Macmillan.

Wylie, Ian. (1989) *Young Coleridge and the Philosophers of Nature*, Oxford: Clarendon Press.

37 Coleridge and the new unconscious

Alan Richardson

Given [Samuel Taylor] Coleridge's influential defense of a unitary, transcendentalist conception of mind, it seems ironic that "Kubla Khan" is becoming a standard example within cognitivist accounts of a modular and material brain-mind. The pioneering cognitive psychologist Allan Paivio, for one, cites Coleridge's narrative of the poem's composition for its intuitive glimpse into the fundamental "duality" that empirical research would later establish between the visual and verbal systems, supporting two distinct "modes of thought."[1] Steven Pinker, in his popular book *The Language Instinct*, also cites Coleridge's description of poetic "composition in which all the images rose up before him as *things*, with a parallel production of the correspondent expressions," in discussing his conception of "mentalese," a preverbal and unconscious representational system probably closer to computing languages than to any human dialect.[2] The Artificial Intelligence researcher Margaret Boden, for her part, takes issue with Coleridge's "romantic" account of spontaneous composition in her study of cognition and creativity, noticing the introduction to "Kubla Khan" only to dismiss it. Yet Boden also finds in Coleridge's scattered remarks and poetic practice the outlines of a computational approach to unconscious mental composition, recuperating his revisionist account of associationist theory as an inspired premonition of neural network models of creative cognition.[3] What, one wonders, would Coleridge himself make of all this?

The question, it turns out, isn't quite as idle as it might sound. For had Coleridge happened to look into the July 1831 issue of *The Quarterly Review*, he would have found a much earlier citation of "Kubla Khan" in support of a brain-based conception of mind. In the course of a wide-ranging response to John Abercrombie's *Inquiries Concerning the Intellectual Powers* – with the running head "Connexion of the Intellectual Operations with Organic Action" – the reviewer (Sir David Brewster) takes up the novel dream theory advanced by, among others, [Pierre-Jean-George] Cabanis, called here the theory of "mental excitation." In contrast to the notion (held by most "metaphysicians") that dreams are provoked only by external causes (like street noise) or simple bodily discomfort (a cricked neck or dyspeptic stomach), the revisionist theory advanced by Cabanis holds that the "mind never sleeps," that cognition can proceed without conscious awareness, that the "operations carried on by the mind during the sleep of the body" can produce coherent and even novel ideas despite the suspension of the will and the temporary dissolution of the conscious subject. Brewster lists anecdotal evidence concerning such notables as Benjamin Franklin and Henry Mackenzie, Condorcet, and – Coleridge. "When Coleridge composed that exquisitely melodious piece of versification, which he calls 'a psychological curiosity,' – it is not easy to admit that operations so purely intellectual had their origin in abdominal or external uneasiness."[4]

With his lifelong interest in medical matters, all the more as they touched on mental phenomena, Coleridge may well have discovered in 1831 how readily his publication of "Kubla Khan" as a "psychological curiosity" would be enlisted in the service of brain-based psychologies.[5] Might he, in fact, have worried that his visionary poem, with the brief composition history he attached to it, would be put to just such a use? This question too is far from idle. For if Coleridge did fear that his dream poem, allegedly composed under the influence of a narcotic in the absence of waking consciousness, might become a textbook example of unconscious, involuntary, or automatic artistic creation, his well-founded anxiety might go far toward resolving a longstanding mystery concerning the publication history of "Kubla Khan." Why did Coleridge hold back one of his most powerful poems for nearly twenty years? Why, in contrast to "Christabel" or "The Pains of Sleep," other poems that long remained in manuscript, did he fail to transcribe or even mention it in a letter, to discuss it in his notebooks, to read it aloud to more than a select few auditors (almost exclusively poets he trusted and admired)?[6] Did Coleridge's reticence surrounding this "vision in a dream" stem, at least in part, from his ambivalence regarding unconscious cognition and the fragmented, naturalistic model of mind it had come to exemplify?

Coleridge had participated in the 1790s vogue for what he called the "corporeality of *thought*," going so far as to describe himself (in another 1794 letter to [Robert] Southey) as an "Advocate for the Automatism of Man" (*STCL* I: 137, 147).[7] Yet Coleridge no sooner makes such pronouncements than he begins to distance himself from them. His remarks on [David] Hartley and the corporeal mind are immediately followed, for example, by a joking, pseudo-materialist account of the violence inflicted on the "thinking corporealities" of a "certain Uncouth Automaton" upon his being heartily thrashed at school (*STCL* I: 137).[8] The 1800 letter to [William] Godwin outlining a "simply organic" approach to language and consciousness ends with a decidedly less playful qualification: "all the nonsense of the vibrations etc you would of course dismiss" (*STCL* I: 626). [Joseph] Priestley, [Erasmus] Darwin, and others had advanced "corporeal" accounts of thought that were also dismissive of Hartley's vibrations, but Coleridge here might be taken instead as casting physiological models of mind into doubt altogether, while at the same time appealing to connections among language, thought, and the "organic" approach to mind being forged in contemporary brain science.[9] Materialist, naturalistic, and embodied notions of the psyche would continue to play an ambiguous role in Coleridge's thinking throughout his career, particularly in regard to his speculation on the emotions and on the unconscious.

[. . .]

The dreaming body

[. . .]

Coleridge's grappling with the mind–body relation was marked by a good deal of anxiety and vacillation. His ambivalence grows most evident in discussions of dreams and other manifestations of unconscious mental life, as David Miall has demonstrated in an important series of essays on Coleridge, dreams, creativity, and emotion.[10] Darwin, Cabanis, and [F.J.] Gall had all discussed dreams in terms that implied a split or fragmented subject, cognition in the absence of conscious volition or supervision, and the subtle and pervasive influence of bodily processes – not least those related to sexuality – on psychic life.[11] Darwin notes the "ceaseless flow of our ideas in dreams," unhampered by the interference of conscious volition and free to jump from association to association. In the absence of external stimulation, "internal stimuli" are given freer rein and take on a "great vivacity," including the brain's stock of remembered sensations, the ideas variously associated with them, and the "internal senses" of "hunger, thirst, and lust," all making part of the "farrago of our dreams" (*Z*1: 199, 201, 209, 213).[12] For Cabanis, the brain is in "continuous activity," and sleep, rather than constituting a suspension of neural activity, is in fact "produced" by the brain, a startlingly modern formulation.[13] In dreams the "internal impressions" from what we would now call the hormonal and visceral nervous systems are unusually intense, as can be seen with sexual dreams and nocturnal emission (*R*1: 136, 138–9).[14] But the sleeping brain is capable of learned behaviors and even rational activity as well, as seen in the somnambulist's unerring performance of various acts and in the mind's ability to "continue its research in dreams," waking with the solution to an intellectual problem at hand (*R*2: 626). Gall, envisioning the brain as an "assemblage of particular organs" enjoying a certain degree of autonomy, holds that the "sensations and ideas which constitute dreams" arise when some cerebral organs are active while others are "suspended" (*FB* 1: 185).[15] The "plurality of organs" also accounts for the "energy" (vivacity) of dreams: "The whole vital strength is concentrated in a single organ or a small number of organs whilst the others sleep; hence their action must of necessity be more energetic." The dreaming brain does not merely recycle and rearrange waking ideas and perceptions, but may "invent" new material as well, since the "internal sources" that give rise to "sentiments and ideas" are as available in sleep as in wakefulness (*FB* 2: 321). All of these theories presuppose an active brain, the continuity of neural activity during sleep, and unconscious cognitive processes liable (but not limited) to expressing the claims of the body. Perhaps most crucially for a discussion of Coleridge, they also entail the suspension of volition: as Darwin writes in *The Botanic Garden*, "The WILL presides not in the bower of SLEEP."[16] They contribute as well to a materialist, neurological approach to mind that goes back at least to [Denis] Diderot's *Le rêve d'Alembert*, at once a philosophical examination and a fictional representation of the large role of unconscious activity in mental life. Taken together, these neurophilosophical theories of dreaming represent an important (though rarely examined) context for what has been seen as the "discovery of the unconscious" within literary Romanticism.[17]

[. . .]

When placed in the context of the new biological approach to mind represented by Darwin, Gall, [J.G.] Spurzheim, and Cabanis, an approach that constitutes the principal contemporary challenge to the position staked out in the central chapters of the *Biographia*, Coleridge's long and productive fascination with physiological psychology seems continually to skirt the abyss of materialism, to force a renewed engagement with the "corporeality of *thought*." In this context, Coleridge's suppression of "Kubla Khan" for nearly two decades, along with the remarkable story of its composition, appears not mysterious but predictable.

For, after all, what Coleridge describes in the introductory notice to "Kubla Khan" might be seen as the most spectacular psychophysiological experiment of his career, though an unplanned one; a "psychological curiosity" of the highest moment. And when read against the background of Coleridge's fraught relation to contemporary biological accounts of mind, the introductory note becomes a still more remarkable document than before. It raises no fewer than three issues crucial to contemporary debates on the mind and brain: the splitting or fragmenting of the psyche, the status of conscious volition within mental life, and the relationship between mental events and the organic body. Moreover, it raises these issues in ways that seem, from an orthodox or transcendentalist perspective, to give aid and comfort to the materialist adversary. Perhaps even worse, it seems designed to court an "abnormal" reading of the poem it accompanies, like J.M. Robertson's notorious characterization of "Kubla Khan" as one of the "chance brain-blooms of a season of physiological ecstasy."[18] The publication of the introductory note with the poem in 1816 all but guaranteed that "Kubla Khan" would become an object lesson for the biological study of psychology and an irresistible subject for the psychological study of literature.

Poetry and the unwilling suspension of consciousness

[. . .]

Although Kenneth Burke considered "Kubla Khan" the "kind of poem that Coleridge's own aesthetic theories were not much abreast of," it has seldom been remarked that the introductory notice to that poem implies a view of poetic creation very much at odds with the holistic account of imaginative creation in the *Biographia*.[19] Coleridge's alleged composition of the poem in a "profound sleep, at least of the external senses" does little to convey that the "whole soul of man" has been active. Rather, as Brewster would note in the *Quarterly Review* of 1831, it implies exertion of thought in the absence of a conscious thinker, the unconscious workings of a brain-mind compatible with the psychophysiological models of Darwin, Cabanis, and their ilk. The details of Coleridge's description, as Paivio would argue many years later, imply another level of psychic fragmentation into discrete visual and linguistic modules: "if that indeed can be called composition in which all the images rose up before him as *things*, with a parallel production of the correspondent expressions, without any sensation or consciousness of effort." It is difficult to square this account with Coleridge's insistence, contra Spurzheim, that "every" mental act must be the "act of the entire man." Even if one ignores Coleridge's own qualification ("if that indeed can be called composition") and charitably interprets the parallel imagistic and linguistic production as "faculties" in the "metaphysical" sense, working together – though hardly "fusing" – in poetic production, there remains the embarrassing lack of a conscious, voluntary subject directing or even bearing witness to the process.

Coleridge's celebrated account of the poetic imagination, after all, goes on to specify just such volitional activity: "This power, first put into action by the will and understanding, and retained under their irremissive, though gentle and unnoticed, controul (*laxis effertur habenis*) reveals itself in the balance or reconciliation of opposite or discordant qualities" (*BL* 2: 16).[20] These faculties, moreover, remain engaged in an explicitly conscious manner, with "judgement ever awake and steady self-possession" (*BL* 2: 17). According to the introduction to "Kubla Khan," however, the reins are not so much held loosely as either dropped altogether or never taken up. More than one critic has remarked on the imagination's "peculiar independence from . . . conscious control" in "Kubla Khan," an independence already evident in the account of spontaneous, unconscious composition in the introductory note.[21] Of course, the will and understanding can, perhaps must, work in the absence of full consciousness. Elsewhere, Coleridge (closely following Schelling) defines "unconscious activity" as the "Genius in the man of Genius" and describes the work of art as one in which the "*Conscious* is so impressed on the *Unconscious*, as to appear *in* it" (*LL* 2: 221–2).[22] But here conscious activity seems missing altogether; rather than a joint production of conscious and unconscious activity – an "interpenetration," as Coleridge puts it in the *Biographia*, of "*spontaneous* impulse and of *voluntary* purpose" (*BL* 2: 65) – the poem is depicted as having sprung from a "deep" unconscious state with no contribution from the purposeful subject of volition in evidence. Indeed, "*voluntary* purpose" seems, in this signal case, incompatible with poetic production; once the poet's transcription of the lines is interrupted, the rest of the poem is forever unrecoverable. [. . .]

The presence of a psychoactive drug or "anodyne" further vexes the problematic status of the will in the prose introduction. A note in Coleridge's hand added to the Crewe manuscript of "Kubla Khan" specifies "two grains of Opium," the standard anodyne of the time. And opium was notorious for its capacity to suspend or counteract, even to destroy the will.

[. . .]

Not only does opium, a material substance, act on the will; but by acting on the will, it suggests that mental faculties are affected by material changes in the body. Why, then, should mental events not be reducible to a series of physiological dispositions, to "motions"? The longer one looks at it in the context of Romantic brain science, the more the introductory note to "Kubla Khan" begins to read like an anecdotal report expressly designed for the use of Darwin, Gall, or Cabanis. It implies a mind divided into discrete powers and organs, a subject fractured into conscious and unconscious entities, the persistence of cognitive activity in the absence of conscious judgment and volition, the mind's susceptibility to and perhaps ultimate dependence on material changes in the body. As a case history, it is a brain scientist's dream.

Indeed, one critic has cannily described the introductory note as reading like "straightforward clinical description, rather in the manner of an early scientist reporting an experiment that he performed on himself."[23] All the more reason, then, to recall that Coleridge had written a brief report in this very genre, not too long after the year (1797) he claims to have experienced the opium dream or "reverie" that gave rise to "Kubla Khan." In the fall of 1799, Coleridge took part in what has been called the "first controlled scientific exploration of a consciousness-altering drug," Humphry Davy's experiments with nitrous oxide in Thomas Beddoes' notorious Pneumatic Institution in Bristol.[24]

[. . .]

Given the materialist tenor of 1790s radical science, it is not surprising to learn that, despite his idealist outburst while under the influence, Davy interpreted these experiments as further evidence for the material nature of mind. As [Jan] Golinski points out, Davy's notebooks interpret the effects of nitrous oxide in terms of a "clear demonstration of the material basis of human actions, emotions, and perceptions"; issues he had explored in his "Essay to Prove that the Thinking Powers Depend on the Organization of the Body," which he prudently left unpublished.[25] Presciently as well, since Davy (like Coleridge) would later seek to develop a new vitalism calculated to "underwrite the existing social order" that the work with nitrous oxide seemed more likely to undermine.[26] Coleridge himself proved eager to leave the experiments, and their materialist implications, behind. Suzanne Hoover has discussed Coleridge's lifelong "reticence" concerning his experiences with nitrous oxide, comparing it to his "defensiveness" concerning his use of opium. It is remarkable, she concludes, that Coleridge's interests in consciousness, sensation, and mind–body relations did not inspire a more thorough exploration of his first-hand experience with "consciousness-altering" drugs.[27] [Simon] Schaffer, who notes that "galvanism, pneumatics, and mesmerism" were all deployed by materialists to "efface distinctions between mind and body," explains the circumspect character of Davy's published report and the Romantic reaction typified by Coleridge along ideological lines: "The unspeakable relationship between the evidence of the imagination and the power of a material gas proved too vulnerable a resource at a time of fierce conservative reaction."[28] Given their contemporary ideological implications, the nitrous oxide experiments could only have increased Coleridge's anxieties regarding the possible uses of his own psychopharmacological experiment, one that has not lost any notoriety for having been undertaken by accident and in a lonely farmhouse rather than in the controlled (if hilarious) atmosphere of the Pneumatic Institution. If the drug trials carried out with Davy helped to inspire the "clinical" style of Coleridge's note to "Kubla Khan," they may also help to explain why Coleridge kept the experience quiet for so long.

[. . .]

"Need we wonder," he asks in a notebook entry in 1808,

> at Plato's opinions concerning the Body, at least, need that man wonder whom a *pernicious Drug* shall make capable of conceiving & bringing forth Thoughts, hidden in him before, which shall call forth the deepest feelings of his best, greatest, & sanest Contemporaries? and this proved to him by actual experience?

In the context of contemporary brain science, and given the role of narcotics in materialist speculation on the mind going back to the mid-eighteenth century, such striking and immediate evidence of the effect of a psychoactive drug upon latent or "hidden" thoughts seems to demand a neurological explanation. "But can subtle strings set in greater tension do this?" As the entry continues, one can see both the explicitly neuroscientific element in Coleridge's anxious speculation, and also the strategy he will use in the *Biographia* for downplaying the threat of materialist accounts of mind by reverting to a dated model of vibrating strings, as though Hartley's model had not been superseded by the work of Priestley, Galvani, Darwin, Davy, and others. Then he moves to an alternate explanation that looks forward to his resolution of the mind–body question in the 1820s. "Or is it not that the dire poison for a delusive time has made the body, <i.e., the *organization*, not the articulation (or instruments of motion)> the unknown somewhat, a fitter Instrument for the all-powerful Soul" (*CN* [*Coleridge's Notebooks*] 3: 3320).

Was Coleridge thinking of "Kubla Khan" in this entry? His reference to "Thoughts," like his allusion to Plato, remains obscure. Coleridge appears, however, to be working at an analysis of the cognitive effects of opium that, if plausibly developed, would enable him to publish "Kubla Khan" without fear of its enlistment in the cause of biological psychology, or of its subjection to the psychopharmacological readings that have met the poem beginning with Robertson's critique ("an abnormal product of an abnormal nature under abnormal conditions") a century ago.[29] The analysis was never fully worked out, "Kubla Khan" remained in manuscript for almost another decade, and when published, it was accompanied by a statement that constitutes an apology rather than a defense.

[. . .]

If, as John Beer suggests, the "facts surrounding its composition act as a comment upon the very powers which he was investigating," Coleridge's presentation of these "facts" entails a far different commentary on the imagination, memory, volition, and like powers of mind than the theories worked out in the *Biographia* and in the manuscript essays of the 1820s.[30] The picture of the mind suggested by the introductory notice is one much more in tune with the tradition of radical brain science running from the 1790s to the very "London Materialists" whom Coleridge, late in his career, would decry for viewing "individuality, intellect, and moral agency" as "properties or functions of organized matter" [(*SW* 2: 904).][31] [. . .] Far from considering the introduction to "Kubla Khan" as a sort of "confidence-trick" set to trap the unwary, one could place it instead among Coleridge's most brutally honest and genuinely disinterested confessions.[32][. . .]

Xanadu and the new unconscious

Up to now I have been concerned with placing the introduction to "Kubla Khan" in the context of Romantic-era speculation on the relations of mind, body, brain, and nerves, while keeping the poem itself out of consideration. It is tempting to leave things there. "Kubla Khan" has garnered more than its share of allegorical interpretations and I have no interest in developing yet another. Nevertheless, there is a long and rather august tradition of considering the poem in relation to the "psychological" issues so tantalizingly raised in the introductory note and reading it as an "aesthetic representation" of Coleridge's philosophy of art or a meditation upon "*creative inspiration.*"[33] Beer interprets "Kubla Khan" as a poem more specifically "about poetry – in some respects even a poem about itself" and Burke views it as "in effect a poeticized *psychology*, detailing not what the reader is to *see* but what *mental states* he is thus empathically and sympathetically *imitating* as he reads."[34] In light of the poem's reception history, it seems appropriate to consider at least briefly whether Coleridge's concerns with mind–body interaction, unconscious cognition, and volition – and the contemporary scientific, medical, and polemical discourses that help shape them – seep into the text of "Kubla Khan." The result would be not another interpretation of the poem, but rather a supplement to the work of contextualization exemplified by [John Livingston] Lowes' monumental study *The Road to Xanadu*,[35] with an eye to traces not of early travel writing, exploration accounts, ethnographies, and literary exoticism, but rather of the emergent neuroscientific discourse that haunts Coleridge's career and provides so telling a background for the introductory note.

One might well begin with the common observation that the landscape of "Kubla Khan" presents at once a "mental topography" or map of the human psyche and a representation (however fragmented or over-determined) of the human body.[36] This conjunction, generally taken for granted in the criticism, suggests the sort of mind one encounters in the biological psychologies of the time: an embodied mind, a mind that perhaps most blatantly manifests its embodied nature in dreams. Here it may be useful to return to the largely unprecedented emphasis on unconscious mental life found in the brain science of Coleridge's era. Literary Romanticism is frequently credited for anticipating various notions of the unconscious, particularly the unconscious of Freud, but Romantic poets and critics were by no means operating in a cultural vacuum. Peretz Lavie and Allan Hobson have called attention to a "rich pre-Freudian tradition" of scientific work, particularly in eighteenth-and nineteenth-century Britain, on dreams and the unconscious, a tradition that grounds the mind securely in the brain and body and that looks forward to recent work in cognitive psychology and neuroscience rather than to psychoanalysis.[37] Jonathan Miller has more recently sketched out a line from Mesmer, not to Freud (and what Miller characterizes as Freud's "custodial" conception of the unconscious) but to the "alternative, non-Freudian Unconscious" of cognitive science. In contrast to the "almost exclusively withholding function" he attributes to the unconscious of psychoanalytic theory, Miller describes the cognitive unconscious as "altogether productive," enabling the processes "integral to memory, perception, and behavior."[38] These mental activities remain largely inaccessible to conscious introspection not because of any presumed threat to the conscious ego, but rather because a range of mental functions can be performed more quickly and expeditiously in the absence of conscious control and supervision. In Miller's telling, this "new" understanding of the unconscious had been adumbrated by a group of British psychologists in the mid-nineteenth century who in turn drew on earlier formulations in the Mesmeric literature, the phrenological school of Gall and Spurzheim, the French materialist tradition, and the German Romantics with their interest in comparative neuroanatomy and physiology. Herder, to cite one key example, had made a naturalistic argument for the adaptive value of unconscious mental processing more than a century and a half before such a conception became standard in cognitive science. [...][39]

Post-Freudian accounts of the "discovery of the unconscious" suggest how those Romantic-era formulations of unconscious mental processes that most closely anticipate psychoanalysis and other "depth" psychologies form only one subset of a larger discursive field. As Coleridge's scattered remarks on dreaming suggest, writers now associated with literary Romanticism were aware of the "alternate" unconscious outlined by Miller, more productive than repressive, working to a large extent independently of the conscious subject, rendering the mind a theater of instinct, emotion, and desires as well as of reason, perception, and ideas. [...]

[Thomas] De Quincey, in arguing that feelings may crucially convey what "consciousness has not seen"; or [William] Hazlitt, in rooting both genius and "common sense" in an explicitly physiological conception of "unconscious impressions" manifested in bodily "feeling"; or Godwin, in enumerating a surprisingly large range of human activities performed in an irrational state of "reverie" or "human vegetation" – all bear witness to how the "alternative unconscious" of brain science impinges on Romantic writing.[40] In these essays, the material body manifests through "feeling" or "sensibility" an unconscious knowledge of its own, residing in the brain and nervous system and located at once within the body and below conscious awareness. Given his psychosomatic approach to mind–body relations, retaining the traditional primacy of psyche over soma while recognizing their extensive commerce, Coleridge characteristically describes their exchange as running in the opposite direction: "What I keep out of my mind or rather *keep down* in a state of under-consciousness, is sure to act meanwhile with its whole power of poison on my body" (*STCL* 3: 310). But scattered among the notebook entries, particularly those concerning dreams, lie those other passages suggesting that the body may have a mind of its own, that dream images may arise from the "Ganglionic" system or that spontaneous emotions and even speech-acts – guilt and falsehood – may be traced to the "Gastric Life."

The conjunction of dreams and the unconscious, the embodied mind and the "Gastric Life" takes us back to the poem allegedly composed "in a sort of Reverie brought on by two grains of Opium, taken to check a dysentery." The dreamscape of "Kubla Khan," at once detailed and indefinite, has been aptly described as a sexualized, amoral version of the conventional *paysage moralisé*, a psychologized landscape that also suggests a dispersed, erotically charged body.[41] There is a fair amount of agreement among critics that the poem's scenery lends itself to such a reading, though somewhat less about what body part goes where and how precisely to locate gender in an obviously sexualized landscape. Where some oppose the patriarch's "walls of culture – his 'stately pleasure dome' " – to a feminine, maternal landscape – the "primal female caverns and 'fertile ground,'" other critics have (notoriously) seen the pleasure dome instead as a representation of the mother's breast or even an image of the "Mons Veneris."[42] The fountain, though issuing from a "female landscape of caverns and chasms," is often read in terms of a "phallic" or "ejaculatory" force.[43] Yet others note instead a mimesis of "childbirth" in the "'fast thick pants'" with which the fountain bursts forth, possibly connected to the "sunless sea" allegorized as "womb-heaven of the amniotic fluid."[44] One Freudian analyst detects a "fantasy of anal birth" at work in this section of the poem, while another, struck by the bewildering "mixing of sexual symbols," can only compare them to the "bi-sexual" imagery he encountered in the course of his psychiatric work with marijuana "addicts."[45] At the same time, and by the same critics, the landscape with its caverns and chasm is linked with the "subconscious" sources of inspiration, "anti-rational forces associated with nature," the Freudian "id," the guilt-ridden deeps of the "poet's unconscious."[46] These irrational forces and depths are in turn connected with somatic "natural periodicity," "choric pulsions," the involuntary and "mysterious processes that go on inside the body."[47]

Reuven Tsur, in his innovative study of the reception and poetic structure of "Kubla Khan," has trenchantly pointed out that psychological analyses of the poem implicitly grant the relevance of twentieth-century conceptions of the unconscious to a late eighteenth-century poem.[48] Burke develops his psychological reading along "transcendental" lines suggested by Coleridge's own writings and finds his students' Freudian readings unduly "*erotic*" by comparison.[49] One could go a long way toward meeting charges of irrelevance or anachronism, however, by recovering a wider sense of the psychological discourse of Coleridge's era, taking better account of the brain-based approaches to mind that Coleridge flirted with at the beginning and then grappled with until the end of his intellectual career. Connections between unconscious mental activity, a dynamic conception of nature ("fertile ground"), internal bodily processes, spontaneous or unwilled thoughts and behaviors, and sexual life in particular are pervasive, as detailed above, in the pioneering neuroscience of the time. Coleridge often broaches such connections in his unpublished writings, sometimes in the very language of Romantic brain science. To read "Kubla Khan" in terms of a biology of mind – one that pays special attention to instinctive, unconscious, or involuntary aspects of psychic life – need not entail abandoning Coleridge's discursive context in favor of later psychological theories.

Rather, such a reading can underscore the links between Romantic psychologies and the revival of psychodynamic theories later in the nineteenth century.[50]

Even at a more detailed level, such as symbolically equating the pleasure dome with both esthetic culture and the maternal breast, or the stock ejaculatory reading of the "obviously scandalous" fountain, interpretations inspired by psychoanalysis and related depth psychologies could find warrant in the psychological discourses of Coleridge's own era.[51] Darwin had written in *Zoonomia* that the infant's repeated association between pleasure and the dome shaped "form of the mother's breast" provides a lasting psychological template for beauteous forms (*Z*: 145), a notion he would later versify in *The Temple of Nature*:

> Warm from its cell the tender infant born
> Feels the cold chill of Life's aerial morn;
> Seeks with spread hands the bosom's velvet orbs,
> With closing lips the milky fount absorbs;
> And, as compress'd the dulcet streams distil,
> Drinks warmth and fragrance from the living rill;
> Eyes with mute rapture every waving line,
> Prints with adoring kiss the Paphian shrine,
> And learns erelong, the perfect form confess'd
> IDEAL BEAUTY from its Mother's breast.[52]

The milk of Paradise indeed. And the incorrigible fountain? Erotic dreaming accompanied by ejaculation made a prime example for French physiological psychologies of the close links between bodily desires, unconscious mental activity, and spontaneous behaviors, from Diderot (who includes a wickedly amusing scene of nocturnal emission in *Le Rêve d'Alembert*) to Cabanis, who cites "nocturnal emissions" in his discussion of the brain's activity and its enhanced susceptibility to "internal impressions" during sleep (*R* 1: 136–9).[53] Coleridge's anxious notebook jottings regarding the "bad Passions in Dreams" place him surprisingly close to this tradition. The suggestions of polymorphous or ambiguous sexuality that some psychoanalytic critics have located in Coleridge's revision of the Edenic myth also find resonance in Darwin, who postulates an "original single sex" in *Zoonomia* that accounts, among other things, for the human male's possession of seemingly useless nipples.[54] And readers who would relate the "milk of paradise" to Coleridge's experiences with "laudanum and the whole tribe of stimulants," suggesting an Edenic return to the full pleasures of infancy, might profit from the connections between narcotic states and "connate" desires posed by Darwin and others.[55] Coleridge himself poses associations between opium and an embodied mind, a "sort of stomach sensation attached to all my thoughts."[56] He also describes the "divine" effects of opium as "a spot of enchantment, a green spot of fountain and flowers and trees in the very heart of a waste of sands" (*STCL* 1: 394), another example of the contemporary fascination with mind-altering drugs that found such ecstatic expression in the laboratory reports collected by Davy. Rather than calling psychodynamic interpretations of "Kubla Khan" altogether into question on historical grounds, we can draw support for their general drift and even for some of their more outlandish hermeneutical claims by redirecting the historicist gaze to a different, less familiar section of the archive. Readings of Coleridge's dream poem that emphasize the interrelations among body, mind, and natural world, that link spontaneous acts to unconscious and libidinal forces, that posit a fragmented psyche and reject classical notions of the subject, are as much in the spirit of the emergent biological psychologies of the Romantic era as they are of later "depth" psychologies, though by an accident of literary history such readings became widespread only in the wake of Freud.

[. . .]

Some of the most persuasive readings of "Kubla Khan" to date have gestured, though without explicit attention to the brain science of the era, toward an understanding of Romanticism as a cultural movement throwing notions of conscious volition and the integral self into crisis and acknowledging the irrational, bodily, and instinctual elements of mental life in unprecedented ways. Burke, who ties his reading of the River Alph as a "stream of consciousness" fed from "*below*" to Coleridge's own musings on the "streamy" nature of association and subconscious inspiration, sees a "'problematical' element implicit" in the "romantically spontaneous waywardness" that drives the poem.[57] Sandra Gilbert and Susan Gubar, more ambitiously, argue that "when the chasm of romanticism opened culture to the revolutionary and anti-rational forces associated with nature, with imagination, with unconsciousness, and with spontaneity – that is, to all the terms that had been repressed" by patriarchal culture – male poets like Coleridge felt "threatened" by the irruption of "the feminine" within themselves.[58] For Tsur, this threatening sensation is felt instead by the poem's readers and critics, who deploy a whole range of "cognitive strategies" for dealing with the "irruption of the irrational into our ordered world."[59] Bringing the neuroscientific context to bear on British Romanticism only intensifies the widespread sense of its "problematical" aspects, its anxious subversion of traditional valuations of mind over body, spirit over matter, reason over passion, conscious judgment over unconscious spontaneity. This is a problematic that marks Coleridge's intellectual career and that marks "Kubla Khan" and its confessional introduction as well. Whatever else the poem signifies – and both its amazingly wide range of reference and the seemingly inexhaustible resonance of its imagery have been amply attested to by Lowes and many since – it touches squarely and inescapably on issues that were no less central for Romantic brain science than for Romantic poetry.

[. . .]

Notes

1 Allan Paivio, "The Mind's Eye in Arts and Science," *Poetics* 12 (1983), 16.
2 Steven Pinker, *The Language Instinct: How the Mind Creates Language* (New York: Harper, 1994), 70. Quotations from the relevant poems and Coleridge's introductory notice follow the facsimile reprint of the 1816 edition of *Christabel: Kubla Kahn, A Vision; The Pains of Sleep*, ed. Jonathan Wordsworth (Oxford: Woodstock Books, 1991).
3 Margaret A. Boden, *The Creative Mind: Myths and Mechanisms* (New York: Basic Books, 1990), 18–19.
4 Sir David Brewster, "The Connexion of Intellectual Operations with Organic Action," *Quarterly Review* 45 (1831): 357.
5 For discussions of Coleridge's interest in contemporary medicine and science, see John Harris, "Coleridge's Readings in Medicine," *The Wordsworth Circle*, 3 (1972): 85–95; Trevor Levere, *Poetry Realized in Nature: Samuel Taylor Coleridge and Early Nineteenth-Century Science* (Cambridge: Cambridge University Press, 1981); Ian Wylie, *Young Coleridge and the Philosophers of Nature* (Oxford: Clarendon Press, 1989); Marilyn Gaull, "Coleridge

and the Kingdoms of the World," *The Wordsworth Circle*, 22 (1991): 47–52; and Jennifer Ford, *Coleridge on Dreaming: Romanticism, Dreams, and the Medical Imagination* (Cambridge: Cambridge University Press, 1998).

6   Among the few known to have read the poem or heard Coleridge recite it are Mary Robinson (who had herself written a poem, "The Maniac," in an opium-induced reverie), Charles Lamb, Lord Byron (a recitation just missed by Leigh Hunt) and, almost certainly, William and Dorothy Wordsworth. See Elisabeth Schneider, *Coleridge, Opium, and Kubla Khan* (Chicago: University of Chicago Press, 1953), 22, 83, 216; Molly Lefebure, *Samuel Taylor Coleridge: A Bondage of Opium* (London: Victor Gollancz, 1974), 254; and Edmund Blunden, *Leigh Hunt: A Biography* (London: Cobden-Sanderson, 1930), 93–4.

7   [Samuel Taylor Coleridge, *Collected Letters of Samuel Taylor Coleridge*, ed. E.L. Griggs, 6 vols (Oxford: Oxford University Press, 1956–71), cited parenthetically in text as *STCL*.] For a pioneering account of Coleridge's early interest in the theories of Darwin, Priestley, and other radical scientists, see H.W. Piper, *The Active Universe: Pantheism and the Concept of Imagination in the English Romantic Poets* (London: Athlone Press, 1962), 29–51.

8   This distancing strategy is noted by both K.M. Wheeler, *The Creative Mind in Coleridge's Poetry* (Cambridge: Harvard University Press, 1981), 12–13 and Jerome Christensen, *Coleridge's Blessed Machine of Language* (Ithaca: Cornell University Press, 1981), 63–4.

9   [. . .] In his useful discussion of the letter to Godwin, J.A. Appleyard argues that "organic" would have had "no special meaning" for Coleridge in 1801 but would connote instead the "physiological functioning of an organ, as in the Hartleyan system," *Coleridge's Philosophy of Literature: The Development of a Concept of Poetry* (Cambridge: Harvard University Press, 1965), 81. James McKusick, in his important book on Coleridge and language, reads "organic" in terms of the "materialistic" linguistic theories being advanced at the time, *Coleridge's Philosophy of Language* (New Haven: Yale University Press, 1986), 41. Neither mentions the crucial significance of terms like "organ" and "organic" in the brain science of the time.

10 See especially David Miall, "The Meaning of Dreams: Coleridge's Ambivalence," *Studies in Romanticism*, 21 (1982): 57–87; "Coleridge on Emotion: Experience into Theory," *The Wordsworth Circle*, 22 (1991): 35–9; and "'I See It Feelingly': Coleridge's Debt to Hartley," *Coleridge's Visionary Languages: Essays in Honor of J.B. Beer*, eds Tim Fulford and Morton D. Paley (Cambridge: Brewster, 1993), 151–63.

11 See my essay "Romanticism, the Unconscious, and the Brain," in *Romantic Prose*, eds Virgil Nemoainu and Steven Sondrup, a [. . .] volume of the *Comparative History of Literatures in European Languages*.

12 [Erasmus Darwin, *Zoonomia: or, The Laws of Organic Life*, 2 vols (London: J. Johnson, 1794–96), cited parenthetically in text as *Z*.]

13 The 1801 account of Cabanis' views in the *Monthly Review* stressed this very point: "The result of his chain of reasoning is that sleep, as well as thought, is produced by a real and peculiar action of the brain," review of *Mémoires de l'Institut National*, 302.

14 [Pierre-Jean-George Cabanis, *On the Relations Between the Physical and Moral Aspects of Man*, tr. Margaret Duggan Saidi, ed. George Mora, 2 vols (Baltimore: Johns Hopkins University Press, 1981), cited parenthetically in text as *R*.]

15 [François Joseph Gall, *On the Functions of the Brain and of Each of Its Parts: With Observations on the Possibility of Determining the Instincts, Propensities, and Talents, or the Moral and Intellectual Dispositions of Men and Animals by the Configuration of the Brain and Head*, tr. Winslow Lewis, 6 vols (Boston, MA: Marsh, Capen, and Lyon: 1835), cited parenthetically in text as *FB*.]

16 *The Botanic Garden*, book III, line 74; from *The Poetical Works of Erasmus Darwin, M.D., F.R.S.*, 3 vols (London: J. Johnson, 1806).

17 See especially Henri Ellenberger, *The Discovery of the Unconscious: The History and Evolution of Dynamic Psychiatry* (New York: Basic Books, 1970) and Catherine Belsey, "The Romantic Construction of the Unconscious," in *Literature, Politics, and Theory: Papers from the Essex Conference 1976–84*, eds Francis Barker *et al.* (London: Methuen, 1986), 57–76.

18 John Mackenzie Robertson, *New Essays Towards a Critical Method* (London: John Lane, 1897), 140, 190.

19 Kenneth Burke, *Language as Symbolic Action: Essays on Life, Literature, and Method* (Berkeley: University of California Press, 1966), 218.

20 [Samuel Taylor Coleridge, *Biographia Literaria, or Biographical Sketches of My Literary Life and Opinions*, eds James Engell and W.J. Bate, 2 vols (Princeton: Princeton University Press, 1983), cited parenthetically in text as *BL.*]
21 Wheeler, *Creative Mind*, 26.
22 [Samuel Taylor Coleridge, *Lectures 1808–19 on Literature*, ed. R.A. Foakes, 2 vols (London and New York: Routledge & Kegan Paul, Princeton University Press, 1987), cited parenthetically in text as *LL.*]
23 Jack Stillinger, *Coleridge and Textual Instability: The Multiple Versions of the Major Poems* (New York: Oxford University Press, 1994), 78.
24 Suzanne R. Hoover, "Coleridge, Humphry Davy, and Some Early Experiments with a Consciousness-altering Drug," *Bulletin of Research in the Humanities* 81 (1978): 10.
25 [Jan] Golinski, *Science as Public Culture [: Chemistry and Enlightenment in Britain, 1760–1820* (Cambridge: Cambridge University Press, 1992)], 172.
26 [Christopher] Lawrence, "[The] Power and the Glory [: Humphry Davy and Romanticism," in *Romanticism and the Sciences*, eds Andrew Cunningham and Nicholas Jardine (Cambridge: Cambridge University Press, 1990)], 223.
27 Hoover, "Coleridge, Humphry Davy," 19, 22.
28 Simon Schaffer, "Self Evidence," [*Critical Inquiry* 18 (1992):] 358–9.
29 Robertson, *New Essays*, 187; cf. Eli Marcovitz, "Bemoaning the Lost Dream: Coleridge's 'Kubla Khan' and Addiction," *International Journal of Psychoanalysis* 45 (1964): 411–25.
30 [John] Beer, *Coleridge's Poetic Intelligence* [(London: MacMillan, 1977)], 118.
31 [Samuel Taylor Coleridge, *Shorter Works and Fragments*, eds H.J. Jackson and J.R. de J. Jackson, 2 vols (London and New York: Routledge & Kegan Paul, Princeton University Press, 1995), cited parenthetically in text as *SW.*]
32 Lefebure, *Samuel Taylor Coleridge*, 257.
33 Wheeler, *Creative Mind*, 38; Reuven Tsur, *The Road to Kubla Khan: A Cognitive Approach* (Jerusalem: Israel Science Publishers, 1987), 74.
34 Beer, *Coleridge's Poetic Intelligence*, 118; Burke, *Language*, 208–9.
35 [John Livingston Lowes, *The Road to Xanadu: A Study in the Ways of the Imagination* (Boston: Houghton Mifflin, 1927).]
36 Wheeler, *Creative Mind*, 26.
37 Peretz Lavie and J. Allan Hobson, "Origin of Dreams: Anticipations of Modern Theories in the Philosophy and Physiology of the Eighteenth and Nineteenth Centuries," *Psychological Bulletin* 100 (1986): 230.
38 Jonathan Miller, "Going Unconscious," *New York Review of Books*, April 20, 1995, 64.
39 Lancelot Law Whyte, *The Unconscious Before Freud* (New York: Basic Books, 1960), 117.
40 *De Quincey's Works*, ed. David Masson, 14 vols (Edinburgh: A. and C. Black, 1896–7), 10: 390; *HW* [William Hazlitt, *The Complete Works of William Hazlitt*, ed. P.P. Howe, 21 vols (London, Dent: 1930–4),] 8: 31–2, 35; William Godwin, *Thoughts on Man, His Nature, Productions, and Discoveries* (London: Effingham Wilson, 1831), 152, 159.
41 Sandra Gilbert and Susan Gubar, "The Mirror and the Vamp: Reflections on Feminist Criticism," in *The Future of Literary Theory*, ed. Ralph Cohen (New York: Routledge, 1989), 162.
42 Gilbert and Gubar, "Mirror," 162; Marcovitz, "Lost Dream," 414; Eugene Sloane, "Coleridge's *Kubla Khan:* The Living Catacombs of the Mind," *American Imago* 29 (1972): 106–7; [Norman] Fruman, *Coleridge[, the Damaged Archangel* (New York: George Braziller, 1971)], 400.
43 Gilbert and Gubar, "Mirror," 160; William Benzon, "Articulate Vision: A Structuralist Reading of 'Kubla Khan,'" *Language and Style* 18 (1985): 11.
44 Wheeler, *Creative Mind*, 34; Burke, *Language*, 206.
45 Sloane, "Coleridge's *Kubla Khan*," III; Marcovitz, "Lost Dream," 416.
46 Wheeler, *Creative Mind*, 26; Gilbert and Gubar, "Mirror," 163; M.W. Rowe, "'Kubla Khan' and the Structure of the Psyche," *English* 41 (1992): 150; Fruman, *Coleridge*, 399.
47 Benzon, "Articulate Vision," 10; Gilbert and Gubar, "Mirror," 161; Marcovitz, "Lost Dream," 414.
48 Tsur, *Road to Kubla Khan*, xxxi.

49 Burke, *Language*, 210, 220.

50 Links between Freud and Romantic biology and medicine have been posited by Iago Galdston, "Freud and Romantic Medicine," *Bulletin of the History of Medicine* 30 (1956): 489–507; for a broader study, see Frank J. Sulloway, *Freud, Biologist of the Mind: Beyond the Psychoanalytic Legend* (New York: Basic Books, 1983).

51 Burke, *Language*, 220.

52 Darwin, *The Temple of Nature*, book III, lines 167–76.

53 Cabanis adds that "men of letters" are especially subject to these "disturbing" visitations, thanks to the heightened activity of their nerves and brains (*R* 1: 136).

54 Ashton Nichols, "The Anxiety of Species: Toward a Romantic Natural History," *The Wordsworth Circle* 28 (1997): 135.

55 Fruman, *Coleridge*, 401.

56 Schneider, *Coleridge, Opium*, 318, n. 75.

57 Burke, *Language*, 221.

58 Burke, *Language*, 221; Gilbert and Gubar, "Mirror," 163.

59 Tsur, *Road to Kubla Khan*, xiii.

38 John Clare's dark ecology

Timothy Morton

> I am here, sitting by the fire, wearing a dressing gown, holding this page in my hand[1]

Place, and in particular, the local, have become key terms in romantic ecocriticism's rage against the machine. This rage is as impotent as it is loud – indeed rhetorical affect is here in direct proportion to marginalization.[2] Moreover, this impotent rage is itself an ironic barrier to a genuine (sense of) interrelationship between beings – the kind desired, posited and/or predicted by ecological thinking itself. Elsewhere I have called it "beautiful soul syndrome" after Hegel's brilliant characterization of Romantic subjectivity as a "beautiful soul" that perceives a chasm between consciousness and the world. This chasm cannot be fully bridged; not, at any rate, without compromising the beauty of the soul itself.[3] Ideas such as "place" and "the local," let alone "nation," entail subject positions – "places" from which Romantic ideas of place make sense. For this reason, it is all the more important for us to consider deeply the idea of place, and in general the Romantic attitude to "nature" prevalent today (we are still, in effect, within the Romantic period). We should not throw the baby of place out with the Romantic bathwater.

Instead of wondering how to bridge the unbridgeable gap, ecological thinking might pose another kind of question. Indeed, to *pose* a *question* is to reveal how our sense of place and what we mean by terms such as *question, aporia* or *wonder* are interconnected. What if globalization, via an ironic negative path, revealed that place was never very coherent *in the first place?*

Notice the difference between stating that place as such does not exist at all, and saying that its existence is not as an independent, definable object "over there" somewhere. Place, if anything, is slippery *because* it exists, but not in the way in which, conventionally, mathematical axioms or empirical objects, or, indeed, ideals structurally beyond our reach, exist. Globalization compels us to rethink the idea of place, not in order to discard it, but indeed to strengthen it, and to begin to use it properly in a yet more thorough critique of the world that brought about mass hunger, monocultures, nuclear radiation, global warming, mass extinction, pollution and any number of harmful ecological phenomena.

Place is always caught up in a certain *question*, assuming the form of a questioning, or questioning attitude. (Notice, incidentally, that place, when properly considered, undoes the distinction between subject and object.) Phenomenology has come closest to understanding place as a provisional yet real "thing" (*thing* in its original sense, and some of its more recent ones, implies *place* as *meeting place*). Martin

Heidegger powerfully described place as open and in some ways opaque. But Heidegger, infamously, solidifies this very openness, turning history into destiny and leaving the way open for an extreme right-wing politics, which can easily assimilate ecological thinking to its ideological ends. Instead of running away from Heidegger, scholarship should encounter him all the more rigorously in seeking to demystify place, in the very name of a politics and poetics of place. In short, we must put the idea of place into question. Hence the idea of "depthless ecology": an ecological criticism that resists the idea that there is a solid metaphysical bedrock (Nature or Life, for instance) beneath which thinking should not delve.

In the rush to embrace an expanded view, the plangent, intense rhetoric of localism, the form of ecological thinking that seems the most opposed to globalization and the most resistant to modern and postmodern decenterings and deconstructions, must not be left on the shelf and allowed to fall into the hands of reactionaries. Instead, scholarship must examine the central fixations upon which localism bases its claims. A left ecology must "get" even further "into" place than bioregionalism and other forms of Romantic localism.[4]

Only then can progressive ecocriticism establish a firm basis for an exploration of environmental justice issues such as environmental racism, colonialism and imperialism. This firm basis is indeed a strong "theoretical approach." If we restrict our examination to the citation of ecological "content" – listing what is included and excluded in the thematics of the (literary) text – we hand over aesthetic form, the aesthetic dimension and even theory itself, to the reactionary wing of ecological criticism. The aesthetic, and in a wider sense, perception, must form part of the foundation of a thoroughly transnational ecological criticism. If we do not undertake their task, virulent codings of place will keep rearing their ugly heads.

Let us commence, then, by considering how place need not be a *thing*. Indeed, it is with the idea of *thing* that Heidegger's famous meditation on the work of art as a special kind of place begins. In brief, Heidegger tries to de-reify the idea of the thing. One of the senses of *thing* in Old English is "meeting place," and this is somewhat the conclusion to which Heidegger comes, without stating it as such. The work of art tells us something about the nature of the thing, precisely that it is an opening, a "place" where phenomena become available to us; a sense of the "thingliness" of things covered over or denied in the notion of the thing as formed matter (a derivation, claims Heidegger, from the status of equipment), or the thing as a perceptual manifold of substance and accident. Heidegger's famous reading of the peasant shoes, as painted by Van Gogh, poetically renders the way in which these humble things gather together the entire environment, the social and natural place, of the peasant woman. Heidegger's description opens the shoes to the "earth" (the things that are not worked on by or with human hands), and to the "world" (the historical/cultural dimension in which the shoes are used and gain significance):

> There is nothing surrounding this pair of peasant shoes in or to which they might belong – only an undefined space. There are not even clods of soil from the field or the field-path sticking to them, which would at least hint at their use. A pair of peasant shoes and nothing more. And yet –
> From the dark opening of the worn insides of the shoes the toilsome tread of the worker stares forth. In the stiffly rugged heaviness of the shoes there is the accumulated tenacity of her slow trudge through the far-spreading and

ever-uniform furrows of the field swept by a raw wind. On the leather lie the dampness and richness of the soil. Under the soles slides the loneliness of the field-path as evening falls. In the shoes vibrates the silent call of the earth, its quiet gift of the ripening grain and its unexplained self-refusal in the fallow desolation of the wintry field. This equipment is pervaded by uncomplaining anxiety as to the certainty of bread, the wordless joy of having once more withstood want, the trembling before the impending childbed and shivering at the surrounding menace of death. This equipment belongs to the *earth*, and it is protected in the *world* of the peasant woman. From out of this protected belonging equipment itself rises to its resting-within-itself.[5]

Similarly, the Greek temple, a product of the "world" of Greek cultural/historical projects, opens the space that it inhabits such that we perceive the "earth," the stoniness of the stone, the "skyey" quality of the sky (it is hard not to employ a Shelleyan adjective here; "Origin" 41–2). Likewise, in another essay, it is the bridge that makes possible the riverbank as a specific place. Poetry *is* place, for Heidegger.[6] In some deep sense, it actually saves the earth – sets it "free into its own presencing" ("Building Dwelling Thinking" 150).

On a Heideggerian reading, any place other than the peasant woman's farm – say the city, and its manifold urban spaces – make[s] possible certain experiences of space and place, revealing the "earth" that resists instrumentalization, along with the "world" of instruments. This must be the case, otherwise Heidegger's distinction of earth and world would cease to be generalizable. There is nothing in Heidegger that compels us to only seek the earth outside the instrumental world. If the avatar of deep ecology himself can be used in this way, how much more could other philosophers not so averse to modernity?

Art simultaneously opens up the *earth* just as it carves out a *world* in that earth. There is a tendency, then, for Heidegger to secretly be on the side of technology rather than of Being, despite his stated intentions. Taken to an extreme, in fact, his view could be parodied by declaring the obvious truth that the environment (*earth*) has become more present to us precisely because humans have been carving it up and destroying it so effectively. What remains of earth, on this view, is really a ghostly resonance in the artwork itself. Perhaps, then, all the environmental art being produced both in high art and in kitsch (from experimental noise music to Debussy for relaxation, for instance) is actually a symptom of the loss of the actually existing environment as non-cultural, non-historical *earth*. Heidegger, the philosopher invoked in deep ecological assaults on modern times, turns out to be working for the other side. As Avital Ronell has brilliantly demonstrated, the Heideggerian call of conscience, that which reminds us of our earthbound mission, is imagined in *Being and Time* as a telephone call.[7]

In an extraordinary invagination, Heidegger literally turns the shoes inside out to reveal the environment in which they come to exist. But why, historical details aside, did he choose a dirty pair of peasant shoes rather than, say, something like a fresh pair of sneakers made in a sweatshop and worn in the projects? The environmentalness of the shoes is a function of modern capitalist society despite Heidegger's best efforts to disguise this fact. There is an ideological flavor to the substance of Heidegger's description. It is a form of Romanticism: of countering the displacements of modernity with the politics and poetics of place. On its own terms, the gesture is always aware of its futility: it is a cry of the heart in a heartless world, a declaration that if we just think hard enough, the hard rain of modern life will stop falling.

This may be an obvious point, but it is nevertheless worth making. Romanticism is itself a flavor of modern consumerist ideology. It is in this respect thoroughly urban, as are many aspects of forms of environmentalism, which are often quintessentially Romantic. So Heidegger tries to bring place back: among other philosophers in the twentieth century, he tries to re-establish the idea of place. He goes so far, in his re-assertion, to state that we could not have space without place: the sureness of place is what enables us to glimpse the openness of space ("Building Dwelling Thinking" 154). This is ironic, since his idea of place is one of the most open and seemingly non-reified ones we could think of. This is why we should reconsider him in any revision of the idea of place. His notion of place is very compelling for certain influential forms of ecological thinking, and it seems so rich, so inviting, so downright earthy.

Indeed, for Heidegger, place is at once the very opposite of closing or closure. Place is the aperture of Being ("Origin" 54–5), and yet it is at risk of becoming a component of fascist ideology, of the sort suggested by the idea of *Lebensraum,* a locality *meant* for a certain race or class. The shoes, in this case, are not randomly chosen. Heidegger could have used a photograph of a dam, but the peasant shoes are the ideological fantasy objects of a certain backwards-looking strain in nationalism.

Let us now consider the issue of language and art. Since a poem happens to the body, it happens to the environment – the voice resonates in air; the eyes fall across the page in actually existing space. The marks and sounds have a certain *timbre,* a specific way of vibrating or squiggling – a *Stimmung* or "attunement," "tone" (the term *Stimmung* is significant across a range of philosophical views from Humboldt to Kant). In this sense we could view the poem, any poem, as a constructivist object in which the reader is embedded. All poems, whether they are explicitly "about" a certain kind of environment or not, positively evoke an actually existing environment – this one, right here – in their very existence. All poems, then, are occupied at some level (or many) with issues of place and space. This insight is significant, since poetic form is seen as capable of evoking the world and earth of the reader, as much as any thematic "content." Poems put us in our place. But before we think that this is an authoritarian statement, we should ask, where is that, exactly?

[. . .]

When I am "here," here includes a sense of "there": here is precisely not there. Even if we are not living in a point-based universe, this idea of "there" is intrinsic to "here": it *is* here, in some way, such that *here* is shot through with *there*. Here is not a solid thing. I mean this much more strongly than Heidegger when he claims that "man is the creature of distance."[8] This idea of distance ultimately aestheticizes the idea of *here*. *Here* itself becomes an object we are gazing at through the glass shop window of aestheticization. Quite the opposite: we are so involved in *here* that it is constantly dissolving and disappearing. It fails to be where we look for it. *Here is a question*; indeed, *here is question*.

The environment is that which cannot be indicated directly. We could name it apophatically. It is not-in-the-foreground, in the terms given to us by Gestalt psychology. It is the background, caught in a relationship with a foreground. As soon as we concentrate on it, it turns into something in the foreground. In ecological terms, "nature" becomes rabbits, trees, rivers and mountains – we lose its environmental quality, but this is what we wanted to convey. We are compelled to rely on a list that gestures towards infinity. The environment is sublime. It *is* the "what-is-it?" – the objectified version of our question. As soon as it becomes an exclamation it has been disappeared. And the shopping list itself is perilous in this regard, because it will necessarily exclude something (cities, pylons, certain races and classes, certain gender identities). Simply adding something to the list that ends in an ellipsis and the word "nature," is wrong from the start.

In sum, *environment is theory* – theory not as answer to questions, or as an instruction manual (what is the theory behind that dishwasher?) but as question, and question-mark, as *in question*, questioning-ness. The best environmental art, then, is deconstructed from the inside. As theory it retains its fullest existence as questioning – internally fractured by a doubt, stronger than English skeptical empiricism (we know the ideological uses of that) or Germanic peasant wondering (we know the ideological uses of *that*). When we start to think about what ecocriticism excluded, eco-criticism's very concept of environment and the rhetorical gestures it makes to evoke it must give way to something more theoretical.

Arne Naess's idea of deep ecology is based on an idea of the encounter of a (little /s/) self with a (big /S/) Self:

> Organisms and milieux are not two things – if a mouse were lifted into absolute vacuum, it would no longer be a mouse. Organisms presuppose milieux. Similarly, a person is a part of nature to the extent that he or she is a relational junction within the total field. The process of identification is a process in which the relations which define the junction expand to comprise more and more. The "self" grows towards the "Self."[9]

It sounds like secular science, with its talk of organisms and fields. But Naess' idea is a version of Hinduism. The mouse would remain a mouse. It would just be a dead mouse. There is a slip between the sentences here. If they are to survive, organisms presuppose certain milieux. To argue in this way, to reformulate the self as a "relational junction" is to push the issue of identity back a stage further, but not to get rid of it. And I remain uncertain of the extent to which a "relational junction" gets rid of the dualism that Naess sees as the problem. The logic is still that something must relate to something else. The "total field" continues the idea of environment as a different thing to these relational junctions, the background to their foreground as it were, however much the ideas of field and totality strive to submerge difference.

Naess's figuration is also interesting for its reliance on highly non-organic language, more reminiscent of electromagnetism and cybernetics, if not cyberpunk, than trees and roots. The way in which Naess reduces the self to a (zero-dimensional) point in a field, as David Harvey rightly puts it in his reading of this passage,[10] actually resembles nothing so much as the Cartesian reduction itself, the limitation of identity to a dot of doubt. Like Pascal's before him, Naess's prose is ironically an experiential rendering of what it *feels like* to inhabit a Cartesian universe.

How about basing ecological poetics and politics on no-self (and thus on no-nature)? Wherever I look for my self, I only encounter a potentially infinite series of alterities: my body, my arm, my ideas, place of birth, parents, history, society. . . . The same goes for nature. Wherever we look for it, we encounter just a long metonymic string of chipmunks, trees, stars, space, toothbrushes, skyscrapers. . . . Of course, where the list ends is telling. Basing a politics and philosophy on a view of self, however sublimated and radically "alternative" to a "Cartesian" view, involves us in an aporia. These "new improved" versions of identity never entirely get rid of the paradoxes of the idea of self from which they deviate. And yet the ultimate paradox is that wherever we look for the self, we will not find it.

That we will not find the self where we look for it is the message of Buddhism and deconstruction, but it is also the message of Lacan's sustained reading of Descartes' own cogito, which he develops into this outrageously convoluted statement: "I am not wherever I am the plaything of my thought. I think of what I am where I do not think to think."[11] This convolution is eloquent, for it speaks to the radical way in which displacement exists at the very kernel of the self itself.

Place as question has become a question *internal* to the very question of self, of that which is located in place. This is of supreme importance, since place is the consequence of Naess's view of self. Thus we return to the epigraph, and Descartes' act of situating himself at the start of the *Meditations*, in a way that, retroactively, should remind us ironically of any phenomenologist worth his ecological salt: "I am here, sitting by the fire, wearing a dressing gown, holding this page in my hand" (19). I venture the provocative, probably heretical and certainly, to many ecological ears, blasphemous idea that Descartes, the whipping boy of ecological discourse, may have something to tell us about place. Wasn't it Descartes who helped to get us into this mess, with his idea of the skin-encapsulated ego, as so many ecologically minded writers have observed (Harvey 167–8)? Their names are legion.

The movement of Descartes' thought ending with the cogito, transitioning through a phase of radical doubt, commences in this innocent seeming scene, where the warm ambience of the fire and the satisfaction to the body that it bestows enable the thinking process to take place. The self, in other words, depends upon its environment. "I think" depends upon the "I am" of "I am here, sitting by the fire." Moreover, the very philosophy of the self depends upon this environment, as Descartes starts to subject his innocent situatedness to a series of doubts that hollow out that comfortable place by the fire. "I am here" depends upon a sense of doubt, which leads us to the cogito. We are on a Moebius strip whose either side twists about the other such that it is impossible to designate one (either "self" or "place") as ontologically prior.

The Cartesian situation contains a kind of double-take, which Descartes registers by wondering why he shouldn't be dreaming that he is beside a fire – surely a question that any satisfied, comfortable person may ask, relatively unaware of their bodily determinacy. Alleviated of suffering, the self stops to wonder whether it is dreaming or not. Place is a function of suffering. "This land is my land" is a symptom of injustice. The politics of place, then, is a struggle to achieve a state in which the question of place, the question that is place, can emerge *as* a question. Utopia, from this point of view, would look more like critique and debate than an affirmation.

To use Descartes' situatedness rhetoric in the manner suggested is thus not to assert that one must have achieved a certain level of comfort in order to theorize. And this is where John Clare's profound poems of depression come to mind. Clare is usually framed as a proto-ecological poet of minute particulars, a genuine and genuinely disturbing working-class presence in the revised Romantic canon. Far from being tangential to the general nature poetry project, the depression poems are essential to it. They stage the idea of *being here* in its most profound, formal way. Beyond any specific ecological content, indeed, often in spite of it, the narrator remains. Of all the humors, melancholy is the closest to the earth. In his study of German tragic drama, Walter Benjamin explores the heavy materialism of the baroque, whose emotional analogue, he claims, is the relentless melancholy of the drama's protagonists.[12] For Freud, melancholy is a refusal to digest the object, a sticking in the throat, an introjection. It is now old fashioned to think that melancholia is an irreducible component of subjectivity, rather than one emotion among many. But it seems undeniable. Melancholia is precisely the point at which the self is separated from, and forever connected to, the mother and the body of the earth. Isn't this lingering with something painful, disgusting, grief-striking, exactly what we need right now, ecologically speaking?

   Take the poem "I Am."

> I am – yet what I am, none cares or knows;
> My friends forsake me like a memory lost: –
> I am the self-consumer of my woes; –
> They rise and vanish in oblivion's host,
> Like shadows in love's frenzied stifled throes: –
> And yet I am, and live – like vapours tost
>
> Into the nothingness of scorn and noise, –
> Into the living sea of waking dreams,
> Where there is neither sense of life or joys,
> But the vast shipwreck of lifes esteems;
> Even the dearest, that I love the best
> Are strange – nay, rather stranger than the rest.
>
> I long for scenes, where man hath never trod
> A place where woman never smiled or wept
> There to abide with my Creator, God;
> And sleep as I in childhood, sweetly slept,
> Untroubling, and untroubled where I lie,
> The grass below – above the vaulted sky.[13]

The title's Cartesian reference should be obvious. Now one might think that this was Cartesian subjectivity at its darkest hour – the subject as pure empty self-reference. And this thought would be right, in a sense. At first glance, the closest we get to ecology is the last couplet, where the narrator wishes for an impossible relief. And even here there is an ambiguity in the sense of "above": is the narrator lying with the sky above him, or lying "above . . . the sky" in heaven? But it is the very form of this yearning and impossibility that is precisely the *most* ecological thing about the poem. The narrator's (I want to say Clare's) identity has shrunk to the pure open empty set of blank consciousness, filled with ambient noises and disturbing otherness. There is an extraordinary enactment of this between the first and second stanzas, where the reader's eyes have to "toss" themselves into the nothingness of an immense gap between lines in order to arrive at the end of the phrase (6–7). The narrator is so untogether, as they'd say in California, compared with Heidegger's peasant woman, whose shoes connect her to feudal rhythms. Here they are, *right here*, on the earth, feeling like shit (hence melancholia). Why did we think that the deepest ecological experience would be full of love and light? I am, therefore I doubt, therefore I think, therefore I am, therefore I doubt – I wish life were simple.

The doubt in the poem is so very corrosive, that before we get to the grass and sky, we have a ghostly, ambient version of an environment formed from the narrator's scooped-out insides (7–12). The narrator is painfully aware that the Otherness that surrounds him does not truly exist; it is a "nothingness of scorn and noise" (7). Does this "I am," like an Old English riddle in which the poem declares itself to be something ("I am . . . an onion"), not point out the status of the poem itself, a spectral quasi-object suspended in nothingness, an inconsistent bunch of squiggles that cannot ever know itself as such?[14] This depressive Romantic poem comes curiously close to Mallarmé's experiments with crossed-out words. In both cases, the sheer opacity of the poem becomes its very subject, involving us in a paradox, since it is precisely the "lack of content" that gives the poem its opacity. Thus behind the vapor and mist we glimpse a dull inertia, symbolized by the dash, that quintessential gesture of sensibility, and hence the illusion of deep subjectivity. In the printed text, the dash becomes the sheer inert breath between signs, making us aware of the throat in which that breath is sticking. Wherever you go, here, even here, you are. In other words, the poem's inertia, its gravitational field, does not allow the doubting part to escape into some abstract realm beyond grass and sky, but in an extraordinary way, connects grass and sky to depression and doubt. We are a long way from traditional, organicist readings of Clare. We are also a long way from the therapeutic poetics of John Stuart Mill's reading of Wordsworth, celebrated in Jonathan Bate's *Romantic Ecology*. Clare wants us to stay in the mud, rather than pull ourselves out of it. If we read the last line of "I Am" literally, this is exactly where we are.[15]

We are now in a position to read Clare's ecological-poetic career backwards from the startling event of "I Am." At first, it might appear that "I Am" stands for a drastic, even tragic departure from an original ecological sensibility. That is, Clare seems to embody the latest form of his poetic selfhood as an empty nothingness that can only yearn for an earth minimalistically conceived as grass and sky, like a character in a Beckett play looking out of a window. "I Am," however, has a retroactively corrosive effect on Clare's oeuvre. It helps us to see how, even from the point of view of the supposed self-contained, organic, feudal village, Clare was writing poetry *for another.* Jonathan Bate's biography of Clare makes this very point, perhaps inadvertently and ironically, in that it ostensibly tries to put a certain ecology firmly at the heart of Clare's poetics – an ecology marked by close, local observation of a feudal vestige of community and custom obliterated by capitalist procedures such as enclosure. Writing itself, publication, editors in London, and circulation of writing, all come to stand in for these obliterating processes. But even when he was writing without a view to publication, Clare's work was displaced *from the inside* by an awareness of the other. He read his poems anonymously to his relatives out of an embarrassed fear that they would despise his work if they knew it was by him.[16] It had to sound as if it came from somewhere else in order to receive validation. Rusticity was itself a poetic trope of which Clare was well aware. And his poetic love of nature was itself a displacement from normative village life (206). As a self-taught poet living in misery, Clare had a deep understanding of the complexities of his situation. He did not need a formal knowledge of Descartes to voice a sense of radical doubt.

It all comes down to the question of writing, which, confirming Derrida's view, carries the burden of all that seems wrong about language: it's never really *yours*, it is always dispersed, differential, and so forth. Recent textual criticism has sought to discover an original, authentic Clare behind or before the corruption

of London, capitalism, and so on, metonymies (or metaphors?) for the spacing
and displacing actions of grammar. Ecological literary criticism has assumed this
task as its own, discovering a natural Clare beneath the artificiality.[17] But Bate
himself observes that the image of an authentic ungrammatical Clare corrupted
by revision is in fact part of a fantasy of ownership in which Clare the primitive
becomes an object of consumerism (563–75). A painful awareness of grammar
always bisected Clare's poetics, even (especially) in those moments when he was
angry about grammar.

   The space of the village, even if it was indeed feudal, was always already crisscrossed
with otherness. There was no *there* there that was not already aware of *another there.*
"I Am" is thus the stunning moment at which this otherness is perceived as intrinsic
to the self, at a terrible cost. Clare does not know who he is, as a horribly vivid letter
from the asylum indicates (Bate, *Biography* 506). But this not knowing is also a hard-
won moment of actual subjectivity, in which, if we are to take Clare as an ecopoet
seriously, we have lost nature, but gained ecology.

   Clare actually gives us the feeling of environment as open mind. For example,
consider the weird ending of "Mouse's Nest," which opens up the landscape:

   I found a ball of grass among the hay
   And progged it as I passed and went away
   And when I looked I fancied something stirred
   And turned agen and hoped to catch the bird
   When out an old mouse bolted in the wheat
   With all her young ones hanging at her teats
   She looked so odd and so grotesque to me
   I ran and wondered what the thing could be
   And pushed the knapweed bunches where I stood
   When the mouse hurried from the crawling brood
   The young ones squeaked and when I went away
   She found her nest again among the hay
   The water oer the pebbles scarce could run
   And broad old cesspools glittered in the sun

What Clare helps us to feel here is the existential quality of doubt. This is by no
means ecoskepticism – quite the opposite in fact. The poetic language is tied irrevocably to the earth's emotional gravitational field. Doubt – the effect of things ceasing
to be what you expect – is here mingled with a heavy sadness, a lingering quality, even
of dread, especially in the final couplet, which situates the sonnet in an oppressive
summer sunlight, an intense sense of environment from which there is no escape.
Faith is no longer a question of belief, of cleaving to ideas in your head, but of an
existential remaining in place. The existential "thisness" of the glittering cesspools is
surely an environmental analogue for the anti-aesthetic grotesqueness of the close up
view of the mouse and her young, which surprises the narrator and defeats trite ecological sentimentality.[18] This is life, as Giorgio Agamben would now put it, reduced to
bareness, just as the mother mouse and her children are metonymically reduced to a
trickle of water and a stagnant pool.

   This is incredibly good news for ecocriticism. Even here, even at the limits
of subjectivity, we find closeness to the earth. It is quite the opposite of what we

might expect: that environment as theory, as wonder, as doubt, does not achieve escape velocity from the earth, but, in fact, is a sinking down into it further than any wishful thinking, any naïve concept of interconnectedness could push us. This is the place reached in Shelley's extraordinary essay "On Love," where the very feelings of loneliness and separation, rather than narcissistic fantasies of interconnectedness, put us in touch with a surrounding environment.[19] I am calling it dark ecology, after Frost ("The woods are lovely dark and deep"), but also after Gothic culture, from *Frankenstein* to The Cure, a reminder that we can't escape our minds. Far from giving us a liturgy for how to get out of our guilty minds, how to stick our heads in nature and lose them, Clare actually helps us to stay right here, in the poisoned mud. Which is just where we need to be, right now.

Notes

1 René Descartes, *Meditations and Other Metaphysical Writings*, trans. and intro. Desmond M. Clarke (Harmondsworth: Penguin, 1998, 2000), 19.
2 For a comprehensive survey, see Edward Casey, *The Fate of Place: A Philosophical History* (Berkeley: U of California P, 1999).
3 Timothy Morton, "Environmentalism," in Nicholas Roe, ed., *Romanticism: An Oxford Guide* (Oxford and New York: Oxford UP, [2005]). Georg Wilhelm Friedrich Hegel, *Hegel's Phenomenology of Spirit*, trans. A.V. Miller, analysis and foreword by J.N. Findlay (Oxford: Oxford UP, 1977), 383–409.
4 I use the language of the title of Edward Casey, *Getting Back into Place: Toward a Renewed Understanding of the Place-World* (Bloomington: Indiana UP, 1993).
5 Martin Heidegger, "The Origin of the Work of Art." *Poetry, Language, Thought*, trans. Albert Hofstadter (New York: Harper and Row. 1971), 15–87 (33–4).
6 Martin Heidegger, "Building Dwelling Thinking," *Poetry, Language, Thought*, 143–61 (152–3).
7 Avital Ronell, *The Telephone Book Technology, Schizophrenia, Electric Speech* (Lincoln and London: U of Nebraska P, 1989), 26–83 (28).
8 Martin Heidegger, "Supplement," *Metaphysical Foundations of Logic*, trans. M. Heim (Bloomington: Indiana UP, 1984), 221.
9 Arne Naess, *Ecology, Community and Lifestyle* (Cambridge and New York: Cambridge UP, 1989), 56.
10 David Harvey, *Justice, Nature and the Geography of Difference* (Oxford, UK and Malden, MA: Blackwell, 1996), 167–8.
11 Jacques Lacan, "The Agency of the Letter in the Unconscious or Reason Since Freud," *Écrits: A Selection*, trans. Alan Sheridan (London: Tavistock Publications, 1977), 146–78 (166).
12 Walter Benjamin, *The Origin of German Tragic Drama*, trans. John Osborne, intro. George Steiner (London: New Left Books. 1977), 153, 230.
13 John Clare, *John Clare*, eds Eric Robinson and David Powell (Oxford and New York: Oxford UP, 1984).
14 *Anglo-Saxon Poetry*, trans. and ed. S.A.J. Bradley (London, Melbourne and Toronto: Dent, 1982), 372.
15 I am grateful to Tim Fulford for discussing this with me.
16 Jonathan Bate, *John Clare: A Biography* (London: Picador, and New York: Farrar, Straus and Giroux, 2003), 91.
17 James C. McKusick, *Green Writing: Romanticism and Ecology* (New York: St. Martin's, 2000), 77–94 (especially 89, 91).
18 John Goodridge has indicated to me that "cesspools" is a textual crux. Some scholars, including Goodridge and Robert Heyes, prefer "sexpools" (small pools formed in the hole left by turf cutting). I do not believe this affects my reading.
19 Percy Bysshe Shelley, "On Love," *Shelley's Prose: The Trumpet of a Prophecy*, ed. David Lee Clark (London: Fourth Estate, 1988), 169–71 (170).

39 The monster in the rainbow

Keats and the science of life

Denise Gigante

At Benjamin Haydon's "immortal dinner" party of 28 December 1817, Keats agreed with Charles Lamb that Newton "had destroyed all the poetry of the rainbow, by reducing it to the prismatic colors" (Haydon [1927:] 231).[1] At about the same time, the physiologist John Abernethy (1764–1831), whom Keats knew from his medical training at Guy's Hospital in London, was claiming that materialist practitioners of the "science of life" were destroying all the poetry of the living organism by reducing it to the sum of its functions. Just as the physical sciences had eliminated the life of the rainbow, in other words, radical physiologists, such as Abernethy's rival William Lawrence (1783–1867), were threatening to dissolve the mystery of life itself. Scientific discourse between 1780 and 1830 was preoccupied with the idea of a "living principle" that distinguished living matter from nonliving. The focal point for the dispute between Abernethy and Lawrence over this possibility of a supervenient vital principle was the work of the British physiologist John Hunter (1728–93). Although Hunter was not the first to renounce the mechanical application of Newtonian principles to the living organism, he lent the weight of extensive empirical experimentation to the idea that life was something superadded to – or in excess of – physical organization.[2] Against the materialism represented by Lawrence, vitalists in the wake of Hunter sought to define the science of life beyond the mechanistic sphere of Newtonian science that had dominated the physiology of the first half of the eighteenth century.[3] The paradox, which Keats brilliantly brings to light in *Lamia* (the site of his famous attack on the Newtonian tendency to "[u]nweave a rainbow" [*Complete Poems* 342–59; 2.237]), is that the same philosophy that would reduce life to the sum of its bodily functions helped to generate a countertheory of life as excess. The theory of a self-propagating vital power, which could extend beyond the physical borders of the organism, found creative expression in the various guises of Romantic monstrosity: a radically new aesthetic that emerged from the natural philosophy of the late eighteenth and early nineteenth centuries.

The aesthetic definition of monstrosity changed significantly during this period, from an Enlightenment concept of defect or deformity to a Romantic notion of monstrosity as too much life. Hunter, whose notion of a living principle was at the source of the controversy between Abernethy and Lawrence, posited an even more speculative "principle of monstrosity" (*Essays* 240), which held that rather than something gone awry during formation, monstrosity was the result of the formative capacity.[4] Hunter's principle of monstrosity was nothing other than the principle of life propagating itself to excess from within. This concept of a self-propagating vital power, developed in physiological discourse of the late eighteenth century, had its equivalent in the natural philosophy of early German Romanticism, where it was discussed by Johann Friedrich Blumenbach in 1780 as a "formative force" (*Bildungstrieb*), or *nisus formativus*.[5] It was subsequently imported into Romantic aesthetics by way of Kant's third critique, where the Hunterian-Blumenbachian notion of what Kant calls a "self-propagating formative power" informs his aesthetic definition of monstrosity as that which exceeds representation ([Kant 1952,] 2: 22). Kant blends natural philosophy with aesthetics to articulate the emergent concept of Romantic monstrosity. Such monstrosity does not remain on the level of theory but becomes the motivation for a new kind of monster in the literature of the Romantic period, one whose life force is too big for the matter containing it.

In the early-nineteenth-century debate over the controversial principle of life, Lawrence asserted against Abernethy that "[a]n immaterial and spiritual being could not have been discovered amid the blood and filth of the dissecting-room" (*Lectures* 18). Yet this is the space that Romantic writers used as their mental workshop of filthy creation. As Mary Shelley records in her 1831 introduction to *Frankenstein*, a single evening's conversation at Villa Diodati in June 1816 over the so-called principle of life prompted two of the period's most famous monsters: Frankenstein's creature and the Byronic vampire. Coleridge, who wrote his *Theory of Life* (*Shorter Works* 485–557) in response to Lawrence in the final months of 1816, portrays the climactic scene of *The Rime of the Ancyent Marinere* as an encounter with monsters of the deep. And Keats answers Newton with his "rainbow-sided" monster Lamia (1.54). Whether we consider Shelley's creature of perverted physiology, the Byronic vampire, Coleridge's "water-snakes" (*Rime*, line 265), or Keats's vivified rainbow, the contemporary scientific concern that life could propagate itself was the condition of possibility for Romantic monstrosity.

In what follows, I sketch the theoretical background for the kind of monstrosity Keats brings to life in *Lamia* and then suggest how such monstrosity answers the Romantic, and particularly Keatsian, concern with what it means to be born – or to die – into life. Keats's fragmentary epic *Hyperion* (*Complete Poems* 248–69), composed in the final months of 1818, notoriously breaks off at the moment when the ascendant poet-hero, the golden boy Apollo, is about to "[d]ie into life" (3.130). *Lamia* and *The Fall of Hyperion* (*Complete Poems* 361–73), written contemporaneously from July through September 1819, respond to that abyss of the unknown, the unwritten mystery of "life" at the end of *Hyperion*. But whereas *The Fall of Hyperion* portrays the heavy physicality of bodies barely able to sustain life, *Lamia* portrays an excessive vitality that is finally too much for the feeble frame of the ostensible hero, Lycius. When Lamia vanishes with a "frightful scream" at the end of the poem, "Lycius' arms were empty of delight, / As were his limbs of life, from that same night" (2.306–8). Viewed in this light, *Lamia* is no mere narrative swerve from Keats's epic ambitions; rather, it is an overexuberant response to the problem of life posed at the end of the first *Hyperion* and worked through, to opposite effect, in the second. Lamia represents the consummate Romantic monster, a vision of life conceived beyond the material fact of organization.

I

When Keats conceived his rainbow-sided monster in the summer of 1819, the debate between Abernethy and Lawrence over the principle of life had reached its peak. In a series of public lectures at the Royal College of Surgeons between 1814 and 1819,

Abernethy proposed, and his onetime student Lawrence denied, that what Hunter had called a *materia vitae diffusa* was nothing other than an invisible vital fluid, which was the source, or the "principle," of life (Abernethy [1814:] 32).[6] Updating the premodern concept of ether, Abernethy claimed in his opening lecture, *Enquiry into the Probability and Rationality of Mr. Hunter's Theory of Life* (1814), that

> a subtle substance of a quickly and powerfully mobile nature, seems to pervade every thing, and appears to be the life of the world; and therefore it is probable that a similar substance pervades organized bodies, and produces similar effects in them.
>
> (51)

In March 1816, Lawrence responded with *An Introduction to Comparative Anatomy and Physiology*, denying the presence of a supervenient vital fluid and insisting that life was simply a matter of organization, or "the assemblage of all the functions" (120). Unlike more strictly mechanistic models of human physiology – which saw life as "an assemblage of pipes, canals, levers, pulleys, and other mechanism," as Lawrence put it (speaking of the school of Hermann Boerhaave) – Lawrence's brand of materialism drew a distinction between life as an assemblage of functions and life as an assemblage of parts (*Lectures* 67). According to Lawrence, the latter would be the study of anatomy, rather than physiology, since it could not account for certain vital phenomena present only in living bodies. Unlike his more radical French counterparts, Lawrence recognized that after the mid-century discovery of sensibility and irritability by Albrecht von Haller, it was no longer possible to embrace uncritically a mechanistic Newtonian physiology. His definition of life as an "assemblage of all the functions" was thus a materialist, not a mechanistic, theory of life. The distinction is significant, for the new vitalist monstrosity that sprang forth against it would not have been possible in the mechanistic world of Newton.

In a series of papers published throughout the 1770s, Hunter defined the methods and techniques of modern physiology, grounding them on the central assumption that "[w]hatever Life is, it most certainly does not depend upon the structure or organization" (*Essays* 114). Instead, Hunter believed that life was the result of a supervenient, and moreover formative, power. As Abernethy put it, "Hunter was the first who deduced the opinion, as a legitimate consequence of legitimate facts, that life actually constructed the very means by which it carried on its various processes" (*Hunterian Oration* 42). This Hunterian notion of a self-propagating vital power, which could assert itself beyond the physical border of the organism, effectively enabled the transformation of an Enlightenment concept of monstrosity as an ill assemblage of parts into a vitalist concept of monstrosity as an extension of the living principle.

Hunter's study of monsters in the three divisions of mineral, vegetable, and animal matter contains the logic for understanding this swerve from an established notion of monstrosity as defect or deformity to a Romantic view of monstrosity as a troubling overflow of the living principle. Hunter's observations on monsters (*Essays* 239–51), published with his posthumous papers in 1861, set out from the prior understanding of monstrosity as malformation:

> Nature being pretty constant in the kind and number of the different parts peculiar to each species of animal, and also in the situation, formation, and

construction of such parts, we call *everything that deviates from that uniformity a "monster,"* whether [it occur in] crystallization, vegetation, or animalization.

(239; my emphasis)

Monstrosity was predicated on a deviation from uniformity, just as beauty had been predicated throughout the eighteenth century on "Uniformity amidst variety" (Hutcheson [1725:] 11). In his 1814 lectures on aesthetics, Coleridge writes, "The BEAUTIFUL [. . .] is that in which *the many*, still seen as many, becomes *one*" (*Shorter Works* 371). He calls the result "*multeity in Unity*," and two years later in his *Theory of Life* he defines life similarly (but with a difference) as "the *power* which discloses itself from within as a principle of *unity* in the *many*," or "the principle of unity in *multeity*" (510). Just as beauty had been conceived as a static harmony of parts, life becomes conceived as a principle of harmony among parts. And monstrosity emerges as a principle opposed to their harmonious convergence in form.

Whereas the Enlightenment conceived monstrosity as a static, ill assemblage of parts – in other words, according to a mechanistic Newtonian physiology – Hunter paves the way for a Romantic rethinking of monstrosity as an extension of the living principle. He observes that "every animal is formed from a portion of animal matter endowed with life and actions, being [. . .] so arranged in itself as only to require new matter for it to expand itself according to the principle inherent in itself." Rather than a deviation from uniformity, monstrosity now came to represent more of – indeed, too much of – the same. Hunter's principle of monstrosity was nothing other than the power of the animal to continue propagating itself or of its "first arrangements to go on expanding the animal according to the first principles arising out of them" (*Essays* 239–40). This is not to say that Hunter completely dismisses the former concept of monstrosity as an irregular assemblage of parts. But he observes that "[a] deficiency and a mal-conformation are much more easily conceived than the formation of an additional part" (244). And it is to the latter, unthinkable kind of monstrosity that he devotes most of his attention.

[. . .]

Just as vegetable monstrosities arise from aggregations, extensions, and a multiplication of parts, animal monstrosities occur when the living principle fails to stay within the formal bounds of the organism. Monstrosity, as Hunter describes it, in animals and vegetables – in all that contain the living principle – is the result of too much life. This is a revised, vitalist concept of monstrosity, according to which monsters are no longer mechanical malformations. After the decline of mechanistic physiology in the late eighteenth century, they become products of the animal's uncontainable vitality.

This theory of monstrosity as an excess of the living principle influenced scientists of the 1820s, whose deliberate creation of monsters from chick embryos had odd parallels with Romantic fiction. The French zoologist Etienne Geoffroy Saint-Hilaire, building on the work of Georges Cuvier and Jean Baptiste de Lamarck, founded a school of philosophical anatomy on the concept of "unity of composition." The concept allowed Geoffroy and his leading disciple, Etienne Serres, like Hunter, to define monstrosity as something gone awry during "recapitulation," or self-repetition (Desmond [1989:] 52–3). The conservative Cuvier rightly feared that these experiments with chick monstrosities would ultimately subordinate human beings to an autonomous law of nature. Indeed, the ground of modern evolutionary theory had already been prepared by Erasmus Darwin, who speaks in *Zoonomia* (1794) of

> changes produced probably by the exuberance and nourishment supplied to the fetus, as in monstrous births with additional limbs; many of these enormities are propagated, and continued as a variety at least, if not as a new species of animal.
>
> (501)

The physiologist William Carpenter would similarly explain exceptions to natural law, such as "monsters," in his *Principles of General and Comparative Physiology* (1839) as part of an experimental self-extension by self-propagating matter (Winter [1997:] 36). For practitioners of the post-Hunterian science of life, monstrosity was not malformed but overexuberant living matter.

Such monstrous profusion was the necessary result of a universe conceived against the mechanistic model. Whereas in Newton's cosmos each part worked in harmony with the rest toward the functioning of a greater whole, Kant argued in "The Critique of Teleological Judgement," the second half of *The Critique of Judgement* (1790), that "this is not enough [. . .]. On the contrary the part must be an organ producing the other parts – each, consequently, reciprocally producing the others." Following a renewed vitalist natural philosophy, Kant believed that "an organized being possesses inherent *formative* power, and such, moreover, as it can impart to material devoid of it – material which it organizes. This, therefore, is a self-propagating formative power, which cannot be explained by the capacity of movement alone, that is to say, by mechanism" (2: 21–2). Against the static Newtonian world-clock, whose parts were synchronized according to a mechanistic plan, Kant's "*formative* power" exceeds organization.[7] Spilling out of the ontological container of the organism, it extends itself to external matter, which it shapes to its own purposes.

In "The Critique of Aesthetic Judgement," Kant claims, "An object is *monstrous* where by its size it defeats the end that forms its concept" (1: 100). [. . . I]n Kant's aesthetic ontology, things in nature exhibit purposiveness; they orient themselves toward a telos that defines them as organized beings.[8] Like Hunter's formative force, pushing out as "so many monsters" through momentary gaps in the organism, the aesthetic magnitude that nullifies its own purpose extends outward to obliterate the telos of form. [. . .] This vitalist concept of a living principle that can assert itself in a monstrous profusion underwrites the Romantic aesthetics of monstrosity. It remains to be shown how this vital force takes creative shape in *Lamia*.

II

When Keats lamented the Newtonian propensity to "[u]nweave a rainbow" in the summer of 1819, during the tail end of the Abernethy–Lawrence debate, his real target may not have been the mechanistic philosophy of the physical sciences so much as its application to the science of life. For to deny the poetry of the "awful rainbow" (*Lamia* 2.231) would be to deny Lamia the living principle that in the end constitutes her monstrosity.[9] Her first appearance in book 1 is as a "rainbow-sided," serpentine seductress (1.54). She enters a dialogue with the god Hermes, who is searching for a nymph whom he adores and whom Lamia has made invisible. Lamia promises that if he will agree to change her into human form she will make the nymph visible to him. Lamia is in love with the Corinthian youth Lycius, whom she marries after her metamorphosis. The main tension in the poem is Lamia's resistance to her public wedding, for she foresees her destruction under the analytic gaze of Lycius's tutor, Apollonius. Keats's original phrase for "Unweave a rainbow" was "Destroy a rainbow" (*Poetry Manuscripts* 215), and when Lamia first appears in the poem,

> She was a gordian shape of dazzling hue,
> Vermilion-spotted, golden, green, and blue;
> Striped like a zebra, freckled like a pard,
> Eyed like a peacock, all crimson bar'd [. . .].
> (1.47–50)

Keats portrays his rainbow as a she, yet instead of a cleanly divided spectrum, rigidly defined by "rule and line" (2.235), she appears as an explosion of color that can only occur in language. As the rigid stripes and bars of color are disrupted with spots, freckles, and eyes, Lamia becomes difficult, if not impossible, to contain in aesthetic representation. [. . . A]s a rainbow imbued with vital power, she is a monstrous object of not Newtonian physics but rather the science of life.

Two weeks after Haydon's immortal dinner party, where Keats and Lamb toasted "Newton's health, and confusion to mathematics" (Haydon [1927:] 231), Hazlitt remarked that scientific investigation tended to "clip the wings of poetry," which had already received "a sensible shock from the progress of experimental philosophy" ([1930–4:] 9). In *Lamia* Keats accuses (experimental or natural) philosophy of something similar:

> There was an awful rainbow once in heaven:
> We know her woof, her texture; she is given
> In the dull catalogue of common things.
> Philosophy will clip an Angel's wings,
> Conquer all mysteries by rule and line,
> Empty the haunted air, and gnomed mine –
> Unweave a rainbow [. . .].
> (2.231–7)

This is the same tendency Wordsworth refers to as "murder[ing] to dissect" in "The Tables Turned," and as the elder poet's metaphor of vivisection indicates, it is not Newton's analytic procedures but their application to life that is cause for concern in this period.

Keats observes of *Lamia* that "there is that sort of fire in it which must take hold of people in some way – give them either pleasant or unpleasant sensation" ("To George and Georgiana Keats," 27 Sept. 1819, letter 199 of *Letters* [189]), and several forms of fire – "electric fire," "animal fire," "fire-air" – had currency at the time as signifiers for the principle of life. Hunter proposed an analogy between life and fire in his essay "On Life and the Living Principle" (*Essays* 113–21): "I would consider Life as a Fire, or something similar, which might for distinction's sake be called Animal Fire" (113). [. . .] Keats's description of the monster sparkles with electric life. She is "dazzling," "crimson," "full of silver moons," and burning bright – a "brilliance feminine" (1.47–52, 92). Slightly later in book 1, she "[f]lash'd phosphor and sharp sparks" (1.152). This electric fire animating Lamia would have resonated at a time when electricity was figuratively, if not literally, the spark of life.

The theory that Lawrence referred to derisively in his debate with Abernethy as the "electro-chemical hypothesis of life" held that an electric life force, or a power analogous to electricity, sparked and sustained living matter (*Lectures* 22). In the late 1780s, Luigi Galvani had popularized the notion of "animal electricity" as an innate vital force or property, distinct from "natural" electricity ([1953:] 59–88). This contemporary preoccupation with the idea of an electric life force has received plenty of critical attention, though mostly with respect to *Frankenstein*.[10] Through Mary Shelley, we are familiar with the numerous experiments with galvanic electricity performed on vegetables, animals, human beings, and (as Shelley writes in her introduction to *Frankenstein*) even vermicelli. But Keats's brightly colored, antimechanistic creature, flashing phosphor and sharp sparks, was also at the crossroads of this debate.

Lamia's transformation into a human being is a scene of creation strangely analogous to the one in *Frankenstein*, and her electric birth anticipates film versions of *Frankenstein* better than does Shelley's novel, where the creature comes to life behind closed doors. Unlike Shelley, Keats renders visible the details of electric animation:

> Her eyes in torture fix'd, and anguish drear,
> Hot, glaz'd, and wide, with lid-lashes all sear,
> Flash'd phosphor and sharp sparks, without one
>   cooling tear.
> The colours all inflam'd throughout her train,
> She writh'd about, convuls'd with scarlet pain:
> A deep volcanian yellow took the place
> Of all her milder-mooned body's grace;
> And, as the lava ravishes the mead,
> Spoilt all her silver mail, and golden brede;
> Made gloom of all her frecklings, streaks and bars,
> Eclips'd her crescents, and lick'd up her stars:
> So that, in moments few, she was undrest
> Of all her sapphires, greens, and amethyst,
> And rubious argent: of all these bereft,
> Nothing but pain and ugliness were left.
>   (1.150–64)

Lamia's short-circuiting colors, her "sharp sparks" and "scarlet pain," all suggest a galvanic experiment gone awry. As in the cinematic *Frankenstein's* fiat by thunderbolt, the electrochemical experiment described above defeats its purpose by giving too much life. Both scenes of creation were intended to produce objects of beauty, and both erupt in monstrosity.

Like Hunter's principle of monstrosity conceived as the principle of life taken to a radical extreme, Lamia is too much to be contained in a "woman's shape, and [. . .] woman's form" (1.118–20). As her sudden explosion into life overwhelms her "dazzling" exterior, she defeats her own purpose and hence her status as beautiful: "Nothing but pain and ugliness were left." But what are we to make of this ugliness at the core of Keats's living rainbow? Slavoj Žižek suggests,

In the case of beauty, the outside of a thing – its surface – encloses, overcoats, its interior, whereas in the case of ugliness, this proportionality is perturbed by the excess of the interior stuff that threatens to overwhelm and engulf the subject.

([1997:] 22–3)

Lamia is ugly insofar as she is a vital force with the capacity to perturb her proportionality by extending past the limits of form.[11] The excess of her electric life singes her a "deep volcanian yellow."

Keats refers directly to the contemporary obsession with the possibility of an electric life force in his notes from an anatomy course with Astly Cooper and Henry Cline, Jr. He mentions the effects of "animal electricity" in those strangely charged organisms *Gymnoti electrici*, or electric eels:

> The opinion of late years entertained concerning the Cause of nervous energy was started by Mr J. Hunter. He examined y̆ Body of a Gymnotus Electricus he found it provided with abundance of Nerves sufficient to account for its electric properties. From this he inferred that the Nerves were conductor of electric fluid. ~~Cavallo~~ Galvani found that a<n> action of y̆ Nerves was produced by applying Metal thereto. The present opinion therefore is that a fluid, like that of the electric is secreted in y̆ brain which is thence communicated along the Nerves.
>
> (*Note Book* 58)

Attempting to penetrate the mystery of life, Hunter cut into the bowels of the electrically charged eel and discovered its vital powers. In his account of this experiment in the *Philosophical Transactions of the Royal Society* of 11 May 1775, he remarks that the *Gymnotus electricus* "may be considered, both anatomically and physiologically, as divided into two parts; *viz.* the common animal part; and a part which is superadded, *viz.* the *peculiar organ*" ([1775:] 395). This "peculiar organ" is the particular object of his study, for it has "peculiar powers" that extend beyond "the common animal part" of the organism. Hunter does not claim to have discovered "animal electricity" but credits the physician John Walsh (1725–95), who performed some of the first experiments with electrical therapy in England and who provided Hunter with an electric eel for dissection.[12] Yet Hunter brings to light the "peculiar property" of the eel, the ability to extend its powers throughout – and beyond – its physical organization (much like the monstrous "*formative* force" informing Kantian aesthetics). And this power of the *Gymnotus electricus* enacts literally Hunter's principle of monstrosity.

[. . .]

III

As *Lamia* suggests, to exceed the mechanistic spectrum of colors from red to violet is to erupt in pain and ugliness. Just as other Romantic-era monsters, such as Frankenstein's creature and the Byronic vampire, prove too big for their narrative frames and emerge as cultural icons or myths, Lamia will not be contained within the allegorical web of the poem. Although the narrative seems to invite allegorical interpretations, none have proved completely satisfactory, and what has caused the most confusion of all is the seemingly unnecessary opening frame in which Lamia interacts with the god Hermes and his love object, a soon-to-be-ravished nymph. Read not as a narrative digression but as a sequel to the abruptly terminated *Hyperion*, Keats's monstrous vision of life as excess in *Lamia* provides an alternative vision of what happens to the ravished nymph left out of the end of *Hyperion*.

The only existing holograph of the *Hyperion* fragment contains an analogy – omitted from the published poem of 1820 – comparing Apollo to a "ravish'd Nymph" (*Manuscript Poems* 55). Keats was enraged that his publishers, John Taylor and James Hessey, should add an "Advertisement" to the volume, without his knowledge, that asserted,

> If any apology be thought necessary for the appearance of the unfinished poem of HYPERION, the publishers beg to state that they alone are responsible, as it was printed at their particular request, and contrary to the wish of the author.
>
> (Lamia)[13]

It was also likely contrary to the wish of the author that the printed version of Apollo's metamorphosis (3.124–30) eliminated the third through the fifth lines below from Keats's manuscript:

> And soon wild commotions shook him, and
>   made flush
> All the immortal family of his limbs
> Into a hue more roseate than sweet pain
> Gives to a ravish'd Nymph when her warm tears
> Gush luscious with no sob. Or more severe;
> More like the struggle at the gate of death,
> Or liker still to one who should take leave
> Of pale immortal death and with a pang
> As hot as death is chill, with fierce convulse
> Die into life.
>
> (*Manuscript Poems* 55)

The first edition condenses (and changes) the second to sixth lines above as follows: "All the immortal fairness of his limbs; / *Most* like the struggle at the gate of death" (3.125–6; my emphasis). In calling attention to the elision, I do not wish to suggest a direct transference, namely that the "ravish'd Nymph" who disappears from *Hyperion* reappears as the nymph who "cower'd, nor could restrain / Her fearful sobs" as she gives herself up to Hermes in *Lamia* (1.137–8) or that she becomes Lamia, who, "[r]avish'd [. . .] lifted her Circean head" to Hermes shortly before her metamorphosis (1.115). Rather, I propose that in response to *Hyperion*'s dangling question of what it means to "[d]ie into life," Keats imagined two scenarios. On the one hand, if, as so many readers have supposed, Apollo dies into the poet-speaker of *The Fall of Hyperion*, he dies into a material world seemingly stripped of all vitality. While the deposed Titans are "nerveless, listless, dead" (1.323), the speaker struggles "hard to escape / The numbness": "Slow, heavy, deadly was my pace: the cold / Grew stifling, suffocating, at the heart" (1.127–31). *The Fall of Hyperion* hardly augurs life beyond the material – and barely grants the speaker that. Keats knew himself to be writing against death, and the despair of the poem is in part a metaphysical despair of life's ever being anything more than a mechanism of heavy limbs. On the other hand, to imagine more than this – to imagine life as an autonomous power with the capacity to exceed its material dimensions – is to imagine something monstrous.

Unlike the uncanny, ghostly figures inhabiting Gothic fiction, the monsters who spring forth from the Romantic imaginary are literally bursting with life. Just as Lamia breaks out of the mechanical bars of the rainbow, Frankenstein's creature spills out between the fissures in his skin as another figure of excessive vitality. Even the Romantic vampire is gorged with too much life. John Polidori writes in his introduction to *The Vampyre* (1819) that "these human bloodsuckers fattened – and their veins become distended to such a state of repletion, as to cause the blood to flow from all the passages of their bodies, and even from the very pores of their skins" ([1990:] xx). Frankenstein refers to his monster as "my own vampire, my own spirit let loose from the grave" (Shelley [1994:] 105), and Lamia too has been perceived as vampiric (e.g., Stevenson [1972]; Twitchell [1981]).

[. . .]

Because Lamia will not be contained by the formal telos of the beautiful – or its teleological expression in the form of organized life – she appears monstrous in her own magnitude. Nevertheless, she exhibits the seductive appeal of monstrosity as a Romantic version (or perversion) of sublimity. Lycius's first encounter with her is described as follows: "And soon his eyes had drunk her beauty up, / Leaving no drop in the bewildering cup, / And still the cup was full" (1.151–3). As Lamia overruns "the bewildering cup" of her beautiful form in an abundance that Lycius can never fully consume, she becomes a devouring presence who inverts the rules of aesthetic contemplation. She tells her lover Lycius (as if in warning) that she desires a place "Where I may all my many senses please, / And by mysterious sleights a hundred thirsts appease" (1.284–5). Instead of the five senses by which we register sensation, Lamia boasts an unbounded "many." In the place of a single thirst, she has "a hundred," which she must try to appease by "mysterious sleights," since by all standard means they are unappeasable. She spills over the brim of "the bewildering cup" in more ways than one, and the feast she offers her guests is likewise conceived as an extravagant excess. Keats describes the banquet hall "[t]eeming with odours," "[t]he fretted splendour of each nook and niche," and every square inch of wall space erupting with uncontainable vitality as "there burst / Forth creeping imagery" (2.133–40). One suspects that this is indeed "the symbolic extroversion of her innate qualities in the banquet décor" (Stewart [1976:] 31). Asserting herself as an unconsumable overabundance, Lamia is more than human – or more than material organization alone would allow.

If Lamia represents a vital – if monstrous – response to the looming question of what it means to "[d]ie into life," Lycius comes to embody the other extreme. In the final line of the poem, after Lamia's sudden disappearance (under the stern gaze of Apollonius), he is reduced to an "it," a "heavy body" (2.311). As Keats would have known, experimental natural philosophy grew out of Newton's experiments showing that heavy bodies falling to earth follow the same laws of gravitation as heavenly bodies in orbit. Lycius's "heavy body" would fit all too well into Newton's schema, which had no place for an intangible, unquantifiable life force. From this perspective, Lycius becomes the poem's material remainder, a heavy body that would sink naturally into the shady vale of *The Fall of Hyperion* alongside all the other heavy bodies of the fallen gods. In a materialist world, deprived of all hope of redemption, one's pace is necessarily "[s]low, heavy, deadly." Yet I submit that the final tragedy of Keats's unfinished epic is not the reduction of the human to a mechanistic collection of limbs, a heavy body deprived of its living principle like Newton's rainbow deprived of its poetry. Rather, it is the possibility that to die into anything more than this is to become too much – to become monstrous in the eyes of a calculating world.

Notes

1 Newton's major works, *Philosophiae naturalis principia mathematica* (1687) and *Opticks; or, A Treatise of the Reflexions, Refractions, Inflexions, and Colours of Light* (1704), established the principles and methods of quantitative natural philosophy. Schofield [(1970)] and Thackray [(1970)] demonstrate the numerous scientific schools of thought emanating from Newton that were operative throughout the eighteenth century.

2 The notion of a supervenient vital power that could animate matter was nothing new; in response to seventeenth-century iatrochemical and iatromechanical models of human physiology (themselves responses to animistic and scholastic models), theorists from George Ernst Stahl (1660–1734) to Paul Joseph Barthez (1734–1806) proposed various *causae vitae*, including "forces," "powers," "properties," and "principles." Brown [(1974)], de Almeida ([1991:] 87–110), Gode-von Aesch ([1941:] 183–203), Goodfield-Toulmin [(1969)], Hall ([1969,] 2: 5–278), and Schofield ([1970:] 191–231) provide helpful accounts of the rise of vitalism.

3 From 1740 the practice of physiology began to swerve from Newtonian mechanistic techniques toward a new vitalism whose central concern was the nature of the living principle. [. . .].

4 For a related argument, which I encountered after completing this essay, see Hagner [(1999)], who focuses on the epigenetic redefinition of monstrosity by Caspar Friedrich Wolff and its application by Samuel Thomas Soemmerring.

5 Blumenbach introduced the idea of a formative force, by which living creatures take a certain form, maintain it, and reproduce it in case of destruction, in his 1780 essay "Über den Bildungstrieb (*Nisus Formativus*) und seinen Einsfluß auf die Generation und Reproduction" ("On the Formative Force and Its Influence on Generation and Reproduction"; my trans.). The essay was later expanded into *Über den Bildungstrieb und das Zeugungsgeschäfte* (1781), which was translated into Latin in 1785 and issued in English in 1792 as *An Essay on Generation*. On the fertility of the concept of the formative force for German Romanticism, see Gode-von Aesch ([1941:] 198).

6 Hunter's *materia vitae* was an invisible hypothetical substance, unlike the visible vital matter that microscopists (e.g., C.F. Wolff, Otto Fredrik Müller, Abraham Trembley) were investigating and that became, under the designation "protoplasm," the *materia vitae* of the nineteenth century.

7 As Walter D. Wetzels points out, "The word *mechanisch* became [. . .] in general the polemic adjective in the battle against the old [Newtonian] and for the new organic physics" ([1976:] 46).

8 While for Kant the power of self-formation was sufficient to distinguish living from non-living matter, Blumenbach came to believe that it was one of three vital (as opposed to "dead" – i.e., physical, chemical, or mechanical) powers, namely "[o]rganic *formation* and increase; *motion* in the parts when formed; *sensation* from the motion of certain similar parts" (*Institutions* 18). On Blumenbach's influence on Kant, see Lenoir [(1982)].

9 As the mechanistic Newtonian worldview was on the decline and vitalist theories were on the rise, Christopher Smart [(1990)] also attempted to put some poetry back into Newton's rainbow, in fragment B (648–59) of *Jubilate Agno* (1758–63). Epstein and Greenberg [(1984)], Jones [(1966)], and Nicolson [(1946)] discuss the effect of Newton's *Opticks* on eighteenth-century poetry.

10 An accomplished and rapidly growing literature on Shelley and science commences with Crouch [(1978)], Mellor ([1988:] 89–114), and Vasbinder [(1984)].

11 On this concept of the ugly in *Frankenstein*, see Gigante [(2000)].

12 Such experiments began at mid-century; in 1748 the British physician Henry Baker made
    a case for the medicinal use of electricity as practiced elsewhere in Europe ([1748:] 270).
13 Rollins records that in one copy of the volume, Keats scratched out the advertisement,
    writing above it, "This is none of my doing – I w{as} ill at the time" (Keats, *Letters* 277n).
    Jack Stillinger, in the introduction to the Keats holograph, interprets this to mean that
    "Keats did not want *Hyperion* included in the volume" (xi). I read the publishers' claim that
    the volume was printed "at their particular request" to mean that Keats gave his consent
    but was embarrassed by the announcement that an apology might be thought necessary.
    Ironically, *Hyperion* was the best-received poem in the volume throughout the nineteenth
    century.

Bibliography

Abernethy, John. *An Enquiry into the Probability and Rationality of Mr. Hunter's Theory of Life.*
    London: Longman, Hurst, Rees, Orme, and Brown, 1814.
Abernethy, John. *The Hunterian Oration for the Year 1819.* London: Longman, Hurst, Rees,
    Orme, and Brown, 1819.
Baker, Henry. "A Letter from Mr. Henry Baker F.R.S., to the President, Concerning Several
    Medical Experiments of Electricity." *Philosophical Transactions of the Royal Society* 45 (1748):
    270–5.
Blumenbach, Johann Friedrich. *The Institutions of Physiology.* Trans. John Elliotson. Philadelphia:
    Benjamin Warner, 1817.
Blumenbach, Johann Friedrich. "Über den Bildungstrieb (*Nisus Formativus*) und seinen
    Einfluß auf die Generation und Reproduction." *Göttingischen Magazin* (1780): 247–66.
Brown, Theodore M. "From Mechanism to Vitalism in Eighteenth-Century English Physiology."
    Journal of the History of Biology 7 (1974): 179–216.
Coleridge, Samuel Taylor. *The Rime of the Ancyent Marinere. Lyrical Ballads.* William Wordsworth
    and Coleridge. 2nd ed. Eds R.L. Brett and A.R. Jones. London: Routledge, 1991. 9–35.
Coleridge, Samuel Taylor. *Shorter Works and Fragments.* Eds H.J. Jackson and J.R. de J. Jackson.
    Vol. 11, pt. 1. *The Collected Works of Samuel Taylor Coleridge.* Princeton: Princeton UP, 1995.
    14 vols.
Crouch, Laura E. "Davy's *A Discourse, Introductory to a Course of Lectures on Chemistry:* A Possible
    Scientific Source of *Frankenstein.*" *Keats-Shelley Journal* 27 (1978): 35–44.
Daruwala, Maneck H. "Strange Bedfellows: Keats and Wollstonecraft, Lamia and Berwick."
    Keats-Shelley Review 11 (1997): 83–132.
Darwin, Erasmus. *Zoonomia; or, The Laws of Organic Life.* Vol. 1. London: J. Johnson, 1794. 2 vols.
Davy, Humphry. *The Collected Works of Sir Humphry Davy.* Vol. 2. London: Smith, Elder, 1839–40.
    9 vols.
de Almeida, Hermione. *Romantic Medicine and John Keats.* New York: Oxford UP, 1991.
Desmond, Adrian. *The Politics of Evolution: Morphology, Medicine, and Reform in Radical London.*
    Chicago: U of Chicago P, 1989.
Epstein, Julia L., and Mark L. Greenberg. "Decomposing Newton's Rainbow." *Journal of the
    History of Ideas* 45 (1984): 115–40.
Galvani, Luigi. *Commentary on the Effects of Electricity on Muscular Motion.* Trans. Margaret Glover
    Foley. Ed. I. Bernard Cohen. Norwalk: Burndy Lib., 1953.
Gigante, Denise. "Facing the Ugly: The Case of *Frankenstein.*" *ELH* 67 (2000): 565–87.
Gode-von Aesch, Alexander. *Natural Science in German Romanticism.* New York: Columbia UP,
    1941.
Goodfield-Toulmin, June. "Some Aspects of English Physiology: 1780–1840." *Journal of the
    History of Biology* 2 (1969): 283–320.
Hagner, Michael. "Enlightened Monsters." *The Sciences in Enlightened Europe.* Eds William Clark,
    Jan Golinski, and Simon Schaffer. Chicago: U of Chicago P, 1999.

Hall, Thomas S. *Ideas of Life and Matter: Studies in the History of General Physiology, 600 B.C.–1900 A.D.* 2 vols. Chicago: U of Chicago P, 1969.

Hanafi, Zakiya. *The Monster in the Machine: Magic, Medicine, and the Marvelous in the Time of the Scientific Revolution.* Durham: Duke UP, 2000.

Haydon, Benjamin Robert. *The Autobiography and Memoirs of Benjamin Robert Haydon, 1786–1846.* Ed. P.D. Penrose. London: Bell, 1927.

Hazlitt, William. *The Complete Works of William Hazlitt.* Ed. P.P. Howe. Vol. 5. London: Dent, 1930–4. 21 vols.

Hunter, John. "An Account of the *Gymnotus Electricus.*" *Philosophical Transactions of the Royal Society* 65 (1775): 395–407.

Hunter, John. *Essays and Observations on Natural History, Anatomy, Physiology, Psychology, and Geology.* Vol. I. London: John van Voorst, 1861. 2 vols.

Hunter, John. *A Treatise on the Blood, Inflammation, and Gun-Shot Wounds.* London: John Richardson, 1794.

Hutcheson, Francis. *An Inquiry into the Original of Our Ideas of Beauty and Virtue.* London: J. Darby, 1725.

Jones, William Powell. *The Rhetoric of Science: A Study of Scientific Ideas and Imagery in Eighteenth-Century English Poetry.* Berkeley: U of California P, 1966.

Kant, Immanuel. *The Critique of Judgement.* Trans. James Creed Meredith. Oxford: Clarendon, 1952.

Keats, John. *Anatomical and Physiological Note Book.* Ed. Maurice Buxton Forman. New York: Haskell, 1970.

Keats, John. *Complete Poems.* Ed. Jack Stillinger. Cambridge: Harvard UP, 1978.

Keats, John. Lamia, *"Isabella," "The Eve of St. Agnes," and Other Poems.* London: Taylor and Hessey, 1820.

Keats, John. *The Letters of John Keats.* Ed. Hyder Edward Rollins. Vol. 2. Cambridge: Harvard UP, 1958. 2 vols.

Keats, John. *Manuscript Poems in the British Library: Facsimiles of the* Hyperion *Holograph and George Keats's Notebook of Holographs and Transcripts.* Ed. Jack Stillinger. Vol. 5 of *The Manuscripts of the Younger Romantics.* Donald H. Reiman, gen. ed. New York: Garland, 1988.

Keats, John. *Poetry Manuscripts at Harvard.* Ed. Jack Stillinger. Cambridge: Harvard UP, 1990.

Lawrence, William. *An Introduction to Comparative Anatomy and Physiology; Being the Two Introductory Lectures Delivered at the Royal College of Surgeons on the 21st and 25th of March, 1816.* London: J. Callou, 1816.

Lawrence, William. *Lectures on Physiology, Zoology, and the Natural History of Man, Delivered at the Royal College of Surgeons.* Salem: Foote and Brown, 1828.

Lenoir, Timothy. *The Strategy of Life: Teleology and Mechanics in Nineteenth-Century German Biology.* Dordrecht: Reidel, 1982.

Mellor, Anne K. *Mary Shelley: Her Life, Her Fiction, Her Monsters.* New York: Methuen, 1988.

Nicolson, Marjorie Hope. *Newton Demands the Muse: Newton's* Opticks *and the Eighteenth-Century Poets.* Princeton: Princeton UP, 1946.

Polidori, John William. Introduction. *The Vampyre.* 1819. Oxford: Woodstock, 1990. xix–xxv.

Schofield, Robert E. *Mechanism and Materialism: British Natural Philosophy in an Age of Reason.* Princeton: Princeton UP, 1970.

Shelley, Mary Wollstonecraft. *Frankenstein; or, The Modern Prometheus: The 1818 Version.* Eds D.L. Macdonald and Kathleen Scherf. Peterborough, ON: Broadview, 1994.

Smart, Christopher. *Selected Poems.* Eds Karina Williamson and Marcus Walsh. London: Penguin, 1990.

Stevenson, Warren. "*Lamia:* A Stab at the Gordian Knot." *Studies in Romanticism* 11 (1972): 241–52.

Stewart, Garrett. "*Lamia* and the Language of Metamorphosis." *Studies in Romanticism* 15 (1976): 3–41.

Stillinger, Jack. Introduction. Keats, *Manuscript Poems* ix–xvi.

Stoker, Bram. *Dracula*. Ed. Maurice Hindle. New York: Penguin, 1993.

Thackray, Arnold. *Atoms and Powers: An Essay on Newtonian Matter-Theory and the Development of Chemistry*. Cambridge: Harvard UP, 1970.

Twitchell, James B. *The Living Dead: A Study of the Vampire in Romantic Literature*. Durham: Duke UP, 1981.

Vasbinder, Samuel Holmes. *Scientific Attitudes in Mary Shelley's* Frankenstein. Ann Arbor: UMI Research, 1984.

Wetzels, Walter D. "Aspects of Natural Science in German Romanticism." *Studies in Romanticism* 10 (1976): 44–59.

Winter, Alison. "The Construction of Orthodoxies and Heterodoxies in the Early Victorian Life Sciences." *Victorian Science in Context*. Ed. Bernard Lightman. Chicago: U of Chicago P, 1997. 24–50.

Wordsworth, William. "The Tables Turned." *Lyrical Ballads*. Wordsworth and Samuel Taylor Coleridge. 2nd ed. Eds R.L. Brett and A.R. Jones. London: Routledge, 1991. 105–6.

Žižek, Slavoj. "The Abyss of Freedom." *"The Abyss of Freedom"* / Ages of the World. By Žižek and F.W.J. von Schelling. Trans. Judith Norman. Ann Arbor: U of Michigan P, 1997. 1–104.

40 Romantic transformation

Literature and science

Sharon Ruston

The French Revolution rouses the character called the Solitary in Wordsworth's *Excursion* from his dejection and he describes how from the horrid wreck of the Bastille there rose, or seemed to rise, a new, golden palace in its place. At this moment in time, the event seems to augur a new beginning and the Solitary claims: 'The potent shock / I felt: the transformation I perceived' (Wordsworth 1836: III, 716–17). Speaking from France itself, Helen Maria Williams also considered the Bastille ruins to be 'transformed, as if with the wand of necromancy, into a scene of beauty and of pleasure' (1794: 21). In this essay, I consider the potency of the idea of transformation during the Romantic period, finding it used not only in reference to the historical events and politics of the age, but also – and significantly – in the period's scientific writings. Transformation entails a change in 'form, shape, or appearance' (*OED*). As much as literature, scientific writing is a product of its historical moment and inflected with political meaning. The elements that make up the subject that is transformed are not lost or added to, but reorganized to create something new. I here examine developments in biology, chemistry, geology, and astronomy for this sense of the elements of the world being already in existence rather than being continually created anew.

The word 'transformation' is a useful term in political writing, since it can convey the notion that change is the same but different, as well as more decisively heralding a radical, new beginning. Mary Ashburn Miller, in her book *A Natural History of Revolution*, notes that the language used to describe the French Revolution is particularly drawn from natural history, using tropes such as earthquakes, lightning, mountains, and volcanoes. She finds that revolutionary transformation was explained and justified by reference to the eighteenth-century understanding of the natural world, which demonstrated that violence and disorder could lead to restored equilibrium and even positive regeneration (Miller 2011). This essay extends her argument, finding that the trope of transformation used to figure revolutionary politics can also be traced in other scientific fields.

Interconnections between literature and science are not unique to the Romantic period, and nor is the figuring of a new political order as a kind of transformation in the terms set out above. The word allows for the communication of scepticism with regard to the new world order. When Andrew Marvell seemingly commends Cromwell on his ability to 'cast the Kingdoms old / Into another mould', for example, playing with alchemical allusion, he suggests by means of this metaphor that not much has changed (2003: 275, ll. 35–6). Marvell's ambivalence about Cromwell's achievement becomes explicit in his metaphor. According to Jerome de Groot, 'The nation is recast – not essentially changed, but reshaped or reconfigured [. . .] Is this historical break actually decisive, and is this actually freedom?' (2004: 172). By the time Marvell is writing, alchemy has been exposed as fraudulent because all it does is recast metal into a new mould, retaining the volume but changing its shape. Lydia Maria Child, the American Abolitionist, in her novel *The Rebels; or Boston before the Revolution*, perhaps uses the word transformation in a similar way: 'On the whole it is evident that another transformation will soon take place. Pitt seems to have the power to lord it over king and parliament' (1825: 203–4). The fictional letter in which this is written is dated 12 June 1766, a month before William Pitt was given the king's permission to choose whomever he liked to form the Chatham ministry, which in the event only lasted for a few years (until 1768). Writing with hindsight in 1825, Child perhaps expresses the apathy of the moment. A new ministry means 'another transformation' but perhaps not much real political change.

The *Oxford English Dictionary* makes the differences discernible between these two possibilities of the word. The first meaning given is 'The action of changing in form, shape, or appearance; metamorphosis'. A number of the entries here refer to unnatural or monstrous transformations – one alludes to Ovid's *Metamorphoses* – and this meaning is very present in Romantic-period writing, as Denise Gigante has also shown (*OED*; Gigante 2002). For example, Edmund Burke speaks of King Louis XVI's horror at 'the strange and frightful transformation of his civilized subjects' with the onset of revolutionary fever (1986: 168–9). This accords with Burke's insistence that revolution has degraded the French people to monsters and his characterization of them as 'swinish multitude', hybrids of pig and human (1986: 173). Byron's unfinished drama *The Deformed Transformed* (1824) features both the so-called glorious transformation of the 'deformed' Arnold, born with 'hunchback' and 'cloven-foot', and the devious transformation of the Mephistophelean 'Stranger' into Arnold's old body (1824: I. 1.1, l. 105). Here Byron appears at first to subvert one common understanding of the idea of transformation; instead of being transformed into a monstrous version of himself, Arnold assumes the beautiful (though flawed) body of Achilles. However, because the Stranger then changes his appearance to assume that of the old Arnold, his old self continues to haunt him, reminding him of the Faustian pact he has made: 'you shall see / Yourself for ever by you, as your shadow' (Byron 1824: I. 1. 447–8). This device realizes the idea that during transformation all component parts are present but reorganized: here Arnold is never allowed to escape his former appearance or to notice how others react to it. This also accords with the understanding that any transformation is only one of appearance; in other words, that change only appears or seems to have taken place. Mary Shelley's short story 'Transformation' (1830) also features the swapping of bodies, one handsome and one a 'monster', in order to teach the handsome youth the true value of life (1990: 127).

The second definition offered by the *Oxford English Dictionary* is presented as a transferred meaning, or a new application, of the word. In this definition, 'transformation' is taken to mean a complete change in person or character, so that nothing of the old is recognizable. For Coleridge, it is the peculiar quality of poetry to transform in this manner. Using John Davies' poem on the soul, but replacing the idea of the soul with the imagination, Coleridge writes that the imagination can be likened to the chemical trope of sublimation, which transforms matter from one state to another (1983: II, 17). Alan Richardson notes how Coleridge worked 'eclectically and brilliantly with ideas developed (and sometimes borrowed wholesale) from his readings' in science and philosophy, including 'Davy's chemistry' (2001: 43). Davies' poem was originally published in 1599 and thus refers to an alchemical rather than a chemical process. With Coleridge's change of subject, it is the imagination that 'transforms' 'gross matter' and 'things' into her own form, 'abstract[ing]' the universal 'kinds' from individual 'states', which are then 're-clothed' and communicated to us through poetry (1983: II, 17). This transformation again involves a reorganization of finite material, but the change is not merely superficial. Other Romantic writers were convinced that poems had the capacity to change and transform their historical moment: for example, think of Shelley's 'Mask of Anarchy' and its call for peaceful protest and reform.

Comparing the act of writing to painting, William Hazlitt declares that 'transferring our ideas to canvas; they gain more than they lose in the mechanical transformation':

> One is never tired of painting, because you have to set down not what you knew already, but what you have just discovered. In the former case, you translate feelings into words; in the latter, names into things. There is a continual creation out of nothing going on.
>
> (1824: I, 7)

Hazlitt's words exist in a debate that had troubled ancient philosophy but which seems to gather force in the science of the Romantic period: the question of whether something can be created from nothing (*ex nihilio*) or whether nothing can be created from nothing. Hazlitt's definition of 'transformation' is opposite to those I have looked at previously: in this act of transformation, something is created from nothing. A limited number of elements mean that transformation is the only means for change. These terms and ideas reappear in the scientific writings of the Romantic period too. We can see them in the competing ideas of preformation versus epigenesis, the 'organic particles' of Buffon, the 'formative nisus' of Blumenbach, and the debate concerning vitalism in Britain (Buffon 1780: II, 41; Blumenbach 1792: 20). In chemistry, it was becoming clear that elements could change state – from solid to liquid to gas and back again – but during this process would remain the same element with the same chemical properties. In geology, some began to see that the world had changed and transformed over time rather than having been created anew with each catastrophic disaster.

In non-fiction travel writing, Richard Joseph Sulivan's 1794 *A View of Nature* offered, as his subtitle asserted, '*reflections on atheistical philosophy now exemplified in France*' and gives a distinctly conservative account of the ability of matter to transform. Retracing this debate, Sulivan notes that, since ancient times, philosophers have thought that 'nothing can be derived from nothing; that nothing can be annihilated' (1794: I, 106). Even though he acknowledges the ability of, say, powdered lead to return to solid lead with the application of heat, he does not regard this as a transformation. He writes that this and other instances show that 'Matter is capable of many seeming transformations, but no real transmutations have ever been discovered' (Sulivan 1794: I, 112). He compares this with the way that plants and animals return to the earth after death and dissolution, because this is only a 'return to the same sort of vegetable earth out of which they arose' rather than a genuinely new existence (Sulivan 1794: I, 113). Given that Sulivan's principal aim was to 'expose the fallacy of the *aethestical* philosophy' in France, it makes sense that he expresses sentiments unlike some of the contemporary natural philosophers examined below (1794: 1, v). A mere change in appearance accords with a divinely ordained world that evinces God's design in nature; whereas the ability of matter to transmute into another kind of matter signifies radical and genuine change.

The dominant theory of generation until the mid-eighteenth century was that bodies were preformed, in miniature, in the ovaries. This theory asserted that God had designed all species at the beginning of time and implanted them within each other. As late as the 1750s Albrecht von Haller was calculating that Eve 'must have stored 200,000 million diminutive human beings in her ovaries' (Gigante 2009: 11). In this theory, then, and in the terms of this essay, all the elements of living beings already exist in the world and they merely emerge with the aid of nutrition in a mechanical way when their time comes. Botanists thought the same, that 'the plant was already present, preformed in the seed [. . .] It therefore needed only to grow' (Roger 1997: 119). Gigante traces the emergence of a new idea of 'vital power' to the 1740s and to John Turberville Needham's sightings of microscopic creatures that appeared to be capable of self-generation (Gigante 2009: 12). These were not interpreted as having been spontaneously generated but as proof that matter was active and had powers within itself to generate life. The discovery of the polyp also challenged the preformation theory; each part of the polyp was capable of becoming an entirely new, whole life form after it was cut up: it could regenerate at will (Roe 2003: 9–12). The most significant challenge to preformation theories came with Georges Louise Leclerc, Compte de Buffon's *Natural History*, which, according to Jacques Roger, 'incited passionate controversies across Europe, [. . .] that would echo until the end of the century' (1997: 116).

From the outset of the second volume of *Natural History*, Buffon makes a clear distinction between organic and inorganic matter; the latter is 'perfectly inert, and deprived of every vital or active principle' (1780: II, 1). The faculty of 'reproduction' he finds to be 'peculiar to animals and vegetables' and it is in the 'successive renovation' of the species 'that Nature assumes an aspect altogether inconceivable and astonishing' (Buffon 1780: II, 2–3). Buffon continues in this volume to make a distinction between '*living* and *dead matter*' (1780: II, 36). The key to reproduction for Buffon was suggested by the powers of digestion; the body's ability to assimilate food to its own matter was identical to the vital powers needed to create a living body from its parts: 'An animal body is a kind of internal mould, in which the nutritive matter is so assimilated to the whole, that, without changing the order or proportion of the parts, each part receives an augmentation' (Buffon 1780: II, 39). Buffon decides that 'there are in nature infinite numbers of living organic particles', which Gigante describes as 'indissoluble, rudimentary building blocks of organized life' (Buffon 1780: II, 41; Gigante 2009: 14). A force like gravity brings these together. The cause, then, of why living bodies grow and generate is this 'penetrating force', which works the same way in digestion as it does in reproduction (Buffon 1780: II, 1). Akin to Newton's law of gravity, it attracts the 'organic particles of food' so that they move into the internal 'mould' of parts of the body, filling the moulds and increasing the body's bulk. The power that animals have to assimilate their food is 'the same [. . .] power which is the cause of reproduction' (Buffon 1780: II, 38). Although Buffon imagines these 'organic particles' to be infinite in number, it seems that they are continually changing in organization rather than being created or destroyed:

death is only the 'separation of the organic particles of which [organized bodies] are composed. These particles continue to separate till they again be united' by the active power of this 'penetrative force' (1780: II, 37). The idea of a life force gains momentum after Buffon's intervention, and its manifestations include Casper Friedrich Wolff's *vis essentialis* and, in the 1790s, Blumenbach's *Bildungstreib*, which Coleridge thought would make a good metaphor for the imagination (Coleridge 1957–92: III, 3744).

Gigante translates *Bildungstreib* as 'formative drive' (2009: 16). In a contemporary translation of 1792, it is 'formative nisus', where *nisus* (a Latin word) is understood as the impulse or tendency of organic matter to form itself (Blumenbach 1792: 20). Blumenbach sets out in his work to prove that '*there is no such thing in nature, as pre-existing organized germs*' (1792: 20). This '*Formative Nisus*' is the '*chief principle of generation, growth, nutrition and reproduction*' (1792: 20). Blumenbach's theory of a vital power was important for Kant's idea of organic purpose (Gigante 2009: 21). Coleridge describes epigenesis when he compares literary creation to organic living beings:

> The organic form on the other hand is innate, it form shapes as it developes itself from within, and the fullness of its developement is one & the same with the perfection of its outward Form. Such is the Life, such the form.
>
> (1969–2002: V, 495)

For Gigante, epigenesis, or 'the ideology of organic form' is the ideology of Romanticism itself (2009: 34).

In chemistry and geology, emerging disciplines at this time, there is evidence of a strand of thought that also privileged change and transformation over the idea of new creation. Perhaps the 'decisive innovation' in chemistry in the eighteenth century was the recognition that matter can change state while not changing its chemical properties: great progress was made in the study of gases in Britain and France during these years with the growing 'realization that substances could be made into gases by the addition of heat without changing their chemical nature' (Golinski 2003: 376). By the date of Percy Shelley's 'Preface' to *Prometheus Unbound* (1820), in which he declares that poetry creates 'by combination and representation', there is an understanding that there is a finite quantity of matter in the world continually circulating but not being created anew. For Shelley, 'Poetical abstractions' are not 'beautiful and new' because they have never existed before 'in the mind of man or in Nature' (2003: 231). In 1808, John Dalton had written that this understanding was the limit of what chemistry could achieve:

> No new creation or destruction of matter is within the reach of chemical agency. We might as well attempt to introduce a new planet into the solar system, or to annihilate one already in existence, as to create or destroy a particle of hydrogen.
>
> (1808: I, 212)

In 1794, Joseph Priestley defined the object of 'experimental philosophy' as the 'knowledge of nature in general, or more strictly, that of the properties of natural substances, and of the changes of those properties in different circumstances' (1794: 1). While he concerns himself with the transformations that natural elements go through with the application of heat or water, he is hampered by his belief in the invisible, imponderable phlogiston. First put forward by the vitalist Georg Stahl, phlogiston was the principle of fire that was released during combustion in the form of light and heat. Priestley worked within these parameters: 'we say, universally, that all metals consist of a peculiar earth and phlogiston' (1794: 4). More than this, he identified new gases according to the degree to which they held phlogiston. In 1794, he presents the argument that there are a limited number of elements that 'compose all natural substances', namely, 'dephlogisticated air, or the acidifying principle [which Lavoisier would later call oxygen]; phlogiston, or the alkaline principle; the different earths; and the principles of heat, light, and electricity' (Priestley 1794: 8–9). Other such 'principles' which 'have not been proved to be substances' included 'attraction, repulsion, and magnetism' (Priestley 1794: 9). William Nicholson, in his *First Principles of Chemistry* (1790), was diplomatic, deciding to present both Priestley's theory and alternative theories, noting that Lavoisier was the first to 'reject the theory of phlogiston altogether' (1790: 90).

Lavoisier challenged the unhelpful and vague theory of phlogiston, replacing it with his own theory of heat, which he called caloric. He thought that gases should not be regarded as having different chemical properties to liquids or solids, and argued that elements possessed identical properties regardless of their state. He came to the conclusion that air was a state produced by heat rather than an entirely new chemical element after recognizing that liquid and gaseous states shared characteristics: they were both elastic fluids *en expansion* (see Morris 1972). The discovery had important implications: it suggested that a finite number of different elements existed, while emphasizing their ability to change and adapt into new forms. Lavoisier had found the presence of both 'pure air' (oxygen) and 'inflammable air' (hydrogen) in water. In 1785, Lavoisier separated water into hydrogen and oxygen and then recombined them to create water again (Golinski 1992: 133). Many in Britain received Lavoisier's ideas with scepticism and the idea of caloric was resisted (Golinski 1992: 138). Priestley remained convinced of the existence of phlogiston throughout his life. Rumford's innovative experiments in 1798, which suggested that heat was the result of friction, did not succeed in changing the outmoded ideas that were then current (Rumford 1798: 81). He asked whether there was any material 'thing' that could 'with propriety be called caloric', framing the question in terms of whether caloric or heat was, really, a 'thing' at all (Rumford 1798: 98). In the debate on the nature of vitality between John Abernethy and William Lawrence decades later, the same terms were used. Abernethy, complaining of Lawrence and the group of 'Modern Sceptics' to whom he claimed Lawrence belonged, seemed to wish him 'to consider life to be nothing' (1814: 44; see Ruston 2005: 54). Alternatively, Hunter, Abernethy, Keats, and others, as Gigante has shown, represent the vital principle as something: 'life as something superadded to – or in excess of – physical organization' (Gigante 2002: 433).

Though speaking of Charles Darwin's generation, Rob Pope notes that 'it was chiefly work in the newer "natural" sciences (notably geology and biology) that put change and transformation firmly back on the cultural agenda' (2005: 41). Even in the early nineteenth century, in the emerging field of geology, there was a growing sense that the key to the past could be seen in the present. While debates continued about whether the great geological changes that had clearly taken place on earth were the result of fire (for the Vulcanists) or flood (for the Neptunists), fossils showed that different kinds of creatures had lived during different epochs of the earth's history (see Rudwick 1985: ch. 3). In the 1790s, George Cuvier persuasively argued that extinction had taken place during the earth's history. Such discoveries called into question God's purpose and design but many, including Cuvier himself, refused to believe that this meant that species were capable of change. Many – like Cuvier – worked hard to reconcile geological discoveries with Biblical accounts of creation. Conversely, James Hutton in 1795 controversially claimed that there was 'no occasion for having recourse to [. . .] any preternatural cause in explaining what actually appears' (1795: 1, 165). Though this claim was far from being accepted by the majority, the movement of land mass caused by extreme heat was beginning to be used to explain the changes that had occurred on earth rather than having recourse to God's actions.

Hutton's *Theory of the Earth* was much criticized upon publication in 1795 but it does begin to describe a process not unlike what is now known as the rock cycle. As his friend and explicator John Playfair put it in 1802, there is a 'great geological cycle, by which the waste and reproduction of entire continents is circumscribed', which he compared to the process we would now call photosynthesis (Playfair 1822: 1, 139). Playfair tried to reconcile Hutton's theory with religious views when he wrote that Hutton's theory in fact demonstrated 'an order, not unworthy of Divine wisdom' when it revealed that 'seas and continents' are created 'not by accident, but by the operation of regular and uniform causes' (Hutton 1795: 1, 6; Playfair 1822: 129). Hutton was convinced of the importance of 'subterraneous fire', in bringing about changes on earth but it was still the case, in England at least, that natural philosophers referred to the Biblical flood (Hutton 1795: 1, 38; Rudwick 1985: 111). James Parkinson writes in 1804, for example, that

> Scripture [. . .] corroborated by the collateral evidence of all human tradition, supplies us with the grand leading facts; that after the complete formation and peopling of this globe, it was subjected to the destructive action of an immense deluge of water.
>
> (1820: 1, 13)

For Parkinson, the geologists' task was 'to endeavour to find out the ways of God, in forming, destroying, and reforming the earth' (1820: 1, 13). So, while it was rarely the case that natural philosophers could countenance the idea of living species as anything other than fixed and immutable, geology was beginning to see the earth as having undergone gradual change over vast periods of time. As is well known now, the uniformitarianism of Charles Lyell helped Charles Darwin towards the idea of human evolution. Catastrophic theories were popular in the late eighteenth century; Cuvier concluded that extinctions such as that of the mammoth could only have occurred by means of a 'sudden and drastic event' (Rudwick 1985: 110). The history of the earth, then, was one of violent change and transformation, with the slow action of the continual circulation of land being pushed up and submerged.

Finally and briefly, in astronomy the work of William Herschel and Pierre Simon, Marquis de Laplace, helped bring about a similar shift in thinking. In 1796, Laplace referred to Cuvier's discovery of extinction as revealing 'a tendency to change in things' and argued that the 'magnitude and importance of the solar system ought not to except it from this general law' (1830: II, 333). There is evidence too of an interest in creation myths. Lucretius's *De Rerum Natura* was republished four times between 1799 and 1813; his theory of the circulation of atoms is particularly apt for the ideas discussed in this essay. His story of how the world came to be influenced Erasmus Darwin and Shelley, among others (see Priestman 2007). The composer Joseph Hadyn wrote *The Creation* between 1796 and 1798, with the original libretto offering a mixture of the creation myths found in the Book of Genesis and in Milton's *Paradise Lost*; in 1803 or 1804, Anne Home Hunter (wife of the surgeon John Hunter) wrote a new English libretto for it, maintaining this mix rather than returning to the source texts (Hunter 2009: 69–72).

When Shelley referred to the French Revolution as the 'master theme of the epoch in which we live', he was identifying the time in which he lived as one that had certain characteristics that distinguished it from other epochs (1964: 1, 504). He was also potentially borrowing a term from geology, since Playfair had used 'epocha' a number of times in his illustration of Hutton's theory in 1802 (1822: 1, 133, 367, 464). For Shelley in *A Defence of Poetry*, 'manners and institutions' characterize an epoch, and these determine the kind of poetry that is produced (2003: 686). The French Revolution was represented in the language of natural history as a transformation: those who supported the French Revolution saw it as a genuine transformation, while its critics saw it as only a temporary reorganization of political powers. The ambivalence of the word's meaning allowed for both possibilities. In accounts of natural phenomena, we also find evidence that supports an ancient philosophy, the idea that there were a limited number of elements in the world, which though they could be reorganized, could not be added to or destroyed.

Works cited

Abernethy, J. (1814) *An Enquiry into the Probability and Rationality of Mr. Hunter's Theory of Life*, London: Longman, Hurst, Rees, Orme and Brown.

Blumenbach, J.F. (1792) *An Essay on Generation*, trans. A. Crichton, London: T. Cadell.

Buffon, G.L.L. (1780) *Natural History, General and Particular, by the Count de Buffon*, 8 vols, Edinburgh: William Creech.

Burke, E. (1986) *Reflections on the Revolution in France*, ed. Conor Cruise O'Brien, Harmondsworth: Penguin.

Byron, G. (1824) *The Deformed Transformed*, Philadelphia: H.C. Carey and I. Lea.

Child, L.M.F. (1825) *The Rebels; or Boston before the Revolution*, Boston: Cummings, Hilliard and Co.

Coleridge, S.T. (1957–92) *The Notebooks of Samuel Taylor Coleridge*, ed. K. Coburn, 5 vols, London: Routledge and Kegan Paul.

Coleridge, S.T. (1969–2002) *The Collected Works of Samuel Taylor Coleridge*, gen. ed. K. Coburn, 23 vols, Princeton: Princeton University Press.

Coleridge, S.T. (1983) *Biographia Literaria*, eds J. Engell and W. Jackson Bate, Princeton: Princeton University Press.

Dalton, J. (1808) *A New System of Chemical Philosophy*, 2 vols, London: R. Bickerstaff.

De Groot, J. (2004) *Royalist Identities*, Basingstoke: Palgrave Macmillan.

Gigante, D. (2002) 'The Monster in the Rainbow: Keats and the Sciences of Life', *PMLA*, 1117: 3, 433–48.

Gigante, D. (2009) *Life: Organic Form and Romanticism*, New Haven: Yale University Press.

Golinski, J. (1992) *Science as Public Culture: Chemistry and Enlightenment in Britain, 1760–1820*, Cambridge: CUP.

Golinski, J. (2003) 'Chemistry', *Eighteenth-Century Science*, in *The Cambridge History of Science*, ed. Roy Porter, 8 vols, Cambridge: CUP, IV, 375–96.

Hazlitt, W. (1824) 'On the Pleasure of Painting', in *Table-Talk; or, Original Essays on Men and Manners*, 2nd edn, 2 vols, London: Henry Coburn.

Hunter, A. (2009) *The Life and Times of Anne Hunter: Hadyn's Tuneful Voice*, ed. C. Grigson, Liverpool: Liverpool University Press.

Hutton, J. (1795) *Theory of the Earth [. . .]*, 2 vols, Edinburgh: Cadell, Junior, and Davies.

Laplace, P.S. (1830) *The System of the World*, trans. H.H. Harte, 2 vols, Dublin: Rees, Orme, Brown and Green.

Marvell, A. (2003) *The Poems of Andrew Marvell*, ed. Nigel Smith, Harlow: Pearson.

Miller, M.A. (2011) *A Natural History of Revolution: Violence and Nature in the French Revolutionary Imagination, 1789–1794*, Ithaca, New York: Cornell University Press.

Morris, R.J. (1972) 'Lavoisier and the Caloric Theory', *British Journal for the History of Science*, 6: 1–38.

Nicholson, W. (1790) *The First Principles of Chemistry*, London: G.G.J. and J. Robinson.

Parkinson, J. (1820) *Organic Remains of a Former World*, 3 vols, London: Sherwood, Neely, and Jones.

Playfair, J. (1822) *Works*, 4 vols, Edinburgh: Archibald Constable and Co.

Pope, R. (2005) *Creativity: Theory, History, Practice*, London: Routledge.

Priestley, J. (1794) *Head of Lectures on a Course of Experimental Philosophy*, London: J. Johnson.

Priestman, M. (2007) 'Lucretius in Romantic and Victorian Britain', in *The Cambridge Companion to Lucretius*, eds S. Gillespie and P. Hardie, Cambridge: CUP, 289–305.

Richardson, A. (2001) *British Romanticism and the Sciences of the Mind*, Cambridge: CUP.

Roe, S.A. (2003) 'The Life Sciences', in *Eighteenth-Century Science* in *The Cambridge History of Science*, eds Roy Porter, 8 vols, Cambridge: CUP, IV, 397–416.

Roger, J. (1997) *Buffon*, trans. S.L. Bonnefoi, Ithaca, New York: Cornell University Press.

Rudwick, M.J.S. (1985) *The Meaning of Fossils: Episodes in the History of Palaeontology*, 2nd edn, Chicago: University of Chicago Press.

Rumford, B.T. (1798) 'An Inquiry Concerning the Source of the Heat which is Excited by Friction', *Philosophical Transactions*, 88: 80–102.

Ruston, S. (2005) *Shelley and Vitality*, Basingstoke: Palgrave Macmillan.

Shelley, M. (1990) *Collected Tales and Stories with Original Engravings*, Baltimore: Johns Hopkins University Press.

Shelley, P.B. (1964) *The Letters of Percy Bysshe Shelley*, ed. F.L. Jones, 2 vols, Oxford: Clarendon Press.

Shelley, P.B. (2003) *The Major Works*, eds Z. Leader and M. O'Neill, Oxford: OUP.

Sulivan, R.J. (1794) *A View of Nature*, 6 vols, London: T. Becket.

Williams, H.M. (1794) *Letters Written in France, in the Summer 1790*, 4th edn, London: T. Cadell.

Wordsworth, W. (1836) *The Excursion*, London: E. Moxon.

Part 11

Literature, media, mediation

Introduction

This final section of essays looks into history and also into our present and the future as it relates Romanticism to the field of media studies. In many respects, critics of Romanticism for generations have needed to be keenly aware of media history, perhaps because their most treasured objects of attention make issues of mediation – that is, how a text is presented in terms of specific genres, publishing venues, and material constructions – so central to their self-conception. For instance, it is hard to read Wordsworth's Preface to *Lyrical Ballads* without taking note of the way he situates his collaborative venture with Coleridge in relation to the popular media of his day in order to specify what he takes its unique contribution to be. And it is likewise difficult to ignore the fact that William Blake's work, which makes each volume of poetry into a distinct work of art, differing not only from other books on the market but also from other embodiments of the "same" words, is intended to occupy a very specific – and perhaps critical – position in the exploding eighteenth-century marketplace for printed books. The section on audiences (as in Kevin Gilmartin's essay on Hannah More) and the section on authority (as in Margaret Russett's essay on Blake) emphasize how discussions of authors and their readers have increasingly found it necessary to account for the precise means through which works of art are constructed and mediated.

When many influential critics noted facts of media history – for instance, when Harold Bloom credited Blake with inventing "a new art form" (Bloom 1971: 6) – such observations were not entirely specific about what was new about that form (and what was old about it as well). Other notable commentators went somewhat further, suggesting that Romantic writers engaged in a deeply fraught relationship with the material fact of written or published text: the result is a sense of defeat, triumph, or some anxious state in between. Mary Jacobus's deconstructionist analysis of *The Prelude*'s book 5, for instance, reveals Wordsworth's dream of the Arab to be an encounter with the materiality of books and writing; the episode conveys "the anxiety about the representability of the self that is always by definition 'Of texture midway between life and books' " (Jacobus 1989: 98).

Jacobus's analysis focuses mainly on "bookishness" as "literariness," and literariness as a potential undoing of the stable imaginative self (Jacobus 1989: 100). Recent work on the bookishness of Romanticism (such as Andrew Stauffer's work on anxieties about paper and print [Stauffer 2006]) implicitly views even this kind of emphasis on the material support for writing to be too abstract. The critics in this section seek to situate Romantic writing and publication in a more densely described history of the production of books and other printed media, even as (in some instances) they have connected this history of media to our present digital media environment. Modifying the kind of claim that Jacobus made about the anxious relationship between media and Romantic imagination, more recent critics show how media are not objects of anxious aversion or avoidance; they are the necessary conditions for the existence of literary expression and transmission.

A great deal of research has been necessary in order to uncover specifics about media practices. William St. Clair, for instance, argues that the specific forms and regulations (through copyright) of works written during the age need to be carefully understood in order to get a sense of what people were reading and how they were reading it (St. Clair 2004); Nicholas Mason exposes the dependency of Romantic authorship on an expanding culture of advertising (Mason 2013). But the impact of this research is interpreted differently among the critics represented here, and some of the differences can be connected with other major theoretical differences in orientation that can be seen elsewhere in this volume. The section begins with two contrasting arguments about ballad writing. Maureen McLane, in a selection from her article eventually incorporated into chapter 4 of her book *Balladeering, Minstrelsy, and the Making of British Romantic Poetry*, considers media primarily in terms of how the printed "literate" aspect of poetry mediates a fiction of orality. Her readings of major Romantic ballad writers, building on work by structuralist anthropologists, thus analyze various permutations of an "oral-literate conjunction" in which print does not merely communicate an emphasis on individual orality and oral folk cultures; the function of a readable text is to create "orality effects" in which the significance of the oral is framed, analyzed, and interpreted.

The chapter excerpt on Sir Walter Scott from Andrew Piper's *Dreaming in Books: The Bibliographic Imagination in the Romantic Age* acknowledges the importance of this "mediality" of the ballad revival through which the ballad is constructed in order to gesture toward an original, natural, oral culture. And following the arguments by McLane and Steve Newman (2007), he emphasizes the "bookishness" of the genre. But the point of locating this important Romantic genre in print culture is quite different. The fact that Scott was not only an author but also an editor of ballads opens up important questions about ownership and borders, in Piper's view. He claims that print produces problems of authority – of determining what parts of the text belong to whom. And he continues his chapter by turning from ballad editions to Scott's *The Heart of Midlothian*, a novel which orchestrates confessions and problematizes the ownership of speech. In Piper's account, print culture introduces a deconstruction of authority, and this selection could be compared and contrasted usefully with Andrew Bennett's selection on Keats in this volume, with which it shares some methodological features.

The contextualization of Romanticism in print culture provokes an obvious question: since the explosion of print in fact precedes what is familiarly known as the Romantic age, how does this mode of analysis affect our understanding of Romanticism as a unique phenomenon? As discussed in the introductory essay, questions about this uniqueness have been posed with great frequency within historicist scholarship in general, which tends to tie typically Romantic concerns with selfhood, imagination, and political revolution to wider developments that sweep across the eighteenth and nineteenth centuries, such as the industrial revolution and imperial expansion. An analysis of print culture is now playing an important role in such reconsiderations. Scholars such as Elizabeth L. Eisenstein trace the "revolution" in print culture (and the ideology of progressive individualism it encouraged) to the early modern age (Eisenstein 1983); Sue Zemka shows how important print was in furthering the ambitions of Christian missionaries throughout the empire in the nineteenth century (Zemka 1997). In a similar spirit, Clifford Siskin and William

Warner, in their conference paper, show how a revolution in print culture preceded the Romantic age and laid the groundwork for it. They demonstrate how print, during the American revolution, allowed people to be considered within a communication "network"; Romanticism was thus an "eventuality" that appeared only after the earlier installation of an "operational platform" of a vibrant print culture.

If Siskin and Warner's argument resonates with the rhetoric of digital technology, Tom Mole's new essay for this volume explicitly demonstrates how large-scale databases enabled by that technology can procure new kinds of analyses of Romantic texts and their reception history. This application of new technology to explore new areas of research is fundamental to work in "digital humanities." Employing but modifying the techniques of "distant reading" that allow for views of general trends and patterns among many texts, Mole takes a broad and illuminating view of the way that Romantic poetry was anthologized throughout the nineteenth century. By examining the ways in which these anthologies lyricized Romantic narrative poems and excerpted passages out of politicized contexts, Mole shows how crucial the practices of mediation were for shaping our long-standing views of Romanticism's legacy.

Works cited

Bloom, Harold. (1971) *The Visionary Company: A Reading of English Romantic Poetry*, rev. ed. Ithaca: Cornell University Press.

Eisenstein, Elizabeth L. (1983) *The Printing Revolution in Early Modern Europe*, Cambridge: Cambridge University Press.

Jacobus, Mary. (1989) *Romanticism, Writing, and Sexual Difference: Essays on The Prelude*, Oxford: Clarendon Press.

Mason, Nicholas. (2013) *Literary Advertising and the Shaping of British Romanticism*, Baltimore: Johns Hopkins University Press.

Newman, Steve. (2007) *Ballad Collection, Lyric, and the Canon: The Call of the Popular from the Restoration to the New Criticism*, Philadelphia: University of Pennsylvania Press.

Stauffer, Andrew. (2006) "Romanticism's Scattered Leaves," *Romanticism on the Net* 41–2.

St. Clair, William. (2004) *The Reading Nation in the Romantic Period*, Cambridge: Cambridge University Press.

Zemka, Sue. (1997) *Victorian Testaments: The Bible, Christology, and Literary Authority in Early Nineteenth-Century British Culture*, Stanford: Stanford University Press.

Further reading

Christensen, Jerome. (2000) *Romanticism at the End of History*, Baltimore: Johns Hopkins University Press.

Connell, Philip, and Nigel Leask, eds. (2009) *Romanticism and Popular Culture in Britain and Ireland*, Cambridge: Cambridge University Press.

Fraistat, Neil. (1985) *The Poem and the Book: Interpreting Collections of Romantic Poetry*, Chapel Hill: University of North Carolina Press.

Khalip, Jacques, and Robert Mitchell. (2011) *Releasing the Image: From Literature to New Media*, Stanford: Stanford University Press.

Langan, Celeste. (2001) "Understanding Media in 1805: Audiovisual Hallucination in The Lay of the Last Minstrel," *Studies in Romanticism* 40: 49–70.

Levy, Michelle. (2008) *Family Authorship and Romantic Print Culture*, Houndmills: Palgrave Macmillan.

Otto, Peter. (2011) *Multiplying Worlds: Romanticism, Modernity, and the Emergence of Virtual Reality*, Oxford: Oxford University Press.

Viscomi, Joseph. (1993) *Blake and the Idea of the Book*, Princeton: Princeton University Press.

41 Ballads and bards

British romantic orality

Maureen McLane

In *Tristes Tropiques*, Claude Lévi-Strauss tells us that we should think of so-called primitive peoples not as "peoples without history" but as "peoples without writing."[1] The British poets of the late eighteenth and early nineteenth centuries discovered themselves to be indisputably and perhaps regrettably both historical and literate. Not that Chaucer, Spenser, or Milton lacked either a sense of history or the resources of writing; but none of these luminaries had to consider, as did so many of the English and Scottish Romantics, the fate of poetry as a cultural project set adrift from its imagined origins in speech and gesture, in what Percy Shelley called a "vitally metaphorical" language.[2] To restore poetry to those origins, or at the very least to remind readers of those origins, was the explicit aim of such poets as William Wordsworth and Walter Scott. Shelley described poetry as "connate with the origin of man"; Wordsworth lauded the almost mystical connection between the first bards and their audiences; and Scott derived his own poetic genealogy from minstrels who, he maintained, served the Scottish "National Muse" even as Homer served that of the Greeks.[3]

It is not surprising that the ballad emerged as the genre most implicated in the romantic exploration of primitivity, modernity, and historicity. In *Crimes of Writing*, her critical study of literature in the age of industrial and print capital, Susan Stewart cites the ballad of the romantic period as one of several "distressed genres" (among others mentioned are the epic, fable, and proverb).[4] Antiqued, imitated, simulated, composed during walking tours in the case of Wordsworth, collected from old Scottish women in the case of Scott, transliterated from the Albanian in the case of Lord Byron, the increasingly vexed ballad may be seen as a symptom of the distressing of poetry itself.

Many scholars of English literary history have documented the so-called ballad craze, which Bishop Thomas Percy launched with his phenomenally successful edition, *Reliques of Ancient English Poetry*, in 1765. Percy's title suggests the complex fortunes of the ballad in the eighteenth and nineteenth centuries: collected and corrected as literary antiquities, ballads in these editions became the signifiers both of literary historicity and of an apparently obsolete orality. Ballads thus acquired value as national, historical, cultural, and linguistic "relics." Of the many collectors and inventors of poetic antiquities in Britain, the most spectacularly successful was surely James Macpherson, who in the 1760s published a series of fragments and "translations" of third-century Scottish Gaelic poetry known as the Ossian poems; they prompted the most infamous scandal in English literary history.[5] Macpherson and the pathetic boy-poet Chatterton both understood that antiquity could be not only imitated but indeed simulated (with pseudo-archaic spelling, locution, syntax; antiqued papers and inks; and elaborate stories of transmission and editing).[6] Whether this simulation was acknowledged, as in Coleridge's "Ancyent Marinere" (which was "professedly written in imitation of the *style*, as well as of the spirit of the elder poets," as Wordsworth noted),[7] or dissembled, as in Macpherson's and Chatterton's pseudo-antique poems, the literary fix was in. With the notable exception of William Blake, who developed what he called his own "infernal method" of printing his books, poets in this period turned to the sophisticated resources of print culture to satiate the nostalgia for a poetry and an epoch that preceded print.

The proliferating editions of ballads, and the simultaneous eruption of ballad scandals, were signal moments in a transformation of poetic possibility in eighteenth-century Britain: the emergence of a new literary orality. It was not of course orality per se but rather a variety of orality effects that these poets strove to attain. The English-language epic had long been an irremediably and gloriously literary form; the ballad, however, offered to the most modern and literary of poets the romance and techniques of a popular, apparently collective, still living oral tradition. In his landmark collection of 1802–3, *Minstrelsy of the Scottish Border*, Walter Scott classified ballads as "historical," "romantic," and "imitations of these ballads by modern authors" – including Scott himself. With the benefit of work by Walter Ong, Eric Havelock, and other theorists of oral poetry and the primitive, we may propose for this period another poetic spectrum, one which carefully ranges through the cultural meanings and stylistic possibilities of literary orality.[8] In this article I will select cases, "ballad instances" as it were, from the following works: Blake's *Songs of Innocence* (1789), Byron's *Childe Harold* (cantos 1 and 2, 1812), and Wordsworth and Samuel Taylor Coleridge's *Lyrical Ballads* (1798). [. . .] I choose these works, and passages from them, to illustrate certain aspects of the complex oral–literate conjunction in the period. The usual discussion of these works, both in their own day and in current scholarship, relies on an array of distinctions: "antiquarian" versus "modern," fakes versus originals, tradition versus originality, and editing versus authoring. I will argue that it is more fruitful to consider these works as part of a poetic complex revolving around multiple oral–literate axes. [. . .] I will try to sketch in a necessarily brisk and preliminary fashion the relations of the "oral" to the "literate" and the "literary" as figured within romantic literary poems.

[. . .]

I From piping to print: Blake's allegory of poetic mediation

Blake's "Introduction," the first poem in his *Songs of Innocence*, will allow me to establish some coordinates for talking about romantic orality. Although not labeled a ballad, this and the other poems in the collection straddle that fertile ground between song, ballad, and nursery rhyme, the generic and formal definitions of which seem to vary depending on the sociohistorical and formal commitments of the classifier.[9] Blake's inaugurating song establishes the occasion, scene, and mode of poetic composition: we first see and hear the poet as a piper casually "piping down the valleys wild."[10] As if to anticipate John Stuart Mill's dictum that lyric poetry is not heard but rather overheard, Blake introduces a fey child who has apparently overheard the piper. Asked by the child to "pipe a song about a Lamb," the Pan-like piper obliges. We may assume that, since he pipes and thus occupies his mouth, the poet-figure pipes a tune of pure music, devoid of words (and yet the child through his request has already made the song "about a lamb"). This assumption (that the song begins as purely or primarily instrumental tune) is confirmed by the child's next request for a song to be sung, not piped: "Drop thy pipe thy happy pipe! / Sing thy songs of happy chear" (lines 9–10). The poet again obliges, singing, as he asserts, "the same" (line 11). (Yet we are induced to wonder: in what way is the song, sung and no longer piped, "the same"?) The child then exhorts the poet: "Piper sit thee down and write / In a book that all may read" (lines 13–14). Again, the poet obliges, plucking a hollow reed: "And I wrote my happy songs, / Every child may joy to hear" (lines 19–20).

Blake's "Introduction" is a lovely fable about the origin of the *Songs of Innocence*; the poem is also a whimsical allegory about performance, composition, and mediation. The poem imagines the preconditions of its existence: the book in our hands was desired, requested, by a child "on a cloud" (line 3). The child here serves as an imagined audience and as a kind of media muse: his requests usher us through a set of poetic mediations. The inner stanzas each mark a new moment and a different medium of performance. Music as pure sonority becomes a kind of program music ("a song about a Lamb" [line 5]), which in turn becomes sung text and finally the written song. This sequence could be seen as a progressive sophistication of the acoustic and verbal arts, culminating in the written poem; these transformations would then appear in sequence as a kind of unfolding hierarchy of technologies and arts. Unmediated piping, a kind of primitive pastoral, gives way to verbal articulation and ultimately to writing. Yet both the imagined origin and destination of the work remain somewhat ambiguously in the oral despite this progressive displacement toward writing, literacy, and the literary. Note the closing lines: "And I wrote my happy songs, / Every child may joy to hear." The potentially pleased children, the imagined future audiences, are imagined as auditors, not readers.

Yet these songs are now explicitly written, albeit with a "rural pen." Blake's song invites us to consider what is gained and what is lost in the fixing of form implied by writing. The child urges the piper to write "in a book that all may read" (line 14). The book form amplifies the potential audience (to include "all") but also decisively sunders the "song," the poem, from the scene of performance. We see that as soon as the piper begins to write, the child "vanish'd from" the piper's sight. No longer is the child's presence necessary to inspire or guarantee the offering and occasion of song. The very turn to writing banishes the child; in terms of the internal drama of the poem, both muse and audience are gone. Or rather, the audience is implicitly transformed; just as piping yields to writing, so too the single child-interlocutor gives way to the imagined community of child auditors.

Yet for children "to hear" this song, it must be read or recited aloud. One must get one's hands on this book, or must learn by heart this poem, for it to be transmitted as Blake envisions. Blake's poem thus indicates other potential scenes than the dramatized dialogue, the scene of reading and the scene of recitation. Blake prefers to imagine children as auditors, not readers; yet he slyly tips his writing hand in the fourth stanza, in which he rhymes "read" – the deciphering operation which will presumably bring the book to "all" – with "reed," the instrument which allows him to transcribe his song. The homonym captures in miniature one aspect of the oral–literate conjunction: as the grammar school definition has it, homonyms are words that sound alike but are spelled differently. Such a definition, and such a pun, depends on a fixed orthography. We are clearly far from primitive orality, clearly *après la lettre*. The lexical puns have the fullest force for the reader who sees but also hears the joke. Yet the imagined children still remain relatively in the oral, relying on a literate interlocutor to recite this poem so that they "may joy to hear."

Thus we see that a song of innocence is also a song about a complex oral–literate conjunction. The poem takes into account the acoustic and cognitive dimensions of speech, the rhetorical uses of orthography in its puns, and the vital interaction of reading, writing, and hearing. Readers are after all made not born. Blake both acknowledges the mediation of reading and represents a viable preliterate audience of children. In this way he gestures toward the social, generational aspect of the oral–literate conjunction: we have both children in the oral domain and the unrepresented but implicitly mediating literate elders.

A final word on Blake's oral–literate conjunction: a word about pictures. The second and third plates of *Songs of Innocence* – the plates which immediately precede the poem, "Introduction" – illustrate almost perfectly the transition from the orally oriented world of piping to the literarily mediated scene of reading. It is as if Blake gives us a preview, as it were, of the cultural allegory to follow in words. On the frontispiece (Figure 41.1), the Adamic piper looks up to the child, who has apparently just addressed him (the piper pauses, as it were, mid-stride). On the title page that follows (Figure 41.2), we see children leaning on their seated nanny or mother who holds a book – a volume, quite possibly, of these songs. [. . .]

Before we even arrive at the first poem, then, Blake offers us images of the transition he will soon encode in words as well as pictures. To invoke another medium anachronistically, it is as if Blake gives us two silent film stills, which retrospectively become intelligible as a "before" (piping) and an "after" (print). We might say, then, that the frontispiece conjures an oral prehistory (replete with pastoral iconography – Pan, pipers, Arcadia, the conventions of the idyll). Such a prehistory is, of course, an invention of literature. The title page conjures, by contrast, a "contemporary" and highly mediated oral sphere, the one inhabited by pre- and semiliterate children then and now. [. . .] It is, interestingly, under the relatively domesticated scene of reading and not under the sculpted, striding, frontal body of the piper that Blake puts his title, his name, and his joint occupation, author and printer. However primitivist his allegiances, Blake had no particular nostalgia for the "piping" phase of poetry, just as he had no longing for the infantine preserve of innocence, which he in other works derided as the saccharine land of Beulah. It was the *Songs of Experience*, after all, that ultimately gave the *Songs of Innocence* their dialectical spin; so too it was Blake, as author, printer, and urban poet, who reached back across the divide separating him from primary orality to conjure and critique the primarily oral world of pipers, lambs, and children.

II The romance of orality: "balladizing" the primitive spectacle

We can ascertain a whole other domain of romantic orality in Byron's *Childe Harold*, the first two cantos of which were published in 1812. A fabulously self-promoting travel poem, *Childe Harold* ushers its eponymous and self-exiled hero through wide-ranging European terrain. Harold, like Byron, fancies himself a true-born son of Greece,

Figure 41.1 William Blake, Male figure and cherub © The British Library Board,
C.71.d.19 page 2

and as he nears the imagined cradle of his much-loved civilization he offers many
observations about the peoples now dwelling in the formerly Hellenized mountain
region. The world-weary Harold is especially delighted by the primitive hospitality
afforded him by the motley crew of soldiers loyal to the Ali Pasha. As he rests in a
military camp, the Albanian soldiers begin their war chant. Harold assures us that "In
sooth, it was no vulgar sight to see / Their barbarous, yet their not indecent, glee."[11]
Of the Albanians he notes "the long wild locks that to their girdles stream'd, / While
thus in concert they this lay half sang, half scream'd" (*CH*, 2.72). The song then
begins,

Figure 41.2 William Blake, Songs of innocence and experience © The British
Library Board, C.71.d.19 page 3

Tambourgi! Tambourgi! Thy 'larum afar
Gives hope to the valiant, and promise of war;
All the sons of the mountains arise at the note,
Chimariot, Illyrian, and dark Suliote!

(*CH*, 2.649–52)

In Harold's pleased contemplation of the chanting soldiers, we have an ethnographic
scene made literary. The Albanians' performance is notably unrefined – the soldiers "half
sang, half scream'd" the song. The piling on of ethnographic detail – the "wild locks," the
"kirtled" style of dress (*CH*, 2.58, 71) – helps to establish the scene of ballad recitation.

The Albanians, specified throughout as exotic "Mussulmans," conveniently generate a song assimilable to Byron's loose generic categories. Formally, the Tambourgi song (tambourgi being the name of the war drum) is a ballad specimen isolated within a larger poetic romance composed in Spenserian stanzas. For the war song itself Byron resorts to a ballad stanza, four lines of four stresses each in running rhythm. His assignment of a new numbering series to the war song – resuming the suspended numbering sequence, as well as the Spenserian stanza, after the song – further marks the war song as a set piece. The formal and numerical shifts constitute a new poetic moment in the poem, in which the ballad serves handily as the form appropriate for rendering, indeed translating and transposing, the Albanians' "barbarous, yet not indecent, glee."

This ballad moment, both embedded in and set off from what is already a notably archaizing romance, allows us to make several observations about genre, form, and the sociocultural code of romantic poetry. When Byron chose the Spenserian stanza for his long romance, he paid homage to the Renaissance master of what was already in Spenser's hands a medievalizing genre, the romance epic. As Byron wrote in his "Preface to the First and Second Cantos," "The stanza of Spenser, according to one of our most successful poets, admits of every variety."[12] To sustain the complex music of this stanza was to establish one's claim to a certain poetic pedigree: learned, aristocratic, masterful. Spenser's intricately rhymed nine-line stanza, with its closing alexandrine, is decidedly literary and classically allusive; the use of the stanza clearly signifies both Byron's comprehensive familiarity with literary history and the nature of his poetic ambition. To choose to write in Spenser's stanza was also to avail oneself of its sweetly archaic, and to Byron poetical, potential. Indeed, his hero's very epithet – Childe – is only one of a series of archaisms that Byron employed. As he observed, "It is almost superfluous to mention that the appellation 'Childe,' as in 'Childe Waters,' 'Childe Childers,' &c. is used as more consonant with the old structure of versification which I have adopted."[13]

Yet even as the versification and such diction as "wight," "in sooth," and "whilome" (all these coming as early as the second stanza of the first canto) left long before 1812 an archaic taste on the tongue, the poetic project of *Childe Harold* was decidedly modern, journalistically contemporary and immediate. As Byron declared, "The following poem was written, for the most part, amidst the scenes which it attempts to describe."[14] The devastation of the Peninsular War, the sexiness of Spanish girls, the degradation of modern Greeks, the outrage of Lord Elgin's appropriation of the marbles – these are only a sampling of the topics Byron addressed in his versified travels. [. . .]

In the Albanian war song, the disjunction between archaizing verse technique and modern self-production arises in another form. Byron calls the Albanian war song a "lay" – a notably archaic term suggestive of medieval minstrels and their songs. The distance between Harold, the entertained and apparently scribbling guest, and the unselfconscious and dancing Albanians, is rendered in part as a difference in poetic forms. Harold, we might say, speaks Spenser; the Albanians scream ballad. The ballad stanza, unlike the Spenserian, lacks a proper name; it is a quintessentially popular stanza; its serviceability for this scene reveals how closely allied was the concept of the ballad with the oral, the exotic, and the primitive.

Of course, Byron's fluency in ballad forms came in part through his deep acquaintance with Walter Scott's collection: as he wrote in his preface, he modeled another ballad in *Childe Harold*, the "Good Night" song, upon " 'Lord Maxwell's Good Night,' in the Border Minstrelsy, edited by Mr. Scott."[15] The extensive scholarship on oral poetry, with its emphasis on composition during performance, its debates over the status of memorization, and its demoting or erasing of the category "author," allows us to distinguish between these two ballad instances in *Childe Harold*.[16] Byron represents Harold as the sole singer spontaneously moved by his grief to sing and perhaps compose his "Good Night" ballad, whereas the Albanians sing as an undifferentiated wild group. Of course, Byron authored each ballad, however indebted he was to his literary and ethnographic sources. Yet he very carefully orchestrated the respective scenes of their occasion in the poem. These two instances suggest how the ballad could simultaneously uphold literary conceptions of authorship and romantic theories of collective folk utterance; the ballad as a form could mark out a continuum from primitive to civilized in one long poem. So we see that the ballad could be used to signify both the alterity of another primitive culture, such as the Albanians', and the primitive within one's own culture, as in the case of Scott's border ballads and Harold's "Good Night."

The ballad form in *Childe Harold* acquires its cultural meaning, then, from its contextualization in the larger romance. If it is true that, as Ong says, "popular ballads . . . develop on the edge of orality," we may say that literary ballads explore the cultural meaning of that edge and indeed render it a quasi-anthropological trope – ballad form as the figure of the primitive, the popular and the authentically emotive, whether encountered at home or abroad.[17]

The significance of this ballad specimen increases when we turn to the notes to *Childe Harold*. Byron published his cantos with notes; the poem was read and reviewed in light of these notes, which feature Byron *in propria persona* relating various details of and observations from his actual travels in 1810 and 1811. Byron's notes might be read as a late and decisive intervention in the discourse and practice of antiquarian documentation and annotation, consolidated most notably through the publication of ballad collections (e.g., by Percy, Joseph Ritson, and a contemporary of Byron, Scott). [. . .] [The notes'] series of transcriptions, transliterations, and translations provides extremely suggestive material for thinking about the oral, the written, and (to invoke Ong) the technologies of the word. Moreover, Byron's two-tiered structure of poem and notes juxtaposes the war song as a kind of ballad signifier against an ethnographic and linguistic signified. Crucial to the interest of the war song and of the Albanians themselves, in both the poem and the notes, is their "picturesque" primitivity. In the poem, the Albanians appear as a "barbarous" people; in the notes, we are informed that they are also an oral people. Byron observes that

> the Arnaout is not a written language: the words of this song, as well as the one which follows, are spelt according to their pronunciation. They are copied by one who speaks and understands the dialect perfectly, and who is a native of Athens.[18]

In Byron's case, as in the case of Walter Scott's *Border Minstrelsy*, the ballad with its apparatus of notes provides an opportunity both for literary intervention and for establishing ethnographic and linguistic bona fides. In his use of the ballad as a literary, linguistic, and ethnographic resource, Byron resembles many of his contemporaries; special to Byron is the harnessing of those resources to yet another project, the production of a specific public poetic persona. Constantly emphasizing the cultural and historical distance between himself and the people he encounters, Byron anoints himself as cultural mediator and commentator, as a poetic tour guide. He will present their barbarity for us; he will ventriloquize their wild songs for us; and he will suffer conspicuously from historically induced melancholia as a result of such encounters. Indeed, the Albanian war song segues immediately into Byron's signal lament: "Fair Greece! sad relic of departed worth!" [*CH*, 2.73].

Such differently oriented theorists of ethnographic writing as James Clifford and Michel de Certeau might both say, with good reason, that Byron produces and aestheticizes the gap between himself as civilized and the Albanians as savages.[19] Yet, recalling my opening quotation from Lévi-Strauss, we can foreground another rift between poet-observer and Albanian-observed – between the literate writer and the apparently nonliterate Albanians. And we note as well the presence of that wonderfully shadowy character in so much ethnographic writing, the native informant, who in this case is a "native of Athens" – not an Albanian – who nevertheless "understands the dialect perfectly." With his fluency in Albanian and his skill at transcription, the informant is the embodiment, the personification as it were, of a complex oral–literate conjunction. This conjunction, imagined in Blake as taking place both within language and across generations, appears here as an ethnographic and linguistic encounter across a multiple mediated and aesthetically useful divide. This divide, and the multiple literary and linguistic realizations of it, are characteristic of what I would propose we call the ethnographic strain of romantic orality.

III The oral at home: Wordsworth's ballads

A poet did not need to travel to Greece or Albania to find examples of poeticizable primitivity; fascination with orality and the primitive (so often confounded) could be indulged at home, as Wordsworth's oeuvre suggests. I will conclude my discussion with an account of Wordsworth's poetics of encounter, revealed in such ballads as "We are Seven" and "Simon Lee." The child, that famously Wordsworthian subject, is also a perpetually oral subject. [...] The rustic, while not illiterate, offered Wordsworth another kind of primitive figure than the child – a figure, as it were, of speech. Praising what he called the rustic's "plainer and more emphatic language," Wordsworth turned to rustic speech as a cure for the maladies of the poetic diction of his day.[20] In different but thematically related ways, then, the rustic and the child furnished Wordsworth with alternate resources of speech and mind. Imagined as relatively "in the oral," these interlocutors allowed Wordsworth to refigure the relation of "poetry" to the literate and the literary.

Throughout *Lyrical Ballads*, encounters are modeled as embodied exchanges of speech. This produces and sustains the illusion of orality. In "We are Seven," the narrator comes across "a little cottage girl" clad in "rustic" dress; she is eight years old, presumably a-, pre-, or at most partially literate. Her status as both rustic and child flags her as one of Wordsworth's local and domestic primitives. The poem explores in deceptively simple language a metaphysical and cognitive problem. The speaker poses to himself a question: "A simple child, dear brother Jim / That lightly draws its breath / And feels its life in every limb / What should it know of death?"[21] The rest of the poem is an investigation of the little maid's conception of death, revealed quite soon to be different from the ideas of her increasingly pompous interlocutor, whom she politely addresses as Master. Their conversation begins,

> "Sisters and brothers, little maid,
> How many may you be?"
> "How many? Seven in all," she said,
> And wondering looked at me.
>   ("Seven," lines 13–16)

We soon learn that among the seven the maid counts are two children "who in the church-yard lie" ("Seven," line 21). The Master spends the rest of the poem trying to force the little girl to concede that, since these siblings are dead, they don't count: "You run about, my little maid, / Your limbs they are alive / If two are in the church-yard laid, / Then ye are only five" ("Seven," lines 33–6). Yet the maid patiently resists the Master's imprecations, explaining that she sits by their graves, eats by them, plays near them, talks to them. Her siblings, though dead, retain a vitality for her, a vitality registered in her counting them as present in her insistent refrain: we are seven, we will always be seven.

The poem reaches its comic impasse in the last two stanzas, when the Master with blithe condescension asks again,

> "How many are you then," said I,
> "If they two are in Heaven?"
> The little Maiden did reply,
> "O Master! We are seven."
>
> "But they are dead; those two are dead!
> Their spirits are in heaven!"
> 'Twas throwing words away; for still
> The little Maid would have her will,
> And said, "Nay, we are seven!"
>   ("Seven," lines 61–9)

The little maid's "Nay!" appears as the final assertion of her "will": she will not be moved or persuaded; she will not adopt the Master's categories of spirit, Heaven, or death. Her negation is a comic triumph, if one sides with the maid's resistance. The Master gets his comeuppance, and his sentimental indulgence quickly turns sour. By assessing their impasse in terms of "her will," the Master shows that he will inevitably reduce any encounter to a contest, all communication to assertion.

The poem, however, suggests and enacts a modest alternative to this impasse: a sustaining of the encounter. Whereas the Master reads this encounter as an impasse of "will," I suggest that we read "We are Seven" as a seriocomic investigation of the impasse between what we might call an oral mind and a self-satisfiedly literate mind. However exasperating the Master finds the maid, nevertheless he must, to put it colloquially, deal with her. On the level of the poem, the ballad formalizes their dealings and slyly allies us with the maid. Indeed the very title, "We are Seven," may be read as an endorsement of the maid's accounting; had the Master prevailed the poem might be called "Ye are only five." Unlike Byron's use of the ballad for the Albanian war song, the ballad in Wordsworth's hands becomes the space for encounter, not the sign of the exotic or of primitivity per se. Nor is the ballad reserved for especially "romantic" utterance, as in Harold's swooning "Good Night." Instead the ballad in Wordsworth's corpus provides the metric for increasingly serious poems of counterenlightenment.

Throughout *Lyrical Ballads* Wordsworth explores how poetry might address the complex relations across generations, sexes, classes, and registers of diction. His poems also diagnose the oral–literate conjunction as a symptom of literature itself. "Simon Lee" begins as a kind of popular yarn, with Wordsworth emphasizing the sometimes dubious nature of oral transmission:

> In the sweet shire of Cardigan,
> Not far from pleasant Ivor-hall,
> An old man dwells, a little man,
> I've heard he once was tall.
> Of years he has upon his back,
> No doubt, a burthen weighty;
> He says he is three score and ten,
> But others say he's eighty.[22]

Simon Lee – the man and the poem – seems to come from an oral world of rumor, report, and long if arguable communal memory. Yet the poet – clearly not a rustic and probably more sure of his age than Simon is – also moves in this world, speaking to Simon Lee as the old man struggles to cut a tangled root, and ultimately lending "poor Simon" a hand. Speech and contact appear as the very formal condition for the generation and indeed the transmission of this ballad.

Wordsworth complicates the orality effect of this poem when in the ninth of thirteen stanzas he addresses the "gentle reader." Wordsworth introduces the mediation of reading even as he promotes an orality effect through his jaunty versification, the rustic social space of the poem, and his simulation of talk. He apostrophizes the reader as a possible transmitter of the poem in the future. In his comically circumlocutory address the poet says,

> What more I have to say is short
> I hope you'll kindly take it;
> It is no tale; but should you think,
> Perhaps a tale you'll make it.
>   ("Lee," lines 77–80)

What follows then is the account of the poet's lending his hand to Simon, and Simon's astonishing gratitude after. This is "no tale," Wordsworth insists, yet it may become one: this claim reads several ways. Wordsworth may be suggesting that the pathetic scene with Simon should not be cheerfully assimilated into the category of "tale"; he may also be suggesting that the printed account may yet be circulated as a "tale" among a community of readers, hearers, overhearers, and raconteurs. The poem imagines its other lives as a printed object (thus "O Reader!" [line 73]) and less assuredly as a told "tale" ("Perhaps a tale you'll make it"). Wordsworth would not have his "tale" passively transmitted, as if the reader were a mindlessly memorizing conduit: only if she should "think" will the reader "make" it a tale. Here the reader becomes, like the poet, a "maker," which is, as Walter Scott and Percy Shelley both noted, the

English approximation of the term "poetas."[23] The future of the poem, then, involves a collaboration between the author, the reader, and possible auditors. Expanding upon Wordsworth's apostrophe, we could also describe the life of the poem through an array of linguistic and social practices – composing, writing, printing, bookselling, reading, reciting, revising, and indeed, photocopying.

"Simon Lee" imagines several avenues of poetic transmission, and in doing so the poem also reveals mutually permeable domains of orality, semiliteracy, and sophisticated literacy. These terms, after all, are reifications – the "oral" and the "literate" are not in the end abstractions but rather markers of the complex linguistic, cognitive, and technological capacities and orientations of individuals and communities. Even more than my example from Blake, who keeps his oral–literate conjunction mostly on the plane of fanciful imagination, Wordsworth's ballads gesture to a complex social and linguistic reality. The rustics and children of his poems show habits of mind and speech that linguistic and cultural anthropologists would designate as partially "oral," yet it is also crucial to Wordsworth's vision that these characters freely interact with more literate interlocutors. And if these poems run the risk of condescending to or sentimentalizing the aliterate or preliterate figure, as Coleridge and other critics then and now have claimed, nevertheless Wordsworth's poems consistently and compassionately reach across a divide that other poets and theorists of the human sciences would have kept rigorously unbridgeable.

In sum, the oral–literate conjunction appears in Wordsworth's *Lyrical Ballads* not as a border between primitivity and modernity, or between Scotland and England, or between the contemporary and the residual, but rather as a lived and living speech situation. Of course, these are "balladized" speech situations, as Scott would say. Moreover, Wordsworth's ballads could be seen as instituting another rift – that between child and adult, or between rustic and sophisticate – which would obscure the oral–literate conjunction. Yet in refusing to relegate "orality" to the margins or footnotes, in refusing to make the literate Master triumph over the more orally inflected thinking of the maid, in refusing to regard Simon as a merely picturesque other, Wordsworth's poems offer a way to rethink the relation of orality to literacy and more specifically the relation of the oral to the literate within literature.

Given the primacy of speech in these ballads, we can also reassess the oft-quoted Wordsworthian ambition to write a poetry from "a selection of the real language of men." The circumscribed and orally inflected world of the rustic, as perceived by Wordsworth and pointedly noted as a defect by Coleridge, thus appears as a great asset. "Real" language, as circulated in the poems, appears as a spoken, embodied language. When Wordsworth invokes the ideal poet as "a man speaking to men," we should place as strong an emphasis on his choice, "speaking," as on his insistence on horizontal relations among men.[24] For among the many issues Wordsworth addresses in his preface is the very futurity of poetry when confronted with its exile from speech.

Poetry still bears, in this period and perhaps in ours (as in the proliferation of "spoken word" and "performance art"), the promise of speech and immediacy. In terms of the writing and circulation of romantic poetry, some anecdotes may illuminate the persistence of the oral and the immediate as still-vital elements of composition and transmission. The circuit of *Lyrical Ballads* often runs from oral to literate to oral: the poet tells us in his notes, for instance, that he actually met the little girl who appears in "We are Seven." Their conversation became the stuff of the poem, ultimately a written document, but first composed – as usual – in Wordsworth's head as he walked in the Lake District. To invoke another case, one of Mary Shelley's earliest memories was of hiding behind her father's couch as Coleridge thundered the stanzas of "The Ancient Mariner"; a stanza from that poem later appeared in her novel *Frankenstein*. She experienced the poem as a recited piece, a memorable acoustic event; like most children, she was introduced to "literature" through the medium of speech. Another instance: Coleridge himself alluded to the long-standing circulation of "Christabel" in manuscript; before the poem was ever printed it had inspired two imitations by Scott and Byron – which irked Coleridge so much that he protested in print, "During the many years which intervened between the composition and publication of Christabel, it became almost as well known among literary men as if it had been on common sale." This intermediate mode of circulation – in manuscript – was complicated by Coleridge's and others' recitations, which further exposed "literary men" to the poem.[25] These anecdotes do not of course revise the general condition of romantic poetry as a linguistic practice in early industrial capital; but the stories show that the oral persisted as a vital and, in some cases, the most vital mode of circulation.

Poetry was, and indeed is, circulated in several ways: in speech, in written manuscripts, in printed books, and now on the Internet. Just as Ruth Finnegan suggests that there is no "oral poetry" per se but rather a range of oral poetries,[26] so too I would argue that there were multiple romantic oralities and poetries. However inexact the notion of an "oral–literate conjunction," it is a useful if imprecise tool for wedging open the critical vise around accounts of poetry in English.

Notes

1 [. . .] Claude Lévi-Strauss, "A Writing Lesson," in *Tristes Tropiques*, trans. John and Doreen Weightman (New York, 1992). p. 298.
2 For this phrase, see Percy Bysshe Shelley, *A Defence of Poetry*, in *Shelley's Poetry and Prose*, eds Donald Reiman and Sharon Powers (New York, 1977), pp. 481, 482.
3 Ibid., p. 480. For Wordsworth's ruminations on "the earliest poets of all nations" see his "Appendix on Poetic Diction," appended in 1802 to William Wordsworth and Samuel Taylor Coleridge's *Lyrical Ballads*, eds R.L. Brett and A.R. Jones (London, 1991), pp. 317–18. After a brief discourse on Homer and his imagined editor Pisistratus, Walter Scott informs us that Scottish ballads offer a glimpse of "the National Muse in her cradle." See his "Introductory Remarks on Popular Poetry and on the Various Collections of Britain, particularly those of Scotland" (1830), in *Minstrelsy of the Scottish Border* (1802–3), 4 vols, ed. T.F. Henderson (Edinburgh, 1902), 1: 2–7.
4 Susan Stewart, *Crimes of Writing: Problems in the Containment of Representation* (Durham, N.C., 1994). See especially her third and fourth chapters, "Notes on Distressed Genres" and "Scandals of the Ballad."
5 For a lucid and measured survey of the Ossian controversy, its "three phases" (p. 99), and more broadly of Macpherson's career, see Paul J. de Gategno, *James Macpherson* (Boston, 1989). [. . .]
6 Yet [Fiona] Stafford, in her introduction to *Poems of Ossian*, cautions us: "In academic discussions of eighteenth-century literature, James Macpherson is frequently mentioned alongside Chatterton, even though the Rowley poems and their manuscripts were entirely created by Chatterton" [Introduction. *The Poems of Ossian and Related Works* by James Macpherson. Ed. Howard Gaskill (Edinburgh, 1996), p. viii]. I here elide the particulars of each case, as the contemporary commentators did, in order to emphasize Macpherson's and Chatterton's similar status as poet-experimenters with antiquities.
7 See Wordsworth's 1798 "Advertisement" to *Lyrical Ballads*, p. 8.
8 Some essential texts for this discussion are Walter J. Ong's classic *Orality and Literacy: The Technologizing of the Word* (London, 1982); Ruth Finnegan's disputed but still useful *Oral Poetry: Its Nature, Significance, and Social Context* (1977; rev. ed., Bloomington, Ind., 1992); Jack Goody's *The Domestication of the Savage Mind* (Cambridge, 1977); and Eric A. Havelock's *The Muse Learns to Write: Reflections on Orality and Literacy from Antiquity to the*

Present (New Haven, Conn., 1986). Albert B. Lord's *The Singer of Tales* (Cambridge, Mass., 1964) and the work of Milman Parry (e.g., *The Making of Homeric Verse*, ed. Adam Parry [Oxford, 1971]), on which Lord builds, together constitute the most important twentieth-century rethinking of Homeric epic and of oral poetry in general.

9 A brief glance at some standard books on English metrics and poetic forms confirms this elasticity: John Hollander in *Rhyme's Reason: A Guide to English Verse* (New Haven, Conn., 1989) has several witty and exemplary definitions of the generic ballad stanza and its variants, but none for "song." Hollander first introduces the term "quatrain" and then specifies "ballad" as a special kind of quatrain. In *Poetic Meter and Poetic Form* (New York, 1979), Paul Fussell similarly informs us that the "simplest quatrain is the ballad stanza" (p. 133). Like Hollander, Fussell offers no entry for "song," which seems to be a far more elastic term than "ballad"; this may derive from the literary ballad's stronger association with poetry as an art of arranged words, whereas "song" powerfully connotes a tune. Perhaps the most useful distinction between popular and literary ballads may be found in their differing relations to music, tunes, and transmission. Such a distinction would resemble that between "folk song" and "art song," a distinction which has itself come under assault as scholars become more sophisticated about the interpenetrability of "high" and "low" musical culture. In *Fakesong*, [Dave] Harker aims "to show how concepts like 'folksong' and 'ballad' were produced, historically" [*Fakesong: The Manufacture of British "Folksong," 1700 to the Present Day* (Milton Keynes, U.K., 1985), p. xv]. Harker emphasizes that these categories and materials have complex class histories and cultural resonances which collectors and scholars – expropriating workers' song-culture for their own bourgeois editions – have tended to displace and indeed efface.

10 William Blake, "Introduction," *Songs of Innocence*, in *Songs of Innocence and of Experience* (Oxford, 1967), pl. 4. line 1. Hereafter cited parenthetically in the text.

11 George Gordon, Lord Byron, *Childe Harold's Pilgrimage*, in *The Poetical Works of Lord Byron* (London, 1966), p. 204 [2.72]. Hereafter cited parenthetically in the text by book and line number as *CH*.

12 Byron, "Preface to the First and Second Cantos," *Childe Harold's Pilgrimage*, in *The Poetical Works*, p. 179.

13 Ibid.

14 Ibid.

15 Ibid.

16 For one partisan version of the contentious history of this scholarship, see Finnegan; Ong's critical assessment of the term, "oral literature," launches a series of useful observations in his *Orality and Literary*, pp. 10–15.

17 Ong (n. 8 above), p. 159.

18 [Byron, Notes to *Childe Harold*, in *the Poetical Works*, p. 879.]

19 On the links between ethnographic writing, historiography, and poetry, see James Clifford, *The Predicament of Culture: Twentieth-Century Ethnography, Literature, and Art* (Cambridge, Mass., 1988) and Michel de Certeau, *The Writing of History*, trans. Tom Conley (New York, 1988). [. . .]

20 Wordsworth, Preface to *Lyrical Ballads* (n. 3 above), p. 245.

21 Wordsworth, "We are Seven," in *Lyrical Ballads*, pp. 66–8 (lines 1–4). Hereafter cited parenthetically in the text by line number as "Seven."

22 Wordsworth, "Simon Lee," in *Lyrical Ballads*, pp. 60–3 (lines 1–8). Hereafter cited parenthetically in the text by line number as "Lee."

23 Scott notes that "the bards of Greece [earned] the term 'POETAS,' which, as it singularly happens, is literally translated by the Scottish epithet for the same class of persons, whom they term the *Makers*." See Scott (n. 3 above), 1: 4.

24 See the passage from Wordsworth's 1802 Preface to the *Lyrical Ballads*: "What is a Poet? To whom does he address himself? And what language is to be expected from him? He is a man speaking to men . . . " (p. 255). That Wordsworth's "men" may not have included women, or may in fact have subsumed women under a problematic "human universal" (Man = men and women), is a possibility I will let readers ponder at their leisure.

25 Samuel Taylor Coleridge, *Biographia Literaria: or Biographical Sketches of My Literary Life and Opinions*, ed. George Watson (London, 1991), p. 282. In his notes on that passage, Watson discusses the circulation of the poem between 1800 and 1816.

26 Finnegan (n. 8 above), pp. 1–29.

42 Processing

Andrew Piper

[In omitted sections from this chapter excerpt, Piper explores the relationship between authoring and editing in the Romantic age, using Ludwig Tieck, Friedrich von der Hagen, and Karl Lachmann as examples.]

[E]ditors produced authors in the romantic age and for long after. [. . . E]diting and authoring nearly overlapped. To understand [. . . this] I want to turn the clock back to a time (the 1790s), an author (Walter Scott), and a genre (the ballad) where we can see how issues [of editing and authoring] were being worked out in very concrete and often deeply paradoxical ways. [. . .]

During the late 1790s, Walter Scott began touring the border regions of Scotland with his friend, John Leyden, to collect recitations of Scottish ballads. Such activity mirrored with remarkable fidelity a similar project undertaken by [J.W.] Goethe and [Johann Gottfried] Herder over twenty years earlier, when they traveled to the region of Alsace and began recording the folksongs that would eventually contribute to Herder's *Volkslieder* (1778).[1] Two decades later one could find the same exploratory poetic ethnography in the work of Charles Nodier, who, as the municipal librarian in Ljubljana under Napoleon, began recording and promoting Illyrian ballads in his periodical, *Télégraphe officiel* (1812–13).

Such renewed interest in the ballad as an articulation of an often distressed local culture – one believed to be imminently passing away – was not simply a transnational phenomenon that took place at different times and in different places. It was also crucially an inter-national one of influence and circulation, especially between German and Scottish culture.[2] During the years of his ballad-collecting excursions, Scott was also at work translating German balladeers like Gottfried August Bürger, and both Scott and Bürger were inspired by Herder's edition of folksongs and ballads from across Europe that had appeared two decades earlier, an edition which itself derived from Herder's initial interest in [Thomas] Percy's *Reliques* [*of Ancient English Poetry* (1765)]. [. . .] Scott's reimportation of such Anglo-inspired Germanic balladeering would then be imported *back* into the German states as his *Minstrelsy of the Scottish Border* would serve as a key influence on [Clemens] Brentano and [Achim von] Arnim's *Des Knaben Wunderhorn* [(1805–8)].[3]

As a witness to the new international attention to the local, the ballad would go on to play an essential generic role in the development of romantic poetry.[4] [. . .] With its inherent appeal to the oral and the medium of the body (ballad comes from the Provençal *ballada*, or dance tune [*Tanzlied*]), the ballad came to stand in a post-Rousseauean fashion for all things natural, original, and prelapsarian.[5] [. . .] If the ballad was on the one hand one of the most emphatic signs of a greater romantic fascination with orality and the originary, it was also a key index of a romantic attention to intermediality.[6]

[. . .]

Despite a wealth of research today that is attuned to the mediality of the romantic ballad revival, what much of this work has overlooked is the ballad's bookishness and, by extension, the way the ballad was a key object in early-nineteenth-century editorial debates. As Steve Newman has shown, in the new critical context of the mid-twentieth century the ballad was thought to be *the* literary genre to initiate readers into reading literature in books precisely because it was imagined to be a *non*-bookish genre, a critical move imported wholesale from the romantic era.[7] But few genres were as tied to debates about making books as the ballad was by the early nineteenth century. The ballad revival was always intensely mediated through the bibliographic practices of collection and correction. The ballad was in this sense not the genre where we learn to read in books, but the one where we learn to read the logic of *books* themselves.

In her groundbreaking work on categorizing the ballad as a "distressed genre" – as that which has been made old – Susan Stewart has shown how the ballad's cultural work during the long eighteenth century was its capacity to "mean historically," to mean time.[8] But I want to add to Stewart's claim and argue that the ballad's other significance, at least to the romantic project at the end of Stewart's timeframe, was the way it dramatized the problem of textual transmission through books, the way it signified as a genre not just time itself but the dual problems of literary ownership and textual stability that were at the heart of an expanding early-nineteenth-century editorial culture. The ballad foregrounded a range of problems surrounding the commonality of literary property in an age of the printed book and the editor's role in producing, protecting, and pirating such poetic commons. As a translator of German ballads, an editor of Scottish ones, and an author of historical novels that straddled both English and Scottish culture, Walter Scott was one of the great mediating figures of the nineteenth century. In returning to Scott's early editorial project, *Minstrelsy of the Scottish Border* (1802–3), I want to show how his editorial work was not a phase through which Scott passed on his way to becoming a full-fledged author but offered instead the conditions upon which such authorship would later be achieved. [. . .] I want to suggest that it was the problematic ownership of narrative property that surrounded editorial work and that Scott's *Minstrelsy* itself dramatized that became a key "source" for Scott's poetry and novels. As Maureen McLane has suggested, it was precisely the impossible presence of minstrelsy as a poetic practice that necessitated and in some sense authorized the figure of the editor.[9] Not only did the figure of minstrelsy and the genre of the ballad highlight with unusual clarity the contests of textual attribution during the romantic period, but Scott's figure of the "border" as the location of such poetic creations also drew attention to the difficulties of such literary specification.

Scholars of Scott's work have repeatedly drawn attention to the way it participated in a greater nineteenth-century obsession with borders, whether of time or space, from the making of national or imperial borders, to the borders of history, to those of language (most notably between Scots and English).[10] But while we have been vigorously debating Scott's role in shaping the nineteenth-century consciousness of nation, empire, or time, we have been ignoring Scott's place in a literary culture that was overwhelmingly concerned with *textual* borders, with the boundaries within and between books. We have overlooked not only the origins of Scott's own career, which began in the editor's laboratory, but also the larger concerns of a literary market that was increasingly beset by an editorial culture that was ransacking its textual past and debating how to do it. With so much material reappearing and so many hands involved, how was one to tell the difference between what belonged to whom, especially in an environment in which the very categories of belonging and authenticity were at the heart of such nationalist editorial projects? What were the visual and discursive protocols that were to determine the successful transmission and attribution of writing in the nineteenth century, whether to a person or a place?

It was precisely this problematic relationship of the specificity of poetic language to either person, place, or book that would be dramatized in the making of Scott's ballad edition and that would then reemerge in his novelistic productions, indeed would become the ground of his writerly fame. Rather than trace an intra-genre genealogy of the novel that passes through the complex intersections of romance, national tale, gothic and historical novel as others have already done,[11] I want to understand the way the novel, and Scott's novels in particular, emerged in the early nineteenth century within a bibliographic context that was programmatically attentive to the transcription, correction, and reproduction of historical narrative material. [. . . F]or Scott the novel – and the historical novel in particular – took shape in its negotiation with the bibliographic format of the edition and its investment in marginalizing the mediating practices of the editor. The novel thus represented less the prosification of poetic genres like the ballad as it did an engagement with the intense process of bookification that such genres underwent at the turn of the century.

The borders of books: *Minstrelsy of the Scottish Border*

Walter Scott's edition of Scottish ballads, *Minstrelsy of the Scottish Border* (1802–3), began to take shape as a book when he wrote to the printer John Ballantyne: "I have been for years collecting old Border ballads, and I think I could, with little trouble, put together such a selection from them as might make a neat little volume, to sell for four or five shillings."[12] Both Ballantyne and Scott were at the beginning of their careers, and the *Minstrelsy* was to serve as a showcase of Scott's editorial and Ballantyne's printing ability. Unlike the relative lack of splendor that surrounded the publication of Herder's *Volkslieder*, for example, Scott's ballads were printed in octavo with an elegant title page that combined a noticeably large amount of text (there are twenty-one lines of text versus seven for [Karl] Lachmann's Wolfram [von Eschenbach] edition or eight for [Friedrich von der] Hagen's *Nibelungen Lied* [1807]) with a typographical uniformity that also utilized an array of alternating font sizes [. . .]. The pages for the texts were then characterized by a vast amount of white space, a true sign of bookish luxury. [. . .] Unlike early-modern editions with their encircling layers of commentary, the romantic edition was supposed to free the reader's imaginative engagement with the text.

At the same time, such typographical exclusivity of Scott's edition (in both the elegance and the relative absence of type) included another level of omission: that of musical notation. [. . .] Scott's collection [unlike Joseph Ritson's *Scotish Songs* (1794)] excluded [. . .] calls to musicality. There was no musical notation, and the frontispiece illustration was of a castle ruin, emphasizing instead the material fragments that underlay this print artifact. The *Minstrelsy* visually foregrounded the editorial work of textual archaeology on which such collections were based instead of the primary orality from which they derived. It drew attention through its visual semantics to the collective practices of making artifacts instead of the singular practices of melodic performance.

This tension between singularity and collectivity in the physical make-up of the edition was also enacted through the title Scott chose for it. When Scott used the word "Minstrelsy" in his title he was explicitly drawing on Percy's theory of ballad production from the *Reliques*.[13] According to the Minstrel theory, ballads were not the work of some collective folk but the product of individual bards who performed for chiefs or lords. [. . .] The Minstrel theory emphasized the fact of sovereignty – of both production and reception – over against any sharedness or collectivity that might surround such traditional songs.

At the same time, by referring to his collection as "of the Scottish Border," Scott was following Percy's lead in another way – in Percy's suggestion that the Border region was the cradle of Scottish balladry.[14] In grounding his ballad collection in a single local culture, Scott was participating in a larger trend of publishing folksongs and ballads whose monocultural or nationalist trajectory stood in stark contrast to the cosmo-provincialism of someone like Herder's collection.[15] Again, the emphasis was on singularity and not plurality. But while the "border" signified, on the one hand, a particular geographical and political region within Anglo-Scottish history, the border also signified, in a more general sense, no space at all.[16] The very site, the very particularity on which this edition was supposed to be based, was in fact ungrounded. Its singularity was simultaneously constituted as liminality.

The genre of the ballad that formed the core of Scott's collection of minstrelsy exhibited at the level of genre the same tension found at the level of both book and title. As a deeply narrative poetic form, the ballad favored third-person narrators and the direct speech of characters over and above the lyrical "I" for which romantic poetry would become so famous. There were no heart-felt lamentations, no single guiding consciousnesses, no interiors here. As tales told in the third person according to a standard and mostly unwavering rhyme scheme, they were designed for collective ownership, to be passed around from person to person.

When we turn to the content of this form, a similar focus emerges. Taken together, the ballads dramatize a relatively homogenous body of material that concerns tales of battles, stealing, and revenge, tales of fairies and elves, tales of mothers who kill their children or knights who steal their brides or wives who cheat on their husbands. As Max Kommerell has pointed out about the ballad in general, what all of these themes have in common is the problem of legitimacy, as they enact the transgression of various ethical, corporeal, or property boundaries.[17] The border ballads were most often, and not unsurprisingly, about the problematic status of cultural, social, and personal borders. They were about the difficulties of establishing – and protecting – singularity and ownership.

Moving further into the text, we can see how this delicate balancing act between the proprietary and the commons is further enacted in the margins of Scott's edition. The *Minstrelsy* opened with a long, 110-page introduction, and each ballad was accompanied by introductory notes as well as endnotes. Like the editor of the emerging critical edition, the editor here was overwhelmingly present at the bibliographic frames of Scott's edition. The individual introductions to the ballads described the numerous sources from which Scott had drawn, putting on display the collating as well as completing that he did as an editor. [. . .]

Scott's footnotes, on the other hand, departed from what would become the standard use of footnotes in the critical edition. Instead of explaining the variant readings that supported his ballads – they did not record the exclusions and corruptions that the editor of multiple sources invariably faced – Scott's footnotes were only used to translate or explicate foreign (most often Scottish) words. The paratextual elements of Scott's edition thus suggested a gradual, if incomplete, movement of the editor beyond the boundaries of his primary text and towards the margins. He was largely concerned with collating and comparing his primary sources, but he was also concerned with translating and completing his text according to aesthetic criteria. He was both at the margins and in the text at the same time, mirroring the editor of both the *Erneuung* and the critical edition at once. The *Minstrelsy* thus not only captured a certain spatial liminality of the Scottish border, it also represented a temporally liminal moment between competing notions of editorial practice. Like the middling heroes that would populate so many of his novels (Edward Waverley or Henry Morton), Scott was once again crucially in the middle.

In order to illustrate how this friction between the commons and the singular achieved an ultimately revelatory intensity within the works themselves, I want to concentrate on one ballad in particular, "The Sang of the Outlaw Murray," which Scott chose to open the first edition of his ballad collection (later replaced by "Sir Patrick Spens"). It tells the story of how John Murray became the Sheriff of Ettrick Forest in the sixteenth century, which we know was a remarkably autobiographical choice, as Scott had been appointed Deputy Sheriff just three years earlier. According to Scott's introduction, on the other hand, it was said to be at the head of the collection because "this Ballad appears to be among the most ancient offered to the Public in the present collection."[18] Instead of autobiography, then, the ballad apparatus offered another competing motivation, that of chronology, for the placement of "Murray" at the outset of the collection. By placing the oldest first, the ballad collection was lent a developmental logic [. . .]. At the same time, when we look more closely at the content of this ballad, a third possible motivation emerges as to why it was chosen as the frame to the collection. As the tale of an "outlaw," "Murray" was essentially about the problem of property and legitimacy, about the difficult operations involved in moving from out-law to in-law. In this sense, it was a ballad about ballad collections and thus an ideal ballad to begin one.

It is when we turn to the poem itself, and specifically Scott's rendering of the poem, that we find a fourth, and by far the most significant, possible reason for this ballad's location at the head of the collection. Stanzas forty-nine to fifty-one do not appear in any other version of the ballad prior to Scott's version (Scott himself writes in a note that "this and the three following verses [49–51] are not in some copies" [23]), and can thus be read in some sense as proprietary material, as Scott's personal contribution to this collective text (whether Scott personally authored them is not my concern here, but is the subject of considerable debate). In these three stanzas, a character named Sir Walter Scott, Lord of Buccleuch, appears, who challenges Murray's acquisition of the Forest. The stanzas read:

Then spak kene lair of Buckscleuth,
A stalworthye man, and sterne was he –

"For a King to gang an Outlaw till,
Is beneath his state and his dignitie.

"The man that wons yon Foreste intill,
He lives by rief and felonie!
Wherefore, brayd on, my Sovereign liege,
Wi' fire and sword we'll follow thee;
Or, gif your Courtrie Lords fa' back,
Our Borderers sall the onset gie."

Then out and spak the nobil King,
And round him cast a wilie ee –
"Now haud thy tongue, Sir Walter Scott,
Nor speik of reif nor felonie:
For had everye honeste man his awin kye,
A right puir clan thy name wad be!"

(16)

In the very lines that are unique to Scott's edition, we find that Scott's name appears ("Now haud thy tongue, Sir Walter Scott"). It is in fact one of several instances in Scott's edition where a character from the Scott family emerges, most often when the ownership of property is at stake. On one level, we could say that Scott's construction of this ballad makes its autobiographical function even more explicit, serving as a means of suggesting his own genealogical rights to the property whose stewardship he has just been accorded. But on a more general level, the appearance of Scott's name in lines unique to Scott's edition – lines that appear at the transactional center of the opening ballad where the ownership of property is being negotiated – performs an authorial function. The name functions like a kind of signature here, marking this text, and this collection, in some sense as *Scott's* text and *Scott's* collection. The sovereignty of the fictional "sir" in "Sir Walter Scott" (it would be many years before Scott acquired his baronetcy) only underscored the supposed sovereignty of this edition. In the opening ballad to Scott's collection questions of personal and familial property are deeply intertwined with questions of literary property.

And yet when we look at the last four lines spoken by the king to Sir Walter Scott, this very possibility of sovereignty is precisely what the language of the ballad calls into question. At the moment that the editor's name appears in the text to make a claim of ownership, he is instructed to remain silent ("Now hand thy tongue"). However, the passage does not tell us that he has no right to claim ownership, but that the very category of ownership and ownness upon which such claims are based has been suspended. He cannot speak of "reif" (robbery) or "felonie" because he is operating in a state of the *absence* of legitimate ownership, of the possibility of possessing one's "awin kye" (own cattle). Scott is making an important point here about the inherent difficulties or contradictions of applying commercial notions of private ownership to a space of collective goods. In a world of cattle rustling – or ballad collecting – how was one to ground oneself in a notion of legitimate property? Better to hold one's tongue on that score. At the same lime, the very line that suggests the commonality, not the singularity, of property is metrically distinct from the rest of the ballad with five feet instead of four. In the passage that stands out in Scott's edition, the line about one's own property literally stands out from the rest of the ballad. And yet the final word that participates in the stanza's rhyme, "kye," the word that denotes property, is a distinctly Scottish word, pointing to a common space whose singularity and cultural uniqueness is what the ballad collection is designed both to capture and to produce.

This otherwise simple passage thus performs a series of complex, and importantly contradictory, operations. In invoking the name of Walter Scott in a passage unique to Scott's edition, the passage confers a kind of authoriality on the edition. It emphatically endorses the uniqueness of this particular edition. And yet in the sovereign's command for the editor to hold his tongue, it also anticipates the emerging early-nineteenth-century consensus of the marginalization of the editor. It enacts, in other words, Lachmann's principle of immaculate reception.[19] The editor was precisely the figure who should not speak in a poem. At the same time, the sovereign's speech calls into question the very conditions of sovereignty, the possibilities of ownness and ownership ("For had everye honeste man his awin kye"). It highlights the internal contradictions of asserting principles of proprietariness within an *edition*. [. . . N]owhere was the conflict between the proprietary and the commons more pronounced in this passage than in the fifth line of the third stanza cited above, where we experience rhythmic singularity alongside semantic commonality.

It was precisely in the *addition* where we can see Scott offering his readers a crucial moment of self-reflection about the nature of the *edition*, about the contradictions and the tensions that surrounded textual ownership in the practice of editing in the early nineteenth century. It was in the transactional heart of the opening entry in a collection of ballads about the border where Scott teases out the contradictions surrounding the uncertain boundaries of literary property inherent in the "edition." Whether here or on the title page, the name of Walter Scott was enmeshed in the competing imperatives of the proprietary and the common *in a world of common property*. The passage enacted precisely the editor's dilemma between producing an *original* edition, something his own, and an *authentic* edition, something decidedly not his own. The editor was caught between making too many and too few changes to his material, thereby assuming either the position of author or that of the reprinter, or worse, the plagiarist. The editor was always there, like the Walter Scott who discretely emerged in the body of the text, but he was also not there, like the Walter Scott instructed to hold his tongue. According to the logic of this passage, the editor's activity was supposed to efface its very presence. [. . .]

Narrating editing: the historical novel and the *Tales of My Landlord*

When Scott invented the persona of Jedediah Cleishbotham as the fictive editor of the novels that would appear under the heading *Tales of My Landlord*, he was not only drawing attention to a professional continuity in his own life, he was also participating in a long and illustrious novelistic tradition. [. . .]

[W]hat makes the prefaces and opening chapters (which served as prefaces) to the *Tales of My Landlord* series so important to the history of the novel is not the singular figure of Cleishbotham but the *accumulation* of narrative personae responsible for the tales that he oversees. Not only do we have Peter, or Patrick, Pattieson, who is the compiler of these tales, which Cleishbotham has merely selected and sent to a bookseller (who is himself a "counterfeiter of voices"), but we have the various narrators Pattieson cites, such as Old Mortality, Mr. Dunover, Halkit, Hardie, Dick Tinto, and of course the Landlord himself, to whom these tales somehow belong, along with a host of nameless corroborating narrators such as the weavers, tailors, moorland farmers, traveling merchants, honorable families, bishops, gamekeepers, and "a laird or two" that Pattieson names in the opening chapter of *Old Mortality*, to which we could add the "real" sources that Scott later cites in the introductions to the *Magnum Opus* edition, such as Joseph Train, Helen Lawson, Mrs. Goldie, and the volume *Sketches from Nature* by John M'Diarmid. [. . .]

Fiona Robertson has made the point that the Waverley Novels were intimately concerned with problems of historical and political legitimacy.[20] In highlighting the question of legitimacy in Scott, Robertson has drawn our attention to one of the central recurring themes that run throughout Scott's work. But in her analysis Robertson does not address the ways in which the Waverley Novels and the *Tales of My Landlord* series in particular were also thinking through questions of *textual* legitimacy. The prefaces to the *Tales* creatively frame the problem of textual ownership, the difficulty of attributing speech to a particular individual, which we already saw prefigured in the primal scene surrounding the name of "Sir Walter Scott" in the opening ballad of Scott's *Minstrelsy*. They highlight the way the "achievement of literary authority," as Ina Ferris titled her study of Scott,[21] was a product of one's relationship to a given textual tradition.

[. . .]

Such contractual ambiguities of possession [. . .] are then amplified not only in the first series in *Old Mortality*, which concerns the fate of a covenant, but again in the second series in *The Heart of Mid-Lothian*, where in the first chapter the singular narrator of Old Mortality, after whom the novel in the first series is named, is replaced by the triumvirate of Mr. Dunover, Halkit, and Hardie. When the narrator shifts from an external to a character-bound narrator through the introduction of the narrative "I" in the opening of *Mid-Lothian's* second chapter, the reader is faced with the dilemma of whom this "I" refers to, where possibilities range from the three overturned narrators named in chapter 1 to the two compilers, Pattieson and Cleishbotham, named in the preface. A similar trajectory away from the singularity of direct speech towards increasing degrees of indirection could be typographically observed in the first series' use of quotation marks to surround the entire first chapter – to affirm that the chapter's contents belonged to the single character Peter Pattieson – which are then absent from the opening chapter of *The Heart of Mid-Lothian* in the second series. When poststructuralists like Deleuze and Guattari write that "language in its entirety is indirect discourse,"[22] we can see how such seemingly universal sentiments about the nature of language and narration were being prepared in the historical cauldron of the romantic historical novel.

The empty "I" that stands over, or at the heart of, *The Heart of Mid-Lothian* not only captured a fundamental feature of Scott's authorial project that dated back to his injunction to Walter Scott the editor to hold his tongue in the *Minstrelsy* and continued through his enduring anonymity in the Waverley Novels. It also, I want to suggest, captured a fundamental feature of the narrative organization of this signal romantic novel in particular, where the plural significations articulated through the empty "I" are graphed onto the figure of the "heart" that is at the heart, so to speak, of both this novel and of a nineteenth-century notion of subjectivity that was increasingly being produced through the reading of novels.

In the reconceptualizations of the human body that took place around 1800, the identity of the heart was, not surprisingly, integral to such corporeal reconfigurations and the communicative poetics they subtended.[23] The question that surrounded the human heart was whether it was to be understood as the center or core of the human body or as a circulatory relay. In the opening chapter of Scott's novel in which the figure of the heart is put through a rapid series of puns, we learn that the "Heart of Mid-Lothian" refers to an architectural structure that is both a prison and a toll-booth, a container *and* a relay.

[. . .]

The figure of the heart was [. . .] connected to a variety of communicative practices that would emerge as central points of tension during the early nineteenth century and that would include the categories of confession, sympathy, and sentimentality, as well as those of memory, memorialization, collection, and commonality. As Andrea Henderson has highlighted in her reading of the novel, Scott's *Heart* was intensely concerned with the tensions between legitimate and illegitimate circulation,[24] participating in what Deidre Lynch has identified as a longer novelistic tradition defined by an attention to both the commercial and social circulations that inhered in an emergent market economy.[25] Just as in Scott's historical narrative poem *Marmion*, for example, one could break down the characters of the *Heart of Mid-Lothian* into two groups, those that embodied illegitimate movements (Madge, Staunton, Effie) and those that remained "steadfast" (Jeanie, Butler, Jeanie's father), where the former seemed to disappear and the latter always to return home, completing the circuit that they began like Scott's first hero, Edward Waverley. As Jane Millgate has argued, "journeys in [Scott's] fiction rarely follow the unidirectional pattern of the simple picaresque. Coming home to the father or the place of the fathers is an essential element in his characteristic design. . . . London cannot provide a conclusion."[26] This sense of circularity and closure that informed so many of Scott's novels, and *The Heart of Mid-Lothian* in particular, has no doubt been one of the reasons why much recent scholarship on *The Heart of Mid-Lothian* has focused on its participation in constructing British nationalism.[27] The closed routes of the characters' travels in the novel are meant to reenact the closing of the nation's (or empire's) borders.

What I want to focus on instead is not the way such circulatory logic reinforced emerging national or imperial mentalities or, as Henderson and Lynch have suggested, facilitated romantic subjects' adaptation to the commercial circulations of an ever-expanding market economy. Rather, I want to focus on the way these questions of circulation and circularity, transmission and reliability, were deployed by Scott to address the increasingly urgent problem of textual circulation and ownership, of how to attribute language to a person (or a nation) as so much material passed out of a literary commons and into the hands of editors and authors. And here the punning passage on the heart in the novel's first chapter is again instructive. When Hardie asks, "Why should not the Tolbooth have its 'Last Speech, Confession, and Dying Words'?"[28] the question that this question poses is, What are the rhetorical and technological conditions that are capable of generating the speech act of "confession" itself, of aligning the heart – and by association the novel that was called a heart – away from speaking *by heart* and towards speaking *from the heart*? In place of the numerous narrators that the novel deploys at its opening, how can the heart speak *itself*?

"By heart" v. "from the heart" in *The Heart of Mid-Lothian*

In order to try to answer these questions I would like to concentrate on two key scenes that concern the performance of a confession – that concern, in other words, the very production of singularity that would provide the conditions of both *The Heart of Mid-Lothian's* success and of course Scott's own career. The novel tells the story of Jeanie Deans, whose sister, Effie, has been accused of murdering the child she had out of wedlock and who sits in the "Heart of Mid-Lothian" awaiting her fate. Jeanie can free her sister on a legal technicality if she perjures herself in court, but she ultimately does not. Instead, after her sister is sentenced, she undertakes a voyage on foot to London to gain a pardon for her sister from the queen, where the eventual overturning of the judicial decision mirrors the overturning of the coach at the novel's opening that led to its being written down in the first place. The overturned case, in both cases, leads to a new narrative reordering of existing documents. Upon being freed, Jeanie's sister will once again disappear, as the novel continues to rehearse two different forms of being "wayward."

In chapter 2, volume 2, Jeanie responds to a written communiqué that requests her to meet her sister's seducer, George Staunton, late one night at Muschat's Cairn in St. Leonard's Chase. We are told in the novel that this enclosed space is also crucially a storied space, [. . .] and while there are numerous legends that belong to this space, the Cairn in particular is named after Nicol Muschat, who brutally murdered his wife. "With all of these legends Jeanie Deans was too well acquainted, to escape that strong impression which they usually make on the imagination" (*HM*, 135). [. . . I]t is the natural setting in Scott that is denoted by the presence and power of such oft-repeated tales. Landscape is marked as a narrative archive. [. . . T]he conversation between Jeanie and her interlocutor will revolve around the status and the utility of what one has been told [(*HM*, 140–1)]. [. . .] In distinction to the very tales that make a "strong impression" on Jeanie in this cavernous landscape, George Staunton's tale does not make a lasting impression on Jeanie because she has not heard it before ("But I cannot remember that which Effie never told me"). In invoking frames of reference such as "it is in your own hands" or "nothing is so natural," Staunton attempts to reverse the very unnaturalness of facts such as Effie's own act of child-murder at the heart of this dialogue, Muschat's act of murdering his wife that was memorialized where the dialogue occurs, or the prospect of a future dialogue where she will say what she has not been told. Alongside this invocation of ownness at the heart of the confession, Staunton will nevertheless reveal the indirection at the heart of his method ("the blow which the law aims cannot be broken by directly encountering it") – not just indirectly freeing Effie by a legal loophole, but also the use of indirection itself to achieve this end, that is, the control of Jeanie's speech through his own. Staunton's project is not simply to control Jeanie's confession but to control confession itself. "In saying what I have said, you will only speak the simple truth." And yet unlike the oft-repeated tales that make a "strong impression" on Jeanie – that bear some truth value – Staunton's tale is a *novel* statement and therefore must remain untrue.

Staunton's project of trying to control Jeanie's confession, staged of course in the middle of the night in a space of illicit backdrop, is threatening not because of its illegality – the perjury at its heart – but because of its communicative rationale, that it would redefine *confession* as the speech of *someone else*. [. . .]

If we turn to the famous confrontation between Jeanie and the queen in chapters 10 through 12 of volume 3, we see a similar moment of an attempt to control Jeanie's confession, only this time the operation is far more successful (it results in the desired pardon for her sister). In place of Staunton as the directorial figure, it is now the Duke of Argyle who will orchestrate Jeanie's confession, and in place of the Scottish court of law as the site of this confession, it is now the court of the English king to which Jeanie will petition her sister's case. We must remember that the very conditions upon which Jeanie acquires the duke's assistance as a mediating figure in the first place depended on her own capacity to properly utilize mediation. It was only when she presented the document entrusted to her by her fiancé, Butler, which explained the Argyle family's indebtedness to Butler's family, that the effect of her presentation to the duke achieved its desired goal. In repayment for being entrusted with this document, Jeanie will perform another act of mediation in return by writing in Butler's Bible (*HM*, 247).

In response to this media performance, the duke agrees to arrange an audience with the queen, who refers to herself as a "medium": "Your Grace is aware, that I can only be the medium through which the matter is subjected to his Majesty's superior wisdom" (*HM*, 334). The mediality of the queen is the further continuation of *all* of the characters' mediality in this scene, as both Jeanie and the duke function, each in their own way, as media (to which one could add the queen's attendant, Lady Suffolk, who was then sleeping with the king but was also the former lover of Argyle). "Now I have done for you," says the duke to Jeanie,

> what I would certainly not have done to serve any purpose of my own – I have asked an audience of a lady whose interest with the king is deservedly very high. It has been allowed me, and I am desirous that you should see her and speak for yourself. You have no occasion to be abashed; tell your story simply as you did to me.
>
> (*HM*, 328)

Yet the duke will continue:

> Just say what you think is likely to make the best impression – look at me from time to time – if I put my hand to my cravat so – (shewing her the motion) – you will stop; but I shall only do this when you say anything that is not likely to please.

To which Jeanie replies, "But, sir, your Grace, if it wasna ower muckle trouble, wad it na be better to tell me what I should say, and I could get it by heart?" "No Jeanie," the duke concludes, "that would not have the same effect."

Who is the medium here? The duke arranges the connection ("I have asked an audience of a lady") but also orchestrates the performance ("look at me from time to time"). Jeanie is merely the vehicle for her sister's case, but she is supposed to speak *from* the heart, not *by* heart ("tell your story as simply as you did to me"). The success of the performance depends, as it will for the queen who will communicate it further to the king and as it did for Jeanie's handling of someone else's document to gain the queen's audience in the first place, on the delicate balance between mediation and originality, saying someone else's story *as though it were your own.* It depends, in other words, on the delicate balance of the "by heart" and the "from the heart." In place of George Staunton's "In saying what I have said, you will only speak the simple truth," we have the duke's assurance to Jeanie's question, "wad it na be better to tell me what I should say, and I could get it by heart?": "No Jeanie, that would not have the same effect." In moving from Staunton to the duke, from the Cairn to the Court, we are always moving in the direction of increasing direction, but such direction is always still fundamentally coupled in *The Heart of Mid-Lothian* with the art of indirection. Only in this way [. . .] will one's listeners be moved to "collection": in both the sense of giving alms for such a narrative performance and in terms of becoming a collective. It is this particular type of media performance that will result in both financial reward for the author and the generation of a reading public.

In exchange for her performance of mediation as origination, Jeanie will be rewarded with "a little pocket-book" (*HM*, 343). James Chandler has identified this scene as a paramount example of the romantic investment in the "case" as the essential genre of historiographical discourse, to which Scott's historical novels become some of the most important narrative contributions [. . .].[29] But rather than see the case here as a representation of a more universal notion of the case, I want to unpack this object in Scott in a more literal and material sense, to look inside, as it were, what is actually there on the page. [. . .] When Jeanie writes in Butler's Bible, she is highlighting the way writing in books at the turn of the nineteenth century continued to play a crucial role in establishing a network of reciprocal obligations through books, nowhere more prevalent than in "little pocket-books." When the queen gives Jeanie this book in which we later learn she has inscribed her own name, "Caroline," she is not only participating in a popular nineteenth-century bibliographic practice, she is also drawing attention to the complex mixture of sharing and owning that surrounded such medial practices of inscription.

When we turn to the inside of the book as case, we see how the contents correspond to the container in which they appear. Inside the pocket-book we find, along with the queen's inscription, the "usual assortment of silk and needles" and "a bank-bill for fifty pounds." To put it more abstractly but no less suggestively, what we find inside the book is handwriting (the inscription), printed writing (the bill), and the tools for producing texts/textiles (the silk and needles). We could organize these symbolic items even more concretely by saying that what this book does that is given in exchange for Jeanie's oral performance is replace the oral performance itself with a written one that is based on the practices of collection (the silk and needles that are used to piece together the textile), circulation (the bank-bill), and *shared* ownership (the inscription).

[. . .T]he exchange of the "little pocket-book" for Jeanie's oral [. . .] models a mode of text-making and text-transmitting that *combined* the principles behind these two regimes and that were associated with the figure of the heart. Jeanie's audience with the queen highlights the profound ways in which speaking *from the heart* was not opposed to, but necessarily incorporated with, speaking *by heart.* Scott's novel dramatized, in other words, the necessary overlap between the practices of preservation, transmission, and attribution that were underwriting the novel's rise to prominence in the nineteenth century.

[. . .]

Notes

1 For a record of Goethe's work, see J.W. Goethe, *Volkslieder in Elsaß aufgezeichnet: Faksimile-Ausgabe*, ed. Louis Pinck (Heidelberg: Elsaß-Lothringische Wissenschaftliche Gesellschaft, 1932).

2 On the translatability of bardic and balladic imaginaries from one local culture to another, see Katie Trumpener, *Bardic Nationalism: The Romantic Novel and the British Empire* (Princeton: Princeton University Press, 1997).

3 See Reinhold Steig, ed., *Achim von Arnim und die ihm nahe standen*, vol. 1 (Stuttgart: Cotta, 1894), 95, where Arnim writes to Brentano during his trip to London in July 1803 about buying a copy of Scott's *Minstrelsy*.

4 For a recent treatment of the ballad's role in the development of romantic poetry, see Steve Newman, *Ballad Collection, Lyric, and the Canon: The Call of the Popular from the Restoration to the New Criticism* (Philadelphia: University of Pennsylvania Press, 2007).

5 See David Wellbery, "Primordial Orality," *The Specular Moment: Goethe's Early Lyric and the Beginnings of Romanticism* (Stanford: Stanford University Press, 1996), 187–221, and Maureen McLane, "Ballads and Bards: British Romantic Orality," *Modern Philology* 98, no. 3 (2001): 423–43.

6 See Maureen McLane, "Tuning the Multi-Media Nation, or, Minstrelsy of the Afro-Scottish Border ca. 1800," *European Romantic Review* 15, no. 2 (June 2004): 289–305.

7 Steve Newman, *Ballad Collection, Lyric, and the Canon*, 185.

8 Susan Stewart, "Notes on Distressed Genres," *The Journal of American Folklore* 104 (1991): 5–31.

9 "However he was placed, however he was dated, the minstrel raised methodological problems of dating and placing." Maureen McLane, "The Figure Minstrelsy Makes: Poetry and Historicity," *Critical Inquiry* 29, no. 3 (2003): 429–52, at 434.

10 Franco Moretti writes that Scott's historical novels produce a "phenomenology of the border." Franco Moretti, *Atlas of the European Novel, 1800–1900* (London: Verso, 1998), 35. [. . .]

11 See Katie Trumpener, *Bardic Nationalism*; Fiona Robertson, *Legitimate Histories: Scott, Gothic, and the Authorities of Fiction* (Oxford: Clarendon, 1994); Ian Duncan, *Modern Romance and Transformations of the Novel: The Gothic, Scott, and Dickens* (Cambridge: Cambridge University Press, 1992); and Ina Ferris, "From 'National Tale' to 'Historical Novel': Edgeworth, Morgan and Scott," in *The Achievement of Literary Authority: Gender, History and the Waverley Novels* (Ithaca: Cornell University Press, 1991), 105–36.

12 Cited in J.G. Lockhart, *Memoirs of the Life of Sir Walter Scott, Bart.*, 9 vols (Boston: Ticknor and Fields, 1861), 2: 39. For discussion of the making of the ballad edition, see Jane Millgate, "The Early Publication History of Scott's Minstrelsy of the Scottish Border," *The Papers of the Bibliographical Society of America* 94, no. 4 (2000): 551–64.

13 Percy writes:

> The word Minstrel is derived from the French Menestrier; and was not in use before the Norman conquest. . . . The Minstrels continued a distinct order of men, and got their livelihood by singing verses to the harp, at the houses of the great.
>
> Thomas Percy, ed., *Reliques of Ancient English Poetry: Consisting of Old Heroic Ballads, Songs, and Other Pieces of our Earlier Poets (Chiefly of the Lyric Kind); Together with some few of later Date*, 3 vols (London: Dodsley, 1765), xv–xvi.

14 In the fourth edition, which was reissued in 1794, Percy writes: "The scene of the finest Scottish Ballads is laid in the South of Scotland; which should seem to have been peculiarly the nursery of Scottish Minstrels" (lii).

15 For a discussion of the difference between Herder's project and later editions of ballads and folksongs, see Max Kommerell, "Das Volkslied und Das Deutsche Lied," *Jahrbuch des freien deutschen Hochstifts* (1922/23): 3–51.

16 The choice of the border assumes even more richness given that a majority of the ballads Scott included in his collection were from the northern regions of Scotland, although we do not know whether Scott was aware of this fact. See David Buchan, *The Ballad and the Folk* (London: Routledge, 1972).

17 Max Kommerell, "Das Volkslied und Das Deutsche Lied," 17.

18 Walter Scott, *Minstrelsy of the Scottish Border*, 2 vols (Kelso: Ballanryne, 1802), 1: 4.

19 [Karl Lachmann, "Vorrede," *Iwein*, 2nd edn (1843), v.]

20 "The term 'legitimate,' therefore, most immediately conjures up the political context of Scott's work, asking what counts as a legitimate history for Britain within the rapidly changing European framework of Scott's time." Fiona Robertson, *Legitimate Histories*, 12.

21 Ina Ferris, *The Achievement of Literary Authority*.

22 Gilles Deleuze and Félix Guattari, *A Thousand Plateaus: Capitalism and Schizophrenia*, trans. Brian Massumi (Minneapolis: University of Minnesota Press, 1987), 84.

23 Albrecht Koschorke, *Körperströme und Schriftverkehr. Mediologie des 18. Jahrhunderts* (München: Fink, 1999).

24 Andrea Henderson, "Centrality and Circulation in *The Heart of Mid-Lothian*," in *Romantic Identities: Varieties of Subjectivity 1774–1830* (Cambridge: Cambridge University Press, 1996), 130–62.

25 Deidre Shauna Lynch, *The Economy of Character: Novels, Market Culture, and the Business of Inner Meaning* (Chicago: University of Chicago Press, 1998).

26 Jane Millgate, *Walter Scott: The Making of the Novelist* (Toronto: University of Toronto Press, 1980), 159.

27 Charlotte Sussmann, "The Emptiness at the Heart of Midlothian: Nation, Narration and Population," *Eighteenth-Century Fiction* 15, no. 1 (2002): 103–26; Caroline McCracken-Flesher, "Narrating the (Gendered) Nation in Scott's *The Heart of Mid-Lothian*," *Nineteenth-Century Contexts* 24, no. 3 (2002): 291–316; David Hewitt, "The *Heart of Mid-Lothian* and the People," *European Romantic Review* 13, no. 3 (2002): 299–309.

28 Walter Scott, *The Heart of Mid-Lothian*, Edinburgh Edition of the Waverley Novels, eds David Hewitt and Alison Lumsden (Edinburgh: Edinburgh University Press, 2004), 14. Parenthetical citations in this section are to this edition.

29 James Chandler, *England in 1819: The Politics of Literary Culture and the Case of Romantic Historicism* (Chicago: University of Chicago Press, 1998), 304–5.

43 If this is Enlightenment then what is Romanticism?

Clifford Siskin and William Warner

[. . .]

[. . .] With [Immanuel] Kant's essay ["What is Enlightenment?"], a conversation started that has now dominated inquiries into Enlightenment for over 200 years.[1] And much of that conversation for those *centuries* has entailed, per [Francis] Bacon, *repeating* the question: What is Enlightenment? What was Enlightenment? What's left of Enlightenment? We've learned much, including the fact that asking that question again, and yet again, turns Enlightenment into a *problem* – into something that is guilty from the get-go of being hard to find and easy to judge. And the more times we pose the question, the more the mystery deepens: "When did Enlightenment occur?" "Where did it occur?" "Did it really occur at all?" If we go cold turkey and stop the repetition, we can, with the help of our new databases, identify the early 1730s as the moment of the first clustering articulation of the term and concept of Enlightenment in Britain, France, and Germany, as well as growing testimony to a sense at the time of a new kind of knowledge environment. We argue that by the time Kant wrote his essay in 1784, his formulation of a self that dares to know – that has the courage to use – as he emphasized – its own understanding – is less a description of Enlightenment than a product of it.

To provide a sense of what's at stake in making this claim, we contrast the ways that Francis Bacon and Kant use the word "machine." To push his readers into taking the dare to know, Kant ends "What is Enlightenment?" with a before-and-after of what they will become: if they use their own reason, "men" will be "more than machines" (Kant 2007, 37). This binary – man vs. machine – became, of course, a staple of modernity, and thus a barrier to our thinking of Enlightenment in terms that precede Kant's ideal of individual, courageous selves – a model for knowing that we still hold dear. In Bacon, those terms are radically different: machines are not what we don't want to be; they are the means for men to do what they should be doing – making "advances worthy of mankind" (Bacon 1994, 8).[2]

Whether moving a "heavy obelisk" or "advancing" knowledge, daring to depend on one's own strength or one's own understanding, as Kant demands, was not courageous in Bacon's view, but an "act of utter lunacy" (Bacon 2000, 28–29). Sanity, for Bacon, then, was accepting the necessity of tools – tools that work. We can't create – at least create very well – on our own. The problem of the "renewal" of knowledge – of why knowledge had stalled and what to do about it – was thus fundamentally for Bacon a problem of "mediation." We use "mediation" here in its broadest sense as shorthand for the work done by tools, by what we would now call "media" of every kind – everything that intervenes, enables, supplements, or is simply in-between – emphasizing the Baconian stipulation that media of some kind are always at work.

By casting knowledge as necessarily mediated, Bacon found a way to identify and articulate change: mediation was always necessary but the forms of mediation differ over time. There *is* a history of mediation. "Mediation," we want to emphasize, is the *inclusive* term for the history we propose; it can include what we now call "media," but [. . .] it is not restricted to them. The history of mediation can thus engage "media history" and "media theory," but its wide range of objects, forms, technologies, agency, and interactions – and thus its chronological scope – differentiates it from both of those established enterprises.

So how can we put Romanticism into this history [. . .]? Our strategy is to do some mediating of our own: not just in number – putting our two heads together with many others – but in kind. Genres change by mixing with *other* genres, so let's fill up this plenary with other forms, starting with one that many of us have read, and even taught, but rarely use. If you clicked on our title on the Conference website, you would have seen this tractate: *see Figure 43.1* [. . .].

A tractate is a form that "handles" a particular topic, one that manages it in a particular way. For William Blake, it was a particularly useful form for manhandling what he saw as an intellectual bad habit of the late eighteenth century: natural religion. We've updated it here to provide the means of managing a bad habit of our own – the tendency to naturalize Romanticism: to be Romantic rather than to put Romanticism into history. The message of our parody is that there's no need to go into rehab: the remedy is not to change ourselves – that's exactly what Romantic discourse prescribes – but to change our histories.

Turning to a history of mediation, allows us to bring very different kinds of questions to the problem of periodization. In the case of Enlightenment, we have to ask "how do we describe an event?" In the case of Romanticism, the central question is "how do we describe the condition of being *after* an event?" *This Is Enlightenment* provides a detailed framework for answering the first question. For each of three chronological markers for the event, we engage a particular kind of change:

1   To map the "delay" between Bacon's formulations in the early seventeenth century and the conventional start of Enlightenment in the 1730s/40s we project a historical hierarchy of mediations. It is historical in that it highlights certain forms of mediation as not inherently "better" but as enabling – in particular times and particular places – of others. We call those mediations cardinal mediations.

2   To identify Enlightenment as a chronologically specific "event" – one that conventionally occupies roughly a half century between the 1730s/40s and the 1780s – we take a quantitative turn, focusing on the number as well as the kinds of mediation enabled by the early eighteenth century. Enlightenment emerged, we argue, as an effect of mediations proliferating and coalescing.

3   To understand how that event came to an end – and why it was at that same moment retroactively labeled by Kant's subject – we couple the concept of saturation to proliferation. The Enlightenment, we argue, can be best understood not as failed, or interrupted by revolution or Romanticism, but as an event that was "successful" in two ways. First, it performed as our label for it advertises: Enlightenment mediations produced change. Second, in detailing the effects of

---

All Histories Are Not One OR There Is A History of Mediation

I The title of this Conference ["Romantic Mediations"] tells us, at least grammatically, that some mediations are Romantic and others are not.

II To the extent that "Romantic" references temporality, "Romantic Mediations" needs a *"history of mediation"* – everything is always already mediated, but the forms of mediation change.

III Since mediation embraces both the technological and the human – it does not discriminate between any particular form of agency – the *history of mediation* steers us clear of the unproductive binaries of the "technodeterminism" debate. (Print technology and Samuel Johnson are both forms of mediation.)

IV The *history of mediation* turns instead to how mediations of all kinds interact. Because they can be more easily pinned down to particular times and places than "ideas," we can track mediations more accurately – and thus more readily identify changes in their interactions.

V The *history of ideas*, like classical physics, gets its stories wrong when it tries to scale too far up or too far down. Our narratives and anthologies record those stumbles as "periods." ("Enlightenment," for example, has been either one idea extended across thousands of years, as in the Frankfort School version, or it has been fragmented into multiple Enlightenments, each one tied to different ideas and/or different locations [e.g., "Radical Enlightenment" or "Scottish Enlightenment."])

VI The *history of mediation*, like post-classical physics, foregrounds the notion of an "event" to clarify contingencies of time, place, and scale.

VII In science, an event is a single coordinate in the fabric of four-dimensional spacetime; the "universe" is mapped as "just the set of all events – every point in space, at every moment of time."

VIII In the *history of mediation*, an event is a singularity in a multidimensional fabric of mediation; the past is mapped as the set of events that are the effects, not the products, of those mediations.

IX The relationship of "effect," by foregrounding contingency of time and place, admits the multiplicity and specificity of that contingency without sacrificing both to the reductive linearity of causality.

APPLICATION. "Enlightenment is an event in the history of mediation" (*This Is Enlightenment*, Chicago, 2010).

CONCLUSION. When the "Study of Romanticism" focuses on ideas and themes, the "Romantic" becomes as we are, so that we may be as it was. In order not to repeat the same dull round over again, "Romantic Mediations" requires a *history of mediation* that links mediations to each other, to the events they effect, and to the effects that one event has on what follows. (We are here focusing upon the specific ways an event ends (Enlightenment) – i.e., how something e-vents, "comes out" – and how the outcome of one event mediates what follows. At stake is the problem of change: on a local scale, how to describe the continuities and discontinuities between Enlightenment and the Romantic; on a larger scale, how to establish a hierarchy of change.)

Figure 43.1 An abstract in the form of an argument

saturation on key mediations, we show how Enlightenment contained the formal conditions for its own demise: in a strange way, it succeeded in ending itself.

We won't test your patience here by reciting detailed analyses of these kinds of mediations, but here's a very brief sampling. The cardinal mediations include changes in infrastructure, genres and formats, associational practices, and protocols:

- *Infrastructure,* for example, entails the formation of the postal system, including the setting of uniform postal rates, the development of fixed mail routes, and the formation of private trusts to fund and administer the turnpikes. In addition to new tools for mediating motion, the second half of the seventeenth century also saw new forms for gathering in one place, including the number and kinds of public houses from inns to coffee houses.

- New *genres and formats* were developed that extended the reach of print and speech and enabled more of both. These became the "content" for the new infrastructures: the newspapers not only provided much of the discourse that circulated through the new infrastructure of the post and turnpike and coffee houses, they also became a new interface for mediating the users' knowledge of events, opinions, and even the speech of public figures.

- New infrastructure and new genres and formats became crucial to the promotion of new *associational practices*. The Enlightenment emerged in part from the creation of a remarkable number and variety of voluntary associations, each promoting a distinctive discourse: from political gatherings (like the Whig Kit Kat club) and secret societies (like the Freemasons) to scientific corresponding societies, political committees of correspondence, and gendered intellectual clubs.

- New *protocols* also emerged to underwrite the infrastructure, genres, formats, and associational practices we describe. Protocols are enabling constraints: the rules, codes, and habitual practices that help to secure the channels, spaces, and means of production and communication. They control for the sake of growth. We address, in particular, the postal principle, public credit, and the regime of copyright.

The "magazines" that first proliferated in Britain during the 1730s, such as *The Gentleman's Magazine* founded by Edward Cave in 1731, exemplify how these cardinal mediations then enabled the proliferation of other kinds of mediations. As "storehouses" of previously printed materials, magazines were literally filled with the output of the mediations described above, including the newspaper and the periodical and the new clubs and coffeehouses in which they circulated. What the scope and gathering intensity of all of these proliferations demonstrate is that the mediations we describe had not only enabled many new forms of mediation; they had also added a new dimension to the very act of mediation itself. With new channels and stopping places for new genres and formats to circulate through new social matrices sustained by new protocols, possibilities and expectations for what mediation could accomplish changed. The very medium of mediation – its architecture of forms and tools, people and practices – became load-bearing. On this new *platform,* each individual act came to be understood – and the result deployed – as working not only in its own terms, but as a part of a cumulative, collaborative, and ongoing enterprise.

What emerged, that is, was the experience of Enlightenment as a historical event – an event *in* the history of mediation. And what happened after that event, happened *on* that platform. The relationship of the Romantic period to Enlightenment is that of an eventuality to an event: Romanticism took shape as a contingent possibility, a coming to terms with what had just happened *in* the terms that event had platformed – had turned into a platform.

The American Revolution offers a particularly useful example of the event of Enlightenment becoming a platform for Romantic eventualities. Yes, the American Revolution not the French. With good reason, given the impact of events in France on Britain, Romanticists have habitually gazed across the Channel in their efforts to make sense of Romanticism. But underwriting the many valuable results has been an assumption about the nature of the political: that we can best use it in order to map British politics into "radicals" and "conservatives." We argue, however, that if one turns from ideas to mediations, one finds that it was the communications innovations of the American Whigs as they coalesced during the American Revolution that became a new platform for the very practice of politics in Britain.

This new politics of change was grounded in the cardinal mediations we have described. It began with a new associational practice. In the fall of 1772, the Town of Boston appointed the first standing committee of correspondence. This committee and the many committees that followed were based in town, county, and provincial government, but because they were "standing committees," that is, committees that convene at any time and on their own authority, they separated themselves from the instituted hierarchies of Royal government. The main activity of these committees was to write: to each other and to the public. To do this, the Boston committee also invented a new genre, the popular declaration. There are two decisive features of this genre. First, they incorporate two elements of the ancient petition of authority: a statement of rights and a list of grievances (violations of those rights). But the declaration was not, like the petition, written with humility toward an addressee whose authority the petition gracefully affirmed: Royal Governor, King or Parliament. Instead, the declaration was addressed to "the people" in a bold and fearless tone. The change of the direction of address in the rewriting of the petition as a declaration – from vertical to horizontal, from up to out – carried revolutionary potential.

What made this public address possible were the infrastructure of a post and the public and open formats of public print: newspaper, pamphlet, and broadside. Second, the popular declarations observe certain protocols: of legal procedure, of corporate action, of public access, of a systematic and general address to the people, and of evidencing virtuous initiative. Between 1772 and 1776, Whig committees wrote and distributed literally hundreds of declarations. While each declaration offered its own remix of Whig political ideas, the binding effect of these declarations came from the common protocols they observed. And, crucially, that binding effect produced a new associational practice: a *network* of American Whigs that successfully acted together in opposing the measures of the King, Whitehall, and Parliament.

While the committee had written declarations that had used the first person plural, "we," it was the transformation of number into network that gave the "we" the operational power to make revolution. The successful scaling up of this network was signaled by what happened in the weeks before 4 July 1776. The group that had formed to resist administration and Parliament morphed into a new institution of government. Separation from Britain became operationally possible.

We describe the Revolution in this way and in these terms for a very specific purpose: to develop a high-contrast picture of the roles ideas play in the history of ideas versus the history of mediation. In the history of ideas, ideas themselves are seen as operational. The revolutions in North America, France, and Haiti have thus been portrayed primarily as wellsprings of ideas – of the modern value of critiquing authority; of liberty, equality, and popular sovereignty; and of a distinctly modern experimental and optimistic orientation toward the future. These ideas are either granted their own agency or put into the hands of agents – heroic subjects who change the world.[3] Foregrounding mediation offers a fundamental revision of this picture.

It is the open media-communications of British America that is the condition of the possibility of the public resistance to British rule in America; it is the committee of correspondence that launches the decisive critique of instituted systems of authority; it is the new genre of the popular declaration that gives the ideas of liberty, equality, and popular sovereignty articulate force; and it is the inter-colonial Whig network of committees that pulls off an experimental and optimistic orientation toward the future by forming a committee of committees, the Continental Congress, which organized the colonies in its struggle with Britain, and eventually evolve into the United States.

The American Revolution became, in a sense, an operating system for Romantic political change in Britain. The operational success of the American Revolution meant that by 1780 – even before the end of the war – its innovations in communication could serve as a platform for the Association movements that begin in Ireland and England and received new force in the wake of the start of the French Revolution. These include the formation of committees, the writing of declarations, the observation in both meetings and declarations of the five protocols of legal procedure, corporate action, public access, a systematic address to the people, performed to evidence virtuous initiative. Finally, these committees seek to associate so that they can become a dispersed network that can act together.

Our turn to the Revolution that has been less central to the study of Romanticism – the American rather than the French – and our focus in turning to that Revolution on how specific cardinal mediations coalesced into an operational platform are strategies with a twofold purpose. First, we're trying to get us and you used to thinking about the Romantic as something that comes after: an eventuality that comes after an event. Second, by specifying that this is an event in the history of mediation, we are trying to highlight what we see as the advantages of that history versus our conventional histories of ideas. Given the time that we're spending [. . .] on mediation, we don't want to be accused of mounting a straw-man argument against the history of ideas. So just as we turned back to Bacon and Kant to make our argument about the history of mediation, let's take a moment to put the history of ideas *into* history.

We can take advantage here of recent work on historiography, especially Pomata and Siraisi's *Historia: Empiricism and Erudition in Early Modern Europe* (2005). This remarkable volume forcefully reminds us of the importance of understanding "history" as consisting historically of different kinds with different functions – history is, that is, a genre that, like all genres, is always already mixed. And those mixtures of features and uses change over time. *Historia* is extraordinarily helpful in its tracking of the genre's shifting mix of the empirical and the chronological. The volume as a whole demonstrates in detail that it was not until the late eighteenth century that temporality "moved" to the "core" of history. Many kinds of histories were simply not concerned with the passage of time. As late as 1771, *Encyclopædia Britannica* defined "history" as "a description or recital of things as they are, or have been" (*Encyclopædia Britannica* 788).

Notice that "have been" – the past tense – is only an option. In the last decades of the eighteenth century, that began to change as the primary use of historia moved from the plural to a collective singular – a singularity that was energized by the notion that " 'history' might itself have a 'story.' " The playing out of this self-reflexivity brackets the Romantic period, from the stadial conceptions of civil society, with its built-in story of stages that surfaced in late eighteenth-century Scotland to the large-scale teleological and dialectical epics of Hegel and Marx in the second quarter of the nineteenth century.

As history's own stories of historical change stretched temporally and geographically from local reports on things as they *are* to universalizing tales of things as they *were*, are, and must become, gaps in the narratives were filled in two primary ways. "Ideas," which had been, in Donald Kelley's words, "rational and universally valid concepts independent of time," became, in the context of these new kinds of history, things that "lived in time" – and thus capable of explaining how times changed.[4] In retrospect, all that was necessary to give us that most familiar form of modem history – the "history of ideas" – was a companion for this new form of life: a subject capable of generating and carrying ideas forward *in* time.

That developmental subject – a subject now defined and made deep by the capacity to change *over* time – advertised its newly intimate relationship with ideas in a wide range of genres, from the philosophical – as in Kant's "dare to know" "motto" for Enlightenment – to the lyric forms *we* Romanticists know so well.[5] But here's where the history of ideas is deeply implicated in Romanticism itself. We've known for some time that there's something funny in the fact the essay so many of us use to periodize Enlightenment – based on Kant's claim that Enlightenment was in process – appeared at the very moment that we think Enlightenment ended and the Romantic period began. The answer that we argue in detail in *This Is Enlightenment* is that Kant's daring subject was *not* in need of Enlightenment; it was the *product* of Enlightenment. By 1784, the year of Kant's famous essay, man had already become, in Bacon's terms, a new kind of tool – a tool whose power after so many Enlightenment mediations now lay in its insistence on using its own understanding to change itself.

This embodiment of agency – what we know as the Romantic subject – is, from the perspective offered by the history of mediation, *the self on the platform of Enlightenment*. Let us say that again: the Romantic subject is the self on the platform of Enlightenment. As it used that platform as a bully pulpit *for* itself, the hegemony of agency over history – the assumption that history was something that told of causal relationships between past and present – was secured. And the history of ideas became the dominant form of this causal history as its narratives came, during the Romantic period, to be driven by two kinds of persons: personifications of ideas themselves, such as "liberty" and "capitalism," and individuals whose own, daring ideas changed history: Marx and Carlyle. And that's exactly the shape our own literary histories of that time have taken: an "ism" – "Romanticism" – of daring individuals.

Variations on the history of ideas can't solve the problem of historicizing Romanticism because it is itself Romantic. The history of mediation provides us with distance now even as it helps us to reassess the proximity back then of Romanticism to Enlightenment: the Romantic is about the condition of being after an event – about what happens after the coalescing of a new operational platform. To grasp what it means to think of the Romantic as being on that platform, just visit Wordsworth and Coleridge trying to decide what to do with themselves during the 1790s. The "what" turned out to be the easy part – almost a given: "to deliver upon authority a system of philosophy," a task that Coleridge later simply referred to as "what I have been all my life doing."[6] Philosophical system-making, of course, was exactly what the Enlightenment had been doing. The real choice was how to mediate that effort so that it could be delivered with maximum authority in a crowded marketplace. The answer was to mediate through generic change – to switch from prose to verse. When, years later, Hazlitt singled out Wordsworth's "genius" as a "pure emanation of the Spirit of the Age," the pedestal he put him on was that same platform: Wordsworth's "genius," Hazlitt claimed, was "to compound a new system of poetry." Being on an operational platform makes new kinds and compounding of mediations possible. Everything can and does operate differently; even when you're trying to repeat, you can't. Enlightenment proceeded in different ways . . . and this is Romanticism.

Let's be as clear as possible about what is at stake here. We don't need a history of mediation to tell us what came chronologically first. But chronology is just the start. What are we sequencing? What are the things that change in that sequence? Are all changes on the same scale? In the histories of ideas, Enlightenment and Romanticism are periods, and periods are marked by changes in ideas, and – with ideas as the common denominator across periods – the issue of a hierarchy of changes just doesn't come up. And that has kept the peace between period specialists: we can all make equal claims of difference from each other – Victorian as different from Romantic as Romantic from Enlightenment.

The big irony here is that the flip side of idea-based periods is that assumptions of difference easily collapse into claims of continuity or of outright *a*historicity, especially when, for example, our favorite ideas appear to pop up at different times. Let's mix another genre into this talk – the thought experiment – to help us to visualize this problem: *see Figure 43.2* [. . .].

A history of mediation does not ignore ideas but adds another dimension to our encounter with them. Instead of engaging them in the standard terms of representation and interpretation: it always asks, "In what?" How are they always already mediated? And if the history of mediation points to an event where the outcome is on the scale of a new operational platform, as we have just described, then we can begin to talk about the elephant in the room: some of the changes that we have been using to mark periods are bigger than other changes. And the difference in scale and scope can and should alter how we understand the periods themselves.

So let's acknowledge the elephant in the room: all changes and thus all periods are *not* one. If this is Enlightenment scaled to a hierarchy of change [*open hands wide*] then this is Romanticism [*open hands not as wide*]. Enlightenment is an event, Romanticism is an eventuality, and the Victorian is a variation. This is *not* a judgment of how important the study of any of these periods should be to any of us. Depending on when we're working and to what ends, attention to any one of these kinds can be equally or more valuable. Let's put this concluding point in compact and practical terms.

From the vantage point of the long history of mediation, not all periods have the same purchase upon change. If one scales up – scaling up being a challenge felt across all of the disciplines today – from decades, with which we usually divide periods, to centuries, and if one focuses on one axis of the history of mediation – changes in the technium, the domain of tools – one can discern two first-order transformations over the past few hundred years in the West. First, what we are calling the event of Enlightenment saw the coalescing of a new operational platform from mediations that had first appeared during the Renaissance. This entailed the formation of what we now call print cultures – societies saturated by what Raymond Williams called "writing," his shorthand for the forms and practices of writing, silent reading, and print. The momentum of that change, one that was crucial to the formation of literary study, has extended through every subsequent period to the present day. At the same

---

Can Periodization Be Aperiodic?

According to the Physics arXiv Blog of 25 March 2010:

> the problem of tiling a plane has fascinated builders and mathematicians alike since time immemorial. At first glance, the task is straightforward: squares, triangles, hexagons all do the trick producing well known periodic structures. Ditto any number of irregular shapes and combinations of them. A much trickier question is to ask which shapes can tile a plane in a pattern that does not repeat. . . . The problem of finding a single tile that can do the job is called the einstein problem; nothing to do with the great man but from the German for one – "ein" – and for tile – "stein." But the search for an einstein has proved fruitless. Until now.

> The solution required quite literally thinking out of the box – allowing the tile a 3D shape.
>   [. . .]
> Claiming no value beyond the heuristic, what if we thought of our history-making as tiling the past with periods? So many of our efforts would point to the same problem of repetition – of the various ways our laying out of periods has turned out to be periodic. Think of how many histories have been constructed of Aristotle and Plato tiles. Think of how many histories find themselves finding modernity in earlier periods (e.g., the modern self is Shakespearean). In fact, it's hard to think of a kind of period that doesn't repeat – that is aperiodic. So let's take a clue from the einstein solution: what dimensions can we bring to our tiling that will get the job of difference done? [Hint from Siskin and Warner: how would attention to medium and mediation change the shape of our histories?]

Figure 43.2 An abstract in the form of a thought experiment

time, starting with the electronic telegraph in the fourth decade of the nineteenth century, electronic tools began to take hold, but their transformative power did not coalesce until they became computable – that is, uploaded onto a new operational platform in the late twentieth century.

Now, for the first time since the Enlightenment, many of the institutions that started back then – modern disciplines and their departments, schools and universities, libraries and galleries, clubs and learned societies, journals and presses – all find themselves experiencing the vertigo of being *up* on a new load-bearing platform. That's why a group of us have joined together to pursue what we see as a historic opportunity: the opportunity to play a role in the transformation of our Enlightenment inheritance. The Re:Enlightenment Project is using the history we presented to you tonight as a map of mediations past and present – a guide to how, like the Romantics, to find our way into and through the aftermath of an event. To figure out what runs on the new operating system, we are recovering and remediating associational practices, by conducting protocoled exchanges, and repurposing genres, including the declarations that will make up a sister genre to this talk: *The Re:Enlightenment Report*. [. . .]

Notes

1 We quote from Lewis White Beck's translation of "Was ist Aufklärung," originally published in *Foundations of the Metaphysics of Morals,* but now conveniently reprinted together with Foucault's lectures on *Kant and Enlightenment* in Foucault, *The Politics of Truth.* Hereafter cited as Kant (2007).

2 [We have used two different translations of Bacon (1994 and 2000) to help us best capture what we understand to be the meaning and force of his arguments. For the full version of our argument about Bacon and Kant, see *This Is Enlightenment.*]
3 For an influential example of the intellectual history of the American Revolution, see Bailyn (1967); for an example of blending intellectual history with founder studies, see Wills (1978).
4 Donald R. Kelley, "Between History and System," in Pomata and Siraisi (2005: 231).
5 See Siskin (1988: 3–36).
6 Coleridge (1971–2001: 14.2: 177).

References

Bacon, Sir Francis. *Novum Organon with Other Parts of The Great Instauration.* Trans. and eds P. Urbach and J. Gibson. Chicago: Open Court, 1994. Print.

Bacon, Sir Francis. *The New Organon.* Eds L. Jardine and M. Silverthorne. Cambridge Texts in the History of Philosophy. Cambridge: Cambridge UP, 2000. Print.

Bailyn, Bernard. *The Ideological Origins of the American Revolution.* Cambridge, MA: Harvard UP, 1967. Print.

Coleridge, Samuel Taylor. *Table Talk.* Ed. Carl Woodring. 2 vols. Vol. 14 of *The Collected Works of Samuel Taylor Coleridge.* Ed. Kathleen Coburn. 16 vols. Bollingen Series. Princeton and London: Princeton UP and Routledge, 1971–2001. Print.

Encyclopædia Britannica; or, a dictionary of arts and sciences, compiled upon a new plan . . . Illustrated with one hundred and sixty copperplates. By a Society of Gentlemen in Scotland. 3 vols. Edinburgh: Macfarquhar, 1771. Print.

Kant, Immanuel. "Was Ist Aufklärung?" *The Politics of Truth.* Eds Sylvere Lotringer and Lysa Hochroth. New York: Semiotext(e), 2007. Print.

Pomata, Gianna and Nancy G. Siraisi, eds. *Historia: Empiricism and Erudition in Early Modern Europe. Transformations: Studies in the History of Science and Technology.* Ed. Jed Z. Buchwald. Cambridge: MIT P, 2005. Print.

Siskin, Clifford. *The Historicity of Romantic Discourse.* New York: Oxford UP, 1988. Print.

Siskin, Clifford and William Warner, eds. *This Is Enlightenment.* Chicago: U of Chicago P, 2010. Print.

Wills, Garry. *Inventing America: Jefferson's Declaration of Independence.* New York: Viking, 1978. Print.

44 Romantic long poems in Victorian anthologies

Tom Mole

In 1867, Charles Mackay published *A Thousand and One Gems of English Poetry*. This anthology went through twenty-three editions by the end of the century. Its depiction of poems as gems – small, attractive, and timelessly valuable – was a common trope among nineteenth-century literary anthologies. I have counted over thirty with the word 'gems' in the title. It suggests the premium placed on short forms in the anthologies, and their dedication to lyrics above all. This raises a problem for the anthologies' handling of Romantic poetry, since many of the most famous Romantic poems are long, narrative, or even epic. The problem here was not thematic, but formal. Even if the subjects and ideas of Romantic poetry continued to appeal to Victorian readers, there was a mismatch between the formats in which that poetry originally appeared – usually as individual poetry volumes – and the formats in which poetry from earlier periods mostly circulated to wide audiences in the later nineteenth century – in giftbooks, annuals and anthologies. This chapter investigates how Victorian anthologies handled book-length Romantic poems, using examples by Lord Byron, Felicia Hemans, and Percy Shelley.

I base my arguments on a corpus of 210 literary anthologies, published in Britain between 1822 (when Shelley died) and the end of the century, and now in the British Library. There were certainly other literary anthologies published in Britain in this seventy-eight-year period, but these books provide a substantial sample. Having identified the corpus, I examined each of the 210 books, with the help of student assistants, and recorded information about each poem, or extract from a poem, by Byron, Hemans, or Shelley that appeared in them. The resulting database is a powerful research tool. It contains details of 210 anthologies, containing 1055 poems or extracts from Byron, 554 from Hemans and 402 from Shelley. These data allow us to see which sections of long poems were anthologised. Developing a variant on the 'distant reading' advocated by Franco Moretti, this approach nonetheless involves careful examination of the volumes in the corpus, attention to textual variants, and close reading of the anthologies' paratexts (Moretti 2005, 2009). It is therefore a contribution to what scholars like Martin Mueller (2012) have now begun to call 'scalable reading'.

Anthologists developed several strategies for handling book-length Romantic poems that they could not reprint in their entirety. They often began by dis-embedding the lyrics that had been embedded in long poems. John Wesley Hales introduced his very popular anthology *Longer English Poems* (1872) with a discussion of Walter Scott's poem 'Rosabelle', without once mentioning that these lines were originally part of *The Lay of the Last Minstrel* (1805), where they appeared as one of several lyrics sung by different poets taking part in a competition (Hales 1872: xvii–xxxvii; see also Elfenbein 2009: 186–92). Francis Jeffrey had already excerpted 'Rosabelle' in his review of the *Lay* in the *Edinburgh Review*, where he called it 'one specimen of the songs which Mr. Scott has introduced into the mouths of the minstrels', but in Hales's anthology the lines were treated as a fully independent poem, floating free of their poetic context (Jeffrey 1805: 16).

Similarly, 'Childe Harold's Good Night' (reprinted thirteen times in the anthologies surveyed) and 'The Castled Crag of Drachenfels' (reprinted nine times) were dis-embedded from Byron's *Childe Harold's Pilgrimage*. Two anthologies presented 'The Castled Crag' as addressed to Byron's sister, an assumption for which the poem provides no support (*Poets* 1853: 263–4; Shorter 1861: 202). Four songs were dis-embedded from Hemans' *The Siege of Valencia*: the opening ballad sung by Ximena (reprinted twice), Theresa's song 'Why is the Spanish maiden's grave / So far from her own bright land?' (reprinted once), the nuns' chant beginning 'A sword is on the land' (reprinted twice), and the eight-line funeral hymn beginning 'Calm on the bosom of thy God' (reprinted once). These kinds of embedded lyrics were a common feature of Romantic long poems and some novels and were often reprinted in nineteenth-century anthologies.

In some cases, embedded lyrics had always been understood to be detachable. In *The Siege of Valencia*, the embedded lyrics are typically treated not as extempore effusions by the characters, but as songs they already know. Characters repeatedly draw attention to the particular circumstances in which the song is sung or heard, and the effect of this context on its meaning. Theresa, Ximena's maid, indicates that her song is already well known to her and her mistress when she introduces it with the words 'Rest here, ere you go forth, and I will sing / The melody you love' (V.40–1). The song she sings, 'Why is the Spanish maiden's grave / So far from her own bright land?', which Hemans wrote for the play, has many of the characteristics of Hemans' most popular short poems: it tells the story of a woman's death in a faraway land, as a result of her devotion to her husband and her faith. After hearing the song, Ximena remarks:

> Those notes were wont to make my heart beat quick,
> As at a voice of victory; but to-day
> The spirit of the song is changed, and seems
> All mournful.
>
> (V.86–9)

Ximena acknowledges that the song's current context is only one of its possible contexts. Its meaning is inflected differently when it is heard in different circumstances. *The Siege of Valencia*, then, is self-conscious about how its songs can be detached from the contexts in which they are presented. Even familiar lines, Ximena suggested, gained new dimensions of meaning from this redeployment, because 'The spirit of the song [was] changed' by the circumstances in which it was encountered. When 'Why is the Spanish maiden's grave' was reprinted in the anthology *Lyrical Gems* (1825) under the generic editorial title 'Ballad', with no reference to the play in which it first appeared, the editor was extending an understanding of the poem already implicit in Hemans' verse drama (*Lyrical Gems* 1825: 253–4).

But the anthologies also dis-embedded lyrics that were clearly not presented as detachable from their first publication contexts. 'The Isles of Greece' was reprinted twenty-three times in the volumes surveyed, making it by far the most often-quoted section of *Don Juan*. The anthologies handled 'The Isles of Greece' as though it were a freestanding lyric, abstracted from its poetic context and detached from its specified speaker. In *Don Juan*, Canto Three, Byron spends seventy lines explaining that context, introducing the poem's speaker – 'a sad trimmer' (3.82) – and locating the poem as the utterance of a particular man, at a specified time in his life, occupying a particular social situation, in a stated location, for a particular audience, and with a specific set of (mixed) motives. Jerome McGann (2002) has argued that the poem's speaker blends elements of Robert Southey and Byron himself, creating a complex, layered, mobile and self-conscious poetic utterance. In the anthologies, however, this careful specification of the poem's speaking voice and the occasion of its utterance were sheared off. Lyric abstraction was not an inherent property of 'The Isles of Greece', but something ascribed to it by the anthologies' handling of it as, in the words of the *Lyrical Gems'* editor, 'one of the first lyrical compositions of modern times' (461).

Dis-embedding lyrics that had been embedded in long poems provided a paradigm for the anthologies' approach to Romantic long poems more generally. Anthologies extracted sections from long poems and treated them as though they were independent short poems. Examples from Byron include the description of the dying gladiator and the address to the ocean from *Childe Harold*, Canto Four; the description of a thunderstorm from *Childe Harold*, Canto Three; and the lines beginning ''Tis sweet' from *Don Juan*, Canto One. Speeches from plays could also be dis-embedded in this fashion and treated as though they were independent monologues; this happened to Manfred's soliloquy on the Jungfrau on nine occasions in the anthologies surveyed.

When passages that suited their purposes did not exist, editors intervened to create them. Five speeches by the priest Hernandez in Scene Two of Hemans' *The Siege of Valencia* were stitched together into one long monologue in *Lyrical Gems* (84–7). In it, Hernandez tells Elmina how his son deserted Spain's armies to fight for the Moors and how Hernandez later met his son in battle and slew him in ignorance of his identity. In the anthology version, Elmina's interjections were elided, as well as all remarks Hernandez addressed to her directly, including a whole speech of twenty lines. In each elision, the first half of one line was stitched to the second half of another, with the intervening lines silently omitted. In some cases the text was altered to fill up the metre. The editor called the resulting poem 'The Monk's Tale', although Hernandez is not a monk. This synthetic poem is a monologue of eighty-nine lines carved out of 122 lines in the source, a compressed oriental tale in blank verse and a ready-made piece for speech-day declamations.[1] Having been created in *Lyrical Gems*, it was then reprinted in *The Diadem* with identical elisions and variants (*Diadem* 1830: 186–8). In excerpting these sections, anthologists were effectively creating short poems that did not exist before. When several anthologies followed each other in excerpting the same passage from a longer poem and treating it as though it were an independent poem, they collectively reshaped an author's oeuvre, and the canon of English literature as a whole.

The anthologies thus promoted an 'anthological' approach to long poems, which encouraged readers to view them as collections of short highlights connected by more prosaic or undistinguished linking passages (Lethbridge 2000). In this, they followed and extended a Romantic line of thought developed by writers such as Coleridge, who asserted that 'a poem of any length neither can be, nor ought to be, all poetry' (Coleridge 1983: II, 15). Monique Morgan (2009) has shown how nineteenth-century long poems, including *The Prelude* and *Don Juan*, embed suspended moments of lyricism in their narrative form. Literary anthologies gave an independent existence to such lyrical passages. Anthologies treated long poems as collections of short set-pieces, nuggets for extraction, and marginalized poetry that could not be made to conform to anthological modes of presentation and reading.

These modes were displayed in the editors' handling of *Childe Harold's Pilgrimage*, which was consistently popular in the anthologies surveyed. Two thirds of the poem's lines – 67 per cent – were quoted at least once in the anthologies surveyed.[2] The most popular sections of the poem were lyrical passages that combined descriptions of sublime natural phenomena with heightened emotional states: the address to ocean from Canto Four (which appeared forty times in the anthologies surveyed); the thunderstorm from Canto Three (nineteen times); the description of Lake Leman (seventeen times); and the evening reflection from Canto Two beginning ''Tis night, when Meditation bids us feel / We once have loved, though Love is at an end' (sixteen times).

Roughly one third of *Childe Harold*, however, was never quoted in any anthology surveyed.[3] Some of these unquoted lines were apparently censored. Not a single book reprinted Byron's attack on British foreign policy at the Convention of Cintra from Canto One (a section of 144 lines from 315 to 458). His description of Albania from Canto Two was never reprinted, perhaps because of its persistent homoerotic undertones (458 lines from 235 to 692). And part of Byron's reflection on his own fall from grace in Canto Four was also judged to be unsuitable for anthology readers (140 lines from 41 to 180). These preferences and exclusions suggest that the anthologies helped to confirm the centrality of *Childe Harold's Pilgrimage* to Byron's oeuvre, but that in the process they reshaped how new generations of readers would encounter the poem. Readers of the anthologies would be less likely, on the whole, to consider *Childe Harold* as a poem of political, sexual, or social dissent, and more likely to read it as a disjointed series of lyrical or descriptive set-pieces prompted by natural sights.

When the anthologies reprinted parts of *Childe Harold* that dealt with current events, such as Byron's stanzas on the Battle of Waterloo from Canto Three, they minimised their political dimensions. Thirty-five of the anthologies surveyed quote some of the Waterloo section, making it the second most popular section of the poem (after the address to ocean). After its abrupt beginning, 'Stop! – for thy tread is on an Empire's dust!' (3.17), this section of the poem modulates through several phases: it starts with four broadly political stanzas (3.17–20) which oppose the Congress of Vienna's restoration of pre-Revolutionary monarchies ('What! shall reviving Thraldom again be / The patched-up idol of enlightened days? / Shall we, who struck the Lion down, shall we / Pay the Wolf homage?' [3.19]); it then moves on to the ball held by the Duchess of Richmond and the 'mounting in hot haste' as officers rushed from the ball to the battle beginning at Quatre-Bras (3.21–8); it continues with Byron's singling out of Frederick Howard among the fallen (3.29–31); this leads him to reflect on mourning ('the heart will break, yet brokenly live on' [3.32]) and memory ('And this is much, and all which will not pass away' [3.35]); and the whole thirty-stanza section concludes with ten stanzas (3.36–45) sympathetically invoking Napoleon as 'the greatest, nor the worst of men' (3.36). Throughout, the section is scrupulously balanced between the glamour and valour of the soldiers ('Battle's magnificently-stern array' [3.28]) and the sorrow of those who mourn the fallen, between the individual such as Howard and the collective of which he forms a part, and between description of the battle and reflection on its political significance.

This balance and modulation, however, is missing from the anthologies. Most anthologies – twenty-one out of the thirty-five that quoted this section of *Childe Harold* – restricted themselves to eight stanzas or fewer describing the Duchess of Richmond's ball and its sequel: fifteen of the thirty-five began at 'There was a sound of revelry by night' (3.21) and ended at 'Rider and horse, – friend, foe, – in one red burial blent!' (3.28), while a further six quoted a shorter extract from the same eight stanzas. For twenty-one out of the thirty-five anthologies that quoted some of the Waterloo stanzas, then, Byron's treatment of the battle included no political polemic about 'reviving Thraldom', no meditation on mourning, and no mention of Napoleon at all. Nine anthologies did include the four political stanzas that open the Waterloo section, but only one included the stanzas on Napoleon.

Anthologists performed similar surgery on three of Shelley's longer poems: *Queen Mab*, *Alastor*, and *The Cenci*. In each case, the lines most often anthologised from these poems were passages of natural description. With its youthful radicalism and outspoken attacks on religion, monarchy, and contemporary society, *Queen Mab* was especially difficult for anthologists to handle. Its publishers had been successfully prosecuted in the past, and so there were good reasons for editors and publishers to be cautious about excerpting it in anthologies. Nonetheless, extracts from it appeared in eleven books. The most commonly anthologised passage from *Queen Mab* was the opening of Canto Four, which was reprinted eight times. *The Literary Gazette*, in its otherwise very hostile review of 1821, singled this passage out as 'the noblest piece of poetry the author ever imagined' (Anon 1821: 305–8, repr. Barcus 1975: 77). It begins with this description of night:

> How beautiful this night! the balmiest sigh,
> Which vernal zephyrs breathe in evening's ear,
> Were discord to the speaking quietude
> That wraps this moveless scene. Heaven's ebon vault,
> Studded with stars unutterably bright,
> Through which the moon's unclouded grandeur rolls,
> Seems like a canopy which love had spread
> To curtain her sleeping world.

> (4.1–8)

The passage goes on to describe the snowy hills surrounding the speaker, and the castle visible in the distance, 'Whose banner hangeth o'er the time-worn tower / So idly, that rapt fancy deemeth it / A metaphor of peace' (4.13–15). These lines provide the only hint of discord in the scene, in their faint suggestion that only 'rapt fancy' would see the flag as a metaphor of peace, while a more clear-eyed and disenchanted observer would see it as a sign of strife. The speaker then reflects that this scene is one:

> Where musing solitude might love to lift
> Her soul above this sphere of earthliness;

> Where silence undisturbed might watch alone,
> So cold, so bright, so still.

(4.16–19)

Five anthologies stopped there, while another three extended the extract to line 70. As a whole, *Queen Mab* employs what Mark Sandy (2002) calls 'an introduction of fantastical reverie for the narrative's mainstay of religious and political polemic'. Fantastical elements arguably appear throughout the text, alongside the polemic that appears both in the poem's central cantos and in the prose notes on free love, necessity, atheism, Christian dogma, and vegetarianism. The *Literary Gazette* found this passage acceptable, even 'noble', because it bore no trace of Shelley's opinions on these topics. By extracting calm moments such as this description of the night, anthologies inoculated themselves against *Queen Mab's* radical content, protected themselves against prosecution, and reiterated their focus on Shelley's lyrical and descriptive poetry.

Alastor featured in ten of the anthologies surveyed. One quoted the whole poem, but, apparently for reasons of space, elided a section of 132 lines (492–624) describing the Poet's physical decline. The other nine books all excerpted the poem, quoting seven distinct passages, six of which were only included in one or two books. One passage, however, was quoted in five books: a description from the middle of the poem of a well in a shady forest. Four books quoted this whole section (420–68), while one quoted only the last fifteen lines (454–68). In a dense, slow-moving passage of lush description, Shelley enumerates the trees in the wood – the oak, beech, cedar, ash, and acacia – the flowers that grow around them, '[s]tarred with ten thousand blossoms' (440), the intertwining leaves in the canopy, which 'make net-work of the dark blue light of day' (446), and the mossy forest floor '[f]ragrant with perfumed herbs' (450). He then turns to the well, whose liquid surface reflects the forest canopy, the stars twinkling through the branches, the birds asleep in the trees, and the insects of the wood (459–68). Immediately after this passage, the Poet re-enters the poem on his quest, but the anthologies were not concerned with him. Their interest in *Alastor* was in its passages of natural description, especially those that took place in a suspended lyrical present, free from narrative, tension, and decay. In this, they followed some of the poem's first reviewers. *The Eclectic Review* called *Alastor* a 'heartless fiction' that failed 'in accomplishing the legitimate purposes of poetry' but it conceded that '[i]t cannot be denied that very considerable talent for descriptive poetry is displayed in several parts' (*Eclectic* 1816: 391–3, repr. Barcus 1975: 99).

The most anthologised passage from *The Cenci* was also a natural description. Seven anthologies included lines from the play, with some including more than one extract. They quoted six distinct passages. Five of those were only quoted once, but one was quoted five times: a description of a rocky landscape from Act Three (III.i.242–65). Beatrice speaks these lines, describing to Lucretia and Orsino the spot where Count Cenci can be ambushed and killed. Like the passage from *Alastor*, this passage describes a wooded landscape, with 'Cedars, and yews, and pines', and a place of shadows. 'At noonday here / 'Tis twilight, and at sunset blackest night' (264–5). But this landscape is sinister, with a 'mighty rock' (247) which hangs over a gulf 'with terror and with toil' (249), 'Even as a wretched soul hour after hour, / Clings to the mass of life' (252–3). In his preface to *The Cenci*, Shelley singled this passage out as the only one in the play that could be described as 'mere poetry', writing that:

> I have avoided with great care in writing this play the introduction of what is commonly called mere poetry, and I imagine there will scarcely be found a detached simile or a single isolated description, unless Beatrice's description of the chasm appointed for her father's murder should be judged to be of that nature.

Passages of 'isolated description' were something Shelley sought to avoid in *The Cenci*, but they were exactly what the anthologies valued most in his poetry. In *Queen Mab*, *Alastor*, and *The Cenci*, the only passages excerpted in several anthologies were passages of natural description, extracted from their narrative or dramatic contexts. By reprinting these passages, the anthologies acknowledged Shelley's achievement as an author of long poems – even though they reprinted his short lyrics much more often – while insulating their readers against the political radicalism of *Queen Mab*, the 'heartless' poetic quest-narrative of *Alastor*, and the horror and moral complexity of *The Cenci*.

Whether they excerpted the Waterloo stanzas from *Childe Harold*, Canto Three, or the 'Monk's Tale' from *The Siege of Valencia*, or extracted passages of natural description from *Queen Mab*, *Alastor*, or *The Cenci*, the anthologists weren't seeking a manageable part that faithfully represented the whole. Leah Price writes that 'each anthology-piece functions (at least in theory) as a representative synecdoche for the longer text from which it is excerpted' (2000: 68). But all these examples suggest that the approach of nineteenth-century anthologists to Romantic long poems was not fundamentally synecdochic. In extracting these lines from the long poems in which they first appeared, the anthologists sought not a synecdochic excerpt from the longer poem but a standalone substitute for it.

Some sections of *Don Juan* appeared regularly in the anthologies, most notably the embedded lyric 'The Isles of Greece' from Canto Three, but over three-quarters of the poem – 12,500 out of its 16,000 lines – was never quoted in any anthology.[4] The selections that appeared in the anthologies were skewed drastically towards the earlier cantos of the poem, plus some parts of the English cantos (Figure 44.1). Three-quarters of all quotations from *Don Juan* in the anthologies came from the first four cantos. For those nineteenth-century readers who only experienced *Don Juan* through anthologies – and there must have been many who were disinclined to read the poem as a whole because of its length and its reputation for immorality – Juan's adventures in the slave market, the Sultan's harem, the siege of Ismail, and the court (and bed) of Catherine the Great might as well have never been written. The preference for the earlier cantos reflects in part a Victorian aversion to the harder satirical edge and dissenting politics that Byron brought to the poem's later cantos. For most Victorian readers of the anthologies, *Don Juan* ends somewhere in the third canto.

Don Juan resisted extracting at multiple levels, and anthologists had to work hard to contain it within their operating procedures. As well as being highly selective in their treatment of *Don Juan*, the anthologies tended to present the poem in very short gobbets of text. Almost 90 per cent of extracts from the poem consisted of twelve stanzas or less (eighty-eight out of 100). (These figures exclude the embedded lyric 'The Isles of Greece'.) The usual way for a Victorian reader of anthologies to encounter *Don Juan*, then, was in disjointed fragments with little sense of the poem's narrative or its

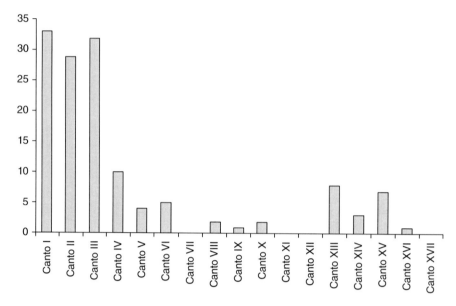

Figure 44.1 Number of extracts from *Don Juan* reprinted in anthologies surveyed, by canto

recurrent concerns. The result was often to make short passages from *Don Juan* read like separate lyrics. One anthology – James Blackwood's *Selections from the Poets* – printed three extracts from *Don Juan*, all less than six stanzas long and appearing in the first four cantos, under the editorial titles 'First Love', 'The Lovers', and 'A Dream'.[5] It did not identify any of the lines as coming from *Don Juan*. On either side of these extracts, the anthology reprinted several of Byron's lyrics under their original titles, giving the impression that the passages from *Don Juan* were short lyrics in their own right.

This approach provided the anthologies with a strategy for neutralising the supposedly immoral content of *Don Juan* without censoring it altogether, similar to their handling of *Queen Mab*. This approach had been adopted by the poem's first reviewers: *Blackwood's* was 'willing to quote a few of the passages which can be read without a blush' on the understanding that 'the comparative rarity of such passages will, in all probability, operate to the complete exclusion of the work itself, from the libraries of the greater part of our readers' (repr. Mason 2006: V, 319). An 1873 anthology echoed this judgement when it justified its inclusion of two short passages from *Don Juan* ('The Isles of Greece' and a description of Haidee):

> The work was roundly abused for its immorality, but all acknowledged its marvellous power, and the brilliant gems of poetry which thickly studded the production throughout – they were the stars which gave their light to good and bad impartially. [. . .] Notwithstanding, it is only selected portions, such as the above, that may be safely read by those whose judgement has not obtained complete control of passion.
>
> (Gibbon 1873: 173)

Although *Don Juan* was, overall, one of the poems by Byron most often quoted in the anthologies, they tended to treat it as a string of 'brilliant gems' – that word again – which could be detached, re-cut, and reset. They reproduced only a tiny fraction of the poem, divided that fraction into small, disjointed gobbets of text, and effectively detached those fragments from their poetic context, making them into short, standalone poems.

Like other cultural products that mediated or remediated Romantic writing to Victorian audiences, nineteenth-century literary anthologies faced the challenge of accommodating Romanticism to new readerly expectations, new social contexts, and new media of cultural transmission. In the examples discussed here, we can see anthologists, often heavily dependent on the selections of previous anthologists, scanning the long works of Romantic authors in search of passages that could be removed from their poetic contexts, shorn of specific narrative and political references, detached from their individualised speakers, and made into independent lyrics, treating universal themes, and spoken in the depersonalised lyric voice of 'pure' poetry. As a result, nineteenth-century anthologies occluded most of the lines in most of the long poems that we now think of as among the central texts of Romanticism. The lines from these long poems that *were* included could be dis-embedded lyrics, passages of natural description, detachable *bon mots*, poetic highlights such as Byron's stanzas on Waterloo, or even synthetic poems created by stitching together lines of poetry across silent elisions. Whatever their provenance, in the anthologies these lines were stripped of their poetic context, encouraging readers to approach them as though they were short poems of the kind the anthologies preferred. This anthological reading protocol could be carried over to the long poems as a whole, or even to an author's collected works; both could be treated as strings of brilliant gems to be experienced discreetly.

Notes

1 *The Siege of Valencia*, II.274–83, 311–28, 333–44, 353–74, 377–96.
2 3119 lines out of a total of 4655.
3 1450 lines, including the openings of Cantos One and Four, are never reprinted in the anthologies surveyed.
4 I calculate that out of a total of 16,068 lines in the poem (including the Dedication, but not including unincorporated stanzas), 12,533 do not appear in any anthology surveyed.
5 The sections reprinted in Blackwood from *Don Juan* are: 1.123–7 ('First Love', pp. 296–7), 4.11–16 ('The Lovers', pp. 298–9) and 4.31–4 ('A Dream', p. 300).

Works cited

Anon., review of 'Queen Mab', *The Literary Gazette and Journal of Belles Lettres*, 226 (May 1821), 305–8.

Barcus, James E., ed., *Shelley: The Critical Heritage* (London: Routledge and Kegan Paul, 1975).

Blackwood, James, ed., *Selections from the Poets: Popular Poems from the Most Eminent Authors, Illustrated with Fine Steel Engravings* (London: n.p., [1850]).

Coleridge, Samuel Taylor, *Biographia Literaria: or, Biographical Sketches of my Literary Life and Opinions, The Collected Works of Samuel Taylor Coleridge*, VII, eds James Engell and W. Jackson Bate (Princeton, NJ: Bollingen Series, Princeton University Press, 1983).

Elfenbein, Andrew, *Romanticism and the Rise of English* (Stanford, CA: Stanford University Press, 2009).

Gibbon, Charles, ed., *The Casquet of Literature: Being a Selection in Poetry and Prose from the Works of the Most Admired Authors* (London, Glasgow: n.p., 1873).

Hales, J.W., ed., *Longer English Poems, with Notes, Philological and Explanatory, and an Introduction on the Teaching of English* (London: Macmillan, 1872).

Jeffrey, Francis, 'Review of *The Lay of the Last Minstrel: a Poem*', *Edinburgh Review*, 6 (1805), 1–20.

Lethbridge, Stefanie, 'Anthological Reading Habits in the Eighteenth Century: The Case of Thomson's Seasons', in *Anthologies of British Poetry: Critical Perspectives from Literary and Cultural Studies*, eds Barbara Corte, Ralf Schneider, and Stefanie Lethbridge (Amsterdam: Rodopi, 2000), pp. 89–104.

Lyrical Gems: A Selection of Moral, Sentimental, and Descriptive Poetry, from the Works of the Most Popular Modern Writers (Glasgow: Richard Griffin, 1825).

Mason, Nicholas, gen. ed., *Blackwood's Magazine, 1817–25: Selections from Maga's Infancy*, 6 vols (London: Pickering & Chatto, 2006).

McGann, Jerome J., 'Mobility and the Poetics of Historical Ventriloquism', in *Byron and Romanticism*, ed. James Soderholm (Cambridge: Cambridge University Press, 2002), pp. 36–52.

Moretti, Franco, *Graphs, Maps, Trees: Abstract Models for A Literary Theory* (London: Verso, 2005).

Moretti, Franco, 'Style, Inc. Reflections on Seven Thousand Titles (British Novels, 1740–1850)', *Critical Inquiry*, 36.1 (2009), 134–158.

Morgan, Monique R., *Narrative Means, Lyric Ends: Temporality in the Nineteenth-Century British Long Poem* (Columbus: Ohio State University Press, 2009).

Mueller, Martin, 'Scalable Reading', 29 May 2012. Available at https://scalablereading.northwestern.edu/scalable-reading/ (accessed 23 July 2013).

Poets of England and America; Being Selections from the Best Authors of Both Countries (London: Whittaker & Co., 1853).

Price, Leah, *The Anthology and the Rise of the Novel: From Richardson to George Eliot* (Cambridge: Cambridge University Press, 2000).

Sandy, Mark, 'Queen Mab', in *The Literary Encyclopedia*. First published 20 September 2002. Available at www.litencyc.com/php/sworks.php?rec=true&UID=2505 (accessed 20 July 2012).

Shorter, Thomas, ed., *A Book of English Poetry; for the School, the Fireside, and the Country Ramble* (London: n.p., 1861).

The Diadem; or, Poetical Scraps: Comprising a Selection of Lyric, Moral, Sentimental and Humorous Poetry, from the Most Admired Authors (Leith: Commercial List Office, 1830).

The Eclectic Review, review of *Alastor* (October 1816), 391–3.

Index

Abernethy, John 557–61
abolition *see* slavery
Abrams, M.H. 4–5, 7, 105, 421, 422, 439, 464, 479, 529
Adorno, Theodor 39–40, 73, 103–13
aesthetics 34–5, 71–3, 102–13
affect 280–93, 363–417
Agamben, Giorgio 555
Aikin, John 352
Althusser, Louis 7, 78, 482–3
Altick, Robert 129
Anderson, Benedict 210–11, 305, 351, 487, 508
Aristotle 363
Armstrong, Nancy, 115
Arnold, Matthew 3, 91, 481, 491
atheism 425
audience 63–67, 129–79
Austen, Jane 2, 4, 299–300; works: *Persuasion*, 494–504; *Sense and Sensibility*, 280–93
authority 183–241

Bacon, Francis 615–16
Baillie, Joanna 146–51, 352
ballad 587–614
Barbauld, Anna Letitia 9, 134; works: *Eighteen Hundred and Eleven* 349–59, 391–93; "Epistle to William Wilberforce" 390–91, "A Summer Evening's Meditation" 386–90
Barker-Benfield, G.J. 363
Barrell, John 8, 61, 63, 216, 354
Barthes, Roland 82, 183, 529
Bate, Jonathan 530
Beardsley, M.C. 129
Baudrillard, Jean 81
Beccaria, Cesare 120
Beer, John 539
Bender, John 124
Benedict, Barbara M. 410
Benjamin, Walter 483, 553
Bennett, Andrew 72, 130, 184, 198–208
Bentham, Jeremy 9, 104, 107, 116, 117, 146, 245, 318

Berlin, Isaiah 305
Bewell, Alan 306, 336–48
Bible 465–66
Blake, William 185,476–77; works: *The Book of Urizen* 227–30; *The Four Zoas* 229; *The Marriage of Heaven and Hell* 224–25, 323–35; *Milton* 221–41; *Songs of Innocence and of Experience* 323–35, 518–26
Bloom, Harold 5, 103, 141, 173–4, 421, 583
Blumenbach, Johann Friedrich 575
body 202–3,205
Bourdieu, Pierre, 75,83
brain *see* cognitive science
Bromwich, David 20
Brooks, Cleanth 4, 170, 171, 173–74, 177
Buffon, Comte de 574–75
Burke, Edmund 9,335–36,351,367–68,369
Burns, Robert 137, 140, 199, 200, 205
Butler, Judith 245, 401, 398–99
Butler, Marilyn 7, 118, 129, 133, 191, 453
Byron, George Gordon, Lord 135–36, 138, 572, 626–29; works: *Childe Harold's Pilgrimage* 593–95; *Don Juan* 46–55;

Cabanis, Pierre-Jean-Georges 533, 535
calculation, 103, 105–6
Canuel, Mark 1–22, 73, 114–25
Carlson, Julie 246
Caruth, Cathy 476, 501
Chandler, James 9, 19, 20–21, 46–56, 476
Chatterton, Thomas 36, 137, 201–2
Child, Lydia Maria 572
Christensen, Jerome 72, 138, 476, 479–93, 518–19
Clare, John 9, 530, 547–56
Clarkson, Thomas 339–40
class 20, 25, 34, 41, 44, 146–57, 158–69, 216–17, 265–67, 291–93, 309–22, 327, 410, 452, 458
Clery, E.J. 306,349–59
Cobbett, William 353
cognitive science 533–46

Coleridge, S. T. 1–2, 140, 250–51, 355–57, 530, 558; works: *Biographia Literaria* 479–93, 537; "Hymn Before Sunrise" 426–7; "Kubla Khan" 533–46; "The Rime of the Ancient Mariner" 336–44
Collings, David 364–65, 409–17
colonialism *see* imperialism
copyright 183, 226, 227, 232, 235, 490, 584, 618
cosmopolitanism 162, 353
Cowper, William 9, 11, 246, 265–79, 345, 353, 495, 496
Cox, Jeffrey, 184
Craciun, Adriana 353
Cragwall, Jasper 422
critique, social 35, 42, 104, 146
Croker, John Wilson 36, 37, 137, 187, 198, 393
cultural criticism 75–87
culture, 24, 28, 30, 34, 40–41, 49; conservative 165; popular 162, 315, 453; specificity 75–87, 209, 245, 507, 512
Curran, Stuart 72
Cuvier, George 577

Darnton, Robert 77
Darwin, Erasmus 535, 542, 551
Deane, Seamus 19
de Certeau, Michel 75, 82
deconstruction 6, 71, 88–101, 129, 130, 171, 184, 475, 476, 519, 530, 548, 552, 583, 584
de Man, Paul 3, 6, 72, 92–96, 99, 170–75, 479, 496, 501, 523
Denham, John 25
De Quincey, Thomas 10, 140, 209–20; works: *Confessions* 219–20; "The English Mail Coach," 210–19; *Suspiriia De Profundis* 142–4; "Traveling in England in Old Days" 213–14, 540
Derrida, Jacques 6, 184, 198, 199, 520, 530, 554
de Staël, Anne Louise Germaine 1
Descartes, René 552
detail 76–77
discretion 285–86
disease 336–48
Dissent (Protestant) 421, 451–63
Doody, Margaret 281
Duncan, Ian 476, 505–17

ecocriticism 548
editing 603–7
Edgeworth, Maria 187–97, 298–99, 490
Edwards, Bryan 319
Eilenberg, Susan 184
Elfenbein, Andrew 11, 246, 265–79

Eliot, T. S. 3–4, 170,172
Ellison, Julie 10, 364, 382–94, 396
emotion *see* affect
enlightenment 19, 50, 81, 103, 105–6, 108–9, 120, 123, 187, 192, 305, 306, 315, 331, 351–2, 396–7, 471, 476, 490, 506–7, 511–15, 557–60, 615–24
enthusiasm (religious) 438–50
environment 551
Equiano, Olaudah 9,342
Erdman, David 7
ethics 146–57,363–65

Fairchild, Hoxie Neale 421
fancy 382–94
Favret, Mary 11,476,494–504
feminism 161, 163, 292; *see also* gender
Ferguson, Frances 5, 72–73, 88–101
Ferris, Ina 183–84, 187–97
Finch, Ann 245
form, literary 1–12, 71–73, 88–101, 102–13, 176, 557–69
Foucault, Michel 7, 40, 75, 84, 124, 183–84, 223, 226, 227, 230, 246, 268, 290, 422
Franta, Andrew 130–31, 170–79
Fraser, Nancy 129
free indirect style *see* narrative
French Revolution *see* revolution, French
Freud, Sigmund 82,379,487–88,553
Frey, Anne 209–21, 304
Fukuyama, Francis 476
Fulford, Tim 530

Gall, F.J. 535
Gallagher, Catharine 7, 8
Galperin, William 8
Geertz, Clifford 75–76, 77, 83
gender 146–57, 245–302,
genius 265–79, 326, 357
George III 57–67
Gigante, Denise 11, 530, 557–69, 574
Gilbert, Sandra 245
Gilmartin, Kevin 10, 130, 158–69
Gittings, Robert 199
Godwin, William 9, 73; works: *Caleb Williams*, 114–25, 443, 451–63; *Memoirs*, 458–61; *Political Justice*, 454–58
Greenblatt, Stephen 7, 8
Gubar, Susan 245

Habermas, Jürgen 129, 422
Hamilton, Elizabeth 2, 196
Hamilton, Paul 10, 19, 20, 33–45
Hartley, David 534
Hartman, Geoffrey 6, 30, 79, 305, 363
Hayley, William 230, 272
Hazlitt, William 134–5, 199,540,573

Hegel, G.W.F. 34, 82,476,480,487,547
Heidegger, Martin 548–50
Hemans, Felicia 249,254–62,625
Herder, Johann Gottfried 466
Heringman, Noah 530
Hertz, Neil 475
Hickey, Alison 8, 184
history 25, 28, 29, 50–51, 480, 505–16; see
    also new historicism
Hofkosh, Sonia 246
Home, John 196
Howard, John 120
Hume, David 397–98
Hunt, Leigh 428, 431, 441
Hunter, Ann 383–4
Hunter, John 557–60, 564, 576, 578
Hutton, James 576

ideology 8, 19, 35, 89–90, 102, 104, 199, 329.
    349, 396, 480, 481–3, 490–91, 522, 550,
    575
imagination 8, 35, 89–90, 102–13, 173, 211,
    215–16, 250–51, 256, 274, 385–6, 404–5,
    439, 445, 573, 575
imperialism 209–21,305–7,323–59, 382
Inchbald, Elizabeth 153–57
Ingram, Anne 246
irony 40, 44, 93, 130, 170–79

Jacobus, Mary 397, 403, 406, 583–84
Jager, Colin 422, 464–72
Jameson, Fredric 103, 476, 480, 506, 518
Janowitz, Anne 305
Jay, Martin 103
Jewsbury, Maria Jane 249, 251–54

Kant, Immanuel 33, 73, 103, 104,561,615–16
Kaufman, Robert 10, 73, 102–13,125
Keats, John 33–45, 198–208, 476–77;
    Endymion 36–42; *Hyperion* 43, 565–6; *The
    Fall of Hyperion* 43–44,565–66; *Lamia*
    557–69; Odes 204–5, 518–26; "On Seeing
    the Elgin Marbles" 203–4; "On Visiting the
    Tomb of Burns" 199; "To Haydon" 204
Keen, Paul 476
Kelly, Gary 115
Khalip, Jacques 364,395–408
Kitson, Peter 530
Klancher, Jon P. 129
Knapp, Steven 73, 79–80
Krimmer, Elisabeth 294

Labbe, Jacqueline 246–7, 294–302
Lacan, Jacques 482
Lavoisier, Antoine 576
Lawrence, William 557–61
Leader, Zachary 184

Leavis, F.R. 4, 114
Lee, Debbie 306,530
Lentricchia, Frank 6
Levinson, Marjorie 7, 19,20, 23–32, 34, 91,
    171,421
liberalism 11, 317, 476, 479–93
Liu, Alan 20, 72, 75–87,439
Locke, John 225–26
Lovejoy, Arthur O., 77
Lynch, Deidre Shauna 246, 290, 609
Lyotard, François 75, 80–81, 82, 475

MacLeish, Archibald 3
Macpherson, C.B. 486–7
Makdisi, Saree 305, 323–35
Malchow, H.L. 306,309–22
materiality 226, 537–41
Malthus, Thomas 9, 141, 142
Manning, Peter 8
Marcus, Leah 81
Marvell, Andrew 571–72
Marxism 76, 79, 83, 102, 229, 309, 480,
    481–88, 490, 505, 519, 621
Mason, Nicholas 574
McCusik, James 530
McGann, Jerome J. 7, 8,20, 72, 75, 79, 89–92,
    96, 99, 171,337, 363, 476, 481–82
McLane, Maureen N. 72, 584, 587–600
media, and mediation 10, 209–21, 583–634
Mee, Jon 363, 422, 438–50
melancholy 395–408
Mellor, Ann K. 130, 146–57, 305, 306
Methodism, 440, 442
Miall, David, 534
Michaels, Walter Benn 79–80
Mill, John Stuart 3
Miiller, Jonathan 540
Milnes , Richard Monckton 199–201
Milton, John 2, 5, 103–110, 221–41
Mitchell, W.J.T. 482–83
modernity 140–44, 327, 464, 475–526, 549,
    598, 615
Mole, Tom, 584
More, Hannah 142, 151–53, 158–69
mortality 198–208
Morton, Timothy 11, 530, 547–56
Murphy, Peter 184

Naess, Arne 551
narrative 283–91
national tale 187–97
nationalism 148, 156–7, 305–59; *see also*
    imperialism
New Criticism 3–5, 12, 114, 171, 173,
new historicism 7–8, 10, 19–21, 71–2, 79,
    171, 439, 445, 475–6; *see also* Levinson,
    Marjorie, and McGann, Jerome J.

new pragmatism 79
Newlyn, Lucy 130, 133–45, 176, 183
novel: gothic 114, 115, 147, 284, 309–22, 367–81, 384, 392, 409–17, 483, 511–12, 566
    historical, 187–97; history of, 114–16

orality 466, 587–600
Orientalism 323–35
Otway, Thomas 59–64
O'Quinn, Daniel 21, 57–68

Park, Mungo 310–11, 312
patriotism 349–59
Peacock, Thomas Love 105
performance 57–68
Pfau, Thomas 20, 413
Philp, Mark 453
Pinch, Adela 364, 367–81, 410, 411
Piper, Andrew 584,601–14
Plato 363
Polidori, John 566
politics 19, 35, 57–68, 158–69; see also history, imperialism, nationalism
Poovey, Mary 6
Pope, Alexander 353
postmodernism 79–80, 518–26
Potkay, Adam 12
practice 84
Priestley, Joseph 575
print culture 584; *see also* media, mediation
property *see* copyright
Protestantism 421
public *see* audience

race 305–7, 309–22, 332, 340–41, 382–3
Radcliffe, Ann 364 367–81, 410
Rajan, Tilottama 72, 124
Regier, Alexander 72
reading public *see* audience
reform 161, 163
religion 421–72
reviews 35, 129–30, 134, 203, 254, 280
revolution 110–111, 213–14, 619–20; French 7, 25, 44, 48, 57, 68, 118, 146. 158–69, 283, 294, 305, 367, 406, 414, 445, 452, 578
Reynolds, Joshua 82
Richardson, Alan 529–30,533–46
Ricoeur, Paul 482
Robinson, Mary 298
Roe, Nicholas 19, 199
Romanticism, defined 1–2, 615–24
Rorty, Richard 75, 76, 80
Rose, Mark 226–27
Rousseau, Jean-Jacques 92–96
Rubin, Gayle 245

Russett, Margaret 184, 221–41
Ruston, Sharon 530, 571–9
Ryan, Robert 421–2, 425–37
Rzpeka, Charles 20, 469

Schoenfield, Mark 130
Schor, Naomi 75, 82
sciences 10,529–79
Scott, Grant 199
Scott, Sir Walter 46–56, 187–97, 476; *The Heart of Midlothian* 607–12; *Minstrelsy of the Scottish Border* 603–7; *Rob Roy* 505–17
secularization 464–5,469
Sedgwick, Eve Kosofsky 281–2
sensibility 458–61, *see also* affect
sentiment *see* affect
sexuality 54–5, 270–7
Shaffer, Elinor, 445
Shaftesbury, Anthony Ashley Cooper, Earl of 443–44
Shakespeare, William 494
Shelley, Percy Bysshe 6, 33, 73, 327–28, 575, 578, 629–33; *Adonais* 137; *A Defence of Poetry* 103–13; *Hellas* 431–6; "Mont Blanc" 426–30; "Ode to the West Wind" 170–9; *Prometheus Unbound* 430
Shelley, Mary 9, 139–40; *Frankenstein* 299–300, 305, 309–22; *The Last Man* 299–300
Sheridan, Richard Brinsley 57–68
Simpson, David 20, 305, 345
Siskin, Clifford, 10, 124, 294, 584, 615–24
slavery 339–40, 342
Smith, Adam 507–10
Smith, Charlotte 9, 295–7, 383
Soni, Vivavsan 73, 476
Southey, Robert 9
spirituality 467–71
St. Clair, William 574
Sulivan, Richard Joseph 573–74
sympathy 3, 102–13, 146, 188, 211, 286–9, 382–94, 395–408, 440, 446–8, 457

Tate, Allen, 4
theater 57–68, 146–57
Thelwall, John 60, 62
Thomson, James 351, 354
Tomko, Michael 422
trade 349–59
transcendence 75–87, 89, 214, 334, 411
transformation 571–79
trauma 267, 338, 343–4, 476, 496
Trumpener, Katie 476
Tuite, Clara 72, 246, 280–93, 363

United States 351
utility 116–25

Victorians 2–3, 11–12, 625–34
vitality 557–69
Virioli, Maurizio 351

Wahrman, Dror 294
Wang, Orrin N.C. 476–7, 518–26
war 336, 350, 494–504
Warner, William 10, 584, 615–24
Wasserman, Earl 5
White, Daniel E. 184, 422, 451–63
Wilson, John 140
Wimsatt, W.K. 3–4, 129, 529
Wolfson, Susan 72, 246, 249
Wollstonecraft, Mary 2, 5, 142, 245, 363,
    367, 458–61; *Letters Written During a Short
Residence* 404–7; *A Vindication of the Rights of
Woman* 395–408
women *see* gender
Woodring, Carl 7
Wordsworth, William, 1, 12, 88–101,
    142, 174, 383, 490; *The Excursion*
    571; "Intimations" Ode, 23; *The
    Prelude*, 136, 438–50; "Resolution and
    Independence," 137 ; *The Ruined Cottage*
    344–46; "Simon Lee" 595–97; "The
    Thorn" 422, 464–72; "Tintern Abbey"
    23–32, 409–17; "We are Seven" 96–100,
    595–7

Žižek, Slavoj 563